"The study of heroes and exemplars is generating increasing excitement throughout the social sciences at the present time, and for good reason. We live in a time of diminished expectations for moral leadership and true heroism. This innovative *Handbook of Heroism and Heroic Leadership* draws on the best available science to help us understand the conditions that foster heroic leadership, and how it works across a variety of social contexts. The volume is an essential contribution to the study of human lives in all their full potential."
—**William Damon**, Professor and Director, Stanford Center on Adolescence, Stanford University

"Studying heroism is challenging for scientists, yet Allison, Goethals, and Kramer have assembled 29 chapters by knowledgeable authors who explore varied aspects of heroism. The result is a thoroughly impressive volume that surely is the key resource in this developing area of science. Professors could organize an outstanding course or seminar on heroism around these excellent chapters."
—**Alice Eagly**, Professor of Psychology and James Padilla Chair of Arts & Sciences at Northwestern University

"Allison, Goethals, and Kramer's *Handbook* marks the emergence of the study of heroes and heroism as a central concern of the social sciences. A handbook in the truest sense, the book's well-organized and executed chapters—written by leading experts in the field—combine to form a foundation for the study of heroic leadership; they summarize current scholarly thinking, build thematic connections between subareas, suggest novel interpretations and insights, and identify future directions for theory, research, development, and application. This book is a goldmine of information essential for anyone seeking to better understand the ethical, psychology, interpersonal, and spiritual bases of heroism."
—**Donelson R. Forsyth**, Colonel Leo K. and Gaylee Thorsness Endowed Chair in Ethical Leadership, University of Richmond

"This handbook is a comprehensive, informative, and exciting contribution to the literature on heroism and heroic leadership. Material on heroism tends to be scattered in many different places, and it is wonderful to have it at last in one place, in readable and engaging prose. I recommend the handbook most highly."
—**Robert J. Sternberg**, Professor of Human Development, Cornell University

"Editors Scott Allison, George Goethals and Roderick Kramer have assembled an outstanding team of contributors whose expertise ranges from neurobiology and evolutionary psychology to developmental approaches as well as spirituality, leadership, and career development. In addition to the variety of topics and approaches featured in this volume, readers will appreciate the uniform clarity of the presentations and their engaging style of academic storytelling."
—**Phil Zimbardo**, Professor Emeritus, Stanford University, and Founder of the Heroic Imagination Project

Handbook of Heroism and Heroic Leadership

Over the past decade, research and theory on heroism and heroic leadership has greatly expanded, providing new insights into heroic behavior. The *Handbook of Heroism and Heroic Leadership* brings together new scholarship in this burgeoning field to build an important foundation for further multidisciplinary developments. In its three parts, "Origins of Heroism," "Types of Heroism," and "Processes of Heroism," distinguished social scientists and researchers explore topics such as morality, resilience, courage, empathy, meaning, altruism, spirituality, and transformation. This handbook provides a much-needed consolidation and synthesis for heroism and heroic leadership scholars and graduate students.

Scott T. Allison is Professor of Psychology at the University of Richmond. He has published numerous books and articles on heroism, villainy, heroic leadership, and underdogs.

George R. Goethals holds the E. Claiborne Robins Distinguished Professorship in Leadership Studies at the University of Richmond and studies heroes and presidential leadership.

Roderick M. Kramer is the William R. Kimball Professor of Organizational Behavior at Stanford University and is the author or coauthor of more than a dozen academic books.

Handbook of Heroism and Heroic Leadership

Edited by Scott T. Allison, George R. Goethals, and Roderick M. Kramer

NEW YORK AND LONDON

First published 2017
by Routledge
711 Third Avenue, New York, NY 10017

and by Routledge
2 Park Square, Milton Park, Abingdon, Oxon, OX14 4RN

Routledge is an imprint of the Taylor & Francis Group, an informa business

© 2017 Taylor & Francis

The right of the editors to be identified as the authors of the editorial material, and of the authors for their individual chapters, has been asserted in accordance with sections 77 and 78 of the Copyright, Designs and Patents Act 1988.

All rights reserved. No part of this book may be reprinted or reproduced or utilized in any form or by any electronic, mechanical, or other means, now known or hereafter invented, including photocopying and recording, or in any information storage or retrieval system, without permission in writing from the publishers.

Trademark notice: Product or corporate names may be trademarks or registered trademarks, and are used only for identification and explanation without intent to infringe.

Library of Congress Cataloging in Publication Data
Names: Allison, Scott T., editor. | Goethals, George R., editor. | Kramer, Roderick M. (Roderick Moreland), 1950- editor.
Title: Handbook of heroism and heroic leadership / edited by Scott T. Allison, George R. Goethals, and Roderick M. Kramer.
Description: 1 Edition. | New York : Routledge, 2017. | Includes bibliographical references and index.
Identifiers: LCCN 2016013497| ISBN 978-1-138-91563-3 (hardback : alk. paper) | ISBN 978-1-138-91565-7 (pbk. : alk. paper) | ISBN 978-1-315-69010-0 (ebook)
Subjects: LCSH: Leadership—Psychological aspects.
Classification: LCC BF637.L4 H336 2017 | DDC 158/.4—dc23LC record available at https://lccn.loc.gov/2016013497

ISBN: 978-1-138-91563-3 (hbk)
ISBN: 978-1-138-91565-7 (pbk)
ISBN: 978-1-315-69010-0 (ebk)

Typeset in Bembo by
FiSH Books Ltd, Enfield

Contents

Contributors   x
Foreword   xxi

Introduction: Setting the Scene: The Rise and Coalescence of Heroism Science   1
Scott T. Allison, George R. Goethals, and Roderick M. Kramer

PART I
Origins of Heroism   17

1. Attributes and Applications of Heroes: A Brief History of Lay and Academic Perspectives   19
   Elaine L. Kinsella, Timothy D. Ritchie, and Eric R. Igou

2. Why Heroism Exists: Evolutionary Perspectives on Extreme Helping   36
   Sara Kafashan, Adam Sparks, Amanda Rotella, and Pat Barclay

3. Adaptive Foundations of Heroism: Social Heuristics Push Advantageous Everyday Ethical Behavior to Heroic Extremes   58
   Gordon T. Kraft-Todd and David G. Rand

4. The Evolution and Neurobiology of Heroism   74
   Stephanie D. Preston

5. Character Development and the Emergence of Heroic Leadership: Towards a Relational Developmental Systems-Based Model   88
   Kristina Schmid Callina, Richard M. Lerner, Ettya Fremont, Brian Burkhard, Danielle Stacey, and Shaobing Su

6. The Moral Character of Heroes   99
   Lawrence J. Walker

7. Why and How Groups Create Moral Heroes   120
   Ari Decter-Frain, Ruth Vanstone, and Jeremy A. Frimer

Contents

8   The Hero Organism: Advancing the Embodiment of Heroism Thesis in the Twenty-First Century   139
Olivia Efthimiou

PART II
Types of Heroism   163

9   Everyday Heroes: Determinants of Moral Courage   165
Anna Halmburger, Anna Baumert, and Manfred Schmitt

10   Heroism in Times of Crisis: Understanding Leadership during Extreme Events   185
Zeno E. Franco

11   Holocaust Heroes: Heroic Altruism of Non-Jewish Moral Exemplars in Nazi Europe   203
Stephanie Fagin-Jones

12   Heroism and Wisdom in Medicine   229
Margaret Plews-Ogan, Justine E. Owens, Natalie May, and Monika Ardelt

13   Deviant Heroes and Social Heroism in Everyday Life: Activists and Artists   249
Mihaly Csikszentmihalyi, Michael Condren, and Izabela Lebuda

14   To Become or Not to Become? Existential Courage and the Quest for Identity   262
Roderick M. Kramer

15   Heroism in the Networked Society   283
Dana Klisanin

16   A Training Program in Spiritually Oriented Leadership: Inner Growth for Outer Change   300
Elsa Lau, Sarah B. Sherman, and Lisa Miller

17   Career Development and a Sense of Calling: Contexts for Heroism   316
Bryan J. Dik, Adelyn B. Shimizu, and William F. O'Connor

18   Underdogs as Heroes   339
Joseph A. Vandello, Nadav Goldschmied, and Kenneth Michniewicz

19   Whistleblowers as Heroes: Fostering "Quiet" Heroism in Place of the Heroic Whistleblower Stereotype   356
A. J. Brown

PART III
Processes of Heroism — 377

20 The Hero's Transformation — 379
    Scott T. Allison and George R. Goethals

21 Moral Transformation: The Paths to Heroism, Villainy, and Victimhood — 401
    Amelia Goranson and Kurt Gray

22 The Impact of Heroism on Heroes and Observers: Stories of Elevation and Personal Change — 417
    Jeanne Nakamura and Laura Graham

23 Accidental and Purposeful Impediments to Heroism — 438
    Craig D. Parks

24 Heroic Empathy: The Heart of Leadership — 459
    Ronald H. Humphrey and Laural L. Adams

25 Heroic Leaders and Despotic Tyrants: How Power and Status Shape Leadership — 476
    Anika Stuppy and Nicole L. Mead

26 The Intersection of Purpose and Heroism: A Study of Exemplars — 495
    Kendall Cotton Bronk and Brian R. Riches

27 Heroism and the Pursuit of Meaning — 507
    Jeffrey D. Green, Daryl R. Van Tongeren, Athena H. Cairo, and Nao Hagiwara

28 Psychopathy and Heroism: Unresolved Questions and Future Directions — 525
    Brett A. Murphy, Scott O. Lilienfeld, and Ashley L. Watts

29 The Courage of One's Moral Convictions: Exploring the Two Sides of Heroism — 547
    Ronnie Janoff-Bulman and Prerana Bharadwaj

Index — *561*

Contributors

Editors

Scott T. Allison is Professor of Psychology at the University of Richmond, where he has published extensively on heroism and leadership. His other books include *Heroes, Heroic Leadership, Reel Heroes and Villains, Conceptions of Leadership,* and *Frontiers in Spiritual Leadership*. His work has appeared in *USA Today*, National Public Radio, the *New York Times*, the *Los Angeles Times*, *Slate Magazine*, MSNBC, CBS, *Psychology Today*, and the *Christian Science Monitor*. He has received Richmond's Distinguished Educator Award and the Virginia Council of Higher Education's Outstanding Faculty Award.

George R. Goethals holds the E. Claiborne Robins Distinguished Professorship in Leadership Studies at the University of Richmond. His research focuses on heroes and presidential leadership. He is co-author with Scott Allison of *Heroes: What They Do and Why We Need Them* (2011) and *Heroic Leadership: An Influence Taxonomy of 100 Exceptional Individuals* (2013). His most recent book is *Presidential Leadership and African Americans: "An American Dilemma" from Slavery to the White House* (2015).

Roderick M. Kramer is the William R. Kimball Professor of Organizational Behavior at Stanford University's Graduate School of Business. He is the author of more than 150 scholarly articles and 17 books, including most recently, *Restoring Trust in Organizations and Leaders* and *Contemporary Conceptions of Leadership*. He has been a Visiting Scholar at numerous institutions, including the London Business School, Oxford University, Harvard Business School, Harvard Kennedy School, Bellagio Center, and Stanford's Hoover Institution.

Authors

Laural L. Adams teaches organizational and intercultural communication at Virginia Commonwealth University. Her research explores the rhetorical aspects and implications of "meaningful work" for both leaders and followers, as well as the role of mental models in constructing and circulating expertise in knowledge ecologies. Her forthcoming publications include research on the rhetorical construction of the "green university" and a model for extending higher education's participation in the development of open educational resources.

Monika Ardelt, Ph.D. is Associate Professor of Sociology in the Department of Sociology and Criminology & Law and an Advisory Board Member of the Center for Spirituality and Health at the University of Florida. She is a Brookdale National Fellow, a Fellow of the Gerontological Society of America, and the Executive Secretary of the Society for the Study of Human Development. Her research focuses on successful human development across the life course with particular emphasis on the relations between wisdom, religion, spirituality, aging well, and dying well.

Pat Barclay is an Evolutionary Psychologist at the University of Guelph, Canada. He studies the evolution of human cooperation, especially the role of reputation-based partner choice. He draws his theory from the literature on animal behavior and evolutionary biology, especially biological markets and costly signaling theory. He then uses experimental economic games and mathematical modeling to predict when cooperation will arise and be maintained. In 2015, he won the Early Career Award from the Human Behavior and Evolution Society.

Anna Baumert is an Assistant Professor for Personality and Psychological Assessment at the University of Koblenz-Landau, Germany. Her research focuses on cognitive, emotional, and behavioral reactions to perceived injustice. A particular focus lies on moral courage, meaning the intervention of uninvolved bystanders to stop or redress moral norm violations. Currently, she receives funding for research projects on justice sensitivity and information processing as well as on the stability of social and political trust.

Prerana Bharadwaj is a graduate student in the Social Psychology Program at the University of Massachusetts, Amherst. Her research focuses on the intersection of morality, social justice, and social class.

Kendall Cotton Bronk is an Associate Professor of Psychology at the Claremont Graduate University. She is a developmental psychologist who studies positive youth development and the moral growth of young people. Most recently, she has investigated these topics through the lens of young people's purposes in life. She is currently focused on creating tools that effectively cultivate purpose among youth. She has published a book on purpose (*Purpose in Life: A Critical Component of Positive Youth Development*, Springer), and her work has been generously supported by the John Templeton and Spencer foundations.

A. J. Brown is Professor of Public Policy and Law, and program leader, public integrity and anti-corruption in the Centre for Governance and Public Policy at Griffith University, Brisbane, Australia. He is also a board member of Transparency International Australia, Fellow of the Australian Academy of Law, and member of the International Whistleblowing Research Network. Formerly a senior investigation officer with Australia's Commonwealth Ombudsman, judicial associate, and state ministerial policy advisor, he is currently project leader on the Australian Research Council Linkage Project "Whistling While They Work #2: Improving managerial responses to whistleblowing in the public and private sectors." His authored and co-edited works include *Whistleblowing in the Australian Public Sector* (Australian National University Press, 2008), *Promoting Integrity: Evaluating and Improving Public Institutions* (Ashgate, 2008), *Whistling While They Work: A Good Practice Guide* (ANU Press, 2011), and the *International Handbook on Whistleblowing Research* (Edward Elgar, 2014).

Brian Burkhard is a researcher at the Institute for Applied Research in Youth Development (IARYD) and a doctoral student in the Eliot-Pearson Department of Child Study and Human Development at Tufts University. Before coming to IARYD, Brian worked as a school therapist in the Philadelphia public school system and as a behavior specialist consultant and therapist at The Institute for Behavior Change. Most recently he managed research for the Boy Scouts of America in conjunction with the Tufts Character and Merit Project. Brian has a B.A. in Psychology and Classical Studies and an M.S. in Counseling and Human Relations from Villanova University.

Contributors

Athena H. Cairo received a B.A. in Psychology from the University of Richmond and an M.S. in Psychology from Virginia Commonwealth University, where she is currently a doctoral candidate. Her research emphasizes factors promoting social and emotional connections in relationships, particularly the antecedents and effects of emotional empathy, attachment security, and the perception of meaning. Her personal heroes include William James, Eleanor Roosevelt, and her parents.

Kristina Schmid Callina is a Research Assistant Professor at the Institute for Applied Research in Youth Development in the Eliot-Pearson Department of Child Study and Human Development at Tufts University, where she also received her Ph.D. in 2013. Dr. Callina uses a strengths-based perspective to better understand the positive development of military-connected adolescents and young adults. In collaboration with colleagues at the United States Military Academy, Dr. Callina is investigating the development of character and leadership among cadets at West Point (a project funded by the Templeton Religion Trust, 2015).

Michael Condren, M.A., is a doctoral student in Positive Organizational Psychology at Claremont Graduate University. His primary research interests are creative change agents, and in particular their interaction with organizational cultures and structures, and social heroism.

Mihaly Csikszentmihalyi is currently the Co-Director of the doctoral program in Positive Developmental Psychology at Claremont Graduate University. He is the Co-Founder of the field of Positive Psychology, and the author or co-author of over 250 peer-reviewed articles and 19 books, including *Flow* (translated into 26 languages), *Good Business*, and *Creativity*.

Ari Decter-Frain is an honors psychology student at the University of Winnipeg. His research interests center on the psychological processes by which people develop their beliefs and defend them from threat. After graduation, he intends to complete a postgraduate degree in law or economics, or a multidisciplinary degree with themes centered on moral and scientific epistemology.

Bryan J. Dik is Associate Professor of Psychology at Colorado State University and Co-Founder and Chief Science Officer of jobZology. His research explores perceptions of work as a calling; meaning, purpose, religion and spirituality in career decision-making and planning; measurement of vocational interests; and career development interventions. He is co-author of *Make Your Job a Calling: How the Psychology of Vocation Can Change Your Life at Work*, and co-editor of two other books: *Psychology of Religion and Workplace Spirituality* and *Purpose and Meaning in the Workplace*. Dr. Dik is an American Psychological Association Fellow and received an Early Career Professional Award from the Society for Vocational Psychology. He lives with his wife Amy and their four sons in Fort Collins, Colorado.

Olivia Efthimiou is a transdisciplinary Researcher at Murdoch University, Perth, and Associate Researcher at the Australian National Academy of Screen and Sound. Her current research focuses on the emerging field of heroism science, embodiment, transdisciplinarity, the philosophy of science, and creative play in social, locative, and mobile spaces. She is the website creator and administrator of "Heroism science: Promoting the transdisciplinary study of heroism in the 21st century". She is Editor of *Heroism Science*, the first cross-disciplinary journal dedicated to advancing heroism research.

Stephanie Fagin-Jones is a scholar-practitioner who has published several articles on heroic altruism during the Holocaust, beginning with her doctoral dissertation awarded with distinction at Columbia University Teachers College, where she subsequently taught in the Counseling and Clinical Psychology Masters Program. She completed a Stanley Foundation Post-Doctoral Fellowship in Affective Disorders Research at North-Shore Long Island Jewish Medical Center and is a graduate of the Stephen Mitchell Center for Relational Psychotherapy and Psychoanalysis. She has a full-time private practice in New York City where she works on transgenerational trauma with first-, second-, and third-generation Holocaust survivors.

Zeno E. Franco, Ph.D., is an Assistant Professor in the Department of Family and Community Medicine and the Center for Clinical and Translational Science at the Medical College of Wisconsin. Dr. Franco is a former US Department of Homeland Security Fellow, a member of the Board of Directors at the International Association for Information Systems for Crisis Response and Management (ISCRAM), and an external science advisor to EU and Canadian projects addressing community level crisis management, responder mental health, and military reintegration. Dr. Franco has written extensively on heroism with his senior colleague, Dr. Philip Zimbardo, over the past decade.

Ettya R. Fremont is a doctoral student and researcher at the Institute for Applied Research in Youth Development at Tufts University. Her current research interests center around exploring resilience, empathy and identity development in adolescents, particularly those afflicted by chronic illnesses. Although she once considered medical school, her passion for mental health, policy, and advocacy inspired her to pursue doctoral work instead. She has a broad educational background, which includes a B.A. in Field Studies in Psychology from Wichita State University, an M.P.P. from Brown University, and a post-bac pre-med certificate from Bryn Mawr College.

Jeremy A. Frimer is an Assistant Professor of Psychology at the University of Winnipeg in Winnipeg, Canada. His research investigates the social psychology of ideological groups. Findings from over a dozen empirical studies suggest that committing to any ideological belief system—ranging from environmentalism to radical Islam—biases social cognition and behavior in reliable and non-rational ways. Among these biases is a tendency to create moral heroes. Frimer's research findings have received widespread international press coverage, including in the *Guardian*, *Wall Street Journal*, and *Huffington Post*. He currently holds an Insight Grant from the Social Sciences and Humanities Research Council of Canada (SSHRC).

Nadav Goldschmied is an Assistant Professor of Psychology at the University of San Diego. He received his Bachelor's from the University of Bar-Ilan in Israel and his Ph.D. from the University of South Florida. His research focuses on how inequality and disadvantage shape social perceptions of competitors and groups in contention, as well as topics in sport psychology and the forensic psychology.

Amelia Goranson is a second-year Ph.D. student at the University of North Carolina at Chapel Hill. She is interested in moral transformation, perceptions of death, and the power of narrative. She also studies how moral typecasting can make people feel healthier and happier.

Laura Graham is a doctoral student in Positive Developmental Psychology at Claremont Graduate University where she works in the Quality of Life Research Center. Her research interests include narrative identity, positive emotions, eudaimonic well-being, and meaning-making throughout the life course. Specifically, she explores moral elevation, the emotional response to witnessing an act of moral excellence, in relation to eudaimonic well-being and personal narratives that emphasize growth.

Contributors

Kurt Gray is an Assistant Professor at The University of North Carolina at Chapel Hill who studies mind perception and morality. Together with Daniel Wegner, he is the author of *The Mind Club: Who Thinks, What Feels and Why it Matters* (Viking).

Jeffrey D. Green is a social psychologist whose research focuses on: (a) the interplay of affect and the self, such as nostalgia and the influence of affective states on self-views, (b) the processes by which individuals process and remember threatening self-relevant information (mnemic neglect), (c) close relationships, particularly forgiveness (e.g., the "third-party forgiveness effect") and attachment processes (e.g., attachment and exploration), and (d) how individuals create and defend meaning in life. He is currently an Associate Professor of Psychology at Virginia Commonwealth University.

Nao Hagiwara is an Assistant Professor of Psychology. She joined the Department of Psychology at Virginia Commonwealth University in 2012 with affiliations with both the Health (primary) and Social (secondary) Psychology programs. She received her Ph.D. in Social/Personality Psychology from Michigan State University in 2010 and her two-year postdoctoral training in health disparities research at Karmanos Cancer Institute/Wayne State University School of Medicine. Her research bridges basic social psychology of intergroup bias and applied research of health disparities.

Anna Halmburger is a Research Scientist of an interdisciplinary research network on Communication, Media, and Politics of the University of Koblenz-Landau. In her work, she addresses the impact of norm violations of politicians and citizens on emotions, trust, and behavior. As part of the research network, she investigated how much negative media reports on politicians threaten citizens' political trust. Currently, she is particular interested in what motivates people to engage in bystander interventions against norm violations. She teaches seminars in the interface between Personality, Social, and Political Psychology as well as Psychological Assessment for students from psychology and social sciences.

Ronald H. Humphrey is a Distinguished Professor of Leadership in the Lancaster University Management School in the United Kingdom. Before joining Lancaster University in October 2015, he was a professor at Virginia Commonwealth University, where he won the 2014 VCU School of Business Distinguished Researcher award. He recently published *Effective Leadership: Theories, Cases, and Applications (Sage, 2013)*. He previously edited a special issue of *The Leadership Quarterly* on emotions and is currently co-editing a special issue of the *Academy of Management Review* on emotions and management.

Eric R. Igou is a Senior Lecturer at the Department of Psychology at the University of Limerick in Ireland. Dr. Igou's primary research interests are person perception, existential psychology, and biases in judgment and decision making. He frequently teaches decision making, attitude change, and cognition.

Ronnie Janoff-Bulman is Professor of Psychology at the University of Massachusetts-Amherst, where she has been since receiving her Ph.D. in 1977. She is the recipient of teaching and research awards, including the University Distinguished Teaching Award, the Aaron T. Beck Award for Excellence in Psychological Research, and the Morton Deutsch Award. Dr. Janoff-Bulman's research in recent years has focused on morality and has been supported by the National Science Foundation. Since 2010 Dr. Janoff-Bulman has been the editor of *Psychological Inquiry*, an international journal for the advancement of theory in psychology.

Sara Kafashan is a Ph.D. Candidate in the Department of Psychology at the University of Guelph. She uses evolutionary theory to understand and predict human social and interpersonal behavior. Specifically, her research interests include applying costly signaling and biological markets theory to cooperation, generosity, kin and non-kin relations, friendships, and social status.

Elaine L. Kinsella is a Lecturer at the Department of Psychology at Mary Immaculate College, University of Limerick in Ireland. Dr. Kinsella's primary research interests include the relations between the self and identity, memory, and psychological wellbeing. She frequently teaches social psychology, biological psychology, and abnormal psychology.

Dana Klisanin is a Research Psychologist and Integral Theorist investigating the evolution of heroism in an age of interconnectivity and the impact of information and communication technologies on present and future social evolution. She is CEO at Evolutionary Guidance Media R&D, Inc., and Executive Board member of the World Futures Studies Federation. Her work has been cited in news outlets including BBC, Time, USA Today, and Huffington Post. She has authored book chapters and journal articles and has received the *Distinguished Early Career Award for Scientific Achievement in Media Psychology* from the American Psychological Association's Society for Media Psychology and Technology.

Gordon T. Kraft-Todd is a Ph.D. student in Psychology at Yale University. He is interested in understanding how individuals can spread cooperative behavior. Types of cooperative behavior he is interested in include environmental (e.g. installing solar panels), mundane (e.g. holding a door open), charitable (e.g. giving to charity), and heroic (e.g. donating a kidney). He aims to conduct research that is both of theoretical and practical interest, and is therefore interested in combining laboratory experiments with interventions and field studies.

Elsa Lau is doctoral student in clinical psychology with an interest in spirituality, psychoneuroimmunology, and post-materialist science. Her previous research at McGill University and Memorial Sloan Kettering Cancer Center investigated psycho-oncology across the lifespan, from prevention to biomarkers and psycho-spiritual outcomes in palliative care. Her current work at Columbia University explores cross-cultural spirituality and mind-body medicine.

Izabela Lebuda, Ph.D., is Assistant Professor at Creative Education Lab, the Maria Grzegorzewska University, Poland. Her main research interests are the psychology of creativity, especially the social context of eminent artists and scientists' development.

Richard M. Lerner is the Bergstrom Chair in Applied Developmental Science and the Director of the Institute for Applied Research in Youth Development at Tufts University. He received his Ph.D. in developmental psychology from the City University of New York. His work integrates the study of public policies and community-based programs with the promotion of positive youth development and youth contributions to civil society.

Scott O. Lilienfeld is Samuel Candler Dobbs Professor of Psychology at Emory University. He received his Ph.D. in psychology (clinical) from the University of Minnesota in 1990; he completed his clinical internship at Western Psychiatric Institute and Clinics (University of Pittsburgh Medical School) from 1986 to 1987. His primary research interests include the assessment and etiology of personality disorders, especially psychopathic personality, the classification and diagnosis of psychopathology, scientific thinking in psychology, and the role of evidence-based practice in clinical psychology.

Contributors

Natalie May, Ph.D., is Associate Professor of Research at the University of Virginia Department of Medicine. She is also the lead author of *Appreciative Inquiry in Healthcare: Positive Questions to Bring Out Your Best* and a faculty member in the UVA Center for Appreciative Practice. She has conducted numerous qualitative research studies in education and healthcare and is currently the curriculum coordinator for the Phronesis Project at UVA School of Medicine.

Nicole L. Mead received her Ph.D. in Social Psychology and is currently Associate Professor of Marketing Management at Rotterdam School of Management, Erasmus University. Broadly, one of her research streams focuses on uncovering when and why people act antisocially. To that end, her work has helped determine when, why, and who power corrupts. Her spare time is devoted to exploring the great outdoors and the fascinating world of wine. Consequently, she is increasingly trying to understand how to facilitate self-control.

Kenneth Michniewicz joined Muhlenberg College as an Assistant Professor of Psychology in 2015. He received his Bachelor's from the University of Central Florida and his Ph.D. from the University of South Florida. His research interests include gender, gender dichotomization, group identification motives, and perceptions of social status.

Lisa Miller, Ph.D., is Professor and Director of Clinical Psychology, as well as the Director of the Spirituality and Mind Body Institute. Dr. Miller is Editor of the *Handbook of Psychology and Spirituality* (Oxford University Press) and Editor-in-Chief of the journal *Spirituality in Clinical Practice*. She is a Fellow of the American Psychological Association and has been awarded the Virginia Sexton Mentoring Award from APA. Dr. Lisa Miller obtained her B.A. from Yale University and her Ph.D. from the University of Pennsylvania, where she studied under Dr. Martin Seligman. Her research and scholarly interests are in spirituality and mind-body pathways to wellness, basic science at multiple levels of analysis on spirituality development, and prevention and treatment interventions for children and adolescents in poverty, increased access to treatment among low SES populations, intergenerational transmission of risk and resilience factors, and development of spirituality in children and adolescents. Dr. Miller's lab over the past fifteen years has been funded by a William T. Grant Faculty Scholars Award, an NIMH K-Award and a number of corporate and family foundations.

Brett A. Murphy is a doctoral student in the Department of Psychology at Emory University. He received his B.A. in History from Rice University in 2004 and his law degree from Harvard University in 2011. His primary research interests include the conceptualization and assessment of morality-related personality traits, particularly psychopathic traits, interpersonal dominance traits, and empathy traits. In addition to his work in psychology, he has also worked extensively within non-profit and social justice advocacy organizations.

Jeanne Nakamura is Associate Professor of Psychology, Claremont Graduate University, where she codirects the Quality of Life Research Center. She investigates positive psychology in adulthood, including meaning and engagement, mentoring and good work, and aging well. Her publications include *Good Mentoring* and (as coeditor) *Applied Positive Psychology*. She currently directs an exemplar study of social purpose as a form of positive aging.

William F. O'Connor is a doctoral student in counseling psychology at Colorado State University. His research interests focus on how emotional processes impact meaning making in life and in work. He is passionate about practicing as a therapist and teaching students interested in counseling, and performs both of these duties at Colorado State. Buddhism, social justice, relationships, dancing, and the human condition are frequently on his mind. He is most at peace in the mountains and reading books only tangentially related to his formal education.

Justine E. Owens, Ph.D., is a cognitive psychologist and Associate Professor in the University of Virginia Department of Medicine, serving on the UVA faculty for the past twenty-six years. She was research director for the NIH-funded Center for the Study of Complementary and Alternative Therapies at UVA from 1995 to 1999 and is the author of numerous publications on integrative therapies for pain management. Her research focuses on the interaction of cognition, affect, and spirituality, especially as it relates to self-regulation, symptom management, and wisdom.

Craig D. Parks is Assistant Provost and Professor of Psychology at Washington State University. His area of expertise is cooperative interpersonal and group behavior. He has published over 50 articles and four books in these areas. His research focuses specifically on two topics: How willingness to cooperate, and extent of cooperation, are affected by personality traits and individual differences, social comparison processes, and person-situation interactions; and why people harbor mixed feelings about those who are group-oriented. He is interested in relating cooperative choice processes to problems of resource consumption and conservation, community activity, and engagement in socially good works.

Margaret Plews-Ogan, M.D., is Associate Professor of Medicine at the University of Virginia, where she has recently served as Director of the UVA Institute for Quality and Patient Safety and the UVA Center for Appreciative Practice. She began studying wisdom and suffering when she was an undergraduate student, and it has been the focus of her research and teaching for many years. With Justine Owens and Natalie May, she is the lead author of *Choosing Wisdom: Strategies and Inspiration for Growing through Life-Changing Difficulties*. She is currently the director of the Phronesis Project, a medical school curriculum at UVA designed to foster wisdom in young physicians.

Stephanie D. Preston is a tenured Associate Professor of Psychology with an interdisciplinary background that has shaped her unique approach to complex basic and applied psychological problems. Dr. Preston obtained an M.A. and Ph.D. in Behavioral Neuroscience with Lucia Jacobs at the University of California, Berkeley, where she investigated the role of social stress and competition on food-storing decisions in animals. During this time she also published her influential review on empathy with Frans de Waal in *Behavioral and Brain Sciences*. After graduate school she held a post-doctoral fellowship in the Department of Neurology at the University of Iowa Hospitals and Clinics with Drs. Bechara, Damasio, and Anderson, where she studied the neuroanatomy of decision making, resource hoarding, and empathy. Since 2005 Dr. Preston has been a professor at the University of Michigan where she has focused on the mechanisms of emotion processing, empathy, altruism, and resource decisions.

David G. Rand is an Associate Professor of Psychology, Economics, and Management at Yale University and director of Yale's Human Cooperation Laboratory. His research asks (1) what prosocial and antisocial decisions people will make in particular situations and social environments, (2) the cognitive mechanisms that determine how these decisions are actually made (often looking at conflicts between intuition and deliberation), and (3) the ultimate explanations for why our decision-making processes have come to function as they do (in terms of evolution, cultural, and learning). In doing so, David combines empirical observations from behavioral experiments with predictions generated by math models and computer simulations using evolutionary game theory.

Contributors

Brian R. Riches is a doctoral student in the Positive Developmental Psychology program at Claremont Graduate University. He also teaches part-time at California State University, Fullerton, and online at Brigham Young University, Idaho. As an applied developmental scientist, his research interests include heroism, moral development, and purpose in life as avenues to positive youth development. He has recently been creating and evaluating interventions that foster heroism and purpose in life in young people.

Timothy D. Ritchie is an Associate Professor and Chairperson of the Department of Psychology at Saint Xavier University. Dr. Ritchie's primary research interests include the relations between the self and identity, memory, and emotion. He frequently teaches statistics, research methods, social cognition, and biological psychology.

Amanda Rotella is a SSHRC-funded Ph.D. student in the Department of Psychology at the University of Guelph, advised by Pat Barclay. She uses evolutionary approaches to investigate social behavior, such as trust, cooperation, and generosity. Specifically, she is interested in individual differences in cooperative and moral decision making, situational influences on cooperative behavior, and trust (or skepticism of) displays of generosity.

Manfred Schmitt teaches Personality and Psychological Assessment at the University of Koblenz-Landau. Prior to his current affiliation, he was professor of Developmental Psychology (Saarbruecken), Statistics (Magdeburg), and Social Psychology (Trier). His research interests include emotion (guilt, shame, anger, jealousy, anxiety, disgust), social justice, personality and information processing, nonlinear person x situation interaction, objective personality testing, the joint impact of implicit and explicit dispositions on behavior, and the simultaneous modelling of traits and states. Manfred Schmitt has served as associate editor of *Social Justice Research*, *Psychologische Rundschau*, *Diagnostica*, the *European Journal of Psychological Assessment*, and the *European Journal of Personality*.

Sarah B. Sherman is a doctoral student in Interdisciplinary Studies, within the departments of Counseling and Clinical Psychology, and Organization and Leadership at Teachers College, Columbia University. Her research focuses on spirituality in educational and professional contexts. She is director of the Spirituality Mind Body Institute's Master's Degree Program.

Adelyn B. Shimizu is a doctoral student in counseling psychology at Colorado State University specializing in occupational health psychology. Her research strives to promote occupational health and well-being within the workplace through the framework of applied positive psychology. The focus of her current research is on perceptions of work as a calling. Ms. Shimizu is an international traveler who enjoys the beauty of the Rocky Mountains and keeping her golden retriever and parrot amused.

Adam Sparks is a postdoctoral fellow at the Center for Behavior, Evolution and Culture and the Department of Anthropology at the University of California, Los Angeles. He is generally interested in evolutionary approaches to the study of human social behavior. Specific research interests include situational influences on generosity and selfishness, emotional mechanisms of cooperation and conflict, moral and political judgments, and social status.

Danielle Stacey is a researcher at the Institute for Applied Research in Youth Development and a doctoral student in the Eliot-Pearson Department of Child Study and Human Development at Tufts University. Danielle uses a developmental approach to explore the use of digital media to promote positive outcomes among youth and their families. In partnership with WGBH

Digital Kids, Danielle is evaluating the Arthur Interactive Media Buddy Project, a digital media-based program to promote character development in elementary school age children. Danielle earned a B.S. in Psychology from University of Wollongong, Australia, and an M.A. in Applied Developmental Science from Tufts University.

Anika Stuppy is a Ph.D. candidate at the Marketing Department of Rotterdam School of Management, Erasmus University. Her research explores how social status influences consumption behavior. More specifically, Anika investigates what makes consumers feel like their social status is threatened and how they boost status through strategic purchases. A second line of research explores how negative emotions like guilt and feelings of undeservingness change consumption preferences and experiences.

Shaobing Su is a Research Assistant at the Institute for Applied Research in Youth Development and a doctoral student in the Eliot-Pearson Department of Child Study and Human Development at Tufts University. Driven by interests in research on human development, Ms. Su has actively engaged in many research projects since her sophomore year. Her dedication to research has resulted in a rich publication record (over 20 peer-reviewed publications) and an impressive number of scholarly presentations at important scientific meetings. Ms. Su's research interests focus on mixed-methods research on positive youth development (PYD) among immigrant children in the U.S.

Daryl R. Van Tongeren is a social psychologist who earned his Ph.D. in Experimental Social Psychology from Virginia Commonwealth University in 2011. Currently, he is an Assistant Professor of Psychology at Hope College. His research interests include meaning, religion/spirituality, virtues, and morality. His research has been funded by The John Templeton Foundation, and he has published research in journals such as *Journal of Personality and Social Psychology*, *Personality and Social Psychology Bulletin*, *Journal of Experimental Social Psychology*, and *Social Psychological and Personality Science*.

Joseph A. Vandello is Professor of Psychology at the University of South Florida, where he has taught since 2002. He received his Bachelor's from the University of Iowa and his Ph.D. from the University of Illinois at Urbana-Champaign. His research interests include gender, culture, conflict and violence, social perceptions of disadvantaged groups, prejudice, morality and moral judgments, and work and family issues.

Ruth Vanstone is an honors psychology student at the University of Winnipeg. She is currently conducting her honors thesis, which investigates how the facial orientation of moral heroes influences followers' behavior. She received the Philip Joseph Rogers Brickman Memorial Scholarship in Psychology and holds an undergraduate degree in Conflict Resolution Studies.

Lawrence J. Walker, Ph.D. (University of Toronto), is Professor of Psychology and Senior Associate Dean of Graduate and Postdoctoral Studies at the University of British Columbia, Vancouver. His program of research focuses on the psychology of moral development, particularly in terms of moral reasoning, personality, and identity. This research has been aimed at developing a more full-bodied account of moral functioning that may help explain the psychological dynamics in exemplary moral action, including heroism. Toward that end, Dr. Walker examines individuals' conceptions of moral excellence as well as the psychological functioning of a range of actual moral exemplars.

Contributors

Ashley L. Watts is a doctoral student in the Department of Psychology at Emory University in Atlanta, Georgia. She received her B.S. in psychology from the University of Georgia in 2011. Her primary research interests include the assessment and etiology of personality, particularly psychopathic and narcissistic traits, and the extent to which normal-range personality traits contribute to personality disorders and psychopathology more broadly.

Philip Zimbardo is internationally recognized as a leading "voice and face of contemporary psychology" through his widely seen PBS-TV series, *Discovering Psychology*, his media appearances, best-selling trade books on shyness, and his classic research, *The Stanford Prison Experiment*. Zimbardo has been a Stanford University professor since 1968 (now an Emeritus Professor), having taught previously at Yale, NYU, and Columbia University. He continues teaching graduate students at the Pacific Graduate School of Psychology, and at the Naval Post Graduate School (Monterey). He has been given numerous awards and honors as an educator, researcher, writer, and service to the profession. Recently, he was awarded the Havel Foundation Prize for his lifetime of research on the human condition. Among his more than 300 professional publications and 50 books is the oldest current textbook in psychology, *Psychology and Life*, now in its 18th Edition, and *Core Concepts in Psychology* in its 5th Edition.

Foreword

"Heroes do not walk on mortal soil." That view of heroism is as a category containing special, unique individuals who organize their entire lives around personal sacrifice for a moral, social, or political cause, and who are willing to die in their pursuit of that justice. Some exemplars would be Jesus, Martin Luther King, Nelson Mandela, Mother Teresa, and others whose names we know because of their lifelong heroic endeavors. In addition, we have long honored male warriors, such as Agamemnon and Achilles, as well as those generals from nations that have won wars against formidable enemies. This male-oriented bias can also be seen among comic and movie superheroes, which, with few exceptions, are dramatically masculine.

An alternative, or supplementary, category is that of heroes who are ordinary people but who engage in extraordinary actions to help others in need or in defending a moral cause, doing so aware of personal risk and loss, and without expectation of material gain for their action. In this democratic view, heroism is both practical and teachable, contained within a related series of attitudes, skills, habits, and analytical lenses. One goal of education in every society should be to promote this knowledge and to spread a way of living that incorporates a pattern of daily deeds of heroism along with individual and social growth. Ultimately, education can activate and empower the hidden hero within each of us. If anyone can become a hero, then it follows that everyone should aspire to become a person who does heroic deeds daily—of kindness and empathy that transform compassion into social action. Heroes put their best selves forward in service to humanity; they are willing to make personal sacrifices that help make the world a better place.

In a sense, Joseph Campbell's treatise on the nature of heroes in his classic *The Hero with a Thousand Faces* (1949) encompasses both categories of classic and mundane heroes. In addition, his highlighting of the special journey any person takes on the path to becoming a true hero has been the heart and soul of storytelling in movies, classical drama and literature.

Christopher Vogler has encompassed this wisdom in *The Writer's Journey* by focusing on the mythic structure of the hero's journey that is the core of compelling storytelling. Consider his view on what the Hero's journey is all about:

> At heart, despite its infinite variety, the hero's story is always a journey. A hero leaves his comfortable, ordinary surroundings to venture into a challenging, unfamiliar world. It may be an outward journey to an actual place: a labyrinth, forest or cave, a strange city or country, a new locale that becomes the arena for her conflict with antagonistic, challenging forces.
>
> But there are as many stories that take the hero on an inward journey, one of the mind, the heart, the spirit. In any good story the hero grows and changes, making a journey from one way of being to the next: from despair to hope, weakness to strength, folly to wisdom, love to hate, and back again. It's these emotional journeys that hook an audience and make a story worth watching.
>
> *(Vogler, 2007, p. 7)*

Foreword

As fascinating as such literary views are to consider, what has long been missing from our deeper understanding of the nature of heroism is researched-based conclusions from social scientists. It is curious that the terms hero and heroism are not contained in any textbook in introductory psychology, nor in the lexicon of Martin Seligman's positive psychology.

So it is with considerable delight that I am finally able to see the needed remedy appear in the form of this wonderful *Handbook of Heroism and Heroic Leadership*. More than forty authors have contributed a wide range of perspectives that enable us to more fully appreciate the breadth and depth of what heroism means. Editors Scott T. Allison, George R. Goethals and Roderick M. Kramer have assembled an outstanding team of contributors whose expertise ranges from neurobiology and evolutionary psychology to developmental approaches, as well as spirituality, leadership, and career development. I found particularly intriguing the chapters on psychopathology and heroism, collaborative heroism, underdog heroes, as well as new takes on status and power, and also on moral and existential courage as hero predispositions. In addition to the variety of topics and approaches featured in this volume, readers will appreciate the uniform clarity of the presentations and their engaging style of academic storytelling.

Philip Zimbardo, Ph.D.
Professor Emeritus, Stanford University
Founder/President, The Heroic Imagination Project

References

Campbell, J. (1949). *The hero with a thousand faces*. New York: Pantheon Books.
Vogler, C. (2007). *The writer's journey: Mythic structure for writers* (3rd edition). Studio City, CA: Michael Wiese Productions.

Introduction
Setting the Scene
The Rise and Coalescence of Heroism Science

Scott T. Allison, George R. Goethals, and Roderick M. Kramer

Words move people, examples compel them.

(Latin proverb)

The goal of humanity lies in its highest specimens.

Friedrich Nietzsche (Hollingdale, 2001, p. 102)

Heroism represents the pinnacle of human behavior. The most noble act that a human being can perform is a heroic act, and the most distinguished life that a human being can lead is a heroic life. More than the pinnacle, heroism occupies a *central* place in human experience. Scottish philosopher Thomas Carlyle (1841) opined that "society is founded on hero worship" (p. 19). William James (1899) observed quiet heroism among the entire working class, noticing "the great fields of heroism lying round about" him (p. 2). Modern treatments of heroism emphasize that heroes serve fundamental human needs (Allison & Goethals, 2014; Kinsella, Ritchie, & Igou, 2015a), and that all of humanity—not just a select group of moral elite—is capable of heroism (Franco, Blau, & Zimbardo, 2011). Heroes are "fascinating to people in everyday life," (Kinsella, Ritchie, & Igou, Chapter 1, this volume), "literally commanding our attention" (Franco et al., 2011, p. 99). So central to our humanity is heroism that it may even be imprinted into our DNA (Efthimiou, 2015; Chapter 8, this volume).

Yet this centrality of heroism to our lives remains a well-kept secret. All of us may harbor the potential for heroism, but we tend to reserve the label of "hero" for the best of humanity. Perhaps we relish occupying the role of spectator; it leaves us clean, unharmed, and able to savor the feelings of elevation that sweep over us upon witnessing others' heroic acts (Csikszentmihalyi, Condren, & Lebuda, Chapter 13, this volume). For Carlyle (1841), "no nobler or blessed feeling dwells in man's heart" than the feeling of hero worship. The veneration of heroes serves as the catalyst for self-enrichment, as "every true man" feels that "he is himself made higher by doing reverence to what is really above him" (p. 23). Each human being, according to Carlyle, "in some sense or other, worships heroes; that all of us reverence and must ever reverence Great Men" (p. 24). The allure of heroism taps into a deeply rooted archetype of god-like individuals who are "the creators" and "the soul of the whole world's history" (p. 6). Hero worship, from Carlyle's perspective, is:

the deepest root of all; the tap-root, from which in a great degree all the rest were nourished and grown ... Worship of a hero is transcendent admiration of a Great Man ... No nobler feeling than this of admiration for one higher than himself dwells in the breast of men.

(Carlyle, 1841, pp. 18–19)

Carlyle's assertions about our depth of feeling for heroes are not mere hyperbole. The deep veneration of heroes permeates every segment of our post-modern society, from the adoration of pseudo-hero celebrities to the sobering reverence of consummate heroes who sacrifice their lives to save others. Our thirst for heroes runs so deep that people are quick to attribute heroism to those who are famous, muscular, or talented, or to anyone who performs *any* action considered "good," such as saving a slice of pizza from hitting the ground. One cannot help but stumble upon daily news stories about dogs, cats, and even parakeets who are deemed heroes by the media (People, 2009). Some bemoan this dilution of the term hero, and there is reason for concern if the reckless use of the "hero" nudges it from the pinnacle of human experience. But we interpret the liberal and generous use of the hero label as exposing people's profound hunger for heroes in a world that so desperately needs them.

Descriptions of Heroism

Early conceptions of heroes emphasized the qualities of power, apotheosis, and masculinity (see Hughes-Hallett, 2004). Heroes in antiquity were revered for their strength, courage, resourcefulness, and ability to slay enemies (Schein, 1984). The human tendency to assign god-like characteristics to heroic leaders can be traced to Beowulf and Achilles, and it later became manifest as the divine right of kings during the Middle Ages and Renaissance. Carlyle (1841) believed that hero worship was a small leap from divine worship, observing that "there needs not a great soul to make a hero; there needs a god-created soul which will be true to its origin; that will be a great soul!" (p. 194). From this perspective, "worship of a hero is transcendent admiration of a Great Man" (p. 19). Max Weber (1919) argued that great men are endowed with charisma, which he called "a certain quality of an individual personality, by virtue of which he is set apart from ordinary men and treated as endowed with supernatural, superhuman, or at least specifically exceptional powers or qualities." The word *charisma*, of course, stems from the Greek phrase "divine gift of grace" (Riggio & Riggio, 2008), and in that sense it includes a religious element. In fact, Weber noted that the qualities of charismatic heroic leaders "are regarded as of divine origin or as exemplary."

In the same vein, Freud (1922) noted that the leader of early human groups, "at the very beginning of the history of mankind, was the *Superman* whom Nietzsche only expected from the future ... The leader himself need love no one else, he may be of a masterly nature, absolutely narcissistic, but self-confident and independent" (p. 3). Intrigued by Darwin's view of the primal horde leader, Freud was fascinated by the tendency of these leaders to become deified in death. He observed how we respond to charismatic leaders with reverence and awe. Leaders who invoke religious feelings and ideation, he noted, are viewed as especially charismatic. People in groups crave heroic leadership but those who would be leaders must not only be powerful and charismatic, they must themselves "be held in fascination by a strong faith (in an idea) in order to awaken the group's faith." Freud expanded on Gustave Le Bon's (1895) crowd theory and suggested that "leaders make themselves felt by means of the ideas in which they themselves are fanatical believers" and that through "the truly magical power of words" leaders acquire a "mysterious and irresistible power" which acts as "sort of domination exercised over us" (p. 5).

Sadly, throughout most of human history heroism has been a decidedly male activity denied to the vast majority of women. Men's advantage in the heroic realm stems from their greater physical prowess, highly entrenched patriarchal social forces, and the restrictions that women's reproductive activities place on their activities in many settings (Becker & Eagly, 2004; Wood & Eagly, 2002). Most classical descriptions of heroism have thus emphasized male behavior and masculine attributes. Carlyle (1841) wrote that heroes possess "a sort of savage sincerity—not cruel, far from that; but wild, wrestling naked with the truth of things" (p. 193). As a result, "the history of the world is but the biography of great men" (p. 12). Freud (1922), as we have noted, invoked an evolutionary basis for male heroic leadership, arguing "that the primitive form of human society was that of a horde ruled over despotically by a powerful *male*" (p. 122; emphasis added). Evolutionary psychologists have argued not only that men evolved a tendency to take risks but also that women evolved a tendency to avoid them (Campbell, 1999). Baumeister (2010) has made the similar argument that because men have faced a more daunting challenge in reproducing, they may have evolved to be more risk-taking than women. To attract mates, nature designed men to take chances, try new things, be creative, and explore bold heroic possibilities. Today it has become clear that biology is not destiny. Women are men's equals in all realms of heroism, and in fact women occupy the majority of occupational positions (e.g., teachers) in the category of "unsung" heroes (see Goethals & Allison, 2012).

Perhaps the most famous description of heroes comes from the seminal work of Joseph Campbell (1949), a comparative mythologist who noticed a distinct pattern within hero myths from around the world. In virtually all mythological stories from every time period in human history, a hero embarks on a journey that begins when he or she is cast into a dangerous, unfamiliar world. The hero is charged with accomplishing a daunting task and receives assistance from unlikely sources. There are formidable obstacles along the way and villainous characters to overcome. After many trials and much suffering, the hero learns an important truth about herself and about the world. Succeeding on her journey, the hero is forever changed and returns to her original world. There she bestows some type of gift to that society, a gift that is only made possible by her own personal journey of growth and change. In short, heroes undergo a personal transformation that includes the development of a motive to improve the lives of others (Allison & Goethals, Chapter 20, this volume).

Campbell proposed that this prototypical heroic path, which he called the hero *monomyth*, consists of three parts: *departure*, *initiation*, and *return*. The initial *departure* phase refers to the forces that set the hero's journey in motion. Heroes embark on their journeys to achieve a goal that requires the acquisition of an important quality that the hero lacks. All heroes start out "incomplete" in some sense. They are missing some essential inner strength or quality that they must develop to succeed. This quality can be self-confidence, humility, courage, compassion, faith, resilience, a moral compass, or some fundamental insight about themselves and the world. The second phase, *initiation*, refers to the challenges, obstacles, and foes that must be overcome for the hero to prevail. Heroes cannot triumph over these obstacles without help from others. Campbell calls these helpers *mentors*, who bear a resemblance to the Jungian archetype of the *wise old man*. These mentors can be friends, teachers, love interests, sidekicks, or father figures. The role of the mentor is to help the hero discover, or recover, the missing quality that is needed to overcome challenges and obstacles on the journey (Allison & Smith, 2015). Good mentors are leaders in the classic sense; they help others discover their strengths and raise them to new levels of competence and morality (Burns, 1978). Campbell believed that the most satisfying heroes we encounter in mythic storytelling are heroes who are transformed by the mentoring they have received. Transforming mentorship is a pivotal component of the hero's journey.

Of central importance in the hero monomyth is the phase involving the hero's *return* to his or her original world. Upon returning, the hero brings a great boon, or benefit, to the world. Having been personally transformed, the hero is drawn to a higher calling of giving back to his or her group, organization, or society. This transition from self-transformation to a desire for a wider, social transformation is similar to Maslow's (1943) distinction between the need for self-actualization and the need for self-transcendence. It also bears a resemblance to the progression from Erik Erikson's (1975) stage of identity formation to the later stages of generativity and integrity. The hero's journey is the human journey, replete with struggle, growth, learning, transformation, and an ascendency from followership to heroic leadership (Goethals & Allison, 2017).

Metaphors of Heroism

Scientists have long used metaphors to guide their worldviews, theories, hypotheses, and experimental designs (Leary, 1994). William James (1878/1983) claimed that the use of metaphor undergirds all human understanding, and this assertion is supported by contemporary research suggesting that metaphors may form the basis for all thought, perception, language, and social experience (Allison, Beggan, & Midgley, 1996; Lakoff & Johnson, 2003; McPherson, 1992; Olson & Haynes, 2008). Metaphors assist us in grasping the complexities of the world by providing, in James' words, vivid examples and "similar instances" which operate as "pegs and pigeonholes—as our categories of understanding" (p. 12). Leary (1994) has argued, moreover, that the use of metaphor throughout the history of science has led to revolutionary breakthroughs by offering scientists fresh frameworks for identifying new phenomena worthy of scrutiny. As new fields of inquiry are born and begin cutting their teeth, metaphors are proposed and take root in the emerging literature, energizing researchers. These metaphors are then replaced, or augmented, with new ones, and the process keeps repeating itself. Heroism science is no exception to this pattern.

One could argue that Carlyle's (1841) *great man* theory of heroic leadership offered the first metaphor of human agency as paramount in understanding heroic action. From this perspective, heroism derives entirely from the motives and abilities of the hero, and situational forces that may have given rise to the heroism are largely neglected. Kinsella, Ritchie, and Igou's (2015b) prototype analysis of a hero's characteristics serves as an example of research that follows in this metaphorical tradition. Campbell's (1949) monomyth of the hero's journey represents another metaphor of heroism. The idea that heroism is a journey of growth would seem to underlie research on heroism as a lifelong developmental process (Allison & Goethals, 2016; Goethals & Allison, 2012, 2017). Franco and Zimbardo have composed two metaphors of heroism. The banality of heroism metaphor (Franco & Zimbardo, 2006) underscores the human universality of heroism and opens doors to researching the heroic potential in everyone. The metaphor of *heroic imagination* (Franco et al., 2011) "can be seen as mind-set, a collection of attitudes about helping others in need, beginning with caring for others in compassionate ways, but also moving toward a willingness to sacrifice or take risks on behalf of others or in defense of a moral cause" (p. 111). From this metaphorical perspective, unleashing the heroic imagination involves fostering the development of new mental scripts and enhancing people's heroic self-efficacy.

Two additional metaphors have recently appeared on the horizon. Allison and Goethals (2014, 2016) have recently proposed a model called *the heroic leadership dynamic* (HLD). Central to the HLD is the idea that people need heroes and that one's life circumstances determine which specific heroes one needs. Young soccer players need professional soccer heroes, and cancer victims need cancer survivor heroes. Also crucial to the model is the idea that need-based heroism shifts over time, explaining people's occasional repudiation of heroes. There is more to the HLD than simply need-based heroism, but for our purposes we will focus on the two metaphors inherent in the model. First, the HLD describes humans as creatures of needs and motives. These needs developmentally follow Maslow's (1943) hierarchy of needs, with each level of the hierarchy corresponding to a different type of hero that someone at that level may adopt. The second metaphor of the HLD is the image of humans as dynamic beings. People change. Our heroes evolve to reflect our own maturation process across the lifespan.

One final metaphor that we will discuss is that of the hero organism as proposed recently by

Efthimiou (Chapter 8, this volume). The organism metaphor places heroic actors in their biological, psychological, social, and cultural contexts as living entities that grow, respond, and regenerate within complex systems. According to Efthimiou:

> The concept of the heroic actor as a dynamical hero organism self-system is born out of the notion of the "heroic body as biological organism" which can only be fully comprehended in unison with the broader ecological, cultural, social and phenomenological aspects of the heroic body.
>
> *(Chapter 8, this volume)*

In short, the heroic actor is a "functioning biological organism that can perceive, move within, respond to, and transform its environment" (Johnson, 2008, p. 164). Efthimiou's hero organism metaphor adopts and extends a systems theory approach toward understanding human organisms in multiple contexts. Imbedded within her organism framework is the additional metaphor of *regeneration* or *restoration*, an acknowledgment of an organism's ability to grow, heal, and re-create itself (Chapter 8, this volume). Efthimiou's metaphors are bold, provocative, and subsume several other hero metaphors that have been proposed, such as the metaphors of agency, needs, development, and dynamism.

Definitions of Heroism

In discussing the definition of *hero*, we first make the obvious observation that there are many different subtypes of heroes, each with its own unique definition. Scholars have made distinctions between heroes who are *impulsive reactive* versus *reflective proactive* (Zimbardo, 2015); *episodic* versus *everyday* (Kerrigan, 2015); *personal* versus *cultural* (Allison & Goethals, 2012); *proper* versus *dark* (Kruger, Fisher, & Jobling, 2003); *transformed* versus *untransformed* (Allison & Smith, 2015); *emergent* versus *sustained* (Kraft-Todd & Rand, Chapter 3, this volume); *civil* versus *martial* (Franco et al., 2011); and *brave* versus *caring* (Walker & Frimer, 2007). The list of hero dichotomies could fill several pages, and scores of other hero tropes have been identified in film, television, and literature (TV Tropes, 2016). We will discuss different taxonomic structures of heroes in the next section of this chapter, each outlining and defining many subcategories of heroes. In this section, for the sake of simplicity, we will address attempts to construct one single definition of the broad category of *hero*. From our review of the literature, we observe that efforts to define a hero fall into one of two camps: those who believe that the term can be defined objectively, and those who believe that heroism defies an objective approach and is ultimately in the eye of the beholder. We describe the objective and subjective approaches below.

Objective Approach

Scholars who adopt the objective approach to defining heroism tend to converge on several core ideas. First, heroism involves taking one or more actions that are deemed to be morally good, or that are directed toward serving a noble principle or the greater good. Second, these good actions must be exceptional, not minor or ordinary. Third, heroism involves making a significant sacrifice. Fourth, heroism involves taking a great risk. Franco et al. (2011) thus offer this definition: "Heroism is the willingness to sacrifice or take risks on behalf of others or in defense of a moral cause" (p. 13). Kohen (2014) tweaks this definition slightly in stating that heroes are "people who faced the fact of their mortality, who took serious risks and/or overcame major hardship, and who did so in service of a principle" (see also Kohen, 2015). Merriam-Webster's definition of hero also adds that a hero attracts admiration from others, a *recognition* aspect of heroism that Franco et al. acknowledge in their observation that heroism is "a social attribution."

Most objective attempts to define heroism, however, do not include this idea that a hero must be admired by others for her work to be considered heroic. A more thorough discussion of previous objective efforts to define heroism can be found in Chapter 1 of this volume, by Kinsella et al.

Subjective Approach

Scholars who challenge the objective approach point out that most of the criteria for heroism listed above are open to vast subjective interpretation. If heroism is good, who defines what is good? And how much good is a *heroic* amount? Moreover, even if a standard of goodness were found and applied, who determines the criteria for judging a *heroic* level of exceptionality, sacrifice, and risk? Advocates of the subjective approach claim that there exist no absolute standards or criteria for determining a threshold by which sufficient levels of goodness, exceptionality, sacrifice, or risk can merit a heroic designation.

Campbell (1988), in discussing his hero monomyth, acknowledged the weakness of an objective approach: "You could be a local god, but for the people whom that local god conquered, you could be the enemy. Whether you call someone a hero or a monster is all relative …" (p. 156). The World War II German soldier who died, said Campbell, "is as much a hero as the American soldier who was sent over there to kill him." Allison and Goethals (2011) mince no words in claiming that "heroism is in the eye of the beholder" (p. 196). These scholars have discovered in their research that people's needs and motives determine whom they choose as heroes, a finding consistent with their HLD model. Maturity and development play a role in hero selection, with younger people tending to choose heroes known for their talents, physical skills, and celebrity status. Older people tend to favor moral heroes. As we get older and wiser, our tastes in heroes evolve, an idea captured in the subtype of *transitional heroes* (Goethals & Allison, 2012). Franco et al. (2011) also hint at the subjective nature of heroism in their observation that heroism is a "social construction" and that "heroes of one era may prove to be villains in another time when controverting evidence emerges … Moreover, the very same act accorded hero status in one group, such as suicide bombing, is absolutely abhorrent to many others" (p. 99).

Not coincidentally, there is also a subjectivist approach to evil and villainy. This perspective is evident in Baumeister's (2012) views of evil, which tends to be a label for behavior assigned by victims and witnesses of evil but not by perpetrators. "It is therefore necessary," wrote Baumeister, "to define evil as in the eye of the beholder, who may be victim or observer but is probably not the perpetrator. And this means that evil is defined in a way that is not strongly tethered to objective reality" (p. 374). Schoenewolf (2014) has identified "a particularly toxic variety" of "person or group that abuses others and not only thinks it's quite normal to do so, but very often thinks their abuse is an act of heroism" (p. 1). During the Nazi era, when millions of Germans persecuted Jews, they felt justified in doing so and believed they were acting for the greater good. The subjective approach uncomfortably reminds us there exists a fine line between heroism and villainy.

Scholars who adopt the subjective approach to heroism focus less on attempting to define heroism themselves and more on studying how the general population perceives and defines heroism. Allison and Goethals (2011) asked participants to list as many traits as they could that best describe heroes. These traits were then sorted by other participants into piles based on similarity, and the resultant piles were subjected to exploratory multivariate factor analyses and cluster analyses. The resultant factors and clusters revealed the following eight categories of traits describing heroes: *intelligent, strong, reliable, resilient, caring, charismatic, selfless,* and *inspiring*. Allison and Goethals called these trait categories *the great eight*. Kinsella, Ritchie, and Igou (2015b) improved on this methodology by using a prototype analytic approach toward discerning people's conceptions of heroic traits. Their analysis yielded 12 central characteristics of heroes and 13 peripheral characteristics. Kinsella et al.'s central characteristics are *brave, moral integrity, conviction, courageous, self-sacrifice, protecting, honest, selfless, determined, saves others, inspiring,* and *helpful*. The peripheral characteristics of heroes are *proactive, humble, strong, risk-taker, fearless, caring, powerful, compassionate, leadership skills, exceptional, intelligent, talented,* and *personable*. What is important to keep in mind with regard to Allison and Goethals' great eight traits, and with Kinsella et al.'s central and peripheral traits, is that these characteristics are not necessarily the actual characteristics of heroes. They reflect perceptions of heroes.

The weakness of the subjective approach is that it can potentially legitimize any claim to heroism, even behaviors that are acknowledged by nearly everyone to be abhorrent. Kohen, an ardent supporter of the objectivist approach to defining heroism, makes the following point:

> If someone claims that Stalin is a hero or a cactus is a hero and a researcher says, "well, heroism is in the eye of the beholder," then the researcher's implicit argument is that absolutely anyone or anything is a hero because there's no way to judge one person's claim from another person's without taking sides, being partial.
>
> *(Kohen, 2013)*

Kohen argues that the subjectivist approach "might suggest that people have a lot of different ideas about heroism, but it might also suggest that people simply aren't thinking very critically or carefully about heroism." We take the position that both the objective and subjective approaches to understanding heroism are useful in different ways. The objective approach is useful in scientifically identifying and defining the phenomenon, fine-tuning our understanding of it, and distinguishing it from other related phenomena. The subjective approach is useful in illuminating lay-perceptions of heroism that, regardless of their accuracy, are no doubt important to know because these perceptions drive people's decisions, social judgments, and everyday behavior.

Taxonomies of Heroes

Carlyle (1841) observed that "Nature does not make all great men, more than all other men, in the self-same mould" (p. 108). As heroes are packaged into different types, there is a need to develop a classification scheme. Carlyle identified six different "classes" of heroes: *divinity, prophet, poet, priest, man of letters,* and *king*. Klapp (1954) suggested the following eight types of heroes: *conquering, clever, Cinderella, quest, deliverer, popular benefactor, cultural,* and *martyr*. Several contemporary investigators have since proposed taxonomies of heroism based on situational demands of the heroism (Franco et al., 2011), the social influence exerted by the hero (Goethals & Allison, 2012), and the social structure of heroism (Allison & Smith, 2015). We examine these models below.

A Situational Demand-Based Taxonomy: Franco et al. (2011)

Franco et al. (2011) were the first contemporary investigators to propose a taxonomic framework. Their model is based on the relationship between heroic individuals and the situations that drive these individuals' heroic actions (Franco & Zimbardo, 2006). The taxonomy contains twelve heroic subtypes along with the situations that give rise to heroism. Two forms of heroism are included that involve physical risk: *military heroes* and *civilian heroes*. To be considered heroes, military heroes must go beyond the call of duty, and civilian heroes must knowingly put their lives at risk. The remaining ten types of heroism require social sacrifice: *religious figures, politico religious figures, martyrs, political leaders, adventurers, scientific heroes, good Samaritans, underdogs, bureaucracy heroes,* and *whistleblowers*.

In describing these eight social heroes, Franco et al. (2011) argue that religious heroes must perform life-long service embodying the highest principles of living. Politico religious figures turn to politics to affect sweeping change or they apply deep spiritual practices to enact wide political reform. Martyrs put their lives at risk in the service of a cause or to spotlight an injustice. Political leaders successfully lead a nation during times of war or disaster. Adventurers explore unfamiliar geographic areas. Scientific heroes use novel methods to make discoveries valuable to humanity. Good Samaritans help others in need when there are significant deterrents to altruism. Underdogs prevail by overcoming obstacles or difficult conditions and serve as social role models for others. Bureaucracy heroes stick with principles despite severe pressures to conform or blindly obey higher authorities. Whistleblowers report insider knowledge of illegal activities occurring in an organization, and they report the activity publicly to effect change, without expectation of reward. Overall, Franco et al.'s taxonomy provides a thorough and compelling typology of heroes that remains the gold standard in the field of heroism science today.

A Social Influence-Based Taxonomy: Goethals and Allison (2012)

Goethals and Allison (2012) developed a taxonomy of heroism based on their observation that a hero's influence can differ on many significant dimensions. Influence can vary along the continua of *weak* versus *strong*, *short-term* versus *long-term*, *widespread* versus *limited*, *waxing* versus *waning*, *hidden* versus *exposed*, and *constructed* versus *genuine*. These dimensions of influence are reflected in the various categories of heroism contained in the taxonomy. Goethals and Allison's taxonomic structure features the following subtypes of heroes: *trending, transitory, transitional, tragic, transposed, transparent, traditional, transfigured, transforming,* and *transcendent*. Trending heroes are either on a trajectory toward becoming heroes or losing their heroic status. Transitory heroes are "hero today, gone tomorrow," exerting only brief heroic influence. Transitional heroes are heroes that we outgrow over time. Tragic heroes self-destruct due to a personal shortcoming. Transposed heroes undergo rapid change from either villain to hero or from hero to villain. Transparent heroes are the invisible, unsung heroes. Traditional heroes follow the conventional Campbellian hero's journey. Transfigured heroes are individuals whose heroism is constructed or exaggerated into legend. Transforming heroes tend to transform entire societies. Transcendent heroes wield such great influence that they defy placement into only one of these hero categories.

A Social Structure-Based Taxonomy: Allison and Smith (2015)

Allison and Smith (2015) have recognized a larger social structure of heroic actors that includes heroes as individuals, dyads, small group ensembles, large organizations, and societies. Individual heroes in hero narratives include the hero as one's self, the leader of a group, or "the face" of an organization. Dyadic heroes in film and literature include buddy heroes, romantic heroes, divergent heroes, and a hero and sidekick. Group ensembles can include teams, police or military units, family units, or fraternity units. Larger social systems include governments, corporations, organizations, or institutions. Another important feature of Allison and Smith's taxonomy is its emphasis on the transformations that heroes undergo while on their hero's journeys. Heroes can undergo one of five types of transformation: *moral, emotional, mental, physical,* and *spiritual*. One sees parallels here to Carlyle's (1841) classes of heroes, with the priest being Carlyle's *moral* hero, the poet occupying the *emotional* role, the man of letters corresponding to *mental*, the king *physical*, and the divine *spiritual*. Allison and Smith also propose seven different transformational arcs describing the hero's trajectory during her journey. Depending on the arc, heroes can be designated as *enlightened, irredeemable, untransformed, regressed, fallen, classic,* or *redeemed*. Central to their taxonomy is the idea that heroes of any scale unit (individual, dyad, small group ensembles, large organizations, and societies) can traverse the path of the hero.

Themes in Heroism Science and Heroic Leadership

Although heroism science is only a decade old, several recurring themes are emerging that have attracted attention, debate, theorizing, and empirical work. In this section, we describe four such themes. The first frequently encountered issue, situationism versus dispositionism, has a longstanding history in the study of myriad other social science phenomena. Carlyle (1841), as we have noted, set the dispositional ball in motion with his great man theory. Shortly after Carlyle's book appeared, Herbert Spencer threw down the gauntlet by counter-arguing that great men are a mere artifact of social conditions (Carneiro, 1981). Tolstoy (1869), moreover, wrote that "kings are the slaves of history," suggesting that events shape leaders more than leaders shape events. Thus was born the nature-nurture debate that has wracked the field of leadership studies for many decades. It was only inevitable that heroism scientists would confront the issue, too. In this handbook, we see either implicit or explicit treatments of the situationism-dispositionism schism in chapters by Walker (Chapter 6), Parks (Chapter 23), Decter-Frain, Vanstone, and Frimer (Chapter 7), Janoff-Bulman and Bharadwaj (Chapter 29), Halmburger, Baumert, and Schmitt (Chapter 9), and Franco (Chapter 10).

A second recurring theme in heroism science research is the issue of whether heroic action precedes, or is the result of, prosocial thoughts and feelings. The preliminary answer to this question is that the causal path is bi-directional, with heroism triggering specific meaningful mindsets and also occurring as a result of those mindsets, depending on contextual factors. The pervasiveness of *reciprocal causal influence* has deep roots in psychology (see Bandura, 1986). Heroism scientists who address this issue in this volume, either directly or indirectly, include Bronk and Riches (Chapter 26), Green, Van Tongeren, Cairo, and Hagiwara (Chapter 27), Janoff-Bulman and Bharadwaj (Chapter 29), and Nakamura & Graham (Chapter 22).

A third recurring theme in heroism research addresses whether mental images and conceptions of heroism are learned (e.g., cognitive scripts and prototypes) or are hardwired into us (e.g., Jungian archetypes). Campbell (1949) championed the latter approach, and other contemporary theorists have built on Campbell's ideas (e.g., Allison & Goethals, 2011; Moxnes, 1999). In addition, Preston (Chapter 4, this volume) and Kafashan, Sparks, Rotella, and Barclay (Chapter 2, this volume) use principles of evolution to illuminate the biological correlates of heroism. Efthimiou (Chapter 8, this volume), moreover, argues for a transdisciplinary understanding of heroism which includes the biological basis as a central feature. With regard to heroism as a learned activity, Callina et al. (Chapter 5, this volume) elucidate a life-span approach to the study of the development of a heroic character. Kraft-Todd and Rand (Chapter 3, this volume) also put forward a clever and surprising argument for the learned nature of heroism. In addition, Kramer (Chapter 14, this volume) shows how he may have devised an exercise for helping people acquire existential courage and for fostering the development of heroic personal identities.

A fourth, related theme we see emerging is the portrayal of heroism as resulting from deep, deliberative thought processes versus shallow, perhaps even automatic mental processes. This distinction has a voluminous presence in the scientific literature in psychology (e.g., Bargh & Ferguson, 2000), and it veers close to the *free will* versus *determinism* debate endemic to both psychology and philosophy. Joseph Campbell hints at this issue in several of his books, citing an essay written in 1840 on the foundations of morality by Arthur Schopenhauer. Paraphrasing Schopenhauer, Campbell writes that a hero may act

> out of an instinctive recognition of the truth that he and that other in fact are one. He has been moved not from the lesser, secondary knowledge of himself as separate from others, but from an immediate experience of the greater, truer truth, that we are all one in the ground of our being … For a moment one is selfless, boundless, without ego.
>
> *(Campbell, 1972, p. 150)*

This issue about the degree of deliberation necessary for heroism to unfold is addressed in this volume either directly or indirectly by Goranson and Gray (Chapter 21), Allison and Goethals (Chapter 20), Humphrey and Adams (Chapter 24), Franco (Chapter 10), and Efthimiou (Chapter 8), among others. No doubt there are many more themes in heroism science beyond these four that merit inclusion in this chapter. Unfortunately, we do not have the time and space here to give all these issues the attention they deserve. We list these four themes as a starting point of discussion and we invite other heroism scientists to examine these and other recurring themes, and their resolution, in greater depth.

Overview of the Chapters in This Volume

This inaugural *Handbook of Heroism and Heroic Leadership* has assembled scholarly contributions about heroism from a variety of distinguished social scientists from around the world. Our volume begins with a thoughtful foreword by Phil Zimbardo. We do not exaggerate when we say that none of the editors of this volume, nor any of its contributors, would be producing a handbook about heroic behavior without Zimbardo's groundbreaking vision and accomplishments. The nature and scope of his farsighted thinking in the field is described in several of the chapters in this volume. There is much more to Zimbardo's indelible impact on the newly emerging science of heroism than can be told in a single page, chapter, or handbook. His leadership in fostering people's heroic imagination, establishing heroism as a science, and galvanizing a strong activism branch of the heroism movement, all borders on the heroic. We hope you take a few moments to read his thoughtful reflections in his foreword to this volume.

The main body of the *Handbook of Heroism and Heroic Leadership* is partitioned into three conceptually distinct parts that reflect the current state of theory and research on heroism and heroic leadership:

- Part I: Origins of Heroism;
- Part II: Types of Heroism; and
- Part III: Processes of Heroism.

Below we briefly highlight the contributors and content of each of these sections.

Origins of Heroism

Part I of this volume focuses on the formation, causes, and antecedents of heroic action. Elaine Kinsella, Timothy Ritchie, and Eric Igou lead us off with an overview of existing research on heroism with particular focus on the audience for heroes, and their perception of hero characteristics and heroic influence. Kinsella and her colleague discuss three categories of psychological functions that heroes fulfill for others: enhancing, moral modeling, and protecting others—together forming the hero functions framework. Next, Sara Kafashan, Adam Sparks, Amanda Rotella, and Pat Barclay show us how evolutionary biology, and its subfield evolutionary psychology, can offer an understanding of the genesis of heroism. Kafashan and her colleagues use relevant evolutionary literatures to develop compelling explanations for the phenomenon of heroism, and they suggest some practical implications of evolutionary perspectives on heroism.

In the next chapter, Gordon Kraft-Todd and David Rand show us how heroism may be adaptive ethical behavior taken to the extreme by over-generalization. Because this behavior is *typically* adaptive for individuals, it becomes automatized as social heuristics, and these heuristics may then be (mis)applied to produce heroism. Next, Stephanie Preston examines the evolutionary and neural bases of heroism. She argues that research on altruistic behavior cannot be applied to heroism because of heroism's unique qualities. Preston describes how accumulating evidence on the neural bases of offspring care can be applied to heroism, and she argues for a homology between offspring care and heroism. Next, Kristina Schmid Callina, Richard Lerner, Ettya Fremont, Brian Burkhard, Danielle Stacey, and Shaobing Su examine the formation of heroism from the perspective of human development. They introduce a relational developmental systems-based model that conceptualizes character in regard to mutually influential and mutually beneficial individual-context relations. The authors offer a model that may account for the emergence of leadership and heroism across diverse settings.

We next offer a chapter by Lawrence Walker, who explores aspects of the moral character of heroes that may help explain their extraordinary actions. Walker examines recipients of awards for moral action or historical figures who were notable for their moral character. His research findings indicate that the distinctive character of moral heroes clearly emerges from the data and that character is causally operative, supporting a dispositional explanation for their behavior and challenging a situational one. Next, Ari Decter-Frain, Ruth Vanstone, and Jeremy Frimer describe the motives and mechanisms underlying the tendency of groups to turn ordinary individuals into moral heroes. Followers give leaders titles and awards, encouraging leaders to give charismatic speeches that specify a threat, speak of sacrifice for sacred values, and contain themes of agency and communion. Our section on the origins of heroes concludes with a chapter by Olivia Efthimiou, who defines heroism as a distinct state of embodied consciousness accessible to all human agents in everyday lived experience. She maps out the *lived heroic body* across five spheres: the biological; the ecological; the social; the cultural; and the phenomenological. Efthimiou's chapter concludes with a transdisciplinary epistemological and methodological framework, the *hero organism*, which focuses on the development and functioning of the heroic embodied mind.

Types of Heroism

In Part II of this volume our contributors address phenomena associated with different categories of heroism and how these hero types affect individuals and society. Anna Halmburger, Anna Baumert, and Manfred Schmitt focus on everyday heroes to illustrate the phenomenon of moral courage. They distinguish moral courage from heroism and helping behavior, and they propose an integrative model of moral courage as well as practical implications for its promotion in organizations and society. Next, Zeno Franco shows us how disasters offer a rare chance to examine heroic leaders in action. His chapter takes a situationist perspective, offering theories of crisis as critical elements in understanding the dynamics that set the stage for leadership failure or daring success. Franco describes five specific tactics used repeatedly by crisis leaders, and he shows how these tactics distinguish good leaders from those who are truly heroic in the midst of disaster.

Next, Stephanie Fagin-Jones provides an overview of the social psychological research on the rescue of Jews by non-Jews during the Holocaust. She finds that rescuers were a demographically heterogeneous population who showed strong care-based moral courage. Their moral exemplarity was likely an ordinary extension under extraordinary circumstances of the natural progression of moral identities formed in childhood. Our next chapter, by Margaret Plews-Ogan, Justine Owens, Natalie May, and Monika Ardelt, addresses the topic of medical heroes. These scholars describe the journey of physicians who have made a medical error and who, rather than retreating, acknowledged their mistakes, reached out to care for the patient and family with honesty and humility, learned deeply from the experience, and allowed it to change them for the better. Next, Mihaly Csikszentmihalyi, Michael Condren, and Izabela Lebuda examine the heroism of social activists and dissident artists, with the goal of illuminating the role of social influence in the decision to engage in heroic behavior. Interviews with these heroes yielded support for the importance of role models in fostering epiphany moments, elevation, and empowerment for the activists, and in providing examples, initiators, and comrades for the artists.

Our next chapter, by Roderick Kramer, explores the antecedents and consequences of existential courage in the specific context of individuals' pursuits of desired but challenging identity attributes. Drawing from the results of a pilot study, Kramer identifies identity-relevant concerns students view as salient and significant, as well as experiments in existential risk-taking that students design to "nudge" themselves toward successful pursuit of those coveted identities. Next, Dana Klisanin shows us how digital connectivity and social media have forever altered the expression and potential for collaborative heroism. She describes various tools of collaboration in an age of transition from a mythos of exclusion, separation, and boundaries, into a mythos of inclusion, relationship, and openness. Klisanin portrays heroism as evolving, becoming more digital, complex, interdependent, collaborative, communal, and planetary.

We then present a chapter by Elsa Lau, Sarah Sherman, and Lisa Miller, who contribute an overview of work on spiritually-oriented leadership. These scholars review the intrapsychic, interpersonal, organizational, and societal implications that have been investigated up to date. They propose a model of core pedagogical mechanisms in spiritual leadership, and they introduce a spiritually-oriented academic training program that portrays the processes and outcomes of spiritually-oriented leadership and training. Next, Bryan Dik, Adelyn Shimizu, and William F. O'Connor explore the theoretical links between heroism, career development, and a sense of calling in one's work and career. These authors show how a sense of calling overlaps conceptually with heroism, and their analysis underscores the value of adapting an integrative approach to understanding the interaction of work environments and personal characteristics. Our section on types of heroes continues with a chapter by Joseph Vandello, Nadav Goldschmied, and Kenneth Michniewicz. These scholars address why people love to root for and venerate underdogs. Vandello and his colleagues evaluate various explanations for the underdog phenomenon, focusing on aversion to inequality and the belief in a just world, and they show how an understanding of underdogs informs our understanding of heroes.

In the final chapter in this section, A. J. Brown unpacks the conventional image of the whistleblower as an organizational or social hero. By reviewing when and why whistleblowers tend to be portrayed as heroes, he posits that we can begin to identify a more nuanced and useful approach to identifying what is (or can be) heroic about whistleblowing, and what may not be, or isn't. Given the very real prospect of unintended consequences, and even institutional and societal harm that whistleblowers might cause in an increasingly tightly-coupled world, this is a much-needed perspective.

Processes of Heroism

Part III of the *Handbook* examines the functions, processes, and consequences of heroism. This section begins with a chapter on the hero's transformation by Scott Allison and George Goethals. These authors argue that the hero's transformation is the most central yet most overlooked component of the hero's journey. They describe the many triggers, dimensions, processes, and consequences of the hero's transformation. Next, Amelia Goranson and Kurt Gray focus specifically on moral transformation. These scholars explore six different varieties of moral transformation. They argue that the route to heroism is not through extraordinary deeds, but through everyday acts of kindness that can change not only our mental character but also our physical power. We then present a chapter by Jeanne Nakamura and Laura Graham, who examine the impact of narratives of heroism on heroes themselves and on witnesses of heroism. These authors show how remembering stories of witnessed heroism elicits the moral emotion of elevation, and how feeling elevated, or uplifted, becomes the mechanism through which heroism changes those who observe heroic actions.

Next, Craig Parks reviews phenomena that can, and often do, suppress a person's impulse to act heroically. He distinguishes between *accidental* impediments, which arise as a result of social factors, and *purposeful* impediments, which arise when people desire to prevent victims from receiving relief from their plight. Parks concludes with a consideration of the distinction between thwarted heroism and cowardice. Ronald Humphrey and Laural Adams then explore the role of empathy in heroic leadership. These scholars review research on empathy that supports the empathy-altruism hypothesis, and they show how empathy explains why heroes take risks on behalf of others and make personal sacrifices for people. Humphrey and Adams also examine heroic empathy from a distributed cognition perspective that positions heroic leaders in the larger context of organization and systems. Next, Anika Stuppy and Nicole Mead elucidate how two central aspects of social hierarchies—status and power—influence heroic leadership. These scholars show how status and power are both *antecedents* of leadership and *individual motivations* reflecting different desires to obtain power or status. Stuppy and Mead's chapter encourages scholars to differentiate between power and status and investigate them as separate yet interacting constructs.

Our next chapter, by Kendall Cotton Bronk and Brian Riches, introduces a framework that outlines two ways that purpose and heroism overlap in the lives of real heroes. Drawing from two case studies, Bronk and Riches make an interesting and useful distinction between *purpose-guided heroism* and *heroism-guided purpose*. Next, Jeffrey Green, Daryl Van Tongeren, Athena Cairo, and Nao Hagiwara propose that meaning is a likely motivator of heroism as well as a natural consequence of heroic actions. These scholars discuss how virtues of humility, prosociality, self-control, and gratitude are relevant to heroism and meaning. Seeking meaning and affirmation of meaning via virtuous behavior may be a key to unlocking the latent hero that exists in all of us. Our next chapter, authored by Brett Murphy, Scott Lilienfeld, and Ashley Watts, focuses on the link between heroism and psychopathic traits. These scholars argue that some psychopathic traits can help us achieve success in life, and perhaps even allow us to act heroically when the situation calls for it. Their conclusion is that psychopathic traits may sometimes be conducive to heroism, or at the very least adaptive in some cases. We wrap up our Handbook with a chapter by Ronnie Janoff-Bulman and Prerana Bharadwaj, who address extended acts of morality that involve considerable personal risk. These authors argue that strong moral conviction may motivate heroism at the outset but may also develop gradually, even unwittingly, from more ordinary moral actions that transform motivation and justify increasingly costly, principled behavior. They conclude with some caveats regarding human tribalism and moral exclusion.

Looking Ahead: The Future of an Emerging Science

Hero worship ... cannot cease until man himself ceases.

(Thomas Carlyle)

It is our deepest hope, as scholars of pro-social behavior, that this inaugural *Handbook of Heroism and Heroic Leadership* offers you, the reader, some enjoyment, insights, and inspiration about the zenith of human behavior. In our view, the chapters in this volume have laid some sturdy foundations for the development of a multidisciplinary and even transdisciplinary perspective on the antecedents and consequences of heroic behavior. In aggregate, these chapters chart the landscape of what we currently know about heroism-related phenomena, covering a panoply of human experiences. The chapters encompass such diverse topics as courage, empathy, resilience, hope, meaning, purpose, spirituality, morality, altruism, character strengths, wisdom, development, regeneration, and transformation. Looking ahead, we anticipate future editions of this handbook will push the borders of our understanding even further, by going both deeper and broader in their inquiry. We imagine future volumes might separate the study of heroism per se from heroic leadership, perhaps into two different volumes. We can also envision future handbooks that splinter into specialized volumes corresponding to particular components of heroism, such as its evolutionary, biological, motivational, or cultural components. Attempting to peer into the crystal ball of heroism science might seem a futile endeavor, as the growth of this nascent field will no doubt spawn new research areas that we cannot even imagine today. We are encouraged, however, by the breadth of theoretical perspectives which have already been brought to bear on this enterprise, as well as the diversity of methodological approaches employed, and the distinctive kinds of empirical evidence they have spawned.

In a world that produces more than its share of bystander apathy and villainous behavior, we pause to rejoice that there are ample gifted and enlightened individuals whose behavior has embodied the most exquisite qualities of humanity. The world, as we know all too well, desperately needs heroes. We dedicate this handbook to all those who answer the call, to these awakened heroic individuals—past, present, and future. With equal appreciation, we wish to acknowledge those dedicated researchers who have taken on the challenge of furthering our understanding of the well-springs of such heroism and its impact. It is clear the embryonic science of heroism is off to a sound start and has a bright future ahead of it.

References

Allison, S. T., Beggan, J. K., & Midgley, E. H. (1996). The quest for "similar instances" and "simultaneous possibilities": Metaphors in social dilemma research. *Journal of Personality and Social Psychology*, 71, 479–497. doi: 10.1037/0022-3514.71.3.479

Allison, S. T., & Goethals, G. R. (2011). *Heroes: What they do and why we need them*. New York: Oxford University Press.

Allison, S. T., & Goethals, G. R. (2012). Personal versus cultural heroes. Retrieved from https://blog.richmond.edu/heroes/2012/09/12/personal-versus-cultural-heroes

Allison, S. T., & Goethals, G. R. (2014). "Now he belongs to the ages": The heroic leadership dynamic and deep narratives of greatness. In G. R. Goethals et al. (eds), *Conceptions of leadership: Enduring ideas and emerging insights*. New York: Palgrave Macmillan. doi: 10.1057/9781137472038.0011

Allison, S. T., & Goethals, G. R. (2016). Hero worship: The elevation of the human spirit. *Journal for the Theory of Social Behaviour*.

Allison, S. T., & Smith, G. (2015). *Reel heroes & villains*. Richmond, VA: Agile Writer Press.

Bandura, A. (1986). *Social foundations of thought and action: A social cognitive theory*. Englewood Cliffs, NJ: Prentice-Hall.

Bargh, J. A., & Ferguson, M. L. (2000). Beyond behaviorism: On the automaticity of higher mental processes. *Psychological Bulletin*, 126, 925–945.

Baumeister, R. F. (2010). *Is there anything good about men?* New York: Oxford University Press.

Baumeister, R. F. (2012). Human evil: The myth of pure evil and the true causes of violence. In R. F. Baumeister, M. Mikulincer, & P. R. Shaver (eds), *The social psychology of morality: Exploring the causes of good and evil* (pp. 367–380). Washington, DC: American Psychological Association. doi: 10.1037/13091-020

Becker, S. W., & Eagly, A. H. (2004). The heroism of women and men. *American Psychologist*, 59, 163–178.

Burns, J. M. (1978). *Leadership*. New York: Harper & Row.

Campbell, A. (1999). Staying alive: Evolution, culture, and women's intrasexual aggression. *Behavioral and Brain Sciences*, 22, 203–252.

Campbell, J. (1949). *The hero with a thousand faces*. New York: New World Library.

Campbell, J. (1972). *Myths to live by*. New York: Viking Press.

Campbell, J. (1988). *The power of myth*. New York: Anchor Books.

Carlyle, T. (1841). *Heroes, hero worship, and the heroic in history*. Philadelphia, PA: Henry Altemus.

Carneiro, R. L. (1981). Herbert Spencer as an anthropologist. *Journal of Libertarian Studies*, 5, 171–172.

Efthimiou, O. (2015). The search for a hero gene: Fact or fiction? *Heroism Science*, 1, 106.

Erikson, E. H. (1975). *Identity and the life cycle*. New York: W. W. Norton & Company.

Franco, Z. E., & Zimbardo, P. G. (2006). The banality of heroism. *The Greater Good*, 3, 30–35.

Franco, Z. E., Blau, K., & Zimbardo, P. G. (2011). Heroism: A conceptual analysis and differentiation between heroic action and altruism. *Review of General Psychology*, 15(2), 99–113. doi: 10.1037/a0022672

Freud, S. (1922). Group psychology and the analysis of the ego. In J. Strachey (ed.), *The standard edition of the complete works of Sigmund Freud, Vol. 28: Beyond the pleasure principle, group psychology, and other works*. London: Hogarth Press.

Goethals, G. R., & Allison, S. T. (2012). Making heroes: The construction of courage, competence and virtue. *Advances in Experimental Social Psychology*, *46*, 183–235. doi: 10.1016/B978-0-12-394281-4.00004-0

Goethals, G. R., & Allison, S. T. (2017). Transforming motives and mentors: The heroic leadership of James MacGregor Burns. In G. R. Goethals (ed.), *Politics, ethics and change: The legacy of James MacGregor Burns*. Northampton, MA: Edward Elgar Publishing.

Hollingdale, R. J. (2001). *Nietzsche: The man and his philosophy*. Cambridge, UK: Cambridge University Press (p. 102).

Hughes-Hallett, L. (2004). *Heroes*. London: HarperCollins.

James, W. (1878/1983). Brute and human intellect. In *Essays in psychology* (pp. 1–37). Cambridge, MA: Harvard University Press.

James, W. (1899). *Talks to teachers on psychology: And to students on some of life's ideals*. New York, NY: Henry Holt & Company.

Johnson, M. (2008). "What makes a body?" *The Journal of Speculative Philosophy*, *22*, 159–169. doi: 10.1353/jsp.0.0046

Kerrigan, M. J. (2015). Episodic vs. everyday heroes. Retrieved from http://characterbuildingproject.com/2015/12/14/3846/#.Vsk7hxh_3AE

Kinsella, E. L., Ritchie, T. D., & Igou, E. R. (2015a). Lay perspectives on the social and psychological functions of heroes. *Frontiers in Psychology*, *6*, 130. doi: 10.3389/fpsyg.2015.00130

Kinsella, E. L., Ritchie, T. D., & Igou, E. R. (2015b). Zeroing in on heroes: A prototype analysis of hero features. *Journal of Personality and Social Psychology*, *108*, 114–127.

Klapp, O. E. (1954). Heroes, villains and fools, as agents of social control. *American Sociological Review*, *19*, 56–62.

Kohen, A. (2013). Heroism and relativism. Retrieved from http://kohenari.net/post/53764408412/heroism-and-relativism

Kohen, A. (2014). Heroism and subjectivity. Retrieved from http://kohenari.net/post/99653156590/heroism-not-subjective

Kohen, A. (2015). *Untangling heroism: Classical philosophy and the concept of the hero*. New York: Routledge.

Kruger, D. J., Fisher, M., & Jobling, I. (2003). Proper and dark heroes as dads and cads: Alternative mating strategies in British Romantic literature. *Human Nature*, *14*, 305–317.

Lakoff, G., & Johnson, M. (2003). *Metaphors we live by*. London: University of Chicago Press.

Le Bon, G. (1895). *Psychology of crowds*. Southampton: Sparkling Books.

Leary, D. L. (1994). *Metaphors in the history of psychology*. Cambridge: Cambridge University Press.

Maslow, A. H. (1943). A theory of human motivation. *Psychological Review*, *50*, 370–396.

McPherson, J. M. (1992). *Abraham Lincoln and the second American Revolution*. New York: Oxford University Press.

Moxnes, P. (1999). Deep roles: Twelve primordial roles of mind and organization. *Human Relations*, *52*, 1427–1444.

Olson, J. M., & Haynes, G. A. (2008). Leadership and persuasion. In C. Hoyt, G. Goethals, & D. Forsyth (eds), *Leadership at the crossroads*. New York: Palgrave Macmillan.

People (2009). Pet hero! Parokeet saves choking toddler's life. *People*, March 24. Retrieved from www.peoplepets.com/people/pets/article/0,,20492258,00.html

Riggio, R. E., & Riggio, H. R. (2008). Social psychology and charismatic leadership. In C. L. Hoyt, G. R. Goethals, & D. R. Forsyth (eds), *Leadership at the crossroads, Vol. 1: Leadership and Psychology* (pp. 30–44). Westport, CT: Praeger.

Schein, S. (1984). *The mortal hero: An introduction to Homer's Iliad*. Berkeley, CA: University of California Press.

Schoenewolf, G. (2014). People who think their meanness is heroic. Retrieved from http://blogs.psychcentral.com/psychoanalysis-now/2014/12/people-who-think-their-meanness-is-heroic/

Schopenhauer, A. (1840). *On the basis of morality*. Indianapolis, IN: Hackett Publishing.

Tolstoy, L. (1869). *War and peace*. London: Penguin Classics.

TV Tropes (2016). The hero. Retrieved from http://tvtropes.org/pmwiki/pmwiki.php/Main/TheHero

Walker, L., & Frimer, J. (2007). Moral personality of brave and caring exemplars. *Journal of Personality and Social Psychology*, *93*, 845–860.

Weber, M. (2015/1919). Politics as Vocation. In T. Waters & D. Waters (eds), *Weber's Rationalism* (pp. 129–198). New York: Palgrave Macmillan.

Wood, W., & Eagly, A. H. (2002). A cross-cultural analysis of the behavior of women and men: Implications for the origins of sex differences. *Psychological Bulletin*, *128*, 699–727.

Zimbardo, P. (2011). What makes a hero? *The Greater Good* (January 11). Retrieved from http://greatergood.berkeley.edu/article/item/what_makes_a_hero

Zimbardo, P. (2015). *Philip Zimbardo on the two types of heroes.* Retrieved from http://bigthink.com/videos/those-who-resist-philip-zimbardo-on-the-two-types-of-heroes-2

Part I
Origins of Heroism

1

Attributes and Applications of Heroes

A Brief History of Lay and Academic Perspectives

Elaine L. Kinsella, Timothy D. Ritchie, and Eric R. Igou

Research on heroism typically seems fascinating to people in everyday life: they ask insightful and interesting questions about the research, offer their personal reflections on heroes, and sometimes share details of significant life events triggered by the conversation. Heroism is an approachable topic that appears to influence individuals and groups in extraordinary ways. Indeed, heroes have been described as "support for all human life and the inspiration of philosophy, poetry, and the arts" and function as "a vehicle for the profoundest moral and metaphysical instruction" (Campbell, 1949, p. 257). Campbell further suggests that the metaphors by which heroes live have been "brooded upon, searched, and discussed for centuries: they have served whole societies, furthermore, as the mainstays of thought and life" (p. 256).

Scholars convey similar ideas about the ways that heroes shape and represent culture (Hegel, 1801/1975), and act as source of social control (Klapp, 1954). Other philosophers highlight hero-worship as a way to re-establish meaning and idealism (Früchtl, 2009). Not only do heroes help people to survive physical dangers, but also they can evoke eudemonistic questions of "How should I live? What do I really want?" (Früchtl, 2009). Further still, individuals may seek to achieve symbolic immortality and a meaningful existence by worshiping the lives of their heroes (Becker, 1973). In an essay entitled "What makes a life significant?" William James wrote:

> What excites and interests the looker-on at life, what the romances and the statues celebrate and the grim civic monuments remind us of, is the everlasting battle of the powers of light with those darkness; with heroism, reduced to its bare chance, yet ever and anon snatching victory from the jaws of death.
>
> *(James, 1899, pp. 5–6)*

These influential writings about heroes hint about the psychological importance of heroes to individuals and groups, and are suggestive of the role heroes can play in movements, institutions, political regimes, historical periods, and everyday life (Klapp, 1954). However, until very recently the associated systematic empirical investigations have been scarce in the social science literatures.

Addressing this gap, contemporary social scientists have turned their attention to finding answers to important and unanswered empirical questions about heroes, such as: What are the most essential characteristics of a hero? Why are heroes important? What psychological and social functions do heroes provide to individuals and groups? How does heroism differ from altruistic behaviors? What are the conceptual differences between heroes, leaders, and role models? In this chapter, we highlight the contribution of psychology so far to our understanding of this ancient and complex subject.

First, we briefly summarize the existing research on heroism with particular focus on the audience for heroes, and their perception of hero characteristics and influence. Second, a new model, the hero functions framework (Kinsella, Ritchie, & Igou, 2015a), is presented and the three categories of psychological functions that heroes seem to fulfill for others are discussed. Third, we outline three areas that we believe should be prioritized when planning future research. Fourth, we provide examples of how to use citizen heroes as a tool for positive change in health, well-being, rehabilitation, and education contexts.

What is a Hero?

Heroes come in many forms: some real and some fictional. The term hero derives from the Greek word *heros*, meaning protector or defender. Historical views of heroism emphasize the importance of nobility of purpose or principles underlying a heroic act (see Zimbardo, 2007), but definitions of heroes have changed over generations. The term hero is used on a daily basis in the media (Sullivan & Venter, 2010) and many people readily name their personal heroes (Kinsella et al., 2015a). However, the term hero has been described as "radically ambiguous" in contemporary life (Gill, 1996, p. 98). For example, heroes have been described as those who reflect societal values (Campbell, 1949; Smith, 1976), provide standards of conduct (Pretzinger, 1976; Wecter, 1941), represent an ideal self-image (Caughey, 1984), in terms of their exceptional behavior, unusual merits or attainments (Boorstin, 1987; Klapp, 1954), and acting in an altruistic or courageous way despite physical risk (Becker & Eagly, 2004).

Becker and Eagly (2004), however, were criticized for narrowing the definition of hero to exclude heroism in the service of ideas (Martens, 2005). Heroes are also described as individuals concerned with protecting and promoting the well-being of future generations (McAdams, 2008). Schwartz (2009) describes heroes as individuals who demonstrate practical wisdom, showing the desire to do good for others and the capacity to do the right thing in a particular situation.

Franco, Blau, and Zimbardo (2011) distinguish between heroism and other prosocial behaviors, such as altruism: Heroism typically involves greater levels of risk and self-sacrifice, and unlike altruism, health benefits are rarely associated with heroism due to the high levels of personal sacrifice involved. Those authors note that heroes reliably choose a challenging particular course of action even when it may be psychologically easier to exit the situation (e.g., in the case of whistleblowers and political activists), whereas bystander intervention typically involves an actor who feels they have no psychological choice but to save, rescue, or help another person in an emergency situation (see Franco et al., 2011).

A number of scholars have suggested that a common heroic ideal exists (Jung, 1969; Allison & Goethals, 2011). To examine stereotypes of heroes, researchers refocused the meaning of heroism, by examining lay conceptions of heroes; a means to understand the defining features of heroism and how the term is applied in daily life (Allison & Goethals, 2011; Kinsella et al., 2015a; Sullivan & Venter, 2010). This approach converges with some of the central goals of empirical research; namely, construct conceptualization and quantification, method and results replication, and practical applications.

The first of such studies included pilot work with children to identify the characteristics of their preferred hero characters (Gash & Conway, 1997). The 24 characteristics derived from this work were: active, beautiful, brainy, brave, brilliant, caring, confident, dresses well, famous, friendly, funny, gentle, good, good-looking, helpful, honest, important, kind, loving, loyal, rich, skillful, strong and warrior. The children named heroes who originated from diverse domains such as family, film, TV, politics, community, religion, music, sport and other broad categories. It is interesting that children selected beautiful, famous, good-looking, and rich as important features of heroism. However, perhaps it is not surprising given that fairy tales, cartoons, or movies often portray good people and heroic figures as beautiful, pretty, or attractive (Eco, 2004; Klein & Shiffman, 2006). The findings from Gash and Conway (1997) indicate that children do show some bias, such that "beautiful people are good," or in this example, heroic. At a later developmental stage, children may develop an ability to acknowledge good and heroic behavior with less regard for a person's physical appearance, however adults do still have a tendency to assume that beautiful people possess more socially desirable traits (Dion, Berscheid, & Walster, 1972).

In another study, students based at a Catholic university in the USA were asked to define a hero and were provided with one half of a page to write an open response. Participants' responses were compared with six categories of hero definitions existing in the literature (see Sullivan & Venter, 2010, p. 437). Most commonly, participants defined heroes as "providing standards of conduct/being a role model" ($n = 81$) and "representing an ideal self-image" ($n = 85$). Fewer individuals defined heroes in terms of their accomplishments ($n = 57$), specific altruistic acts ($n = 48$), embodying social values ($n = 16$), or allowing individuals to vicariously reach new experiences ($n = 1$). Many persons' responses reflected how they relate to their hero, in other words, viewing the hero as a role model or viewing the hero as an idealized version of the self.

In a second study, Sullivan and Venter (2010) requested students recruited from a Southern Baptist university in the USA. Participants were asked to identify one of their heroes and to provide reasons to explain why this person is a hero. Participants were provided with 9 blanks for them to record their reasons as well as an example: "Hero: George Washington, US President; Reasons: Honest, intelligent, great leader, brave." Participants' responses were coded to account for synonyms or unique phrasing, and features were compiled according to frequency of each term's use. The results indicated that the participants described heroes as intelligent, loving, caring, talented, hardworking, a role model, creative, motivated, and religious (Sullivan & Venter, 2010). One wonders whether adults sampled from a secular setting would prioritize different hero features. The authors acknowledged that the example of George Washington may have primed participants to think and respond in a particular way, thus calling to question the validity of the list of hero features generated. The issue of using specific hero examples in research is a key methodological challenge facing hero researchers.

Allison and Goethals (2011) asked a sample of college students in the USA to list the traits that they believed described heroes. Next, a sample of students sorted the traits, identified in the first study, into groups based on how similar or different they thought the traits were to each other. Data analysis suggested eight trait clusters of heroes: smart, strong, caring, selfless, charismatic, resilient, reliable, and inspiring (the "Great Eight"; Allison & Goethals, 2011). One could argue that "loving" is an aspect of "selfless" and that "creative" is included in the "smart" category. The characteristics smart/intelligent and caring were also mentioned by Sullivan and Venter (2010), but the characteristics loving, talented, hardworking, a role model, creative, motivated, and religious did not appear in this more recent study. Given the discrepancies between the findings in the studies described above, one could wonder whether the differences were arising as a result of the different methods employed as well as the populations sampled. Further, one could ask whether non-USA and non-student samples respond similarly to the question, "what makes a hero?"

To address these questions we (Kinsella et al., 2015a) conducted seven independent studies using prototype methods, in an attempt to understand how people think about the characteristics of heroes, and to decipher how those features compare with leader and role model characteristics. The samples were drawn predominantly in Europe and the USA from community samples, online communities, and among student populations. Research on everyday social phenomena is dependent on the availability of a conceptual definition (Cronbach & Meehl, 1955). To meet this requirement, a theoretical definition must ensure rigor and coverage of the topic (Gregg, Hart, Sedikides, & Kumashiro, 2008). A method that balances both scientific rigor and captures the complexity of everyday phenomena is prototype analysis (e.g., Hassebrauck, 1997; Gregg et al., 2008). We employed this method to identify how a hero is viewed and to characterize the features that are more or less prototypical of that person.

In our studies, the first step was to generate open-ended descriptions of the *characteristics* of heroes and heroic behavior (Study 1, $n = 189$). These descriptions were later grouped together into 26 categories of hero features by independent coders to determine if such features were identical, semantically-related, or meaning-related. The second step was to identify which of these characteristics were most central to the concept of hero using a ratings scale method (Study 2, $n = 365$), a reaction time task (Study 3, $n = 33$), and a surprise recall task (Study 4, $n = 25$). The findings from these four studies indicate that the central features of heroes are: brave, moral integrity, conviction, courageous, self-sacrifice, protecting, honest, selfless, determined, saves others, inspiring, and helpful. Less common than the central features but frequently included peripheral features are: proactive, humble, strong, risk-taker, fearless, caring, powerful, compassionate, leadership skills, exceptional, intelligent, talented, and personable. Interestingly, the list of central and peripheral features represents characteristics that area stereotypically masculine (brave, protecting, strong, fearless) and female (helpful, selfless, caring, compassionate) which perhaps challenges a view that heroes are conceptualized in exclusively masculine terms. Next, in our Study 5 ($n = 89$) of that project, participants most strongly identified a hero when the target was described with central features (vs. peripheral or neutral features). The findings support the idea that people's conceptions of heroes are matched on the basis of a cognitive construction process (Goethals & Allison, 2012).

The third stage involved teasing apart the characteristics that were most closely associated with heroes when pitted against leaders or role models using rating scales. Both Study 6 ($n = 212$) and Study 7 ($n = 307$) indicated that the prototypical or central features of heroes did not fit conceptually as well for role models and leaders. In other words, heroes were more likely to be described as brave, showing moral integrity, saving others, willing to sacrifice, altruistic, compassionate, selfless, courageous, and protecting, than leaders or role models.

Lay conceptions of heroes encompass both planned, learned, controlled heroic everyday acts, as well as heroic acts that include spontaneous, involuntary, reactive, and unplanned acts. These findings suggest that participants (aged between 18 and 73 years), sampled predominantly in Europe and the USA, were able to communicate clear conceptual differences between heroes, leaders, and role models. What is particularly noteworthy is that lay conceptions of a hero, sampled across 25 different countries, reflect its original Homeric meaning—pertaining particularly to moral integrity, bravery, and self-sacrifice. Thus, a person described as brave, showing moral integrity, conviction, courage, self-sacrifice and who is willing to protect others is likely to evoke the schema of hero, if at least in Europe and the USA. It is interesting to note that lay theories about risk and personal sacrifice associated with heroes are consistent with previous concerns about the physical risk, financial consequences, loss of social status, social ostracism, or possible long-term health problems associated with heroic behavior (Franco et al., 2011; Glazer & Glazer, 1999; Shepela et al., 1999).

Participants described martial heroes, civil heroes, and social heroes (discussed later in this chapter; for full discussion see Franco et al., 2011) in their survey responses, and notably, both male and female heroes were named as personal heroes. While gender differences in conceptions of heroes were not apparent (both male and female participants agreed on the central characteristics of heroes), there were differences in participants' naming of their personal heroes. For instance, there was a slight tendency for participants to name female family members and lesser known or "unsung" heroes (e.g., mother, grandmother, teacher), as well a limited number of female social heroes (e.g., Rosa Parks, Aung San Suu Kyi). The male heroes named by participants tended to fit the more traditional stereotype of a hero that includes physical risk heroism (including both martial and civil heroism), superheroes (e.g., Batman, Spiderman, Iron Man), as well as famous heroes and political activists (e.g., Nelson Mandela, Martin Luther King). Cultural views about heroes are shifting and educational initiatives such as Giraffe Heroes Project (www.giraffe.org) and Moral Heroes (http://moralheroes.org) serve to remind audiences of the many inspirational examples of female and male heroes around the world.

Opportunities for explicit, implicit, or subliminal priming of heroic behavior are now possible using the central and peripheral characteristics of heroes. By means of various priming techniques, researchers can learn how to use heroes to influence individuals' physiological, cognitive, motivational, emotional, or behavioral responses. Future research could assess how priming people with heroic images or characteristics might influence their internal states, goals, and behavior. In fact, such techniques might also prime people to display their own heroic characteristics (e.g., strength, bravery, integrity, and self-sacrifice), if at least temporarily. We encounter positive caricatures and ideal forms of heroes in books, comics, television programs, movies or video games, however, little is known about the priming influence of these superheroes: How do these everyday heroic encounters shape our daily lives?

What about Warmth and Competence?

Warmth and competence are universal dimensions in person perception (Fiske, Cuddy, & Glick, 2006). Judgments about politicians and leaders, for example, typically involve perceptions of warmth and competence (Chemers, 2001). Deductions about heroes may also rely on these dimensions. The central and peripheral characteristics of heroes (Kinsella et al., 2015a) reveal that heroes are described as warm (and the closely related dimension of moral; Wojciszke, 2005) and competent (Fiske, Xu, Cuddy, & Glick, 1999). People who are judged to be warm and competent tend to evoke positive emotions and behavior in others (Fiske et al., 2006). Interestingly, admiration is the emotional response that people experience following an encounter with someone who is warm and competent (Cuddy, Glick, & Beninger, 2011), giving clues about the psychological influence of heroes. Some prototypical features of heroes map onto the dimensions of warmth (e.g., helpfulness, trustworthiness, moral integrity) and competence (e.g., intelligence, talent, exceptional). Other central heroic characteristics (e.g., protecting, self-sacrificing, saving, inspiring) fit less well within those two dimensions, reinforcing the idea that heroism is multi-dimensional and complex. Therefore, evidence of high morality/warmth and high competence are not sufficient for promotion to traditional hero status according to lay conceptions.

What are the Physical Characteristics of Heroes?

There may be particular physical characteristics associated with heroism. Research suggests that leaders who are taller, more attractive, and display a greater physique are more successful (Van Vugt & Ahuja, 2011); however, the physical features of heroic individuals are not well understood and need clarification. Research on face perception suggests that individuals make instantaneous facial judgments about other individuals and their intentions, often drawing conclusions about the trustworthiness of a person (Willis & Todorov, 2006). For instance, recent evidence suggests that men with wide faces tend to be more sacrificial (Stirrat & Perrett, 2012). Other studies have shown that facial width-to-height ratio can be used to judge aggressiveness (Carré, McCormick, & Mondloch, 2009). Do we make decisions about heroic or non-heroic people based on facial and other physical attributes? If so, to what extent do such attributes correspond with actual heroic behavior?

Anecdotal evidence suggests that heroes are often described as strong, larger-than-life, someone to look up to, and standing out from the crowd: each of these phrases suggest that, at least in abstract terms, individuals believe that heroes are larger than the average person. Heroes may appear larger due to their physical size or social size (fame, authority, prestige, social influence). This idea is consistent with research on embodiment by Landau and colleagues (2011), who found that exposure to an expanding physical image led participants to report higher levels of self-actualization. The relationship to heroism becomes clearer by considering the items of the Jones and Crandall's (1986) self-actualization scale that was used. Some of these items relate to feeling a sense of responsibility to help others, fearlessness, having a purpose in life and as such could be viewed as a proxy for heroism.

Similarly, physical size typically correlates with strength (Lakoff & Johnson, 1980); therefore, if people consider heroes as "larger than life" it is not surprising that associated adjectives of strength are common. These ideas are reiterated in heroic journeys of hardship and challenge (see Campbell, 1949), which call for physical and mental strength. Some heroes are known for their physical size but other heroes are celebrated for their mental strength and determination (e.g., Harriet Tubman, Rosa Parks). When an individual encounters a hero directly, they may feel overwhelmed by their extraordinary behaviors, stature, physique, or size resulting in an experience of awe and perceived vastness (Keltner & Haidt, 2003). Considering the physical attributes of popular heroic figures and embodied perceptions may prove a fruitful and interesting direction for future research.

There is likely to be a relationship between the features of heroes and the types of heroes that exist. Perhaps heroic features may be grouped together in a way that different types of heroes emerge. Next, we will turn our attention to examining different types of heroes.

Types of Hero

Three broad categories of heroes have been outlined in the literature (Franco et al., 2011): martial heroes, civil heroes, and social heroes. Some individuals, including police officers, firefighters and paramedics, are bound to a code of conduct where they are trained to protect and rescue others from danger, referred to as martial heroes. Civil heroes, or physical-risk, non-duty-bound heroes, also risk themselves for others but there is no military code or training to help them deal with the unfolding scenarios. An example of a civil hero could include a bystander performing an emergency rescue, in other words a Good Samaritan. Not all heroism involves immediate physical risk. For instance, social heroism is associated with serious personal sacrifices. Examples of social heroism include whistleblowers, scientific heroes, martyrs, Good Samaritans, underdogs, political figures, religious figures, adventurers, politico-religious figures, and bureaucratic heroes (Zimbardo, 2007). The prototypical features of heroes identified in our own research (Kinsella et al., 2015a) are relevant and applicable to almost all types of heroes. In fact, these central and peripheral features can be applied and used to describe each of the three broad heroic types, namely, martial heroism, civil heroism, and social heroism (Franco et al., 2011).

Taking a different position, Allison and Goethals (2013) have developed a detailed taxonomy of heroes differentiating heroes on the basis of the type of influence they have on others. The authors note that heroic influence can differ along various dimensions including weak–strong, short-term–long-term, widespread–limited, waxing–waning, hidden–exposed, or constructed–authentic (Allison & Goethals, 2013), and suggest ten subtypes of heroes. Trending heroes, for example, are those heroes whose impact is rising or falling. Examples of trending heroes include Lady Gaga and Arnold Schwarzenegger. Transitory heroes are those individuals who are deemed heroic and celebrated but quickly forgotten—Joe Darby, the whistleblower of Abu Ghraib, for example. Transitional heroes are those are particularly influential in our lives during particular phases of development. Examples of transitional heroes include Iron Man and Captain James T. Kirk. Tragic heroes are those whose character failings bring about his or her downfall. Famous examples of tragic heroes include Tiger Woods and Oedipus the King. Transposed heroes are described as individuals who are heroes or at least appear to be heroes, but then convert to villain status (e.g., Harvey Dent). Transparent heroes are those individuals who humbly perform heroic deeds outside of the public spotlight. Examples of transparent heroes include supporting cast in hero narratives and many parents. In one of their studies, Allison and Goethals found that 65 percent of the heroes were perceived to be transparent heroes. Transparent heroes are everyday heroes such as nurses, teachers, fire fighters, first respondents in emergency situations, whose achievements often remain unnoticed.

Traditional heroes, according to Allison and Goethals (2013), are those individuals who come from humble origins, experience early setbacks, and receive assistance from unlikely sources, overcome obstacles, and returns with gifts to society, akin to the classic hero journal described by Campbell (1949). Examples of traditional heroes include the Dalai Lama and Irena Sendler. According to Allison and Goethals' research, traditional heroes made up only 13 percent of their participants' hero choice. Transfigured heroes are those who are declared heroic despite only partial evidence to determine whether their status has been exaggerated (e.g., Amelia Earhart, Sherlock Holmes). Transforming heroes are those individuals whose actions have transformed the hero and the society in which they live (Mahatma Gandhi, Nelson Mandela). Finally, there are transcendent heroes who are made up of a mixture of the subtypes of the taxonomy. Examples of transcendent heroes include Jesus of Nazareth and Harry Potter. This taxonomy highlights the diversity of heroes, and the next step then is to identify exactly how heroes act as agents of social influence, and to use this taxonomy to help structure the process.

Functions of Heroes

On an individual level, heroes can be viewed as norms for social comparison where individuals can emulate (e.g., observing the charitable work of Mother Teresa and looking for opportunities to volunteer in one's local charity shop) or avoid (e.g., observing a bystander emergency rescue and then seeking to avoid putting one's own life at risk in the future by putting in place better safety processes and equipment in the workplace) their behavior (Klapp, 1954). Individuals rarely live up to the standards of the hero, according to Klapp, but they do benefit from affirming themselves vicariously through their personal heroes. On a group level, Klapp suggests that heroes organize and simplify collective responses by enlisting interest in causes and creating mass followings, heightening a sense of "we," and strengthening morale by focusing collecting efforts and complexities on one individual.

Groups of people may draw together to praise and support a hero, which reaffirms group values. Heroes may also perpetuate collective values and socially necessary virtues (such as courage, self-sacrifice, hatred of evil) across generations. In fact, Klapp (1954) describes a hero as an heirloom, a symbol or metaphor for values and codes of behavior that can be passed on to others. More recently, Allison and Goethals (2015) proposed the heroic leadership dynamic, a framework that describes both the epistemic (i.e., imparting knowledge and wisdom to others) and energizing (i.e., inspiring and promoting personal growth) functions of heroes. Each of these potential functions, for groups and individuals, seem plausible and fascinating, and complement our own ideas and research about heroic functions (see Kinsella, Ritchie, & Igou, 2015b). In our own analyses of writings about heroes in philosophy, sociology, and psychology, the functions of heroes tend to map onto three key areas of influence: uplifting and enhancing the lives of others (Klapp, 1954; Algoe & Haidt, 2009; Cialdini, 2007), modeling morals and values (Carlyle, 1840; Pretzinger, 1976; Cohen, 1993; Flescher, 2003; Schwartz & Schwartz, 2010), and protecting others from physical or psychological harm (Becker, 1973; Hobbs, 2010; Goethals & Allison, 2012).

To our knowledge, the first psychological study on this topic was conducted by Gash and Conway in 1997 with children (mostly aged between 9 and 10 years) in an attempt to understand what *functions* heroes provide to others, and the results were as follows: to entertain, to be the best at what they do, to give a good example, to do good, to protect against bad things, to risk their lives for others, to show how well things can be done, and there was an open-ended category (full details not provided). While interpreting these responses it is worth noting that the children sampled by Gash and Conway (1997) were most likely operating at the pre-conventional and conventional levels of moral development (see, for example, Kohlberg, Levine, & Hewer, 1983). The children's responses reflect heroes as figures of authority on good behavior and viewing heroes as a means of promoting interpersonal harmony, rather than representing more abstract principles of social contracts and universal ethical principles (a stage of moral development that typically occurs later in life). Some children may have selected celebrities or sports players as their personal heroes, which in turn influenced their descriptions of heroic functions (for instance, to entertain others). In our view, many celebrities and sports players entertain others, as well as serving as (positive or negative) role models for others, yet few of those well-known individuals display qualities such as bravery, moral integrity, conviction, courage, and self-sacrifice, which are central characteristics of heroism (Kinsella et al., 2015a). A number of the functions identified by these elementary school children relate to themes of enhancing, modeling morals, and protecting others (consistent with our literature review), and spurred us to begin our own investigations of heroic functions.

Building on this work, we designed and conducted four studies in an attempt to identify lay perspectives about the psychological functions provided by heroes (Kinsella et al., 2015b). As part of our initial research project, we asked participants (n = 189) to share open-ended descriptions of hero *functions*, which were then sorted by independent coders into 14 categories, including to instill hope, to guide others, to improve morale, and to act against evil or danger. In Study 2, participants (n = 249) rated how each function resembled their personal views about heroes. Both exploratory and confirmatory factor analysis techniques revealed that a three-factor model of hero functions fit the data well: Participants described how heroes enhanced the lives of others, promoted morals, and protected individuals from threats (themes that we had previously identified in the literature). In Study 3 (n = 242), participants rated heroes as more likely to provide a protecting function than either leaders or role models. In Studies 4a (n = 38) and 4b (n = 102), participants indicated that thinking about a hero (compared to a leader or an acquaintance) during psychological threat fulfilled enhancement, moral modeling, and protection needs, as predicted by the three-factor model (we call the hero functions framework).

The Hero Functions Framework

Our analysis of the literature and empirical studies (see Kinsella et al., 2015b) provided support to the idea that hero functions can be mapped into three categories: Uplifting and enriching the lives of others (*enhancing*), promoting morals and virtues (*moral modeling*), and protecting individuals from physical or psychological threats (*protecting*): Together these ideas posit the hero functions framework.

- **Enhancing.** Lay persons describe the enhancing function of heroes: to motivate, to be a role model, to inspire, to instill hope, to improve morale and camaraderie, and to guide others. Heroes boost, energize, and inspire us (e.g., the energizing function of heroes; Allison & Goethals, 2015), and likely boost positive emotions such as awe, gratitude, or admiration (Algoe & Haidt, 2009). People experience positivity when they feel a part of their hero's exceptional accomplishments (Allison & Goethals, 2011) and while basking in their reflected glory (Cialdini, 2007). Heroes raise awareness of ought selves and ideal selves (Klapp, 1969), perhaps occasionally motivating individuals toward being a better person.

- **Moral modeling.** We noted earlier that previous hero definitions describe them as modeling the values and virtues of society (Carlyle, 1840) and acting as comparison targets for the masses (Pretzinger, 1976), consistent with the moral modeling function of heroes. Heroes impart wisdom by supplying mental models or scripts for how one could, or should, lead one's life (epistemic function of heroes; Allison & Goethals, 2015), as well as helping people to understand the norms and values within society (Erikson, 1977; Cohen, 1993). Heroes prompt people to do what they can for those who need help (Flescher, 2003). Heroes are moral exemplars and although it may not be realistic to imitate heroes that show moral fortitude, the encounter may trigger a moment of reflection where the individual questions their moral decision-making and behaviors, avoiding moral complacency (Flescher, 2003).
- **Protecting.** Consistent with the etymology of the word, heroes are protectors (Becker & Eagly, 2004) and our research suggests that heroic functions reflect this theme: protecting, doing what no one else will, helping, saving, guiding, and acting against evil or danger (Kinsella et al., 2015b). Some philosophers and psychologists have alluded to the idea that heroes protect against threats to perceptions about one's own meaning or purpose in life. For example, Hobbs (2010) suggested that heroes offer resources to adults who feel dejected. Heroes who represent cultural values and norms may also serve as a resource for dealing with threats to uncertainty, meaning, or other existential dilemmas (Becker, 1973).

The hero functions framework organizes existing information about hero functions, and enables researchers and practitioners to generate hypotheses about the influence of heroes on individuals and groups. The next step is to consider the extent that heroes enhance, protect, and provide moral guidance in a variety of controlled laboratory settings. For instance, researchers could design an intervention where individuals are requested to think, read, or write about a hero every day over time and monitor changes in their levels of enhancement (e.g., using measures of positive affect, motivation, inspiration), moral guidance (e.g., using measures of ethics and integrity, moral decision making), and protection (e.g., using measures of depression, anxiety, meaningfulness, perceived control, and mortality salience) over time. Besides analyzing the effectiveness of heroes in providing these functions, the extent that heroes affect people in everyday life is an interesting point of inquiry for future researchers.

In Allison and Goethals' (2013) taxonomy of heroes, transparent heroes are the "nurturers" of society: heroic individuals who appear in the roles of nurses, teachers, coaches, and mentors who each guide us somehow and aim to clarify how we heal, learn, succeed, and be good persons and citizens. Their contributions tend to go unrecognized and remain unsung because nurturing and enhancing activities are less newsworthy than the more glamorous and attention-grabbing protecting activities. Future research might conduct careful analyses using these complementary frameworks about which type of heroes (e.g., transitory heroes, traditional heroes, transparent heroes) provide greater enhancing, moral modeling and protecting functions, and whether these hypothesized effects differ by individuals (e.g., strength of identification with hero, perceived similarity to hero) and differ by groups (e.g., shared group membership, identification with group represented by hero). If this distinction of hero-intervention is supported empirically, the model could be applied to school curricula, psychotherapy, rehabilitation and elsewhere. More broadly, future researchers may opt to study the role of heroic individuals and how their stories communicate moral messages within a given culture.

Heroism Research: Some Questions

Building on these findings, there are many opportunities for interesting and useful research and applications about heroes. For instance, there is a need for more global cross-cultural research on heroism, and a closer examination of the vicissitudes of the Western bias in heroism research. In the past and occasionally in the present, the term hero was synonymous with the masculine and masculinity, generally. An important direction for future research is to clarify the extent that gender bias impacts upon how researchers perceive hero concepts, measures, and applications. Heroism research remains a nascent discipline and as such it can be difficult to determine how to priorities research resources when so many avenues are unexplored. Next, we outline three areas of research that we believe should be prioritized.

Individual Differences and Hero Identification

One study found that people who rated themselves higher on integrity also chose heroes who were characterized by principled commitment, authenticity, beneficence towards others, non-self-absorption, and spirituality (Schlenker, Weigold, & Schlenker, 2008). The authors adopted the following definition: integrity is the steadfast adherence to a strict moral or ethical code (taken from the *American Heritage Dictionary*). People who self-reported with lower integrity (e.g., putting profits over telling the truth, willing to compromise principles for possible gain) evaluated their hero as intelligent, likeable, and similar to them. The authors concluded that the people with higher (vs. lower) levels of integrity use different criteria to judge the actions of others and decide whom to admire. Furthermore, when asked to judge the behavior of a central character, participants who were higher on integrity were guided by principles (ethical/not-ethical) rather than the outcome (successful/not-successful).

These findings suggest that people who claim greater commitment to ethical principles are more likely to admire heroes with similarly high standards for integrity and values, even if the hero's efforts are not objectively successful. Also, the authors proposed that people with heroes who model high moral standards are more likely to adopt their hero's ethical ideologies and emulate the hero's behavior. Further research needs to be carefully designed to assess the extent that individual differences influences judgments about heroic figures, and also, the extent that hero identification may actually influence judgments about the self.

Indeed, humility varies from person to person: some individuals may feel humble more often than others. Humility includes an understanding of oneself through awareness of personal identities, strengths and limitations, as well as perspective of the self's relationship with others (Nielsen, Marrone, & Slay, 2010). Humility enables a realistic assessment of one's strengths and weaknesses (Ryan, 1983). Heroes often deny their own heroic status, saying they just did what needed to be done or did what anyone would do in that situation, modeling humility (e.g., Worthington, 2007; heroes of humility). In our own research, humility is one of the defining characteristics of heroism (Kinsella et al., 2015a).

Furthermore, we believe that encounters with heroes who display extraordinary behaviors sometimes induce humility in onlookers. Humble individuals may seek out heroes in order to experience humility. For others, encounters with heroes are likely to provoke a humble state, at least temporarily. When experiencing humility as a result of a heroic encounter the individual may be more likely to get an accurate sense of self (instigating a period of self-focus; Bryant & Veroff, 2007) than they would experience in their usual daily lives without a heroic encounter. This shift of perspective may help to motivate the individual towards personal goals and make people aware of what they need to do to achieve their own success. Future research could consider the match and associations between types of heroes and individual preference for heroes, and hero effectiveness as a function of the match.

Self-Discrepancies and Regulatory Focus

Mark Twain (1835–1910) famously claimed, "If everybody was satisfied with himself, there would be no heroes," expressing unfulfilled needs that are projected onto others. The idea of regulatory foci has origins in self-discrepancy theory (Higgins, 1987) which suggests that during a person's life, self-guides (ideal or ought) are formed and provide the basis for self-assessment. One's own ought self may tend to represent the duties and obligations that a person feels that they should be going in the present. A discrepancy between one's actual self and ought self sometimes results in negative, self-focused affect is likely to ensue (rumination, anxiety). Conceptualizations of the ideal self tend to be associated with the achievements and aspirations of the individual. When a discrepancy between actual and ideal self occurs, a person will experience a sense of loss, such as rumination, depression and disappointment. Heroes may remind some individuals about an ideal self or an ought self, motivating us to keep striving to pursue personal goals.

For instance, according to regulatory focus theory (Higgins, 1987) individuals are typically driven to strive towards making good things happen, maximizing gains (promotion focus) or to avoid opportunities for negative events to occur, minimizing threats (prevention focus). These two orientations influence the behaviors, emotions, cognitions, and preferences of individuals and may also provide a useful lens for examining people's identification with heroes. For example, individuals with a promotion focus may be more attracted to heroes who show attributes that are similar to their ideal self. Promotion-focused individuals are concerned with values, ideals, goals, which in turn could provoke associations with accomplishment, advancement, and nurturance; however, individuals with prevention focus may be more likely to choose a hero that reduces the discrepancy between ought and actual self—such heroes are likely to represent safety, security, duties, and obligations.

Heroic Influence: A Case of Upward Social Comparison?

Social comparison theory (Festinger, 1954) suggests that individuals often look to other individuals as a reference for comparing one's own behavior. Downward social comparisons involve comparing the self to a person who is considered worse than one's self on some attribute. Upward social comparison, on the other hand, involves comparing oneself to someone else whose abilities and attributes are better than one's self. It is often through upward social comparisons that individuals improve themselves and learn how to perform like those who are more knowledgeable, skilled or experienced (Butler, 1992; Helgeson & Mickelson, 1995; Taylor, Neter, & Wayment, 1995; Wood, 1989).

Self-improvement is one of the four central processes, along with self-enhancement, self-assessment, and self-verification, each part of the self-system, operating together to promote well-being and social functioning (Sedikides & Strube, 1997; Gaertner, Sedikides, & Cai, 2012). People actively pursue upward social comparisons when pursuing self-improvement goals. For instance, dieters have placed images of thinner individuals on the refrigerator to remember dietary goals and desired changes (Helgeson & Taylor, 1993). The decision to actively seek upward social comparisons occurs when the available comparison provides important learning benefits in relation to motives. In such circumstances, exposure to successful others (including heroes), can be motivational, inspiring, and mood elevating (Taylor & Lobel, 1989). Social comparisons must be "cognitively digested, actively worked on, and made sense of" (Collins, 1996, p. 66) and in doing so, the individual can consciously prevent upward social comparisons from hurting evaluations about the self. For example, one might expect that social comparisons with heroes might result in feeling bad about the self (e.g., "I could never go through the hardship encountered by Aung San Suu Kyi in her pursuit of democracy in Burma") or perhaps instead one decides to feel inspired by her efforts and decide to show more courage and determination modestly in one's own daily life.

Additional research will need to uncover the extent to which the positive influence of heroes can be explained by contemporary ideas about social comparisons. Key factors, such as personal relevance, closeness to the self (Tesser, 1988), shared social identity, and individual differences need to be carefully assessed. Our observations suggest that heroes may sometimes trigger a period of self-focus and self-improvement goals, but at other times heroes trigger an outward focus, where the individual is more concerned with others than the self (world-focused; Bryant & Veroff, 2007); however, this has not been investigated empirically.

Heroes Applied: Some Examples

As much of the previous sections have focused on theory and the conceptualization of heroic attributes, the aim of the next section is to focus on the pragmatic and usefulness of heroism research, particularly the many functions that heroic individuals provide to others. There are numerous examples of practical applications for heroes in health, education, rehabilitation and organizational settings.

Heroes for Health, Well-being, and Rehabilitation

Given the multiple positive psychological benefits that people can gain from interacting with and thinking about heroes, there is great potential to create interventions that promote positive emotions, well-being, growth, creativity, and social connections. Indeed, studies have shown that failing to adequately cope with stressful life events contributes to a variety of clinical disorders (Kross, Davidson, Weber, & Ochsner, 2009) and impedes subjective well-being (Ritchie, Sedikides, Wildschut, Arndt, & Gidron, 2011). Knowledge about the ways in which people use heroes to self-regulate (e.g., using a personal hero as a metaphor to help a client to make links between values, goals, and behaviors) may be important for people who work in mental healthcare, such as psychotherapists. Broadly, the findings from the present research could be used to inform clinical therapists and those who work in mental healthcare, such as to refine psychological interventions that aim to decrease personal negativity and also promote psychological well-being and positive affect.

For instance, broad-minded affective coping (BMAC; Tarrier, 2010) is a technique that builds on Fredrickson's (1998) broaden-and-build theory. The BMAC approach aims to promote positive emotions by prompting individuals to recall positive autobiographical memories for their own lives. Even brief, transient experiences of positive emotions have been found to increase resilience (measured one month later), suggesting a role for clinical interventions that foster positive affect. An adapted BMAC technique would focus specifically on those autobiographical memories that involve encounters with heroic persons. Such positive memorial activity may prompt individuals to feel a greater sense of protection (from negative feelings), and enhancement of positivity towards self and humanity, in addition to positive affect, generally.

Another approach, appreciative inquiry (e.g., Johnson & Leavitt, 2001; Martinetz, 2002), encourages individuals, organizations, or communities to contemplate and extend their most effective behaviors or practices rather than dwelling on the problems. The aim of this technique is to focus on the stories, metaphors, or symbols that inspire hope, change, purpose, joy, camaraderie, compassion, and innovation (e.g., Fitzgerald, Murrell, & Miller, 2003). Such aims are associated closely to the characteristics and functions of heroic influences. Appreciative inquiry opposes other approaches that focus on problems and difficulties; indeed, negative foci can reduce motivation and persistence (e.g., Whitney, 1998). Extending appreciative inquiry further, individuals could be asked to contemplate heroic qualities or actions that they have witnessed in others or in themselves, and then share these observations with others. Individuals or groups work together to formulate plans to utilize, share, and remember these uplifting initiatives and practices. For instance, initiatives that promote gratitude promote positive emotions and psychological well-being (e.g., Seligman, Steen, Park, & Peterson, 2005). As a personal development exercise, a person might write a letter of gratitude to each of the heroic people who have entered their lives. Such expressive writing may increase gratitude, which promotes emotion regulation (e.g., Pennebaker & Chung, 2011) and ultimately could boost psychological well-being.

Metaphoric identity mapping (MIM; Ylvisaker, McPherson, Kayes, & Pellett, 2008) is an approach to identity construction and goal setting that draws upon theories of possible selves (Markus & Nurius, 1986), metaphors, and interacting cognitive subsystems (Barnard, 1985). This approach was designed to help survivors of acquired brain injury (ABI), such that individuals with brain injuries could construct a new sense of identity, in part, by identifying a hero that unifies the self and offers a sense of emotional power to their strong characteristics, and opens up action strategies associated with the identity schema (Ylvisaker et al., 2008). The action strategies purportedly identify meaningful and realistic goals, overcome resistance and other obstacles that the individual is struggling with. One advantage of MIM is that the heroic metaphor unites the elements of a person's cognitive representation of the self into an organized unit of thought (e.g., hero, symbol, metaphor), helping them to effectively encode and retrieve this information in memory.

Heroes for Education and Socio-Cultural Change

In educational settings, heroes can inspire, motivate, and offer moral guidance to students of all ages. For instance, the Hero Construction Company (www.heroconstruction.org) and the Heroic Imagination Project (http://heroicimagination.org) offer classroom presentations, educational modules, and large group assemblies that convey stories, images, and interactive discussion about heroes. These initiatives aim to convince young students that they too are "heroes in waiting" and that they have the potential to behave heroically—showing bravery, self-sacrifice, moral integrity—when the situation arises. Teaching students and teachers about the characteristics of heroes and sharing examples of heroic behavior may help them to increase awareness of heroism. Images, videos, classroom discussions, keywords or quotes (i.e., environmental cues) could be strategically placed around the immediate and virtual learning environments. New creative initiatives in schools, colleges, and universities could be designed in an effort to promote and celebrate heroic behaviors. Given our research findings that indicate that heroes can sometimes provide many social and psychological benefits, it seems reasonable to encourage faculty, teachers, educators, instructors, and students to identify and learn about heroes.

On a related note, the explicit instruction about the bystander effect, groupthink, and other social psychological phenomena that result in poor decision-making could increase the likelihood that individuals take action to intervene, to prevent potential malfeasance and even thwart disaster. If heroes represent virtuous traits such as strength, bravery, integrity, doing what no-one else will, protecting others, and showing leadership qualities, then such qualities are worthy of modelling to our young people. Furthermore, action research (Lewin, 1946) or participatory action research on specific hero-related topics (e.g., speaking out against bullying, speaking out against wrong-doing) could be useful, such as educating children about relevant skills for solving real-life problems.

Historically, heroes have played an important role in inter-group conflict scenarios, particularly those involving racial, political, and religious tensions. Heroic figures, such as Martin Luther King, Rosa Parks, Mahatma Gandhi, Aung San Suu Kyi, and Nelson Mandela, have each been instrumental in influencing conflict scenarios. Indeed, a variety of heroes may be powerful and influential in different types of public crises and across historical eras (see Klapp, 1969). Perhaps learning from the past, we could assess what heroes are needed to reduce tension between groups and increase co-operation. There are heroic figures of the past that seemed useful; however, more research is needed to elucidate how historical heroes can influence the present and the future.

Conclusions

Heroes exemplify rare agentic and moral virtues. Heroes can be spatio-temporally remote, even dead, and yet these figures continue to influence the lives of others. Despite the power of heroic figures to act as a positive and everyday source of influence, heroes are currently an underused resource in health, education, and rehabilitation settings. In this chapter, we examined the literature and recent research, considered the practical and theoretical implications for understanding heroes and their influences on individuals, and we suggested ways to use this information to create new hero initiatives. We are honored to be part of the growing collective of researchers who are passionate about the empirical study of heroism, and hope that our chapter will inspire other researchers to continue this exciting advancement of ideas and practices. We hope that this chapter will provoke self-reflection among readers, regarding their own potential for heroic behavior and ability to recognize and celebrate in the heroic behavior that exists around them: "Wishing for heroism and the spectacle of human nature on the rack, I had never noticed the great fields of heroism lying round about me, I had failed to see it present and alive" (James, 1899).

References

Algoe, S., & Haidt, J. (2009). Witnessing excellence in action: The other-praising emotions of elevation, admiration, and gratitude. *Journal of Positive Psychology, 4*, 105–127. doi: 10.1080/17439760802650519
Allison, S. T., & Goethals, G. R. (2011). *Heroes: What they do and why we need them.* New York: Oxford University Press.
Allison, S. T., & Goethals, G. R. (2013). *Heroic leadership: An influence taxonomy of 100 exceptional individuals.* Abingdon: Routledge.
Allison, S. T., & Goethals, G. R. (2015) Hero worship: The elevation of the human spirit. *Journal for the Theory of Social Behaviour.* doi: 10.1111/jtsb.12094.
Barnard, P. (1985). Interacting cognitive subsystems: A psycholinguistic approach to short-term memory. In A. Ellis (ed.), *Progress in the Psychology of Language* (pp. 197–258). Hove, UK: Lawrence Erlbaum Associates Ltd.
Becker, E. (1973). *The denial of death.* New York: Simon & Schuster.
Becker, S. W., & Eagly, A. H. (2004). The heroism of men and women. *American Psychologist, 59*, 163–178. doi: 10.1037/0003-066X.59.3.163
Boorstin, D. J. (1987). *The image: A guide to pseudo-events in America.* New York: Vintage Books.
Bryant, F. B., & Veroff, J. (2007). *Savoring: A new model of positive experience.* Mahwah, NJ: Lawrence Erlbaum Associates.
Butler, R. (1992). What young people want to know when: Effects of mastery and ability goals on interest in different kinds of social comparisons. *Journal of Personality and Social Psychology, 62*, 934–943.
Campbell, J. (1949). *The hero with a thousand faces.* Princeton, NJ: Princeton University Press.
Carlyle, T. (1840). *On heroes, hero-worship and the heroic in history.* London: Chapman & Hall.
Carré, J. M., McCormick, C. M., & Mondloch, C. J. (2009). Facial structure is a reliable cue of aggressive behaviour. *Psychological Science, 20*, 1194–1198. doi: 10.1111/j.1467-9280.2009.02423.x.
Caughey, J. L. (1984). *Imaginary social worlds: A cultural approach.* Lincoln, NE: University of Nebraska Press.
Chemers, M. M. (2001). Leadership effectiveness: An integrative review. In M.A. Hogg & R.S. Tindale (eds), *Blackwell handbook of social psychology: Group processes* (pp. 376–399). Oxford, UK: Blackwell.
Cialdini, R. B. (2007). *Influence: The psychology of persuasion.* New York: Collins.
Cohen, S. (1993). Lessons in moral behaviour: A few heroes. *Childhood Education* (Spring), 168–170.
Collins, R. L. (1996). For better or worse: The impact of upward social comparison on self-evaluations. *Psychological Bulletin, 119*, 56–69. doi: 10.1037/0033-2909.119.1.51

Cronbach, L. J., & Meehl, P. E. (1955). Construct validity in psychological tests. *Psychological Bulletin, 52*, 281–302.

Cuddy, A. J. C., Glick, P., & Beninger, A. (2011). The dynamics of warmth and competence judgements, and their outcomes in organisations. *Research in Organizational Behaviour, 31*, 73–98. doi: 10.1016/j.riob.2011.10.004

Dion, K. K., Berscheid, E. & Walster, E. (1972). What is beautiful is good. *Journal of Personal and Social Psychology, 24*, 285–290.

Erikson, E. H. (1977). *Toys and reasons: Stages in the ritualization of experience.* London, UK: Marion Boyars.

Eco, U. (2004). *On beauty: A history of a Western idea.* London: Secker & Warburg.

Festinger, L. (1954). A theory of social comparison processes. *Human Relations, 7*, 117–140. doi: 10.1177/001872675400700202

Fiske, S. T., Cuddy, A. J. C., & Glick, P. (2006). Universal dimensions of social cognition: warmth and competence. *Trends in Cognitive Science, 11*(2), 77–83.

Fiske, S. T., Xu, J., Cuddy, A. J. C., & Glick, P. (1999). (Dis)respecting versus (dis)liking: Status and interdependence predict ambivalent stereotypes of competence and warmth. *Journal of Social Issues, 55*, 473–489.

Fitzgerald, S. P., Murrell, K. L., & Miller, M. G. (2003). Appreciative inquiry: Accentuating the positive. *Business Strategy Review, 14*, 5–7.

Flescher, A. M. (2003). *Heroes, saints, and ordinary morality.* Washington, DC: Georgetown University Press.

Franco, Z., Blau, K., & Zimbardo, P. (2011). Heroism: A conceptual analysis and differentiation between heroic action and altruism. *Review of General Psychology, 5*(2), 99–113. doi: 10.1037/a0022672

Fredrickson, B. L. (1998). What good are positive emotions? *Review of General Psychology, 2*, 300–319. doi: 10.1037/1089-2680.2.3.300

Früchtl, J. (2009). *The impertinent self: A heroic history of modernity.* Stanford, CA: Stanford University Press.

Gaertner, L., Sedikides, C., & Cai, H. (2012). Wanting to be great and better but not average: On the pancultural desire for self-enhancing and self-improving feedback. *Journal of Cross-Cultural Psychology, 43*, 521–526. doi: 10.1177/0022022112438399

Gash, H., & Conway, P. (1997). Images of heroes and heroines: How stable? *Journal of Applied Developmental Psychology, 18*, 349–372. doi: 10.1016/S0193-3973(97)80005-6

Gill, C. (1996). *Personality in Greek epic, tragedy and philosophy: The self in dialogue.* Oxford, UK: Clarendon Press.

Glazer, M. P., & Glazer, P. M. (1999). On the trail of courageous behavior. *Sociological Inquiry, 69*, 276–295. doi: 10.1111/j.1475-682X.1999.tb00503.x

Goethals, G. R., & Allison, S. T. (2012). Making heroes: The construction of courage, competence and virtue. *Advances in Experimental Social Psychology, 46*, 183–235. doi: 10.1016/B978-0-12-394281-4.00004-0

Gregg, A. P., Hart, C. M., Sedikides, C., & Kumashiro, M. (2008). Everyday conceptions of modesty: A prototype analysis. *Personality and Social Psychology Bulletin, 34*, 978–992. doi: 10.1177/0146167208316734

Hassebrauck, M. (1997). Cognitions of relationship quality: A prototype analysis of their structure and consequences. *Personal Relationships, 4*, 163–186. doi: 10.1111/j.1475-6811.1997.tb00137

Hegel, G. W. F. (1801/1975). *Aesthetics: Lectures on fine art.* Oxford, UK: Clarendon Press.

Helgeson, V. S., & Mickelson, K. D. (1995). Motives for social comparison. *Personality and Social Psychology Bulletin, 21*, 1200–1209.

Helgeson, V. S., & Taylor, S. E. (1993). Social comparisons and adjustment among cardiac patients. *Journal of Applied Social Psychology, 23*, 1171–1185.

Higgins, E. T. (1987). Self-discrepancy: A theory relating self and affect. *Psychological Review, 94*, 319–340.

Hobbs, A. (2010). Heroes and heroism [radio broadcast]. In J. Cook (Producer), *Free thinking festival* (November 8). Gateshead, UK: BBC Radio 3. Retrieved from www.bbc.co.uk.

James, W. (1899). *Talks to teachers on psychology: And to students on some of life's ideals.* New York: Henry Holt & Company.

Johnson, G., & Leavitt, W. (2001). Building on success: Transforming organizations through an appreciative inquiry. *Public Personnel Management, 30*, 129–136.

Jones, A., & Crandall, R. (1986). Validation of a short index of self-actualization. *Personality and Social Psychology Bulletin, 12*, 63–73.

Jung, C. G. (1969). *Collected works of C. G. Jung: Archetypes and the collective unconscious* (Vol. 9). Princeton, NJ: Princeton University.

Keltner, D., & Haidt, J. (2003). Approaching awe: A moral, spiritual, and aesthetic emotion. *Cognition and Emotion, 17*, 297–314. doi: 10.1080/02699930302297

Kinsella, E. L., Ritchie, T. D., & Igou, E. R. (2015a). Zeroing in on heroes: A prototype analysis of hero features. *Journal of Personality and Social Psychology, 108*, 114–127. doi: 10.1037/a0038463

Kinsella, E. L., Ritchie, T. D., & Igou, E. R. (2015b). Lay perspectives on the social and psychological functions of heroes. *Frontiers in Psychology, 6*, 130. doi: 10.3389/fpsyg.2015.00130

Klapp, O. E. (1954). Heroes, villains and fools, as agents of social control. *American Sociological Review, 19*, 56–62. doi: 10.2307/2088173

Klapp, O. E. (1969). *Collective search for identity*. New York: Holt, Rinehart, & Winston.

Klein, H., & Shiffman, K. S. (2006). Messages about physical attractiveness in animated cartoons. *Body Image, 3*, 353–363.

Kohlberg, L., Levine, C., & Hewer, A. (1983). *Moral stages: A current formulation and a response to critics*. Basel, NY: Karger.

Kross, E., Davidson, M., Weber, J., & Ochsner K. (2009). Coping with emotions past: The neural bases of regulating affect associated with negative autobiographical memories. *Biological Psychiatry, 65*, 361–366.

Lakoff, G., & Johnson, M. (2003). *Metaphors we live by* (2nd ed.). Chicago, IL: University of Chicago Press.

Landau, M. J., Vess, M., Arndt, J., Rothschild, Z. K., Sullivan, D., & Atchley, R. A. (2011). Embodied metaphor and the "true" self: Priming entity expansion and protection influences intrinsic self-expressions in self-perceptions and interpersonal behavior. *Journal of Experimental Social Psychology, 47*, 79–87.

Lewin, K. (1946). Action research and minority problems. *Journal of Social Issues, 2*(4), 34–46.

Markus, H., & Nurius, P. (1986). Possible selves. *American Psychologist, 41*, 954–969.

Martens, J. W. (2005). Definitions and omissions of heroism. *American Psychologist, 60*, 342–343.

Martinetz, C. F. (2002). Appreciative Inquiry as an organizational development tool. *Performance Improvement, 41*, 34–39.

McAdams, D. P. (2008). Generativity, the redemptive self, and the problem of a "noisy" ego in American life. In H. Wayment, and J. J. Bauer (eds), *Transcending self-interest: Psychological explorations of the quiet ego* (pp. 235–241). Washington, DC: American Psychological Association.

Nielsen, R., Marrone, J. A., & Slay, H. S. (2010). A new look at humility: Exploring the humility concept and its role in socialized charismatic leadership. *Journal of Leadership & Organizational Studies, 17*, 33–43.

Pennebaker, J. W., & Chung, C. K. (2011). Expressive writing and its links to mental and physical health. In H. S. Friedman (ed.), *Oxford handbook of health psychology* (pp. 417–437). New York: Oxford University Press.

Pretzinger, K. (1976). The American hero: Yesterday and today. *Humboldt Journal of Social Relations, 4*, 36–40.

Ritchie, T. D., Sedikides, C., Wildschut, T., Arndt, J., & Gidron, Y. (2011). Self-concept clarity mediates the relation between stress and subjective well-being. *Self and Identity, 10*, 493–508. doi: 10.1080/15298868.2010.493066

Ryan, D. S. (1983). Self-esteem: An operational definition and ethical analysis. *Journal of Psychology and Theology, 11*, 295–302.

Schlenker, B. R., Weigold, M. F., & Schlenker, K. A. (2008). What makes a hero? The impact of integrity on admiration and interpersonal judgment. *Journal of Personality, 76*, 323–355. doi: 10.1111/j.1467-6494.2007.00488.x

Schwartz, B. (2009). Barry Schwartz on our loss of wisdom [Video file]. February. Retrieved from www.ted.com.

Schwartz, J. A., & Schwartz, R. B. (2010). *The wounds that heal: Heroism and human development*. Lanham, MD: University Press of America.

Sedikides, C., & Strube, M. J. (1997). Self-evaluation: To thine own self be good, to thine own self be sure, to thine own self be true, and to thine own self be better. *Advances in Experimental Social Psychology, 29*, 209–269.

Seligman, M. E. P., Steen, T., Park, N., & Peterson, C. (2005). Positive psychology progress: Empirical validation of interventions. *American Psychologist, 60*(5), 410–421.

Shepela, S. T., Cook, J., Horlitz, E., Leal, R., Luciano, S., Lutfy, E., … Warden, E. (1999). Courageous resistance. *Theory and Psychology, 9*, 787–805. doi: 10.1177/0959354399096004

Smith, G. J. (1976). An examination of the phenomenon of sports hero worship. *Canadian Journal of Applied Sport Sciences, 1*, 259–270.

Stirrat, M., & Perrett, D. I. (2012). Face structure predicts cooperation: men with wider faces are more generous to their in-group when out-group competition is salient. *Psychological Science, 23*(7), 718–722.

Sullivan, M. P., & Venter, A. (2005). The hero within: Inclusion of heroes into the self. *Self and Identity, 4*, 101–111. doi: 10.1080/13576500444000191

Sullivan, M. P., & Venter, A. (2010). Defining heroes through deductive and inductive investigations. *Journal of Social Psychology, 150*, 471–484. doi: 10.1080/00224540903366602

Tarrier, N. (2010). Broad minded affective coping (BMAC): A "positive" CBT approach to facilitating positive emotions. *International Journal of Cognitive Therapy, 3*, 64–76.

Taylor, S. E., & Lobel, M. (1989). Social comparison activity under threat: Downward evaluation and upward contacts. *Psychological Review, 96,* 569–575.

Taylor, S. E., Neter, E., & Wayment, H. (1995). Self-evaluation processes. *Personality and Social Psychology Bulletin, 21,* 1278–1287.

Tesser, A. (1988). Toward a self-evaluation maintenance model of social behaviour. In L. Berkowitz (ed.), *Advances in experimental social psychology* (Vol. 20, pp. 181–227). New York: Academic Press.

Van Vugt, M., & Ahuja, A. (2011). *Selected: How evolution has shaped our leadership psychology.* London: Profile Books/Harper Collins.

Wecter, D. (1941). *The hero in America: A chronicle of hero worship.* New York: Scribner.

Whitney, D. (1998). Let's change the subject and change our organization: an appreciative inquiry approach to organization change. *Career Development International, 3,* 314–319.

Willis, J., & Todorov, A. (2006). First impressions: Making up your mind after 100 ms exposure to a face. *Psychological Science, 17,* 592–598

Wojciszke, B. (2005). Affective concomitants of information on morality and competence. *European Psychologist, 10,* 60–71.

Wood, J. V. (1989). Theory and research concerning social comparisons of personal attributes. *Psychological Bulletin, 106,* 231–248.

Worthington, E. J. (2007). *Humility: The quiet virtue.* West Conshohocken, PA: Templeton Foundation Press.

Ylvisaker, M., McPherson, K., Kayes, N., & Pellett, E. (2008). Metaphoric identity mapping: Facilitating goal setting and engagement in rehabilitation after traumatic brain injury. *Neuropsychological Rehabilitation, 18,* 713–741. doi: 10.1080/09602010802201832

Zimbardo, P. (2007). *The Lucifer effect.* New York: Random House.

2

Why Heroism Exists

Evolutionary Perspectives on Extreme Helping

Sara Kafashan, Adam Sparks, Amanda Rotella, and Pat Barclay

On June 17, 2014, thirteen-year-old Robert Pritchard Junior rushed into a burning mobile home to rescue a six-year-old girl from being engulfed by the flames. Almost a year earlier, Christopher Ihle saved an eighty-four-year-old male and his seventy-eight-year-old wife from being struck by a train. A year prior to this incident, Kyle Hardman attempted to save three men and two children from drowning in the Mississippi River. Pritchard Junior, Ihle, and Hardman are recipients of the prestigious Carnegie Medal. These heroes were awarded their medals for voluntarily and knowingly risking their lives to attempt to save others. Why would anyone do such a thing? Why would one incur a cost—such as risk their life—to benefit others? Why would anyone be a hero?

From an evolutionary perspective, incurring any such costs appears puzzling at first glance. Natural selection favors traits that increase the propagation of one's genetic material into future generations, and it ruthlessly eliminates any costly traits that provide no net reproductive advantage. This logic prompts the following crucial questions: do heroes receive any benefits that counteract the costs of their actions (thus providing a net selective advantage for heroic traits), and if so, what is the nature of those benefits?

Evolutionary explanations solve the puzzle of prosociality (i.e., behaviors that involve benefiting others) by focusing on the inclusive fitness benefits (i.e., the survival and reproduction of one's offspring and the offspring of close genetic relatives) for the prosocial individual. For example, kin selection theory offers a strong evolutionary explanation for prosociality directed towards kin (Hamilton, 1963, 1964), because the personal fitness costs of providing such help are compensated by fitness benefits to kin (i.e., the survival and reproduction of copies of our genes in other bodies). Similarly, costly signaling theory (Zahavi, 1990, 1995; Zahavi & Zahavi, 1997) suggests that extreme forms of prosociality, such as heroism, might have evolved because heroes are able to gain elevated status for their remarkable actions, which in turn allows them access to previously unattainable social benefits.

Although prosocial individuals may be acting in ways to increase their inclusive fitness, they are not necessarily conscious of it. That is, people do not need to be aware of the link between prosociality and fitness to engage in these actions, any more than they need to think about their inclusive fitness every time they have sex, eat, sleep, or defecate. Self-sacrifice, cooperative sentiments, and empathy are *proximate mechanisms*, which motivate helpful behaviors within an individual to achieve the *ultimate function* of increasing the actor's survival and reproduction (proximate and ultimate causes are reviewed in Tinbergen, 1963; also see Scott-Phillips et al., 2011).

Throughout this chapter, we will address the evolutionary functions (ultimate causes) of being a hero (actor-side) and distinguishing someone as a hero (judger-side). We specifically take note of the observers (also termed "judges") because these individuals play a crucial role in determining who a hero is and what kinds of status benefits one receives for their heroism. These two perspectives—the hero's and the judge's—are both necessary to explain why heroism exists. We begin by reviewing some general evolutionary theories of "typical" prosociality, or what biologists would call theories of cooperation. We then discuss how these and other theories can be used to explain extreme prosociality such as heroism. But, before we attempt to explain the existence of heroism through an evolutionary lens, we must first provide a working definition of heroism.

What Is a Hero?

Heroism is an *extreme* form of prosociality, a category of behavior that involves benefiting another.[1] By definition, "typical" prosociality involves the actor delivering *average*—or *expected*—levels of benefits to others. Here we define heroes as those who incur costs (e.g., risk of injury or death; or significant sacrifices such as time, money, or other forms of personal loss) to deliver *greater-than-expected* benefits to others (Baumard & Boyer, 2013). That is, among many actors who engage in behaviors of a given cost, heroes are those who deliver *many more* benefits to others. Typically these costs are incurred by the hero without certainty and/or negotiated expectation of direct future rewards.

There are various types of heroes. Prototypical heroes are characterized by physical feats, bravery, and high risks of serious injury or death, such as war heroes or individuals who save others from peril. Folklore heroes such as Superman and Batman are deemed heroic for similar reasons: Their (fictive) willingness and superior ability to incur potentially high costs (e.g., deadly fights with various villains) to save others from danger and threat. Much like these fictive heroes, many may view famous athletes as heroic. Sports heroes gain status because they incur similar costs to other players but deliver greater-than-expected benefits (i.e., wins and entertainment).

Moving beyond prototypical heroism, some people may be deemed heroic because of their ability to offer greater-than-expected benefits in other ways. Heroic fictional detective Sherlock Holmes, for example, did not usually incur physical costs to save others. Instead he used superior reasoning and logical thinking to solve crimes and save lives. Others may even be deemed heroic because of incidental consequences of overtly self-beneficial acts. For example, vigilance may be primarily motivated by concern for protecting oneself and one's family from enemies, predators, or other threats. If such vigilance incidentally provides major protection benefits to others in the community, they may regard the watchman as a hero.

This list of hero-types is not exhaustive, but hopefully illustrates the idea that many different types of acts involve a delivery of greater-than-expected benefits to another, hence meeting our definition of heroism. Our definition of heroism may not perfectly map on to definitions used by others, but it does heavily overlap with conventional usage of the term. At the least, our definition is tractable, allowing us to offer useful evolutionary-minded insights into the heroism phenomenon. We invite readers to substitute their own term for the phenomenon we are examining if our definition does not fit their understanding of heroism.

Now that we have defined heroism, we can begin examining this phenomenon in greater detail. Our first line of inquiry answers the following question: If heroes are people who deliver many more benefits than would normally be expected, how much helping is normally expected of people? The answer to this question is a necessary first step to explaining the persistence of heroism, and will be addressed in the following section.

Expected Levels of Helping

Prosocial sentiments (e.g., feelings, attitudes) can evolve when providing help causes helpers to receive benefits that outweigh the costs of helping, on average. By using evolutionary theory to identify what kind of benefits helpers receive under normal circumstances, we can make predictions about the normal level of helping (i.e., the expected level of benefit-conferral). In this section, we focus on four categories of help by which benefits can accrue to helpers or their genes:

1 help directed towards close kin who share copies of the same genes (kin selection theory: Hamilton, 1963, 1964);
2 help that is exchanged reciprocally between individuals or within groups (reciprocity: Nowak & Sigmund, 2005; Trivers, 1971);
3 help towards recipients in whom one has vested interests due to interdependence or shared fates (Brown & Brown, 2006; Roberts, 2005; Tooby & Cosmides, 1996); and
4 help that evades punishment (Yamagishi, 1986).

Kin Selection

Legendary biologist J. B. S. Haldane famously quipped that he would willingly "jump into the river to save two brothers or eight cousins." Why? Kin selection (Hamilton, 1964) is a form of natural selection whereby costly helping to kin can evolve if the fitness costs to the helper are less than the fitness benefits to the recipient, discounted by the likelihood of the two sharing rare genes. This applies to all forms of helping, from help that incurs minor costs to extreme costs like sacrificing one's life. Haldane's cousins were more likely to share his genes than strangers, and his brothers even more likely, providing an inclusive fitness rationale for his (hypothetical) extreme sacrifices. Honeybees famously sacrifice their own lives for their hive-mates and their queen, all of whom are close relatives (e.g., sisters). In humans, it is now well established that help is preferentially directed towards kin (Mateo, 2015), particularly in high-cost situations (Stewart-Williams, 2007, 2008).

Heroism, as presented in this chapter, is going *beyond* the expected benefits, and as described above, kin are expected to help kin. We expect that people will help kin in need, especially in high-cost, hero-esque contexts, such as parents rescuing their children from a house fire. Parent rescuers receive inclusive fitness benefits that non-kin rescuers do not. Accordingly, extreme helping directed toward kin are often not viewed as heroic—or at least the bar is much higher for help towards kin to be called "heroic." Notably, the Carnegie Medal does not recognize individuals who helped save members of their immediate family, except in cases of outstanding heroism where the rescuer loses his or her life or is severely injured. Conversely, when heroic feats are directed towards a non-relative (i.e., when the hero receives no kin-selected benefits), they are widely recognized.

Reciprocity

Reciprocal interactions are an integral part of our daily life. In repeated interactions, such as friendships, we exchange help for mutual benefit (e.g., Barclay, 2013, 2016; Noë & Hammerstein, 1994, 1995). Prosocial actions can prompt two kinds of reciprocal interactions:

1 help that is directly returned by the person we previously helped ("direct reciprocity": Axelrod, 1984; Trivers, 1971); or
2 help that allows us to establish a good reputation such that benefits are returned indirectly by third-party observers ("indirect reciprocity": Nowak & Sigmund, 2005).

Experience with such interactions sets the expectation that once you help someone, benefits will eventually be returned either directly or indirectly. So, if you have been helped, the expectation is that you will return the favor. For instance, if a co-worker buys you coffee or sweets, or a neighbor helps you with your groceries, there may be an expectation that you should return the favor (or a different favor) at a later time. If this is people's expectation—conscious or otherwise—then people will not consider it heroic when people help each other at normal levels within an established relationship. Even large amounts of help are not considered heroic if they are close to the range of what is normally given within the relationship (direct reciprocity) or within the society more generally (indirect reciprocity).

Vested Interest

Sometimes helpers directly benefit from helping someone because they have a stake or vested interest in the recipient's welfare. We can think of many instances of this: giving coffee to your tired driver so he does not crash, participating in a collective defense of your own group, and making a donation to a local politician who is fighting a plan to build a polluting factory in your neighborhood. In these cases, the helper has a "stake" in the well-being of the beneficiary. When two or more people are interdependent, we'd expect helpers to deliver benefits to the recipient because the helper's welfare is necessarily linked to the recipient's (e.g., Brown & Brown, 2006; Roberts, 2005; Tooby & Cosmides, 1996). In such cases, the costs of providing help are less than the fitness benefits received, and we can expect that benefits would be directed towards those whose well-being is valuable to the helper. These vested interests can explain even large delivery of benefits to other people, if the donor has a correspondingly large stake in the recipient(s), such as when health insurance companies in the United States donated millions of dollars to politicians who opposed universal care. Hero judgments are sensitive to such vested interests in others: people who are perceived to benefit directly by helping others tend to be rated as less heroic by observers (Lin-Healy & Small, 2013).

Punishment

Not all help is freely provided to others. Punishment can be used to motivate continual compliance with cooperative expectations. For instance, laboratory experiments have consistently established that people within groups contribute more money to a fund that benefits everyone in the group (the fund is a "public good") if a system is available to sanction those who do not contribute (for a review, see Balliet, Mulder, & Van Lange, 2011). In the real world, community-owned public goods resources are best sustained when the community can impose sanctions on those who overuse the resource or who do not pay for its maintenance (Ostrom, 1990). Other real-world examples of contributing to public goods include taking your turn at completing household chores or, on a more extreme scale, billionaires paying millions in taxes to avoid tax evasion charges. In all these examples, imposing costs on selfish individuals helps maintain cooperation because the benefits for conforming exceed the costs of receiving punishment. Thus, sanctioning systems set others' expectations of compliance: benefits are expected to be delivered when failure to comply can lead to punishment.

How does punishment relate to heroism? Well, if one delivers the amount of benefits necessary to evade punishment, such behavior would not be considered heroic. Such helping is expected because evading punishment could save oneself from severe fitness costs, such as losing one's good reputation, being shunned or ostracized by one's community, and/or receiving high financial fines. So, given the potentially high fitness costs of *not* helping, help in such circumstances do not generally fit most people's conception of heroism.

Exceeding Expected Levels of Helping: Why Be a Hero?

We can predict others' helping based on kinship, reciprocity, vested interests, and avoidance of punishment—these all set our expectations of how much person A might help person B. But why might someone *exceed* these expectations? That is, why might someone perform heroic acts by incurring costs to deliver higher-than-expected benefits to others? Why—in an evolutionary sense—do heroes exist? One answer comes from costly signaling theory (Zahavi, 1975, 1990, 1995; Zahavi & Zahavi, 1997).

Costly signaling theory relies on the notion that observable displays (i.e., signals) are associated with unobservable qualities (i.e., one's underlying genetic or phenotypic characteristics; Zahavi, 1975, 1990, 1995; Zahavi & Zahavi, 1997). Accordingly, people can use cooperative behavior as signals to communicate their underlying qualities to others. For example, the hero risking his life to rescue a non-related child may be (not necessarily consciously) signaling his superior physical prowess and his willingness to help others.

A costly signaling communication system is important because individuals vary in their possession of desirable qualities (McNamara, Barta, Frohmage, & Houston, 2008), and many desirable qualities are unobservable (Gintis, Smith, & Bowles, 2001). Moreover, one's qualities can affect one's willingness, ability, and availability to provide others with social benefits (Barclay, 2013; Noë & Hammerstein, 1994, 1995). Costly signals provide evidence of underlying characteristics that could inform fitness-enhancing decisions about who to interact with as a mate, ally, or competitor (McNamara et al., 2008).

A key question, and heavily debated issue, of costly signaling theory is what specifically keeps signals honest. In other words, what ensures the association between signal and quality, such that this communication system is not destabilized by cheaters (i.e., signaling dishonestly about underlying qualities; e.g., Getty, 1998, 2006; Higham, 2013; Hurd, 1995; Számadó, 1999, 2011)? Two theoretical possibilities have been offered. Originally, signals were thought to "handicap" the signaler by being extremely costly to perform, such as peacocks carrying heavy tails (the "handicap principle": Grafen, 1990; Zahavi, 1975, 1990, 1995; Zahavi & Zahavi, 1997). This logic suggests that all signalers incur costs (e.g., anyone with a heavy tail incurs a weight cost), but those who truly possess high enough quality ("honest" signalers) pay a lower marginal cost for that signal (e.g., can more easily carry a tail's weight), such that they can afford to send a stronger signal (e.g., a heavier tail) (Grafen, 1990). Recent developments in the theory, however, have shown that the honesty and reliability of signals can be maintained even if no one pays a cost for honestly signaling their quality, as long as there are potential costs for dishonest signaling (i.e., advertising a higher quality level than one actually possesses) (Getty, 1998, 2006; Számadó, 1999, 2011). For example, an individual who falsely presents oneself as having high status would be challenged by more formidable opponents than he could defend against, and it is this "punishment" that prevents individuals from claiming higher status than they actually possess (Tibbetts & Izzo, 2010).

Regardless of whether signaling systems are kept honest and reliable by costs or by potential costs (see Számadó, 2011 for a review), the fundamental logic of costly signaling theory is that producing a given signal has more net fitness benefits for honest signalers than dishonest signalers. Specifically, high quality individuals would incur fewer costs than lower quality individuals to produce a given signal. Or, framed in terms of benefits, producing a given signal allows high quality individuals to reap greater benefits than lower quality individuals.

When signals are honestly linked to the actor's quality, information sharing is mutually beneficial (e.g., Gintis et al., 2001; Zahavi & Zahavi, 1997). Signalers are able to use costly signals to honestly convey their underlying desirable traits to responders. Responders pay attention to these signals to assess the signaler's difficult-to-observe qualities, and then use such information to make fitness-enhancing decisions about who to interact with as potential cooperative partners, mates, or competitors (McNamara et al., 2008). This shifts the responder's behavior in a way that benefits the signaler, such as being chosen as a partner or avoided as a competitor. Therefore, in turn, signalers and responders gain from being on opposite, but complementary, ends of the signal.

To apply the logic of this theory to heroism, some heroes are essentially costly signalers—high quality individuals who incur fewer costs (or reap greater gains) for advertising desirable traits to observers by providing higher-than-expected benefits to others. Other people pay attention to heroic acts because they gain useful information about the hero's qualities. But, if heroes are costly signalers, what exactly are they advertising? What desirable traits do heroes possess? And is the advertising of some traits deemed more heroic than others? The upcoming sections will attempt to address these questions.

Signaling Hard-to-Fake Traits

Individuals can advertise various traits through costly help. In this section, we will discuss the most prominently advertised traits: Physical abilities, resources, and intelligence. Each of these traits is difficult-to-fake, ensuring that only those who honestly possess them could profitably incur potential costs to produce a signal to others.

Signaling Physical Abilities

In various hunter–gatherer societies, males hunt meat. Although several types of prey may be targeted, males consistently hunt big game (e.g., Hawkes, 1991, 1993; Hawkes & Bliege Bird, 2002; Smith & Bliege Bird, 2000; Wiessner, 2002). Targeting one's foraging efforts towards large game is puzzling because acquiring such prey is dangerous and time-consuming, and success is often unpredictable. Furthermore, big game hunting creates a surplus of meat, which is frequently distributed publicly, rather than monopolized by the hunter. It seems males can better nourish their immediate kin through less risky forms of hunting (e.g., small animals) and gathering (e.g., plant matter) (Hawkes, 1991, 1993; Hawkes & Bliege Bird, 2002).

So why do males hunt big game? Many have argued that hunting big game and sharing the meat publicly serves as a costly signal (e.g., Hawkes, 1991, 1993; Hawkes & Bliege Bird, 2002; Smith & Bliege Bird, 2000; Wiessner, 2002). A successful big game hunter needs skill, strength, and agility. And showing off such traits to others has great benefits for both signalers and observers. Several studies have shown that successful big game hunters enjoy social, political, and reproductive benefits, and that observers who respond to signals benefit as well (reviewed in Hawkes & Bliege Bird, 2002).

Meriam turtle hunters of the Torres Strait, in Australia, benefit from gaining a reputation as a successful big game hunter. Hunting turtles is costly, risky, and potentially dangerous. Hunters not only absorb the monetary costs to fuel boats (approximately 60 Australian dollars for each hunt), but also risk their safety by diving into ocean waters to wrestle and capture 200-pound turtles. Despite all the costs to acquire turtle meat, hunters regularly share and gift the meat to community members, without receiving formal repayment. These successful hunters, however, do not go unnoticed. Instead, they gain hero-like status in the eyes of their community, and such elevated status has perks. Hunters have higher reproductive success than similarly aged non-hunters. Specifically, compared to non-hunters, turtle hunters mate with higher quality females, have more offspring, and gain sexual access to females at a younger age (Smith, Bliege Bird, & Bird, 2003). Hunters are not the only ones that benefit from signaling: Responding to the hunters' signals and interacting with such hunters is also advantageous. Female partners of hunters have also been shown to have higher cumulative reproductive success than other females, suggesting that the costly signals allowed them to accurately assess mate quality.

The Meriam are not the only foragers to place their successful big game hunters on heroic pedestals. Like the natives of the Torres Strait, the Ache big game hunters of Paraguay gain reproductive and social benefits from their risky foraging strategies. Good Ache hunters have more extra-marital affairs and illegitimate children, and have their children more likely to survive, than do worse hunters (Hill & Kaplan, 1988). This general pattern holds true for hunters in other parts of the world, such as the Tanzanian Hadza and !Kung bushmen of the Kalahari desert (reviewed in Hawkes & Bliege Bird, 2002). Older Hadza men who are more successful at hunting have younger wives than other age-matched males (reviewed in Hawkes & Bliege Bird, 2002). And compared to non-hunters, Hadza hunters gain access to younger and more hard-working females, traits that are used as a criterion for a high quality female mate (Hawkes, O'Connell, & Blurton Jones, 2001). Similarly, good !Kung hunters have higher fertility and more surviving offspring than poor hunters (Wiessner, 2002).

The field research on big game hunters in traditional societies appear to be in line with the logic of costly signaling, and these hunters fit our definition of heroism. Why? Because each of them go beyond their expected level of delivered benefits by not just providing a surplus of meat that feed kin and non-kin, but also by engaging in risky and dangerous foraging strategies to do so. So, their acts fit the bill of heroism in two crucial ways. First, their foraging is risky, posing a potential threat to their safety—this can impose large costs. And second, they are also generous, enabling others to gain from their actions.

Big game hunting is not the only way males can show off their physical abilities and be deemed heroes. Males can engage in various other forms of risk-taking, which serve as equally good signals of superior health, vigor, strength, and skill. And these behaviors gain them substantial social status and reproductive benefits. Kelly and Dunbar (2001), for example, showed that men who were brave (i.e., took risks) were more attractive as short-term and long-term romantic partners than men who did not do so, especially when the bravery benefited others (heroism) and was voluntary rather than part of someone's job. Adding to this literature, Farthing (2005) specified that heroic risky behaviors were more valued than other risky behaviors. Farthing distinguished between four types of risk-taking: (a) Risks that pose a threat to one's physical safety and benefit another (e.g., rescuing a person from a burning building; saving a drowning child in a raging river), (b) acts that involve a physical risk but no benefit to others (e.g., risky sports), (c) risky alcohol or drug use, and (d) financial risks. Not unexpectedly, only certain forms of risk-taking were deemed valuable in a mate and ally. In particular, results illustrated that females were most attracted to males who engaged in acts that were physically risky and benefited others. If the benefits to others were removed from the equation, however, the pattern evidently reversed. Specifically, females preferred males who *avoided* physical-only, drug, and financial risk. Thus, it appears that females prefer helpful men, but have a higher preference for men who show heroic helpfulness (i.e., acts that involve physical risks and benefit others). Men, in turn, are aware of this and are more likely to display courage, strength, and bravery through helpful acts when primed with mating motives (Griskevicius et al., 2007).

In sum, engaging in potentially physically risky behavior that benefits others, whether in the form of big game hunting or rescuing a person from a burning building, signals valuable information to others about the actor's quality. When this information is highly beneficial and valuable to observers, all parties to the signaling equation receive gains. Actors use their superior quality to share greater-than-expected benefits with others, leading them to receive reproductive benefits and other perks of elevated status by being deemed heroes. And, observers can increase their reproductive success by associating with these heroes.

One factor that has been prominent in this section is the notion that heroism is defined by *physically* risky behaviors that benefit another individual or others. This definition is consistent with the popular conception of superheroes, such as Superman and Batman, who put themselves in *physical* harm's way to help others. And, as mentioned earlier, the Carnegie Medal is awarded to those who incur *physical* costs to save others. But, does one necessarily need to have advanced *physical* abilities, health, strength, and/or skill to be heroic? Isn't the person who donates millions of dollars to help find the cure for sleeping sickness as much of hero as an individual who carries the parasite-ridden child to the hospital to receive medical attention? Isn't the individual who diffuses a bomb to save the lives of many equally as heroic as the person who uses his body to shield others from the explosion? We would argue yes. We define a hero as someone who goes *above and beyond the expected levels of delivered benefits*, regardless of whether these benefits were delivered through one's superior physical abilities, excessive wealth, or intelligence. The next two sections discuss the notion of heroism as costly signals of wealth and intelligence.

Signaling Resources

Philanthropists can achieve great fame. John Rockefeller, for example, contributed over $500 million of his wealth to humanitarian causes such as The Rockefeller Foundation, which seeks to promote the well-being of humanity throughout the world by advancing more inclusive economies (New York Times, 1937). Bill Gates is renowned for sizeable donations to several causes, including his $50 million contribution to Save the Children, a global campaign dedicated to saving the lives of newborns, and the billions of dollars that founded the Bill and Melinda Gates Foundation (Diamond, 2015). Mark Zuckerberg, the founder of Facebook, is also known for his generosity, and has contributed $100 million dollars to Newark, the New Jersey Public School System (Inside Philanthropy, 2015). All three of these philanthropists provided above expected levels of help to millions around the world through their extravagant financial contributions. And providing such supererogatory help can give such philanthropists hero-like status (e.g., Lane, 2013; Lewis, 2015; Snyder, 2011).

By taking a financial risk or giving away a portion of their wealth, philanthropists are not just benefitting many individuals; they are also sending a (not necessarily conscious) costly signal to observers about their access to resources. The whole world knows that John Rockefeller, Bill Gates, and Mark Zuckerberg are incredibly rich. We know this to be true because the reputational benefits accrued from donating millions of dollars would not be worth the crippling financial effects on their lifestyle if they did not truly possess such wealth. That is, there is a better benefit-to-cost ratio for honest signalers, compared to dishonest signalers, for signaling at a given level (e.g., donating $100 million dollars to charity). And, thus, only those who honestly possess such wealth are willing and able to accept financial costs or risks to deliver greater-than-expected benefits to others.

You might be wondering if such million dollar donations are truly considered generous given the wealth of these philanthropists. After all, how generous is a million dollar donation when one is worth several billions? To answer this question, we must remember that generosity is a relative, as opposed to absolute, concept (Barclay, 2013). Accordingly, whether one's actions will be deemed generous is not just dependent on one's level of helping, but also on the level of helping exhibited by others. Take for example, a population whereby everyone gives x units to charity per month. Because donating x units is the norm, doing so would not make one appear generous in this population, even though donating to charity may be a generous act in absolute terms. Donating $x + 1$ units, however, allows one to be viewed generous because this show's one's ability and willingness to go beyond the norm of giving to charity. Conversely, donating $x - 1$ units may make one appear selfish. Using similar logic, philanthropists' donations may be a small portion of their wealth, but in comparison to other rich individuals who rarely donate their wealth to the less fortunate, such millionaire donors are very generous. Furthermore, regardless of whether such donors are seen as "generous," they are certainly seen as "wealthy" (for the former, see further below).

Generous displays that signal access to resources are also common in traditional cultures and societies. The Kwakiutl of Vancouver Island, for example, host extravagant ceremonies called "potlatches" whereby chiefs of tribes use conspicuous generosity to compete with each other for status and prestige. To maintain or elevate their status, chiefs must give away costly resources, such as food, canoes, and blankets to other tribes (Goldman, 1937; Piddocke, 1965). These potlatches are extremely costly and appear to serve as a reliable and honest signal of a chief's access to resources (Goldman, 1937; Piddocke, 1965).

Similarly, several New Guinean tribes, such as the Metlpa, Enga, and Gawil, engage in pig exchange ceremonies known as "mokas" (Brown, 1978). During mokas, pigs are exchanged among tribes to signal wealth and resources, and maintain status. Pigs are the main means of exchange because they are difficult to rear, time-consuming, and costly. Many pigs die before reaching adulthood, and fattened pigs, which are highly valued at mokas, require tribes to have a surplus of food to feed and sustain the weight of these large animals. Thus, much like potlatches, mokas are a costly signal of a tribe's wealth.

Signaling Intelligence

If you ask individuals "who is your hero," some of the answers will be of people with great physical ability or wealth. But many answers will be of people who have contributed greatly to our artistic or intellectual culture, such as musicians, artists, scientists, and inventors. This is because heroism need not involve the delivery of benefits through superior physical ability or wealth. Instead, one could confer above expected levels of benefits by using one's intelligence. Alexander Graham Bell, for example, might not have physically risked his life to help others the way the Meriam turtle hunters do, but he revolutionized the lives of millions across the world with the invention of the telephone. Likewise, Charles Babbage, a British engineer, changed the world and the way people live when he developed the first computer. Bell and Babbage may not be considered heroes in the conventional sense, but these two men have incurred costs and risks to deliver greater-than-expected benefits to others. And given the benefits they have conferred on others, Bell and Babbage could be deemed *intellectual* heroes—people who have used their *intelligence* to confer above expected levels of benefits to others.

Although little empirical work has explored the notion of intellectual heroism, research to date has revealed some related findings. Theoretical work has suggested that intelligence is costly and difficult-to-fake, suggesting that it may be a valuable trait to signal to others. The idea here is that the human brain—and the phenomena it produces—is like a peacock's tail for display to others (Miller, 2000). Brains, much like peacocks' tails, are difficult to build and maintain, and cannot be faked. Developing a large brain is not only time-consuming, it is also energetically expensive and anatomically complex (Dunbar & Shultz, 2007). Because of the high costs associated with building and maintaining brain tissue, some researchers have argued that intelligence may be a reliable indicator of genetic quality and may have been a target of sexual selection (e.g., Furlow, Armijo-Prewitt, Gangestad, & Thornhill, 1997; Haselton & Miller, 2006; Luxen & Buunk, 2006; Miller, 2000).

Displays of intelligence could also be useful for indicating that one has the capability to confer benefits on others (Barclay, 2013, 2016). In fact, studies show that intelligence and competence (e.g., Anderson & Kilduff, 2009; Driskell, Olmstead, & Salas, 1993), as well as generosity and commitment (e.g., Hardy & Van Vugt, 2006; Willer, 2009), consistently predict elevated status, in terms of ability to sway and determine the direction of group decisions (for a review, see Cheng, Tracy, Foulsham, Kingstone, & Henrich, 2013). Furthermore, intelligent people may be valued as social partners because others will have the opportunity to learn useful skills simply by observing them (Henrich & Gil-White, 2001) or because they can use their intelligence to access resources.

Thus, while scientists sitting comfortably in research labs might not fit most heroic prototypes, such individuals can be consistent with our definition of heroism in two fundamental ways. First, these individuals use their intellect to deliver greater-than-expected benefits to others through their inventions. These inventions can, and have, changed the lives of many in revolutionary ways. Second, such intellectual heroism can be risky. Of course, intellects are not necessarily risking their lives like conventional heroes. But, scientists are risking their time on potentially fruitless inventions that may never succeed, let alone amount to anything useful. So, the risk of science is that one's time is wasted on experimenting with non-useful inventions instead of bringing in a steady income that could better allow financially stability and increase reproductive success.

Signaling a Willingness to Help

Two of the most important things to know about others are the likelihood that they will help you and the likelihood that they will harm you (Barclay, 2016). If someone is known for helping others in your in-group, then there is an increased likelihood that they will help you. Thus, large displays of heroism can function to (unconsciously) signal a hero's cooperative intent, such that audiences are more cooperative and more trusting with the hero. This benefits the hero, creating a selection pressure for mechanisms that cause extreme helping.

What maintains the honesty of such signals of cooperative intent? Long-term interactions are crucial, because people who are cheated will generally cease cooperating with the cheater. The benefits of "suckering" someone are thus short-term benefits. A costly public cooperative gesture would not be worth it for anyone who intended to cheat someone at the first opportunity: the cost of the public help would outweigh the short-term benefits of "suckering" someone (André, 2010; Barclay, 2016; Bolle 2001; Ohtsubo & Watanabe, 2009; Smith & Bliege Bird, 2005). Conversely, such cooperative displays would be worth it for someone with genuine cooperative intent, because the long-term benefits of mutual cooperation can outweigh the cost of the public help. This form of signaling remains honest even if everyone pays the same fitness cost for helping, because the honest signalers receive larger long-term benefits than the dishonest signalers. In the past, this type of signaling was used to explain more "mundane" types of helping that everyone could do equally well, like volunteering one's time (Barclay, 2013; Barclay & Reeve, 2012), but could in principle apply to more "extravagant help" including heroism.

Do people treat helpful behavior as a signal of cooperative intent? According to multiple studies, it pays to be nice (e.g., Barclay, 2004, 2006; Clark, 2002; Milinski, Semmann, & Krambeck, 2002). Specifically, behaving generously can serve as a signal of one's cooperative intent, i.e., the degree to which one is likely and willing to cooperate with, instead of exploit, another individual. And, showcasing one's cooperative intent appears to benefit signalers by giving them access to social partners and opportunities. For instance, those who behave generously are deemed to be of high status and perceived as highly trustworthy (Barclay, 2004; Hardy & Van Vugt, 2006; Price, 2003; Van Vugt & Hardy, 2010; Willer, 2009). Furthermore, those who contribute more than their fair share towards a common good are generally preferred as interaction partners (Barclay & Willer, 2007; Sylwester & Roberts, 2010), leaders (Milinski et al., 2002), and long-term romantic partners (Barclay, 2010). As a result, engaging in various acts of generosity also increases the status and reputation of the signaler (reviewed by Kafashan, Sparks, Griskevicius, & Barclay, 2014).

Using Generosity to Compete

One way that almost anyone can increase their value as a cooperative partner or mate is to be generous. Behaving generously increases one's desirability as a partner because it displays one's enhanced ability and willingness to offer and/or share benefits within a partnership (Barclay, 2013; Noë & Hammerstein, 1994, 1995). This fact incentivizes individuals (not necessarily consciously) to act *more* generously than others in their social environment. By being more generous than others, individuals can signal *greater* qualities to potential partners, allowing them to out-compete others to access to the most beneficial partnerships (Barclay, 2013, 2016; Noë & Hammerstein, 1994, 1995; Roberts, 1998). This notion of escalating one's generosity to be *more* generous than those around you is known as competitive altruism or competitive helping (Barclay, 2004, 2011; Barclay & Willer, 2007; Roberts, 1998; Van Vugt, Roberts, & Hardy, 2007).

Findings from many lab studies support the signaling logic of competitive altruism. For example, people give more to their partners in economic games when such contributions are public instead of private (e.g., Hardy & Van Vugt, 2006; Milinski et al., 2002), and, most importantly, if public contributions are coupled with the opportunity for partner choice, then people escalate their contributions even further (e.g., Barclay, 2004; Barclay & Willer, 2007; Sylwester & Roberts, 2010). This suggests that people are actively competing with others for interaction partners by being more generous (see also Raihani & Smith, 2015). Additional studies have shown that being more generous than others allows one to gain a reputation for trustworthiness and high status (Barclay, 2004; Hardy & Van Vugt, 2006; Price, 2003; Van Vugt & Hardy, 2010; Willer, 2009).

Researchers have applied the logic of competitive altruism to understanding extravagant forms of helping (e.g., Barclay, 2010; Van Vugt et al., 2007), suggesting that heroism is one way to compete for status, which in turn enables one access to social benefits. And, heroes may be more inclined to such competitive altruism than the average individual because they pay a lower marginal cost to provide greater-than-expected benefits to others. Of course, individuals do not need to be conscious of the link between competitive altruism and fitness to engage in such prosocial behaviors.

Non-Adaptive Explanations of Heroism

So far we have discussed adaptive explanations for heroism, by showing that the benefits of extravagant helping can outweigh the costs for actors involved. Of course, there are many non-adaptive instances of generosity. That is, people sometimes help others in situations where the benefits of being helpful do not outweigh the costs, and such heroic behavior does not increase the inclusive fitness of the generous individual. Contrary to popular misconceptions, evolutionary theory does not predict helpful behavior will only be used adaptively. For any given decision making process, errors and mistakes are inevitable (Johnson et al., 2013). Evolved mechanisms do not perform perfectly all the time. There are instances where mechanisms break down, leading to unintended consequences for one's behavior. Although a thorough review of non-adaptive explanations of generosity is beyond the scope of this chapter (instead, see Barclay & Van Vugt, 2015), it is worth briefly mentioning three non-adaptive explanations to add to our discussion of evolutionary perspectives on heroism.

Mistakes

Our decision-making mechanisms have evolved to be *adaptive on average*. That is, on average, over time and across situations, adaptive mechanisms will yield more benefits than costs, increasing the inclusive fitness of the actor. However, *mistakes* are inevitable (Johnson et al., 2013). Because mechanisms are only adaptive on average, there might be certain situations or circumstances where one does not receive benefits from helping. As examples, one may help an individual who does not reciprocate, or one may perform help in private when reputational benefits are not possible.

Mistakes resulting in extreme forms of helping are also possible. Although many may receive fitness benefits for their heroic deeds, some heroes, unfortunately, pay the ultimate price. That is, heroes occasionally lose their lives by attempting to rescue non-relatives from danger. In such situations, the costs may far exceed the benefits of extreme helping, such that the heroic act does not increase the inclusive fitness of the individual.[2]

If there are such high potential costs associated with heroism, what sort of decision making process might lead one to be a hero? Recent research reveals that heroic action may, in fact, be a result of mistakes in a given decision making process. Specifically, Rand and Epstein (2014) found that recipients of the Carnegie Medal acted heroically without deliberate thought, but instead with extremely quick, intuitive, and automatic processing. Rand and Epstein argue that such findings are consistent with the Social Heuristics Hypothesis (Rand et al., 2014), which suggest that heroes may be wrongfully overgeneralizing the gains from low-stake cooperation (i.e., helping in low-stake situations is a long-term fitness enhancing strategy) to more extreme, dangerous forms of helping (where low-stake cooperative gains do not apply). Thus, under this line of thought, it is possible that heroism is a product of a mistake in a decision making process. But, despite this, some heroes might have been able to reap more gains than costs in performing heroic action. And, as long as such non-adaptive instances of giving are outweighed by adaptive instances (i.e., when help is reciprocated at a time of need, one performs helping that results in reputational benefits, and/or one lives to reap the social benefits of heroism), then prosocial sentiment would still be adaptive and genetic variation associated with such sentiment will increase in frequency over generations (Delton, Krasnow, Cosmides, & Tooby, 2013).

Outliers

Individuals vary in countless ways, from their genetic make-up, to their environment of upbringing, past experiences, and learning ability. For any trait that involves variation, the distribution of that trait resembles a bell curve (Tooby & Cosmides, 1990), especially when multiple genes are involved. Although there may be an optimal level of a trait, random variation inevitably exists. Such variation can be a result of random mutations, recombination of different genes, and selection pressures being imperfect. Most people will exhibit near-optimal levels of the trait (e.g., helping not much more or less than needed to receive benefits to outweigh the costs), while others will be on the tail end of this distribution, either being overly helpful or overly selfish. Thus, if one is extremely generous and performs heroic deeds without gaining the fitness benefits to compensate for the costs of such kindness, one might just be on the tail end of the distribution.

Breakdown of mechanisms

Perturbations or accidents during development can also lead to a *breakdown of mechanisms*. Humans are subject to various pathologies throughout development, and exposure to perturbations, such as pathogens, genetic mutations, or physical trauma, could result in non-adaptive forms of helping. For example, stroke victims sometimes display pathological generosity and become completely selfless, even though doing so harms them and their relationships (Ferreira-Garcia, Fontenelle, Moll, & de Oliveira, 2014). Is it possible that some heroes have experienced some brain damage that causes them to be so selfless? This remains a theoretical possibility.

Why Call Someone a Hero?

So far, we have focused on understanding heroism from the hero's perspective: We've argued that the costs borne by heroes can be compensated by status benefits delivered. But, a thorough investigation of the evolutionary existence of heroism requires examination of the observer or judge—those who call others heroes and bestow status benefits on these heroes. In this section, we look at the other side of the transaction and examine heroism from the judge's perspective. In other words, we offer tentative answers to the general questions: what is in it for the observer or judge, and why might someone deem another a hero?

One type of explanation for hero judgment is that heroes can serve as role models—imitating them can be a path to success. Seeing Michael Jordan achieve fame and fortune through his basketball heroics (and urged on by the famous Gatorade commercial), many young athletes wanted to "be like Mike." But imitating successful people does not require publicly declaring their heroism; one's choice of role model could be purely private. Most hero judgments, however, are often not private matters—why? In this section we focus on explaining hero judgments that are publicly declared, defended, and acted upon.

Although little empirical work has directly investigated this issue, we use well-defined evolutionary-minded theoretical concepts to speculate about this topic. In doing this, we begin by examining the costs of making heroism judgments, and then move on to consider when benefits might offset these costs.

The Costs of Heroism Judgments

High status allows heroes greater access to social rewards and a greater share of finite resources. So a judgment that someone is a hero is equivalent to a judgment that the heroic person should be granted elevated status and its accompanying rewards—implying that the judge herself should have relatively less status and reduced access to valued resources. Thus, hero judgments can involve suppressing one's own status and thereby future access to resources. Current resources are also on the line. People give gifts to their heroes, spend time honoring them, and argue about who is or isn't heroic, using precious time and social capital. Declaring some people to be heroes (e.g., NSA whistleblower Edward Snowden) could limit your access to certain social opportunities (e.g., jobs with intelligence agencies). These resource costs and forgone opportunities represent some of the meaningful costs of making hero judgments.

Further, people often must incur costs to defend their hero judgments, sometimes leading to costly conflict between those with differing judgments. After MSNBC journalist Chris Hayes expressed discomfort with the widespread practice of automatically calling deceased United States military members heroes, a panel of pundits on *NBC Today* condemned his comments and added that Hayes "looks like a weenie" (Drennan, 2012). Hayes apologized for his comments and kept his job. For disputing the heroic status of his country's military, Australian sports commentator Scott McIntyre was fired by Special Broadcasting Services and harshly criticized by Communications Minister Malcolm Turnbull (Whitbourn, 2015).

Why do people risk their jobs to voice their opinion about who is or isn't a hero? Why will people condemn, insult, or even threaten the livelihood of someone who disagrees with their hero judgments? Incurring costs to confer benefits on someone else is the definition of (costly) cooperative behavior, so our explanations of heroism judgment are specific implementations of a broader explanatory framework for explaining costly cooperation. As such, the theoretical concepts about cooperation on which we base the following discussion are generally well-established (Barclay & Van Vugt, 2015), but our application to the specific topic of heroism is speculative.

Benefits of Heroism Judgments

Just as the costs borne by heroes present an evolutionary puzzle—are there corresponding benefits for heroes?—the costs borne by judgers of heroism demand functional explanation—why incur costs to bestow status upon others? In this section, we discuss the various benefits that can accrue to those who make good heroism judgments (i.e., those who receive a higher benefit-to-cost ratio for their heroic judgments).

Reciprocity Benefits: Heroism Judgments as Prestige-for-Help Transactions

My hero!

Damsel in distress to her rescuer

Heroism judgments can be half of a mutually-beneficial transaction—a hero performs some special deed that directly benefits the judge and receives prestige in return (Chapais, 2015). This could be a one-time transaction, or part of an ongoing series of exchanging help as in an alliance. Endorsing the heroism of someone who helps you personally can thus be a form of reciprocity, perhaps a very efficient form. Rather than help your ally (or rescuer) with a direct transfer of your own resources (especially difficult if a monster has you captive in its lair), you instead will convince others to grant prestige and resources to your ally by proclaiming the ally's heroism. In addition to maintaining the relationship (and/or your reputation, see below) by meeting your reciprocal obligation, your ally is then in a stronger position to provide further benefits to you, and can be more confident that you'll continue returning the favour.

Nepotistic Benefits: Heroism Judgments as Helping

Humans show nepotistic biases in a variety of their cooperative behaviors (e.g., Stewart-Williams, 2007, 2008), suggesting that people might bias their heroism judgment in favor of kin. A recent Harris poll seems supportive (Pollack, 2014). Over two thousand and five hundred American adults spontaneously named three heroes; more people named at least one family member (32%) than any other category, including military (21%), religious figures (19%), medical and emergency services personnel (18%), US presidents (17%), activists and humanitarians (12%), and celebrities (11%).

The costs invested in promoting the heroism of family members can be repaid in inclusive fitness benefits if the heroic kin convert their status gains into reproductive success (Hamilton, 1964). Furthermore, our kin are the people most likely to provide help to us when we need it, so enhancing their status and resource access may indirectly create future benefits for us. Additionally or alternatively, having heroic kin or allies might elevate our own status. For example, we might gain resources and opportunities from people seeking the favor of our heroic sibling.

Reputational Benefits: Heroism Judgment as Costly Signaling

Costly signals honestly advertise the ability and willingness of the signaler to provide benefits to partners, and the potential costs of such advertising can be compensated by the benefits associated with increased access to quality partners. We have argued that acts of heroism can function as costly signals; here we argue that judgments about heroism can function similarly. It is probably quite clear why heroes make desirable partners: who *wouldn't* want a friend with exceptional ability and/or willingness to deliver benefits? Alas, most of us are unexceptional (by definition) and will therefore be unlikely to attract exceptional partners—but we still want the best available partners from our pool of non-exceptional folks (Barclay, 2013, 2016). Heroism judgments can facilitate partnerships by revealing honest information about the partner quality of the judge.

What desirable abilities underlie heroism judgments? Naming a hero requires understanding and applying the concept of heroism. Someone who earnestly asserts that a puddle or a rock is heroic has demonstrated a basic misunderstanding and is therefore probably not a desirable partner. Good hero judgments that actually contribute to the status of heroes require more than the simple ability to distinguish humans from non-living entities. Recognizing who are exceptional deliverers of benefits requires the ability to understand and track complex social behaviors and relationships, such as who did what to whom, how these behaviors affected everyone involved, how this history will be perceived by others, etc. Convincing others to recognize the status of heroes, or at least respect our judgment, requires abilities of persuasion and influence. For example, to successfully argue that Charles Darwin was a hero might require special abilities like general knowledge about science and history, expertise in evolutionary biology and its influence on other fields, and the verbal and reasoning skills to make a compelling case.

In addition to demonstrating these types of abilities that make us potentially valuable to our partners, heroism judgments can also signal willingness to help our partners. We can adhere to partners' expectations about what is fair, good, and reasonable by not exhibiting unjustifiable selfish biases (DeScioli et al., 2014). Relentless advocacy of the heroism of in-group members could demonstrate loyalty to the group, which may enhance the advocate's access to group benefits.

Political Benefits: Heroism Judgments as Social Niche Construction

Niche construction (Laland, Odling-Smee & Feldman, 2000) is a process whereby an organism modifies its immediate environment—its niche. Widespread recognition of a hero sets a precedent, incentivizing certain kinds of behaviors by implying they can be rewarded with prestige. To the extent such precedents are widely known, heroism judgments have social/political consequences that can shape our environments and can be regarded as a form of social niche construction. Changes to a feature of a social/political environment will have different effects on different people within that environment, depending on their own personal ability to exploit the change for their own benefit (DeScioli et al., 2014; Weeden & Kurzban, 2014). People's attitudes towards these influential features of the social environment, features such as what kinds of behaviors are rewarded with prestige, can be expected to reflect their varying interests and abilities relevant to those behaviors.

This type of social niche construction perspective on the function of social judgments has received support in recent studies showing that moral condemnation judgments reflect the interests of the judge. For example, those more vulnerable to pathogens and exploitation more intensely condemn disease-spreading behaviors (van Leeuwen et al., 2012) and exploitative acts (Petersen, 2013; Sparks & Barclay, 2015), respectively. The connection between a judgment and the judge's interest can be more subtle. For example, dedicated monogamists tend to condemn recreational drug use (Kurzban, Dukes, & Weeden, 2010). Drug use doesn't directly harm the monogamists, but drug users also tend to be promiscuous. Promiscuous people do threaten the interests of monogamists—their sexual availability may tempt the partners of monogamists into infidelities. Monogamous people's condemnation of drug users thus functions as moral pretense for imposing costs upon reproductive rivals (Kurzban et al., 2010).

Heroic praise (e.g., moralization of political heroes like Gandhi and Martin Luther King, Jr.) is roughly the opposite of moral condemnation (e.g., disapproval of political villains like Hitler and Pol Pot). And thus, these two forms of judgment can be expected to follow roughly similar functional logic. Heroism judgments can benefit the judge if the judgments lead to changes in the judge's social environment that the judge is well-positioned to exploit. For example, the authors of this chapter might endorse the Nobel Prize candidacy of an evolutionary biologist, not because we work with her or have been directly helped by her work, but because her academic heroism might cause Universities to become more interested in hiring and supporting other academics who study evolution ... like us!

Context-Specificity of Hero Judgments

Heroism judgments can be made in a wide variety of different contexts: telling children a story, applauding at a ceremony, making a charitable donation, debating sports over beers in a pub, considering a job offer from a prestigious employer, deciding whether to support a revolutionary leader against an oppressive regime. The magnitude(s) and source(s) of costs and benefits can vary widely among these circumstances, so we expect judgment to be based on some kind of integration of context-specific estimates of the various payoffs. For example, people tend to care about the intentions of others, preferring to partner with those who cooperate without the appearance of self-interested calculation (Hoffman, Yoeli & Nowak, 2015). This suggests that heroism judgments of those who expect to benefit from future reciprocity with the hero will be influenced by what the judge believes to be the hero's intentions. In contrast, for judgments that capture political benefits, the hero's intentions are only relevant insofar as they influence the judge's ability to change the social environment.

Thus, an evolutionary scientist may claim Darwin as her hero if she's asked while interviewing for an academic job. But, the same scientist might proclaim Miles Davis as her hero if she is trying to join a band. Hero judgments may be different when writing a eulogy than when chatting on a first date. The judgments may be different depending on who is in the casket and the audience for the eulogy, and whether the date is with a solider or a peace activist.

Real-World Applications

We have now reviewed various evolutionary concepts related to heroism, and addressed the evolutionary function of performing heroic acts (actor's perspective) and calling someone a hero (judge's perspective). All of this information is well and good, but knowledge is only useful if it can be applied to effect change. So, how can we apply these ideas about heroism to promote heroic behavior?

We have argued that heroism may function to signal desirable qualities to observers of the heroic acts; now we cautiously recommend harnessing these forces of reputation to encourage more societal cooperation (see also Barclay, 2012). Field experiments show that reputation can help solve many real-world problems where cooperation otherwise breaks down, including littering, energy overuse, and underfunded charities (reviewed by Kraft-Todd et al., 2015). The same thing can happen with many other types of heroism we have discussed. When heroism is better publicized, it enhances the reputational incentives necessary for heroism to spread. This is more than people blindly imitating what others do: audiences will also see the recognition that heroes receive, which gives them good reason to preferentially imitate heroes. Important note: we are not suggesting explicitly providing rewards to heroes—instead we are suggesting providing opportunities for heroes to gain recognition for their actions, and audience's natural responses will naturally provide those rewards.

Slate.com used to publish the *Slate 60*, a list of the 60 biggest personal charitable contributions in each year—these are all multi-million dollar donations that truly deserve to be called heroic. Although slate.com apparently no longer publishes this list, other news agencies now do so. Such lists not only encourage hero-sized donations, but also create competition among philanthropists to be a *bigger* hero than others. People like to compete with each other, so why not harness that urge for good by inciting competitive helping (Barclay, 2004, 2013; Barclay & Willer, 2007; Roberts, 1998)? Such lists of "biggest heroes" could apply to any domain where we need people to lead the way, whether it is personal philanthropy, corporate philanthropy, environmental sustainability, pollution control, or social, ethical, and moral responsibility. Many magazines publish lists of companies that do the most for their employees or to protect the environment; we can imagine similar lists in these other domains as well. It is better to have people compete in these domains than in less beneficial ways such as overconsumption. And why must people always compete nationally to be the biggest heroes? Local lists in local publications may be most effective at promoting "everyday heroism," given that people compare themselves most with the people they interact with the most. The positive effects of countless "everyday heroes" might well outweigh the effects of focusing on a select few "uber-heroes."

When publicizing heroism in any domain, we would encourage larger lists like Slate's 60 biggest donations, rather than smaller lists like the 10 biggest donations. Large lists encourage competitive philanthropy among givers who would not make the top 10 but could still gain wide recognition for being, say, the 48th biggest donor (who gave over $20 million in 2010). Much heroism would go unrecognized if we only ever know the single biggest donors, and signaling theory predicts that those who cannot win a competition (e.g., be the biggest hero) may stop trying (e.g., Barclay, 2016; Dessalles, 2014). Larger lists could still focus more on the biggest donors in order to encourage ultra-philanthropy among the uber-rich, while giving some recognition to others whose philanthropy is only slightly less heroic.

While we recommend harnessing the power of reputation to promote heroism, it would be irresponsible of anyone to make recommendations without providing appropriate cautions and limitations. The science of reputation is still relatively new, so there are still several unknowns, as well as some known limitations (Barclay, 2012).

The biggest risk of promoting heroism with reputational incentives is that such attempts will accidentally undermine prosocial goals (Barclay, 2012). It is hard to decipher someone's motives if they have extrinsic incentives for their behavior. Who would you trust more: someone who jumped into a dangerous river to save a baby even though no one was looking, or someone who did so in front of a live television audience? We suspect the former. While both baby-savers may have equally heroic character, it is hard to know whether the second one risked his life because he genuinely wanted to help or because he knew the cameras were rolling. Research shows that people who help others are viewed as less charitable if the helper receives direct benefits for her actions or if the recipient was a close friend of the helper (Lin-Healy & Small, 2012, 2013). A similar effect could occur with reputational benefits: audiences might attribute less charitable motives to heroes if it is common knowledge that heroes will be publicly rewarded. People might then be less heroic if they anticipate public questioning of their motives (Barclay, 2012; Bénabou & Tirole, 2006).

This may be an example of how extrinsic incentives can undermine intrinsic incentives for action (Deci, Koestner, & Ryan, 1999). One famous example is when daycares introduced small fines for parents who picked up their children late, and parents' lateness got *worse* (Gneezy & Rustichini, 2000a; see also Kraft-Todd et al., 2015). The fines made it unclear whether parents arrived on time to be nice to the daycare workers or simply to avoid the fines—the extrinsic incentives undermined the signaling value of arriving on time, thereby undermining the social incentives to arrive on time (Bénabou & Tirole, 2006). In a similar vein, explicit intrinsic incentives for heroism may undermine its value for signaling the hero's good character, and thus inadvertently undermine heroism (Barclay, 2012).

Barclay (2012) suggests some ways to prevent this undermining. For example, rather than explicitly rewarding heroes, would-be social engineers could simply create opportunities for heroes to acquire a good reputation from others. They need not mention any benefits when doing so, and indeed should *not* mention such benefits! Furthermore, they could compare heroes with people who incur similar costs for less noble causes (e.g., starting charities versus buying bigger houses). If explicit top-down incentives are ever used, they need to be big enough to fully repay the cost of heroism or else they will be counter-productive—as the title of Gneezy and Rustichini's classic paper (2000b) says, "Pay enough or don't pay at all." A mixed design that involves both explicit material rewards and reputational rewards may have the beneficial effects of neither.

Summary and Conclusion

We began this chapter by first defining heroism as an extreme form of prosociality, whereby heroes deliver greater-than-expected benefits for a given cost. We then examined how and why evolutionary theory sets expected levels of benefits for cooperation by reviewing models of kin selection, reciprocity, vested interest, and punishment. Establishing expected levels of benefits then enabled us to explore evolutionary reasons for why heroes go above expectations and why observers bestow status on these individuals. Under a costly signaling interpretation, heroes are viewed as high quality individuals that pay lower potential costs (or reap greater benefits) for delivering supererogatory benefits to others. Field and lab evidence supports this logic. We extended this logic beyond the displays of physical ability exhibited by archetypal heroes, to the displays of resources and intelligence of philanthropic and intellectual heroes. The judge's side is equally relevant in the discussion of heroism, as observers willingly bestow great status on heroes, allowing heroes access to precious finite resources. Although judges may incur costs by deeming someone a hero (e.g., suppressing one's own status and access to future resources; limiting opportunities), there could be potential benefits that surpass such costs. We speculate that these benefits could increase one's fitness via reciprocity, nepotism, reputation, and social niche construction.

To conclude this chapter, we cautiously offered examples of how to apply evolutionary perspectives on extreme helping to encourage more heroic behavior. It may be particularly important to create opportunities for people to observe and acknowledge heroism: such opportunities enable observers to bestow status on heroes, further incentivizing and reinforcing heroism. Publicizing and making lists larger could also ensure that no hero goes unnoticed, again creating motivation to be a hero. As mentioned, there are potential risks of harnessing the power of reputation to promote heroism (e.g., Barclay, 2012). But, with careful implementation and further investigation, these risks may be well worth the gains.

Notes

1. In this chapter, several terms, such as generosity, kindness, cooperation, altruism, and helpful acts, will be used interchangeably to refer to the above definition.
2. Losing one's life may not be a "mistake" in that the act could still increase the inclusive fitness of the hero if the rescued individual is a close relative (i.e., kin selection: Hamilton, 1964) or if kin receive benefits from others because of the hero's dying act, e.g., increased status or money to relatives (Blackwell, 2006; CBSNews.com, 2002).

References

Anderson, C., & Kilduff, G. J. (2009). Why do dominant personalities attain influence in face-to-face groups? The competence-signalling effects of trait dominance. *Journal of Personality and Social Psychology, 96*, 491–503.

André, J.-B. (2010). The evolution of reciprocity: Social types of social incentives? *The American Naturalist, 175*, 197–210.

Axelrod, R. (1984). *The evolution of cooperation*. New York: Basic Books.

Balliet, D., Mulder, L. B., & Van Lange, P. A. M. (2011). Reward, punishment, and cooperation: A meta-analysis. *Psychological Bulletin, 137*, 594–615.

Barclay, P. (2004). Trustworthiness and Competitive Altruism Can Also Solve the "Tragedy of the Commons." *Evolution & Human Behavior, 25*(4), 209–220.

Barclay, P. (2006). Reputational benefits for altruistic punishment. *Evolution and Human Behavior, 27*, 325–344.

Barclay, P. (2010). Altruism as a courtship display: Some effects of third-party generosity on audience perceptions. *British Journal of Psychology, 101*, 123–135.

Barclay, P. (2011). Competitive helping increases with the size of biological markets and invades defection. *Journal of Theoretical Biology, 281*, 47–55.

Barclay, P. (2012). Harnessing the power of reputation: strengths and limits for promoting cooperative behaviours. *Evolutionary Psychology*, *10*(5), 868–883.

Barclay, P. (2013). Strategies for cooperation in biological markets, especially for humans. *Evolution & Human Behavior*, *34*(3), 164–175.

Barclay, P. (2016). Biological markets and the effects of partner choice on cooperation and friendship. In press at *Current Opinion in Psychology*.

Barclay, P., & Reeve, H. K. (2012). The varying relationship between helping and individual quality. *Behavioral Ecology*, *23*(4), 693–698.

Barclay, P., & Van Vugt, M. (2015). The evolutionary psychology of human prosociality: adaptations, mistakes, and byproducts. In D. Schroeder & W. Graziano (eds) *Oxford Handbook of Prosocial Behavior* (pp. 37–60). Oxford, UK: Oxford University Press.

Barclay, P., & Willer, R. (2007). Partner choice creates competitive altruism in humans. *Proceedings of the Royal Society of London Series B*, *274*, 749–753.

Baumard, N. & Boyer, P. (2013). Explaining moral religions. *Trends in Cognitive Sciences*, *17*, 272–280.

Bénabou, R., & Tirole, J. (2006). Incentives and prosocial behavior. *The American Economic Review*, *96*, 1652–1678.

Blackwell, A. (2006). Terrorism, heroism, and altruism: the behavioral ecology of Palestinian suicide attacks as a model for the evolution of self-sacrificial behavior in humans. Unpublished Master's thesis, University of Oregon, Eugene, OR.

Bolle, F. (2001). Why to buy your darling flowers: On cooperation and exploitation. *Theory and Decision*, *50*, 1–28.

Brown, P. (1978). New Guinea: Ecology, society, and culture. *Annual Review of Anthropology*, *7*, 263–291.

Brown, S. L., & Brown, M. (2006). Selective investment theory. *Psychological Inquiry*, *17*, 1–29.

CBSnews.com. (2002). Salaries for suicide bombers. *CBS News* (April 3). Retrieved from www.cbsnews.com/stories/2002/04/03/world/main505316.shtm.

Chapais, B (2015). Competence and the evolutionary origins of status and power in humans. *Human Nature 26*, 161–183.

Cheng, J. T., Tracy, J. L., Foulsham, T., Kingstone, A., & Henrich, J. (2013). Two ways to the top: Evidence that dominance and prestige are distinct yet viable avenues to social rank and influence. *Journal of Personality and Social Psychology*, *104*, 103–125.

Clark, J. (2002). Recognizing large donations to public goods: an experimental test. *Managerial and Decision Economics*, *23*, 33–44.

Deci, E. L., Koestner, R., & Ryan, R. M. (1999). A meta-analytic review of experiments examining the effects of extrinsic rewards on internal motivation. *Psychological Bulletin*, *125*, 627–668.

Delton, A. W., Krasnow, M. M., Cosmides, L., & Tooby, J. (2011). Evolution of direct reciprocity under uncertainty can explain human generosity in one-shot encounters. *Proceedings of the National Academy of Sciences*, *108*, 13,335–13,340.

DeScioli, P., Massenkoff, M., Shaw, A., Petersen, M., & Kurzban, R. (2014). Equity or equality? Moral judgments follow the money. *Proceedings of the Royal Society B*, *281*, 20142012.

Dessalles, J.-L. (2014). Optimal investment in social signals. *Evolution*, *68*, 1640–1650.

Diamond, D. (2015). Bill Gates will try to save 2 million children from dying this year—here's how. *Forbes* (January 22). Retrieved from www.forbes.com/sites/dandiamond/2015/01/22/bill-gates-says-we-can-save-millions-of-children-from-dying-heres-how/

Drennan, K. (2012). NBC "Today" panel rips Chis Hayes: "He looks like a weenie" after anti-military comments. *Media Research Center NewsBusters* (May 29). Retrieved from http://newsbusters.org/blogs/kyle-drennen/2012/05/29/nbc-today-panel-rips-chris-hayes-he-looks-weenie-after-anti-military-c

Driskell, J. E., Olmstead, B., & Salas, E. (1993). Task cues, dominance cues, and influence in task groups. *Journal of Applied Psychology*, *78*, 51–60.

Dunbar, R. I. M., & Shultz, S. (2007). Evolution in the social brain. *Science*, *317*, 1344–1347.

Farthing, G. W. (2005). Attitudes towards heroic and nonheroic risk takers as mates and as friends. *Evolution and Human Behaviour*, *26*, 171–185.

Ferreira-Garcia, R., Fontenelle, L. F., Moll, J., & de Oliveira, R. (2014). Pathological generosity: An atypical impulse control disorder after a left subcortical stroke. *Neurocase: The Neural Basis of Cognition*, *20*, 496–500.

Furlow, F. B., Armijo-Prewitt, T., Gangestad, S. W., & Thornhill, R. (1997). Fluctuating asymmetry and psychometric intelligence. *Proceedings of the Royal Society B*, *264*, 823–829.

Getty, T. (1998). Handicap signalling: When fecundity and viability do not add up. *Animal Behaviour*, *56*, 127–130.

Getty, T. (2006). Sexually selected signals are not similar to sports handicaps. *Trends in Ecology & Evolution*, *21*, 83–88.

Gintis, H., Smith, E. A., & Bowles, S. (2001). Cooperation and costly signalling. *Journal of Theoretical Biology*, *213*, 103–119.
Gneezy, U., & Rustichini, A. (2000a). A fine is a price. *Journal of Legal Studies*, *29*, 1–17.
Gneezy, U., & Rustichini, A. (2000b). Pay enough or don't pay at all. *The Quarterly Journal of Economics*, *115*, 791–810.
Goldman, I. (1937). The Kwakiutl Indians of Vancouver Island. In M. Mead (ed.), *Cooperation and Competition Among Primitive People* (pp. 180–209). Boston, MA: Beacon Press.
Grafen, A. (1990). Biological signals as handicaps. *Journal of Theoretical Biology*, *144*, 517–546.
Griskevicius, V., Tybur, J. M., Sundie, J. M., Cialdini, R. B., Miller, G. F., & Kenrick, D. T. (2007).Blatant benevolence and conspicuous consumption: When romantic motives elicit strategic costly signals. *Journal of Personality and Social Psychology*, *93*, 85–102.
Hamilton, W. D. (1963). The evolution of altruistic behaviour. *The American Naturalist*, *97*, 354–356.
Hamilton, W. D. (1964). The genetical evolution of social behavior. *Journal of Theoretical Biology* 7, 1–52.
Hardy, C. L., & Van Vugt, M. (2006). Nice guys finish first: The competitive altruism hypothesis. *Personality and Social Psychology Bulletin*, *32*, 1402–1413.
Haselton, M. G., & Miller, G. F. (2006). Women's fertility across the cycle increases the short-term attractiveness of creative intelligence. *Human Nature*, *17*, 50–73.
Hawkes, K. (1991). Showing off: Tests of a hypothesis about men's foraging goals. *Ethology and Sociobiology*, *12*, 29–50.
Hawkes, K. (1993). Why hunter-gatherers work: An ancient version of the problem of public goods. *Current Anthropology*, *34*, 341–361.
Hawkes, K., & Bliege Bird, R. (2002). Showing off, handicap signaling, and the evolution of men's work. *Evolutionary Anthropology*, *11*, 58–67.
Hawkes, K., O'Connell, J. F., & Blurton Jones, N. G. (2001). Hadza meat sharing. *Evolution and Human Behaviour*, *22*, 113–142.
Henrich, J., & Gil-White, F. J. (2001). The evolution of prestige: freely conferred deference as a mechanism for enhancing the benefits of cultural transmission. *Evolution and Human Behavior*, *22*, 165–196.
Higham, J. P. (2013). How does honest costly signalling work? *Behavioural Ecology*, *25*, 8–11.
Hill, K., & Kaplan, H. (1988). Tradeoffs in male and female reproductive strategies among the Ache: part 1. In L. Betzig, M. Borgerhoff Mulder, & P. Turke (eds), *Human Reproductive Behaviour: A Darwinian Perspective* (pp. 277–289). Cambridge, UK: Cambridge University Press.
Hoffman, M., Yoeli, E., & Nowak, M. A. (2015). Cooperate without looking: Why we care what people think and not just what they do. *Proceedings of the National Academy of Sciences*, *112*, 1727–1732.
Hurd, P. L. (1995). Communication in discrete action response. *Journal of Theoretical Biology*, *174*, 217–222.
Inside Philanthropy (2015). Tech philanthropists: Guide to top funders in the technology industry. Retrieved from www.insidephilanthropy.com/guide-to-individual-donors/mark-zuckerberg.html.
Johnson, D. D. P., Blumstein, D. T., Fowler, J. H., & Haselton, M. G. (2013). The evolution of error: error management, cognitive constraints, and adaptive decision-making biases. *Trends in Ecology and Evolution*, *28*, 474–481.
Kafashan, S., Sparks, A., Griskevicius, V., & Barclay, P. (2014). Prosocial behaviour and social status. In J. T. Cheng, J. L. Tracy, & C. Anderson (eds) *The Psychology of Social Status* (pp. 139–158). New York: Springer.
Kelly, S., & Dunbar, R. I. M. (2001). Who dares, wins: Heroism vs. altruism in women's mate choice. *Human Nature*, *12*, 89–105.
Kraft-Todd, G., Yoeli, E., Bhanot, S., & Rand, D. (2015). Promoting cooperation in the field. *Current Opinion in Behavioral Sciences*, *3*, 96–101.
Kurzban, R., Dukes, A., & Weeden, J. (2010). Sex, drugs, and moral goals: Reproductive strategies and views about recreational drugs. *Proceedings of the Royal Society B*, *277*, 3501–3508.
Laland, K. N., Odling-Smee, J., & Feldman, M. W. (2000). Niche construction, biological evolution, and cultural change. *Behavioral and Brain Sciences* 23, 131–175.
Lane, R. (2013). The 50 philanthropists who have given away the most money. *Forbes* (November 18). Retrieved from www.forbes.com/sites/randalllane/2013/11/18/the-50-philanthropists-who-have-given-away-the-most-money.
Lewis, J. (2015). Why Bill Gates is a true hero. *The Telegraph* (January 9). Retrieved from www.telegraph.co.uk/technology/bill-gates/11334128/Why-Bill-Gates-is-a-true-hero.html.
Lin-Healy, F., & Small, D. A. (2012). Cheapened altruism: discounting personally affected prosocial actors. *Organizational Behavior and Human Decision Processes*, *117*, 269–274.
Lin-Healy, F., & Small, D. A. (2013). Nice guys finish last and guys in last are nice: the clash between doing well and doing good. *Social Psychology and Personality Science*, *4*, 692–698.
Luxen, M. F., & Buunk, B. P. (2006). Human intelligence, fluctuating asymmetry and the peacock's tail:

General intelligence (g) as an honest signal of fitness. *Personality and Individual Differences, 41*, 897–902.
Mateo, J. M. (2015). Hamilton's legacy: Mechanisms of kin recognition in humans. *Ethology, 121*, 419–427.
McNamara, J. M., Barta, Z., Frohmage, L., & Houston, A. I. (2008). The coevolution of choosiness and cooperation. *Nature, 451*, 189–192.
Milinski, M., Semmann, D., & Krambeck, H.-J. (2002). Reputation helps solve the "tragedy of the commons." *Nature, 415*, 424–426.
Miller, G. F. (2000). *The mating mind: How sexual choice shaped the evolution of human nature.* New York: Anchor Books.
New York Times (1937). Rockefeller gifts total $530,850,632. *The New York Times* (24 May). Retrieved from www.nytimes.com/books/98/05/17/specials/rockefeller-gifts.html
Noë, R., & Hammerstein, P. (1994). Biological markets: Supply and demand determine the effect of partner choice in cooperation, mutualism, and mating. *Behavioural Ecology & Sociobiology, 35*, 1–11.
Noë, R., & Hammerstein, P. (1995). Biological markets. *Trends in Ecology & Evolution, 10*, 336–339.
Nowak, M. A., & Sigmund, K. (2005). Evolution of indirect reciprocity. *Nature, 437*, 1291–1298.
Ohtsubo, Y., & Watanabe, E. (2009). Do sincere apologies need to be costly? Test of a costly signalling model of apology. *Evolution and Human Behaviour, 30*, 114–123.
Ostrom, E. (1990). *Governing the Commons: The Evolution of Institutions for Collective Action.* Cambridge, UK: Cambridge University Press.
Petersen, M. B. (2013). Moralization as protection against exploitation: do individuals without allies moralize more? *Evolution and Human Behavior 34*, 78–85.
Piddocke, S. (1965). The potlatch system of the Southern Kwakiutl: A new perspective. *Southwestern Journal of Anthropology, 21*, 244–264.
Pollack, H. (2014). Many Americans find their heroes in family members. Retrieved from www.harrisinteractive.com/NewsRoom/HarrisPolls/tabid/447/ctl/ReadCustom%20Default/mid/1508/ArticleId/1518/Default.aspx
Price, M. E. (2003). Pro-community altruism and social status in a shuar village. *Human Nature, 14*, 191–208.
Raihani, N. J., & Smith, S. (2015). Competitive helping in online giving. *Current Biology, 25*, 1183–1186.
Rand, D. G., & Epstein, Z. G. (2014). Risking your life without a second thought: Intuitive decision making and extreme altruism. *PLoS ONE, 9*, e109467.
Rand, D. G., Peysakhovich, A., Kraft-Todd, G. T., Newman, G. E., Wurzbacher, O., et al. (2014). Social heuristics shape intuitive cooperation. *Nature Communications, 5*, 3677.
Roberts, G. (1998). Competitive altruism: from reciprocity to the handicap principle. *Proceedings: Biological Sciences, 265*, 427–431.
Roberts, G. (2005). Cooperation through interdependence. *Animal Behaviour, 70*, 901–908.
Rockefeller Archive Center (2015). 100 years: The Rockefeller Foundation. Retrieved from http://rockefeller100.org/exhibits/show/health/yellow-fever.
Scott-Phillips, T. C., Dickins, T. E., & West, S. A. (2011). Evolutionary theory and the ultimate–proximate distinction in the human behavioral sciences. *Perspectives on Psychological Science, 6*, 38–47.
Smith, E. A., & Bliege Bird, R. L. (2000). Turtle hunting and tombstone opening. *Evolution and Human Behavior, 21*, 245–261.
Smith, E. A., & Bliege Bird, R. (2005). Costly signalling and cooperative behaviour. In H. Gintis, S. Bowles, R. Boyd, & E. Fehr (eds) *Moral Sentiment and Material Iinterest: The Foundations of Cooperation in Economic Life* (pp. 115–148). Cambridge, MA: MIT Press.
Smith, E. A., Bliege Bird, R., & Bird, D. W. (2003). The benefits of costly signaling: Meriam turtle hunters. *Behavioral Ecology, 14*, 116–126.
Snyder, B. (2011). Bill Gates, not Steve Jobs, is the real hero. November 3. Retrieved from www.infoworld.com/article/2621430/techology-business/bill-gates—not-steve-jobs—is-the-real-hero.html
Sparks, A., & Barclay, P. (2015). No effect on condemnation of short or long exposure to eye images. *Letters on Evolutionary Behavioral Science, 6*, 13–16.
Stewart-Williams, S. (2007). Altruism among kin vs. nonkin: effects of cost of help and reciprocal exchange. *Evolution and Human Behaviour, 28*, 193–198.
Stewart-Williams, S. (2008). Human beings as evolved nepotists: exceptions to the rule and effects of cost of help. *Human Nature, 19*, 414–425.
Sylwester, K., & Roberts, G. (2010). Cooperators benefit through reputation-based partner choice in economic games. *Biology Letters*, 659–662.
Számadó, S. (1999). The validity of the handicap principle in discrete action response games. *Journal of Theoretical Biology, 198*, 593–602.
Számadó, S. (2011). The cost of honesty and the fallacy of the handicap principle. *Animal Behaviour, 81*, 3–10.

Tibbetts, E. A., & Izzo, A. (2010). Social punishment of dishonest signalers caused by mismatch between signal and behavior. *Current Biology, 20,* 1637–1640.

Tinbergen, N. (1963). On aims and methods of ethology. *Zeitschrift für Tierpsychologie, 20,* 410–433.

Tooby, J., & Cosmides, L. (1990). On the uniqueness of human nature and the uniqueness of the individual: the role of genetics and adaptation. *Journal of Personality, 58,* 17–67.

Tooby, J., & Cosmides, L. (1996). Friendship and the Banker's Paradox: Other pathways to the evolution of adaptations for altruism. *Proceedings of the British Academy, 88,* 119–143.

Trivers, R. L. (1971). The evolution of reciprocal altruism. *The Quarterly Review of Biology, 46,* 35–57.

van Leeuwen, F., Park, J.H., Koenig, B.L., & Graham, J. (2012). Regional variation in pathogen preference predicts endorsement of group-focused moral concerns. *Evolution and Human Behavior, 33,* 429–437.

Van Vugt, M., & Hardy, C. L. (2010). Cooperation for reputation: Wasteful contributions as costly signals in public goods. *Group Processes & Intergroup Relations, 13,* 101–111.

Van Vugt, M., Roberts, G., & Hardy, C. (2007). Competitive altruism: A theory of reputation-based cooperation in groups. In R. Dunbar, & L. Barrett (eds), *Oxford Handbook of Evolutionary Psychology* (pp. 531–540). Oxford, UK: Oxford University Press.

Weeden, J., & Kurzban, R. (2014). *The hidden agenda of the political mind: How self-interest shapes our opinions and why we won't admit it.* Princeton, NJ: Princeton University Press.

Whitbourn, M. (2015). SBS presenter sacked Scott McIntyre sacked over "inappropriate" Anzac Day tweets. *The Sydney Morning Herald* (April 26). Retrieved from www.smh.com.au/national/ww1/sbs-presenter-scott-mcintyre-sacked-over-inappropriate-anzac-day-tweets-20150426-1mtbx8.html

Wiessner, P. (2002).Hunting, healing, and *hxaro* exchange: A long-term perspective on !Kung (Ju/'hoansi) large-game hunting. *Evolution and Human Behaviour, 23,* 406–437.

Willer, R. (2009). Groups reward individual sacrifice: The status solution to the collective action problem. *American Sociological Review, 74,* 23–43.

Yamagishi, T. (1986). The provision of a sanctioning system as a public good. *Journal of Personality and Social Psychology, 51,* 110–116.

Zahavi, A. (1975). Mate selection: A selection for handicap. *Journal of Theoretical Biology, 53,* 205–214.

Zahavi, A. (1990). Arabian babblers: The quest for social status in a cooperative breeder. In P. B. Stacey, & W. D. Koenig (eds), *Cooperative breeding in birds* (pp. 105–130). Cambridge, U.K.: Cambridge University Press.

Zahavi, A. (1995). Altruism as a handicap: The limitations of kin selection and reciprocity. *Journal of Avian Biology, 26,* 1–3.

Zahavi, A., & Zahavi, A. (1997). *The handicap principle: A missing piece of Darwin's puzzle.* New York: Oxford University Press.

3

Adaptive Foundations of Heroism
Social Heuristics Push Advantageous Everyday Ethical Behavior to Heroic Extremes

Gordon T. Kraft-Todd and David G. Rand

The potential to be a hero is in all of us. This is no mere platitude; it reflects a deep and simple truth: heroism is an extreme form of everyday ethical behavior. Heroes, by our definition, are people who make great personal sacrifices for the benefit of others. From an evolutionary perspective, heroes have a mysterious origin story: how did the "self-interested" process of natural selection give rise to self-sacrifice? Extreme self-sacrificing behavior seems particularly maladaptive: wouldn't heroes have died out by now? We will argue that this puzzle can be resolved by considering the evolutionary logic supporting milder forms of self-sacrifice, the sort of ethics we see in our everyday lives.

We will specifically discuss three types of ethical principles: justice, solidarity, and pacifism. By *justice,* we mean behaviors concerned with fairly distributing resources; by *solidarity*, we mean behaviors concerned with group-beneficial self-sacrifice; and by *pacifism,* we mean behaviors concerned with the avoidance of harming others. These three ethics are not meant to be an exhaustive list, but rather a sample of key ethical principles with the properties of being (a) cooperative (i.e., individually costly but beneficial to others); (b) adaptive (i.e., individually long-run payoff maximizing) in the context of everyday life; but (c) not in one's self-interest (and therefore "heroic") when taken to the extreme.

There is something seemingly counterintuitive about the evolutionary nature of our thesis: how could costly other-benefiting behavior have evolved through a process that is inherently self-interested? The answer has to do with the timescale of evolution. Self-interested behaviors are often thought about in the short term: if I steal money from you today, I will be richer. It is important, however, to consider both the short- *and* long-term consequences of behavior: if I steal from you today, I will be richer today, but you will avoid me in the future and I will miss out on joint ventures with you that will make me richer in the long-term. Not stealing from you, therefore, may *seem* virtuous, but really it is in my long-term self-interest not to do so. If I started as a thief and learned the hard way, it may be that I stop stealing from you not because I am concerned about *you*, but because I am concerned about *myself*. It is therefore important to consider the consequences of behaviors not only in the short-term but in the long-term as well.

Evolution is generally considered in biological terms, as a process that involves environmental and social pressures selecting for adaptive traits which arise from randomly varying genes. But for humans, evolution can occur in the domain of culture, wherein natural selection acts not on genes, but on "memes," or units of culture such as rituals, behaviors, symbols, and strategies (Dawkins, 2006; Richerson & Boyd, 2008). Cultural evolution works via "social learning":

people imitate the actions and beliefs of those whom are seen as successful. Therefore, memes that cause their adopters to succeed (i.e., that increase cultural "fitness") will spread through the population. We will discuss the evolution of heroic ethics mainly in terms of learning, though we will provide evidence of their biological origins as well.

We adopt the dual process model of cognition (Kahneman, 2003; Sloman, 1996), and argue that *social heuristics*, or rules of thumb for thinking about social interaction, play a key role in the transition from adaptive everyday ethicality to heroism. Heuristics can increase long-run payoff-maximizing behavior because they avoid the time and cognitive cost of deliberating when in familiar situations (Gigerenzer, Todd, & Group, 1999; Gilovich, Griffin, & Kahneman, 2002). Applying the general idea of heuristics to social interaction leads to the concept of cooperative intuitions that we develop through our everyday social interactions–because cooperation typically benefits our long-term self-interest (Bear & Rand, 2016; Rand et al., 2014). While cooperative intuitions may typically be adaptive—because the (often long-term) benefits generally outweigh the short-term costs—there are situations in which this is not the case. Also, because social heuristics are automatic, non-reflective processes, they are less sensitive to contextual complexity; that is, they respond similarly in situations where cooperation is advantageous as well as those where it is not. When cooperative intuitions are applied in non-advantageous contexts (i.e., where the short-term costs outweigh the long-term benefits), we often see the resulting behavior as heroic. In other words, everyday ethics are self-sacrificial helping behaviors that benefit the actor in the long run, whereas heroism is self-sacrificial helping behavior that *does not* benefit the actor in the long run.

Heroism, we therefore argue, occurs when cooperative intuitions are over-generalized to situations where they are net costly (for the individual hero). One might object, however, that not all heroism is intuitive in nature—some heroism is quite deliberate. Indeed, we identify two types of heroism: *emergent* and *sustained*. Emergent heroism is an act of self-sacrifice that occurs "without a second thought," exemplified by many of the people honored as Carnegie Heroes who jump in front of trains or into raging rivers to save strangers (Rand & Epstein, 2014). This type of heroism arises directly from the intuitive over-generalization logic laid out above.

Sustained heroism, on the other hand, involves a long-term, often life-long commitment to self-sacrifice, exemplified by the "moral saints" of history such as Mother Teresa or Mahatma Gandhi. We believe this type of heroism could also arise from the logic above, but via a less direct route: it may be that heroic, individually costly cooperative *goals* are set via automatic processes, and this goal setting is based on over-generalization, but then deliberative processes are recruited to pursue these goals (Cushman & Morris, 2015). In other words, it could be that automatic processes lead to the establishment of (heroic) extreme goals, and then deliberative processes enact these goals, leading to sustained heroism over time. For example, many sustained heroes have a distinct moment of inspiration, as Mother Teresa did on a retreat in 1946 (Langford, 2008). It could be that her concept of justice changed to a (heroic) extreme in this moment, driven by an intuitive process, and that the rest of her life was effectively spent pursuing this heroic goal. Alternatively, it could be that deliberative processes contribute to sustained heroism by anticipating guilt for not acting in accordance with intuitive responses favoring extreme prosociality. In other words, it could be that when we deliberate and evaluate our cooperative intuitions, we consider not only the material costs and benefits of cooperating, but also the future psychological costs imposed on us by our intuitive cognitive processes: for example, we might anticipate that we would feel guilty if we do not behave cooperatively (Battigalli & Dufwenberg, 2007). Thus, whether heroism is emergent or sustained, i.e., enacted via intuition or deliberation, it may be that over-generalized cooperative intuitions are at its root.

Importantly, the claim we make here is descriptive, rather than normative. We do not argue that heroism is *bad* because it is individually non-advantageous; on the contrary, we hold that the source of heroism's virtue—the reason it is so *good*—is that it is so remarkably selfless (i.e., costly to the individual). Indeed, exploring the evolutionary roots of moral psychology (Kurzban & DeScioli, 2015) to discover when seemingly altruistic behavior pays off in the long-run (e.g., by benefitting one's reputation, as in Yoeli, Hoffman, Rand, and Nowak, 2013) allows us to identify when cooperation actually is extraordinary and worthy of being called *heroic*.

In sum: we argue that the everyday ethics of justice, solidarity, and pacifism arise from adaptive mechanisms. When these cooperative behaviors are typically individually adaptive, they become automatized as social heuristics. The automaticity of social heuristics makes cooperative behavior prone to over-generalization, and when this occurs in individually costly contexts, the resulting behavior is heroic. Having laid this foundation for the origins of heroism, we now provide a more detailed survey of evidence that justice, solidarity, and pacifism are adaptive and automatic.

Justice

Moral codes in spiritual and secular traditions have long hailed the virtue of justice. Around 800 BC, the Sanskrit epic the Mahabharata stated: "As a man himself sows, so he himself reaps; no man inherits the good or evil act of another man. The fruit is of the same quality as the action" (Hopkins, 1906). Similarly, the Bible says: "Evil men do not understand justice, but those who seek Yahweh understand it fully" (Proverbs 28:5, World English Bible). Social systems are built on conceptions of justice and much of the disagreement in civil society centers on what exactly justice entails. Nearly synonymous with morality itself, justice invokes the idea of right and wrong, and the appropriate respective response of reward and punishment. But justice concerns not only "just deserts" for right and wrong, but encompass more broadly the fair distribution of resources, including the allocation of rewards and punishments. We treat justice as this broad category of behaviors that is concerned with distributing resources fairly. Justice is a puzzling ethical principle to get off the ground in an evolutionary sense, though, because treating others—particularly strangers—fairly may require self-sacrifice. As we will argue, though, justice is adaptive in everyday life, it is often automatic, and in its extreme, it is heroic.

Justice is Adaptive

The logic behind the adaptive value of justice is captured by the idiom "you scratch my back and I'll scratch yours," or, colloquially, "tit-for-tat." This logic was formalized using game theory, which demonstrates how cooperation could evolve among non-kin via a tit-for-tat strategy with initially cooperates, and then imitates its partners move in the previous interaction (Axelrod & Hamilton, 1981). The underlying principle, *direct reciprocity*, is the idea that when individuals interact repeatedly and can remember previous interactions, cooperation among non-kin can be evolutionarily stable (Trivers, 1971). In a world in which you do not see your interaction partners again (e.g., tipping a waiter while on vacation in a foreign country), it is possible to cheat (not tip) because your interaction partner has no recourse. However, in a world in which you repeatedly interact (e.g., tipping a waiter at your favorite local restaurant), it is more difficult to cheat because your interaction partner can reciprocate the behavior (e.g., spit in your food) at your next meeting. Trivers formalized the wisdom of the folk concept of tit-for-tat, demonstrating that it can account for diverse behavior among animals of all stripes, from warning cries in birds to cooperation among humans. Here, we can see how the timescale of evolutionary analysis creates a conflict: while it is our *short-term* (i.e., one-shot interaction) self-interest to defect on others in social dilemmas, it is in our *long-term* (i.e., repeated interaction) self-interest to cooperate with them. The theory of direct reciprocity has been supported by numerous experiments in humans (Dal Bo, 2005; Fudenberg, Rand, & Dreber, 2012) as well as non-human animals (e.g., food sharing among vampire bats: Wilkinson, 1984; grooming in primates: Schino,

2007; but see Clutton-Brock, 2009 for the limitations of direct reciprocity in explaining non-human animal cooperation).

While direct reciprocity may seem straightforwardly applicable to relationships like those found among friends or business partners (and even family), it still does not seem to extend to strangers. That is, when we know our interactions are repeated (as in friendship or business or family), we may cooperate by the logic of tit-for-tat, but what about when we interact with people with whom we are uncertain about the repeated-ness of our future interactions? How could we establish friendships and business partnerships in the first place? And why would we ever be nice to strangers with whom we know we will *not* interact again (like the foreign waiter)?

Folk wisdom again captures the answer: "your reputation precedes you." Formally, the mechanism of reputation is called "indirect reciprocity" and the logic is this: when individuals can track each other's reputations, cooperation can be in the long-term self-interest of individuals even in non-reciprocal interactions because it affects future interaction partners' behaviors (Nowak & Sigmund, 2005). In other words, even if I do not expect to interact with someone again, if someone sees me being mean to them, they might tell others about what a bad guy I am. The nonconformist might rebut: "who cares what other people think?" Well, most of the time most of us ought to, and for selfish reasons. When other people know what a bad guy I am, they might avoid interacting with me and tell others to do likewise, and thus I pay an opportunity cost in missed future joint ventures. And worse, they may seek me out to punish me (Fehr & Fischbacher, 2004)! Cooperating for this reason, selfish as it may be, could even spark positive relationships by the logic of tit-for-tat. Here again, we see the strategic conflict of evolutionary timescale: when there is a chance that I may be observed by others, it is in my *long-term* self-interest to cooperate with non-reciprocal interaction partners, though it is still in my *short-term* self-interest to defect on them. Note that even "observation" may be indirect; that is, my reputation can be affected not only by what others' see me do, but what others say about what I did. Thus indirect reciprocity does not require another agent to observe the interaction, but merely the ability of the recipient of the interaction to communicate the actor's behavior. In a population of agents with a certain degree of memory and communicative ability (like humans), then, even private interactions can become public record, thus motivating cooperation by the power of indirect reciprocity. Indeed, there is extensive evidence of indirect reciprocity promoting cooperation in humans (e.g., Milinski, Semmann, & Krambeck, 2002; Yoeli et al., 2013) and there has even been some evidence in non-human animals (e.g., in sparrows: Akçay, Reed, Campbell, Templeton, & Beecher, 2010; and in capuchins: Anderson, Takimoto, Kuroshima, & Fujita, 2013).

So far, we have seen how the mechanisms of direct and indirect reciprocity explain how it could be adaptive for people to cooperate in social dilemmas with their (reciprocal and non-) interaction partners. But consider again the case of the foreign waiter: suppose the waiter does not know anyone I may interact with in the future, does not speak my language, and does not even know who I am (I paid in cash, so there's no identifying check or credit card)—what possible reason would I have to tip him then? Upon reflection, the answer may be: "none," yet still people do (at least, it does not seem as if there is a world-wide problem of foreigners not tipping). What could explain this seemingly irrational behavior?

Justice is Automatic

To the extent that justice, or distributing resources fairly, is typically adaptive, it would be efficient to not have to think about whether to act justly at every juncture. In other words, where interactions are repeated and/or reputation is known, developing a cooperative social heuristic for just behavior can save cognitive resources. Innocuous though this logic may sound, the assertion that people may be intuitively cooperative seems to fly in the face of commonly held wisdom about human nature. After all, does the Bible not speak of original sin? And evolution of "nature, red in tooth and claw" (Tennyson, 2004)? And the rational actor model of our pursuit of self-interest?

Which perspective is correct is an empirical question—and there is evidence to support the claim that justice is automatic (Zaki & Mitchell, 2013). For example, consider experiments that manipulate cognitive processing of people playing economic cooperation games. In these games, participants choose how much money to keep for themselves versus give up to be evenly distributed between themselves and others (Peysakhovich, Nowak, & Rand, 2014). To test for automatic justice, participants were made to either decide more intuitively or to deliberate more when making their decisions (e.g., by applying time pressure or enforced delay, or by having them recall a time from their life where intuitive versus deliberative thinking worked out well). Consistent with the concept of automatic justice and the existence of social heuristics, inducing participants to rely on intuition makes them more likely to cooperate and benefit others (e.g., Rand, Greene, & Nowak, 2012; Rand et al., 2014).

In addition to social heuristics offering efficient routes to typically advantageous outcomes, there is another reason to expect justice to be automatic: reputational costs to be seen as deliberative when deciding whether to cooperate. If I see that you have to think hard before deciding to help me, it signals that next time I'm relying on you, you might come to a different decision (if the costs of helping or the benefits of betrayal turn out to be large). If you help automatically, however, then I know that you won't stop to consider the costs and benefits, and that I can trust you. This logic of "cooperating without looking" has been formalized with a game theoretic model (Hoffman, Yoeli, & Nowak, 2015), and is supported by empirical evidence that people who make moral decisions quickly are evaluated more positively than those who choose to deliberate first (Critcher, Inbar, & Pizarro, 2013). Cooperating without looking may explain some forms of emergent heroism, where people do not to deliberate over whether to engage in an extremely costly behavior on behalf of someone else. When deciding whether to jump in front of a train or bus or save someone from drowning when there is a crowd (especially of people who know each other), it may be that the reputational benefit of quick cooperation motivates heroic action.

While there is reason to believe that learning and cultural evolution play an important role in the development of social heuristics and reputational concerns, there is also some evidence that automatic justice may be hard-wired. A growing body of research demonstrates that pre-verbal infants demonstrate prosocial tendencies, including preferring nice to mean characters (Hamlin, Wynn, & Bloom, 2007) and voluntarily providing instrumental helping behavior (Warneken & Tomasello, 2006); although when it comes to distributing actual resources, young children tend to be quite selfish (Blake & Rand, 2010; Fehr, Bernhard, & Rockenbach, 2008).

Whether a product of genetic or cultural evolution (or both), we argue that the long-held view of a selfish human nature requiring restraint to benefit others—e.g., "For the laws of nature (as justice…) of themselves, without the terror of some power, to cause them to be observed, are contrary to our natural passions, that carry us to partiality, pride, revenge and the like" (Hobbes & Curley, 1994)—might have it backwards. Instead, it appears that we may often act with an intuitive sense of justice.

Justice in the Extreme

Because a justice heuristic is automatic, it is susceptible to over-generalization, or being applied in contexts where it is *not* individually advantageous—that is, situations where the costs of cooperating will not actually be recouped in the future. For example, consider Julio Diaz, who was mugged on his way home from work one day. Feeling compassion for the teenage boy mugging him, he offered up his coat and then treated the boy to dinner (StoryCorps, 2008). It seems unlikely that the boy would be a good long-term interaction partner, yet Diaz's explanation perfectly follows the logic of direct reciprocity: "I don't know, I figure, you know, you treat people right, you can only hope that they treat you right." While this act demonstrates how a justice heuristic may be over-generalized in a single instance—an example of *emergent* heroism—it may also be the case that justice heuristics are over-generalized in setting goals that lead to *sustained* heroic justice. For example, consider kidney donors who, in a very extreme form of justice, fairly distribute their two healthy kidneys, keeping one for themselves and giving the other to people in danger of having none. Certainly they cannot expect reciprocation—particularly in-kind—from the beneficiaries of their sacrifice, nor can they expect other forms of (adequate) recompense, as engaging in this act itself can serious health consequences (Segev et al., 2010). One suggestion that such heroic commitment may originate with a justice heuristic is neurological evidence that their decisions to donate are driven by automatic, rather than deliberative, processes (Marsh et al., 2014). Alternatively, consider extreme charitable givers (MacFarquhar, 2015) like Julia Wise and Jeff Kaufman who currently live on 6 percent of their income and give the rest to charity. They cannot reasonably expect reciprocation from the beneficiaries of their donations, and the amount they donate is so extreme that any reputational benefits are quite unlikely to outweigh the cost they are incurring. (Further, their giving principle is based on how much they need, and so they would presumably also give away any material benefit due to improved reputation.) Yet they feel compelled to give nonetheless. These are two examples of how the typically-adaptive principle of justice may be over-generalized to set heroic goals that deliberative processes are recruited to pursue. Because these acts are not in the actor's long-term self-interest, we call this ethical behavior *extreme* and the actors *heroes*.

Solidarity

The virtue of solidarity, like justice, has appeared throughout human cultures:

- Confucius (*c*.500 BC): "the noble man ... takes loyalty and good faith to be of primary importance, and has no friends who are not of equal (moral) caliber" (Muller, 1990).
- Cicero (*c*.50 BC): "piety admonishes us to do our duty to our country or our parents or other blood relations" (Wagenvoort, 1980).
- The Bible: "He who pursues righteousness and loyalty finds life, righteousness and honor." (Proverbs 21:21, New American Standard Bible).

Solidarity is the bedrock of loyalty to groups of all sizes and kinds, including towns, businesses, churches, and states. But how could such group loyalty have evolved by such a supposedly selfish process as natural selection? As with justice, we will argue that solidarity is adaptive in everyday life, that it has become automatic, and in its extreme, it is heroic.

Solidarity is Adaptive

There are numerous direct fitness benefits that come from being a member of a group. Group living reduces risk of predation (e.g., Treherne & Foster, 1980), improves the ability to defend oneself (e.g., Bertram, 1978). Groups also create the opportunity for specialization and division of labor, allowing positively-non-zero sum gains from trade (Durkheim, 2014). Other major benefits of group living involve improved yield to foraging (e.g., Clark & Mangel, 1986) and increasing mechanical efficiency (e.g., in movement: Herskin & Steffensen, 1998; or in staying warm: Andrews & Belknap, 1986). These are only a few examples of the extensive literature on the individual fitness benefits of group living in the animal literature (for a review, see Krause & Ruxton, 2002).

Being a member of a group is clearly adaptive, but why engage in self-sacrifice on behalf of that group? We have discussed one answer already: *indirect reciprocity*; if I am seen helping someone in the group, others will think that I am a good future interaction partner (Nowak & Sigmund, 2005). And this logic doesn't only apply to dyadic interactions; it also applies to situations where an individual's action benefits the group (Milinski et al., 2002; Panchanathan & Boyd, 2004). Crucial to the indirect reciprocity explanation, however, is that individuals have information about past behavior of other agents. (Without accurate information about the reputations of others, obviously reputation systems cannot function.) To the extent that behavior is more likely to be observable (either directly or through reputation) among ingroup members, indirect reciprocity could support greater cooperation with the ingroup than the outgroup (Masuda, 2012). Furthermore, it can be adaptive to cooperate with members of your group because they are more similar to you, and therefore more likely to have the same strategy as you—leading to the evolution of ingroup bias as a form of *tag-based* cooperation (Fu et al., 2012).

We note that some have also argued that solidarity may have evolved via *group selection* (Choi & Bowles, 2007): if intergroup competition is common, then groups whose members engage in costly cooperation within the ingroup and aggression towards the outgroup can outcompete groups that don't. However, there is a great deal of controversy regarding whether intergroup competition was intense enough over human history to actually allow selection at the level of the group to function effectively (Burnham & Johnson, 2005, p. 14; Williams, 1966, p. 3576; West et al., 2007, p. 218). Therefore we do not build our adaptive argument on group selection.

Instead, we conclude that solidarity is another example of sacrificing *short-term* self-interest for *long-term* self-interest. Costly behavior on behalf of ingroup members may not be reciprocated immediately, but by solidifying one's ingroup identity, one gains access to group benefits, such as avoiding predation, increasing the gains of trade and foraging, and achieving mechanical efficiency. In sum, solidarity is adaptive: while the price of group membership may be a short-term cost, it is well worth the long-term benefits of group living.

Solidarity is Intuitive

Given the benefits of group living, a social heuristics perspective would predict that preference for one's group should become automatized. And indeed, the automaticity of ingroup preferences has been demonstrated repeatedly (for a review, see Hewstone, Rubin, and Willis, 2002). Intergroup bias has been explored (following distinctions made by Mackie & Smith, 1998) through cognition/stereotyping (e.g., Hilton and Hippel, 1996), attitudes/prejudice (e.g., Allport, 1979), and behavior/discrimination (e.g., Tajfel, 1982). Because there are many reasons that people might be motivated not to report bias (e.g., social desirability: Crowne and Marlowe, 1960), a number of implicit measures of bias have been developed (e.g., the implicit associations test, Greenwald, McGhee, and Schwartz, 1998).

Although attitudes (implicit and explicit) are shaped by the accrual of experience (e.g., Smith and DeCoster, 2000), there is substantial evidence that ingroup bias emerges early in development (for a review, see Dunham, Baron, & Banaji, 2008). For example, newborns prefer their mothers' native language (Moon, Cooper, & Fifer, 1993), three-month-olds prefer people of the same race (Bar-Haim, Ziv, Lamy, & Hodes, 2006), and cross-culturally, six-year-olds demonstrate implicit bias favoring people of the same race (Dunham, Baron, & Banaji, 2006). Further, implicit attitudes have been shown to develop with very little experience (Otten & Moskowitz, 2000), employing "minimal group" paradigms in which individuals are randomly sorted into groups using non-meaningful distinctions (often with false feedback) such as differences in how images are perceived (Brewer, 1979).

Solidarity is intuitive: we have briefly surveyed evidence that we have implicit ingroup bias and that this emerges early in development. Everyday solidarity predicts loyalty to group members: we have automatic cognitions favoring ingroup members and adaptive reasons for cooperating with them. When this automatic solidarity is over-generalized to extremes that are not in the actor's self-interest, it is heroic.

Solidarity in the Extreme

Given the multitude of benefits to group living, solidarity heuristics are adaptive in most contexts. Here, an individual paying a short-term cost on behalf of an ingroup stands to gain future benefits; thus doing so is in their long-term self-interest. One way in which solidarity may be *over*-generalized, however, is when the short-term cost is so great as to eliminate the possibility of future benefit; in other words, when the usually short-term sacrifice becomes the *ultimate* sacrifice. This type of heroism—*emergent* heroic solidarity—is often seen in military heroes who jeopardize (and sometimes knowingly sacrifice) their lives to protect their comrades, and in a larger sense, their countrypeople's way of life. In contrast to the decision to give up *resources* for the good of a nation (e.g., via taxes or participation in the political process), which may bring future benefits (or avoid future penalties), offering one's life for the sake of one's group invites the possibility of sacrifice that can never be repaid. To promote this kind of heroic behavior, military training places a large emphasis on acting to help one's fellow soldiers automatically without deliberation, facilitating the over-generalization of solidarity to settings of ultimate sacrifice (Grossman, 2009). More acutely, consider cases of "altruistic suicide"—when a soldier jumps on a hand-grenade to save the group. Here, the decision not merely of risking death, but of almost certain death to benefit others is more common among lower-ranking servicepeople in more cohesive groups—a finding consistent with an account explaining this behavior as an overgeneralization of reputational concerns within a well-defined and tight-knit group (Blake, 1978). Heroic solidarity may also be *sustained*. For example, consider Aung San Suu Kyi, who, leading a movement to bring democratic rule to her home country of Burma, was arrested on July 20, 1989 by the military-led government. She refused freedom in exile, enduring twenty years of house arrest and numerous attempted attacks on her person in the name of her people. Two years after her release, she said, "I'm not the only one working for democracy in Burma—there are so many people who have worked for it because they believe that this is the only way we can maintain the dignity of our people" (BBC News UK, 19 June 2012, BBC. Available at: www.bbc.com/news/uk-18509455) It is difficult to imagine that her people could ever repay Suu Kyi for her sacrifice, yet still she gave it willingly. Such sustained heroic solidarity may be the result of solidarity heuristics becoming over-generalized in setting the goals that deliberative processes carry out. A small sacrifice on behalf of one's group is the stuff of everyday ethics; the *ultimate* sacrifice or a lifetime of sacrifice, may have a similar evolutionary basis, but because it is *not* in the individual's long-run self-interest, it is an example of an ethical extreme, and the person who makes it, a hero.

Pacifism

Pacifism, or the aversion to causing physical harm, also has a long tradition as a virtue in human culture. For example, consider the Hippocratic oath, *c.*400 BC, still given by American doctors today: "either help or do not harm," (Lloyd, 1983) and well as the Christian tradition, e.g.: "Love does no harm to a neighbor; therefore love is the fulfillment of the law" (Romans 13:10, New International Version). Aggressive cultures and massive wars are, of course, ubiquitous in our history too, yet still the virtue of "not harming others" remains present in diverse cultures and throughout time. In a certain way, it seems trivial to assert pacifism as a virtue, as most of us most of the time are being nonviolent. What is virtuous about pacifism, however, is when it appears in contexts in which we would expect violence, like in Gandhi's political protests where people did not defend themselves when being attacked. Of course, in most of today's large industrialized societies, there are not many situations in which we would expect violence, as violence seems to be on the decline (Pinker, 2011). But consider early human societies, which were on a much smaller scale, and lacked professional armies, police forces, or formal institutions to settle disputes. Or, to strip away even more potential mechanisms that could mitigate violent conflict (e.g., language, theory of mind, etc.), consider non-human animals—why might it be in their self-interest *not* to fight?

Pacifism is Adaptive

When two animals fight for access to a resource, an individual does best if she goes for the resource while the other individual retreats. If both animals approach, conflict ensues, which is costly for both parties. Thus, if you think the other will approach, you should retreat; but if you think the other will retreat, you should approach. This kind of interaction is formally modelled in game theory as the "Hawk–Dove" game, a type of anti-coordination game (Smith & Price, 1973), or "Chicken"/"Snowdrift" in the human literature (Rapoport & Chammah, 1966). The basic model assumes the individuals have symmetrical fighting abilities and so there is no single best strategy; instead, the best strategy is *mixed* (i.e., it alternates between approaching and avoiding). In nature, however, there is variation in fighting ability, or formally: *resource holding potential* (RHP; Parker, 1974). Building on this, other heterogeneities have been argued to influence the outcome of conflicts, namely motivation or *resource value*, V (Hammerstein, 1981), and *daring* (Barlow, Rogers, & Fraley, 1986). Because there is variation in RHP (and V and daring; we'll summarize these in the following as "strength"), strong individuals could beat weak individuals in a fight, thus incurring a lower marginal cost of fighting. Still, fighting is costly, and so it would be in the interest of strong individuals to take the resources without having to fight. Thus, it can be adaptive to signal one's strength, intimidating the other party and avoiding actual conflict.

Many animal species signal their RHP rather than fight (for a review, see Davies, Krebs, & West, 2012), from beetles (West-Eberhard, 1979) to narwhals (Silverman & Dunbar, 1980) to musk ox (Wilkinson & Shank, 1976). This can be accomplished by a number of means: ritualized displays, as in red deer who assess each other through a sequence of behaviors—roaring, walking in parallel and pushing antlers against each other (Clutton-Brock, Albon, Gibson, & Guinness, 1979); visual "badges" of status, as in the plumage of the Harris sparrow, where darker plumage indicates greater RHP (Rohwer & Rohwer, 1978); or through auditory cues, as in frogs and toads, whose croak frequency is determined by body size (Davies & Halliday, 1978). Humans also have reliable signals of fighting ability: anger is perceived as a credible signal of threat (Reed, DeScioli, & Pinker, 2014), and anger is more effectively used as a signal by stronger individuals in bargaining situations (Sell, Tooby, & Cosmides, 2009). Further, people can accurately assess upper-body strength by looking at facial structure alone (Sell, Cosmides, et al., 2009).

While it is certainly in the weaker individual's interest to avoid fighting if possible (after all, they wouldn't win!), it is also in the stronger individual's interest to avoid fighting because via signaling, they can still gain the contested resources without paying the cost of fighting. Thus, pacifism, even for the strong, is adaptive. What is the short-term v. long-term tradeoff here? Weaker parties cede the contested resource, but they live to forage another day. Stronger parties do not eliminate the competition (after all, a fight would be *more* costly for the weaker party), but by doing so, also do not risk their own injury (and perhaps a David and Goliath moment).

Pacifism is Automatic

If it is adaptive to *not* harm others, even among strong individuals in a competition over resources, we might expect harm aversion to be automatic. Even in the extreme case of war, many soldiers have trouble actually pulling the trigger (Grossman, 2009). Furthermore, it is enough to mentally *simulate* actions that have harmful outcomes (e.g., smacking a baby doll on a table, but *not* smacking a broom on a table) to elicit a biophysiological stress response (Cushman, Gray, Gaffey, & Mendes, 2012). And people are willing to pay more to avoid delivering electric shocks to other people than to themselves (Crockett, Kurth-Nelson, Siegel, Dayan, & Dolan, 2014).

The automaticity of pacifism may come from our capacity for empathy. There is extensive neuroimaging evidence that feeling others' pain is associated with empathy (for reviews, see de Vignemont & Singer, 2006; Hein & Singer, 2008). On the flip side, deficits in empathy have been associated with violent criminal offense (Jolliffe & Farrington, 2004). Further, neurobiological studies of abnormal brain functioning confirms the association of specific brain areas with (non)empathic behavior, e.g., reduced empathy following brain injury to the right ventromedial prefrontal cortex (Shamay-Tsoory, Tomer, Berger, & Aharon-Peretz, 2003), reduced empathy in patients with autism spectrum disorder (Baron-Cohen & Wheelwright, 2004), and in reduced empathy in psychopaths (Blair, Jones, Clark, & Smith, 1997). It has been argued that psychopaths' particular empathy deficit—decreased response to distress cues—may play a role in their disproportionately committing violent crimes (Blair, 1995).

Empathic harm aversion is not only found in the automatic processing of adults—it has also been found to emerge early in development. One-day-old babies cry when they hear tape-recorded crying of other babies (e.g., Martin & Clark, 1982). At around two months, babies begin to show emotional synchrony with their mothers during play (e.g., Stern, 1985). At six months, babies demonstrate a preference for puppets who help (rather than harm) another puppet (Hamlin et al., 2007). Finally, preverbal children at eighteen months can infer when an adult is struggling with a physical task and offer spontaneous help (Warneken & Tomasello, 2006).

Thus we have seen that empathic harm aversion is automatic, that it is linked with affective empathy, and that it emerges early in development. When this automatic pacifism is overgeneralized to extremes that are not in the actor's self-interest, it is heroic.

Pacifism in the Extreme

Pacifism is adaptive in many situations, and for humans, it is automatic. But if it happens all the time without our thinking about it, how could it be heroic? Pacifism in situations of *potential* harm, when either a weak party cedes a resource to a strong party or when a strong party signals rather than fights a weaker party, do seem commonplace. Pacifism in situations of *certain* harm, however, are more remarkable. Consider for example that you are attacked and you do not respond by attacking back—here, you risk incurring a greater cost because your self-defense could precipitate the end of the fight or mitigate the ability of your opponent to harm you. This sort of pacifism, in the face of *certain* rather than *potential* harm, is heroic, especially when exercised on behalf of another.

Our automatic aversion to harming others may serve us well in most situations—whether we are weak or strong—to help us avoid harm to ourselves. But like other heuristics, a pacifism heuristic may be insensitive to context, and applied in situations where it is not in our long-term self-interest. Consider willfully incurring physical harm, especially on behalf of others; for example, when people interpose their bodies between assailants and victims, such as when Benie Kaulesar attempted to separate his friend from a man that friend was fighting, and received a fatal blow to the head (Thorbourne, 2015). In situations of potential harm, pacifism may serve to avoid the costs of fighting, but once the fight has begun and harm is certain, pacifism may incur greater costs, and unnecessary ones to individuals outside the fight who exhibit it on behalf of others. When putting oneself in harm's way in the context of a fight, it may be that the same automatic aversion to harm that prevents us from engaging in fights in situations of potential harm prevents us from engaging in fights when harm is certain. Therefore, we might call this *emergent* heroic pacifism due to its intuitive nature. On a grander scale, there are many examples of *sustained* heroic pacifism, as in the nonviolent political resistance led by Mahatma Gandhi. Protesting British colonial rule, 2,500 Indians marched to Dharasana Salt Works on May 21, 1930 and were met by a police force of 400. Journalist Webb Miller observed:

> Police charged, swinging their clubs and belaboring the raiders on all sides. The volunteers made no resistance. As the police swung hastily with their sticks, the natives simply dropped in their tracks … The watching crowds gasped, or sometimes cheered as the volunteers crumpled before the police without even raising their arms to ward off the blows.
>
> *(Miller, 1930)*

Typically, pacifism is a strategy for avoiding harm, but here, Indian protestors did not resist the use of force, at great physical risk. Here, it may be that an automatic aversion to harm has set a goal of nonviolent resistance that protestors execute recruiting more deliberative processes. Pacifism, then, is an everyday ethical principle for the weak and strong alike when harm is uncertain, but when pacifism is exhibited in the face of certain harm—especially on behalf of others—it is extreme, and the people who do it, heroic.

Conclusion

In this chapter, we have presented an adaptive theory of heroic ethics—distributing resources fairly (justice), group-beneficial self-sacrifice (solidarity), and not harming others (pacifism)—that explains heroic behavior as an extreme form of more common "everyday heroism" that all of us exhibit, and with good reason.

For each of these ethics—justice, solidarity, and pacifism—we have argued that there are adaptive reasons to engage in the associated ethical behaviors. We then surveyed evidence that cognitions supporting these behaviors are automatic, and often emerge early in development. We argue that due to the automatic nature of the cognitive processes driving these behaviors, they are less sensitive to context and thus prone to over-generalization: these behaviors sometimes get deployed in situations where it is *not* in the individual's long-run self-interest to behaving ethically. In particular, people sometimes act ethically even when it is extremely individually costly to do so, or when no future benefits exist. That is, social heuristics sometimes take ethical behavior to the extreme. It is these extreme actions that earn the title of "heroic."

One way to interpret our argument is that heroism is foolish or irrational; after all, we have argued that heroism is about applying typically advantageous behaviors to situations in which they are actually disadvantageous (in terms of the hero's personal outcome). However, that does *not* mean that the overall strategy that leads to heroism is maladaptive. It is cognitively efficient and advantageous to sometimes rely on heuristics and intuitive processes—hence their maintenance as a key piece of human cognition (as shown, for example, in evolutionary models of dual-process agents; Tomlin, Rand, Ludwig, & Cohen, 2015; Toupo, Strogatz, Cohen, & Rand, 2015). And as discussed above, there can be reputational benefits to "cooperating without thinking." Thus it is not foolish to adopt a strategy that leads one to sometimes in engage in heroic agents—on the contrary, selection can in fact favor such strategies (Bear & Rand, 2016; Hoffman et al., 2015).

Relatedly, the large body of literature explaining other-benefiting behavior using long-term self-interest (for a review, see Rand and Nowak, 2013) has led to disillusionment over whether there is such a thing as "pure altruism" (Lichtenberg, 2010). Here, there are two important distinctions to be made. First, cooperation is (by definition) beneficial to others, and to the extent that "action benefiting others" constitutes moral goodness, cooperation is good, whether ultimately self-interested or not. Second, however, the "self-interested cooperation is not pure altruism" argument may gain some of its condemnatory strength by confusing levels of analysis. Specifically, arguments about the evolutionary mechanisms favoring cooperation are *ultimate* explanations, that is, they explain *why* cooperation could be advantageous to individuals subject to natural selection. Critics, however, may have in mind self-interested *proximate* explanations for cooperation, that is, explanations of *how* cooperation is implemented in a given situation. In other words, altruism may be tainted when the proximate mechanism is consciously self-interested, as in the politician who gives to charity knowing the reputational benefits of doing so. The self-interestedness of evolutionary ultimate mechanisms, on the other hand, is often not in conscious awareness (when cheering for one's home sports team, does the division of labor come to mind?), and so the moral standing of cooperative behaviors motivated by them seem less in jeopardy.

We have not presented an exhaustive account of heroism, but rather a suggestion for a theory of heroism that raises interesting questions for future work. For example, there are many models that attempt to carve morality at its joints—one question that arises from our exploration is: what are other ethical principles have evolutionary origins? For example, Moral Foundations Theory (Graham et al., 2011) posits five fundamental areas of moral concern—harm, fairness, ingroup, authority, and purity. While attempts have been made to link these domains of morality to their evolutionary origins (e.g., Graham et al., 2012), an exploration of morality "from the bottom-up" that begins with adaptive challenges may refine such theories and potentially introduce new domains of moral concern. Regarding the connection of these moral domain theories to heroism, another question is: are there types of heroism not captured by these theories? And related to our argument: are there other types of heroism that result from over-generalization of evolutionarily adaptive intuitions? And are there types of heroism that do not?

In addition to these broad questions, many specific questions might be asked to follow up on our argument. For example, regarding justice, what differences are there in the psychology of distributing resources evenly with regard to time (e.g., in vampire bats, and in common accounts of direct reciprocity) as opposed to money (e.g., in the case of wealth redistribution)? Regarding solidarity, how does group membership affect perceptions of heroism? And is heroic solidarity a solely within group phenomenon or is it recognized across group boundaries? Finally, regarding pacifism, does the connection of empathy and violence also go in the positive direction; i.e., are individuals inclined toward nonviolence more empathic? And while it has been argued that nonviolent protest is more effective than violent protest because it engenders higher participation (Chenoweth & Stephan, 2011), what is the mechanism of this contagion? Zooming out again, and of great theoretical and practical interest: when does heroism inspire others toward similar behavior?

In sum, we have argued that heroism is typically adaptive everyday ethical behavior taken to the extreme by over-generalization. Short-run sacrifices on behalf of others are typically in our long-run self-interest, and so we may develop cooperative intuitions. Whether these proximately motivate our behavior or help set long-term cooperative goals, their automaticity makes them less context-dependent, occasionally resulting in cooperative behavior that is *not* in our long-run self-interest. This truly selfless behavior, then, is different from our everyday ethical behavior not in kind, but in degree. The potential to be a hero, therefore, is in all of us.

References

Akçay, Ç., Reed, V. A., Campbell, S. E., Templeton, C. N., & Beecher, M. D. (2010). Indirect reciprocity: Song sparrows distrust aggressive neighbours based on eavesdropping. *Animal Behaviour*, *80*(6), 1041–1047. doi: 10.1016/j.anbehav.2010.09.009

Allport, G. W. (1979). *The nature of prejudice*. New York: Basic Books.

Anderson, J. R., Takimoto, A., Kuroshima, H., & Fujita, K. (2013). Capuchin monkeys judge third-party reciprocity. *Cognition*, *127*(1), 140–146. doi: 10.1016/j.cognition.2012.12.007

Andrews, R. V., & Belknap, R. W. (1986). Bioenergetic benefits of huddling by deer mice (*Peromyscus maniculatus*). *Comparative Biochemistry and Physiology Part A: Physiology*, 85(4), 775–778. doi: 10.1016/0300-9629(86)90294-X

Axelrod, R., & Hamilton, W. (1981). The evolution of cooperation. *Science*, 211(4489), 1390–1396. doi: 10.1126/science.7466396

Bar-Haim, Y., Ziv, T., Lamy, D., & Hodes, R. M. (2006). Nature and nurture in own-race face processing. *Psychological Science*, 17(2), 159–163. doi: 10.1111/j.1467-9280.2006.01679.x

Barlow, G., Rogers, W., & Fraley, N. (1986). Do Midas cichlids win through prowess or daring? It depends. *Behavioral Ecology and Sociobiology*, 19(1), 1–8. doi: 10.1007/BF00303836

Baron-Cohen, S., & Wheelwright, S. (2004). The empathy quotient: An investigation of adults with Asperger syndrome or high functioning autism, and normal sex differences. *Journal of Autism and Developmental Disorders*, 34(2), 163–175. doi: 10.1023/B:JADD.0000022607.19833.00

Battigalli, P., & Dufwenberg, M. (2007). Guilt in games. *American Economic Review*, 97(2), 170–176. doi: 10.1257/aer.97.2.170

Bear, A., & Rand, D. G. (2016). Intuition, deliberation, and the evolution of cooperation. *Proceedings of the National Academy of Sciences*. doi: 10.1073/pnas.1517780113

Bertram, B. C. (1978). Living in groups: Predators and prey. In J. R. Krebs & N. B. Davies (eds), *Behavioural ecology* (pp. 64–96). Oxford: Blackwell Scientific Publications.

Blair, R. J. R. (1995). A cognitive developmental approach to morality: investigating the psychopath. *Cognition*, 57(1), 1–29. doi: 10.1016/0010-0277(95)00676-P

Blair, R. J., Jones, L., Clark, F., & Smith, M. (1997). The psychopathic individual: A lack of responsiveness to distress cues? *Psychophysiology*, 34(2), 192–198. doi: 10.1111/j.1469-8986.1997.tb02131.x

Blake, J. A. (1978). Death by hand grenade: Altruistic suicide in combat. *Suicide and Life-Threatening Behavior*, 8(1), 46–59.

Blake, P. R., & Rand, D. G. (2010). Currency value moderates equity preference among young children. *Evolution and Human Behavior*, 31(3), 210–218. doi: 10.1016/j.evolhumbehav.2009.06.012

Brewer, M. B. (1979). In-group bias in the minimal intergroup situation: A cognitive-motivational analysis. *Psychological Bulletin*, 86(2), 307.

Burnham, T. C., & Johnson, D. D. (2005). The biological and evolutionary logic of human cooperation. *Analyse und Kritik*, 27(1), 113.

Chenoweth, E., & Stephan, M. J. (2011). *Why civil resistance works: The strategic logic of nonviolent conflict*. New York: Columbia University Press.

Choi, J.-K., & Bowles, S. (2007). The coevolution of parochial altruism and war. *Science*, 318(5850), 636–640. doi: 10.1126/science.1144237

Clark, C. W., & Mangel, M. (1986). The evolutionary advantages of group foraging. *Theoretical Population Biology*, 30(1), 45–75. doi: 10.1016/0040-5809(86)90024-9

Clutton-Brock, T. (2009). Cooperation between non-kin in animal societies. *Nature*, 462(7269), 51–57. Retrieved from www.nature.com/nature/journal/v462/n7269/pdf/nature08366.pdf.

Clutton-Brock, T. H., Albon, S. D., Gibson, R. M., & Guinness, F. E. (1979). The logical stag: Adaptive aspects of fighting in red deer (*Cervus elaphus* L.). *Animal Behaviour*, 27(Part 1), 211–225. doi: 10.1016/0003-3472(79)90141-6

Critcher, C. R., Inbar, Y., & Pizarro, D. A. (2013). How quick decisions illuminate moral character. *Social Psychological and Personality Science*, 4(3), 308–315. doi: 10.1177/1948550612457688

Crockett, M. J., Kurth-Nelson, Z., Siegel, J. Z., Dayan, P., & Dolan, R. J. (2014). Harm to others outweighs harm to self in moral decision making. *Proceedings of the National Academy of Sciences*, 111(48), 17,20–17,325. doi: 10.1073/pnas.1408988111

Crowne, D. P., & Marlowe, D. (1960). A new scale of social desirability independent of psychopathology. *Journal of Consulting Psychology*, 24(4), 349.

Cushman, F., & Morris, A. (2015). Habitual control of goal selection in humans. *Proceedings of the National Academy of Sciences*, 112(45), 13,817–13,822. doi: 10.1073/pnas.1506367112

Cushman, F., Gray, K., Gaffey, A., & Mendes, W. B. (2012). Simulating murder: the aversion to harmful action. *Emotion*, 12(1), 2. Retrieved from http://psycnet.apa.org/journals/emo/12/1/2.

Dal Bo, P. (2005). Cooperation under the shadow of the future: experimental evidence from infinitely repeated games. *The American Economic Review*, 95(5), 1591–1604. Retrieved from www.jstor.org/stable/4132766.

Davies, N. B., & Halliday, T. R. (1978). Deep croaks and fighting assessment in toads *Bufo bufo*. *Nature*, 274(5672), 683–685. doi: 10.1038/274683a0

Davies, N. B., Krebs, J. R., & West, S. A. (2012). *An introduction to behavioural ecology*: Chichester: John Wiley & Sons.

Dawkins, R. (2006). *The selfish gene*. Oxford, UK: Oxford University Press.

de Vignemont, F., & Singer, T. (2006). The empathic brain: How, when and why? *Trends in Cognitive Sciences*, *10*(10), 435–441. doi: 10.1016/j.tics.2006.08.008

Dunham, Y., Baron, A. S., & Banaji, M. R. (2006). From American city to Japanese village: A cross-cultural investigation of implicit race attitudes. *Child Development*, *77*(5), 1268–1281. doi: 10.1111/j.1467-8624.2006.00933.x

Dunham, Y., Baron, A. S., & Banaji, M. R. (2008). The development of implicit intergroup cognition. *Trends in Cognitive Sciences*, *12*(7), 248–253. doi: 10.1016/j.tics.2008.04.006

Durkheim, E. (2014). *The division of labor in society*: New York: Simon & Schuster.

Fehr, E., & Fischbacher, U. (2004). Third-party punishment and social norms. *Evolution and Human Behavior*, *25*(2), 63–87. doi: 10.1016/S1090-5138(04)00005-4

Fehr, E., Bernhard, H., & Rockenbach, B. (2008). Egalitarianism in young children. *Nature*, *454*(7208), 1079–1083. Retrieved from www.nature.com/nature/journal/v454/n7208/suppinfo/nature07155_S1.html.

Fu, F., Tarnita, C. E., Christakis, N. A., Wang, L., Rand, D. G., & Nowak, M. A. (2012). Evolution of in-group favoritism. *Scientific Reports*, *2*, 460.

Fudenberg, D., Rand, D. G., & Dreber, A. (2012). Slow to anger and fast to forgive: Cooperation in an uncertain world. *American Economic Review*, *102*(2), 720–749. doi: 10.1257/aer.102.2.720

Gigerenzer, G., Todd, P. M., & Group, A. R. (1999). *Simple heuristics that make us smart*. Oxford, UK: Oxford University Press.

Gilovich, T., Griffin, D., & Kahneman, D. (2002). *Heuristics and biases: The psychology of intuitive judgment*: Cambridge, UK: Cambridge University Press.

Graham, J., Haidt, J., Koleva, S., Motyl, M., Iyer, R., Wojcik, S. P., & Ditto, P. H. (2012). Moral foundations theory: The pragmatic validity of moral pluralism. *Advances in Experimental Social Psychology*. Retrieved from http://ssrn.com/abstract=2184440.

Graham, J., Nosek, B. A., Haidt, J., Iyer, R., Koleva, S., & Ditto, P. H. (2011). Mapping the moral domain. *Journal of Personality and Social Psychology*, *101*(2), 366. Retrieved from www.ncbi.nlm.nih.gov/pmc/articles/PMC3116962/pdf/nihms246870.pdf.

Greenwald, A. G., McGhee, D. E., & Schwartz, J. L. (1998). Measuring individual differences in implicit cognition: The implicit association test. *Journal of Personality and Social Psychology*, *74*(6), 1464. Retrieved from http://psycnet.apa.org/journals/psp/74/6/1464.

Grossman, D. (2009). *On killing: The psychological cost of learning to kill in war and society*. New York: Little, Brown & Company.

Hamlin, J. K., Wynn, K., & Bloom, P. (2007). Social evaluation by preverbal infants. *Nature*, *450*(7169), 557–559. Retrieved from www.nature.com/nature/journal/v450/n7169/suppinfo/nature06288_S1.html.

Hammerstein, P. (1981). The role of asymmetries in animal contests. *Animal Behaviour*, *29*(1), 193–205. doi: 10.1016/S0003-3472(81)80166-2

Hein, G., & Singer, T. (2008). I feel how you feel but not always: The empathic brain and its modulation. *Current Opinion in Neurobiology*, *18*(2), 153–158. doi: 10.1016/j.conb.2008.07.012

Herskin, J., & Steffensen, J. F. (1998). Energy savings in sea bass swimming in a school: Measurements of tail beat frequency and oxygen consumption at different swimming speeds. *Journal of Fish Biology*, *53*(2), 366–376. doi: 10.1111/j.1095-8649.1998.tb00986.x

Hewstone, M., Rubin, M., & Willis, H. (2002). Intergroup bias. *Annual Review of Psychology*, *53*(1), 575–604. doi: 10.1146/annurev.psych.53.100901.135109

Hilton, J. L., & Hippel, W. v. (1996). Stereotypes. *Annual Review of Psychology*, *47*(1), 237–271. doi: 10.1146/annurev.psych.47.1.237

Hobbes, T., & Curley, E. (1994). *Leviathan: with selected variants from the Latin edition of 1668*. Indianapolis, IN: Hackett Publishing.

Hoffman, M., Yoeli, E., & Nowak, M. A. (2015). Cooperate without looking: Why we care what people think and not just what they do. *Proceedings of the National Academy of Sciences*, *112*(6), 1727–1732. doi: 10.1073/pnas.1417904112

Hopkins, E. W. (1906). XXI. Modifications of the Karma Doctrine. *Journal of the Royal Asiatic Society of Great Britain & Ireland* (new series), *38*(03), 581–593.

Jolliffe, D., & Farrington, D. P. (2004). Empathy and offending: A systematic review and meta-analysis. *Aggression and Violent Behavior*, *9*(5), 441–476. doi: 10.1016/j.avb.2003.03.001

Kahneman, D. (2003). A perspective on judgment and choice: Mapping bounded rationality. *American Psychologist*, *58*(9), 697.

Krause, J., & Ruxton, G. D. (2002). *Living in groups*. Oxford, UK: Oxford University Press.

Kurzban, R., & DeScioli, P. (2015). Morality. In D. M. Buss (ed.), *The Handbook of Evolutionary Psychology, Vol. 2: Integrations* (2nd ed., pp. 770–787). Chichester: John Wiley.

Langford, J. (2008). *Mother Teresa's Secret Fire*. Huntington, IN: Our Sunday Visitor.

Lichtenberg, J. (2010). Is pure altruism possible? *New York Times*, October 19.
Lloyd, G., ed. (1983). *Hippocratic writings* (2nd Edition). London: Penguin.
MacFarquhar, L. (2015). *Strangers drowning: Grappling with impossible idealism, drastic choices, and the overpowering urge to help*. London: Penguin.
Mackie, D. M., & Smith, E. R. (1998). Intergroup relations: Insights from a theoretically integrative approach. *Psychological Review*, *105*(3), 499. Retrieved from http://psycnet.apa.org/journals/rev/105/3/499.
Marsh, A. A., Stoycos, S. A., Brethel-Haurwitz, K. M., Robinson, P., VanMeter, J. W., & Cardinale, E. M. (2014). Neural and cognitive characteristics of extraordinary altruists. *Proceedings of the National Academy of Sciences*, *111*(42), 15,036–15,041. doi: 10.1073/pnas.1408440111
Martin, G. B., & Clark, R. D. (1982). Distress crying in neonates: Species and peer specificity. *Developmental psychology*, *18*(1), 3.
Masuda, N. (2012). Ingroup favoritism and intergroup cooperation under indirect reciprocity based on group reputation. *Journal of Theoretical Biology*, *311*, 8–18. doi: 10.1016/j.jtbi.2012.07.002
Milinski, M., Semmann, D., & Krambeck, H.-J. (2002). Reputation helps solve the "tragedy of the commons." *Nature*, *415*(6870), 424–426. Retrieved from www.nature.com/nature/journal/v415/n6870/pdf/415424a.pdf.
Miller, W. (1930). Natives beaten down by police in India salt bed raid. *The New York World-Telegram* (May 21). Retrieved from www.upi.com/Archives/1930/05/21/Natives-beaten-down-by-police-in-India-salt-bed-raid/5882104113261.
Moon, C., Cooper, R. P., & Fifer, W. P. (1993). Two-day-olds prefer their native language. *Infant Behavior and Development*, *16*(4), 495–500. doi: 10.1016/0163-6383(93)80007-U
Muller, C. (1990). The analects of Confucius. Retrieved from www.acmuller.net/con-dao/analects.html.
Nowak, M. A., & Sigmund, K. (2005). Evolution of indirect reciprocity. *Nature*, *437*(7063), 1291–1298. Retrieved from www.nature.com/nature/journal/v437/n7063/pdf/nature04131.pdf.
Otten, S., & Moskowitz, G. B. (2000). Evidence for implicit evaluative in-group bias: Affect-biased spontaneous trait inference in a minimal group paradigm. *Journal of Experimental Social Psychology*, *36*(1), 77–89. doi: 10.1006/jesp.1999.1399
Panchanathan, K., & Boyd, R. (2004). Indirect reciprocity can stabilize cooperation without the second-order free rider problem. *Nature*, *432*(7016), 499–502. Retrieved from www.nature.com/nature/journal/v432/n7016/suppinfo/nature02978_S1.html.
Parker, G. A. (1974). Assessment strategy and the evolution of fighting behaviour. *Journal of Theoretical Biology*, *47*(1), 223–243. doi: 10.1016/0022-5193(74)90111-8
Peysakhovich, A., Nowak, M. A., & Rand, D. G. (2014). Humans display a "cooperative phenotype" that is domain general and temporally stable. *Nature Communications*, *5*. doi: 10.1038/ncomms5939
Pinker, S. (2011). *The better angels of our nature: Why violence has declined*. New York: Viking.
Rand, D. G., & Epstein, Z. G. (2014). Risking your life without a second thought: Intuitive decision-making and extreme altruism. *PLoS ONE*, *9*(10), e109687. doi: 10.1371/journal.pone.0109687
Rand, D. G., & Nowak, M. A. (2013). Human cooperation. *Trends in Cognitive Sciences*, *17*(8), 413–425. doi: 10.1016/j.tics.2013.06.003
Rand, D. G., Greene, J. D., & Nowak, M. A. (2012). Spontaneous giving and calculated greed. *Nature*, *489*(7416), 427–430. Retrieved from www.nature.com/nature/journal/v489/n7416/abs/nature11467.html#supplementary-information.
Rand, D. G., Peysakhovich, A., Kraft-Todd, G. T., Newman, G. E., Wurzbacher, O., Nowak, M. A., & Greene, J. D. (2014). Social heuristics shape intuitive cooperation. *Nature Communications*, *5*. doi: 10.1038/ncomms4677
Rapoport, A., & Chammah, A. M. (1966). The game of chicken. *American Behavioral Scientist*, *10*(3), 10–28. doi: 10.1177/000276426601000303
Reed, L. I., DeScioli, P., & Pinker, S. A. (2014). The commitment function of angry facial expressions. *Psychological Science*, *25*(8), 1511–1517. doi: 10.1177/0956797614531027
Richerson, P. J., & Boyd, R. (2008). *Not by genes alone: How culture transformed human evolution*: University of Chicago Press.
Rohwer, S., & Rohwer, F. C. (1978). Status signalling in Harris sparrows: Experimental deceptions achieved. *Animal Behaviour*, *26*, 1012–1022. doi: 10.1016/0003-3472(78)90090-8
Schino, G. (2007). Grooming and agonistic support: A meta-analysis of primate reciprocal altruism. *Behavioral Ecology*, *18*(1), 115–120. doi: 10.1093/beheco/arl045
Segev, D. L., Muzaale, A. D., Caffo, B. S. et al. (2010). Perioperative mortality and long-term survival following live kidney donation. *JAMA*, *303*(10), 959–966. doi: 10.1001/jama.2010.237
Sell, A., Cosmides, L., Tooby, J., Sznycer, D., von Rueden, C., & Gurven, M. (2009). Human adaptations for the visual assessment of strength and fighting ability from the body and face. *Proceedings of the Royal*

Society of London B: Biological Sciences, 276(1656), 575–584. doi: 10.1098/rspb.2008.1177

Sell, A., Tooby, J., & Cosmides, L. (2009). Formidability and the logic of human anger. Proceedings of the National Academy of Sciences, 106(35), 15,073–15,078. doi: 10.1073/pnas.0904312106

Shamay-Tsoory, S., Tomer, R., Berger, B., & Aharon-Peretz, J. (2003). Characterization of empathy deficits following prefrontal brain damage: The role of the right ventromedial prefrontal cortex. Journal of Cognitive Neuroscience, 15(3), 324–337. doi: 10.1162/089892903321593063

Silverman, H. B., & Dunbar, M. J. (1980). Aggressive tusk use by the narwhal (Monodon monoceros L.). Nature, 284(5751), 57–58. Retrieved from http://dx.doi.org/10.1038/284057a0.

Sloman, S. A. (1996). The empirical case for two systems of reasoning. Psychological Bulletin, 119(1), 3.

Smith, E. R., & DeCoster, J. (2000). Dual-process models in social and cognitive psychology: Conceptual integration and links to underlying memory systems. Personality and Social Psychology Review, 4(2), 108–131. doi: 10.1207/s15327957pspr0402_01

Smith, J. M., & Price, G. (1973). The logic of animal conflict. Nature, 246, 15.

Stern, D. N. (1985). The interpersonal world of the infant: A view from psychoanalysis and developmental psychology: London: Karnac Books.

StoryCorps (2008). Julio Diaz [Audio podcast]. StoryCorps (March 28). Retrieved from https://storycorps.org/listen/julio-diaz.

Tajfel, H. (1982). Social psychology of intergroup relations. Annual Review of Psychology, 33(1), 1. Retrieved from http://search.ebscohost.com/login.aspx?direct=true&db=bth&AN=11268157&site=ehost-live&scope=site.

Tennyson, A. (2004). In memoriam. The Norton Anthology of English Literature. New York: Norton, 1962), II, 1141.

Thorbourne, K. (2015). Jersey City man who tried to break up fight dies, authorities say. The Jersey Journal, August 23. Retrieved from www.nj.com/hudson/index.ssf/2015/08/jersey_city_man_who_tried_to_break_up_fight_dies_a.html.

Tomlin, D. A., Rand, D. G., Ludwig, E., & Cohen, J. D. (2015). The evolution and devolution of cognitive control: The costs of deliberation in a competitive world. Scientific Reports, 5, 11002.

Toupo, D. F. P., Strogatz, S. H., Cohen, J. D., & Rand, D. G. (2015). Evolutionary game dynamics of controlled and automatic decision-making. Chaos, 25(7), 073120. doi: 10.1063/1.4927488

Treherne, J. E., & Foster, W. A. (1980). The effects of group size on predator avoidance in a marine insect. Animal Behaviour, 28(4), 1119–1122.

Trivers, R. L. (1971). The evolution of reciprocal altruism. The Quarterly Review of Biology, 46(1), 35–57. Retrieved from www.jstor.org/stable/2822435.

Wagenvoort, H. (1980). Pietas: Selected studies in roman religion. Leiden: Brill.

Warneken, F., & Tomasello, M. (2006). Altruistic helping in human infants and young chimpanzees. Science, 311(5765), 1301–1303. doi: 10.1126/science.1121448

West, S. A., Griffin, A. S., & Gardner, A. (2007). Evolutionary explanations for cooperation. Current Biology, 17(16), R661–R672.

West-Eberhard, M. J. (1979). Sexual selection, social competition, and evolution. Proceedings of the American Philosophical Society, 123(4), 222–234. Retrieved from www.jstor.org/stable/986582.

Wilkinson, G. S. (1984). Reciprocal food sharing in the vampire bat. Nature, 308(5955), 181–184. doi: 10.1038/308181a0

Wilkinson, P. F., & Shank, C. C. (1976). Rutting-fight mortality among musk oxen on Banks Island, Northwest Territories, Canada. Animal Behaviour, 24(4), 756–758. doi: 10.1016/S0003-3472(76)80004-8

Williams, G. C. (1966). Natural selection, the costs of reproduction, and a refinement of Lack's principle. The American Naturalist, 100(916), 687–690.

Yoeli, E., Hoffman, M., Rand, D. G., & Nowak, M. A. (2013). Powering up with indirect reciprocity in a large-scale field experiment. Proceedings of the National Academy of Sciences, 110(Supplement 2), 10,424–10,429. doi: 10.1073/pnas.1301210110

Zaki, J., & Mitchell, J. P. (2013). Intuitive prosociality. Current Directions in Psychological Science, 22(6), 466–470. doi: 10.1177/0963721413492764

4

The Evolution and Neurobiology of Heroism

Stephanie D. Preston

Heroism is an inherently exciting topic that has unfortunately enjoyed only sporadic attention over the years from the academy. Most people enjoy hearing stories of both everyday and exceptional heroes through friends and the media; moreover, anecdotes of heroic rescues quickly spread in the public consciousness. Such stories are likely compelling because they allow us to marvel in and relish the amazingly altruistic and risky actions of our fellow man—elevating our very sense of the human capacity to give. These stories also allow us to experience vicarious relief for those rescued from harm. They may even indulge our seemingly maudlin need to process others' potential life-threatening events, similar to the way people "rubber neck" at car accidents on the side of the road, seeking an "eyeful" and information about the sources of potential danger in life.

Heroism is also inherently interesting to academics for multiple reasons. Heroic acts have been documented throughout human history and even in other species (e.g., see de Waal, 1996; O'Connell, 1995; Preston & de Waal, 2002a), demonstrating that there is potentially something "natural" or "instinctual" about these amazing acts, which are not restricted to particular cultures, time periods, or forms of teaching (even if some traditions do encourage it more than others). However, one of the defining characteristics of a heroic act is also its infrequency. When someone performs an act of assistance that is considered "doable" by most people, or when the act is one that occurs fairly frequently, people do not consider it heroic *per se*, but rather classify it under the more general category of being helpful or "altruistic" (that is, benefitting another at a current cost to the self). Acts are usually only considered heroic in lay parlance when they involve a high level of risk to the helper—usually physical risk—while also providing immediate aid to someone who may have died were it not for the uncommonly helpful stranger. Thus, from an evolutionary and psychological perspective, it is not easy to explain why acts that appear so risky for the actor nonetheless would be deeply rooted in our evolutionary heritage and psychology.

The Paradox of Heroism as a Specific, Unusual Case of Altruism

Heroism is also paradoxical to scientists because it defies the most common biological explanations for the more general class of human altruism. On the surface of it, any seemingly selfless act of giving could be considered irrational from a biological perspective, because one assumes that organisms should only act to improve their own fitness—to help their "selfish genes" (cf., Dawkins, 1976/2006). However, most biologists assume—after W. D. Hamilton and Robert Trivers—that it can benefit an organism to help another if the target of aid is either somewhat related (inclusive fitness; cf., Hamilton, 1964) or will return the favor down the line (reciprocal altruism; cf., Trivers, 1971). Modern theories of such "reciprocity" (when one returns favors in kind, usually in an almost rule-based or normative process) further assume that even if the recipient cannot personally return the favor, the reputational benefits of being observed helping can still result in a net benefit if observing individuals then assist the altruist during his or her time of need (Bauman, 1993) or because people are more likely to give after someone gives to them (Pfeiffer, Rutte, Killingback, Taborsky, & Bonhoeffer, 2005; Yamagishi, Jin, & Kiyonari, 1999), termed "generalized reciprocity." Generalized reciprocity is strong and has been found in humans (Yamagishi et al., 1999) and rats (Rutte & Taborsky, 2007). Still other reciprocity theories assume that being helpful is adaptive for group-living individuals because tribes that evolved to be supportive of one another were more likely to survive and thrive during resource bottlenecks or against warfaring outside groups. This is called "strong reciprocity" because it does not require that any one altruistic act be adaptive as long as being generous or cooperative as a species was historically adaptive (Bowles & Gintis, 2004; Gintis, 2000). Some psychologists, economists, and philosophers make a more specific process-level argument about the nature of reciprocity by assuming that people "calculate" in some explicit and rational way the degree to which their gift will benefit them in the future, comparing the costs and the benefits when deciding whether or not to act in any given situation (e.g., see Milinski & Wedekind, 1998). It is highly unlikely that reciprocity requires such explicit calculation, especially given that it can be exhibited in other species that people do not assume are capable of such deliberative decision making (e.g., see de Waal & Brosnan, 2006; de Waal, 2000; de Waal & Luttrell, 1988; Wilkinson, 1984, 1988). It is more plausible that emotionally-mediated or attitudinal forms of reciprocity that are available across mammals pervade most situations (see Aureli & Schaffner, 2002; Brosnan & de Waal, 2014; Preston & de Waal, 2011), even if people do sometimes make explicit calculations. Regardless of this process-level debate, most biological work on why altruism is adaptive assumes that inclusive fitness benefits and reciprocity, which can exist at many levels, largely explain the evolution and persistence of altruism. But these may not apply as well to heroism *per se*, evoking the paradox of heroism once again.

Most of the assumptions underlying the adaptive benefits of inclusive fitness and reciprocity cannot be applied to heroic altruism and we need to consider whether there are alternative or distinct origins for the evolution of an instinct to rush into danger to help perfect strangers compared to more common and rational acts like sharing food with relatives and group mates. Heroic altruism by its very nature usually involves a highly dangerous and life-threatening act that is undertaken to save another, usually a complete stranger, who is unlikely to share genes or cross paths with the giver in the future. This greatly minimizes the expected benefits of inclusive fitness or reciprocity. They could possibly play a role if nearly all group members that one would encounter historically were actually somewhat related through inbreeding and if dying or significant injury were extremely rare during heroic aid, or if groups lauded heroes to the point where even injury or death would come at some significant reward to kin. But the mathematical trade-off of costs to the giver and benefits to the recipient is typically highly skewed in human heroism in a direction that seems to eradicate the potential or likely long-term benefits, which were supposedly providing the act with its "adaptive" quality.

In most descriptions of human altruistic aid in the literature, the gift or support is usually only "costly" in a nominal sense of not being free from negative consequences for the giver; however, the costs to the giver in the examples are still typically much lower than the benefit enjoyed by the recipient. For example, if I have a large share of food from a successful hunt or foraging expedition, I probably can't even eat it all by myself before it spoils and, thus, giving some to a group mate is not particularly costly. Of course I am, in a literal sense, giving up something I possess, which does count as a cost. However, for the recipient—a group mate who failed to secure a hunt or foraged food perhaps—the extra bit that he or she received could mean the difference between dying of starvation and living to see another day. Such is the case in vampire bats, who are considered altruistic because they do share food, even with non-relatives. Research into the gift exchanges in vampire bats shows that the gifts usually come from successful, adult foragers who share food with juveniles that failed their own independent hunt and could not survive the night without the gift (Wilkinson, 1990). As another example, if a human group member is weak or injured and cannot carry his or her supplies as the group moves from one campsite to another, an altruistic individual may carry his or her supplies along with their own—which is surely costly because it requires extra energy and effort—but there is an important gap between the additional fatigue endured by the good Samaritan compared with the benefit received by the injured party who can only move with the group because of this gift. In more typical modern scenarios, people usually altruistically donate money to worthwhile causes but, whether they are giving tens or hundreds or even millions of dollars, the philanthropists are usually careful only to give to the point where they still know there is plenty left over for themselves and their family, to purchase or acquire whatever they need for the foreseeable future. Thus, such commonly referenced altruistic gifts are adaptive because the giver clearly does not, in the long run, give up more of their own resources than would make sense in relation to the benefit accrued by the other, who ideally is even genetically related or interrelated due to shared group membership.

Heroism by its very nature incurs a much more serious cost than these examples, with an appreciable risk of something catastrophically bad happening to the hero during the act, including dying. As evidence for this very real risk, 20 percent of Carnegie Hero Medals were awarded posthumously because the hero died while trying to save another (Becker & Eagly, 2004). Dying is clear evidence that you have sacrificed your direct genetic fitness. And unless you have saved approximately two of your own biological children plus at least a niece or nephew from dying in the act (because each child shares half of your genes plus you share a quarter of the genes with your sibling's children) you will not recoup those benefits to your genes in the next generation.

The fact that the target in a heroic act is usually a stranger, and often a child or otherwise helpless victim (like an elderly, sick, or injured individual), additionally limits the victim's future potential to reciprocate when you need help. Perhaps you could argue—as some do (e.g., Haley & Fessler, 2005; Hardy & Van Vugt, 2006; Manfred, Semmann, & Krambeck, 2002)—that the benefits of heroism derive instead from the public adulation piled onto heroes, who do, after all, receive a "hero's welcome" that often comes with prizes, monetary gifts, or at least wide-spread attention as evidenced by our cultural attention to such stories as referenced in the opening to this chapter. Adulation is surely a benefit to successful heroism and one that is usually observed by others, but it is not a benefit that can overcome the catastrophic cost of dying during a failed attempt. Thus, unless a potential hero is certain they will successfully save the other, and will not be seriously injured or killed while trying, then it does not make good statistical sense to intervene. (Genes are, after all, all about statistics.) And since when can we be sure of the outcome in a rapidly changing, dynamic, dangerous situation? Yet people do, sometimes, rush into aid. Why do they do this?

These clear differences from more mundane or typical examples of human altruism, when compared with heroic altruism *per se*, indicate that heroism does not clearly abide by key assumptions in the common biological argument for adaptive altruism. Thus, heroism is fairly mysterious from an evolutionary standpoint. The black hole surrounding our intellectual understanding of heroism only deepens when we consider that there is almost no direct empirical research in psychology or neuroscience on heroism. There were extensive early empirical studies on how people respond to another's urgent need, but those studies were designed to demonstrate why people fail to respond in such emergency need situations—also known as "bystander apathy" (Darley & Latané, 1968; Latané & Rodin, 1969)—rather than what causes people to rise to the challenge. There are a few qualitative studies into the nature of heroes or people who act in unusual circumstances, including an excellent paper on gender differences in heroism by Becker and Eagly (Becker & Eagly, 2004) and a book chapter on the "extraordinary acts of ordinary people" (Oliner, 2002) that examines the attributes and life experience of heroes through case studies and surveys to predict when people do respond. However, there are almost no coherent psychological, evolutionary, or neuroscientific accounts of heroism that predict when people will respond, and who is most likely to act.

The remainder of this chapter describes my integrated ultimate and proximate level model for heroic altruism. Typically people present arguments that are posited at either the "ultimate level"—explaining why the behavior is adaptive and how it evolved in evolutionary history—or at the "proximate level," by explaining how the behavior or phenomenon is instantiated in the nervous system, how it develops within the individual, or which environmental or situational cues elicit the response. According to Mayr, ultimate and proximate explanations are separate levels of analysis and, thus, do not compete with one another directly (Mayr, 1961). Thus, different people's models to explain a behavior could be perfectly compatible with one another, as long as they exist at different levels of analysis (e.g., ultimate or proximate). In my integrated ultimate and proximate approach, it is assumed that the nervous system itself evolves, and shows great conservation of mechanism across generations, such that pre-existing neural circuits and mechanisms for solving key problems across mammalian species are preserved over time and also strongly influence the form of any novel behavioral innovation or genetic adjustment. As such, if you assume that it was adaptive for mammals with altricial offspring to provide careful, attentive, active care and protection of their young, so that their genetic half relatives would survive into the next generation, then existing scientific knowledge about the neurohormonal system employed by mammals to care for offspring also provides a window into the proximate mechanism of active care of human others since, after all, humans are caregiving mammals as well.

This model is consistent with other work in the social and biological sciences that assume empathy for distressed others evolved from the need for mammalian or early human parents to provide sensitive and tailored care to their own offspring (which surely abides by the rules of inclusive fitness). For example, Frans de Waal writes extensively about how behaviors in primates like consolation, reconciliation, empathy, and helping evolved in the context of the mother–offspring bond (de Waal, 2010). This view was also mentioned previously in early work in human ethology (Bowlby, 1969; Eibl-Eibesfeldt, 1971/1974) and even hundreds of years earlier in moral philosophy (e.g., see Hume, 1739–1740/1990; Smith, 1759). Similarly, Sarah Hrdy has written a book describing in detail how human evolved from a context of group living animals who cared for one another, which helped to form the basis for our cooperative nature (Hrdy, 2009), much like the strong reciprocity view described above (Gintis, Bowles, Boyd, & Fehr, 2003). However, my offspring care model of heroic altruism (Preston, 2013) augments these caregiving models of prosocial behavior with additional proximate-mechanism level evidence about active offspring care and retrieval, which is particularly well adapted to explain *heroic* forms of altruism, above and beyond the consoling, succorant, passive and abstract aid that has been studied to date.

An Offspring Care Model of Altruism

The parental care literature in rodents describes and examines a very specific behavior required to care for litters of young pups. In a typical scenario, a dam (female rodent mother) is huddling and nursing pups in the nest when one of them starts to wander off, perhaps exploring and practicing new-found walking skills or seeking a nearby food source. When the dam notices the separated pup, or hears its ultrasonic distress calls, she approaches the pup and carries it back to the nest in her mouth. This behavior prevents the helpless, separated pup from encountering danger, like predators who can better access the pups when they are not in the protection of the nest; it also ensures that the pup has continuous access to the substantial early benefits of passive care received in the nest from the mother dam like licking, grooming, and nursing (e.g., see Champagne, 2008). Pup retrieval is a highly stereotyped behavior in rodent dams. For example, one experiment found that even after three hours, experimental dams were still willing to bar press to receive and then retrieve to the nest an endless series of unrelated pups down a chute into the testing chamber, creating a veritable assembly line of helpless pups (Wilsoncroft, 1969). Eventually the exhausted researchers had to terminate the experiment, after determining that the "pup retrieval" sequence was not prone to extinction or habituation. Moreover, indicating an almost fixed nature of the pup retrieval response, parenthetic reports in multiple older studies on maternal care describe confused dams who occasionally even try to retrieve their own tail back to the nest, particularly after cortical damage that experimenters applied to determine the neural locus of caregiving behavior (Beach, 1937; Slotnick & Nigrosh, 1975). Thus, the motivation to retrieve pups, particularly in the days and weeks after parturition (giving birth), is strong, it is not restricted to related pups, and it is characterized by stereotypies that suggest a powerful and innate aspect of the behavior. (The term "innate" only means that the behavior is built into the genetic code, but it still requires situational, hormonal, and neural changes to be induced, usually through pregnancy and parturition.)

The neural control of pup retrieval—as first described by the innovative neuroethologist Jay Rosenblatt, and then later in more detail by his postdoctoral scholar Michael Numan—is described as a natural opponency between approaching the target in need and avoiding the novel stimulus. In the complete neural circuit described by Michael Numan (Numan, 2007; Stolzenberg & Numan, 2011), perception of the target under both approach and avoidance conditions activates the amygdala. But in the "default" mode, the circuit is initially set for non-maternal rodents to avoid pups through neural activity that proceeds from the amygdala to the anterior hypothalamus (AHN) and on to the periaqueductal gray (PAG) where it produces downstream effects on the body, such as increased sympathetic arousal and behavioral avoidance. This is the avoidance route. However, when a female is in a maternal state, or when a virgin female or a male has become habituated to pups over time, this avoidance system becomes inhibited and connections from the amygdala instead project to the MPOA/vBST and on to the dopaminergic ventral striatal system, which in turn motivates the active approach and care of pups. This approach-avoidance opponency is not reserved for offspring care, but rather appears to be a specific instantiation of a more general sense in which the brain and mind pair and oppose motivations to approach versus avoid all stimuli. This fundamental characteristic of biopsychology was initially described by Rosenblatt's mentor Theodore Christian Schneirla (Schneirla, 1959), but has since been extended to explain a wide variety of phenomena including individual personality differences, psychopathologies like anxiety, hemispheric lateralization in the brain, and even collective group behavior (see reviews in Elliot & Thrash, 2002; Roth & Cohen, 1986).

Pup retrieval is extremely adaptive because it provides multiple fitness benefits to the pup and to the dam. As mentioned above, retrieving separated pups back to the nest reduces the chances of predation. It also conveniently pairs the safety of the pups with their nourishment and physiological need for warmth and stimulation—all of which are required by altricial mammals to survive and adapt to early developmental conditions. Keeping the pups together in the nest also allows the dam to efficiently feed many pups at a time, providing them with key nutrients and important antibodies from the mother. The close contact from huddling and the stimulation from licking and grooming by the dam is also known to improve the neurophysiological development of the pup by upregulating neurobiological and immune systems, which develop rapidly during this period (Champagne, 2008; Champagne, Francis, Mar, & Meaney, 2003; Meaney, 2003). Thus, the active retrieval behavior that retains pups in the nest combined with the passive nurturant care that take place in the nest like nursing, huddling, and grooming all combine to increase the direct fitness of the pup and the indirect fitness of the dam. Because of this, pup retrieval is not just a cute or odd behavior that scientists can elicit in the lab, it is a stereotyped and caricaturized form of a natural and powerful instinct that is extremely important for the survival and flourishing of altricial species under typical, ecological conditions.

What can these studies tell us about the human instinct to help? Most people are probably sympathetic to the idea that pup retrieval is an important, evolved behavior that ensures the safety and health of neonatal rodents and their offspring. A goodly proportion of that majority would further acknowledge an evolutionary link among mammals such that not only rodents but also people possess this evolved tendency to be attracted to and to protect one's own, helpless neonates. But what about human altruism? How is the retrieval of neonates relevant to human prosocial behavior, human altruism, or even human heroism? There are a few strong reasons to assume that mammalian parental care is highly relevant to our understanding of human prosociality. There is even reasonably strong evidence—some direct and plenty indirect—that retrieval behavior *per se* is related to human heroism.

By extrapolating the form, function, and underlying mechanism of pup retrieval to other forms of offspring care, and even the care of even unrelated individuals, we can actually begin to understand why people seem to possess a seemingly irrational but remarkable motivation to save perfect strangers from immediate harm—to plunge into icy waters and burning buildings, to hide Jewish children from Nazi soldiers during the Holocaust, or to donate money to starving children on the other side of the planet. The offspring care model proposes that mammalian offspring care formed the basis for many human prosocial acts, including the mysterious examples of human heroism, which heretofore have really only been the subject of speculation and wonder in the sciences.

A Homology between Offspring Retrieval and Human Heroism

Functional Characteristics in Common between Retrieval and Rescue

On the surface of it, descriptions of the way that rodent female dams quickly and urgently approach and retrieve helpless neonates to return them to the comfort and safety of the nest bear a striking physical, functional, and phenomenological resemblance to the most active and heroic forms of altruism.

Pup retrieval and human heroism both involve a vulnerable, distressed, endangered individual who is usually alone and emitting calls of distress and need. In both cases, a nearby individual observes these signals and feels some subsequent compulsion to rush to the victim's assistance and retrieve them from danger. In addition, in both pup retrieval and human heroism the rescued individual is often cuddled, hugged, or held close after the rescue, which not only ensures the continued safety of the target but also comforts both parties, as the helper also becomes somewhat contagiously distressed by the event. Pup retrieval descriptions also convey an intense and maybe even irrational strength and fixed nature of the drive to respond to helpless, endangered targets, pointing to a strong and often unpremeditated evolved response in much the same way that human heroes describe their "urge" to respond to a stranger in need. Thus, descriptions of pup retrieval are highly similar to descriptions of human heroism in the types of targets involved, the form and function of the behavior, and the phenomenological sense of urgency and immediacy despite the costs to the giver.

Most of these similarities exist at a level that is fairly easily and directly observed, which could represent an analogy that, in reality, is only coincidental, convenient, or perhaps poetic. In biology, the term "analogy" is used to refer to behaviors or adaptations that look similar in two distinct species or genetic lines despite not having emerged from a shared, common ancestor. When there is a biological analogy, the behavior or morphological adaptation is assumed to have simply arisen independently in the two cases because both species faced a similar problem that was most readily solved with a similar solution. In contrast, sometimes two behaviors that look similar in disparate species actually result from a common, shared ancestor that possessed the shared trait and passed it on to both emerging lines. In these cases, the similarity is more than a coincidence or an "analogy" and instead reflects an evolutionary "homology." Thus, while we can feel fairly certain that there is an interesting analogy between pup retrieval and human heroism, is there a homology? There are strong reasons to assume that there is, which I turn to next.

Mammalian Brains and Mechanisms of Offspring Care are Highly Conserved

Extensive data in evolutionary neurobiology demonstrates that the overall nervous system design is highly conserved across mammalian species. This means that most mammals have nervous systems that are highly similar, with nearly the same neural regions, processing the same neurotransmitters, through many of the same interconnections across species. Thus, from a mechanistic standpoint at least, there is clear evidence that we do share most neural mechanisms with species like rodents, which are also mammals, even if, to most people, we do not look similar on the surface. In addition, proximate-level data on parental care *per se* suggests that the mechanisms that have been discovered and described for parental care in rodents (the most often studied animal for practical reasons) are also largely present in other mammalian species that have been investigated to date (see review in Preston, 2013). For example, the way that pregnancy and parturition induce neurohormonal, psychological, and behavioral states that are highly attuned to neonates (and sometimes specific neonates likes one's own offspring, depending upon the ecology of the species), has been observed in sheep (Kendrick et al., 1997; Nowak, Keller, Val-Laillet, & Lévy, 2007), monkeys (Maestripieri, 1999; Maestripieri & Roney, 2006), and to some extent humans (e.g., see Barrett et al., 2011; Delahunty, McKay, Noseworthy, & Storey, 2007; Stallings, Fleming, Corter, Worthman, & Steiner, 2001). Many of the same hormonal transitions into motivated offspring care have even been observed in males and caregiving virgin females in rodents (Rosenblatt, 1992), monkeys (Maestripieri, 1999), and human fathers (Delahunty et al., 2007; Fleming, Corter, Stallings, & Steiner, 2002; Rilling, 2013; van Anders, Tolman, & Volling, 2012). Thus, there are substantial reasons to assume that the evolution and neurohormonal basis of offspring care are actually conserved across caregiving mammals and derive from a common ancestor that also provided extensive care for altricial, slowly developing offspring.

The Approach-Avoidance Opponency in Retrieval and Rescue

The approach-avoidance opponency that was described above for offspring care also supports a biological homology between pup retrieval and human altruism because people also avoid helping strangers any time they feel intimidated or concerned about the target's need, the situation, or their capacity to successfully respond. In contrast, when people are socially bonded to the other and feel confident that they can perform the necessary response—successfully and in time—they will respond, even in situations that appear scary and dangerous to less competent onlooking peers.

This avoidance that humans exhibit under uncertain, intimidating, or overwhelming conditions is actually one of the most highly studied aspects of human prosocial behavior, perhaps only bested in number of articles by research on the link between empathic feelings and the motivation to help (cf., Batson, 2011). The tradition of research on what is most commonly called "bystander apathy" emerged from a post-Second World War movement where the forefathers of social psychology tried to determine why humans appeared to be so apathetic and sometimes even willing to participate in the mass genocide of Jews in Europe. We would like to think that if someone in our environment was doing wrong—hurting and killing people who did not pose an immediate, violent threat—that we would say something ... that if they asked us to hurt them, even instructed us to hurt them, we would refuse. But the body of social psychological research performed after the war revealed that perhaps, as a people, we often fail to meet our own elevated expectations for moral behavior under distinct conditions when we feel intimidated or fearful for our own safety, despite a simultaneous capacity to care for and even heroically assist others under more favorable conditions.

The most well-known research on bystander apathy was performed by Darley & Latané (Darley & Latané, 1968; Latané & Rodin, 1969). In a typical bystander apathy study, a confederate research assistant feigns injury or pain in a public place or the subject hears the sound of someone in pain or distress from an adjacent room while they perform an unrelated experiment. The experimenters then measure whether participants will leave their ostensive task to approach the target in need and offer help. The most common interpretation of these studies is that the presence of bystanders prevents people from acting because the probability of help goes down with the number of bystanders due to a "diffusion of responsibility." For example, this research tradition often makes conceptual links to real-life events by referring to the popular case of Kitty Genovese from 1964, in which it was reported that 37 or 38 people all witnessed or heard the screams of Ms. Genovese, who was stabbed repeatedly with a knife in the alley behind her building, without anyone intervening or offering help. This story has since been subject to criticism, and it may be that more like a dozen people heard or observed portions of the attack but not clearly or for very long, and one man did actually call out to help (see Manning, Levine, & Collins, 2007; Rasenberger, 2006). The story is so tightly linked to the phenomenon of bystander apathy that the effect is sometimes referred to as "Genovese syndrome."

However, a strict "diffusion of responsibility" interpretation of the bystander effect seems to be an oversimplification that misses many key nuances in those older experiments. For one thing, people actually do show themselves to be moderately and impressively helpful in those studies, particularly when there is no "rule" enforced upon them to stay where they are or to refrain from acting. In the original studies by Darley and Latané, the subjects actually respond uniformly and quickly when they feel free to react and when they saw the person in distress earlier in the experiment and feel some connection to them. For example, nearly every subject in their 1968 study who faced the target alone helped, the vast majority in fewer than ten seconds, with few reporting any thoughts between hearing the distress and acting (Darley & Latané, 1968). Such redeeming responses are also true of the Holocaust itself, as many people actually did rescue and hide victims in their own homes, particularly when they had to directly face the distress of the other, felt empathy, love, compassion, and a personal responsibility that simply compelled action, without "considering risk or thinking about being either lauded or maligned" (Oliner, 2002, p. 127). The fact that people particularly failed to act when they felt constrained by the experimental situation in the bystander studies and even in the Second World War is perhaps better taken as evidence for the powerful influence of authority, as was studied by Milgram and colleagues in the same post-Second World War tradition (Milgram, 1974).

Thus, the bystander apathy literature in general may be better encapsulated by a broader theme of approach-avoidance processes, as was described in the offspring care model, in which people fail to respond when inaction is actually the adaptive response, such as when the observer feels intimidated by the situation, unqualified to help as in a real medical emergency, or when others are present who seem more capable or may pressure the observer to remain in place.

The case of Kitty Genovese aptly encapsulates this conflict. Not only were there many potential helpers present in the surrounding apartments—the sheer number of which may have made people feel complacent like someone else would surely help—there were clearly other factors at play, like the fact that the perpetrator was a violent criminal who was not afraid to hurt someone in a public place. In this case, intervening could be seen as clearly putting one's own self into danger, which is not adaptive and may seem to represent the appropriate avoidance arm of the offspring care mechanism.

Despite these complexities, bystander apathy experiments still have something interesting to teach us because, even in the Genovese case, calling the police would seem to be at least a warranted and relatively safe course of action. And in the classic bystander apathy psychology experiments, there is no knife-wielding maniac. There is usually just one single adult victim who is either observed lying on the ground moaning in pain or someone heard from the next room crying for help. A man lying on the ground in pain does not pose an immediate danger to the potential altruist, who you would think could at least walk near him and ask him if he needs help or could walk the opposite way to find help. There are even demonstrations of bystander apathy constructed by the media on television shows like *Dateline 20/20* or *What Would You Do?* in which someone poses as an injured or sick person on the steps of a highly populated building, like a train station, and the show films passers-by as they glance down at the purported victim and continue walking, not even checking to see if the victim is ok. While people are not in much literal or objective risk when they intervene to help an injured or sick person, especially when the help just requires a phone call to a trained professional, this apathy can also be viewed as adaptive in that it reflects a more general heuristic to avoid myriad forms of uncertainty: uncertainty about what is wrong with the victim, whether the observer really can do anything to help, whether the victim would react well to intervention, and whether intervening will negatively impact the observer's own personal goals (e.g., *What if the person writhing on the ground in public is a crazy drug addict and comes after me? What if they have a contagious illness? What if helping them ends up taking the rest of the day and I miss my appointment and get demoted at work?*). The default assumption appears to be that someone else will be more qualified to help and that it is best not to add chaos into one's own difficult life by intervening, especially for a victim they do not even know. These appear to be adaptive decisions according to the inclusive fitness and reciprocity arguments, even if the judgment is a conservative one that greatly overestimates the risks.

Interesting research in evolutionary psychology can add something to this conundrum by demonstrating that people may have a sort of innate disease-avoidance mechanism that helps them avoid potentially infectious pathogens, by causing them to generally avoid any people or even foods that have attributes that may be associated with illness, in a very conservative manner that clearly includes avoiding things that are not due to illness per se but do follow a general heuristic of avoiding or being disgusted by people and foods that are in any way "different" or "affected" (Huang, Sedlovskaya, Ackerman, & Bargh, 2011; Mortensen, Becker, Ackerman, Neuberg, & Kenrick, 2010). As such, in cases like the apathetic bystanders on television passing by someone moaning on the ground, the disease avoidance mechanism may further tilt the scales toward avoidance of the target in need causing people to wait ... like in a game of chicken ... hoping that someone else will be the first to intervene so that they can remain "off the hook."

The neural and behavioral opponency built into both offspring retrieval and heroic altruism appropriately explains bystander apathy and the discrepancy between when people act and when they do not. But this homology is also critical from a comparative perspective. People usually assume that humans are more thoughtful, planful, and rational than non-human animals, while also assuming that rodents are simple stimulus–response machines that cannot maximize the effectiveness of their behavior. But the homology suggests that the truth is actually somewhere in between, such that the evolved, biological mechanism that we share with rodents and other caregiving mammals naturally pairs caring with competency and security while prohibiting foolhardy and reckless heroism that could endanger the helper.

Thus, through a sophisticated and sensible evolved mechanism, both rodents and humans can be extremely helpful when it would benefit them the most while also being alarmingly apathetic or even aggressive in cases where, on average, it would hurt them unnecessarily to help. The approach-avoidance opponency is also well suited to explain prominent gender differences in altruism, with most passive, succorant, and tireless givers being more often female while the most publicly lauded heroes who rush into danger are more often males who are confident that they can succeed under these highly physical conditions. These canonical "heroes" are usually stronger and feel sufficiently in control in even risky situations to enact the approach, for example, to drag someone out of a dangerous fire or flood—situations where the avoidance response is potentiated in all but the most physically adept individuals, and for good reason.

The Neural and Hormonal Bases of Offspring Care Overlap with those of Human Altruism

The most compelling reason to assume that active offspring retrieval and human heroism are connected derives from data on the human neuroscience of prosocial giving. Most existing neuroscience studies have not examined heroism *per se*. But when researchers do examine the neural and hormonal bases of more general decisions to give (e.g., to donate money to a preferred charity or help a peer during an experiment) the brain areas and hormones associated with the altruistic response overlap considerably with those required for offspring care, particularly engaging the amygdala, nucleus accumbens, anterior cingulate, and medial prefrontal cortex and involving the related hormones like oxytocin and prolactin (see review in Preston, 2013). This neural circuit is not only associated with pup retrieval, it is part of a more general dopaminergic mesolimbocortical system associated with the motivation to seek all rewarding substances, from drugs of abuse to money to delicious prepared foods and sexual partners. The response in the case of offspring care or human heroism is just applied to endangered, helpless individuals, instead of consumable rewards. The offspring retrieval response also requires a few additional proximate mechanisms beyond those associated with approaching consumable rewards, like the neurohormonal changes that shift individuals from the avoidance to the approach arm of the circuit (associated with pregnancy and parturition or habituation). In addition, pup retrieval is thought to require the medial preoptic area of the hypothalamus (MPOA), which is not implicated in responses to consumable rewards like food and drink but does seem necessary for the active response to pups. This is a very small region of the brain that is hard to image in a brain scanner or to study using human neuroscientific methods. Therefore, it is currently unknown whether this particular nucleus is also required for human offspring care or active altruism, but time will tell.

There is also interesting research on "exceptional" human altruists, who donate their own organs to strangers in need that further supports a homology between offspring care and human helping. In this line of work, Dr. Abigail Marsh and colleagues follow people who, for example, donate their kidneys to strangers on the organ donation list. When the researchers examine the responses of these extraordinary altruists in behavioral and neuroimaging experiments they find that altruistic kidney donors are more sensitive to observed facial distress and fear in others and have stronger amygdala responses and larger gray matter volume in that region (Marsh et al., 2014). In contrast, individuals with psychopathic tendencies tend to have lower responses to such stimuli and reduced activation and gray matter volume in the amygdala (Marsh & Blair, 2008; Vieira et al., 2015). This research is important not only because it helps support the presumed homology between neural regions required for offspring care and altruism, but also because it examines a more risky altruistic response than most research and, thus, comes closer to testing hypotheses about risky heroism *per se*.

Thus, there are strong reasons to assume that there is indeed an evolved, biological homology between caring for offspring and helping human strangers, particularly between pup retrieval and human active or heroic altruism. There are also many benefits to applying the offspring retrieval model to human altruism at this particular point in time, which we turn to now.

The Current Importance of an Ultimate and Proximate Model of Heroism

As stated above, the offspring care model could provide a proximate-level explanation for active human altruism, which had largely been ignored by the field to date. It also places altruism into a more ecological context than is typically the case in the social sciences. Whereas most experimental treatments of altruism in economics and psychology involve giving money to strangers in the laboratory—a situation that is not really similar to anything in our ancestral heritage—one can easily imagine early human ancestors having to pull genetic relatives and group mates back from potential falls or dangerous conditions. This homology also emphasizes the role of overt motor responses in the evolution of a human behavior that is too often characterized in abstract, cognitive terms. Emphasizing a link between offspring retrieval and active human altruism also supports the long-standing assumption in psychology and biology that empathy and prosocial behavior evolved as extensions of the drive to care for one's own offspring (e.g., see Churchland, 2008; Eibl-Eibesfeldt, 1971/1974; Hrdy, 2009; Preston, 2013; Preston & de Waal, 2002b). However, the specificity of the rodent offspring retrieval research in neurobiology permits more specific predictions about how offspring care and altruism are related at the proximate and ultimate level than was possible before. Most prior theories about how altruism evolved from the motivation for mothers to care for their own offspring were just assertions unaccompanied by empirical tests, counter-theories, or specifications. For example, existing caregiving theories of altruism were too general to make predictions about when females or mothers would help compared to non-mothers, or when people would exhibit the potent and remarkable capacity for aid versus embarrassing apathy. In contrast, we can now make specific predictions about when and why people will be compelled to help based on specifications from the neuroscientific literature.

This inclusive approach recasts potentially problematic paradoxes—like the concurrent ability to be compassionate and apathetic or gender differences in passive versus active care—as opportunities for scientific growth. Like a litmus test, only if a model of altruism explains these conundrums can we be sure it is explanatory. By carefully considering situations where responses are potentiated versus inhibited in animals and humans we can fully understand how nature, nurture, and the situation interact to influence the altruistic response, in ways that are usually adaptive—at least under natural conditions like those in which our ancestors evolved.

There are multiple reasons that I choose to focus on the analogy between active offspring care and human altruism. The superficial functional and structural similarities between pup retrieval and heroic altruism require that we at least examine the analogy more closely. Heroism is also the least-well understood aspect of prosocial giving, because it is so different from other forms of giving like alarm calls, grooming, food sharing, and giving gifts or money, and because it is so hard to study in the laboratory. But because of these factors, we have much to gain in the current moment by focusing on the potential homology between active offspring care and heroic human altruism. The potential homology between pup retrieval and human heroism in particular is important for our understanding of human altruism because, to date, this is the only proximate level or evolutionary story that has been offered to explain why people sometimes take extreme risks to help even complete strangers. The goal of this offspring care model is to correct this imbalance, by considering how active offspring care may be related to human altruism—particularly heroic altruism—and to provide some fairly detailed predictions about how human heroism should operate and be instantiated in the brain and body if the model is correct. Some of these ideas may turn out to be wrong. But at least providing them with specific commitments and testable hypotheses we will advance the field beyond where it too often lays—in speculation without the benefit of empirical evidence.

By deeply exploring the messy details regarding when humans or non-humans actually exhibit this behavior, we can develop a more accurate and comprehensive model that makes more precise predictions about when someone will help. If we are lucky, this information can even be applied to encourage helping where it is most needed, in the real world.

References

Aureli, F., & Schaffner, C. M. (2002). Relationship assessment through emotional mediation. *Behaviour*, *139*(2/3), 393–420. doi: 10.1163/156853902760102726

Barrett, J., Wonch, K. E., Gonzalez, A., Ali, N., Steiner, M., Hall, G. B. et al. (2011). Maternal affect and quality of parenting experiences are related to amygdala response to infant faces. *Social Neuroscience*, *7*(3), 252–268. doi: 10.1080/17470919.2011.609907

Batson, C. D. (2011). *Altruism in humans*. New York: Oxford University Press.

Bauman, Z. (1993). *Postmodern ethics*. Oxford: Blackwell.

Beach, F. A. J. (1937). The neural basis of innate behavior. I. Effects of cortical lesions upon the maternal behavior pattern in the rat. *Journal of Comparative Psychology*, *24*(3), 393–440. doi: 10.1037/H0059606

Becker, S. W., & Eagly, A. H. (2004). The heroism of women and men. *American Psychologist*, *59*(3), 163–178. doi: 10.1037/0003-066x.59.3.163

Bowlby, J. (1969). *Attachment and loss* (Vol. 1). New York: Basic Books.

Bowles, S., & Gintis, H. (2004). The evolution of strong reciprocity: cooperation in heterogeneous populations. *Theoretical Population Biology*, *65*(1), 17–28. doi: 10.1016/j.tpb.2003.07.001

Brosnan, S. F., & de Waal, F. B. M. (2014). Reciprocity in primates. In S. D. Preston, M. L. Kringelbach & B. Knutson (eds), *The interdisciplinary science of consumption* (pp. 3–32). Cambridge, MA: MIT Press.

Champagne, F. A. (2008). Epigenetic mechanisms and the transgenerational e ects of maternal care *Frontiers in Neuroendocrinology*, *29*, 386–397. doi: 10.1016/j.yfrne.2008.03.003

Champagne, F. A., Francis, D. D., Mar, A., & Meaney, M. J. (2003). Variations in maternal care in the rat as a mediating influence for the effects of environment on development. *Physiology & Behavior*, *79*(3), 359–371. doi: 10.1016/S0031-9384(03)00149-5

Churchland, P. S. (2008). The impact of neuroscience on philosophy. *Neuron*, *60*(60), 409–411. doi: 10.1016/j.neuron.2008.10.023

Darley, J. M., & Latané, B. (1968). Bystander intervention in emergencies: Diffusion of responsibility. *Journal of Personality and Social Psychology*, *8*(4), 377–383. doi: 10.1037/h0025589

Dawkins, R. (1976/2006). *The selfish gene* (30th anniversary ed.). Oxford: Oxford University Press.

De Waal, F. (1996). *Good natured: The origins of right and wrong in humans and other animals*. Cambridge, MA: Harvard University Press.

De Waal, F. (2000). Attitudinal reciprocity in food sharing among brown capuchin monkeys. *Animal Behaviour*, *60*(2), 253–261. doi: 10.1006/anbe.2000.1471

De Waal, F. (2010). *The age of empathy: Nature's lessons for a kinder society*. New York: Random House.

De Waal, F., & Brosnan, S. (2006). Simple and complex reciprocity in primates. In P. S. Kappeler & P. Carel (eds), *Cooperation in primates and humans: Mechanisms and evolution* (pp. 85–105). New York: Springer.

De Waal, F., & Luttrell, L. M. (1988). Mechanisms of social reciprocity in three primate species: symmetrical relationship characteristics or cognition? *Ethology & Sociobiology*, *9*, 101–118. doi: 10.1016/0162-3095(88)90016-7

Delahunty, K. M., McKay, D. W., Noseworthy, D. E., & Storey, A. E. (2007). Prolactin responses to infant cues in men and women: Effects of parental experience and recent infant contact. *Hormones and Behavior*, *51*(2), 213–220. doi: 10.1016/j.yhbeh.2006.10.004

Eibl-Eibesfeldt, I. (1971/1974). *Love and hate* (G. Strachan, Trans. 2nd ed.). New York: Schocken Books.

Elliot, A. J., & Thrash, T. M. (2002). Approach-avoidance motivation in personality: approach and avoidance temperaments and goals. *Journal of Personality and Social Psychology*, *82*(5), 804.

Fleming, A. S., Corter, C., Stallings, J., & Steiner, M. (2002). Testosterone and prolactin are associated with emotional responses to infant cries in new fathers. *Hormones and Behavior*, *42*(4), 399–413. doi: 10.1006/hbeh.2002.1840

Gintis, H. (2000). Strong reciprocity and human sociality. *Journal of Theoretical Biology*, *206*(2), 169–179. doi: 10.1006/jtbi.2000.2111

Gintis, H., Bowles, S., Boyd, R., & Fehr, E. (2003). Explaining altruistic behavior in humans. *Evolution and Human Behavior*, *24*(3), 153–172. doi: 10.1016/S1090-5138(02)00157-5

Haley, K. J., & Fessler, D. M. T. (2005). Nobody's watching? Subtle cues affect generosity in an anonymous economic game. *Evolution and Human Behavior*, *26*(3), 245–256. doi: 10.1016/j.evolhumbehav.2005.01.002

Hamilton, W. D. (1964). The genetical evolution of social behavior, I and II. *Journal of Theoretical Biology*, *7*(1), 1–52. doi: 10.1016/0022-5193(64)90038-4

Hardy, C. L., & Van Vugt, M. (2006). Nice guys finish first: The competitive altruism hypothesis. *Personality and Social Psychology Bulletin*, *32*(10), 1402–1413. doi: 10.1177/0146167206291006

Hrdy, S. B. (2009). *Mothers and others*. Cambridge, MA: Harvard University Press.

Huang, J. Y., Sedlovskaya, A., Ackerman, J. M., & Bargh, J. A. (2011). Immunizing against prejudice effects of disease protection on attitudes toward out-groups. *Psychological Science*, *22*(12), 1550–1556.

Hume, D. (1739–1740/1990). *A treatise of human nature* (7th impression of 2nd ed.). Oxford: Clarendon Press.

Kendrick, K. M., Da Costa, A. P., Broad, K. D., Ohkura, S., Guevara, R., Levy, F. et al. (1997). Neural control of maternal behaviour and olfactory recognition of offspring. *Brain Research Bulletin*, *44*(4), 383–395. doi: 10.1016/S0361-9230(97)00218-9

Latané, B., & Rodin, J. (1969). A lady in distress: Inhibiting effects of friends and strangers on bystander intervention. *Journal of Experimental Social Psychology*, *5*(2), 189–202. doi: 10.1016/0022-1031(69)90046-8

Maestripieri, D. (1999). The biology of human parenting: Insights from nonhuman primates. *Neuroscience & Biobehavioral Reviews*, *23*(3), 411–422. doi: 10.1016/S0149-7634(98)00042-6

Maestripieri, D., & Roney, J. R. (2006). Evolutionary developmental psychology: Contributions from comparative research with nonhuman primates. *Developmental Review*, *26*(2), 120–137. doi: 10.1016/j.dr.2006.02.006

Manfred, M., Semmann, D., & Krambeck, H.-J. (2002). Reputation helps solve the "tragedy of the commons." *Nature*, *415*(6870), 424–426. doi: 10.1038/415424a

Manning, R., Levine, M., & Collins, A. (2007). The Kitty Genovese murder and the social psychology of helping: The parable of the 38 witnesses. *American Psychologist*, *62*(6), 555–562. doi: 10.1037/0003-066X.62.6.555

Marsh, A. A., & Blair, R. J. R. (2008). Deficits in facial affect recognition among antisocial populations: A meta-analysis. *Neuroscience and Biobehavioral Reviews*, *32*, 454–465. doi: 10.1016/j.neubiorev.2007.08.003

Marsh, A. A., Stoycos, S. A., Brethel-Haurwitz, K. M., Robinson, P., VanMeter, J. W., & Cardinale, E. M. (2014). Neural and cognitive characteristics of extraordinary altruists. *Proceedings of the National Academy of Sciences*, *111*(42), 15,036–15,041.

Mayr, E. (1961). Cause and effect in biology. *Science*, *134*(3489), 1501–1506. doi: 10.1126/science.134.3489.1501

Meaney, M. J. (2003). Maternal care, gene expression, and the transmission of individual differences in stress reactivity across generations. *Annual Review of Neuroscience*, *24*(1), 1161–1192. doi: 10.1146/annurev.neuro.24.1.1161

Milgram, S. (1974). *Obedience to authority: An experimental view*. New York: Harper & Row.

Milinski, M., & Wedekind, C. (1998). Working memory constrains human cooperation in the Prisoner's Dilemma. *Proceedings of the National Academy of Sciences*, *95*(23), 13,755–13,758.

Mortensen, C. R., Becker, D. V., Ackerman, J. M., Neuberg, S. L., & Kenrick, D. T. (2010). Infection breeds reticence the effects of disease salience on self-perceptions of personality and behavioral avoidance tendencies. *Psychological Science*, *21*, 440–447.

Nowak, R., Keller, M., Val-Laillet, D., & Lévy, F. (2007). Perinatal visceral events and brain mechanisms involved in the development of mother–young bonding in sheep. *Hormones and Behavior*, *52*(1), 92–98. doi: 10.1016/j.yhbeh.2007.03.021

Numan, M. (2007). Motivational systems and the neural circuitry of maternal behavior in the rat. *Developmental Psychobiology*, *49*(1), 12–21. doi: 10.1002/dev.20198

O'Connell, S. M. (1995). Empathy in chimpanzees: Evidence for theory of mind? *Primates*, *36*(3), 397–410. doi: 10.1007/BF02382862

Oliner, S. P. (2002). Extraordinary acts of ordinary people. In S. Post, L. G. Underwood, J. P. Schloss & W. B. Hurlburt (eds), *Altrusim and altruistic love : Science, philosophy, and religion in dialogue* (pp. 123–139). Oxford: Oxford University Press.

Pfeiffer, T., Rutte, C., Killingback, T., Taborsky, M., & Bonhoeffer, S. (2005). Evolution of cooperation by generalized reciprocity. *Proceedings of the Royal Society of London B*, *272*(1568), 1115–1120.

Preston, S. D. (2013). The origins of altruism in offspring care. *Psychological Bulletin*, *139*(6), 1305–1341. doi: 10.1037/a0031755

Preston, S. D., & de Waal, F. (2002a). The communication of emotions and the possibility of empathy in animals. In L. G. U. Stephen G. Post, Jeffrey P. Schloss, William B. Hurlbut (ed.), *Altrusim and altruistic love* (pp. 284–308). Oxford: Oxford University Press.

Preston, S. D., & de Waal, F. (2002b). Empathy: Its ultimate and proximate bases. *Behavioral and Brain Sciences*, *25*(1), 1–71. doi: 10.1017/S0140525X02000018

Preston, S. D., & de Waal, F. (2011). Altruism. In J. Decety & J. T. Cacioppo (eds), *The handbook of social neuroscience* (pp. 565–585). New York: Oxford University Press.

Rasenberger, J. (2006). Nightmare on Austin Street. *American Heritage*, *57*, 1–2.

Rilling, J. K. (2013). The neural and hormonal bases of human parentalcare. *Neuropsychologia*, *51*(4), 731–747. doi: 10.1016/j.neuropsychologia.2012.12.017

Rosenblatt, J. S. (1992). Hormone-behavior relations in the regulation of maternal behavior. In J. B. Becker, S. M. Breedlove & D. Crews (eds), *Behavioral endocrinology* (1st ed., pp. 219–259). Cambridge, MA: MIT Press/Bradford Books.

Roth, S., & Cohen, L. J. (1986). Approach, avoidance, and coping with stress. *American Psychologist*, *41*(7), 813.

Rutte, C., & Taborsky, M. (2007). Generalized reciprocity in rats. *PLoS Biol*, *5*(7), e196.

Schneirla, T. C. (1959). An evolutionary and developmental theory of biphasic processes underlying approach and withdrawal. In M. R. Jones (ed.), *Nebraska symposium on motivation* (pp. 1–42). Lincoln, NE: University of Nebraska Press.

Slotnick, B. M., & Nigrosh, B. J. (1975). Maternal behavior of mice with cingulate cortical, amygdala, or septal lesions. *Journal of Comparative and Physiological Psychology*, *88*(1), 118–127. doi: 10.1037/h0076200

Smith, A. (1759). *A theory of moral sentiments*. Oxford: Clarendon Press.

Stallings, J., Fleming, A. S., Corter, C., Worthman, C., & Steiner, M. (2001). The effects of infant cries and odors on sympathy, cortisol, and autonomic responses in new mothers and nonpostpartum women. *Parenting-Science and Practice*, *1*(1–2), 71–100. doi: 10.1207/S15327922par011&2_5

Stolzenberg, D. S., & Numan, M. (2011). Hypothalamic interaction with the mesolimbic DA system in the control of the maternal and sexual behaviors in rats. *Neuroscience & Biobehavioral Reviews*, *35*(3), 826–847. doi: 10.1016/j.neubiorev.2010.10.003

Trivers, R. L. (1971). The evolution of reciprocal altruism. *Quarterly Review of Biology*, *46*, 35–57. doi: 10.1086/406755

Van Anders, S. M., Tolman, R. M., & Volling, B. L. (2012). Baby cries and nurturance affect testosterone in men. *Hormones and Behavior*, *61*(1), 31–36. doi: 10.1016/j.yhbeh.2011.09.012

Vieira, J. B., Ferreira-Santos, F., Almeida, P. R., Barbosa, F., Marques-Teixeira, J., & Marsh, A. A. (2015). Psychopathic traits are associated with cortical and subcortical volume alterations in healthy individuals. *Social Cognitive and Affective Neuroscience*, *10*(12), 1693–1704. doi: 10.1093/scan/nsv062

Wilkinson, G. S. (1984). Reciprocal food sharing in the vampire bat. *Nature*, *308*(5955), 181–184. doi: 10.1038/308181a0

Wilkinson, G. S. (1988). Reciprocal altruism in bats and other mammals. *Ethology and Sociobiology*, *9*(2–4), 85–100. doi: 10.1016/0162-3095(88)90015-5

Wilkinson, G. S. (1990). Food sharing in vampire bats. *Scientific American*, *262*(2), 76–82. doi: 10.1038/scientificamerican0290-76

Wilsoncroft, W. E. (1969). Babies by bar-press: Maternal behavior in the rat. *Behavior Research Methods, Instruments and Computers*, *1*, 229–230. doi: 10.3758/BF03208105

Yamagishi, T., Jin, N., & Kiyonari, T. (1999). Bounded generalized reciprocity: Ingroup boasting and ingroup favoritism. *Advances in group processes*, *16*(1), 161–197.

5

Character Development and the Emergence of Heroic Leadership

Towards a Relational Developmental Systems-Based Model

Kristina Schmid Callina, Richard M. Lerner, Ettya Fremont, Brian Burkhard, Danielle Stacey, and Shaobing Su

Heroism may be a topic having broad boundaries, ones pertinent to the diverse accomplishments of humankind (Carlyle, 1993). Although the concept of heroism has been discussed in great detail in such fields as history, political science, religion, and psychology (Carlyle, 1993; Cole, 2005; Jayawickreme & Di Stefano, 2012), little theory—and even less empirical research—has focused on the formation of heroism from the perspective of human development. Nevertheless, researchers can look to a burgeoning literature on the development of character and prosocial behaviors to understand how heroism and heroic leadership may emerge across the life course.

Accordingly, as a means to promote developmental research on leadership and heroism, this chapter focuses on the role of character development in the formation of these constructs. We introduce a relational developmental systems-based model that conceptualizes character in regard to mutually influential and, as well, mutually beneficial individual-context relations (Lerner & Callina 2014; Overton, 2015). We present a life-span approach to the study of the development of character, with the aim of offering a model that may account for the emergence of leadership and heroism in the diverse settings involved in human endeavors.

The Relational Developmental Systems Metamodel: An Overview

To formulate our character-based model of leadership and heroism, we draw from the metatheoretical approach framing much of the contemporary research in human development, relational developmental systems (RDS) (Overton, 2015). RDS metatheory emphasizes the study and integration of different levels of organization as a means to understand life-span human development (Lerner, 2012; Overton, 2015). The conceptual emphasis in all models derived from RDS metatheory is placed on the nature of bidirectional relations between individuals and contexts; these mutually influential exchanges are represented as individual ↔ context relations.

All levels of the relational developmental system itself are integrated within theories constructed within this metatheory (Overton, 2015), including biological/physiological, behavioral, and social relationship processes, as well as physical, ecological, cultural, and historical ones (Bronfenbrenner & Morris, 2006). The embeddedness of all levels of organization and processes within history imbues temporality into individual ↔ context relations, meaning there is the potential for plasticity, for organized and systematic change in these relations, across person, time, and place (Elder, Shanahan, & Jennings, 2015).

Models constructed within the frame of RDS metatheory focus on the processes that regulate exchanges between individuals and their contexts. Brandtstädter (1998) terms these relations *developmental regulations* and notes that, when developmental regulations involve mutually beneficial individual ↔ context relations, they constitute *adaptive developmental regulations*. These regulations, or rules, may change over the ontogenetic course of individual ↔ context relations. The possibility of adaptive developmental relations between individuals and their contexts, and the potential plasticity of human development, are distinctive features of this approach to human development.

We shall use RDS metatheory to understand character development and its role in the formation of leadership and heroism, and—given that individual ↔ context relations are the primary unit of analysis for understanding *any* developmental phenomenon within RDS-based models—we will conceptualize leadership and heroism as arising from the dynamic, bidirectional relations among the multiple levels of human ecology (Bronfenbrenner & Morris, 2006; Elder et al., 2015; Overton, 2015).

Of particular concern in our RDS-based approach to leadership and heroism is the person component of adaptive individual ↔ context relations. RDS metatheory points to the diverse contributions individuals may make to the relational developmental system in which they are embedded; in other words, people influence all levels of the ecology that are influencing them (Brandtstädter, 1998, 2006). Humans are, then, producers of their own development (Lerner, 1982), in that, to survive and, indeed, to thrive, they must contribute to the setting that is contributing to them (Lerner, 2004). We have already noted that, when individuals' contributions benefit both themselves and their contexts, they are contributing to adaptive developmental regulations (Brandtstädter, 1998). These person-based contributions underscore the role of human agency in promoting adaptive exchanges between individuals and settings. In effect, agency moderates individual ↔ context relations. As we shall explain below, such agency is central to the understanding of the link between the RDS-based conception of character that we will present and our ideas about the nature of heroic leadership.

RDS Metatheory and Definitions of Leadership and Heroism

The individual's agentic contributions to adaptive developmental regulations, (i) when marked by initiative to improve or enhance their social or physical ecology and (ii) when functioning to influence other individuals through modeling, motivating, or inspiring others' adaptive individual ↔ context relations, constitutes *leadership*. When such leadership is manifested in settings wherein the probability of subsequent adaptive individual ↔ context relations for others substantially exceeds the probability of subsequent adaptive individual ↔ context relations for the leader, *heroism* may be said to exist. In such situations, the leader's future adaptation (and perhaps even survival) is substantially compromised, for example, they may be contending with existential threat or risk of substantial loss.

Our RDS-based conceptions of leadership and heroism are consistent with definitions of these constructs found in non-developmental literatures. For instance, heroism is frequently viewed as a complex, even contradictory, human behavior (Franco, Blau, & Zimbardo, 2011). Nevertheless, fundamentally, it seems clear that heroes are people who act prosocially, and do so voluntarily and despite personal risk (Becker & Eagly, 2004; Franco et al., 2011). Risk and service/sacrifice are considered two indispensable attributes in the definition of heroism, as actions with either attribute are far less likely to yield heroic status than actions with both attributes (Becker & Eagly, 2004). In other words, taking risks merely for pleasure should not be considered as heroic. Similarly, service to a socially valued goal without taking risks is not heroic.

These attributes of risk-taking and prosocial orientation are consistent with our views of the nature of adaptive individual ↔ context relations reflecting leadership and heroism. Nevertheless, the constructs of risk taking and pro-social orientation are necessary but insufficient to define heroism (Franco et al., 2011). To better understand heroism and heroic leadership, we believe that an RDS-based view of its development is needed.

For instance, leadership and heroism may vary across time and place (Elder et al., 2015). According to Franco et al. (2011), heroism "is historically, culturally, and situationally determined, thus heroes of one era may prove to be villains in another time when controverting evidence emerges; yet some heroes endure across the centuries. Moreover, the very same act accorded hero status in one group, such as suicide bombing, is absolutely abhorrent to many others" (Franco et al., 2011, p. 99).

The embeddedness of leadership and heroism within time and place raises a problematic issue for our RDS-based conception of these constructs. That is, if leadership and heroism can show such historical and contextual variation, then it must be that adaptation itself is relative to time and place. We believe it is. That is, to understand what makes developmental regulations adaptive (and, therefore, what makes the developmental regulations associated with instances of leadership and heroism adaptive), one needs both conceptual and empirical criteria. Conceptually, developmental regulations are adaptive when, and only when, they are beneficial to the maintenance of positive, healthy functioning of the components of a bidirectional relation (e.g., both individual and context). Empirically, assessments of positive and/or healthy functioning must be conducted with the recognition that contexts are complex, for example, they exist at multiple levels of organization. Bronfenbrenner's (1979) notions of the micro-, meso-, exo-, and macro-systems within the ecology of human development illustrate this complexity. Individuals cannot necessarily act in ways that benefit all levels and all components of the context at all times and places (Elder et al., 2015).

Thus, one may need to treat adaptation—and, in turn, leadership and heroism—not as a categorical concept (as something that either exists or not) but, instead, as a multivariate concept composed of ordinal or interval dimensions. As such, researchers studying adaptation, in general, or leadership or heroism, more specifically, should ask questions such as, how beneficial is the developmental regulation (the individual ↔ context relation) for specific people or specific social institutions of the context, at specific times and in specific places (e.g., see Bornstein, 2006)?

In other words, then, heroes of one era may not be exemplary figures any more in another era; even within the same era and culture, standards for a hero may differ across contexts. For example, heroes among police officers and fire fighters may be different from heroes among civilians. Considering the contextually sensitive nature of heroism, Franco et al. (2011) utilized a conceptual analysis approach to describe three broad forms of heroic action: martial (military) heroism, civil heroism, and social heroism. Martial heroes refer to people who take physical risks for the sake of others above and beyond the call of their duties. Civil heroes are comparable to martial heroes in the style of engagement and potential sacrifices, but are not driven by duties. Social heroism may involve risk and sacrifice in other dimensions of life (e.g., serious financial consequences, long-term health problems, and social ostracism) rather than physical risks. Based on the different forms of heroism noted above, Franco et al. (2011) offered the following operational definition of heroism, which is consistent with the RDS-based conception we have offered:

> a social activity ... (a) in service to others in need—be it a person, group, or community, or in defense of socially sanctioned ideals, or new social standard; (b) engaged in voluntarily (even in military contexts, heroism remains an act that goes beyond actions required by military duty; (c) with recognition of possible risks/costs, (i.e., not entered into blindly or blithely, recalling the 1913 Webster's definition that stated, "not from ignorance or

inconsiderate levity"); (d) in which the actor is willing to accept anticipated sacrifice, and (e) without external gain anticipated at the time of the act.

(Franco et al., 2011, p. 101)

In sum, it is clear from both our RDS-based conceptions of leadership and heroism and from conceptions found elsewhere in the literature pertinent to these constructs (e.g., Franco et al., 2011), that these attributes involve adaptive regulatory relations between individuals and their setting and, in particular, the social portions of their ecology comprised of other people. These relations thus benefit self and others and may, as well, transform from functioning for such mutual, individual-other benefits to functioning to benefit others to the detriment of the self. What may moderate the transformation of leadership into heroism? More fundamentally, what may engender leadership? We believe answers here pertain to character development.

An RDS-Based Model of Character Development

Beyond merely contributing to their contexts in the service of regulating a developmental system, humans may contribute in ways that enhance the context for both themselves and others (leadership) and, in some cases, for others much more than for themselves (which may be an instance of generosity) and, finally, individuals may contribute to their contexts in ways that endanger their future adaptiveness or survival (heroism). That is, it is a commonplace observation that some exemplary individuals contribute to their physical or social ecology—for instance, to their families, institutions, and societies—in ways that reflect leadership and heroism. Ideas from RDS-metatheory inform a model of character development that may explain how such desirable and, in the case of heroism, extraordinary behavior emerges within the course of life.

Within RDS metatheory, character may be conceived of as a specific set of mutually beneficial individual ↔ context relations and, in particular, individual ↔ individual relations that may vary across ontogenetic time and contextual location (place) (Lerner & Callina, 2014). Adapting the ideas of moral development and character education theorist Nucci (2001, p. 7), Lerner and Callina believe that a fundamental feature of character development involves "human welfare, justice and rights, which are a function of inherent features of interpersonal relations." That is, character development—which may be comprised of several distinct features of individual-context relations—invariantly involves interpersonal relations that, according to character education scholar, Berkowitz (2012, p. 249), reflect "a public system of universal concerns about human welfare, justice, and rights that all rational people would want others to adhere to." Thus, when character is viewed from the lens of contemporary, cutting-edge theory in developmental science character arises through the agentic processes involved in a living, open, self-constructing (autopoietic), and integrated, holistic system (Molenaar, 2014; Overton, 2015; Witherington, 2014, 2015.) This RDS-based approach to character development reflects contemporary thinking in both human development and related fields, such as organizational behavior, that recognize leadership as a multilevel phenomenon. For instance, according to Hannah and colleagues:

> Leadership research has increasingly recognized that leadership is a collective and multilevel process or system that entails the interactions between leaders, followers, and peers at multiple levels of an organization, each dependent to differing extents and at differing times on the other to produce leadership.
>
> *(Hannah, Campbell, & Matthews, 2010, p. S158)*

As Hannah and colleagues indicate, the bidirectional relations between a person and his/her context, and especially *between the individual and other individuals* that comprise the context, are important for understanding heroic leadership. That is, whereas an RDS-based model of human development always focuses on mutually influential, individual ↔ context relations, in the realm of character development we "privilege" one domain: mutually beneficial individual ↔ individual relations. Leadership and, especially, heroic leadership cannot exist without a person's actions contributing to individual ↔ individual relations. Thus, as noted earlier, human agency is key to both character development and to the occurrence of heroic leadership.

To reiterate, adapting the ideas of Nucci (2001, p. 7), we believe that a fundamental feature of character development involves "human welfare, justice and rights, which are a function of inherent features of interpersonal relations." Character development—which may be comprised of several distinct features of individual ↔ context relations—invariantly involves interpersonal relations that reflect "a public system of universal concerns about human welfare, justice, and rights that all rational people would want others to adhere to" (Berkowitz, 2012, p. 249). Hannah et al. (2010, p. S159) likewise state that "the first tenet that should guide future research is that the goals, purposes, and problems that require and produce leadership emerge from complex intrasystem social dynamics and from interactions between the social system and its environment."

In sum, RDS metatheory (Overton, 2015) may be able to productively frame the study of the links between character development and the emergence of leadership and heroism. We believe that RDS-based ideas about the role of an individual's agency, within the context of a living, open, self-constructing (autopoietic), and integrated/holistic system (Molenaar, 2014; Overton, 2015; Witherington, 2015), may provide a lens for understanding the relations among character, leadership, and heroism.

The Role of Agency

RDS metatheory focuses on the processes which govern, or regulate, exchanges between individuals and their contexts. Such processes are the *function* of the developmental system. An RDS program of research might seek to understand the nature of relations between individuals and their contexts, including the dynamics of those relations across the life course. Heroes are viewed as agents of change representing the human attempt to expand present abilities towards new, greater levels of skill or application (Polster, 1992, p. 48). However, we have noted that the definition of heroism varies across historical time, culture, and place (Franco et al., 2011). An RDS-based program of research might therefore ask how specific features of the individual and specific features of the ecology coalesce to influence the substantive course of individual ↔ individual relations, thereby allowing for a contextualized understanding of the development of leadership and heroism.

Self-regulation is a key variable for understanding a range of behaviors, from basic physiological functions to complex intentional cognitive processes (e.g., Bandura, 2001; Brandtstädter, 1998; McClelland et al., 2015). Gestsdottir et al. (2015) note that self-regulation is a multi-dimensional construct pertaining to all aspects of adaption, as people alter their thoughts, attention, emotions, and behaviors to react to contextual events and, as well, to influence selected features of the contexts. Here, culture plays a key moderating role. Trommsdorff (2012, p. 19) notes that self-regulation "is assumed to develop by organizing inner mental processes and behavior in line with cultural values, social expectations, internalized standards, and one's self-construal."

However, whereas all adaptive developmental regulations must involve individual ↔ context relations, not all exchanges between an individual and context are adaptive developmental regulations; not all developmental regulations maintain (sustain) and enhance *both* individual and context. When such maintenance and enhancement exist, then a person is contributing (through his/her agency, his/her self-regulatory processes) to a context that supports him or her. We have emphasized that mutually beneficial *individual* ↔ *individual* regulations may constitute specific instances of adaptive developmental regulations that reflect character attributes particularly pertinent to leadership and heroism.

The role of human agency proposed in RDS metatheory is consistent with a vision for thriving found in the character education literature. That is, the individual has agency in producing a life *that is good for one to live within one's community* (Narvaez, 2008). Therefore, character develops through a RDS-framed process involving person ↔ context relations (Berkowitz, 2011; Lapsley & Narvaez, 2006; Lerner, 2004; Seider, 2012; Sokol et al., 2010). However, as we have emphasized, the *individual* ↔ *individual* instantiation of individual ↔ context relations may be the key facet of developmental regulations involved in character development. Indeed, Walker (2013, p. 27) indicates that "moral action is not merely other-regarding; it also can, and should be, self-regarding ... moral exemplars do synergistically integrate their self-promoting agentic motivation in service to their other-promoting communal values." Walker underscores the importance of a focus on adaptive developmental regulations that, in particular, involve mutually beneficial individual ↔ individual relations in the study of character development.

This view of character, then, emphasizes the moral virtue of contributing to the welfare of others through one's actions and, as such, provides the foundation for leadership. When such virtues reach a tipping point wherein benefits to others are pursued in ways that privilege others' welfare over the welfare of the self, then the seeds of heroism may be planted.

What may create this tipping point in individual ↔ context relations? Agency may take the form of the intentional self-regulatory attributes involved in selecting and managing goals; in recruiting resources, or employing strategic thinking or other attributes of executive functioning, to optimize opportunities for successfully attaining goals; or in compensating effectively when strategies fail or goals are blocked (e.g., Baltes, Lindenberger, & Staudinger, 2006; Brandtstädter, 1998; Freund & Baltes, 2002; Gestsdottir & Lerner, 2008; Mascolo & Fischer, 2010, 2015). Intentional self-regulation and related features of agentic individual functioning, including "autonomy, perspective taking and moral reasoning, and ... empathy and emotional competence" (Sokol et al., 2010, p. 584), or moral sensitivity, moral judgment, moral motivation, and moral character (Bebeau, Rest, & Narvaez, 2014; Rest & Narvaez, 1994), may fuse with time- and place-specific features of the context to afford (Gibson, 1969) or shape trajectories of character across the life span (Elder et al., 2015). However, it may be that actions reflecting heroic leadership might emerge when these other-oriented character attributes encompass altruism and courage, and when the circumstances of a situation require great sacrifice to the individual's well-being to instantiate these virtues.

Of course, agency may transform character-based attributes other than altruism and courage into heroic leadership. Several scholars have presented lists of several character or character-related attributes that mark a hero. For instance, Goethals and Allison (2012) identified the "Great Eight" attributes of heroism; they suggest that heroes are caring, charismatic, inspiring, reliable, resilient, selfless, smart, and strong. Similarly, Kinsella, Ritchie, and Igou (2015) conducted a study in which participants rated heroes higher than either role models or leaders on nine characteristics: brave, moral integrity, saves, willingness to sacrifice, altruistic, compassionate, selfless, courageous, and protecting. Moreover, at times, the attributes associated with being a leader reflect also features of character- or character-related constructs that are linked to *heroic* leaders. For instance, Kinsella et al. (2015) noted that the participants in their research saw leaders as powerful, strong, fearless, demonstrating conviction, proactive, determined, intelligent, inspiring, and willing to take risks that others may be loath to pursue. However, Goethals and Allison (2012) distinguish between leaders *per se* and heroes by noting that, whereas leaders often have a requisite following, heroes may not possess such groups. Their acts of selflessness may occur suddenly, in an emergency situation, may take place on an isolated battlefield, or may involve an act of solitary performance.

In turn, not all acts of leadership are associated with moral virtues. Some leaders may drive others in amoral quests, through their power and charisma, and because of their willingness to take risks. However, individuals regarded as heroic leaders are distinguished by their adherence to morals. Wansink, Payne, and van Ittersum (2008) surveyed Second World War veterans about their military leadership, risk-taking behaviors, and cohesion behaviors during combat. Veterans who had received medals for heroism rated themselves higher on leadership characteristics, loyalty, and risk taking behaviors than their peers (Wansink et al., 2008). Similarly, Hannah et al. (2010) identified self-efficacy, hardiness, resiliency, and courage as character strengths necessary for leadership in dangerous contexts. Finally, hope might help individuals make sense of dangerous or challenging situations and cope with the stress of risky or negative events associated with heroism and heroic leadership (Schmid & Lopez, 2011).

From Character Development to the Development of Leadership and Heroism

Acts of heroism and courage can range from the extraordinary to the everyday (Pury & Starkey 2010), but the origin of the capacity for heroic action is worth investigating regardless of the magnitude of the outcome. Can the beginnings of heroism be reduced to merely a unique combination of latent individual attributes, or action potentials, dormant within select people? Conversely, do the proper circumstances summon forth an act of heroism no matter the person? Is heroism merely a matter of a person being at the "right place and the right time?"

Viewed within the RDS metatheory framework, character attributes that predict heroism may develop as the individual gains experience through social relations both with other people and with their environment over the life span (Lerner & Callina, 2014). That is, heroism may come about as a result of processes undertaken by an individual to navigate and understand his/her environment and, ideally, contribute to its betterment (Lerner, 2004). According to RDS metatheory, the capacity for heroism may develop through specific life lessons and experiences (e.g., about the virtues of generosity and of future mindedness, of a perspective that goes beyond one's self, e.g., of "planting tress under whose shade one will never sit"). The adoption of such life lessons, of such character virtues, might ultimately be manifested in courageous action when the context is aligned properly with one's own strengths.

To illustrate, consider the example of the development of courage and altruism, two important components of heroic leadership (Franco et al., 2011). Courage encompasses the notion of willful action despite fear or potential risk, and altruism involves motivation fueled by the desire to do good for the benefit others (Rate et al., 2007). Understanding the development of courage and altruism as they contribute to heroism is important, as constant trials and tribulations across both work/professional and family life often call for heroic action. Opportunities for heroism abound whether as firefighters or parents, soldiers or teachers. A better grasp on what developmental processes lead to these heroic acts might contribute to helping to foster these laudable characteristics in others (through modeling or inspiration), and might also contribute to more effective and intentional training and education where appropriate.

Lester et al. (2010) outline four methods, heavily grounded in Bandura's (1977) social learning theory, by which courage may systematically develop: mastery experience, vicarious learning, social persuasion, and physiological and emotional arousal. Mastery experiences refer to both guided and intellectual instruction with the aim to better prepare one for potential crises by way of quick decision-making and practiced reactions. Examples of this type of development abound in emergency medical education and military training. Vicarious learning is the observation of a competent role model, all the more enhanced by the presence of that individual's own personal strengths such as integrity or justice. Imagine watching a respected paragon of heroism like Gandhi or Dr. Martin Luther King in action, and thus learning from them what to do when faced with similar trying experiences. Social persuasion may facilitate the development of courage when counseling, guidance, and coaching are utilized in social groups. Finally, one's physiological or emotional arousal can be leveraged to promote courageous or heroic action. Lester et al. (2010) give the example of Kennedy's call to, "ask what you can do for your country," as an explicit example of arousing one's emotions to develop courage.

Similar examples of the bidirectional relations between person and context emerge from research on altruism. In a study of Carnegie Medal Heroes, the expectation of parents of heroes to help others was significantly differentiated from the parents of a random sample. This expectation to help at an early age may create a sense of responsibility to help others, even in dangerous situations (McNamee & Wesolik, 2014).

In short, then, heroic leadership involves agency and character. It involves attributes of the person and features of the context that, in mutually influential and beneficial ways, contribute to self and others, even under conditions wherein the future adaptiveness of the person may be compromised (or sacrificed). How may this RDS-based conception of heroic leadership be tested? We conclude with some ideas for, and challenges to, bringing data to bear on our conception of heroic leadership.

Conclusions: Towards a Research Agenda Investigating the Development of Heroic Leadership

On describing his definition of a hero, Senator John McCain, a Vietnam War veteran and former prisoner of war, said that heroes are "those that inspired us to do things we wouldn't have otherwise been capable of doing" (MSNBC, 2015). Senator McCain reflects the individual ↔ individual relations we have privileged in the character-based model of heroic leadership we have mentioned. Moreover, and as suggested by both the definition offered by Senator McCain and, as well, the literature we have discussed in this chapter, the links among character, leadership, and heroism are not unique to our thinking. Nevertheless, despite some agreement about the nature of these links, no systematic, prospective studies of the development of heroic leadership framed by RDS-based ideas exist to our knowledge. No research exists about how these links come about and how they impact people's actual behavior pertinent to leadership and heroism.

Of course, such an absence of developmental data may not be surprising. Randomized control trials assigning people to conditions wherein heroic leadership compromises one's adaptiveness are neither feasible nor ethical. Similarly, simulation studies, perhaps like those associated with the sorts of contrived conditions used in Milgram's (1963) studies of obedience to authority or Zimbardo's (1971; Haney, Banks, & Zimbardo, 1973) Stanford prisoner study, are similarly unethical under the ethical standards prevalent at this writing. In any event, however, neither randomized control trails nor simulation studies involve developmental analyses of the individual ↔ individual processes we have discussed. Indeed, given that opportunities for leadership and especially heroism cannot necessarily be arranged in advance, and may arise serendipitously in the life span (Napolitano, 2013), multiple strategies for understanding the development of the links among character, leadership, and heroism must be pursued in order to attain a comprehensive understanding of the bases of character development, its links to leadership, and the tipping point between leadership and heroism.

One obvious methodological route to studying the development of heroic leadership is to conduct a prospective longitudinal study. Here, theoretically relevant individual and contextual variables pertinent to character may be assessed in the context of addressing a set of interconnected questions derived from the Bornstein (2006) specificity principle. That is, in order to understand how facets of character may enable an individual to engage in adaptive developmental regulations that reflect leadership, and that may move the person beyond a tipping point and become heroic leadership, researchers may collect longitudinal data to ask:

1. What cognitive, emotional, and behavioral facets of a person; possessing
2. What age, gender, race, etc., demographic characteristics; living in
3. What place and time; and engaging in
4. What social activities and relationships; and experiencing
5. What normative and non-normative life and historical events; are associated with
6. What instances of adaptive developmental regulations; that are linked to
7. What character virtues, instances of leadership, or heroic leadership?

Assuming that such a prospective study would encompass a sufficient portion of the life span and involve a relatively large sample of people, framing one's empirical assessments in the service of answering such questions might provide a sample of instances of character development → leadership → heroism sufficient to formulate generalizations about the developmental pathways leading to the emergence of such acts.

Of course, analyses of existing longitudinal data sets can be used as yet another means to address the above-noted, multi-part what question. In addition, such archival data sets can be used to explore the bases of heroic leadership, to cross-validate findings from other longitudinal studies, and/or to assess if there may be a longitudinal counterpart to cross-sectional data.

A third methodological strategy that may be used to assess the development of heroic leadership is to employ an exemplar approach, as has been done in the study of moral and character development (Colby & Damon 1992; Damon & Colby, 2015). Here, people whose life achievements include heroic leadership, for example, individuals such as Senator McCain, General Eric Shinseki, or Malala Yousafzai (the Pakistani activist in female education and the youngest-ever Nobel Peace Prize laureate), can be interviewed about their lives. Such interviews may lead to formulations of individual ↔ context relations common across exemplars. Independent of such generalizations, the accounts provided by exemplars can be triangulated with data derived from other research about heroic leaders to determine if any generalizations may be made.

In sum, the common thread across these examples of methods that may be useful in studying the development of heroic leadership is that research must be able to identify the course of adaptive individual ↔ context relations that provide the foundation of character development and, potentially, its transformation into heroic leadership. Heroic leaders contribute to the greater good by acting in ways that enhance the adaptiveness of others, even when their own adaptiveness may be diminished or lost.

As citizens, we should celebrate such extraordinary people. As developmental scientists, we should strive to learn how such heroic leadership may be nurtured and promoted.

Acknowledgement

This chapter was supported in part by grants from the John Templeton Foundation.

References

Baltes, P. B., Lindenberger, U., & Staudinger, U. M. (2006). Life span theory in developmental psychology. In W. Damon & R. M. Lerner (eds), *Handbook of child psychology: Vol. 1. Theoretical models of human development* (6th ed., pp. 569–664). New York: Wiley.

Bandura, A. (1977). *Social learning theory*. Englewood Cliffs, NJ: Prentice-Hall.

Bandura, A. (2001). Social cognitive theory: An agentic perspective. *Annual Review of Psychology, 52*, 1–26.

Bebeau, M. J., Rest, J. R., & Narvaez, D. (2014). Beyond the promise: A perspective on research in moral education. *Educational Researcher, 28*(4), 18–26.

Becker, S. W., & Eagly, A. H. (2004). The heroism of women and men. *American Psychologist, 59*(3), 163.

Berkowitz, M. W. (2011). What works in values education. *International Journal of Educational Research*, 50(3), 153–158.

Berkowitz, M.W. (2012). Moral and character education. In K. R. Harris, S. Graham, T. Urdan, S. Graham,

J. M. Royer, & M. Zeidner (eds), *APA educational psychology handbook, Vol. 2: Individual differences and contextual factors* (pp. 247–264). Washington, DC: American Psychological Association.

Bornstein, M. H. (2006). Parenting science and practice. In K. A. Renninger & I. E. Sigel, (eds), *Handbook of child psychology and developmental science, vol. 4: Child psychology in practice* (6th ed., pp. 893–949). Hoboken, NJ: Wiley.

Brandtstädter, J. (1998). Action perspectives on human development. In R. M. Lerner (ed.), *Handbook of child psychology and developmental science, vol. 1: Theoretical models of human development* (5th ed., pp. 807–866). New York: Wiley.

Brandtstädter, J. (2006). Adaptive Resources in Later Life: Tenacious Goal Pursuit and Flexible Goal Adjustment. In M. Csikzentmihalyi & I. Selgea (eds), *A life worth living: Contributions to positive psychology* (pp. 143–164). New York: Oxford University Press.

Bronfenbrenner, U. (1979). *The ecology of human development: Experiments by nature and design.* Cambridge, MA: Harvard University Press.

Bronfenbrenner, U., & Morris, P. A. (2006). The bioecological model of human development. In R. M. Lerner (ed.). *Handbook of child psychology and developmental science, vol. 1: Theoretical models of human development* (6th ed., pp. 795–828). Hoboken, NJ: Wiley.

Carlyle, T. (1993). *On heroes, hero-worship, and the heroic in history.* Berkeley, CA: University of California Press.

Colby, A., & Damon, W. (1992) *Some do care: Contemporary lives of moral commitment.* New York: Free Press.

Cole, T. (2005). The political rhetoric of sacrifice and heroism and US military intervention. In L. Artz & Y. R Kamalipour (eds), *Bring 'em on: Media and politics in the Iraq War* (pp. 139–154). Lanham, MD: Rowman & Littlefield.

Damon, W., & Colby, A. (2015). *The power of ideals: The real story of moral choice.* New York: Oxford University Press.

Elder, G. H., Shanahan, M. J., & Jennings, J. A. (2015). Human development in time and place. In M. H. Bornstein and T. Leventhal (eds), *Handbook of child psychology and developmental science, vol. 4: Ecological settings and processes in developmental systems* (7th ed., pp. 6–54). Hoboken, NJ: Wiley.

Franco, Z. E., Blau, K., & Zimbardo, P. G. (2011). Heroism: A conceptual analysis and differentiation between heroic action and altruism. *Review of General Psychology, 15*(2), 99–113.

Freund, A. M., & Baltes, P. B. (2002). Life-management strategies of selection, optimization, and compensation: Measurement by self-report and construct validity. *Journal of Personality and Social Psychology, 82*, 642–662.

Gestsdottir, G., & Lerner, R. M. (2008). Positive development in adolescence: The development and role of intentional self regulation. *Human Development, 51*, 202–224.

Gestsdottir, S., Geldhof, G. J., Paus T., Freund, A. M., Aðalbjarnardóttir S., Lerner, J. V., & Lerner, R. M. (2015). Self-regulation among youth in four Western cultures: Is there an adolescence-specific structure of the Selection-Optimization-Compensation (SOC) model? *International Journal of Behavioral Development, 39*(4), 346–358.

Gibson, E. J. (1969). Principles of Perceptual Learning and Development. In R. M. Lerner, *Concepts and theories of human development* (3rd ed., p. 557). Hillsdale, NJ: Lawrence Erlbaum.

Goethals, G. R., & Allison, S. T. (2012). Making heroes: The construction of courage, competence, and virtue. *Advances in Experimental Social Psychology, 46*, 183–235.

Haney, C., Banks, W. C., & Zimbardo, P. G. (1973). A study of prisoners and guards in a simulated prison. *Naval Research Review, 30*, 4–17.

Hannah, S. T., Campbell, D. J., & Matthews, M. D. (2010). Advancing a research agenda for leadership in dangerous contexts. *Military Psychology, 22*(S1), S157–S189.

Jayawickreme, E., & Di Stefano, P. (2012). How can we study heroism? Integrating persons, situations and communities. *Political psychology, 33*(1), 165–178.

Kinsella, E. L., Ritchie, T. D., & Igou, E. R. (2015). Lay perspectives on the social and psychological functions of heroes. *Frontiers in psychology, 6*, 130.

Lapsley, D. K., & Narvaez, D. (2006). Character education. A. Renninger & I. Siegel (eds), *Handbook of child psychology and developmental science, vol. 4: Child psychology in practice* (6th ed., pp. 248–296). Hoboken, NJ: Wiley.

Lerner, R. M. (1982). Children and adolescents as producers of their own development. *Developmental Review, 2*(4), 342–370.

Lerner, R. M. (2004). *Liberty: Thriving and civic engagement among american youth.* Thousand Oaks, CA: Sage Publications, Inc.

Lerner, R. M. (2012). Essay review: Developmental science: Past, present, and future. *International Journal of Developmental Science, 6*(1–2), 29–36.

Lerner, R. M., & Callina, K. S. (2014). The study of character development: Towards tests of a relational developmental systems model. *Human Development, 57*(6), 322–346.

Lester, P. B., Lester, G. V., Hannah, S. T., & Kimmey, T. (2010). Developing courage in followers: Theoretical and applied perspectives. In C. L. S. Pury & S. J. Lopez (eds) *The psychology of courage: Modern Research on Ancient Virtue* (pp. 187–207). Washington, DC: American Psychological Association.

Mascolo, M. F. and Fischer, K. W. (2010). The dynamic development of thinking, feeling, and acting over the life span. In W. F. Overton (eds), *Handbook of Life-Span Development, Vol. 1: Cognitive, biology and methods* (pp. 149–194). Hoboken, NJ: John Wiley.

Mascalo, M. F., & Fischer, K. W. (2015). The dynamic development of thinking, feeling, and acting: Infancy through adulthood. In W. F. Overton and P. C. M. Molenaar (eds), *Handbook of child psychology and developmental science, vol. 1: Theory And method* (7th ed., pp. 113–161). Hoboken, NJ: Wiley.

McClelland, M. M., Geldhof, G. J., Cameron, C. E., & Wanless, S. B. (2015). Development and self-regulation. In W. F. Overton & P. C. Molenaar (eds), *Handbook of child psychology and developmental science, vol. 1: Theory and method* (7th ed., pp. 523–565). Hoboken, NJ: Wiley.

McNamee, S., & Wesolik, F. (2014). Heroic behavior of Carnegie Medal Heroes: Parental influence and expectations. *Peace and Conflict: Journal of Peace Psychology*, 20(2), 171–173.

Milgram, S (1963). Behavioral study of obedience. *Journal of Abnormal and Social Psychology* 67(4): 371–378.

Molenaar, P. C. (2014). Dynamic models of biological pattern formation have surprising implications for understanding the epigenetics of development. *Research in Human Development*, 11(1), 50–62.

MSNBC (2015). Morning Joe. *MSNBC*, July 20. Retrieved from: on.msnbc.com/1IdPyvX

Napolitano M. C. (2013). More than just a simple twist of fate: serendipitous relations in developmental science. *Human Development*, 56, 291–318.

Narvaez, D. (2008). Human flourishing and moral development: Cognitive and neurobiological perspectives of virtue development. In L. Nucci and D. Narvaez (eds), *Handbook of moral and character education* (pp. 310–327). Abingdon: Routledge.

Nucci, L. P. (2001). *Education in the moral domain*. Cambridge, UK: Cambridge University Press.

Overton, W. F. (2015). Process and relational developmental systems. In W. F. Overton & P. C. Molenaar (eds), *Handbook of child psychology and developmental science, vol. 1: Theory and method* (7th ed., pp. 9–62). Hoboken, NJ: Wiley.

Polster, M. F. (1992). *Eve's daughters: The forbidden heroism of women*. San Francisco, CA: Jossey-Bass.

Pury, C. L. S., & Starkey, C. B. (2010). Is courage an accolade or a process? A fundamental question for courage research. In C. L. S. Pury & S. J. Lopez (eds), *The psychology of courage: Modern research on an ancient virtue* (pp. 67–87). Washington, DC: American Psychological Association.

Rate, C. R., Clarke, J. A., Lindsay, D. R., & Sternberg, R. J. (2007). Implicit theories of courage. *The Journal of Positive Psychology*, 2(2), 80–98.

Rest, J., & Narvaez, D. (eds) (1994). *Moral development in the professions: Psychology and applied ethics*. Hillsdale, NJ: Lawrence Erlbaum.

Schmid, K. L., & Lopez, S. (2011). Positive pathways to adulthood: The role of hope in adolescents' constructions of their futures. In R. M. Lerner, J. V. Lerner, & J. B. Benson (eds), *Advances in child development and behavior, vol. 41: Positive youth development* (pp. 72–89). London: Academic Press.

Seider, S. (2012). *Character compass: How powerful school culture can point students toward success*. Cambridge, MA: Harvard Education Press.

Sokol, B. W., Hammond, S. I., & Berkowitz, M. W. (2010). The developmental contours of character. In T. Lovat, R. Toomey, & N. Clement (eds), *International research handbook on values education and student wellbeing* (pp. 579–603). Dordrecht, The Netherlands: Springer.

Trommsdorff, G. (2012). Development of "agentic" regulation in cultural context: The role of self and world views. *Child Development Perspectives*, 6(1), 19–26.

Walker, L. J. (2013). Exemplars' moral behavior is self-regarding. In M. K. Matsuba, P. E. King, & K. C. Bronk (eds), *Exemplar methods and research: Strategies for investigation: New Directions for Child and Adolescent Development*, 142, 27–40.

Wansink, B., Payne, C. R., & van Ittersum, K. (2008). Profiling the heroic leader: Empirical lessons from combat-decorated veterans of World War II. *The Leadership Quarterly*, 19(5), 547–555.

Witherington, D. C. (2014). Self-organization and explanatory pluralism: Avoiding the snares of reductionism in developmental science, *Research in Human Development*, 11, 22–36.

Witherington, D. C. (2015). Dynamic systems in developmental science. In W. F. Overton & P. C. Molenaar (eds), *Handbook of child psychology and developmental science, vol. 1: Theory and method* (7th ed., pp. 63–112). Hoboken, NJ: Wiley.

Zimbardo, P. G. (1971). The power and pathology of imprisonment. *Congressional Record* (Serial No. 15, 1971-10-25). Hearings before Subcommittee No. 3, of the United States House Committee on the Judiciary, Ninety-Second Congress, First Session on Corrections, Part II, Prisons, Prison Reform and Prisoner's Rights: California. Washington, DC: U.S. Government Printing Office.

6

The Moral Character of Heroes

Lawrence J. Walker

What psychological processes realistically explain the extraordinary moral actions of heroes? These courageous individuals engage in behavior that promotes others' betterment but, at the same time, invariably involves considerable cost for them. Their behavior fascinates and inspires us because it is largely outside of our own lived experience. Heroism is so enigmatic, but its study has the potential for considerable advances in our understanding of human nature, its development, and our collective efforts to promote civil and caring societies. In this chapter I intend to examine aspects of the moral character of heroes.

It may be appropriate right at the outset to advance the case for the study of the character of moral heroes. First, heroism entails real-world behaviors that have obvious validity and significance (in contrast to behaviors in the lab involving inconsequential experimental manipulations). Second, the study of the character of heroes has the potential to enlarge the moral domain, particularly if it entails a broadband assessment of their functioning. Because the approach fosters a focus on persons, rather than mere variables, it forces us to consider the breadth of psychological functioning. The study of persons has the potential to draw our attention to aspects of the domain that may be obscured or overlooked by a conceptual focus on particular variables that are core to competing theoretical perspectives. Third, understanding the character of heroism helps to inform our ethical ideals by revealing what is humanly attainable and what various forms that might take. Fourth, empirical comparisons contrasting heroes with ordinary folk essentially serve to amplify effects (since these represent relatively extreme groups), allowing operative processes to be more clearly identified. Fifth, within-person analyses capture the "dynamic organization within the individual" (Allport, 1937, p. 48) and so can yield more holistic understandings of the complexities of heroism and the balancing of various virtues. And sixth, the study of heroes is conducive to an investigative process of "reverse engineering" in which we initially identify and analyze the "finished product" and then work backwards in deconstructing it to gain understandings of the trajectories and causal processes in development.

This chapter is organized around ten issues, pivotal to our understanding of heroism, and presented in a progressively unfolding manner:

1 Do heroes have distinctive aspects to their character, evidence of the operation of personality dispositions?
2 Is moral character a causally operative force underlying heroic action or is it merely a post hoc descriptive accounting?
3 Is heroism characterized by a single ideal personality profile or might there be a variety of ideal forms?

4 What is the role of religiosity, spirituality, and transcendent faith in moral heroism?
5 Do characterological variables contribute toward bridging the explanatory gap between judgment and action?
6 Is it possible to identify a set of foundational personality variables underlying moral heroism?
7 What are the developmental roots that may foster a moral character that is predisposed to heroism?
8 Is individuals' style of construing life events an important aspect of the moral character of heroes?
9 What fundamentally motivates moral heroes to pursue others' well-being when that action entails significant cost? Are they able to meaningfully integrate the seemingly oppositional motives of self-promoting agency and other-promoting communion?
10 What are the developmental trajectories of moral motivation—the relationship between agency and communion—across the life span?

To these issues we now turn.

Distinctive Personalities

This chapter's remit is to explore the moral character of heroes, but perhaps a prior assumption—that moral heroes actually do have distinctive aspects to their character or personality—needs to be considered. This is not a trite or uncontested issue. Within both psychology and philosophy, there are notable cadres of scholars (e.g., Doris, 2002; Franco & Zimbardo, 2006; Harman, 2009; Zimbardo, 2007) who contend that behavior, both nefarious and heroic, is primarily determined by situational rather than characterological factors; indeed, personality dispositions in this view are either relegated to a relatively inconsequential role or regarded as entirely epiphenomenal.

This situationalist perspective was first prominently voiced in the conclusions of Hartshorne and May's (1928–1930) *Character Education Inquiry* which indicated that pretty well anyone could be induced to transgress on measures of moral behavior if the situational pressures and opportunities were sufficiently compelling. Then, in the wake of the abject horrors of the Second World War and the Holocaust, further analyses served to reinforce this situationalist view. Arendt's (1963) study of Adolf Eichmann, the architect of the Holocaust, advanced the notion of the "banality of evil" by minimizing his character flaws and instead referencing his context. Latané and Darley's (1970) analysis of bystander intervention in emergency situations demonstrated the significant power of situational factors (such as the often inhibiting presence of others). Milgram's (1974) social-psychological studies of obedience to authorities again implicated various situational factors in people's willingness to deliver painful electrical shocks to a "learner." Zimbardo's Stanford prison experiment (Zimbardo, Banks, Haney, & Jaffe, 1973) demonstrated that ordinary people quickly displayed the malevolent behaviors of the respective roles to which they had been assigned. And the list of classic studies could go on—see any social psychology textbook.

The situationalist perspective has not only been advanced to explain moral failure but also to explain moral heroism; in other words, situational factors can serve not only to undermine socialization but also to scaffold it. Zimbardo's (2007) more recent arguments are illustrative in that regard: "The banality of evil is matched by the banality of heroism. Neither is the consequence of dispositional tendencies" (p. 275). So there is good reason to scrutinize the fundamental premise of this chapter that moral heroes have distinctive personalities, ones that are not banal.

Our empirical strategy in addressing this issue was to determine whether a distinctive personality of heroism would arise from the data. Previous research within the situationalist perspective has largely relied on the "variable approach" in which mean-level differences between conditions or groups on individual variables are of primary interest. In contrast, the "person approach" focuses on the structure of variables within the individual, reflecting the composition of the personality. Magnusson (2003), in advocating the person approach, argued that "the psychological significance of a certain component for the functioning of an individual cannot be understood … out of its context with other, simultaneously operating components of the individual" (p. 11). The analytic strategy that bests encapsulates the person approach is cluster analysis, a statistical technique which groups cases (i.e., participants) into "clusters" based on the pattern of interrelationships among the whole set of variables.

In one such study, Dunlop, Walker, and Matsuba (2012) examined whether there is a distinctive personality characteristic of caring exemplars. Participants included recipients of the Canadian Caring Award, a national award given to volunteers who have demonstrated extraordinary and long-term commitment in providing care to others or in supporting community service or humanitarian causes, often in the face of considerable adversity and challenge. A sample of comparison participants, drawn from the general community and individually matched to the exemplars on demographic variables, was also recruited. All participants completed a broadband assessment of their personality, including self-report measures of behavioral dispositions and personal goals as well as a life story interview that was coded for a variety of personological themes.

With these personality data in hand, a cluster analysis was conducted to classify participants into clusters based on the interrelationships among the personality variables considered. In such an analysis the two most homogeneous cases are grouped first and then it proceeds in the same manner through the successive cases. The clustering process is stopped when further grouping would entail a substantial loss of information (because very dissimilar clusters are being combined). Using this decision rule, Dunlop et al. (2012) found that a two-cluster solution best fitted the data.

Strikingly, one of these clusters predominantly comprised caring heroes (76%) and the other cluster predominantly comprised comparison participants (69%). Recall that the cluster analysis was based exclusively on the assessment of personality variables, with no indication of whether the participant was a caring award recipient or not. Yet the analysis accurately detected a distinctive personality exemplifying caring heroes (and discussion of that personality profile will be deferred to later).

An identical analytic strategy was undertaken by Dunlop and Walker (2013), but with a different type of moral hero—recipients of the Canadian Medal of Bravery, a civilian award given to those who have shown exceptional bravery in risking their own lives in an attempt to save others. In addition to these brave heroes, comparison participants included demographically matched individuals, all of whom responded to a broadband assessment of their personality. Again, a cluster analysis of these participants was undertaken based on the variables in the personality dataset and, again, a two-cluster solution was found to be appropriate with one cluster largely comprising brave heroes (67%) and the other, comparison participants (70%). In other words, a distinctive personality profile, characteristic of brave heroes, emerged from the data, seemingly *ex nihilo* (discussion of that distinctive brave personality will be deferred to later).

This evidence of distinctive moral personalities lends credence to the perspective that personality causally contributes to moral action and challenges the claim that heroism is, at its core, fundamentally banal. However, it is acknowledged that the person × situation issue has many nuances, some of which we will return to in subsequent sections. Regardless, the extant evidence supports the basic assumption and gives license to now explore the distinctive aspects of the moral character of heroes.

Causal Personalities

One of the major methodological challenges in studying heroes is that assessment of their psychological functioning is typically only undertaken subsequent to their heroic action and the recognition that such heroism garnered them. Engaging in such momentous action and receiving public approbation may very well have a significant impact on one's personality. The concern, then, is that the distinctive personalities evidenced by heroes may not be a primary cause of their behavior but rather a mere consequence.

The situationalist perspective would advance the argument that situational factors, not personological ones, are the fundamental cause of the heroic behavior, and that the subsequent operation of self-perception processes (Bem, 1972) activate a reformulation of aspects of personality to align them with behavior, ex post facto. In this formulation, personality is akin to a *documentary* which retroactively scripts a dispositional account to reflect the observed behavior. The dispositional perspective, in contrast, regards personality as akin to an *operator's manual* which interprets contexts and then functionally and causally guides behavior.

Are there data that might shed light on these competing claims regarding the causal power of personality dispositions? Indeed there are, but before discussing those data an explication of levels of personality description is relevant. Although the study of traits has dominated contemporary personality science, personality comprises much more. McAdams (1995, 2009) has advanced a typology that references three broad levels of personality description, each having its own particular strengths and weaknesses but together yielding a comprehensive profile. This typology has been increasingly accepted as a heuristic framework for the field (Dunlop, 2015).

The first level entails the familiar *dispositional traits*—broad, nonconditional, and decontextualized dimensions that are implicitly comparative (e.g., extraversion). The second level is that of *characteristic adaptations*—the motivational and strategic aspects of personality that are typically contextualized in role, place, and time (e.g., goal motivation). The third level refers to *integrative life narratives*—the psychosocial construction of a personal identity that imparts a sense of coherence, continuity, meaning, and purpose in life (e.g., identity). McAdams (2013) illustrates the meaning of these three levels of personality description by referencing different roles that people commonly assume in life: the role of *actor* for dispositional traits, *agent* for characteristic adaptations, and *author* for integrative life narratives.

These different levels of personality are, not surprisingly, typically assessed with different types of measures. Dispositional traits are usually assessed with personality inventories in which respondents indicate the extent to which various trait terms are self-descriptive. The motivational aspects of personality, central to the level of characteristic adaptations, are typically tapped by having participants generate in some way their personal goals in life. Integrative life narratives are typically assessed by eliciting the telling of a life story and exploring critical life events, features of which can be analyzed for largely projective aspects of personality.

It should be evident that the lower levels of personality (behavioral traits and characteristic adaptations), assessed by relatively transparent self-report measures, should be more (consciously or unconsciously) malleable in the wake of heroic action and recognition than the deeper and more subtle level of integrative life narratives. For example, if someone has recently been lauded as an exemplar of extraordinary caring, self-perception theory would suggest that this person would likely document his or her dispositional traits by strongly endorsing items such as "tenderhearted," "sympathetic," and "kind," and by proffering personal goals such as "I typically strive to help the needy." It is not so readily apparent how one would reframe an integrative life narrative and project into it different personality themes. Thus, the view that personality is merely a post hoc descriptive accounting and not a causal force underlying behavior would predict that differences between moral heroes and comparison participants would be most apparent in the more surface-level aspects of personality and less apparent at the deeper levels.

Walker and Frimer (2007) have data relevant to this issue. The sample comprised moral heroes (recipients of either the Caring Canadian Award or the Medal of Bravery) and individually matched comparison participants. They responded to an assessment of their personality functioning involving multiple measures tapping all three levels of personality description, with a total of 14 personality variables being retained for analysis. Tests of the mean-level differences between the moral hero and comparison groups revealed significant effects on seven personality variables, all favoring heroes (who had more adaptive personalities) and all at the deeper life-narrative level of personality description, clearly contrary to the view that personality merely is a descriptive accounting of behavior that has actually been caused by situational factors. Rather, the present data better accord with the dispositional perspective that regards moral character as causally operative in action.

It is revelatory that the evidence most clearly distinguishing moral heroes from ordinary people was found at the life-narrative level of personality description, given the theorizing that moral motivation arises less from moral understandings and moral emotions and more from the formation of a moral identity (Blasi, 1993, 2004; Hardy & Carlo, 2005; Walker, 2014). This moral identity is essentially one that incorporates morality as central to the self. The characterological processes that constitute a moral identity are optimally assessed in terms of individuals' self-narratives.

Varieties of Moral Heroes

Assuming the viability of the notion of the moral character of heroes, we can now ask whether exemplary character is embodied by a single form or might there be different varieties. The situationalist perspective, of course, denies any causal significance for characterological factors. Scholars within the dispositionalist perspective agree among themselves that personality is operative but diverge in their understanding of its nature. Some define a single ideal type (either entailing the full complement of virtues or reifying a single superintending virtue), whereas others advance a variety of ideal forms.

The Aristotelian tradition in moral philosophy (Aristotle, 350 BC/1962; Watson, 1984) characterizes moral heroes as possessing the full array of virtues which are interdependent; one cannot really embody one cardinal virtue without also possessing the others (the unity-of-the-virtues doctrine), each depends on the other for its true realization. Empirically, this perspective implies a single ideal type with moral heroes exhibiting highly adaptive functioning across the full complement of morally relevant personality variables.

Another variation of the dispositionalist perspective, while also holding that there is a single ideal type, contends that it entails not the full array of virtues but rather a single, general-purpose moral principle or virtue. Enlightenment-era philosophers eschewed the characterological basis for moral heroism and instead held that a superintending principle was sufficient for dictating the morally good life and compelling moral action (e.g., the categorical imperative of Kant, 1785/2002; the utilitarian rule of Bentham, 1789/1970). Examples of contemporary formulations of such a superintending principle would be Kohlberg's (1981) advocacy for the principle of justice and Gilligan's (1982) popularization of the ethic of care. Regardless of the formulation here, empirically this perspective implies a single ideal type with moral heroes exhibiting high functioning on the definitional superintending virtue (and agnostic regarding their functioning on other virtues).

Although moral philosophers typically advocate for a singular moral ideal, some more recently have advocated for the notion of moral pluralism. Flanagan (1991, 2009), for example, has advanced a dispositionalist perspective that posits varieties of moral personality and explicitly rejects the idea of a single ideal type. Similarly, Blum (1988) contends that moral paragons "are of irreducibly different types" (p. 197). Certainly, ordinary folk conceptions of moral exemplarity reference a range of psychological profiles (Walker & Hennig, 2004). Empirically, this perspective implies that multiple types of moral heroes will be evidenced, with each embodying a different and partial set of virtues (although they may share features as well).

These competing perspectives on the number and the nature of exemplary moral personalities were examined by Walker, Frimer, and Dunlop (2010). In the first step of their examination of the issue, they conducted a (person-level) cluster analysis with a sample of moral heroes (recipients of either the Caring Canadian Award or the Medal of Bravery) who had completed a comprehensive assessment of their personality, and found that a three-cluster solution best fit the data. Note that the analysis did not simply bifurcate the sample in terms of the type of heroism (caring vs. brave); rather, three different clusters of heroes were derived.

Having established that there were three varieties of moral heroism—clearly supporting the varieties perspective and challenging the views that heroism is best encapsulated by a single ideal type—the next step in Walker et al.'s (2010) analytic strategy was to determine which personality variables contributed most to the definition of each cluster. The first cluster of heroes was characterized by themes of communion in life stories, behavioral traits of nurturance, and goal motivation that exemplified interpersonally relational and generative strivings—together warranting the label *communal* for this cluster. A second cluster was characterized quite differently, by variables somewhat more "in the head," to use colloquial parlance: advanced epistemic and moral reasoning, goal motivation that entailed self-development strivings, and behavioral traits that exemplified openness to experience—together suggesting the label *deliberative* for this cluster. The third cluster of heroes had low scores on most personality variables relative to other clusters and was consistently unremarkable—implicating the label *ordinary* for this cluster.

Having established that the data are more consistent with the varieties perspective ("moral pluralism") than the notion of a single ideal type, we now revisit the dispositionalist versus situationalist claims. To do so, each exemplar cluster was contrasted with its associated comparison participants to determine whether each cluster was indeed exemplary in some way. The exemplars in the communal and deliberative clusters outscored their comparison participants not only on the personality variables that defined each cluster but also on several other variables, confirming that their personalities were anything but banal and indeed indicating that they were highly adaptive, albeit in different ways. These two types of moral heroes exemplified distinct moral ideals: either a moral character of social interdependence or one of thoughtful meaning-making and personal growth. The situationalist perspective would not predict these exceptional moral personalities. In contrast, analyses indicated that the cluster of "ordinary" exemplars did not differ significantly from their comparison participants at all, confirming their banality and, by default, according with the situationalist perspective.

This cluster of psychologically commonplace people who have engaged in extraordinary heroism challenges the framing of this chapter. What sense can be made of this finding? It turns out that this so-called ordinary cluster predominantly comprised bravery award recipients, whereas the other two clusters either predominantly comprised caring award recipients or were more balanced in their composition. Recall that the brave awardees were recognized for a single heroic rescue. This may suggest that one-off heroic action may frequently be instigated by powerful and compelling situational factors, as often exist in emergency (or otherwise strong) situations, whereas a "moral career" may be more dependent on the operation of sustained dispositional factors that entail moral motivation and continuity of purpose. It is not particularly remarkable that a long-term pattern of behavior is more readily predicted by moral character than is a single behavior in a context with strong situational cues (Epstein, 1983).

Fleeson (2004) argued that both of these competing perspectives on the person × situation debate have some validity: The situationalist perspective may better explain single, momentary behaviors whereas the dispositionalist perspective may better account for longer-term behavioral trends. Thus, a singular focus on the situation or the personality is probably misguided if one is interested in a comprehensive and valid test of moral heroism. Increased attention to the interplay between persons and situations (e.g., how people of differing moral dispositions tend to construe situational cues) is most likely to advance the field.

Transcendence in the Lives of Moral Heroes

Of the many factors often considered in explaining moral heroism, the potential relevance of religion, spirituality, and transcendent faith has often been overlooked, perhaps reflecting the secular skew that characterizes the social sciences in general. Certainly Kohlberg (1967), whose theory framed the field for a generation, was insistent that the moral and religious domains were independent. However, it is not difficult to make the case for the role of the transcendent. All religious and spiritual traditions reference not only the vertical dimension of relating to the divine or the transcendent but also the horizontal dimension of leading a morally good life and interacting appropriately with others, and provide explicit directives in that regard. Numerous scholars (Blasi, 1990; Fernhout, 1989; Kunzman, 2003) contend that, for some people, morality acquires its meaning and impetus primarily within the context of religious faith.

Although for many people transcendent faith acts to motivate moral functioning, it is important to acknowledge the complexity of the relationship and, in particular, the obvious counterexamples where religious motivation has gone awry, resulting in blatantly immoral behavior (as in religious persecution). All of this suggests the possibility of multiple paths to mature moral functioning, both secular and transcendent. Additionally, it is worth considering that causal influence may operate in both directions: Not only may transcendent faith impact and enhance morality, but morality may also influence faith. Higher forms of moral functioning may prompt fundamental questions about the meaning of life and the ultimate purpose of morality, and the realm of transcendent faith may be best able to proffer answers to such issues of ultimate concerns.

A check on such theorizing can be provided by ordinary folk conceptions of the relationship between morality and religiosity/spirituality. Prototype theory (Rosch, 1978) suggests a way to examine the relationship between concepts; in this approach, concepts are represented in people's understandings in terms of typical examples (i.e., prototypes) rather than by definitional boundaries. Prototypes are structured, then, with some attributes being central to the concept and others being peripheral or irrelevant.

Walker and Pitts (1998) used people's evaluations of the attributes of moral, religious, and spiritual exemplars to explore the relationships across these domains. Such folk evaluations are salient and operative in everyday life. The important feature of these attributes in this study is that, across domains, some attributes were uniquely applied to a particular concept (e.g., *just* was unique to the moral domain and *traditional* was unique to the religious domain), whereas other attributes were shared between domains (e.g., *devout* was common to both the religious and spiritual domains). In other words, these domains are overlapping to some extent. In this study participants were asked to rate the prototypicality (i.e., the accuracy) of these attributes in describing each type of exemplar. The evaluations of the unique versus the shared attributes can inform the relationships among these domains.

The findings of Walker and Pitts's (1998) study revealed that these domains are related in people's understandings, but in an asymmetrical pattern. The unique attributes ascribed to the moral exemplar garnered higher prototypicality ratings than the attributes shared with either the religious or the spiritual exemplar. Thus, in these data at least, foundational moral virtues are relatively independent of religious and spiritual ones. So, to be a moral hero, one does not necessarily need to embody the core characteristics of either religiosity or spirituality.

In contrast, the unique attributes of both the religious and spiritual exemplars received lower prototypicality ratings than the attributes shared with the moral exemplar. Thus, in people's ordinary understandings, pivotal to what it means to be a highly religious or spiritual person is the embodiment of moral virtues. Stated more succinctly, people consider it more probable that someone can function as a moral hero but be functionally irreligious or unspiritual than it is that someone can be a religious or spiritual exemplar but be characteristically immoral in their behavior. This accords with the fundamental premise of William James's classic text, *The Varieties of Religious Experience* (1902; Walker, 2003), in which he argued that the virtuous life should be the evident reflection of an authentic spirituality.

At the zenith of Kohlberg's (1981, 1984) influence on the field, when the moral and religious domains were fervently demarcated, Colby and Damon (1992) reported a serendipitous and surprising finding regarding the significance of faith and spirituality in their case-study analysis of moral heroes who had been identified for their extraordinary moral commitment and action: almost 90 percent of their sample attributed the value commitments underlying their moral action to their religious faith or spirituality. This finding was quite unexpected given that religious faith was not among the selection criteria for the sample and that the interview did not entail an explicit probing in that regard; rather insights about faith emerged rather spontaneously.

More recently, Damon and Colby (2015) undertook a case-study analysis of several notable historical figures of the twentieth century (e.g., Eleanor Roosevelt, Nelson Mandela), including both religious and secular leaders, and were again struck by the observation that religious faith was apparent for all. It is instructive that they consider such faith to entail grappling with questions about the nature of ultimate reality, meaning and purpose, and what is good and true; and that they found both religious and secular manifestations of faith as foundations for moral actions, a faith that was tempered by humility and truthfulness.

Colby and Damon's (1992) and Damon and Colby's (2015) findings are intriguing, but caution regarding a definitive conclusion is warranted given the lack of both objective measures (i.e., no operationalization of the concepts) and comparison groups in their analyses. And there is a critical need to disambiguate the related constructs of religiosity, spirituality, and faith. Scholars of the psychology of religion (Hill & Hood, 1999) make critical and nuanced distinctions among these concepts.

In an attempt to provide more definitive data regarding transcendence in the lives of moral heroes, Walker and Frimer (2008) designed a study using a matched comparison group and objective methodology. Two different types of moral heroes participated (brave and caring award recipients), as the relationship may differ across types of moral action. Three aspects of the transcendent domain were differentiated: religiosity, spirituality, and faith. Religiosity was defined as "the creedal and ritual expressions of belief associated with institutional religion;" spirituality referred to "the more personal affirmation of a higher power that is beyond oneself;" and faith was defined as "the process of meaning-making and an epistemic stance toward the transcendent" (Walker & Frimer, 2008, pp. 317–318).

Religiosity was assessed by a self-report measure of extrinsic religiosity and the frequency of religious strivings in participants' goal motivation. Spirituality was assessed by a self-report measure of intrinsic spirituality and the frequency of spiritual strivings. Faith was assessed with an interview measure tapping stage of faith development (Fowler, 1981), reflecting processes in meaning-making and the epistemic understanding of the transcendent.

Walker and Frimer's (2008) analyses revealed no relevant effects for the measures of religiosity and spirituality; nor was there a difference in faith development between brave exemplars and their comparison group. However, caring exemplars evidenced a more mature level of faith development than did any other group. This cognitive-developmental measure of faith development is most appropriately considered a measure of epistemic development as applied to one's worldview and beyond. It is possible, then, that the relationship between faith development and moral heroism is mediated by some aspect of socio-cognitive development rather than reflecting a relatedness to the transcendent. However, subsequent analyses controlling for cognitive-developmental status (as indicated by stage of moral reasoning development) did not eliminate the relationship between faith development and moral exemplarity. A further suggestion considered was that religiosity or spirituality might mediate the relationship, but neither was found to do so.

Collectively, these findings indicate that the moral and faith domains have important interconnections, challenging the strict demarcation view. However, mature moral functioning certainly does not require high levels of religiosity or spirituality, thereby suggesting that there are multiple pathways to moral heroism. The evidence regarding the psychological functioning of moral heroes (Walker & Frimer, 2008) clearly accords with the findings regarding people's ordinary conceptions of these domains (Walker & Pitts, 1998). The findings also converge with those of Matsuba and Walker (2004) who found that their sample of young adult moral exemplars (who were identified for their extraordinary commitment to social service agencies) evidenced more mature faith development than did comparison participants. Indeed, of the numerous personality variables assessed in Matsuba and Walker's study, faith development was the one that best discriminated the groups.

When it comes to moral heroism, it seems that the relevant psychological dimension is neither religiosity nor spirituality, but rather transcendent faith development. Walker and Frimer (2008) found that caring, but not brave, exemplars had a more mature level of faith development, indicating that the role of faith is differentially implicated for various types of moral action and perhaps reflecting the fact that caring exemplars had engaged in long-term volunteer service whereas brave exemplars had engaged in a single heroic act. More mature faith development entails openness to the complexity and ambiguity of multiple dimensions of reality. It recognizes that this multidimensional reality can be apprehended through different methods and metaphors. It reflects an expanded inclusiveness of groups other than one's own (resonating with Staub's notion of inclusive caring, the humanizing of all people; Staub, 2005). And it embodies an evident striving towards a transcending vision of the good, which is grounded in a critical self-awareness. Collectively, these aspects provide a foundation for an expanded circle of concern that characterizes committed moral action.

Bridging the Judgment–Action Gap

The challenge of identifying the source of motivation for moral exemplarity or heroic action permeates this chapter. The cognitive-developmental paradigm, which long dominated the field, advanced the view that the fundamental basis for moral functioning entailed processes of deliberative moral judgment (Kohlberg, 1984; Piaget, 1932/1977; Rest, 1979; Turiel, 1983). This view reflected the philosophical mindset of the Enlightenment Era which construed human nature dualistically, standing rationality against personality (Kant, 1785/2002). Moral rationality was exalted, not only because it was essential for defining the moral quality of situations but also because it was held to be auto-motivating, following Plato's aphorism that to know the good is to do the good. In contrast, aspects of personality were regarded as contaminating influences that should be somehow overcome in order to follow the purer dictates of reason. Cognitive-developmentalists would have nothing to do with notions of character: witness Kohlberg's (1981) dismissive comments regarding the "bag of virtues" (p. 78) and Turiel's (1983) segregation of personal concerns from the moral domain.

Conceptually, this claimed motivational power of moral rationality is rather suspect given that it essentially requires one to act out of drear duty, onerous obligation, and selfless sacrifice—and seemingly against one's personal interests and dispositional inclinations. It presumes that moral action should not be self-regarding (Walker, 2013). That does not seem psychologically viable as it undermines any motivation to be moral. Furthermore, this conceptual skewing, with a focus on moral cognition and neglect of moral personality, unnecessarily constrains what is undoubtedly a broader and more complex phenomenon. In sharp contrast, Flanagan (1991) contends that people are rightly partial to their own interests, projects, and commitments, all of which imbue life with meaning, and that such meaning is integral to and constitutive of morality; a position which references a more characterological, Aristotelian view of morality.

Empirically, the validity of this claim of the auto-motivating power of moral judgment came into question with the accumulating evidence that moral cognition typically is a weak predictor of moral action (Blasi, 1980; Krebs & Denton, 2005; Walker, 2004), what became known as the judgment–action gap (Straughan, 1986). Stating the obvious, this implies that the singular emphasis on moral cognition may be overlooking something important in moral functioning. If, indeed, moral judgment is inadequate in explaining moral action, the question then becomes, do personality variables go some way toward bridging that judgment–action explanatory gap? My hunch is that personality variables are not irrelevant or redundant with moral judgment; rather they may contribute a substantial portion of the explanatory equation.

Data regarding this question were provided by Walker and Frimer's (2007) study of brave and caring moral heroes who, along with comparison participants, not only responded to a comprehensive assessment of their personality but also discussed a moral dilemma from their own experience which was coded for stage of moral reasoning (Colby & Kohlberg, 1987). Analyses were conducted for the brave and caring groups separately because each type of heroism may have different predictors.

For the brave groups, analyses indicated that stage of moral reasoning contributed nothing to the prediction of moral heroism (i.e., did not differentiate the exemplar and comparison groups), but the addition of the personality variables substantively improved the explanatory equation (with 68% of the variability explained). For the caring groups, analyses indicated that moral reasoning was a significant but relatively modest predictor of moral heroism (with caring exemplars evidencing higher moral reasoning than their comparisons), explaining 20 percent of the variability, but that the personality variables powerfully improved the prediction of moral heroism beyond that yielded by moral reasoning alone (now explaining 87% of the variability). The fact that moral reasoning was a predictor for caring but not for brave heroism may reflect the fact that caring exemplars had developed a lifestyle of moral commitment, whereas brave exemplars had engaged in a single act of heroism which would seem less dependent upon processes of moral cognition.

Thus, the findings of Walker and Frimer's (2007) study indicate that aspects of moral character do help to bridge the explanatory gap between judgment and action. Personality variables do provide a unique and substantial contribution to our understanding of moral heroism. This is not to minimize the role of moral cognition, but rather to broaden our conceptualization of moral functioning to incorporate aspects of moral character that have not received due attention.

A Foundation for Moral Heroism

Having amassed some considerable support for the dispositional account of moral character, the question then arises, what are the foundational personality variables, relevant to moral heroism, to which we should direct our focus? Ideally, the research strategy would entail casting a wide net—a comprehensive and broadband assessment of characterological variables. This issue of the "psychological essentia" of moral heroism was one addressed by Walker and Frimer (2007). To provide a fair test of the psychological foundation for moral heroism their study employed multiple measures, including several personality inventories and an extensive life-story interview, collectively tapping all three levels of personality description (dispositional traits, characteristic adaptations, and integrative life narratives; McAdams, 1995, 2009). A process of data reduction winnowed the set of personality variables for analyses to 14.

Walker and Frimer (2007) assessed the personality functioning of two quite different types of moral heroes (brave vs. caring), albeit ones vetted through the same honors system with similar numbers typically being recognized annually. The brave heroes had engaged in a single, momentous act where they had risked their own lives to save others. The caring heroes had engaged in long-term caring action in support of individuals, groups, communities, or humanitarian causes. On the basis of that description, one might certainly expect that their personality profiles would differ dramatically; but are there any aspects of their personality that they share and which, at the same time, distinguish them from their respective comparison groups—the "psychological essentia" of moral heroism? Such commonalities in personality functioning implicate some basic aspects of moral heroism.

In their analysis, Walker and Frimer (2007) only considered a personality variable as foundational if, for that particular variable, brave exemplars differed from their comparison group and, similarly, caring exemplars differed from their comparison group. In other words, both of these disparate types of heroism needed to evidence the same personality exemplarity for a variable to be counted. Of the set of personality variables analyzed, five were identified as foundational, all at the life-narrative level of personality description: both agentic and communal motivation, themes of redemption, and intimation of formative relationships in early life as evidenced by secure attachments and the presence of "helpers" who scaffolded development. (Two other variables distinguished caring heroes, but not brave ones, from their respective comparison groups: optimistic affective tone throughout the life story and sensitization to the needs of others in early life.)

One of the more intriguing findings was that these disparate types of moral heroes evidenced strong themes of *both* agency and communion (and not, as might be expected, that brave heroes were primarily agentic whereas caring heroes were communal). The agentic aspects of heroes' character reflect their bold action in challenging and often difficult circumstances, action that necessitates self-control, independence, a need for achievement, a sense of responsibility, persistent pursuit of goals, and a sense of empowerment. The communal aspects of heroes' character reflect an empathic orientation to others, concern for their well-being, interpersonal sensitivity, and positive emotionality. These fundamental types of motivation are typically conceptualized as being in tension: "getting ahead" versus "getting along" (Hogan, 1982). That both form the basis for heroism is a significant finding that will be further examined in the "Agency and Communion Integrated" and "Developmental Trajectories" sections of this chapter.

Another foundational personality variable of moral heroism was the prevalence of redemption sequences in life stories (and the relative absence of contamination sequences). McAdams (2006) contends that it is not so much the recalled events in themselves that are important for assessing personality, but how they are construed and the meaning derived from them. Themes of redemption entail the positive construal of life events in which some benefit is discerned out of negative experiences; the event is redeemed or salvaged in some way. Complementarily, themes of contamination entail the negative construal of life events in which an initial positive situation is irreconcilably contaminated or ruined by an outcome that is viewed as pervasively negative. The suggestion here is that the ability or conscious choice to construe some benefit out of challenge may be adaptive and help sustain heroic action. This foundational aspect of moral character will be further discussed in the "Redemption" section of this chapter.

Finally, two related aspects of early life experiences figured prominently in the personological foundation of moral heroism, reflecting beneficial and formative relationships in childhood. One variable that characterized both brave and caring heroes was evidence of secure attachments in their childhood relationships; the other was the identification of "helpers" who influenced them in an explicitly positive way (and the relative absence of "enemies" who were detrimental to their well-being). To these developmental roots of moral heroism we now turn.

Developmental Roots

Obviously, formative relationships in childhood may very well be indicative of the developmental roots of moral heroism (Dunn, 2014; Thompson, 2009; Walker & Frimer, 2011), particularly secure relationships and influential mentors. McAdams, Diamond, de St. Aubin, and Mansfield (1997) first articulated the notion of an early advantage in life that can contribute to a "commitment story," a life narrative in which one recalls a positive and benevolent childhood and in which one constructs a personal ideology centered on prosocial commitments, personal goals that expand one's circle of care for others. McAdams et al. identified a cluster of themes indicative of early life advantage, including secure attachments in significant relationships, the presence of helpers who in some way scaffold development (and the relative absence of enemies), and sensitization to the needs of others.

In Walker and Frimer's (2007) analysis of early advantage in the lives of moral heroes (in contrast to comparison participants) it is important to note that there was no explicit questioning in that regard and, indeed, these notions arose unprompted in the interview, mitigating concerns about demand characteristics. Coding of these variables was based on spontaneous and incidental recall of important relationships and experiences in the early-life portion of the interview. The first variable was the quality of attachments, which was assessed for six different significant relationships. The second variable coded was the frequency of explicitly identified helpers versus enemies. And the third variable rated the extent to which participants reported being exposed to the needs of others in early life.

It cannot be determined from Walker and Frimer's (2007) data whether these recollections of childhood represent actual experiences or rather construals made in the framing of present understandings; regardless, there are clear indications of early advantage. Irrespective of their factual veracity, such intimations do reflect important components of moral character. In contrast to comparison participants, both brave and caring heroes were rated as evidencing more secure attachments in early-life relationships; the frequency of helpers in their life stories was almost three times greater; and the caring exemplars' life stories evidenced greater exposure and sensitization to the needs of others.

Obviously, in exploring the developmental roots of moral heroes, the methodological ideal would be to conduct prospective longitudinal studies to identify personality and demographic precursors to moral action, but the rarity of heroes, by definition, likely constrains this approach to less consequential behaviors (see, for example, Hart, 2005, for a review of large-scale longitudinal surveys that have been used to predict volunteerism).

The developmental roots for moral heroism suggest a positively valenced childhood characterized by secure, nurturing, and scaffolding relationships. Such a context for development may prompt an early realization that one is in some way advantaged and that realization may serve to foster an identity that encompasses a sense of efficacy, prosocial motivation, and a pervasive commitment to moral concerns.

Redemption

At the foundational core of moral functioning, Walker and Frimer's (2007) data revealed not only aspects of early-life advantage but also the personality variable of redemption. In assessing the impact on personality of various transformative life events, McAdams (2006) contends that it is not so much the concrete details of these recounted events themselves that are important but rather how these events are construed and what personal meanings are discerned from them. In his conceptualization, redemption is considered to be the construal of transformative life events such that a demonstrably negative situation is salvaged or redeemed in some way that reveals a positive benefit. In a contrasting manner, contamination refers to the construal of an initially positive state such that it is irreconcilably tainted or contaminated by a perceived negative outcome.

McAdams's (2006) review of the available evidence suggested that redemptive construals are associated with well-being whereas contaminative construals tend to be more associated with psychological distress. Further, redemption seems to be a prevalent theme in the psychological functioning of generative adults (McAdams et al., 1997; McAdams, Reynolds, Lewis, Patten, & Bowman, 2001).

As noted earlier, Walker and Frimer (2007) found that common to both brave and caring types of moral heroes (and in contrast to their comparison groups) was the prevalence of redemption sequences in their life stories and the relative absence of contamination sequences. Quite strikingly, the narratives of moral heroes had 66 percent more redemption and 51 percent less contamination than the narratives of comparison participants. The finding references the significance of the capability and often intentional choice to construct some positive benefit from critical personal experiences. The dispositional tendency for reframing, either of emergencies in which people's lives were gravely endangered or of situations in which people suffered disadvantage or adversity, was an important feature of the character of moral heroes. Note that it was not the case that these heroes were minimizing or delusional about the challenges they encountered, rather they had a propensity to "spin" these challenges redemptively and optimistically to feature some positive benefit. This adaptive form of psychological functioning helps to both instigate and sustain moral action in difficult situations.

Another personality variable, related to redemption, that was assessed in Walker and Frimer's (2007) study of moral heroes was the overall affective tone of the life narrative; that is, the degree of optimism versus pessimism expressed. There is considerable evidence that dispositional optimism is associated with adaptive coping and better psychological adjustment (Peterson, 2000; Zaslavsky et al., 2015). Certainly, the case studies reported by Colby and Damon (1992) and Oliner (2003) suggest the significance of hopefulness, forgiveness, and positivity as factors underlying extraordinary moral commitment. In Walker and Frimer's analysis, caring exemplars evidenced a generally more optimistic affective tone to their life stories than brave exemplars whose narratives tended to be more neutral or mixed in affectivity.

Pervasive optimism in the context of heroic caring service may be somewhat surprising given that these volunteers often labored in situations that entailed destitution, disenfranchisement, and despair. These caring heroes defy their environments in engendering positivity. This implies the working of an agentic personality that transduces the negativity of trying circumstances into behaviors that exude hope and affirmation.

A serendipitous and quite unanticipated finding from Walker and Frimer's (2007) study was that a disproportionate number of the caring heroes had experienced the death of one or more of their children (more than their comparison group and more than the brave heroes). The death of a child is an out-of-time, out-of-sequence traumatic life event with which most people typically have great difficulty coping, even over the long term; often falling into despair, anger, and self-absorption (Janoff-Bulman, 1992). These extraordinary people seemed to have coped with this personal tragedy by discerning some meaning or benefit from it and deliberately fostering a positive attitude toward their life circumstances. But herein is a question for future research: Does this pattern indicate that these caring heroes were predisposed to such optimistic construals throughout life or is it suggestive of some form of posttraumatic growth (Vollhardt, 2009)?

A case-study analysis of one of these caring award recipients who had suffered the death of her adult child (Dunlop, Walker, & Wiens, 2015) intimated that the construction of a redemptive narrative—one in which the tragic death is framed as contributing to prosocial behavior—and incorporating it into one's life story is essential to sustaining this behavior pattern following a traumatic experience. It does so because it imparts moral action with a sense of meaning and purpose.

Agency and Communion Integrated

The pivotal issue with which we are grappling in this chapter centers on the source and nature of moral motivation. What fundamentally motivates moral heroes to pursue others' well-being when that action entails seemingly considerable cost to themselves?

The final pair of personality variables found to characterize the foundational core of moral heroism in Walker and Frimer's (2007) study—agency and communion—references the fundamental duality of human existence (Bakan, 1966) and it is their relationship that we explore in this section. That both agency and communion characterize moral heroism accords with findings of the conceptions of ordinary folk where both themes are ubiquitous (Hardy, Walker, Olsen, Skalski, & Basinger, 2011; Walker & Hennig, 2004; Walker & Pitts, 1998), although that research paradigm provides no insights regarding whether and how these motives might be coordinated in actual psychological functioning.

Agency and communion are basic themes in motivation (Bakan, 1966; McAdams, 1988) where they are frequently conceptualized as dualistic and competing (Hogan, 1982); one motive being expressed at the "expense" of the other. This is well-illustrated in Schwartz et al.'s (2012) values circumplex where these motives are placed in opposing quadrants and are explicitly conceptualized as mutually interfering.

The strong themes of both agency and communion among moral heroes could, of course, simply mean that heroes are simply strongly motivated in general. So the critical question becomes: Is the relationship between agency and communion among moral heroes merely a byproduct of the higher levels of each motive or is there evidence of an interactive effect that reflects some synergy between the motives? Walker and Frimer (2007) addressed the question of the relationship between agency and communion in their sample of moral heroes and comparison participants. Although the moral heroes evidenced considerably stronger themes of both agency and communion than comparison participants (with 68% more agency and 82% more communion), no evidence was found of a statistical interaction between these motives after controlling for baseline levels, failing to support the notion of synergistic integration.

Frimer, Walker, Dunlop, Lee, and Riches (2011) revisited this question with the same dataset, introducing both a conceptual clarification and an analytical refinement. The conceptual clarification entailed more precise definitions of agency and communion. As meta-constructs they have acquired a wide range of meanings (Paulhus & Trapnell, 2008) which has introduced some imprecision. Frimer et al. (2011) defined agency as self-promoting motives of power and achievement and defined communion as other-promoting motives of benevolence and universalism (in contrast to other definitions that focus on psychological distance, for example). Their analytical refinement was to examine the relationship between agency and communion at the within-person level. A person-level analysis is able to detect the meaningful co-occurrence of the motives within individuals' thought structures, rather than merely detecting a statistical interaction as in the variable-level approach. Armed with these innovations, Frimer et al. found that the moral heroes, indeed, did evidence greater motivation that integrated agentic and communal themes than did comparison participants whose extent of integration did not differ from what would be expected by chance. This was the first compelling evidence of the adaptive integration of what are often considered competing motives.

However, an ambiguity remained. Frimer et al. (2011) had assessed the co-occurrence of agency and communion within individuals' thoughts on a topic, but did not determine the direction of the relationship between these two motives. These motives could co-occur in the form of agency promoting communion (e.g., "I'm trying to use my resources and skills to help the disadvantaged") or in the form of communion promoting agency (e.g., "I tried to help that drowning man so that people would think of me as a hero"). These two forms of integration should rightly garner quite different moral approbation. In considering the relationship between these motives, Rokeach (1973) helpfully distinguished between instrumental and terminal values, with an instrumental value being a means to something else and a terminal value being an end in itself.

A clarification of the instrumental–terminal relationship between agency and communion was undertaken by Frimer, Walker, Lee, Riches, and Dunlop (2012). They took a different tack to identifying moral heroes. Their target subjects were highly influential people of the past century, as identified by *Time* magazine. These are leaders, revolutionaries, heroes, and icons who have had enormous impact, and are of both positive and negative renown. First, these researchers had a large sample of social scientists rate these influential figures on several dimensions of moral character. The top-ranking of these figures were thus classified as moral heroes (e.g., Nelson Mandela, Aung San Suu Kyi, Mother Teresa) and the bottom-ranking comprised a comparison group of similarly influential people but ones not regarded as particularly prototypic of moral exemplarity (e.g., Kim Jong-il, Adolf Hitler, Vladimir Putin).

Second, the motivational functioning of these historical figures was assessed by systematic content analysis of archival materials such as their interviews and speeches (because, of course, these subjects were not available for direct research participation). Excerpts of these materials were coded for motives of agency (power, achievement) and communion (benevolence, universalism), and then the relationships between motives were assessed by determining which were instrumental to each terminal value voiced.

The analyses were revelatory: The comparison figures unmistakably embodied unbridled agency, what Bakan (1966) labeled "the villain" (p. 14), with considerably more agency than communion at both the instrumental and terminal levels (i.e., agency in service to more agency). The moral heroes also displayed abundant agency at the instrumental level; they are, of course, hugely impactful figures. However, at the terminal level, they displayed overwhelming levels of communion. These moral heroes were using their considerable agency in the potent promotion of communal causes; they had integrated their agentic motivation hierarchically into communal ends. In their functioning, agency imparts life to communion and communion imbues agency with a greater purpose. So it seems that, in moral heroism, personal impact, achievement, and fulfillment are actualized in an integrated manner of motivation through promoting others' welfare—the appropriation of morality to the self. This renders the distinction between self-interest and morality a false dichotomy (Frimer & Walker, 2009), and highlights the motivational mechanism that undergirds moral heroism.

Developmental Trajectories

Research reviewed in the previous section indicated that moral heroes have integrated the typically oppositional motives of agency and communion, by appropriating agentic means in service to communal goals. We now turn to the question of how this moral motivation develops across the life span. This, of course, represents an investigative process of reverse engineering where, in the first step, we identified the "finished product"—moral heroes—and assessed aspects of their character that might explain their action. The next step is to examine the developmental trajectories that lead to this end-point integration of agentic and communal motivation. And, of course, subsequent steps, left to future research, would be to determine the psychological mechanisms that influence these differing developmental trajectories and end states, as well as to implement appropriate interventions in that regard.

Frimer et al. (2012) made the important distinction between instrumental and terminal motives. Instrumental motives were predominantly agentic for both the historical figures identified as moral heroes and for comparison figures. These were hugely influential, goal-oriented people. The attainment of goals (whatever they may be) is dependent upon agentic motives of power and achievement. Terminal motives, in contrast, may be somewhat more variable and may be better predictive of behavior. So, then, how do instrumental and terminal motives of agency and communion develop across the life span?

Dunlop, Walker, and Matsuba (2013, Study 2) undertook a comparison of the motivational profiles of moral heroes at different points in the life span. Their participants were young adults (18–30 years) who had been identified as moral heroes because of their extraordinary commitment to social service agencies, as well as a matched comparison group (see Matsuba & Walker, 2004, 2005); they were then contrasted with the older influential figures from Frimer et al.'s (2012) study. The young adult sample completed an interview which, among other things, explored their life goals that were subsequently coded for agency and communion within an instrumental–terminal framework.

Dunlop et al. (2013) found initial evidence that the relationship between agentic and communal motivation does change over the course of development. The older comparison figures clearly exemplified unmitigated agency; the younger comparison participants also were predominantly agentic at both the instrumental and terminal levels, although the effect was weaker at the terminal level. The older moral heroes used motives of instrumental agency to advance terminal communal concerns; the younger moral heroes had not yet attained that endpoint state. These younger moral heroes were predominantly agentic at the instrumental level (as is typical) but, at the terminal level, advanced agentic and communal concerns with equal vitality, exemplifying a somewhat divided state.

To more systematically examine developmental trajectories of agentic and communal motivation across the life span, Walker and Frimer (2015) conducted a cross-sectional study with a community-based sample comprising four age groups that may mark developmental transitions: childhood (8–12 years), adolescence (14–18 years), emerging adulthood (20–28 years), and mid-adulthood (35–45 years). Participants responded to a semi-structured interview intended to assess their value motivation in various aspects of everyday living and to explore the instrumental–terminal structure of their thinking (by probing how their current endeavors might be instrumental to their terminal goals).

Walker and Frimer (2015) found that, in all age groups from childhood to mid-adulthood, motivation at the instrumental level was primarily agentic, which is as expected given its instrumentality. Motivation at the terminal level was also primarily agentic in the younger age groups, but the effect diminished by mid-adulthood, albeit far from being completely extinguished. Terminal agency decreased with age whereas terminal communion increased with age. The significance of communion as a terminal motive increased markedly from childhood to mid-adulthood, and the critical pattern of motivational integration—instrumental agency advancing terminal communion—similarly became more prominent. At the terminal level in mid-adulthood, goals tended to be about equally split between agency and communion.

Integrating Walker and Frimer's (2015) findings with that of Dunlop et al. (2013) and Frimer et al. (2012) yields some pertinent observations. First, the children in Walker and Frimer's study and the nonmoral comparison figures in Frimer et al.'s study were strikingly similar in their motivational profiles, displaying unmitigated agency, and suggesting that these influential figures who were lacking in moral character were developmentally delayed. Second, the emerging adults in Walker and Frimer's cross-sectional study and the similarly aged comparison participants in Dunlop et al.'s study evidenced the same motivational profile, providing a partial replication despite the different methodology. Third, the midlife adults in Walker and Frimer's study and the young-adult moral heroes in Dunlop et al.'s study both evidenced a balanced mixture of agentic and communal motivation at the terminal level, suggesting that the younger group of moral heroes was developmentally advanced; however, both groups had not yet attained the pattern of instrumental agency for terminal communion exemplified by the moral heroes of historical renown.

Collectively, these findings suggest that moral motivation continues to develop across the life span and is typically not fully integrated in many adults. Further, these findings imply that the fundamental objective in fostering moral heroism is to displace agential desires with communal concerns as the terminal value.

Concluding Thoughts

In this chapter my intent was to explore the moral character of heroes, but we first had to deal with the validity of the premise that there actually is something to discuss in that regard. Support for this prior assumption was readily amassed with distinctive heroic personalities being readily apparent in the data. Furthermore, the research evidence was consistent with the notion that aspects of character do causally operate in enacting heroism and do not merely represent a post hoc descriptive accounting.

Heroism is not characterized by a single personality profile; rather multiple types of personality profiles were found to be associated with heroism with the dynamic interplay between situational and personological variables being implicated. There is good reason to contend that, in strong situations with obvious contextual pressures, heroic action may be readily triggered by certain situational cues for people who are predisposed to act. However, the instigation and maintenance of a "moral career" of heroism is more likely dependent upon the continual functioning of personality dispositions.

One of the personality dispositions implicated in heroism for at least some people references the role of transcendent faith (as distinguished from religiosity) in universalizing the circle of concern and engendering an open-minded search for a greater good. Psychological variables associated with character, in general, were found to explain much of the variability in heroic action, certainly beyond what is provided by moral cognition alone.

Despite the evidence for a variety of personality profiles associated with different types of heroism, it was possible to identify some core personality variables that were shared by these disparate types but which, at the same time, distinguished them from ordinary folk. These variables include ones pointing to the developmental roots of heroism in secure relationships and influential mentors—a beneficial childhood that cultivates an enduring sense of being advantaged. Also core to heroism is a redemptive disposition that tends to construe some positive benefit out of transformative life events and, presumably, fosters prosocial action in the face of challenge. And, finally, foundational to moral heroism is the tendency to meaningfully integrate the typically opposing motives of agency and communion: Agency gives communal values motivational oomph and communion guides agency with a higher moral purpose.

Thus, the motivational end-point of development is an integrated pattern of instrumental agency serving terminal communion. The relationship between agency and communion typically changes across the life span. Young-adult moral heroes and ordinary middle-aged adults have developed partway toward the pattern of integration that is more fully apparent in mature moral heroes. Thus, the research evidence suggests that the objective for development is to displace self-promoting agentic goals, as a terminal value, with other-promoting communal ones.

Of course, the more we explore an issue, the more apparent it becomes that there are many other important, but as yet unanswered, questions. For example, this chapter focused on a limited range of heroes whose actions were relatively uncontroversial in their moral valence. But there are, of course, many other types of heroism to consider, being mindful of the adage that one person's saint can be another's scoundrel (e.g., witness the controversy regarding Edward Snowden's whistle-blowing on the National Security Agency's surveillance activities; MacAskill & Dance, 2013). The present focus was also on the positive characterological aspects of moral heroism, but attention also needs to be directed to the potential shadow-side that might be implicated. What are the maladaptive aspects of some forms of moral heroism (e.g., pathological altruism, hypermoralism, zealotry)? Are there costs to self or others in being heroic?

Sensitivity to cultural and ethnic group differences is similarly warranted, as heroism may take different forms and have different meanings in individualistic and collectivist cultures, for example. Caution should be using in drawing inferences about human behavior, in general, based on data from WEIRD samples (*W*estern, *e*ducated, *i*ndustrialized, *r*ich, and *d*emocratic; Henrich, Heine, & Norenzayan, 2010), as the field is wont to do.

One obvious future research direction is to continue the process of reverse engineering by examining, for example, the psychological mechanisms underlying divergent developmental trajectories: those that lead to moral heroism versus those that inhibit such behavior. We currently understand much more about the end-point than the developmental roots, trajectories, and processes. What influences the various critical turning-points, progressions, stagnations, and end-points along the path of development? Prospective longitudinal data from early childhood to late adulthood are ideal for assessing these individual patterns of change in the relationship among relevant characterological variables and for ruling out cohort effects (Twenge, Campbell, & Freeman, 2012). There are various psychological mechanisms that also need more extensive examination in exploring the bases for heroism, including parenting, community, media, and other socialization factors; the development of sociocognitive understandings and identity (Walker, 2014); and the potential contribution of neuroscience (Killen & Smetana, 2008) and biological predispositions (Pinker, 2008). Once these psychological processes are better understood, we will be in a better position to answer the question, "How can we make moral heroism the norm rather than the exception?"

References

Allport, G. W. (1937). *Personality: A psychological interpretation*. New York: Holt.
Arendt, H. (1963). *Eichmann in Jerusalem: A report on the banality of evil*. New York: Viking.
Aristotle (350 BC/1962). *Nicomachean ethics* (M. Ostwald, Trans.). Indianapolis, IN: Bobbs-Merrill.
Bakan, D. (1966). *The duality of human existence: An essay on psychology and religion*. Chicago, IL: Rand McNally.
Bem, D. J. (1972). Self-perception theory. In L. Berkowitz (ed.), *Advances in experimental social psychology* (Vol. 6, pp. 1–62). New York: Academic Press.
Bentham, J. (1789/1970). *An introduction to the principles of morals and legislation*. London: Athlone.
Blasi, A. (1980). Bridging moral cognition and moral action: A critical review of the literature. *Psychological Bulletin, 88*, 1–45. doi: 10.1037/0033-2909.88.1.1
Blasi, A. (1990). How should psychologists define morality? Or, the negative side effects of philosophy's influence on psychology. In T. Wren (ed.), *The moral domain: Essays in the ongoing discussion between philosophy and the social sciences* (pp. 38–70). Cambridge, MA: MIT Press.
Blasi, A. (1993). The development of identity: Some implications for moral functioning. In G. G. Noam & T. E. Wren (eds), *The moral self* (pp. 99–122). Cambridge, MA: MIT Press.
Blasi, A. (2004). Moral functioning: Moral understanding and personality. In D. K. Lapsley & D. Narvaez (eds), *Moral development, self, and identity* (pp. 335–347). Mahwah, NJ: Erlbaum.
Blum, L. A. (1988). Moral exemplars: Reflections on Schindler, the Trocmes, and others. In P. A. French, T. E. Uehling, Jr., & H. K. Wettstein (eds), *Midwest Studies in Philosophy: Vol. 13. Ethical theory: Character and virtue* (pp. 196–221). Notre Dame, IN: University of Notre Dame Press. doi: 10.1111/j.1475-4975.1988.tb00122.x
Colby, A., & Damon, W. (1992). *Some do care: Contemporary lives of moral commitment*. New York: Free Press.
Colby, A., & Kohlberg, L. (1987). *The measurement of moral judgment* (Vols. 1–2). New York: Cambridge University Press.
Damon, W., & Colby, A. (2015). *The power of ideals: The real story of moral choice*. New York: Oxford University Press.
Doris, J. M. (2002). *Lack of character: Personality and moral behavior*. Cambridge, UK: Cambridge University Press.
Dunlop, W. L. (2015). Contextualized personality, beyond traits. *European Journal of Personality, 29*, 310–325. doi: 10.1002/per.1995
Dunlop, W. L., & Walker, L. J. (2013). The personality profile of brave exemplars: A person-centered analysis. *Journal of Research in Personality, 47*, 380–384. doi: 10.1016/j.jrp.2013.03.004

Dunlop, W. L., Walker, L. J., & Matsuba, M. K. (2012). The distinctive moral personality of care exemplars. *Journal of Positive Psychology, 7*, 131–143. doi: 10.1080/17439760.2012.662994

Dunlop, W. L., Walker, L. J., & Matsuba, M. K. (2013). The development of moral motivation across the adult lifespan. *European Journal of Developmental Psychology, 10*, 285–300. doi: 10.1080/17405629.2012.746205

Dunlop, W. L., Walker, L. J., & Wiens, T. K. (2015). The redemptive story: A requisite for sustaining prosocial behavioral patterns following traumatic experiences. *Journal of Constructivist Psychology, 28*, 228–242. doi: 10.1080/10720537.2014.917444

Dunn, J. (2014). Moral development in early childhood and social interaction in the family. In M. Killen & J. G. Smetana (eds), *Handbook of moral development* (2nd ed., pp. 135–159). New York: Psychology Press.

Epstein, S. (1983). Aggregation and beyond: Some basic issues on the prediction of behavior. *Journal of Personality, 51*, 360–392. doi: 10.1111/j.1467-6494.1983.tb00338.x

Fernhout, H. (1989). Moral education as grounded in faith. *Journal of Moral Education, 18*, 186–198. doi: 10.1080/0305724890180303

Flanagan, O. (1991). *Varieties of moral personality: Ethics and psychological realism*. Cambridge, MA: Harvard University Press.

Flanagan, O. (2009). Moral science? Still metaphysical after all these years. In D. Narvaez & D. K. Lapsley (eds), *Personality, identity, and character: Explorations in moral psychology* (pp. 52–78). New York: Cambridge University Press.

Fleeson, W. (2004). Moving personality beyond the person–situation debate: The challenge and the opportunity of within-person variability. *Current Directions in Psychological Science, 13*, 83–87. doi: 10.1111/j.0963-7214.2004.00280.x

Fowler, J. W. (1981). *Stages of faith: The psychology of human development and the quest for meaning*. San Francisco, CA: Harper & Row.

Franco, Z., & Zimbardo, P. (2006). The banality of heroism. *Greater Good, 3*(2) (Fall/Winter), 30–35.

Frimer, J. A., & Walker, L. J. (2009). Reconciling the self and morality: An empirical model of moral centrality development. *Developmental Psychology, 45*, 1669–1681. doi: 10.1037/a0017418

Frimer, J. A., Walker, L. J., Dunlop, W. L., Lee, B. H., & Riches, A. (2011). The integration of agency and communion in moral personality: Evidence of enlightened self-interest. *Journal of Personality and Social Psychology, 101*, 149–163. doi: 10.1037/a0023780

Frimer, J. A., Walker, L. J., Lee, B. H., Riches, A., & Dunlop, W. L. (2012). Hierarchical integration of agency and communion: A study of influential moral figures. *Journal of Personality, 80*, 1117–1145. doi: 10.1111/j.1467-6494.2012.00764.x

Gilligan, C. (1982). *In a different voice: Psychological theory and women's development*. Cambridge, MA: Harvard University Press.

Hardy, S. A., & Carlo, G. (2005). Identity as a source of moral motivation. *Human Development, 48*, 232–256. doi: 10.1159/000086859

Hardy, S. A., Walker, L. J., Olsen, J. A., Skalski, J. E., & Basinger, J. C. (2011). Adolescent naturalistic conceptions of moral maturity. *Social Development, 20*, 562–586. doi: 10.1111/j.1467-9507.2010.00590.x

Harman, G. (2009). Skepticism about character traits. *Journal of Ethics, 13*, 235–242. doi: 10.1007/s10892-009-9050-6

Hart, D. (2005). The development of moral identity. In G. Carlo & C. P. Edwards (eds), *Nebraska Symposium on Motivation, Vol. 51: Moral motivation through the life span* (pp. 165–196). Lincoln, NE: University of Nebraska Press.

Hartshorne, H., & May, M. A. (1928–1930). *Studies in the nature of character* (Vols. 1–3). New York: Macmillan.

Henrich, J., Heine, S. J., & Norenzayan, A. (2010). The weirdest people in the world? *Behavioral and Brain Sciences, 33*, 61–83. doi: 10.1017/S0140525X0999152X

Hill, P. C., & Hood, R. W., Jr. (1999). *Measures of religiosity*. Birmingham, AL: Religious Education Press.

Hogan, R. (1982). A socioanalytic theory of personality. In M. M. Page (ed.), *Nebraska Symposium on Motivation: Vol. 30. Personality: Current theory and research* (pp. 55–89). Lincoln, NE: University of Nebraska Press.

James, W. (1902). *The varieties of religious experience*. New York: Longmans, Green, & Company.

Janoff-Bulman, R. (1992). *Shattered assumptions: Towards a new psychology of trauma*. New York: Free Press.

Kant, I. (1785/2002). *Groundwork for the metaphysics of morals* (A. W. Wood, Trans.). New Haven, CT: Yale University Press.

Killen, M., & Smetana, J. (2008). Moral judgment and moral neuroscience: Intersections, definitions, and issues. *Child Development Perspectives, 2*, 1–6. doi: 10.1111/j.1750-8606.2008.00033.x

Kohlberg, L. (1967). Moral and religious education and the public schools: A developmental view. In T. Sizer (ed.), *Religion and public education* (pp. 164–183). Boston, MA: Houghton Mifflin.

Kohlberg, L. (1981). *Essays on moral development: Vol. 1. The philosophy of moral development*. San Francisco, CA: Harper & Row.

Kohlberg, L. (1984). *Essays on moral development: Vol. 2. The psychology of moral development.* San Francisco, CA: Harper & Row.

Krebs, D. L., & Denton, K. (2005). Toward a more pragmatic approach to morality: A critical evaluation of Kohlberg's model. *Psychological Review, 112,* 629–649. doi: 10.1037/0033-295X.112.3.629

Kunzman, R. (2003). Religion, ethics, and the implications for moral education: A critique of Nucci's Morality and religious rules. *Journal of Moral Education, 32,* 251–261. doi: 10.1080/0305724032000136671

Latané, B., & Darley, J. M. (1970). *The unresponsive bystander: Why doesn't he help?* New York: Appleton-Crofts.

MacAskill, E., & Dance, G. (2013). Edward Snowden's surveillance revelations explained. *The Guardian* (November 1). Retrieved from www.theguardian.com/us-news/the-nsa-files.

Magnusson, D. (2003). The person approach: Concepts, measurement models, and research strategy. *New Directions for Child and Adolescent Development, 101,* 3–23. doi: 10.1002/cd.79

Matsuba, M. K., & Walker, L. J. (2004). Extraordinary moral commitment: Young adults working for social organizations. *Journal of Personality, 72,* 413–436. doi: 10.1111/j.0022-3506.2004.00267.x

Matsuba, M. K., & Walker, L. J. (2005). Young adult moral exemplars: The making of self through stories. *Journal of Research on Adolescence, 15,* 275–297. doi: 10.1111/j.1532-7795.2005.00097.x

McAdams, D. P. (1988). *Power, intimacy, and the life story: Personological inquiries into identity.* New York: Guilford Press.

McAdams, D. P. (1995). What do we know when we know a person? *Journal of Personality, 63,* 365–396. doi: 10.1111/j.1467-6494.1995.tb00500.x

McAdams, D. P. (2006). *The redemptive self: Stories Americans live by.* New York: Oxford University Press.

McAdams, D. P. (2009). The moral personality. In D. Narvaez & D. K. Lapsley (eds), *Personality, identity, and character: Explorations in moral psychology* (pp. 11–29). New York: Cambridge University Press.

McAdams, D. P. (2013). The psychological self as actor, agent, and author. *Perspectives on Psychological Science, 8,* 272–295. doi: 10.1177/1745691612464657

McAdams, D. P., Diamond, A., de St. Aubin, E., & Mansfield, E. (1997). Stories of commitment: The psychosocial construction of generative lives. *Journal of Personality and Social Psychology, 72,* 678–694. doi: 10.1037/0022-3514.72.3.678

McAdams, D. P., Reynolds, J., Lewis, M., Patten, A. H., & Bowman, P. J. (2001). When bad things turn good and good things turn bad: Sequences of redemption and contamination in life narrative and their relation to psychosocial adaptation in midlife adults and in students. *Personality and Social Psychology Bulletin, 27,* 474–485. doi: 10.1177/0146167201274008

Milgram, S. (1974). *Obedience to authority: An experimental view.* New York: Harper & Row.

Oliner, S. P. (2003). *Do unto others: Extraordinary acts of ordinary people.* Boulder, CO: Westview.

Paulhus, D. L., & Trapnell, P. D. (2008). Self-presentation of personality: An agency–communion framework. In O. P. John, R. W. Robins, & L. A. Pervin (eds), *Handbook of personality psychology: Theory and research* (3rd ed., pp. 492–517). New York: Guilford Press.

Peterson, C. (2000). The future of optimism. *American Psychologist, 55,* 44–55. doi: 10.1037/0003-066X.55.1.44

Piaget, J. (1932/1977). *The moral judgment of the child* (M. Gabain, Trans.). Harmondsworth, UK: Penguin.

Pinker, S. (2008). The moral instinct. *New York Times Magazine* (January 13), pp. 32–37, 52–58.

Rest, J. R. (1979). *Development in judging moral issues.* Minneapolis, MN: University of Minnesota Press.

Rokeach, M. (1973). *The nature of human values.* New York: Free Press.

Rosch, E. (1978). Principles of categorization. In E. Rosch & B. B. Lloyd (eds), *Cognition and categorization* (pp. 27–48). Hillsdale, NJ: Erlbaum.

Schwartz, S. H., Cieciuch, J., Vecchione, M., Davidov, E., Fischer, R., Beierlein, C., & ... Konty, M. (2012). Refining the theory of basic individual values. *Journal of Personality and Social Psychology, 103,* 663–688. doi: 10.1037/a0029393

Staub, E. (2005). The roots of goodness: The fulfillment of basic human needs and the development of caring, helping and non-aggression, inclusive caring, moral courage, active bystandership, and altruism born of suffering. In G. Carlo & C. P. Edwards (eds), *Nebraska Symposium on Motivation, Vol. 51: Moral motivation through the life span* (pp. 33–72). Lincoln, NE: University of Nebraska Press.

Straughan, R. (1986). Why act on Kohlberg's moral judgments? (Or how to reach Stage 6 and remain a bastard). In S. Modgil & C. Modgil (eds), *Lawrence Kohlberg: Consensus and controversy* (pp. 149–157). Philadelphia, PA: Falmer.

Thompson, R. A. (2009). Early foundations: Conscience and the development of moral character. In D. Narvaez & D. K. Lapsley (eds), *Personality, identity, and character: Explorations in moral psychology* (pp. 159–184). New York: Cambridge University Press.

Turiel, E. (1983). *The development of social knowledge: Morality and convention.* Cambridge, UK: Cambridge University Press.

Twenge, J. M., Campbell, W., & Freeman, E. C. (2012). Generational differences in young adults' life goals, concern for others, and civic orientation, 1966–2009. *Journal of Personality and Social Psychology, 102,* 1045–1062. doi: 10.1037/a0027408

Vollhardt, J. R. (2009). Altruism born of suffering and prosocial behavior following adverse life events: A review and conceptualization. *Social Justice Research, 22,* 53–97. doi: 10.1007/s11211-009-0088-1

Walker, L. J. (2003). Morality, religion, spirituality—The value of saintliness. *Journal of Moral Education, 32,* 373–384. doi: 10.1080/0305724032000161277

Walker, L. J. (2004). Gus in the gap: Bridging the judgment–action gap in moral functioning. In D. K. Lapsley & D. Narvaez (eds), *Moral development, self, and identity* (pp. 1–20). Mahwah, NJ: Erlbaum.

Walker, L. J. (2013). Exemplars' moral behavior is self-regarding. *New Directions for Child and Adolescent Development, 142,* 27–40. doi: 10.1002/cad.20047

Walker, L. J. (2014). Moral personality, motivation, and identity. In M. Killen & J. G. Smetana (eds), *Handbook of moral development* (2nd ed., pp. 497–519). New York: Psychology Press.

Walker, L. J., & Frimer, J. A. (2007). Moral personality of brave and caring exemplars. *Journal of Personality and Social Psychology, 93,* 845–860. doi: 10.1037/0022-3514.93.5.845

Walker, L. J., & Frimer, J. A. (2008). Being good for goodness' sake: Transcendence in the lives of moral heroes. In F. Oser & W. Veugelers (eds), *Getting involved: Global citizenship development and sources of moral values* (pp. 309–326). Rotterdam, The Netherlands: Sense Publishers.

Walker, L. J., & Frimer, J. A. (2011). The science of moral development. In M. K. Underwood & L. H. Rosen (eds), *Social development: Relationships in infancy, childhood, and adolescence* (pp. 235–262). New York: Guilford Press.

Walker, L. J., & Frimer, J. A. (2015). Developmental trajectories of agency and communion in moral motivation. *Merrill-Palmer Quarterly, 61,* 412–439. doi: 10.13110/merrpalmquar1982.61.3.0412

Walker, L. J., & Hennig, K. H. (2004). Differing conceptions of moral exemplarity: Just, brave, and caring. *Journal of Personality and Social Psychology, 86,* 629–647. doi: 10.1037/0022-3514.86.4.629

Walker, L. J., & Pitts, R. C. (1998). Naturalistic conceptions of moral maturity. *Developmental Psychology, 34,* 403–419. doi: 10.1037/0012-1649.34.3.403

Walker, L. J., Frimer, J. A., & Dunlop, W. L. (2010). Varieties of moral personality: Beyond the banality of heroism. *Journal of Personality, 78,* 907–942. doi: 10.1111/j.1467-6494.2010.00637.x

Watson, G. (1984). Virtues in excess. *Philosophical Studies, 46,* 57–74.

Zaslavsky, O., Palgi, Y., Rillamas-Sun, E., LaCroix, A. Z., Schnall, E., Woods, N. F., & Shrira, A. (2015). Dispositional optimism and terminal decline in global quality of life. *Developmental Psychology, 51,* 856–863. doi: 10.1037/dev0000018

Zimbardo, P. G. (2007). The banality of evil, the banality of heroism. In J. Brockman (ed.), *What is your dangerous idea? Today's leading thinkers on the unthinkable* (pp. 275–276). New York: Harper Perennial.

Zimbardo, P. G., Banks, W. C., Haney, C., & Jaffe, D. (1973). The mind is a formidable jailer: A Pirandellian prison. *The New York Times Magazine* (April 8), Section 6, pp. 38–46.

7

Why and How Groups Create Moral Heroes

Ari Decter-Frain, Ruth Vanstone, and Jeremy A. Frimer

Tenzin Gyatso is no ordinary man—he is a living, breathing moral hero. Gyatso, also known as His Holiness, the 14th Dalai Lama of Tibet, received the Nobel Peace Prize in 1989 for his leadership role in the non-violent struggle for Tibet's independence from China (Aarvik, 1989). A community of 100,000+ exiled Tibetans look to Gyatso for guidance and view him as their spiritual champion. Even Americans approve of the Dalai Lama more so than any other world leader—including their own (Corso, 2013). Drawing crowds of more than 10,000 people at a time, the Dalai Lama's sustained plea for compassion draws in his followers, giving the impression that the Dalai Lama has an inner glow or a "special something."

The Dalai Lama's story raises the possibility that moral heroism is earned. Perhaps moral heroes have their standing because of their sophisticated ability to reason through complex moral problems (Kohlberg, 1984) or narrate heart-warming life stories about their lives (Colby & Damon, 1992; McAdams & Guo, 2015; Walker & Frimer, 2007). This notion that moral heroes have an inner greatness has seemed self-evidently true to both the public and scholars (Carlyle, 1840; Woods, 1913).

We propose an alternative explanation for the existence of moral heroes. Rather than thinking of moral heroes as superb individuals that followers discover, we propose that followers *manufacture* the perception of moral heroism in rather ordinary individuals. That is, followers may turn these ordinary individuals into moral heroes in the eyes of followers by shaping followers' perceptions. The idea that moral heroes are "Great Men" may overestimate the inner goodness of these leaders, and underestimate the active role of followers in the *perception* of the moral hero's greatness. We will set out the view that moralistic groups create moral heroes out of surprisingly ordinary persons.

Once again, the Dalai Lama's story is apt. His beginnings as a spiritual leader were hardly earned in any meritocratic sense. Rather, they were astonishingly arbitrary. The 13th Dalai Lama died in 1933. According to Buddhist tradition, when a Dalai Lama dies, he reincarnates to another body. His followers' task is to find that body. A search team followed a series of symbols, which led to a house. There, they found a two-year-old boy (Aarvik, 1989). The search team tested the toddler, for example, by presenting him with a series of two items, one of which the previous Dalai Lama had owned. His task was to select the correct one. Two-year-old Gyatso correctly identified every object (Thondup & Thurston, 2015).

The Dalai Lama's followers anointed him at age four, and he became the official political leader of Tibet at age 15, almost a decade before he completed his education in Buddhist philosophy (Marcello, 2003). That is, he had ascended to the rank of spiritual and political leader of his people without having achieving expertise in his people's politics and philosophy. Hence, at least some of the Dalai Lama's influence may have arisen not from his own intellectual and moral greatness, but rather through social processes—such as arbitrarily granting of titles like "his holiness" to a 2-year-old toddler.

We suggest that groups may catapult relatively ordinary individuals into moral heroism. To our knowledge, no experimental evidence exists that directly establishes that groups do create moral heroes. However, we rely on a circumstantial approach by describing the motive and mechanism by which groups might do so. Followers may elevate relatively ordinary individuals into the role of symbols of moral heroism by giving them titles and awards, propagating heroic portraits, and encouraging them to give inspiring speeches. Creating a moral hero may benefit a tribe by giving its members a rallying point around which to unite and fight. Finally, we explain how impressing a few can lead to population-wide endorsement.

Definitions and Theoretical Underpinnings

We define heroes as symbols, and leaders as agents. We see heroism as a perception in the eyes of followers, one that symbolizes the desires and values of the collective they represent. Heroes need not necessarily act on any of these values; the defining feature of heroism is that followers attribute symbolic status to them. In contrast, we characterize leaders by their engagement in concrete acts of leadership. Leaders actively manage people, give advice, make decisions, and so on. In this way, heroism and leadership are independent; leadership is possible without heroism, and heroism is possible without leadership. CEOs illustrate the independence of heroism and leadership. To their executive team, CEOs act as leaders by chairing meetings, delegating tasks, and making critical decisions. To the broader organization, CEOs can function as heroes by symbolizing the values of the organization, giving inspiring speeches, and appearing on the cover of the organization's annual report.

Heroes can be of different sorts, ranging from celebrities (e.g., Michael Jackson) to athletes (e.g., Michael Jordan) to social leaders (e.g., Martin Luther King, Jr.). We distinguish heroes that are known for their competence, ability, and agency (e.g., celebrities and athletes) from those who are known for both their agency and their communal focus (e.g., Martin Luther King, Jr.) by labeling the latter kind "moral heroes."

Our approach to understanding heroism aligns with follower-centric approaches to heroism. Social constructivist approaches posit that the hero is a construction in the minds of the observer. Followers play an active role in selecting and shaping an individual into a symbol of the goals of the group, and the qualities that the followers deem ideal (Adams, 2006; Gardner & Avolio, 1998). Guiding this process is the hero schema, a shared notion of what the prototypic hero is like as a person and that which he/she represents. Followers' schemas can influence both the discovery of heroes, and shape the development of a hero embedded within a group of followers (Goethals & Allison, 2012).

This notion of active followership is also consistent with social identity theory. Followers may recognize a prototypical quality in a certain group member and elevate that individual to hero status (Hogg, 2001). Even within organizational settings, people may have a romanticized notion of leadership whereby groups over-attribute success and failure to leaders and under-attribute outcomes to followers (Pfeiffer, 1977; Meindl, Ehrlich, & Dukerich, 1985; Bass & Bass, 2009). Following in these traditions, our approach aims to specify a set of specific social processes by which followers elevate individuals into heroic status.

Moral Heroes Benefit from their Group Standing

Moral heroes derive material and psychological benefits from their role. In many societies, prestigious people are both wealthy, reproductively successful, and happy (Frimer & Brandt, 2015; Irons 1979; Borgerhoff Mulder, 1988). Nobel Prize winners tend to live longer than Nobel nominees (Rablen & Oswald, 2008).

Moral heroes can influence adherents' behavior to benefit the group, but also to the benefit of their own personal interests (Bligh, Kohles & Pillai, 2011). The story of Blake Mycoskie illustrates how a hero can benefit from a prosocial cause. Mycoskie is the founder of the company TOMS, a for-profit shoe company. TOMS's policy is to donate one pair of shoes to impoverished children for each pair they sell. Some consumers may approve of the company's model because they regard it as a charity. Despite its charitable appearance, Mycoskie recently sold half of the company for $300 million (O'Connor, 2014). While some may think of Mycoskie and TOMS as an exemplar of corporate morality, he is also a multi-millionaire, reaping financial benefits from his station.

Groups Benefit from having Moral Heroes

Groups also benefit from having moral heroes. As the global population grows and competition for finite resources increases, belonging to a cohesive moral community becomes increasingly important for individuals to survive and thrive (Atran & Norenzayan, 2004). Group belonging confers physical and psychological resources to members. People with a strong sense of belongingness tend to be physically and emotionally healthy (Begen & Turner-Cobb, 2015; Hagerty et al., 1996; Hale, Hannum, & Espelage, 2005). Simply belonging to an online dating community may satisfy a physical need by increasing an individual's number of potential mates. The existence of heroes may benefit group members in three ways.

Heroes Strengthen Ingroup Ties

Groups become more productive and members feel greater belonging when they bind together into a tight-knit moral community (Haidt, 2012). The presence of a hero may strengthen the bonds among group members. Occupying the leadership position may help maintain the group's social structure (Fiske, 1992). Their position at top of the hierarchy grant heroes sacred status, just as religious groups sacralize deities (Atran & Norenzayan, 2004). Sacralizing mundane objects, practices, or people binds people together (Tetlock, 2003).

Heroes may also bind groups together simply by bringing attention to a dividing characteristic between "us" and "them," such as when Ronald Reagan referred to the Soviet Union as the "evil empire" and highlighted philosophical differences between the U.S.S.R. and the U.S.:

> the Soviet leaders have openly and publicly declared that the only morality they recognize is that which will further their cause, which is world revolution… they must be made to understand: we will never compromise our principles and standards. We will never give away our freedom.
>
> *(Reagan, 1983)*

Drawing attention to more superficial distinctions between the ingroup and outgroup is sufficient to create group behavior. Mere preferences, such as a preference for one painter's work over another, are sufficient to establish group identity (Tajfel, 1970; see Diehl, 1990 for a review). By describing themselves and their followers as belonging to the same team, and drawing attention to some other group of non-like-minded outsiders, moral heroes may stoke ingroup favoritism.

Heroes Enforce Cooperation

Moral heroes play a critical role in promoting large-scale group cooperation by punishing free riders, both directly and indirectly (Richerson & Boyd, 1998). Punishment need not be physical or even aggressive. When in the role of leader, moral heroes may simply express disappointment or withdraw resources and opportunities from followers who are not behaving appropriately. And the mere presence of moral heroes as symbols may cause some followers to enforce group norms by punishing misbehavers. Without individuals that punish selfish individuals, group cohesion breaks down. A classic example of this comes from research in public goods. The reciprocal tit-for-tat strategy suffices to establish norms of cooperation in dyads (Axelrod and Hamilton, 1981). Prompt and limited retaliation works because, in effect, each person punishes the other' selfishness, and thus encourages a return to cooperation. However, in larger group interactions, direct reciprocity becomes insufficient to sustain cooperation (Boyd & Richerson, 1992) because punishing a selfish group member has the side effect of punishing all the other group members, the cooperative ones included. The result is social entropy, leading to outcomes like the "tragedy of the commons." Groups can achieve generalized reciprocity and maintain cooperation by adopting a moralistic model, in which a small number of punishers (e.g., moral heroes) exact rents from selfish group members. With the addition of just one punisher, cooperation eventually becomes the norm within the group (Boyd & Richerson, 1992; Fehr & Gächter, 2002).

Taken to the extreme, punishment can lead to fascism. However, heroes can use gentle (social, rather than physical) disincentives to reduce selfishness (Richerson & Boyd, 1998). Like punishment, the threat of gossip and ostracism induce cooperation (Feinberg, Willer, & Schultz, 2014). Followers may augment the threat of disincentives for selfishness by demanding obedience to authorities who share their ideology (Frimer, Gaucher, & Schaefer, 2014). By enforcing pro-group behavior, moral heroes solve the "free rider problem" and maintain cooperation among group members. Without enforcement, prosocial behavior would be limited to instances of dyadic, and therefore direct, reciprocity.

Heroes Model Behavior that Followers Copy

Heroes inspire followers to act as they do. When asked to list the traits that describe heroes, people consistently list eight traits: *smart, strong, selfless, caring, charismatic, resilient, reliable,* and *inspiring* (Allison & Goethals, 2011). Followers emulate these traits, which signals their commitment to the group (Gardner, 2003). Regardless of the behavior of other group members, the addition of a single person who contributes consistently to the group's welfare can cause generosity to spread (Weber & Murnighan, 2008). Gandhi's non-violent resistance to British rule encouraged similarly non-violent resistance from followers. For example, along with Gandhi, 78 citizens marched for weeks to the sea to collect their own salt, an act forbidden by the British government. The march attracted more than 1000 followers, and inspired other Indian citizens to protest against unjust laws in a peaceful manner (Engler & Engler, 2014).

Hero Creation

How do individuals become moral heroes? Is most of the action in the hero, with the hero raising awareness of a cause and mobilizing (otherwise passive) followers for action? Or might followers play a more active role in the emergence of heroes? We entertain the latter possibility, positing that group members create the perception of moral heroism in their leaders.

People tend to have a romantic notion of their leaders, over-attributing the success of a group to the leader's actions (Meindl, 1985). Rather than being primarily responsible for the group's success, moral heroes may exist within a complex, bidirectional relationship between the leader and his/her followers. Leaders' messages may simply put into words an existing, widespread moral sentiment within a group. Reactions from followers may trim off the messages that resonate less, and reinforce the messages that resonate more with the movement. In this way, followers may play an active role in sculpting the hero's message (Howell & Shamir, 2005). Exerting this influence over their leaders may also enhance followers' sense of agency (Avolio & Reichard, 2008), which makes followership feel volitional (Stech, 2008).

Followers may create the perception of moral heroism in their leaders by giving them titles and awards, propagating heroic portraiture, and encouraging their leaders to give heroic speeches. Whether followers are aware of the social effects of these actions remains unclear, and worthy of future research.

Titles and Awards

The Dalai Lama's official name is Jetsun Jamphel Ngawang Lobsang Yeshe Tenzin Gyatso, which translates to Holy Lord, Gentle Glory, Compassionate, Defender of the Faith, Ocean of Wisdom, Tenzin Gyatso. Heroes' titles can signal to followers that the hero has moral virtue and will bring about important changes for their followers. Awards can have a similar effect, such as when Barack Obama won the Nobel Peace prize in 2009, with the closing date for nominations being just 12 days into his presidency. Asked why Obama received the prize, Nobel Committee head Thorbjorn Jagland explained that "it was because we would like to support what he is trying to achieve … It is a clear signal that we want to advocate the same as he has done" (BBC, 2009). Obama's Nobel Peace Prize was less so a recognition for a past achievement than it was a mandate to help Obama carry out his vision in the future.

Does receiving such an award succeed in changing the recipient's behavior? Or does it merely elevate other people's perception of the leader? We are aware of no evidence that directly addresses this question. However, research on the effects of awards in other social arenas tentatively suggests that awards enhance reputation, but do little to the recipient's behavior. For example, winning a teaching award bolsters teachers' reputations but does not change their behavior; moreover, teaching awards seem to have little effect on the teacher's students (Huggett et al., 2012). Future research should test the effects of moral titles and awards on recipients' behavior and reputation. One possibility is to examine changes in behavior and reputation of winners and nominees of awards for youth activism.

Portraits

Followers may create the perception of heroism by propagating heroic images of their leaders. The quintessential posture of the moral hero depicts the hero looking up and to the viewer's right (Frimer & Sinclair, 2015; see Figure 7.1 for examples).

Internet images of moral heroes (e.g., Martin Luther King, Jr.; Mother Teresa) tend to portray them looking up and to the viewer's right more often than one would expect if their gaze varied at random, and also more often than did non-heroic celebrities such as Brad Pitt and Elvis Presley (Frimer & Sinclair, 2015, Study 1). One explanation for this curious occurrence is that moral heroes adjust their posture when posing for photographs. That is, the action may be in the hero. Another possibility locates the action in the hero's follower. Evidence supports this latter possibility. When tasked with selecting a portrait of a leader for promotional materials, people selectively choose the up-and-right posture (Frimer & Sinclair, 2015, Study 2).

Followers may select the up-and-right posture because it depicts the leader as calm and rational. In the up-and-right posture, the subject's right side of the face is more visible than the more emotionally expressive left side. The right cerebral hemisphere, which controls the hidden

Why and How Groups Create Moral Heroes

Figure 7.1 Portraits of moral heroes often portray the individual gazing up and to the viewer's right (hero's left). Left to right: the Dalai Lama, Ronald Reagan, and Malala Yousafzai

Source: Photo credits: Right: K. Krug, 2009, retrieved from www.flickr.com/photos/kk/3959577856; Centre: National Archives, catalog.archives.gov; Left: C. Powers, 1988, retrieved from www.washingtontimes.com/multimedia/image/106_2014_beltway-ronald-reag8201jpg

left side of the face, processes more emotional information than the left cerebral hemisphere. As a result, the displayed right side of the face is less emotionally expressive than the left (e.g., Sackeim, Gur, & Saucy, 1978). The up-and-right posture may conceal the more emotionally expressive side of the face, and thus give the impression that the moral hero is calm and level-headed, and thus ready to make sound decisions.

A second explanation for why followers select portraits of their leaders looking up-and-right is that these images activate a network of conceptual metaphors that connect direction with personal virtue. This network and its prescriptions about directionality are evident in the term *upright citizen*. The word *right* connotes correctness whereas the origin of the word *left* is an old English term meaning *idle, weak,* or *useless*. In Latin, the word *sinister* means left. Terms like *uplifting* and *heaven above* imply morality and strength to the upward direction (Haidt & Algoe, 2004). Social status also implies vertical elevation. For example, seeing the word *king* causes people to search the top of their visual field, whereas the word *servant* has the opposite effect (Zanolie et al., 2012). Resultantly, posing in the up-and-right posture makes a person look warm, proud, and future-minded (Frimer & Sinclair, 2015, Study 3).

A recent example of the social consequences of the hero pose was Barack Obama's 2008 presidential campaign. Shepard Fairey's stylized portrait of Obama—with Obama gazing up and to the viewer's right—came to symbolize hope, progress, and change, and enhance the hysteria surrounding his presidential campaign. The origin of the image is telling about the active role of followers in the emergence of the hero. Fairey's iconic image was the product of the artist selecting a particular image, cropping out most of it, and stylizing the rest. Mannie Garcia, working for the Associated Press, took the original image in 2006, depicting Obama apparently listening to someone speak while sitting beside George Clooney at a media event. Obama's attention seems to focus entirely on the speaker, and away from the photographer, suggesting that Obama was not posing for the photograph. Rather, evidence of active followership is in abundance, for instance in Fairey's selecting this particular image and cropping out George Clooney. Other followers contributed to the hysteria as well. The media presented the portrait frequently. And posters, stickers, and T-shirts displaying it sold by the hundreds of thousands. We suggest that part of the hysteria and Obama's resultant electoral success was his followers selecting and propagating heroic imagery.

Speeches

Speeches represent a third way in which groups create the perception of moral heroism in their leaders. Some of the most meaningful and salient memories followers have of their heroes are associated with speeches. For example, when people think about Martin Luther King, Jr., the following words likely come to mind:

> I have a dream that one day ... the sons of former slaves and the sons of former slave owners will be able to sit down together at the table of brotherhood ... I have a dream that my four little children will one day ... not be judged by the color of their skin.
>
> *(King, 1963)*

Hearing or reading these words leaves an impression—the man who uttered these words was a *good* man.

Warm, charismatic language leaves a lasting impression about the speaker, as a person. But are these impressions accurate? That is, do audiences draw meaningful inferences about the speaker's underlying character from the words they hear? We suggest that they may not. Language may be a surprisingly poor means of learning about a person's underlying traits. For example, narcissists do *not* talk about themselves more often than non-narcissists do (Carey et al., 2015). And people who describe prosocial personal goals do not behave especially generously toward strangers (Frimer, Zhu, & Decter-Frain, 2015).

This dissociation between language and inner disposition may be a consequence of the *correspondence bias*, wherein audiences erroneously think that people's words *correspond* to their inner personality. In the classic illustration of the correspondence bias, audience members read pro-Castro speeches and guessed the true attitudes of the speaker. Even when the audience learned that the speaker was told that he/she *had* to write a pro-Castro speech, the audience still made pro-Castro attitudinal attributions to the speaker (Jones & Harris, 1967). Audiences fail to fully take into account the pressures that unseen situational pressures exert on people speaking, and mistakenly think that people's words are telling of who they are as people.

While not particularly telling of the inner character of the speaker, language can have a powerful persuasive effect on audiences. Movement leaders may intuit this and carefully select charismatic orators as movement leaders. For example, key movers within the Democratic Party—Jack Corrigan and Mary Beth Cahill—chose Barack Obama to give his 2004 Convention speech because of his youth, African American roots, and oratory charisma (Bernstein, 2007). Followers may also encourage moral heroes to focus on certain themes in their speeches.

The persuasive effect can be so profound that audiences sometimes endorse leaders whose ideology conflicts with their own. This may be because the speaker's warm, fuzzy language induces the audience to endorse the speaker without knowing precisely the speaker's ideological stance. A poignant illustration of this is the widespread American approval of the Dalai Lama (64% according to a 2013 Harris poll). However, the Dalai Lama openly identifies as a Marxist, an ideology that just 11 percent of Americans feel should be implemented as system of government (Rasmussen Reports, 2011). That is, the vast majority of American Dalai Lama supporters do not actually support his objective.

Charismatic speeches follow a formula, which include: threat, personal sacrifice for sacred values, agency, and communion. The narrative goes as follows: Something is terribly wrong (*threat*). Something that we hold dear is under threat—we must defend it at any cost (*personal sacrifice for sacred values*). Everyone will have to work hard (*agency*) to make the world a more fair, compassionate place again (*communion*).

Threat

Heroes often make reference to a threat or conflict in their speeches. For example, Ronald Reagan launched his political career in 1964 when he described how national debt and Communism threatened American freedom:

> We're at war with the most dangerous enemy that has ever faced mankind in his long climb from the swamp to the stars, and it's been said if we lose that war, and in so doing lose this way of freedom of ours, history will record with the greatest astonishment that those who had the most to lose did the least to prevent its happening.
>
> *(Reagan, 1964)*

Moral heroes on the political left also identify threat. The day before his assassination, Martin Luther King, Jr. raised an alarm about the state of the world in his "mountaintop" speech: "The world is all messed up. The nation is sick. Trouble is in the land; confusion all around" (King, 1968).

Moral heroes may signal threat because leaders become increasingly influential during times of crisis (Bligh, Kohles, & Meindl 2004). When people feel threatened, they accept their (low) position in the social hierarchy (Jost, Banaji & Nosek, 2004) and seek protectors (Atran & Norenzayan, 2004; Klapp, 1948). Reminders of one's mortality make people feel antipathy toward opposing views, as well as support for those who validate one's own beliefs (Greenberg & Arndt, 2011). Hence, when heroes make reference to outside threat, they may strengthen group members' allegiance to the group and their willingness to follow their leader.

Sacred Values

Can heroes raise the alarm about threats to anything of value? Or must the threat be to a specific subtype of values? To illustrate, imagine that the government raised taxes on almonds. Almond-growers aside, most people are unlikely to react strongly because they merely value almonds, thinking of them as a means to an end (of eating nuts) and interchangeable with other nuts (such as pecans). In contrast, raising taxes on a single racial group (e.g., African Americans) would elicit a much stronger reaction, especially from the political left. Raising taxes on gun purchases would have the same effect on from some people on the political right.

A key distinction is between values and sacred values (Tetlock, 2003). Values are things that are important to a person because they are useful. A valuable thing is a means to an end. As a result, people will sacrifice them when the benefits of doing so outweigh the costs. A sacred value is a type of values that is not a means to an end, but rather an end in itself. People treat their sacred values as not open to trading off or exchanging for other goods, even when doing so makes sense.

A common example of a sacred value in Western culture is life, which the U.S. Declaration of Independence enshrines as an "inalienable right." Most Westerners would feel disgusted at the thought of sacrificing one ill child to harvest his organs to save five other ill children. Pro-lifers cite the "sanctity of life" as a consideration that trumps all others in the abortion debate. And modern healthcare practices aim to keep alive terminally ill patients, even when they desire to die. However, not all cultures (e.g., radical Islam) thinks of life as sacred.

Sharia Law is sacred to radical Islamists. Life is sacred to Westerners. Personal freedom is sacred to libertarians. And social justice is sacred to liberals. The cultural relativity of sacred values serve a functional purpose—their unique correspondence to a particular tribe enhances their fidelity as signal of group identity. Their costly, irrational (i.e. not amenable to rational cost/benefit calculus) and often outlandish nature (e.g., sacred cows) raises their fidelity as a signaling device. No one in his or her "right mind" would accidentally defend another group's sacred values. Sacred values are like a secret password: they function like a high-fidelity signal as to whether a person is an insider or an outsider.

To become a symbol for the group's struggle, moral heroes signal their allegiance to the group's sacred values. Ronald Reagan communicated his commitment to protecting American freedom from escalating debt and Communism in his first inaugural address:

> The economic ills we suffer have come upon us over several decades. They will not go away in days, weeks, or months, but they will go away. They will go away because we as Americans have the capacity now, as we've had in the past, to do whatever needs to be done to preserve this last and greatest bastion of freedom.
>
> *(Reagan, 1981)*

Left-wing heroes also defend sacred values, such as social justice and the environment (Frimer, Tell, & Haidt, 2015). While on trial for treason for waging guerrilla warfare against the apartheid government, Nelson Mandela appealed to the Left's sacred value of social equality:

> During my lifetime I have dedicated my life to this struggle ... I have cherished the ideal of a democratic and free society ... It is an ideal for which I hope to live for ... But, My Lord, if it needs be, it is an ideal for which I am prepared to die.
>
> *(Mandela, 1964)*

Personal Sacrifice

The quotes from both Reagan and Mandela highlight how the defense of sacred values requires personal sacrifice. Reagan called for the American people to "do whatever needs to be done" (Reagan, 1981), and Mandela expressed his willingness to die for the cause. Personal sacrifice is common in the stories of moral heroes. Like Mandela and Reagan, Martin Luther King, Jr. also declared his willingness to become a martyr for the cause of social equality in a speech the day before his assassination: "Like anybody, I would like to live a long life. Longevity has its place. But I'm not concerned about that now. I just want to do God's will" (King, 1968). Similarly, Malala Yousafzai's rise as a moral hero came after she survived an assassination attempt.

Enduring personal hardship for the cause may make people seem like moral heroes for several reasons. First, martyrs no longer have the opportunity to fall from grace, and so they cement their legacy when they die. To illustrate, the public consistently rates John F. Kennedy more favorably (~70th percentile among presidents) than they do George W. Bush (~20th percentile). However, examining their public approval ratings (Figure 7.2) suggests that the two presidents were on a *similar* trajectory—their public approval ratings correlate positively and strongly ($r = +.58$). Both Kennedy and Bush faced an outgroup threat (the Cuban Missile Crisis and September 11th attacks, respectively) early in their presidencies. And then public approval began to decline as fear dissipated and day-to-day governance commenced.

Whether Kennedy's plunge in public approval would have continued as Bush's did is not clear. However, the steep downward trajectory of Kennedy's approval ratings at the time of his death suggests that his legacy as a great American president may, in part, be because he died young.

People generally rate heroes who were assassinated at a young age as the most influential heroes of their time (Allison & Goethals, 2011). The longer heroes remain in the spotlight, the more likely they are to reveal their banality. Illustratively, Nelson Mandela's performance as

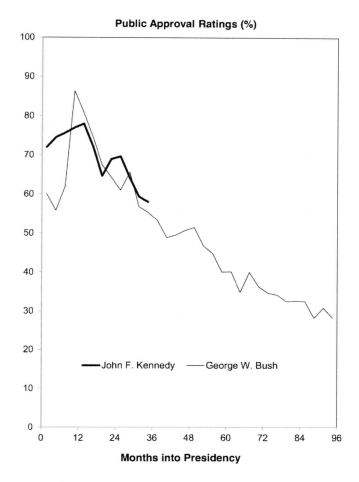

Figure 7.2 Public approval ratings of Presidents John F. Kennedy and George W. Bush show a similar pattern

president of South Africa was surprisingly lackluster. And once elected, Barack Obama could no longer merely symbolize his message of hope. By both expert and public opinion, his presidency has been about average.

Without some criteria for discriminating between genuine and selfish/manipulative leaders, groups remain vulnerable to exploitation. Sacrifice is a high-fidelity signal of commitment to the group. Natural selection may have shaped cultural learning such that people pay greater attention to messages containing themes of personal sacrifice (Henrich, 2009). Hence, humans may have evolved a means by which to grant greater credence to people who set aside their own self-interest in the name of the cause.

Audiences attend more closely to those who demonstrate their commitment to a cause through self-sacrifice. Speakers that set aside their own interests are more convincing than ones who displays their vested interest (Eagly, Wood, & Chaiken, 1978; Newman & Cain, 2014; Walster, Aronson, & Abrahams, 1966). Impressing upon an audience that the speaker him/herself behaves charitably enhances the success of pleas for charitable donations (Bryan, Redfield, & Mader, 1971).

Suicide bombers represent a salient contemporary example of self-sacrificial behavior, and the motive behind it. While researchers originally hypothesized that pathology was responsible for suicide bombings, attempts to identify any such pathologies have come up empty (McCauley, 2007). Moreover, suicide bombers are not necessarily of a low socio economic status (Krueger & Maleckova, 2002). People who are ready to self-sacrifice for a cause tend to be committed, passionate and altruistic, but not necessarily depressed, suicidal, or fatalistic (Bélanger, Caouette, Sharvit, & Dugas, 2014). Suicide bombers understand their actions through a moral lens, seeing it as a necessary and justifiable means to an end of defending their sacred values and family (Atran, Sheikh, & Gomez, 2014; Whitehouse, McQuinn, Buhrmester, & Swann, 2014). Motives for suicide attacks may seem rational within the perpetrator's worldview (Kruglanski, Chen, Dechesne, Fishman, & Orehek, 2009; Wintrobe, 2006). A normal individual, placed in exacting circumstances, can end up a martyr.

Agency and communion.

When communicating a call for action, moral heroes explain how the group will succeed (agency) as well as the social objective (communion). Agency and communion are the two primary dimensions of social judgment (Bakan, 1966; Cuddy, Fiske, & Glick, 2008). Agency refers to a striving to get ahead, and concerns competence, intelligence, skill, empowerment, and creativity. Barack Obama's rallying cry to voters, delivered during the 2008 New Hampshire Primary Race, illustrates agency in the hero's speech:

> For when we have faced down impossible odds, when we've been told we're not ready or that we shouldn't try or that we can't, generations of Americans have responded with a simple creed that sums up the spirit of a people: Yes, we can. Yes, we can. Yes, we can.
>
> *(Obama, 2008)*

Communion refers to the desire to get along and concerns friendliness, helpfulness, sincerity, interpersonal warmth, trustworthiness and morality. Communicating a communal message induces others to come to one's aid (Cuddy, Fiske, & Glick, 2008). An example of communion in the hero's speech is the Dalai Lama Nobel Peace Prize acceptance speech (1989). The Dalai Lama received the prize for his continued efforts to achieve a non-violent, conciliatory resolution between China and Tibet. In his speech, he shared a communal message:

> Although I have found my own Buddhist religion helpful in generating love and compassion, even for those we consider our enemies, I am convinced that everyone can develop a good heart and a sense of universal responsibility with or without religion.
>
> *(Dalai Lama, 1989)*

Folk conceptions of heroes (Allison & Goethals, 2013) draw from both agency (*smart*, *strong*, *resilient*, *charismatic*, and *inspiring*) and communion (*selfless*, *caring*, and *reliable*). Brands portraying both agency and communion belong to the "golden quadrant" of marketing success. The absence of either dimension elicits negative emotions in consumers. Brands lacking agency elicit pity, whereas brands lacking a communal message elicit envy (Aaker, Garbinsky, & Vohs, 2012).

While moral heroes' speeches may have the greatest influence when they integrate both agency and communion (Frimer, Walker, Dunlop, Lee & Riches, 2011; Frimer, Walker, Lee, Riches, & Dunlop, 2012), communion is the primary dimension of social judgment (Cuddy, Fiske, & Glick, 2008). Communal language is among the most powerful tools of mass social persuasion. For example, a text analysis of all the words spoken in U.S. Congress over the past 20 years found that levels of communal language strongly predicted public approval 6 months later, even when controlling for exogenous factors such as the 9/11 attacks and the economy (Frimer, Aquino, Gebauer, Zhu, & Oakes, 2015). Warm, communal language was a stronger predictor of public approval than more substantive factors, such as the economy and the productivity of Congress. Warm, fuzzy words work.

Social Contagion

Would-be heroes give speeches, appear in iconic portraits, and win awards. Yet, sometimes only a few people hear the speeches, see the images, or are present for the award ceremony. How then does leaving an impression on just a few people in the audience have an upward spiraling effect on a larger group? To illustrate the problem, consider the following words:

> With malice toward none; with charity for all; with firmness in the right, as God gives us to see the right, let us strive on to finish the work we are in … to do all which may achieve and cherish a just and a lasting peace, among ourselves, and with all nations.
>
> *(Lincoln, 1865)*

To many people living in the year 2015, these words are familiar. Yet, for a person living today to have heard the original speaker utter these words, they would have to be at least 150 years old. Abraham Lincoln delivered these words to sum up his post-Civil War agenda in his second inaugural address. Given that the oldest person alive is 116, not a single person living today ever heard Lincoln utter these words. Yet these words remain etched in memory. Social contagion is likely at play.

Social contagion refers to the viral spreading of an emotion, message, or behavior throughout a group (Levy & Nail, 1993). Contagion works because group members interact regularly. One person changes another, who changes another, and so on until a whole group has changed. In the contemporary era of social media, a hero's message can spread quickly and recruit millions of followers in days. This process was evident when Invisible Children launched a video titled "Kony 2012," which became the most viral video in history, quickly accumulating more than 50 million views, causing Invisible Children's annual donations to nearly double, from $14 million in 2011 to $27 million in 2012 (Invisible Children, 2014). Similar social contagion was at play in various Arab Spring movements.

People often become followers after hearing of or witnessing a hero standing up against an external norm (e.g., segregation laws in the U.S.). Heroes differentiate themselves by their refusing to conform to external norms, and thus establishing a new set of acceptable practices. A new norm spreading within a group can resolve inner conflicts that group members feel about whether to conform to the old or new norm—an effect called disinhibitory contagion (Levy, 1992).

Asch's (1952, 1956) seminal conformity paradigm demonstrates how disinhibitory contagion works. Participants viewed a target line and were tasked with identifying which among a series of lines of varying lengths matched the target. Performance on the task was excellent. However, when confederates were present and consistently selected an incorrect line, participants' performance plummeted, in conformity with group norms. Conformity was but one solution to the conflict between responding correctly or as the rest of the group responded.

The disinhibiting power of a nonconformist became evident when Asch had one of the confederates give the correct answer while all of the others continued to give incorrect ones. The presence of this single nonconformist decreased incorrect answers by a factor of four (see Bond & Smith, 1996 for a review). A single individual deviating from the norm was sufficient to resolve most participants' conformity conflict, thereby helping them undertake the more honest behavior.

Rosa Parks is an example of a moral hero who performed the function of disinhibitory contagion. Her refusal to sit at the back of a Montgomery, Alabama bus represented a key moment for the American Civil Rights movement. Parks may have become symbolic of the movement because she resolved people's inner conflict about a practice that they understood to be unjust, yet felt compelled to do to fall in line with popular norms. Other passengers on the bus and other people who heard about the incident may have experienced a resolution of a conflict, which spiraled upwards into protest against racial inequality. Rosa Parks receives much credit for countering and eliminating segregation laws, and many think of her as the moral hero for doing so.

Emotional contagion can also bolster a hero's popularity. The earliest contagion research focused on the spread of emotion through crowds (McDougall, as cited in Levy & Nail, 1993). However, the spread of mood and emotion via contagion occurs across species, including in pigs (Reimert, Bolhuis, Kemp, & Rodenburg, 2015) and dogs (Yong & Ruffman, 2014; Sümegi, Oláh, & Topál, 2014). An illustrative moment of social contagion is when a speaker finishes speaking. If some members of the audience begin a standing ovation, the result can be social contagion if a cascade of people begin to stand up as well.

Social contagion also occurs over social media. Emotional content of people's Facebook news feeds causes corresponding changes in the content of their own status updates in both positive and negative valence (Kramer, Guillory, & Hancock, 2014). A leader giving a charismatic speech may initiate a first wave of emotional elevation. The wave propagates when followers attribute their emotions to the hero's moving rhetoric.

Critical players in social contagion.

Contagion may spread non-uniformly through a social network. That is, certain individuals tend to contribute more than others to the growth of a hero's popularity. To illustrate this, consider the recent case of Malala Yousafzai. In 2012, Yousafzai (aged 15) was promoting girls' education in Pakistan when a Talibani militant shot her in the face at close range. She survived the attack and quickly became a modern day moral hero, winning the Nobel Peace Prize two years later. The prize, however, came at the end of a complex social drama that involved two types of critical players in social networks—mavens (trusted experts) and connectors (Bailey, 2014).

The BBC's editorial staff acted as mavens when they first published Yousafzai's diary entries (under the alias Gul Makai) in 2009. *The New York Times*' Adam Ellick, who made a documentary about her, was also a maven. Archbishop Desmond Tutu then publicly recognized her greatness by nominating her for the International Children's Peace Prize in 2011.

Following her assassination attempt, connectors like celebrities Angelina Jolie and Madonna spread the word about Malala with slogans like "we are all Malala." By the time the Nobel Committee cemented Malala's legacy as the youngest Nobel Peace Prize laureate, the mavens and connectors had already done their work.

Mavens

Trusted experts—or mavens—play a critical role in manufacturing a hero. Mavens are knowledgeable, curious, critical, and prone to gossip (Boster, Kotowski, Andrews, & Serota, 2011; Feick & Price, 1987). Because of their expertise, mavens are often be the first in a group to recognize a new hero and spread word of them. Mavens are quite unlike scientists trying to discover a new species in that mavens' political agenda plays a critical role in their "discoveries." Mavens "discover" heroes that can give a face and a voice to their own ideology. Illustratively, consider the mavens Jack Corrigan and Mary Beth Cahill. Seeking a young, charismatic, African American to deliver an optimistic Keynote address in 2004, they "discovered" Barack Obama.

And Edgar Nixon was a maven. After Rosa Parks' arrest, he sought a young civil rights advocate with a history free of antagonizing the white establishment to lead the Montgomery bus boycott. He "discovered" a reverend named Martin Luther King, Jr.

Mavens may influence followers by sharing information about the newly discovered moral hero. They may also create opportunities for the moral hero. Early speeches, awards, and portraits may give rise to invitations to speak again, more awards for greatness, and more images. In this way, mavens may start a snowball effect, wherein the hero's greatness becomes increasingly well known and exaggerated.

Connectors

Connectors are the cool kids; they have and maintain large numbers of acquaintances by, for example, sending Christmas cards to their entire address book (Gladwell, 2000). Some people center their lives are "strong ties," a small set of people whom to trust and share one's life. Connectors' insight is their dedicated maintenance of many "weak-tie" relationships, which involve minimal, sometimes superficial communication but often bridge gaps between social groups (Granovetter, 1973). For example, connectors may have friends of a multitude of interests, which allows them to propagate information from one social group to another (Boster, Carpenter, & Kotowski, 2015; Boster, Kotowski, Andrews, & Serota, 2011; Flynn, Goldsmith & Eastman, 1996). Connectors play a similar role in multiple domains, including fashion, marketing, and public affairs (Katz & Lazarsfeld, 1955).

Connectors have often served as powerful agents of change. In the early 1990s, when the AIDS epidemic was beginning, connectors facilitated one of the first successful community-wide AIDS prevention interventions. Kelly et al. (1992) entered primarily gay bars and identified the patrons who conversed with the most different people and received the most greetings. They then educated and trained these individuals on AIDS prevention. Three months later, bar patrons reported significantly more use of condoms and significantly less engagement with multiple sexual partners. In comparison locations, condom usage declined over the same time period. Three years later, bar patrons showed further increases in condom use (St Lawrence et al., 1994).

The critical role of connectors also became evident in Travers and Milgram's (1969) small world experiment. Letters mailed from all over the United States to a particular home in Omaha reached their destination in an average of six steps. Of the letters that reached their destination, half of them traveled through just three connectors—a neighbor and two colleagues. Their widespread influence makes connectors critical to the development of the hero's reputation.

Conclusion

Are moral heroes innately glowing people? Or might groups create moral heroes? In this chapter, we provided evidence of motive—groups benefit from turning one of their own into a moral hero. The presence of moral heroes increase group cohesion, enforce cooperation, and inspire group members to live up to their standard. We have also described three mechanisms—titles and awards, portrait images, and charismatic speeches—along with an explanation of how local efforts can have a global influence.

However, we have not provided a "smoking gun." To our knowledge, no existing experimental evidence establishes that groups create moral heroes out of ordinary persons. However, we anticipate that such evidence will be forthcoming in the coming years. Under the right conditions, a group of like-minded people may spontaneously catapult a group member into the role of leader, and deify the leader as a moral hero.

References

Aaker, J. L., Garbinsky, E. N., & Vohs, K. D. (2012). Cultivating admiration in brands: Warmth, competence, and landing in the "golden quadrant." *Journal of Consumer Psychology*, *22*(2), 191–194.
Aarvik, E. (1989). Award ceremony speech. Norwegian Nobel Committee. Retrieved from www.nobelprize.org/nobel_prizes/peace/laureates/1989/presentation-speech.html. Copyright © The Nobel Foundation (1989).
Adams, P. (2006). Exploring social constructivism: Theories and practicalities. *Education 3–13*, *34*(3), 243–257. doi: 10.1080/03004270600898893
Allison, S. T., & Goethals, G. R. (2011). *Heroes: What they do and why we need them*. New York: Oxford University Press.
Allison, S. T., & Goethals, G. R. (2013). Our definition of "hero" [Blog post]. January 22. Retrieved from https://blog.richmond.edu/heroes/2013/01/22/our-definition-of-%E2%80%9Chero%E2%80%9D.
Asch, S. E. (1952). Group forces in the modification and distortion of judgments.
Asch, S. E. (1956). Studies of independence and conformity: I. A minority of one against a unanimous majority. *Psychological monographs: General and applied*, *70*(9), 1.
Atran, S., & Norenzayan, A. (2004). Religion's evolutionary landscape: Counterintuition, commitment, compassion, communion. *Behavioral and Brain Sciences*, *27*, 713–770. doi: 10.1017/S0140525X04000172
Atran, S., Sheikh, H., & Gomez, A. (2014). Devoted actors sacrifice for close comrades and sacred cause. *Proceedings of the National Academy of Sciences of the United States of America*, *111*(50), 17,702–17,703. doi: 10.1073/pnas.1420474111
Avolio, B., & Reichard, R. J. (2008). The rise of authentic followership. In R.E. Riggio, I. Chaleff & J Lipman-Bulmen (eds), *The art of followership: How great followers create great leaders and organizations* (pp. 325–337). San Francisco, CA: Jossey-Bass.
Axelrod, R., & Hamilton, W. D. (1981). The evolution of cooperation. *Science*, *211*(4489), 1390–1396. doi: 10.1126/science.7466396
Bailey, G. (2014). The power of Malala. *International Social Work*, *57*(1), 75. doi: 10.1177/0020872813511910.
Bakan, D. (1966). *The duality of human existence: An essay on psychology and religion*. Chicago IL: Rand McNally.
Bass, B. M., & Bass, R. (2009). *The Bass handbook of leadership: Theory, research, and managerial applications*. New York: Simon & Schuster.
BBC (2009). Obama wins Nobel Peace Prize. Retrieved from http://news.bbc.co.uk/2/hi/europe/8298580.stm
Begen, F. M., & Turner-Cobb, J. M. (2015). Benefits of belonging: Experimental manipulation of social inclusion to enhance psychological and physiological health parameters. *Psychology & Health*, *30*(5), 568–582. doi: 10.1080/08870446.2014.991734.
Bélanger, J. J., Caouette, J., Sharvit, K., & Dugas, M. (2014). The psychology of martyrdom: Making the ultimate sacrifice in the name of a cause. *Journal of Personality and Social Psychology*, *107*(3), 494–515. doi: 10.1037/a0036855.
Bernstein, D. (2007). The speech. Retrieved from www.chicagomag.com
Bligh, M. C., Kohles, J. C., & Meindl, J. R. (2004). Charisma under crisis: Presidential leadership, rhetoric, and media responses before and after the September 11th terrorist attacks. *The Leadership Quarterly*, *15*, 211–239. doi: 10.1016/j.leaqua.2004.02.005
Bligh, M. C., Kohles, J. C., & Pillai, R. (2011). Romancing leadership: Past, present, and future. *The Leadership Quarterly*, *22*, 1058–1077. doi: 10.1016/j.leaqua.2011.09.003
Bond, R., & Smith, P. B. (1996). Culture and conformity: A meta-analysis of studies using Asch's (1952b, 1956) line judgment task. *Psychological Bulletin*, *119*(1), 111–137. doi: 10.1037/0033-2909.119.1.111.
Borgerhoff Mulder, M. (1988). Behavioral ecology of traditional societies. *Trends in Ecology and Evolution*, *3*, 260–264.
Boster, F. J., Carpenter, C. J., & Kotowski, M. R. (2015). Validation studies of the maven scale. *Social Influence*, *10*(2), 85–96. doi: 10.1080/15534510.2014.939224
Boster, F. J., Kotowski, M. R., Andrews, K. R., & Serota, K. (2011). Identifying influence: Development and validation of the connectivity, persuasiveness, and maven scales. *Journal Of Communication*, *61*(1), 178–196. doi: 10.1111/j.1460-2466.2010.01531.x
Boyd, R., & Richerson, P. J. (1992). Punishment allows the evolution of cooperation (or anything else) in sizable groups. *Ethology & Sociobiology*, *13*(3), 171–195. doi: 10.1016/0162-3095(92)90032-Y
Bryan, J. H., Redfield, J., & Mader, S. (1971). Words and deeds about altruism and the subsequent reinforcement power of the model. *Child Development*, *42*(5), 1501–1508.
Carey, A. L., Brucks, M. S., Küfner, A. P., Holtzman, N. S., Große Deters, F., Back, M. D., & … Mehl, M.

R. (2015). Narcissism and the use of personal pronouns revisited. *Journal of Personality and Social Psychology, 109*(3), e1–e15. doi: 10.1037/pspp0000029

Carlyle, T. (1840). *On heroes, hero-worship and the heroic in history*. London: Chapman and Hall.

Colby, A., & Damon, W. (1992). *Some do care: Contemporary lives of moral commitment*. New York: Free Press.

Corso, R. A. (2013). The Dalai Lama, President Obama and Pope Francis at Highest Levels of Popularity in U.S. and Five Largest European Countries. Retrieved from www.prnewswire.com/news-releases/the-dalai-lama-president-obama-and-pope-francis-at-highest-levels-of-popularity-in-us-and-five-largest-european-countries-209304431.html.

Cosmides, L. (1989). The logic of social exchange: Has natural selection shaped how humans reason? Studies with the Wason selection task. *Cognition, 31*(3), 187–276.

Cuddy, A. C., Fiske, S. T., & Glick, P. (2008). Warmth and competence as universal dimensions of social perception: The stereotype content model and the BIAS map. In M. P. Zanna, feinM. P. Zanna (eds), *Advances in experimental social psychology, Vol 40* (pp. 61–149). San Diego, CA: Elsevier Academic Press. doi: 10.1016/S0065-2601(07)00002-0

Dalai Lama. (1989). Nobel Prize acceptance speech. December 10. Retrieved from www.dalailama.com/messages/acceptance-speeches/nobel-peace-prize. Copyright © The Nobel Foundation (1989). Reprinted with Permission. www.nobelprize.org/nobel_prizes/peace/laureates/1989/presentation-speech.html

Diehl, M. (1990). The minimal group paradigm: Theoretical explanations and empirical findings. *European Review of Social Psychology, 1*(1), 263–292.

Eagly, A. H., Wood, W., & Chaiken, S. (1978). Causal inferences about communicators and their effect on opinion change. *Journal of Personality and Social Psychology, 36*(4), 424–435. doi: 10.1037/0022-3514.36.4.424

Engler, M., & Engler, P. (2014). How did Gandhi win? Retrieved from http://wagingnonviolence.org/feature/gandhi-win.

Fehr, E., & Gachter, S. (2002). Altruistic punishment in humans. *Nature, 415*, 6868, 137–40.

Feick, L. F., & Price, L. L. (1987). The market maven: A diffuser of marketplace information. *Journal Of Marketing, 51*(1), 83–97. doi: 10.2307/1251146

Feinberg, M., Willer, R., Schultz, M. (2014). Gossip and ostracism promote cooperation in groups. *Psychological Science, 25*(3), 656–664, doi: 10.1177/0956797613510184

Fiske, A. P. (1992). The four elementary forms of sociality: Framework for a unified theory of social relations. *Psychological Review, 99*, 689–723. doi: 10.1037/0033-295X.99.4.689

Flynn, L. R., Goldsmith, R. E., & Eastman, J. K. (1996). Opinion leaders and opinion seekers: Two new measurement scales. *Journal of the Academy of Marketing Science, 24*(2), 137–147. doi: 10.1177/0092070396242004

Frimer, J. A. (in press). Groups create moral superheroes to defend sacred values. In J. Forgas, P. van Lange, & L. Jussim (eds), *The social psychology of morality*. Psychology Press, New York.

Frimer, J. A., & Brandt, M. J. (2015). The ideological happiness gap favors the party in power. Manuscript under review.

Frimer, J. A., & Sinclair, L. (2015). Moral heroes gaze up and right. Manuscript under review.

Frimer, J. A., Aquino, K., Gebauer, J. E., Zhu, L., & Oakes, H. (2015). A decline in prosocial language helps explain public disapproval of the U.S. Congress. *Proceedings of the National Academy of Sciences of the United States of America, 112*, 6591–6594. doi: 10.1073/pnas.1500355112

Frimer, J. A., Gaucher, D., & Schaefer, N. K. (2014). Political conservatives' affinity for obedience to authority is loyal, not blind. *Personality and Social Psychology Bulletin, 40*, 1205–1214. doi: 10.1177/0146167214538672

Frimer, J. A., Tell, C. E., & Haidt, J. (2015). Liberals condemn sacrilege too: The harmless desecration of Cerro Torre. *Social Psychological and Personality Science, 6*, 878–886. doi: 10.1177/1948550615597974

Frimer, J. A., Walker, L. J., Dunlop, W. L., Lee, B., & Riches, A. (2011). The integration of agency and communion in moral personality: Evidence of enlightened self-interest. *Journal of Personality and Social Psychology, 101*, 149–163. doi: 10.1037/a0023780

Frimer, J. A., Walker, L. J., Riches, A., Lee, B., & Dunlop, W. L. (2012). Hierarchical integration of agency and communion: A study of influential moral figures. *Journal of Personality, 80*, 1117–1145. doi: 10.1111/j.1467-6494.2012.00764.x

Frimer, J. A., Zhu, L., & Decter-Frain, A. (2015). Do givers leak their social motives through what they talk about? Maybe not. Unpublished manuscript, Department of Psychology, University of Winnipeg, Winnipeg, Canada.

Gardner, W. L. (2003). Perceptions of leader charisma, effectiveness, and integrity: effects of exemplification, delivery, and ethical reputation. *Management Communication Quarterly, 16*(4), 502–527. doi: 10.1177/0893318903251324

Gardner, W. L., & Avolio, B. J. (1998). The charismatic relationship: A dramaturgical perspective. *The Academy of Management Review, 23*(1), 32–58. doi: 10.2307/259098

Gladwell, M. (2000). *The tipping point: How little things can make a big difference*. Boston, MA: Little, Brown.

Goethals, G. R., & Allison, S. T. (2012). Making heroes: The construction of courage, competence, and virtue. In J. M. Olson and M. P. Zanna (eds), *Advances in Experimental Social Psychology*, (Vol. 46, pp. 183–235). San Diego, CA: Elsevier.

Granovetter, M. S. (1973). The strength of weak ties. *American Journal of Sociology, 78*(6), p.1360–1380.

Greenberg, J., & Arndt, J. (2011). Terror management theory. *Handbook of Theories of Social Psychology, 1*, 398–415. Thousand Oaks, CA: Sage Publications Ltd.

Hagerty, B. M., Williams, R. A., Coyne, J. C., & Early, M. R. (1996). Sense of belonging and indicators of social and psychological functioning. *Archives of Psychiatric Nursing, 10*(4), 235–244. doi: 10.1016/S0883-9417(96)80029-X

Haidt, J. (2012). *The righteous mind: Why good people are divided by politics and religion*. New York: Pantheon Books.

Haidt, J., & Algoe, S. (2004). Moral amplification and the emotions that attach us to saints and demons. In J. Greenberg, S. L. Koole, T. Pyszczynski, J. Greenberg, S. L. Koole, & T. Pyszczynski (eds), *Handbook of experimental existential psychology* (pp. 322–335). New York: Guilford Press.

Hale, C. J., Hannum, J. W., & Espelage, D. L. (2005). Social support and physical health: The importance of belonging. *Journal of American College Health, 53*(6), 276–284. doi: 10.3200/JACH.53.6.276-284

Henrich, J. (2009). The evolution of costly displays, cooperation and religion: Credibility enhancing displays and their implications for cultural evolution. *Evolution and Human Behavior, 30*(4), 244–260. doi: 10.1016/j.evolhumbehav.2009.03.005

Hogg, M. A. (2001). A social identity theory of leadership. *Personality and Social Psychology Review, 5*(3), 184–200. doi: 10.1207/S15327957PSPR0503_1

Hogg, M. A. (2008). Social identity process and the empowerment of followers. In R. E. Riggio, I. Chaleff & J. Lipman-Bulmen (eds), *The art of followership: How great followers create great leaders and organizations* (pp. 267–276). San Francisco, CA: Jossey-Bass.

Howell, J. M., & Shamir, B. (2005). The role of followers in the charismatic leadership process: relationships and their consequences. *The Academy of Management Review, 30*(1), 96–112. http://dx.doi.org.libproxy.uwinnipeg.ca/10.2307/20159097

Huggett, K. N., Greenberg, R. B., Rao, D., Richards, B., Chauvin, S. W., Fulton, T. B., & ... Simpson, D. (2012). The design and utility of institutional teaching awards: A literature review. *Medical Teacher, 34*(11), 907–919. doi: 10.3109/0142159X.2012.731102

Invisible Children. (2014). Financials. Retrieved from http://invisiblechildren.com/financials.

Irons, W. (1979). Cultural and biological success. In N.A. Chagnon and W. Irons (eds), *Evolutionary biology and human social behavior* (pp. 257–272). North Scituate, MA: Duxbury Press.

Jones, E. E., & Harris, V. A. (1967). The attribution of attitudes. *Journal of Experimental Social Psychology 3*(1): 1–24. doi: 10.1016/0022-1031(67)90034-0

Jost, J. T., Banaji, M. R. and Nosek, B. A. (2004). A decade of system justification theory: Accumulated evidence of conscious and unconscious bolstering of the status quo. *Political Psychology, 25*, 881–919. doi: 10.1111/j.1467-9221.2004.00402.x

Katz, E., & Lazarsfeld, P. F. (1955). *Personal influence: The part played by people in the flow of mass communications*. New York: The Free Press.

Kelly, J. A., St Lawrence, J. S., Diaz, Y. E., Stevenson, L. Y., Hauth, A. C., Brasfield, T. L., Kalichman, S. C., Smith, J. E., & Andrew, M. E. (1992). HIV risk behavior reduction following intervention with key opinion leaders of population: an experimental analysis. *American Journal of Public Health, 81*(2), 168–171.

King, M. L. (1963). I have a dream. August 28. The King Center. Retrieved from: www.thekingcenter.org/archive/document/i-have-dream-1.

King, M. L. (1968). I've been to the mountaintop. April 3. The King Center. Retrieved from www.thekingcenter.org/archive/document/ive-been-mountaintop-1.

Kinsella, E. L., Ritchie, T. D., & Igou, E. R. (2015). Zeroing in on heroes: A prototype analysis of hero features. *Journal of Personality and Social Psychology, 108*(1), 114–127. doi: 10.1037/a0038463

Klapp, O. (1948). The creation of popular heroes. *American Journal of Sociology, 54*(2), 135–141. Retrieved from www.jstor.org/stable/2771362.

Kohlberg, L. (1984). *Philosophy of moral development*. New York: Harper & Row.

Kramer, A. D. I., Guillory, J. E., & Hancock, J. T. (2014). Experimental evidence of massive-scale emotional contagion through social networks. *Proceedings of the National Academy of Sciences of the United States of America, 111*(24), 8788–8780. doi: 10.1073/pnas.1320040111

Krueger, A. B., & Maleckova, J. (2002). *Education, poverty, political violence and terrorism: Is there a causal connection?* No. w9074. Washington, DC: National Bureau of Economic Research.

Kruglanski, A. W., Chen, X., Dechesne, M., Fishman, S., & Orehek, E. (2009). Fully committed: Suicide bombers' motivation and the quest for personal significance. *Political Psychology*, *30*(3), 331–357.

Levy, D. A. (1992). The liberating effects of interpersonal influence: An empirical investigation of disinhibitory contagion. *The Journal Of Social Psychology*, *132*(4), 469–473. doi: 10.1080/00224545.1992.9924726

Levy, D. A., & Nail, P. R. (1993). Contagion: A theoretical and empirical review and reconceptualization. *Genetic, Social, and General Psychology Monographs*, *119*(2), 233–284.

Lincoln, A. (1865). Second Inaugural Address. March 4. Abraham Lincoln Online. Retrieved from www.abrahamlincolnonline.org/lincoln/speeches/inaug2.htm

Mandela, N. (1964). I am prepared to die: Nelson Mandela's statement from the dock at the opening of the defence case in the Rivonia Trial. April 20. Nelson Mandela Foundation. Retrieved from www.nelson-mandela.org/content/page/speeches

Marcello, P. C. (2003). *The Dalai Lama: A biography*. Santa Barbara, CA: Greenwood Press.

McAdams, D. P., & Guo, J. (2015). Narrating the generative life. *Psychological Science*, *26*(4), 475–483. doi: 10.1177/0956797614568318

McCauley, C. (2007). Psychological issues in understanding terrorism and the response to terrorism. In B. Bongar, L. M. Brown, L. E. Beutler, J. N. Breckenridge, P. G. Zimbardo, B. Bongar, ... P. G. Zimbardo (eds), *Psychology of terrorism* (pp. 13–31). New York: Oxford University Press.

Meindl, J. R. (1995). The romance of leadership as a follower-centric theory: A social constructionist approach. *The Leadership Quarterly*, *6*(3), 329–341. doi: 10.1016/1048-9843(95)90012-8

Meindl, J. R., Ehrlich, S. B., & Dukerich, J. M. (1985). The romance of leadership. *Administrative Science Quarterly*, 78–102. doi: 10.2307/2392813

Newman, G. E., & Cain, D. M. (2014). Tainted altruism: when doing some good is evaluated as worse than doing no good at all. *Psychological Science*, *25*(3), 648–655. doi: 10.1177/0956797613504785

Obama, B. (2008). Barack Obama's New Hampshire Primary speech. January 8. Retrieved from www.nytimes.com/2008/01/08/us/politics/08text-obama.html?pagewanted=all.

O'Connor, C. (2014). Bain deal makes TOMS shoes founder Blake Mycoskie a $300 million man. *Forbes*. Retrieved from www.forbes.com/sites/clareoconnor/2014/08/20/bain-deal-makes-toms-shoes-founder-blake-mycoskie-a-300-million-man.

Pfeffer, J. (1977). The ambiguity of leadership. *Academy of Management Review*, *2*(1), 104–112. doi: 10.5465/AMR.1977.4409175

Rablen, M. D., & Oswald, A. J. (2008). Mortality and immortality: The Nobel Prize as an experiment into the effect of status upon longevity. *Journal of Health Economics*, *27*(6), 1462–1471.

Rasmussen Reports (2011). 11% Say Communism Better Than U.S. System of Politics and Economics. Retrieved from www.rasmussenreports.com/public_content/politics/general_politics/march_2011/11_say_communism_better_than_u_s_system_of_politics_and_economics.

Reagan, R. (1964). A time for choosing. October 27. Ronald Reagan Presidential Library & Museum. Retrieved from www.nationalcenter.org/ReaganChoosing1964.html.

Reagan, R. (1981). Inaugural Address. January 20. Retrieved from www.presidency.ucsb.edu/ws/?pid=43130.

Reagan, R. (1983). Remarks at the Annual Convention of the National Association of Evangelicals in Orlando, Florida. March 8. The Public Papers of President Ronald W. Reagan, Ronald Reagan Presidential Library. Retrieved from https://reaganlibrary.archives.gov/archives/speeches/1987/061287d.htm.

Reimert, I., Bolhuis, J. E., Kemp, B., & Rodenburg, T. B. (2015). Emotions on the loose: shermanEmotional contagion and the role of oxytocin in pigs. *Animal Cognition*, *18*(2), 517–532. doi: 10.1007/s10071-014-0820-6

Richerson, P. J., & Boyd, R. (1998). The evolution of human ultra-sociality. Retrieved from www.researchgate.net/publication/2314563_The_Evolution_of_Human_Ultra-sociality.

Sackeim, H. A., Gur, R. C., & Saucy, M. C. (1978). Emotions are expressed more intensely on the left side of the face. *Science*, *202*, 434–436. doi: 10.1126/science.705335

St Lawrence, J. S., Brasfield, T. L., Diaz, Y. E., Jefferson, K. W., Reynolds, M. T., & Leonard, M. O. (1994). Three-year follow-up of an HIV risk-reduction intervention that used popular peers. *American Journal of Public Health*, *84*(12), 2027–2028.

Stech, E. L. (2008). A new leadership-follower paradigm. In R.E. Riggio, I. Chaleff & J Lipman-Bulmen (eds), *The art of followership: How great followers create great leaders and organizations* (pp. 41–52). San Francisco, CA: Jossey-Bass.

Sümegi, Z., Oláh, K., & Topál, J. (2014). Emotional contagion in dogs as measured by change in cognitive task performance. *Applied Animal Behaviour Science*, *160*, 106–115. doi: 10.1016/j.applanim.2014.09.001

Tajfel, H. (1970). Experiments in intergroup discrimination. *Scientific American*, *223*(5), 96–102.

Tetlock, P. E. (2003). Thinking the unthinkable: Sacred values and taboo cognitions. *Trends in Cognitive Sciences*, *7*, 320–324. doi: 10.1016/S1364-6613(03)00135-9

Thondup, G., & Thurston, A. F. (2015). *The noodle maker of Kalimpong: The untold story of my struggle for Tibet* (1st ed.). Philadelphia, PA: PublicAffairs.

Travers, J., & Milgram, S. (1969). An experimental study of the small world problem. *Sociometry*, *32*(4), 425–443.

Walker, L. J., & Frimer, J. A. (2007). Moral personality of brave and caring exemplars. *Journal of Personality and Social Psychology*, *93*, 845–860. doi: 10.1037/0022-3514.93.5.845

Walster, E., Aronson, E., & Abrahams, D. (1966). On increasing the persuasiveness of a low prestige communicator. *Journal of Experimental Social Psychology*, *2*, 325–342.

Weber, J. M., & Murnighan, J. K. (2008). Suckers or saviors? Consistent contributors in social dilemmas. *Journal of Personality and Social Psychology*, *95*(6), 1340–1353.

Whitehouse, H., McQuinn, B., Buhrmester, M., & Swann, W. B., Jr. (2014). Brothers in arms: Libyan revolutionaries bond like family. *Proceedings of the National Academy of Sciences*, *111*(50), 17,783–17,785. doi: 10.1073/pnas.1416284111

Wintrobe, R. (2006). *Rational extremism: the political economy of radicalism*. Cambridge, UK: Cambridge University Press.

Woods, F. A. (1913). *The influence of monarchs: Steps in a new science of history*. New York: Macmillan.

Yong, M. H., & Ruffman, T. (2014). Emotional contagion: Dogs and humans show a similar physiological response to human infant crying. *Behavioural Processes*, *108*, 155–165. doi: 10.1016/j.beproc.2014.10.006

Zanolie, K., van Dantzig, S., Boot, I., Wijnen, J., Schubert, T. W., Giessner, S. R., & Pecher, D. (2012). Mighty metaphors: Behavioral and ERP evidence that power shifts attention on a vertical dimension. *Brain and Cognition*, *78*(1), 50–58.

8

The Hero Organism
Advancing the Embodiment of Heroism Thesis in the Twenty-First Century

Olivia Efthimiou

> [C]ontrary to the idea of the heroic elect ... most people are capable of heroism with the *right mindset* and under *certain conditions* that call for heroic action ... The *banality of heroism* argument ... asks the question, "*what if the capability to act heroically is also fundamentally ordinary and available to all of us?*"
>
> (Franco, Blau & Zimbardo, 2011, p. 100; emphasis added)

Heroic accounts have captured the human imagination throughout history. In postmodern times the academic community has witnessed a resurgence in the intellectual and empirical pursuit of the concept of heroism—the advent of the multiple disciplinary field of heroism science signals the end of the monopoly of myth, fiction and popular culture on the study of heroism, offering a multi-perspective lens for the active and rigorous observation of this enduring phenomenon. Research efforts to date, however, have largely focused on its psychosocial aspects, without addressing the interaction with and relationship to the body in sufficient depth. This chapter aims to contribute to growing heroism research by considering the sidelined role of the body, and embodiment more broadly in the heroic process and experience.

First, I will contextualize this agenda in broader significant intellectual shifts. Second, the joint reading of contemporary and traditional phenomenological embodiment schools of thought, in particular Merleau-Ponty's (1962, 1964) address of contemporary heroism and his legacy, together with Allison and Goethals' (2014) *heroic leadership dynamic*, is used to form an "embodiment of heroism thesis"—heroism is defined as a distinct state of embodied consciousness accessible to all human agents in everyday lived experience. The idea of heroism as embodied skill acquisition is used as an example. This thesis rests on the notion of the body as compatible with, but distinct from traditional biological conceptualizations. In the third section, the application of Johnson's (2008) outline of the five facets of a body to heroism results in two transdisciplinary conceptual frameworks: the *heroic body* (as biological organism; the ecological; the social; the cultural; and the phenomenological), and the *hero organism*. In the fourth and final section, I map the epistemological and methodological contours of the "dynamical hero organism self-system." This is a preliminary investigation of organisms against cutting-edge theories that demonstrate peak states, agency and embodiment—physical intelligence and flow—resulting in the definition of the heart of heroism as biopsychosocial resilience and transformation. As Allison and Goethals (2014) surmise, we are all wired for heroism—to uncover this we must develop an intimate understanding of the processes, functions and consequences of the "heroic embodied mind."

Olivia Efthimiou

The Dissolution of Disciplinary Boundaries, the Return of the Body and the Rise of Heroism Science

Heroism science seeks to reconceptualize heroism and reinvigorate its relevance in the twenty-first century, by using a broad range of epistemological and methodological tools to promote widespread holistic well-being. The timing of its emergence is not coincidental—it is representative of a broader shift in intellectual thought towards greater "multiple disciplinarity" (Choi & Pak, 2006, p. 358). The opening up of the study of heroism beyond the humanities to increasingly "integrative" disciplines such as psychology (Bandura, 2001, p. 12) is in many ways revolutionary. It reflects the breakdown of "disastrous" (Johnson, 2010) dualisms in which our history is deeply, but thankfully not irreversibly, steeped. Most prevalent is the mind-body dichotomy, or the long-held view that the mind and body are to be looked at separately, with the brain's development remaining fixed following our formative years (Johnson, 2010). Kinsella (2012, p. 85) highlights the sweeping "physical, psychological, and social benefits provided by heroes." Researchers (Kafashan, Sparks, Rotella, & Barclay, Chapter 2, this volume; Preston, Chapter 4, this volume; Rusch, Leunissen & van Vugt, 2015; Smirnov, Arrow, Kennett & Orbell, 2007) are just beginning to embark on important work that investigates the biological and evolutionary aspects of heroism, with the physical aspects only having been addressed peripherally in the literature (e.g. physical attributes, physical strength, gender).

This renewed interest in the centrality of the body has been gaining considerable ground by a new generation of scholars since the mid-twentieth century. Tremendous advances in the cognitive sciences spanning a vast array of disciplines from "genetics" to "linguistics" (Johnson, 2008, p. 160) are now making it possible for us to begin to construct novel conceptualizations of human behaviors. Heroism is no exception—Gray (2010), for example, is in the early stages of demonstrating the remarkable links between the heroic mindset and its impact on our bodies. In what is perhaps the most fascinating unfolding story of "genomics meets heroism," The Resilience Project led by Dr Stephen Friend at Sage Bionetworks and Dr Eric Shadt at the Icahn School of Medicine at Mount Sinai is a groundbreaking global study looking for "genetic heroes" who have demonstrated unusual immunity to debilitating diseases and "genetic mutations" (Giller, 2014). This is prime evidence that the way we are looking at disease, well-being and the human condition is shifting ground at the nexus of science and culture.

This increasing momentum stands to have far-reaching impacts not only for the study of heroism, but research overall. Bandura (2001, p. 12) highlights the "changing face of psychology," the primary field presently engaged in the rigorous analysis of heroism. Chemero (2013, p. 145) notes that "there have been two ways to do psychology" from its inception: the mainstream "Structuralist," and the nascent "Functionalist" approach. The functionalist view of the "whole is greater than the sum of its parts" was born out of a dissident tradition of scholars seeking a deeper understanding of how individuals function in their broader environment, and how this in turn affects them at the deepest sensorial and embodied level of consciousness. The emerging field of "Radical embodied cognitive science is an interdisciplinary approach to psychology that combines ideas from the phenomenological tradition with ecological psychology and dynamical systems modeling" (Chemero, 2013, p. 145). The timeless, intricate and deeply enduring nature of heroism figures as a prime candidate for this multi-spectrum framework. Heroism science therefore has the potential to radicalize the face of psychology, cognitive sciences and beyond, re-shaping and challenging fundamental notions of what it means to be human in the process.

The mind–body connection and the vital role of the body, however, still remain largely absent from emerging perspectives on heroism, despite the significant strides that have occurred in only a decade. The embodiment of heroism thesis presented here aligns with radical embodied cognitive science's agenda in a number of ways. At its very core, it aims to supplant "the current trend of supplementing standard cognitive psychology with occasional references to the body"

(Chemero, 2013, p. 145). Franco et al. (2011, p. 106) highlight "the role of physical risk as a determining element in the public's view of prototypical heroic action," noting that social heroes are not commonly perceived *as heroic* as "physical risk heroes," such as firefighters and soldiers. The embodiment of heroism thesis differs in its proposition that *all types of heroism encompass a physiological and embodied basis or aspect of experience*. In this critical point of departure we cannot distinguish between "physical" and "non-physical" heroism. It is the aim of this thesis to counteract such public pre-conceptions and empirical observations of the phenomenon.

The Heroic Embodied Mind: Heroism as an Embodied State of Consciousness

What precisely *is* a "body"? This is perhaps the most poignant question any embodiment theorist can ask, and an enterprise that is far from simple given the intricate layers with which our corporeality is intimately interwoven—from the cultural, to the biological, the spiritual, the psychological and so forth. Addressing this question becomes an inevitable focal point on our journey to developing a deep appreciation of the heroic experience. Smyth (2010) and Moya (2014) provide illuminating interpretations of some of the core theories set out by the "father" of embodiment, French phenomenological philosopher Maurice Merleau-Ponty. In particular, Smyth's (2010) elucidation of Merleau-Ponty's (1964) essay "Man, the Hero" (originally published in 1948) serves as a critical insight into the vital contribution embodiment theory can make to contemporary understandings of heroism.

Merleau-Ponty (1964 and 2012, cited in Moya, 2014, p. 1) argued that "there is no hard separation between bodily conduct and intelligent conduct; rather, there is a unity of behavior that expresses the intentionality and hence the meaning of this conduct." This is a non-reductionist view of the brain and body; this idea of an "*embodied mind* [emphasis added] or a minded body" (Gallagher & Zahavi, 2008, p. 153) integrates and "transcends the physiological and psychological" (Merleau-Ponty, 1964 and 2012, as cited in Moya, 2014, p. 1) dismantling the mind-body dichotomy. Accordingly, the concept of a "body" in the embodiment of heroism thesis is not confined to traditional biological interpretations. Rather, it is a transdisciplinary understanding that embraces biology and evolution, but transcends it to consider the critical inter-relationship with the mind, broader environment, and metaphysical experiences beyond these. As will be discussed, the physical, mental, social *and* spiritual modes of experience are co-present in, dynamic and integral to the embodiment of heroism and the heroic body.

In this integrative conceptual framework the body appropriates "itself a form of *embodied consciousness* [emphasis added]" (Merleau-Ponty, 1964 and 2012, as cited in Moya, 2014, p. 1). The foundation of this embodied state of consciousness that gives expression to the intentionality and meaning of embodied action, according to Merleau-Ponty (2012, as cited in Moya, 2014, p. 2), is *habit*:

> the situated character of the person explains that there is, at the same time, a "general" existence as well as an existence that is linked with the effectiveness of action, and which we can call "personal." Being anchored in the world makes the person renounce a part of his or her protagonism because he or she already possesses a series of habitualities.

This concordance of the general and personal nature of situated embodiment reminds us of the paradoxical universal and context-specific property of heroism (Franco et al., 2011; Kinsella, 2012). Heroic protagonists' actions may be theorized as being deeply embedded in a readily accessible habitual apparatus, invoking Allison and Goethals' (2014, p. 175) proposition that any person is "developmentally equipped" for heroic action, which can be adjusted according to the sociocultural setting.

Crucially, for Merleau-Ponty (1962, as cited in Smyth, 2010, p. 177) "*the locus of heroic action is the habitual body.*" This notion of habituality provides a fundamental link between embodiment, Carl Jung's innateness of archetypes theory proposed over 50 years ago, and heroic leadership or action. Merleau-Ponty (2012, as cited in Moya, 2014, p. 2) makes a distinction between "the habitual body—that of general and pre-reflexive existence—from the actual—that of personal and reflexive existence." The habitual body corresponds with Jung's conceptualization of archetypes as innate, universal and pre-conscious, which has been the focus of rigorous debate by analytical psychologists (for examples see Goodwyn, 2010; Knox, 2004). This powerful correlation between the habitual body, archetypes and their pre-reflexivity lends credence to the "hypothesis of shared generic dimensions of embodiment," with archetypes figuring as an explanation for the "bodily grounding of our conceptual systems" and "key concepts in languages and symbol systems around the world" which feature so prominently in hero stories (Johnson, 2008, p. 162). The archetypal habitual heroic body is so firmly embedded in "*deep time*" (Allison & Goethals, 2014, p. 171) and the pre-conscious that it is impossible to ignore its perpetuity, as is manifested in the endurance of cultural tropes. Its form may change across contexts with the *actual* heroic body's conscious domain of lived situated experience, but the universality of its *habituality* demands due attention.

Situating the heroic body in pre-conscious habitualities and supporting its rootedness in the innateness of the hero archetype could be viewed as an annihilation of our reflexive capacity and free will. How can we possibly be active participants in our life choices and wilful heroic actors if we are driven by pre-programmed archetypal bodily scripts drilled into us by evolution? But speaking of an embodied heroic mind and archetypal locus of heroic action is by no means a static view of the body. Despite the possibilityof the existence of such pre-conscious mental and bodily schemas, there is a perpetual "*dialog* between environment and subject," and an "understanding that both always co-penetrate each other" (Merleau-Ponty, 2012, as cited in Moya, 2014, p. 2). For Merleau-Ponty (1962, as cited in Smyth, 2010, p. 177) the localization of heroism in the habitual body is not a mindless and tragic thrusting of "one's body into a lethal situation" signaling some temporal dislocation from our rational faculties. Merleau-Ponty's (1962, as cited in Smyth, 2010, p. 168) "contemporary hero" always operates in the ever-present dynamic exchange between the habitual pre-reflexive and actual reflexive body. The heroic actor is constantly negotiating meaning between her instinctual patterns and lived environment. This is exemplified in Merleau-Ponty's (1964 and 2012, as cited in Moya, 2014, p. 1) notion of the "*lived* or *own* body and of *lived* space." In an embodied reading the heroic actor is seen "as subject, as experiencer, as agent" (Gallagher & Zahavi, 2008, p. 155).

There is a crucial link between this concept of lived heroism, embodiment and emerging notions of everyday heroism. According to Smyth (2010, p. 167), Merleau-Ponty's (1964) brief essay on heroism aimed "to supply experiential evidence attesting to the latent presence of human universality," reminiscent of Campbell's (1949) seminal work on the universality of the "hero's journey" as a pervasive mythical structure through culture and time. Merleau-Ponty (1964, as cited in Smyth, 2010, p. 170) had a very specific agenda: "to define 'the existential attitude (as a general phenomenon of our times, and not as a school of thought)'." The definition of this existential attitude is exemplified in his notion of the contemporary hero. For Merleau-Ponty (1964), like Campbell (1949), the exaltation of heroes is a timeless cultural phenomenon. Merleau-Ponty (1964) notes a poignant shift in the hero in history from the Christian notion of sacrifice and the transcendental, to its grounding in the everyday individual with Hegel. It is in these Hegelian roots that we find the birth of the concept of the "everyday hero": "*living contact with the present* as the germinal origins of the future" (Merleau-Ponty, 1964, as cited in Smyth, 2010, p. 174). This central feature of Hegelian heroism can be said to be the core premise of the emerging field of heroism science and the "new heroism" (Zimbardo & Ellsberg, 2013), characteristic of the increased infiltration of heroism as an "embodied and embedded" (Gallagher & Zahavi, 2008, p. 74) form of core human action and civic engagement.

Allison and Goethals (2014, p. 170) have introduced the *heroic leadership dynamic* (HLD) to gain a deeper understanding of the universal profundity of heroism and hero stories through time. The central premise of the HLD is the notion that "hero stories fulfill important cognitive and emotional needs" (Allison & Goethals, 2014, p. 169). The profundity of this need for story has been theorized by Price (1978, p. 3) as vital to the "species *Homo sapiens*—second in necessity apparently after nourishment and before love and shelter." The HLD suggests that hero narratives serve two core functions: "*epistemic*" and "*energizing*." The former "refers to the knowledge and wisdom that hero stories impart to us"; the latter "to the ways that hero stories inspire us and promote personal growth" (Allison & Goethals, 2014, p. 170).

Can Allison and Goethals' (2014) HLD model be expanded to biological needs and situated in an embodied sense of self? The primacy of the attainment of knowledge and wisdom in heroic leadership's epistemic function takes on a profound significance with the concept of a *lived heroic body* and its extension to the corporeal. The habitual property of human action suggests a type of "corporeal *knowledge*" as generator and distributor of bodily meaning (Merleau-Ponty, 1964 and 2012, as cited in Moya, 2014, p. 1). This is the original and truly embodied notion of the gaining of wisdom in the experiential terms and deep altering of consciousness that was implied by the ancient Greeks. It predates the school of thought of Plato and Aristotle in which the roots of contemporary Western culture may be traced, which gave primacy to knowledge acquisition as an exercise that is driven by pure reason and logic (Kingsley, 1999). This potentially profoundly transformative effect of the epistemic function of hero stories which lies in their "*transrational*" qualities (Allison & Goethals, 2014, p. 170; Rohr, 2011) speaks to the notion of the lived body as "a constitutive or transcendental principle, precisely because it is involved in the very possibility of experience" (Gallagher & Zahavi, 2008, p. 153). This grounds the everyday heroic experience in our bodies and the immediacy of the world around us, in meanings that cannot be reduced to conventional logic.

The energizing function of heroic leadership also takes on a heightened meaning in an embodied reading of everyday heroism. Moya (2014, p. 2) highlights that Gallagher and Zahavi (2008) demonstrate how perception "is not a passive reception of information, but instead implies activity, specifically, the movement of our body." In this "*enactive*" approach to embodied cognition (Varela, Thompson & Rosch, 1991, p. xx) we can use embodiment theories to apply the notion of personal growth to the idea of heroic action as skill acquisition. Heroism is being reconceptualized as a behavior that can be trained and instilled in people of all ages, especially the younger generation. Initiatives such as the Heroic Imagination Project (http://heroicimagination.org) and The Hero Construction Company (www.heroconstruction.org) which aim at educating school children on Campbell's (1949) hero's journey, and inspiring and energizing heroic behavior to combat bullying, social injustice and promote civic action, evoke this emerging understanding of everyday heroism as a skill that can be acquired. In this spirit, Zimbardo (2015) has made a call for a public commitment to heroic action, and ordinary people to think of themselves as "heroes-in-training." For embodiment theorists skill acquisition is centered in the "corporealization of habit" (Moya, 2014, p. 3); any skill that was once external and unfamiliar to us penetrates our corporeality when fully grasped, connoting "beginner" through to "expert" stages of heroic embodied skill acquisition (Dreyfus & Dreyfus, 1999, pp. 105, 109). The energizing function of heroism permeates all aspects of our interiority, transcending the mental and psychological arenas—it is a property innate to us all which we can learn to master until it becomes fully embodied and integrated into our corporeality, accentuating our corporeal knowledge.

This embodied contextualization of the contemporary hero questions readings of heroic acts as "spontaneous" (for example, "subway heroes" in New York who save commuters about to be struck by an oncoming train). One might begin to consider the events that led the individual to commit the heroic act as the product of a trained and astute embodied consciousness, culminating in the perfect unison of innateness and preparedness, or nature and nurture. This is contrary to what others might perceive as virtually seamless, even insane or irrational, reflecting the "junction of madness … and reason" in the contemporary hero (Merleau-Ponty, 1964, p. 324f/183; cf. p. 9/4). According to Smyth (2010, p. 177), for Merleau-Ponty (1962) "heroic action precisely instances the coincidence of" the actual and habitual body; "This is the condition of absolute knowledge, 'the point at which consciousness finally becomes equal to its spontaneous life and regains its self-possession'." The interchanging of heroism with this embodied condition of absolute knowledge aligns with the grounding of Allison and Goethals' (2014) core epistemic function of the HLD in the acquisition of knowledge and wisdom.

This is a remarkably complex view of heroic action which cannot be reduced to any one aspect of existence or reference point. The point at which consciousness joins with its innateness is not a debilitating one that robs us of our self-determinism, according to Merleau-Ponty (1962, as cited in Smyth, 2010). By contrast, it may be the most profoundly liberating experience; Merleau-Ponty (1962 and 1964, as cited in Smyth, 2010, p. 178) states that "the hero is fully invested in the realization of freedom, *understood in universal terms*," rendering the contemporary hero an "exemplary *vivant*, or living person." This point of unison between the habitual and actual body is where heroic "*operant intentionality*" (Merleau-Ponty, 2012, as cited in Moya, 2014, p. 1) and sensibility "meets its maker" at its purest, both conscious and preconscious, embodied form. If we speak of heroism as an embodied acquired skill, this reading of Merleau-Ponty's contemporary hero foreshadows the manifestation of heroism at its peak state.

This embodied engagement with our surroundings implies an active meaning-making process and understanding of the lived heroic body as always "coming to be" (Merleau-Ponty, 2012, as cited in Moya, 2014, p. 1). It is in direct agreement with the "Temporal and Dynamic Components" of Allison and Goethals' (2014, p. 177) HLD "in which the psychology of heroism unfolds over time." This can be extended to the lived corporeal experience of heroism—we may thus speak of an embodied *hero-in-process* or *hero-becoming*. In the embodiment of heroism thesis *heroic action is conceived as a simultaneously universal, yet deeply personal, distinct state of embodied consciousness and intentionality. The lived heroic body is grounded in corporeal knowledge generated both from a pre-reflexive or transrational set of innate habitualities, and conscious dynamic inquiry within lived space*. This phenomenologically-informed definition suggests that heroism must assume its rightful place on the stage of consciousness in the cognitive sciences.

What Makes a Heroic Body?

What is the makeup of a lived heroic body? Founded on Johnson's (2008) five-dimensional framework of a generic body, the embodiment of heroism is staged across the biological, the ecological, the social, the cultural and the phenomenological spheres of experience. Below is a preliminary outline of each of these dimensions.

The Heroic Body as Biological Organism

The concept of a heroic body travels far beyond certain physical characteristics, behavioral or physiological patterns reduced to traditional notions of personality and biology. This is a dynamic view of the heroic actor as a:

> functioning biological organism that can perceive, move within, respond to, and transform its environment … It is this whole body, with its various systems working in marvellous coordination, that makes possible the qualities, images, feelings, emotions, and thought

patterns that constitute the ground of our [heroic] meaning and understanding.

(Johnson, 2008, p. 164)

This provides a foundation for the re-conceptualization of human organisms in their behavior, biology *and* culture, as *hero organisms*, to employ a transdisciplinary terminology.

The heroic body as biological organism is grounded in the "*body schema*," or the "preconscious capacities" and "system of sensory-motor functions" of the habitual body (Gallagher, 2005, p. 26; Johnson, 2008, p. 164). This is an extension of Allison and Goethals' (2014, p. 170) description of the epistemic function of hero stories in imparting "wisdom by providing mental models, or scripts" of heroic action, to embodied existence and bodily scripts pre-dating language and the construction of these stories in written or oral form. All action and perception is grounded in the corporeal for embodiment theorists such as Gallagher and Zahavi (2008). The attainment of wisdom in the process of heroic action is therefore no exception. We may ask for example: do heroic actors talk, think, move, perceive, and sense their environments in common patterns? How is this "set of structural patterns" (Johnson, 2008, p. 164), capabilities or scripts dynamically transforming and evolving with their interaction with the environment? Are modern sensory-motor manifestations of heroic action similar to or significantly different from ancient ones? These are just some cursory questions that setting a transdisciplinary framework for the reading of the heroic body can spark further inquiry into.

Johnson (2008, p. 161) states, "It is not surprising to find shared dimensions of bodily experience underlying all aspects of meaning and thought. Indeed, this is exactly what we would expect, given our animal nature and our bodily capacities for perception and action." Allison and Goethals (2014, p. 171) highlight the significance of the epistemic function of metaphor, especially in the work of thinkers such as James (1878) who centralize it as a vehicle of human meaning: "heroic narratives and their meaningful symbols serve as metaphors for easing our understanding of complex, mysterious phenomena." The function of metaphor is a central tenet in embodiment literature; one of the main drivers of Johnson's (2008, p. 160) body of work, for example, has been to demonstrate "how imaginative processes like conceptual metaphor make it possible for us to do all of our most amazing feats of abstract reasoning, from moral deliberation to politics to logic." Metaphor could therefore be the key to unravelling the shared body schemas of the heroic body, its pre-conscious and evolutionary roots.

Lobel (2014a, 2014b, 2014c) illustrates how the cognitive sciences are beginning to enrich our understanding of the embodied aspects of meaning-making processes. Lobel (2014c) defines embodied cognition as "the idea that the body and the mind work together and that our bodily feelings, our physical sensations influence our thoughts, our decisions, our behaviors, our emotions, and what is more important often without our awareness"—this is an "indissoluble link." Lobel (2014c) denotes the critical importance of metaphor in establishing associations between physical objects, behaviors and perceptions of others—this is "embodied cognition in language," and the premise that we use concrete objects to describe abstract concepts. Physical intelligence researchers are demonstrating that metaphors are more than just figures of speech—they are grounded in embodied experience. Indeed, Johnson (2008, p. 161) notes that a number of:

> cognitive linguists have argued that it is ... shared sensorimotor structures of generic bodies that underlie much of the syntax and semantics of our natural languages and symbolic interactions, including spoken and written languages ... art, ritual practice, and many other forms of symbolic expression.

This can extend to myth-making and the creative construction of hero stories.

Lobel (2014b) agrees that some metaphors are universal and cross-cultural, pointing to fertile ground for joint research initiatives between the field of heroism science and physical intelligence to better understand the connection between story, language, metaphor (to name only a few) and heroism, and their shared embodied knowledges. Two pertinent questions that may drive the joint investigative enterprise between embodied cognition and heroism science, could be how can we apply the emerging theory of physical intelligence to: (a) heroic metaphors and understand their origins in embodied experience, and shared sensorimotor archetypal structures (e.g. via the use of Functional Magnetic Resonance scans); and (b) cellular behavior in relation to the hero's journey to demonstrate the concept of the mind-body journey in heroism as a continuous, indissoluble process.

The Ecological Heroic Body

This dimension is premised on the notion that "The body does not, and cannot, therefore, exist independent of its environment" (Johnson, 2008, p. 164). This is an acknowledgement of the dynamic formation of identity in the intricate web of organismal-environmental systems. Indeed, researchers such as Lerner and Schmid Callina (2014) theorize a "relational developmental systems model" of "character development." Our senses, bodily sensations and awareness, perceptions, inner thoughts, neurochemistry, non-conscious percepts, cellular behavior, physical expressions, language and so forth are constantly transmuted by this interactive dance. We may therefore speak of the broader *ecology of the hero organism* and its "ecology of suffering" (to borrow the latter term from Krassnitzky's 1994 eponymous thesis). Thus, in the embodiment of heroism thesis an "organism" is understood as a transdisciplinary concept, across all spheres of experience. This notion is developed further in the next section.

The Social Heroic Body

This dimension recognizes that the environment or ecology in which the hero organism moves in is not simply biological in nature, and gives primacy to the premise that the "*brain* and the entire bodily organism are being trained up through deep interpersonal transactions" (Johnson, 2008, p. 165). Zimbardo and Ellsberg (2013) articulate the powerful effect group dynamics and social forces can have on fostering heroism. Franco et al. (2011, p. 101) have developed a multi-level operational definition of heroism "as a social activity." The function of narrating hero stories as a primary social activity that affects us profoundly through our interaction with others, helps us grow as heroic actors and imparts knowledge, dates back to our earliest ancestors (Allison & Goethals, 2014). In the twenty-first century this process is facilitated now more than ever with the rise of social media, a space in which we can reflect on, debate and be inspired into action by heroic accounts across all spheres of human activity. In many cases the universal character of hero stories provides a lifeline and shared ground for people across cultures, dismantling cultural, racial, language and other barriers.

The social dimension of the heroic body comes with the recognition that some of our bodily capabilities are rooted in evolutionary processes such as natural selection. The deep-seated need for hero stories (Allison & Goethals, 2014; Price, 1978), as well as pro-social behaviors that are thought to play at least some part in the development of heroism in our species, are being framed by contemporary authors as evolutionary in nature. The potential evolutionary origins of heroism in connection with ancestral warfare and altruism are now being addressed in scientific literature (Kelly & Dunbar, 2001; Rusch et al., 2015; Smirnov et al., 2007), as well as emerging heroism science research (Kafashan et al., Chapter 2, this volume; Preston, Chapter 4, this volume). These preliminary studies can provide the foundation for building a sociobiological epistemology of heroism.

The Cultural Heroic Body

This dimension considers the cultural constructions of identity such as "gender, race, class (socioeconomic status), aesthetic values, and various modes of bodily posture and movement" (Johnson, 2008, pp. 165–166). We may indeed speak of a universal heroic culture that transcends local nuances (Allison & Goethals, 2014; Campbell, 1949; Kinsella, 2012). However, intricacies in specific cultural constructions of heroism are already beginning to be revealed. Franco et al. (2011) point out this complexity—heroes are both constructed and contested by a specific cultural setting, time and place of the act, usually in its aftermath when viewed as part of a sequence of events, and can be fleeting or enduring, positive or negative. The myth of a hero can take on a life far greater than the original act or achievement. It can be surmised that different historical and cultural periods need and give rise to specific types of heroes, a notion reflected in Allison and Goethals' (2014, p. 178) concept of the "need-based origin of heroism."

The complexity of the phenomenon is enhanced by gendered dimensions, addressed by some of the psychological literature (Becker & Eagly, 2004; Eagly & Becker, 2005; Martens, 2005; Rankin & Eagly, 2008). Other surreptitious factors have been highlighted by DeAngelis (2002, p. 1280), who points out that common definitions of heroism have never considered the issues of power and money. A critical analysis of heroism in popular culture must address the sensationalist tendencies of the reporting of events, potentially contributing to the over-saturation of heroic ascriptions, and their impact on our perceptions of the phenomenon. The political nature and discourse often underlying heroism forms a further important cultural aspect. The "new heroism" (Zimbardo & Ellsberg, 2013) is, at its very core, radically and inexorably political in nature. The increasing momentum being witnessed in a campaign to spread heroism into numerous facets of society—from education, to health, business, science, psychology, the arts and so forth—reflects a truly global phenomenon that can be dubbed an emerging twenty-first century heroism movement. The broad sociocultural and political impacts of this movement deserve systematic study.

The Phenomenological Heroic Body

This aspect of embodied heroic experience is vastly incomprehensible by the rational conscious mind. It is grounded in the "pre-reflective, nonconscious structures that make it possible for us to have any bodily awareness" (Johnson, 2008, p. 165). This proposed phenomenological aspect of the heroic body aligns with emerging understandings of heroism—Allison, for example, describes the hero's journey as "a spiritual journey marked by encounters with transrational phenomena" (S. T. Allison, personal communication, November 7, 2014). Allison and Goethals (2014, p. 170) support the function of hero narratives as "far more than simple scripts prescribing prosocial action," stating "that effective hero stories feature an abundance of *transrational* phenomena, which ... reveal truths and life patterns that our limited minds have trouble understanding using our best logic or rational thought." Smyth (2010, p. 187) argues that "Merleau-Ponty's heroic myth in effect marginalizes heroism by confining it to a transcendental role." This is arguably not a failing, but rather an accurate statement of the inherent transrational and energizing property of hero mythologies "which Haidt calls *elevation*" (Allison & Goethals, 2014, p. 173).

In a 1988 interview Campbell defined a hero as "someone who has given his or her life to something bigger than oneself." This transformative property and function of heroic action is captured by Wade's (1998, p. 174) interpretation of Joy's (1979) conceptualization of transformation as "a metaphysical event. Energy fields not only permeate the physical body, but extend for some distance beyond." This expansion of consciousness is a deeply regenerating event, felt across the physical *and* spiritual plane, illustrating a critical connection between heroism and the transformative process. The phenomenological heroic body is marked by transrational phenomena which "beg to be understood but cannot be fully known using conventional tools of human reason. Hero stories help unlock the secrets of the transrational" (Allison & Goethals, 2014, p. 171).

This phenomenological property of the heroic body is critical because it gives us permission to delve beyond the confines of contemporary orientations of heroism towards morality or pro-social behavior, both from a psychosocial (e.g. group dynamics) and evolutionary (e.g. cooperation and altruism) perspective. Although it is important to acknowledge these aspects as part of the broader ecology of a hero organism, they cannot be regarded as definitive of the heroic process—this can be a deeply personal experience that takes place in the darkest, most quiet corners of life, and has little or no impact on other people. Does this make the act any less heroic? A pro-social attribution to heroism implies that the heroic act will be shared, and others will benefit in some form (as is indeed represented in Campbell's hero's journey cycle; Campbell, 1949). It arguably necessitates by definition that unsung heroes are sidelined, with their acts going unnoticed, unheard of and unrewarded. The transrational phenomenological lived heroic body is a recognition and validation of these silent heroic acts in real time—these *do* take place, eliminating the necessity for an audience or the presence of others for these acts to gain meaning. Rather, they carry an inherent meaning of their own, a corporeal knowledge that is bound to the lived experience of the heroic actor and does not require rational validation to assert its significance.

Out of all the dimensions of the heroic body, the phenomenological is perhaps the most problematic. Its transrational properties suggest that the domain of embodied heroic consciousness is never completely communicable, observable or quantifiable, and its ultimate knowledge is preserved only for those who venture beyond the realm of the known. Ultimately, the energizing force of heroism is geared towards one thing—emancipation (Merleau-Ponty, 1962, as cited in Smyth, 2010). The embodiment of heroism thesis asserts that if we are to truly understand the full gamut of this complex phenomenon we must widen its scope and definition. Indeed, not doing so goes against the very premise of the "banality of heroism" (Franco & Zimbardo, 2006). The phenomenological aspect of the heroic body lends support to the premise of the embodiment of heroism thesis to look beyond simple accounts of heroism as pro-social behavior or an exemplar of a moral ideal, and enhance its appreciation as a deeply personal, multi-sensorial and transrational experience.

Similar to Johnson's (2008, pp. 164, 166) alert to the complexities of the notion of the body, the multi-dimensional schematic of the heroic body sketched out above offers "a cautionary tale" such that we must consider "multiple nonreductive levels of explanation" to fully appreciate the heroic embodied mind and the human condition. Accordingly, as Johnson (2008, p. 166) notes, we must be careful not to fall into the trap of "deconstructivist accounts of the body as a fabric of textuality ... The body bleeds, feels, suffers, celebrates, desires, grows, and dies before and beyond texts"; *all* five interlaced aspects of the heroic body must be taken into account if we are to recognize the significance of the embodied nature of the heroic state. This cannot be reduced to a mere discussion grounded in biology, brain anatomy and genes (as scientistic accounts would offer), *nor* pure culture and relativism (as postmodern critiques would offer), *nor* traditional personality psychology with its deep emphasis on the behavioral aspects of an individual divorced from social, physical *and* spiritual forces. A reading of heroism must be accompanied by a deep interpretative proficiency in a multitude of discourses, as well as in our own and others' life stories as part of a larger fabric.

A New Epistemological and Methodological Narrative: The Hero Organism

How may we begin to outline the parameters of the *hero organism* (HO) under an embodiment of heroism thesis as a valid epistemological and methodological narrative? Landau (1984, pp. 267, 268) asks: "Are narratives testable" and "an appropriate form of scientific hypothesis"? In an attempt to offer a critical rationale for the bridging of the sciences and the humanities Landau (1984, p. 268) asserts that, "Rather than avoid [narratives], scientists might use them as they are used in literature, as a means of discovery and experimentation. Treating scientific theories as fictions may even be a way of arriving at new theories." The implicit assumption of myth and story as fundamentally inferior to scientific and rational inquiry must be a key consideration in any future multi-level reading of heroism, especially in light of the core roots of heroism in the former.

Allison and Goethals' (2014) HLD offers a solution to Landau's question on the testability of narratives as suitable forms of scientific hypothesis. The HLD is a "science of story"—but not one that pushes myth to the corner as a second-order epistemology. It is a framework that preserves the integrity and "life-supporting nature of myths" (Campbell, 1972, p. 12) and function of hero stories, presenting a methodological baseline from which we can begin to dissect, review and expand on the mechanics of heroism, and story at large. Allison and Goethals (2014, p. 177) note that, "The HLD and its temporal component can be viewed as a story itself." In a similar fashion, the HO can be approached as a base (life) narrative on which we can apply the central components of the HLD, embodiment theory and other emerging innovative frameworks. We may thus begin to develop a transdisciplinary epistemology and methodology for the theoretical observation and empirical assessment of the core functions, processes and consequences of the HO as a testable narrative (see Table 8.1).

In this integrative framework the heroic embodied mind may be applied across multiple layers of narratives or contexts. Stephens and McCallum (1998, p. 6) define a "metanarrative" as "a global or totalizing cultural narrative schema which orders and explains knowledge and experience." This is a narrative *about* a narrative, incorporating other smaller stories forming a whole. The embodiment of heroism thesis considers how seemingly different types of stories can enrich and enhance each other. To achieve this, this section considers traditional, as well cutting-edge theories, in a preliminary attempt to hone in on the contours of heroism as a distinct state of embodied consciousness. It builds on the five-dimensional model of the heroic body, using it as a foundation for embarking on an embodied reading and expansion of Allison and Goethals' (2014) HLD at greater depth. By doing so, it provides a preliminary outline of the parameters of the HO, offering a narrative mechanism to gain a comprehensive and integrative understanding of heroism in the field of heroism science. A reflection of the fluid, dynamic state of the embodied mind, the HO framework rests on the following four key tenets: *heroism as process*; *crisis as the core activator of heroism* with *embodied transformation* lying at the heart of the heroic process; and the notion of the *HO as a dynamical self-system*.

The Dynamical Hero Organism Self-System and the Relationship Between the Ecology of Suffering and the Ecology of Heroism

The concept of the heroic actor as a dynamical HO self-system is born out of the notion of the "heroic body as biological organism" which can only be fully comprehended in unison with the broader ecological, cultural, social and phenomenological aspects of the heroic body. Chrisley and Ziemke (2006, p. 1102) argue that:

> An understanding of how cognition is realized or instantiated in a physical system, especially a body, may require or be required by an account of a system's embedding in its environment, its dynamical properties, its (especially phylogenetic) history and (especially biological) function …

To apprehend the dynamical properties and other key parameters of the HO self-system, we turn to our systems-inspired HLD. The energizing function of hero stories in Allison and Goethals'

(2014, p. 173) HLD is broken down into three sub-components; hero narratives achieve this function "by healing our psychic wounds, by inspiring us to action, and by promoting personal growth." The epistemic function is also premised on a tri-part vehicle that reveals "deep truths," "paradox" and develops "emotional intelligence," resulting in "wisdom" gaining as its core impact (Allison & Goethals, 2014, p. 171). The role of each of these in relation to the proposed epistemology of the HO will be considered at further detail.

How is the HO energizing? In an embodied reading, the healing of our psychic wounds takes on a core meaning. For Merleau-Ponty (1964), according to Smyth (2010, p. 179), "*normal human existence is constitutively "sick" on account of the schizoidal duality of being-in-itself and being-for-itself to which anthropogenetic reflective self-consciousness leads.*" The contemporary hero plays a crucial role in alleviating this state of malaise, revealing the energizing function: "Through his complete internalization of the negativity of death, the hero effectively *heals* this split by achieving a self-coincidence that amounts to a condition of pathological health" (Merleau-Ponty, 1964, as cited in Smyth, 2010, p. 179). The key component that activates heroism and this crucial opportunity for healing, action and personal growth, is crisis or struggle. It is the premise of the embodiment of heroism thesis that the deeper the suffering and crisis, the deeper the potential for transformation and change. Crisis, as Franco and others theorize and incorporate into holistic community crisis management strategies (for examples see Franco, Hayes, Lancaster & Kisaaack, 2012; Franco, Zumel, Blau & Ayhens-Johnson, 2008; Gheytanchi et al., 2007), serves as a key activator that spins all aspects of heroism into motion.

As Begley (2007) reveals, persistence, intensive focus and hard work in the face of struggle and trauma appear to figure as prominently in neuroplasticity—the emerging cognitive science detailing the astounding capacity of the mind and body to work together in the healing process—as they do in hero stories. These traits can be used to describe heroism. This is reflective of the rehabilitation journey of the most difficult cases of brain damage, such as stroke, where the view of the brain's hardwiring is most persistent—the stories of these patients who struggle to regain the function of their paralysed limbs can be pinpointed as an example of a heroic day-to-day activity aiding the survival and evolution of the organism. Emerging literature cites the conflation of trauma and personal growth, and how challenges may feature as an essential pathway for building resilience, and the development of a heroic mode of being. Nelson (2011, p. 26) describes how PTSD sufferers can connect with the heroic domain by "creating their own unique meaning that can be brought out of the experience, writing their own ending to the trauma narrative." The experience of trauma and the demonstration of resilience, which "is generally defined as one's ability to bounce back after a traumatic experience" (Nelson, 2011, p. 7) is instrumental to this process:

> What makes our characters heroic is their perseverance through the trickery and shadows, finding or creating light to guide them through the darkness instead of getting lost in it. Heroes are formed through transformative suffering and immortalized in legends throughout time.
>
> *(Nelson, 2011, pp. 26–27)*

Likewise, Fosha (2002, p. 2) writes of September 11 survivors: "sometimes trauma awakens extraordinary capacities that otherwise would lie dormant, unknown and untapped … Crisis is opportunity." Nelson (2011, p. 6) refers to September 11 as an example of "the potential for a national crisis to provide an opportunity for positive growth." The "huge *transformational potential*" (Fosha, 2002, p. 4) of trauma is the foundation of the hero's journey, as it is to the neuroplastic journey.

Monteiro and Mustaro's (2012) representation of the hero's journey utilizing bifurcation theory is a prime example of a scientific (in this case mathematical) analysis of the hero's journey and the cross-fertilization of epistemologies. Crucially, a hero figure's evolution is measured against the "cumulative suffering" experienced throughout the journey as the "control parameter" of the proposed context specific "discrete-time dynamical system," rendering change inevitable (Monteiro & Mustaro, 2012, pp. 2233). It is notable that Monteiro and Mustaro (2012, p. 2233) state that this suffering is either self-imposed, or imposed by the environment or "unknown world." This idea that an organism sets itself up for suffering as a conscious or unconscious learning and evolving process merits further investigation, in relation, for example, to its situatedness in the habitual and/or actual heroic body. According to Monteiro and Mustaro (2012, p. 2234) "in the bifurcation diagram, the first critical moment of the hero's journey coincides with the transition from fixed point to chaos; the second one with the transition from limit cycle to fixed point," with these "two crucial moments in every hero's journey" regarded as "unique."

Merleau-Ponty's (1964, p. 330/186) contemporary hero is also grounded in chaos and disequilibrium:

> Today's hero is not skeptical, dilettantish, or decadent ... it is simply the case that he has experienced chance, disorder, and failure ... He has a better experience than anyone has ever had of the contingency of the future and the freedom of man.

This transdisciplinary historical juncture gives rise to the notion of the lived heroic body as a *dynamical self-system*. Indeed, as Allison and Goethals (2014, p. 169) explicate, "The HLD includes the term *dynamic* ... intentionally"; this denotes "an interactive *system* [emphasis added] or process that unfolds over time ... that is energizing and always in motion," consistent with Campbell's (1949) conceptualization of the hero's journey as a parallel for the stages of human development. The hero or HO is always defined in relation to chaos and crisis, but *capable* of (by being developmentally wired according to the HLD) organizing herself around it and overcoming it. Thus, the hero's journey and heroic lived experience is, in essence, a regenerative and restorative cycle.

The grounding of a hero in the critical relationship between suffering and healing, or crisis and order, is clearly not unique to our times. However, for Merleau-Ponty (1964, as cited in Smyth, 2010, p. 177) the contemporary hero is in a distinct position due to the heightened diversity of our historical period—this is a "time neither of faith nor of reason, but rather of a world out of joint. Events exhibit no clear overarching pattern ... for there are no absolute reference points for historical action." In this age of increased uncertainty it is tempting to revert to old beliefs and dogmas, which has been demonstrated by the rise of religious fundamentalism and deep distrust in science. But it is precisely this heightened state of chaos that calls for the development of a deeper faith to facilitate our survival and self-organizing capabilities—one in ourselves, and our inner hero. This is not mindless faith; it is firmly planted in lived experience, in the examples of everyday heroism we can see all around us in their various typologies, settings and intensities. Smyth (2010, p. 180) notes that "For Merleau-Ponty, the hero provides such evidence." Indeed, in the new heroism and heroism science the potency of the phenomenon is evidence-based, paving the way for the in-depth empirical assessment of heroism for the first time in the history of its study. This realizes Merleau-Ponty's (1964, as cited in Smyth, 2010, p. 170) existential agenda for heroism "(as a general phenomenon of our times, and not as a school of thought)," validated "positively and on the basis of examples."

Developing a nuanced understanding of the embeddedness of the HO within its broader ecology of suffering and its dynamic inter-relationship with healing and growth, is critical to an embodied reading of heroism and the advancement of heroism science. Cutting-edge enterprises such as the Flow Genome Project (which will be explored in greater detail) are founded on the notion of "*knowing* how to suffer" and understanding its mechanics as crucial to well-being and human greatness. Within the context of a HO self-system suffering may be defined as the *degree of disruption of equilibrium* (positive or negative) in organisms, whether internally caused, or external/environmental (the "mythical call to adventure"), and the *degree of challenge posed to the organism* (the "mythical rites of passage"). The immediate spin-off effect is the commencement of some form of transformation (or regeneration in biological terms), complete or incomplete, which may have repercussions for the immediate environment and broader macro social scale. This transformative process is bound to the language of suffering and resilience in the bearing (trauma) or shedding (healing) of an emotional and/or physical wound. It is notable that Campbell's (1949) hero cycle necessitates the passage through trauma in order to achieve healing of a wound (though the end of a cycle might mean the accumulation of new wounds, which require the repetition of the cycle, and so on and so forth). Further, the nature of the journey/cycle implies that there is no guarantee of a positive outcome (the risk factor associated with the hero's journey).

This dynamic process denotes a scale of *degrees of suffering* ranging from mild discomfort to extreme life-threatening pain. Therefore, in the embodiment of heroism thesis heroism is understood as transformation through struggle, experienced and expressed in the everyday in varying degrees or forms. Specifically, in this working definition a hero, or hero-becoming, is understood as:

- any person who has the ability, capacity or willingness to accept or endure—and in some cases impose on oneself and self-propagate—varying degrees of struggle throughout one's lifespan;
- be shaped by this struggle and, under certain conditions, overcome or rise above it;
- resulting in its elimination or reduction at a particular instance of one's life-cycle, and a deep irreversible transformation.

In short, the above parameters can be conceptualized as *biopsychosocial* (to borrow the term from Engel's 1977 biopsychosocial model of illness and well-being) *resilience*, echoing research trends in the sciences zeroing in on broad-spectrum resilience biomarkers that may enhance well-being overall (Giller, 2014; Lawrence, Phillips & Liu, 2007), as well as contemporary efforts to spread heroism training and foster psychosocial resilience. This is the capability of resilience across multiple spheres—the widespread biopsychosocial impacts of heroism asserted by Kinsella (2012) and the heroic body's five-dimensional framework suggest the requirement of this type of resilience that is canvassed in the HO's broader ecology. Heroism is the ultimate journey inwards; the prototypical definition of a hero is arguably the figure that is faced with the deepest and darkest conditions who should, by all accounts, be doomed to fail. Yet, they somehow rise up despite all odds and return (or are "resurrected" in transcendental terms); the very definition of resilience requires (a) adversity and (b) the capacity to return from it, as described by Nelson (2011).

The proposed definition suggests that there are multiple hero journeys within the lifespan of a single organism, with varying degrees of suffering, healing and transformation. The energizing property of the dynamical HO self-system denotes its "*operant intentionality*" in agreement with Merleau-Ponty's (2012, as cited in Moya, 2014, p. 1) embodiment thesis. It is the premise of the embodiment of heroism thesis that behind every instance and story of human greatness is a deep hero's journey founded on these principles of the HO and heroism-as-process, and grounded in a dynamic relationship between suffering and healing. Assessing the role inflammation and stress play on the immune system and how the organism reacts is thus likely to be critical to this enterprise. Medical research centers such as the Center for Inflammation and Regeneration Modeling (CIRM) at the McGowan Institute for Regenerative Medicine (2014) state as their central mission "optimizing the regenerative potential intrinsic to many organ systems ... [and]

understand[ing] how we can facilitate the body's ability to heal itself." Understanding the "pivotal role of inflammation" is cited as central to realizing this goal (CIRM, 2014). Strategies for defining, teaching and fostering heroism in the everyday must therefore be centered on life coping and stress management skills to be effective and resonate with individuals and communities in a post-millennium era, and acknowledge the paramount importance of the complex ecology of suffering for HO self-systems and the realization of their inherent energizing properties.

Physical Intelligence, Embodied Agency and Leadership in the Ecological System of the Hero Organism

An important consequence of the epistemic function of narratives of heroism is the development of "emotional intelligence" (Allison & Goethals, 2014, p. 171). But can we extend this notion to the emerging science of physical intelligence (PI)? First, we must consider the question: why *intelligence* in relation to heroism? Allison and Goethals (2011, pp. 61–62) propose "the Great Eight" behavioral properties of heroism: "Smart, Strong, and Selfless, Caring and Charismatic, Resilient and Reliable, and finally, Inspiring." "Smart" is indeed one of the properties directly related to heroism in this research. However, all the above characteristics suggest a degree of intelligence—researchers are increasingly recognizing the presence of multiple types of intelligences (Gardner, 1983).

As discussed earlier, the heroic body as biological organism is housed in the pre-conscious, the habitual body and the body schema. The role of PI therefore takes on a central role in the embodied discussion of heroism and the HO. Lobel (2014c) discusses how our "sensory-motor experiences," including little considered aspects of our physical world such as color, temperature and surface textures, influence us in unimaginable and unexpected ways. Emergent understandings of these affective aspects and their likely role as determinants of heroism and the heroic body, call for the expansion of the function of hero stories and heroic action from the domain of emotional to physical intelligence. Empirical findings in PI that our everyday physical experiences can "have subtle but profound influences on our thoughts, perceptions, and judgments" (Lobel, 2014a, p. 4) are situated firmly in the history of embodiment literature. This provides a solid foundation on which to begin to appreciate the role of physical intelligence, or how our sensory and embodied reality affects our perception, cognition and so forth, in heroic sensibility and action.

In the embodiment of heroism thesis the conceptualization of heroic physical intelligence is situated in the ecology of organisms—this endeavor is accurately reflected in Turvey and Carello's (2012) exploration of "Intelligence from First Principles" offering a set of "Guidelines for Inquiry into" PI. Turvey and Carello (2012) have been proponents of a more integrative brand of psychology for over 30 years and are joined by a stream of emerging thinkers. This is a transdisciplinary approach that seeks to unify culture and science in its conceptualization of the term "organism." It is not a conventional concept of the organism reduced to an analysis of its biological properties (e.g. brain, neurons) as isolated "crude matter," but rather as part of a larger dynamic eco-system, aptly mirrored in the Johnson (2008) based concept of the ecological body and Engel's (1977) biopsychosocial model. The foundation of ecological psychology "is the question of how organisms make their way in the world (and not the historically popular question of how a world is made inside of organisms)" (Turvey & Carello, 2012, p. 4), suggesting an "organism's journey." Ecological psychology joins embodiment literature in the battle against the mind-body dualist tradition and attempts to ameliorate its damage:

> It is clear that for the past 50 years, an alternative paradigm has developed within psychology that does not suppose that the brain is the seat of intelligence ... Once James Gibson became disaffected with the dominant paradigm (which really dates to the 1600s ...) and

questioned the assumptions on which it rested, a natural-physical approach to perceiving, acting, and knowing proceeded inexorably.

(Turvey & Carello, 2012, p. 25)

This could provide the foundation for the concept of the ecology of hero organisms, linking it to PI as explored preliminarily in Lobel's (2014a, 2014b, 2014c), as well as Turvey and Carello's (2012) work.

This highly embodied view of organisms is not limited to the study of the microcosm as applicable to traditional biology—it is one that views this microcosm in the context of the macrocosm it is situated in and how it functions within it. This is the core tenet of the embodiment of heroism thesis, the HO and its ecology. It reflects an *"approach to intelligence that is physically grounded* [emphasis added]" (Turvey & Carello, 2012, p. 3). Significantly, the ecological approach does not suggest that any particular set of organisms is privileged over another, and that there are "laws" underlying the behavior of organisms. Ecological psychology seeks to uncover these laws which "underlie intelligent capabilities" by offering "guidelines for how one might address intelligence not as the special province of the neurally endowed but as physically generic" (Turvey & Carello, 2012, pp. 3, 4). In line with this approach, heroism is proposed to be physically generic or embedded and embodied in the very makeup of organisms operating under baseline parameters, advancing the re-conceptualization of humans (and cells overall as the foundational unit of organisms) as hero organisms and dynamical self-systems.

Aside from the advancement of deep intelligence across emotional and physical parameters in the heroic embodied mind, the function of the HO is further illuminated by the critical connection between the concept of *leadership* and the resulting "inspiring … to action" (Allison & Goethals, 2014, p. 173) impact of the energizing function of hero narratives in the HLD, and *agency* in PI theory. Allison and Goethals' (2014, p. 169) Dynamic is strategically framed around the notion of "*heroic leadership* rather than as simply heroism" based on their focal premise expounded in previous works (Allison & Goethals, 2011, 2013; Goethals & Allison, 2012) "that although not all leaders are heroes, all heroes are leaders." Turvey and Carello (2012, p. 4) highlight that "Agency, scientifically explained, is the goal of ecological psychology: the manifest capability of all organisms to exhibit some degree of autonomy and control in their encounters"—this implies a degree of leadership exhibited in organism behavior, a critical property identified in heroism by Allison and Goethals (2014).

The key elements of agency according to Turvey and Carello (2012, pp. 4–5) are: "(a) variation of means to bring about an end (*flexibility*), (b) coordinating current control with emerging states of affairs (*prospectivity*), and (c) coordinating current control with prior states of affairs (*retrospectivity*)." By implication, we may speak of the *flexibility, prospectivity* and *retrospectivity* of the *heroic body, and heroic action or agency*—an agency which "is likely emergent from *spontaneous self-organization*" (Turvey & Carello, 2012, p. 5) of the dynamical HO self-system. These three properties roughly correspond with the three-fold working definition of "heroism-as-process" and as biopsychosocial resilience introduced in page 152: (a) any person who has the ability, capacity or willingness to accept or endure varying degrees of struggle throughout one's lifespan (retrospectivity); (b) be shaped by this struggle and, under certain conditions, overcome or rise above it (prospectivity); (c) resulting in its elimination or reduction at a particular instance of one's lifecycle (flexibility). This further suggests a high degree of operant intentionality and agency within an ecology of suffering, fostering the self-organizing quality of the heroic embodied mind and HO around disorder and discomfort to eventuate a state of transformation and healing.

Here, the call for a connection between the ecological psychological notion of PI and heroism takes the theory of different types of intelligences in relation to Allison and Goethals' (2011) Great Eight traits of heroism to another level. All these traits are representative of agency, or the "manifest capability of all [hero] organisms to exhibit some degree of autonomy and control in their encounters" (Turvey & Carello, 2012, p. 4). This embodied reading of multiple intelligences, the depths of which we are clearly only beginning to comprehend, places the epistemic function of the HLD in the advancement of knowledge center-stage in the HO and the ecological heroic body:

> Characterizing knowing as coordinating organism and environment demands the kind of serious treatment of environment that is absent from the prevailing view of knowing as a property of mind. The emphasis on the ecological scale highlights the centrality of perception and action to defining the essence of effective, intelligent behavior. Characterizing knowing as a natural phenomenon is at once acknowledging intelligence as physical while dismissing business-as-usual explanations that are satisfied with borrowing intelligence as a means to explain it.
>
> (Turvey & Carello, 2012, p. 7)

The lived heroic body is grounded in this deeper sense of *embodied knowing* that coordinates its actions as an organism within its broader ecology, in which knowledge and the epistemic function is physical. This is the lived heroic actor and heroic "body as subject, as experiencer, as agent" (Gallagher & Zahavi, 2008, p. 155) and, by implication, as leader. The heroic body's perceptions and actions define effective and intelligent heroic behavior. The epistemic function of hero stories and heroism in the suggested advancement of physical intelligence and knowledge, and the energizing function with its thrusting of the HO into heroic action, agency or leadership, are therefore inexorably linked within an embodiment of heroism thesis.

For Turvey and Carello (2012) the ecological enterprise that seeks to uncover the laws that underlie intelligent capabilities is far-reaching—an approach to intelligence that is physically grounded is applicable not only to humans, but animals, micro-organisms, and even non-sentient beings. This tenet allows us to expand the concept of the HO to other living, and non living organisms. As Turvey and Carello (2012, pp. 3–4) put it, "The change of focus from inside-the-head to outside-the-head ... means that ecological psychology is *not human-centric*"—this driver of ecological psychology "as a psychology for all organisms" gives us permission to conceptualize hero organisms not only in the human species, but beyond, revealing a vast network of life grounded in heroic properties and evolution. We may thus begin to conceive of a radical notion of *cells as physically intelligent entities that demonstrate heroic leadership*. In her exposition of the "apparatus of bodily production," Haraway (1988, pp. 592, 595) advocates that "Situated knowledges require that the object of knowledge be pictured as an actor and agent." This three-dimensional, interactive and unorthodox view of our own body as an "active entity," a "witty agent" and "a most engaging being" (Haraway, 1988, pp. 593, 594), can greatly contribute to the (re)telling of scientific stories of regeneration via the lens of heroic embodied intelligences.

Although this chapter does not outline what the specific base laws governing the HO might be, it is clear that ecological psychology and PI are strongly linked to the embodiment of heroism thesis, and can provide a platform on which we may begin to significantly contribute to the advancement of the field of heroism science in its transdisciplinary scope. This section provides a cursory indication of the room for collaborative research and joint inquiry between PI, heroism and heroic leadership; this is likely to culminate in innovative narratives of heroism and heroic embodied intelligence, as for example, a re-reading of the hero's journey as a "complex, open thermodynamic system" (Turvey & Carello, 2012, p. 25). Given that we are still at the very early stages of heroism science, this allows researchers scope for creativity and flexibility in the frameworks that are yet to be developed. In this sense, the concepts of the HO as a dynamical self-system and the ecological heroic body provide pillars on which heroism science may join ecological psychology in this enterprise of deepening our knowledge of complex intelligent behaviors and systems—one that is for many "obligatory and serves as an engine of discovery" (Turvey & Carello, 2012, p. 25).

Flow, Deep Embodiment and the Hero's Journey—the Conditions and Mindset of Heroism-as-Process

Merleau-Ponty (1962, as cited in Smyth, 2010, p. 178) suggested, "the hero is someone who 'lives to the limit ... his relation to men and the world'." Allison and Goethals (2014, p. 167) concur, noting, "The human tendency to bestow a timeless quality to heroic leadership is the culmination of a pervasive narrative about *human greatness* [emphasis added] that people have been driven to construct since the advent of language." We can thus surmise that *hero stories are stories of peak human performance, activity and agency*. It is interesting that the build-up of momentum in the study of heroic leadership and heroism is coinciding with the burgeoning of emerging advanced narratives in optimal human functioning. Perhaps the most prominent narrative of peak performance pervading both science and culture is the Flow Genome Project (www.flowgenomeproject.co). Co-founder Steven Kotler has reinvigorated a field of research that has had a history of almost 150 years. Drawing on Csikszentmihalyi (1990) and over 10 years of research, Kotler (2014a, 2014b) explores the mechanics of flow in its most heightened manifestations in adventure sports. In particular, Kotler (2014a) investigates how cutting-edge technologies are facilitating an unprecedented understanding of the mechanics of the flow state at the neurochemical level.

This is an innovative enterprise that aims to "hack" the science behind this elusive "quasi-mystical" state and bring it into the everyday (Kotler, 2014b), similar to contemporary efforts centering on the notion of the banality of heroism. Kotler (2014b) notes that traditionally the activation of flow has involved the presence of extreme risk and danger—this provides a critical link between the instrumental presence of danger in hero stories (Allison & Goethals, 2014), risk in contemporary understandings of heroism (Anderson, 1986; Franco et al., 2011; Eagly & Becker, 2005; Stenstrom & Curtis, 2012; Weinstein, 2012), and the mechanics of peak states of human performance. Further, Kotler (2014a, pp. 97–98) notes that "In the world of philanthropy, *helper's high* is the term for an altruism-triggered flow state, literally brought on by the act of helping another." Although altruism may not be a definitive aspect of or synonymous with heroism, with recent empirical data indicating that "that there are fundamental perceived differences between heroism and altruism" (Franco et al., 2011, p. 108), there is still debate and significant areas of overlap (e.g. see Shepela et al., 1999). The enduring centering of heroic behavior in relation to a surrender or "service" to an "other" (Campbell, 1988; Franco et al., 2011, p. 101), whether that be a person, a group, an ideal, or something else, spells a critical connection between selfless flow states and heroism. The premise of emerging research is that if the mastery of flow can be realized without the presence of extreme physical risk, this could result in a critical "paradigm shift" on an evolutionary scale, marked by a "whole-body transformation" in the human species (Kotler, 2014a, pp. 24, 74). We can thus begin to reconceptualize heroism and the hero's journey as peak flow states and key evolutionary processes.

The notion of heroism as an evolutionary process geared towards achieving a peak state of human performance or "transformations of consciousness of one kind or another" (Campbell, 1988, p. 155) is in direct alignment with the HLD's energizing function of hero narratives in advancing human evolution and development, as well as increasing agency and PI in the HO as part of the embodiment of heroism thesis. This "common theme of an expanded consciousness" in transformation has been described as "an evolutionary process" for centuries (Wade, 1998, p. 714). The process of personal transformation, like the hero's journey, "is circular and expanding. Each transformation brings the individual to higher levels of being," through the confronting of pain, struggle and reordering of identity (Wade, 1998, p. 714). This is a view of every individual as a hero-in-process or hero-becoming, suggesting heroism's evolutionary property from a psychosomatic standpoint given the deeply experiential and complex nature of the transformative journey.

How can cutting-edge flow research enhance our understanding of heroism as a deeply embodied, energizing and action-oriented transformative developmental process? Kotler, who went through a radical transformative journey of this type curing himself from a debilitating autoimmune disease, sets out to demonstrate that the *re*formation and *trans*formation of neural networks lies at the heart of this process. Kotler (2014a, pp. 65–69; 2014b) outlines the specific neurochemicals involved in the flow process, the "Big Five" ("dopamine," "norepinephrine," "endorphins," "anandamide," and "serotonin"), which can have profound healing properties and enhance the immune system when released on a regular basis. This is a bona fide and very specific state of embodied consciousness with precise parameters and descriptors, which have the capacity to rewire and transform the self and being—this aligns with the conceptualization of the hero's journey as grounded in the lived heroic body. In an evolutionary sense, it is the hero's journey from "sub-par" or sub-optimal, to normal, to super-normal or "super-human." Kotler (2014b) joins emerging understandings of the embodied mind and neuroplastic inspired narratives by stating that "the brain can radically alter consciousness to improve performance." Many of our publicized heroes are successful leaders, consistent with Allison and Goethals' (2014, p. 167) statement that the "timeless quality" attributed to heroic leadership is rooted in "a pervasive narrative about human greatness."

Kotler (2014b) outlines the intellectual tradition of flow research—the broad consensus is that this "ubiquitous" state can manifest in anyone "provided certain initial conditions are met," once again mirroring Franco and Zimbardo's (2006) hypothesis of the banality of heroism. Since 1990 neurobiology with advanced imaging of the brain has been brought into the conversation to better understand and "see" this state of consciousness, contributing to the literature of embodied cognition. But perhaps the most crucial connecting rod of flow to heroism is *struggle*—struggle, pain and suffering in its varying degrees is the primary activator of the transformative flow process and its evolutionary cycle (Wheal, 2013). This is the ultimate state of human performance, when "life and limb is on the line" (Kotler, 2014b); a quality that also appears to be the core instigator of heroism, heroic action and the hero's journey, and entrenched in the heroic body's ecology of suffering. In light of the above, it is evident that the renewed interest in flow research, the focus of which is precisely the study of human greatness and its unique properties, stands to offer critical clues to the embodied state of heroism and the heroic embodied mind.

Franco et al. (2011, p. 100) propose that everyone is "capable of heroism with the right mindset and under certain conditions"—what are this mindset and those conditions? The Flow Genome Project is premised on the notion that "flow states have triggers; these are preconditions" (Kotler, 2014b). Kotler (2014b) identifies three keys to unlocking this potential: "deep embodiment," "high consequences" and "rich environments." Aside from deep embodiment, high consequences and rich environments also lend directly to a critical conflation between heroism and flow in the presence of a degree of risk which is instrumental to heroic action. Rich environments result in heightened risk, awareness and perception. This precondition of flow directly correlates with Zimbardo's (2015) call for the development of "situational awareness" as part of our heroic training and the primacy of "opportunity" (Zimbardo, 2011) for the activation of heroism; notably, situational awareness is also a key property in the state of flow (Kotler, 2014a, p. 72), as are "*affordances* (J. J. Gibson …): organism-specific opportunities for action encountered in the environment" to ecological psychology (Turvey & Carello, 2012, p. 5). Not focusing in these heightened environments can pose a threat to our physical and mental well-being, and at extremes, survival. We can thus infer that rich environments activate the flow embodied state of heroism and facilitate quick response time in the HO for situations that call for heroic action. Learning to recognize these opportunities and environments ultimately lies in the *"natural purposiveness"* (Merleau-Ponty, 1964, as cited in Smyth, 2010, p. 179) that is exemplified in the astutely trained habitual heroic body.

These powerful synergies among the hitherto disparate fields of embodiment, heroism and heroic leadership, flow, PI, ecological and mainstream psychology, systems theory, and potentially many more, make a strong case for the possibility of joint research ventures between the Flow Genome Project, The Resilience Project searching for genetic heroes, and a "Heroic Body or Hero Genome Project."[1] These may help to identify synergies between the Big Five, Great Eight, PI in metaphor, the embodied state of heroism and other mutually beneficial research avenues. The cursory linkages outlined above between flow research, embodiment theory and heroism lead us to consider: can we apply these triggers, and demonstrate their presence and critical importance in specific case studies to support the notion of heroism as a distinct state of embodied consciousness or *flow*?

These emerging connections directly lead into the idea that we can manipulate the environment to induce the Big Five neurochemicals of flow states, and by implication instill heroic action and heroic consciousness, thereby altering our cellular and genetic profile. This *is* dynamic heroism-in-process, and the neurobiology and culture of the HO and its ecology. By uncovering the inter-relationship between the pre-conditions of the flow state, and the mindset and conditions of heroism as a peak state, we may begin to expose the laws governing the physical and emotional intelligence of hero organisms and their ecological properties, which are embodied and physically generic to all of us. Decoding and "hacking" heroism alongside flow can provide invaluable insights for the field of heroism science in their emerging role as transdisciplinary sciences of peak states of human performance, and achieve Merleau-Ponty's (1962, as cited in Smyth, 2010) highest end of lived embodied heroism with the absolute self-realization of humanity and its accession to the universal.

Heroism: The Final Frontier

This chapter has attempted to demonstrate heroism as embedded and embodied in the everyday. By positing heroism as a distinct state of embodied consciousness comprising specific parameters we may begin to appreciate and dissect its complex architecture. It is proposed that the ubiquity, and concurrently, elusiveness of the phenomenon lies in that there is *never* a complete absence of heroism, but rather low, middle or peak expressions—every individual is a "hero-in-waiting"(Zimbardo, 2015) demonstrating various levels of biopsychosocial resilience at any given point, as an organism embedded in a larger ecological structure. This transdisciplinary framework of heroic transformation aims to reconceptualize cognitive and cellular agents (and therefore potentially both human and non-human agents) as hero organisms and dynamical self-systems capable of demonstrating fluidity, leadership and heightened organizational awareness in times of crisis and stress. This is a system in which everyone is biologically, psychologically, socially and spiritually equipped to be a hero. For Franco et al. (2011, p. 112) "the question of what the term "hero" will mean for this generation is yet to be answered." Zimbardo's (2006) idea of the banality of heroism, originally presented in the *Edge* in response to the intellectual challenge "What is your dangerous idea?," is precisely that—a provocative notion which could have wide-reaching and lasting impacts for this generation, and generations to come. If these vibrant emerging research linkages are any indication, the central question posed by the authors (Franco et al., 2011, p. 100) as to whether heroism is "fundamentally ordinary and available to all of us" may well be the holy grail of our species.

Table 8.1 The Parameters of the Hero Organism, the Heroic Body and their Ecological Landscape

		THE 5 PROPERTIES OF THE HEROIC BODY		
Biological Organism	Ecological	Social	Cultural	Phenomenological/Transnational
ECOLOGY OF SUFFERING		HERO ORGANISM DYNAMICAL SELF-SYSTEM		ECOLOGY OF HEALING

FUNCTIONS OF THE HEROIC BODY
 	
1. Epistemic:
  a. Reveals deep truths
  b. Reveals paradox
  c. Develops emotional and physical intelligence
2. Energizing:
  a. Heals psychic and physical traumas
  b. Inspires us to heroic action
  c. Promotes biopsychosocial growth, regeneration and transformation
3. Ecological:
  a. Manages the regulation of suffering and healing, or crisis and order, within the broader ecology of the hero organism
	PROCESSES OF THE HEROIC BODY AND THE HEROIC EMBODIED MIND:
	HEROISM-AS-PROCESS
	
	Conditions for the activation of the embodied state of consciousness of heroism and the heroic embodied mind
	1. Deep embodiment
	2. High consequences, risk, crisis, struggle, trauma, stress, inflammation (physical, mental and emotional)
	3. Heightened or dynamic environments, fluidity and change making the occurrence of suffering and trauma high
		Mindset of the embodied state of consciousness of heroism and the heroic embodied mind
		1. Function(ality)
		2. Self-organization
		3. Physical Intelligence
		4. Flow
		5. Agency, heroic leadership, operant intentionality
		6. Heightened perception, sensory experience, emotion, heroic action
			CONSEQUENCES OF THE HEROIC EMBODIED MIND AND HEROIC AGENCY:
			DEEP EMBODIED TRANSFORMATION AND BIOPSYCHOSOCIAL REGENERATION
			
			1. Heightened embodiment and embodied engagement with oneself and the everyday – the lived heroic body
			2. Heightened heroic flow state – heroism as a peak state of experience, human performance, expanded consciousness and evolutionary process
			3. Heightened physical and emotional intelligence, or heroic embodied intelligence
			4. Heightened stress management, resilience and coping abilities
			5. Heightened agency or heroic leadership:
			  a. Flexibility
			  b. Prospectivity
			  c. Retrospectivity
			6. Heightened experiential based knowledge and wisdom, or embodied knowing
			7. Heightened personal (and eventually social, by virtue of the hero's actions) growth
			8. Heightened state of risk and dis-ease followed by a heightened state of well-being and pathological health.	

ADVANCEMENT OF BIOPSYCHOSOCIAL RESILIENCE = EMBODIED HEROISM				

Sources: a transdisciplinary framework drawing from Allison and Goethals (2014); Engel (1977); Kotler (2014a, 2014b); Merleau-Ponty (1962, 1964); Turvey and Carello (2012)

Note

1   Table 8.1 outlines these preliminary connections and the transdisciplinary parameters of the epistemological concept of the hero organism, as well as the functions, processes and consequences of embodied heroism.

References

Allison, S. T., & Goethals, G. R. (2011). *Heroes: What they do and why we need them*. New York: Oxford University Press.

Allison, S. T., & Goethals, G. R. (2013). *Heroic leadership: An influence taxonomy of 100 exceptional individuals*. New York: Routledge.

Allison, S. T., & Goethals, G. R. (2014). "Now he belongs to the ages": The heroic leadership dynamic and deep narratives of greatness. In G. R. Goethals, S. T. Allison, R. M. Kramer, & D. M. Messick (eds), *Conceptions of leadership: Enduring ideas and emerging insights* (pp. 167–183). New York: Palgrave Macmillan.

Anderson, J. W. (1986). Military heroism: An occupational definition. *Armed Forces & Society, 12*(4), 591–606. doi:10.1177/0095327X8601200406

Bandura, A. (2001). The changing face of psychology at the dawning of a globalization era. *Canadian Psychology, 42*(1), 12–24.

Becker, S. W., & Eagly, A. H. (2004). The heroism of women and men. *American Psychologist, 59*(3), 163–178. doi:10.1037/0003-066X.59.3.163

Begley, S. (2007). *Train your mind, change your brain: How a new science reveals our extraordinary potential to transform ourselves*. New York: Ballantine Books.

Campbell, J. (1949). *The hero with a thousand faces*. Princeton, NJ: Princeton University Press.

Campbell, J. (1972). *Myths to live by*. New York, NY: Viking Press.

Campbell, J. (1988). *The power of myth, with Bill Moyers*. New York: Doubleday.

Chemero, A. (2013). Radical embodied cognitive science. *Review of General Psychology, 17*(2), 145–150. doi:10.1037/a0032923

Choi, B. C. K., & Pak, A. W. P. (2006). Multidisciplinarity, interdisciplinarity and transdisciplinarity in health research, services, education and policy: 1. definitions, objectives, and evidence of effectiveness. *Clinical and Investigative Medicine, 29*(6), 351–364.

Chrisley, R., & Ziemke, T. (2006). Embodiment. In *Encyclopedia of Cognitive Science*. doi: 10.1002/0470018860.s00172

CIRM (2014). Center for Inflammation and Regeneration Modeling. Retrieved from www.mirm.pitt.edu/cirm.

Csikszentmihalyi, M. (1990). *Flow: The psychology of optimal experience*. New York: Harper & Row.

DeAngelis, C. D. (2002). Heroism. *JAMA, 288*(10), 1280. doi:10.1001/jama.288.10.1280

Dreyfus, H. L., & Dreyfus, S. E. (1999). The challenge of Merleau-Ponty's phenomenology of embodiment for cognitive science. In G. Weiss & H. F. Haber (eds), *Perspectives on embodiment: The intersections of nature and culture* (pp. 103–120). London: Routledge.

Eagly, A. H., & Becker, S. W. (2005). Comparing the heroism of women and men. *American Psychologist, 60*(4), 343–344. doi:10.1037/0003-066X.60.4.343

Engel, G. L. (1977). The need for a new medical model: A challenge for biomedicine. *Science, 196*(4286), 129–136.

Fosha, D. (2002). Trauma reveals the roots of resilience. *Constructivism in the Human Sciences, 6*(1/2), 7–15.

Franco, Z., & Zimbardo, P. (2006). The banality of heroism. Retrieved from http://greatergood.berkeley.edu/article/item/the_banality_of_heroism.

Franco, Z. E., Blau, K., & Zimbardo, P. (2011). Heroism: A conceptual analysis and differentiation between heroic action and altruism. *Review of General Psychology, 15*(2), 99–113. doi:10.1037/a0022672

Franco, Z., Hayes, A., Lancaster, J., & Kisaaack, A. (2012). Disaster medical education and simulated crisis events: A translational approach. In L. Rothkrantz, J. Ristvej, & Z. Franco (eds), *Proceedings of the 9th International ISCRAM Conference, Vancouver, Canada, April*. Retrieved from www.iscramlive.org/ISCRAM2012/proceedings/145.pdf.

Franco, Z., Zumel, N., Blau, K., & Ayhens-Johnson, K. (2008). Causality, covariates and consensus in ISCRAM research: Towards a more robust study design in a transdisciplinary community. *International Journal of Emergency Management, 5*(1), 100–122. doi: 10.1504/IJEM.2008.019909

Gallagher, S. (2005). *How the body shapes the mind*. Oxford: Clarendon Press.

Gallagher, S., & Zahavi, D. (2008). *The phenomenological mind: An introduction to philosophy of mind and cognitive science*. New York: Routledge.

Gardner, H. (1983). *Frames of mind: The theory of multiple intelligences.* New York: Basic Books.

Gheytanchi, A., Joseph, L., Gierlach, E., Kimpara, S., Housley, J., Franco, Z. E., & Beutler, L. E. (2007). The dirty dozen: twelve failures of the hurricane Katrina response and how psychology can help. *American Psychologist, 62*(2), 118–130. doi: 10.1037/0003-066X.62.2.118

Giller, G. (2014). "Genetic heroes" may be key to treating debilitating diseases. *Scientific American* (May 30). Retrieved from www.scientificamerican.com/article/genetic-heroes-may-be-key-to-treating-debilitating-diseases.

Goethals, G. R., & Allison, S. T. (2012). Making heroes: The construction of courage, competence and virtue. In J. M. Olson & M. P. Zanna (eds), *Advances in Experimental Social Psychology* (Vol. 46, pp. 183–235), San Diego, CA: Elsevier Inc.

Goodwyn, E. (2010). Approaching archetypes: Reconsidering innateness. *Journal of Analytical Psychology, 55*(4), 502–521. doi: 10.1111/j.1468-5922.2010.01862.x

Gray, K. (2010). Moral transformation: Good and evil turn the weak into the mighty. *Social Psychological and Personality Science, 1*(3), 253–258. doi: 10.1177/1948550610367686

Haraway, D. (1988). Situated knowledges: The science question in feminism and the privilege of partial perspective. *Feminist Studies, 14*(3), 575–599. doi: 10.2307/3178066

James, W. M. (1878). Brute and human intellect. *The Journal of Speculative Philosophy, 12*(3), 236–276.

Johnson, M. (2008). What makes a body? *The Journal of Speculative Philosophy, 22*(3), 159–169. doi:10.1353/jsp.0.0046

Johnson, M. (2010). The meaning of the body: Aesthetics of human understanding [video file]. October 4. Retrieved from www.youtube.com/watch?v=HaMeGdrKnEE.

Joy, W. B. (1979). *Joy's way: A map for the transformational journey.* Los Angeles, CA: Tarcher.

Kelly, S., & Dunbar R. I. M. (2001). Who dares, wins. *Human Nature, 12*(2), 89–105.

Kingsley, P. (1999). *In the dark places of wisdom.* Dorset, UK: Element Books Limited.

Kinsella, E. L.. (2012). A psychological perspective on the features and functions of heroes. Retrieved from ProQuest Dissertations and Theses Global.

Knox, J. (2004). From archetypes to reflective function. *Journal of Analytical Psychology, 49*(1), 1–19. doi: 10.1111/j.0021-8774.2004.0437.x

Kotler, S. (2014a). *The rise of superman: Decoding the science of ultimate human performance.* Seattle, WA: Amazon Publishing.

Kotler, S. (2014b). The rise of superman: Decoding the science of ultimate human performance [video file]. May 5. Retrieved from www.youtube.com/watch?v=y1MHyyWsMeE

Krassnitzky, O. (1994). The ecology of suffering (an ecological-anthropological analysis of the experiences of victims of transfusion-related HIV and viral hepatitis infections in Canada). Retrieved from ProQuest Dissertations and Theses Global.

Landau, M. (1984). Human evolution as narrative: Have hero myths and folktales influenced our interpretations of the evolutionary past? *American Scientist, 72*(3), 262–268.

Lawrence, M. S, Phillips, K. J., & Liu, D. R. (2007). Supercharging proteins can impart unusual resilience. *Journal of the American Chemical Society, 129*(33), 10,410–10,112. doi: 10.1021/ja071641y

Lerner, R. M., & Schmid Callina, K. (2014). The study of character development: Towards tests of a relational developmental systems model. *Human Development, 57*(6), 322–446. doi: 10.1159/000368784

Lobel, T. (2014a). *Sensation: The new science of physical intelligence.* New York: Atria Books.

Lobel, T. (2014b). Sensation: The new science of physical intelligence [video file]. May 14. Retrieved from www.youtube.com/watch?v=R33dwl9vjQs.

Lobel, T. (2014c). Hack your brain with sense science, part 1: Introduction and temperature [video file]. July 24. Retrieved from www.youtube.com/watch?v=qLaK2ONM5jc.

Martens, J. W. (2005). Definitions and omissions of heroism. *American Psychologist, 60*(4), 342–343. doi:10.1037/0003-066X.60.4.342

Merleau-Ponty, M. (1962). *Phenomenology of perception* (C. Smith, Trans.). London: Routledge & Kegan Paul. (Original work published 1945).

Merleau-Ponty, M. (1964). *Sense and non-Sense* (H. L. Dreyfus and P. A. Dreyfus, Trans.). Evanston: Northwestern University Press. (Original work published 1948).

Merleau-Ponty, M. (2012). *The phenomenology of perception* (D. A. Landes, Trans.). New York: Routledge.

Monteiro, L. H. A., & Mustaro, P. N. (2012). Hero's journey in bifurcation diagram. *Communications in Nonlinear Science and Numerical Simulation, 17*(6), 2233–2236. doi:10.1016/j.cnsns.2011.09.035

Moya, P. (2014). Habit and embodiment in Merleau-Ponty. *Frontiers in Human Neuroscience, 8*(542), 1–3. doi:10.3389/fnhum.2014.00542

Nelson, S. D. (2011). The posttraumatic growth path: An emerging model for prevention and treatment of trauma-related behavioral health conditions. *Journal of Psychotherapy Integration, 21*(1), 1–42. doi:10.1037/a0022908

Price, R. (1978). *A palpable god*. New York: Atheneum.

Rankin, L. E., & Eagly, A. H. (2008). Is his heroism hailed and hers hidden? Women, men, and the social construction of heroism. *Psychology of Women Quarterly, 32*(4), 414–422. doi: 10.1111/j.1471-6402.2008.00455.x

Rohr, R. (2011). *Falling upward: A spirituality for the two halves of life*. Richmond: Union Theological Seminary.

Rusch, H., Leunissen, J. M., & van Vugt, M. (2015). Historical and experimental evidence of sexual selection for war heroism. *Evolution and Human Behavior, 36*(5), 367–373. doi: 10.1016/j.evolhumbehav.2015.02.005

Shepela, S. T., Cook, J., Horlitz, E., Leal, R., Luciano, S., Lutfy, E., Miller, C., Mitchell, G., & Worden, E. (1999). Courageous resistance: A special case of altruism. *Theory & Psychology, 9*(6), 787–805. doi: 10.1177/0959354399096004

Smirnov, O., Arrow, H., Kennett, D., & Orbell, J. (2007). Ancestral war and the evolutionary origins of "heroism." *The Journal of Politics, 69*(4), 927–940. doi:10.1111/j.1468-2508.2007.00599.x

Smyth, B. (2010). Heroism and history in Merleau-Ponty's existential phenomenology. *Continental Philosophy Review, 43*(2), 167–191. doi:10.1007/s11007-010-9138-5 © Springer Science+Business Media B.V. 2010 "With permission of Springer"

Stenstrom, D. M., & Curtis, M. (2012). Heroism and risk of harm. *Psychology, 3*(12A), 1085–1090. doi: 10.4236/psych.2012.312A160

Stephens, J., & McCallum, R. (1998). *Retelling stories, framing culture: Traditional story and metanarratives in children's literature*. New York, NY: Garland.

Turvey, M. T., & Carello, C. (2012). On intelligence from first principles: Guidelines for inquiry into the hypothesis of physical intelligence (PI). *Ecological Psychology, 24*(1), 3–32. doi:10.1080/10407413.2012.645757 Reprinted by permission of the publisher (Taylor & Francis Ltd, www.tandfonline.com).

Varela, F. J., Thompson, E., & Rosch, E. (1991). *The embodied mind: Cognitive science and human experience*. Cambridge, MA: MIT Press.

Wade, G. H. (1998). A concept analysis of personal transformation. *Journal of Advanced Nursing, 28*(4), 713–719. doi:10.1046/j.1365-2648.1998.00729.x

Weinstein, H. (2012). Beyond courage: The psychology of heroism. Retrieved from ProQuest Dissertations and Theses Global.

Wheal, J. (2013). Hacking the GENOME of flow: Jamie Wheal at TEDxVeniceBeach [video file]. December 26. Retrieved from www.youtube.com/watch?v=WqAtG77JjdM.

Zimbardo, P. (2006). The banality of evil is matched by the banality of heroism. Retrieved from https://edge.org/response-detail/10421.

Zimbardo, P. (2011). The heroic imagination [video file]. August 20. Retrieved from www.youtube.com/watch?v=mWQq0E8ENSc.

Zimbardo, P. (2015). Philip Zimbardo and Matt Langdon at the Hero Round Table 2014: What makes a hero? [video file]. January 21. Retrieved from www.youtube.com/watch?v=ujtkIaAfiSM.

Zimbardo, P., & Ellsberg, D. (2013). Psychology and the new heroism [video file]. Retrieved from www.thepromiseofgrouppsychotherapy.com/psychologyandthenewheroism.html.

Part II
Types of Heroism

9

Everyday Heroes
Determinants of Moral Courage

Anna Halmburger, Anna Baumert, and Manfred Schmitt

On November 15, 2014, 22-year-old Tuğçe Albayrak tried to help two girls who were being harassed by a young man in the restroom of a fast-food restaurant. The dispute escalated in the parking lot where the 18-year-old offender beat Tuğçe down, resulting in severe skull and brain injuries caused by her fall. Eleven days later, she fell into a coma. On November 28, her 23rd birthday, life-support was switched off. Hundreds of people joined silent protests and solemn vigils, and German and international media reports celebrated her as a heroine of moral courage. This example shows that the public protection of moral values, such as physical integrity, is a highly desired but also risky behavior.

The kind of behavior shown by Tuğçe Albayrak in stopping a man from harassing the young women has been termed *moral courage*. It is viewed as highly desirable for the functioning of human societies (Fehr & Gächter, 2002; Kennedy, 1955). However, scientific knowledge about its determinants is relatively scarce. To develop an in-depth understanding of this phenomenon, different forms of moral courage need to be considered, and their underlying processes need to be reviewed. This involves becoming aware of the situational and person factors that promote or inhibit a person from acting in a morally courageous way. Only then will we have the potential to design effective interventions to promote this kind of behavior.

The present chapter provides an overview of the literature on moral courage. First, the phenomenon of moral courage will be introduced and a definition provided. In particular, we will discuss the ways in which it is both similar to and different from heroism. Second, on the basis of theoretical models on helping (Latané & Darley, 1970) and whistleblowing (Gundlach, Douglas, & Martinko, 2003), we will discuss an integrative model of moral courage. Thereby, we will focus on the underlying processes and antecedents of this behavior as revealed in different fields of research. Third, the present chapter will address necessary next steps in research on moral courage as well as practical implications for its promotion.

What is Moral Courage?

Most obviously, the term moral courage involves two central aspects: *morality* and *courage*. This kind of behavior is aimed at protecting moral values and standards, but it also requires courage to overcome barriers and to face potential negative consequences related to this behavior. In general, moral courage (*Zivilcourage* in German, von Keudell, 1901; *courage civique* in French, Le Gall, 1889/2010) is seen as a subtype of *prosocial behavior* specifically aimed at stopping a perpetrator from violating ethical norms (Jonas & Brandstätter, 2004; Voigtländer, 2008). For example, moral courage is directed at stopping the unfair treatment or degradation of people and violence and aggression against weaker individuals (Frey, Schäfer, & Neumann, 1999). More generally, moral courage is morally relevant because it is directed toward reinforcing moral standards and values (Miller, 2000; Skitka, 2011). Such standards involve a variety of issues such as the protection of human rights, the principles of equality and justice, or the rights of minorities. They all represent a common understanding of what is "wrong" and what is "right" according to societal consensus and culturally specific proscriptions (Tangney, Stuewig, & Mashek, 2007). Most important, moral courage reflects not only a passive inclination to embrace moral values (i.e., perceiving a norm violation as wrong) but the active (and potentially public) protection of such values. Especially in the organizational context, a body of literature has investigated morally courageous behavior under the term *whistleblowing*. This behavior has been defined as "the disclosure by organizational members (former or current) of illegal, immoral, or illegitimate practices under the control of their employers, to persons or organizations that may be able to effect action" (Near & Miceli, 1985, p. 4). Whistleblowing can be aimed at stopping sexual harassment, abuse, mobbing, or illegal business practices (Anand, Ashforth, & Joshi, 2004). By integrating previous empirical findings on whistleblowing in organizations, we are able to extend our knowledge of important situational and personal antecedents of morally courageous behavior. As the following case exemplifies, this kind of behavior is highly desirable but also involves potential negative (social) consequences.

In 2007, New Jersey State Trooper Justin Hopson became the witness of an unlawful arrest of a citizen and false reports made by his training officer (New York Times, 2007). When he refused to testify in favor of this arrest in court, he received threatening notes and was physically assaulted by a group of troopers known as the "Lords of Discipline." When Hopson discovered that this group had been bullying fellow troopers for decades, he officially lodged a complaint. As a result of a 2-year investigation, 14 victims identified themselves, and seven troopers who had been involved in harassing the victims were suspended. This case is still known as one of the largest internal investigations in U.S. state police history, and the report of the investigation is publicly available (Department of Law and Public Safety, 2005).

This example illustrates the second of the two core aspects of moral courage: Courage is needed for a person to intervene in a fight or stop a thief on the street, to speak out for foreigners in a group of hostile nationalists, or to report to a supervisor that a colleague mobbed another employee. This is especially the case as such behavior will likely not be welcomed by the perpetrators, supervisors, or other observers (Dyck, Morse, & Zingales, 2010; Miceli, Dozier, & Near, 1991; Monin, Sawyer, & Marquez, 2008). In fact, a person who engages in morally courageous behavior typically has to face severe consequences, for example, vengeful acts, insults or attacks committed by the perpetrator (Greitemeyer, Fischer, Kastenmüller, & Frey, 2006; Kidder, 2005; Meyer & Hermann, 2000), the loss of social approval (Miller, 2000), social exclusion, or discrimination (Parmerlee, Near, & Jensen, 1982). According to Dyck and colleagues (2010), about 80 percent of named whistleblowers were either fired, quit their job under duress, or found their responsibilities significantly altered as a consequence of their engagement. In this sense, moral courage is courageous because this kind of behavior is enacted despite an inherent uncertainty about the reactions of the perpetrator or other bystanders and potential negative social consequences for the intervening person (Batson, 1998; Fischer et al., 2004; Niesta Kayser et al., 2010).

Besides the aim of protecting moral values and the need for courage, researchers have also discussed additional characteristics of morally courageous behavior. According to Greitemeyer, Osswald, Fischer, and Frey (2007), morally courageous behavior is often directed toward a more powerful person or group and is thus characterized by an imbalance with the disadvantages falling on the side of the morally courageous person (Lopez, O'Byrne, & Peterson, 2003). Skitka

(2011) additionally argued that moral courage is rare because the intervening person often has to overcome the strong influences of *social obedience* by declining to adhere to the rules of the authorities or of *group conformity* as regulation through a social majority. To act disobediently or to break social rules emphasizes another important characteristic of morally courageous behavior. Although it is based on morality, it can be seen as antisocial behavior because it usually violates norms (e.g., privacy) for a greater good.

What Makes Moral Courage Heroic?

The case of Tuğçe Albayrak is only one case of many where morally courageous behavior was termed a heroic act by the public. Indeed, moral courage and heroism have some strong conceptual overlapping qualities. Franco and Zimbardo (2006) defined heroism as behavior directed toward a noble purpose, involving the willingness to accept negative consequences. Thus, moral courage and heroism can be seen as highly similar. However, scholars have discussed their distinctness on the basis of the precise nature of the values at stake as well as the kinds of costs that are (potentially) involved (Osswald, Greitemeyer, Fischer, & Frey, 2010a). Moral courage has been repeatedly found to be related to a person's inclination to embrace justice values (Baumert et al., 2013; Osswald et al., 2010a; Waytz, Dungan, & Young, 2013). For example, Osswald and colleagues (2010a, Study 5) found that an experimental activation of justice values (compared with a neutral condition) increased participants' likelihood of being willing to participate in discussions with young right-wing extremist delinquents. By contrast, heroism was shown to be strongly associated with loyalty (e.g., Wansink, Payne, & Ittersum, 2008). In more detail, Wansink and colleagues (2008) found that veterans of World War II were more likely to have received medals for heroism if they reported valuing loyalty compared with those who did not. As a further distinction, Osswald and colleagues (2010a) argue that moral courage should be associated with potential social costs, whereas heroism primarily involves potential physical costs such as physical harm or death. Indeed, when empirically comparing different scenarios in which prosocial behaviors occur, the authors found that moral courage was more strongly related to potential social costs than heroism was. By contrast, heroism scenarios were perceived as more dangerous than moral courage scenarios. However, as the example of Tuğçe Albayrak shows, such theoretical distinctions between heroism and moral courage on the basis of the type of negative consequences often do not represent our everyday understanding. By contrast, it can be assumed that the distinction between moral courage and heroism is rather gradual: A broad range of morally courageous behaviors involve potential social and physical risks. From this point of view, we suggest that moral courage be viewed as "everyday heroism" as it represents the courageous standing up for moral values across a range of daily norm violations and conflicts.

An Integrative Model of Moral Courage

Whereas the previous sections addressed the question of what morally courageous behavior is, in the following, we draw attention to the question of why some people engage in morally courageous behavior, whereas others stand and watch or turn away. However, the development of theoretical models as well as empirical studies on moral courage is still scarce. For this reason, we adapted a psychological model by Latané and Darley (1970) that was initially developed to explain helping behavior. We use this adapted model to identify processes that are potentially involved in the determination of morally courageous behavior. Speaking in favor of the applicability of this model, moral courage and helping represent two subtypes of prosocial behavior (e.g., Jonas & Brandstätter, 2004). Whereas moral courage is aimed at stopping or redressing a norm violation (Jonas & Brandstätter, 2004; Voigtländer, 2008), *helping behavior* benefits others in need (Batson, 1998; Hinde & Groebel, 1991). Examples of prototypical helping behaviors are social support, giving assistance, or donating (Batson, 1998). A body of literature has suggested that determinants of helping might also be useful for predicting moral courage (e.g., Kuhl, 1986; Labuhn, Wagner, van Dick, & Christ, 2004; Niesta Kayser et al., 2010). For example, empathic feelings for a victim of a norm violation were found to be positively related to morally courageous behavior intentions (Labuhn et al., 2004) and have been identified as a motivational source of helping (Batson, 1998; Eisenberg & Miller, 1987). In addition, results from Niesta Kayser and colleagues (2010, Study 3) suggest that moral courage and helping are both related to a person's moral beliefs or convictions. Thus, it is plausible to use findings on helping behavior as a starting point from which to investigate morally courageous behavior.

However, despite the similarities regarding the above-mentioned findings, research has revealed crucial differences in the psychological processes involved in moral courage and helping. The empirical findings by Osswald and colleagues (2010a) indicate that moral courage is more strongly based on a person's inclination to embrace justice (i.e., honesty, fairness), whereas helping reflects a person's inclination to care (i.e., compassion, helpfulness). Although empathic feelings were found to be related to morally courageous intentions (Labuhn et al., 2004), they seem to be less central to moral courage than to helping (Greitemeyer et al., 2006). As a situational factor, the bystander effect, which has been found to reduce helping (Latané & Nida, 1981), does not appear to affect moral courage (Fischer, Greitemeyer, Pollozek, & Frey, 2006; Harari, Harari, & White, 1985; Schwartz & Gottlieb, 1976).

For helping to occur, five stages of psychological processes need to be established:

1 An incident has to be witnessed, and
2 it has to be interpreted as an emergency
3 the witness has to assume personal responsibility, and
4 he or she must feel able to help
5 to make a final decision, the benefits have to outweigh the anticipated costs

This model can easily be adapted to morally courageous behavior by focusing on the detection and interpretation of a behavior as a norm violation instead of an emergency. On the basis of these differences, the applicability of the helping model to moral courage needs to be carefully reviewed.

In addition to the helping model (Latané & Darley, 1970), we draw on a social information processing model by Gundlach and colleagues (2003) employed to explain the whistleblower's decision-making process. In line with the helping model, the social information processing model (Gundlach et al., 2003) proposes that morally courageous behavior is the result of a person's detection (Stage 1), interpretation (Stage 2), and cost-benefit analyses (Stage 5). Whereas the helping model focuses on the role of an observer's perceived responsibility to intervene (Stage 3), the social information processing model instead considers the strength with which the observer attributes responsibility to the wrongdoer. As a main extension, Gundlach and colleagues (2003) emphasized the importance of observers' emotional reactions to a wrongdoing in their willingness to engage in morally courageous behavior. By considering the two theoretical models, our integrative model of moral courage includes cognitive and emotional processes as well as their interplay. In the following, we will shed light on the processes underlying moral courage in more detail. Thereby, we aim to achieve a more complete understanding of the situational and personal determinants of morally courageous behavior. Moreover, we aim to extend the scope of the integrated model by applying it to all types of moral courage instead of focusing on related concepts (i.e., helping) or subforms (i.e., whistle-blowing). For this purpose, empirical findings from different fields will be reviewed.

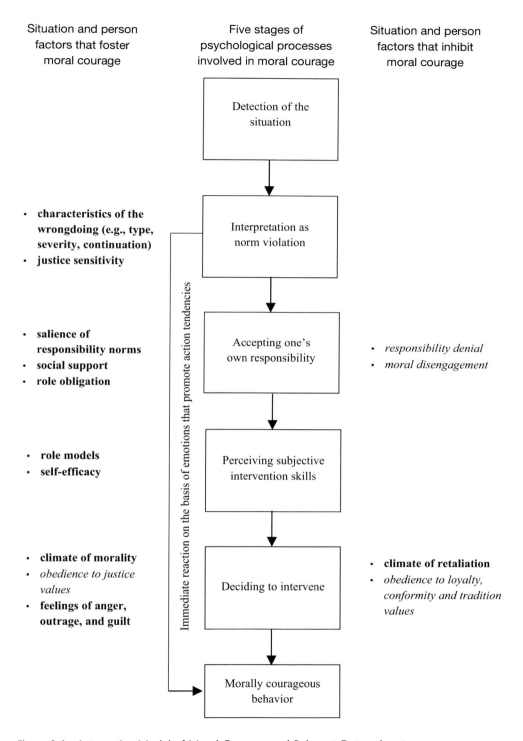

Figure 9.1 Integrative Model of Moral Courage and Relevant Determinants

Note: The integrative model of moral courage exclusively contains situation and person factors that were empirically found to be related to either moral courage intentions (in italic) or morally courageous behavior (in bold).

Stage 1: Detection

In accordance with both theoretical models (Gundlach et al., 2003; Latané & Darley, 1970), a situation has to be witnessed to initiate a certain behavior as a reaction. It is plausible that diverse kinds of situational circumstances can reduce the probability that a person will focus his/her attention on an acute norm violation. As Darley and Batson (1973) demonstrated in their empirical studies on helping behavior, *time pressure* potentially shifts a person's attention from the occurrence of an emergency to personal aims. More specifically, they provided evidence that the probability of helping a person in need dropped by 50 percent when participants were put (compared with not put) under time pressure beforehand. On the basis of post-experimental interviews with the participants, the authors interpreted their findings to mean that most participants simply did not even see the person who was in need. In line with this, it is highly plausible that circumstances that limit a person's attention prevent morally courageous behavior.

Stage 2: Interpretation

Once a person observes a certain incident, he or she has to interpret it as a norm violation to engage in morally courageous behavior. This is particularly important as such situations are often highly ambiguous. For example, at first glance, if a female applicant was not hired, it would not be easy to see whether this was because of her gender or because of her skills. Thus, situation and person factors that influence a person's interpretation should be very important for moral courage.

In accordance with the social information processing model (Gundlach et al., 2003), a person's *attribution* of an observed behavior is crucial at this stage. To the extent that an observer attributes behaviors that endanger moral values to the bad intentions of an actor or actors rather than to situational circumstances (e.g., Weiner, 1985), the observer will be more likely to show behavior that is aimed at protecting these values. A behavior that is interpreted as due to the internal characteristics of the wrongdoer, controllable by this party, and stable over time will more likely result in whistleblowing (Gundlach et al., 2003). In support of these assumptions, Near and Miceli (1985, 1996) provided evidence that *characteristics of the wrongdoing* as type, severity, and continuation influence the interpretation of a situation as a norm violation and promote a person's willingness to engage in behavior to protest against a norm violation in an organization. In line with empirical findings from helping behavior (Shotland & Huston, 1979), we assume that severe wrongdoings should be more likely to be detected and interpreted as norm violations because they differ more strongly from normal behaviors. It is also highly plausible that the more often a perpetrator violates norms, the more likely such norm violations will be detected as well as attributed to the internal and stable characteristics of the perpetrator rather than to situational circumstances (e.g., Carroll, Perkowitz, Lurigio, & Weaver, 1987; Feather & Souter, 2002).

If a setting leaves no room for (re-)interpretation at all (i.e., it is clearly a norm violation), the probability that a witness will intervene will be high compared with ambiguous settings. Especially in such ambiguous settings, witnesses tend to rely on additional information drawn from the reactions of other witnesses. Depending on the behavior of other witnesses, this could either promote or decrease a person's tendency to interpret a perpetrator's behavior as a norm violation. In the latter case, this phenomenon has been called *pluralistic ignorance* in research on helping behavior, meaning that the inaction of other bystanders is employed as information that speaks against viewing the incident as an emergency (Latané & Nida, 1981; Thornberg, 2007). As a broad body of literature on pro-environmental behavior showed, the behavior of others are viewed as descriptive norms and therefore influence how likely a person perceive the respective behavior as morally accepted (e.g., Cialdini, 2005; Nolan, Schultz, Cialdini, Goldstein, &

Griskevicius, 2008). Thus, transferred to morally courageous behavior, the action or inaction of other witnesses might influence a person's interpretation of a potential norm violation.

In a series of empirical studies, Gino and Bazerman (2009) tried to answer the question: Under what conditions do people ignore unethical behaviors in organizations? The results of their studies suggest a *slippery-slope effect*, meaning that gradual erosions of ethical standards are less likely to be detected compared with an abrupt change. In this sense, norm violations might not be detected due to the implicit bias of the observers. As one explanation, Ashford and Anand (2003) argued that unethical acts can evolve as part of a daily routine to such an extent that employees are unable to detect them. Moreover, Anand et al. (2004) identified *rationalization structures*, which collectively undermine the interpretation of behaviors as wrongdoing. For example, harm is denied and corruption is downplayed or argued as necessary for realizing higher-order goals, or in order to protect the reputation and functioning of an organization.

According to van den Bos, Müller, and van Bussel (2009), social mechanisms that inhibit a person's action can be overridden by *behavioral disinhibition*. Behavioral disinhibition describes a person's predisposition to act with no inhibitions toward a specific goal (Carver & White, 1994; Gray, 1972). In their study, van den Bos and colleagues (2009) found that experimentally increasing participants' disinhibition by instructing them to act freely and with no bounds reduced the bystander effect on helping behavior. Transferred to the context of moral courage, it could be assumed that others' inactions or rationalizations lead a person to conclude that nothing has gone wrong. However, this interpretational bias can be reduced by a witness' predisposition to disinhibit such social restrictions.

Besides situational factors, personality dispositions that reflect a person's readiness to perceive and interpret situations as involving a norm violation should promote moral courage. Two personality dispositions have been found to be especially important: justice sensitivity and moral convictions. The personality disposition *justice sensitivity* (Baumert & Schmitt, in press; Schmitt, Baumert, Gollwitzer, & Maes, 2010) can be argued to be an important determinant of moral courage as it has been found to involve a perceptual readiness for the violation of justice norms as well as the interpretation of ambiguous situations as unjust (Baumert, Gollwitzer, Staubach, & Schmitt, 2011; Baumert, Otto, Thomas, Bobocel, & Schmitt, 2012). According to Mikula (1980), a norm violation can be witnessed from different perspectives. In accordance with these perspectives, justice sensitivity is represented by a person's observer sensitivity, victim sensitivity, beneficiary sensitivity, and perpetrator sensitivity (Schmitt et al., 2010). All these perspectives represent a person's perceptual threshold for injustice, meaning that a highly justice-sensitive person detects injustice even if only a few or rather ambiguous cues point toward injustice (Thomas, Baumert, & Schmitt, 2012). Most important, empirical studies have provided evidence that a person's justice sensitivity is related to his/her morally courageous behavioral intentions (e.g., Krettek, 2007; Niesta Kayser et al., 2010; Pfetsch, Steffgen, & Schiffhauer, 2009) and real behavior (Baumert et al., 2013). For example, a person's beneficiary sensitivity predicted the strength with which participants intervened to stop a thief from stealing a mobile phone (Baumert et al., 2013).

Besides justice sensitivity, previous findings on *moral convictions* indicate that this disposition also influences people's interpretations of a potential norm violation. Moral convictions can be understood as fundamental beliefs about right and wrong, morality and immorality (Skitka & Wisneski, 2011; Skitka, 2011). For example, a person's strong conviction that life is sacred could involve the belief that abortion is wrong under any circumstances. Thus, such a conviction is not limited to justice principles but refers to all kinds of moral domains. Moral convictions have been found to reduce conformity with group behavior and other forms of social influence on a person's judgment (Skitka, 2011). Thus, it can be argued that strong convictions should lead to interpretations and moral judgments that are less likely to be influenced by social and situational factors. In line with this idea, empirical findings have provided evidence that people reject the decisions of authorities when such decisions were not consistent with their own moral convictions (Bauman & Skitka, 2007; Skitka, Baumann, & Lytle, 2009; Skitka & Mullen, 2002). In one of these studies (Skitka et al., 2009), people with strong moral convictions against physician-assisted suicide more often interpreted the U.S. Supreme Court decision as illegitimate compared with people with no such moral convictions.

Stage 3: Accepting One's Own Responsibility

If a person interprets a situation as involving a norm violation, it is important to know whether the person sees him- or herself as responsible for the redressing of this norm violation. Again, situation and person factors likely determine the relevant processes at this stage and thus influence the probability that a person will exhibit morally courageous behavior.

With regard to situation factors, previous studies have indicated that a person's perceived responsibility can be increased when *norms of responsibility* are situationally emphasized (Levine & Crowther, 2008; Osswald, Greitemeyer, Fischer, & Frey, 2010b; Rutkowski, Gruder, & Romer, 1983). In addition, two empirical studies showed that the activation of prosocial norms via film material fostered participants' subsequent intervention against the (staged) discrimination of a foreign student (see Osswald et al., 2010b). Furthermore, the results of Near and Miceli's (1996) study suggest that people are more likely to blow the whistle in organizations if they reported not having a role-related obligation due to their job position.

Previous research on helping provided evidence that the reaction of other bystanders influence a person's interpretation of the situation (pluralistic ignorance). In addition, the presence of other bystanders might decrease a person's willingness to accept own responsibility. The *bystander effect* has also been investigated with regard to moral courage. These findings have indicated that the number of bystanders has no impact on moral courage (Bleda, Bleda, & White, 1976; Fischer et al., 2006). The lack of relation between the number of bystanders and the probability that people will exhibit morally courageous behavior is highly plausible. On the one hand, research on helping behavior has repeatedly shown that an increasing number of bystanders leads to a greater likelihood of *diffusion of responsibility* (Blair, Thompson, & Wuensch, 2005; Solomon, Solomon & Stone, 1978; Thornberg, 2007). On the other hand, the availability of bystanders can be perceived as *social support*, especially in dangerous situations, and might thereby promote moral courage. Empirical field experiments speak in favor of this claim, showing that whistleblowing was more likely to occur when there were many compared with only a few observers (Miceli et al., 1991). Similarly, interventions against a fictitious rape were more frequently by groups than individual bystanders (Harari, Harari, & White, 1985).

Whether personal responsibility will be assumed in a situation in which a norm violation occurred may also be determined by a person's dispositional tendency to deny or accept responsibility in general. One important disposition in this context is *moral disengagement* (Bandura, Barbaranelli, Caprara, & Pastorelli, 1996). This disposition captures individual differences in how strongly people disengage from their own moral standards by (among other strategies) attributing responsibility to others or to situational circumstances (Bandura et al., 1996). In order to avoid self-censure and feelings of guilt, people with a high tendency toward moral disengagement attribute their failure to stop or redress a norm violation to external sources such as social pressure or a potential victim. Therefore, high moral disengagement should reduce a person's inclination to adhere to moral norms and display morally courageous behavior. Although this relation is theoretically plausible, previous studies have provided only preliminary empirical support. Vignette studies found a negative relation between moral disengagement and the self-reported willingness to engage in morally courageous behavior (i.e., stopping a student from teasing her classmate; Paciello, Fida, Cerniglia, Tramontano, & Cole, 2013; Baumert et al., 2013). By contrast, the empirical results of a study by Baumert and colleagues (2013) showed no relation between moral disengagement and intervening in a real theft situation. This mixed pattern of result suggests that further research is needed to clarify the role of moral disengagement in moral courage.

Similarly to moral disengagement, the personality disposition *responsibility denial* can be seen as highly plausible predictor of morally courageous behavior. According to Schwartz and Howard (1981), responsibility denial reflects a person's stable tendency to deny norm violations or emergencies, relativize the importance of norms, play down negative consequences of own behavior, as well as pass the buck to others (Schwartz, 1977). In general, Schwartz and Howard (1980) found that persons with low compared with high responsibility denial more likely acted consistently with their personal norms. Results of vignette-studies furthermore provided empirical evidence that a person's inclination to deny own responsibility is negatively related to his/her morally courageous behavioral intentions (Krettek, 2007; Labuhn et al., 2004).

Stage 4: Subjective Intervention Skills

A person confronted with a norm violation might feel responsible for acting but might still withdraw from the situation if the person perceives him- or herself as unable to intervene due to situational or personal constraints.

Empirical evidence for the relevance of situation factors at this stage of moral courage is rather scarce. It seems plausible that previous experiences with similar situations or the availability of successful role models should increase a person's willingness to engage. Results from interviews with whistleblowers in organizations support this assumption, suggesting that *role models* help people to anticipate efficient and inefficient ways to stop a norm violation (Henik, 2008).

As a person factor, generalized *self-efficacy* beliefs might be important determinants of perceived intervention skills as they reflect the degree to which people see themselves as capable of coping effectively with challenges in everyday life (Bandura, 1997). On the basis of fictitious scenarios, Kuhl (1986) found that self-assurance was positively related to intentions to engage in behavior reflecting moral courage. More important, previous studies have provided evidence that self-efficacy is positively related to whistleblowing behavior (MacNab & Worthley, 2008; Miceli, van Scotter, Near, & Regh, 2001).

Stage 5: Decision to Act

As proposed by both theoretical models discussed above (Gundlach et al., 2003; Latané & Darley, 1970), people are assumed to conduct cost-benefit analyses in order to make a decision about whether to intervene or not. In addition, Eisenberg (1991) argued that salient moral norms as well as emotions shape a person's decision to act. Therefore, the importance and interplay of norms and emotions will also be discussed in this section.

As mentioned before, morally courageous behavior is characterized by potential negative (social or physical) consequences a person has to face. Such potential costs involve retaliation by the perpetrator, physical harm, social exclusion, job loss, or defamation of the person's own character. In addition, observers might benefit from nonintervention as they spare time and effort. By contrast, however, a nonintervention might also be costly as important values are at stake or a victim might be harmed, both of which can lead to potential experiences of self-censure, such as feelings of guilt and shame. Moreover, people might benefit from acting in accordance with their own moral standards, thus increasing public or workplace safety or protecting the victims who are involved, as well as gaining a sense of self-consistency (Blasi, 1999; DeQuervain, Fischbacher, Treyer, Schellhammer, Schnyder, Buck, & Fehr, 2004). Assumedly, the costs and benefits of intervening and not intervening will be weighed against each other to make a decision. If the anticipated benefits of intervention and the anticipated costs of nonintervention outweigh the costs of intervention and the benefits of nonintervention, people should be more likely to decide to intervene. In the following, we will discuss situation and person factors that could influence the perception of costs and benefits in a situation that requires morally courageous behavior. In line with Gundlach and colleagues (2003) as well as Eisenberg (1991), the importance of values and emotions will be stressed.

The Anticipated Costs of Intervening

The costs of morally courageous behavior have been found to be related to the degree to which moral standards are perceived to be shared and protected on the one hand and the fear of retaliation on the other hand. For example, people are more likely to blow the whistle on a wrongdoing if they perceive that their organization has a *climate of morality* that is responsive and supportive of such behavior (Miceli & Near, 1988; Near & Miceli, 1995). By contrast, they will be less likely to report wrongdoings when they perceive a *climate of retaliation* for potential whistleblowers (Keenan, 1995; King, 1999; Near & Miceli, 1996). Thus, expectations of others' reactions to a person's morally courageous behavior should be very important to his/her decision.

Plausibly, feelings of *anxiety* may lower the likelihood of intervention. In line with this idea, observers of norm violations probably fear negative consequences from the perpetrator or other observers as reactions to their engagement (Karakashian, Walter, Christopher, & Lucas, 2006). As a result, they should be highly motivated to withdraw from the situation instead of stopping a wrongdoer. Up to now, previous research has neglected to explore the influence of state feelings of anxiety on morally courageous behavior. By contrast, previous studies have considered the impact of the personality trait of *social anxiety* on prosocial behavior. In general, highly social anxious people tend to more often and more strongly react with feelings of anxiety in anticipated or real threat situations than low social anxious ones (e.g., Kashdan & Steger, 2006). With regard to moral courage situations, social anxiety should chronically increase concerns about negative social consequences (e.g., vengeful reactions of the perpetrator), thus inhibiting moral courage. As indicated by previous studies, dispositional anxiety inhibits prosocial behavior (Karakashian et al., 2006), especially in situations of social threat (McGovern, 1976). Thus, it is theoretically plausible that highly socially anxious people will be less likely to engage in morally courageous behavior.

By contrast, research on helping has revealed that social anxiety might also accentuate the negative consequences of nonintervention if the situation contains cues that trigger reputational concerns (van Bommel et al., 2012). When situations contained cues that indicated that nonintervention might be scrutinized, social anxiety was found to increase rather than decrease prosocial behavior (Garcia, Weaver, Darley, & Spence, 2009). Accordingly, a person's social anxiety could either foster or decrease morally courageous behavior, depending on the person's perception of the respective situation. In line with these two opposing effects, Baumert and colleagues (2013) found a negative but nonsignificant relation between social anxiety and intervening in a theft situation.

The Anticipated Cost of Not Intervening

The costs of not intervening can roughly be distinguished in two categories: costs that involve the observer, not acting in line with his/her moral values, and costs that involve the harm of the victim.

According to Skitka (2011), people are likely to experience a deep threat to their personal sense of moral authenticity if they fail to defend their core moral convictions. In line with this, it can be argued that not intervening in a norm violation situation involves high costs for the observer if these norms are important to him/her. This should especially be the case when personal values are highly salient in the respective situation (Eisenberg, 1991). In general, a violation of important norms has been found to be accompanied by a state of cognitive and emotional distress for the respective person (Tangney et al., 2007). Empirical findings by Skitka and Wisneski (2011) indicate that people's moral convictions towards an issue (i.e., war, physician-assisted suicide) are strongly related to negative emotions. Similarly, people who are highly sensitive to injustice have been found to intensively ruminate and experience negative emotions about a perceived injustice (Schmitt, Neumann, & Montada, 1995). More important, a threat to personally important values will most likely promote value-restoring behavior (e.g., Wenzel, Okimoto, Feather, & Platow, 2008). When moral values are violated with great severity, a person should experience this threat as particularly dreadful and should hence be very likely to engage in restoring such values. Indeed, Near and Miceli's (1985, 1996) empirical results indicated that people are more likely to blow the whistle on wrongdoings they perceive as severe as opposed to minor.

When witnessing a norm violation, people have been found to respond with *anger* and *outrage* toward the perpetrator (Batson et al., 2007; Hoffman, 2000; Mikula, Scherer, & Athenstaedt, 1998; Montada & Schneider, 1989). In line with previous findings, it can be argued that such emotions interact with processes at different stages, thus, affecting moral courage. On the one hand, the interpretation of a situation as a norm violation (Stage 2) should promote strong anger reactions (e.g., Batson et al., 2007; Hoffman, 2000; Montada & Schneider, 1989). Speaking in favor of this claim, Nelissen and Zeelenberg (2009) found that a person's anger about a norm violation was strongly related to how much he/she perceived the wrongdoer's behavior as intentional. On the other hand, anger and outrage should directly affect morally courageous behavior because such emotions have been found to promote action and approach tendencies (Harmon-Jones & Sigelman, 2001; Mackie, Devos, & Smith, 2000). In other words, a person who experiences anger as a response to a norm violation should be more likely to engage in value-protecting behavior and less likely to withdraw from the situation. Although this has not yet been systematically investigated, it can be argued that anger and outrage emphasize the benefits of value-protecting behavior while reducing its perceived costs. Indeed, anger has been found to be a motivator of value-reaffirming action tendencies such as retribution (Carlsmith, Darley, & Robinson, 2002; de Rivera, Gerstmann, & Maisels, 2002) and protesting (Rothmund, Baumert, & Zinkernagel, 2014; Valentino, Brader, Groenendyk, Gregorowicz, & Hutchings, 2011). An important point is that anger has been found to promote value-reaffirming behavior even when the respective behavior was related to high personal costs (Nelissen & Zeelenberg, 2009). Empirical findings from both vignette studies (Krettek, 2007; Greitemeyer et al., 2006) and studies involving real behavior (Halmburger et al., 2014; Niesta Kayser et al., 2010, Study 3) have supported this claim, providing evidence that anger fosters moral courage. For example, when participants were confronted with a theft, their experience of anger and their facial expressions predicted the intensity with which they immediately tried to stop the thief (Halmburger et al., 2014).

Feelings of *guilt* are also typically involved when people witness norm violations. They can serve the function of acting as a person's emotional barometer, providing feedback if his/her behavior is congruent with social and moral norms (Tobey-Klass, 1978; Nelissen, Leliveld, Van Dijk, & Zeelenberg, 2011; Tangney et al., 2007). Such discrepancies are not restricted to a person's own wrongdoings but can also be experienced from the perspective of an uninvolved bystander (Mikula, 1980). If a person feels responsible for stopping or redressing a norm violation, a failure to intervene should induce feelings of guilt. Hence, the other way around, anticipated guilt can be expected to promote a person's morally courageous behavior. An empirical study on bargaining scenarios provided evidence that emphasizing participants' responsibility for the outcome of a situation increased feelings of guilt and, through this, their willingness to punish the unfair allocator (Nelissen & Zeelenberg, 2009). This study also indicated that anger and guilt independently affected value-reaffirming behavior (Nelissen & Zeelenberg, 2009). With regard to moral courage, Halmburger and colleagues (2014) showed that self-reported acute guilt was positively related to participants' interventions in stopping a thief. However, the results also suggested that in direct comparison with anger, guilt seems to play only a minor role in determining moral courage.

Besides the costs of nonintervention that are directly linked to the moral values of the observer, further costs exist when concrete victims of norm violations are present. Observing the suffering of others was found to induce feelings of *empathy* (Batson & Shaw, 1991). Empathy is directed toward the feelings of others, promoting prosocial engagement to improve a victim's condition (Eisenberg, Guthrie, Cumberland, Murphy, & Shepard, 2002). Thus, nonintervention should be less likely when an observer feels empathy toward the victim of a norm violation. In particular, people with high *dispositional empathy* should more often engage in morally courageous behavior in order to reduce the costs of nonintervention for the victim. However, results on the effects of empathy on morally courageous behavior have been mixed. In vignette studies, empathy was found to enhance self-reported moral courage (Labuhn et al., 2004; Paciello et al., 2013). When actual behavior was observed, dispositional empathy predicted only helping but not moral courage (Niesta Kayser et al., 2010). A preliminary conclusion might be that morally courageous behavior is indeed more about the protection of moral values and less about the harm inflicted on a concrete victim. Thus, a plausible explanation for this pattern of results might be that only in situations when a victim is in the bystander's focus of attention, feelings of empathy as well as dispositional empathy foster morally courageous behavior. However, our understanding of moral courage will truly benefit from a more systematic investigation of the importance and the interplay of the emotions that are involved.

The present section addressed different costs and benefits of intervening and not intervening. However, in many cases, a strict distinction between costs and benefits is not possible because they are closely related to each other. For example, when people detect norm violations, they often experience a conflict between different values: For example, their obligation to uphold justice values pushes them to intervene, whereas their conformity, loyalty, and tradition values urge them to remain calm (Bardi & Schwartz, 2003; Waytz et al., 2013). When asking participants to recall a situation when they did not report a wrongdoing, Waytz and colleagues (2013) found that they often stated that this decision was driven by their loyalty to their organization, colleagues, and superiors. Similarly, Bardi and Schwartz (2003) demonstrated that normative pressures to obey conformity and tradition values decrease the probability to intervene. Thus morally courageous behaviors involve the benefits of acting in congruence with justice values, but are genuinely related to the costs of violating one's values of loyalty, conformity, and tradition. In sum, a person's decision to intervene in a norm violation situation should be the result of a complex weighing of costs and benefits, accompanied by potential conflicting values and emotions.

Future Research and Practical Implications

After we summarize the most important point of the present chapter, this last section will address ideas about future steps in research on moral courage as well as the practical implications of recent findings.

What We Can(not) Learn from the Research on Moral Courage

Taken together, moral courage is based on morality, and depends on situation and person factors that shape the predisposition to act in accordance with moral values. Moreover, a person's courage is needed to overcome barriers and the fear of negative (social or physical) consequences. As both characteristics are also central to heroism, morally courageous behavior can be understood as a less risky form of heroism. In other words, moral courage represents everyday heroism. As the integrative model of moral courage reflects (Figure 9.1), this kind of behavior is the result of a complex interplay of a person's cognitions, judgments, and emotions regarding a norm violation. At all stages, situation and person factors can either promote or inhibit a person's willingness to engage in morally courageous behavior. Our review furthermore indicates that some stages might be of higher importance in forming morally courageous behavior in comparison with others. Whereas empirical results clearly supported the relevance of the detecting and interpretation of an incident as norm violation, results on an observer's responsibility and skills are either mixed or scarce. In line with theoretical claims, we furthermore found that empirical findings provide strong evidence for the involvement of emotions in morally courageous behavior.

Still, some important barriers need to be overcome in future research to find answers to the question of why some people engage in morally courageous behavior whereas others do not. As findings on cost-benefit analyses exemplified, the different processes, antecedents, and their interplay are rather complex and should be in the focus of future research. Besides this, one major challenge lies in transferring previous empirical findings that were based on retrospective self-reports or fictitious scenarios to real behavior. Surprisingly, this central point has often been neglected in previous research. Most empirical studies have been based on the assessment of *intentions* to engage in behavior reflecting moral courage rather than the assessment of real behavior (Greitemeyer et al., 2006; Hornsey, Majkut, Terry, & McKimmie, 2003; Meyer & Hermann, 2000; Osswald et al., 2010a). This is partly due to the fact that it is much less economical and much more difficult to examine real moral courage compared with self-reports and vignette studies. Furthermore, it is challenging to generate credible situations or to make observations in everyday life. As ethical considerations prohibit an exposure of participants to danger or to unreasonable psychological stress, some prototypical situations cannot be examined (e.g., situations that involve physical harm to victims or observers). Still, it is important to investigate real morally courageous behavior instead of behavioral intentions. It has been repeatedly criticized that self-reported intentions on the basis of hypothetical descriptions have only limited validity (Back & Egloff, 2009; Baumeister, Vohs, & Funder, 2007; Baumert et al., 2013). Most important, comparative studies by Voigtländer (2008) provided evidence that people strongly overestimate their own inclination to show moral courage. In more detail, participants' self-reported morally courageous behavioral intention rates were significantly higher than their actual behavior in the same kind of situation. Similarly, the results of a meta-analytic study on whistleblowing showed extremely low relations between behavioral intentions and real behavior (Mesmer-Magus & Viswesvaran, 2005). Moreover, this meta-analysis and empirical studies by Baumert and colleagues (2013) suggest that self-reported intentions and real behaviors are influenced by different situational and personal factors. One explanation for this pattern has been provided by van Boven, Lowenstein, and Dunning (2005). They assume that people misjudge their intervention rates as their ability to imagine the emotional state in the respective situation is limited. This idea has been supported by studies on bystander interventions against racism (Kawakami, Dunn, Karmali, & Dovidio, 2009). The authors found that participants who watched a video or read about an act of racism strongly overrated how emotional distressed they would feel compared with a group of participants that experiences this respective situation. The central conclusion from these studies is that "wanting to be a hero" is not the same as "being a hero." Thus, future research on moral courage has to find ways to investigate persons' real behavior instead of just their behavioral intentions.

How Can People Become Everyday Heroes?

Although the phenomenon of moral courage is not yet fully understood, the present chapter adds to its understanding as we systematically reviewed empirical findings and discussed them under the light of one integrative model. The development of interventions aimed at promoting moral courage is an important step toward a better society. In the following, some important practical implications from the present summary of findings will be discussed. On the basis of previous findings on the impact of a moral personality (Baumert et al., 2013; Skitka, 2011), the importance of supporting the development of moral convictions that are in line with human ethics should be emphasized. Most important, each individual should be encouraged to overcome social or personal restrictions that hamper them from acting in accordance with their own moral convictions. In particular, on the basis of empirical findings on whistleblowing (e.g., Keenan, 1995; King, 1999; Miceli & Near, 1988; Near & Miceli, 1995, 1996), it can be argued that it is important for organizations and society to cultivate a climate of morality that encourages citizens and employees to act in accordance with moral values. For example, leaders must demonstrate moral courage in their daily tasks to act as role models (Furnham, 2002; Kidder, 2005; Murray, 2007). This means that they must make decisions about alternatives on the basis of moral considerations rather than on the basis of pure economic considerations. Furthermore, leaders should encourage their citizens or employees to openly express ethical concerns. Citizens or employees can help others to engage in morally courageous behavior by supporting them in taking the risks of actions that go against the status quo but are necessary to protect superior values (Walston, 2003). In short, one message that can be taken from the present chapter is: The more everyone contributes to the protection of moral values in their daily lives, the fewer heroes will be needed to show morally courageous behavior.

References

Anand, V., Ashforth, B. E., & Joshi, M. (2004). Business as usual: The acceptance and perpetuation of corruption in organizations. *Academy of Management Executive*, *18*(2), 39–53. doi: 10.5465/AME.2004.13837437

Ashforth, B. E., & Anand, V. (2003). The normalization of corruption in organizations. *Research in Organizational Behavior*, *25*, 1–52. doi:10.1016/S0191-3085(03)25001-2

Back, M. D., & Egloff, B. (2009). Yes we can! A plea for direct behavioral observation in personality research. *European Journal of Personality*, *23*, 403–405. doi: 10.1002/per.725

Bandura, A. (1997). *Self-efficacy: The exercise of control*. New York, NY: Freeman.

Bandura, A., Barbaranelli, C., Caprara, G. V., & Pastorelli, C. (1996). Multifacet impact of self-efficacy beliefs on academic functioning. *Child Development*, *67*, 1206–1222. doi:10.2307/1131888

Bardi, A., & Schwartz, S. H. (2003). Values and behavior: Strength and structure of relations. *Personality and Social Psychology Bulletin*, *29*, 1207–1220. doi: 10.1177/0146167203254602

Batson, C. D. (1998). Altruism and prosocial behavior. In D. T. Gilbert, S. T. Fiske, & G. Lindzey (eds), *Handbook of social psychology* (Vol. 2, pp. 282–316). New York: McGraw Hill/Oxford University Press.

Batson, C. D., & Shaw, L. L. (1991). Encouraging words concerning the evidence for altruism. *Psychological Inquiry*, *2*, 159–168. doi: 10.1207/s15327965pli0202_17

Batson, C. D., Kenedy, C. L., Nord, L.-A., Fleming, D. A., Marzette, C. M., Lishner, D. A., Ayes, R. E., Kolchinsky, L. M., & Zerger, T. (2007). Anger at unfairness: Is it moral outrage? *European Journal of Social Psychology*, *37*, 1272–1285. doi: 10.1002/ejsp.434

Bauman, C. W., & Skitka, L. J. (2007). *Procedural and moral influences on fairness judgments and group rejection*. Paper presented at the annual meeting of the International Association for Conflict Management, Budapest, Hungary.

Baumeister, R. F., Vohs, K. D., & Funder, D. C. (2007). Psychology as the science of self-reports and finger movements. *Perspectives on Psychological Science*, *2*, 396–403. doi: 10.1111/j.1745-6916.2007.00051.x

Baumert, A., & Schmitt, M. (in press). Justice sensitivity. In M. Schmitt & C. Sabbagh (eds), *Handbook of Social Justice Theory and Research*. New York: Springer.

Baumert, A., Gollwitzer, M., Staubach, M. & Schmitt, M. (2011). Justice sensitivity and the processing of justice-related information. *European Journal of Personality*, *25*, 386–397. doi:10.1002/per.800

Baumert, A., Halmburger, A., & Schmitt, M. (2013). Intervention against norm violations: Dispositional determinants of self-reported and real moral courage. *Personality and Social Psychology Bulletin, 39*, 1053–1068. doi:0.1177/0146167213490032

Baumert, A., Otto, K., Thomas, N., Bobocel, D. R. & Schmitt, M. (2012). Processing of unjust and just information: Interpretation and memory performance related to dispositional victim sensitivity. *European Journal of Personality, 26*, 99–110. doi:10.1002/per.1844

Becker, S. W., & Eagly, A. H. (2004). The heroism of women and men. *American Psychologist, 59*, 163–178. doi: 10.1037/0003-066X.59.3.163

Berry, B. (2004). Organizational culture: A framework and strategies for facilitating employee whistleblowing. *Employee Responsibilities and Rights Journal, 16*, 1–11. doi: 10.1023/B:ERRJ.0000017516.40437.b1

Blair, C. A., Thompson, L. F., & Wuensch, K. L. (2005). Electronic helping behavior: The virtual presence of others makes a difference. *Basic and Applied Social Psychology, 27*, 171–178. doi:10.1207/s15324834basp2702_8

Blasi, A. (1999). Emotions and moral motivation. *Journal for the Theory of Social Behaviour, 29*, 1–19. doi: 10.1111/1468-5914.00088

Bleda, P. R., Bleda, S. E., & White, L. A. (1976). Bystander reactions to a petty crime. *Criminology, 14*, 287–290. doi: 10.1111/j.1745-9125.1976.tb00022.x

Bleda, P. R., Bleda, S. E., Byrne, D., & White, L. (1976). When a bystander becomes an accomplice: Situational determinants of reactions to dishonesty. *Journal of Experimental Social Psychology, 12*, 9–25. doi: 10.1016/0022-1031(76)90083-4

Brauer, M., & Chekroun, P. (2005). The relationship between perceived violation of social norms and social control: Situational factors influencing the reaction to deviance. *Journal of Applied Social Psychology, 35*, 1519–1539. doi: 10.1111/j.1559-1816.2005.tb02182.x

Carlsmith, K. M., Darley, J. M., & Robinson, P. H. (2002). Why do we punish? Deterrence and just deserts as motives for punishment. *Journal of Personality and Social Psychology, 83*, 284–299. doi: 10.1037//0022-3514.83.2.284

Carroll, J.S., Perkowitz, W.T., Lurigio, A.J., & Weaver, F.M. (1987). Sentencing goals, causal attributions, ideology, and personality. *Journal of Personality and Social Psychology, 52*, 107–118. doi: 10.1037/0022-3514.52.1.107

Carver, C. S., & White, T. L. (1994). Behavioral inhibition, behavioral activation, and affective responses to impending reward and punishment: The BIS/BAS scales. *Journal of Personality and Social Psychology, 67*, 319–333. doi: 10.1037/0022-3514.67.2.319

Chaiken, S., & Trope, Y. (1999). *Dual process theories in social psychology.* New York, NY: Guilford.

Cialdini, R. B. (2005). Basic social influence is underestimated. *Psychological Inquiry, 16*, 158–161. doi: 10.1207/s15327965pli1604_03

Darley, J. M., & Batson, C. D. (1973). From Jerusalem to Jericho: A study of situational and dispositional variables in helping behavior. *Journal of Personality and Social Psychology, 27*, 100–108. doi: 10.1037/h0034449

Department of Law and Public Safety (2005). Lords of Discipline Task Force—Report of Investigation and Findings. Retrieved from www.nj.gov/oag/newsreleases06/lod-report.pdf.

DeQuervain, D. J.-F., Fischbacher, U., Treyer, V., Schellhammer, M., Schnyder, U., Buck, A., & Fehr, E. (2004). The neural basis of altruistic punishment. *Science, 305*, 1254–1258. doi: 10.1126/science.1100735

de Rivera, J., Gerstmann, E., & Maisels, L. (2002). Acting righteously: The influence of attitude, moral responsibility, and emotional involvement. In M. Ross & D. T. Miller (eds), *The justice motive in everyday life* (pp. 271–288). New York: Cambridge University Press.

Dyck, A., Morse, A., & Zingales, L. (2010). Who blows the whistle on corporate fraud? *Journal of Finance, 65*, 2213–2254. doi: 10.1111/j.1540-6261.2010.01614.x

Eisenberg, N. (1991). Meta-analytic contributions to the literature on prosocial behavior. *Personality and Social Psychology Bulletin, 17*, 273–282. doi: 10.1177/0146167291173007

Eisenberg, N., & Miller, P. A. (1987). The relation of empathy to prosocial and related behaviors. *Psychological Bulletin, 101*, 91–119. doi: 10.1037/0033-2909.101.1.91

Eisenberg, N., Guthrie, I. K., Cumberland, A., Murphy, B. C., & Shepard, S. A. (2002). Prosocial development in early adulthood: A longitudinal study. *Journal of Personality and Social Psychology, 82*, 993–1006. doi: 10.1037/0022-3514.82.6.993

Epstein, S., Lipson, A., Holstein, C., & Huh, E. (1992). Irrational reactions to negative outcomes: Evidence for two conceptual systems. *Journal of Personality and Social Psychology, 2*, 328–339. doi: 10.1037/0022-3514.62.2.328

Feather, N. T., & Souter, J. (2002). Reactions to mandatory sentences in relation to the ethnic identity and criminal history of the offender. *Law and Human Behavior, 26*, 417–438. doi: 10.1023/A:1016331221797

Fehr, E., & Gächter, S. (2002). Altruistic punishment in humans. Nature, 415, 137–140. doi: 10.1038/415137a

Fischer, P., Greitemeyer, T., Pollozek, F., & Frey, D. (2006). The unresponsive bystander: Are bystanders more responsive in dangerous emergencies? *European Journal of Social Psychology, 36*, 267–278. doi: 10.1002/ejsp.297

Fischer, P., Greitemeyer, T., Schulz-Hardt, S., Frey, D., Jonas, E., & Rudukha, T. (2004). Zivilcourage und Hilfeverhalten. Der Einfluss negativer sozialer Konsequenzen auf die Wahrnehmung prosozialen Verhalten [Moral courage and helping behavior: The impact of negative social consequences on the perception of prosocial behavior]. *Zeitschrift für Sozialpsychologie, 35*, 61–66. doi: 10.1024/0044-3514.35.2.61

Franco, Z., & Zimbardo, P. (2006). The banality of heroism. *Greater Good, 3*(2), 30–35.

Frey, D., Schäfer, M., & Neumann, R. (1999). Zivilcourage und aktives Handeln bei Gewalt: Wann werden Menschen aktiv? [Moral courage and intervention in cases of violence: When do people become active?] In M. Schäfer & D. Frey (eds), *Aggression und Gewalt unter Kindern und Jugendlichen* (pp. 265–284). Göttingen: Hogrefe.

Frohloff, S. (2001). *Gesicht Zeigen! Handbuch für Zivilcourage* [*Do not hide yourself! Handbook for moral courage*]. Bonn: Bundeszentrale für Politische Bildung.

Furnham, A. (2002). *The psychology of behaviour at work: The individual in the organization.* New York: Psychology Press.

Garcia, S. M., Weaver, K., Darley, J. M., & Spence, B. T. (2009). Dual effects of implicit bystanders: Inhibiting vs. facilitating helping behavior. *Journal of Consumer Psychology, 19*, 215–224. doi:10.1016/j.jcps.2009.02.013

Gino, F., & Bazerman, M. H. (2009). When misconduct goes unnoticed: The acceptability of gradual erosion in others' unethical behavior. *Journal of Experimental Social Psychology, 45*, 708–719. doi: 10.1016/j.jesp.2009.03.013

Goldberg, J. H., Lerner, J. S., & Tetlock, P. E. (1999). Rage and reason: The psychology of the intuitive prosecutor. *European Journal of Social Psychology, 29*, 781–795. doi: 10.1002/(SICI)1099-0992(199908/09)29:5/6<781::AID-EJSP960>3.0.CO;2-3

Gray, J. A. (1972). The psychophysiological basis of introversion-extraversion: A modification of Eysenck's theory. In V. D. Nebylitsyn & J. A. Gray (eds), *The biological bases of individual behaviour* (pp. 182–205). New York: Academic Press.

Greene, J. D. (2009). Dual process morality and the personal/impersonal distinction: A reply to McGuire, Langdon, and Mackenzie. *Journal of Experimental Social Psychology, 45*, 581–584. doi: 10.1016/j.jesp.2009.01.003

Greitemeyer, T., Fischer, P., Kastenmüller, A., & Frey, D. (2006). Civil courage and helping behavior: Differences and similarities. *European Psychologist, 11*, 90–98. doi: 10.1027/1016-9040.11.2.90

Greitemeyer, T., Osswald, S., Fischer, P., & Frey, D. (2007). Civil courage: Implicit theories, related concepts, and measurement. *The Journal of Positive Psychology, 2*, 115–119. doi: 10.1080/17439760701228789

Gundlach, M. J., Douglas, S. C., & Martinko, M. J. (2003). The decision to blow the whistle: A social information processing framework. *Academy of Management Review, 28*, 107–123. doi:10.5465/AMR.2003.8925239

Halmburger, A., Baumert, A., & Schmitt, M. (2014). Anger as driving factor of moral courage in comparison with guilt and global mood: A multimethod approach. *European Journal of Social Psychology, 45*, 39–51. doi: 10.1002/ejsp.2071

Harari, H., Harari, O., & White, R. V. (1985). The reaction to rape by American male bystanders. *Journal of Social Psychology, 125*, 653–658. doi: 10.1080/00224545.1985.9712039

Harmon-Jones, E., & Sigelman, J. (2001). State anger and prefrontal brain activity: Evidence that insult-related relative left prefrontal activation is associated with experienced anger and aggression. *Journal of Personality and Social Psychology, 80*, 797–803. doi: 10.1037/0022-3514.80.5.797

Henik, E. G. (2008). Mad as hell or scared stiff? The effect of value conflict and emotions on potential whistleblowers. Dissertation, University of California, Berkeley.

Hinde, R. A., & Groebel, J. (1991). *Cooperation and prosocial behavior.* Cambridge: Cambridge University Press.

Hoffman, M. L. (2000). *Empathy and moral development: Implications for caring and justice.* New York: Cambridge University Press.

Hornsey, M. J., Majkut, L., Terry, D. J., & McKimmie, B. M. (2003). On being loud and proud: Non-conformity and counter-conformity to group norms. *British Journal of Social Psychology, 42*, 319–335. doi: 10.1348/014466603322438189

Jonas, K. J., & Brandstätter, V. (2004). Brennpunkt Zivilcourage: Definitionen, Befunde und Maßnahmen

[Focus on moral courage: Definitions, findings, and intervention]. *Zeitschrift für Sozialpsychologie, 35*, 185–200. doi: 10.1024/0044-3514.35.4.185

Karakashian, L. M., Walter, M. I., Christopher, A. N., & Lucas, T. (2006). Fear of negative evaluation affects helping behavior: The bystander effect revisited. *North American Journal of Psychology, 8*(1), 13–32.

Kashdan, T. B., & Steger, M. F. (2006). Expanding the topography of social anxiety—an experience-sampling assessment of positive emotions, positive events, and emotion suppression. *Psychological Science, 17*, 120–128. doi: 10.1111/j.1467-9280.2006.01674.x

Kawakami, K., Dunn, E., Karmali, F., & Dovidio, J. F. (2009). Mispredicting affective and behavioral response to racism. *Science, 323*, 276–278. doi: 10.1126/science.1164951

Keenan, J. P. (1995). Whistleblowing and the first-level manager: Determinants of feeling obliged to blow the whistle. *Journal of Social Behavior and Personality, 10*(3), 571–584.

Kennedy, J. F. (1955). *Profiles in courage*. New York: Harper & Brothers.

Kidder, R. M. (2005). *Moral courage: Taking action when your values are put to the test*. New York: HarperCollins.

King, G. (1999). The implications of an organization's structure on whistleblowing. *Journal of Business Ethics, 20*, 315–326.

Krettek, C. (2007). Sensibilität für beobachtete Ungerechtigkeit und ihr Einfluss auf die Bereitschaft zu zivilcouragiertem Verhalten [Observer sensitivity and its influence on the willingness to engage in morally courageous behavior]. Unpublished diploma thesis. Landau: University of Koblenz-Landau.

Kuhl, U. (1986). *Selbstsicherheit und prosoziales Handeln [Self-assurance and prosocial behavior]*. Munich: Profil.

Labuhn, A., Wagner, U., van Dick, R., & Christ, O. (2004). Determinanten zivilcouragierten Verhaltens: Ergebnisse einer Fragebogenstudie [Determinants of civil courage: Results of a questionnaire study]. *Zeitschrift für Sozialpsychologie, 35*, 93–103. doi: 10.1024/0044-3514.35.2.93

Latané, B., & Darley, J. (1970). *The unresponsive bystander: Why doesn't he help?* New York: Meredith Corporation.

Latané, B., & Nida, S. (1981). Ten years of research on group size and helping. *Psychological Bulletin, 89*, 308–324. doi: 10.1037/0033-2909.89.2.308

Le Gall (1889/2010). *Du courage civique: Discours*. Whitefish, MT: Kessinger.

Lerner, J. S., & Tiedens, L. Z. (2006). Portrait of the angry decision maker: How appraisal tendencies shape anger's influence on cognition. *Journal of Behavioral Decision Making, 19*, 115–137. doi: 10.1002/bdm.515

Levine, M., & Crowther, S. (2008). The responsive bystander: How social group membership and group size can encourage as well as inhibit bystander intervention. *Journal of Personality and Social Psychology, 95*, 1429–1439. doi: 10.1037/a0012634

Lopez, S., O'Byrne, K. K., & Petersen, S. (2003). Profiling courage. In S. Lopez & C. R. Snyder (eds), *Positive psychology assessment: A handbook of models and measures* (pp. 185–197). Washington, DC: American Psychological Association.

Mackie, D. M., Devos, T., & Smith, E. R. (2000). Intergroup emotions: Explaining offensive action tendencies in an intergroup context. *Journal of Personality and Social Psychology, 79*, 602–616. doi: 10.1037/0022-3514.79.4.602

MacNab, B. R., & Worthley, R. (2008). Self-efficacy as an intrapersonal predictor for internal whistle-blowing: A US and Canada examination. *Journal of Business Ethics, 79*, 407–421. doi: 10.1007/s10551-007-9407-3

McGovern, L. P. (1976). Dispositional social anxiety and helping behavior under three conditions of threat. *Journal of Personality, 44*, 84–97. doi: 10.1111/j.1467-6494.1976.tb00585.x

Mesmer-Magnus, J., & Viswesvaran, C. (2005). Whistleblowing in organizations: An examination of correlates of whistleblowing intentions, actions, and retaliation. *Journal of Business Ethics, 62*, 277–297. doi: 10.1007/s10551-005-0849-1

Meyer, G. (2004). Was heißt mit Zivilcourage handeln? [What does it mean to act in a morally courageous way?] In G. Meyer, U. Dovermann, S. Frech, & G. Gugel, (eds). *Zivilcourage lernen* (pp. 22–41). Bonn: Bundeszentrale für Politische Bildung.

Meyer, G., & Hermann, A. (2000). Zivilcourage im Alltag. Ergebnisse einer Fragebogenstudie [Moral courage in everyday life]. *Aus Politik und Zeitgeschichte, 7–8*, 3–13.

Miceli, M. P., & Near, J. P. (1988). Individual and situational correlates of whistle-blowing. *Personnel Psychology, 41*, 267–282. doi:10.1111/j.1744-6570.1988.tb02385.x

Miceli, M. P., Dozier, J. B., & Near, J. P. (1991). Blowing the whistle on data fudging: A controlled field experiment. *Journal of Applied Social Psychology, 21*, 271–295. doi: 10.1111/j.1559-1816.1991.tb00521.x

Miceli, M. P., van Scotter, J. R., Near, J. P., & Regh, M. T. (2001). Individual differences in whistleblowing. *Academy of Management Proceedings, 1*, C1–C6. doi: 10.5465/APBPP.2001.6133834

Mikula, G. (1980). On the role of justice in allocation decisions. In G. Mikula (ed.), *Justice and social interaction* (pp. 127–166). Bern, Switzerland: Huber.

Mikula, G., Scherer, K. R., & Athenstaedt, U. (1998). The role of injustice in elicitation of differential

emotional reactions. *Personality and Social Psychology Bulletin*, *24*, 769–783. doi: 10.1177/0146167298247009
Miller, W. I. (2000). *The mystery of courage*. Cambridge, MS: Harvard University Press.
Monin, B., Sawyer, P. J., & Marquez, M. J. (2008). The rejection of moral rebels: Resenting those who do the right thing. *Journal of Personality and Social Psychology*, *95*, 76–93. doi: 10.1037/0022-3514.95.1.76
Montada, L., & Schneider, A. (1989). Justice and emotional reactions to the disadvantage. *Social Justice Research*, *3*, 313–344. doi: 10.1007/BF01048081
Murray, J. S. (2007). Creating ethical environments in nursing. *American Nurse Today*, *2*(10), 48–49.
Near, J. P., & Miceli, M. P. (1995). Effective whistle-blowing. *Academy of Management Review*, *20*(3), 679–708.
Near, J. P., & Miceli, M. P. (1985). Organizational dissidence: The case of whistleblowing. *Journal of Business Ethics*, *4*, 1–16. doi: 10.1007/BF00382668
Near, J. P., & Miceli, M. P. (1996). Whistleblowing: Myth and reality. *Journal of Management*, *22*, 507–526. doi: 10.1177/014920639602200306
Nelissen, R. M. A., & Zeelenberg, M. (2009). Moral emotions as determinants of third-party punishment: Anger and guilt and the functions of altruistic sanctions. *Judgment and Decision Making*, *4*, 543–553.
Nelissen, R. M. A., Leliveld, M. C., Van Dijk, E., & Zeelenberg, M. (2011). Fear and guilt in proposers: Using emotions to explain offers in ultimatum bargaining. *European Journal of Social Psychology*, *41*, 78–85. doi:10.1002/ejsp.735
New York Times (2007). The lords of disorder. *The New York Times* (October 7). Retrieved from www.nytimes.com/2007/10/07/opinion/nyregionopinions/NJtrooper.html?_r=0.
Niesta Kayser, D., Greitemeyer, T., Fischer, P., & Frey, D. (2010). Why mood affects help giving but not moral courage: Two types of prosocial behaviours. *European Journal of Social Psychology*, *40*, 1136–1157. doi: 10.1002/ejsp.717
Nolan, J. M., Schultz, P. W., Cialdini, R. B., Goldstein, N. K., & Griskevicius, V. (2008). Normative social influence is underdetected. *Personality and Social Psychology Bulletin*, *34*, 913–923. doi: 10.1177/0146167208316691
Osswald, S., Greitemeyer, T., Fischer, P., & Frey, D. (2010a). Moral prototypes and moral behavior: Specific effects on emotional precursors of moral behavior and on moral behavior by the activation of moral prototypes. *European Journal of Social Psychology*, *40*, 1078–1094. doi: 10.1002/ejsp.728
Osswald, S., Greitemeyer, T., Fischer, P., & Frey, D. (2010b). What is Moral Courage? Definition, Explication and Classification of a Complex Construct. In C. Pury & S. Lopez (eds), *Psychology of Courage* (pp. 149–164). Washington, DC: American Psychological Association.
Paciello, M., Fida, R., Cerniglia, L., Tramontano, C., Cole, E. (2013). High cost helping scenario: The role of empathy, prosocial reasoning and moral disengagement on helping behavior. *Personality and Individual Differences*, *55*, 3–7. doi: 10.1016/j.paid.2012.11.004
Parmerlee, M. A., Near, J. P., & Jensen, T. C. (1982). Correlates of whistleblowers' perceptions of organizational retaliation. *Administrative Science Quarterly*, *27*, 17–34. doi: 10.2307/2392544
Pavey, L., Greitemeyer, T., & Sparks, P. (2012). "I help because I want to, not because you tell me to": Empathy increases autonomously motivated helping. *Personality and Social Psychology Bulletin*, *38*, 681–689. doi: 10.1177/0146167211435940
Pfetsch, J., Steffgen, G., & Schiffhauer, S. (2009). *Gerechtigkeitswahrnehmungen und Zivilcourage [Sense of justice and civil courage]*. Talk given at the 12th Tagung der Fachgruppe Sozialpsychologie der Deutschen Gesellschaft für Psychologie (DGPs). Luxembourg: University of Luxembourg.
Piliavin, J., Dovidio, J., Gaertner, S., & Clark, R. (1981). *Emergency intervention*. New York: Academic Press.
Rehg, M., Miceli, M., Near, J., & Scotter, J. (2008). Antecedents and outcomes of retaliation against whistle-blowers: Gender differences and power relationships. *Organization Science*, *19*, 221–240, 378–379. doi: 10.1287/orsc.1070.0310
Rothmund, T., Baumert, A., & Zinkernagel, A. (2014). The German "Wutbürger"—How justice sensitivity accounts for individual differences in political engagement. *Social Justice Research*, *27*, 24–44. doi: 10.1007/s11211-014-0202-x
Rutkowski, G. K., Gruder, C. L., & Romer, D. (1983). Group cohesiveness, social norms, and bystander intervention. *Journal of Personality and Social Psychology*, *44*, 545–552. doi: 10.1037/0022-3514.44.3.545
Schmitt, M., Baumert, A., Gollwitzer, M., & Maes, J. (2010). The Justice Sensitivity Inventory: Factorial validity, location in the personality facet space, demographic pattern, and normative data. *Social Justice Research*, *23*, 211–238. doi:10.1007/s11211-010-0115-2
Schmitt, M. J., Neumann, R., & Montada, L. (1995). Dispositional sensitivity to befallen injustice. *Social Justice Research*, *8*, 385–407. doi: 10.1007/BF02334713
Schwartz, S. H. (1977). Normative influences on altruism. In L. Berkowitz (ed.), *Advances in experimental social psychology* (Vol. 10, pp. 221–279). New York: Academic Press.
Schwartz, S. H., & Gottlieb, A. (1976). Bystander reactions to a violent theft: Crime in Jerusalem. *Journal of*

Personality and Social Psychology, 34(6), 1188–1199.

Schwartz, S. H., & Howard, J. A. (1980). Explanations of the moderating effect of responsibility denial on the personal norm-behavior relationship. *Social Psychology Quarterly, 43*, 441–446. doi: 10.2307/3033965

Schwartz, S. H., & Howard, J. A. (1981). A normative decision-making model of altruism. In J. P. Rushton & R. M. Sorentino (eds), *Altruism and helping behavior* (pp. 189–211). Hillsdale, NJ: Erlbaum.

Shotland, R. L., & Huston, T. L. (1979). Emergencies: What are they and do they influence bystanders to intervene. *Journal of Personality and Social Psychology, 37*, 1822–1834.

Skitka, L. J. (2011). Moral convictions and moral courage: Common denominators of good and evil. In M. Mikulincer & P. R. Shaver (eds), *The social psychology of morality: Exploring the causes of good and evil* (pp. 349–365). Washington, DC: American Psychological Association.

Skitka, L. J., & Mullen, E. (2002). Understanding judgments of fairness in a real-world political context: A test of the value protection model of justice reasoning. *Personality and Social Psychology Bulletin, 28*, 1419–1429. doi: 10.1177/014616702236873

Skitka, L. J., & Wisneski, D. C. (2011). Moral conviction and Emotion. *Emotion Review, 3*, 328–330. doi: 10.1177/1754073911402374

Skitka, L. J., Bauman, C. W., & Lytle, B. L. (2009). The limits of legitimacy: Moral and religious convictions as constraints on deference to authority. *Journal of Personality and Social Psychology, 97*, 567–578. doi: 10.1037/a0015998

Skitka, L. J., Bauman, C. W., & Sargis, E. G. (2005). Moral conviction: Another contributor to attitude strength or something more? *Journal of Personality and Social Psychology, 88*, 895–917. doi: 10.1037/0022-3514.88.6.895

Solomon, L. Z., Solomon, H., & Stone, R. (1978). Helping as a function of number of bystanders and ambiguity of emergency. *Personality and Social Psychology Bulletin, 4*, 318–321. doi:10.1177/014616727800400231

Tangney, J. P., Stuewig, J., & Mashek, D. J. (2007). Moral emotions and moral behavior. *Annual Review of Psychology, 58*, 345–372. doi: 10.1146/annurev.psych.56.091103.070145

Thomas, N., Baumert, A., & Schmitt, M. (2012). Justice sensitivity as a risk and protective factor in social conflicts. In E. Kals & J. Maes (eds), *Justice and conflicts* (pp. 107–102). Heidelberg: Springer. doi: 10.1007/978-3-642-19035-3_6

Thornberg, R. (2007). A classmate in distress: Schoolchildren as bystanders and their reasons for how they act. *Social Psychology of Education, 10*, 5–28. doi: 10.1007/s11218-006-9009-4

Tobey-Klass, E. (1978). Psychological effects of immoral actions: The experimental evidence. *Psychological Bulletin, 85*, 757–771. doi: 10.1037//0033-2909.85.4.756

Uleman, J. S., Newman, L. S., & Moskowitz, G. B. (1996). People as flexible interpreters: Evidence and issues from spontaneous trait inference. *Advances in Experimental Social Psychology, 28*, 211–280. doi: 10.1016/S0065-2601(08)60239-7

Valentino, N. A., Brader, T., Groenendyk, E. W., Gregorowicz, K., & Hutchings, V. L. (2011). Election night's alright for fighting: The role of emotions in political participation. *Journal of Politics, 73*, 156–170. doi: 10.1017/S0022381610000939

Van Bommel, M., Van Prooijen, J., Elffers, H., & Van Lange, P. A. M. (2012). Be aware to care: Public self-awareness leads to a reversal of the bystander effect. *Journal of Experimental Social Psychology, 48*, 926–930. doi:10.1016/j.jesp.2012.02.011

Van Boven, L., Loewenstein, G., & Dunning, D. (2005). The illusion of courage in social predictions: Underestimating the impact of fear of embarrassment on other people. *Organizational Behavior and Human Decision Processes, 96*, 130–141. doi: 10.1016/j.obhdp.2004.12.001

Van den Bos, K., Müller, P. A., & van Bussel, A. A. L. (2009). Helping to overcome intervention inertia in bystander's dilemmas: Behavioral disinhibition can improve the greater good. *Journal of Experimental Social Psychology, 45*, 873–878. doi10.1016/j.jesp.2009.03.014

Van den Bos, K. (2007). Hot cognition and social justice judgments: The combined influence of cognitive and affective factors on the justice judgment process. In D. de Cremer (ed.), *Advances in the psychology of justice and affect* (pp. 59–82). Greenwich, CT: Information Age Publishing.

Voigtländer, D. (2008). Hilfeverhalten und Zivilcourage: Ein Vergleich von antizipiertem und realem Verhalten. [Helping and moral courage: A comparison of anticipated and real behavior]. Dissertation, University of Göttingen, Germany.

Von Keudell, F. M. L. R. (1901). Fürst und Fürstin Bismarck: Erinnerungen aus den Jahren 1846 bis 1872 [Prince and Princess Bismarck: Memories of the years 1846 to 1872]. Berlin, Germany: W. Spemann.

Walker, L. J., & Hennig, K. H. (2004). Differing conceptions of moral exemplarity: Just, brave, and caring. *Journal of Personality and Social Psychology, 86*, 629–647. doi: 10.1037/0022-3514.86.4.629

Walston, S. F. (2003). Courage and caring: Step up to your next level of nursing excellence. *Patient Care Management, 19*(4), 4–6.

Wansink, B., Payne, C. R., & van Ittersum, K. (2008). Profiling the heroic leader: Empirical lessons from combat-decorated veterans of World War II. *The Leadership Quarterly, 19,* 547–555. doi: 10.1016/j.leaqua.2008.07.010

Waytz, A., Dungan, J., Young, L. (2013). The whistleblower's dilemma and the fairness–loyalty tradeoff. *Journal of Experimental Social Psychology, 49,* 1027–1033. doi:10.1016/j.jesp.2013.07.002

Weiner, B. (1985). An attribution theory of achievement motivation and emotion. *Psychological Review, 92,* 548–573. doi: 10.1037/0033-295X.92.4.548

Wenzel, M., Okimoto, T. G., Feather, N. T., & Platow, M. J. (2008). Retributive and restorative justice. *Law and Human Behavior, 32,* 375–389. doi: 10.1007/s10979-007-9116-6

10
Heroism in Times of Crisis
Understanding Leadership during Extreme Events

Zeno E. Franco

Too often companies become complacent. They begin to feel almost invincible. Their financial performance is strong, and they fall into the trap of believing they have little to worry about. Then they're blindsided by a crisis and don't have a response plan in place ...
(Alsop, 2006)

Every human crisis demands a hero, an individual or small group of individuals who are not only aware of impending chaos, but in the vernacular are, "ready, willing, and able" to act decisively. Their decisive actions are understood to be the very barrier that holds back destruction—whether it is physical, financial, emotional, or philosophical. While the phrase "ready, willing, and able" sounds trivial in common use, the reason heroes are valuable in crisis events is precisely because most people are unable or unwilling to act. Thus, in moments of crisis, the risks involved and the decision making authority to address those risks, typically become concentrated in an individual or small group. This is often a tacit transaction wherein a heroic actor becomes the agent of the larger group (Desmond, 2008a, 2008b), and thus this individual no longer able to rely on the psychological and social crutches that allow others the "out" of inaction.

While heroes and heroism have long seemed the realm of myth and legend, recent scholarship on the social psychology of heroism is beginning to systematically address the phenomenon, focusing initially on taxonomies of heroic types (Allison & Goethals, 2011, 2013b; Franco, Blau, & Zimbardo, 2011), perceptions of the general public toward various forms of heroic action and archetypes (Franco et al., 2011; Kinsella, Ritchie, & Igou, 2015), examining differences between individuals publically recognized for heroism versus normal controls (Walker, Frimer, & Dunlop, 2010), and self-reported engagement in heroic acts over the course of a life time (Zimbardo, Breckenridge, & Moghaddam, 2013). However, this focus on individual heroes and how these heroes are perceived by others has not fully addressed the situational dynamics that call forth heroic action in organizational leaders.

This chapter explores three deeply interrelated areas of inquiry: crisis events, leadership within these crises, and the tactical behaviors crisis leaders use to effect heroic outcomes. In taking a largely situationist perspective, the ideal of heroic leadership can be illustrated in actions taken (or not taken) to reduce the crisis or to transform it in an unanticipated way. Examining heroes and heroism on their own is important, but there have also been calls within the field of leadership psychology to develop a better understanding of "heroic leadership" (Allison & Goethals, 2013a, 2015). For example, in the introductory article to an *American Psychologist* special issue on leadership, Warren Bennis noted that, "Heroic or charismatic leadership is still an essential, unsolved part of the puzzle" (Bennis, 2007). Various forms of heroic leadership occur on a daily basis in crises, large and small. Heroic leaders act in closed board rooms, in hospital operating theaters, in military engagements, and in our neighborhoods and communities—but we still know relatively little about how these leaders react to the contours of crisis, and at what threshold good leadership becomes heroic. Leaders who are able to take the risks required to respond in the face of disaster remain an area in need of considerable theoretical and empirical exploration.

Dr. Philip Zimbardo and I have argued elsewhere that heroic leadership involves:

> leaders who take on extraordinary personal, corporate, or national risks. It is easy to conflate the ideas of heroism and heroic leadership with the simpler idea of charismatic leadership, and much of the leadership and management literature can be accused of making this mistake (Arnulf, Mathisen, & Hærem, 2012; Carney, 2007). As noted earlier, at its core, the term hero implies the acceptance of significant personal risk, engaged in voluntarily. This is not the risk that a charismatic leader might face, for example, that by using powerful persuasive techniques the leader alienates some followers. Instead, the term "heroic leader" should be reserved for larger-than-life figures, who take larger-than-life gambles to advance socially just ideals, transform societies, lead soldiers into battle (Wansink, Payne, & Van Ittersum, 2008), place companies at financial or security risk to prove a moral point (e.g., the *Charlie Hebdo* satirical newspaper, which refused to give into threats ultimately resulting in deaths of 12 of its journalists is arguably one exemplar; Somaiya, 2015) or lead nations out of existential crisis (Allison & Goethals, 2015).
>
> *(Franco & Zimbardo, 2016)*

While we stressed the idea of the larger-than-life leader, heroic leadership is also shown in "small" ways as well, in quieter forms, in less public encounters. Just as the stories of the most heroic soldiers are often never known, the most profound corporate and government battles often happen in obscure venues, outside of the public eye. These battles are won and lost, and good or bad outcomes from them impact all of us, although we rarely know the names of the individuals who successfully fought for what was right, or those who "died trying," even though in this case the death may have been figurative, in the form of resignation from an important post, being fired, or losing the blessing of supervisors. Just as important as considering the transformative change heroic leaders can create, examining the impact when no hero appears in a corporate or government crisis warrants deep consideration. We often neglect the fact that there are real costs, often deep financial costs, to what has been termed "heroic failure" (Franco, 2014; Franco & Langdon, 2012). By *heroic failure* what is meant is not that someone tried to be heroic and failed in the process, but rather than a leader's "heroic imagination" failed, thus not allowing her to see the unfolding crisis events as requiring a heroic response (Zimbardo, 2007). Failure to act heroically can cripple corporations, governments and other organizations, leading to devastating financial and human costs that can ultimately result in existential threats to the very organizations the leader was sworn to guide. Ultimately, the financial costs associated with the disasters that occur when heroic leadership is absent suggests that governments, corporations, and other structured systems should not only value, but foster heroic leadership as one type of human asset that is critical to effective contingency management (Kakabadse, Kouzmin, Kakabadse, & Mouraviev, 2012).

This chapter deliberately focuses on the situations that call forth heroic efforts in leaders. In so doing, the point is not to fall in to the false dichotomy often engendered by the person/situation debate, but to more fully characterize the dynamics of the complex crisis events leaders face. Through this exploration of the crisis situation and some of the specific tactical approaches leaders employ to impact these events, it is possible to deeply explore the interactions between individual leadership traits and heroic leadership activities in the most trying circumstances faced by those entrusted significant responsibility.

The first goal of this chapter is to provide an introduction to the theoretical underpinnings of crisis research in order to deliberately and systematically ground the discussion in the realities of complex disasters. Second, throughout the chapter a set of detailed examples of recent major crises are offered, as well as the stories of the heroes and heroic failures illustrated by these events. These example crisis events include the grounding of the *Costa Concordia*; the interlocking contingencies that nearly cost the lives of three astronauts aboard the Apollo 13 mission; aspects of the recent global economic crisis; the story of how the Thalidomide disaster was largely averted in the U.S. by a female physician in the fledgling FDA; the ice-bound survival of the Captain Shackleton and the crew of the *Endurance* in Antarctica; a fictional story from *Star Trek* describing a desperate interplanetary search for survivors; among others. Third, some of the specific tactical behaviors heroic leaders exhibit are examined in detail, as these actions are likely the window into how leaders' cognitive, emotional, and behavioral traits are expressed in interaction with the disaster event. In this third section, these actions are also tied to key theoretical aspects of crisis response behaviors including concepts such as catastrophic leadership failure, distributed situational awareness, option awareness, and improvisation. Finally, thoughts about future theoretical and empirical research that may drive the exploration of heroic behavior in new directions are offered as part of the discussion.

Understanding the Situational Dynamics of Crisis

In prior work, Dr. Philip Zimbardo and I have advanced a largely situationist view of heroism. Again, to be clear, this is not meant to discount individual factors in engaging in heroic acts, but to emphasize the importance of the specific situational elements that call for heroic action. The situations that call for heroism are almost always aberrations from normal daily life, and in many cases they are considered to be *crises* or *disasters*. An entire domain of research has grown up around crisis events, which remains largely unincorporated in modern psychology. Yet, the role of the heroic leader is largely that of a broker or edge worker (Cross & Prusak, 2002) between one (or multiple) external contingencies and the social group they are charged with leading (broadly, their followers, employees, etc.). Especially with regard to crisis events, the goal of the leadership process can be seen as either acting on the situation in ways intended to force a return to normalcy or to shape the response of followers to effectively adapt to an uncomfortable, but inevitable, new reality. Leaders in these crisis situations are forced work with political mechanisms, social structures, and physical assets that are poorly aligned with the contours of the crisis (Wagner-Pacifici, 2000), resulting in improvisations that are unfamiliar and novel (Mendonça, Beroggi, & Wallace, 2001; Mendonça & Wallace, 2007). In this sense, systematically examining heroic leadership holds the potential to identify personal leadership and decision-making strategies that may offer important efficiencies in other complex organizational contexts.

Definitions and Theories of Crisis

The definitions of crisis events are varied and complex, but nonetheless illuminating when considering the situational aspects of human behavior that occur during these moments of chaos and uncertainty. When faced with a crisis, it is the hero's ability to act differently than many of her companions—i.e. not responding with panic, indecision, inaction, or flight—that in part defines her actions as heroic. One of the simplest definitions of a "crisis" emerged from the disaster management literature and can be summarized as follows:

Zeno E. Franco

> A crisis is an event or occasion in which things that are widely valued by human social systems are deeply threatened in an unanticipated manner, and the demand for resources to address the catastrophic event outstrips available capacity.
>
> *(paraphrasing Quarantelli, 1985)*

This definition underscores the idea that crisis events are different than "normal emergencies" because they:

- involve fundamentally unanticipated shock to a system;
- exceed the capabilities of pre-positioned emergency assets and resources; and
- cause profound disruption in social life.

These basic ideas are inculcated into many contemporary policy statements offered by organizations charged with managing disasters and major crisis events. For example the UN Office for Disaster Risk Reduction (UNISDR) defines a disaster as:

> A serious disruption of the functioning of a community or a society involving widespread human, material, economic or environmental losses and impacts, which exceeds the ability of the affected community or society to cope using its own resources ... Disasters are often described as a result of the combination of: the exposure to a hazard; the conditions of vulnerability that are present; and insufficient capacity or measures to reduce or cope with the potential negative consequences. Disaster impacts may include loss of life, injury, disease and other negative effects on human physical, mental and social well-being, together with damage to property, destruction of assets, loss of services, social and economic disruption and environmental degradation.
>
> *(UNISDR, 2007)*

Crisis events are also understood to occur in different phases and sub-phases, often with prodromal warning signs that are difficult to detect (Hensgen, Desouza, & Kraft, 2003; Samarajiva, 2005), interlocking contingencies that result in cascading events and sudden escalations in problem complexity (Peters, Buzna, & Helbing, 2008); peak phases where resource demand profoundly exceeds capacity (Petak, 1985); and, in worst case scenarios, an event horizon or "point of criticality" beyond which catastrophic loss becomes not just a possibility, but a harsh reality (Sornette, 2002).

Theories and conceptual structures describing the situational and organizational aspects of disasters and crisis events include normal accident theory (NAT; Perrow, 2011), high reliability organizations (HROs; Rochlin, La Porte, & Roberts, 1987; Weick, Sutcliffe, & Obstfeld, 2008); and latent human failures (Reason, 1990), among others. Generally, these theories acknowledge a range of disaster types involving simple, predictable "component failures" to broader "systems failures" in which the complex interaction between social and technical systems may prevent accurate prediction of disaster, or even preclude *an understanding* of the events that brought on the crisis.

NAT in particular emphasizes the importance of system "coupling" suggesting that *tightly coupled* systems are those in which automated processes may occur before humans are capable of acting to avert crisis, where *loosely coupled* systems allow greater time for human control over events because of compartmentalization. Both coupling approaches have their own strengths and weaknesses, and different failure points emerge in organizations in part because of the systems coupling strategies employed. The ideas contained in NAT and HRO deal extensively with how human systems are organized to exert control over crisis events, typically in centralized, decentralized, or mixed hierarchies, and which type of leadership approach work best for each disaster context. Other sociological theories have emphasized the importance of combined latent and active human error in complex systems. For example, while a nuclear power plant operator may make an error that initiates a catastrophic chain of downstream events, there are often a set of less well understood set of prior (latent) engineering errors that did not anticipate this particular eventuality (Reason, 1990).

In practical terms, the contours of disasters often result in leaders experiencing a tangle of contingencies or "catch-22" situations (Berariu, Fikar, Gronalt, & Hirsch, 2015) that gradually remove degrees of freedom to act. While outside resources may be requested, the immediate resource environment becomes increasingly diminished. The candle is literally burning at both ends as options and assets are removed, leaving the crisis leader and her team on ever shrinking safe-ground. In organizations, these problems are often amplified by misinformation or pressure to act in irrational ways (Clements & Washbush, 1999). Yet despite this complexity, the crisis leader must swiftly devise creative, sometimes daring action strategies, and convince her team to follow her despite the very human desire to retreat.

Examples of Crisis Events, Heroic Failure and Heroic Leadership

The Costa Concordia Disaster

One of the key reasons disasters at sea, in the wilds on land, and in limitless space are easily to transliterate to the screen in TV and movies is because they distil the idea that crises lead to diminished option availability as interlocking contingencies mount (Pfaff et al., 2013). Quite simply, there is no safe pace to run, there are few last resort options, and it is often impossible to effect rescue or move additional assets into place in time to avert loss of life. Thus, the crisis leader is on her own, forced to take rapid action to try to save passengers, crew, and, if possible her own life in the process.

The recent *Costa Concordia* disaster, involving a luxury cruise liner that ran aground off the cost of Italy provides one example of how quickly things can go terribly wrong in maritime operations, even close to shore. The ship was carrying 3,000 passengers and 1,000 crew members when Captain Schettino steered toward the coast just for show—close enough to allow a crew member to waive to friends on shore. While this error in judgment was bad enough, the Captain then waited for 40 minutes between realizing there was a hull breach and issuing the order to abandon ship. During that 40 minute delay, there are indications that the Captain was discussing the situation with the company that owned the ship, possibly trying to jointly make decisions about whether to declare an emergency or not. While the Captain claimed to have improved the situation by maneuvering his ship closer to shore, this delay to take the dramatic but necessary step of sounding the alarm to abandon ship meant that one of the most precious commodities in a disaster—time—was lost. With more warning time and clear crisis messaging from the Captain, passengers and crew could have organized a more orderly evacuation before the ship began to violently list. But instead, by failing to imagine the consequences of not acting decisively and by worrying about a mistake that he could no longer control, Captain Schettino ran down the clock, leaving very few options for those in the bowels of the ship. Instead of facing his own initial failure and taking the next set of actions the situation demanded, Captain Schettino abandoned his vessel before all passengers and crew had evacuated—despite intense verbal pressure over the radio from an Italian coast guard officer insisting that as the Captain he needed to remain aboard to fulfill his duty:

> CAPTAIN SCHETTINO: In this moment, the boat is tipping ...
> [COAST GUARD] DE FALCO: ... There are people coming down the pilot ladder...You go up that ladder...tell me if there are children, women or people in need of assistance ... you

saved yourself from the sea, but I am going to ... really do something bad to you ... Go on board, [expletive]!

(Associated Press, 2012)

In a discussion of the lack of heroic leadership on the *Costa Concordia*, my colleague Matt Langdon and I noted:

It is a heroic tradition as old as the Sea itself—in a crisis, the captain is the last person to leave the ship. The privilege of being the master of a vessel also comes with the "burden of command"—the responsibility for every soul aboard.

(Franco & Langdon, 2012)

Ultimately this "heroic failure" of leadership cost 32 lives among passengers and crew, billions of dollars in salvage and insurance losses (Veysey, 2013), and deep ecological injury to the coast.

Apollo 13—Finding a Way Home through Distributed Crisis Problem Solving and Option Awareness

The disaster aboard the Apollo 13 mission, triggered by an explosion in a service module oxygen tank, is a quintessential example of a disaster in a High Reliability Organization (Casler, 2014), meaning groups that are charged with routinely performing complex, often dangerous tasks, with an absolute minimum of error. The deeply interlocking contingencies between sub-systems on the Apollo missions or what is often referred to in disaster science as a "tightly coupled system" (Weick et al., 2008), and failure of these systems relatively few options for the astronauts and their support team on Earth after an explosion on the craft. The group was forced to rapidly improvise in order to avert complete loss of the mission and the lives of its crew. The drama of the events was so compelling that it created rapt attention in the U.S. and worldwide at the time, and was latter made into a major film. It is worth briefly summarizing what disaster science describes as "problem cascades" (Peters et al., 2008) and how these occurred aboard the vessel to understand how disasters box in leaders, and how critical crisis leadership is to working out alternative paths of action.

Take a moment to consider for yourself what the astronauts and ground controllers had to work with in the three major components of the Apollo 13 craft. To make it feel as real as possible, I have deliberately offered more detail than would usually be afforded in a chapter of this type, encouraging you to "walk a mile in the shoes" of these astronauts and the engineers who worked to save them.

The components of the craft included the *Service Module*, the *Command Module* and the *Lunar Module*, and each of these segments of the space craft had limited assets (oxygen, electrical power generation, food, water, etc.) and each had particular liabilities (energy consumption, damage, mass, etc.). Under optimal conditions, the three components of the craft were designed to work seamlessly together, but during the Apollo 13 crisis, this carefully orchestrated dance began to break down. A partial list of the many considerations and their implications is offered below. Again, rather than skimming them, take a moment to really let yourself feel the weight of each "catch-22" these issues presented. They were responding not just one problem, but rather a set of interlocking problems, each tightening the situational knots, limiting action:

- The pre-planned Direct Abort trajectory approach required that the Lunar Module be jettisoned, but the crew's survival depended on the resources in the Lunar Module during the trip back toward earth.
- An alternative would have involved burning remaining fuel in in the Service Module, then

jettison the Service Module, and make a final burn with the Lunar Module engines, but the team wanted to keep the Service Module attached as long as possible as it provided additional heat shielding to the Command Module.
- The craft was almost at the point where the direct abort trajectory would switch to the circumlunar abort trajectory, which was more complex, but also allowed more time for the control team on earth to evaluate options.
- Because of the explosion, project engineers were also concerned that using the engines aboard the Service Module could cause further problems because of decreased structural integrity of that segment of the vessel.
- Low power levels aboard the vessel made voice communication to Earth difficult.
- Carbon dioxide scrubber cartridges were critical to keeping the atmosphere in the vessel breathable, but because all three crew members were in the Command Module for the duration of the attempt to get back to Earth, CO_2 scrubbers from the Lunar Module were needed.
- Unfortunately, the CO_2 scrubber cartridges used in the Lunar Module had been engineered differently than those in the Command Module, leaving the crew unable to repurpose the Lunar Module CO_2 scrubbers and thus they were vulnerable to death from this poisonous gas that they were producing every time they exhaled.
- The low power state required to conserve energy also dropped the temperature in the vessel, resulting in condensation of water vapor, increasing the chances of an electrical short, fire and death of the crew.
- The Lunar Module had to be separated from the Command Module at the last moment. Yet, applying too little pressure to the Lunar Module would not move it far enough away, and too much pressure could damage the Command Module hatch, exposing the crew to the vacuum of space.

(Lovell & Kluger, 2006)

Interestingly, in the case of the Apollo 13 mission, it wasn't just that there was one leader acting heroically, but that an entire team, with many leaders and a distributed leadership approach was able to work through the situation, balancing risk and options to ward off disaster. From a crisis research perspective, this scenario is a classic example of *distributed situation awareness* (Stanton et al., 2006) and *option awareness* (Pfaff, Drury, Klein, & More, 2010). Situation awareness revolves around three main cognitive processes, perception, comprehension, and projection into the future. Interestingly, over 90 percent of leadership decision errors in experimental crisis or command simulations occur during the first two processes, perception and comprehension (Endsley, 2000). Option awareness, or an understanding of the actions that can be taken given the constraints of the situation is also key. Option awareness largely relies on the same three processes found in situational awareness, but applied to the decision and action space leaders must occupy once the situation has been assessed (Pfaff et al., 2013). In addition to the leader needing to correctly put all of these situation and option awareness elements into a cognitive map of the crisis, she also must be able to communicate the key pieces of information to others within the team or facilitate critical communication between stakeholders (Franco, Zumel, Holman, Blau, & Beutler, 2009; Salmon et al., 2008).

Economic Crisis

The "Great Recession" of 2007 served as a powerful reminder of how fragile our economic systems can be when fundamentals are not carefully attended to. Millions of lives were impacted by unscrupulous investment, inflated housing valuations, and failure to call market hype into question (Jenkins, Brandolini, Micklewright, & Nolan, 2012). Psychologists often suggest that panic is not something that is likely to occur. But crisis events, especially those that are poorly understood, provide exactly the context for panic to set in (Beutler, Reyes, Franco, & Housley, 2006; Pastel, 2002; Slovic, 2002).

In this case, chaos in securities markets predictably led to panicked selling, huge economic losses, and personal financial ruin for many people. More than 100 mortgage lenders failed in the U.S., and the major investment house Bear Stearns was sold on an emergency basis, just to illustrate a few of the specific contours of this crisis event. While unscrupulous activities were rampant and largely unchecked, numerous stories of heroic risk taking also emerged from this crisis, ranging heroic whistleblowers who risked internal retribution for trying to stop illegal or unethical activity within some of the lending companies (Goldstein, 2014), to the actions of the three central bankers in the U.S. and Europe charged with stopping the run away damage to global economies and restoring order in the aftermath of the crisis.

The economic collapse of the great recession provides a striking example of how central bankers in the U.S. had to contend not only with the crisis itself, but the need to move a convoluted bureaucracy from its usual lumbering pace, to a rapid-fire structure capable of improvising in order to respond to huge market fluctuations occurring in real time. While the personal risks faced by the Central Bankers were limited, and some blame them for not taking steps to prevent the crisis from happening in the first place, the tasks given to them within the heart of the crisis were nonetheless laden with risk. A set of false moves could have easily deepened the crisis and resulted in much greater instability. Business periodicals noted this heroic status given to the Central Bankers, with Bloomberg summarizing this as: "Dominant Social Theme: Central bankers are unlikely heroes, but they're all we've got" (Daily Bell, 2014).

The events of the financial crisis also underscore the importance for crisis leaders to rapidly move out of "business as usual" to put into place solutions that would seem impossible under normal circumstances. The gritty reality of this move toward rapid action and role expansion is best conveyed in journalistic coverage of the events and the actions of the central banks. For example:

> Over two continents, five years, thousands of conference calls, and trillions of dollars, euros, and pounds deployed to rescue the world financial system, central bankers would take the primary role in grappling with the global panic that began in earnest on August 9th, 2007. They would act with a speed and on a scale that presidents and parliaments could never seem to muster ... this committee of three knew better than anyone else just how high the price of failure could be.
>
> *(Irwin, 2013, pp. 8, 13)*

Again, one of the hallmarks of crisis situations in tightly coupled systems is that their complexity defies easy understanding. As our society becomes increasingly sophisticated, it is possible for us to build systems that no single individual, or even a team of experts fully understand. For example, in the early hours and days of the Great Recession the central bankers charged with bringing order to the financial systems of the world had to seek out expertise from individuals who had created some of the investment instruments that were causing the problems, as well as seeking input from teams with sophisticated computer models of these securities markets (Irwin, 2013).

Yet despite this expert input, Ben Bernanke and the other bankers did not and quite possibly *could not* fully understand what was occurring because of the number of inter-relationships within the securities markets. Yet they acted anyway. Ultimately, in the U.S., numerous actions were taken by the Fed, including Credit Easing (creation of money to stimulate the economy), tightening of mortgage lending rules, a number of broad programs such as TARP, Dollar Swap Lines, facilitating overnight bridge loans to major mortgage companies while sales of these companies to larger organizations were facilitated, and so on (Klyuev, De Imus, & Srinivasan, 2009). In some cases, driven by fear of catastrophe, the Fed put into place contingency arrangements with large financial companies that were never used as the crisis event came under control, a point that will be taken up in more detail in the next section.

As we enter the early recovery period after this crisis, historians and others are beginning to try to understand the actions of the central bankers and the success or failure of their efforts as crisis leaders. In an article titled "Central Bankers Weren't Meant to Be Heroes," Bloomberg's editorial board noted:

> The most effective central banks stretched the limits of their mandate. The fact remains that QE [quantitative easing] requires more bravery of the ECB's president, Mario Draghi, than it did of Ben Bernanke at the Fed or Mervyn King at the Bank of England.
>
> *(Bloomberg, 2014)*

Thus, in addition to speed and creative action, the actions taken by the central bankers were daring enough to be controversial, speaking directly to the crisis leader's need to engage in role expansion. This role expansion almost inevitably results in push-back from other players, often the very people or institutions that were unwilling to take on the risks they asked the crisis leader to shoulder. For example, in reviewing the actions of Ben Bernanke at the U.S. Federal Reserve, Senator DeMemit argued for greater political oversight of the Fed, stating, "Americans don't trust the Federal Reserve…[it has expanded its] mission well beyond anything that was ever discussed" (Reddy, 2009). Yet without these bold actions, it is unclear what the outcome of the crisis would have been.

In considerations of heroism, Rand & Epstein (2014) have performed experiments that suggest heroic action is largely driven by intuitive, automatic thought. This evidence suggests that heroes, at least in facing physical risk situations, may depend largely on automatic, intuitive cognition and recognition-primed decision making (Klein, 1993; Sorensen, Øvergård, & Martinsen, 2014). However, a careful examination of the strategies used by heroic leaders forces us to think about how much resourcefulness and creativity is required under duress to affect successful, heroic outcomes. An under-explored aspect of heroism is the ability to think creatively under pressure. As described in the introduction, crisis situations involve complex events, often with interlinking contingencies that rapidly reduce options and degrade assets available to address the emergency event.

In an article on corporate leadership during crisis events, Fred Garcia Helios described the nexus point between situational awareness and improvisation, noting one of the classic reasons why improvisation must occur—the fact that standard operating procedures are no longer meaningful:

> leaders demonstrate situational awareness in a crisis, grasping the significance of the underlying event and its likely impact … [leaders] mobilize a quick response and protect the company's enterprise value … the New Orleans flood and Exxon's early response to the Valdez spill demonstrated lack of … situational awareness … discipline and command focus …
>
> *(Helio, 2006)*

In crisis events, heroic leaders must be able to creatively cobble together other resources in new ways to create a set of "work arounds" that allow their team to respond immediately, before reinforcements arrive. This is a critical skill set in affecting a heroic response as an organization. The leader's ability to *improvise* (i.e., to engage in rapid succession of considered actions) suggests deep situational awareness, an understanding of the constraints and options available, and an ability to develop and modify an action plan as necessary in a rapidly changing environment, is key to heroic leadership in times of crisis (Mendonça et al., 2001; Mendonça & Franco, 2013; Mendonça & Wallace, 2007).

Action Strategies of Heroic Leaders Facing Crisis

We often observe individual crisis events as "one-offs" or rare situations, with equally rare leaders who took exceptional actions that were driven by that particular event. But in examining many disasters, researchers have developed a deeper understanding of the characteristics of crisis that emerge over and over again. Similarly, I argue here that beyond the personal, idiosyncratic leadership strategies employed by a single crisis leader, there is a group of specific techniques or action strategies used by most leaders we come to view as heroic. Crisis leaders deploy these tactical responses when the usual options fail, and these approaches enable them to become maverick actors when the situation requires daring, unflinching action. A great deal more effort will be needed to fully characterize the range and nuances of these tactics, but those that I have thought about the most are offered here as a way to begin the process of systematically examining heroic leadership in action:

The Stand-off

While good leaders typically try to resolve conflict and allow for "smoothness" in social relationships, heroic leaders also know when to dig their heels in to address an underlying, often under-recognized, or deliberately hidden crisis. Some issues need to come to a head in order to be resolved clearly and decisively, and sometimes stand-offs can also be used to create important compromise that ultimately move groups and even nations forward in ways that might not be achievable without putting a spotlight on the unspoken crisis, temporarily creating a sharp dividing line on the issues.

Although not much more than a footnote in history and medical textbooks now, the Thalidomide crisis of the late 1950s and early 1960s offers a compelling example of a quiet leader electing to raise the stakes to a stand-off rather than simply acquiescing and allowing a medical tragedy to strike the U.S. Thalidomide, a drug that was marketed throughout much of the world as a way to suppress morning sickness in pregnant women was ultimately found to be a teratogenic agent, responsible for thousands of deformed babies, with missing limbs and organs, as well as deaths.

A female pharmacologist and physician, Dr. Frances Kelsey, newly hired to the Federal Drug Administration (FDA) was skeptical about the science supporting the drug manufactures safety claims and did not approve the drug in the U.S. Dr. Kelsey's recent death in 2015 brought her story once again to the fore, showing in clear detail the pressure she faced to "go-along-to-get-along," and her response, tirelessly fighting with the company through bureaucratic procedures (referring to my earlier note that crisis leaders often have to be able to effect action using the complex political and organizational mechanisms that seem to slow others to a standstill) to track down doses of the drug that had been delivered to physicians in the U.S. in a quiet, but desperate effort to prevent personal catastrophes for pregnant women throughout the nation (Mintz, 1962a, 1962b).

Consider the context: a woman physician in a male dominated field in the early 1960s, working her first project for a newly created federal agency struggling to gain its footing with little congressional support; and rather than approving the drug application, Dr. Kelsey scuttles the application again and again, despite increasing pressure from the manufacturer, not just levied against her, but her bosses. In a conversation with the investigative journalist, Morton Mintz, who broke the story in 1962, Mr. Mintz noted that, "the company even threatened her with a libel lawsuit" and when asked how she appeared to be responding at a personal level when Mr. Mintz interviewed Dr. Kelsey, he described her as "resolute and steadfast" in her position (Mintz, personal communication, August 19, 2015). A synopsis of the events described in her recent New York Times obituary provides some historical perspective on the struggle to keep the drug off the market:

> [Merrell pharmaceuticals] made glowing claims for Kevadon's [Thalidimide] safety and effectiveness…But Dr. Kelsey…found the evidence for claims about Kevadon to be insufficient. Letters, calls and visits from Merrell executives ensued. She was called a fussy, stubborn, unreasonable bureaucrat. But she refused to be hurried, insisting that there was insufficient proof.
>
> *(McFadden, 2015)*

Ultimately, as reports of horrific limb disfigurement began to be associated with the drug, Merrell withdrew its FDA application and Dr. Kesley's steadfast position was vindicated. By refusing to change her position and allowing a stand-off to occur, Dr. Kesley prevented what could have been a widespread tragedy in the U.S. She was recognized as a hero by her government and the general public at the time, ultimately being awarded the President's Award for Distinguished Federal Civilian Service in 1962 (NIH, undated).

The Gamble

Often when the stand-off is with an inanimate opponent, for example an accident or disaster situation, the heroic leader is faced with what is often described with phrases such as a "no-win situation" or a binary option set in which one can only pick the "best of two evils." A powerful historical example of this comes in the form of Sir Ernest Shackleton, the commander of the vessel *Endurance*, during an Antarctic exploration mission. The vessel became stuck in polar ice as he and his crew tried to reach Vahsel Bay, Antarctica. Shackleton and his crew survived for months on the ice-bound ship hoping to wait out the cold until Spring arrived, but the pressure of the ice-floes ultimately crushed the vessel, forcing the crew to abandon the *Endurance*. Shackleton created a base camp on an ice floe until it broke up, at which point he and his men used life boats to reach the unpopulated Elephant Island. Recognizing that reaching a whaling station 830 miles away was their only hope of rescue, Shackleton decided to attempt an open boat crossing in the largest of the life boats, with five other men, leaving the rest of the crew on Elephant Island.

This profound gamble—staking his own life and the lives of five men as the only option to save the others is highlighted in historical accounts which note that Shackleton refused to pack more than 4 weeks provisions for this last ditch effort, recognizing that if he had not made it to the whaling stations within that time, he and the men with him would have perished in the attempt (Alexander, 1998). Shackleton sailed for 15 days in high seas before reaching the island where the whaling stations were, only to have to hike an additional 32 miles over icy terrain to reach civilization. Shackleton returned to Elephant Island, personally overseeing the rescue of the crew who had remained behind. A later explorer who retraced some of Shackleton's steps stated, "I do not know how they did it, except that they had to—three men of the heroic age of Antarctic exploration with 50 feet of rope between them—and a carpenter's adze" (Fisher & Fisher, 1957, p. 386).

While these situation may have more options than initially recognized, senior decision makers may not have time to fully analyze the problem space, and often will try to narrow the options to two or three alternative courses of action (Bonn & Rundle-Thiele, 2007). In this case, the heroic leader's job is often to serve as a tie-breaker for a team, selecting one path forward even though the outcome is unclear. In effect, this absolves the team members of the responsibility of a negative result and allows the group to take action rather than being stymied. This is an important role particularly when there is a point of no return (criticality) and the stance of indecision and inaction can only lead to further losses of options, escalation of the crisis event, or death. Thus, *option narrowing* and a final "go/no go" decision is a skill that is crucial to embody. Teaching leaders when to be prepared to make a gut decision on a small number of apparently equally bad alternatives is fundamental to understanding the heroic stance.

The logic of the gamble in a "do or die" situation is that it is better to have done something, even if the result is ultimately negative, than to have done nothing and met the same fate. It is important to note that in many academic and non-academic reflections on heroism, the idea that heroism is paradoxical in nature emerges (Franco et al., 2011). This particular idea of action in the face of a no-win situation has been referred to as the "Stockdale paradox" after another man of the sea, decorated U.S. Navy officer James Stockdale who withstood multiple tortures while imprisoned by the Vietnamese government. Stockdale is quoted as offering a dual philosophical view on resilience in crisis, "You must retain faith that you will prevail in the end, regardless of the difficulties. And at the same time, you must confront the most brutal facts of your current reality, whatever they might be" (Maxwell, 2007).

Systematic Use of Luck

Ralph Waldo Emerson is quoted as having said, "Good luck is another name for tenacity of purpose" (Emerson, 1888). As with many aspects of heroism, this can be interpreted simply as an inspirational passage to encourage people to do good work. But a deeper reading points to the strategies of heroic leaders in *prolonging* the crisis situation long enough that more chance events can occur. Luck is at its core a set of binary outcomes offered by events outside of our control that impact our fate (Wagner-Pacifici, 2000). When the chances of success are zero to start with, extending the time-scale can allow for the limited assets available to be repositioned to take advantage of chance events that can be parleyed into better odds.

Exploring psychology through popular culture and television shows is gaining increasing recognition as a key way to teach these concepts to students. Similarly, for mature audiences focused on learning the art of crisis leadership, examining high quality TV and film can be very useful because it provides rich contextual information and the opportunity for leaders to reflect and explore contingencies in hypothetical scenarios (Langley, 2016). Borrowing from film, a classic example of a crisis leader relying heavily on luck is an episode of Star Trek called "The Galileo Seven" (Season 1, Episode 13), in which Spock and six other crew members are marooned on a hostile planet. Their shuttle craft is disabled, and the transporters on the *Enterprise* are malfunctioning. To complete the set of contingencies and constraints facing Captain Kirk, the starship is also required to abandon the search for the lost crew members at a specific time in order to comply with orders from Commissioner Ferris (a higher ranking officer, temporarily aboard the ship) to respond to a medical emergency on another planet. Captain Kirk, clearly frustrated with the Commissioner's desire to leave orbit and abandon the search says:

> KIRK: Look, these people are my friends and my shipmates. *I intend to continue the ship's search for them until the last possible moment.* [Emphasis added; the line implicitly notes Captain Kirk's reliance on luck]

Then later, in assuring his own transporter chief in the strategic value of "luck":

> CHIEF: Captain, it's a big planet. It'll be sheer luck if our landing parties find anything.
> KIRK: I'm depending on luck, Lieutenant. It's almost the only tool we have that'll work.

Here Captain Kirk explicitly acknowledges his reliance on improving odds from zero to something above zero as the only available course of action, and within that he has done everything possible to maximize chance encounters with the away team by sending multiple search parties. Where others under his command have already begun to relax their stance because they assume failure is inevitable, Kirk never lets down his vigil. Instead, he constantly searches for small opportunities that might tip the scales in favor of his lost crew. In these moments Kirk seems most alive, drawing together all of his leadership experience into an orchestrated balance between strategy and tactics, creating deep operational poise throughout the *Enterprise*. In this adventure, Captain Kirk's actions show the crisis leader's ability to "snatch victory from the jaws of defeat" is not simply blind luck, but rather the use of systematic strategies that position a team to use the limited and unpredictable opportunities the crisis situation affords to strike at just the right moment to turn certain failure into a surprising success.

The Gambit

Where the gamble involves selecting from a few bad options, the gambit takes the crisis leader a step further, playing one set of contingencies off of another. Most leaders would fear giving up any available resources, preferring to stabilize as best as possible to a known, safe position, but heroic leaders recognize that the contours of the crisis may eat away at their position over time. In response they may deliberately sacrifice some key assets in the hopes of gaining others. A gambit can be defined as a move that trades off one resource to gain something else, so the crisis leader effectively accepts a further loss of precious resources to buy time, to bridge to another set of resources, or diffuse the resources of an opponent to create situational disadvantage for the opposing force. An example of this can be found by returning to the story of Apollo 13, where the mission control team on Earth elected to give up the easy and immediate abort options in favor of the more complex circumlunar approach in order to buy time and improve option awareness.

Order of Magnitude

During crises, there is often a sense that the event is inevitably carrying the individuals involved toward a certain eventuality that no one wants to see come to pass—the event horizon. In these moments, one leadership strategy is to try to "get ahead of" the event by dramatically changing the scale of the response. Often typical response is limited by a failure of imagination of what the implications of the disaster are. For example, in the Japanese sarin gas attacks, the responders failed to consider that a deliberate exposure to a toxic agent had been perpetrated, and this limited the scale and appropriateness of response (Pangi, 2002). Alternatively, leaders can experience a failure of imagination about how available, but often latent, resources could be dynamically repositioned to outpace events by increasing the scale of response by an order of magnitude above that of the threat. This requires stepping away from simple heuristic responses (Gigerenzer & Gaissmaier, 2011) to being creative even under pressure, and improvising systematically (Mendonça et al., 2001; Mendonça & Wallace, 2007), in a way that goes so far beyond the scale of the crisis, and to respond with such overwhelming force that the crisis is immediately extinguished. While these approaches can ultimately be costly, dangerous, or have other unintended consequences, they can ensure relief from the immediate crisis. In many instances, this allows time for the unintended consequences to be resolved through later actions that can be taken in a more measured fashion.

One historical example of this approach was Abraham Lincoln's expansion of Presidential war powers during the Civil War to set all slaves free. Rather than using normal channels, the war itself presented an opportunity to get ahead of the issue, by declaring the property of Southern slave holders, including the slaves themselves, to be appropriated by the Union army as a necessity of war. President Lincoln's interpretation of his war powers (which were and to this day remain deeply controversial in times of conflict) allowed him to consider creative action an order of magnitude above that achievable in political decision making, where the question of what to do with the slaves had long been stymied. The action was decisive in many ways, yet it left the legal status of the slaves open, ultimately requiring Lincoln to push toward the 13th Amendment. It was also expeditious in the moment both because the Union army needed the support of freed slaves in its ranks, but more importantly because it achieved the desired outcome immediately and with finality (Berdahl, 1921). Again, as with almost all heroic leadership decisions, this action was deeply controversial at the time, and the issue of Presidential war powers remains an open Constitutional issue, with many viewing such authority as resting with Congress, not the President.

Another more contemporary example of dramatic role expansion and going up an order of magnitude to get ahead of crisis comes from the actions the Fed took in the Global Economic Crisis, as discussed earlier. Some of the specific actions taken by the Fed included making provisions to stabilize the life insurance operations of the major financial company AIG and a multi-billion dollar loan to Bank of America. Interestingly, neither of these instruments was ultimately used, because a set of smaller actions started to bring the situation under control. But these measures were put in place anyway, as another line of defense. Through them, it is possible to see that the Fed recognized that it was impossible to fully understand the scale of the emergency, and that the Fed attempted to account for this with interventions set at an extreme level.

Discussion—Areas for Future Research

Bennis' (2007) admonition that we need a great deal more understanding of heroic leaders must be extended to deeply understand the specific individual traits that come to the fore in the heart of crisis events. These are the moments that discriminate good leaders from the truly exemplary expression of leadership in the line of fire—whether that fire is taken on the field of battle, or in a boardroom.

While the main focus of this chapter has been on understanding the dynamics of crisis situations and the heroic action strategies leaders deploy during these events, future work will need to consider the individual characteristics of crisis leaders from the perspective of disaster science. Crisis leaders must be able to maintain situational awareness; tolerate ambiguity; foster shared situational awareness with other leaders and team members; they must foster trust—often blind trust—in their decision making abilities in their subordinates; they must be willing to rapidly and boldly step into leadership voids that occur above them in the hierarchy; they must maintain option awareness and be able to reconfigure assets to create options that ostensibly would not exist in the absence of creative decision making under extreme duress; and simultaneously, a crisis leader must be willing to reduce options to affect action when others are paralyzed by fear.

While these are all "positive" traits, heroic leaders also may be forced to call on darker skills as well (Resick, Whitman, Weingarden, & Hiller, 2009), for example, systematically limiting information available to subordinates to ensure that they do not panic, use of personal force to ensure discipline in the ranks, and the willingness to sacrifice individuals to ensure the greater good. Crisis leaders may also have impulsive tendencies, the ability to act intuitively in ways that are not easily understood by others, be annoyingly dedicated to principles in ways that alienate other team members, have the ability to sacrifice their own career—or at the extreme—their own life in a "moment of truth" (Friedman, in press). These factors suggest that what are often considered to be pathological or anti-social traits may be of fundamental importance to effective crisis leadership. In terms of hiring, retention, and promotion policies, corporations and government employers may suffer long-term consequences by encouraging only "nice" leaders, because other skill sets may be required when the chips are down.

Ultimately, whether perceived positively or negatively by their bosses, colleagues, and subordinates in the moment of crisis, heroic leaders unwaveringly attend to individual and group moral hazards in an effort to take actions that may be costly in the moment that prevent even greater costs at a later time. In so doing, Kakabase and colleagues suggest that crisis leaders avoid setting morally destructive precedents, attend to things like conflict of interest and regulation to ensure good decision making, do not mask failures in corporate governance, take steps to avoid hubris and group think, and do not seek to sanitize language or reduce transparency even in the midst of crisis (Kakabadse et al., 2012). While all of this sounds easy, it is much more difficult when one is personally facing a disaster. As noted earlier, while it is simple for us to excoriate Captain Schettino, there are also indications that during the 40 minutes he delayed ordering the evacuation, he was under pressure from corporate leadership of the cruise line to minimize the event if possible.

The question in many fields, ranging from clinical psychology to artistic endeavors, has remained "are great talents born or taught," and the answer as with all things is not simple (Ericsson, Krampe, & Tesch-Römer, 1993). Heroic leadership doubtlessly is in some cases an expression of innate aptitude and acumen, but experience and even reflection on prior failure to act heroically are also powerful teachers. Examining the contours and dynamics of crisis events can deeply inform our understanding of how these leaders act, what personality characteristics enable action, and what action strategies they apply in these high risk environments. But most leaders are not trained to think about low-base rate, high consequence events as part of their normal business routine (Smith, 2004). By incorporating opportunities for leaders and their teams to encounter the situational constraints that crisis create, in business conditions that are based on the real, embedded activities of daily organizational life, it is possible to foster what Smith (2004) describes as a "crisis-prepared culture" (p. 347).

In order for leaders to be able to explore their core assumptions, the ability of their teams to make sense out of the chaos of the disaster event, examine how protocols will and will not hold up under the stress of crisis, and develop a better understanding of how normal communication channels within the organization may not work during a disaster, crisis leaders must be encouraged to explore the possibility of catastrophic organizational failure, something that most organizational leadership teams are afraid to do. However, this willingness to foster creativity, courage, and to accept risk on a daily basis is key to creating healthy, dynamic, innovative organizations for routine tasks (Kashdan, Barrios, Forsyth, & Steger, 2006; Kashdan, Rose, & Fincham, 2004), and can make them profoundly more resilient in the face of disaster.

References

Alexander, C. (1998). *The Endurance: Shackleton's legendary Arctic expedition*. London: Bloomsbury.

Allison, S. T., & Goethals, G. R. (2011). *Heroes: What they do and why we need them*. New York: Oxford University Press.

Allison, S. T., & Goethals, G. R. (2013a). *Heroic leadership: An influence taxonomy of 100 exceptional individuals*: Routledge.

Allison, S. T., & Goethals, G. R. (2013b). *True heroes: An influence taxonomy of 100 exceptional individuals*. New York: Routledge.

Allison, S. T., & Goethals, G. R. (2015). *"Now he belongs to the ages": The heroic leadership dynamic and deep narratives of greatness*. New York: Palgrave Macmillan.

Alsop, R. J. (2006). *The 18 immutable laws of corporate reputation: Creating, protecting and repairing your most valuable asset*. London: Kogan Page Publishers.

Arnulf, J. K., Mathisen, J. E., & Hærem, T. (2012). Heroic leadership illusions in football teams: Rationality, decision making and noise-signal ratio in the firing of football managers. *Leadership*, 8(2), 169–185.

Associated Press (2012). Costa Concordia transcript: Coastguard orders captain to return to stricken ship. Retrieved from www.theguardian.com/world/2012/jan/17/costa-concordia-transcript-coastguard-captain.

Bennis, W. (2007). The challenges of leadership in the modern world: Introduction to the special issue. *American Psychologist*, 62(1), 2–5.

Berariu, R., Fikar, C., Gronalt, M., & Hirsch, P. (2015). Understanding the impact of cascade effects of natural disasters on disaster relief operations. *International Journal of Disaster Risk Reduction*, 12, 350–356.

Berdahl, C. A. (1921). *War powers of the executive in the United States*. New York: Johnson Reprint Corporation.

Beutler, L. E., Reyes, G., Franco, Z., & Housley, J. (2006). The need for proficient mental health professionals in the study of terrorism. *Psychology of Terrorism*, 32–55.

Bloomberg (2014). Central bankers weren't meant to be heroes. *Bloomberg* (December 22). Retrieved from www.bloomberg.com/view/articles/2014-12-22/if-only-all-central-banks-could-be-like-the-federal-reserve.

Bonn, I., & Rundle-Thiele, S. (2007). Do or die—Strategic decision-making following a shock event. *Tourism Management*, 28(2), 615–620.

Carney, S. (2007). Reform of higher education and the return of "heroic" leadership: The case of Denmark. *Management Revue*, 18(2), 174–186.

Casler, J. G. (2014). Revisiting NASA as a high reliability organization. *Public Organization Review*, 14(2), 229–244.

Clements, C., & Washbush, J. B. (1999). The two faces of leadership: considering the dark side of leader-follower dynamics. *Journal of Workplace Learning*, 11(5), 170–176.

Cross, R., & Prusak, L. (2002). The people who make organizations go-or stop. *Harvard Business Review*, 80(6), 104–112.

Daily Bell (2014). Bloomberg shock: All central bankers are heroes now. *Daily Bell* (December 23). Retrieved from www.thedailybell.com/news-analysis/35935/Bloomberg-Shock-All-Central-Bankers-Are-Heroes-Now/#sthash.jXkEJZfX.dpufhttp://www.thedailybell.com/news-analysis/35935/Bloomberg-Shock-All-Central-Bankers-Are-Heroes-Now.

Desmond, M. (2008a). The lie of heroism. *Contexts*, 7(1), 56–58.

Desmond, M. (2008b). *On the fireline: Living and dying with wildland firefighters*. Chicago, IL: University of Chicago Press.

Emerson, R. W. (1888). *Select Writings of Ralph Waldo Emerson* (Vol. 33): London: W. Scott.

Endsley, M. R. (2000). Theoretical underpinnings of situation awareness: A critical review. In M. R. Endsley & D. J. Garland (eds), *Situation Awareness Analysis and Measurement* (pp. 3–32). Mahwah, NJ: Lawrence Erlbaum Associates.

Ericsson, K. A., Krampe, R. T., & Tesch-Römer, C. (1993). The role of deliberate practice in the acquisition of expert performance. *Psychological Review*, 100(3), 363.

Fisher, M., & Fisher, J. (1957). *Shackleton*. London: James Barrie Books.

Franco, Z. (2014). Heroism in crisis events. Paper presented at the Hero Round Talbe, Flint Michigan. Retrieved from www.youtube.com/watch?v=y1oipKVrh4Q.

Franco, Z., & Langdon, M. (2012). The captain who fell into the lifeboat: What the *Costa Concordia* disaster reveals about heroism—and how we can train ourselves to be heroes. *The Greater Good Magazine*. Retrieved from http://greatergood.berkeley.edu/article/item/the_captain_who_fell_into_the_life_boat.

Franco, Z., & Zimbardo, P. (2016). The psychology of heroism: Extraordinary champions of humanity in an unforgiving world. In A. Miller (ed.), *The Social Psychology of Good and Evil* (2nd ed.). New York: Guilford Press.

Franco, Z., Blau, K., & Zimbardo, P. G. (2011). Heroism: A conceptual analysis and differentiation between heroic action and altruism. *Review of General Psychology*, 15(2), 99–113.

Franco, Z., Zumel, N., Holman, J., Blau, K., & Beutler, L. E. (2009). Evaluating the impact of improvisation on the incident command system: A modified single case study using the DDD simulator. Paper presented at the ISCRAM2009, Gothenburg, Sweden.

Friedman, H. (in press). Everyday heroism in practicing psychology. *Journal of Humanistic Psychology – Special Issue on Heroism and the Human Experience*.

Gigerenzer, G., & Gaissmaier, W. (2011). Heuristic decision making. *Annual Review of Psychology*, 62, 451–482.

Goldstein, M. (2014). Whistle-blower on Countrywide mortage misdeeds to get $57 million, *New York Times* (December 17). Retrieved from http://dealbook.nytimes.com/2014/12/17/countrywide-whistle-blower-to-receive-more-than-57-million/?_r=1.

Helio, F. (2006). Effective leadership response to crisis. *Strategy & Leadership*, 34(1), 4–10.

Hensgen, T., Desouza, K. C., & Kraft, G. D. (2003). Games, signal detection, and processing in the context

of crisis management. *Journal of Contingencies and Crisis Management, 11*(2), 67–77.
Irwin, N. (2013). *The Alchemists: Three Central Bankers and a World on Fire.* New York: Penguin.
Jenkins, S. P., Brandolini, A., Micklewright, J., & Nolan, B. (2012). The Great Recession and its consequences for household incomes in 21 countries. In S. P. Jenkins, A. Brandolini, J. Micklewright, & B. Nolan (eds), *The Great Recession and the Distribution of Household Income* (pp. 33–89). Oxford: Oxford University Press.
Kakabadse, A., Kouzmin, A., Kakabadse, N. K., & Mouraviev, N. (2012). Auditing moral hazards for post-global financial crisis (GFC) leadership. In A. Kouzmin, M. T. Witt, & A. Kakabadse (eds), *State crimes against democracy: Political forensics in public affairs* (pp. 79–106). Basingstoke: Palgrave Macmillan.
Kashdan, T. B., Barrios, V., Forsyth, J. P., & Steger, M. F. (2006). Experiential avoidance as a generalized psychological vulnerability: Comparisons with coping and emotion regulation strategies. *Behaviour Research and Therapy, 44*(9), 1301–1320.
Kashdan, T. B., Rose, P., & Fincham, F. D. (2004). Curiosity and exploration: Facilitating positive subjective experiences and personal growth opportunities. *Journal of Personality Assessment, 82*(3), 291–305.
Kinsella, E. L., Ritchie, T. D., & Igou, E. R. (2015). Zeroing in on heroes: A prototype analysis of hero features. *Journal of Personality and Social Psychology, 108*(1), 114.
Klein, G. A. (1993). A recognition-primed decision (RPD) model of rapid decision making. In G. A. Klein, J. Orasanu, R. Calderwood, & C. E. Zsambok (eds), *Decision making in action: Models and methods* (pp. 138–147). Norwood, NJ: Ablex Publishing Corporation.
Klyuev, M. V., De Imus, P., & Srinivasan, M. K. (2009). *Unconventional choices for unconventional times: Credit and quantitative easing in advanced economies.* Washington, DC: International Monetary Fund.
Langley, T. (2016). *Star Trek psychology: The mental frontier.* New York: Sterling.
Lovell, J., & Kluger, J. (2006). *Apollo 13.* New York: Houghton Mifflin Harcourt.
Maxwell, J. C. (2007). *The 21 irrefutable laws of leadership: Follow them and people will follow you.* New York: Thomas Nelson Inc.
McFadden, R. D. (2015). Frances Oldham Kelsey, who saved U.S. babies From Thalidomide, dies at 101. *New York Times* (August 8), p. A1. Retrieved from www.nytimes.com/2015/08/08/science/frances-oldham-kelsey-fda-doctor-who-exposed-danger-of-thalidomide-dies-at-101.html?_r=0.
Mendonça, D., & Franco, Z. (2013). Improvising. In K. Penuel, M. Statler & R. Hagen (eds), *Encyclopedia of crisis management* (pp. 496–499). Thousand Oaks, CA: Sage.
Mendonça, D., & Wallace, W. A. (2007). A cognitive model of improvisation in emergency management. *Systems, Man and Cybernetics, Part A: Systems and Humans, 37*(4), 547–561.
Mendonça, D., Beroggi, G. E., & Wallace, W. A. (2001). Decision support for improvisation during emergency response operations. *International Journal of Emergency Management, 1*(1), 30–38.
Mintz, M. (1962a). Drug compay aroused ire of Dr. Kelsey, *Washington Post* (September 16).
Mintz, M. (1962b). "Heroine" of FDA keeps bad drug off of market, *Washington Post* (July 15).
NIH (undated). Dr. Frances Kathleen Oldham Kelsey—biography. Retrieved from www.nlm.nih.gov/changingthefaceofmedicine/physicians/biography_182.html.
Pangi, R. (2002). Consequence management in the 1995 sarin attacks on the Japanese subway system. *Studies in Conflict and Terrorism, 25*(6), 421–448.
Pastel, R. H. (2002). *Collective behaviors: mass panic and outbreaks of multiple unexplained symptoms.* Washington, DC: DTIC.
Perrow, C. (2011). *Normal accidents: Living with high risk technologies.* Princeton, NJ: Princeton University Press.
Petak, W. J. (1985). Emergency management: A challenge for public administration. *Public Administration Review, 45*, 3–7.
Peters, K., Buzna, L., & Helbing, D. (2008). Modelling of cascading effects and efficient response to disaster spreading in complex networks. *International Journal of Critical Infrastructures, 4*(1–2), 46–62.
Pfaff, M. S., Drury, J. L., Klein, G. L., & More, L. D. (2010). Decision support for option awareness in complex emergency scenarios. *Advances in Cognitive Ergonomics*, 87.
Pfaff, M. S., Klein, G. L., Drury, J. L., Moon, S. P., Liu, Y., & Entezari, S. O. (2013). Supporting complex decision making through option awareness. *Journal of Cognitive Engineering and Decision Making, 7*(2), 155–178.
Quarantelli, E. L. (1985). What is disaster? The need for clarification in definition and conceptualization in research. *Disasters and Mental Health Selected Contemporary Perspectives.*
Rand, D. G., & Epstein, Z. G. (2014). Risking your life without a second thought: Intuitive decision-making and extreme altruism. *PLoS One, 9*(10), e109687.
Reason, J. (1990). The contribution of latent human failures to the breakdown of complex systems. *Philosophical Transactions of the Royal Society B, 327*(1241), 475–484.
Reddy, S. (2009). Bernanke foes seek to curtail fed, *Wall Street Journal* (December 16). Retrieved from

www.wsj.com/articles/SB126091294891892399.
Resick, C. J., Whitman, D. S., Weingarden, S. M., & Hiller, N. J. (2009). The bright-side and the dark-side of CEO personality: examining core self-evaluations, narcissism, transformational leadership, and strategic influence. *Journal of Applied Psychology*, *94*(6), 1365.
Rochlin, G. I., La Porte, T. R., & Roberts, K. H. (1987). The self-designing high-reliability organization: Aircraft carrier flight operations at sea. *Naval War College Review*, *40*(4), 76–90.
Salmon, P. M., Stanton, N. A., Walker, G. H., Baber, C., Jenkins, D. P., McMaster, R., & Young, M. S. (2008). What really is going on? Review of situation awareness models for individuals and teams. *Theoretical Issues in Ergonomics Science*, *9*(4), 297–323.
Samarajiva, R. (2005). Policy Commentary Mobilizing information and communications technologies for effective disaster warning: lessons from the 2004 tsunami. *New Media & Society*, *7*(6), 731–747.
Slovic, P. (2002). Terrorism as hazard: A new species of trouble. *Risk Analysis*, *22*(3), 425–426.
Smith, D. (2004). For whom the bell tolls: Imagining accidents and the development of crisis simulation in organizations. *Simulation & Gaming*, *35*(3), 347–362.
Somaiya, R. (2015). The men behind the cartoons at Charlie Hebdo. *The New York Times* (January 8). Retrieved from www.nytimes.com/2015/01/08/world/europe/the-men-behind-the-cartoons-at-charlie-hebdo.html.
Sorensen, L. J., Øvergård, K. I., & Martinsen, T. J. (2014). Understanding human decision making during critical incidents in dynamic positioning. *Contemporary Ergonomics and Human Factors*, *2014*, 359–366.
Sornette, D. (2002). Predictability of catastrophic events: Material rupture, earthquakes, turbulence, financial crashes, and human birth. *Proceedings of the National Academy of Sciences*, *99*(suppl 1), 2522–2529.
Stanton, N. A., Stewart, R., Harris, D., Houghton, R. J., Baber, C., McMaster, R., ... Young, M. S. (2006). Distributed situation awareness in dynamic systems: theoretical development and application of an ergonomics methodology. *Ergonomics*, *49*(12–13), 1288–1311.
UNISDR (2007). Definition of disaster. Retrieved from www.unisdr.org/we/inform/terminology.
Veysey, S. (2013). Costa Concordia disaster is costliest marine loss of all time for insurers, *Business Insurance* (August 11). Retrieved from www.businessinsurance.com/article/20130811/NEWS07/308119976.
Wagner-Pacifici, R. (2000). *Theorizing the standoff: Contingency in action*. Cambridge: Cambridge University Press.
Walker, L. J., Frimer, J. A., & Dunlop, W. L. (2010). Varieties of moral personality: Beyond the banality of heroism. *Journal of Personality*, *78*(3), 907–942.
Wansink, B., Payne, C. R., & Van Ittersum, K. (2008). Profiling the heroic leader: Empirical lessons from combat-decorated veterans of World War II. *The Leadership Quarterly*, *19*(5), 547–555.
Weick, K. E., Sutcliffe, K. M., & Obstfeld, D. (2008). Organizing for high reliability: Processes of collective mindfulness. *Crisis Management*, *3*, 81–123.
Zimbardo, P. (2007). *The Lucifer effect: Understanding how good people turn evil*. New York: Random House LLC.
Zimbardo, P. G., Breckenridge, J. N., & Moghaddam, F. M. (2013). "Exclusive" and "inclusive" visions of heroism and democracy. *Current Psychology*, *32*(3), 221–233.

11

Holocaust Heroes
Heroic Altruism of Non-Jewish Moral Exemplars in Nazi Europe

Stephanie Fagin-Jones

> Whosoever preserves one life is as though he has preserved the entire world.
> *Inscription, borrowed from the Talmud, on the medallion bestowed by Yad Vashem to The Righteous Among the Nations (cited in Bauminger, 1983, p. 12)*

Genocide, defined as "the co-ordinated and planned annihilation of a national, religious, or racial group by a variety of actions aimed at foundations essential to the survival of the group" (Lemkin & Power, 2005), has emerged as a weapon of choice by the Islamic State (ISIS or ISIL). In June 2014, ISIS, with the help of local Sunni tribes, killed at least 1,700 Shiite unarmed Iraqi Air Force cadets. Ali Hussein Kadhim miraculously survived. After clawing his way to the top of a pile of dead bodies, he escaped to the river. Thereafter, two Sunni families took him in and risked their lives to feed, clothe and shelter him, until he was able to reach the town of Al Alam. There, Sunni tribal Sheikh Khamis al-Jubouri, who had been operating an underground railroad-like system that successfully rescued at least 40 escaped Shiite soldiers, provided false identification, shelter for two weeks, and transportation to Erbil, where Ali safely reunited with his baby son and daughter (Arrango, 2014).

"Every time that he came to rape me, he would pray," said 15-year-old "F," one of 40,000 Yazidis trapped on Mount Sinjar where over 5000 people were massacred in August 2014, who was sold to an Iraqi fighter in his twenties (Callimachi, 2015). Despite the unbelievable cruelty of ISIS, Callimachi reports, "There were a couple of instances of people within the Islamic State who showed kindness or who helped these women escape or put together some of the key logistics needed for escape" (Allen, 2015). Yazidi businessman Osman Hassan Ali posed as a buyer and successfully smuggled out numerous Yazidi women and girls. After nearly a year in captivity, these young girls who were rescued were far more fortunate than the 3,144 girls still being held as "sabayas," or slaves, today (Callimachi, 2015).

Assuming that the aid undertaken was without expectation of reward, the heroic actions of Sheikh Khamis al-Jubouri, Osman Hassan and the morally courageous Sunni Iraqi families who risked almost certain death by ISIS, parallel those of the Gentile rescuers of Jews during the Holocaust who defied Hitler and the Nazi regime's efforts to render the world *Judenrein* (literally, "purified of Jews"). While the vast majority living in Nazi-occupied territory during the Second World War were passive bystanders, a minute handful of heroic individuals—even the highest estimate of which represents only approximately one half of 1 percent of the non-Jewish population (Oliner & Oliner, 1988)—"risked his or her life, freedom and safety, in order to rescue one or several Jews from the threat of death or deportation to death camps without exacting in advance monetary compensation" (Gutman, 2003).

Despite repeated avowals by policy makers and civilians alike to "Never Again" allow the atrocities perpetrated by the Nazis against the Jewish people to be repeated, the twentieth and twenty-first centuries have witnessed no end to the proliferation of genocide resulting in 262 million deaths since 1900 (Staub, 2011) and, contributing currently to a staggering 60 million refugees worldwide. Given the global crisis in which we find ourselves today, it is morally imperative that we urgently persist in our efforts to both understand and undertake heroic altruism. Thus it is vital that we examine heroic altruism during the Holocaust, with the goal of translating moral exemplarity into the moral norm over time, lest we allow history to continue to repeat itself.

January 27, 2015 marked the 70th anniversary of the liberation of Auschwitz concentration camp where nearly one million Jews were starved, tortured, and killed in the Nazi gas chambers. Most of the survivors are now in their nineties and few are expected to live to see the 75th anniversary. The same holds true for most Gentile rescuers of Jews who are also quite elderly (e.g., Sir Nicholas Winton, British rescuer of 669 children, died on July 1, 2015 at 106 years old), and few opportunities remain to learn from and bear witness to their heroism. While scores of rescue narratives have been amassed and examined to understand who these people were and why they risked their lives to help while the vast majority remained bystanders in the face of evil, only a few systematic studies of rescue during the Holocaust have been undertaken.

Subsequent to the end of the Second World War, the focus of social psychological research centered on understanding the vicissitudes of authoritarianism and evil (Adorno, Frenkel-Brunswick, Levinson & Sanford, 1950; Milgram, 1974; Zimbardo, Banks, Haney, & Jaffe, 1973). In 1963, nearly twenty years after the Second World War, the founding of The Institute for Righteous Acts by the late Rabbi Harold Schulweis to "search out and conduct interviews with the rescuers, probing the motivation for their acts" (Baron, 1985–1986, p. 241) prompted the first systematic studies of Holocaust rescue (London, 1970). These early naturalistic studies had several limitations including small sample sizes, the absence of control groups, and few, if any, psychometrically reliable and valid instruments (Gordon, 1984; Wolfson, 1975). Nonetheless, they provide some insight into factors impacting the decision to participate in Holocaust rescue.

To date, the largest systematic study of rescue during the Holocaust was the Oliners' "Altruistic Personality Project" (1988). The Oliners interviewed a sample of 700 Holocaust-era rescuers and non-rescuers and used quantitative analyses to arrive at several meaningful conclusions, which are discussed further below. Subsequently, Midlarsky (1985) examined correlates of Holocaust rescue among a sample of 80 verified rescuers and 73 bystanders, building upon the Oliners' pioneering study by (1) including subjects who *had not yet been honored* for their heroism; (2) deepening the focus on the dispositions of participants; (3) utilizing more psychometrically valid and reliable instruments to assess constructs predicated on the findings of numerous laboratory studies on altruism; and (4) including a comparison group of 43 demographically similar pre-war immigrants who emigrated to the United States and Canada prior to the onset of the Second World War. Using Midlarsky's data-set, a robust series of secondary analyses were conducted by Ganz (1993), Midlarsky, Fagin-Jones and Corley (2005), and Fagin-Jones and Midlarsky (2007). These studies examined the relationship between rescue and family upbringing, prosocial and proactive personality characteristics, and the relative importance of positive personality traits examined in the context of potentially important situational and demographic factors, respectively.

Before going further into depth about the factors underpinning rescue during the Holocaust, a brief discussion of where this phenomenon resides in the literature on heroism is warranted. The advent of the positive psychology movement that evolved in direct response to the overwhelming focus on pathology within the field of psychology brought with it a renewed focus on character strengths and virtues that highlight the maximization of human potential and happiness (Peterson and Seligman, 2004; Seligman & Csikszentmihalyi, 2000). Consequently, perhaps in response to increasing incidences of global violence, terrorism and genocide, heroism has been one area of inquiry receiving a recent surge in attention.

An example of the shift away from the examination of evil in favor of understanding the basis of good can be seen in the work of Philip Zimbardo whose classic Stanford Prison Experiment (Zimbardo et al., 1973) revealed how ordinary college students, under certain conditions, conformed with role expectations as prison guards, adopting authoritarian attitudes and behaviors toward the "prisoners." More recently, Franco, Blau and Zimbardo (2011), positing a common underlying "core concept" of heroism, aimed to systematically differentiate the constructs of heroism and altruism, and conducted a study in which participants were asked to determine whether an act of helping was either heroic or altruistic. In so doing, three problems arise.

First, Hawley (2014) alerts us to the tendency among psychologists to conflate terms and to use imprecise language when defining and examining prosocial behavior. She refers to the "jingle fallacy" or the common error of labeling different psychological, behavioral, or theoretical constructs, such as using the terms "altruistic" and "prosocial" interchangeably. Imprecision, she contends, can "impede effective communication, cloud a domain, or perturb paths of connection," (p. 44) and, "will quickly control—often in unrecognized ways—the way we think," (Block, 1995, p. 211).

Hence when attempts are made to operationally define a broad construct such as "heroism," it is important that language and concepts are distinct. This distinction becomes blurred in the positing of the core concept of heroism by Franco et al. (2011) who operationally define heroism as a social activity: (a) in service to others in need; (b) engaged in voluntarily; (c) with recognition of possible risks/costs; (d) in which the actor is willing to accept anticipated sacrifice, and (e) without external gain anticipated at the time of the act.

While arguing that heroism and altruism represent a "fundamentally different class of behaviors," (p. 6), paradoxically, their operational definition of heroism in fact, *subsumes* the construct of altruism, in its inclusion criteria that helping must be undertaken *voluntarily*, is *motivated without expectation of reward* and includes *the potential for sacrifice*. A proposed operational definition of heroism that includes voluntary, intentional, motivational, and potentially sacrificial aspects of behavior is *predicated* upon the construct of altruism, *not distinguished* from it.

Fundamentally, altruism refers to voluntary behavior that is intended to benefit another at personal cost motivated without expectation of reward (Batson et al., 2002). Some theorists add that the behavior can stem from internalized values (Eisenberg, 1991) or a strong moral identity (Eisenberg, Shea, Carlo & Knight, 1991). Expectations of reward, reciprocation, or self-interest are not motives of altruistic behavior (Batson, 2011). Indeed, the honor of *hasidei umot ha-olam*, or "The Righteous Among the Nations" proposed by Yad Vashem, The Holocaust Martyrs' and Heroes' Remembrance Society established in Jerusalem in 1953, requires verification of helping that included great personal risk *and* altruistic motives:

1. Active involvement of the rescuer in saving one or several Jews from the threat of death or deportation to death camps.
2. Risk to the rescuer's life, liberty or position.
3. The initial motivation being the intention to help persecuted Jews: i.e. not for payment or any other reward such as religious conversion of the saved person, adoption of a child, etc.
4. The existence of testimony of those who were helped or at least unequivocal documentation establishing the nature of the rescue and its circumstances (Yad Vashem, 2016a).

Second, the authors articulated three broad subtypes of heroism: civil (physical risk/non duty-bound), martial/ military (physical risk/duty bound), and social heroism. According to this model, Holocaust rescue is considered, along with whistleblowing and other forms of courageous resistance (Shepela, Cook, Horlitz, Leal, Luciano & Lufty, 1999), an example of social heroism that is often controversial, enacting an "extra-community" standard that has not yet been accepted, typically non-dramatic, typically not involving physical danger, and typically eliciting other often-increasing costs over time. Holocaust rescue was among the most dramatic episodes in human history and was defined by extremes of morality and risk (Staub, 2011). Furthermore, in contrast to acts of courageous resistance (Shepela et al., 1999), studies of rescue during the Holocaust examine helping behavior that was undertaken by individuals whose altruistic motives were *verified* by the recipients of their actions, archival records, and corroborating reports (Fagin-Jones & Midlarsky, 2007).

Third, the results indicated that higher risk helping behaviors were more likely to be defined as heroism, whereas lower risk forms of helping were more likely to be defined as altruism. One acknowledged yet significant limitation to the validity of this study is the forced categorical format of the questionnaire (i.e., heroism vs. altruism). Respondents were not given the option to characterize an act of helping as both heroic *and* altruistic, or to determine the relative degree of perceived heroism and altruism in an act of helping. While not all altruistic behavior can be considered heroic in that it does not occur in the context of endangerment to the self, when combined with extreme risk to the actor, whether physical, social or psychological, the altruistically-motivated act can be considered heroic (Becker & Eagly, 2004). The dichotomy of heroism versus altruism, in the case of Holocaust rescue disappears.

The rescue of Jews during the Holocaust was undertaken at the highest levels of risk and involved the highest levels of moral courage on behalf of others without expectation of reward or recognition. Other forms of resistance activity during the Holocaust could be heroic but not altruistic. For example, Polish resistance fighters risked their lives to save lives but helped members of their own group. Individuals who risked their lives to rescue Jews but were compensated were not considered altruistic.

Holocaust rescue was not egoistically motivated to avoid personal distress, in fact, rescue activity sometimes sustained over a period of two to five years with chronic risk of being betrayed or discovered, thus increasing personal distress (Batson, 1991). Moreover, escape from the situation was not only easy but normative, and helping was socially and physically imperiling. Those who turned in Jews were rewarded with cash compensation (Oliner & Oliner, 1988), whereas those who engaged in even minor helping acts toward a Jew received harsh punishment (Bartoszewski & Lewin, 1969; Gilbert, 2003), as illustrated in the following proclamation from November, 10, 1941, by Dr. Ludwig Fischer, the German district governor of Warsaw:

> *Concerning the Death Penalty for Illegally Leaving Jewish Residential Districts* ... Any Jew who illegally leaves the designated residential district will be punished by death. Anyone who deliberately offers refuge to such Jews or who aids them in any other manner (i.e., offering a night's lodging, food, or by taking them into vehicles of any kind, etc.) will be subject to the same punishment.
>
> *(Yad Vashem archives; cited in Paldiel, 1993, p. 3)*

Thus rescue during the Holocaust should be considered both heroic *and* altruistic. Moreover, this behavior is morally distinguishable from other forms of helping in that the help was directed toward people being persecuted on the basis of their ethnicity and religion, beyond one's own ethnic group. It is therefore appropriate to characterize this phenomenon of humanitarian behavior as *heroic altruism*.

Another model of heroism referred to as the "Great Eight" offered by Allison and Goethals (2011) more closely captures the exceptional character of Gentile rescuers of Jews during the Holocaust. Allison and Goethals interviewed a sample of 75 college students who were asked to posit traits associated with heroism that were, in turn, sorted into eight factors: *smart, strong, selfless, caring, charismatic, resilient, reliable,* and *inspiring.* The caring, selfless, inspiring traits reflect heroes' care-based morality, whereas the resilient, reliable, charismatic, smart, and strong traits reflect heroes' competence. The combination of care-based moral courage and competence were the defining characteristics of Holocaust rescuers (Staub, 2011) and were exemplified by Irena Sendler, the courageous and ingenious Polish non-Jewish rescuer of thousands of children from the Warsaw Ghetto.

Allison and Goethals (2011) introduce their discussion of heroism with the case of Sendler, who was arrested, tortured and sentenced to death (but was later rescued) for her participation in helping Jews. Sendler and her colleague Irena Schultz put their lives on the line to hide and extricate children from the ghetto by ambulance, toolboxes, body bags, potato sacks, and even coffins (Allison & Goethals, 2011). In so doing, Sendler and Schultz exemplified the "Great Eight" traits, which closely align with "Traits that Transcend" enumerated by The Jewish Foundation for the Righteous (https://jfr.org) to portray the personalities of the rescuers: *compassion, cooperation, courage, ingenuity, integrity, moral leadership, self-sacrifice,* and *social responsibility.*

Who were these righteous few, and why did they engage in heroic altruism? This chapter will review the research on demographic, situational, socialization, and personality variables associated with the non-Jewish rescue of Jews during the Holocaust. Thereafter, implications and suggestions for future research will be discussed.

Demographics

The vast body of Holocaust literature reveals that the population of rescuers was demographically heterogeneous consisting of both men and women; the very young and the very old; the extremely rich and the poverty stricken; Catholics, Protestants, and Muslims; the highly educated and the illiterate; diplomats and sewer workers. Rescuers honored by Yad Vashem originated from 54 countries ranging from Indonesia and Ecuador to China and Peru. Rescuers were represented in every Nazi-occupied territory such as Poland, Denmark, France, and Holland; Axis power countries, such as Italy and Japan; neutral countries such as Switzerland, Spain and Sweden, and non-occupied Allied countries such as the United States and England.

Both archival and empirical studies have examined whether certain trends in regard to gender, age, occupation, religion, socio-economic status, education or occupation may have made rescue more likely (Fagin-Jones & Midlarsky, 2007). The results suggest that while certain demographic factors such as occupation or age may have favored a few rescuers, these were not a critical factor (Geras, 1995; Gushee, 1993; Fagin-Jones & Midlarsky, 2007).

Age

In regard to age, some evidence suggests that older adults may have been more likely to engage in rescue, particularly in Germany (Fagin-Jones & Midlarsky, 2007; Oliner & Oliner, 1988). Older individuals may have had access to more resources, such as the cultivation of networks through educational or vocational channels, were less likely to be inducted into the army, may have had more firmly established identities and been less vulnerable to conform to Nazi propaganda. Both Henry (1984) and Wolfson (1975) found the majority of rescuers in their samples were born before 1910 and achieved adulthood prior to the Nazi takeover, and the majority of a sample of Dusseldorf rescuers were older Germans (Gordon, 1984).

Still, considerable evidence for child and teenage rescue has been found, for example, among Polish partisans who participated in underground networks (Tec, 2003). Younger rescuers often participated in familial rescue efforts (Fogelman, 1994) such as Serbian Margica Baic, age 12, who assisted her mother Clara in rescuing the Denenberg children by providing shelter, food, and false identities, and by keeping their secret until the liberation in 1944. Thus age did not likely influence the decision to rescue with any meaningful consistency.

Gender

Gushee (1993) suggests that the prediction of rescue or kinds of rescue activities on the basis of gender may not be relevant. While, both Wolfson (1975) and Gordon (1984) found that males were disproportionately represented in their respective samples of German helpers; Henry (1984) reports that more females than males participated in rescue, and Fagin-Jones and Midlarsky (2007) found no significant gender differences between the rescuers and the bystanders.

Friedman (1980) assumed that women may have played a more significant role in rescue, particularly in the rescue of children, based on their tendency to be more emotional and more empathic than males. Some empirical support for Friedman's theory was found by Anderson (1991) whose secondary analysis of the Oliners' dataset based on gender revealed that female rescuers had a more highly developed relational capacity with others and received more encouragement by both parents to be other-oriented than male rescuers. Fogelman and Lewis Wiener (1985) reported that more female rescuers attributed their motivation to an emotional or personal identification with the victim. Still, in subsequent studies (i.e., Fagin-Jones & Midlarsky, 2007; Fogelman, 1994), both male and female rescuers were found to exhibit the highest levels of care-based moral reasoning and empathic concern.

Despite evidence that some female rescuers attributed their motivation to more traditional gender-based stereotypes, in actuality, many female rescuers used these stereotypes to their advantage and successfully engaged in less traditional, high-risk rescue activities such as transporting and smuggling Jews (Baron, 1985–1986). For example, Belgian school teacher Jeanne Daman began her rescue efforts by procuring families with which to hide Jewish children. Over time, her activities grew more clandestine and dangerous escorting children throughout Belgium, and eventually joining the Belgian intelligence, establishing an undercover identity, and transporting arms (YadVashem, 2016b).

Women who were empathically moved by the plight of the Jews, and in particular, the suffering of children, defied imprisonment and torture and would stop at nothing to protect their charges. French socialite Suzanne Spaak jettisoned the comforts of her private life including her husband and two children and participated in Parisian intelligence activities to save numerous Jewish children and adults. Spaak was eventually arrested and executed by the Germans in 1944, one week before the liberation of Paris. Dutch rescuer Marion Pritchard shot and killed a Dutch Nazi and survived a seven-month-long imprisonment to save the lives of some 150 (mostly) children she rescued. Hence, in addition to the deepest levels of compassion, women rescuers exhibited the highest levels of courage and self-sacrifice.

Occupation and Socio-economic Status

No single type of occupation or social class significantly influenced the decision to rescue, although some occupations or social status may have favored rescue in some circumstances (Fagin-Jones & Midlarsky, 2007; Oliner & Oliner, 1988). Peasants, diplomats, sewer workers, nannies, mayors, farmers, physicians, maids, principals, soccer players, factory owners, soldiers, nuns, thieves, businessmen, bishops, teachers, students, Nazi officers, a Russian Princess, and a Romanian Queen were among the varied occupations held by rescuers of Jews during the Second World War (Paldiel, 1993).

Among government employees in Nazi-occupied France, where levels of pre-war anti-Semitism were high, it was "unclear where the borderline of unavoidable co-operation ended and active collaboration began (Limore, 2004, p. 111)." However, recently discovered archival evidence suggests that some individuals who held government positions, such as prefects, police agents, low-level administrators and social workers defied orders and engaged in acts of civil disobedience on behalf of Jewish rescue (Limore, 2004). In the unoccupied Vichy zone of Malzieu, for example, Lieutenant Marcellin Cazal, head of the gendarmerie, alerted Jews to anticipated Gestapo roundups, thus enabling them to flee and saving more than 100 lives. These findings converge with Fogelman's (1994), who described a special class of rescuers as *concerned professionals* such as doctors or social workers for whom helping Jews was a natural extension of their professional activities.

Inconsistencies emerge regarding the relationship of occupation, social class and rescue. Lower middle-class workers represented the majority of rescuers in one sample of rescuers (Henry, 1984), while affluent white-collar, independently employed individuals characterized the majority in another (Gordon, 1984). Moreover, Wolfson (1975) and Tec (1986) found that socioeconomic class and occupation was only weakly, if at all, related to rescue in Germany and Poland, respectively. Both Oliner & Oliner (1988) and Fagin-Jones and Midlarsky (2007) found no significant pre-war differences between rescuers and bystanders regarding pre-war perceived social class, perceived socioeconomic status, work, and occupational status.

Religious Affiliation

Members of the clergy in many but not all cases were strongly moved to provide shelter and security to Jews as an expression of their religious duty. Among the most noteworthy was self-effacing French Capuchin monk Father Marie-Benoit, dubbed "Father of the Jews," whose herculean efforts succeeded in saving thousands of Jewish lives. Certain subgroups of non-clergy-affiliated rescuers attributed religion as the basis of their motivation to undertake rescue. For example, Fogelman (1994) identified a proportion of rescuers in her sample who felt a moral obligation to follow the religious tenets inherent in Catholicism or Protestantism, and fifteen percent of the rescuers in the Oliners' sample reported that they were motivated by religion, God or Christianity (Oliner & Oliner, 1988). Examples of religious motivations include (Paldiel, 1993):

> It was a Christian act done in Christian love. We felt it was our duty because they were God's people.
>
> *Henrietta Wiechertjes-Hartmenik, Netherlands*

> By helping Jews during the Second World War we were only doing our duty and putting into practice our Gospel and the teachings of the prophets.
>
> *Louisa Mercier, Belgium*

Still, it is not likely that religious affiliation per se significantly influenced the decision to act, as Christians in proportionate numbers of various denominations engaged in heroic altruism (Paldiel, 1988). Moreover, religious affiliation did not consistently distinguish the rescuers from the bystanders (Fagin-Jones & Midlarsky, 2007; Fogelman, 1994). In fact, whether the majority of rescuers were Protestant or Catholic was strongly influenced by the dominant religious affiliation of the region of residence (Paldiel, 1988). In Italy, for example, home of the Roman Catholic Church, most rescuers were predominantly Catholic. Despite its alliance with Germany and Pope Pius XII's notorious passivity in the face of Hitler's reign of terror against the Jews, the Italian rescue effort succeeded in saving an astounding 85 percent of its Jewry. No other occupied Catholic country engaged in as widespread a humanitarian effort led by Catholic bishops, priests, and nuns who opened their houses of worship to shelter, hide, and protect Jewish victims slated for decimation.

In south-central France, however, where French Huguenots had suffered persecution as a religious minority in Catholic France since the seventeenth century, empathic identification and the heroic leadership of Pastor Andre Trocmé and his wife, Magda, may have predisposed some Protestant villagers to engage in extraordinary acts of collective rescue. Cousin Daniel Trocmé, who aided many of the Jewish children whose parents had been deported, was killed in Madjanek along with "his" Jewish children in June, 1943 (Hallie, 1979). Interestingly, alongside the Chambonais stood a handful of Catholics who represented, "a minority within a minority," joining actively in the rescue effort (Sauvage, 1984, p. 255).

In addition, lesser known cases of Muslims rescuing Jews occurred, in particular, in Albania, which succeeded in rescuing nearly their entire prewar population of Jews (Satloff, 2006). Based on the Islamic principle of *besa* ("the promise"), Muslims such as 15-year-old Refik Veseli, an Albanian apprentice photographer, defied the Nazis and saved seven people including the entire Mandil family. Jews were so welcome in the homes of Muslims that Muslim women often did not cover their faces in front of Jewish men in their homes because they considered these men family.

Thus, consistent with findings associating religiosity and moral exemplarity (Colby & Damon, 1992–1995), it seems that more than religious affiliation, the *quality* of an individual's religiosity, or how a person interprets religious teachings, may have played a more influential role (Gushee, 1993). Indeed, Oliner & Oliner (1988) contend that the rescuers in their sample were more likely than bystanders to have subscribed to religious tenets emphasizing the common humanity of all people. Notably, the propensity to invest in humanistic ideology and to live one's life according to those foundational principles and beliefs was likely introduced in childhood.

Family Upbringing/Socialization

The parents of rescuers and bystanders were a demographically heterogeneous group and differed in the degree to which they fostered family closeness; expressed warmth and affection, predicated their own and their family values on inclusiveness, care, kindness and consideration for others; used reasoning and empathy as the basis of child discipline; and modeled altruistic behaviors toward others (Ganz, 1993; Oliner & Oliner, 1988).

Closeness/Cohesiveness

Familial closeness and parental warmth are thought to facilitate secure attachments, which in turn, impact prosocial development and behavior (Shaver & Mikulincer, 2012). Family cohesion, defined as the degree of commitment, help and support family members provide for one another, emerged as the strongest predictor among a set of family upbringing variables that significantly discriminated Holocaust rescuers from bystanders (Ganz, 1993). Nonetheless, parental warmth and family cohesion were neither necessary nor sufficient to promote rescue. A small percentage of rescuers in the Oliners' study recalled their early childhood relationships with their families and their fathers as "not at all" close (Oliner & Oliner, 1988). Nevertheless, warmth and cohesion may have impacted the degree to which rescue activities were sustained once undertaken. In one of the earliest studies, London (1970) found that the most committed rescuers reported having loving, supportive relationships in early childhood, and the least committed rescuers depicted relationships with their family of origin as cool, negative, avoidant and ambivalent.

More rescuers than bystanders recalled their parents as affectionate and engaged in praising, hugging, kissing, joking around, and smiling (Ganz, 1993). Indeed, strong family attachments were the central component characterizing one of four types of extensive orientations in the Oliners' rescuer sample based on a factor analysis of 100 variables (Oliner & Oliner, 1988). These early cohesive family bonds fostered other-oriented relationships based on tolerance, inclusion, and openness. The family unit as a relational model, once internalized, became a source of psychological ego strength which, in turn, engendered the development of independence, potency, risk-taking, decisiveness, and tolerance in the rescuers. In contrast, more bystanders recalled a lack of both early and later familial closeness that fostered a sense of impotence, indecisiveness and passivity, and may have influenced their wartime bystander behavior.

Discipline

Still, as Eisenberg notes, "Warmth alone is not enough to develop empathy. In fact, warmth alone can encourage selfishness in a child. Children also need a firm parental hand setting limits and guidelines," (in Goleman, 1990). Hoffman asserts that prosocial behavior emerges as result of an internal altruistic predisposition and moral norms internalized by parental upbringing, specifically inductive and victim-centered discipline based on reasoning and explanation (Hoffman, 1975, 1984).

Significantly more rescuers recalled their parents using both inductive and victim-centered discipline including (1) using clear, emotionally charged explanations, less punishment and more reasoning in response to their mistakes; and (2) encouraging them to make reparations for harm they caused. More bystanders recalled their parents using more power-assertion techniques (Ganz, 1993), and only rescuers reported that where physical punishment was used, it was always contingent on behavior as an occasional "follow-up" to explanation and was never used gratuitously as a non-behavior related release of aggression (Oliner & Oliner, 1988). The rescuers' parents communicated implicitly both the presumption of *error* rather than the *evil intent* of the child, as well as their faith in the child's ability to learn and improve. Moreover, in choosing inductive over power-assertive approaches to discipline, the rescuers' parents modeled benign behavior by the powerful over the vulnerable. Hence the rescuers may have had more opportunity than bystanders to internalize an interpersonal script based on parental tolerance, emotion regulation, and care-based attitudes by the more powerful toward the less powerful, needy and vulnerable.

In contrast, many bystanders may have responded to their parents' occasional gratuitous punitive discipline with fear. This fear, in turn, may have prompted withdrawal, reduction of personal agency, preoccupation with self-protection, avoidance of responsibility for others, and aversion to risk. Thus, when confronted with the decision whether to engage in high-risk, other-oriented helping behavior such as the rescue of Jews, these bystanders may not have been equipped with the requisite psychological, emotional and interpersonal tools with which to undertake and sustain extreme high-risk helping behavior.

Parental Values and Role Modeling

Prosocial development can be influenced by parental values and role modeling consistent with kindness and care (Eisenberg & Spinrad, 2014). Rescuers reported an intense identification with, and strong admiration for, a parent or a role-model characterized by strong moral conduct (London, 1970). More rescuers than bystanders reported that their most influential role models were kind and hospitable, were praised for kindness, took risks, encouraged them to take risks, participated in anti-Nazi activities, and helped Jewish people very much (Ganz, 1993). Rescuers learned early in life to tolerate differences in others, and these inclusive parental values influenced rescuers' decisions to help (Fogelman, 1987; Oliner & Oliner, 1988; Tec, 1986).

Parents of rescuers were less likely than bystanders' parents to express negative Jewish stereotypes such as "dishonest," "untrustworthy," and "too powerful," and talked about Jews no different from others (Klingerman, 1985). The rescuers were socialized toward *extensivity*: qualities of involvement, commitment, care, and responsibility for others, which they naturally continued to express on behalf of Jews during the Holocaust (Oliner & Oliner, 1988, p. 186). In contrast, some bystanders' parents attributed demonic qualities to Jews or suggested the Jews deserved their fate.

Rescuers whose strong family bonds were the cornerstone of their value systems were raised by parents who valued dependability, caring for others, and independence, often in the context of religious values (Oliner & Oliner, 1988, p. 184). A second group of rescuers derived their extensive orientation primarily from having had close relationships with Jews, both personally and professionally, which may have been influenced by their role models' tolerant attitudes toward Jews. Their close relationships sensitized these rescuers to Jews as human beings with different perspectives and cultures. Socialized to stand up for their beliefs and to engage in socially responsible behaviors, a third group of rescuers were more likely to feel more abstractly connected to Jews as an extension of a sustained commitment to ensuring the welfare of society in general. A fourth group of rescuers were the egalitarians, who "derived their sense of responsibility to others from their strong feelings of psychological similarity to humankind generally and empathy for persons in pain" (Oliner & Oliner, 1988, p. 185).

In contrast, the bystanders' childhood upbringings predisposed them toward *constrictedness* or attitudes of detachment, dissociation and self-orientation (Oliner & Oliner, 1988). Four types of non-rescuer non-extensive equivalents were interpreted based on results of a factor analysis. The first bystander subgroup was distinguished by a lack of family closeness, close relationships and a sense of impotence; the second group viewed Jews as distant, irrelevant objects; the third group was primarily self-oriented and avoided social involvement and responsibility; and the fourth group were considered true ethnocentrics who viewed people as alien to them, especially "outsiders." In the first study to examine the combined effect of an empirically derived set of family upbringing variables to discriminate a sample of rescuers from bystanders (Ganz, 1993), a discriminant function analysis (DFA) correctly classified 79.7 percent of subjects. The function was best accounted for by family cohesiveness, followed by victim-centered discipline, father's values, mother's values, inductive discipline, parental affection, and father as role model.

Situational Variables

In November 1942, Anne Frank, along with seven others, began their 25 months in hiding behind the bookcase in the attic before they were betrayed by an informer on August 4, 1944. With the exception of Otto Frank, there were no survivors. Would Otto Frank have survived without the attic, or if he and his Gentile rescuers hadn't had prior ties, or if the character of Miep Gies (who bravely marched into Gestapo headquarters and demanded the release of the eight Jews upon their arrest) was less exemplary?

A *social psychological* approach to the study of rescue during the Holocaust has been undertaken wherein it is assumed that the decision to engage in rescue likely results from the interaction of personal dispositional factors and external social environmental situations. Personality variables refer to personality characteristics and individual values. Situational variables refer to immediate or past external environmental conditions over which the actor has no control but nonetheless may affect the decision to act. Among the situational variables empirically investigated thus far are wartime living arrangements, the degree to which an individual had previous experience with Jews, a history of persecution and the opportunity to help.

Wartime Living Arrangements

The decision to engage in rescue activity may have been influenced by the availability of resources and the ability to manage risk. Indeed, some rescuers acted only when they felt that circumstances favored their prospects for helping successfully (Huneke, 1980). Adequate shelter and potential hiding places, the proximity and helpfulness of neighbors, the type of dwelling, renting versus owning, living in an urban or rural setting, number of occupants in the household, and in particular the presence children, significantly influenced engagement in rescue activity.

Whether an individual lived in a rural or urban setting, a home or a rented apartment, very near to or very distant from neighbors may have influenced the degree of risk and the choice to undertake rescue in some circumstances, but research suggests that no consistent patterns emerged in regard to wartime setting. In one study, half of both the rescuers and the bystanders lived in a large city, but more rescuers than bystanders reported living in a village or a farm during the war (Oliner & Oliner, 1988). Regardless of setting, having helpful neighbors was advantageous and may have increased the likelihood of rescue activity. Rescuers such as Belgian Josephine Mans, who hid a Jewish mother and her newborn, was betrayed by a neighbor, and severely beaten by the Gestapo (Paldiel, 1933), were willing to engage in rescue *despite* having unhelpful neighbors who lived very nearby. This, and the fact that more rescuers than bystanders reported living with their own children during the war thus exponentially increasing their risk, underscores the rescuers' moral courage (Fagin-Jones & Midlarsky, 2007).

Previous Experience with Jews

More than a third of a sample of Polish rescuers identified friendship with Jews as their primary motivation for rescue (Tec, 1986), and personal and professional employer/employee prewar relationships were the predisposing factors that led some people to help Jews in a small German town (Henry, 1984). Furthermore, Fogelman (1994) identified a subgroup of rescuers as *judeophilic* who tended to have had a special relationship with or a feeling of closeness to a Jewish person or to the Jews as a whole.

The rescuers in the Oliners' sample reported having had significantly more Jewish friends before the war and had lived near and worked with Jews, and almost 75 percent of the rescuers in an earlier study helped Jews they already knew personally or professionally (Oliner, 1984). Individuals who had more direct exposure to the plight of the Jews through personal and professional relationships were more likely to have a higher comprehension of the need for aid, and prior exposure to Jewish culture and values may have enhanced a sense of familiarity with Jewish people and diminished perceptions of "otherness" (Huneke, 1985–1986). Moreover, having had previous relationships with Jews increased the likelihood that an individual was asked to help, which, in turn, made rescue more likely. The Epstein family lived one floor below Henri and Suzanne Ribouleaus. When the police came for the Epsteins on July 19, 1942, they were allowed to contact the Ribouleaus', who willingly took in their nine- and four-year-old children whom they raised as their own, subsequent to the murder of the Epsteins in the death camps (Paldiel, 1993).

Having had close personal ties, including friendships, employer-employee relationships and interfaith marriages may have facilitated rescue activity which later broadened to helping others with whom a rescuer had no relational history. This "foot-in the door- phenomenon" (Varese & Yaish, 2000), in some cases, may have been influenced by what Paldiel labeled *evolutionary altruism* wherein moral obligations between non-Jews and pre-war Jewish acquaintances deepened and developed over time, and, in turn, may have prompted some rescuers to help others with whom they had no prior history. One of the most famous instances of this type was the heroic altruism of Herman "Fritz" Graebe, a German engineer who initially undertook rescue to help one of his Jewish suppliers and thereafter established a rescue network culminating in the rescue of hundreds of Jews, dissidents and peasants (Huneke, 1985–1986).

Still, having personal ties with Jews did not guarantee rescue. For example, more than 90 percent of the rescuers in the Oliners' project reported having helped at least one stranger and only 16 percent of rescuers said they were motivated to act on the basis of care for a personal

Jewish friend (Oliner & Oliner, 1988). Indeed, a more recent study found that having had a history of relationships with Jews was not significantly more common for rescuers than for bystanders (Fagin-Jones & Midlarsky, 2007), where more bystanders than rescuers reported having had more previous experience with Jews. These results suggest that simply having had previous relationships with Jews may not be as significant as the subjective experience of the relationship. While bystanders may have had more previous experience with Jews, they may also have held more negative attitudes toward Jews. In countries such as Poland, where levels of pre-war anti-Semitism were strikingly high, the percentage of Jews that survived the Nazi onslaught were abysmally low. Conversely, in countries where pre-war attitudes toward Jews were more tolerant such as Denmark, instances of the heroic altruism were remarkably high.

History of Persecution

Most of the rescuers interviewed by Huneke (1981–1982) had significant personal experience with suffering and death that likely enhanced their ability to empathize with Jews. As a child, Fritz Graebe stuttered terribly and endured years of bullying, which rendered him more capable in adulthood of empathizing with the plight of the Jews and prompted him to take action. In addition, many rescuers reported having witnessed the persecution of Jews. Irena Gut, the Polish rescuer who hid 12 Jews in the cellar of a German Major's house, saw a Nazi toss a baby in the air and shoot the child dead.

Rescuers more than bystanders reporting significantly higher levels of having both experienced and witnessed persecution (Fagin-Jones & Midlarsky, 2007; Oliner & Oliner 1988). While both groups reported witnessing the Jews being forced to wear the Yellow Star of David, significantly more rescuers reported *being deeply distressed by* its implications, and while both groups were reportedly distressed by the Nazi pogrom against the Jews on *Kristallnacht* on November 9, 1938 (literally, "night of broken glass"), more bystanders did not believe or fully understand the Nazi intentions to annihilate the Jews (Henry, 1984). More rescuers acknowledged awareness of the full extent of the Nazi's intentions regarding Jews *before* the Nazi takeover, whereas more bystanders reported full awareness of the Nazi's intentions only *after* the liberation.

Many bystanders, having chosen to remain passive in the midst of the massacre of six million Jews, may deny having understood the "harmful implications of the persecutory acts" they witnessed as well as having had prewar and wartime awareness of the Nazi genocidal machine. Hence, despite some researchers' attempts to control for the impact of social desirability, the number of bystanders who were reportedly aware of the Nazi's intentions both before and during the war was likely higher (Oliner & Oliner, 1988). Nevertheless, a handful of bystanders, among them some true ethnocentrics, were more than willing to report full awareness of Nazi intentions prior to and during the war and were unmoved by the plight of persecuted Jews to act on their behalf (Fagin-Jones & Midlarsky, 2007; Oliner & Oliner, 1988).

Still, having experienced or witnessed persecution was neither necessary nor sufficient to motivate rescue. In Le Chambon several villagers had neither previous exposure to Jews nor had witnessed their persecution but engaged in rescue because they were asked to help by their highly regarded leader (Hallie, 1979). Indeed, rescue was more likely to occur when an individual was asked to help either directly or by an intermediary (Fagin-Jones & Midlarsky, 2007; Freedman, 1993; Varese & Yaish, 2000).

Opportunity to Help

Paldiel (1988) observed, "with the exception of a handful, the rescuers' actions were not the product of their own initiative, assertion, and initial determination," (p. 190). Varese and Yaish

(2000) found that a direct request for help made rescue 17 times more likely. More rescuers more than bystanders were asked by a Jew or an intermediary on their behalf to help (Fagin-Jones & Midlarsky, 2007; Oliner & Oliner, 1988).

When requested either directly or indirectly, help was more likely to be given to a stranger (Varese & Yaish, 2000), and when spontaneous, help was twice as likely to be offered to a friend or family member. The choice of person whose help was being requested was often carefully considered by the requester. Those who were asked were likely selected based on their compassionate and courageous dispositions. Potential rescuers often very cautiously communicated their willingness to help and were subsequently asked. Once rescuers agreed to help, they became among only a sacred few to whom victims and their intermediaries could trust to turn to for support for their survival. Thus, given the scarcity of individuals who were known to be willing to help, after the initial request was granted, opportunities to help grew exponentially in response to the increased frequency of requests (Varese & Yaish, 2000). Still, approximately one third of the rescuers in the Oliners' sample initiated helping activities without having been asked, and when empirically examined alongside prosocial personality traits, "opportunity to help" did not remain a significant discriminator of group membership (Fagin-Jones & Midlarsky, 2007).

Personality variables

Studies examining personality correlates of rescue during the Holocaust (see Fagin-Jones & Midlarsky, 2007; Midlarsky, Fagin-Jones & Corley, 2005; Oliner & Oliner, 1988) are necessarily retrospective and assume the relative stability of personality over the life-span (Koestner, Franz & Weinberger, 1990; McCrae, Costa, Terraciano, Parker, Mills, De Fruyt & Mervielde, 2002). While the literature on Holocaust rescue offers no single operational definition of "personality," the construct can be viewed as "those distinctive personal attributes and predispositions developed during childhood and relatively stable through adulthood that are fundamental in shaping a person's consciousness and behavior" (Gushee, 1993, p. 382). The war itself, as well as subsequent post-war life experiences could have significantly impacted respondents' personalities. Indeed, some psychologists argue that individual dispositions can change markedly over time (Smith & Baltes, 1999). Still, evidence suggests that personality remains relatively stable particularly once adulthood is achieved (McCrae & Costa, 2003).

Empathic Concern

The research provides strong empirical support for the vast archival evidence gathered from rescuers' memoirs, letters and case studies testifying to a preponderance of rescuers' motivation to act out of compassion for the suffering of the Jews. More than bystanders, the rescuers possessed the highest levels of empathic concern (Fagin-Jones & Midlarsky, 2007; Oliner & Oliner, 1988), defined as the human capacity to put oneself in the place of the other and viscerally experience his or her pain and sorrow (Gushee, 1993), and considered to be a critical factor in altruism and high cost helping (Bierhoff, Klein & Kramp, 1991; Hoffman, 2000; Tice & Baumeister, 1985).

Fogelman (1994) found that Christian rescuers driven by "emotional morality" responded to an internal sense of compassion or pity for the plight of others. Tec (1986) found that Polish rescuers shared a "universalistic perception" of Jews defined as helpless beings and totally dependent on the protection of others, while rescuers in Huneke's sample (1981–1982) possessed "an empathic imagination and the ability to place oneself in the actual situation or role of another person and to imagine the effect and the long-term consequences of the situation or the role on the person" (p. 324).

The rescuers scored higher on a measure of empathic concern than both bystanders and a comparison group of non-Jewish immigrants (Midlarsky et al., 2005). In a separate study examining the relative power of the set of personality variables to distinguish these same rescuers from bystanders in the context of other potentially significant variables (Fagin-Jones & Midlarsky, 2007), empathic concern emerged as one of a set of four personality variables, including social responsibility, altruistic moral reasoning, and risk-taking that differentiated rescuers from bystanders over and above significant situational and demographic variables.

In contrast to much of the research on empathy suggesting individuals are more likely to help victims who are similar to them (Batson et al., 2002), non-Jewish rescuers of Jews during the Holocaust helped members of a persecuted ethnic "out-group." Indeed, even prior to the Nazi propaganda which portrayed Jews as vermin, pre-war attitudes toward Jews by many non-Jews were often highly stereotyped and negative. Biased individuals were less likely to identify with and to help others perceived as inhuman.

Rescuers may have identified with the Jews they rescued (Midlarsky, 1985–1986). More rescuers than bystanders reported greater feelings of similarity to both Gypsies and Jews, and more bystanders reported feeling "not at all like" Jews (Oliner & Oliner, 1988). The rescuers were characterized by a felt connection to others through a perception of common humanity. While both rescuers and bystanders subscribed to social conventional values and norms, the rescuers were willing to extend these norms to include members of a persecuted out-group (Oliner & Oliner, 1988).

Where rescuers identified with the Jews on political, theological, and socioeconomic grounds, such as in Denmark, where non-Jewish Danes strongly identified with Jewish Danes, 96 percent of the Jewish population was successfully rescued. In contrast, in Eastern European countries such as Poland and Lithuania, where less than one-half of 1 percent of the Jewish population survived, differences between Jews and non-Jews in appearance, theology, and politics were marked. Hence, the relative paucity of non-Jewish identification with Jews in much of Nazi-occupied Europe may have contributed meaningfully to their annihilation.

Social Responsibility

In most cases, in addition to compassion, an individual was compelled to action by a felt sense of social responsibility. Social responsibility is a personal norm requiring concern with broader ethical issues beyond the self and characterized by an obligation to a common good (Peterson & Seligman, 2004). Individuals with high levels of social responsibility feel compelled to aid those who are dependent on them for help in society, because it is the right thing to do (Berkowitz & Lutterman, 1968). Numerous studies have found Holocaust rescuers and other helpers, such as Carnegie heroes, philanthropists, and hospice volunteers to be characterized by high levels of social responsibility (Monroe, 2002; Oliner, 2003). Furthermore, Tec (1986) found that rescuers from Poland maintained a strong sense of personal commitment to the helpless and needy.

Social responsibility emerged as the strongest predictor among a set of positive personality variables that correctly classified 96.1 percent of participants over and above situational and demographic variables. Bystanders reported feeling lower levels of social responsibility than both the rescuers and the comparison group of pre-war immigrants (Midlarsky et al., 2005). Rescuers scored higher than bystanders on the Social Responsibility Scale (Berkowitz & Lutterman, 1968) and on *prosocial action orientation*, which assessed the degree to which individuals are likely to help others based on their emotional empathic response to pain and feelings of social responsibility. American journalist Varian Fry epitomized the height of social responsibility, relinquishing the safety of the U.S. to lead a rescue network in Vichy France that helped approximately 2,000 to 4,000 anti-Nazi and Jewish refugees.

Locus of Control

Rescuers tended to possess a more "internal" locus of control, believing that they could influence outcomes in their environments, and bystanders were more "external," believing that control over outcomes was experienced as outside of the self (Fagin-Jones & Midlarsky, 2007). Moreover, rescuers scored higher on a measure of locus of control than a demographically similar group of pre-war immigrants suggesting that rescuers might have been especially high in this trait. Rescuers were surrounded by the overwhelming force of the Nazi killing machine, the power of colluding local governments such as the Arrow Cross of Hungary, and the anti-Semitic attitudes of neighbors. Jews were being deported by the thousands per day, and yet rescuers continued to believe that they could make a difference. Unlike many bystanders, who felt a sense of helplessness in response to the overwhelming fear and authority perpetrated by the Nazis, rescuers took control of life events around them. These findings cohere with other moral exemplars who were rarely discouraged by obstacles toward their goal of helping others (Colby & Damon, 1992–1995).

Autonomy

Holocaust rescuers have been characterized as "persons with especially strong forms of autonomy" (Jones, 1999, p. 223), defined as independence and resistance to social controls. In one of the earliest studies of Holocaust rescuers, London (1970) described a small number of Christian rescuers he interviewed as characterized by strong moral principles, a subjective sense of marginality, autonomy, and a willingness to take risks.

Indeed, Midlarsky et al. (2005) found that rescuers scored significantly higher than both bystanders and pre-war immigrants on a measure of autonomy. Some Holocaust heroes, such as German industrialist Oscar Schindler, Polish professor Jan Karsky, and Dutch Montessori school principal Joop Westerweel, who was brutally tortured and executed by the Nazis in 1944 at age 45, were highly autonomous and epitomized Western notions of heroes, which are predicated on ideas of rugged individualism. Still, not all rescuers were highly autonomous and not all bystanders were exceptionally passive. Numerous bystanders compelled by feelings of resistance to Nazi occupation engaged in resistance activities but did not rescue Jews. Various rescuers, such as Calvinist farmers in the Niewlande region of the Netherlands, who were highly influenced by religious leader Johannes Bogaard, participated in collective rescue activity as a member of a group, not as an individual. Bogaard, along with his father, brother and son, reportedly perished in a German concentration camp in 1942.

Risk-Taking

The unique type of bravery possessed by rescuers can be characterized as *moral courage*, "the willingness and ability to act according to one's values in the face of opposition and potential harm to oneself," (Staub, 2011, p. 391). The rescuers were far more predisposed to undertake a task involving danger than were the bystanders who scored significantly lower on a measure of risk-taking than both rescuers and a comparison group of pre-war immigrants (Midlarsky et al., 2005). Rescuers were no less afraid than the bystanders, but they were more courageous. Bystanders who felt compassion for Jews and who reported wanting to but not helping often attributed inaction to the fear of being caught. The vast majority of rescuers engaged in ongoing rescue activity. In some cases, rescuers hid entire families in their own homes for a period of several years under increasing threat of discovery or betrayal. Rescuers learned how to cope with extreme fear, using humor, togetherness, secrecy, duplicity, and sheer will.

Among the most noteworthy and courageous rescuers was Swedish Diplomat Raoul Wallenberg, who in 1944, succeeded in saving the lives of tens of thousands of Hungarian Jews by brazenly confronting the SS and Hungarian police and issuing *schutzbriefes* (safe papers) to Jews already boarded on trains destined for concentration camps or left to die in ditches on the side of the road under the horrific toll of the Death March. On January 17, 1945, Wallenberg was arrested by the Russian army and was never seen or heard from again.

Altruistic Moral Reasoning

Compared with the bystanders, the rescuers saw themselves as having personal integrity: as being honest and helpful, able to take responsibility, and as willing to stand up for their beliefs (Oliner & Oliner, 1988). Rescuers who broke the law, lied, stole, cheated and killed to save Jewish lives are recognized and honored as *hasidei umot ha-olam*, "Righteous among the Nations," a term which refers to people who live by the highest of moral standards.

In addition to possessing the highest levels of principle-based moral judgment (Gross, 1994), rescuers demonstrated the highest levels of moral development based on values of caring and compassion. Fagin-Jones and Midlarsky (2007) found that use of the highest level of abstract care-based moral reasoning to solve moral dilemmas emerged as the strongest predictor among a set of positive personality variables that defined a function on which rescuers and bystanders were more than three standard deviations apart. This finding lends strong empirical support for the exceptional moral character of rescuers (Jones, 1999).

Authoritarianism/Tolerance

Authoritarianism, the tendency to be rigid, intolerant, and ethnocentric has been associated with the perpetration of genocide (Adorno et al., 1950; Butler, 2000). The two largest studies found that bystanders were significantly more anti-Semitic and authoritarian than rescuers, whereas more rescuers reported feeling openness toward Jews and were more likely to have Jewish friends and acquaintances. No rescuers reported feeling antipathy toward Jews (Midlarsky et al., 2005; Oliner & Oliner, 1988).

Summary and Discussion

What, then, does the research on Holocaust rescue reveal about the rescuers? While certain trends emerged, rescuers were a demographically heterogeneous population representing all walks of life. The rescuers came from more cohesive families and had more affectionate parents who valued inclusion, used reason-based inductive and victim-centered discipline, and were prosocial role models who did not endorse Jewish stereotypes. In turn, rescuers attained more securely-attached mature ego development defined by the highest levels of care-based moral reasoning, social responsibility, empathic concern and courage.

On the basis of these exceptional traits, which closely adhere to both the "Great Eight" (Allison & Goethals, 2011) and "Traits that Transcend," the rescuers were differentiated from bystanders as well as from a "comparison group" of non-Jewish European immigrants (Fagin-Jones & Midlarsky, 2007). The bystanders, with the exception of their feelings of personal responsibility toward others and their propensity to undertake risks, generally did not differ from the "norm." Conversely, as indicated by the minute proportion of rescuers in Nazi-Europe, the rescuers, who performed two standard deviations over and above both groups, were *dispositionally exceptional*. Of course, no single dispositional trait or set of traits characterized *all* rescuers. For example, while most rescuers were genuinely caring and concerned for the Jews, examples of anti-Semitic Christian rescuers suggest that these helpers did not care about the victims they saved (Staub, 2012). Nevertheless, *the results reveal a strong dispositional trend characterized by care-based moral courage manifesting in heroic altruism.*

Notably, the traits underlying heroic altruism significantly predicted group membership over and above significant situational factors (Fagin-Jones & Midlarsky, 2007), including wartime living arrangements, whether an individual was asked for help, had witnessed or experienced persecution, and had previous relationships with Jews. These results strongly support the theory that situational factors might be more explanatory of "one-shot" acts of heroism, and that dispositional factors are more salient in long-term helping by moral exemplars (Fleeson, 2004; Walker, Frimer & Dunlop, 2010).

The Dalai Lama (2002) differentiated between two types of people: those who wish to see others free from suffering and those who help others to be free from suffering. The latter individual possesses courage, which was evident in the rescuers' strong tendency towards a willingness to undertake risk and to sustain rescue activity over time despite the constant threat of torture, deportation and death. Such high risk character traits have emerged among other samples of moral exemplars, including a subsample of recipients of a Canadian national honor award (Walker & Frimer, 2007). Despite strong contextual pressures to comply under the threat of death to oneself and to one's family, the rescuers refused to engage in harmful behaviors even when it was the prevailing cultural norm. These results are consistent with lesser-known findings from Milgram's classic electric shock experiments in which almost all individuals (83%) who *refused* to obey orders, such as Jan Rensaleer, who stood up to Milgram saying, "I do have choice!" possessed the highest levels of moral reasoning (as cited in Baum, 2008).

A still lesser-known study conducted by Elms and Milgram (as cited in Baum, 2008) examined the context effects of two confederates who *resisted* administering shocks. Under these conditions, a full ninety percent of subjects resisted the authority of the experimenter and refused to obey orders. Indeed, genocide expert Ervin Staub (2012) asserts that bystanders can influence each other and were as likely to have followed orders for peace. Conformity, obedience and passivity were the hallmarks of the bystanders, who represented the vast majority of individuals living in Nazi-occupied Europe.

The bystanders' families were generally less cohesive. Their parents tended to be less affectionate and more likely to use authoritarian power-based discipline techniques and occasional gratuitous aggression, and to model conventional norms and stereotypical attitudes toward Jews and other out-groups. Consequently, the bystanders attained average levels of ego development, demonstrated more anxious/avoidant patterns of attachment; were more concerned with social acceptance and conformity; and were more passive, self-centric, and less inclined to take risks (Baum, 2008). Bystanders preferred to distance themselves from distress arising from awareness of persecution and empathy toward the victims and rationalized their need to protect themselves from perceived threats to their sense of self by the "others" (Monroe, 2012). This "distancing" often grew into extreme dissociation, psychic numbing (Lifton, 2000), and dehumanization leading some bystanders to become perpetrators (Staub, 2012).

Bystanders, argues Baum (2008), are more likely to prioritize their social identity over individualism and to conform with peer and authority pressure in order to fit in. They tend to be less emotionally, cognitively and morally developed. Rescuers, on the other hand, exist at the opposite extreme of this continuum of social-individual identity, and are more likely to defy group norms. Interestingly, one sample of bystanders scored lower than both rescuers *and* a comparison group of non-Jewish immigrants on measures of social responsibility *and* risk-taking. Hence, *bystanders exhibited a dispositional aversion to risk and avoidance of responsibility toward others.*

Underscoring the significance of the moral failure of the bystander, Martin Luther King admonished that our generation would not only repent for the hateful words and deeds of the perpetrators but for the unconscionable silence of the good people. Most "good people" rationalize their inaction, desensitize themselves, and routinize victimization (Baum, 2008). Such individuals have great difficulty overcoming psychological and situational constraints against heroic altruism (Bar-On, 2001; Browning, 1992). Yet, some who possess moral courage choose to resist the extraordinary seductions and pressures of the situation contradicting Zimbardo's contention that:

> The banality of evil is matched by the banality of heroism. Neither is the consequence of dispositional tendencies … Both emerge in particular situations at particular times, when situational forces play a compelling role in moving individuals across the line from inaction to action.
>
> *(Zimbardo, 2007, p. 275)*

The situational forces surrounding genocide, particularly the diffusion of responsibility among bystanders (Latané & Darley, 1970) are powerful, but compliance is not inevitable (Goldhagen, 1997; Staub, 2012), and cases of noncompliance may be underreported or underemphasized. In the notorious murder case of 28-year-old Kitty Genovese that prompted research on "the bystander effect," where "37 who saw murder didn't call the police," later reports revealed that some people did call the police, and one person comforted the victim as she was dying (Anderson, 2015). In the Stanford Prison Experiment (see www.prisonexp.org) there were "good guys" who did favors for the prisoners and never punished them, and when replicated by the BBC, the Stanford Prison Experiment was cancelled because the prison "guards" did not conform (Bartels, 2015; Reicher & Haslam, 2006). In Solomon Asch's (1955) classic study of conformity at University of Pennsylvania, some 25 percent of subjects were "independents" who would not conform. Indeed, Hannah Arendt remarked:

> Under conditions of terror most people will comply but *some people will not*, just as the lesson of the countries to which the Final Solution was proposed is that "it could happen" in most places but *it did not happen everywhere*. Humanly speaking, no more is required, and no more can reasonably be asked, for this planet to remain a place fit for human habitation.
>
> *(Arendt, 1963, p. 233)*

Moral Exemplarity

The rescuers' early socialization experiences may have fostered the development of a strong moral identity (Blasi, 1984; Damon, 1984) defined by both strong agency and communal orientations (Walker, 2014) underpinning their non-conformity. Moral centrality has been associated with heroic altruism in other samples of moral exemplars (Colby & Damon, 1992–1995) and with a need to engage in behavior that is consistent with the moral identity in the self (Walker & Frimer, 2007). Individuals who internalize morality as central to their identity have been found to possess a broad sense of moral obligation toward out-groups (Reed & Aquino, 2003).

Assor (2012) asserts that an important determinant of moral behavior is *integrated moral motivation*, or the propensity to act morally because the act is experienced as reflecting one's core self, central values, and identity. Furthermore, Assor wisely contends that integrated moral motivation is a crucial determinant of highly moral behavior, such as Holocaust rescue, as motivation anchored to the core self provides strength to endure the personal costs of helping. Moral centrality, then, may underpin integrated moral motivation which, in turn, may facilitate heroic altruism.

Rescuers' moral identities did not begin and end with the Holocaust but likely pre-dated the Second World War and persisted thereafter, reflecting the deeper level of moral integration into their characteristic adaptations and life narratives (McAdams, 1995, 2009; McAdams & Cox, 2010; Walker & Frimer, 2007). Rescuers, more than bystanders, for example, were still volunteering in late life feeding the sick, providing counseling, and raising money for a cause, despite their overall poorer health (Midlarsky, 1985; Oliner & Oliner, 1988). This finding is consistent with "lifespan" volunteers who view prosocial values as a core component of the self (Piliavin, Grube, & Callero, 2002).

Rescuers overwhelmingly reported that helping was a "natural" thing to do, asserting that they "had no choice" but to help. Such testimony suggests that rescuers were indeed motivated by integrated moral principles reflecting "deep-seated instincts, predispositions, and habitual patterns" related to their central identity (Fogelman, 1994; Monroe, 2012, p. 256). The strong moral identity of Holocaust rescuers was further manifested by their humility. That these exemplars did not envision themselves as heroes subsequent to the rescue activity, in most cases eschewed the epithet and were even reluctant to be honored, is emblematic of their exemplary moral identities. In fact, most rescuers claimed that they did not do enough to help or that what they did was but an infinitesimal fraction of what needed to be done to right the unimaginable wrongs perpetrated by the Nazi regime. For example, Ukrainian Baptist rescuer Ivan Jaciuk:

> I am told that a tree will be planted in my honor in that majestic city of Jerusalem ... but I am not worthy of it or of any honor ... There is a blot on my conscience. Perhaps I could have done more for your people during those terrible days when I saw your starved brethren carrying heavy stones and begging for a crumb of bread from passersby—so-called Christians!
>
> *(Cited in Paldiel, 1993, p. 277)*

Implications and Suggestions for Future Research

Given the perpetuation of genocide into the twenty-first century, it is vital to translate *exemplary* moral action into *normative* moral action, especially toward members of out-groups, including Jews. According to the Anti-Defamation League-sponsored first global survey of anti-Semitic attitudes and opinions in over 100 countries from 2013–2015 (see http://global100.adl.org), some 1.09 billion people harbor anti-Semitic attitudes, and of these, 74 percent have never met a Jewish person. Two out of every three people surveyed never heard of the Holocaust or do not believe historical accounts to be accurate, perhaps in part due to shame-induced silence and denial (Zerubavel, 2015). There is reason to hope, however, given that only 16 percent of Germans surveyed in 2015 held anti-Semitic beliefs, suggesting that meaningful change can occur over time, even in the heart of darkness.

Still, some 74 percent of Middle Easterners and 93 percent of Palestinians harbor anti-Semitic attitudes. In his work with Palestinians and Israelis, social psychologist Herbert Kelman (2007) emphasizes the importance of mutual acknowledgement and accommodation of the identity of the other, in order to develop tolerance and empathy. Contact theory suggests that merely having contact between social groups is insufficient to reduce intergroup biases based on greed, fear, and mistrust (Allport, 1954; Brown & Hewstone, 2005). Recall that merely having had pre-war exposure to Jews was insufficient to promote rescue: an individual had to embrace the other. Hence future efforts should focus on increasing opportunities to bring together groups who negate the other and foster understanding, accommodation and identification under optimal conditions (Brown & Hewstone, 2005; Pettigrew & Tropp, 2011). Our collective goal to promote the universality of humanity, one of six virtues that is considered cross-culturally consistent (Peterson & Seligman, 2004) will be influenced by the degree to which we can apply what we have learned from the research on heroic altruism during the Holocaust to promote prosocial development among our youth.

Parenting is considered the most impactful factor on child social development (Grusec, 2006; Padilla-Walker, 2014). Indeed, the rescuers Fritz Graebe, Miep Gies, and Marion Pritchard all recalled being raised with complete love, respect and understanding in a child-oriented home environment. Allison and Goethals (2011) examine the theory that one's capacity for morality may be innate (Hauser, 2006), and that parental upbringing plays a critical role in elaborating this innate moral capacity. Hence, heroic altruism may be an innate predisposition that can be elaborated "phenotypically" in response to environmental forces (Hoffman, 1975; Monroe, 2012; Warneken & Tomasello, 2009).

Parenting practices that focus on the development of moral identity maximize our chances of cultivating heroic altruists among our youth. The research on Holocaust heroes and moral development (Shaver & Mikulincer, 2012) converge to suggest that this process should begin via the early development of empathic concern, which is fostered via the establishment of secure attachments (Ainsworth, Blehar, Waters & Wall, 1978; Bowlby, 1988) and "good-enough" infant-caregiver attunement (Stern, 1985; Winnicott, 1965). Once a secure base of warmth, safety, and trust has been established (Erikson, 1950; Grusec & Davidov, 2010), parenting should focus on creating environments that facilitate the cultivation of social responsibility, care-based moral identity, and courage, via role modeling, discipline, vicarious learning, and reinforcement (Allison & Goethals, 2011).

Specific parenting and teaching practices, such as autonomy support practices (ASP) may be more likely to influence specific prosocial behaviors (Bergin, 2014). ASP have been associated with the development of integrated moral motivation and prosocial behavior in children and teens, who (1) report feeling a stronger sense of volition, happier and more alive; (2) provide empathic support and engage in prosocially motivated behavior; and (3) demonstrate improved affect regulation (Assor, 2012; Roth, 2008; Roth & Assor 2012). Examples of ASP include support of reflective values and goal examination, fostering inner-directed valuing processes, taking the child's perspective, providing rationales for expected behaviors, demonstrating positive valuing of modeled expected behaviors, encouraging critical thinking, and providing choices (Assor, 2012; Roth & Assor, 2000).

Parents can be trained to use victim-centered and inductive discipline techniques and be educated about the potential negative outcomes of coercive power-based discipline and the use of gratuitous aggression, including reduction in perceived physiological and psychological safety, love, trust, tolerance, playfulness, spontaneity, creativity, independence and the increased likelihood of bullying (Espelage, Low, Rao, Hong & Little, 2014). Indeed, the deleterious impact of bullying on the behavioral, mental, social and academic health of victims, bullies and witnesses has been verified (Bradshaw, Waasdorp, Goldweber, & Johnson, 2013; Rivers, Poteat, Noret & Ashurst, 2009).

The phenomenon of bullying includes the adoption of certain roles including "the bully," "the victim," "assistants," "reinforcers," "outsiders," and "defenders," (Richards et al., 2008). "Outsiders" most closely resemble the "bystander" who may experience an intention to intervene but lacks the courage to do so, and subsequently may be especially vulnerable to vicarious traumatization as a result of cognitive dissonance (Craig & Pepler, 1997). Efforts to increase empathic concern and moral courage among "outsiders" might predispose them to undertake the role of the "defender," who offers support, comfort, and intervention to the victim (Richards et al., 2008; Salmivalli, Voeten, & Poskiparta, 2011). Potential "defenders" should be identified as those students who demonstrate behaviors associated with moral exemplarity in schools including standing up for others, providing emotional support, helping others develop skills, providing encouragement, using humor, being inclusive, and keeping the peace (Bergin, Talley & Hamer, 2003).

Finally, optimal contact conditions when established in the workplace can improve tolerance and integration of employees with minority status including individuals with psychiatric and general disabilities (Novak, Feyes, & Christensen, 2011; Vezzali & Capozza, 2011). Kindness and courage among leaders who are open to establishing "high-risk/high-care" environments can effect positive change in the workplace (Kohlreiser, Goldsworthy, & Coombe, 2012). Clinical psychologist, hostage negotiator and leadership expert George Kohlreiser recommends providing a "secure base" of kindness and security from which employees can be pushed beyond their comfort zones to unleash their potential. Those who "care to dare," Kohlreiser asserts, regulate their distress, express kindness, connect to the pain and the humanity in others, and establish bonds through a common goal in the workplace. Such corporate cultures are less likely to induce shame and are more likely to encourage vulnerability, trust, honesty, openness, and helping behavior (Brown, 2012).

Conclusion

On January 9, 2015, in the wake of the *Charlie Hebdo* massacre two days earlier—where two Islamic militants opened fire, killing 12 people—terrorist Amedy Coulibaly, claiming allegiance to the Islamic State and the Levant, attacked a kosher market at the Porte de Vincennes, killing four Jewish hostages and holding 15 others in a siege (Mackey, 2015). A 24-year-old Malian-born Muslim shop assistant, Lassana Bathily, risked his life and ushered several of the store's customers to hide in a freezer in the basement. Needing to inform the police, he slipped out of the building via an elevator shaft, whereupon he was detained for an hour and a half by the French police who suspected him of being an accomplice. Once cleared, Bathily was able to assist police by describing the layout of the shop and providing an extra key to the front gate, which the police rammed in without harming the hostages, and shot and killed Coulibaly. Subsequently awarded French Citizenship and the Legion of Honor, Bathily rejected the hero label, stating, "Yes, I aided Jews. We're brothers. It's not a question of Jews, Christians, or Muslims. We're all in the same boat. We need to help each other to get out of this crisis."

Bathily, like most non-Jewish rescuers of Jews in Nazi occupied Europe, embraced the "other" as brother, and although he could have easily chosen to save himself alone, he risked his life on behalf the others because it was the right thing to do. Hence, Bathily's actions suggest that he possessed the care-based moral courage to engage in heroic altruism.

Historically, the international political response to genocide has been egregiously passive. Individual countries, notably the United States, have lacked the collective integrated moral motivation and courage to act to eradicate genocide and terrorism perpetrated by ISIS and other militant Islamic extremists (Power, 2002). Few international leaders seem to possess the moral identity and altruistic dispositions of the rescuers, especially in pluralistic countries in the Middle East that lack pluralism (Friedman, 2015). Recall that most bystanders will likely conform to ideologies of inclusiveness as readily as those of prejudice and hate (Staub, 2012). Until leaders emerge across the globe to promote these ideologies, genocide will likely persist.

If heroic altruism is a trait without which society cannot survive (Rushton, 1980), it is vital that ordinary citizens who possess the exemplary traits raise their voices and take action. Efforts to promote moral exemplarity among our youth are critical (Staub, 2002a, 2002b), as are efforts to model other-oriented prosocial behavior toward out-groups in schools, the workplace and the community. Above all, we must "never forget" the non-Jewish rescuers of Jews during Nazi-occupied Europe whose heroic altruism must shine as an eternal example for humanity as we continue to struggle with genocide and the forces of evil. For, as Yehuda Bauer of the U.S. Holocaust Memorial Museum memorably commanded, "Thou shalt not be a perpetrator; thou shall not be a victim; and thou shall never, but never, be a bystander" (quoted in Skog, 2011, p. 57).

References

Adorno, T. W., Frenkel- Brunswick, E., Levinson, D. J., & Sanford, R. N. (1950). *The authoritarian personality*. New York: Harper.

Ainsworth, M., Blehar, M. C., Waters, E., & Wall, S. (1978). *Patterns of attachment: A psychological study of the strange situation*. Hillsdale, NJ: Erlbaum.
Allen, E. (2015). Kidnapping and sex slavery: Covering ISIS' religious justification for rape. *The New York Times* (August 14). Retrieved from www.nytimes.com/2015/08/14/insider/kidnapping-and-sex-slavery-covering-isiss-religious-justification-for-rape.html.
Allison, S. T., & Goethals, G.R. (2011). *Heroes: What they do and why we need them*. New York: Oxford University Press.
Allport, G. W. (1954). *The nature of prejudice*. Reading, MA: Addison-Wesley.
Anderson, V. L. (1991). Gender difference in altruism: A psychological study of Non-Jewish German Holocaust rescuers. (Doctoral dissertation, Massachusetts School of Professional Psychology, 1990/1991). *Dissertation Abstracts International, 51*(9-B), 4631.
Anderson, J. (2015). *Kitty Genovese killing is retold in the film "37."* New York Times, Movies, July 26.
Arendt, H. (1963). *Eichmann in Jerusalem: A report on the banality of evil*. New York: Viking Press.
Arrango, T. (2014). Escaping death in Northern Iraq. *The New York Times* (September 3), International Section, Middle East. www.nytimes.com/2014/09/04/world/middleeast/surviving-isis-massacre-iraq-video.html
Asch, S. E. (1955). Opinions and social pressure. *Scientific American, 193*(5), 31–35.
Assor, A. (2012). Autonomous moral motivation: Consequences, socializing antecedents, and the unique role of integrated moral principles. In M. Mikulincer & P.R. Shaver (eds), *The social psychology of morality* (pp. 239–256). Washington, DC: American Psychological Association.
Baron, L. (1985–1986). The Holocaust and human decency: A review of research on the rescue of Jews in Nazi occupied Europe. *Humboldt Journal of Social Relations, 13*, 237–251.
Bar-On, D. (2001). The bystander in relation to the victim and the perpetrator: Today and during the Holocaust. *Social Justice Research, 14*, 125–148.
Bartels, J. (2015). The Stanford prison experiment in introductory psychology textbooks: A content analysis. *Psychology Learning & Teaching, 14*(1), 36–50.
Bartoszewski, W., & Lewin, Z. (1969). *The righteous among the nations*. London: Earl's Court.
Batson, C. D. (1991). *The altruism question: Toward a social psychological answer*. Hillsdale, NJ: Lawrence Erlbaum.
Batson, C. D. (2011). *Altruism in humans*. New York: Oxford University Press.
Batson, C. D., Ahmad, N., Lishner, D. A., & Tsang, J.-A. (2002). Empathy and altruism. In C. R. Snyder & S. J. Lopez (eds), *Handbook of positive psychology* (pp. 485–498). New York: Oxford University Press.
Baum, S. K. (2008). *The psychology of genocide: Perpetrators, bystanders, and rescuers*. New York: Cambridge University Press.
Bauminger, A. L. (1983). *The Righteous*. Jerusalem: Yad Vashem.
Becker, S., & Eagly, A. (2004). The heroism of women and men. *American Psychologist, 59*, 163–178.
Bergin, C. (2014). Educating children to be prosocial at school. In L. M. Padilla-Walker & G. Carlo (eds), *Prosocial Development* (pp. 279–301). New York: Oxford University Press.
Bergin, C., Talley, S., & Hamer, C. (2003). Prosocial behaviours of young adolescence: A focus group study. *Journal of Adolescence, 26*, 13–32.
Berkowitz, L., & Lutterman, K.G. (1968). The traditionally socially responsible personality. *Public Opinion Quarterly, 32*, 169–187.
Bierhoff, H., Klein, R., & Kramp, P. (1991). Evidence for the altruistic personality from data on accident research. *Journal of Personality, 59*, 263–279.
Blasi, A. (1984). Moral identity: Its role in moral functioning. In W. M. Kurtines & J. L. Gewirtz (eds), *Morality, moral behavior, and moral development* (pp. 128–139). New York: Wiley.
Block, J. (1995). A contrarian view of the five-factor approach to personality description. *Psychological Bulletin, 117*, 187–215.
Bowlby, J. (1988). *A secure base: Parent–child attachment and healthy human development*. London: Routledge.
Bradshaw, C. P., Waasdorp, T. E., Goldweber, A., & Johnson, S. L. (2013). Bullies, gangs, drugs, and school: Understanding the overlap and the role of ethnicity and urbanicity. *Journal of Youth and Adolescence, 42*, 220–234.
Brown, B. (2012). *Daring greatly: How the courage to be vulnerable transforms the way we live, love, parent, and lead*. New York: Gotham.
Brown, R., & Hewstone, H. (2005). An integrative theory of intergroup contact. In M. Zanna (ed.), *Advances in experimental social psychology* (Vol. 37, pp. 255–343). San Diego, CA: Academic Press.
Browning, C. R. (1992). *Ordinary men: Reserve police battalion 101 and the Final Solution in Poland*. New York: Harper Perennial.
Callimachi, R. (2015). ISIS enshrines a theology of rape. *The New York Times* (August 13). Retrieved from www.nytimes.com/2015/08/14/world/middleeast/isis-enshrines-a-theology-of-rape.html?_r=0.

Colby, A., & Damon, W. (1992). *Some do care: Contemporary lives of moral commitment*. New York: Free Press.
Colby, A., & Damon, W. (1995). The development of extraordinary moral commitment. In M. Killen & D. Hart (eds). *Morality in everyday life: Developmental perspectives* (pp. 342–370). New York: Cambridge University Press.
Craig, W., & Pepler, D. (1997). Observations of bullying and victimization in the schoolyard. *Canadian Journal of School Psychology*, *2*, 41–60.
Dalai Lama (2002). Understanding our fundamental nature. In R.J. Davidson & A. Harrington (eds). *Visions of compassion: Western scientists and Tibetan Buddhists examine human nature* (pp. 66–80). New York: Oxford University Press.
Damon, W. (1984). Self-understanding and moral development from childhood to adolescence. In W. M. Kurtines & J. L. Gewirtz (eds), *Morality, moral behavior, and moral development* (pp. 109–127). New York: Wiley.
Eisenberg, N. (1991). Values, sympathy, and individual differences: Toward a pluralism of factors influencing altruism and empathy. *Psychological Inquiry*, *2*, 128–131.
Eisenberg, N., & Spinrad, T. L. (2014). Multidimensionality of prosocial behavior: Rethinking the conceptualization and development of prosocial behavior. In L. M. Padilla-Walker & G. Carlo (eds), *Prosocial Development* (pp. 17–42). New York: Oxford University Press.
Eisenberg, N., Shea, C. L., Carlo, G., & Knight, G. P. (1991). Empathy related responding and cognition: A "chicken and the egg" dilemma. In W. Kurtines & J. Gewirtz (eds), *Handbook of moral behavior and development: Vol. 2. Research*. 63–88. Hillsdale, NJ: Erlbaum.
Erikson, E. H. (1950). *Childhood and society*. New York: Norton & Co.
Espelage, D. L., Low, S., Rao, M. A., Hong, J. S., & Little, T. D. (2014). Family violence, bullying, fighting, and substance use among adolescents: A longitudinal mediational model. *Journal of Research on Adolescence*, *24*(2), 337–349.
Fagin-Jones, S., & Midlarsky, E. (2007). Courageous altruism: Personal and situational correlates of rescue during the Holocaust. *Journal of Positive Psychology*, *2*(2), 136–147.
Fleeson, W. (2004). Moving personality beyond the person-situation debate: The challenge and the opportunity of within-person variability. *Current Directions in Psychological Science*, *13*(2), 83–87.
Fogelman, E. (1987). The rescuers: A social psychological study of altruistic behavior during the Nazi era. Unpublished doctoral dissertation. Ann Arbor. *University Microfilms International*.
Fogelman, E. (1994). *Conscience and courage: Rescuers of Jews during the Holocaust*. New York: Anchor Books/Doubleday.
Fogelman, E., & Lewis Wiener, V. (1985). The few, the brave, the noble. *Psychology Today*, *19*, 126.
Franco, Z., Blau, K., & Zimbardo, P. G. (2011). Heroism: A conceptual analysis and differentiation between heroic action and altruism. *Review of General Psychology*, *15*(2), 99–113.
Freedman, R. B. (1993). Give to charity?—Well. Since you asked. Unpublished paper. LSE conference on the economics and psychology of happiness and fairness. (4–5). November.
Friedman, P. (1980). Righteous Gentiles in the Nazi era. In A.J. Friedman (ed.), *Roads to extinction: Essays on the Holocaust*. New York: Jewish Publication Society.
Friedman, T. L. (2015). *Contain and amplify*. New York Times, Op. Ed. May 27. www.nytimes.com/2015/05/27/opinion/thomas-friedman-contain-and-amplify.html
Ganz, I. (1993). *Personal and familial predictors of altruism under stress*. Columbia University, ProQuest Dissertations Publishing. 9318238.
Geras, N. (1995). *Solidarity in the conversation of humankind*. London: Verso.
Gilbert, M. (2003). *The righteous: The unsung heroes of the Holocaust*. New York: Holt.
Goldhagen, D. J. (1997). *Hitler's willing executioners: Ordinary Germans and the Holocaust*. New York: Random House.
Goleman, D. (1990). Studies on development of empathy challenge some old assumptions. *The New York Times* (July 12), Science Section. www.nytimes.com/1990/07/12/us/health-studies-on-development-of-empathy-challenge-some-old-assumptions.html?pagewanted=all
Gordon, S. (1984). *Hitler, Germans, and the Jewish question*. Princeton, NJ: Princeton University Press.
Gross, M. L. (1994). Jewish rescue in Holland and France during the Second World War: Moral cognition and collective action. *Social Forces*, *73*, 463–496.
Grusec, J. E. (2006). The development of moral behavior and conscience from a socialization perspective. In M. Killen & J. Smetana (eds), *Handbook of moral development* (pp. 243–262). Mahwah, NJ: Erlbaum.
Grusec, J. E., & Davidov, M. (2010). Integrating different perspectives on socialization theory and research: A domain specific approach. *Child Development*, *81*, 687–709.
Gushee, D. P. (1993). Many paths to Righteousness: An assessment of research on why Righteous Gentiles helped Jews. *Holocaust and Genocide Studies*, *7*, 372–401.
Gutman, I. (ed.) (1990). *Encyclopedia of the Righteous Among the Nations: Rescuers of Jews during the Holocaust*. Jerusalem: Yad Vashem.

Hallie, P. (1979). Lest *innocent blood be shed: The story of Le Chambon and how goodness happened there*. New York: Harper & Row.
Hauser, M. D. (2006). *Moral minds: How nature designed our universal sense of right and wrong*. New York: HarperCollins.
Hawley, P. H. (2014) Evolution, prosocial behavior, and altruism: A roadmap for understanding where the proximate meets the ultimate. In L. M. Padilla-Walker & G. Carlo (eds), *Prosocial Development* (pp. 43–69). New York: Oxford University Press.
Henry, F. (1984). *Victims and neighbors: A small town in Nazi Germany remembered*. South Hadley, MA: Bergin & Garvey.
Hoffman, M. L. (1975). Altruistic behavior and parent–child relationship. *Journal of Personality and Social Psychology*, *31*, 937–943.
Hoffman, M. L. (1984). Parent discipline, moral internalization, and development of prosocial motivation. In E. Staub, D. Bar-Tal, J. Karylowski, & J. Reykowski, (eds), *Development and maintenance of prosocial behavior: International perspectives on positive behavior* (pp. 117–137). New York. Plenum Press.
Hoffman, M. L. (2000). *Empathy and moral development: Implications for caring and justice*. New York: Cambridge University Press.
Huneke, D. K. (1980). *In the darkness ... glimpses of light: A study of Nazi era rescuers*. Portland, OR: Oregon Committee for the Humanities.
Huneke, D. K. (1981–1982). A study of Christians who rescued Jews during the Nazi era. *Humboldt Journal of Social Relations*, *9*, 144–150.
Huneke, D. K. (1985–1986). The lessons of Herman Graebe's life: The origins of a moral person. *Humboldt Journal of Social Relations*, *13*, 320–332.
Jones, D. H. (1999). *Moral responsibility in the Holocaust: A study in the ethics of character*. New York: Rowman & Littlefield.
Kelman H. C. (2007). Social-psychological dimensions of international conflict. In I. W. Zartman (ed.), *Peacemaking in international conflict: Methods and techniques* (revised ed., 61–107). Washington, DC: United States Institute of Peace.
Klingerman, V. (1985). The study of rescuers of Jews in Berlin: A progress report. Paper presented to the eighth annual scientific meeting of the International Society of Political Psychology, Washington, DC, June.
Koestner, R., Franz, C., & Weinberger, J. (1990). The family origins of empathic concern: A 26-year longitudinal study. *Journal of Personality and Social Psychology*, *58*, 709–17.
Kohlreiser, G., Goldsworthy, S., & Coombe, D. (2012). *Care to dare: Unleashing astonishing potential through secure base leadership*. Chichester: John Wiley & Sons.
Latané, B., & Darley, J. (1970). *The unresponsive bystander: Why doesn't he help?* New York: Appleton-Crofts.
Lemkin, R., & Power, S. (2005). *Axis rule in occupied Europe: Laws of occupation, analysis of government, proposals for redress*. Clark, NJ: Lawbook Exchange.
Lifton, R. J. (2000). *The Nazi doctors: Medical killing and the psychology of genocide*. New York: Basic Books.
Limore, Y. (2004). Rescue of Jews: Between history and memory. *Humboldt Journal of Social Relations*, *28*(2), 105–138.
London, P. (1970). The rescuers: Motivational hypotheses about Christians who saved Jews from the Nazis. In J. Macaulay & L. Berkowitz (eds), *Altruism and helping behavior* (pp. 241–250). New York: Academic Press.
Mackey, R. (2015). Muslim employee of kosher market in Paris praised for hiding customers from gunman. *The New York Times* (January 10). Retrieved from www.nytimes.com/2015/01/11/world/europe/charlie-hebdo-kosher-supermarket-hostage-crisis.html.
McAdams, D. P. (1995). What do we know when we know a person? *Journal of Personality*, *63*, 365–396.
McAdams, D. P. (2009). The moral personality. In D. Narvaez & D. K. Lapsley (eds), *Personality, identity, and character: Explorations in moral psychology* (pp. 11–29). New York: Cambridge University Press.
McAdams, D. P., & Cox, K. S. (2010). Self and identity across the lifespan. In M. E. Lamb, A. M. Freund, & R. M. Lerner (eds), *Handbook of life-span development, Vol. 2: Social and emotional development* (pp. 158–207). Hoboken, NJ: Wiley.
McCrae, R. R., & Costa, P. T. Jr. (2003). *Personality in adulthood: A five-factor theory perspective* (2nd ed.). New York: Guilford Press.
McCrae, R. R., Costa, P. T. Jr., Terraciano, A., Parker, W. D., Mills, C. J., De Fruyt, F., & Mervielde, I. (2002). Personality trait development from age 12 to age 18: Longitudinal, cross-sectional and cross-cultural analyses. *Journal of Personality and Social Psychology*, *83*, 1456–1468.
Midlarsky, E. (1985). Heroes of the Holocaust: Their health and well-being 40 years later. Paper presented at the 93rd Annual Convention of the American Psychological Association, Los Angeles, CA, August 23–27.

Midlarsky, E., Fagin-Jones, S., & Corley, R. (2005). Personality correlates of heroic rescue during the Holocaust. *Journal of Personality*, *73*(4), 907–934.

Midlarsky, E., Fagin Jones, S., & Nemeroff, R. K. (2006). Heroic rescue during the Holocaust: Empirical and methodological perspectives. In R. R. Bootzin & P. McKnight (eds). *Measurement, methodology, and evaluation* (pp. 29–45). Washington, DC: American Psychological Association.

Midlarsky, M. I. (1985–1986). Helping during the Holocaust: The role of political, theological, and socioeconomic identifications. *Humboldt Journal of Social Relations*, *13*, 285–305.

Milgram, S. (1974). Obedience *to authority: An experimental view*. New York: Harper & Row.

Monroe, K. R. (2002). Explicating altruism. In S.G. Post, L. G. Underwood, et al. (eds), Altruism *and altruistic love: Science, philosophy, & religion in dialogue* (pp. 106–122). New York: Oxford University Press.

Monroe, K.R. (2012). Ethics *in an age of terror and genocide: Identity and moral choice*. Princeton, NJ: Princeton University Press.

Novak, J., Feyes, K., Christensen, K. (2011). Application of intergroup contact theory to the integrated workplace: Setting the stage for inclusion. *Journal of Vocational Rehabilitation*, *35*(3), 211–226.

Oliner, S. P. (1984). The unsung heroes in Nazi-occupied Europe: The antidote for evil. *Nationalities Papers*, *12*, 129–136.

Oliner, S. P. (2003). *Do unto others: Extraordinary acts of ordinary people*. Boulder, CO: Westview Press.

Oliner, S. P., & Oliner, P. M. (1988). *The altruistic personality: Rescuers of Jews in Nazi Europe*. New York: Free Press.

Padilla-Walker, L. M. (2014). Parental socialization of prosocial behavior: A multidimensional approach. In L. M. Padilla-Walker & G. Carlo (eds), *Prosocial Development* (pp. 131–155). New York: Oxford University Press.

Paldiel, M. (1988). The altruism of the Righteous Gentiles. *Holocaust and Genocide Studies*, *3*, 187–196.

Paldiel, M. (1993). *The path of the righteous: Gentile rescuers of Jews during the Holocaust*. Hoboken, NJ: KTAV Publishing House.

Peterson, C., & Seligman, M. E. P. (2004). *Character strengths and virtues*. Oxford and New York: Oxford University.

Pettigrew, T. F., & Tropp, L. R. (2011). *When groups meet: The dynamics of intergroup contact*. New York: Psychology Press.

Piliavin, J. A., Grube, J. A., & Callero, P. L. (2002). Role as resource for action in public service. *Journal of Social Issues*, *58*(3), 469–485.

Power, S. (2002). *A problem from hell: America and the age of genocide*. New York: Basic Books.

Reed II, A., & Aquino, K. F. (2003). Moral identity and the expanding circle of moral regard toward out-groups. *Journal of Personality and Social Psychology*, *84*(6), 1270–1286.

Reicher, S., & Haslam, S. A. (2006). Rethinking the psychology of tyranny: The BBC prison study. *British Journal of Social Psychology*, *5*(1), 1–40.

Richards, A., Rivers, I, & Akhurst, J. (2008). A positive psychology approach to tackling bullying in secondary schools: A comparative evaluation. *Educational & Child Psychology*, *25*(2), 72–90.

Rivers, I., Poteat, V. P., Noret, N., & Ashurst, N. (2009). Observing bullying at school: The mental health implications of witness status. *School Psychology Quarterly*, *24*(4), 211–223.

Roth, G. (2008). Perceived parental conditional regard and autonomy support as predictors of young adults' self-versus other-oriented prosocial tendencies. *Journal of Personality*, *76*, 513–533.

Roth, G., & Assor, A. (2000). The effect of conditional parental regard and intrinsic value demonstration on academic and prosocial motivation. Paper presented at the Conference of the European Association for Learning and Instruction, Malmö, Sweden, June.

Roth, G., & Assor, A. (2012). The costs of parental pressure to express emotions: conditional regard and autonomy support as predictors of emotion regulation and intimacy. *Journal of Adolescence*, *35* (4), 799–808.

Rushton, J. P. (1980). *Altruism, socialization, and society*. Englewood Cliffs, NJ: Prentice-Hall.

Salmivalli, C., Voeten, M., & Poskiparta, E. (2011). Bystanders matter: Associations between reinforcing, defending, and the frequency of bullying behavior in classrooms. *Journal of Clinical Child & Adolescent Psychology* *40*(5), 668–676.

Salmivalli, C., Lagerspetz, K., Björkqvist, K., Österman, K., & Kaukiainen A. O. (1996). Bullying as a group process: Participant roles and their relations to social status within the group. *Aggressive Behavior*, *22*, 1–15.

Satloff, R. B. (2006). *Among the righteous: Lost stories from the Holocaust's long reach into Arab lands*. New York: Public Affairs.

Sauvage, P. (1984). Faith in humankind: Rescuers of Jews during the Holocaust. Address presented at the U.S. Holocaust Memorial Council conference, Washington, DC, September.

Seligman, M. E. P., & Csikszentmihalyi, M. (2000). Positive psychology: An introduction. *American Psychologist*, *55*(1), 5–14.

Shaver, P. R., & Mikulincer, M. (2012). An attachment perspective on morality: Strengthening authentic forms of moral decision making. In M. Mikulincer & P. R. Shaver (eds), *The Social psychology of morality* (pp. 257–274). Washington, DC: American Psychological Association.

Shepela, S. T., Cook, J., Horlitz, E., Leal, R., Luciano, S., Lufty, E., Miller, C., Mitchell, G., & Worden, E. (1999). Courageous resistance: A special case of altruism. *Theory and Psychology, 6,* 787–805.

Skog, J. (2011) *The legacy of the Holocaust.* Mankato, MN: Compass Point Books.

Smith, J., & Baltes, P. B. (1999). Trends and profiles of psychological functioning in very old age. In P. B. Baltes & K. U. Mayer (eds), *The Berlin aging study: Aging from 70 to 100* (pp. 197–226). New York: Cambridge University Press.

Staub, E. (2002a). The psychology of bystanders, perpetrators, and heroic helpers. In L. S. Newman & R. Erber (eds), *Understanding genocide: The social psychology of the Holocaust* (pp. 11–42). New York: Oxford University Press.

Staub, E. (2002b). Emergency helping, genocidal violence, and the evolution of responsibility and altruism in children. In R. J. Davidson & A. Harrington (eds), *Visions of compassion: Western scientists and Tibetan Buddhists examine human nature* (pp. 165–181). New York: Oxford University Press.

Staub, E. (2011). *Overcoming evil: Genocide, violent conflict and terrorism.* New York: Oxford University Press.

Staub, E. (2012). Psychology and morality in genocide and violent conflict: Perpetrators, bystanders, and rescuers. In M. Mikulincer & P. R. Shaver (eds), *The social psychology of morality* (pp. 381–398). Washington, DC: American Psychological Association.

Stern, D. N. (1985). *The interpersonal world of the infant: A view from psychoanalysis and developmental psychology.* New York: Basic Books.

Tec, N. (1986). *When light pierced the darkness: Christian rescue of Jews in Nazi-occupied Poland* (pp. 150–164). New York: Oxford University Press.

Tec, N. (2003). *Resilience and courage: Women, men, and the Holocaust.* New Haven, CT: Yale University Press.

Tice, D. M., & Baumeister, R. F. (1985). Masculinity inhibits helping in emergencies: Personality does predict the bystander effect. *Journal of Personality and Social Psychology, 49,* 420–428.

Varese, F., & Yaish, M. (2000). The importance of being asked: The rescue of Jews in Nazi Europe. *Rationality and Society, 12,* 307–334.

Vezzali, L., & Capozza, D. (2011). Reducing explicit and implicit prejudice toward disabled colleagues: effects of contact and membership salience in the workplace. *Life Span and Disability, 14*(2), 139–162.

Waasdorp, T. E., Bradshaw, C. P., & Duong, J. (2011). The link between parents' perceptions of the school and their responses to school bullying: Variation by child characteristics and the forms of victimization. *Journal of Educational Psychology, 103,* 324–335.

Walker, L. J. (2002). Moral exemplarity. In W. Damon (ed.), *Bringing in a new era in character education* (pp. 65–83). Stanford, CA: Hoover Institution Press.

Walker, L. J. (2014). Prosocial exemplarity in adolescence and adulthood. In L.M. Padilla-Walker & G. Carlo (eds), *Prosocial Development* (pp. 433–453). New York: Oxford University Press.

Walker, L. J., & Frimer, J. A. (2007). Moral personality of brave and caring exemplars. *Journal of Personality and Social Psychology, 93,* 845–860.

Walker, L. J., Frimer, J. A., & Dunlop, W. L. (2010). Varieties of moral personality: beyond the banality of heroism. *Journal of Personality, 78,* 907–942.

Warneken, F., & Tomasello, M. (2009). The roots of human altruism. *British Journal of Psychology, 100,* 455–471.

Winnicott, D. W. (1965). *Maturational processes and the facilitating environment: Studies in the Theory of emotional development.* London: Hogarth Press.

Wolfson, M. (1975). Zum Widerstand gegen Hitler: Umriss eines Gruppenportrats deutscher Retter von Juden [Opposition to Hitler: Profile of the German rescuers of Jews]. *Tradition und Neubeginn 20,* 391–407.

Yad Vashem (2016a). The righteous among the nations: FAQs. Retrieved from www.yadvashem.org/yv/en/righteous/faq.asp. Reprinted with Permission.

Yad Vashem (2016b). Jeanne Daman-Scaglione. Retrieved from www.yadvashem.org/yv/en/exhibitions/righteous-women/daman.asp.

Zerubavel, E. (2015). *The elephant in the room: Silence and denial in everyday life.* New York: Oxford.

Zimbardo, P. G. (2007). The banality of evil, the banality of heroism. In J. Brockman (ed.), *What is your dangerous idea? Today's leading thinkers on the unthinkable* (pp. 275–276). New York: Harper Perennial.

Zimbardo, P. G., Banks, W. C., Haney, C., & Jaffe, D. (1973). The mind is a formidable jailer: A Pirandellian prison. *The New York Times Magazine* (April 8), Section 6, pp. 38–46.

12

Heroism and Wisdom in Medicine

Margaret Plews-Ogan, Justine E. Owens, Natalie May, and Monika Ardelt

---

Heroes are made by the paths they choose, not the powers they are graced with.
Brodi Ashton, Everneath (2012)

The heroic doctor sacrifices everything to help the needy.
(ABC News, 2006)

The heroic, tragic story of the doctor who saved Nigeria from Ebola.
(Cohn, 2014)

[Doctors Without Borders volunteers] treat the sick and wounded and try to uphold modern standards of care in rough and sometimes horrifying circumstances.
(New York Times, 2010)

Heroic nurse, shot 27 times, saves lives.
(CBS News, 2009)

These ripped-from-the-headlines tales of medical heroism describe extraordinary acts of heroism by doctors and nurses, stories worthy of news reports and documentaries: risking one's own life to save others; treating a disease from which one cannot protect oneself; standing up for justice for one's patients. These are all acts of heroism and often acts of heroism uniquely suited to someone with a medical degree.

Heroism in Medicine

Who is the greatest medical hero who ever lived? Typically, this honor is given to one of the greatest minds in medicine—Hippocrates, Galen, Harvey, Jenner—those who left legacies of foundational thought and breakthrough discovery. One might argue, however, that the greatest heroes are born from singular acts of courage, when a doctor sacrifices his or her own life to save the lives of others, whether on the battlefield, in life-threatening epidemics, or other beyond the call of duty situations. More recently, the idea of the "wounded hero" has resurfaced, a more complex formulation of the hero with roots in Greek tragedy and philosophy (McCoy, 2013).

Reviewing the history of medical heroism sets the stage for a fusion of the multiple images of heroism in medicine and for recognizing singular acts of bravery in what might appear an unlikely place, in the wake of a medical mistake.

"A Medical Hero" was a recurrent feature of the *British Medical Journal* since the mid-1800s and excerpts offer vivid descriptions of "the practitioner who sacrifices ease, health, and often life in the faithful discharge of his mission of relieving suffering." For example:

> A striking example of heroism of this kind has recently been afforded by an Irish doctor who in his unselfish devotion to patients of the humblest class has died of disease contracted in the course of his ministrations. The sad, yet glorious story is of Dr. William Smyth, the medical officer to the Burton Port Dispensary District, which includes the island of Arranmore. The island was visited by an epidemic of typhus fever. Owing to the terror inspired by the disease, Dr. Smyth could get no help in fighting the epidemic. Alone each day he rowed his boat across the stormy waters of the Sound to the island, a distance of four miles. Alone he tried to be at once nurse and doctor to the poor stricken people in their miserable homes. When at length he succeeded in persuading them that their only chance of recovery lay in removal to the mainland, he was confronted by the difficulty that no one would help him, or even lend him a boat. Fortunately Dr. Brendon McCarthy, Medical Inspector to the Local Government Board, arrived on the scene. Without any other help, these two devoted men brought the patients down to the beach, embarked with them in a crazy boat, and rowed them across the Sound. The boat was only kept afloat by the continuous bailing of the strongest of the patients, and sank five minutes after reaching her destination. Happily all the patients were safely transferred, and are all now on the way to recovery. But Dr. Smyth has fallen a martyr to his devotion to duty, having himself contracted the disease which he had fought so manfully. Such a man as William Smyth is a glory to the whole profession, and his death in the prime of manhood in the circumstances related must be counted more truly heroic than a death in battle. Soldiers die for their country in the fierce joy of combat; William Smyth died for his fellow men with nothing to cheer him on but the sense of professional duty.
>
> *(BMJ, 1901, p. 1709)*

The debate about which acts of medical bravery are the more heroic is a continued theme in these accounts, as in the description of doctors who lost their lives in the treatment of diphtheria:

> Almost the only serious disease of an epidemic character that doctors and nurses have still to face is diphtheria and there is no disease in which more heroism has been displayed. ... In the Paris Hospital for Sick Children there is a tablet commemorating the names of house-surgeons who have lost their lives in consequence of sucking the tube after tracheotomy for this frightful disease.
>
> *(BMJ, 1908, p. 1128)*

The battlefield cases of medical heroism appeared regularly as in a description of the first battle of the First Boar War and, all told, far outnumber the other cases:

> The bright example of Arthur Jermyn Landon, who, while continuing to dress the wounded amid a shower of balls in the action on Majuba Hill, was in turn mortally wounded by a bullet; and calling out to his assistants, "I am dying; do what you can for the wounded", only desired for himself that his friends might be told that "he fell doing his duty".
>
> *(BMJ, 1881, p. 488)*

Seventy years later, a description of "Medical Heroes" following World War II stated that 6 percent of all decorations awarded for meritorious service and gallantry went to medical department personnel. While all of the Congressional Medals of Honor were given to enlisted officers, thousands of doctors were also cited for conspicuous bravery. Doctors went through "brutal machine gunfire" to rescue men, they performed operations under mortar attack, and they chose to remain in enlisted men's barracks in prisoner of war camps to care for thousands in "filthy and louse-infested" rooms (Krieghbaum, 1946, p. 76).

No overview of medical heroism would be complete without mention of the "unsung hero" and the heartfelt essays written in their praise for well over a century. These works extol the softer side of heroism, praising the multitudes that silently labor and quietly support the more singular moments of discovery (Elmore & Feinstein, 1994; AMJ, 1855), the consistently cheerful hospital employees that steadfastly sustain the heroes in the spotlight (Merenstein, 2013), and the physicians who serve as inspiration and role models in caring for difficult patients and their families (Radetsky, 2015).

A recent effort in reframing medical heroism draws upon Homer and Sun Tzu to transform the epic and angry medical metaphor with its love of war to a pastoral image that extols reflection, moral courage, empathy, and a more "productive, warm-hearted engagement" (Bleakley, Marshall, & Levine, 2014, p. 22). The authors examine the language of warfare that infuses the medical world today: battling cancer, drugs and surgeries as weapons in the arsenal against disease, invading bugs, and magic bullets. They suggest that these pervasive metaphors form a tough-minded masculine Procrustean bed in need of tempering into a more peaceful, collaborative, and reflective occupation. This brings us back to the idea of the wounded hero and how the process of coming to terms with making a serious medical error—even one that cost rather than saved a life—can be embraced and viewed as heroic.

The Wounded Healer

The wounded hero archetype is rooted in Greek epic and philosophy (McCoy, 2013), although it plays a central role in myths cross-culturally as well (Campbell, 2008). The hero's journey inevitably involves the overcoming of obstacles, with the most difficult and potentially transformative being the hero's own vulnerability (McCoy, 2013). This vulnerability is not merely a physical vulnerability but primarily a psychological vulnerability, containing the emotional wounds that are an inescapable part of life. The courageous response to suffering and weakness is at the core of the hero's journey. When the wounded hero is also a healer, the narrative centers on the relationship of the healer to the patient and the power that arises when the vulnerabilities of both the healer and patient are acknowledged. Jung was the first to propose the wounded healer as essential to the success of a therapeutic relationship, and it is still a useful construct today in helping physicians heal and be healed (Daneault, 2008). The image of the wounded healer is in striking contrast to the notion of an all-powerful physician, who makes no mistakes and can heal all disease. It goes beyond this unrealistic ideal and allows the imperfect doctor to heal.

When Physicians Make a Mistake

When we talk about the wounded healer in medicine, we encompass all forms of the healer's suffering. Caring for others in the face of one's own illness, grief, or suffering is an act of great selflessness, even courage. Yet, there is another kind of wound that might make it even more difficult to continue as an effective and compassionate healer: The most difficult experience doctors can face is to know that they hurt and caused harm to one of their patients. Even today, this is not widely discussed in private and certainly not publicly. This culture of silence was pervasive in 1984 when David Hilfiker published his ground-breaking story and reflection about his own medical error in the prestigious *New England Journal of Medicine*. In his article, "Facing our Mistakes," Hilfiker (1984) shared in detail his story of aborting a woman's fetus in error.

Following four negative pregnancy tests, he performed a D & C, judging that this was what his patient needed. Tragically, he was wrong. The patient and her husband were Hilfiker's friends; as a family physician in a small Minnesota town, he had delivered their first child two years earlier. In addition to the death of her baby, the patient experienced physical pain, expensive medical treatments, and was unable to become pregnant for two more years. Hilfiker was overcome by guilt and anger. He argues that the consequences of doctors' mistakes are so grave that it's a rare physician who can deal with error in a healthy manner. The wounds, or the consequences of a medical mistake, carry with them an overlay of shame and guilt, making them the most difficult circumstance of suffering (Christensen, Levinson, & Dunn, 1992; Kohn, Corrigan, & Donaldson, 1999; Wachter, 2010).

In 1993, Albert Wu and his colleagues studied the psychological impact of making a medical error on young physicians and found "the large majority describing remorse, anger, guilt, and feelings of inadequacy" (Wu, Folkman, Mcphee, & Lo, 1993, p. 567). Several years later, Wu gave a name to these physicians who experienced devastation in the wake of a medical error: "the second victims" (Wu, 2000). Of course, he wrote, "patients are the first and obvious victims of medical mistakes, [but] doctors are wounded by the same errors: they are the second victims" (Wu, 2000, p. 726). He elaborates further, describing the loneliness and despair that physicians experience when they have made a serious error. Physicians often obsess over the event, replaying it over and over again in their mind. Many doubt their competence and worry that they will be found out, even punished.

Multiple studies have described the negative emotional impact of errors on physicians, which include guilt, shame, emotional distress, fractured relationships, isolation, and negative adaptive behaviors (Delbanco & Bell, 2007; Newman, 1996; Waterman et al., 2007). Physicians experience depression, anxiety, and professional burn-out, which might cause them to leave their medical practice or even lead to thoughts of suicide (Wears & Wu, 2002; West et al., 2006). Not surprisingly, studies that focus on trainees—resident physicians—find similar distress among young doctors (Engel, Rosenthal, & Sutcliffe, 2006; Fischer et al., 2006). Wu's editorial was so powerful because he captured not only the emotional distress of physicians but also the dysfunctional manner in which they coped in the aftermath. Anger, blame, and callousness become magnified when legal action comes into play. In the worst cases, Wu disclosed, physicians give up, burn out, or turn to alcohol and drugs (Wu, 2000).

Until recently there have been no available avenues for healing for the physician. Rather than focusing directly on the emotional needs of physicians, the current patient safety movement aims at preventing the predictable aspects of human factor error. In a move away from the traditional "blame and shame" mentality around error, we adopted a systems approach to address the problem of medical error directly (Haynes et al., 2009; Leonard, Graham, & Bonacum, 2004). To fundamentally improve the safety of medical care, we must address systems that fail to protect against inevitable human failings and their potential consequences. Every error that occurs is an opportunity to learn from the human vulnerability to mistakes and to better design systems that help human beings function as safely as possible. This requires laying to rest the old notion of the perfect doctor, the idea that if we try hard enough we will not make mistakes. Experts agree that confronting mistakes transparently and promoting open communication after an error is critical to organizational learning (National Quality Forum, 2010). This means that acknowledging and talking about the mistake is the only way to ensure that the mistake does not happen again. Openly acknowledging and talking about error may also be central to an individual clinician's ability to learn and grow following harmful mistakes. As Hilfiker observed, like sins, "it is permissible to talk about them only when they happen to other people" (Hilfiker, 1984, p. 121).

But acknowledging "the imperfect doctor" has been a challenging cultural shift. Progress is occurring slowly. Yet recent reforms and innovations around medical error disclosure to patients and support for providers who are coping with the impact of the error are promising (Bell,

Moorman, & Delbanco, 2010; Christensen et al., 1992; Delbanco & Bell, 2007; Fischer et al., 2006; Gallagher, Denham, Leape, Amori, & Levinson, 2007; Newman, 1996; Scott et al., 2009; Waterman et al., 2007; Wu, 2000). With the emotional stakes so high, it is not surprising that peer support programs that help physicians cope in the aftermath of an error are gaining national momentum (Shanafelt et al., 2011; Wu, Boyle, Wallace, & Mazor, 2013).

Despite these gains in preventing error by making systematic improvements in healthcare safety, the growth of peer support programs in hospitals and medical centers, and improvement in disclosure training and processes, the toll on physicians remains high. For example, the suicide rate among physicians is 2.45 times higher than that of their peers in other professions (Stack, 2004). Schernhammer & Colditz (2004) conducted an extensive study of reported suicide rates among physicians, discovering high rates of suicide among doctors, especially among women. Factors that might account for the higher suicide rate among physicians are a higher prevalence of depression, a higher rate of psychiatric disorders, including substance abuse disorders, social isolation, and neglect of their own psychiatric, emotional, and medical needs (Schernhammer, 2005). It is not surprising then that coping with a medical error further increases physicians' vulnerability.

A Hero's Journey

We cannot think of anyone more heroic in our professional realm than a physician who bears the mantle of shame, guilt, and loneliness resulting from a medical mistake and makes the choice to be honest and open, face their mistake head on, learn, and become transformed by the experience. Outside of medicine, we all know individuals—either personally or by reputation—who manage to derive meaning and initiate profound positive change out of their own personal tragedy. Think of parents who create foundations and awareness campaigns following the loss of their child (e.g., Mothers Against Drunk Driving). Or those relatives who, in the face of their own grief, work with determination to serve the greater good to prevent the same suffering in other families. One powerful example is Sorrel King, the mother of a toddler, Josie, who died at Johns Hopkins when staff administered the wrong drug. Consumed with rage and grief, Sorrel King began a journey, fueled by her desire to punish the doctors, hospital, and health system that had allowed this tragedy to happen. Yet somewhere along the way, she had a seismic shift of heart and saw the bigger picture. With the settlement money, she created the Josie King Foundation. In her daughter's name, her foundation has prevented countless deaths caused by medical errors (see www.josieking.org). These and so many other remarkable individuals transformed their suffering into what looks like compassion for others and meaning for themselves.

In her work as a patient safety expert, Dr. Plews-Ogan has seen first-hand the devastating effects of medical error, on not only patients and families, but also on the physicians. Yet she also witnessed that some doctors are able to move through this experience of medical error and emerge as better healers. Some demonstrate more humility and compassion, are more mindful of their limitations, and are better able to see the big picture. Some become leaders with a stronger sense of purpose and commitment to the greater good of medicine and teaching.

We typically think of heroes running toward the bullets instead of away from them, or in the case of healers, running toward diseases such as diphtheria, Ebola, or AIDS. These heroes do not run away; they put themselves in harm's way in order to save a life or many lives. In medicine, we would argue, facing mistakes and dealing with the shame, guilt, and anger that result from the mistake is similarly placing oneself in harm's way.

In the study we describe here, we wanted to know how physicians were able to move through this experience and emerge as better healers. What did it take for them to choose the hero's path? How is it that one physician, in the wake of a medical error, chooses a path of anger and despair, or even suicide, and another chooses the path that leads toward growth and wisdom? We wondered if we could learn from their journeys to help other physicians confront their mistakes in a positive way, a way that increases their capacity for learning, promotes humility and compassion, and even instills a dedication to the greater good.

Post-Traumatic Growth

Research in post-traumatic growth laid the groundwork for the questions we asked, although this construct is relatively new to the conversation in medicine. As discussed earlier, health care has identified the "second victim" of medical error (Wu, 2000), acknowledging the healer's emotional suffering in the wake of a mistake. In the examples such as Sorrel King, the Komen family, and others who transform grief into a focus on the greater good, "victims" frame their post-event suffering in a heroic way, rather than merely "coping" or "surviving."

The construct of post traumatic growth suggests that adversity might not only be endured but also presents an opportunity to reawaken us to the uncertainty of life, remind us of the limits of what we know, help us connect with others who are suffering, and open us up to the possibility of change both within ourselves and within the broader world. Adversity presents the greatest of all challenges to what we know about ourselves and the meaning of our lives. Empathy and compassion are often borne of suffering.

According to post-traumatic growth researchers, an unexpected and difficult turn of events reminds us of the uncertainty of life, and trauma can be a catalyst not just for learning but also for major growth and perhaps even wisdom (Calhoun & Tedeschi, 2014; Tedeschi & Calhoun, 2004). Post-traumatic growth is a relatively new understanding of what can happen as a result of trauma (an alternative to either post-traumatic stress or simple recovery), in which people coping with a traumatic event move through a process of rumination and, with self-disclosure and the right social supports, are able to re-work their understanding of themselves, learning and growing in the process. The outcome of post traumatic growth is postulated to be wisdom.

We wondered whether such principles could apply to medical error and if physicians who chose the heroic path through the traumatic event and reached a place of compassion, openness, and focus on the greater good might exemplify a quality beyond "survivor" or "resilient." Might they indeed exemplify a quality that could be described as wisdom?

Wisdom in Medicine

Despite its implicit role in training programs, wisdom is not routinely discussed in medicine (Branch & Mitchell, 2011). One of the reasons might be the elusive nature of wisdom (Ardelt, Achenbaum, & Oh, 2013). Despite continued effort to study the nature, origin, and development of wisdom (Sternberg, 1990), a consensus definition of wisdom does not exist. However, most lay people and wisdom researchers agree that wisdom is a multidimensional construct, comprising cognitive, reflective, and benevolent elements (Bangen, Meeks, & Jeste, 2013; Bluck & Glück, 2005; Jeste et al., 2010; Staudinger & Glück, 2011). For example, Walsh (2015, p. 282), synthesizing cross-cultural and cross-disciplinary contemporary, philosophical, and contemplative approaches to wisdom, defines wisdom as "deep accurate insight and understanding of oneself and the central existential issues of life, plus skillful benevolent responsiveness."

We used the Three-Dimensional Wisdom Model (Ardelt, 1997, 2003, 2004) to conceptualize wisdom as an integration of cognitive, reflective, and compassionate dimensions. This model was derived from earlier research by Clayton and Birren (1980) on lay conceptions of wisdom but is compatible with most prevailing definitions of wisdom by both lay people and wisdom researchers in the East and West. The cognitive dimension of wisdom refers to the ability to understand the deeper meaning of the inter-personal and intrapersonal aspects of life, tolerate ambiguity and uncertainty, and understand the limits of knowledge. The reflective dimension is characterized by wise individuals' capacity to engage in self-reflective practice and perceive things from many different perspectives, which reduce self-centeredness and make it possible to see through the illusion of one's subjectivity and projections (McKee & Barber, 1999). Reduced self-centeredness and a more thorough and accurate understanding of oneself and the existential and social aspects of life result in greater tolerance, understanding, empathy, and compassion for others, which describe the compassionate wisdom dimension (Ardelt, 2003, 2004; Sternberg, 1990; Sternberg & Jordan, 2005).

Wisdom is inherently connected with wise conduct in life and with applying accurate insight and understanding to right action. Hence, wisdom is most easily recognizable in the decisions we make in challenging life situations (Sternberg, 2000). Although the experience of a medical error can be devastating for patients and physicians alike, this challenging life situation might also provide opportunities for the development of wisdom (Ardelt, 2005; Pascual-Leone, 2000). We wanted to find out whether physicians might be able to not just survive the experience of making a harmful error but also learn something essential about themselves that promotes growth. We explored these issues in the *Wisdom in Medicine* study, a three-year project investigating how physicians cope, learn, and change following a medical error (Plews-Ogan et al., 2016; Plews-Ogan, Owens, & May, 2012; Plews-Ogan, Owens, & May, 2013). Hoping to provide insight for our colleagues and institutions about educational and peer support programs, this study explored what helped doctors to respond positively to such a difficult experience.

We did not initially set out to study examples of medical heroism, the journey of doctors who chose paths to wisdom rather than despair. What we are presenting here is a slice and reframing of our larger *Wisdom in Medicine* study. As part of this study, we interviewed 61 physicians who had made a serious medical error. The goal was to identify "exemplars" or individuals who despite experiencing adversity also experienced growth, even wisdom.

Over an 18-month period, we conducted interviews with physicians in three regions of the country (southeast, northeast, and west). The majority (41) were face-to-face interviews and the remaining 20 were conducted by telephone. Interviews lasted from 45 minutes to two hours, and each interview was audiotaped and transcribed verbatim. We began each interview by asking physicians to share their story of coping with a medical error, including the events leading up to the error as well as events that happened in the aftermath. Interviews followed an open-ended interview guide that we had developed to reflect the research literature on coping with adversity, post-traumatic growth, and wisdom. We thought it was important to learn details about what people, events, and structures helped physicians to cope with this experience and what hindered their journey. What was the actual cause of the error? What was the medical impact of the mistake? Did they disclose the event to the patient or family? If yes, how did the family respond? Whom did the physicians turn to for advice or support? What coping strategies did they use, such as talking, their religion or spiritual practice, or journaling? What role did forgiveness play in their journey? How would they say the experience changed them as a physician or a person? What advice would the physician give to another physician if they experienced something similar? And finally, did the doctors feel that they had gained wisdom as a result, and if yes, what did that mean?

We have published a book and several articles that describe the "path through adversity" that emerged in our research, as well as a detailed description of what helped physicians cope and the role of talking and keeping silent in moving through the experience of a medical error (May & Plews-Ogan, 2012; Plews-Ogan et al., 2016; Plews-Ogan et al., 2012; Plews-Ogan et al., 2013). We also produced a PBS documentary film, *Choosing Wisdom*, which describes the path leading to wisdom as experienced by the physicians in our study (Roberts, 2012).

Characteristics of physicians in the study

Of the 61 physicians included in the study, 54 percent were male, 46 percent female, and their mean age was 46 years. Sixty-nine percent practiced in an academic medical center, and 31 percent were in private practice. Their levels of experience in medical practice ranged from less than two years to over 30 years. Although 39 percent were internal medicine physicians, eleven other specialties, including surgery, were represented. The physicians reported disclosure of the error to patients or family members in 60 percent of the cases, although only 10 percent said that they had previously been trained in disclosure. Doctors reported that a lawsuit was filed in 21 percent of the cases.

We categorized three-quarters of the physician narratives as "exemplars," physicians whose response to an error and their path out of the crisis resembled what we view as wisdom. In our original study, we analyzed these exemplar stories to see if we could identify a common path through adversity. We have written on this path leading to wisdom elsewhere (Plews-Ogan et al., 2012; Plews-Ogan et al., 2013). Of these exemplar narratives, we have identified several themes that not only exemplify wisdom but also heroic responses to the most difficult circumstance a doctor can face. In this chapter, we first describe illustrative stories of our physicians' responses to their mistakes and then consider specific heroic responses to medical error: taking responsibility, disclosure and apology, and focusing on the greater good.

Physician responses to medical error[1]

The physicians in our study reflected the guilt, shame, and anger of responses to error described up to 26 years earlier by Hilfiker (1984) and Wu (2000). In one case, Dr. H's error as a pediatric surgeon resulted in a patient's death. He tells the story of assisting in the surgery of a two-year-old boy when the boy suddenly died during what was supposed to be a relatively routine heart-valve repair.

> My role in this resuscitation included multiple units of blood and cracking open his chest— I mean the whole nine yards—his not surviving and hearing the attending tell the family and hearing them fall apart. It was the most horrible nightmare I could imagine. This little boy had gone from somebody who maybe needed this repaired and maybe didn't—he was asymptomatic—to dead.
>
> The rest of the month I felt like I was just getting by. Somebody bumped into me in the hall and said, "Hi, how are you doing?" and I just start crying. I mean, I couldn't stop. I think everything had been bottled up. I couldn't even walk, so they sent me home.

In our film, *Choosing Wisdom*, Lawrence Calhoun used the metaphor of the aftermath of an earthquake to describe the emotional devastation left in the wake of a fatal medical mistake. He speaks over footage of earthquake victims looking dazed and grief-stricken, often standing motionless and seeming unable to process fully what has just happened. Similarly, after making a critical medical error, physicians sometimes describe their immediate reactions as numbness, confusion, emotional distress, and the natural impulse to get some respite from it. In Dr. H's words:

> I think that time allows you not to think about things. I mean the next day I couldn't work, and part of it was I wanted that bad thing to go away, and I think I pushed it back, so it wasn't so raw. I wanted it to be very private. I didn't want other people to know that I had made a mistake.
>
> Well, the whole time that this was going on, the lawsuit was happening and I couldn't sleep. I would wake up at night. I would sit up at night and my heart was pounding. I was

beside myself with anxiety, fear, guilt. I felt terrible. For days, it was just turmoil—very distracted by the fact that someone had died on my watch, probably for a reason that was preventable.

You go through the looking glass. It's just a very bizarre world.

Many of the physicians we interviewed experienced the earth-shattering impact of a medical error by remaining distracted, devastated, and often withdrawn. Some stopped practicing medicine. Others became filled with distrust, fearful that patients might be "out to sue" them, or bitter that administrators or supervisors had not supported them following the event. Some relied on drugs or alcohol to cope with the shame and other complex emotions in the wake of their mistake.

Other physicians followed a different path, a path that we believe led to wisdom. We wanted to learn from these physicians who became better healers, teachers, colleagues, and leaders. We sought to learn, "How did they do that?"

The path through adversity to wisdom

We identified a path through adversity to wisdom following a serious medical error that included five major elements in the process of coping positively: acceptance, stepping in, integration, new narrative, and wisdom.

Acceptance

The first path element to emerge was acceptance. Exemplar physicians described facing their circumstances directly and accepting, in a clear-eyed way, the reality of events. Some described quickly seeking out a colleague who could help them look at the event with clarity. Acceptance also involved recognizing and taking in the true emotional and psychological impact of the situation, including the recognition that it would take time to move through it and to understand it. It involved accepting responsibility, rather than blaming others. One physician explained:

> Like any other big event in your life, you don't immediately fix it, you can't gloss it over, you know, being able to recognize, okay, I am just going to feel wrong about this no matter what, and I am not going to be able to fix it. Time will put some space there and make it less tender, but I will always feel, you know, like I was the proximate cause of that because it was up to me to make that decision.

Stepping In

The second element we identified in the exemplar narratives was termed "stepping in." Stepping in often involved taking hold of a situation. It was an active, empowering step that often seemed to catalyze the next steps toward growth. Common themes within this element included taking responsibility for the next steps, disclosure and apology, learning about the mistake, doing the right thing, and reaching out to others. For example, one physician told us,

> Talking those things through is very helpful. It's not weak and it's not weird, it's not bad to find somebody to let that emotional energy out on so that you can move ahead…get it all out and then move…it's a grieving process in a way.

Because this step was often a difficult and courageous step, we discuss this at length later in this chapter.

Integration

The next element, the process of integrating the realities and implications of the mistake, necessitated that the physicians revised or expanded their views of themselves and the world. This step captures the process of integrating the realities and the implications of the mistake, often a challenging and prolonged process. Within the context of this element, we saw physicians deal with their own imperfection, forgive without forgetting, find meaning, and experiment with new ways of doing their work. For example, physicians almost universally described wrestling with the issue of imperfection and its implications. Many spoke of how difficult this was. For example, one physician said, "Well, I actually stepped away from clinical medicine for two years after residency … I didn't know how to be an imperfect doctor."

Physicians also wrestled with forgiveness as they struggled to integrate events. Forgiveness was a key to moving forward, but physicians worried that forgiveness was somehow letting themselves off the hook or diminishing the important lessons they needed to learn. One physician managed self-forgiveness this way:

> I think it honors the memory of those patients if you share these things, if you are willing to carry them with you and never forget. So, I like to say I carry a little graveyard in my head of all the patients that have passed and of all the people I wish I had done things differently for, and, when the opportunity comes up I honor those people.

Finding meaning in the experience—making them not just better doctors, but better people—allowed physicians to integrate the error into their expanded view of themselves.

> The humility I gained was not just in the professional domain. That was, that was deep down in my core. I used to try to separate them (the professional and the personal), I don't try to do that anymore.

Finally, integration involved exploring new ways of doing things that were coherent with what physicians had learned about themselves. They explored talking about things more freely, sharing their imperfections, being more assertive, working more closely with colleagues, spending more time with patients, any number of things that helped them to incorporate the things they had learned into their lives as doctors.

New Narrative

As the physicians integrated their experiences of errors, they developed new or revised narratives for themselves as physicians, new ways of thinking about themselves, and new ways of doing things. The first new narrative theme we identified, *the imperfect but good doctor*, referred to a self-understanding that incorporated imperfection into the physicians' notions of being a good doctor. They described incorporating humility, continuous learning, and honesty into how they are as doctors. Second, in *changing their work to enhance safety*, physicians developed different ways of incorporating what they had learned from their mistakes, such as working as a team, being open to others' opinions, paying attention, and developing systems to safeguard against their own fallibility. Third, in *changing the work to enhance meaning*, some took more time with patients, shared more of themselves with patients, or paid more attention to their relationship with patients. We called the final theme "*the humble expert*," in which physicians described learning to temper their expertise with humility and learning to have confidence without being cocky.

Wisdom

The last path element, wisdom, emerged as physicians reflected on the changes that had occurred in them as a result of the medical error experience. We identified six themes related to the development of wisdom. First, the physicians described an increased sense of strength, a sense that in the future they would be able to face difficult experiences in their lives and face them well. Second, they described an increased sense of humility, an acute awareness of the limitations of their knowledge and their own imperfection and a desire to balance humility with confidence. They viewed this as an important and very positive element in their maturity as physicians. Third, they described being more compassionate and able to connect more deeply with their patients. This compassion seemed facilitated by an increased capacity for forgiveness brought about through their experience of a devastating mistake. As one physician recounted, "And I certainly am absolutely more understanding and forgiving of the frailties of others, whether my coworkers or the nurses." Fourth, the physicians talked about being open to learning not just about that mistake, but in an ongoing and deep way. This kind of learning necessitated being open to others' ideas and to what they might be missing. Fifth, exemplars described being better able to deal with uncertainty, ambiguity, and complexity and to be more resistant to black and white thinking. For example, one physician said, "So I do think I am a lot more tolerant of uncertainty … because you realize that you can't fix it all …" And finally, physicians described how their experience had helped them to focus on the deeper meaning of what they do and to recognize, appreciate, and foster that in their work. Much of this deeper meaning stemmed from their closer relationship with patients.

Two other points are worth mentioning. First, in examining the path elements and how physicians moved through the various phases in their journey, a thread that was woven through each of these path elements was the concept of "choosing." These changes were not passive but rather active, precipitated by choices made by the physicians, choices to actively pursue positive changes and to learn rather than avoid or deny what had happened. As one physician put it,

> I realized that I had a choice. I could stay in that dark place, blaming myself and feeling that life really wasn't worth living, or I could get out of it and use that situation for the betterment of the world.

Second, the process of moving through the experience of a serious error to a place of wisdom was not linear, but rather iterative and circular, with elements being revisited many times. Every element may not be emphasized in a particular person's journey, and often one element was more prominent, more difficult, or more transformative.

Three heroic responses to a medical error

Taking responsibility

It is hard to imagine the anguish that Dr. C felt when she learned that she had failed to diagnose her patient's lung cancer. She thought she might have to quit practicing medicine. "I can't be a doctor anymore," she thought. "I don't want to hurt people. I want to help people." Although the patient's oncologist assured Dr. C that the two- or three-month delay in the diagnosis was not going to have an impact on how well the patient did, Dr. C did not feel any better. "How many other mistakes have I made that I don't know about?" she wondered. She was too ashamed to tell her colleagues, afraid that she was not up to standards and that she was not a good enough doctor to care for their patients.

When she broke the terrible news to her patient, he was justifiably angry and upset. "How could you do this to me? I'm going to die now because you didn't follow up on this fast enough." For over a month, Dr. C followed her patient's progress from a distance. She stayed in touch with the oncologist as the patient underwent cancer treatments. Finally she realized that she needed to apologize to him. "It took all the courage I could muster to go back and see him," she said. "I thought he was just going to lash out at me again, but I felt such a strong need to ask him to forgive me and to check on him and to let him know that I care about him and that I would never mean him any harm." Standing outside his hospital door that day, seeking his forgiveness, she was certain that this was the hardest thing she had ever done.

She went into his room, filled that morning with his family members, and before she could even say a word, the patient told her he was so happy to see her and so touched that she had come to visit. "I know that you care about me," he said, and he even apologized for being so angry with her before. His family told her that he spoke so often about how she took such good care of him.

Seeking forgiveness from her patient allowed Dr. C to take that first step toward healing. It was a long and difficult journey for her, but ultimately she became more sensitive and alert to the privilege of her profession. "From then on, it made me much more awed at the power that physicians do have, and to be very respectful of that, and not to take it for granted."

Disclosure and Apology

Response to an error sometimes meant not only actively taking responsibility for the error that had occurred but also having the courage to face devastated patients and families. This often resulted in the process of disclosure, or talking honestly with the patient or family about what had happened. As seen in Dr. C's story, this process can be extremely difficult. Disclosure is a very complex process involving multiple layers and many reasons why it takes courage.

The first layer is the legal system. Although not as common a practice as it was a decade ago, lawyers have traditionally instructed doctors to keep silent, with the concern that disclosing or apologizing to a patient will result in a lawsuit. Therefore, many doctors struggle with errors that could easily have remained hidden from the patient. What if an error was made that had no adverse outcome? In that situation, should the doctor disclose to the patient? A doctor may think, "If I tell you about what I did, you may sue me for something you wouldn't have known about if I hadn't told you." Yet many doctors adhere to a code that requires them to do the right thing, even at risk to themselves.

Dr. Q delayed his diagnosis of a patient's pancreatic cancer; the patient, an eighty-year-old woman, died. Although an earlier diagnosis would not have changed the ultimate outcome, he felt compelled to speak to the family, to tell the woman's family about the delay in identifying her disease correctly as cancer. Dr. Q said:

> Keeping stuff inside festers and feels really bad and really dishonest. Confession is important to me. It would have been okay if they had been furious with me. It would have been well within their rights also.

Many doctors agree with this approach of facing the family rather than hiding and holding onto secrets. One insisted on talking with his patient's family, against the legal advice of the hospital.

> I felt like the right thing to do was to go and talk to them and tell them what had happened. And if they felt like they needed to sue me, then we would just have to deal with that.

Another layer of, or barrier to, disclosure is the shame in having made a mistake. We have all felt the shame of making an error, but few of us have made a mistake that resulted in someone's death or injury. Physicians who have erred must face their patients, their colleagues, themselves, and sometimes lawyers and lawsuits. Moreover, many physicians in this position carry the weight of this shame for years. Dr. C's shame kept her locked in silence at a time when she most needed the support of her peers.

> I was too ashamed to tell any of my colleagues, so I suffered in silence for probably a week or two. Because, I thought, if I tell them, they're not going to trust me to cover their patients, they're not going to think I'm smart anymore—all of those things go through your head. I mean, you really feel defective, you feel like you're not up to standards.

A third layer of disclosure is the doctor's realization that revealing the error could result in a broken relationship with one's patient. In the best doctor-patient relationships, an intimacy and caring develop, often over the course of many years and the highs and lows of a patient's health history. Just as a patient would be saddened by the loss of this relationship so, too, would a doctor. Dr. T is an ob-gyn who enjoys her close relationships with her patients, their newborn babies, and their families. She often cares for patients through multiple pregnancies and "really significant events in their life." Living in a small town, she enjoys watching the babies she's delivered grow up. For her, one of the hardest aspects of an error during childbirth and the ensuing lawsuit was the destruction of the relationship with her patient.

> We had a really good relationship before this. I delivered her first child, too, and watched her deal with some pretty difficult stuff during this second pregnancy. I think probably the mother and certain family members pushed her into the lawsuit. There's very little available for a special needs child, so this is the American mechanism to make this happen. But based on her deposition, I don't think she was really angry with me.

Dr. T remembers that she and the patient even shared a smile over an inside joke during the hearing.

Another physician, Dr. D, had a similar experience with a delayed diagnosis. Shortly after the correct diagnosis was revealed, she was invited to attend an event that the patient and his family also attended. Several physicians were in the patient's family, and one of them asked, "How could you miss that?" Dr. D told another family member, a family physician like herself, that she wished more than anything she had done the ultrasound when the patient had complained of stomach pain the year before. He told her, "Our lives are full of shoulda coulda woulda." His attempt at kindness was helpful, but "it was definitely a hard place to go. I felt like whatever I got, I would deserve. But I stood there. I stood there."

Standing there and listening to the anger of a distraught patient or family member or waiting outside a patient's hospital door with the intent of seeking forgiveness is never easy. Both acts require exceptional courage and resolve. Dr. Jo Shapiro, speaking in the film, talked about facing her patient following a surgical error. She explained everything to him and his family. She apologized. She was very careful to tell him exactly what happened and what their plans were to repair the damage. It was helpful to be able to face him and explain it all to him. "That said," she reflected, "all of those feelings of being very, very sad about what happened would bubble up and would make it hard for me to even want to go in the room and see him." Overcome with feelings of inadequacy, she remembered forcing herself to visit him twice a day. "Every part of me was saying, *'Don't go in there. It will just remind me of all that went wrong.'*" But ultimately she realized, "I didn't want my emotions and my needs to get in the way of helping him get through this process."

Approaching the patient and the family rather than avoiding them is critical to healing, and facing mistakes is what our exemplar physicians encouraged other physicians to do in similar situations. An experienced physician, Dr. G, accidentally gave her patient too much medication in preparation for a test while in the hospital. The elderly and already fragile patient became unresponsive and had to be resuscitated. Dr. G, who immediately went to the patient's waiting children to report what she had done, underscored the importance of facing the family in this healing process. She pointed out,

> I would encourage people not to run from this process. I think people don't want to talk about it, but I've never had a bad experience when we've been able to get families back in and talk about unexpected bad outcomes with them. Some physicians want to hide from those meetings, and I try to encourage them not to, because it's a way for the families to heal, it's a way for us to heal.

Dr. T, the surgeon, agreed:

> You've got to live with your complications. One of my old attendings taught me that many years ago. When you have a complication, the natural tendency is avoidance. You want to stay away from it with some surrealistic hope that it'll just go away if you ignore it.

But after years of experience, she concluded:

> As hard as it is, you have to suck it up and you have to walk in that room every day and see your patient and take care of her and address her needs and get through this just like she's got to get through it. And you'll both get better.

There are also other forms of disclosure that do not involve these open conversations with patients. Sometimes doctors are unable to talk with patients or families, perhaps because the patient has died and has no surviving family. In these cases, disclosing to a mentor, peer, or friend is a helpful form of disclosure. In the film, Dr. Matt Goodman revealed that telling a trusted colleague about his mistake enabled him to move beyond the error to constructive healing:

> I think the disclosure was the thing that helped me most. Telling the story and just mulling it over. However I processed it, it's just incredibly painful. Then a couple of days later it's not quite as painful, and then I can start to intellectualize and learn about it and figure out what concrete steps to take to try to keep it from happening again.

Compassion and the Greater Good

Some physicians responded in ways that increased their own compassion and shifted their focus to changing institutional systems, helping others, and promoting the greater good. Physicians described how their experience had given them a greater capacity for relating to patients and greater compassion for suffering patients. Some found that sharing their own experiences and emotions allowed them to connect with patients in a completely different and deeper way.

Up until her experience with a mistake in the operating room, Dr. J had never been able to share her own experiences of difficulty with her patients, even though she understood that her patients might benefit from seeing someone who was coping well with a circumstance similar to their own. Somehow the experience of her mistake eventually allowed her to be comfortable sharing her personal challenges with her patients. As Dr. J related:

> With patients I think I have developed a much better sense of compassion and empathy. Where I used to be ashamed or afraid to talk about any personal experience, I have no

problems sharing these stories now. That's so helpful to them in helping them come to grips with their situation. That's been incredibly empowering for me.

Similarly, Dr. Jamie Redgrave in the film *Choosing Wisdom* described how, after coming to terms with her own difficult experiences, she was more willing to be open with her patients. As she put it, she no longer finds it draining to be with patients in their times of need, because she is able to truly connect with them.

The exemplar physicians also reported a greater compassion for other clinicians who had made mistakes and found themselves to be more forgiving and less judgmental of others. As one physician said, "I am less critical when I hear a story about another physician. And I think I am perhaps a little more sympathetic when bad things do happen."

For some, like Dr. Jo Shapiro in the film, this compassion for their fellow caregivers inspired them to become active in trying to change the culture of medicine from blame and silence to openness and learning. Dr. Shapiro started the Center for Professionalism and Peer Support at the Brigham and Women's Hospital in Boston. This program provides training and support for clinicians at the hospital, preparing them to respond with openness, honesty, and compassion when something goes wrong and supporting clinicians and families in the aftermath of an error. Dr. Shapiro explained:

> There's something so special about talking to peers. I think that colleagues can help us forgive ourselves in a way that we have trouble doing ourselves. And I thought, "*We have to harness this!*" I mean, this is so powerful and also so needed. Harnessing the power of community is something I really learned from this experience.

Many exemplar physicians turned their focus toward determining the cause of the error and changing their practice to ensure the mistake would never happen again. After a wrong-site surgery, a surgeon knew he had to figure out why the mistake had occurred:

> When I got over the shock of what had happened and was sitting at my desk at the end of that day, my thoughts were, *Okay, figure out what happened.* I went through the process that I normally go through to avoid wrong-site surgeries, and I decided, *Okay, there's some things I need to do.* At that point, in addition to making the "Yes" on the correct part, I changed my marking strategy so that when we're doing multiple sites, I'm going to have a mark or an arrow or something to point me to the correct ones. And I added a step to write "No" on the spots where I would do the wrong one. This is all in magic marker. It's probably kept me from doing the wrong site God knows how many times. And I have the patient put the mark on her own body part the night before. No one knows better than the patient where her surgery is.

Some physicians took this root cause of the error and prevention process one step further, determined to make a difference beyond their own medical practice. For some, the logical next step was to share that knowledge with others, even if it meant publicly acknowledging the mistake. For example, Dr. B was devastated when one of his first patients during his internship died. Because no one on the team could come up with a diagnosis, the patient did not receive surgery in time. An autopsy revealed a bowel ischemia. Dr. B recalled:

> One of the things that I have done since then is that I've told the story. Not the emotional part of the story—partially that—but I've told the clinical story probably fifty times. I'd use it as a teaching case so that this might not happen to someone else. At my third-year residents' conference, I did a sort of literature review on this and did a write-up, and then I

used that handout to teach students and residents for twenty years. But you can see why I might want to do my project on it, why I consider myself a minor expert on the condition. That was part of my coping: to learn about it and say, "How can I help other people?"

Some physicians even went so far as to try to address the institutional and wider issues that had a direct or indirect impact on their experience, as we saw earlier with Dr. Shapiro. She saw that there was no forum for peers to help one another through the aftermath of a bad outcome, so she established a peer support program for health care providers. That program has become a model nationwide. Several physicians in our study became involved in patient safety programs in their hospital or practice as a result of their own experience with medical error. According to Dr. Shapiro:

> I see the importance of improving quality of care. To me the solution to both of these problems was to have the appropriate systems in place. Systems are like the ropes that a rock climber uses. If you have appropriate systems in place, it gives you more freedom. Some people worry that if you make everything so systematized, it doesn't give you the freedom to make the choices you need to make. In my mind, if I have the systems in place, then I don't have to have all the details in place. It gives you more processing room in your brain; to use a computer analogy, it frees up more RAM. So I think quality is important. And I think it's important for everybody to be involved.

Dr. T., the ob-gyn whose case ended in a difficult lawsuit, became involved in reforming malpractice policy in the United States. She even served on a roundtable with then-President George W. Bush. "There's got to be reform in medical liability or the cost will keep going up. I think slowly but surely it'll change. It started as a coping strategy, but it turned into kind of a mission."

Heroic leadership in medicine

Some exemplar physicians not only took responsibility for what went wrong but also demonstrated leadership with both their patients and their medical team. In the film *Choosing Wisdom*, Dr. Andy Wolf shared the tragic story of a patient who died in the hospital. It was a sudden and unexpected death that left everyone on the team stunned and devastated. "It was a tragedy for everybody, having this horrible, horrible thing happen." But in the immediate aftermath, he felt an overwhelming sense that he was the "captain of the ship" and that he needed to maintain order and stability for everyone involved:

> I very quickly got the team together in a room and said, "*We have to accept that we have had a tragedy here. We're not sure what happened, but let's process it.*" I just had everybody process it right there.

The focus of that gathering and much of the time in the following days was to process the event emotionally. The medical processing would come later, but for now, Dr. Wolf felt it was important to "try to turn this into a growth experience from the start." After the initial tears and sadness, the result was a team that responded in a healthy way, without defensiveness, blaming, casting aspersions, or anger. Upon reflection, Dr. Wolf stated that the moment of bringing everyone together "was probably the turning point, right there. The rest of it sort of fell into place after that." In the immediate aftermath, they were able to pull together to care for the family and themselves and to focus on how to prevent a similar occurrence in the future. "I feel like the resident physicians came through it, as far as I can tell, without denial of what had happened, but also not feeling like terrible people—that they are incompetent, terrible people." Dr. Wolf believed that his leadership had come from a combination of his personal and professional maturity. He had learned "how to handle tragic events in one's life [and] that I had evolved to the point where I could handle it in real time pretty, pretty well."

Heroic leadership may also be reflected in compassionate behaviors, not in a moment of crisis but during life's more mundane moments. Exemplar physicians exhibited quiet leadership on a daily basis that had an impact on the greater good in ways we cannot begin to know. For example, as a young physician, Dr. K was shown compassion by her teacher when she made a mistake—a sutured cut that became infected. She has been very intentional about sharing that same compassion with her patients and her students. Her experience with error also had a tremendous impact on her view of the world and her place in it, which she tries to impart to her patients, many of whom are college students:

> This is all fleeting. It's helped me keep the big picture of life in mind, and it's really helped me relate to my patients in helping them keep the big picture of life in mind, rather than dealing with a small problem they have. At the end of the day, if they got a little ankle sprain, it is a problem for them, but in the big picture, it's all about perspective, right? Think about Sudan, think about Darfur, and think about all these kids dying there and think about all that you have—everything you've been blessed with. I remind them about this stuff. This experience has made me very humble, and I can relate that humility to them and give them some perspective. When my professor gave me this perspective, I was able to translate that perspective into sharing with someone else. This relatively small mistake changed the way I feel about things. It's amazing how a little incident in your life can really change things for you.

Finally, heroic leadership often stemmed from the sense of medicine as a calling, a calling that came with a sense of something larger than themselves, drawing them to a profession that involved subsuming their own needs and desire to those of their patients. This larger purpose for their role as doctors pulled them into a life of true service to others. The professional code of ethics, as well as a deeper sense of service, honor, and justice, compelled them to do the right thing in situations where their own self-interest would have had them do otherwise. Dr. Alan Alfano, a rehabilitation physician in *Choosing Wisdom*, described his response to an error this way:

> I decided that I should go over and talk with the patient, although everything in me just wanted to run the other way. In the end, that is not who we are as physicians. We care for the patient, even when—especially when—things have not gone well.

Conclusion

Let us make one thing clear: The physicians in this study would not consider themselves to be heroes. In fact, they would probably object to this characterization. However, we believe that their stories teach us some important lessons about heroism that are more difficult to see in other, more obvious stories of medical heroism.

The first lesson is that some of the most courageous acts that human beings can perform involve facing our own failings and vulnerabilities and allowing that experience to change us for the better. We are accustomed to seeing what we would call cowardly responses to a mistake, consisting of failure to acknowledge, take responsibility, face the consequences, and most importantly, failure to change because of it. Yet we do not often talk about the courage, even the heroism, it takes to walk straight into the fire of our own failings. The risk here is not physical but existential, and some would argue all the more dreadful. Shame and guilt are powerful forces and can shape our lives in sinister ways. Compassion can be the first casualty when shame and guilt create a wall around our soul. The act of facing, even embracing, their failings and vulnerabilities allowed exemplar physicians to stay open, to grow, and to find a deep and authentic way to connect with their colleagues and patients.

The second lesson is that heroes are made in our everyday choices and can be found in the most unlikely of circumstances, where we feel anything but heroic. Many of the mistakes the physicians recounted were simple common human failings, failures of memory or perception, in situations where it might be hard to imagine that anyone could have done better. These physicians could have avoided the emotional toll of disclosure and apology, made excuses, or hidden behind their lawyers or a wall of silence. They, like other heroes, chose a different path, a path that led them straight into the fire of conflict and risk, and in that dark and unlikely place of shame and guilt, they found the hero's way, a way to grow and change for the better.

We all make choices every day that represent opportunities to be small heroes in our own lives. These choices shape who we are, both individually and in community. In medicine, the choice to acknowledge our mistakes, talk openly about them, and learn from them can change us for the better.

Note

1   This material has been adapted from *Choosing Wisdom: Strategies and Inspiration for Growing through Life-Changing Difficulties* (Plews-Ogan et al., 2012).

References

ABC News. (2006). Heroic doctor sacrifices everything to help needy. Retrieved from http://abcnews.go.com/GMA/OnlyinAmerica/print?id=2728557.
AMJ (1855). Medical hero-worship: Its evils, and their remedy. *Association Medical Journal*, 3(107), 47.
Ardelt, M. (1997). Wisdom and life satisfaction in old age. *Journal of Gerontology: Psychological Sciences*, 52B(1), P15–P27. doi: 10.1093/geronb/52B.1.P15
Ardelt, M. (2003). Empirical assessment of a three-dimensional wisdom scale. *Research on Aging*, 25(3), 275–324. doi: 10.1177/0164027503025003004
Ardelt, M. (2004). Wisdom as expert knowledge system: A critical review of a contemporary operationalization of an ancient concept. *Human Development*, 47(5), 257–285. doi: 10.1159/000079154
Ardelt, M. (2005). How wise people cope with crises and obstacles in life. *ReVision: A Journal of Consciousness and Transformation*, 28(1), 7–19. doi: 10.3200/REVN.28.1.7-19
Ardelt, M., Achenbaum, W. A., & Oh, H. (2013). The paradoxical nature of personal wisdom and its relation to human development in the reflective, cognitive, and affective domains. In M. Ferrari & N. M. Weststrate (eds), *The scientific study of personal wisdom: From contemplative traditions to neuroscience* (pp. 265–295). New York: Springer.
Ashton, B. (2012). *Everneath*. New York: Balzer + Bray.
Bangen, K. J., Meeks, T. W., & Jeste, D. V. (2013). Defining and assessing wisdom: A review of the literature. *American Journal of Geriatric Psychiatry*, 21(12), 1254–1266. doi: 10.1016/j.jagp.2012.11.020
Bell, S. K., Moorman, D. W., & Delbanco, T. (2010). Improving the patient, family, and clinician experience after harmful events: The "when things go wrong" curriculum. *Academic Medicine*, 85(6), 1010–1017. doi: 10.1097/ACM.0b013e3181dbedd7
Bleakley, A., Marshall, R., & Levine, D. (2014). He drove forward with a yell: Anger in medicine and Homer. *Medical Humanities*, 40(1), 22–30. doi: 10.1136/medhum-2013-010432
Bluck, S., & Glück, J. (2005). From the inside out: People's implicit theories of wisdom. In R. J. Sternberg & J. Jordan (eds), *A handbook of wisdom: Psychological perspectives* (pp. 84–109). New York: Cambridge University Press.
BMJ (1881). A medical hero. *British Medical Journal*, 2(1081), 488.
BMJ (1901). A true hero of medicine. *British Medical Journal*, 2(2136), 1709.
BMJ (1908). Medical heroes. *British Medical Journal*, 2(2493), 1127–1128.
Branch, W. T., Jr., & Mitchell, G. A. (2011). Wisdom in medicine. *The Pharos*, 74(3), 12–17.
Calhoun, L. G., & Tedeschi, R. G. (eds). (2014). *Handbook of posttraumatic growth: Research and practice*. New York: Psychology Press.

Campbell, J. (2008). *The hero with a thousand faces* (3rd ed.). Novato, CA: New World Library.

CBS News. (2009). Heroic nurse, shot 27 times, saved lives. Retrieved from www.cbsnews.com/news/heroic-nurse-shot-27-times-saved-lives.

Christensen, J. F., Levinson, W., & Dunn, P. M. (1992). The heart of darkness: The impact of perceived mistakes on physicians. *J Gen Intern Med, 7*(4), 424–431. doi: 10.1007/BF02599161

Clayton, V. P., & Birren, J. E. (1980). The development of wisdom across the life-span: A reexamination of an ancient topic. In P. B. Baltes & O. G. Brim, Jr. (eds), *Life-span development and behavior* (Vol. 3, pp. 103–135). New York, N.Y.: Academic Press.

Cohn, J. (2014). The heroic, tragic story of the doctor who saved Nigeria from Ebola. *New Republic*. Retrieved from https://newrepublic.com/article/119956/doctor-stella-adadevoh-isolated-ebola-case-stopped-nigeria-outbreak.

Daneault, S. (2008). The wounded healer—Can this idea be of use to family physicians? *Canadian Family Physician, 54*(9), 1218–1219.

Delbanco, T., & Bell, S. K. (2007). Guilty, afraid, and alone—Struggling with medical error. *The New England Journal of Medicine, 357*(17), 1682-1683. doi: 10.1056/NEJMp078104

Elmore, J. G., & Feinstein, A. R. (1994). Joseph Goldberger: An unsung hero of American clinical epidemiology. *Annals of Internal Medicine, 121*(5), 372–375. doi: 10.7326/0003-4819-121-5-199409010-00010

Engel, K. G., Rosenthal, M., & Sutcliffe, K. M. (2006). Residents' responses to medical error: Coping, learning, and change. *Academic Medicine, 81*(1), 86–93. doi: 10.1097/00001888-200601000-00021

Fischer, M. A., Mazor, K. M., Baril, J., Alper, E., DeMarco, D., & Pugnaire, M. (2006). Learning from mistakes: Factors that influence how students and residents learn from medical errors. *Journal of General Internal Medicine, 21*(5), 419–423. doi: 10.1111/j.1525-1497.2006.00420.x

Gallagher, T. H., Denham, C. R., Leape, L. L., Amori, G., & Levinson, W. (2007). Disclosing unanticipated outcomes to patients: The art and practice. *Journal of Patient Safety, 3*(3), 158–165. doi: 10.1097/pts.0b013e3181451606

Haynes, A. B., Weiser, T. G., Berry, W. R., Lipsitz, S. R., Breizat, A. H., Dellinger, E. P., … Safe Surgery Saves Lives Study, G. (2009). A surgical safety checklist to reduce morbidity and mortality in a global population. *The New England Journal of Medicine, 360*(5), 491–499. doi: 10.1056/NEJMsa0810119

Hilfiker, D. (1984). Facing our mistakes. *New England Journal of Medicine, 310*(2), 118–122. doi: 10.1056/NEJM198401123100211

Jeste, D. V., Ardelt, M., Blazer, D., Kraemer, H. C., Vaillant, G., & Meeks, T. W. (2010). Expert consensus on characteristics of wisdom: A Delphi method study. *The Gerontologist, 50*(5), 668–680. doi: 10.1093/geront/gnq022

King, S. (2009). *Josie's story* (1st ed.). New York: Atlantic Monthly Press.

Kohn, L. T., Corrigan, J. M., & Donaldson, M. S. (eds). (2000). *To err is human: Building a safer health system*. Washington, DC: National Academy Press.

Krieghbaum, H. (1946). Medical heroes. *The Science News-Letter, 49*(5), 74–76. doi: 10.2307/3922583

Leonard, M., Graham, S., & Bonacum, D. (2004). The human factor: The critical importance of effective teamwork and communication in providing safe care. *Quality and Safety in Health Care, 13*(Suppl 1), i85–i90. doi: 10.1136/qhc.13.suppl_1.i85

May, N., & Plews-Ogan, M. (2012). The role of talking (and keeping silent) in physician coping with medical error: A qualitative study. *Patient Education and Counseling, 88*(3), 449–454. doi: 10.1016/j.pec.2012.06.024

McCoy, M. B. (2013). *Wounded heroes: Vulnerability as a virtue in ancient Greek literature and philosophy*. Oxford: Oxford University Press.

McKee, P., & Barber, C. (1999). On defining wisdom. *International Journal of Aging and Human Development, 49*(2), 149–164. doi: 10.2190/8G32-BNV0-NVP9-7V6G

Merenstein, J. H. (2013). Unknown heroes. *Family Medicine, 45*(2), 128–129.

National Quality Forum (2010). *Safe practices for better healthcare–2010 update: A consensus report*. Washington, DC: National Quality Forum.

Newman, M. C. (1996). The emotional impact of mistakes on family physicians. *Archives of Family Medicine, 5*(2), 71–75. doi: 10.1001/archfami.5.2.71

Scott, A. O. (2010). Treating the world's sorrow and pain. *The New York Times* (June 3). Retrieved from www.nytimes.com/2010/06/04/movies/04living.html?ref=movies&_r=1.

Pascual-Leone, J. (2000). Mental attention, consciousness, and the progressive emergence of wisdom. *Journal of Adult Development, 7*(4), 241–254. doi: 10.1023/A:1009563428260

Plews-Ogan, M., May, N., Owens, J. E., Ardelt, M., Shapiro, J., & Bell, S. K. (2016). Wisdom in medicine: What helps physicians after a medical error? *Academic Medicine, 91*(2), 233–241. doi: 10.1097/ACM.0000000000000886

Plews-Ogan, M., Owens, J. E., & May, N. (2012). *Choosing wisdom: Strategies and inspiration for growing through life-changing difficulties*. West Conshohocken, PA: Templeton Press.

Plews-Ogan, M., Owens, J. E., & May, N. B. (2013). Wisdom through adversity: Learning and growing in the wake of an error. *Patient Education and Counseling, 91*(2), 236–242. doi: 10.1016/j.pec.2012.12.006

Radetsky, M. (2015). The hero in medicine. *Journal of the American Medical Association, 313*(17), 1715.

Roberts, P. (Writer). (2012). *Choosing wisdom* [documentary film]. J. Felton, P. Roberts, M. Plews-Ogan, J. E. Owens, & N. May (Producers). Richmond, VA: WCVE.

Schernhammer, E. S. (2005). Taking their own lives—The high rate of physician suicide. *The New England Journal of Medicine, 352*(24), 2473–2476. doi: 10.1056/NEJMp058014

Schernhammer, E. S., & Colditz, G. A. (2004). Suicide rates among physicians: A quantitative and gender assessment (meta-analysis). *The American Journal of Psychiatry, 161*(12), 2295–2302. doi: 10.1176/appi.ajp.161.12.2295

Scott, S. D., Hirschinger, L. E., Cox, K. R., McCoig, M., Brandt, J., & Hall, L. W. (2009). The natural history of recovery for the healthcare provider "second victim" after adverse patient events. *Qual Saf Health Care, 18*(5), 325–330. doi: 10.1136/qshc.2009.032870

Shanafelt, T. D., Balch, C. M., Dyrbye, L., Bechamps, G., Russell, T., Satele, D., ... Oreskovich, M. R. (2011). Special report: Suicidal ideation among American surgeons. *Archives of Surgery, 146*(1), 54–62. doi: 10.1001/archsurg.2010.292

Stack, S. (2004). Suicide risk among physicians: A multivariate analysis. *Archives of Suicide Research, 8*(3), 287–292. doi: 10.1080/13811110490436954

Staudinger, U. M., & Glück, J. (2011). Psychological wisdom research: Commonalities and differences in a growing field. *Annual Review of Psychology, 62*(1), 215–241. doi: 10.1146/annurev.psych.121208.131659

Sternberg, R. J. (ed.). (1990). *Wisdom: Its nature, origins, and development*. New York: Cambridge University Press.

Sternberg, R. J. (2000). Intelligence and wisdom. In R. J. Sternberg (ed.), *Handbook of intelligence* (pp. 631–649). New York: Cambridge University Press.

Sternberg, R. J., & Jordan, J. (eds). (2005). *A handbook of wisdom: Psychological perspectives*. New York: Cambridge University Press.

Tedeschi, R. G., & Calhoun, L. G. (2004). Posttraumatic growth: Conceptual foundations and empirical evidence. *Psychological Inquiry, 15*(1), 1–18. doi: 10.1207/s15327965pli1501_01

Wachter, R. M. (2010). Patient safety at ten: Unmistakable progress, troubling gaps. *Health Affairs, 29*(1), 165–173. doi: 10.1377/hlthaff.2009.0785

Walsh, R. (2015). What is wisdom? Cross-cultural and cross-disciplinary syntheses. *Review of General Psychology, 19*(3), 278–293. doi: 10.1037/gpr0000045

Waterman, A. D., Garbutt, J., Hazel, E., Dunagan, W. C., Levinson, W., Fraser, V. J., & Gallagher, T. H. (2007). The emotional impact of medical errors on practicing physicians in the United States and Canada. *Joint Commission Journal on Quality and Patient Safety, 33*(8), 467–476.

Wears, R. L., & Wu, A. W. (2002). Dealing with failure: The aftermath of errors and adverse events. *Annals of Emergency Medicine, 39*(3), 344–346. doi: 10.1067/mem.2002.121996

West, C. P., Huschka, M. M., Novotny, P. J., Sloan, J. A., Kolars, J. C., Habermann, T. M., & Shanafelt, T. D. (2006). Association of perceived medical errors with resident distress and empathy: A prospective longitudinal study. *Journal of the American Medical Association, 296*(9), 1071–1078. doi: 10.1001/jama.296.9.1071

Wu, A. W. (2000). Medical error: The second victim—The doctor who makes the mistake needs help too. *British Medical Journal, 320*(7237), 726–727. doi: 10.1136/bmj.320.7237.726

Wu, A. W., Boyle, D. J., Wallace, G., & Mazor, K. M. (2013). Disclosure of adverse events in the United States and Canada: An update, and a proposed framework for improvement. *J Public Health Res, 2*(e32), 186–193. doi: 10.4081/jphr.2013.e32

Wu, A. W., Folkman, S., Mcphee, S. J., & Lo, B. (1993). How house officers cope with their mistakes. *Western Journal of Medicine, 159*(5), 565–569.

13

Deviant Heroes and Social Heroism in Everyday Life

Activists and Artists

Mihaly Csikszentmihalyi, Michael Condren, and Izabela Lebuda

In most (or all?) human groups certain actions are considered heroic, and the individuals who act them out are considered heroes. This is an important feature of human societies: to recognize that there are actions that might be more important than life, actions that lift the community above the primal subsistence level where mere survival is the highest goal. When Pliny the Elder in the year 79 decided not to sail away from the erupting Mount Vesuvius, (either because he was curious to understand how eruptions worked, or because he wanted to help his friend Pomponianus, who with his family was living in Stabiae close to the volcano) and because of his asthmatic condition was killed by the fumes of the volcano, he left an example to all humanity with a clear message: if necessary, adding to knowledge, or helping a friend, are worth risking one's life for.

Changes in the way heroism has been conceived during history mirror quite well the evolution of the human species as a whole. Originally, in the first cultures that have left written records, heroism was an attribute of warriors who had risked their lives for the sake of their kin, their community, and later for the sake of country or ideology (cf. e.g., Redfield, 1975). This way of thinking about heroism corresponds to the sequence through which human identity appears to have evolved: first the identity is focused exclusively on the self, then it expands to include family, kin, neighbors, and eventually those other selves who share the language, beliefs, and nationality of the individual (Csikszentmihalyi, 1993).

Recognizing only martial heroes reflects a limited understanding of societal well-being, and in turn limits our understanding of what society needs in order to flourish. Naturally, when a group is threatened with destruction, surrounded by enemies intent on taking away their territory, the material sources of their well-being, or the cultural elements that support the group's identity, it is understandable—even essential—that those individuals who are ready to intervene in defense of their group should be recognized and admired. Under the pressure of socio-cultural competition, the production, recognition, and reward of heroism becomes a survival strategy for the group.

Of course, martial heroism is usually a zero-sum process. The hero of group A is usually the nemesis of group B, and vice-versa (Campbell & Moyers, 1988). Voltaire is thought to have said that on the cages of the wild beasts at the Zoological Garden in Paris they should hang signs warning: *Cet animal est trés méchant; quand on l'attaque, il se defend*; or, "Watch out for this savage beast; when attacked, it will defend itself!" (According to King (1904), however, the phrase more likely originated in a nineteenth-century French music-hall song.)

Actually, among the denizens of the zoo it would be difficult to speak of heroism: they sometimes do act in ways similar to what we would call heroism, as when birds on the fringe of a feeding flock will raise the alarm at the approach of a hawk or other predator, even though by so doing they often attract the attention of the hawk, and end up becoming the prey while the rest of the flock flies away to another tree. But birds, as far as we know, have no way of computing the consequences of their actions; it is just that reproductive groups of birds that have several individuals with genes that make them cry out at the sight of a predator will survive and prosper more than a group where every individual is programmed to watch out only for itself. In humans, we speak of heroism only when an act is the result of considered and conscious choice. Nevertheless, because of the complexity of human survival needs, it is difficult to determine at what point an attack is warranted, or a defense disproportionate.

When Christianity started attracting converts, the Roman Empire was on the brink of being toppled by revolts in the Germanic and Celtic regions, and by waves of nomadic hordes from the East. The emperors had to send the Roman armies from the North Sea to the Black Sea, from Britain to Turkey. At the same time, they interpreted the growth of the new religion as a threat to their supreme authority: Christians gave priority to the commandments of their God over the Emperor's power. So the Emperor tried to staunch the spread of Christianity by increasingly severe punishments, ending with the circus spectacles in which heroic Christians died for their beliefs, praising their God while starving lions devoured them. From the Emperor's point of view, the Christians were a subversive sect that came out of nowhere (or Palestine) to undermine the authority of the most successful political and cultural organization on the face of the earth. Feeding them to lions was seen by them as a humanitarian duty. From the viewpoint of the Christians, and of their successful descendants, however, the Christian martyrs were heroes who chose death rather than the spiritual destruction that would have resulted from forsaking their faith.

More recent historical examples of heroism are more inclusive, less zero-sum in nature. We are beginning to recognize as heroes individuals who risk their lives for the advancement of knowledge—like Pliny is said to have done. Galileo came close to being burned alive because of his insistence that his eyes gave him information that was different from that contained in the Bible. Marie Curie gave up her health, and then her life, in order to continue her research into radiation.

This kind of heroism reflects the work of pioneering individuals opening up new possibilities for being human. As such, it makes sense for psychologists to try to understand them—their motives, their strengths, their strategies for persevering against the forces of inertia and the threats to personal comfort, or even of survival. Yet strangely enough, psychologists have not shown much interest in understanding heroism, or the phenomenology of heroes. Until quite recently: the work of Stanley Milgram foreshadowed that of Philip Zimbardo, and their experimental approach has opened up an influential new branch of social psychology.

Here we present another approach, based on qualitative interviews collected from individuals who have acted out behavior in their everyday lives that could be considered heroic. Izabela Lebuda used interviews with Polish artists who have challenged the repressive post-World War II regime of her homeland, together with their written works, to illustrate what makes people take a stand against what they consider bad government—often reluctantly, and often at great personal cost. What caused them to take a stand? What and who helped them to persevere? How did they come to terms with the dangers and privations that their actions provoked?

The other study, from Michael Condren, describes a more muted but psychologically perhaps more difficult form of heroism: one where a person takes a stand against social conventions and institutions that seem benign or at least neutral to the majority of the population, yet are injurious to a minority. He analyzes interviews with activists involved in the gay liberation movement, who risked their jobs and standing in the community to fight for the recognition of the dangers of AIDS, and the necessity for a more active medical response to the scourge. Again, the questions are similar to those asked by Lebuda: What motivated these activists to take a stand? What and who helped them? How did they develop their strategies, and what impact did their actions have on their lives?

Obviously these two studies are just a beginning, an indication of how psychology can help understand a phenomenon that is of great importance for the health of society, and for the future evolution of humankind. It is to be hoped, I think, that psychologists begin to pursue these concerns more actively in the pursuit of a better society, and better ways of living.

Social Heroism and Civil Disobedience

The two studies discussed in this chapter focus on social heroism, and more specifically on civil disobedience. Franco, Blau, and Zimbardo (2011) describe social heroism as behavior that entails risks and dangers to the actor, which may have serious negative outcomes on a financial, social, emotional or physical level, particularly when the heroic actions are carried out over a long period of time. Social heroes may be motivated to act in order to conserve a value or standard in society that is threatened, or they may act in order to create and instill a new set of values or behaviors that are not currently embraced by the society. Social heroism focused on the defense of the existing values system can fulfill a constructive role in maintaining social order and stability. However, to establish and promote new values a different approach is necessary, and social heroes often employ civil disobedience to achieve social change (Franco, Blau, & Zimbardo, 2011).

Social heroism associated with disobedience and nonconformity is a broad category, ranging from whistleblowers (who publicly report illegal or unethical activity), to discovery heroes (who explore unknown areas of science, use novel and unproven research methods, or discover new scientific information seen as valuable to humanity), to odds beaters or underdogs, who manage to overcome some handicap or adverse condition and succeed in their objectives (Franco, Blau, & Zimbardo, 2011). These social heroes may in turn be critical in triggering social heroism in others. Analysis of the lives of Nelson Mandela, Martin Luther King Jr. and Mohandas K. Gandhi found support for the role of interpersonal relationships with peers and role models in their displays of prosocial disobedience behaviors (Morselli & Passini, 2010). The authors conclude from this that the capacity to act heroically, rather than being specific to the individual, can be seen as social constructs and learned behaviors that can be developed through social interactions.

The importance of role models in enabling individuals to dissent from and oppose the majority, and oppose unjust authorities, is supported by research on conformity, independence and minority dissent. Asch's experiments on conformity (Asch, 1956) found that the presence of a naïve or confederate dissenting partner significantly reduced conformity, and later studies have supported these findings under various conditions (Allen & Levine, 1968). Milgram's experiments also support the idea that a dissenting role model can have an impact on levels of obedience to unjust authorities (Milgram, 1963, 1965). Other studies using the Milgram paradigm (Meeus & Raaijmakers, 1986; Burger, 2009) and a meta-analysis (Packer, 2008) have found similar results. It appears that the dissenter plays an important role in other people's behaviors—in both dissent from the majority, and opposition to authority—and this importance exists in different times and contexts. Rates of obedience have remained stable over time since Milgram's first studies (Blass, 1999) and there appears to be little cross-cultural difference between obedience rates in the US and abroad, between the sexes, or in the conceptualization of the agentic state (Blass, 2012).

One way in which the dissenter may influence another's dissent or opposition is by providing a (perhaps competing) definition of the situation at hand. Latané and Darley's (1968) work on bystander intervention suggested that people look to others to make sense of an emergency situation, or to interpret an event, even when that event is potentially life-threatening to them. Later research (Darley, Teger & Lewis, 1973) found that groups of people do interact to create a definition of an unclear situation, and that inaction is perhaps the outcome of a particular interpretation of the event, rather than conformity with another's inaction. Similarly, researchers have found that helping behavior is increased when people observe others who act in a helpful manner (Bryan & Test, 1967; Test & Bryan, 1969). From this research it appears that the example of another person's behavior—a signaler who communicates his or her definition of the situation—can be a critical element in influencing how people respond to that situation.

Signalers may do this by triggering what Franco, Blau and Zimbardo (2011) call the heroic imagination. Their theoretical construct of the heroic imagination functions in three different ways: through the representation of heroes in classical literature and the public imagination; as a mindset or "mental state of anticipation and readiness for any person to act heroically when opportunities arise for heroic actions" (Franco, Blau & Zimbardo, 2011, p. 13); and as a capacity to both imagine and express a vision for a new form of social organization and standards.

From the above we can see that a range of research supports the role of other people—non-conformists, disobedients, signalers—in enabling others to dissent from the majority, oppose unjust authority, act independently, remain true to the evidence of their own senses, and perhaps in some cases the imperatives of their own values. Often, the ability to act independently, to defy authority, and to act on one's values are necessary elements of heroic actions and behavior. This is particularly true of social heroism, which is concerned with protecting existing community values thought to be threatened, or instituting a new set of social values (Franco, Blau & Zimbardo, 2011). By providing a role model and a competing definition of the status quo, other people may play an important role in facilitating social heroism, which entails more significant risks and costs to the actor, and demands sustained action over long periods of time.

The following two studies—of dissident artists and social activists—look at social heroes who demonstrate both the mindset to act, and the capacity to create alternatives visions and realities. In both groups, the important influence of other people in their decisions to engage in acts of social heroism can be seen.

Social Heroism as Civil Disobedience by Dissident Artists

To understand the social context of heroism among dissident artists, we analyzed the life stories of three artists who actively opposed the Polish Communist Party and regime. The communist regime in Poland limited freedom in most areas of everyday life, including creativity. Censorship replaced professional evaluation in every field, with ideological correctness being the main criterion. Artists were required to express "the party line" and support the existing system. Any objection to or violation of established canons could result in artists being excluded from their field, losing the right to work and publish, repression against their family, and even expulsion from their country.

In-depth biographical interviews were conducted with three artists, as part of a larger project concerning the preconditions of creativity among Polish artists (Lebuda, 2014, in press; Lebuda & Csikszentmihalyi, submitted). Although their experiences opposing the political regime were not the main research question, these participants were extremely engaged in the fight against the single party political system. As a result, the theme of creative disobedience informed a large part of their interviews. It was also a theme in the artist's published works, and appeared in other biographical materials that were also included in this analysis.

Analysis identified three main influences on creative disobedience in each artist's early socialization: accruing benefits from being disobedient early in life; having a disobedient hero in one's close family who acted as a positive role model; and coming from a family with a tradition of "being against." For adult artists, a significant role was played by having a role model with whom they had a personal relationship, and who initiated their involvement in acts of civil disobedience. These initiators were respected in their creative field, and possessed strong, admirable characters that were attractive to the artists. They were already involved in the opposition movement, and introduced these artists into the dissident *milieu*. This is similar to what Hornsey, Smith and Begg (2007) noted, that prosocial disobedience can be triggered by being part of a "counter-conforming group" reacting against the majority.

Another important factor for these artists was social identity. The feeling of belonging to a group of artists who were opposed to the system validated their sense of being on the right path artistically (Karwowski & Lebuda, in press). Being part of such a group provided these artists with opportunities to make a lasting contribution to the world, by creating works of art that had an impact on real life. Being surrounded by other artists who shared their belief that art only has meaning when it changes the world helped them to feel that they were both better persons and better artists. It also enabled them to be innovators, in the vanguard of social change. Their desire to influence a wide number of people also played an important role in their creative disobedience and social heroism. These artists considered wielding such influence to be not just a privilege, but an obligation of the artist in times of external oppression.

Individuals can act heroically without having favorable support and social conditions. However, just as certain conditions are conducive to unethical behavior, other conditions may be conducive to social heroism. Based on these analyses, there appears to be a relationship between the person, the situation requiring heroism, and the social interpretation of that situation as risky, that influences the person's decision to engage in socially heroic behavior. Heroic behavior, then, may result from an interaction between the context, the person and that person's resources. Consequently, another important element in heroic behavior—in addition to internalized shared values and the ability to analyze critically the situation—may be the ability to compare the requirements of the situation to one's own resources, and accurately assess one's ability to respond effectively. This assessment could be described as *heroic self-efficacy*, which is the belief that a person has the necessary resources (e.g. social support, resilience), to deal effectively with a risky situation that calls for social heroism. Bandura (1986) maintained that efficacy beliefs are significant contributors to levels of motivation and performance achievement, and also affect responses to potential threats, through one's perception of one's ability to respond to the threat.

Heroism as Civil Disobedience by Social Activists

For another perspective on the social context of heroism, this second study looks at social activists, and more specifically their decision to engage in civil disobedience. The sample is composed of 34 former leaders of the AIDS activist group ACT UP/NY, who challenged oppressive institutional authorities and social mores over a sustained period of time, often at great personal risk and cost. ACT UP/NY leaders are similar in many ways to Wolf and Zuckerman's (2012) definition of deviant heroes and their role as agents of justice and progressive social change. They define heroic deviance as nonconformity that increases justice, decreases suffering or violates oppressive rules in order to change normative contexts, at personal risk. Deviant heroes violate norms, actively challenge oppressive rules and unjust laws, and entail risk in order to achieve lasting positive social change. This description maps closely to what ACT UP/NY leaders and members did consistently over time.

ACT UP/NY was formed in 1987 to challenge what the group perceived as government and institutional bias, discrimination and resulting incompetence in dealing with the AIDS crisis in New York City and the US. ACT UP/NY opposed what it saw as a "business as usual" approach, based on adherence to traditional strictures and thinking about morality, behavior, sexuality, race, gender and institutional power. This traditional approach resulted in the denial of the rights of people with AIDS, as well as blocking access to life-saving services and the research funding to find effective treatments. The activists used civil disobedience and direct action to challenge the institutions and authorities tasked with handling the crisis. In doing so, members were frequently arrested, jailed and fined; threatened with violence; exposed to ridicule; risked income and jobs; and were often rejected by members of their own community as troublemakers.

The analyses discussed here are based on interviews conducted by the ACT UP Oral History Project (www.actuporalhistory.org). The oral history project captures the stories of surviving ACT UP/NY members, and provides information about their experiences, motivations and methods, as well as personal characteristics and histories. The 34 participants in this study (14 women, 20 men, mean age on joining the group = 31.8 years, age range: 17–53 years) were identified by the archivists as having been influential leaders in catalyzing, defining and leading the actions of ACT UP/NY over a period of several years. In this sense they can be considered to be exemplars who demonstrated a high level of social heroism. Interviews are semi-structured and focus on the participant's particular experiences and contributions to the group. Whilst the interview content varies, almost all interviewees were asked similar questions about their background, personal life, formative influences and experiences. Although the interviews were not focused on this research question, 33 of the 34 interviewees were explicitly asked to describe how they first came to know about and eventually join ACT UP/NY. Their responses provide us with insight into the factors in play when they decided to join ACT UP/NY, and the role the group played in their social heroism. Analysis of these leaders' first encounter with the group and their decision to join suggests that recognizing heroic qualities in others can inspire and evoke one's own heroic capacity, serve as a catalyst to heroic action, and help empower and sustain it over time.

Codes

As part of a previous research study, thirty-four interviews were open-coded to identify broad categories and themes. That open-coding revealed several themes relevant to the role of others in heroic choices and actions. These were: descriptions of epiphany moments when the participants first encountered ACT UP; feeling empowered by associating with other people in the group; and feelings of elevation (Haidt, 2003; Algoe & Haidt, 2009) when they first encountered or interacted with members of ACT UP/NY. For this study, the interviews were coded for three variables: epiphany; empowerment; elevation.

Epiphany was defined as a moment of sudden clarity, recognition, or insight; of finding something that one had been searching for. Often participants described a feeling of "finding my home," "finding my people," "falling in love." Empowerment was defined as feeling more resourceful, powerful and courageous through being part of the group, which enabled them to tap into personal and collective resources more effectively than they could as an individual. Many participants described heightened feelings of camaraderie and community that enabled them to transcend personal limitations. Elevation (Algoe & Haidt, 2009) was defined as feeling emotionally moved by the virtuous acts of ACT UP/NY members, and inspired and motivated to act virtuously oneself. Often this occurred when the participant saw ACT UP/NY marches, members being arrested, or members directly challenging institutional authorities. Table 13.1 shows the percentage of participants who mentioned these three codes.

Epiphany

Thirty-three of the 34 subjects in this analysis were asked by the interviewer to describe how they came to join ACT UP/NY. Often this was the first time they went to a meeting, or when they came across a demonstration or poster on the street. Twenty-two participants (64.7% of the sample) described that experience as being a powerful moment of epiphany, with several

Table 13.1 Frequency of Codes Mentioned

Code	%	n
Epiphany	64.7	22
Empowerment	79.4	27
Elevation	44.1	15

Note: N = 34. Percentage of participants mentioning each code.

common elements. Many participants described it as a moment of clarity: that ACT UP crystallized what they had been feeling or thinking about the AIDS crisis. The majority described the experience as finding the answer that they had been seeking for some time. Another common feature of this epiphany moment was a feeling of finding their place or their home. The following quotes communicate this epiphany experience.

> I remember walking into Cooper Union, in the Great Hall. And I had just never seen anything like that ... And I walked in that room, and you could palpably feel the sense of urgency; that there was nothing hypothetical about it. And it was also, to my very academic mind, just a fabulous militia of thinkers, and people willing to take their strength, and what they could think, and then do something with it. It was pragmatism at the highest level. And I was just thrilled by it ... I was like one of those lost kids, that just found a perfect place, for everything ... I was desperately wanting to be part of the world, in a meaningful way. And here it was. And I think from that spring, of 1990, until the spring of 1993, that's all I really did, was ACT UP. I worked, I had jobs, I found a way to support myself. But it was all to get me to those Monday-night meetings, and all the other meetings I went to, from that point on.
>
> *(Anna Blume)*

> I walked up on that rally, and I heard people talking, and I thought, they are talking about America; they are talking New York; they are talking identity; they are talking about what's wrong—exactly in a way that I want to speak. And, you know, I had been in New York for a year, and couldn't find a place to be a political activist. And there it was.
>
> *(Alexandra Juhasz)*

> I walked in, and there were a couple hundred people at the community center, doing what they did then. And I fell in love. It was truly love at first sight for me, in that room. And I immediately recognized it as a bunch of cranky individualists who clearly couldn't get along with any authority figure anywhere and were just all there, being themselves and arguing with each other, and getting stuff done, and having a great time. I never looked back. I just immediately started going to the meetings regularly and got arrested for the first time, at the end of that month ... And got arrested with a couple of hundred people.
>
> *(Ann Northrop)*

These quotes express the profound impact of this moment of recognition—of home, kindred spirits, a worldview, a way to act that corresponded with and expressed their thoughts and feelings. For many of these individuals, their first encounter with the group was a "light bulb" moment of recognition, as expressed in these quotes:

> So, we went to ACT UP ... And it was then—both of us just went through a real eye-opening transformation on all of these issues. Suddenly, everything we'd kind of been

having—perceiving, but couldn't get the words out about, they had all the words. And the facts and the figures and the data.

(Michelangelo Signorile)

That was a very profound experience for me and it changed a lot of things. First, it was then and there that I decided I would become a citizen of this gay community, whatever that meant… That was the pivotal turning point in my life around that time.

(Greg Bordowitz)

ACT UP/NY's definition of the causes and solutions to the AIDS crisis differed radically from the official discourses about, and traditional social responses to, the disease and to the communities affected by it. As such, it provided a catalyst—and a vehicle—for these individuals to respond to the AIDS crisis in a way that corresponded with their own experiences, beliefs and values.

I watched Vito and a few others get arrested. I'm going to say there were 12 people who were arrested that day. But, it was exciting. I had found an outlet. I had found an articulation of that anger, of that sense of injustice, how to express my feelings.

(Jay Blotcher)

For many this felt like they were coming home, often to a place they had not realized they were seeking:

I remember being really nervous; because I really liked it. And I really thought, I thought, oh, oh, I've got to, I, I, I'm home. This is, I'm home. And then, and that made me really nervous, because I had to figure out, I need to find a place here, and how am I going to do it?

(David Barr)

Interviewer: So, what did you see when you got there [Monday night meeting]?
AJ: Exactly what I wanted to see—exactly what I wanted … I felt like I was in a place where I wanted to be, in a place that I wanted to belong.

(Alexandra Juhasz)

Empowerment

Twenty-seven interviewees (79.4%) mentioned the importance of the empowering effect that ACT UP/NY had on themselves and others. (Often this was mentioned in response to the question: what do you think was the group's greatest achievement?) This empowerment appeared to occur in several ways. The group provided a vehicle through which to act and express, and amplified individual resources, by aggregating and making them available to everyone in the group, as this quote illustrates.

If you did something through ACT UP, it had infrastructure, it had support. If you did it anywhere else, it didn't.

(Alexandra Juhasz)

For others, the sense of camaraderie and deep community that grew up enabled them to surpass their previous limits, take courageous action that they would not have considered themselves capable of previously.

And so you had this feeling, like as long as you could read and think and have your focus on what will actually help people; that you could do this. And that you had to do it, and you needed to do it. Plus, people at very high levels were listening to you, almost immediately. And, people that were affected by the disease wanted to hear what you had to say, and wanted this information to help them make decisions, like tomorrow. And so you didn't get caught up in insecurities and doubts. You didn't really have time for that ... we were immersed ... it was all so integrated that it fueled a sense of urgency and confidence; and the decisions you were making were really about life and death, and we just made them.

(Anna Blume)

As mentioned above, many of these people who went on to become leaders of the group started as individuals dealing with strong emotions of anger, outrage and grief at the injustice they perceived. For them, ACT UP/NY members provided each other with the emotional support they needed to sustain action over time.

I really did feel, I think a lot of us did, like we were saving lives, and I think we actually were. We definitely were. But as anyone who went through it knows, and I think it's worth saying to remind people, that it was a different time. People were slipping through our fingers like grains of sand. There wasn't a day that went by when somebody didn't die. And, I think I really did feel like I could prevent that and wasn't able to, and I don't know what I would have done without ACT UP, because there were other people who felt the same way and helped me through it or made it better or made it slower, the death ...

(Avram Finkelstein)

And slowly but surely, ACT UP became a rock for me. Because when I was in there, it was empowering. Outside of the ACT UP rooms, I was vulnerable ... ACT UP made me feel there was something that could be done. It gave me hope; it was intellectual; it was emotional. I fell in and out of love in those rooms. And that was, that felt good. That was my humanity coming out.

(Patricia Navarro)

For some, their experiences of being activists in ACT UP/NY—articulating and acting on their values and principles, and taking risks to fight oppression—was a means of personal development that was empowering. Many mentioned that the group drew from them courage and personal abilities that they never knew they had, and would not have found on their own, as described by this activist.

It was not long before a hundred to two hundred people were meeting in that room every Monday night. Pretty soon, it would be four hundred and even more. But, when you get a hundred people meeting every week, you have enough there to start something and people become courageous awfully quickly. I certainly am not alone in saying—everyone who was active in ACT UP wound up drawing on resources they had inside them, that they never dreamed they had—just never dreamed they had. But, it only could have come out of them because they were locking arms with a hundred other people, at that point ... So none of it came naturally, but ... within ACT UP so many people found reserves within themselves that they never knew they did.

(Jim Eigo)

Elevation

This empowerment may be linked to the experiences of elevation that were mentioned by 15 activists in this sample (44.1%; see Table 13.1). The example of other ACT UP/NY members behaving in ways that they found morally uplifting inspired these activists to join in and take sustained action.

> I do a lot of First Amendment advocacy, so I was involved with David Wojnarowicz and his estate and Felix Gonzalez-Torres—and all the artists who were dying, and what to do with their art. It was just terribly, terribly, terribly sad. But also, this feeling of—just the courage they gave me, the courage they gave me—these men who were dying, because they had no fear.
>
> *(Mary Dorman)*

> [I]n retrospect, I think I was kind of—I don't know if "timid" is the right word, but I thought this was just so beyond what I could imagine actually being able to pull off. And I would be amazed, time after time, that these things would get pulled off, that these demonstrations would happen the way they were supposed to, and people would come. And the arrests would happen, and the bail would be posted. The way, the machine of it, just amazed me. And just people taking those risks. Over and over again, I was just always awed by it.
>
> *(Risa Denenberg)*

Often this experience of elevation happened when they first encountered the group; for some, it happened or continued to happen through ongoing involvement with the organization. Feelings of awe (mentioned in the second quote above) are associated with elevation experiences, and have been found to prompt prosocial behaviors that are oriented to improving the welfare of others (Piff, Dietz, Feinberg, Stancato & Keltner, 2015).

This morally uplifting inspiration may be a part of what helped sustain their social heroism over long periods, despite great challenges and personal cost. For these leaders, their elevation experiences may have acted as a kind of "heroic booster shot." This idea is similar to Allison and Goethals' (in press) proposed heroic leadership dynamic framework, which says that hero narratives fulfill two functions, epistemic and energizing. Heroes energize us by, among other things, providing moral elevation experiences, and inspiring others to take action. For many of these activists, it may be that energizing boosts of elevation enabled them to sustain their social heroism over time.

Discussion

These studies of artists and activists illustrate the important role that other people can play in an individual's decision to engage in, and sustain, socially heroic behavior. This can take different forms. For the artists, having a personal relationship with a dissenting role model or initiator was an important factor in their decision to act. Their sense of identity as an artist was also closely tied up with their social heroism. For the activists, role models were also important, although having a personal relationship with them was not prominent in their discussions. Instead they functioned as triggers of recognition and action, empowering peers, and inspiring examples, as the analysis of epiphany, empowerment and elevation indicates. For both groups, other people—in the form of families, initiators, exemplars or communities—were instrumental in their decision to engage in and sustain heroic behavior over long periods of time, and endure the serious negative consequences of their defiance. The following theoretical model (Figure 13.1) incorporates the findings from both of these studies in an attempt to conceptually organize the

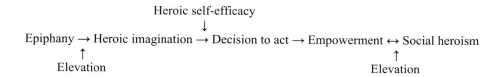

Figure 13.1 Proposed Theoretical Model of the Relationship Between Epiphany Experiences, the Heroic Imagination, Heroic self-efficacy, Empowerment, Elevation and Social Heroism

different elements involved in the decision to engage in social heroism, and sustain that engagement over time.

This model combines elements of cognition (epiphany), affect (elevation), behavior intention (empowerment), and behavior (heroism). The epiphany experience triggers what Franco, Blau and Zimbardo (2011) call the heroic imagination: a mental state of readiness to act heroically, and a capacity to imagine and express a new vision. This epiphany can happen through seeing others acting heroically. The triggering of the heroic imagination may be moderated by the individual's experience of elevation—the extent to which the person is emotionally moved by the virtuous acts of these heroes, and inspired to act virtuously (Haidt, 2003; Algoe & Haidt, 2009). The individual then decides to act; this decision may be moderated by what we earlier termed Heroic Self-Efficacy, the belief that one has the necessary resources to deal effectively with a situation requiring heroism. Taking action with others empowers the individual on his or her path to becoming a social hero, and in turn leads to more heroic action. (Empowerment may also reinforce heroic self-efficacy through enactment experiences of social heroism.) The empowerment process may be moderated by ongoing elevation experiences that energize and inspire the individual's social heroism over time, notwithstanding challenges and negative consequences. Social heroism sustained over time may lead to more empowerment, which in turn enables more social heroism.

Linking this model to the earlier discussion of the role of signaling dissenters in prosocial disobedience, it may be that heroes are extremely powerful signalers because they perform three important functions. First, they define a given situation as one that requires heroic behavior. Second, they provide a model of that behavior and the resources required. Finally, they trigger the heroic imagination in those who have developed a heroic mindset and inspire them to take action. They achieve this by identifying and defining the heroic opportunity, and by doing so, they demonstrate the means by which one's inner beliefs can correspond with one's outer behavior (Nemeth & Chiles, 1988).

Postscript

Over time, both the artists and the activists achieved many of their objectives. In Poland, the Communist Party's control of society gave way to democracy and freedom of creative expression. Although many of its members died of AIDS, ACT UP/NY also saw many of its goals accomplished, such as faster development of effective drug therapies, increased access to treatments and services, and changes in deep-seated social and institutional attitudes towards minorities. The activist leaders discussed here moved on in their lives; most were no longer active in the group, or indeed in social activism. For many, the loss of community, and of the collective power of the group, has been strongly felt on a personal, emotional level. It has also negatively impacted their capacity to act in a socially heroic way. This is poignantly expressed by one of the activists in this quote:

I've gone through very, very sad and dark moments not having something larger than myself to be connected to—very, very difficult moments—extremely painful—feelings of loss, after leaving ACT UP, were very pronounced ... I exist, almost exclusively now, as an individual in the world. I do not have an affinity group, you know—that I can do things with. So, that makes a very big difference in my approach to those kinds of challenges.

(Maria Maggenti)

References

Algoe, S. B., & Haidt, J. (2009). Witnessing excellence in action: the "other-praising" emotions of elevation, gratitude, and admiration. *The Journal of Positive Psychology*, *4*(2), 105–127.

Allen, V. L., & Levine, J. M. (1968). Social Support, Dissent and Conformity. *Sociometry*, *31*(2), 138–149. doi:10.2307/2786454

Allison, S. T., & Goethals, G. R. (in press). Hero worship: The elevation of the human spirit. *Journal for the Theory of Social Behaviour* [online early view]. doi:10.1111/jtsb.12094

Asch, S. E. (1956). Studies of independence and conformity: I. A minority of one against a unanimous majority. *Psychological Monographs: General And Applied*, *70*(9), 1-70. doi:10.1037/h0093718

Bandura, A. (1986). From thought to action: Mechanisms of personal agency. *New Zealand Journal of Psychology*, *15*(1), 1–17.

Blass, T. (1999). The Milgram Paradigm After 35 Years: Some Things We Now Know About Obedience to Authority. *Journal of Applied Social Psychology*, *29*(5), 955–978.

Blass, T. (2012). A cross-cultural comparison of studies of obedience using the Milgram paradigm: A review. *Social and Personality Psychology Compass*, *6*(2), 196–205. doi:10.1111/j.1751-9004.2011.00417.x

Bryan, J. H., & Test, M. A. (1967). Models and helping: Naturalistic studies in aiding behavior. *Journal of Personality and Social Psychology*, *6*(4, Pt.1), 400–407. doi:10.1037/h0024826

Burger, J. M. (2009). Replicating Milgram: Would people still obey today? *American Psychologist*, *64*(1), 1–11. doi:10.1037/a0010932

Campbell, J., & Moyers, B. (1988). *The power of myth*. New York: Doubleday.

Csikszentmihalyi, M. (1993). *The evolving self*. New York: HarperCollins.

Darley, J. M., Teger, A. I., & Lewis, L. D. (1973). Do groups always inhibit individuals' responses to potential emergencies? *Journal of Personality and Social Psychology*, *26*(3), 395–399. doi:10.1037/h0034450

Franco, Z. E., Blau, K. & Zimbardo, P. G. (2011). Heroism: A conceptual analysis and differentiation between heroic action and altruism. *Review of General Psychology*, *15*(2), 99–113. doi: 10.1037/a0022672

Glazer, M. P., & Glazer, P. M. (1999). On the trail of courageous behavior. *Sociological Inquiry*, *69*(2), 276–295., 276–295

Haidt, J. (2003). Elevation and the positive psychology of morality. In C. L. M. Keyes & J. Haidt (eds), *Flourishing: Positive psychology and the life well-lived* (pp. 275–289). Washington, DC: American Psychological Association. doi: 10.1037/10594-012

Hornsey, M. J., Smith, J. R., & Begg, D. I. (2007). Effects of norms among those with moral conviction: Counter-conformity emerges on intentions but not behaviors. *Social Influence*, *2*, 244–268.

Karwowski, M., & Lebuda, I. (in press). Creative self-concept: A surface characteristic of creative personality. In: G. Feist, R. Reiter-Palmon & J. C. Kaufman (eds), *Handbook of creativity and personality*. Cambridge: Cambridge University Press.

King, W. F. H. (1904). *A polyglot manual of historical and literary sayings: Noted passages in poetry and prose, phrases, proverbs, and bons mots*. London: J. Whitaker & Sons.

Latané, B., & Darley, J. M. (1968). Group inhibition of bystander intervention in emergencies. *Journal of Personality and Social Psychology*, *10*(3), 215–221. doi:10.1037/h0026570

Lebuda, I. (in press). Political pathologies and big-C creativity—eminent Polish creators' experience of restrictions under the communist regime. In: V. P. Glaveanu (ed.), *The Palgrave Handbook of Creativity and Culture Research*.

Lebuda, I. (2014). Big-C research—The big challenge? Reflections from research into eminent creativity in the light of the investment theory of creativity. *Creativity: Theories-Research-Application*, *1*, 33–45.

Lebuda, I., & Csikszentmihalyi, M. (submitted). All you need is love: The importance of partner and family relations to eminent creators' well-being and success. Manuscript submitted for publication.

Meeus, W. H., & Raaijmakers, Q. A. (1986). Administrative obedience: Carrying out orders to use psychological-administrative violence. *European Journal of Social Psychology*, *16*(4), 311–324. doi:10.1002/ejsp.2420160402

Milgram, S. (1963). Behavioral study of obedience. *The Journal of Abnormal and Social Psychology*, *67*(4),

371–378. doi:10.1037/h0040525.

Milgram, S. (1965). Some conditions of obedience and disobedience to authority. *Human Relations*, *18*(1), 57–76. doi:10.1177/001872676501800105.

Morselli, D., & Passini, S. (2010). Avoiding crimes of obedience: A comparative study of the autobiographies of M. K. Gandhi, Nelson Mandela, and Martin Luther King, Jr. *Peace and Conflict*, *16*, 295–319.

Nemeth, C., & Chiles, C. (1988). Modeling courage: The role of dissent in fostering independence. *European Journal of Social Psychology*, *18*(3), 275–280.

Packer, D. J. (2008). Identifying systematic disobedience in Milgram's obedience experiments: A meta-analytic review. *Perspectives On Psychological Science*, *3*(4), 301–304. doi:10.1111/j.1745-

Piff, P. K., Dietz, P., Feinberg, M., Stancato, D. M., & Keltner, D. (2015). Awe, the small self, and prosocial behavior. *Journal Of Personality And Social Psychology*, *108*(6), 883–899. doi:10.1037/pspi0000018

Redfield, J. (1975). *Nature and Culture in the Iliad: The Tragedy of Hector*. Chicago, IL: University of Chicago Press.

Test, M. A., & Bryan, J. H. (1969). The effects of dependency, models, and reciprocity upon subsequent helping behavior. *The Journal Of Social Psychology*, *78*(2), 205-212. doi:10.1080/00224545.1969.9922357

Wolf, B., & Zuckerman, P. (2012). Deviant heroes: Nonconformists as agents of justice and social change. *Deviant Behavior*, *33*(8), 639–654. doi:10.1080/01639625.2011.647587

14

To Become or Not to Become?
Existential Courage and the Quest for Identity

Roderick M. Kramer

> There become a few magical moments where you have to have confidence in yourself ... When I dropped out of Harvard and said, "Come work for me," there was a certain kind of self-confidence in that. You have a few moments like that where trusting yourself and saying, "Yes, this can come together"—you have to seize on that because not many come along.
>
> *Bill Gates (2012, p. 110)*

> [H]have the courage to follow your heart and intuition. They somehow already know what you truly want to become. Everything else is secondary.
>
> *Steve Jobs (quoted in Beahm, 2011, p. 89)*

When it comes to both elegance and concision, few definitions rise to the standard of Hemingway's crisp characterization of courage as, "Grace under pressure" (Baker, 2003). In more conventional academic terms, Peterson and Seligman (2004) defined courage in terms of "the exercise of will to accomplish goals in the face of opposition, either external or internal" (p. 199). Regardless of how one defines it, courage has long been counted as among the most revered qualities human beings can possess. Throughout history and across cultures, the veneration of individuals who display courage has been virtually universal (Allison & Goethals, 2011; Campbell, 2008; Coles, 2010; Goethals & Allison, 2012; Moran, 2007; Pury &Lopez, 2010). For reasons both valid and useful, societies celebrate those individuals who display grace under pressure—and especially when that grace is exceptional and exhibited under extreme threat to life, limb or spirit.

In focusing so heavily on extraordinary displays of courage in moments of unusual adversity or threat, however, one might mistakenly conclude that courage is a scarce virtue or an uncommon trait among human beings—an attribute reserved for those who happen to be unusually brave or valorous. As a result, one might fail to consider that, in less extreme or dramatic form, acts of courage may be both prevalent and noteworthy. For example, when a young married woman in her mid-twenties, raised in Japan by a traditional family and expected to fulfill her assigned social role as wife, decides instead to divorce her husband, alienate her family, and moves to the United States in order to pursue her secret longing to acquire an MBA degree and become a high-tech entrepreneur, a genuine act of courage has occurred. To be sure, courageous choices of this magnitude might seem minor and even of trivial import from the perspective of outside observers. For the individual making such choices, however, they may carry all the psychological hallmarks of genuine courage.

In this chapter, I characterize such longings as *identity aspirations* or *strivings* and construe their pursuit as a form of *existential* courage. Further, I propose that such courage is no less important in today's rapidly changing and uncertain world than the more usual acts of physical and moral courage which societies so often venerate. In fact, as I elaborate later in this chapter, identity striving is a form of personal courage whose importance is arguably growing as people around the globe increasingly expect their lives to feel meaningful and consequential, but find the pathway to such lives fraught with uncertainty and challenge (e.g., Emmons, 1999; Seligman, 2011; Wrzesniewski, Rozin, &Bennett, 2003).

More broadly, I suggest that the study of this particular form of courage is important for several reasons. First, by exploring the full range of courageous behaviors in which human beings engage, including those that might seem ordinary or everyday, social scientists might move toward a more comprehensive understanding of courage. In mapping this unexplored territory, for example, scholars may progress toward a more thorough understanding of courage's myriad psychological well-springs, as well as the social processes and situational triggers that prompt courageous action, especially among ordinary individuals pursuing personally meaningful but challenging goals in life. Equally importantly, research on the antecedents and consequences of such courage might contribute to our knowledge of how it might be learned, inculcated, and even taught.

With these diverse considerations in mind, the present chapter has several specific aims. First, it explores the antecedents and consequences of existential courage, operationalized here in terms of individuals' willingness to take psychological and social risks in the pursuit of desired but challenging future identities. A second goal is to explore the potential for such courage to be developed through self-designed behavioral experiments—a process I characterize as "self-nudging." Most simply stated, the question I explore is, "Can individuals nudge themselves towards greater courage in pursuing their identity longings or aspirations?" A third goal of this study is to investigate some of the psychological and social consequences of these experiments in self-nudging. In particular, can such experiments be efficacious with respect to promoting substantive and enduring self-change, and, if so, along what dimensions?

To address these goals, the chapter is organized as follows. I first provide a brief, general overview of the history of research on courage. I then elaborate on why identity striving represents an important but under-studied form of courage. Next, I present the results of a study exploring the kinds of future identities university students aspire to achieve, as well as the specific identity-relevant concerns those strivings make salient. Additionally, the study explores the use of self-designed behavioral experiments aimed at nudging students toward successful pursuit of those longed-for identities. I conclude by discussing some of the theoretical, methodological, and applied implications of this research.

Identity Strivings as a Form of Existential Courage: Some Conceptual Lineage

To lay a foundation for the argument that *identity strivings* constitute a form of existential courage worthy of further scholarly scrutiny, it might be helpful first to briefly survey the landscape of contemporary research on courage. Because space limitations preclude a comprehensive review of the various conceptions of courage that have been proffered by social scientists, interested readers are directed to Pury and Lopez (2010) for an excellent introduction to this literature. In an early contribution, Shelp (1984) defined courage in terms of "the ability to act for a meaningful (noble, good, or practical) cause, despite experiencing the fear associated with perceived threat exceeding the available resources" (pp. 4–5). Subsequently, Pury and Woodard

(2009) advanced the definition of courage as the "intentional pursuit of a worthy goal despite the perception of personal threat and uncertain outcome" (p. 247). Finally, Biswas-Diener (2012) more recently defined courage as "the willingness to act toward a moral or worthwhile goal despite the presence of risk, uncertainty, and fear" (p. 10). Although differing slightly in emphases, these varied definitions converge on the recognition that courage, as a psychological state, entails some mixture of risk, uncertainty, and fear.

Historically, scholars studying courage have generally focused the majority of their attention on either *physical* or *moral* acts of courage (e.g., Coles, 2010; Moran, 2007; Staub, 2015). I briefly consider each of these research streams in turn.

Physical Courage

Acts of physical courage entail individuals risking bodily harm or even death on behalf of other individuals in peril. Not surprisingly, much of the early literature on this form courage focused on displays of physical courage in extreme situations, particularly during wartime (Moran, 2007). As Peterson and Seligman (2004) noted in their discussion of such research, "The historical prototype of the character strength of bravery is the physical valor shown by warriors on the battlefield" (p. 199).

More recent research on physical courage, however, has kept pace with the times, focusing on displays of physical courage in the midst of such events as natural disasters or terrorist attacks (Staub, 2015). As this more recent research amply documents, acts of physical courage often seem to occur somewhat spontaneously, as when an individual bystander reflexively enters a burning building to rescue a trapped child or jumps into the water to rescue a struggling swimmer during a shark attack. Similarly, the New York firefighters who rushed to others' aid during the September 11th terrorist attacks were widely praised for their unhesitating physical courage in ascending the burning towers.

Moral Courage

The study of moral courage has typically focused on individuals exhibiting extreme courage in the face of intense social opposition, ridicule, or risk to their social status or standing in a community (Staub, 2015). Acts of moral courage in this vein include standing up for less powerful but endangered individuals or groups, such as interceding to stop the bullying of victims, and instances of corporate and governmental whistleblowing—thereby risking one's professional livelihood or identity. With such examples in mind, Staub (2015) defined *moral courage* in terms of "the courage to express important values in words and actions, even in the face of opposition, potential disapproval, and ostracism or a violent response" (p. 47). There also exists, it is worth noting, a more narrow but nonetheless relevant genre of research focused on political courage, which explores moral courage within political contexts (see, e.g., Beschloss, 2008; Kennedy, 1955).

The distinction between moral and physical courage, to be sure, is not clear-cut or absolute, as moral courage may sometimes require physical courage, where one literarily "stands up" (or sits down!) to confront one's adversaries, as did Martin Luther King and the civil rights demonstrators during the early 1960s. As Staub (2015) has noted in this regard, "Moral courage may require physical courage, but often it requires only what might be called psychological courage" (p. 47). Irrespective of these variations in its physical or moral manifestations, however, courage entails the willingness to confront and master one's fears and anxieties in the face of an uncertain and dangerous unfolding moment.

With this brief conceptual backdrop of extant research in mind, I turn now to elaborating on the concept of existential courage—especially the particular variant, identity striving, I explore in the present research—and why such merits further attention.

Identity Strivings as Existential Courage

The topic of existential courage, especially when compared to physical and moral courage, has received scant systematic attention from psychologists, despite some early suggestions as to its importance in human development (Maslow, 1962; May, 1975; Rogers, 1961). Indeed, early attempts to conceptualize existential courage are encountered primarily in the philosophical literature, and emphasize its theological moorings. Most prominently, the Christian existentialist Paul Tillich (1952) conceptualized existential courage in terms of "the courage to be." Tillich linked such courage to what he characterized as the "ontological anxiety of human being" (p. 155). In his terms, this *courage to be* is manifested as "the self-affirmation of being in spite of the fact of nonbeing" (p. 155). Tillich goes on to make the vital point that such courage, "always entails a risk ... which is experienced in the anxiety of fate and death [and] which is present in the anxiety of emptiness and meaninglessness" (p. 155).

Subsequently, Maddi (2004) advanced a more psychologically grounded and empirically tractable conception of existential courage. Many consequential life decisions human beings confront, he suggested, "involve choosing a future, unfamiliar path, or repeating a past, familiar path":

> Although choosing the future is most consistent with continuing to elaborate life's meaning, it also brings ontological anxiety, as expressed in fear of uncertainty and possible failure. Consequently ... *to choose the future regularly requires courage.*
>
> (Maddi, 2004, p. 279, emphases added)

Without this requisite courage, Maddi goes on to argue, "one may choose the past regularly, which stagnates the quest for meaning" (p. 279). The hallmark of existential courage, according to this conception, is the individual's willingness to choose that path in life which accepts, even embraces, the prospect of psychological and social risks in order to grow and thrive. In order to pursue a longed-for future self, according to this view, one may have to leave the safe haven of one's familiar harbors in pursuit of a coveted, even if highly uncertain, port.

From the vantage point of Maddi's general conception of existential courage, my research focuses on a specific subset of existentially courageous choices, viz., those manifested in individuals' pursuit of desired or longed-for future identities. As noted earlier, I characterize the pursuit of such desired identities as *identity striving*, and focus particularly on those identities that individuals consider especially central, meaningful and consequential to their sense of self. Thus defined, identity strivings reflect individuals' self-conscious and deliberate pursuit of imagined, valued and desired future identities.

To unpack this construct of identity striving a bit further, I draw a distinction between the pursuit of *holistic future identities* and the cultivation of specific *identity-relevant attributes* associated with those holistic identities. A holistic sense of identity, according to Gardner, Csikszentmihalyi, and Damon (2001), reflects "a person's deeply felt convictions about who she is, and what matters most to her existence as a worker, a citizen, and a human being" (p. 10). A holistic future identity, then, is a "full-fledged," coherent identity one hopes to achieve or attain. For example, one might aspire to become a successful screenwriter, social entrepreneur, hedge fund manager, spouse, parent, or university professor. As these particular examples make clear, the set of holistic future identities encompass consequential *professional identities* as well as *personal* and *social identities* toward which an individual might aspire.

Specific identity attributes, in contrast, are perceived individual components of an individual's holistic identities. For example, an individual might endeavor to become *more of* something that supports the attainment of a given holistic identity. As one illustration, the Japanese student described at the beginning of this chapter (and an actual participant in the study reported here) aspired to become one of Japan's "first globally successful female business entrepreneurs working in the high-tech space" (her holistic identity aspiration as articulated in her own words in her obituary). Achieving this aim, she recognized, would require her to become more *assertive* and more *confident* in her business negotiations and team leadership (two specific identity attributes).

An assumption of the present research is that the successful development of specific identity-relevant attributes, as well as ultimate success in the pursuit of holistic identities, almost always entails some level of psychological and social risk-taking. The risks reside in the very real prospect of some personal or social "costs" associated with that pursuit or striving, such as the prospect of embarrassment, anxiety, disappointment, ridicule, a discomforting sense of heightened public self-consciousness, and even outright failure. As an example, for an extremely introverted or acutely shy individual, learning to lead a company and promote it successfully may constitute a daunting self-perceived bar to clear (cf., Zimbardo, 1990). As I argue next, such psychological and social risk-taking in the pursuit of coveted future identities may have particular salience and relevance for one demographically large and very important population—a population, moreover, of considerable interest to researchers these days.

Identity Strivings among Emerging Adults

Within the past decade, there has been increasing interest in the phase of life broadly construed of as *emerging adulthood* (e.g., Arnett, 2000, 2014; Arnett & Fishel, 2014; Arum & Roksa, 2011, 2014; Settersten, Furstenberg & Ruben, 2005). As defined by Arnett (2014), emerging adulthood is the period of life situated roughly between the end of adolescence and the onset of mature adulthood. Although different studies have employed different age ranges when operationally defining emerging adulthood, generally the periods examined have spanned the years from post-high school through the college years or shortly thereafter (i.e., roughly 18–29-year-old individuals).

More important than chronological age, however, is the "psychological stage" of development, with this phase of life usually conceived of as that period when young people have not reached full financial independence from their parents, have not married, have not had children, have not decided where they will put down their roots geographically, and are still actively deciding what will be their professional identity or work.

As Arnett (2014) has noted, emerging adulthood is a recent phenomenon, and should be thought of less as a distinct, universal phase of human development (in the conventional Eriksonian sense), then as a *cultural product*. Emerging adulthood constitutes a cultural product, Arnett posits, because it reflects a confluence of social and economic conditions which afford, in some societies, the postponement or deferral of true adulthood. In particular, he argues:

> What is mainly required for emerging adulthood to exist is a relatively high median age of entering marriage and parenthood...[allowing] the late teens and most of the twenties to be a time of exploration and instability, a self-focused age, and an age of possibilities.
>
> (Arnett, 2014, p. 21)

It is an age, he goes on to suggest, when identity is both sought and formed, even if only in protean and potentially transient terms. Emerging adulthood, in short, is an intense period of *becoming*, or perhaps more precisely *striving to become*, for many individuals.

This important period of life is thus ripe for exploring the psychology of identity striving for several reasons. First, as obvious from the characterization earlier, emerging adults face a series of vital and exciting choices. They are also choices, however, which may appear potentially daunting. As Settersten aptly noted in this regard:

> The transition into adulthood has, in the span of a few decades, moved from highly standardized to being highly individualized. Individualization brings new freedom to live in ways that are aligned with one's wishes and interests, but it also brings a host of new risks, many of which are not known in advance.
>
> *(Settersten, 2015, p. 122)*

The roads that may be taken may loom excitingly diverse and wide open. Yet, there are few sign posts to guide one's choice at each fork in the road.

With this conceptual preamble in mind, I suggest that Masters of Business Administration students (MBAs) represent ideal candidates for exploring many of these issues associated with identity striving and emergent adulthood. While some individuals return to business school knowing exactly the specific career path they wish to pursue (e.g., careers in private equity or investment banking), a fair number return to school unsure of what they wish to do with their lives, but convinced that the two-years it will take to acquire an MBA degree will provide ample opportunity for self-discovery, as well as the acquisition of the essential skills (e.g., leadership, negotiation, social influence, etc.) needed to pursue whatever avocation they eventually choose. Such individuals, in other words, return to the MBA program not to pursue a chosen path, but to discover, find or create one, much as Erikson (1968) famously suggested when he talked about the college years as a "psychosocial moratorium" (p. 156). They are fully cognizant of being in a stage of emerging (and hopefully nearly incipient!) adulthood as they wrestle with decisions related to their professional identity, choosing a life-partner, deciding on a geographical location, etc.

To recap, the present research had several specific empirical aims. First, it sought to empirically discern the kinds of *identity strivings* students would opt to pursue when afforded the opportunity, with individuals' identity strivings operationalized in terms of both (1) their *holistic* identity aspirations and (2) the specific *identity-relevant attributes* they construed as significant and worthy of further development in the quest to realize their holistic identity aspirations. Second, the research sought to examine the efficacy of an experiential approach to existential risk-taking (viz., behavioral experiments in "self-nudging") in helping students pursue their respective identity aspirations. Third, the study sought to explore the perceived psychological consequences of these behavioral experiments, including whether individuals perceived their experiments as successful in terms of achieving significant and enduring change in the desired direction, and additionally what individuals felt they had learned or gained from their self-designed behavioral experiments, including any perceived cognitive, motivational and/or affective benefits.

Stalking an Elusive Quarry: An Inductive Approach to Studying Identity Strivings

To achieve the empirical aims described in the previous section, I developed an "identity lab" as a supportive setting where students could work individually and collaboratively on their respective identity strivings.[1] In particular, the lab was designed as a reflective and experiential resource where students could (1) identify and research their desired future identities, (2) develop an inventory or assessment of identity-relevant attributes that support the realization of those desired future identities, (3) design behavioral experiments to explore and further develop those self-selected identity attributes, and, finally, (4) consolidate their learnings from their experiments through reflection and assessment.

One hundred and twenty MBAs (including both male and female students, average age 27 years old) participated in the lab. To stimulate students to think holistically about their desired future identities, they were asked first to write their own obituaries. They were told their obituaries should describe in detail the "full and complete" lives they hoped to have lived by the time of their death. To stimulate their thinking about the content of a "good" obituary, students were encouraged to peruse obituaries in the *New York Times* and *The Economist* (both outlets famous for the quality of their obituaries). Students were also asked to write their own eulogies (i.e., the sort of eulogy they hoped that someone would give on their behalf at their funeral).

The obituary and eulogy tasks function much like *gedankenexperiments* or "thought experiments." Importantly, they tend to stimulate and elicit different kinds of imagination with respect to individuals' future selves and lives. In particular, the obituaries tend to elicit more factual and descriptive reportage with respect to laying out the desired major events and achievements in an individual's imagined life and when those events happened (e.g., level of educational attainment, marriage, professional achievements, retirement and pursuit of "second acts" in life). Students' eulogies, in contrast, tend to focus on more global "characterological" aspects, including what kind of person they hoped to become, the sort of reputations they hoped to have built by the end of their lives, and their desired impact on other people (e.g., family and friends) or society in general.

After completing their obituaries and eulogies, students were then asked to analyze both documents in terms of the most important future identities they referenced, including both the significant *personal identities* (e.g., parent, spouse, etc.), as well as the *professional identities* (e.g. social entrepreneur, founder and CEO of a major tech company, etc.) represented in them.

Having identified the holistic identities represented in their write-ups, students were then told to select "one important but challenging or difficult *identity attribute* you perceive as vitally linked to the successful realization of your future identity and on which you would like to work now in the context of the identity lab." This could include, they were told, an identity attribute on which they would like to change by increasing or decreasing where they currently stand with respect to the attribute (e.g., becoming *more* conscientious or *less* impulsive) or even one which they perceived themselves as currently lacking and which they would like to cultivate "from scratch" (e.g., developing tenacity).

Phase 1: Designing the Experiment in Identity Striving

After students had identified the specific attribute identity on which they wanted to work, they then designed a behavioral experiment intended to stimulate them to strive to become or enact the *opposite* of that *current* characteristic or attribute for some time period of their own choosing. For example, if they perceived themselves as too shy or timid in their professional relationships, they should strive to act boldly, confidently, and/or aggressively. Alternatively, if they perceived themselves as too impulsive and reactive, they should strive to act with great restraint and prudence. This self-oppositional "framing" of the task was intended to encourage students to think "outside the box" or "comfort zone" in nudging them toward fuller development of their desired attributes.[2]

To facilitate the richness of their experimental designs, as well as enhance the learning potential of the exercise, students were instructed to research the behavioral science literature pertinent to the attribute on which they had chosen to work, using Google Scholar and other online resources. For example, if a student wanted to work on developing more "grit" (cf., Duckworth, Peterson, Matthews, & Kelly, 2007), they were told to research what is known about the antecedents and consequences of grit. I was also available to guide students towards relevant social science literatures. Indeed, one of the most enjoyable aspects of the identity lab is the close collaboration that forms between the students and me in researching their attributes of choice and designing their behavioral experiments.

Phase 2: Executing and Auditing the Experiment

Students then executed their experiments over the course of the time period they had chosen. Using a journal or other device of their choosing, they were instructed to systematically "audit" the results of their behavioral experiments as they unfolded, including keeping track of what they tried and how well it worked, as well as noting any psychological and social consequences.

Phase 3: Ex Post Assessment of the Results and Consolidating the Learnings

Upon completion of their experiments, students were asked to reflect back on their overall experiences and to attempt to consolidate their learnings from their experiment. They could do this privately or, if desired, in discussion with trusted classmates or friends.

Data Analyses

Students' obituaries and eulogies were used to identify the kinds of holistic identities that students yearned for and sought to achieve during their life-times. Additionally, students prepared reflective accounts or narratives explicating their specific identity strivings, details of their behavioral experiments, and *ex post* reflections on the consequences of those experiments. These narrative accounts were designed to encourage students to capture and consolidate their aggregate learnings, including the perceived benefits from their experiment, as well as what, if anything, worked less perfectly than anticipated. These narrative accounts helped me, as a researcher, assess the perceived impact of, and subjective learnings, from students' experiments.

To analyze these various data, I utilized an inductive, qualitative approach in which content analyses were performed on students' obituaries, eulogies, and narrative accounts. The aim of these content analyses was to derive a set of descriptive categories that reflected (1) the content of students' identity aspirations, (2) the types of behavioral experiments in which they engaged and (3) their perceived psychological consequences. The results of these analyses are reported in the next section.

Profiles in Existential Courage: The Scale and Scope of Students' Identity Aspirations

In this section, I present representative highlights that emerged from this study, beginning with an overview of the major kinds of *identity strivings* students expressed for themselves. I then describe some of the different forms their behavioral experiments took in pursuit of these strivings. Finally, I elaborate on some of the perceived psychological consequences of these behavioral experiments.

Taxonomy of Identity Strivings

Students' identity strivings were expressed in terms of both very general, *holistic identity aspirations*, as well as the specific *identity attributes* on which they sought to work for the purposes of their self-designed behavioral experiments. I begin by discussing students' holistic aspirations.

Holistic Identity Aspirations

Most broadly construed, students' holistic identity aspirations were framed in terms of the imagined and desired future identity they hoped to achieve during their lifetimes. These holistic identities fell into several clusters (all phrases below within quotation marks reflect students' identity aspirations or strivings as expressed in their own words).

The majority of students' identity aspirations fell into two categories, distinguished by fairly concrete and tangible labels. The first of these categories reflect what I will characterize as *personal identity* aspirations. These personal identity aspirations are generally linked to important social roles or statuses that students aspire to achieve in their life-times, such as becoming a "great and supportive spouse," becoming "a caring and effective parent," becoming a "loved and admired friend with a large circle of deep, life-long friendships," or becoming "an outstanding member of my religious community and an active practitioner of my faith." They also included various passions, including athletic quests ("to become a world-class triathlete") and hobbies (e.g., to become "a renowned amateur astronomer").

The second category of expressed aspirations were linked to students' *professional identities*, including the desire, for example, to become a "serial business founder," to become "a successful social entrepreneur," or to "serve as CEO of a Fortune 500 company." There were also many professional aspirations related to students' imagined post-business career successes (so-called "second acts" in life). Interestingly *all* of the students' obituaries reported such rich lives after they had first achieved their initial business successes, suggesting that business success was often perceived as merely a stepping stone to a later happy, meaningful and fulfilling life involving a very different kind of activity. These second-half of life aspirations include such things as becoming "a major philanthropist revered in his country," becoming "an enormously influential business writer whose books changed the way businesses were conducted globally," and becoming "a professor who returned to the classroom to teach at a major university all of the things she had learned as a successful woman leader."

Finally, there was a less frequent cluster of holistic identity strivings related to what might be characterized as *existential aspirations*, along the lines of what Emmons (1999) construed as *personal ultimate concerns*, and defined by him as "multiple personal goals that a person might possess in striving toward the sacred" (p. 6). These include such aspirations as the desire to achieve "a deeply meaningful and significant life," the desire to become "a moral person, universally respected and admired by his business peers, family and friends for his integrity," or becoming "an empathic and altruistic person who leaves a substantial trace of my having been on this planet."

Identity Attributes Selected for Self-Nudging Experiments

Students' choices with respect to the specific identity attributes on which they elected to work in their behavioral experiments generally fell into two primary categories, depending upon how they framed their strivings. The first category represents those strivings that were framed in terms of becoming *more* of something desired or moving *toward* some desired future identity state (e.g., becoming "a *more* conscientious" individual or a person "more *open* to experience" with respect to the conduct of their personal or professional lives). The second major category reflected aspirations that students framed in terms of becoming *less of* something or moving *away from* some undesirable reference point or status quo position (e.g., striving to become "a *less* angry person in my relationships" or "*less* impulsive and rash in my personal and professional decision making"). To provide a better sense of the range of these aspirations, Table 14.1 presents a representative sampling of both categories of identity aspiration.

It is worth noting, as the organization of the table indicates, that students' aspirations fell into several major categories. The first category involved attributes that were linked to desired future *intrapersonal* aspects of their identity, including hedonic goals, such as becoming a more joyous, more fulfilled, or more serene human being. Other student aspirations were linked to what can be construed as *self-regulatory goals*, such as becoming more focused in their goal pursuits, more ambitious, more diligent, more conscientious, more future-oriented, and so forth.

Table 14.1 Representative Identity Attributes Selected for Behavioral Experimentation

Attributes related to *intra-personal* **identity strivings**	**Striving to become** *more* conscientious, perseverant, ambitious, creative, focused, disciplined, goal-oriented, future-focused, analytical, rational, thoughtful, happier, joyful, joyous, spontaneous, present-minded, able to savor positive experiences, optimistic about the future, personal willpower, risk-tolerant (i.e., willing to take risks in personal and business life)	**Striving to become** *less* angry, impatient, volatile, impulsive, regretful, perfectionistic, procrastinating, sad, depressed, anxious, fearful, fragile (especially in response to rejection or negative feedback), ruminative, stuck in the past
Attributes related to *interpersonal* **or relational strivings**	**Striving to become** *more* trusting, open to others, self-disclosing, self-expressive (with others), cooperative, collaborative, socially aggressive, competitive, assertive in pursing own interests when working with others, kinder, empathic, generous, compassionate	**Striving to become** *less* judgmental, harsh, paranoid, obsequious, passive, shy, timid, impatient, envious, jealous, angry (in relationships), judgmental regarding others (including partner and friends)
Attributes related to existential strivings	**Aspiration to become or live a life that is** *more* meaningful, consequential, authentic, ethical, moral, courageous, philosophical, wiser, spiritual, faithful, transcendent, idealistic	**Aspiration to become or live a life that is** *less* superficial, narrow, concerned with physical appearances alone, status-driven, selfish, materialistic, hedonistic, short-term oriented

The second major category were clearly more *interpersonal* or relational in nature, such as becoming "more genuine in my relationships," becoming "a more reliable and giving partner," or becoming "a more empathic and caring parent than my parents had been." There were also interpersonal attributes related to important perceived business leadership goals, such as becoming a "great team builder", "a world-class negotiator", or a leader who was "great at building trust and earning the respect of my co-workers."

Finally, a number of students elected to work on identity attributes that reflected their broader existential goals. Often these aspirations seemed to be linked specifically with students' imagined and consequential "second acts."

Self-Designed Behavioral Experiments in Self-Nudging

To address their specific identity strivings, students undertook a variety of behavioral experiments designed to stretch their current sense of self in the service of their desired future identities. Because of length constraints on this chapter, I will provide only a few examples.

One student elected to work on the goal of becoming "a more deeply trusting human being." This student expressed a life-long difficulty in trusting other people, including not only co-workers but even close friends and family members. Accordingly, she felt closed off and unable to self-disclose fully or connect intimately with others. She perceived her inability to trust as a major impediment to fulfilling her holistic identity aspiration of becoming "an effective business leader" and, eventually, "an impactful community activist." Thus, to address this perceived shortcoming, she committed herself to "taking more social risks by reaching out to people more ... becoming more self-disclosing and more sharing of my own thoughts and feelings." To help her design an experiment in effective trust-taking and trust-building, she reviewed the psychological literatures on trust-building and the benefits of high trust relationships (I should note here that, prior to participating in the identity lab, it had never occurred to her that there was a large literature on trust-building and that, apart from actually participating in therapy, one could work on developing trust on their own; she found it empowering and creatively challenging to engage in this task). As part of her experiment in self-nudging, she resolved to be more open and revealing in every opportunity that presented itself during a three-week period. These opportunities included her conversations with fellow students, professors, friends, and family members. She kept a daily diary of her successes and failures from these experiments in trust-building.

Another student, who had struggled throughout her life with performance anxiety and perfectionistic standards, aspired to become "a more present-minded and serene (and less driven and obsessively future-focused) person." Specifically, she sought to "Slow down and savor my final moments in the MBA program more fully." This student was particularly inspired by, and her experimental design informed by, the slowness movement (Honore, 2004) and research on the benefits of savoring (Bryant & Veroff, 2007; Lyubomirsky, 2007). To pursue her aspirations, she substantially changed a number of her habits and routines as an MBA, including deciding to walk to campus rather than driving so that she could savor the beauty of Palo Alto and the undergraduate part of the campus more fully. She also significantly reduced her schedule to allow more spontaneous encounters, including more leisurely conversations over coffee and meals. Although this may sound like an easy goal to pursue, for this student it was extremely difficult: She saw herself as a Type A individual, a driven, time-urgent individual who took pride in having long, packed days—with every minute scheduled tightly. She feared that "leaning out" from this schedule was extremely risky in so far as she felt she was at risk of sacrificing much of her productivity, her outstanding grades, and her time to strategically network with people in the Silicon Valley. She feared also that even her future employment prospects might be compromised or put at risk, knowing how competitive the market was in her chosen area of post-graduate employment (finance). Thus, she felt genuine anxiety attached to conducting this experiment. At the same time, she had begun to realize how her intense, relentlessly driven, extreme future-focus had caused her to miss out on a lot of the enjoyable social sides of the MBA program. "Now that this [MBA] experience is almost over," she lamented, "and I have only a few months left ... I'm not sure I really enjoyed myself as much as I *should have* or imagined I might have when I started my MBA. *I'm leaving Stanford with some regret, but I hope this experiment will lessen that regret*" (emphasis in original).

Finally, another student elected to experiment with becoming more optimistic and hopeful in his thinking about his future relationships and his career. This student described himself as a life-long pessimist who had approached both his personal relationships and his professional work with a chronically fatalistic attitude. This pessimism, he was quick to note, persisted despite a considerable history of academic success as a Harvard undergraduate and professional achievement at the international consulting firm for which he had worked prior to pursuing his MBA at Stanford. This student did an extensive literature review, becoming quite energized by the research he encountered regarding learned optimism and its benefits (Segerstrom, 2006; Seligman, 2006), as well as research on defensive pessimism (Norem, 2002). Drawing on this research, he was determined to "turn his mind around" and learn to perceive the glasses he encountered in life going forward as "at least half full." Accordingly, he developed a list of personal "mental heuristics" for making more positive attributions regarding his past experiences, as well as setting more positive expectations for both his present and future commitments.

Some of the students' personal identity strivings, I should note, were of a highly personal nature and involved greater levels of perceived psychological and social risks. These included such things as struggling with concealed sexual orientations and striving to "come out" to friends or parents. Other students expressed struggles with depression, anxiety, alcohol or drug abuse, suicidal ideation, etc. Many of these students asked that their obituaries, eulogies, and narratives be regarded as confidential.[3]

These representative examples convey, I hope, some of the flavor of identity strivings on which students elected to work.

Perceived Consequences of Behavioral Experiments

Students' reported an impressive variety of perceived psychological consequences associated with their experiments (as before, the words and phrases enclosed within quotation marks in the following paragraphs reflect students' own descriptive language). I organize the discussion of these consequences in terms of cognitive, motivational, and affective consequences, although recognizing that there is considerable overlap among students' self-reports with respect to these categories.

Perceived Cognitive Benefits

Significantly, the experimental approach was perceived as "powerful," "transformative," "impactful," and "effective" at helping students pursue their identity aspirations. Among the important reported cognitive benefits were enhanced self-perceptions of their "creativity" and "competence" at self-change. Some students also reported feeling "more optimistic" and "hopeful "regarding their ability to change other aspects of their lives going forward. There were also reports of a sense of greater "trust" in themselves and "renewed faith" in their own resources for changing themselves.

A number of students reported feeling "more authentic," "significantly more genuine in my relationships," and "more relaxed about who I am and who I want to be." One student reported that she was very "pleasantly surprised and even thrilled" that "her more honest and deeper self-disclosures to parents, friends, and fellow MBA students had produced a real sense of satisfaction" rather than the anxiety that she had feared.

Relatedly, and more generally, a number of students felt their self-knowledge and self-awareness had increased, especially in terms of a sense of enlarged capacity for personal change, enhanced persistence or tenacity, and the ability to successfully self-regulate themselves. Relatedly, some students reported that they had learned something valuable about themselves. By generating their own experiences, these students experienced an increased sense of mastery and competence. In terms of changes in self-awareness, students also were intrigued by the approach of having to act their way into self-change rather than over-thinking the attempted change process. To this point, a number of students described themselves as tending toward being too "analytical" and "calculating" in their prior self-change efforts, so relished the opportunity to become more experimental and spontaneous. "I enjoyed the experience of just rolling the 'experiential dice'," one student reported.

In addition to these perceived cognitive consequences, students also reported a number of motivational benefits. Among these benefits were feeling enormously energized and re-charged by their successful experiments. There were expressions of enhanced perceptions of personal *self-efficacy* (many students in the lab were interested in Bandura's work on self-efficacy and its effects). Several students reported feeling more *resilient* regarding their prospects for successfully facing future challenges, suggesting a kind of spillover or carry-over effect from their experiments. One student realized that what she termed "Personal Will Power" (something she had heretofore considered as an innate and fixed psychological trait) was better thought of as a habit, skill or mindset that could be cultivated (note that students had read important work in this area as part of their lab work, specifically Baumeister & Tierney, 2012, and Dweck, 2007). Relatedly, another student who had elected to work on increasing her conscientiousness and grit reported great success and felt that her "reservoir" of motivational resources had actually increased substantially. There were also expressions of renewed resolve and/or determination "not to waste my future moments" of opportunity.

Finally, students recounted a number of perceived affective consequences associated with their experiments. I viewed these affective consequences, in part, from the perspective of Russell's (1980) circumplex model of affect. From this model's perspective, students' affective responses can be arrayed in terms of a two-dimensional space with affective valence (positivity versus negativity) on one axis and intensity of affect (high versus low) on the other. Using this scheme as an organizing heuristic for discussing the results—and focusing first on the positive and higher intensity quadrant of this space—students expressed feelings suggestive of exuberance and exhilaration at the perceived success of their experiments. One student described the "intense joy" she experienced from her success with respect to working with her partner on the intimacy of their relationship (both she and her partner were pursuing MBAs, but at different schools, and found the geographical distance and dual-career juggling a relationship challenge and stressor). Another student reported feeling "tremendous zest—especially for the future."

In the positive but lower intensity quadrant, students reported enjoying *savoring* the gains from their experiments, including privately relishing them. Some savored those gains further by discussing them with other students, friends outside the MBA program, and even family members. There were expressions of serenity, including "a quiet but deep sense of personal satisfaction at having done the right thing for myself" and "a completely unexpected calm that followed my successful experiment." In some instances, these lower intensity emotional benefits were also described more in terms of *relief*, a reduction in anxiety, or an appreciation of the fact that their "worst case" fears had not materialized. Construed broadly, such comments reflect the sense that self-chosen acts of psychological and social risk-taking, when undertaken successfully, can be both enjoyable and deeply fulfilling.

Some of the perceived benefits of these experiments can best be characterized as complex psychological states reflecting a mixture of positive cognitive, affective and/or motivational benefits. Numerous students reported feelings of *pride* at having attempted something difficult and succeeding at it, including a sense of self-affirmation. As one student notes, "I felt *enormously proud* of myself for being able to summon up the resources I needed to get through this week" (emphases added). Another reported, "I was *blown away* at how well I had coped, as I had never tried anything quite like this before" (emphases added). In several instances, there were reports of what I will call genuine, pleasant, and even treasured moments of *self-discovery* or *self-surprise*. One student reported, for instance, "I never knew I had it in me to do this. I surprised myself by how well I had done." Another reported, "I felt I had learned something important about myself that I had not known … and I thought I knew myself pretty well." In short, there was sometimes genuine delight in the unexpected effects of the experiments.

I should note that not all of the cognitive, motivational and affective responses reported were positive, although self-reported negative experiences represented fewer than 5 percent of this sample. For instance, there were a few expressions of *regret* for not succeeding with the experiment as much as one had hoped or expected. Along such lines, one student felt he had "given up" too early when his first attempts at change faltered. Another chastised herself for deciding to postpone the experiment until a more opportune or convenient moment presented itself (interestingly, and perhaps somewhat humorously, this student indicated procrastination was an enduring problem in her life and concluded, "Maybe I should have worked on *that* attribute for my experiment!"—as insight that could be coded, I should note, as one positive learning from the experiment). Another student who "kinda blew off the exercise" experienced a sense of disappointment and missed opportunity, after hearing how well other students' experiments had turned out—again, a possible learning or benefit from the experiment. During collective debriefs in the lab, we discussed the literature suggesting that failure can be one of the most useful learning opportunities (e.g., Kelley, 2001), and students found that framing of their experiences quite useful.

Implications and Conclusions

In discussing the importance of the ideas and findings presented in this chapter, I will elaborate first on some of the theoretical contributions made by this research. I will then turn attention to a discussion of some methodological implications. Finally, I will conclude by suggesting some important practical or applied implications.

Theoretical Contributions

With respect to theoretical implications, I would like to suggest first that, construed most broadly, the results of this study contribute to our understanding of the scale and scope of emerging adults' identity aspirations, as manifested in the ambitious and consequential lives they imagine for themselves and that they seek to bring into being. In particular, students' holistic identity strivings, as evident in their detailed obituaries and rich eulogies, speak to the sort of existential yearnings or longings that today's emerging adults entertain. As such, they reflect the ever-ongoing quest for psychological growth and mastery that has long been associated with optimal human development (Baltes, 1968; Kotter-Gruhn, Scheibe, Blanchard-Fields, & Baltes, 2009; Maslow, 1962). As Scheibe et al. (2011) noted in this regard, such longings "shape identity and are part of personal life stories" (p. 615). They go on to posit, on the basis of their own cross-cultural evidence, the pervasiveness of such strivings, noting, "Having ideas about one's optimal, ideal life appears to be a part of daily life in many cultures" (p. 615).

In terms of contributing to our understanding of the life concerns of emerging adults in particular, the results of this study suggest that university students' holistic identity aspirations, as reflected in their obituaries and eulogies, are impressively diverse and ambitious. Every single participant in this research was easily able to articulate a desired future self and the kind of rich personal, social, and professional life such a self would achieve. Moreover, as they imagined the lives that this future self would create, they aimed high and imagined "having it all" in terms of realizing lives that were brimming with substantial professional success, personal happiness and meaning. There is, for example, little evidence of any need to make "trade-offs" between success at work and balance in their personal lives. Elsewhere, I have written about this "winner-want-all" mindset characteristic of MBA students (Kramer, 2003) and note here that this mindset was very much in evidence in the present study. Of course, these lofty aspirations are, in many respects, hardly surprising in light of recent studies documenting that emerging adults' entertain extraordinary, and in many respects quite inspiring expectations with regard to their imagined lives—in many ways they *do* expect to eventually "have it all" (e.g., Arum & Roksa, 2011, 2014; Steinberg, 2014).

Admittedly, the pursuit of such ideal future selves and lives is always a work in progress, vulnerable to derailments, time trapped in unexpected potholes and negotiating unimagined bumps and curves. As Gardner and colleagues (2001) aptly noted along these lines:

> [S]uch an integrated sense of identity remains an ideal: nearly everyone suffers at times from some fragmentation of identity, some diffusion, some confusion. Nor does identity ever completely coalesce. *Rich lives include continuing internal conversations about who we are, what we want to achieve, where we are successful, and where we are falling short.*
>
> (Gardner et al., 2001, p. 10, emphasis added)

The concept of identity striving, as developed here, enjoys conceptual affinities with a number of other recent motivational perspectives in human development, including theory and research on the pursuit of *callings* (Damon, 2008; Wrzesniewski, Rozin, & Bennett, 2003), *ultimate concerns* (Emmons, 1999), *good work* (Gardner et al., 2001), *growth mindsets* (Dweck, 2007), and *mastery* (Halvorson, 2010). Although space constraints preclude further elaboration of these connections, their unpacking merits further attention.

The findings from this research also contribute to our understanding of *why* experiments in "self-nudging" might be efficacious. Framing students' identity strivings simply as creative "experiments," for instance, may be one way for individuals to more easily approach the challenging and otherwise quite daunting aspirations they've set for themselves. To this point, recent research on anxiety suggests that re-framing anxiety as *excitement* might attenuate some of anxiety's more debilitating effects (cf., Brooks, 2013). In a comparable fashion, I would propose, re-framing one's identity strivings as *opportunities* for exploring, expressing and experiencing coveted future attributes might take some of the fear out of the enterprise; the task becomes inherently more play-like as individuals endeavor to just "act as if" they possess a desired attribute. Put differently, it may help students feel that their efforts at self-change feel less like difficult "clinical" or "therapeutic work" and more like playful improvisation or artful self-discovery.

I should note that the experimental approach to self-nudging adopted in this research was inspired, in part, by Frankl's (1959) pioneering method of *paradoxical intention*, which he originally developed in order to treat anxiety and phobia. In particular, Frankl invented this psychotherapeutic technique to encourage his anxious or phobic individuals to "intend, even if only for a moment, precisely that which they fear" (p. 127). To implement this procedure, patients were given guidance on how to strive to experience that very thing which they most dreaded. In theorizing why this approach might be efficacious in reducing anxiety or phobia, Frankl argued that the "procedure consists of a reversal of the patient's attitude, inasmuch as his fear is replaced by a paradoxical wish" (p. 127). As a consequence, he theorized metaphorically, "The wind is taken out of the sails of the [patient's] anxiety" (p. 127). In more concrete terms, paradoxical intention vividly and compellingly reveals to patients that their fears are exaggerated, misplaced, and—importantly—confrontable.

Conceptually, the approach to dynamic or iterative self-change employed in the present study resonates with Fredrickson's (2001) *broaden-and-build model* of positive affectivity. According to Fredrickson's framework, positive affective experiences tend to broaden individuals' repertoire of experiences, generating "virtuous cycles" of positively valenced experiences by building on earlier successes at experiencing positive affectivity. Adapted and applied to the present context, the underlying premise is that deliberately and earnestly engaging in the opposite of generally negative attitudes, feelings, and behaviors might generate *comparatively* more positive experiences—which then support further positive experiences in turn. For example, for a socially anxious, self-conscious student, even the small and simple act of smiling at a social event and spending time in line at a bar waiting for a glass of wine might stimulate some casual social banter in a relatively benign context that can then lead to more sustained and relaxed conversations as the evening wears on and additional social connections are made and deepened (cf., Zimbardo, 1990).

Finally, this self-nudging approach to self-change can also be viewed as consistent with, and even validating, Weick's (1984) "small wins" approach to personal and social change. In motivating his arguments in favor of the efficacy of the small-wins approach, Weick noted that high levels of psychological arousal often impede effective change efforts because "coping responses become more primitive or regressive" (p. 42). In terms of the present context, attempting behavioral experiments involving large-scale self-change, which might be perceived as highly risking and threatening to the present self, might impede effective implementation of the change effort and undermine securing of its desired results. In contrast, focusing on single identity attributes one at a time allows small behavioral and psychological gains to get a psychological toehold, as it were, and accumulate—leading, over time, to aggregate wholesale change. The results of the present study suggest further that individuals' resultant sense of pride in their progress, even if incremental, might infuse their motivation for attempting future acts. Consistent with this line of argument, Williams and DeSteno (2008) found that pride can foster persistence in the pursuit of short-term goals (see also Amabile & Kramer, 2011).

A conventional perspective, derived from social identity theory, is that our extant personal and social identities help us make sense of who we are and also help locate ourselves in the social order via the process of self-categorization (Brewer & Kramer, 1985; Elsbach & Kramer, 1996). I'd like to propose here that, just as our existing identities may help us know where we are at this particular time and place in our lives, our identity aspirations or strivings inform us of where we might go and who we might become. If the inertia of our extant identities pushes us slowly onward in life along a predictable path, our identity strivings may tug us toward longed for even if uncertain futures.

For some readers of this chapter, perhaps, the characterization of identity striving as a form of *existential* courage might seem to pack too much elevated conceptual freight into a very small behavioral container. If such readers prefer to construe identity strivings as examples of *everyday* courage that would be fine—so long as we are careful not to denigrate what it means to be "everyday." Every day is, after all, the only way human beings can and do decide how to live—and it is in that sense that the judgments and choices we make each and every day about who we are and who we wish to become are legitimately considered existential in scale and scope. A useful parallel may be drawn to recent work on the importance of everyday creativity. In a thoughtful discussion of the role such creativity plays in human lives, Richards (2007) observed, "We humans are often 'everyday creatures' ... [and as such] to cope with our changing environments, we improvise, we flexibly adapt, we try this and that" (p.3). It is such everyday creativity, she goes on to argue, that provides us with "a dynamic process and a powerful way of living" (p. 3). So it is, I would posit, with our everyday existential strivings. By bringing the concept of courage down from the Olympian heights, and rendering it as just another important, but learnable and attainable, character strength (*sensu* Peterson & Seligman, 2004), we help ordinary people (and especially emerging adults) imagine how they might engage the concept of existential courage and strive to cultivate it in their own lives. Indeed, I believe it is useful to construe existential courage as a *mindset* rather than a character trait, in much the same way that Dweck (2007) has demonstrated the utility of growth mindsets in learning.

In putting this framing of existential courage in another perspective, I am tempted to echo a comment here that the social psychologist Daniel Gilbert made with respect to displays of human resilience in the face of adversity. After a survey of the extant evidence, Gilbert (2010) concluded, "[Human] resilience is admirable ... but isn't rare. In fact it is quite common." In support of this assertion, Goethals and Allison (2012) noted that individuals they characterized as *transparent heroes*—those relatively invisible individuals among us whose heroic work, while significant, often goes unnoticed (p. 227)—were, in fact, the largest category of heroes to emerge in their typology. So it is, I would argue, with respect to the kind of courage associated with identity striving. Over the course of their lives, many (perhaps most) individuals encounter the occasion to "rise to the occasion"—and do so. Even though the stage on which they act may be largely unlit and their performance unheralded, in doing the right thing *for themselves*, they enlarge their own sense of self. As Streater (2013) asserted along these lines:

> Everyday courage is not exclusive to the fearless or the brave. It forms when action is taken, even in the face of challenge or risk. Whether putting your life on the line or stepping just outside your comfort zone, risk is relative. Acting on your belief is not ... *This is courage.*
>
> *(Streater, 2013, p. 11; emphasis in original)*

In this spirit, the results of the present inquiry suggest that, when supported by a safe and conducive learning environment, individuals can successfully pursue their "becoming" aspirations, very much along the lines that existential psychologists such as Maslow (1962), May (1975), and Rogers (1961) long ago argued. The quest for identity, in short, has both reason and rhyme.

Methodological Contributions

Because this handbook is aimed, at least in part, at a social psychological audience, I would like to make a brief case for the value of inductive research methods, particularly with respect to their potential for producing novel insights regarding the content of emerging adults' identity aspirations. Social scientists have increasingly recognized the potential of qualitative methods to generate data that reveal empirical patterns that might otherwise remain obscured or overlooked using more traditional, quantitative methods (Bartunek, Rynes & Ireland, 2006). Some of this appreciation has been fueled by recent innovations in technologies which afford new ways of collecting, aggregating, and analyzing such data (see Elsbach & Kramer, 2016 for a recent compilation of such methods).

One particularly exciting and attractive aspect of qualitative work is that researchers, by studying real people in real-world contexts, are better able to capture more of the natural variation in their informants' thoughts, feelings, and behaviors. Relatedly, they can more richly and faithfully track the "push and pull" of ambient environmental factors on those thoughts, feelings, and behaviors. In contrast to the controlled and intentionally pared-down variation typical of the laboratory experiment, people in real-world settings are free to respond—quite literally—*ad lib*. Thus, there is an opportunity for researchers to stumble onto unexpected but theoretically significant sources of variance. For some scientists, this approach might seem to put the cart before the hypothesis-testing horse. However, as the distinguished scientist Stuart Firestein (2012) likes to urge his doctoral students, "Let's get the data, and then we can figure out the hypothesis" (p. 19). In the case of the present study, I would argue that by allowing students to identify their own strivings in their own words, I was able to elicit a broader and more faithful representation of the range of identity-relevant concerns with which emerging adults are grappling compared to what might be obtained using a more conventional survey instrument or semi-structured interview format.

Practical Implications and Contributions

Although this research was undertaken with a clear set of theoretical objectives, I was also committed to conducting a study that hopefully might yield practical fruit for those involved in it. In particular, I was interested in developing a pragmatic framework that might be useful for individuals who were confronting *real* existential choices in *real* time in their own lives. I believe, given the enormity of the problems the world confronts—and a world which emerging adults will have to face—that there is a duty to do research that is relevant —probative not only on scholarly grounds, but also potentially consequential in terms of personal and social impact. To this point, the results of the present research suggest that a positive and promotive attitude toward psychological and social risk-taking can be cultivated and, moreover, that the consequences of such an attitude can be substantial from the standpoint of prompting real psychological exploration and growth.

More concretely formulated, the present results suggest that individuals can (1) successfully identify perceived identity-relevant attributes on which they would like to improve, and (2) self-design interventions to "nudge" them in the successful pursuit of such identity goals. Stated more broadly, the results of this study suggests that strategically chosen and carefully constructed behavioral experiments can effectively stimulate individuals to take psychological and social risks in order to challenge their current sense of self in the pursuit of a desired future sense of self. *In short, self-nudging works.*

As noted in the introduction, the sort of existential risk-taking associated with identity strivings constitutes an important form of courage. For the purposes of this research, however, I vigilantly avoided use of the word "courage" in the implementation of the exercises in order to minimize the potential for introducing demand characteristics into students' thinking or behavior. Thus, I deliberately employed the more neutral language of "behavioral experimentation" rather than discussing students' action plans in terms of loftier constructs such as *existential risk-taking* or *courage* per se. However, it is noteworthy that many of the students' reactions to their experiments suggested that they themselves had an awareness of having displayed courage. Moreover, many found the experience of existential risk-taking extremely engaging, sometimes even thrilling, and often deeply satisfying. Although only three students actually used the word "courage" in describing their reactions to their experiments, there were other linguistic variations in which the notion of courage was expressed by students extemporaneously. One respondent, for instance, talked about "being proud to discover that I had the guts to take on such a tough exercise." Another indicated the pleasure of "being willing to choose the most difficult thing I've been avoiding working on, and carry it off." Another found the experiment "challenging ... scary as all hell," but added, "*but I did it!*" (emphasis in original). Finally, one student asserted, "I felt I had reached deep inside myself and pulled out things I didn't know I had in me. It was very gratifying to discover this strength within myself."

These preliminary findings suggest the potency of the self-designed behavioral experiments for eliciting courageous behaviors.[4] In the next study planned for the Identity Lab, I intend to explicitly introduce the construct of *existential courage*, discussing how and why it works, and why it might be worth cultivating in one's conceptual "tool-kit" as a resource for personal growth and change. My *a priori* hunch is that explicitly framing individuals' actions in terms of courage may be even more empowering and effective.

One of the most important practical implications of the present research, perhaps, is that it suggests there can be method rather than mere madness in emerging adults' pursuit of their most cherished aspirations. A number of recent studies of emerging adults have emphasized how many young people today are struggling to find paths to fulfillment. These adults have been characterized as "academically adrift" (Arum & Roksa, 2011), "lost in transition" (Smith, Christoffersen, Davidson, & Herzog, 2011), "motivated but directionless" (Schneider & Stevenson, 1999), problematically "disengaged" (Damon, 2008), or mired in a "quarterlife crisis" (Robbins & Wilner, 2001). The self-nudging approach outlined in this study shows how even a very small intervention can produce significant gains, at least as subjectively reported by the participants involved. In much the same way that Lyubomirsky's (2007) "how of happiness" approach provides a useful roadmap for individuals to match their hedonic aspirations with proven happiness-inducing techniques, so might a more fully developed framework involving guided reflection and behavioral experimentation help students more smoothly stride toward their deepest yearnings and existential aspirations for identity and meaning. Paraphrasing Gilbert (2006), if emerging adults can have a better sense of how and where they might stumble on the road to happiness and meaning, they might avoid some of those missteps and make more rapid and substantive progress toward their aspirational goals.

Notes

1   The research described in this chapter is part of an ongoing program of research I've been doing which focuses on the psychological foundations and 'pragmatics' of identity striving. Conceptually, the lab I've developed for this research is predicated on principles and practices derived largely from design theory

(Kelley, 2001; Kelley & Kelley, 2013), behavioral economics (Thaler & Sunstein, 2009), creativity theory (especially Csikszentmihalyi, 1996) and identity management strategies and tactics (Elsbach & Kramer, 1996). Practically, students' lab work is embedded in three experientially-oriented life-design workshops I teach, entitled, "Mastering Life's Moments," "Lives of Consequence," and "Successful Creativity and the MBA Mind," respectively. Drawing on theories and findings from the social sciences, these workshops explore different facets of what is known about the nature and origins of optimal human experience.

2   Although inspired by Frankl's technique of paradoxical intention, I have to confess that the creation of this exercise was also stimulated, in part, by the famous 86th episode of the television show *Seinfeld*, in which George Costanza decides, while lamenting to Jerry and Elaine, that his life has been a failure because every choice he has ever made has been a disaster. At which point the insight comes to him that if every choice he has ever made has been completely wrong, then the *opposite* of his instinctive choices must be completely right. George's attempts to act on this insight leads to a series of unexpected and hilarious outcomes. Although intended purely as a humorous plot device, philosophers have actually discussed the logic and wisdom behind such a philosophy (see, e.g., Holt, 1999) and its organizational relevance explored as well (Kramer, 2005).

3   Out of respect for those requests, these data are not described in further detail in this chapter. All students indicating any psychological difficulties or discomfort were referred to the appropriate campus counseling resources available to students.

4   In placing the findings of the present study in perspective, it is important to note one possible limitation of these findings. Although the participants in the present study reported an impressive variety of positive consequences associated with their experiments, it is important to contemplate limits to the generalizability of these findings. In particular, it is essential to recognize that, for the most part, the MBA students who participated in this study represent an arguably skewed or "best case" sample for studying existential risk-taking among emerging adults in general. After all, the students who attend the Stanford business school are generally of higher than average intelligence, come from relatively affluent backgrounds, have well-educated parents, and have already accumulated an impressive history of personal successes in their young lives. Additionally, it is reasonable to assume that the average level of emotional and social intelligence possessed by these students are reasonably high, and that their coping skills might also be higher than average. Thus, the generalizability of results to other populations who come from less well-endowed or resource-munificent backgrounds remains an open question. An important extension of this research, therefore, would be to examine the efficacy of this approach with other, more diverse populations. I would argue that the findings presented in this chapter, at the very least, suggest the promise of self-designed behavioral experiments to support emerging adults' identity aspirations and, more generally, desires for individual change.

References

Allison, S. T., & Goethals, G. R. (2011). *Heroes: What they do and why we need them*. New York: Oxford University Press.

Amabile, T., & Kramer, S. (2011). *The progress principle: Using small wins to ignite, joy, engagement and creativity at work*. Boston, MA: Harvard Business Press.

Arnett, J. J. (2000). Emerging adulthood: A theory of development from the teens to the twenties. *American Psychologist, 55*, 469–480.

Arnett, J. J. (2014). *Emerging adulthood: The winding road from the late teens through the twenties*. New York: Oxford University Press.

Arnett, J. J., & Fishel, E. (2014). *Getting to 30: A parent's guide to the 20-something years*. New York: Workman Publishing.

Arum, R., & Roksa, J. (2011). *Academically adrift: Limited learning on college campuses*. Chicago, IL: Chicago University Press.

Arum, R., & Roksa, J. (2014). *Aspiring adults adrift: Tentative transitions of college students*. Chicago, IL: University of Chicago Press.

Baker, C. (2003). *Ernest Hemingway: Selected Letters, 1917–1961*. New York: Scribner.

Baltes, P. B. (1968). Longitudinal and cross-sectional sequences in the study of age and generation effects. *Human Development, 11*, 145–171.

Bartunek, J. M., Rynes, S. L., & Ireland, R. D. (2006). What makes management research interesting, and why does it matter? *Academy of Management Journal, 49*, 9–15.

Baumeister, R., & Tierney, J. (2012). *Willpower*. New York: Penguin.

Beahm, G. (2011). *I, Steve: Steve Jobs in his own words*. New York: Agate.

Beschloss, M. (2008). *Presidential courage: Brave leaders and how they changed America, 1789–1989.* New York: Simon & Schuster.
Biswas-Diener, R. (2012). *The courage quotient: How science can make your braver.* San Francisco: Jossey-Bass.
Brewer, M. B., & Kramer, R. M. (1985). The psychology of intergroup attitudes and behavior. *Annual Review of Psychology, 36,* 219–243.
Brooks, A. (2013). Get excited: Re-appraising pre-performance anxiety as excitement. *Journal of Experiment Psychology: General, 143,* 1144–1158.
Bruckner, P. (2000). *Perpetual euphoria: On the duty to be happy.* Princeton, NJ: Princeton University Press.
Bryant, F. B., & Veroff, J. (2007). *Savoring: A new model of experience.* Mahwah, NJ: Erlbaum.
Campbell, J. (2008). *The hero with a thousand faces* (3rd ed.). New York: New World Library
Coles, R. (2010). *Lives we carry with us: Profiles of moral courage.* New York: The New Press.
Csikszentmihalyi, C. (1996). *Creativity: Flow and the psychology of discovery and invention.* New York: HarperCollins.
Damon, W. (2008). *Paths to purpose: How young people find their calling in life.* New York: Free Press.
Duckworth, A. L., Peterson, C., Matthews, M. D., and Kelly, D. R. (2007). Grit: Perseverance and passion for long-term goals. *Journal of Personality and Social Psychology, 92,* 1087–1101.
Dweck, C. (2007). *Mindset: The new psychology of success.* New York: Ballantine.
Elsbach, K., & Kramer, R. M. (1996). Members' responses to organizational identity threats: Encountering and countering the Business Week rankings. *Administrative Science Quarterly, 41,* 442–476.
Elsbach, K., & Kramer, R. M. (2003). Assessing creativity in Hollywood pitch meetings: A Elsbach dual process model of creativity judgment. *Academy of Management Journal, 46,* 283–301.
Elsbach, K., & Kramer, R. M. (2016). *Handbook of organizational qualitative research: Innovative pathways and methods.* New York: Routledge.
Emmons, R. A. (1999). *The psychology of ultimate concerns.* New York: Guilford.
Erikson, E. H. (1968). *Identity Youth and Crisis.* New York: W. W. Norton.
Firestein, S. (2012). *Ignorance.* New York: Oxford University Press.
Frankl, V. (1959). *Man's search for meaning: An introduction to logotherapy.* Boston, MA: Beacon Press.
Fredrickson, B. L. (2001). The role of positive emotions in positive psychology: The broaden-and-build theory of positive emotions. *American Psychologist, 56,* 218–226.
Gardner, H. (1993). *Multiple intelligences.* New York: Basic Books.
Gardner, H., Csikszentmihalyi, M., & Damon, W. (2001). *Good work.* New York: Basic Books.
Gates, B. (2012). *Impatient optimist: Bill Gates in his own words.* New York: Agate.
Gilbert, D. (2006). *Stumbling on happiness.* New York: Vintage.
Gilbert, D. (2010). *This emotional life* [documentary film]. Boston, MA: PBS Films.
Goethals, G. R., & Allison, S. T. (2012). Making heroes: The construction of courage, competence and virtue. In J. M. Olson & M. P. Zanna (eds), *Advances in experimental social psychology* (vol. 46, 183–235). Amsterdam: Elsevier.
Halvorson, H. G. (2010). *Succeed: How we can reach our goals.* New York: Penguin.
Holt, J. (1999). The Costanza Maneuver: Is it rational for George to 'Do the opposite'?" In W. Irwin (ed.), *Seinfeld and Philosophy* (pp. 121–138). New York: Open Court.
Honore, C. (2004). *In praise of slowness.* San Francisco, CA: Harper.
Kelley, T. (2001). *The art of innovation.* New York: Doubleday.
Kelley, T., & Kelley, D. (2013). *Creative confidence.* New York: Crown Business.
Kennedy, J. F. (1955). *Profiles in courage.* New York: Harper.
Kotter-Gruhn, D., Scheibe, S., Blanchard-Fields, F., and Baltes, P. B. (2009). Developmental emergence and functionality of *schnsucht* (life longings): The same case of involuntary childlessness in middle-aged women. *Psychology and Aging, 24,* 634–644.
Kramer, R. M. (1996). Divergent realities and convergent disappointments in the hierarchic relation: The intuitive auditor at work. In R. M. Kramer & T. R. Tyler (eds), *Trust in organizations: Frontiers of Theory and Research* (pp. 216–245). Thousand Oaks, CA: Sage Publications.
Kramer, R. M. (2003). The harder they fall. *Harvard Business Review, 81,* 58–68.
Kramer, R. M. (2004). The imperatives of identity: The role of identity in leader judgment and decision making. In D. van Knippenberg & M. A. Hogg (eds), *Leadership and power: Identity processes in groups and organizations,* pp. 184–197. London: Sage.
Kramer, R. M. (2005). Flipping without flopping. *Harvard Business Review, 83,* 18.
Lyubomirksy, S. (2007). *The how of happiness.* New York: Penguin.
Maddi, S. (2004). Hardiness: An operationalization of existential courage. *Journal of Humanistic Psychology, 44,* 279–298.
Maslow, A. H. (1962). *Toward a psychology of being.* New York: Van Nostrand Co.
May, R. (1975). *The courage to create.* New York: W. W. Norton.

Moran, L. (2007). *Anatomy of courage*: New York: Basic Books.
Norem, J. (2002). *The positive power of negative thinking*. New York: Basic Books.
Peterson, C., & Seligman, M. E. P. (2004). *Character strengths and virtues: A handbook and classification*. New York: Oxford University Press.
Pury, C. L. S., & Lopez, S. J. (2010). *The psychology of courage: Modern research on an ancient virtue*. Washington, DC: American Psychological Association.
Pury, C. L. S., & Woodard, C. (2009). Courage. In S. J. Lopez (ed.), *Encyclopedia of positive psychology* (Vol. 1, pp. 247–254). Oxford: Blackwell.
Pury, C. L. S., Kowalski, R. M., & Spearman, J. (2007). Distinctions between general and personal courage. *Journal of Positive Psychology*, 2, 99–114.
Richards, R. (2007). *Everyday creativity and new views of human nature*. Washington, DC: American Psychological Association.
Robbins, A., & Wilner, A. (2001). *Quarterlife crisis*. New York: Penguin-Putnam.
Rogers, C. R. (1961). *On becoming a person*. New York: Houghton Mifflin.
Russell, J. A. (1980). A circumplex model of affect. *Journal of Personality and Social Psychology*, 39, 1161–1178.
Scheibe, S., Blanchard-Fields, F., Wiest, M., and Freund, A. M. (2011). Is longing only for Germans? A cross-cultural comparison of *schnsucht* in Germany and the United States. *Developmental Psychology*, 47, 603–618.
Schneider, B., & Stevenson, D. (1999). *The ambitious generation: America's teenagers, motivated but directionless*. New Haven, CT: Yale University Press.
Segerstrom, S. C. (2006). *Breaking Murphy's law*. New York: Guilford.
Seligman, M. E. P. (2006). *Learned optimism*. New York: Vintage.
Seligman, M. E. P. (2011). *Flourish*. New York: Free Press.
Settersten, R. (2015). The new landscape of early adulthood: Implications for broad-access higher education. In M. W. Kirst & M. L. Stevens (eds), *Remaking college: The changing ecology of higher education* (pp. 113–133). Stanford, CA: Stanford University Press.
Settersten, R., & Ray, B. E. (2010). *Not quite adults: Why 20-somethings are choosing a slower path to adulthood, and why it's good for everyone*. New York: Bantam.
Settersten, R., Furstenberg, F. F., & Ruben, G. R. (2005). *On the frontier of adulthood: Theory, research, and public policy*. Chicago, IL: University of Chicago Press.
Shelp, E. E. (1984). Courage: A neglected virtue in the patient-physician relationship. *Social Science and Medicine*, 18, 351–360.
Smelser, N. J. (2009). *Odyssey: Physical, social psychological, and spiritual journeys*. Berkeley, CA: University of California Press.
Smith, C, Christoffersen, K. Davidson, H., & Herzog, P. S. (2011). *Lost in transition: The dark side of emerging adulthood*. New York: Oxford University Press.
Staub, E. (2015). *The roots of goodness and resistance to evil: Inclusive caring, moral courage, altruism born of suffering, active bystandership, and heroism*. New York: Oxford University Press.
Steele, C. (2011). *Whistling Vivaldi*. New York: W. W. Norton.
Steinberg, L. (2014). *Age of opportunity: Lessons from the new science of adolescence*. New York: Houghton Mifflin.
Streater, K. (2013). *The gift of courage: Everyday heroes and the people who share their lives*. Beverly Hills, CA: Streater.
Thaler, R. H., & Sunstein, C. R. (2009). *Nudges: Improving decisions about health, wealth, and happiness*. New York: Penguin.
Tillich, P. (1952). *The courage to be*. New Haven, CT: Yale University Press.
Weick, K. (1984). Small wins: Redefining the scale of social problems. *American Psychologist*, 39, 40–49.
Williams, L. A., & DeSteno, D. (2008). Pride and perseverance: The motivational role of pride. *Journal of Personality and Social Psychology*, 94, 1007–1017.
Woodard, C. R., & Cury, C. L. S. (2007). The construct of courage: Categorization and measurement. *Consulting Psychology Journal: Practice and Research*, 59, 135–147.
Wrzesniewski, A., Rozin, P., and Bennett, G. (2003). Working, playing, and eating: Making the most of most moments. In C. Keyes and J. Haidt (eds), *Flourishing*, pp. 185–204. Washington, DC: American Psychological Association.
Zimbardo, P. (1990). *Shyness: What it is, what to do about it*. Boston, MA: Da Capo Press.

15
Heroism in the Networked Society

Dana Klisanin

> Heroes are most effective not alone but in a network. It's through forming a network that people have the resources to bring their heroic impulses to life.
>
> *(Phil Zimbardo, 2011)*

On a cold February evening in 2012, Canadian teen, Paige Dayal flew across time and space to save the life of young man in England (DiManno, 2012). Later, that same year, frustrated by the maiming and torture of children, over three million individuals set out to capture war criminal, Joseph Kony (Kony Campaign, 2015).[1] In the spring of 2014, distraught by the sudden disappearance of a Malaysian airliner, millions of individuals joined the search and rescue efforts—scanning the seas for signs of the missing airliner and her passengers (Fishwick, 2014).[2]

How does a teenage girl without a private jet conduct such a rescue operation? How do millions of individuals set out to capture a war criminal, or simultaneously scan the ocean to participate in a search and rescue mission? By using the power of interactive technologies to act *collaboratively*—online and in the real world—often simultaneously. Their actions ask us to look again and anew at our perceptions of heroism and heroic archetypes, perceptions that, while historically, culturally, and situationally determined (Franco, Blau, & Zimbardo, 2011, p. 99) have their deepest roots in our mythologies—the filters through which we examine, inhabit, and depart our world (Campbell, 1949).

Mythologies, in turn, arise from our stories—our interpretation of events and experiences—interpretations that depend in large part upon our *technology* (Clark & Chalmers, 1998; Davis, 1998). Cultural anthropologist, Bruno Latour, calls this breeding ground of meaning-making the "anthropological matrix," and suggests that nothing birthed by humanity can be neatly divided between *nature* and *culture*. Everything in the anthropological matrix is composed of hybrids—'speaking things' that are both natural and cultural, real and imagined, subject and object" (Latour, 1993). To simplify, we can think of *nature* as the egg of consciousness and *culture*, the sperm. We and our world—are the product of their procreation. We are often quick to recognize nature's role, but we are less cognizant of culture's pivotal contribution.

To bring attention to this bias, Joseph Campbell, the well-known comparative mythologist, pointed out the important role *technology*—a product of *culture*—plays in expanding human consciousness. In speaking of humanity's journey to the moon and its simultaneous broadcast via television (two extraordinary technological feats), he explained, "The making and the visual broadcasting of that trip transformed, deepened, and extended human consciousness to a degree and in a manner that amount to the opening of a new spiritual era" (Campbell, 1993).

What are the characteristics of that era? Campbell again:

> Our mythology now ... is to be of infinite space and its light ... On our planet itself all dividing horizons have been shattered. We can no longer hold our loves at home and project our aggressions elsewhere; for on this spaceship Earth there is no "elsewhere" any more. And no mythology that continues to speak or to teach of "elsewheres" and "outsiders" meets the requirements of this hour.
>
> *(Campbell, 1993, p. 266)*

Campbell pointed out that within the twentieth century, we went from having no idea how our planet looked to having a beautiful blue-and-white image firmly fixed in our imagination. We learned that our own galaxy is one among millions—that we, here on Earth, are but one strand in a complex web of life. Little by little, we are collectively ushering in a new mythos—*an era of planetary consciousness* (Laszlo, 1997). Planetary consciousness is shorthand for the understanding that everything is interdependent—that our lives and indeed all sentience are engaged in an intimate conversation. The particularities of the conversation sustain the structure of the whole, from the smallest particles to the largest molecule.

The mythos of planetary consciousness, on the horizon of human consciousness, is intimately entwined with advances in technology and unique forms of collaboration—a preview of which is found in the expansive levels of cooperation necessary to space travel. In the years since the first flight to the moon, our rapidly evolving information and communication technologies have come to serve as an external, physical manifestation of the larger web of life. The Internet is now considered to have impacted every dimension of human activity (Negroponte, 1996; Barabasi, 2003; Christakis & Fowler, 2009). From laptops to tablets to smart phones, we have created systems that extend our voices, further our reach, and support greater and greater interconnectivity and interdependence. Renowned communication philosopher, Marshall McLuhan, called this extension of human senses, the "outering" of our nervous systems (McLuhan, 1964). This outering of our sense of self and physical presence has come to be referred to as the "extended mind" (Clark & Chalmers, 1998; Clark, 2003). What does the extended mind mean for scientific inquiry and the study of heroism?

Through each and every technological feat—nature and culture have been mating—the result of their union is a *new level of complex organization*—referred to variously as the global brain, worldwide network, Gaia, collective intelligence (Russell, 1983; Heylighen, 2002, 2011; Lovelock, 1979; Laszlo, 1997). Scientific paradigms being used to explore this new level of complex organization include the systems sciences, network sciences, and complexity science—approaches interested in dynamical properties like self-organization, adaptation, and emergence. These paradigms are both the product and facilitator of the unfurling mythos—they are altering the way we understand and explore our world. Rather than breaking inquiry down into discrete parts and pieces, the methodologies inherent in these paradigms inquire in terms of connections or relationships. This means our understanding of ourselves, as individuals, is determined by our links with others in extensive relational networks—impacting our social identities and cultural attitudes (Christakis & Fowler, 2009) and furthering communal and civic value (Shirky, 2009). These networks and the attitudes they engender are impacting both the methodologies used to explore heroism and the structure of beliefs about the nature of heroism and heroic archetypes (Klisanin, 2012, 2014, 2015, 2016). The emerging field of heroism science speaks to this shift in its resolve "to craft the most inclusive definition of the science as [possible]" one that "is inclusive, transdisciplinary, and risk-taking" (Allison, 2015). Indeed, through acknowledging the extension of our minds via digital technologies, we recognize the need to extend the study of heroism into the milieu of the network—where heroism can expand to include action by the *many*.

During this age of transition, from a mythos of exclusion, separation, and boundaries, into a mythos of inclusion, relationship, and openness the study of heroism is more important than ever. For the tools of the networked society, in the hands of those adhering to an outdated mythos, become weapons of mass destruction—a "Dark Net" used by terrorist groups, drug syndicates, and others with criminal intent (Bartlett, 2014). Combating these threats while transitioning into the new mythos is one of the greatest challenges of the current era. The complexity of tackling such challenges is exemplified in the debate around mass surveillance—a means to track the behavior of terrorists, but an anathema to societies that value privacy.

The contentious nature of this debate is seen most clearly in the ongoing dispute around the actions of Edward Snowden. Vilified by many, and hailed a hero by others, Snowden is a man between countries—unable to find a home in the transition. His actions aim to promote a worldview of 'infinite space and its light' in an era where 'elsewhere and outsiders' dominate the discourse. Rather than disappearing, walls and boundaries are increasingly being erected, or reinforced—as Syrian refugees and other migrants can attest. And yet, in the midst such activities, millions of individuals are using the tools of digital connectivity to collaborate at a level and scale never before possible, contributing to a revolution in the way people perceive heroism. Snowden exists in this hyper-connected milieu—although physically exiled, he is one of the most interconnect people on the planet. According to Pilkington (2015), "Within half an hour of the launch of his verified feed on Tuesday morning from his exile in Russia, Snowden had attracted more than 70,000 followers and counting." Four months later, Snowden has attracted over 1.7 million followers. His "extended mind" is reaching every corner of the globe and his rhetoric reinforcing the "borderless horizons of infinite space," as evidenced by his second tweet to astrophysicist, Neil deGrasse Tyson:

> @neiltyson Thanks for the welcome. And now we've got water on Mars! Do you think they check passports at the border? Asking for a friend.
>
> *(Snowden, 2015)*

The issue of mass surveillance demonstrates the complexity of heroism in the networked era—an era in which the solitary hero and the collective are intimately intertwined.

Extending the Heroic Imagination into the Cloud

> Eternal truth needs a human language that alters with the spirit of the times. The primordial images undergo ceaseless transformation and yet remain ever the same, but only in a new form can they be understood anew.
>
> *(Jung, 1985, p. 196)*

Research on heroism in the networked society began as a consequence of research in the area of *digital altruism*, taking a turn toward heroism when it became increasing apparent that the actions of some digital altruists were resulting in contributions of food, water, and/or medicine to individuals in desperate circumstances. Those digital altruists who were far more active than others, for example, taking action each day, sometimes more than once a day, were posited to represent the emergence of a new form of the hero archetype—the *Cyberhero*. The Cyberhero archetype represents "individuals motivated to act on behalf of other people, animals, and the environment using the Internet and digital technologies in the peaceful service of achieving humanity's highest ideals and aspirations, for example, world peace, social justice, environmental protection, and planetary stewardship" (Klisanin, 2012).

The venture from altruism into heroism was based, in part, upon Rankin and Eagly's (2008) investigation of gender differences in the social construction of heroism; research that cast heroism in a new light, helping the researcher to recognize its' pliability. Soon, the venture was recognized as a step into what Franco, Blau, and Zimbardo (2011) noted to be an "exceedingly complex area of human behavior" (p. 109). The Internet—with its warp of interdependency and weft of interactivity—intensified the complexity. The decision to continue exploring the convergence of heroism and interactive technologies was motivated, in part, by a lack of extant pro-social research—searches of both academic and popular literature consistently turned up a preponderance of research on the negative aspects of its use, for example, cyber-bullies, cyber-crime, and cyber-war. Pro-social research was considered vital, due to research suggesting that human communities are only as healthy as our conceptions of human nature (Maslow, 1971; Hubbard, 1998), and research demonstrating the persuasive nature of interactive technologies (Fogg, 2002, 2008).

Further encouragement came in the form of the "banality of heroism" argument, which asks, "What if the capability to act heroically is also fundamentally ordinary and available to all of us?" as well as the theoretical construct of the "heroic imagination" which suggests the importance and/or possibility of fostering the heroic imagination (Franco & Zimbardo, 2006). Because digital technologies were changing the situation of human life, the possibility that they were also impacting heroism was further supported by Zimbardo's (2007) research showing that "situational factors" play a pivotal role in behavior.

In one of the first investigations, a multiple-case study method was used to explore the impact of social media initiatives on the social construction of heroism (Klisanin, 2015). The research was guided by the premises inherent in the theoretical construct of the heroic imagination (Franco & Zimbardo, 2006), thus criteria for case studies involved selecting social media initiatives in which participants were thought to represent "average citizens" rather than "heroic elect." The Cyberhero archetype was posited as an integral aspect of the "mind-set" of the heroic imagination. However, while the broad field of heroism science requires *heroism* to remain "in the eye of the beholder" (Allison & Goethals, 2015), a networked society transitioning toward a mythos of planetary consciousness, requires the conscious adoption of an ethos that respects diversity, but requires greater inclusivity, one that is fully aware of the "vital interdependence and essential oneness of humankind" (Laszlo, 1997, p. 143). A suicide bomber may yet be hailed a hero within the context of his/her terrorist organization—but in *the eyes of all the world* (i.e., the networked society) the action is seen as an abomination.

Because the networked society requires heroic actions to support the good of the global body, its study required a shared definition of what constitutes the noble, or heroic act. Early on, Csikszentmihalyi (1993) suggested that directing our evolution toward greater complexity would require we find an "appropriate moral code to guide our choices":

> It should be a code that takes into account the wisdom of tradition, yet is inspired by the future rather than the past; it should specify right as being the unfolding of the maximum individual potential joined with the achievement of the greatest social and environmental harmony. The development of this code is no easy task.
>
> *(Csikszentmihalyi, 1993, p. 162)*

Ultimately, a unified view for heroism at the global level is necessary. To address this need, the Universal Declaration of Human Rights (UDHR) and the Earth Charter were posited as consensus documents for research purposes (Klisanin, 2015). The UDHR is a declaration representing a global consensus of rights to which all human beings are entitled and was designed to promote both individual rights and social harmony (United Nations, 1948). The Earth Charter (2015) is a document with a strong focus on environmental protection and stewardship.

In an era when the majority of the world's citizens still lack many of the basic rights described in the UDHR and the natural world is imperiled, actions to secure those rights, and protect our planetary home, that do not violate those selfsame rights, can be consensually recognized as worthwhile, noble and/or heroic goals. While the document asks us to extend our sense of compassion to people of all nations, cultures, and religions, it does not place them all on a level playing field—a caveat that is clearly defined in Article 30 of the UDHR: "Nothing in this Declaration may be interpreted as implying for any State, group or person any right to engage in any activity or to perform any act aimed at the destruction of any of the rights and freedoms set forth herein."

Findings from the case studies indicated that millions of individuals had used interactive tools to take actions with direct correspondence to a variety of Articles within the UDHR. The Kony 2012 campaign primarily addressed Articles 4 and 5 (i.e., prohibiting slavery and torture respectively), while campaigns by members of Avaaz.org addressed seven Articles including, 1, 2, 5, 7, 19, 21, and 25—acting to protect individuals from torture, providing medical care, and more. The research strongly suggested that social media was impacting the social construction of heroism. The "data cloud" was revealed to be a situational factor, placing individuals within an interactive matrix where clear dividing lines between action in the "cyber" world and the "real" world disappeared. Contemporary expressions of heroic behavior were seen to be manifesting in a collaborative form—seamlessly bridging the online and offline worlds (Klisanin, 2015).

To extend the investigation, the method of evolutionary systems design was later used to explore the impact of information and communication technologies on three areas of heroism previously identified by Franco, Blau, and Zimbardo (2011) as martial heroism, civil heroism, and social heroism. That study looked at ten dimensions of human activity and found evidence that digital technologies and cloud computing had impacted heroism in each sector. For example, martial heroism was seen to be impacted by drone warfare, digital surveillance, and counter cyber terrorism, while civil heroism was impacted by crowd-sourcing initiatives, and social heroism by citizen activism (Klisanin, 2014).

But what about the public's perception of the impact of digital technologies on heroism? To explore this question, a study was designed using a survey research approach (Klisanin, 2016). In it 300 participants from 25 countries completed an online survey that consisted of numerous questions about their understanding of heroism and aspects of it. Survey items consisted of statements that the respondents indicated to be more or less true using a four-point response scale. Response data were coded as scale-level data for principal component analysis. A robust five-factor structure emerged, based on five sets of distinct and tightly interrelated subsets of items, as shown in Figure 15.1. Consensus among participants indicated that:

1 collaboration expands heroic potential;
2 Internet technology expands heroic potential;
3 heroes are motivated to serve and protect;
4 heroes are responsive to injustice; and
5 concern for justice is a required ingredient.

The results of the study support a strong collaborative dimension to contemporary and consensus beliefs about the nature of heroic behavior, suggesting that the digital age is contributing to a revolution in the way that people perceive heroism (Klisanin, 2016). While collaboration has always been recognized as essential to the achievement of heroic endeavors, for example, the Salt March led by Mohandas Gandhi, and the March on Washington led by Martin Luther King, Jr., for the most part, research has focused on the actions of the leaders (e.g., Gandhi and King), rather than the collective. While leadership is an essential element of collaborative heroism, in that actions are set in motion by the efforts an individual, a small group of individuals,

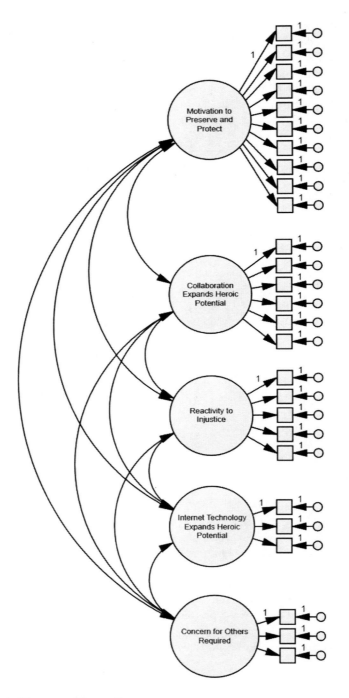

Figure 15.1 Path Diagram of Factor Structure

or through collective decision-making, (Klisanin, 2015), it is now possible to study the behavior of the collective in a manner that was previously impossible (Christakis & Fowler, 2009). When millions of individuals change their profile picture on Facebook to show support for same-sex marriage, or tweet their solidary with a controversial figure such as Edward Snowden, their names become part of networked history. Their vulnerability and/or the personal risks they face largely depend upon the societies in which they live (situation) and their ability to manage the physical, emotional, mental, and spiritual stress associated with participation. At the level of the collective, however risk is often recognized to be social and planetary, rather than personal—thus involving a measure of foresight.

Because the taxonomy of heroism research (Franco, Blau, & Zimbardo, 2011, p. 109) focuses on individual heroes, rather than the collective, a taxonomy for collaborative heroism is warranted (Klisanin, 2014). However, if we focus on the *individuals* engaging in collaborative social heroism (i.e., rather than collaborative marital or civil heroism), and recognize their actions as those that support the adoption of values previously deemed unacceptable (e.g., same-sex marriage, animal rights legislation, environmental protection regulations), we can recognize their resemblance to the individual social hero:

> The true power (and perhaps the final measure of success) of a social hero is that their actions *can* ultimately guide us through the dissonance, *which they themselves produced*, to embrace a challenging new set of values that has the potential to drive further constructive action.
>
> *(Franco, Blau, & Zimbardo, 2011, p. 111)*

The power, risks, and rewards brought about by individuals engaging in other forms of heroism mediated by cloud computing (i.e., soldier maneuvering a drone, individual thwarting cyber terror attack, etc.), require further investigation.

The Psyche of the Networked Hero

What little we know about the psyche of the networked hero is based on a self-report questionnaire generated to explore theoretical research on individuals using digital technologies to help other people, animals, and the environment—described as the Cyberhero archetype (Klisanin, 2012). Archetypes are "collective patterns ... a typos [imprint], a definite grouping of archaic characters containing, in form as well as in meaning, mythological motifs" (Jung, 1968, p. 41). Jung explained these motifs as "appear[ing] in pure form in fairytales, myths, legends, and folklore" and cited "the Hero, the Redeemer, the Dragon," as some of the most well-known (p. 41). In 1938, the hero took another form: the superhero, "secularized forms of supernatural beings that populate folklore and legend and religious literature" (Packer, 2010, p. 23). The Cyberhero is a specialized form of the hero archetype—one that relies upon digital technologies. Because the Internet confers abilities akin to superpowers, the Cyberhero brings the superheroes of sci-fi and/or fantasy—into human embodiment. Thus, as a theoretical construct, the Cyberhero archetype was hypothesized as embodying some of the highest ideals of heroes and superheroes.

An example of this archetype is found in the persons of Paige Dayal, the Canadian teen mentioned in the open line of this chapter. When Dayal learned that a young man in an online chat room had swallowed 36 pills in a suicide attempt, the 14-year-old shared her concerns with her mother. Then "mother and daughter scoured through the Tumblr site" in an attempt to determine the young man's location. After determining his location in Bath, England, they began making phone calls, eventually persuading the police to investigate (DiManno, 2012). Rather than being bystanders, through using the tools of the networked society, Dayal and her mother, set in motion a series of events that ultimately saved the young man's life. The Cyberhero archetype provides a way to recognize such behavior, providing an antithesis to the cyber-bully and related constructs.

To explore the Cyberhero archetype, a study was designed to test premises that (1) individuals are motivated to act on behalf of other people, animals, and the environment using the Internet in the peaceful service of achieving humanity's highest ideals and aspirations, and (2) they embody a transpersonal sense of identity. A total of 298 individuals from 32 countries indicated the degree to which they agreed with 15 statements, with all respondents reporting engagement in one or more form of Internet activism considered beneficial to other people, animals, or the environment (Klisanin, 2012). Results supported both premises. Representative sample statements and results are provided in Figures 15.2 and 15.3.

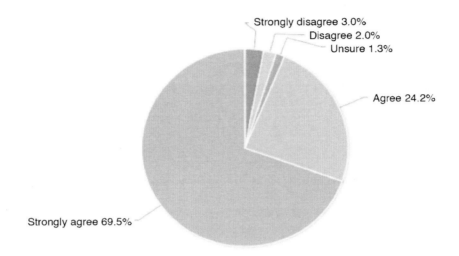

Figure 15.2 Responses to the Statement "I believe my life is interconnected with all the life forms on the planet"

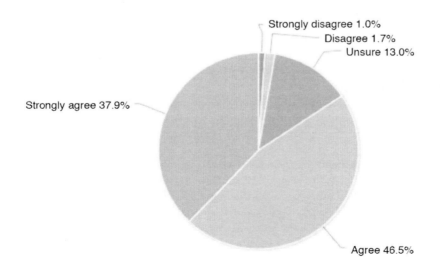

Figure 15.3 Responses to the Statement "Through using the Internet to help others, I am contributing to conditions that create peace in the world"

The transpersonal psyche is to the individual psyche, what planetary consciousness is to the collective. It describes a self or Self that extends "beyond the personal to encompass wider aspects of humankind, life, psyche, and the cosmos" (Walsh & Vaughn, 1993). The psyche brings with it highly developed character strengths and virtues (e.g., altruism, compassion, empathy), the ability to transcend paradox, and a feeling of interdependence, or unity, with all of life. Individuals embodying this psyche have moved beyond the paradox of the "individual" and the "collective"—they understand the "self" as both a strand in the web of life and the web itself.

Traditionally, heroes have been understood as "reactive"—that is, as taking action only when the need to act arises (for example, rescuing a drowning man). Individuals embodying this archetype are however, both reactive and proactive: "reactive" in that they are reaching beyond physical boundaries to address existing problems, and "proactive" in trying to prevent the worst consequence of social inequality and environmental destruction. They recognize global threats to social and ecological wellbeing as personal/collective threats, and rather than requiring a personal confrontation with immediate danger, the individual has a psychological confrontation with current and/or impending species-wide dangers (Klisanin, 2012).

While there is a seeming lack of risk involved and an ease of engagement, traditionally unassociated with heroism, rather than being a solo feat, action arising through the Internet and mobile technologies takes place within a system that is kept online by the actions of a complex network of others. Risks to one individual may be mitigated by the concomitant actions of millions, however the agency of the individual to act is not lost within the matrix, but instead carries tremendous exponential potential. The expansion of the network dramatically decreases risk while inversely increasing individual agency. The level of risk and ease of engagement involved is only determined by the situation in which the individual and/or collective resides. While interactive technology enables some individuals to avoid personal confrontations with immediate danger, this is not true in all circumstances. We have only to look to conflicts in Moldavia, Egypt, and Syria, to bear witness to individuals who have risked their lives by using social media to promote democracy (Bennett, 2011).

Rather than setting out on an epic adventure to faraway lands and encountering life-threatening dangers, as in the traditional heroic narrative (Campbell, 1949), the individual, paradoxically, both stays at home and sets off–into cyberspace with the goal of benefiting others. The "ordinary world" and the "special world" commingle. In this matrix of interactivity, the stages of Campbell's (1949) model of the hero's journey become chaotic, with some of the stages becoming circles in constant motion—concentric circles cycling across multiple dimensions of human action. This hero is called to adventure, but the threshold may move further way, even as it's crossed. For example, the individual may go online to participate in a crowd sourced "search and rescue" mission or to map the territory of a recent Earthquake, and simultaneously receive tweets, posts, or emails, requesting participation in petitions aimed at preventing the execution of an inmate on death row, the protection of an endangered species imperiled by impending development plans, or messages to government officials demanding protection for migrants, or refugees. Likewise, various aspects of these activities may cause an individual to revisit "the descent," continuously meet "tests, allies, and enemies," the "ordeal" may be ongoing (i.e., remain unresolved) and the "rewards" temporary, or solely psychological, as "tangible achievements" may be untenable in the course of a lifetime (depending upon the quest/goal).

The individual's psyche may be bolstered by the tools of networked society—tools which impart abilities and/or powers, historically purview of gods, legends, and superheroes. The latter have been described as including: hyper interconnectivity, super-speed, bi-location/omnipresence, transparency and invisibility, dual persona, avatars & shape shifting (Klisanin, 2012).

- *Hyper Interconnectivity:* The World Wide Web and Social Networks cause Time and Place to converge, giving rise to *hyper interconnectivity*.

- *Super-speed:* Depending on the sped of the server and the size of one's social network, action can be near immediate.
- *Bi-location and/or Omnipresence:* While physically remaining in one location, individuals can extend their senses into other locations. If we consider "cyberspace" as a third, or neutral space accessible to all—the individual can be considered to be "virtually" present in all places—becoming omnipresent.
- *Transparency and Invisibility:* Transparency and invisibility are two distinct approaches to online activities. Opting for one over the other depends largely on the acceptability of the action taking place and the situation within which the individual is acting. Individuals living within democracies may feel comfortable opting for radical transparency—while those living within dictatorships may need to render themselves "invisible" to survive. Examples of software that renders the user invisible (or near invisible) include the Tor Network (www.torproject.org) and Wickr (www.wickr.com).
- *Dual Persona, Avatars and Shape Shifting:* Dual persona and shape shifting are enabled through the use of an avatar. When an individual uses the Internet, or a gamer sits down to play a video game, he selects a digital representation of himself (an avatar). The individual is free to select a gender identity, race, hair color, as well as a variety of other features; depending on the choices available he may choose to "shape shift," identifying, for example, as a mythological creature or a Jedi knight. This ability to create a new identity for oneself, while in reality remaining the same person, mimics the dual-persona and shape-shifting characteristics of the superhero archetype. Research has shown that the type of avatar an individual uses impacts health and other aspects of life (i.e., the Proteus effect; Yee & Bailenson, 2009). The ability to take actions that benefit others in the real world while using an avatar, such as in a video game, will provide interesting opportunities for future research.

In summary, the Cyberhero archetype is an embodiment of some of the best qualities and characteristics of heroes and superheroes—a fusion of the real and the imagined. Harbingers of planetary consciousness, their allegiance is to the health and wellbeing of the Earth and all her inhabitants. While it is unrealistic to suggest that everyone using the Internet to take action across a wide range of "causes" has a transpersonal psyche, or embraces the mythos of planetary consciousness, the research suggests that some individuals do fit this psychological profile. They are best understood as harbingers of the unfurling mythos of planetary consciousness.

Future Horizons

The milieu of collaborative heroism is a situation defined by Cloud computing. While collaboration has always been part of the human experience and is inextricably linked to heroic social movements, in the years since the introduction of interactive technologies, the ability to act on behalf of others has expanded exponentially. Collaborative heroism is a form of heroism arising in, and dependent upon, the networked society. It is emerging in a time of transition and supporting the evolution of higher levels of consciousness, themselves intimately entwined with the outering of our nervous systems (McLuhan, 1964) and extension of our minds (Clark & Chalmers, 1998).

The goals and aspirations of individuals engaging in collaborative heroism include exposing, challenging, and changing untenable conditions around the world, be they social, environmental, economic, political, or otherwise. Rather than standing idly by waiting for the world to change, they are tweeting about the policies of harsh dictators, uploading and sharing videos of human rights abuses, creating accessible online education platforms, signing petitions to save lives, holding virtual rallies on behalf of the natural world, using social media to support charitable causes, creating massive computing grids to solve global challenges, and much more. They appear to be constantly looking for ways to use interactive technology to alleviate suffering.

While they may not all embody the transpersonal psyche of the Cyberhero archetype, future research on the collaborative hero may reveal the presence of one or more of the "eight great traits" described by Allison and Goethals (2011): smart, strong, resilient, selfless, caring, charismatic, reliable, and inspiring. As we move further into a cyborg future (Clark, 2003), the study of heroism will be increasingly important. Indeed, the cost of not pursuing a heroic life may prove disastrous, for although our actions have always impacted others, the nature of "the network" to multiply impact means that individual action carries more weight. At the individual level, we see this in the emotional and psychological ramifications of cyber-bullying—consequences that have included everything from depression to suicide (Goldman, 2012).

At the global level, challenges in a networked society include preventing attacks to the network itself, particularly cyber-attacks and cyber terrorism aimed at disabling critical infrastructure, such as the power grid (Koppel, 2015). The use of digital technologies by those embodying medieval narratives is particularly dangerous. Wood (2015) reports that the Islamic State, which "rejects peace as a matter of principle" and "considers itself a harbinger of—and headline player in—the imminent end of the world" has "toiled mightily" to disseminate propaganda via the Internet. Individuals using the tools of the networked society to stop or prevent cyber-attacks, cyber terrorism, and the use of the Cloud to spread medieval narratives via social media, fall within the *martial sphere of collaborative heroism*—an area for future research.

To a great extent, however, preventing the spread of outdated narratives and affiliated terrorist activities requires supporting the evolution of higher stages of human development (Wilber, 1995). The latter can only be achieved through collective efforts to improve the living conditions of people around the world, such that no strand in the web of life is left to languish in conditions that do not support human flourishing and planetary wellbeing. The 2030 Agenda for Sustainable Development speaks to world resolve to achieve such aims:

> This Agenda is a plan of action for people, planet and prosperity ... *All countries and all stakeholders, acting in collaborative partnership, will implement this plan.* We are resolved to free the human race from the tyranny of poverty and want and to heal and secure our planet. We are determined to take the bold and transformative steps which are urgently needed to shift the world onto a sustainable and resilient path. *As we embark on this collective journey, we pledge that no one will be left behind.*
>
> *(United Nations, 2015; emphasis added)*

Notably, the language of the agreement reflects the understanding that such achievement will require unprecedented levels of collaboration.

The Sustainable Development Goals (SDGs) exemplify the complex nature of the challenges that lie before us (Table 15.1). Achieving these goals will require expanding the heroic mindset in society, such that it encompasses initiatives designed to address such goals, initiatives that are by necessity, collaborative. Many such initiatives exist: a recent example related to SDG 13 is found in the actions leading up to and during the United Nation's Climate Summit in December of 2015 that aimed to bring world leaders to an agreement around climate change. Online and offline activism took place simultaneously, with Avaaz.org (2015) delivering a petition to key German and French ministers signed by 2.7 million individuals around the world. During the Summit, nearly 800,000 people marched at 2,300 events in 175 countries calling for a 100 percent clean energy future (Avaaz.org, 2015). Social media was flooded with images of solidarity, many from the "Earth to Paris" campaign launched by the United Nations Foundation, Good, UNESCO, and a bevy of partners (www.earthtoparis.org). The campaign video had over 1 million views and the hashtag, #EarthtoParis reached over 1.4 billion impressions during the final week of the campaign (Hughes, 2015).

Dana Klisanin

Table 15.1 United Nations Sustainable Development Goals (2015)

1. End poverty in all its forms everywhere.
2. End hunger, achieve food security and improved nutrition and promote sustainable agriculture.
3. Ensure healthy lives and promote well-being for all at all ages.
4. Ensure inclusive and equitable quality education and promote lifelong learning opportunities for all.
5. Achieve gender equality and empower all women and girls.
6. Ensure availability and sustainable management of water and sanitation for all.
7. Ensure access to affordable, reliable, sustainable and modern energy for all.
8. Promote sustained, inclusive and sustainable economic growth, full and productive employment and decent work for all.
9. Build resilient infrastructure, promote inclusive and sustainable industrialization and foster innovation.
10. Reduce inequality within and among countries.
11. Make cities and human settlements inclusive, safe, resilient and sustainable.
12. Ensure sustainable consumption and production patterns.
13. Take urgent action to combat climate change and its impacts
14. Conserve and sustainably use the oceans, seas and marine resources for sustainable development.
15. Protect, restore and promote sustainable use of terrestrial ecosystems, sustainably manage forests, combat desertification, and halt and reverse land degradation and halt biodiversity loss.
16. Promote peaceful and inclusive societies for sustainable development, provide access to justice for all and build effective, accountable and inclusive institutions at all levels.
17. Strengthen the means of implementation and revitalize the global partnership for sustainable development.

By the end of the climate summit, individuals around the world were celebrating: G7 leaders had committed to phase out carbon pollution over the course of the century (Jervey, 2015). The celebration was short-lived, however, with those who participated realizing their real work was far from complete.

> We know this agreement alone will not meet the threat of climate change; that will require continued ambitious action from governments, the private sector, and all of us to limit the global rise in temperature and move more rapidly toward a clean energy future with net zero emissions.
>
> *(Earth to Paris, 2015)*

The hero in the collaborative matrix of the cloud brings rewards to the global society, but another threshold immediately appears. What are the psychological costs? Does the collaborative hero suffer? Are there physical, emotional, mental, and spiritual risks involved in collaborative heroism? Future research will help us answer these questions. One thing appears certain—to flourish in this heroic matrix, an individual will need to recognize himself/herself as part of a larger whole, enfolded in an implicate order that while in flux, has a certain stability. Bohm (1980) explains this type of stability in terms of a forest that maintains its integrity although the trees within it are continually dying and being replaced by new ones (p. 246). Individuals collaborating to tackle global challenges will need to recognize that they may not accomplished their aims in the course of a lifetime, but the larger community—*the forest*—will remain. Although the individual dies and is replaced by another, the heroic journey continues. The scientific paradigm of the networked revolution will support such understanding, for it

Has the promise of reshaping our basic commonsense expectations of the world around us, and may allow us to recognize that we are not a basically individualistic, asocial, and quarrelsome creature that comes in bounded linguistic, ethnic, racial, or religious types, but a social species linked to one another by far-reaching network ties.

(Terrell, Shafie, & Golitko, 2014)

A recent study conducted by Kinsella, Ritchie, and Igou (2015) has underscored the "importance of heroism in everyday life," and suggests wide-reaching effects across a wide range of human experience. Collaborative heroism is poised to expand the heroic imagination in ways that make heroism accessible to all, particularly where education is designed to support the understanding of our interdependence, as well as the skills necessary to support heroic behavior such as currently taught and promoted by the Heroic Imagination Project (http://heroicimagination.org) and the Hero Round Table (www.heroroundtable.com). Because heroes serve as aspirational models of behavior (Allison & Goethals, 2015), such education should be prioritized—for although the space walk was half a century ago, and the World Wide Web has enmeshed us in a global matrix of instant communication, a critical mass of the world's population is yet to evolve beyond the mentality of warring and tribalism (Wilber, 1995).

If we require yet more impetus to explore heroism in the networked society we need only look to Csikszentmihalyi (1993), who reminds us that it is "our responsibility to try imagining what human beings could be at the next stage of its history":

If we do not, evolution will continue to proceed blindly. Yet we have advanced too deeply into the future to simply let things work out as they will. And we cannot chart a hopeful course without meaningful models, without realistic images of what we can become.

(Csikszentmihalyi, 1993, p. 234)

A product of the networked society, collaborative heroism is the child of complexity. Where Chaos Theory tells us that the flapping of a butterfly's wings on one side of the world can affect climate on the other side, collaborative heroism tells us an individual on one side of the world can tweet and set in motion a movement capable of toppling dictators on the other side. With over two billion people yet suffering under dictatorships (Freedom House, 2016) the *heroism of the many* will require courage, leadership, and foresight. In the networked society, *expression* itself carries risk—even in so-called democracies. The Turkish government's detention of academics for signing a petition criticizing military operations exemplifies this risk. The petition called for the government to halt massacres in the south-east region of the country. Individuals signing the petition stated that they "refused to be 'a party to the crime' and called for the resumption of peace efforts with the rebels" (BBC, 2016). Rather than supporting terrorism (as claimed by the government), the signatories aim to address violations of the Universal Declaration of Human Rights. By doing so, they were acting on behalf of the global body and engaging in collaborative heroism.

Collaborative heroism complements more traditional conceptions of heroism. Indeed, some of the individuals who spearhead collaborative initiatives (i.e., the leaders) may best be studied using definitions of heroism such as provided by Allison and Goethals (2011) or Franco, Blau, and Zimbardo (2011). These forms of heroism overlap and support one another. An example of their merging narratives is found in the collaborative effort that brought the Ebola epidemic to an end. In 2014, Time magazine named the "Ebola fighters" as "Person of the Year," (Gibbs, 2014) a designation intended to honor those who voluntarily exposed themselves to the deadly virus—this designation speaks to traditional heroic narratives. However, if we look closely, we find that their efforts were aided by collective intelligence—thousands of volunteers from around the world used OpenStreetMap to create detailed maps and map incoming data. Their actions provided crucial support for the volunteers on the ground (Center for Disease Control, 2016), helping to curtail the spread of Ebola. Time's runner-up selection, "Ferguson protestors—activists" (Altman, 2014) is another example. The "Ferguson protestors—activists" represent a movement for social justice that exemplifies the networked situation of the "cloud"—with thousands of individuals marching in the streets, while sharing and encouraging participation through social media.

> As 2014 closed, stories and unrest regarding police brutality in Ferguson and other parts of the country led to big outcry on social media … #BlackLivesMatter was Tweeted 9 million times this year, and the hashtag that started on social media, has become a social calling card for social justice and racial equality activists across the U.S.
>
> *(Morrison, 2015)*

A final example is Time's 2011, naming of "The Protestors" as "Person of the Year." The "Protestors" included activists across the world, by and large seeking democracy and accountability. The role technology played was instrumental, in the words of the cover story's journalist, Kurt Andersen:

> The degree to which the social media were important in those revolutions, in those protests, has been understated … the way that social media mobilized and directed protestors to this square, at this time, was really extraordinary.
>
> *(Anderson, 2011)*

In each of the movements previously described, each "Person of the Year" took action aimed at accomplishing one or more Articles of the UDHR: the "Ebola Fighters" in providing health care (Article 24); the "Ferguson Protesters—Activists" in seeking equal protection before the law (Article 7); and "The Protesters" in seeking the many benefits of democracy. Those "Protesters" living in the most repressed countries were seeking to accomplish a variety of Articles in the UDHR, while individuals living in more advanced democracies sought a reduction of the influence of corporations on politics, which manifests in issues of access to governance (Article 21) and social and economic inequality (Articles 22, 23, 25).

From Egypt to Greece, Tunisia to Occupy Wall Street, Liberia to Ferguson, the individuals taking action to secure such rights are doing so in the situation of the Cloud. They represent a highly interdependent, globally interconnected body—a global body that is bringing new meaning to heroism. One in which the heroism of the individual is embraced—understood as essential to the heroism of collaboration. Rather than replacing it, individual leadership and heroism are more important and powerful than ever—for the expansion of the network increases individual agency. Efthimiou's (2016) research on the "hero organism," and suggestion that we may one day "manipulate the environment to induce the Big Five neurochemicals of flow states, and by implication instill heroic action and heroic consciousness, thereby altering our cellular and genetic profile," evokes additional directions for future research. For as we move further into the future—of wearable, augmented and virtual realities—we will increasingly be required to recognize the *digital environment of our extended mind as part of our embodiment*. Thus, the study of the manipulation of the digital environment to support states of flow, and potentially support the evolution of heroic consciousness, is warranted. Ultimately, as humanity evolves to embody the emerging mythos and ethos of planetary consciousness, evidence suggests that heroism will become ever more collaborative and the rewards will be communal, societal, and planetary. Where collective intelligence is the global brain, and collaborative heroism the global heart, we will have a global body capable of tackling the complex challenges that lie ahead.

Notes

1 The stated aim of the campaign was to "make Joseph Kony famous," but the purpose, or intent, was to facilitate action toward his capture.
2 The search and rescue attempt was unsuccessful at that time. The purpose here is to introduce new approaches in the sphere of civil heroism.

References

Allison. S. T. (2015). The initiation of heroism science. *International Advances in Heroism Science, 1*, 1–8.
Allison, S., & Goethals, G. (2011). *Heroes: What they do and why we need them*. New York: Oxford University Press.
Allison, S., & Goethals, G. (2015). Defining heroism: Objectively possible or In the Eye of the Beholder? Retrieved from http://works.bepress.com/scott_allison/26
Altman, A. (2014). Protester, the activists. *Time Magazine*. Retrieved from http://time.com/time-person-of-the-year-runner-up-ferguson-protesters
Anderson, K. (2011). Why Time chose "the protesters" [video interview]. Retrieved from http://content.time.com/time/specials/packages/article/0,28804,2101745_2102134_2102355,00.html
Avaaz.org (2015). Avaaz. Retrieved from https://secure.avaaz.org/en/climate_story_loc/?slideshow
Barabasi, A. (2003). *Linked: How everything is connected to everything else and what it means for business, science, and everyday life*. New York: Penguin Group.
Bartlett, J. (2014). *The dark net*. London: William Heinemann.
BBC (2016). Turkey academics held "for criticism of army offensive." Retrieved from www.bbc.com/news/world-europe-35321895
Bennett, B. (2011). Where even cellphones aren't safe: Under authoritarian regimes, texting and emailing can be risky. A U.S. program aims to help. *Los Angeles Times* (April 10), A6. Retrieved May 18, 2013 through ProQuest.
Bohm, D. (1980). *Wholeness and the implicate order*. New York: Routledge.
Boroditsky, L., (2011) How language shapes thought. *Scientific American* (February), 63–65.
Campbell, J. (1949). *The hero with a thousand faces*. Princeton, NJ: Princeton University Press.
Campbell, J. (1993). *Myths to live by*. New York: Penguin Compass.
Center for Disease Control (2016). Retrieved from http://blogs.cdc.gov/publichealthmatters/2015/01/mapping-for-ebola-a-collaborative-effort
Christakis N. & Fowler, J. (2009). *Connected: The surprising power of our social networks and how they shape our lives*. New York: Back Bay Books.
Clark, A. (2003). *Natural-born cyborgs: Minds, technologies, and the future of human intelligence*. Oxford: Oxford University Press.
Clark, A., & Chalmers, D. (1998). The extended mind. *Analysis, 58*(1), 7–19.
Csikszentmihalyi, M. (1993). *The evolving self: A psychology for the third millennium*. New York: Harper Perennial.
Davis, E. (1998) *Techgnosis: Myth, magic, mysticism in the age of information*. New York: Harmony Books.
Detchon, R. (2015). Moving from words to action on climate change. United Nations Blog. Retrieved from http://unfoundationblog.org/moving-from-words-to-action-on-climate-change.
DiManno, R. (2012). Newmarket teen reaches out to save suicidal boy after seeing Tumblr postings. *The Star*. Retrieved from www.thestar.com/news/crime/2012/03/03/newmarket_teen_reaches_out_to_save_suicidal_boy_after_seeing_tumblr_postings.html
Earth Charter (2013). The Earth Charter. Retrieved from www.earthcharterinaction.org/content/pages/What-is-the-Earth-Charter%3F.html
Earth to Paris (2015). About. Retrieved from www.earthtoparis.org/about
Efthimiou, O. (2016). The hero organism: Advancing the embodiment of heroism thesis in the 21st century. In S. T. Allison, G. R. Goethals, & R. M. Kramer (eds), *Handbook of heroism and heroic leadership*. New York: Routledge.
Fishwick, C. (2014). Tomnod—the online search party looking for Malaysian Airlines flight MH370. *The Guardian*. Retrieved from www.theguardian.com/world/2014/mar/14/tomnod-online-search-malaysian-airlines-flight-mh370
Fogg, B. (2002). *Persuasive technology: Using computers to change what we think and do*. Burlington, MA: Morgan Kaufmann Publishers.
Fogg, B. (2008). Mass interpersonal persuasion: An early view of a new phenomenon. In *Proceedings of the Third International Conference on Persuasive Technology*. Berlin: Springer. Retrieved from http://bjfogg.com/mip.html

Franco, Z., & Zimbardo, P. (2006). The banality of heroism. *Greater Good*. Retrieved from http://greatergood.berkeley.edu/article/item/the_banality_of_heroism

Franco, Z., Blau, K., & Zimbardo, P. (2011). Heroism: A conceptual analysis and differentiation between heroic action and altruism. *Review of General Psychology*, *17*(2), 99–113.

Freedom House (2016). Freedom in the World 2015. Retrieved from https://freedomhouse.org/report/freedom-world/freedom-world-2015#.VpqDSrRtCAZ

Gibbs, N. (2014). The choice. *Time Magazine*. Retrieved from http://time.com/time-person-of-the-year-ebola-fighters-choice

Goethals, G., & Allison, S. (2012). Making heroes: The construction of courage, competence and virtue. *Advances in Experimental Social Psychology*, *46*, 183–235.

Goldman, C. (2012). *Bullied: What every parent, teacher, and kid needs to know about ending the cycle of fear*. New York: HarperCollins.

Heylighen, F. (2002). The Global Superorganism: an evolutionary-cybernetic model of the emerging network society. *Journal of Social and Evolutionary Systems*, *6*(1). Retrieved from www.sociostudies.org/journal/articles/140540

Heylighen, F. (2011). Conceptions of a global brain: An historical review. In L. E. Grinin, R. L. Carneiro, A. V. Korotayev, & F. Spier (eds), *Evolution: Cosmic, Biological, and Social* (pp. 274–289). Retrieved from http://softarchive.la/blogs/thebestfreeebooks/evolution_cosmic_biological_and_social.695131.html

Hubbard, B. (1998). *Conscious evolution*. Novato, CA: New World Library.

Hughes, S. (2015). Update: #EarthtoParis reaches over 1.4 billion impressions during COP21. Retrieved from https://hatchexperience.org/earthtoparis-update-over-1-4-billion-impressions-during-cop21

Jenkins, H. (2006). *Convergence culture: Where old and new media collide*. New York: New York University Press.

Jervey, B. (2015). The Paris Agreement is Adopted. Retrieved from http://magazine.good.is/articles/brink-historic-climate-pact

Jung, C. (1968). *Analytical psychology: Its theory & practice*. New York: Vintage Books.

Jung, C. (1985). *The practice of psychotherapy: Essays on the transference and other subjects*. Princeton, NJ: Princeton University Press.

Kinsella, E. L., Ritchie, T. D., & Igou, E. R. (2015). Lay perspectives on the social and psychological functions of heroes. *Frontiers in Psychology*, *6*, 130. doi: 10.3389/fpsyg.2015.00130

Klisanin, D. (2011). Is the Internet Giving Rise to New Forms of Altruism? *Media Psychology Review*, *3*, 1.

Klisanin, D. (2012). The hero and the Internet: Exploring the emergence of the cyberhero archetype. *Media Psychology Review*, *4*, 1.

Klisanin, D. (2014). Changing global mindsets: Convergence & activism. Paper presented at the annual conference of the European Meeting on Cybernetics and Systems Science. Abstract retrieved from http://emcsr.net/book-of-abstracts

Klisanin, D. (2015). Collaborative heroism: Exploring the impact of social media initiatives. *Media Psychology Review*, *9*, 2.

Klisanin, D. (2016). Collaborative heroism: An empirical investigation. *International Advances in Heroism Science*, *1*.

Kony Campaign (2015). The campaign: An experiment. Retrieved from http://invisiblechildren.com/kony/#epic-progress

Koppel, T. (2015). *Lights out: A cyberattack, a nation unprepared, surviving the aftermath*. New York: Crown.

Laszlo, E. (1997). *3rd Millennium: The challenge and the vision*. London: Gaia Books Limited.

Latour, B. (1993). *We have never been modern*. (C. Porter, Trans.). Cambridge, MA: Harvard University Press.

Lovelock, J. (1979). *Gaia: A new look at life on earth*. Oxford: Oxford University Press..

Maslow, A (1971). *The farther reaches of human nature*. New York: Viking.

McLuhan, M. (1964). *Understanding media: The extensions of man*. Cambridge, MA: MIT Press.

Morrison, K. (2015) 2015's top 5 social activism campaigns: #BlackLivesMatter, #LoveWins & More. Retrieved from Adweek, www.adweek.com/socialtimes/2015s-top-5-social-activism-campaigns-blacklivesmatter-lovewins-more/632051

Negroponte, N. (1996). *Being digital*. New York: Vintage Books.

Packer, S. (2010). *Superheroes and superegos: Analyzing the minds behind the masks*. Santa Barbara, CA: Praeger.

Pilkington, E. (2015). Edward Snowden joins Twitter: "Can you hear me now?" *The Guardian* (September 29). Retrieved from www.theguardian.com/us-news/2015/sep/29/edward-snowden-joins-twitter.

Rankin, L., & Eagly, A. (2008). Is his heroism hailed and hers hidden? Women, men, and the social construction of heroism. *Psychology of Women Quarterly*, *32*, 412–422.

Russell, P. (1983). *The global brain*. New York: Tarcher.

Shirky, C. (2009). *Here comes everybody: The power of organizing without organizations*. New York: Penguin.

Snowden, E. (2015) Twitter, September 29, 2015. Retrieved January 9, 2016 from https://twitter.com/Snowden/status/648899559507271680?ref_src=twsrc%5Etfw

Terrell, J., Shafie, T., & Golitko, M. (2014). How networks are revolutionizing scientific and maybe human thought. *Scientific American*. Retrieved from http://blogs.scientificamerican.com/guest-blog/how-networks-are-revolutionizing-scientific-and-maybe-human-thought

Time Magazine (2011). Why Time chose "The Protester." Retrieved from http://content.time.com/time/specials/packages/article/0,28804,2101745_2102134_2102355,00.htm.

United Nations (1948). Universal Declaration of Human Rights. Retrieved fromwww.un.org/en/documents/udhr.

United Nations (2015). Transforming our world: the 2030 Agenda for Sustainable Development. Retrieved from https://sustainabledevelopment.un.org/post2015/transformingourworld

Walsh, R., & Vaughan, F. (1993). *Paths beyond ego: The transpersonal vision*. New York: Tarcher/Putnam.

Wilber, K. (1995). *Sex, ecology, and spirituality: The spirit of evolution*. Boston, MA: Shambhala.

Wood, G. (2015). What ISIS really wants. *The Atlantic* (March). Retrieved from, www.theatlantic.com/magazine/archive/2015/03/what-isis-really-wants/384980

Yee, N. & Bailenson, J. (2009). The difference between being and seeing: The relative contribution of self-perception and priming to behavioral changes via digital self-representation. *Media Psychology, 12*(2). 125.

Zimbardo, P. (2007). *The Lucifer effect: Understanding how good people turn evil*. New York: Random House.

Zimbardo, P. (2011). What makes a hero? Retrieved from http://greatergood.berkeley.edu/article/item/what_makes_a_hero

16

A Training Program in Spiritually Oriented Leadership

Inner Growth for Outer Change

Elsa Lau, Sarah B. Sherman, and Lisa Miller

The Impact of Spiritually Oriented Leadership

The literature on spiritually oriented leadership has emerged primarily from the field of organizational psychology. Spirituality has been defined in many ways, but the aggregate literature generally holds spirituality as a sense of relationship to a greater presence, a force that is positive and guiding. Spirituality can exist within a religious tradition or outside of a religious tradition. Previous work has identified the capacity for spirituality as innate, and its cultivation through religion as one path of socialization (Kendler et al., 1997; Miller, 2015). A recent literature review of 140 articles in the field has provided an overview of the quantitative and qualitative studies supporting the utility of applied spirituality in the workplace (Karakas, 2010). In the twenty-first century, with the growing evidence that spiritual concerns are intrinsic to wellbeing in the professional environment (Beheshtifar & Zare, 2013), there is a great need for leaders and organizations to understand how and why spirituality works, and develop better methods of assessment (Ashmos & Duchon, 2000). Urbanization and increased work hours have transformed the workplace into the primary source of community for many individuals. Although the time and resources for community involvement are limited, aspects of spirituality, such as the drive for connection and meaning, remain to be addressed. As employees search for meaning through the workplace, employers can lead by example, provide support, or ignore spirituality as a critical resource that directly and indirectly supports organizational goals.

Spirituality in the workplace has several aspects which include individual meaning, interpersonal harmony, and value systems (e.g. morality, altruism, and ethics; Beheshtifar & Zare, 2013). Several studies report improved employee productivity and wellness as a consistent outcome of spiritual values-based organizational design (Ajala, 2013; Karakas, 2010). Additionally, employer/organizational spiritual values are positively correlated with group cohesiveness, a sense of belongingness, and employee interpersonal satisfaction (Garcia-Zamor, 2003). In one study, staff ratings of a CEO's spiritual intelligence was significantly correlated with assessment of the CEO's leadership effectiveness, even after controlling for observer ratings on personality and spiritual intelligence as well as differences in company variables (Amram, 2009). This study also provided support for spiritual intelligence as a separate and unique construct from emotional intelligence. Leaders who are open to the guidance and empowerment of ministry and God have been shown to experience positive gains in organizational success (Blackaby & Blackaby, 2001). The growing body of literature on spirituality indicates that there are several areas of the organizational setting that appear to be sensitive to spiritual value systems and application, with positive outcomes.

What Transcendence Has to Do with Spiritual Leadership

Transcendence is a vague term that holds multiple meanings across contexts. In the area of spiritually oriented leadership, the concept of transcendence represents an awareness of self and other in harmonious ways. For example, leaders of an organization can choose to see themselves as the epicenter of a community, and either be aware of the experiences of others or choose to see employees and group members as pieces that revolve around themselves. Awareness of others is critical to sustainable team effort, as the call for creative construction is akin to a song that has many unique notes, each with its specific value and contribution. Beyond organizational skill sets and capacity, spiritual connection (whether as literal or symbolic realities) may provide nourishment for insight and creativity. These are key catalysts to the experience of flow (Csikszentmihalyi, 1997). Transcendence in this chapter, is essentially an awareness of an existence which extends beyond the self; further operationalization of transcendence would include contemplation of a collective consciousness, as Carl Jung proposed (Jung, 1936), or an immortal self and legacy that makes work and creation meaningful in various ways.

Research on spiritually oriented leadership clarifies how spiritual life is often defined in leaders. A review of over 150 studies indicates that spirituality and leadership effectiveness are related through various qualities in addition to ethics and morality, such as humility, respect for others, fair treatment, authentic listening, caring, and reflection (Reave, 2005). Klenke (2007) provides a theoretical model of authentic leadership which points to spirituality and spiritual identity as a core feature of effective leadership. Leaders who value applied spirituality (using spiritual value systems to guide decision-making and action) support both employee meaning-making and work satisfaction, which fosters generativity. Leaders with spiritual practices often develop strong value systems and character, and as a result this fosters a work environment built on authenticity (Sweeney, 2012).

Integration and Application of Transcendence in the Group Context

Research on meaning in spiritually oriented leadership and organizations provides a glimpse into how the early approaches of integrating spirituality in the workplace has led to benefits on well-being, with productivity being a byproduct of well-being. Firstly, both spiritual and values-based organizations focus on individual development and a supportive work environment that encourages proactivity. Work that facilitates individual growth provides acknowledgment, focuses on goals that extend beyond economic gains, results in quality products and services while encouraging a sense of meaning in employees (Fawcett et al., 2008). Faith in work also affects employees' sense of meaningful involvement; believing in one's work as a contribution to a larger collective vision, positively influences employee performance (Javanmard, 2012). In addition, moving from a transactional to a transcendental leadership approach may create a more productive and sustainable work environment (Sanders et al., 2003). These findings support meaning making as a direct and indirect facilitator of personal well-being and enhanced work performance.

Inner Growth for Outer Change

Spirituality that is integrated starts with self-understanding, which then expands to include thoughtful application of awareness in dealing with real life challenges and interpersonal relationships. Positive spiritual action and leadership starts very often with inner work, that is, into the meaning making and expanded contour of the self. A spiritual leader may inspire a collective quest for inner growth, even in a highly pragmatic organization. The guidance of insight, spirit, and collective purpose begins with self-exploration, and defining over time potential answers to existential questions. For example, the symbolic or literal perception of a higher organizing power or creative force can bring a deep sense of existential guidance for an organization in decision making. In addition to enhancing a sense of meaningful contribution and community, spirituality in the organizational vision is also associated with altruism, which in turn supports meaning making and sense of group trust (Javanmard, 2012) in a positive feedback loop. Spiritually oriented leadership and spiritually open and supportive group environments are also associated with altruism, and higher standards of morality and ethics. Spirituality is defined here as an openness to God rather than specific religious affiliations, and this form of awareness in a leader can motivate followers to commit and work cohesively towards goals. Leaders who believe in a higher power can utilize their vision and core values to communicate effectively to their followers and call them to action, invoking engaged membership and continued commitment. (Fry, 2003).

Some scholarly work on the international business environment has suggested that spirituality encourages the exercise of moral imagination and openness to religious and cultural diversity (Jackson, 1999). Leaders and their organizations in the twenty-first century must take into account issues of diversity, as spiritual sensitivity promotes openness and tolerance in place of resistance. Multinational organizations may become more sustainable through education on spiritual sensitivity and flexibility. Spirituality is often defined as an ability to reason both morally and ethically (Ashar & Lane-Maher, 2004). Spiritual leadership also includes an interest in work ethics. In corporate settings where "workaholism" is encouraged, there is often the long term risk of employee burnout. Spiritual leadership brings attention to corporate social responsibility regarding employees' well-being as a solution for sustainability, without detriment to growth and financial performance (Fry & Cohen, 2009). Individual spirituality is also associated with better perception of the ethicality of business practices (Giacalone & Jurkiewicz, 2003).

How Integrated Transcendence Supports Interpersonal Relationships

Spiritually driven organizations encourage individual well-being, which has as a secondary effect of augmenting group productivity. Both spiritual and values-based organizations focus on individual development and a supportive work environment that encourages proactivity. Work that facilitates individual growth provides acknowledgment, focuses on goals that extend beyond economic gains, and results in quality ideas and products while encouraging a sense of meaning in employees (Fawcett et al., 2008). The notion of "Faith in work" is a sense of trust in the deep spiritual values of the workplace and leadership, to be treated and treat others with spiritual value and a pervasive sense that personal contribution to the workplace leads to something valuable for the world. Faith in work affects employees' sense of meaningful involvement; believing that one's work contributes to a larger collective vision positively influences employee performance (Javanmard, 2012). In addition, moving from transactional to a transcendental leadership approach may create a more productive work environment (Sanders et al., 2003). These findings support meaning-making as a direct and indirect facilitator of personal well-being and enhanced work performance.

When the experience and understanding of transcendence is brought into leadership, the unsustainable aspects of group and individual work are brought to light. For example, spiritually oriented leaders often have a deep sense of responsibility, which entails strong values, ethics, and moral codes. Simultaneously, these important beliefs are complemented by an openness to guidance that can arrive in the form of creative and spontaneous conflict and opportunity. The result of the merging of structured beliefs with flexibility and openness, is a leadership approach that is enduring (well regulated and motivated by higher ideals) and sensitive to the needs of different periods of times and contexts (embracing helpful change, letting go of aspects that are no longer useful). Team effort is encouraged and competition is replaced by teamwork and genuine mutual support. Team members are encouraged to become leaders in areas where they have strong skill sets or interests; this is how innovation emerges.

A study on 121 bank branch managers using an independent spirituality assessment scale (iSAS) indicated that spirituality has a significant impact on job satisfaction (Usman & Danish, 2010). Furthermore, spirituality also encourages a sense of interconnectedness and community (Fawcett et al., 2008). This may be one of several pathways that make spiritually driven leaders and organizations more cost-effective. Spirituality's positive correlation to productivity (Dent et al., 2005), may indicate that productivity is a by-product of personal and interpersonal satisfaction, and ongoing work engagement. Spirituality enhances a sense of community and interconnectedness in the workplace (Beheshtifar & Zare, 2013), supporting teamwork and cohesiveness in the group setting.

Transcendent Interpersonal Relationships in the Collective and Societal Level

Spiritually driven organizations demonstrate how to work collectively and harmoniously, how to allow many voices to be heard, and most importantly, how to manage conflicts in a way that goes beyond tolerance and focuses on compromise as well as team-based solution finding. This microcosm affects not only the organization and each individual in their working life, but also has larger scale societal implications. As team members or employees feel supported in working in accordance to values for equality and good work ethics, their well-being and continuously fine-tuned approaches to problem solving demonstrate to their close communities a different way of being. As leaders and organizations move beyond the cut-throat competition model of organizational design, there are certainly ways in which this trickles down into interpersonal and societal contexts, allowing the possibility of transformation to extend beyond the workplace. Spiritual leadership calls for a way of being that is in alignment with human values and environmental awareness, because when the self is seen as interconnected with a transcendent sense of collective selfhood, the responsibility and desire for equality, collaborative and sustainable effort, becomes a call that is too compelling to ignore.

Heroism in Spiritual Leadership

By virtue of adhering to higher ethical and moral standards, spiritually oriented leaders and organizations often become exemplars of heroism. Heroism, as defined by Goethals and Allison (2012), includes eight important traits which capture larger clusters of related traits:

- *caring* (compassionate, empathetic, and kind);
- *charismatic* (dedicated, eloquent, and passionate);
- *inspiring* (admirable, amazing, great, and inspirational);
- *reliable* (loyal, and true);
- *resilient* (accomplished, determined, and persevering);
- *selfless* (altruistic, honest, humble, and moral);
- *smart* (intelligent, and wise); and lastly,
- *strong* (courageous, dominating, gallant, and leader).

These traits sum up the aspects of famous heroic leaders of the past which made them great and larger than life to a degree. The task of upholding such traits and values in the midst of social, political, and/or economic unrest, is no easy goal to maintain.

Historical figures such as Martin Luther King, Mahatma Gandhi, and Mother Teresa, promoted visions of a more harmonious society, each ultimately leaving a unique legacy of hope that inspired many generations to come. Their emphasis on collective progress has an intuitive goodness for all humankind, but the real world decisions they made to promote societies which would be run with equality (Dyson, 2000; Harding, 2008; King, 2000), where human values resolved conflict (Gandhi, 1948), and simple unconditional love is given in total service of God (Teresa, 2007), required sacrifice on many fronts. "Nobility of purpose" is one of the key elements of a leader, along with competency in particular skills (Goethals & Allison, 2012). These leaders can be viewed as spiritual in a sense that is beyond religion, as spirituality can be defined as positive emotions that facilitate our connection to mankind and experience of God (however God is personally defined; Vaillant, 2008). Spiritual leaders heroically apply their beliefs and personal God-connection to the betterment of their in-groups and oftentimes with immense gains for out-groups as well.

Many spiritually oriented leaders in history have met intense push-back for representing the underrepresented and promoting visions that were ahead of their time. An important heroic aspect of spiritual leadership, is the ability to compromise and navigate challenges in a manner which prioritizes long term gain over short term convenience. Keeping with mainstream but outdated practices and social norms is simpler than pushing against the current and changing directions. Additionally, spiritually oriented leaders' prioritization of human values emphasizes brotherhood and sisterhood over a force-against-force approach. Perspective taking and solution-finding generates a form of retaliation and revolution that is more heroic than simple aggression. In the organizational setting, leaders who promote strong human values, community, and equality, face internal and external pressures which counteract values-based progress. Internal pressures may come from co-leaders, who measure net gain as it is solely defined by monetary profit and product/service output. External pressures may similarly come from peer organizations. What spiritually oriented leaders have done and continue to do, is to navigate collective concerns and promote the benefits of collectively oriented decision-making. At times, the heroic aspects of applied spirituality in the workplace can be subtle, and at other times leaders can be faced with challenges that require heroic conviction to bring a cause or vision to fruition.

A Model of Core Pedagogical Mechanisms in Spiritual Leadership

Introduction and Overview of the Spirituality Mind Body Institute Intensive Master's Degree Program

In today's times there is a need for leadership training programs that exist at the intersection of science, psychology and spirituality, integrating with mainstream society. This chapter will will take a close look at one that has emerged, focusing on our discoveries over the ten years of its development.

In 2013 Teachers College, Columbia University launched a Master's Degree concentration in spirituality and psychology. We found an immediate response to the new program of study. Since 2013, enrollment numbers in the Spirituality Mind Body Institute (SMBI) program have rapidly increased each year, tripling in three years while rate of admission is pressed to become more selective. Mid-career leaders and agents of social change are drawn to the program by the notion of "Inner Growth for Outer Change." Students partake in this leadership training at the SMBI's Summer Intensive Master's Degree Program because of its unique content and community of learners. The Master's Degree Program is designed to build a global community of spiritually based leaders from a wide range of fields, including educators, healers, spiritual activists, mental health professionals and visionaries.

Many of the students who joined this program were searching for years or even decades for this form of innovative experiential learning in an institution of higher education, joining from as far away as China, and from fields ranging from finance, education, development and biopsychology. This graduate program marks a genuine pedagogical shift, moving its focus from performance and evaluation, to spiritually based self-reflection, growth, creative leadership, and connection.

SMBI Intensive Master's Degree Program: History, Beginnings, Inspirations

Envisioning

One of our visiting scholars, Benjamin Zander, shares, "In the measurement world, you set a goal and strive for it. In the universe of possibility, you set the context and let life unfold" (Zander & Zander, 2010, p. 21). The envisioning for the SMBI Intensive Master's Degree Program begins in a realm of infinite possibility, the realm of our inner world. It could be compared to the way that we often hear children talking about the world around them, without hindrance. Children often are continuously erupting with boundless energy and curiosity. We no longer have to wait for a far off time when this is possible, we walked into the office and this is exactly what awaited us. Another way of conceptualizing the visioning process is through the language of love, "Listen to lovers build paradise". The talk and vocabulary is of another world, the paradise world. It is a brief preview of the true paradise that will be attained much later by very hard work" (Johnson, 1989, p. 20). The descriptive language that arose when building the SMBI Intensive Master's Degree Program was based in collaboration, connection, union, and oneness. In the visioning process we entered into a field of love, love with a big L, similar to what is described in the quote as a lover's paradise, and then followed with the very hard work needed to bring it into being. When lost on the path or needing guidance and direction, we searched inside, coming back to this space of love as an inner anchor.

We began small and with simplicity, by developing fertile grounds to cultivate a healthy seedling from which we expanded. As stated by Swami Amritaswarupananda Puri in the context of spiritual leadership, "An apple falling down is not a big deal. However, in Sir Isaac Newton's mind it opened up an entire new world, which led to a great discovery. Everything in nature begins small. A huge tree springs forth from a tiny seed" (Amritaswarupananda, 2013, p.54). The elements that created the fertile grounds for our program's seed to grow were those that existed within our time, coming through our own experience. We also attribute the success of the program to the others who have come before us, creating the conditions to make a program such as ours possible. We hold in our awareness and give thanks to the history and context of our program, that which is known and unknown. This includes the many people and programs that broke ground in the U.S., by building the language surrounding spirituality. We recognize that many of these elements have come forward through the work of academics and spiritual teachers over time, slowly breaking down the walls which segregated spirituality from the everyday world.

Initiating Creative Action

> When Mother Teresa opened a school, she did not wait for formal resources to appear first; she initiated creative action by picking up a stick, collecting children and teaching them the alphabet by writing on the ground. Others in the community then helped bring the school into being.
>
> *(Parameshwar, 2005, pp. 715–716)*

This quote illustrates exactly what we did. Without substantial resources we started with creative action, essentially writing the spiritual alphabet in the ground. Although conditions were ripe, when one is embarking into uncharted territory there is much unknown that lies ahead. That moment when Indiana Jones steps off the face of a precipice, not knowing if there will be footing below. What did it take for Mother Teresa to be able to lead an initiative in that way? What we know from our own journey with the SMBI Intensive Master's Degree Program is that we worked with spiritual guidance, vision, faith, and innovation in its simplest form. We metaphorically put a stick in the ground, and community formed around us.

Leveraging Internal Resources and Spiritual Alchemy

Internal creative resources bring about the possibility of spiritual alchemy. A leader needs to be able to inspire others, so they are able to change seemingly simple resources into most prized and valued goods and services.

> In a resource-constrained world, managers need to look at ingenious ways of leveraging spiritual resources. The leaders represent examples of internal resourcefulness that mobilized non-material resources externally (such as the commitment of others), and transmitted tacit knowledge and inspiration (that in turn led others to look within and mobilize themselves).
> *(Parameshwar, 2005, p. 715)*

As a growing program, we have needed to leverage internal resources, much of which came through our administration, faculty and students. Oftentimes, the great gift of presence has been provided by those that have come to teach, as well as through the students' depth of experience. We had faculty join us, and at times waive the fee of $40,000. What we receive is not for personal gain, and is given for a greater good.

Spiritual leaders who have held great positions show examples of this:

> When the Pope gives Mother Teresa a limousine, rather than keeping it for herself or selling it in a straightforward sale, she organizes a raffle which generates more money than a straightforward sale would. When her biographer asks her how she gets such creative ideas, she replies that if he learned to pray he too would get such ideas.
> *(Parameshwar, 2005, p. 716)*

This quote highlights two important aspects that have guided our program's growth. Mother Teresa could have refused the gift, which was not her preferred mode of transportation. Perhaps her lens of a vision beyond her singular self permits her to view this unnecessary gift as a channel to serve others. Mother Teresa's way of leveraging spiritual resources is an example of spiritual alchemy. Another notable aspect of this is to say that the wealth did not materialize out of nothing, in some ways it was a Cinderella story.

At one of our formative meetings, the Vice Provost of the school, Bill Baldwin, said that our program, "Follows the rules and paints outside the lines." In that moment he truly encapsulated the essence of spiritual alchemy that has helped grow our program into what it is today, keeping within the bounds and being able to see the prism of colors beyond. He "got" it, putting a cognitive framework to the process of what was necessary to build a spiritually based program in higher education. Part of the work of SMBI is to recognize what we have, seeing inwards with different eyes and being open to (what are the raw resources) and drawing from our resources in creative spiritually inspired ways.

Coming Together

Swami Amritaswarupananda Puri says:

> There is nothing unsubstantial in this world, everything is substantial, everything is significant. An airplane cannot take off if its engine has a technical problem. Nor will the plane be able to take of if a vital screw is missing. Can we say that the engine is big whereas a screw is small, so let's not bother about it? No, we cannot.
>
> *(Amritaswarupananda, 2013, p. 54)*

The program has a sense of a "we," the necessity of us all working towards a common goal, a higher purpose, a calling. Each faculty and student has an important role and contribution, something different to offer. As Benjamin Zander states, "I settled on a game called 'I am a contribution.' Unlike success and failure, contribution has no other side. It is not arrived at by comparison" (Zander & Zander, 2010, pp. 56–57). That we come together as a community in this way of contribution is significant. Erika Nelson, a student in our program, said that just as great art is meant to be shared to uplift, our spiritual lives are also meant to be shared. We flourish when we do so. There was a deafening silence before arriving together. Each of us and our students had individual experiences and knew a truth from the inside. When we got together, however, there was a collective explosion. This wave of movement is beyond the personal, it is an explosive feeling, erupting, a knowing, I have found you, I see you and you see me, we see we.

SMBI Intensive Master's Degree Program: In Practice

Creating an Applied Language of Spirituality

All of our faculty and students have different words and ways of talking about their spiritual knowing. Some are religious, others monks, and others follow nature-based traditions, Depending on their spiritual path, and where they are coming from, the descriptive language follows accordingly. We have found it important to respect the differences, while connecting on common ground in order to foster interconnectivity. When we come together as a program we practice spiritual multilingualism, perhaps akin to a child growing up with two different languages being spoken at home. Sometimes we come to a mutual understanding and other times we leave a topic open to interpretation and digestion. After all, there is not always an immediate solution, and we see the spiritual path as a continuous journey.

Importance of Experiential Work and Invitations

Due to the nature of our topic, the origins trace back to self-study. People came because of an inner knowing, an intrapsychic experience. Therefore it would be rather isolating to talk about these subjects from a spectator perspective that is descriptive but not at all experiential. We have found that there is a need for the integration of hands-on learning, book learning, skills based learning, and the oral tradition of passing along deep wisdom. This is crucial. Experiential work is like music, and moves through our being. Sometimes it is hard to know if a spiritual practice or approach is personally suitable for us or not until we are in the middle of it, or perhaps even after it is over. To the greatest extent possible, experiential work needs to truly be by invitation, taking into consideration both explicit and implicit pressures involved. There are a number of considerations. For example, since we are in a school where grades are given, we have to be careful about the framing of the grading. To facilitate learning that students are naturally drawn towards, students must feel invited to explore and play, and through the process gain insight.

Ways of Knowing in Organizations

In spiritually based organizations, experiential work is the rich ground through which integrated spirituality can begin to emerge. Through theory and knowledge of the value systems and holistic approaches of spiritual leaders, team members can apply theory in practice, starting with inner work and eventually leading into collective commitments. An individual can intellectually know that altruism and teamwork are beneficial approaches to group work; however, for this knowledge to become wisdom (and therefore a tool for the present and future), they must experience the impact of altruism. Spiritual leaders support this development through example. They practice through ethical and values-based solutions, and when this is applied in a timely manner, the result is a ripple effect. The respect and meaning that leaders generate in their team members allows each individual to consider how they can also allow value systems regarding fairness, hard work, and connection to become their primary focus. Competition steps down in favor of collective work, inspiration, and authentic communication. This merger of head (intellect) and heart (transformational experience) is what allows individuals to step into their work place and into the public with deeper convictions and ability to implement change. This can take place at different levels, for example, the janitor of a multimillion dollar organization can be treated with as much respect and value as the senior CEO. This may sound incredibly foolish or idealistic, and to some organizations run on values-based and spiritually oriented leaders, this may resonate as the truth (particularly in smaller companies that have strong values, and ability to consistently apply and regulate). Both the CEO and janitor can excel at their tasks and goals in the organization, whether it is running a department of hundreds of individuals or systematically maintaining the order and cleanliness of a building, excelling in the organization can take on different faces, each important and with complex levels of impact on others.

One of the first faculty members of SMBI was a true exemplar of the union of intelligence and heart in the organizational setting. In his lifetime, Gary fostered over thirty children, and always demonstrated a deep level of care and commitment to others in both his personal and professional life. The far-reaching impact of Gary's life and work was evident on the day of his memorial service. Hundreds of individuals came to celebrate his life and legacy, from friends and family to many colleagues, along with many unique individuals whose lives intersected with Gary's in diverse contexts over the years. Gary was a clinical psychologist who worked with at-risk youth, and women who have been traumatized and sexually abused, and these were the people who spoke of Gary's love, kindness, and care as catalysts to their healing and transformation. When he came to Columbia University, Gary's seminar on spiritually oriented psychotherapy touched many students and staff. All reported how deeply Gary's support and patience allowed them to experience love, for some it was the first experience of a love they had ever known. Teachers and leaders who courageously allow their hearts to be involved in the work they do allow people to witness and experience new and more sustainable ways of being. In turn, many are then catalyzed to grow and lead similarly in their professional and personal lives. Amritaswarupananda has said:

> One: our life and all our achievements are pointless if we don't have a sense of deep and reverential love toward all of creation. Two: we may have a long list of accomplishments, but none of them are the summit. The peak of existence is love. Three: awakening the dormant love within and realizing it is our innate nature elevates us to the state of pure compassion. When the heart is filled with love, it overflows as compassionate words and actions.
>
> *(Amritaswarupananda, 2013, p. 18)*

To become a successful leader in personal and professional arenas, love and appreciation are key ingredients.

Leader as a Vehicle and Instrument

When we were born, were we given the manual for our brains and bodies? Much of society teaches us to dismiss the rich guidance that our internal world can provide, and we are shown ways to seek fulfillment from the external world. As Ron Young, one of our instructors, asked, "What would it look like, if for as many steps as we took outside, we took the same amount of steps, inside?" When leaders perceive the human body as a compass, both literal (gut knowing) and figurative, then progress is construed in a fundamentally different way.

> Education is not the amount of information that is put into your brain and runs riot there. To me the very essence of education is the concentration of mind, not the collecting of facts. If I had to do my education over again, and had any voice in the matter, I would not study facts at all. I would develop the power of concentration and detachment, and then with a perfect instrument I could collect facts at will.
>
> *(Prasad, 2015)*

As a spiritually oriented leadership training program, we put this way of learning at the forefront. Although knowledge is important, the quality of students' "being" comes first. With their bodies and minds as instruments, our students lead and seek guidance and access information from a variety of resourceful means, such as prayer, religious and spiritual texts, deep spiritual values, visions, inspiration, and the wisdom of elders. This is not uncommon, and highly regarded human rights leaders of our time worked in similar ways, such as Gandhi with prayer, Helen Keller heard voices, Menchu used the bible, Suu Kyi made choices from deeper moral principles, and Mother Teresa heard God's voice. Research is now showing how the inner lives of leaders and spiritual dimensions of their work may parallel. In researching the origin of organizational transformation, other studies have also discovered an unexpected spiritual dimension. According to Neal, Lichtenstein, & Banner (1999), a study was designed to explore the moment of transformation by consultants who had successfully supported organizations in the process of change. The researchers concluded that in all cases they examined, the "cause" of the transformation that the leaders helped to generate was described in spiritual terms as "grace," "magic," or "a miracle" (p. 179). According to their descriptions, the leaders themselves set the stage for change, but a higher power was the source of the actual transformation (Reave, 2005, p. 665).

Working with Inspiration, Creativity, and the Field of Love

Beyond the methodical and calculated planning that we do, there is a deeper reservoir of non-rational space that feeds the developmental progress. As a spiritual leadership training program, we step out of the rational and into inspired space, sometimes also called by us the *creative ocean* and *field of love*. There have been many times we have had plans, an organized structure and yet had to completely let go of that plan and be open to emergence. How many times we have walked into a meeting with a pre-plan, an agenda, and walked out with something else, a sense of awe, wonder, curiosity, and enthusiasm, all of which are transcendent emotions. At times it was not the easy way to redo work that we had already done, but what is easy, is to do what is being called forth, because then it feels good, right, and flows. Meditation practitioners talk about the importance of this space of creativity which can be applied off the meditation cushion, so to speak, but you can experience it on a personal level, which is one thing, and then to work in a team that supports this space and process together, is another thing. This is productivity from another perspective, which could be called *inspired productivity*. When great leaders are asked how they made difficult decisions regarding their organization before they reached success, you will likely hear rational explanations that are partnered with an intuitive gut knowing or guidance that extends beyond intellectual processes, at least in origin.

Need for Master Teachers

In the field of the healing arts and spirituality there are teachers' teachers and master healers, those that have spent a lifetime in the healing arts. There are some people who are gifted healers, and there are others who are gifted healers and teachers, eager to share the hows and the whys. There is a difference between those that are gifted at what they do and those that are gifted teachers, and we have carefully considered this when recruiting our faculty. We invite faculty who can lead and train students on the journey to become healers themselves (psychologists, educators, counselors), rather than only providing students with a personal experience of healing that does not facilitate their path to societal contribution.

In literature on heroism and heroic leadership development, Allison and Goethals highlight the distinction between people who are altruistic, helpers, and leaders versus those that have traits, qualities and characteristics of heroes. Heroes who "behave in ways that benefit others, sometimes at great personal risk, are likely to increase positive feelings towards the hero and others, reminding people of the good in the world" (Allison & Goethals, 2016). Heroes take risks that inspire us. Franco et al. (2011) argue that in addition to sacrifice, risk-taking differentiates heroism from altruism, with heroes taking risks and making self-sacrificing decisions in ways that altruists do not." (Allison & Goethals, 2016) Their distinction is an important aspect of heroic leadership literature, developing a map or lens that sets it apart from literature on spirituality and leadership, which is what we will look into in this section.

We have interviewed two of the SMBI faculty as a way to share a case study of two individuals, marking a difference between spiritual leadership and hero development and the heroes journey. Allison and Goethals note that the concept of hero is not static and that it is also in the eye of the beholder:

> We do not specify the characteristics of heroes, or outline what makes a hero. As mentioned, our conception is not static. We think it is important to remember that heroism is in the eye of the beholder. Different people have different heroes.
>
> *(Goethals & Allison, 2012, p. 186)*

The SMBI faculty would most likely not like to be considered or termed heroes; probably the exact opposite. However, within the specific context of the program and those students in our community that are ignited, inspired by, and look up to our faulty as their mentors, advisors and spiritual teachers, they carry the qualities noted in the literature on heroism and heroic leadership development.

We have found that our faculty are marked with qualities, traits and characteristics that might touch on aspects of heroes literature and the heroes journey. For they have made deep spiritual journeys, both internally and externally. They left the traditional paths that were expected of them, to follow a greater internal calling. Their journeys are marked as having transcendent experiences, or non-local, divine intervention, and higher power. Through this they receive assistance. This is also something that is unique to the heroes journey and stories of heroes:

> Divine intervention on behalf of the hero is a principal element of Campbell's (1949) hero monomyth. The hero in classic mythology is often summoned by a higher power to a great journey, and the catalytic agent of this journey is some type of deficit or wounding suffered by the hero.
>
> *(Allison & Goethals, 2016)*

Within the field of psychology they work in ways that are inclusive of but expand beyond the norm. They share their deepest truths, which many times is outside of what the field deems as acceptable, especially in the field of psychology, where deeply spiritual experiences can be confused with psychopathology. This shows a degree of selflessness and self-sacrifice, to be willing to share when the result is unknown. Our faculty's lives are centered around giving back and inspiring others, also an important characteristic of the heroes journey. "Older adults reach a stage of generativity, which Erikson defines as people's desire to create things that will outlast them and to give back to the society that has given them so much" (Allison & Goethals, 2016).

Interview with SMBI Faculty Mitchell Saskin, Ph.D.

Question: How would you describe your spiritual journey, leading up to your work with SMBI?

Answer: I was trained in psychodynamic psychotherapy and because I had spiritual knowledge, while I was learning I was always translating the psychodynamic psychotherapy concepts into spiritual language, in turn integrating it into who I was, to create a practice and way of working with clients that integrated spiritual beliefs and practices with psychodynamic theory. That is how it began.

I have meditated every day for decades, studied channeling, have sought out spiritual readings, and study astrology. I have become familiar with traditions that have to do with practices of creating intentions, such as the writings of Esther Hicks. These spiritual practices have been integrated into my life, each day I create intentions and meditate.

For most of my career I read spiritual readings, went to workshops, and did other spiritually related work for my own practice and for the people with whom I worked. I see auras when I work with clients and there is both a sense of connection and feeling of an integration, so much so that it is almost that the client's physical body disappears and there is a sense of being together in a spiritual space where what I am saying is coming through me but it is not me. What is coming through me is a wisdom that is connecting exactly where the client is, bringing a sense of instant insight and in turn changes that are miraculous. It is a spiritual moment that transcends psychology, because it is not just psychology, I am the vessel of the energy that is transferred. I am conscious of what is happening but the healing is coming through me from a higher place.

Question: How do you see your role as a teacher?

Answer: With SMBI I feel a great responsibility and that I am a part of a spiritual evolution. I am passing on this knowledge that I have gained through these different methods and my sense is that people are connecting with that because they are ready to hear it, and especially with the students in SMBI because they have come to this, they have realized that this is what they need.

I'm conscious and always aware how the students can take this knowledge and move it on into their own lives, it feels like I am an agent of change and have a spiritual purpose that's very valuable. One of the things I love with SMBI is the different orientations and interests of people. My main orientation is verbal therapy. What I love is that when I express ideas, that students who are more familiar with body therapies translate what I am saying in terms of the body system or the chakra system.

What I really enjoy is sharing my ideas with the students and then have them take it to a different level. They filter it through their own personal and professional experiences and have that come back to me in ways that open my eyes. They have their own experiences and in sharing them it allows me to learn and grow. It is the interaction between myself and the students that I love so much.

Interview with SMBI Faculty Ruth Rosenbaum, Ph.D.

Question: How would you describe your spiritual journey, leading up to your work with SMBI?

Answer: As a child my father worked in the city and we lived out in the suburbs. My father would bring home the NY papers and as a kid, maybe at the age of 8, 9 or 10 I would look at the papers. If it was mentioned that someone was in a car accident and taken to such and such hospital, back then you didn't have Hippa laws, they gave the name, the hospital that the person was taken to. We had a phone down in the basement, and I would sneak down in the basement, and since it was the city that meant it was a 212 area code, which was long-distance for us. Over a period of time I would call the hospitals to find out how the people were because it upset me so much. There was almost no difference to me as to whether it was someone close to me or someone I didn't know. After a while I heard my parents grumble who is making these long distance calls, the phone bill is so high so I finally had to confess. Sensitive people wonder, "Where do you draw the line with compassion and how do you survive as a separate self in the midst of really feeling such compassion and love for the unity of mankind?"

I talk a lot about intersubjective space in the patient therapist bond, and in general, that we all are in a space where there really is no set boundary between ourselves and others. This is a space where the therapist lets go of some of their preconceived theories, own personal structures, and enters into that space with the patient. I feel that is where transformation is more likely to take place. Some people have let me know that notion of being in the intersubjective space rather than the structure helps them.

Transforming people, changing their perspective, has to do with the integration of an existence where we are bound by time and space, where we are very separate, where we are disconnected from not only others, but oftentimes ourselves and this other space where connecting to a larger, whether someone envisions that as a God or cosmic consciousness. It sounds so abstract when people talk about it, but I think what they are talking about, they are getting in a very concrete way, and how that can filter into ones daily life. Once that happens it makes a huge difference.

Question: How do you see your role as a teacher?

Answer: I help students get to know their own source of questioning. In other words, to realize that learning has to do not just with what facts you come across, but with the very process of continuing to open those doors with new questions, with interest, with curiosity, with whatever you think you know, and I am speaking about myself too, whatever I think I know, it just brings me to the next set of questions that I do not know. I feel that in a way that is just as important in a spiritually oriented class as it is in a math class. Sometimes people can feel that once they happen upon a spiritual perspective that it incorporates all of the answers, but it is complex when you think of it. For you and I to talk right now we had to understand what four o'clock means right? We are really bound to local time and space. Therefore, how can a human being in a physical body be in local time and space and then be in the space that has zero definition of those things.

When I create a syllabus I try to really use readings that come from as much of a variety of bodies of knowledge as possible. This includes science, politics, spiritual things, commentaries from different points of view because that's more likely to exercise that part of the mind that keeps asking questions. I think that is where our power comes from as people, that ability to keep making progress and then when we get to the next clearing in the forest to look around and say but what's that over there?

Each person is going to develop a different center for their questioning. Part of it is having them locate that capacity within themselves.

Teachers I grew most from encouraged that kind of thinking, the process of thinking.

Integration and Supportive Structures

We have found that many of our students have come to this training program because they have a sensitivity, heightened perceptions, or as Jung might say, they are the wounded healers. Elizabeth Kubler-Ross says:

> The most beautiful people that we have known are those who have known defeat, known suffering, known struggle, known loss, and have found their way out of the depths. These persons have an appreciation, a sensitivity, and an understanding of life that fills them with compassion, gentleness, and a deep loving concern. Beautiful people do not just happen.
> *(Kubler-Ross, 1988)*

Many have made their way around and through trials, and continue their inner work as part of a lifelong process of committed education and self-exploration. Throughout the program, healing and the journey of self-exploration is like a spiral, where we revisit different aspects of ourselves from different angles and depths at different times. Many of our classes revisit our internal architecture from different theoretical angles, allowing more comprehensive understandings of self, of healing processes, and of wholeness.

Our students come to us from a journey of great challenge, sometimes suffering, and independent sojourning. They are delighted to discover a community of seekers. As a spiritually oriented program that implements experiential work, we have had to put various supportive structures in place. One of these is that we have faculty that are spacious with wisdom and ability to facilitate integration groups. There is a balance that we hold, which is between supporting the inner lives of our students and being an institution of higher education which trains leaders to lead with strong spiritual inner compasses.

Responsibilities and Opportunities of Working in Higher Education

We continuously revisit the platform, the space, and the coordinates of what and where we inhabit. We are an institution of higher education, and that comes with the responsibility and opportunity to bring research, science, and skills-based work together. It is our job to launch students into their careers, and to initiate new conversations. It is our job to provide an incubation space for new thoughts, ideas, visions, and to challenge the status quo. Lastly, it is our responsibility to consider our calling, and how it supports the needs of each new rising generation.

The Future of Spiritual Leadership

The SMBI Intensive Master's Degree Program is an example of what is possible in higher education and can be utilized as an orienting model for other programs and spiritually based organizations. The master's degree program is not meant to emulate, as light shines on all objects that it touches differently and each context is different, but rather to look at the process and glean from it what may be supportive in other group and training contexts. It as an example of what is possible, and in a world of infinite possibility what can be taken further is a leadership from a spiritual lead foot and quality of being. The very thing that this program does is to shift from a perspective of fixed molds and models, to allowing for a space that opens to new possibilities, fresh life, and creativity that stems from applied spiritual resources. However, above and beyond that, this spiritual leadership training program symbolizes a call to action, to look into our inner lives and explore who we are, and to move towards something greater than ourselves in order to lead from this spiritual space. The inclusion of our inner spiritual lives is a fundamental human and social rights issue.

Each time period has its own set of unique needs, leading us to where we are now. With the industrial age, from 1700s until roughly the late twentieth century, economic and social organization moved from the use of hand tools towards power driven machines. At this time, changes took place in the way that goods were produced, there was electric power, running water, changes in the field of medicine, and further advancements in technologies. Shortly after the end of the Second World War, a new conversation began forming around leadership and organizations, this time looking at human capital. Greater value was placed on knowledge, people, and their traits, by society at large. It was understood that organizations and their levels of productivity were only as good as the people and leaders of their organizations.

More recently, with the advent of the Information Age, our economy is increasingly based on information. Most of society engages with technology on a daily basis as a primary form of communication. Companies such as Google do not produce tangible products, but rather are organized to move information. The question becomes, what kinds of needs do leaders of our organizations have in an age of information? How we engage with information and what we do with the information is increasingly important. Furthermore, not only do we have a large amount of information at our fingertips, but it is constantly evolving in complexity. As discussed earlier in this chapter, there are increasingly more conversations stating that in order for an organization to thrive there is great need for innovation, creativity, and values based leadership. In an age of information at our fingertips, globalization, and rapid developments, it is increasingly important to cultivate ourselves as instruments so that we may have a level of embodied wisdom and discernment. The question becomes, "How do we encounter this information and how do we engage?"

We turn to spirituality as it provides an anchor, direction and meaning, a complement to all of this information. Spirituality is an inner sense of a living relationship to a higher power, which may loosely be conceived of as God, nature, spirit, intelligence and the universe—providing a sense of something immortal that is greater than the self. There is a new wave of leaders in the education, mind-body wellness, and business field who value and practice spiritual leadership in visionary ways. They are stepping up, stepping out, voicing their inner truths, and sowing the seeds for a future that is conscious, sustainable, and productive in new and creative ways. These are the heroes who lead with the head, heart, and spirit, with effects that ripple outward, generating futures with less unrest and disparity and greater community and progress.

References

Ajala, E. M. (2013). The impact of workplace spirituality and employees' wellbeing at the industrial sector: The Nigerian experience. *The African Symposium: An Online Journal of the African Educational Research Network, 13*. Retrieved from ncsu.edu/aern/TAS13.2/TAS13.2_Ajala.pdf.

Allison, S. T., & Goethals, G. R. (2016). Hero worship: The elevation of the human spirit. *Journal for the Theory of Social Behaviour.* [Early View] doi: 10.1111/jtsb.12094

Amram, J. Y. (2009). The contribution of emotional and spiritual intelligences to effective business leadership. Doctoral dissertation, Institute of Transpersonal Psychology, Palo Alto, CA.

Amritaswarupananda Puri (2013). *Color of the rainbow: Compassionate leadership.* San Ramon, CA: Mata Amritanandamayi Center.

Ashar, H., & Lane-Maher, M. (2004). Success and spirituality in the new business paradigm. *Journal of Management Inquiry, 13*(3), 249.

Ashmos, D. P., & Duchon, D. (2000). Spirituality at work: A conceptualization and measure. *Journal of Management Inquiry, 9*(2), 134–145.

Beheshtifar, M., & Zare, E. (2013). Effect of spirituality in workplace on job performance. *Interdisciplinary Journal of Contemporary Research In Business, 5*(2), 248.

Blackaby, H., & Blackaby, R. (2001). *Spiritual leadership.* Nashville, TN: Broadman & Holman.

Campbell, J. (1949). *The hero with a thousand faces.* New York: New World Library.

Csikszentmihalyi, M. (1997). *Finding flow: The psychology of engagement with everyday life.* New York: Basic Books.

Dent, E. B., Higgins, M. E., & Wharff, D. M. (2005). Spirituality and leadership: An empirical review of definitions, distinctions, and embedded assumptions. *The Leadership Quarterly*, *16*(5), 625–653.

Dyson, M. E. (2000). *I may not get there with you: The true Martin Luther King, Jr*. New York: Simon & Schuster.

Fawcett, S. E., Brau, J. C., Rhoads, G. K., Whitlark, D., & Fawcett, A. M. (2008). Spirituality and organizational culture: Cultivating the ABCs of an inspiring workplace. *International Journal of Public Administration*, *31*(4), 420–438.

Franco, Z. E., Blau, K., & Zimbardo, P. G. (2011). Heroism: A conceptual analysis and differentiation between heroic action and altruism. *Review of General Psychology*, 1–15. doi: 10.1037/a0022672

Fry, L. W. (2003). Toward a theory of spiritual leadership. *The Leadership Quarterly*, *14*, 693–727.

Fry, L. W., & Cohen, M. P. (2009). Spiritual leadership as a paradigm for organizational transformation and recovery from extended work hours cultures. *Journal of Business Ethics*, *84*(2), 265–278.

Gandhi, M. (1948). *Autobiography: The story of my experiments with truth*. Courier Corporation.

Garcia-Zamor, J. (2003). Workplace spirituality and organizational performance. *Public Administration Review*, *63*(3), 355–363.

Giacalone, R. A., & Jurkiewicz, C. L. (2003b). Right from wrong: The influence of spirituality on perceptions of unethical business activities. *Journal of Business Ethics*, *46*(1), 85.

Goethals, G. R., & Allison, S. T. (2012). Making heroes: The construction of courage, competence, and virtue. *Advances in Experimental Social Psychology*, *46*, 183.

Harding, V. (2008). *Martin Luther King: the inconvenient hero*. Maryknoll, NY: Orbis Books.

Jackson, K. T. (1999). Spirituality as a foundation for freedom and creative imagination in international business ethics. *Journal of Business Ethics*, *19*(1), 61–70.

Javanmard, H. (2012). The impact of spirituality on work performance. *Indian journal of science and Technology*, *5*(1), 1961–1966.

Johnson, R. A. (1989). *She: Understanding feminine psychology: An interpretation based on the myth of Amor and Psyche and using Jungian psychological concepts*. New York: Harper Perennial.

Jung, C. G. (1936). The concept of the collective unconscious. Retrieved from www.cgjungpage.org/learn/articles/analytical-psychology/527-the-concept-of-the-collective-unconscious.

Karakas, F. (2010). Spirituality and performance in organizations: A literature review. *Journal of Business Ethics*, *94*(1), 89–106.

Kendler, K. S., Gardner, C. O., & Prescott, C. A. (1997). Religion, psychopathology, and substance use and abuse: A multimeasure, genetic-epidemiologic study. *American Journal of Psychiatry*, *154*(3), 322–329.

King, M. L. (2000). *Why we can't wait*. New York: Penguin.

Klenke, K. (2007). Authentic leadership: a self, leader, and spiritual identity perspective. International *Journal of Leadership Studies*, *3*(1), 68–97.

Kubler-Ross, E. (1988). Death—the final stage of growth. *Human Survival and Consciousness Evolution*, 274.

Miller, L. (2015). *The spiritual child: The new science on parenting for health and lifelong thriving*. New York: St. Martin's Press.

Mirvis, P. H. (1997). " Soul work" in organizations. *Organization Science*, 193–206.

Neal, J. A., Lichtenstein, B. M. B., & Banner, D. (1999). Spiritual perspectives on individual, organizational and societal transformation. *Journal of Organizational Change Management*, *12*(3), 175–186.

Parameshwar, S. (2005). Spiritual leadership through ego-transcendence: Exceptional responses to challenging circumstances. *The Leadership Quarterly*, *16*(5), 689–722.

Prasad, A. N. (2015). *Blending poetry with philosophy: Swami Vivekananda: The charm of his personality and message*. Mylapore: Adhyaksha Sri Ramakrishna Math.

Reave, L. (2005). Spiritual values and practices related to leadership effectiveness. *The Leadership Quarterly*, *16*(5), 655–687.

Sanders, J. E., Hopkins, W. E., & Geroy, G. D. (2003). From transactional to transcendental: Toward an integrated theory of leadership. *Journal of Leadership & Organizational Studies*, *9*(4), 21–31.

Sen, G. (1988). *The mind of Swami Vivekananda*. Ahmedabad: Jaico Publishing House.

Sweeney, P. J., & Fry, L. W. (2012). Character development through spiritual leadership. *Consulting Psychology Journal: Practice and Research*, *64*(2), 89.

Teresa, M. (2007). *A simple path*. New York: Ballantine Books.

Usman, A., & Danish, R. Q. (2010). Spiritual consciousness in banking managers and its impact on job satisfaction. *International Business Research*, *3*(2), 65–72.

Vaillant, G. (2008). *Spiritual evolution: A scientific defense of faith*. New York: Harmony.

Zander, R. S., & Zander, B. (2010). *The art of possibility: Transforming professional and personal life*. Boston, MA: Vision Australia Information Library Service.

17
Career Development and a Sense of Calling
Contexts for Heroism

Bryan J. Dik, Adelyn B. Shimizu, and William F. O'Connor

March 29, 1869, was a cold, snowy day in Rhode Island, and a fateful one for Ida Lewis. It was on that day that two soldiers, Sergeant James Adams and Private John McLaughlin, hired a 14-year-old boy to pilot their way on a small boat through Newport Harbor toward the army post at nearby Fort Adams. The boy had claimed to know the harbor well, but the waters were rough and the boat soon capsized. The boy, sadly, was swallowed into the icy depths. The soldiers clung for their lives to the overturned boat when they were spotted by Lewis' mother, from her vantage point at the Lime Rock lighthouse. She alerted her daughter, 27-year-old Ida, who immediately ran to her rowboat, not bothering to grab a coat or hat, or even to lace on shoes. With the help of her younger brother, Ida made her way to the wreck and hauled the two men into her boat, returning them to the lighthouse in a frigid but safe condition. Biographer George Brewerton described the rescue this way in 1869:

> The patient toiling girl, immersed in vulgar cares of mending or preparing for the evening meal, becomes the heroine, flying … to the rescue of the perishing. She has no shoes upon her feet, no hat upon her head, no outer garment to protect her slight figure from the storm. A towel is hastily seized and knotted loosely about her neck, and her stocking clad feet are bruised by the sharp rocks and stones, as she speeds her way to the ever-ready boat … Pull bravely … fame, success, and a nation's encomiums wait upon your exertions.
> *(Cited in Adler, 2014)*

"Fame, success, and a nation's encomiums" did indeed await Lewis. Articles in *Harper's Weekly* and *Frank Leslie's Illustrated*, both leading periodicals at the time, publicized the rescue, and stories recounting the event soon appeared all over the United States. Readers found the story captivating, and demand for more about Ida Lewis prompted an influx of attention from writers, photographers, painters, and composers. The city of Newport celebrated the subsequent 4th of July holiday as "Ida Lewis Day," honoring her with a parade and plenty of Ida Lewis souvenirs; hats, ties, and scarves commemorating Lewis adorned the gathering crowds. Lewis was awarded a plush new mahogany rowboat with red velvet cushions and gold-plated oarlocks. A boathouse followed, courtesy of robber baron James Fisk. She became known as the "Bravest Woman in America," and received multiple marriage proposals in the mail, often accompanied by photographs and character references. For their part, the rescued soldiers presented Lewis with a gold watch, and funds from a collection they led among Fort Adams soldiers that totaled $218, a healthy sum in the nineteenth century (Adler, 2014; Clifford & Clifford, 2001).

The recognition Lewis received was well-deserved, because her heroic act that day was remarkable. Just as remarkable, though, is the career development context in which that rescue occurred. Lewis was not a passing bystander who happened upon the soldiers as they called for help, but a member of a family of lighthouse keepers at Lime Rock. Her father, Captain Hosea Lewis, started their tenure as the official keeper of the lighthouse—although just four months into the job, he suffered a stroke that bound him to a wheelchair. His family inherited his duties. Lime Rock is a tiny island in Newport Harbor, reachable only by boat; accordingly, Ida Lewis rowed her younger siblings to school every weekday and became as expert as anyone at handling a rowboat. She was also recognized as the best swimmer in Newport (Clifford & Clifford, 2001). Although her day-to-day duties were fairly mundane, consisting mainly of helping her mother with the light (e.g., filling the lamp with oil, trimming the wick, keeping the reflectors polished) and assisting with her father's care, she was uniquely suited to engage in rescue operations when they were needed.

The 1869 rescue that made her famous was, in fact, far from her first. As a 17-year-old in 1858, Ida Lewis saved four youths who had capsized in the harbor, an event that went nearly unnoticed by the general public. Later, she rescued a pair of inebriated soldiers, followed by a rescue of three men and a sheep, and later another stranded boatman. All of this occurred before her rescue of Adams and McLaughlin. She continued in her rescue efforts long after her rise to fame, as well. After an 1881 rescue in which she used a length of rope to pull out two Fort Adams soldiers who had fallen through the ice into the harbor, the U.S. government awarded Lewis with a gold Congressional medal for lifesaving, making her the first woman to receive the distinction. Her last rescue came at age 63, when she saved a visiting friend who had fallen out of a boat (Clifford & Clifford, 2001). All told, in a career as lighthouse keeper that ultimately spanned a half-century, Lewis was officially credited with rescuing 18 people, although unofficial reports ratchet the number up as high as 36.

Ida Lewis' story highlights how heroism and career development intersect. Lewis was a hero because she performed heroic acts, but she was well-positioned to do so because of her career path—her previous experiences, her personal abilities and skills, her motivation for excellence at her craft, and her desire to provide safety to others, even at great personal risk. While it is unclear precisely how Lewis thought of her work, her obvious commitment to her profession, intrinsic dedication to saving lives, and burden of carrying her father's torch suggest that the work was more than a job to her—it was her calling. This chapter explores the connection between heroism and career development. In it, we make the case that a person's career decisions and sense of calling often function to create the context in which heroic acts occur. After a conceptual and theoretical overview, we articulate possible pathways that may influence the connections between heroism and career development, and propose new directions for scholars to explore.

What Makes a Hero?

Heroism, heroic acts, and heroes represent a core aspect of human history and story-telling. Indeed, stories of heroism throughout history have been told in such a way that there seems to be a common heroic narrative, or monomyth (Campbell, 1949), one that is widely understood across cultures in today's world as well. The narrative consists of a hero leaving the common world of every-day existence, embarking on a journey in which powerful forces are encountered and a period of testing and/or a struggle with dark forces is endured, after which the hero returns to the world changed or transformed, with new insights or power to share and improve life (Campbell, 1949). Curiously, although there appears to be widespread agreement on what makes a hero, there is often considerable disagreement on who warrants the title. This is presumably because although the concept of what constitutes a hero is relatively robust, its application to specific individuals and events within fluid historical contexts is not always straightforward (Allison & Goethals, 2012).

Acknowledging the shared cultural narrative on what constitutes a hero, social science researchers also tend to align in how they conceptualize heroism and heroic actions. Becker and Eagly (2004), for example, suggest that people are considered heroic when there is a convergence of risk taking and service to a socially valued goal. Franco, Blau, and Zimbardo (2011) offer a similar (although narrower) definition, describing heroism as a voluntary social activity in service to others in need, with both recognition and acceptance of possible risks, and without anticipated external gain. They view heroism as the height of positive human behavior. Zimbardo (2007, 2011) adds that heroic acts must be in defense of a moral cause. Paradoxically, heroism often occurs in the context of horrendous acts of evil (Allison & Goethals, 2012), as heroes transform the worst of circumstances into opportunities for good (Zimbardo, 2011).

Functionally, heroes serve to enhance the lives of others, promote morals, and protect individuals from threats (Kinsella, Ritchie, & Igou, 2015). Hearing about heroic acts, especially tales of ordinary people doing extraordinary things, often functions to inspire people to look for opportunities to do good in the world. Campbell (1949) asserted that heroes are uncommon yet serve an important role in casting a vision of a reborn society and teaching lessons of life renewed. Heroes and stories of extraordinary acts inspire otherwise ordinary people toward personal growth and motivate them to do good in the world (e.g., Algoe & Haidt, 2009). Perhaps seeing the apex of human behavior in heroes prompts people to seek opportunities to engage even in small positive acts in everyday life.

Researchers have proposed classification strategies to delineate diverse types of heroes. Franco, Blau, and Zimbardo (2011) proposed 12 hero subtypes based on the types of risks they incur, physical (military personnel, courageous civilians) or social (whistleblowers, scientific heroes, martyrs, good Samaritans, underdogs, political figures, religious figures, adventurers, politico-religious figures, and bureaucratic heroes). Goethals and Allison (2012) proposed a different taxonomic structure consisting of nine hero subtypes that differ across various "dimensions of influence" on the emotions, thoughts, and behavior of people within society. These subtypes are Transforming, Transfigured, Traditional, Transparent, Transposed, Tragic, Transitional, Transitory, and Trending. Transforming heroes are those who are personally transformed and who transform the larger society in positive ways. Transfigured heroes are formed when those around them so desire a hero that they exaggerate or completely construct heroic characteristics or acts. Traditional heroes are those that closely follow Campbell's (1949) monomyth; most examples draw from fictional works. Transparent heroes can be conceptualized as everyday, unsung heroes, quietly doing heroic acts often for only small audiences. Transposed heroes are those who are thought of as heroes, but then commit an act that results in their conversion to villain status. Tragic heroes are heroic individuals who possess some personal flaw which brings about their downfall; examples of this category abound within Greek plays (e.g., Oedipus). The Transitional heroes category conveys the idea that as individuals go through different developmental stages, they evolve different preferences for who warrants the "hero" label; for example, heroes that adolescents admire (e.g., athletes or pop stars) may not retain hero status into adulthood due to the adoption of different or higher standards for what constitutes a hero. Transitory heroes are those who are granted only a brief window of fame for their heroic works. A Trending hero is one whose influence is either steadily rising or falling (e.g., presidents). Adding to these categories is the Transcendent hero, a category reserved for those who are too complex to fit neatly into one of the above categories and instead satisfy multiple criteria (e.g., Jesus of Nazareth).

Walker, Frimer, and Dunlop (2010) proposed another alternative hero classification scheme after surveying 50 "moral exemplars" and 50 normal controls. They identified three types thought to represent personal and situational interactions: a Communal type that is strongly relational and generative; a Deliberative type exhibiting sophisticated moral reasoning and peak levels of self-development motivation; and an Ordinary type exhibiting "a more commonplace personality" (Walker et al., 2010, p. 907). An even simpler means of differentiating among types of heroes contrasts the "proper" hero and the "dark" hero. This distinction, a favorite of literary historians, is outlined by Kruger, Fisher, and Jobling (2003) in their study involving mating selection of female participants. Proper heroes reflect the oft-described cultural narrative, exhibiting characteristics typically accepted by society as heroic, such as those outlined above. In contrast, the dark hero is "dominant, rebellious, frequently a criminal, and often promiscuous" (Kruger et al., 2003, p. 306). While interesting, the notion of dark heroes stretches the commonly accepted understanding of what constitutes a hero within most cultures.

How heroes are perceived by society is a complex process. Typically, it is assumed that heroes are labeled as such by people within a society based on predominant social schemas and shared cultural biases. Accordingly, perceptions of what being a hero entails, which actions are considered honorable, and which unique situational conditions foster heroism all play a role in influencing which individuals are considered heroes within a society. Sometimes there are personal characteristics that make a person more likely to be labeled as a hero. For example, being dead makes it more likely that one is bestowed with hero status, due to what Allison, Eylon, Beggan, and Bachelder (2009) refer to as the "death positivity bias." This bias is as straightforward as it sounds, referring to people's tendency to view deceased individuals more favorably after they are dead. People seem to have a special affinity for martyrs in particular—that is, those who are not only dead, but who died for a noble cause (Goethals & Allison, 2012). Another personal characteristic often associated with heroes is underdog status. While people do not automatically like the underprivileged more, underdogs who prove their worth (i.e., achieving despite disadvantage) tend to generate a positive response to their success. Each of these personal characteristics—death, martyrdom, and underdog status—may at times play into how society assesses heroes and heroic actions.

Finally, Becker and Eagly (2004) assessed the role gender bias may play in how heroism is perceived. They found that women tend to take less dramatic and more relational yet still-risky forms for expressing their heroism (e.g., kidney donation). This finding runs counter to the notion that heroism is a more male-dominated concept because men are more inclined to take risks, and thus more likely to enter into situations in which heroic acts may be necessary. However, Becker and Eagly (2004) argue that the type of heroism typically displayed by men tends to be highly publicized, which accounts for the gender bias associated with what is perceived by society as heroic.

To summarize, although the presence, need for, and function of heroes and heroism are arguably human universals, the particulars regarding what constitutes heroism in its variety of forms are somewhat complex. Regardless of the particular form or type of heroism, the occurrence of a heroic act requires a situation in which such an act is required, a person who has the personal characteristics necessary to identify the need and then carry out the necessary behaviors, and social identification of the act as heroic. The convergence of these factors points to the importance of understanding of their context. Many heroic acts, such as those enacted by Ida Lewis, occur in the context of a career path or work environment. The question of how people choose and interact with particular career paths may therefore be highly relevant to a thorough understanding of heroism, and is the topic to which we now turn.

Career Development as a Context for Heroism

Zimbardo (2007) argued for a situationist view of heroism: moral action is determined not by personality factors but by the confluence of situational factors that lead a person to act heroically.

Although a requisite set of situational factors (e.g., coming across a person in immediate danger who is in need of rescue) must generally be present before a heroic act can occur, research has demonstrated that some people are more inclined to respond to such situations in a heroic manner because of particular features of their personalities. For example, Goethals and Allison (2012) described "the Great Eight" traits of heroism, which share substantial overlap with typical traits of leaders: caring, charismatic, inspiring, reliable, resilient, selfless, smart, and strong. London (1970) examined the personalities of people who rescued Jews from Nazi Germany during the Second World War and found that these heroes possessed a high sense of adventurousness and a secure attachment to a role model. Oliner (2003) found that heroic individuals displayed heightened levels of self-efficacy, optimism, and concern for the welfare of others. In a study extending this line of research by adding a control group, which the previously noted studies did not include, Walker, Frimer, and Dunlop (2010) found that people awarded for moral action displayed comparatively high levels of motivation, reported higher numbers of secure relationships, discussed negative events as leading to positive outcomes, and recalled a high number of people who had helped them personally. These results suggest that personality differences between brave actors and ordinary individuals are distinguished not only on the basis of traits, but also in terms of life narratives (see also Walker & Frimer, 2007). That is, people who find meaning in their life experiences and who reconcile their self-interest with a concern for others seem disproportionately likely to serve as heroes.

Such evidence suggests that some people possess a particular personality and have experienced a particular life narrative that makes them more likely to capitalize on opportunities that may arise to demonstrate heroism. However, some people are also more likely to come upon such situations in the first place, compared to others. For example, some professions regularly place workers in situations in which they are likely to encounter people needing to be rescued. Other professions provide opportunities to have a heroic, transformative influence on struggling students, or on individuals with physical or emotional wounds who are in need of healing. Through which forces and mechanisms do people gravitate toward careers in these fields?

Any understanding of how career choice and development influences, or is influenced by, heroism requires a general understanding of how people make career decisions. It is worth noting that this very question assumes that people have choices to make regarding their career development, an assumption that does not always or even often hold, when one considers the broader global economic context (e.g., Blustein, 2006). Nevertheless, for most people within industrialized nations, at least some level of work volition can be assumed. Vocational psychology has generated a long tradition of theory and research that has targeted the question of why people make the career choices they make. Within this tradition, two paradigms in particular may shed light on understanding what attracts people to jobs that foster heroism: person–environment fit theory (e.g., Dawis & Lofquist, 1984; Holland, 1997) and social-cognitive career theory (e.g., Lent, Brown, & Hackett, 1994).

Person–Environment Fit

The psychological study of career choice and development arguably originated with the deceptively simple trait-and-factor model articulated by Frank Parsons (1909), who proposed that a wise vocational choice required a clear understanding of one's self, a thorough understanding of available opportunities in the world of work, and a good match between the two. This model was proposed just as the study of individual differences and early advances in psychological measurement began to emerge (Dawis, 1992). Early applications of this "person–environment fit" (P-E fit) model focused on assessing vocational interests and subsequently using scores on interest measures to help people identify career paths that they would enjoy and that would permit them to work alongside others with whom they shared key similarities (Dik &

Rottinghaus, 2013). Research on vocational interest measurement has blossomed over the past century and has been described as vocational psychology's most substantial contribution to mainstream psychology (Dik & Hansen, 2008).

The dominant theory that incorporates interests today is John L. Holland's (1959, 1997) theory of vocational types. Holland proposed that both people and work environments can be classified based on how they represent a combination of six vocational types: Realistic (i.e., mechanical, hands-on, outdoor, protective, or adventuring activities), Investigative (i.e., intellectual and scientific pursuits), Artistic (i.e., creative activities that involve self-expression), Social (i.e., activities that involve helping people, such as counseling or teaching), Enterprising (i.e., activities involving persuading people, such in business, law, and politics), and Conventional (i.e., organized, structured, detail-oriented activities). The six types are well-supported by factor and cluster analysis. Also well-supported (by multidimensional scaling and similar procedures) is the circular order or structure of the types, which is intended to convey their relative similarity (Nauta, 2010; Silvia, 2006)—that is, the types that are closest to each other (e.g., Realistic and Investigative) are more similar to each other than those opposite each other (e.g., Realistic and Social), with adjacent types (e.g., Realistic and Artistic) representing a moderate amount of similarity. Holland proposed that people naturally gravitate toward occupations that satisfy their interests, a hypothesis well-supported by predictive validity evidence suggesting that between 54 and 74 percent of people are happily employed in occupations that were predicted from scores on interest inventories administered years earlier (Hansen & Dik, 2004). He also hypothesized that the closer the fit between a person's vocational types and those satisfied by the occupation, the more satisfied the person will be. Although research evidence for this "congruence hypothesis" has been complex and mixed (Dik & Hansen, 2011), it nevertheless guides the use of interest assessment in career counseling.

A conceptually similar model is articulated in the Minnesota Theory of Work Adjustment (TWA; Dawis, 2005; Dawis & Lofquist, 1984). TWA proposes that people have both abilities and needs, and that the degree to which one's abilities corresponds to an occupation's requirements predicts job performance (or "satisfactoriness"), whereas the degree of correspondence between one's needs and an occupation's reinforcers predicts job satisfaction. This "predictive model" has been well-supported by research (e.g., Dawis, 2005; Eggerth, 2008), and conditions of optimal fit may predict optimal psychological states extending beyond job satisfaction (Eggerth, 2008), such as "flow" (Czikszentmihalyi, 1990). TWA also offers an "adjustment model," which goes beyond a static trait-and-factor approach by acknowledging that the fit between a person and a work environment is dynamic, with both "P" and "E" benefitting from working to improve or enhance the fit. When a lack of fit becomes uncomfortable, people can take steps to either change aspects of the environment (an active adjustment style) in ways that better align with their skills or values, or change themselves (a reactive adjustment style) by developing new skills or exploring new work values in ways that permit them to better adapt to the environment. These adjustment styles are very similar to job crafting (Wrzesniewski & Dutton, 2001), a topic within management scholarship that similarly proposes that people can take active steps to shape their work environments in ways that bring it in closer alignment with their interests and values.

Social Cognitive Career Theory

Social Cognitive Career Theory (SCCT) has become perhaps the most vigorously researched career development theory over the last three decades. The theory adapts Bandura's (2001) general social cognitive theory to career choice and development, integrating stable traits with a developmental perspective rooted in the triadically reciprocal model in which persons, situations, and overt behavior interact in mutually causal ways. The core of SCCT consists of three "person variables": self-efficacy (i.e., confidence in one's ability to successfully execute particular tasks), outcome expectations (i.e., beliefs regarding the results of successful completion of particular tasks), and personal goals. According to the theory, these three person variables interact to influence the development of vocational interests, educational and career choice, and work-related performance. Specifically, the theory proposes that people's confidence in their ability to complete tasks related to a particular work domain, paired with the extent to which the person believes that completing those tasks will produce valued outcomes, will work in tandem to influence the likelihood of setting personal goals related to the domain in question. This same dynamic among these three variables, according to SCCT, influences the development of vocational interests, educational and career choice, and work-related performance. A substantial body of research on SCCT, including several meta-analyses (e.g., Brown et al., 2008; Rottinghaus, Larson, & Borgen, 2003), has yielded consistent support for its propositions, including among diverse participant samples.

P-E Fit, SCCT, and Heroism

A key question related to how career development establishes a context for heroism pertains to how people choose to enter career fields in which heroic acts may be comparatively likely to occur. A P-E Fit perspective to addressing this question examines the personal traits that are present among people who enter such occupations. Holland's (1997) theory specifically examines the dominant vocational interest types expressed by people within such careers. TWA (Dawis, 2005; Dawis & Lofquist, 1984) frames the question in terms of people's most salient needs and values, as well as their abilities and skills. There are a variety of ways to identify interests, needs/values, and abilities/skills for a particular occupation, ranging from performing a job analysis to collecting supervisor ratings to gathering "critical incident" data. Perhaps the best approach (e.g., Dik, Hu, & Hansen, 2007) is the incumbent method, in which happily employed members of particular occupations are assessed, and their score profiles summarizing their psychological attributes are reported.

Table 17.1 provides an example of the how these P-E fit approaches apply for six representative "heroic careers": Firefighter, Emergency Medical Technician, Mental Health Social Worker, Police Detective, Special Education School Teacher, and Emergency Management Specialist. For each of these, the characteristic patterns of interests, values, and abilities were obtained from the U.S. Department of Labor's Occupational Information Network, or O★NET (www.onetcenter.org). The O★NET was introduced in 1998, and offers a network of databases, services, and products intended to provide easy access to accurate, continually-updated occupational information (Gore, Leuwerke, & Kelly, 2013). The O★NET database provides detailed information—including interests, values, and skills—for more than 1100 occupational titles, most of which present information that was collected using the incumbent approach. The table reveals that the six occupations differ with respect to which constellation of interests, values, and abilities are satisfied, although some commonalities are evident. For example, Social interests are shared by five of the six, as is a value for Relationships. Abilities required by each of the occupations differ based on the nature of the work, although some commonalities emerge here as well (e.g., Problem Sensitivity). A more thorough list of occupations in which heroic acts are likely to occur is needed, but across the six identified for illustrative purposes here, it appears that individuals with Social interests who value Relationships and have Problem Sensitivity skills may be particularly likely to enter career paths in which the likelihood of a needed heroic act may be relatively high. Although assessment data for Ida Lewis are not available, it is plausible that her psychological profile included these characteristics, given her obvious interest in helping people, her value for being in roles that offer the opportunity to do so, and her ability to quickly identify when a crisis emerged, and act bravely and accordingly. Although one might argue that Lewis fell into the

Table 17.1 Characteristic Interests, Values, and Abilities associated with Six "Heroic" Occupations

Job title	Interests	Values	Abilities
Firefighter	Realistic, social, enterprising	Support, relationships, achievement	Problem sensitivity, reaction time, response orientation
Emergency medical technician	Social, investigative, realistic	Relationships, support	Problem sensitivity, deductive reasoning, inductive reasoning
Mental health social worker	Social, investigative, artistic	Achievement, relationships, independence	Oral comprehension and expression, problem sensitivity
Police detective	Enterprising, investigative	Independence, working conditions, recognition	Deductive reasoning, oral expression, problem sensitivity
Special education school teacher	Social, artistic	Relationships, achievement, independence	Oral comprehension and expression, problem sensitivity
Emergency management specialist	Social, enterprising	Independence, relationships	Deductive reasoning, problem sensitivity, oral comprehension and expression

Note: Information retrieved from the Occupational Information Network (O*NET, www.onetonline.org)

job by virtue of inheriting it from her parents, no one could plausibly suggest that she was anything but an excellent fit for the role.

Closely related to the question of what factors prompt people to enter into heroic careers is the question of how these factors develop, and how they may be reinforced within a particular occupational environment. SCCT provides a framework for answering these questions. In applying SCCT to the life-saving tasks that accompanied nineteenth-century lighthouse keeping, for example, we might consider how Ida Lewis's beliefs in her ability to successfully maneuver a rowboat to reach a flailing swimmer in stormy conditions converged with her beliefs regarding the outcome for doing so (e.g., saving a life). The first of these—self-efficacy beliefs, in this case for engaging in nautical rescue tasks—are influenced by four factors: personal performance accomplishments, vicarious learning, social persuasion, and physiological and affective states (Bandura, 1997). For Lewis, we might imagine that her reputation for being an excellent swimmer and her experience rowing in all weather conditions (personal performance accomplishments) may have boosted her confidence in pulling these experiences together for the purpose of facilitating a rescue. Her experience within a family of lighthouse keepers likely gave her occasion to observe others carry them out successfully (vicarious learning), and it seems likely that even early on, she would have received encouragement and praise for her ability to carry out the behaviors involved in a rescue (social persuasion). Given the poise that Lewis reportedly displayed in the many rescue scenarios she encountered, it seems safe to assume that she could channel her adrenaline into an intense focus while maintaining a cool head (physiological and affective states). All of these factors would have contributed to a high degree of self-efficacy for rescue-related tasks. Whereas self-efficacy answers the question "Can I do this?" outcome expectations answer the question "What will happen if I do (and do I value that?)" The outcome of carrying out a successful rescue was likely enormously rewarding for Lewis, even before the fanfare she eventually came to receive. When self-efficacy is high and outcome expectations are positive, people are likely to set personal goals related to carrying those tasks or producing a desired outcome. It is also worth highlighting that self-efficacy is not global in nature; one can have high self-efficacy for some tasks and low self-efficacy for others. Curiously, for as well-regarded as her life-saving efforts became, Lewis eventually took criticism for what was alleged to be inadequate record keeping (Adler, 2014). From this we might surmise that Lewis had little interest in Holland's Conventional type, and may have had lower self-efficacy and less positive outcome expectations for engaging in such detail-oriented tasks.

Within SCCT, self-efficacy, outcome expectations, and personal goals interact to influence a person's developing vocational interests. If Ida Lewis was selectively encouraged by those close to her to perform tasks related to lighthouse keeping and life-saving, and she came to value the outcomes that she believed would come from these tasks, it is likely that her pattern of likes and dislikes came to reflect strong interests in such activities. Such interests (perhaps Realistic and Social, in Holland's model) would prompt repeated engagement with related activities, resulting in dispositions that become stable over time (Silvia, 2006). This process likely set the stage for Lewis to choose a career in keeping a lighthouse—or to the extent that she had little choice in the matter, it presumably increased the likelihood that she would find such a career satisfying, and keep her from seriously considering alternative paths. SCCT's interest model and choice model predicts these dynamics. The third SCCT model predicts performance, addressing the question how much or how well a person achieves within her or his profession. This model also is governed by the interplay of self-efficacy, outcome expectations, and goals, which work together to predict both the level of performance and the duration or persistence with which a person performs. For Ida Lewis, her record of excellence and her longevity at Lime Rock are testament not only to her objective ability, but to her beliefs in her capacity to perform, her expectation that doing so would result in valuable outcomes, and the goals she set accordingly.

Would Ida Lewis have become widely known for her heroic acts had her circumstances been different, or had her interests, values and abilities prompted her to pursue other opportunities? Although the answer to this is unknowable, it seems likely that she would have encountered fewer opportunities to respond to situations calling for a heroic rescue. In this way, it seems evident that although heroes often emerge from an encounter with situations calling for heroic acts, the likelihood of being present for such situations is at least in part a function of a person's personal characteristics and how these characteristics drive entry into particular career paths. Indeed, arguably few social structures offer the opportunities to for people to express heroic proclivities better than the career domain.

Heroism and Work as a Calling

Beyond questions regarding how people choose a career path, and which factors contribute to those choices, are arguably more complex questions regarding how people experience and interact with their work. Even within a single occupation, people express diverse work orientations. In the mid-1980s, sociologist Robert Bellah and colleagues (1986) described what they perceived to be three dominant work orientations in the United States: job, career, and calling. People with a job orientation view their work as merely a means to paycheck, would take another job in a heartbeat if it paid better, and very much look forward to weekends. Those with a career orientation are focused on meeting achievement needs through promotions, power, and status, and often make great personal sacrifices to achieve such accomplishments. Finally, those with a calling orientation are driven by the intrinsic value of their work, the meaning it provides in life, and the difference it makes in their communities. This job/career/calling distinction is simplistic; some scholars have postulated additional orientations that represent a blend of these more basic orientations, such as craftsmanship, serving, and kinship (Pratt, Pradies,

& Lepisto, 2013). Nevertheless, Bellah et al.'s (1986) three work orientations ignited empirical research on their correlates and consequences (e.g., Wrzesniewski, McCauley, Rozin, & Schwartz, 1997). Eventually, scholars began to focus specifically on the notion that work can be pursued as a calling.

Research on work as a calling has accumulated very rapidly. A decade ago, there were fewer than ten empirical studies on calling; that number has increased approximately tenfold in the intervening years. This short past within the social sciences is the case despite the fact that the work-as-calling concept is centuries old, and has accordingly stimulated volumes of philosophical and theological reflection (e.g., Hardy, 1990; Placher, 2006; Schuurman, 2004). Most empirical research on calling has focused on the role and function of calling within one's work and career, although the construct is relevant within potentially any life domain (e.g., Hunter, Dik, & Banning, 2010).

The meaning of the term "calling" has been the subject of debate; some definitions align with a neoclassical understanding that links to the historic usage of the term and emphasizes a sense of destiny and prosocial duty, whereas other "modern" approaches tend to focus on an inner drive toward self-fulfillment and personal happiness (Bunderson & Thompson, 2009). Given the literal and historic meaning of calling, but with a nod to the ways the term has evolved, we have defined the construct as "a transcendent summons … to approach a particular life role in a manner oriented toward demonstrating or deriving a sense of purpose or meaningfulness and that holds other-oriented values and goals and primary sources of motivation" (Dik & Duffy, 2009, p. 427). These three dimensions—an external summons, purposeful work, and prosocial motivation—distinguish calling from related career development constructs such as work centrality, commitment, engagement, meaningful work, and prosocial work behaviors (Duffy & Dik, 2013).

The idea of work as a calling, and Dik and Duffy's (2009) definition in particular, has some obvious linkages to definitions of heroism. Consider Zimbardo's (2007) four features of a heroic act:

> (a) it must be engaged in voluntarily; (b) it must involve physical risk or potential sacrifice…; (c) it must be conducted in service to one or more other people or community as a whole; and (d) it must be without secondary, extrinsic gain anticipated at the time of the act.
> *(Zimbardo, 2007, p. 466)*

Callings are ordinarily pursued voluntarily. A calling does not require physical risk, although sacrificing some aspects of well-being (e.g., power, prestige, pay) in pursuit of others (making a pro-social difference) frequently occurs when people pursue a calling (Bunderson & Thompson, 2009). Callings, compared to other approaches to work, emphasize the intrinsic value of the work or describe work as serving other-oriented rather than self-focused ends (Dik & Duffy, 2009), consistent with avoidance of extrinsic gain that accompanies a heroic act. Finally, the emphasis on service to others is a core feature of a calling, at least as in neoclassical definitions of the term. We turn next to a summary of research on work as a calling, after which we outline key intersections between calling and heroism, and propose some new directions for research and practice.

Research on Work as a Calling

To date, results from research on calling have been highly consistent despite diverse definitions and measurement approaches. The vast majority of this research has been conducted with college students or employed adults. For both groups, a sense of calling is perhaps surprisingly prevalent, with one-third to one-half of most samples indicating that the concept aligns with how they think about their careers. Some data suggest that women scored slightly higher than men on measures of calling, but no meaningful differences have been found across racial or ethnic identifications (Dik, Eldridge, Steger, & Duffy, 2012; Duffy & Dik, 2013). Among students, the sense that one's career is a calling has been linked with greater vocational self-clarity, career decidedness (e.g., Duffy & Sedlacek, 2007; Hirschi & Hermann, 2012; Steger, Pickering, Shin, & Dik, 2010), career decision self-efficacy, outcome expectations (e.g., Dik, Sargent, & Steger, 2008; Domene, 2012), and academic satisfaction (Duffy, Allan, & Dik, 2011). Similarly, for working adults, perceiving a calling is related to greater levels of commitment to one's career and organization (e.g., Duffy, Dik, & Steger, 2011), greater job satisfaction (e.g., Wrzesniewski et al., 1997), a stronger sense that the work is meaningful (e.g., Hirschi, 2012), and lower scores on measures of turnover intentions (e.g., Cardador, Dane, & Pratt, 2011). Recent studies have also begun to identify mechanisms that govern these relationships; for example, career decision self-efficacy and work hope mediate the relation between perceiving a calling and academic satisfaction (Duffy, Allan, & Dik, 2011), while career commitment and work meaning mediate the link of perceiving a calling and job satisfaction (Duffy, Bott, Allan, Torrey, & Dik, 2012; Duffy, Dik, & Steger, 2011).

Research also has examined how a sense of calling relates to psychological health and well-being, especially life satisfaction and meaning in life. With college students and medical students, perceiving a calling is positively associated with life satisfaction and meaning (e.g., Dik, Eldridge, Steger, & Duffy, 2012; Duffy, Manuel, Borges, & Bott, 2011; Steger et al, 2010). With working adults, several studies have linked calling to life satisfaction (Davidson & Caddell, 1994; Wrzesniewski et al., 1997) and "zest," defined as an approach to life marked by anticipation, energy, and excitement (Peterson, Park, Hall, & Seligman, 2009).

Recent research has established a distinction between perceiving a calling and living a calling. That is, some people may feel that they have a calling but are unable, perhaps due to external (e.g., lack of opportunity) or internal (e.g., lack of confidence) reasons, to actively express or live out their callings. Indeed, evidence suggests that having and living a calling are correlated $r = .46$ (Duffy, Bott, Allan, Torrey, & Dik, 2012), suggesting that there is substantial overlap, but that these are not redundant constructs. Several studies have found that living a calling is a stronger predictor of career-related and general well-being outcomes than is perceiving a calling (Duffy, Allan, Autin, & Bott, 2013; Duffy, Allan, & Bott, 2012). Interaction effects have been found as well. For example, one study found that perceiving a calling was linked to work meaning and career commitment only for those who felt that they were currently living their calling (Duffy, Bott, Allan, Torrey & Dik, 2012); similarly, the relation between perceiving a calling and life satisfaction was shown to be fully mediated by the extent to which participants were living their calling (Duffy et al., 2013). One way to summarize this is to conclude that when it comes to the benefits associated with "calling," it is not only about having it, but living it. Interestingly and perhaps unsurprisingly, evidence suggests that when a sense of calling is examined as a function of income and educational status, no differences are found for perceiving a calling, but people with more privilege and access to opportunity are more likely to say they are living their calling (Duffy & Autin, 2013).

Although the benefits associated with having a calling are well-documented, there is also reason to believe that under some circumstances, a sense of calling can lead to certain vulnerabilities. This "dark side" of calling is not yet well-studied, but theoretically may take several forms. Some people who perceive a calling but who do not feel they are living it may actually be worse off than people without a sense of calling. Evidence suggests, for example, that such individuals are less committed to their careers and have more intention to withdraw from their current jobs (Duffy, Bott, Allan, Torrey, & Dik, 2012). Yet even people who feel they are living their callings may experience downsides. One is workaholism. It is plausible that workers with a sense of calling can potentially feel so strongly about the value of their work, it can become easy to rationalize an unhealthy over-investment in the work (Dik & Duffy, 2012; Duffy & Dik, 2013). Workaholism has many potential drawbacks (Ng, Sorensen, & Feldman, 2007), not the least of which, when linked to an unhealthy pursuit of a calling, is damage to important relationships (Cardador & Caza, 2012). Another vulnerability is goal inflexibility, or "career tunnel vision." In their longitudinal research on elite music students, Dobrow and Tosti-Kharas (2012) found that students with a very strong sense of calling were more likely than other students to ignore advice from their trusted mentors to consider another profession. Finally, Bunderson and Thompson (2009), in their study of zookeepers, found that those with callings often felt a burdensome sense of moral duty—and sometimes felt that they were overworked and possibly denied raises in comparison to co-workers without callings, for whom extrinsic rewards are a more powerful motivator.

Most recently, research on calling has expanded beyond U.S. and other Western samples and has increasingly become a focus of research across diverse cultures. Calling has been investigated in more than a dozen countries within the last half-decade, including Australia (Praskova, Creed, & Hood, 2014), Canada (Domene, 2012), China (Zhang, Dik, Wei, & Zhang, 2015), England (Conway, Clinton, Sturges, & Budjanovcanin, 2015), Germany (Hirschi, 2011), India (Douglass, Duffy, & Autin, in press), Israel (Goldfarb, under review), New Zealand (Lips-Wiersma & Wright, 2012), Romania (Domolescu, Opre, & Ramona, 2015), South Africa (Van Zyl, Deacon, & Rothmann, 2010), South Korea (Shim & Yoo, 2012), and Zambia (Rothmann & Hamukang'andu, 2013). Furthermore, one study (Peterson et al., 2009) included participants from more than 70 nations.

Thus far, the similarities in how calling is experienced and expressed across these diverse cultural contexts have been more striking than the differences. As an example of this, consider two recent studies with Chinese participants. In a qualitative study of 210 Chinese college students, Zhang et al. (2015) asked participants to define the construct, and to describe what it means to view one's career as a calling. Analyses of their responses to these questions revealed that a sense of calling in China (at least using this sample) could be described using four dimensions: Guiding Force, Meaning and Purpose, Altruism, and Active Tendency. These dimensions converge very closely with those found in the United States (e.g., Hunter, Dik, & Banning, 2010), although the label "sense of duty" was found to be unique among Chinese participants, and many more references to religion and spirituality are typically found among U.S. participants. When Zhang and colleagues (in press) designed a measure to assess a sense of calling among Chinese students, the best-fitting measurement model consisted of three dimensions: Altruism, Guiding Force, and Meaning and Purpose, a solution that was extremely similar to the dimensions (i.e., Transcendent Summons, Purposeful Work, Prosocial Orientation) contained in the commonly-used Calling and Vocation Questionnaire (CVQ; Dik, Eldridge, Steger, & Duffy, 2012), which was validated with students in the U.S. It is possible that college student samples may be more similar across cultures than more diverse samples, and other cultural differences in how a calling is expressed seem likely to emerge. For example, base rates are not often compared, but it may be more common to view one's work as a calling in Western cultures with relatively high prevalence of religiously committed individuals (like the U.S.) than in many other cultures. Also, the pro-social dimension of calling may be more salient in collectivist cultures, whereas the emphasis on personal meaning may be more salient in individualist cultures (Dik & Duffy, 2009). Far more remains unknown about cross-cultural differences than known, but to the extent that the quest for meaning in life is a human universal (Frankl, 1969), it reasonable to expect that core features of a sense of calling will prove highly robust across cultures—not unlike core features of the hero narrative.

Three Dimensions of Calling: Connections to Heroism

As the review above demonstrates, research on calling largely explores the construct from a unidimensional perspective, without examining the subcomponents of the construct.

Considering calling's three dimensions, however, offers a nuanced view of how individuals who approach work as a calling may be well-positioned for heroism.

A Summons to Heroism

When people are asked to name their heroes, a third mention fictional characters, a third mention family members, and a third mention real-life statespersons, athletes, agents of social change, or entertainers (Allison & Goethals, 2011). Research has not examined who people identify when asked to name paragons of living a calling, but anecdotally, the examples that frequently emerge share substantial overlap with whom people consider heroes. Biblical examples like Moses or Jesus of Nazareth, religiously-motivated agents of social change like Martin Luther King, Jr., Mother Teresa, or Mahatma Gandhi, and personal connections such as teachers, counselors, or physicians, often are noted. Family members also often come to mind, likely because of their accessibility as role models of perseverance, generosity, and life-giving sacrifice—three of the themes that Allison and Goethals noted as representative reasons for why family members are listed as heroes. Many of these heroes and "calling exemplars" themselves identified the importance of following a "transcendent summons" to approach life in a way that optimizes their ability to express their gifts to glorify God, serve others, or promote the common good.

Among the three components of calling, the transcendent summons dimension is the most controversial, despite also being the "core and most distinctive aspect of calling" (Brown & Lent, 2016, p. 27.16). This may in part be due to a perceived religious connotation. Indeed, the term *calling*, when applied in the work context, originated within a Christian religious context and described a call from God to enter a monastic order. Reformers such as Martin Luther and John Calvin broadened the concept to encompass the full range of vocational possibilities, suggesting that a person could glorify God and serve the greater good within any legitimate occupation (Hardy, 1990). Aspects of this perspective are shared by other world religions, such as Buddhism (Dalai Lama & Cutler, 2004) and Islam (Hermansen, 2004). This religious context for calling is still very salient for people of faith, many of whom identify God or a higher power as the "caller," and the process linked to a more general process of discerning God's will for their lives (e.g., Dik, Duffy, & Tix, 2012). The concept of calling arguably implies a "caller," and the notion of a transcendent summons aligns with how the term has been used historically. However, the concept is no longer tied to religion for many people (Hall & Chandler, 2005). Even so, the sense of being drawn to a particular line of work by someone or something beyond the self is a familiar experience for many people, whether they espouse religious commitments or not. A spirit-stirring awareness of salient social needs may compel some people to pursue opportunities to help others through careers in medicine, education, social work, or biomedical engineering, to cite a few examples. For others, a family legacy functions as a summons, as is often cited by operators of family farms or small businesses—and as was perhaps the case for Ida Lewis.

Regardless of its source, the perception of a transcendent summons is likely a powerful motivator to live a calling. Research on the incremental impact of the transcendent summons dimension has not been reported, and is an important direction for future empirical work on the topic (Duffy & Dik, 2013). Yet to the extent that a sense of being compelled or inspired to approach a particular career path (or to pursue particular objectives within that path) drives a person's career decision-making, its impact is formative. Although research has begun to examine the process through which people perceive and follow a transcendent summons (e.g., McKenna et al., 2015), far more is needed. This is especially the case when considering calling's relationship with heroism. One research question pertains to the extent to which those who experience a summons do so toward career paths that increase the likelihood of heroic acts (e.g., protective services, military careers, emergency services, social activism). Another direction for research is to examine the overlap between personal characteristics that may predict the perception of a calling and also those that may be linked to heroism (e.g., particular personal narratives, social interests, relationship values, problem sensitivity, religious commitments). Framed another way, are people who report that they approach work as a calling more likely to gravitate toward heroic professions (and in turn, heroic behavior) than people who do not report a sense of calling?

Purpose, Meaning, and Heroism

The second dimension of calling refers to an alignment of a person's activity on the job with a broader sense of purpose and meaning in one's life as a whole. Some types of work environments increase the odds of experiencing work as meaningful—in particular, those that offer: autonomy; a chance to use one's skills; recognition of how one's work contributes to a tangible product or service; a sense of how that product or service contributes something of value to society; coworkers who enjoy and value their work; a genuine leader with a clear vision who expresses personal concern and encouragement and who fosters creating problem solving and elicits confidence; and an organizational mission that aligns with one's values (Dik & Duffy, 2012). Such factors are seldom found all at once within a single job, but even a subset can evoke a sense of meaning. These factors are effective in this way because they help a person align her or his work experiences with a broader sense of purpose in life.

Crystal Park's (2012) meaning-making model provides one way to explain this connection between work activity and purpose in life. The model proposes that each person has a worldview—an overarching meaning framework that provides an orientation to the world and directions for living in it. This is the case whether a person articulates that global meaning framework or not. Such meaning systems provide the general scaffold that shapes how people structure their lives (global meaning) and assign specific meanings to every-day encounters with their environments (situational meaning). As this applies to career development, Park (2012) suggests that people experience meaningful work when they find congruence between the components of their global meaning and their daily work experiences, which they achieve through a process of fitting their global beliefs, goals, and values with their work activity and career decisions. This process offers a different type of P-E fit, one focused not on how a person's objective traits (e.g., interests, personality) fit a career path, but rather how what matters most to someone is expressed through, or even derived from, one's work.

This alignment of work purpose with a broader sense of purpose in life is highlighted in the manner in which many individuals describe their underlying motives for doing their jobs. For example, healthcare workers often point to the value of providing healing, clergy to turning people toward matters of ultimate importance, attorneys to seeking justice, garbage collectors to ensuring a sanitary environment and community, or artists to using aesthetics to suggest new ways of thinking about the world. It is plausible that career paths that provide a context for heroism also align with a broader sense of purpose for individuals in such fields. Ida Lewis might have pointed to how her work supports her desire to ensure safe passage for harboring ships and their occupants, for example. Within a particular career path, it is also plausible that this focus on pursuing or expressing a broader sense of meaning primes a person for recognizing and responding to opportunities to act in a heroic manner—expressing both highly competent and highly moral behavior, or both (Goethals & Allison, 2012). Exploring this dynamic is a promising direction for future research.

Social Heroism and Calling

As noted earlier, Zimbardo's (2007) taxonomy of hero types includes those that seldom experience risk of physical peril that is often associated with heroism, such as "bureaucracy heroes" who stand firm in their principles at the risk of social consequences, or "good Samaritans" who help others in ways that often may not involve immediately apparent physical risks. These types of heroes are described as engaged in "social heroism," or heroism that expresses other-oriented values. Franco, Blau, and Zimbardo (2011) explored the complexity of heroism versus non-heroic altruism, asserting that to be considered heroic, altruism must involve some risk and the heroic actor must be under no obligation to complete the heroic act or actions. Given this conceptualization, we can explore how forms of social heroism are expressed through altruistic vocations and thus overlap with the concept of calling.

The third dimension of work as a calling is the sense that one's work is not principally carried out for personal happiness or fulfillment but rather to advance the well-being of others, or the greater good. Such other-oriented motives can potentially be pursued within any legitimate occupation, although they are the core focus within some types of careers (e.g., social work, clergy, teaching, health care). These altruism-focused careers are arguably the contexts in which social heroism is most likely to occur. A career dedicated to altruism not only orients to the greater good, but also often requires significant personal sacrifice. Clavien and Chapuisat (2013), in a philosophical analysis of altruism, defined psychological altruism as "motivations that are causal mechanisms prompting individuals to take care of others' welfare" (p. 6). At what point does altruism become heroic? Kirby (2010) asserted that the development of virtuous character that allows for heroic action involves a re-orienting of one's perspective. Virtuous character in this sense is expressed via an asymmetrical, non-reciprocal commitment to others while sacrificing one's own well-being. This view holds that to become heroic, altruism must go beyond simply helping others to helping others in a way that holds one's own interests as a secondary concern. Given this definition, an examination of heroic altruism and its real-life complexity is warranted. Several work domains and movements serve as examples of social heroism and a commitment to a life of heroic altruism.

Social work is one career path within which heroic altruism is frequently enacted. In a qualitative analysis, Buchbinder (2007) examined the motivations of social workers. The results pointed to themes of existential vulnerability and prosocial values in social workers' family of origin. Specifically, social workers typically observed and experienced the vulnerability of close family members from a young age, then channeled these experiences into a desire to care for others that subsequently shaped their dispositions and, ultimately, their career paths. This pattern raises the question of what constitutes relevant sacrifice; recall Zimbardo's (2007) assertion that no personal gain can be anticipated at the time of heroic action. Buchbinder's findings that some social workers experience significant sacrifice early in life, setting a course in which they later pursue caregiving opportunities, points to a need to broaden the temporal sequence in which sacrifice and heroism are linked.

Beyond early sacrifices impacting later career choices, social work demands personal sacrifice as a norm within the profession. One could argue that the profession itself is heroic by nature, requiring an asymmetrical obligation that fits with Kirby's (2010) definition of heroic virtue. Some social workers, such as those serving suicidal clientele, feel the impact of their work in terms of secondary traumatic stress and overall stress levels even years later (Ting, Jacobson, & Sanders, 2011). Significant exposure to traumatic experiences and behaviors can even lead to permanent changes in one's cognitive schemas (McCann & Pearlman, 1990), illustrating the personal risk involved in the work. The aim of social work is to reduce suffering, but social workers engage with risk that in a way often renders them vulnerable and that is empirically linked to long-term stress (Ting et al., 2011).

Stalker and colleagues (2007) explored the complexity of sacrifice and satisfaction within social work, reviewing multiple studies that report the paradoxical finding of high job satisfaction co-occurring with high rates of emotional exhaustion. Given the deliberate choices involved in developing a career, social workers often anticipate this paradox, consciously choosing to accept personal sacrifice while expecting it to foster a deep sense of meaning. For conceptualizations of heroism that require no secondary gain, this trade-off of hedonic well-being in exchange for eudaimonic well-being would seem to preclude social work as a pathway to heroism. To us, this highlights the limitations of such definitions of heroism.

Further highlighting the limitations of conceptualizations of heroism that require no secondary gain is the Environmental Justice (EJ) movement. The EJ movement integrates social justice values and environmentalist action in response to discriminatory environmental practices and policy based on race and socioeconomic factors (Mohai, Pellow, & Roberts, 2009). Ceaser (2015) pointed to the socioeconomic disadvantage that EJ activists operate from; they are much more likely to face human-caused negative environmental events than more privileged actors. Privileged activists are much more likely to act from a place where they are not impacted by these man-made disasters, thus they would be more likely to fit within Zimbardo's (2007) conceptualization of heroism as activism would elicit less personal gain for these actors. EJ activism, however, as Pulido and Peña (1998) pointed out, is more likely to challenge the status quo to promote broad prosocial goals that simultaneously benefit the activists themselves as they are acting from within impacted communities. Discussing the values and principles of EJ as a movement, Taylor (2000) asserted that the Environmental Justice Paradigm embodies prosocial values of justice for socioeconomically disadvantaged people, future generations, and other species. Given the personal gains for EJ activists, their families, and their communities, conceptualizations of heroism that require no personal gain potentially limit heroism to more privileged actors and thus highlights the need to account for socioeconomic disadvantage when considering the nature of heroic sacrifice.

Social work and environmental justice activists are among many possible examples of people working within professions in which they are keyed on promoting others' well-being and contributing to a healthier society. These values, even when pursued in a way that offers some personal gain, seem likely to drive people to engage in situations that may frequently demand heroism.

Combined with responding to a transcendent summons and forging an alignment of purpose in work with purpose in life, the three dimensions of calling appear to share substantive and functional overlap with heroism. They also likely contribute to a person's entry into, and engagement within, career paths that serve as contexts for heroism. It is likely that both a sense of calling and heroism are linked to the process of navigating the diverse developmental tasks that people confront over the lifespan, such as with an increased emphasis on "giving back" during the later developmental stages in which generativity is a key consideration (e.g., Erikson, Erickson, & Kivnik, 1987). This is one of many promising directions for future research, several of which we explore next.

Directions for Future Research

There are several promising directions for research to pursue that explore the linkages between career development, a sense of calling, and heroism. A few are described above. Beyond these, future research may explore person-situation interactions as an influence on heroism, establish a taxonomy that links types of heroism to occupations, and investigate linkages between a sense of calling and "everyday heroism."

Person–Situation Interactions

One implication of the possible linkages between career development and heroism is that although particular situations are required for heroic acts to occur, there are likely personal characteristics (e.g., personality traits, values) that influence one's proclivity to identify such situations and behave accordingly within them. These characteristics are also likely to influence one's likelihood to enter or create environments in which they are likely to encounter such opportunities in the first place. While some adopt a situationist perspective (e.g., Zimbardo, 2007) and others investigate features of a possible heroic personality (e.g., Goethals & Allison, 2012; Walker, Firmer, & Dunlop, 2012), it seems evident that a dynamic interactionist perspective (e.g., Endler & Parker, 1992) may shed valuable light on antecedents of heroic action.

The situationist perspective is often supported by qualitative methods. For example, in one study, researchers interviewed 63 whistle blowers and 140 activists to gain a richer sense of social capital, cultural commitment to action efficacy, ability to secure strategically placed allies, and other environmental factors that influenced heroic actors (Glazer & Glazer, 1999). Research investigating the heroic personality typically has used personality questionnaires and qualitative interviews that are examined for themes that summarize how personality impacts the framing of heroic actors' life narratives (e.g., Dunlop & Walker, 2013; Walker & Frimer, 2007). Yet Dunlop and Walker's (2013) study, in particular, highlights the potential dynamic interaction between situational and personal factors: they examined personality *after* heroic acts and found that the heroic act itself may alter individuals' personality. Future research should seek to integrate these methods when examining heroic actors. For example, researchers could assess personality factors while also conducting interviews to examine situational factors that influenced heroic action in heroic actors (Reynolds et al., 2010). Longitudinal strategies are another option for examining interactions over time. For example, identifying individuals who display heroic personality traits (such as those found by Dunlop & Walker, 2013) and following them over time, along with a matched control group, to assess the number of heroic actions has potential for disentangling the relationship between persons and environments as influences on heroic acts over time. This design could inform how well heroic personality factors predict heroic action, the amount of variance attributed to situational influence, and answer questions related to the interaction of the two (e.g., what types of situations influence the extent to which personality predicts heroic action?).

Taxonomies of Heroism and Occupations

Another potentially rich direction for future research would be to establish a taxonomy of "heroic occupations," or career paths likely to attract or evoke particular forms of heroism. For example, one might build from Franco, Blau, and Zimbardo's (2011) taxonomy, which examines the relationship between heroic types (e.g. political and military leaders) and the situations in which they are likely to occur (e.g., a time of natural disaster or war), to guide research examining the study of occupation-specific types of heroism. Occupational research on P-E fit could be leveraged in the manner illustrated in Table 17.1 to gain an empirical understanding of how closely individual differences (Dawis, 1992) and vocational types (Holland, 1959, 1997) of those in certain occupations align with heroic characteristics, such as charisma (Goethals & Allison, 2014) or the ability to elicit appraisals from others as skilled, intelligent, and effective (Van Vugt, Johnson, Kaiser, & O'Gorman, 2008). One might also use such a taxonomy to organize reporting of base rates for heroic acts that occur within particular occupations and examine the characteristics that predict entry into those occupations. Obvious challenges in estimating such base rates empirically could be addressed in the near-term by appealing to theory or by employing subject matter experts to provide ratings that could serve to establish connections between heroism and occupational membership. Such connections could permit researchers interested in heroism to draw from the research base within career development and vice-versa.

The title of hero is a social construct (e.g., Rankin & Eagly, 2008), created from social schemas and cultural biases as viewed from within specific temporal lenses. The historical and cultural contexts of these schemas and biases are evident in the frequent lack of consensus on who warrants hero status (Franco et al., 2011), despite the relatively stable and culturally universal structure of the hero concept. Those granted hero status are, in general, those who have strongly activated the hero schema within their particular time and place (Goethals & Allison, 2012). This is another aspect of occupations that may be relevant to understanding heroism. Specifically, certain occupations are likely societally-primed to trigger the hero schema, given stereotypes associated with them and their exposure within popular culture. For example, popular television shows may raise cultural awareness of some types of work, such as counter-terrorism or emergency room healthcare, in a way that leads viewers to expect frequent heroic acts within these professions. The cultural expectations for individuals within such occupations could also be included within the heroism and occupations taxonomy. Such an effort points to the necessity of addressing ongoing challenges such as accounting for gender differences in the ways that heroism is expressed, particularly since "heroic" occupations tend to be male-dominated (Becker & Eagly, 2004; Johnson, 2002).

Callings and Everyday Heroes

Goethals and Allison's (2012) transparent heroes are described as everyday, unsung heroes, quietly doing heroic acts that often go unnoticed. The notion of transparent or "everyday heroes" has deep roots within popular culture. Our university, for example, annually recognizes excellence exhibited within the ranks of the university support staff with an "Everyday Hero Award." Another example is a children's program called *Higglytown Heroes*, which has aired for several years on the Disney Channel, in which four young characters interact with people in their city who share about how their work contributes to the well-being of their community. The show has featured "heroes" representing occupations that include plumber, gardener, mail carrier, librarian, dance instructor, school nurse, tow truck driver, sanitation worker, grocery clerk, and tug boat captain, among many others. Goethals and Allison (2012) note that such transparent heroes warrant their hero status because of their sacrifices and personal investment in others' well-being. They are also perceived to be by far the most prevalent type of hero among Allison and Goethals' (2011) nine subtypes.

We believe that the transparent heroes category represents perhaps the most fruitful starting point for understanding the linkage of heroism and a sense of calling. This is the case because of their relative prevalence and also because of their accessibility—an asset in part for logistic reasons (i.e., they are a comparatively easy population to study) and also because everyday heroes demonstrate that this form of heroism can be pursued and achieved within any career path. This syncs with the way that calling is conceptualized; although some occupations arguably offer a clearer path to living a calling than others, any honest area of work can be pursued as a calling (Dik & Duffy, 2009). Research might begin by examining the overlap between a sense of calling and heroism; for example, to whom do people grant "transparent hero" status, and how many of these also are identified as paragons of living a calling? We suspect substantial overlap in these ratings, which points to opportunities to leverage emerging models of living a calling to understand how people come to express transparent heroism and vice-versa. As basic research on such questions unfolds, interventions designed to foster a sense of calling and heroism can be designed and tested. Empirical research on interventions designed to foster a sense of calling (e.g., Dik & Steger, 2008; Dik, Steger, Gibson, & Peisner, 2012; Dik, Schulljegerdes, Ahn, & Shim, 2015) have lagged behind suggestions and recommendations for such applications (e.g., Dik, Duffy, & Eldridge, 2009; Dik & Duffy, 2015); this has also largely been the case with heroism, such as with efforts to promote heroic imagination (e.g., Franco, Blau, & Zimbardo, 2011). Such applied research promises new pathways to help people cultivate the attributes and express the behaviors that ultimately warrant hero status.

Summary and Conclusion

In this chapter, we sought to explore the linkages between career development in general, and a sense of calling in particular, with heroism. Person-environment fit and social cognitive career theory offer insights into the factors that govern how people choose to enter particular career paths, including those that may increase the likelihood of encountering situations that call for heroic acts. A sense of calling overlaps conceptually with heroism, and its three dimensions—transcendent summons, an alignment of one's work activity with a broader sense of purpose in life, and prosocial or other-oriented motives and goals—each provide a lens through which heroism might be explored. Career paths are just one factor that may offer a context in which heroic acts occur, and the impact of work environments and the personal characteristics they attract and foster point to value of adapting an interactionist approach to disentangling these relationships. Taxonomies of heroes show promise as frameworks for understanding how diverse career paths may influence behavior and how it is perceived within cultures. Ultimately, perhaps anyone can come to express heroic traits and engage in heroic acts within their chosen profession, even if quietly, in largely unsung ways.

References

Adler, M. C. (2014). To the rescue: Picturing Ida Lewis. *Winterthur Portfolio, 48*, 75–104.
Algoe, S., & Haidt, J., (2009). Witnessing excellence in action: The other-praising emotions of elevation, admiration, and gratitude. *Journal of Positive Psychology, 4*, 105–127.
Allison, S. T., & Goethals, G. R. (2011). *Heroes: What they do & why we need them*. New York: Oxford University Press.
Allison, S. T., & Goethals, G. R. (2012). The seven paradoxes of heroism. Retrieved from http://spsptalks.wordpress.com/2012/01/02/the-seven-paradoxes-of-heroism.
Allison, S. T., Eylon, D., Beggan, J. K., & Bachelder, J. (2009). The demise of leadership: Positivity and negativity biases in evaluations of dead leaders. *The Leadership Quarterly, 20*, 115–129.
Bandura, A. (1997). *Self-efficacy: The exercise of control*. Basingstoke: Macmillan.
Bandura, A. (2001). Social cognitive theory: An agentic perspective. *Annual Review of Psychology, 52*, 1–26.
Becker, S. W., & Eagly, A. H. (2004). The heroism of women and men. *The American Psychologist, 59*, 163–178.
Bellah, R., Sullivan, W., Tipton, S., Madsen, R., & Swindler, A. (1986). *Habits of the heart: Individualism and commitment in American life*. New York: Harper & Row.
Blustein, D. L. (2006). *The psychology of working: A new perspective for career development, counseling, and public policy*. Mahwah, NJ: Erlbaum.
Brown, S. D., & Lent, R. W. (2016). Vocational psychology: Agency, equity, and well-being. *Annual Review of Psychology, 67*, 27.1–27.25.
Brown, S. D., Tramayne, S., Hoxha, D., Telander, K., Fan, X., & Lent, R. W. (2008). Social cognitive predictors of college students' academic performance and persistence: a meta-analytic path analysis. *Journal of Vocational Behavior, 72*, 298–308
Buchbinder, E. (2007). Being a social worker as an existential commitment: From vulnerability to meaningful purpose. *The Humanistic Psychologist, 35*, 161–174.
Bunderson, J. S., & Thompson, J. A. (2009). The call of the wild: Zookeepers, callings, and the double-edged sword of deeply meaningful work. *Administrative Science Quarterly, 54*, 32–57.
Campbell, J. (1949). *The hero with a thousand faces*. Princeton, NJ: Princeton University Press.
Cardador, M. T., & Caza, B. B. (2012). Relational and identity perspectives on healthy versus unhealthy pursuit of callings. *Journal of Career Assessment, 20*, 338–353.
Cardador, M. T., Dane, E. I., & Pratt, M. G. (2011). Linking calling orientations to organizational attachment via organizational instrumentality. *Journal of Vocational Behavior, 79*, 367–378.
Ceaser, D. (2015). Significant life experiences and environmental justice: positionality and the significance of negative social/environmental experiences. Environmental Education Research, 21, 205–220. doi: 10.1080/13504622.2014.910496
Clavien, C., & Chapuisat, M. (2013). Altruism across disciplines: one word, multiple meanings. *Biology & Philosophy, 28*, 125–140.
Clifford, M. L., & Clifford, C. (2001). *Women who kept the lights: An illustrated history of female lighthouse keepers*. Alexandria, VA: Cypress Communications.

Conway, N., Clinton, M., Sturges, J., & Budjanovcanin, A. (2015). Using self determination theory to understand the relationship between calling enactment and daily well being. *Journal of Organizational Behavior, 36*, 1114–1131.

Csikszentmihalyi, M. (1990). *Flow: The psychology of optimal experience.* Harper & Row.

Dalai Lama & Cutler, H. C. (2004). *The art of happiness at work.* New York: Riverhead Books.

Davidson, J. C., & Caddell, D. P. (1994). Religion and the meaning of work. *Journal for the Scientific Study of Religion,* 135–147.

Dawis, R. V. (1992). The individual differences tradition in counseling psychology. *Journal of Counseling Psychology, 39*, 7.

Dawis, R. V. (2005). The Minnesota Theory of Work Adjustment. In S. Brown & R. Lent, (eds) *Career development and counseling: Putting theory and research to work* (pp. 3–23). New York: Guilford.

Dawis, R. V., & Lofquist, L. (1984). *A psychological theory of work adjustment.* Minneapolis, MN: University of Minnesota Press.

Dik, B. J., & Duffy, R. D. (2009). Calling and vocation at work: Definitions and prospects for research and practice. *The Counseling Psychologist, 37*, 424–450.

Dik, B. J., & Duffy, R. D. (2012). *Make your job a calling: How the psychology of vocation can change your life at work.* West Conshohocken, PA: Templeton Press.

Dik, B. J., & Duffy, R. D. (2015). Strategies for discerning and living a calling. In P. Hartung, M. Savickas, & B. Walsh (eds), *APA Handbook of Career Intervention* (pp. 305–317). Washington, DC: APA Books.

Dik, B. J., & Hansen, J. I. C. (2008). Following passionate interests to well-being. *Journal of Career Assessment, 16*, 86–100.

Dik, B. J., & Hansen, J. C. (2011). Moderation of P-E Fit—job satisfaction relations. *Journal of Career Assessment, 19*, 21–34.

Dik, B. J., & Rottinghaus, P. J. (2013). Assessments of interests. In K. F. Geisinger (ed.), *APA Handbook of Testing and Assessment in Psychology* (pp. 325–348). Washington, DC: APA.

Dik, B. J., & Steger, M. F. (2008). Randomized trial of a calling-infused career workshop incorporating counselor self-disclosure. *Journal of Vocational Behavior, 73*, 203–211.

Dik, B. J., Duffy, R. D., & Eldridge, B. (2009). Calling and vocation in career counseling: Recommendations for promoting meaningful work. *Professional Psychology: Research and Practice, 40*, 625–632.

Dik, B. J., Duffy, R.D., & Tix, A. P. (2012). Religion, spirituality, and a sense of calling in the workplace. In P. C. Hill & B. J. Dik (eds), *The psychology of religion and workplace spirituality* (pp. 113–133). Charlotte, NC: Information Age Publishing.

Dik, B. J., Eldridge, B. M., Steger, M. F., & Duffy, R. D. (2012). Development and validation of the Calling and Vocation Questionnaire (CVQ) and Brief Calling Scale (BCS). *Journal of Career Assessment, 20*, 242–263.

Dik, B. J., Hu, R. S. C., & Hansen, J.C. (2007). An empirical test of the Modified C Index and SII, O*NET, and DHOC occupational code classifications. *Journal of Career Assessment, 15*, 279–300.

Dik, B. J., Sargent, A. M., & Steger, M. F. (2008). Career development strivings: Assessing goals and motivation in career decision-making and planning. *Journal of Career Development, 35*, 23–41.

Dik, B. J., Scholljegerdes, K. A., Ahn, J., & Shim, Y. (2015). A randomized controlled trial of a religiously-tailored career intervention with Christian clients. *Journal of Psychology and Christianity, 34*, 340–353.

Dik, B. J., Steger, M. F., Gibson, A., & Peisner, W. (2012). Make Your Work Matter: Development and pilot evaluation of a purpose-centered career education intervention. *New Directions in Youth Development, 132*, 59–73.

Dobrow, S. R., & Tosti-Kharas, J. (2012). Listen to your heart? Calling and receptivity to career advice. *Journal of Career Assessment, 20*(3), 264–280.

Domene, J. F. (2012). Calling and career outcome expectations: The mediating role of self-efficacy. *Journal of Career Assessment, 20*, 281–292.

Domolescu, D., Opre, A., & Ramona, B. (2015). "Is your career meaningful?" Exploring career calling on a Romanian students sample. *Procedia—Social and Behavioral Sciences, 187*, 553–558.

Douglass, R. P., Duffy, R. D., & Autin, K. L. (in press). Living a calling, nationality, and life satisfaction: A moderated, multiple mediator model. *Journal of Career Assessment.*

Duffy, R. D., & Autin, K. L. (2013). Disentangling the link between perceiving a calling and living a calling. *Journal of Counseling Psychology, 60*, 219.

Duffy, R. D., & Dik, B. J. (2013). Research on calling: What have we learned and where are we going? *Journal of Vocational Behavior, 83*, 428–436.

Duffy, R. D., & Sedlacek, W. E. (2007). The presence of and search for a calling: Connections to career development. *Journal of Vocational Behavior, 70*, 590–60.

Duffy, R. D., Allan, B. A., Autin, K. L., & Bott, E. M. (2013). Calling and life satisfaction: It's not about having it, it's about living it. *Journal of Counseling Psychology, 60*, 42–52.

Duffy, R. D., Allan, B. A., & Bott, E. M. (2012). Calling and life satisfaction among undergraduate students: Investigating mediators and moderators. *Journal of Happiness Studies, 13,* 469–479.

Duffy, R. D., Allan, B., & Dik, B. J. (2011). The presence of a calling and academic satisfaction: Examining potential mediators. *Journal of Vocational Behavior, 79,* 74–80.

Duffy, R. D., Bott, E. M., Allan, B. A., Torrey, C. L., & Dik, B. J. (2012). Perceiving a calling, living a calling, and job satisfaction: Testing a moderated, multiple mediator model. *Journal of Counseling Psychology, 59,* 50–59.

Duffy, R. D., Dik, B. J., & Steger, M. F. (2011). Calling and work related outcomes: Career commitment as a mediator. *Journal of Vocational Behavior, 78,* 210–218.

Duffy, R. D., Manuel, R. S., Borges, N. J., & Bott, E. M. (2011). Calling, vocational development, and well-being: A longitudinal study of medical students. *Journal of Vocational Behavior, 79,* 361–366.

Dunlop, W. L., & Walker, L. J. (2013). The personality profile of brave exemplars: A person-centered analysis. *Journal of Research in Personality, 47,* 380–384.

Eggerth, D. E. (2008). From theory of work adjustment to person–environment correspondence counseling: Vocational psychology as positive psychology. *Journal of Career Assessment, 16,* 60–74.

Endler, N., & Parker, J. J. (1992). Interactionism revisited: Reflections on the continuing crisis in the personality area. *European Journal of Personality, 6,* 177–198.

Erikson, E. H., Erikson, J. M., & Kivnick, H. Q. (1987). *Vital involvement in old age.* New York: Norton.

Franco, Z. E., Blau, K., & Zimbardo, P. G. (2011). Heroism: A conceptual analysis and differentiation between heroic action and altruism. *Review of General Psychology, 15,* 99–113.

Frankl, V. E. (1969). *The will to meaning.* New York: New American Library.

Glazer, M. P., & Glazer, P. M. (1999). On the trail of courageous behavior. *Sociological Inquiry, 69,* 276–295.

Goethals, G. R., & Allison, S. T. (2012). Making heroes. The construction of courage, competence, and virtue. *Advances in Experimental Social Psychology, 46,* 183–235.

Goethals, G. R., & Allison, S. T. (2014). Kings and charisma, Lincoln and leadership: An evolutionary perspective. In G. Goethals, S. Allison, R. Kramer, & D. Messick (eds), *Conceptions of leadership: Enduring ideas and emerging insights* (pp. 111–124). New York: Palgrave Macmillan.

Goldfarb, Y. (under review). Motivation behind choice of occupation among Charedi women, practical engineers and teachers: Intrinsic, extrinsic and calling factors and their relationship to work satisfaction. Manuscript under review.

Gore, P. A., Leuwerke, N. C., & Kelly, A. R. (2013). The structure, sources, and uses of occupational information. In R. Lent & S. Brown (eds), *Career development and counseling: Putting theory and research to work* (2nd ed., pp 507–538). New York: Wiley.

Hall, D. T., & Chandler, D. E. (2005). Psychological success: When the career is a calling. *Journal of Organizational Behavior, 26,* 155–176.

Hansen, J. C., & Dik, B. J. (2004). Measures of career interests. In M. Herson and J. C. Thomas (eds), *Handbook of psychological assessment, Vol. 4: Industrial/Organizational assessment.* (pp. 166–191). New York: Wiley.

Hardy, L. (1990). *The fabric of this world: Inquiries into calling, career choice, and the design of human work.* Grand Rapids, MI: Eerdmans.

Hermansen, M. (2004). Islamic concepts of vocation. In J. C. Haughey (ed.), *Revisiting the idea lf vocation: Theological explorations* (pp. 77–96). Washington, DC: The Catholic University of America Press.

Hirschi, A. (2011). Callings in career: A typological approach to essential and optional components. *Journal of Vocational Behavior, 79,* 60–73.

Hirschi, A. (2012). Callings and work engagement: Moderated mediation model of work meaningfulness, occupational identity, and occupational self-efficacy. *Journal of Counseling Psychology, 59,* 479–485.

Hirschi, A., & Hermann, A. (2012). Vocational identity achievement as a mediator of presence of calling and life satisfaction. *Journal of Career Assessment, 20,* 309–321.

Holland, J. L. (1959). A theory of vocational choice. *Journal of Counseling Psychology, 6,* 35–45.

Holland, J. L. (1997). *Making vocational choices: A theory of vocational personalities and work environments* (3rd ed.). Odessa, FL: Psychological Assessment Resources.

Hunter, I., Dik, B. J., & Banning, J. (2010.) College student's perception of calling in work and life: A qualitative investigation. *Journal of Vocational Behavior, 76,* 178–186.

Johnson, R. C. (2002). Attributes of persons performing acts of heroism and of the recipients of these acts. *IPT Journal, 12,* 11–16.

Kinsella, E. L., Ritchie, T. D., & Igou, E. R. (2015). Lay perspectives on the social and psychological functions of heroes. *Frontiers in Psychology, 6,* 1–12.

Kirby, K. E. (2010). The hero and asymmetrical obligation: Levinas and Ricoeur in dialogue. *International Philosophical Quarterly, 50,* 157–166.

Kruger, D., Fisher, M., & Jobling, I. (2003). Proper and dark heroes as dad and cads: Alternative mating strategies in British romantic literature. *Human Nature, 14*, 305–317.

Lent, R. W., Brown, S. D., & Hackett, G. (1994). Toward a unifying social cognitive theory of career and academic interest, choice, and performance. *Journal of Vocational Behavior, 45*, 79–122.

Lips-Wiersma, M., & Wright, S. (2012). Measuring the meaning of meaningful work: Development and validation of the Comprehensive Meaningful Work Scale (CMWS). *Group & Organization Management, 37*, 655–685.

London, P. (1970). The rescuers: Motivational hypotheses about Christians who saved Jews from the Nazis. In J. Macaulay & L. Berkowitz (eds), *Altruism and helping behavior: Social psychological studies of some antecedents and consequences* (pp. 241–250). New York: Academic Press.

McCann, I. L., & Pearlman, L. A. (1990). Vicarious traumatization: A framework for understanding the psychological effects of working with victims. *Journal of Traumatic Stress, 3*, 131–149.

McKenna, R.B., Haney, D., Ecker, D., Matson, J., Becker, O., Boyd, T., & Hickory, M. (2015). Calling, the Caller, and being called: A qualitative study of transcendent calling. *Journal of Psychology and Christianity, 34*, 294–303.

Mohai, P., Pellow, D., & Roberts, J.T. (2009). Environmental justice. *Annual Review of Environment and Resources, 34*. 405–430.

Nauta, M. M. (2010). The development, evolution, and status of Holland's theory of vocational personalities: Reflections and future directions for counseling psychology. *Journal of Counseling Psychology, 57*, 11–22.

Ng, T. W. H., Sorensen, K. L., & Feldman, D. C. (2007). Dimensions, antecedents, and consequences of workaholism: A conceptual integration and extension. *Journal of Organizational Behavior, 28*, 111–136

Oliner, S. P. (2003). *Do unto others: Extraordinary acts of ordinary people*. Boulder, CO: Westview.

Park, C. L. (2012). Religious and spiritual aspects of meaning in the context of work life. In P. Hill & B. Dik (eds), *Psychology of religion and workplace spirituality* (pp. 25–42). Charlotte, NC: Information Age.

Parsons, F. (1909). *Choosing a vocation*. New York: Agathon Press.

Peterson, C., Park, N., Hall, N., & Seligman, M. E. P. (2009). Zest and work. *Journal of Organizational Behavior, 30*, 161–172.

Placher, W. C. (ed.). (2006). *Callings: Twenty centuries of Christian wisdom on vocation*. Grand Rapids, MI: Eerdmans.

Praskova, A., Hood, M., & Creed, P. A. (2014). Testing a calling model of psychological career success in Australian young adults: A longitudinal study. *Journal of Vocational Behavior, 85*, 125–135.

Pratt, M. G., Pradies, C., & Lepisto, D. A. (2013). Doing well, doing good, and doing with: Organizational practices for effectively cultivating meaningful work. In B. Dik, Z. Byrne, & M. Steger (eds), *Purpose and Meaning in the Workplace* (pp. 173–196). Washington, DC: APA Books.

Pulido, L., & Peña, D. (1998). Environmentalism and Positionality: The Early Pesticide Campaign of the United Farm Workers' Organizing Committee, 1965–71. *Race, Gender & Class, 6*, 33–50.

Rankin, L. E., & Eagly, A. H. (2008). Is his heroism hailed and hers hidden? Women, men, and the social construction of heroism. *Psychology of Women Quarterly, 32*, 414–422.

Reynolds, K. E., Turner, J. C., Branscombe, N. R., Mavor, K. I., Bizumic, B., & Subasic, E. (2010). Interactionism in personality and social psychology: An integrated approach to understanding the mind and behaviour. *European Journal of Personality, 24*, 458–482.

Rothmann, S., & Hamukang'andu, L. (2013). Callings, work role fit, psychological meaningfulness and work engagement among teachers in Zambia. *South African Journal of Education, 33*, 1–16.

Rottinghaus, P. J., Larson, L. M., & Borgen, F. H. (2003). The relation of self-efficacy and interests: A meta-analysis of 60 samples. *Journal of Vocational Behavior, 62*, 221–236.

Schuurman, D. J. (2004). *Vocation: Discerning our callings in life*. Grand Rapids, MI: Eerdmans.

Shim, Y., & Yoo, S.-K. (2012). Development and validation of the Korean version of the Calling and Vocation Questionnaire (CVQ-K). *The Korean Journal of Counseling and Psychotherapy, 4*, 847–842.

Silvia, P. (2006). *Exploring the psychology of interest*. New York: Oxford University Press.

Stalker, C., Mandell, D., Frensch, K. M., Harvey, C., & Wright, M. (2007). Child welfare workers who are exhausted yet satisfied with their jobs: how do they do it? *Child & Family Social Work, 12*, 182–191.

Steger, M. F., Pickering, N., Shin, J. Y., & Dik, B. J. (2010.) Calling in work: Secular or sacred? *Journal of Career Assessment, 18*, 82–96.

Taylor, D.E. (2000). The rise of the environmental justice paradigm: injustice framing and the social construction of environmental discourses. *American Behavioral Scientist, 43*, 508–580.

Ting, L., Jacobson, J. M., & Sanders, S. (2011). Current levels of perceived stress among mental health social workers who work with suicidal clients. *Social Work, 56*, 327–336.

Van Vugt, M., Johnson, D. D., Kaiser, R. B., & O'Gorman, R. (2008). Evolution and the social psychology of leadership: The mismatch hypothesis. In C. Hoyt, G. Goethals, & D. Forsyth (eds), *Leadership at the crossroads* (pp. 262–282), Westport, CT: Praeger.

Van Zyl, L. E., Deacon, E., & Rothmann, S. (2010). Towards happiness: Experiences of work-role fit, meaningfulness and work engagement of industrial/organisational psychologists in South Africa. *South African Journal of Industrial Psychology, 36,* 1–10.

Walker, L. J., & Frimer, J. A. (2007). Moral personality of brave and caring exemplars. *Journal of Personality and Social Psychology, 93,* 845–860.

Walker, L. J., Frimer, J.A., & Dunlop, W. L. (2010). Varieties of moral personality: Beyond the banality of heroism. *Journal of Personality, 78,* 907–942.

Wrzesniewski, A., & Dutton, J. E. (2001). Crafting a job: Revisioning employees as active crafters of their work. *Academy of Management Review, 26,* 179–201.

Wrzesniewski, A., McCauley, C., Rozin, P., & Schwartz, B. (1997). Jobs, careers, and callings: People's relations to their work. *Journal of Research in Personality, 31,* 21–33.

Zhang, C., Dik, B. J., Wei, J., & Zhang, J. (2015). Work as a calling in China: A qualitative study of Chinese college students. *Journal of Career Assessment, 23,* 236–249.

Zhang, C., Herrmann, A., Hirschi, A. Wei, J., & Zhang, J. (in press). Assessing calling in Chinese college students: Development of a measure and its relation to hope. *Journal of Career Assessment.*

Zimbardo, P. (2007). *The Lucifer effect: Understanding how good people turn evil.* New York: Random House.

Zimbardo, P. (2011). Why the world needs heroes. *Europe's Journal of Psychology, 7,* 402–407.

18
Underdogs as Heroes

*Joseph A. Vandello, Nadav Goldschmied,
and Kenneth Michniewicz*

Here is a plotline of a movie you will never see: a privileged protagonist is given many advantages, is briefly challenged but easily overcomes the opposition, and goes on to great success and adoration. Instead, most films, literature, fairy tales, religious tales, and myths are the retelling of the underdog archetype. These stories venerate the undersized and outmatched, poor, disadvantaged, written off, left for dead, improbable, and never given a chance. Think Harry Potter, Rocky Balboa, Cinderella, Frodo Baggins, Rudy, the Bad News Bears, the Karate Kid, Katniss Everdeen, Seabiscuit, the Little Tramp, David and Goliath, the Tortoise and the Hare, the Little Engine that Could.

Americans love an underdog tale, whether fictional or real. The classic American "rags to riches" tale made popular in the post-Civil War novels of Horatio Alger, Jr. came to exemplify the American Dream. Similarly, American history glorifies heroic underdogs as well. The Mexican Army's siege of the Alamo has come to symbolize (for Americans) the Texans' heroic struggle against impossible odds. The creation story of the U.S. is itself a story of an underdog group of revolutionaries resisting and defeating a more powerful British imperial oppressor.

Championing underdogs is not a uniquely American proclivity, however. Most cultures around the world have well-known and revered underdog stories. A few illustrative examples: Most Filipino children learn the folk tale of The Monkey and the Turtle, in which the slow turtle outwits the quick, nimble monkey who tries to take advantage of him. In Korea, the folktale of Kongji and Patzzi, is essentially a retelling of the Western Cinderella fairy tale, down to the cruel stepmother and ugly step-sisters. In Russian folklore, Ivan the Fool appears as a popular character who, though despite being poor, younger than his brothers, and simple-minded, ends up with good fortune. Nor are these isolated examples. In his seminal exploration of comparative mythology from around the world, *The Hero with a Thousand Faces*, Joseph Campbell (1949) noted that most all cultural myths retell the archetypal hero's journey (what he called the "monomyth"), in which the hero must overcome an extreme challenge against powerful odds. While not all hero myths are underdog stories (Thor, the Iliad and the Odyssey), and not all underdogs are heroic, the ubiquity of these examples makes clear that the underdog as hero touches something deep and universal in the human psyche.

In this chapter, we review theory and research that attempts to unlock the appeal of the underdog. As we will show, while there is plenty of evidence for the powerful draw of underdogs, there is as of yet no consensus about the cause of this appeal. We will also speculate on the conceptual similarities and differences between rooting for underdogs and judging people as heroes.

Searching for the Roots of the Appeal

We define underdogs as disadvantaged parties facing advantaged opponents and unlikely to succeed. Typically the competitors are explicit and the competition is a zero-sum game, as when two athletes face off or two politicians vie for an election. At other times the competition may be more abstract with no identifiable opponent, as when an underprivileged student attempts to become the first person in her family to graduate from college. Having studied the topic for several years, we have found that asking about why people love underdogs makes for spirited discussion at cocktail parties. But while everyone seems to have a theory, seemingly obvious answers often fall apart upon closer examination.

While evidence for the appeal of underdogs is easy to find, the reason for this appeal is far from intuitive. Our initial interest in the psychology of underdogs was sparked several years ago during the first two authors' regular weekly office meeting. We were having a leisurely conversation about the upcoming "March Madness" college basketball tournament. As happens nearly every year, a small little-known school sneaks into the tournament, defying all predictions and becoming a quick fan favorite. Why are people so easily and consistently drawn to underdogs, about whom they knew nothing just a short time before? As we pondered this recurring phenomenon, we first drew upon what we knew about social psychology. However, not only did the social psychological literature fail to provide obvious answers, some of the foundational theories in social psychology seemed to only deepen the mystery. In fact, some classic social psychology research appears to contradict the notion that people would gravitate to underdogs.

For example, a key tenet of social identity theory (Tajfel & Turner, 1986) holds that people form positive senses of self in part by identifying with valued ingroups. That is, successful groups with high status or prestige should be especially attractive sources of self-esteem. This tendency to strengthen our identification with successful groups and conversely distance ourselves from losers is well documented (Cialdini et al., 1976; End, Dietz-Uhler, Harrick & Jacquemotte, 2002; Snyder, Lassegard, & Ford, 1986). Self-esteem grows when we identify with winners. In fact, when groups with which we identify succeed or fail, their performance can become wrapped up in our expectations for our own performance. For example, Hirt and colleagues (1992) had students from Indiana University watch an Indiana basketball victory or loss and then subsequently perform some tasks in a lab (throwing darts, solving anagrams, imagining success with a hypothetical date). Students had greater confidence and self-esteem in their own performance following an Indiana victory compared to a loss.

Research on social status might also seem to suggest the wisdom of distancing from underdogs. High status individuals and groups are seen as more competent, influential and worthy than low status individuals and groups (Ridgeway, 2001, 2003; Sande, Ellard, & Ross, 1986). Similarly, decades of research on stigma suggests that disadvantaged groups are often devalued targets of prejudice (Goffman, 1963; Heatherton, Kleck, Hebl, & Gull, 2000). People take measures to avoid stigma by association (Neuberg, Smith, Hoffman, & Russell, 1994; Pryor, Reeder, & Monroe, 2012) in order to escape the damaging psychological effects.

These studies, then, do not seem to shed light on why a person would willingly choose to hitch his or her wagon to someone who by definition is unlikely to succeed. At the very least, they suggest that rooting for underdogs could be a psychologically risky endeavor. When we began our studies of underdogs, the psychological literature was, in fact, nearly silent on the question of underdogs. We could find almost no research on the topic, with the exception of a few studies in political science on public opinion polling effects (Ceci & Kain, 1991; Simon, 1954), a marketing study on companies' employment of underdog imagery in advertisements to garner support for their products (Gnepa, 1993), and a study of sports observers' rooting tendencies (described more fully below; Frazier & Snyder, 1991).

The lack of research on what seemed like an important question and a ubiquitous phenomenon was puzzling, but also presented an exciting opportunity. We began by testing the basic hypothesis that support for an entity will increase when it is perceived to be an underdog.

In an initial study, we surveyed people in the weeks prior to the 2004 Summer Olympics to examine support preferences in a real-world sporting context (Vandello, Goldschmied, & Richards, 2007). We presented participants with various hypothetical matches between several pairs of countries for which they had no prior affinity or familiarity. To establish underdog or top dog status through past success (or lack thereof), we also gave them information about the total medal winnings of each country. We then asked them to consider an upcoming competition between various pairs and to rate how much they wanted each team to win. In all pairings, participants on average preferred the underdog to win, and this preference was strongest when the disparity in medal totals was greatest. In total, about three quarters of participants supported the underdog.

In a second study, we explored whether people's attitudes about the Israeli–Palestinian conflict could be influenced by a framing manipulation that presented either the Israelis or Palestinians as underdogs. We presented college students (who were mostly uninformed about the conflict) with a brief essay outlining the history of the Israeli–Palestinian conflict. Accompanying the essay was a map of the region. For half of the participants, the map focused on Israel, with the Palestinian Territories taking up a relatively small portion of the visual space; and for half, the map pulled back in perspective to show the entire region of the Middle East, such that Israel was now much smaller in visual space surrounded by the Arab countries of the greater Middle East. This visual perspective manipulation had a sizeable influence on perceptions and attitudes. When Israel was portrayed as larger on the map, the majority saw the Palestinians as the underdog. In contrast, when Israel was portrayed as smaller on the map, the majority saw Israel as the underdog. Furthermore, participants were significantly more likely to support the Israelis (or Palestinians) in the conflict when they saw them as the underdog.

We and others have replicated this basic tendency to support underdogs across a wide variety of contexts, from sports (Vandello, Goldschmied, & Richards, 2007, Studies 1, 3, and 4), to politics (Goldschmied & Vandello, 2009), to international affairs (Vandello, Michniewicz, & Goldschmied, 2011), to businesses (Kim et al., 2008; Goldschmied & Vandello, 2012), to preference for artists (Kim et al., 2008), to potential romantic partners (Michniewicz & Vandello, 2013). In one clever experiment that demonstrates just how ubiquitous the phenomenon is, Kim and colleagues (2008) found that people prefer and sympathize with animated geometric shapes (circles) that appear to struggle up an incline, but particularly when those shapes are paired with a non-struggling shape or a shape that appears malicious (bumping the struggling circle down the incline).

In the sections that follow, we explore several theories for why people show this robust tendency to like and support disadvantaged underdogs.

The Thrill of the Unexpected

Every sports fan can probably think back to a time she or he became deeply invested in the outcome of a match for which she or he held no prior allegiance. Why is it so thrilling to watch a competition with absolutely no material consequence to the self? Part of the answer may lie in the simple thrill itself. We love sports because they can challenge our strongly held expectations about order and predictability. Teams with the most resources get the best players, and the bigger, stronger, faster teams should beat the smaller, weaker, slower teams—except it does not always work out that way. Sometimes what we know to be true is turned on its face, an upending in the natural order of the universe, and this violation of expectations can create an emotional buzz. It seems obvious that at least part of the appeal of watching an underdog is the possibility of witnessing something rare, of introducing a little safe chaos into an otherwise predictable universe.

In an early simple test of the underdog effect, Frazier and Snyder (1991) asked people to imagine two teams in an unspecified sport in which one team was highly favored to win a seven game playoff series. Eighty-one percent chose to root for the underdog. Then, they asked the respondents to imagine that the underdog surprisingly won the first three games of the series, putting them on the brink of winning. About half switched their allegiance and rooted for the original top dog. They interpreted their results as simple emotional economics: "Social support for the underdog reflects a utilitarian perspective that helps maintain an emotional interest in a contest" (Frazier & Snyder, 1991, p. 380).

The logic of maximizing expected emotional outcomes is formalized in Decision Affect Theory (Mellers, Schwartz, Ho, & Ritov, 1997; Shepperd & McNulty, 2002), which proposes that unexpected outcomes have greater emotional impact than expected outcomes. Stated differently, people should get more joy from unexpected successes than expected ones, and conversely they should experience more pain from unexpected than expected failures. Applying this logic to competitions, rooting for an underdog might be seen as a safe emotional investment. If an entity is expected to win, winning will provide only a modest emotional payoff, but losing will be devastating. If an entity is not expected to win, losing will not feel so bad, but winning will feel especially satisfying. This suggests that our allegiances to underdogs are fairly superficial (a "mile wide and an inch deep," according to Kim et al., 2008), driven more by the excitement of seeing something unexpected than in any deep feelings about character.

But there is a logical problem here. If we are simply playing an emotional economics game, trying to maximize our emotional payoff, then rooting for an underdog or favorite should produce the same emotional outcome. If the intensity of emotion we feel is directly inversely proportional to the likelihood of the outcome happening, the expected value of any outcome will be the same. For example, if we feel twice as strongly (say an 80 out of 100 on a feeling thermometer) about a team that has a 25 percent chance of success compared with a team that has a 50 percent chance of success (40 out of 100), the expected value of our emotional outcome ($80 \times .25$, $40 \times .50$), is 20 in either case. Future research might profitably tweak these odds in hypothetical underdog scenarios to see if people in fact are emotional economists whose strength of support is inversely proportional to a target's odds of success. Given that people consistently root for underdogs under circumstances which would yield an irrational emotional payoff under this perspective, people may in fact miscalculate (overvalue) underdogs' chances of success. We explore this possibility further in the next section when we consider the longshot bias.

While the excitement element probably captures part of the appeal, it is not a fully satisfying explanation (particularly outside of the relatively low stakes of sports fandom). Chalking up the underdog appeal to mere entertainment value seems to keep our love at a distance, limiting our emotional investment. It is hard to reconcile this utilitarian account with the strong emotions that underdogs inspire— how many of us cried when watching a triumphant underdog like Rudy? Would we really be brought to tears seeing Rudy win if it was simply about chasing the thrill? We suspect that the fundamental element lacking from this account is morality. The "thrill of the unexpected" fails to capture the heroic element at the core of this handbook. We will return to this idea later in the chapter when we consider the fairness motive.

Hope Springs Eternal

As previously mentioned, if emotional payoffs are inversely proportional to the odds of success, decision affect theory predicts that people will support underdogs and top dogs equally. One way to reconcile our support for underdogs with this theory, then, is to assume that emotional payoffs are *not* inversely proportional to the odds of success. For this to be true, people would either overvalue the emotional payoff of an underdog victory or overestimate an underdog's chances of success.

There is in fact support for the latter. For instance, the "longshot bias" was first identified by Griffith in 1949, who found evidence that betters on horse races overbet on longshots, given how rarely they actually win. Other studies of sports betting (e.g., Sauer, 1998; Thaler & Ziemba, 1988), have replicated this tendency to bet disproportionally on extreme longshots (to the detriment of their wallets). Thus, it seems that the psychological odds (as measured by bets) sometimes exceed true odds.

In a series of recent studies, we found that the underdog label itself can conjure overly optimistic expectations (Goldschmied & Vandello, 2012). We had people read fake newspaper articles about sports teams, politicians, or businesspeople who were labeled as underdogs and given specific unlikely odds (30%) of success by experts. Despite the explicitly stated odds, participants predicted that the targets would exceed expectations, placing their odds of success at significantly greater than 30 percent. We suggest that people's optimistic expectations of underdogs are shaped by the various inspirational archetypal stories to which we are all frequently exposed.

Inspiring underdog success stories fly in the face of the reality that underdogs usually do not win. The power of these underdog stories may draw our attention away from the many more frequent but less vivid examples of underdog losses, creating a type of availability heuristic that can distort our memories as well. Consider the endings of two popular underdog boxing movies: *Rocky* and *Cinderella Man*. As many may remember, James Braddock overcame long odds to become a champion in the latter, but how many people remember that Rocky Balboa actually lost his fight to Apollo Creed at the end of the first Rocky movie? In a recent study by one of the authors, Goldschmied, Olagaray, and Ruiz (2015) asked participants to recall the winners in each movie. Although the majority correctly remembered Braddock winning, most participants failed to remember that Rocky lost his fight. Our memories serve to tell ourselves the stories we want to hear.

Recently, Davidai and Gilovich (2015) documented another type of optimistic distortion of reality. They argue that people are prone to an "upward mobility bias" such that they believe that a rise in rankings is more likely than a decline. For instance, people predicted that low performing sports teams would improve the following year, that low-ranked business schools would improve their standings, that low-performing students would improve their class ranking, and that employees would improve their performance rankings relative to their peers. (They did not however, predict a similar decline among high performing entities). In short, people believe that relative improvements are more likely than relative declines in performance. They argue that this bias occurs because we place too much weight on targets' intentions and motivations (surely low performers are motivated to try hard to improve) and not enough weight on competitors' intentions (those at the top are equally motivated to stay at the top).

The upward mobility bias might play a role in at least some situations of underdog support. People expect underdogs to take actions to improve their performance, and this contributes to an inflated sense of the likelihood of future success. This bias should be especially likely when an underdog's motivation to succeed is made salient. Consider the pre-game interviews with underdog athletes that focus on their will and training despite the odds.

While there is compelling evidence for biased and unrealistic optimism regarding underdogs, not all studies have found such evidence. For instance, Simmons and Nelson (2006) found evidence that people predict favorites more often than underdog sports teams against the point spread, an outcome they attributed to an "intuitive bias" in which it is simply easier to imagine favorites winning. Of course, betting on a team is not the same as emotionally supporting it, and the motivations driving each might be fundamentally different. Future research might attempt to disentangle the conditions under which people overpredict longshots versus favorites.

Other promising directions for future research might attempt to link the optimism associated with underdogs to the self. For instance, might the presentation of a compelling underdog success narrative increase people's optimism about a personal future event, about one's future fortunes, or about the world in general? Conversely, do chronic optimists (Scheier & Carver, 1992; Peterson, 2000) find underdog stories more compelling than pessimists, and are the effects of underdog narratives stronger for the former group?

Identifying with the Little Guy

A commonly held intuition is that we like underdogs because we identify with them. In their struggles, we see our own struggles. After all, who has not had the odds stacked against him or her at one point or another? Direct tests of the identification hypothesis are rare, but Kim and colleagues (2008) did measure identification directly in their study of animated geometric figures mentioned earlier. Participants in this study easily anthropomorphized the inanimate objects, attributing benign or malicious qualities to the circles. The authors found that participants were significantly more likely to identify with a "struggling" circle than a "nonstruggling" circle, particularly when this circle was paired with another nonstruggling circle. Paharia and colleagues (2011) examined the use of underdog stories as marketing tools to enhance liking for brands. In support of identification as a mechanism of support, they found that consumers preferred underdog brands more when they themselves identified as underdogs.

Scott Allison (Allison & Burnette, 2009; Goethals & Allison, 2012) has argued that *identification with struggle* is a prominent theme in reactions to both heroes and underdogs. In their survey of heroes, Goethals and Allison (2012) talk about struggle as an inescapable aspect of human experience and a key theme of the hero narrative: "We identify with struggle precisely because we *know* struggle, both firsthand at the level of personal experience, and also at the deeper archetypal level" (p. 213). Struggle and suffering make eventual success that much nobler; thus, they argue, we may identify with heroic underdogs because they serve as moral guides and inspirational figures.

Struggle as positive and inspirational is also a central theme of Malcolm Gladwell's (2013) popular analysis of underdogs, *David and Goliath*. He proposes a "theory of desirable difficulties" (first articulated in psychology by Robert Bjork, 1988, 1992; Bjork & Bjork, 2011) that argues that seeming disadvantages can in fact foster success; that struggle is important for growth. Gladwell tells the stories of dyslexics who went on to become highly successful entrepreneurs, an undersized novice girls' basketball team that learned how to exploit the conventional play of their more talented opponents, and a legendary oncologist who rose from Depression-era poverty. Although Gladwell's focus is on the transformative possibilities of struggle for the underdogs themselves, there is a parallel to the ways in which observers can take inspiration from these figures.

Also relevant to the identification hypothesis is early work on the "pratfall effect" (Aronson, Willerman, & Floyd, 1966; Helmreich, Aronson, & LeFan, 1970). If underdogs are likeable because people identify with them, it stands to reason that highly competent, advantaged people risk losing sympathy from others because they are unrelatable. How might an exceptionally competent or advantaged person increase his or her attractiveness to others? Aronson and colleagues showed that when mediocre people commit blunders (e.g. clumsily spilling coffee on themselves) it tends to decrease their attractiveness, but when superior people commit blunders, it can humanize them. Bringing them down a peg, it seems, enhances their likeability.

While identification is certainly an intuitively compelling explanation for why people are drawn to underdogs, the identification concept can be murky and loosely defined, overlapping with a number of related but distinct psychological processes such as empathy, imitation, and projection. The identification concept has a long history and a very specific meaning in psychology, elaborated most fully by Freud. According to Freud (1922), identification is the process of unconsciously assimilating the attributes of a valued target into the self. But why do we come to value the target in the first place? Why should we identify more with underdogs than advantaged favorites? Part of the draw may be the universality of struggle, as Allison suggests, but the appeal of witnessing triumph over adversity may have more to do with aspiration and inspiration than identification. That is, we may choose to identify with qualities that we *wish* to have (e.g. courage and perseverance in the face of daunting odds) but are uncertain that we possess, more than we identify with qualities in others that we recognize in ourselves. Without clearly defining identification distinct from liking of underdogs, we risk slipping into circular reasoning. We root for underdogs because we identify with them. But why do we choose to identify with them and not advantaged, high status entities? The answer must be that they have desirable qualities. So, identification follows from underdogs being liked, rather than explaining why underdogs are liked. Future research would do well to disentangle and measure identification separate from attraction to underdogs to elucidate the causal processes involved.

We do not wish to dismiss the importance of identification as an explanation for the psychological appeal of underdogs. However, the explanation in its current form is under-developed. We suspect that to the extent that identification with underdogs is important, it is probably driven by the inspirational modeling that underdogs provide. In a related vein, rooting for underdogs may provide a type of psychological inoculation. That is, people may appreciate or sympathize with the struggles of others, because it helps the observers learn how to explain and adjust to failures themselves, and maybe even overcome them. In other words, sympathizing with underdogs may be a vicarious character builder. This inoculation hypothesis remains speculative at this point as it awaits testing, but it may be another mechanism of identification that could prove illuminating.

Balancing the Scales of Justice

While the theories above each offer compelling reasons why people might sympathize with and support underdogs under certain circumstances, all miss an important element—moral judgments of character. When people root for underdogs, they not only want them to succeed, but they feel it is *right* and *just* for them to do so. It might seem odd, or at least overstated, to suggest that the moral component of underdog competitions is central, especially in the context of sports, which may seem trivial in importance. Why should we care about justice and inequality when watching people play a game with no real social value other than entertainment? We believe a good part of the appeal of sport is the symbolic narrative through which we reflect our world and ourselves. Observing the struggles of smaller, weaker entities against more powerful forces challenges us to confront inequalities in the world around us. Rooting for the underdog is thus expressing a moral view that disadvantaged entities deserve more than they have. Moving outside of the world of sports, it is perhaps easier to appreciate the moral nature of social judgments. Consider people's feelings toward the small, independent "mom-and-pop" store, or the politician that does not enjoy the support of rich corporate benefactors, or even the small, relatively poor nation, and the moral element becomes salient.

We suggest that our tendency to make underdogs into heroes is part of a more general motivation to see the world as a just place (Lerner, 2003; Lerner & Miller, 1978) where people get what they deserve. People generally have finely tuned antennae for inequality and broad desires for social parity (Bolton & Ockenfels, 2000; Dawes et al., 2007; Fehr & Schmidt, 1999; Messick, 1995; Walster, Walster, & Berscheid, 1978; indeed, inequity aversion may be an evolved trait that we share with our primate cousins; see Brosnan & de Waal, 2003). Being presented with inequality can be deeply unsettling because it creates a dissonance between the way we would like to see the world (everybody gets a fair shot) and the way the world is (the deck is stacked in favor of some over others). Short of being able to directly intervene to affect an unequal competition, we may employ psychological strategies to restore a sense of justice. Sympathizing with and favoring the underdog may be one such strategy.

Recall that the definition of underdogs contains two elements: low expectations for success and disadvantage. The distinction between these elements is critical, because disadvantage taps into the justice motive in a way that low expectations alone do not. In one experiment, we explored the strength of each of these elements by presenting people with information about both expectations for a target's future success and its relative resources (Vandello, Goldschmied, & Richards, 2007). Specifically, we presented participants with hypothetical sporting competitions between two teams and we asked them how much they wanted each team to win, and which team (if any) was the underdog. In one version, we manipulated the first component (expectations for success) by simply presented the odds: Team A was described as having a 70 percent chance of victory versus 30 percent for Team B. Not surprisingly, nearly everyone picked the low-expectation team as the underdog, and people wanted them to win more than the high-expectation team. In a second version, we manipulated relative advantage or disadvantage by presenting information about the relative payrolls of each team ($35 million for Team A and $100 million for Team B). Almost everyone chose the small-resource team as the underdog, and they wanted it to win more than the high-resource team. More interesting was what happened when we presented both types of information simultaneously. When a team had both a low payroll and low expectations for success, participants agreed that it was an underdog and they wanted it to win. In a critical condition, we presented a matchup of a team with a relatively low payroll but high probability of winning against a team with a high payroll but low probability of winning. In contrast to the other conditions, when a team with low expectations had high resources, people were reluctant to consider it an underdog (only 55% did so). Allegiance also shifted to the team with low resources, as people wanted the low resources team to win more than the high resources team even though it was expected to do so. In short, when a team with low expectations has ample resources, people no longer see it as disadvantaged and consequently deserving of a win. This study suggests that people's identification of underdogs and their subsequent support for them are not simply about the thrill of unexpected success, but contain a moral judgment informed by disadvantage. We root for underdogs not just because they are unlikely to win, but because they are unjustly disadvantaged and deserving of success.

One non-intuitive implication of the connection between justice and underdog sympathy is that perceptions of underdog status might generate positive attitudes toward stigmatized groups (and conversely, lack of perceived disadvantage may erode support for stigmatized groups). Hettinger and Vandello (2014) explored how perceived disadvantage and deservingness influence Americans' support for gay rights. Gay individuals have long been targets of stigma, prejudice, and negative stereotypes. However, not all stereotypes about gay people are negative. One stereotype endorsed by many Americans is the "gay affluence myth," the (erroneous) belief that gay people are wealthier and have more disposable income than the average American (McDermott, 2014). We reasoned that, to the extent that they endorsed this myth, people might be less inclined to see gays and lesbians as disadvantaged underdogs and therefore might be less likely to support legislation and social policies aimed at protecting them. We found that even after controlling for religiosity and general anti-gay attitudes, support for gay rights legislation decreased among those who endorsed the stereotype that gay people are relatively affluent. This association was moderated by character beliefs about gay people pertaining to wealth deservingness (that is, the negative association was stronger for those who believed gay people lacked the traits associated with wealth deservingness—hard work, honesty, perseverance, etc.). Thus, support and sympathy for stigmatized groups may be contingent upon seeing the groups as disadvantaged. Conversely, even seemingly positive stereotypes (gay people are relatively affluent) can have negative effects.

A related way the justice motivation finds its expression in attitudes toward status differences is in feelings of schadenfreude, the pleasure derived from the misfortune of others. In some ways, this is the flip side of underdog support, but it likely driven by the same desire to perceive the world as just. Research on schadenfreude finds that it tends to be directed at high achievers (Brigham et al., 1997; Feather, 1994; Leach et al., 2003; Smith et al., 1996), supporting the general idea that people are averse to inequality, but more specifically, as Feather and Sherman (2003) have shown, schadenfreude is more closely related to resentment of undeserving success than mere envy of high achievement. Thus, when some people root for the underdog, at least part of that support may be driven less by qualities inherent in the underdog than by wanting to see the advantaged top dog knocked down a peg. Both roads—rooting for the underdog or against the top dog—lead to the same end.

Complementary Justice: Making Good Guys out of Underdogs

The above studies suggest that people's feelings about disadvantaged and advantaged competitors are shaped by moral considerations, and motivations to see the world as just may influence perceptions of entities' actions and character. People create narratives of underdogs such that, whether they ultimately win or lose, they demonstrate bravery and heart by virtue of standing up to a more formidable opponent. Thus, it is not about overcoming unlikely odds so much as *facing* them. The fact that Rocky Balboa did not defeat Apollo Creed did not make his story any less heroic. Constructing positive attributions for underdogs may be a way to reconcile and justify an unequal social system. For instance, people often create complementary stereotypes (e.g. "poor but honest") to make social inequalities more palatable (Kay & Jost, 2003; Kay, Jost, & Young, 2005). That is, by believing that a weakness in one area (e.g. ability) is offset by a strength in another area (e.g. effort), people are able to justify an unequal social system. This motivation to create complementary stereotypes that offset high or low status might explain common inclinations to attribute moral qualities to the disadvantaged ("Blessed are the meek," "The salt of the Earth") and conversely to be suspicious of those in power ("Money is the root of all evil," "Power corrupts").

Admittedly, the hypothesis that we imbue underdogs with moral qualities is somewhat speculative and awaits further direct testing. However, we have found preliminary evidence (some direct, some indirect) that people may employ such a strategy when encountering underdog situations. In several of our studies, we find that portraying a target as an underdog can influence attributions about its performance and perceptions of its moral character. In one dramatic example of how motivation to see underdogs in a positive light can shape perceptions, we explored how underdog status colors the attributions people make for sports teams' performance (Vandello, Goldschmied, & Richards, 2007). We invited people to our lab to watch a video clip of a European pro basketball game between two teams that would be unfamiliar to participants (thus assuring no prior allegiance): Maccabi Tel Aviv and CSKA Moscow. Before watching the game, participants first read a short summary describing the game as the final championship match between two teams with a long, fierce, and lopsided rivalry. Half were told that Moscow was the heavy underdog and half were told that Tel Aviv was the heavy underdog. Following the description, participants watched a 15-minute video clip of an actual televised game. Throughout the clip, the score remained close, with the lead changing several times, and participants never learned who eventually won the game from the segment shown. Following the clip, we asked participants to make ability (how much natural ability did the team have? How much talent?) and effort (how much heart did the team show? How much did they want to win?) attributions for each team. As predicted by the complementary justice perspective, although participants all watched the same clip, they perceived the underdog (for half Moscow and for half Tel Aviv) as having less ability but putting forth more effort than the top dog. Replicating other studies, participants also wanted the underdog to win. This tendency to see underdogs as exerting more effort than top dogs is interesting, given that in fact people may actually work less hard when their individual performance is compared to a higher, as opposed to a lower, status competitor (Pettit & Lount, 2010). People may thus expect underdogs to work harder, when in reality being an underdog may be demotivating.

In another study, we examined how underdog status might influence perceptions of morally ambiguous actions during international conflict (Vandello, Michniewicz, & Goldschmied, 2011). We reasoned that people would be more inclined to give a nation the moral benefit of the doubt when it was portrayed as a disadvantaged underdog in relation to its adversary. We had participants read an account of two fictional countries involved in a long-standing conflict. The story described a violent episode (a bomb detonated at a military parade, killing seventeen soldiers) perpetrated by either the larger, more powerful country or the smaller, weaker country. When the violent act was committed by the less powerful country (the underdog), it was seen as more moral and justified and it was less likely to be seen as terrorism than when the same act was committed by the more powerful country. Furthermore, reading about violence by the underdog country actually increased the favorability of participants' attitudes about aggression and violence in the abstract.

These findings have important implications for international conflicts, because they suggest that the power disparities that usually exist between adversaries can affect moral judgments of groups' actions, particularly by outside parties. As conflicts increasingly involve multiple nations, and as international third-party courts increasingly adjudicate international and regional conflicts (De Baere, Chane, & Wouters, 2015), public approval or disapproval can greatly affect the willingness of nations to engage in conflicts outside of their borders. The studies also suggest that militarily weaker actors may neutralize stronger adversaries' advantages by employing a wider range of actions that may be judged acceptable. In fact, as traditional military battles have been increasingly replaced by asymmetric warfare strategies like terrorism, insurgencies, and guerilla warfare, militarily weaker actors have won with increasing frequency (Arreguin-Toft, 2001).

The motivation to minimize inequalities through compensatory attributions may also influence perceptions of attractiveness. In general, people are attracted to advantage—beautiful, wealthy, high status, popular people do quite well in the dating market. However, under certain circumstances, being an underdog might bolster interpersonal attractiveness. Given motivations to compensate disadvantaged individuals, particularly those perceived to be victims of misfortune through no fault of their own (Haynes & Olson, 2006), people might attribute positive qualities to underdogs that increase their desirability. In a recent study, we explored whether being an underdog could bolster interpersonal attractiveness by having heterosexual men and women read a story about a male or female target who applied for a coveted job (Michniewicz & Vandello, 2013). We manipulated whether the target had a high or low probability of getting the job and whether the advantage or disadvantage was the result of fair or unfair circumstances. In support of the compensation hypothesis, we found that participants judged the unfairly disadvantaged target (i.e., the underdog) as personally desirable and suitable as a date—even as much as a fairly advantaged target and more than a fairly disadvantaged or unfairly advantaged target. We also included photos of the target and found that people even rated the target as more physically attractive when he or she was unfairly disadvantaged (compared to fairly disadvantaged or unfairly advantaged).

The research summarized in this section suggests that people's discomfort with social inequalities motivates them to attribute positive social and moral qualities (bravery, character, heart, effort, attractiveness) to underdogs. These attributions are ultimately what connect underdogs to the main theme of this book: heroism. This "underdogs as heroes" account departs somewhat from typical descriptions of heroes (Franco, Blau, & Zimbardo, 2011) that emphasize placing oneself in personal peril or sacrificing oneself for some greater social good in an act of altruism. The research reviewed here suggests that merely being unfairly disadvantaged can elicit the types of qualities (attributions of character, heart, and bravery) that people associate with heroes.

The Fragility of Underdog Support and the Limits of Justice

Other more self-interested motives may sometimes override our concern for justice. For example, Kim and colleagues (2008) presented survey respondents with a hypothetical scenario in which a community must decide which water testing company should test a community's drinking water supply. They manipulated the stakes such in some scenarios the outcome was both self-relevant (affecting one's own community versus a distant community) and potentially life-threatening (testing for the presence of deadly mercury versus hard water). The respondents had to choose whether to award a contract to a relatively new, small business (the underdog) or a large, well-established business. When the stakes were low, people sympathized and identified with the underdog (though they were equally likely to choose the underdog and top dog business). When the stakes were high, people preferred to go with the top dog. This illustrates the somewhat fragile nature of the underdog effect, but even more importantly it suggests that our concerns for justice and fairness, or our discomfort with inequality may not be enough to overcome self-interest. How often do people lament Walmart opening a store in their town or a Starbucks popping up in the neighborhood of a beloved independent coffee shop, only to end up choosing the convenience and price of the big chain stores over the underdog? The mom-and-pop stores may have our hearts, but the big chains may more often have our wallets.

Similarly, as we discussed earlier, when the chances of underdog success become too remote, it may be difficult to support them. It is one thing to support the politician who trails in the polls by a few points, but when the candidate has no chance of winning, the campaign may take on a quixotic appearance that appears more foolish than reasonable. At what point entities go from lovable underdogs who enjoy support to lost causes is an open question deserving of more research. More generally, while we believe system justifying motivations play a central role in the appeal of underdogs, these motivations must compete with other motivations (e.g. self-interest, ingroup allegiance) that at times can be more salient or powerful.

The Self as Underdog: Motivations and Risks

Thus far, our focus has been on social perceptions of underdogs, arguing that third parties are motivated to see underdogs in the best possible light, even as heroic. The research reviewed suggests that despite the obvious disadvantages of being an underdog, there may also be some less obvious social advantages. Recognizing these social advantages, people sometimes embrace and advertise their own disadvantages as well. This can be a self-presentational strategy or a motivational strategy. Although most existing research considers underdogs from the *observer*'s perspective, it is worth considering the underdog phenomenon from the *actor*'s perspective as well.

In this section, we will briefly consider some ways that people accept or encourage an identity as an underdog and some of the possible motivations for doing so.

Social psychologists have documented a number of motivational and self-presentational strategies in which people intentionally emphasize a personal weakness or disadvantage. As Jones and Pittman (1982) noted in their survey of self-presentational strategies, modest or self-effacing self-presentational tactics (e.g., ingratiation, supplication) can be effective in winning others' approval, while self-presentational strategies that emphasize one's advantage (e.g., self-promotion) can come with significant costs. In fact, people seem to be quite sensitive to the possibility of threatening others with upward social comparisons (Exline & Lobel, 1999, 2001). Claiming or advertising disadvantage can also be a risky strategy, however, as we will detail below.

People sometimes claim to be at a disadvantage or to be the underdog as an impression management tactic. This is a favorite tactic of politicians to seek a populist edge. Barack Obama was able to use an underdog narrative to great effect during his 2008 campaign for president, claiming that "when your name is Barack Obama, you're always an underdog in political races." His biggest rival, Hillary Clinton, countered at about the same time by saying "I'm here asking for your support. I'm the underdog here in South Dakota. I've gotten used to that role" (Goldschmied & Vandello, 2009). Of course, this tactic is only effective if it is believable. An incumbent leading in the polls who claimed to be an underdog would likely be seen as disingenuous at best. In addition, the underdog label is most potent when applied by others than by the self. In a study in which we asked people to read a speech from then Presidential candidate Barack Obama, we manipulated whether he was labeled the underdog or frontrunner. Participants rated him warmer when he was the underdog, but the effect was stronger when a third party labeled Obama's the underdog compared to when he claimed the label for himself (Goldschmied & Vandello, 2009).

High status individuals may feign incompetence or "play dumb" in an attempt to humanize themselves and close the perceived gap between self and others (Aronson, Willerman, & Floyd, 1966; Gove, Hughes, & Geerken, 1980; Helmreich, Aronson, & LeFan, 1970), but this tendency has been linked to poor mental health and low self-esteem. Relatedly, simply acknowledging a negative (such as when a foreign speaker acknowledges a heavy accent or a college applicant acknowledges poor high school grades) can lead to more positive reactions from others (Ward & Brenner, 2006). In competitive situations, people sometimes falsely predict or feign demonstrations of inability, a phenomenon called sandbagging (Gibson & Sachau, 2000; Gibson, Sachau, Doll, & Shumate, 2002). This may be partly an attempt to lower expectations by others, but partly an attempt to reduce performance pressure in the self, particularly when one is favored in a competition.

Of course, targets of stigma do not always choose disadvantaged identities. However, even when stigmatized labels are thrust upon them from dominant groups, they may nonetheless come to embrace the identities in a process called stigma reappropriation (Galinsky, Hugenberg, Groom, & Bodenhausen, 2003; Galinsky et al., 2013). In this process, a stigmatized group may take a derogatory label (e.g. nerd, queer) and claim it as its own as a defiant act of empowerment. When a derogatory term is reappropriated through self-labeling, this can weaken the stigmatizing force and make the group appear more powerful.

The problem with groups claiming or advertising disadvantage is that it can become a competitive, zero-sum game. Norton and Sommers (2011a, 2011b) find, for instance, that as rights have been granted to and gains have been made by traditionally marginalized groups like blacks, even historically empowered groups (i.e. whites) can feel threatened and marginalized themselves. Norton and Sommers (2011b) term this mutual feeling of marginalization "jockeying for stigma," and one consequence is that Whites use a sense of marginalization as a political rallying cry against policies intended to level the playing field. Research on intergroup competitive victimhood (Noor, Shnabel, Halabi, & Nadler 2012; Shnabel, Halabi, & Noor, 2013) similarly demonstrates that groups involved in ongoing violent conflicts often compete to establish who has suffered more, and these efforts can impede conflict resolution. More generally, we suggest that at the intergroup and interpersonal level, people will often engage in a type of competitive "one-downsmanship" to appear to be at a greater disadvantage than a competitor. While such strategies are common (think of the old comedy cliché "I had to walk five miles to school in the snow every day. Uphill. Both ways."), these strategies may have the unintended consequence of creating divisions and animosity that outweigh the intended sympathy one hopes to achieve.

Other self-deprecating strategies may be motivated less by impression management than by personal motivations. For example, when people engaged in competitions for which they are uncertain of the outcome, they may ascribe advantages to competitors, thus making the target inappropriate for social comparison (Shepperd & Taylor, 1999). Exaggerating the abilities of one's opponent can be a mechanism to protect the self against unfavorable social comparisons. Self-handicapping, first proposed by Jones and Berglas (1978), occurs when people claim or create obstacles in anticipation of a failing performance. Although people employ this strategy to protect self-esteem, it is often self-destructive in that it can increases the likelihood of failure and reduce intrinsic motivation (Elliot & Church, 2003). A related phenomenon, defensive pessimism (Norem & Cantor, 1986) occurs when people set low expectation for success in risky, uncertain situations. This can help people cope with performance anxiety and prepare for challenges ahead, but it is also related to lower self-esteem compared to those who do not use the strategy (Norem & Burdzovic Andreas, 2006).

Given the variety of these strategies, there are some important distinctions between them, and some may be more closely related to the psychology of underdogs than others. However, they all have in common a motivation to embrace disadvantage that runs counter to the self-enhancement motive that is often described as a fundamental, ubiquitous, and perhaps universal human motivation (Sedikides, Gaertner, & Toguchi, 2003). While this may be true, we suggest that psychological research has perhaps devoted disproportionate emphasis on self-enhancement and not enough emphasis on these more self-deprecating strategies.

Final Thoughts: Underdogs as Heroes?

Given the ubiquity of underdogs in popular consciousness, it is surprising that there has been limited research on the topic to date. As we hope this review has made clear, there is much fertile ground yet to till. The psychology underlying underdog support goes well beyond rooting for sports teams and has implications for deeper understandings of injustice and morality.

Returning to the theme of this handbook, what is the connection between underdogs and heroes? Certainly not all heroes are underdogs, and not all underdogs are heroic. However, we have argued that people will often imbue underdogs with heroic qualities because people are motivated to see them as moral. Believing the little guy is inherently good helps blunt the discomfort of an unequal world. The heroism of underdogs may not lie in their outcomes so much as in their spirit. Underdogs (whether they are the Texans at the Alamo or the student who is the first in her family to go to college) pursue their goals knowing the long odds against them. The pursuit of a goal, even (or especially) in the face of likely defeat, suggests heroic qualities of perseverance, bravery, and principled integrity.

The links between underdogs and heroes remains under-explored. We have reviewed evidence suggesting that people often believe underdogs have positive personal characteristics and that questionable actions taken by disadvantaged groups are seen as more moral than the same actions taken by advantaged groups. Still, this evidence is rather indirect, and future research would profit from exploring more directly the connections between underdog status and moral and heroic attributions.

We have presented several possible reasons why people are drawn to underdogs. While we treated them as independent explanations, they may be overlapping in reality. For instance, to the extent that people are motivated by moral concerns for fairness, they may wish to see underdogs succeed; And this desire may shape perceptions that underdogs have admirable qualities of character ("heart", effort, perseverance, etc.). Similarly, moral motivations may lead people to identify more strongly with underdogs than top dogs.

As societies wrestle with the realities of social and economic inequality among their citizens, understanding the psychology of people's reactions to advantaged and disadvantaged entities can shed light on populist resentment (or acceptance) of the privileged, such as with the recent "Black Lives Matter" movement or the "Occupy Wall Street" movement that began in the United States and spread to other countries. Most of the time, the resentment and anger felt by societies' underdogs is kept at bay, but at times it surfaces. It would be helpful to better understand the conditions under which these forces work, and the conditions under which people give moral license to groups to express resentment and social grievances.

The themes explored in the current chapter certainly have some theoretical connections to other long-studied psychological phenomenon, such as relative deprivation theory, just world theory, and system justification theory. These connections remain largely unexplored, and represent to us some of the most exciting potential directions for future study. We hope that this chapter can serve as a catalyst for drawing further connections.

References

Allison, S. T., & Burnette, J. (2009). Fairness and preference for underdogs and top dogs. In R. Kramer, A. Tenbrunsel, & M. Bazerman (eds), *Social decision making: Social dilemmas, social values, and ethical judgments* (pp. 291–314). New York: Psychology Press.

Allison, S. T., & Goethals, G. R. (2011). *Heroes: What they do and why we need them*. Oxford: Oxford University Press.

Aronson, E., Willerman, B., & Floyd, J. (1966). The effect of a pratfall on increasing interpersonal attractiveness. *Psychonomic Science*, 4, 227–228.

Arreguin-Toft, A. (2001). How the weak win wars: A theory of asymmetric conflict. *International Security*, 26, 93–128.

Bjork, R. A. (1988). Retrieval practice and the maintenance of knowledge. In M. M. Gruneberg & P. E. Morris (eds), *Practical aspects of memory: Current research and issues: Memory in everyday life* (Vol. 1, pp. 396–410). New York: John Wiley & Sons.

Bjork, R. A. (1992). Interference and forgetting. In L. R. Squire (ed.), *Encyclopedia of learning and memory* (pp. 283–288). New York: Macmillan.

Bjork, E. L., & Bjork, R. A. (2011). Making things hard on yourself, but in a good way: Creating desirable difficulties to enhance learning. In M. A. Gernsbacher and J. Pomerantz (eds), *Psychology and the real world: Essays illustrating fundamental contributions to society* (2nd ed., pp. 56–64). New York: Worth.

Bolton, G. E., & Ockenfels, A. (2000). ERC: A theory of equity, reciprocity, and competition. *American Economic Review*, 90, 166–193.

Brigham, N. L., Kelso, K. A., Jackson, M. A., & Smith, R. H. (1997). The roles of invidious comparison and deservingness in sympathy and schadenfreude. *Basic and Applied Social Psychology*, 19, 363–380.

Brosnan, S. F. & de Waal, F. B. M. (2003). Monkeys reject unequal pay. *Nature*, 425, 297–299.

Campbell, J. (1949). *The hero with a thousand faces*. New York: Pantheon Books.

Ceci, S. J., & Kain, E. L. (1982). Jumping on the bandwagon with the underdog: The impact of attitude polls on polling behavior. *Public Opinion Quarterly*, 46, 228–242.

Cialdini, R. B., Borden, R. J., Thorne, A., Walker, M. R., Freeman, S., & Sloan, L. R. (1976). Basking in reflected glory: Three (football) studies. *Journal of Personality and Social Psychology*, 34, 366–375.

Davidai, S., & Gilovich, T. (2015). What goes up apparently needn't come down: Asymmetric predictions of ascent and descent rankings. *Journal of Behavioral Decision Making*, XX (March 06). doi: 10.1002/bdm.1865

Dawes, C. T., Fowler J. H., Johnson, T., McElreath, R., & Smirnov O. (2007). Egalitarian motives in humans. *Nature*, 446, 794–796.

De Baere, G., Chane, A-L., & Wouters, J. (2015). The contribution of international and supranational courts to the rule of law: a framework for analysis. In G. De Baere & J. Wouters (eds), *The contribution of international and supranational courts to the rule of law* (pp. 19–83). Leuven: Edward Elgar Publishing.

Elliot, A. J., & Church, M. A. (2003). A motivational analysis of defensive pessimism and self-handicapping. *Journal of Personality*, 71, 369–396.

End, C. M., Dietz-Uhler, B., Harrick, E. A., & Jacquemotte, L. (2002). Identifying with winners: A reexamination of sport fans' tendency to BIRG. *Journal of Applied Social Psychology*, 32, 1017–1030.

Exline, J. J., & Lobel, M. (1999). The perils of outperformance: Sensitivity about being the target of threatening upward comparison. *Psychological Bulletin*, 125, 307–337.

Exline, J. J., & Lobel, M. (2001). Private gain, social strain: Do relationship factors shape responses to outperformance? *European Journal of Social Psychology*, 31, 593-607.

Feather, N. T. (1994). Attitudes toward high achievers and reactions to their fall: Theory and research concerning tall poppies. *Advances in Experimental Social Psychology*, 26, 1–73.

Feather, N. T. (1999). Judgments of deservingness: Studies in the psychology of justice and achievement. *Personality and Social Psychology Review*, 3, 86–107.

Feather, N. T., & Sherman, R. (2002). Envy, resentment, schadenfreude, and sympathy: Reactions to deserved and undeserved achievement and subsequent failure. *Personality and Social Psychology Bulletin*, 28, 953–961.

Fehr, E., & Schmidt, K. M. (1999). A theory of fairness, competition and cooperation. *Quarterly Journal of Economics, 114*, 817–868.

Franco, Z. E., Blau, K., & Zimbardo, P. G. (2011). Heroism: A conceptual analysis and differentiation between heroic action and altruism. *Review of General Psychology, 15*, 99–113.

Frazier, J. A., & Snyder, E. E. (1991). The underdog concept in sport. *Sociology of Sport Journal, 8*, 380–388.

Freud, S. (1922). *Group psychology and the analysis of the ego*. London: International Psycho-analytical Press.

Galinsky, A. D., Hugenberg, K., Groom, C., & Bodenhausen, G. B. (2003). The reappropriation of stigmatizing labels: Consequences for social identity. In M. A. Neale, E. A. Mannix, & J. Polzer (eds), *Research on managing in teams and groups* (Vol. 5, pp. 221–256). Greenwich, CT: Elsevier Science Press.

Galinsky, A. D., Wang, C. S., Whitson, J. A., Anicich, E. M., Hugenberg, K., & Bodenhausen, G. B. (2013). The reappropriation of stigmatizing labels: The reciprocal relationship between power and self-labeling. *Psychological Science, 24*, 2020–2029.

Gibson, B., & Sachau, D. (2000). Sandbagging as a self-presentational strategy: Claiming to be less than you are. *Personality and Social Psychology Bulletin, 26*, 56–70.

Gibson, B., Sachau, D., Doll, B., & Shumate, R. (2002). Sandbagging in competition: Responding to the pressure of being the favorite. *Personality and Social Psychology Bulletin. 28*, 1119–1130.

Gladwell, M. (2013). *David and Goliath: Underdogs, misfits, and the art of battling giants*. New York: Little, Brown, and Company.

Gnepa, T. J. (1991). Comparative advertising in magazines: Nature, frequency, and a test of the "underdog" hypothesis. *Journal of Advertising Research, 33*, 70–75.

Goethals, G. R., & Allison, S. T. (2012). Making heroes: The construction of courage, competence, and virtue. *Advances in Experimental Social Psychology, 46*, 183–235.

Goffman, I. (1963). *Stigma: Notes on the management of spoiled identity*. Englewood Cliffs, NJ: Prentice Hall.

Goldschmied, N., Olagaray, L. S. & Ruiz J. (2016). The underdog narrative in movies: When our memory fails us. Paper presented at the 17th Annual Meeting of The Society for Personality and Social Psychology (SPSP), San Diego, CA, January.

Goldschmied, N., & Vandello, J. A. (2009). The advantage of disadvantage: Underdogs in politics. *Basic and Applied Social Psychology, 31*, 24–31.

Goldschmied, N., & Vandello, J. A. (2012). The future is bright: The underdog label, availability, and optimism. *Basic and Applied Social Psychology, 34*, 34–43.

Gove, W. R., Hughes, M., & Geerken, M. R. (1980). Playing dumb: A form of impression management with undesirable side effects. *Social Psychology Quarterly, 43*, 89–102.

Griffith, R. M. (1949). Odds adjustments by American horse-race bettors. *The American Journal of Psychology, 62*, 290–294.

Haynes, G., & Olson, J. (2006). Coping with threats to just-world beliefs: Derogate, blame, or help? *Journal of Applied Social Psychology, 36*, 664–682.

Heatherton, T. F., Kleck, R. E., Hebl, M. R., & Gull, J. G. (2000). *The social psychology of stigma*. New York: Guilford Press.

Helmreich, R., Aronson, E., & LeFan, J. (1970). To err is humanizing sometimes: Effects of self-esteem, competence, and a pratfall on interpersonal attraction. *Journal of Personality and Social Psychology, 16*, 259–264.

Hettinger, V. E., & Vandello, J. A. (2014). Balance without equality: Just world beliefs, the gay affluence myth and support for gay rights. *Social Justice Research, 27*, 444–463.

Hirt, E. R., Zillman, D. Erickson, G. A., & Kennedy, C. (1992). Costs and benefits of allegiance: Changes in fans' self-ascribed competencies after team victory versus defeat. *Journal of Personality and Social Psychology, 63*, 724–738.

Jones, E. E., & Berglas, S. (1978). Control of attributions about the self through self-handicapping strategies: The appeal of alcohol and the role of underachievement. *Personality and Social Psychology Bulletin, 4*, 200–206.

Jones, E. E., & Pittman, T. S. (1982). Toward a general theory of strategic self-presentation. In J. Suls (ed.), *Psychological perspectives on the self* (Vol. 1, pp. 231–260). Hillsdale, NJ: Erlbaum.

Kay, A. C., & Jost, J. T. (2003). Complementary justice: Effects of "poor but happy" and "poor but honest" stereotype exemplars on system justification and implicit activation of the justice motive. *Journal of Personality and Social Psychology, 85*, 823–837.

Kay, A. C., Jost, J. T., & Young, S. (2005). Victim derogation and victim enhancement as alternate routes to system justification. *Psychological Science, 16*, 240–246.

Kim, J., Allison, S. T., Eylon, D., Goethals, G., Markus, M., Hindle, S. M., & McGuire, H. A. (2008). Rooting for (and then abandoning) the underdog. *Journal of Applied Social Psychology, 38*, 2550–2573.

Leach, C. W., Spears, R., Branscombe, N. R., & Doosje, B. (2003). Malicious pleasure: Schadenfreude at the suffering of another group. *Journal of Personality & Social Psychology, 84*, 932–943.

Lerner, M. J. (2003). The justice motive: Where social psychologists found it, how they lost it, and why they may not find it again. *Personality and Social Psychology Review, 7,* 388–399.

Lerner, M. J., & Miller, D. T. (1978). Just world research and the attribution process: Looking back and ahead. *Psychological Bulletin, 85,* 1030–1051.

McDermott, N. (2014). The myth of gay affluence. *The Atlantic* (March 21). Retrieved from: www.theatlantic.com/business/archive/2014/03/the-myth-of-gay-affluence/284570/

Mellers, B. A., Schwartz, A., Ho, K., & Ritov, I. (1997). Decision affect theory: Emotional reactions to the outcomes of risky options. *Psychological Science, 8,* 423–429.

Messick, D. (1995). Equality, fairness, and social conflict. *Social Justice Research, 8,* 153–173.

Michniewicz, K., & Vandello, J. A. (2013). The attractive underdog: When disadvantage bolsters attractiveness. *Journal of Social and Personal Relationships, 30,* 942-952.

Neuberg, S. L., Smith, D. M., Hoffman, J. C., & Russell, F. J. (1994). When we observe stigmatized and "normal" individuals interacting: Stigma by association. *Personality and Social Psychology Bulletin, 20,* 196–209.

Noor, M., Shnabel, N., Halabi, S., & Nadler, A. (2012). When suffering begets suffering: The psychology of competitive victimhood between adversarial groups in violent conflicts. *Personality and Social Psychology Review, 16,* 351–374.

Norem, J. K., & Burdzovic Andreas, J. (2006). Understanding journeys: Individual growth analysis as a tool for studying individual differences in change over time. In A. D. Ong & M. van Dulmen (eds), *Handbook of Methods in Positive Psychology* (pp. 1036–1058). London: Oxford University Press.

Norem, J. K., & Cantor, N. (1986). Defensive pessimism: Harnessing anxiety as motivation. *Journal of Personality and Social Psychology, 51,* 1208–1217.

Norton, M. I., & Sommers, S. R. (2011a). Whites see racism as a zero-sum game that they are now losing. *Perspectives on Psychological Science, 6,* 215.

Norton, M. I., & Sommers, S. R. (2011b). Jockeying for stigma. *New York Times* (May 22). Retrieved from www.nytimes.com/roomfordebate/2011/05/22/is-anti-white-bias-a-problem/jockeying-for-stigma.

Paharia, N., Keinan, A., Avery, J., Schor, J. B. (2011). The underdog effect: The marketing of disadvantage and determination through brand biography. *Journal of Consumer Research, 37,* 775–790.

Peterson, C. (2000). The future of optimism. *American Psychologist, 55,* 44–55.

Pettit, N. C., & Lount, R. B., Jr. (2010). Looking down and ramping up: The impact of status differences on effort in intergroup contexts. *Journal of Experimental Social Psychology, 46,* 9–20.

Pryor, J. B., Reeder, G. D., & Monroe, A. E. (2012). The infection of bad company: Stigma by association. *Journal of Personality and Social Psychology, 102,* 224–241.

Ridgeway C. L. (2001). Gender, status, and leadership. *Journal of Social Issues, 57,* 637–655.

Ridgeway, C. L. (2003). Social status and group structure. In M. A. Hogg & S. Tindale (eds), *Blackwell handbook of social psychology: Group processes* (pp. 352–375). Cambridge, MA: Blackwell.

Sande, G. N., Ellard, J. H., & Ross, M. (1986). Effect of arbitrarily assigned status labels on self-perceptions and social perceptions: The mere position effect. *Journal of Personality and Social Psychology, 50,* 684–689.

Sauer, R. D. (1998). The economics of wagering markets. *Journal of Economic Literature 36,* 2021–2064.

Scheier, M. F., & Carver, C. S. (1992). Effects of optimism on psychological and physical well-being: Theoretical overview and empirical update. *Cognitive Therapy and Research, 16,* 201–228.

Sedikides, C., Gaertner, L., & Toguchi, Y. (2003). Pancultural self-enhancement. *Journal of Personality and Social Psychology, 84,* 60–79.

Shepperd, J. A., & McNulty, J. K. (2002). The affective consequences of expected and unexpected outcomes. *Psychological Science, 13,* 85–88.

Shepperd, J. A., & Taylor, K. M. (1999). Ascribing advantages to comparison targets. *Basic and Applied Social Psychology, 21,* 103–117.

Shnabel, N., Halabi, S., & Noor, M. (2013). Overcoming competitive victimhood and facilitating forgiveness through re-categorization into a common victim or perpetrator identity. *Journal of Experimental Social Psychology, 49,* 867–877.

Simmons, J. P., & Nelson, L. D. (2006). Intuitive confidence: Choosing between intuitive and nonintuitive alternatives. *Journal of Experimental Psychology: General, 135,* 409–428.

Simon, H. A. (1954). Bandwagon and underdog effects and the possibility of election predictions. *Public Opinion Quarterly, 18,* 245–253.

Smith, R. H., Turner, T. J., Garonzik, R., Leach, C. W., Druskat, V. U., & Weston, C. M. (1996). Envy and schadenfreude. *Personality and Social Psychology Bulletin, 22,* 158–168.

Snyder, C. R., Lassegard, M., & Ford, C. E. (1986). Distancing after group success and failure: Basking in reflected glory and cutting off reflected failure. *Journal of Personality and Social Psychology, 51,* 382–388.

Tajfel, H., & Turner, J. C. (1986). The social identity theory of intergroup behavior. In S. Worchel & W. G. Austin (eds), *The social psychology of intergroup relations* (pp. 7–24). Chicago, IL: Nelson Hall.

Thaler, R. H., & Ziemba, W. T. (1988). Anomalies: Parimutuel betting markets: Racetracks and lotteries. *The Journal of Economic Perspectives 2*, 161–174.

Vandello, J. A., Goldschmied, N., & Richards, D. A. R. (2007). The appeal of the underdog. *Personality and Social Psychology Bulletin, 33*, 1603–1616.

Vandello, J. A., Michniewicz, K., & Goldschmied, N. (2011). Moral judgments of the powerless and powerful in violent intergroup conflicts. *Journal of Experimental Social Psychology, 47*, 1173–1178.

Walster, E., Walster, G. W., & Berscheid, E. (1978). *Equity: Theory and research*. New York: Allyn & Bacon.

Ward, A., & Brenner, L. (2006). Accentuate the negative: The positive effects of negative acknowledgement. *Psychological Science, 17*, 959–962.

19

Whistleblowers as Heroes
Fostering "Quiet" Heroism in Place of the Heroic Whistleblower Stereotype

A. J. Brown

Whistleblowing, or the act of speaking up with concerns or information about wrongdoing inside organizations and institutions, can be one of the most important and difficult forms of heroism in modern society. In a complex world where power, decision-making and the lives and work of citizens are tied up with the good governance of public and corporate institutions, the everyday people inside organizations are often the best placed to tell the truth about what went wrong after a disaster—or, even better, to sound the alarm before poor, risky or corrupt practices take hold, and so limit corruption or avert tragedy.

But while *some* whistleblowers can be accurately identified as heroes, is this true of all? *Should* whistleblowing be classed as always, or generally, a heroic act or process? *Why* are key social actors, from the media to whistleblowing advocacy groups, so ready to tag whistleblowers as heroes? How *useful* is this tag when it comes to fully understanding and valuing the vital role that whistleblowing plays in political life, as well as to encouraging and protecting whistleblowers? This chapter dives behind the familiar stereotype of whistleblower as hero, to unpack some of the dilemmas associated with how whistleblowing is, and should be, characterized. These dilemmas revolve especially around the fact that often, as a process, whistleblowing is (or should be) more "normal" than it is "exceptional" in modern institutional life. I will argue that unlike some and perhaps most other forms of heroism, the unexceptional nature of much whistleblowing, the complexity of its motivations, and the options for best recognizing it, can all combine to make the "hero-whistleblower" stereotype as much a hindrance as a help in shaping public discourse, policy, and legal and institutional responses.

By reviewing when and why we tend to identify whistleblowers as heroes, and analyzing this in relation to growing research into whistleblowing behavior and processes, including social attitudes and the self-images of whistleblowers, we can begin to identify a more nuanced approach to identifying what is (or can be) heroic about whistleblowing, and what may not be, or isn't, or is better not depicted in heroic terms even when it is. The first part of the chapter reviews some of the background of what we know about whistleblowing, and when and how heroism becomes associated with it, in order to flesh out the tensions that this association creates for policy choices about how whistleblowing is best recognized. The second part reviews evidence of social attitudes towards whistleblowing in order to provide some new anchors for how the relationship between heroism and whistleblowing should be approached, including results from a large self-selecting sample of whistleblowers, potential whistleblowers and non-whistleblowers, collected through the World Online Whistleblowing Survey (WOWS). In conclusion, given the counterproductive effects that can flow from misrepresentation of all or most whistleblowing as "totally" heroic, these analyses support the need to promote whistleblowing as a "quiet" or everyday form of heroism, recognizing that much of it can and should begin and end with little or no heroism at all.

Background: Why Identify Whistleblowers as Heroes?

Whistleblowing is best understood as the "disclosure by organization members (former or current) of illegal, immoral or illegitimate practices" under the control of that organization, "to persons or organizations that may be able to effect action" (Miceli & Near, 1984, p. 689). While any citizen who speaks up about wrongdoing can sometimes be labelled this way, including victims of crime and accountability activists, the social science focus on the whistleblower as "insider" has a clear rationale—it is insiders who have unique information and are able to form uniquely significant judgments that things are going wrong, and often do so before outsiders become aware, and yet they can be surrounded by heavy institutional and professional barriers, direct and indirect, against reporting their concerns. Depending on the context, the professional and personal costs of whistleblowing can be high, ranging from the simple stress of a reporting and investigation process, through ostracism to career destruction to physical threats, intimidation and loss of life. And yet, people can and do speak up; and are valued for it. Over the last twenty years, reforms aimed at encouraging whistleblowing and/or protecting whistleblowers have become a central part of political and regulatory frameworks on an international basis (Calland & Dehn, 2004; Vandekerckhove, 2006; Lewis, 2010; Vaughn, 2013).

It is no surprise that with great frequency, individual whistleblowers are hailed as heroes, and receive official and unofficial heroism awards. It is also no surprise that the best-known cases, as well as the ones where whistleblowers can appear to have risked or battled the greatest odds, are those which become a *cause celebre* (or *cause infame*) in the public domain. As a result, whistleblowing is often perceived, and sometimes defined even by experts and commentators, as *only* involving the external disclosure of wrongdoing by an individual to the public via the media—as distinct from internal disclosures within organizations, or disclosures via official channels to regulators or other authorities. However, this is a limited window on how whistleblowing occurs and what it involves. Naturally, those whistleblowers who try to go public first, or persevere with their concerns into the public domain; who succeed in winning media and public support; and whose concerns receive at least some level of vindication, are the most likely to be identified as heroes—almost by definition. But research consistently shows that only a small proportion of whistleblowers ascend into these categories, and that an even smaller proportion aspire or intend to do so (see e.g., Miceli, Near, & Dworkin, 2008, pp. 7–10, 85). Rather, the vast bulk of public whistleblowing "heroes" were internal whistleblowing "heroes" long before they went public. Furthermore, the vast bulk of internal whistleblowing "heroes" never go public, especially if their concerns are heard and acted on, obviating the need for public exposure.

Before particular types of whistleblower (if any) can be singled out as fitting the definition of "hero," whistleblowing and whistleblowers therefore need to be understood in its/their full context—as part of a process that includes internal and regulatory disclosures, along with those that make it into the public domain. Why do we readily identify whistleblowers as heroes? If we look to the highest profile *cause celebre* whistleblowers, it is because we see them presented—sometimes accurately—as people who, by disclosing perceived wrongdoing, are (1) acting from a noble purpose, and even a selfless one, by putting the welfare of others or their entire society before their own, (2) exhibiting great bravery or courage by doing so, and (3) are exceptional or unusual by nature, apparently ready to do something others did not or would not. So for example, Allison and Goethals (2013, p. 41) identify US military police sergeant Joe Darby as one of 100 selected "exceptional individuals" who exemplify different forms of heroism. An internal whistleblower, Darby received photos from a friend and peer of prisoner abuse in Iraq's Abu Ghraib jail in 2004, and referred these to the proper authorities. Only publicly identified later as a hero, he "did the right thing" where others in the same position may not have. Perhaps the best known recent example of calls for a whistleblower to be seen as a hero is former US National Security Agency contractor Edward Snowden, for his media revelations of illegal or immoral electronic surveillance activities by US intelligence agencies. Here we can look to Apple co-founder Steve Wozniak's description of Snowden for a definition of what constitutes a "total hero":

> Not necessarily [for] what he exposed, but the fact that he internally came from his own heart, his own belief in ... what democracy and freedom was about ... [and] because he gave up his own life to do it ... he did it for reasons of trying to help the rest of us and not just mess up a company he didn't like.
>
> *(Independent, 2015)*

Immediately, however, there is far greater complexity involved in attaching the "heroism" label to these whistleblowing cases, than the familiarity of the label would tend to suggest. To unpack this complexity, we need to focus on four issues: (1) the importance of, but difference between, pro-sociality and selflessness as attributes of whistleblowing; (2) the problem that images of whistleblowers as brave, selfless and exceptional often have less to do with reality than the search for a positive stereotype, in opposition to negative stereotypes, due to the inherently conflictual nature of whistleblowing as a process; (3) the degree of context dependency that influences when and why the "hero" label is applied; and (4) the policy tensions that flow from these issues.

Prosociality versus Selflessness

Whether internal or external, a great deal of whistleblowing can be identified as largely selfless or altruistic in nature. Certainly, one goal of whistleblowing policies is to encourage individuals to "do the right thing" and speak up for the sake of a wider community, as against following their own self-interest, in circumstances where traditional career preservation is often best served by individuals simply keeping their head down. However, is it accurate to identify *all* speaking up as largely selfless, or any speaking up as ever *wholly* selfless? The issue matters because, frequently, commentators present the designation of whistleblowers as heroes as if this can and should frame all responses to their challenges—not only in the individual case, such as Wozniak's defense of Snowden, but as a general principle that "whistleblowers ... should be celebrated and rewarded like heroes: people who do the right things for the right reasons" (Sehgal, 2014, p. 10). One Canadian religious studies professor goes further, pointing to the "self-sacrificial dedication" of celebrated whistleblowers as something beyond mere heroism, and instead as "the stuff of saints":

> [Whistleblowers] are misunderstood as moral heroes who deserve compensation or even rewards, justified though such compensation may well be, and unjustified as the marginalization and penalties they often suffer are. The most appropriate response to the justified, self-sacrificial whistle blower is the respect and awe elicited by recognition that such saints, who respond to a higher calling, still live among us.
>
> *(Grant, 2002, p. 398)*

The problem in all this is that while altruistic behavior on the part of employees and organizational insiders is to be encouraged, and deserves recognition when it manifests, it is not actually typical of all, or even probably most of the whistleblowing behavior that we value in modern society. It has long been recognized that a myriad of factors may motivate, or trigger, an individual to disclose suspected wrongdoing; and then to persevere with that disclosure where others might not. While some whistleblowing may be mostly altruistic, some also occurs for mostly or wholly self-serving reasons, and the bulk most likely lies in between: "motives rarely are unitary and may be mixed with two parts honesty, one part ambition and one part vengeance" (McCall, 1989, p. 15; Fox, 1993, p. 144; Roberts, 2014). Australian authorities have noted, not only that is it difficult to reliably identify any particular whistleblower's "true motivation," since the answer is mostly "a mixture of emotions and reasons," but that using motivation as a precondition for recognizing the value of whistleblowing can be quite counter-productive: after all, "the public interest in the exposure and correction of illegal and improper conduct is just as well served by an allegation which proves on investigation to be accurate, but which was made *purely* out of spite, malice or revenge" (EARC, 1991, p. 144, par 7.31, emphasis added; Senate Select Committee on Public Interest Whistleblowing, 1994, pp. 170–172).

For thirty years, whistleblowing research has dealt with this conundrum by recognizing whistleblowing as "prosocial behavior," irrespective of motive, altruism or selflessness—that is, behavior "defined by some significant segment of society and/or one's social group as generally beneficial to other people" (Penner et al., 2005, p. 366), irrespective of what particular benefits, if any, were intended in the individual case. Applied to whistleblowing, the prosocial behavior model focuses on the impact of the action rather than motivation, though motivation may play an important role. Behavior does not have to be altruistic to be considered pro-social, such that even if whistleblowers may feel morally compelled to act, they may contemporaneously act—consciously or subconsciously—out of some intended personal gain for themselves (Dozier & Miceli, 1985; Miceli et al. 2001; Miceli et al., 2008, p. 38). Drawing on Latané and Darley's (1970) theory of "bystander effect," when seeking to explain why witnesses to a crime may not intervene, "prosociality" is a useful prism through which to review heroic behavior generally. There may be a range of reasons why people are initially triggered to intervene in a manner that is subsequently defined as altruistic or selfless, by others or themselves; but while all or most heroic behavior might well be identifiably prosocial, it is a mistake to assume that all prosocial behavior is heroic. All whistleblowing has societal value, at some level, and heroic acts of whistleblowing are to be applauded where identified, but only some whistleblowing fulfils the "selflessness" criterion of heroism, and only a much smaller fraction again can be identified objectively or by any degree of social consensus as actually doing so. Hence, assumptions that all or even most whistleblowers are heroes, in the classic sense that underpins public stereotypes, commence on shaky if not dangerous ground.

Oppositional Stereotyping as a Response to Conflict

Where a blanket image of whistleblowers as heroes begins to become directly counterproductive, is in any attempt to apply it to the bulk of whistleblowing cases or processes in practice—as well as any attempt to anchor a more informed public discourse. Unlike some archetypal forms of heroism, what was "the right thing to do" in a given whistleblowing situation remains contested and conflict-ridden within institutions or even whole societies, and not only at the time, but even with full hindsight. Not only is motive not a useful guide to what we value in whistleblowing, therefore, but the inherently conflict-laden nature of the process of disclosing the wrongdoing of others makes the application of concepts of heroism even more complex. Again, circumstances do arise where conflicting perceptions of the value of whistleblowing are minimized, because all or most of those in authority, the wider society, and peers, recognize the value of the disclosure more or less immediately and act accordingly. Especially where those responsible for the wrongdoing are silent or silenced, these are also the circumstances where—whatever the risks may have been of worse outcomes—reprisals, suffering and sacrifice on the part of the whistleblower stand to be minimized, and a hero may emerge not only vindicated but intact. However, most whistleblowing is surrounded by judgement calls and value conflicts on the part of the many players involved, as to the relative significance of the suspected wrongdoing, and the justifications, morality or professionalism of the particular disclosure path chosen by, or forced upon, the whistleblower. The points in the process where it is possible for whistleblowers to be clearly identified as heroes by all or most in their own society are few and far between, sometimes even in hindsight—unlike other archetypes such as the soldier standing victorious on the defeated enemy position, or the fireman emerging with the saved baby from the burning house.

In this context, it needs to be understood that whistleblowers very readily come to be identified as heroes not for the descriptive accuracy of the title—which can be elusive—but for its normative value when navigating this field of contest. When the discourse of heroism is used in relation to whistleblowing, it is usually not as an absolute concept (i.e., a clear presentation or justification of whistleblowing as heroic). Rather, the hero whistleblower is more often presented as an oppositional concept, or stereotype, in counterpoint to equal and opposite stereotypes attaching to the whistleblower in the same case. The Snowden case exemplifies this rhetorical dichotomy. Many may agree with Wozniak's defense of Snowden as a "total hero," but this emphatic defense arises in large part as a response to criticism of the whistleblower as nothing of the sort, but instead as a "cowardly traitor"; far from being unequivocally celebrated, the "Snowden leaks" are also widely seen as perhaps "the most *infamous* example of whistleblowing of all time" (Alati, 2015, p. 92, emphasis added; see also Moretti, 2014). There is nothing new about this dichotomy. Indeed, discourses on whistleblowing have been bogged for decades in the almost unanswerable question of whether whistleblowers are better seen as heroes, or as "villains" or "traitors." One of the earliest US postgraduate theses in the field (Egan, 1988) was titled *Hero or traitor? the ethical dilemma of the whistleblower.* This oppositional frame of reference has tended to dominate the application of concepts of heroism to whistleblowing, in countless publication titles and analyses ever since (e.g., Grant, 2002; Sehgal, 2014).

Here, then, is a first problem for heroism science to solve—how to escape a dichotomy which has confounded if not defeated much scholarship and commentary on whistleblowing over a long period, in which heroism is used not only as a stereotype, but in a manner that lends disproportionate legitimacy to the negative stereotypes against which it is pitted (by suggesting they may represent a valid descriptive option), and which risks being self-defeating because on close scrutiny it is often inapposite. While stereotypes of whistleblowers as "vengeful troublemakers" need to be fought (Lewis, 2001), the answer does not lie in any equal or opposite version. Indeed, the ease with which the hero image collapses under pressure, in most individual cases, can devalue whistleblowing as a whole. As soon as attempts are made to portray the average whistleblower as a hero, it becomes easier for those negatively affected by wrongdoing disclosures to discredit him or her by drawing attention to possible evidence of the opposite (e.g., possible self-interest, even if small or tangential; or workplace unpopularity, even if reasonable in the circumstances). More broadly, managers or even whole organizations that do not understand or accept whistleblowing as a process, can easily be pushed away from supporting or developing it in their own organization because of the obvious inapplicability of the stereotype to cases of which they are aware. Again, some whistleblowers are heroes, and others may become heroes along the path, but others may be prone to have this status thrust upon them (or even to seek it out) when this is, in fact, counterproductive for themselves and others. Even where there is no malice, vengeance, troublemaking or betrayal involved, it can be legitimately contestable whether the benefits and costs of an act of whistleblowing weigh out to serve the greater good, depending on how the whistle is blown, how it is handled, and the nature of the issues and conflicts. These "grey area" debates are themselves a large part of whistleblowing's value.

How might the discourse be shifted to escape this self-defeating battle of stereotypes? As noted above, Grant (2002) suggests overcoming the image of the whistleblower as "tattle-tale, traitor, troublemaker," not by falling back on the image of "tragic hero battling the system," but by elevating him or her to secular sainthood. However, this does not seem to improve the situation, and arguably (since it relies on even greater self-sacrifice) may make it worse. Better insights come from an examination of heroic and anti-heroic narratives surrounding Sherron Watkins, former vice president of Enron Corporation, who along with WorldCom's Cynthia Cooper and the FBI's Coleen Rowley was one of three whistleblowers recognized by *Time Magazine* as its 2002 Persons of the Year. Despite the hero status earned by alerting Enron's CEO to the financial irregularities and frauds that ultimately brought down the company, and then testifying honestly before subsequent inquiries, Watkins was also criticized by some for not herself going to the authorities or going public sooner. Reviewing these conflicting narratives, Hillon, Smith, and Isaacs (2005) argue for "a new prototype" which is neither classical hero nor anti-hero: "the quasi-hero, which possesses some classical hero attributes, yet is devoid of other essential qualities," as a means of understanding the types of corporate spectacles and organizational dynamics within which whistleblowing arises:

> In order for Watkins to adequately portray roles of both hero and anti-hero, she must be perceived to be imbued with multiple conflicting values, with both will to power and will to serve. In essence, her narratives require a new typology, the quasi-hero.
>
> *(Hillon, Smith, & Isaacs, 2005)*

The term "quasi-hero" is also probably not itself helpful, since it signals that any given whistleblower may, or may not actually satisfy different characteristics of a hero (or anti-hero) depending on the organizational and political circumstances. This is accurate, but where does it leave either the public discourse, or policy and regulatory choices? A third way is needed to escape the current battle of stereotypes; one that recognizes the complexity of most whistleblowing contexts.

Context Dependency

For heroism science to offer a better path, we have already seen that the broad context and nature of whistleblowing needs to be grasped. It also helps to identify in more detail the factors that tend to see whistleblowers identified as heroic, in a full spectrum of contexts, in order to be clearer as to what it is that we are trying to value. Of the three factors noted earlier as key characteristics of "classic" heroism (nobility of purpose; exceptionalism; and bravery/risk/sacrifice), we have already seen that altruism or selflessness may or may not feature in a whistleblowing situation—and yet we value most whistleblowing as pro-social, and may even try to thrust altruism onto it as an *ex post facto* rationalization.

In fact, looking more closely at this first factor, we find that what tends to define nobility of purpose, in whistleblowing, may have less to do with the "hero" and their perspective on the situation, than the scale or seriousness of the wrongdoing that would have otherwise gone undisclosed. Here is one possible key to better understanding the Watkins case, or even the Snowden disclosures: for those inclined to describe their role as heroic, the whistleblower's purpose is in fact almost irrelevant relative to the importance of the issues on which they spoke up, and the fact they did so. The same may explain why some of the best recognized, and most valued whistleblowers are nurses, whose disclosures about dysfunctional medical or hospital practices (or worse) touch directly on issues of life and death, as well as the high levels of trust placed by citizens in the professions and institutions involved. The first and as yet only whistleblower to be recognized in Australia's national honors system, as Australia Day "Local Hero" in 2006, was senior nursing unit manager Toni Hoffmann (for a full account see Thomas, 2007). In the United Kingdom, the Francis Inquiry into the National Health System (NHS) has seen multiple nurses hailed as "heroes working in the public interest," thanks to their whistleblowing (Guardian, 2015).

Consequently, we have a first indicator of the type of concept of heroism that may be more apposite, applied to whistleblowing in general—one in which criteria of selflessness or altruism play a much reduced role. The real position suggested by these cases is not: "they did it for the greater good," but rather: "who cares why or how they did it: the important thing was to know what was going on" in these particular instances (but perhaps not others). What becomes exceptional, in fact, is not the whistleblower as an individual, but the wrongdoing against which they reacted, and not simply because it was wrong, but because of the seriousness and scale of its particular implications.

On this second question of exceptionalism, it also stands out that in many such cases, the nature of the wrongdoing relative to the whistleblower's professional training, roles and responsibilities made its disclosure something that was, or should have been, quite unexceptional. Instead, speaking up about it was, or should have been, simply part and parcel of their job. In any whistleblowing case, it is important to recognize that individuals do speak up in a manner or circumstances whether others either did not, or might not; and that some individuals are prepared to speak up sooner, rather than waiting for the wrongdoing to get worse (which could make then seem an even greater hero!) or for it to be uncovered by other means, as is often likely. But broadly, it is far from clear why, and when, we identify whistleblowing as so exceptional, when research repeatedly indicates that almost anyone can and does blow the whistle, depending on the situation. Studies over many years in a range of developed countries including the USA, Australia and Norway, indicate that the proportion of employees who do speak up about wrongdoing, at least internally, can be surprisingly high: several reviews suggest on average approximately half of all observers of wrongdoing are likely to report it in these contexts (Miceli & Near, 2013; Olsen, 2014). Obviously, in other countries or in particular industries or contexts, the proportions can be presumed to vary widely—in some places it may indeed by only the truly exceptional person who dares speak up. But if the proportion can already be that high, and more broadly if one goal of whistleblowing policies is to recognize, value and "normalize" such behavior, then when is it accurate or valuable to define it as exceptional? Here we have another reason to look for a form of recognition that relies less on the broad heroism stereotype than on a concept more capable of varying for its individual and organizational context.

Thirdly, whistleblowing tends to be identified as heroic where there is a high level of risk and either possible or actual sacrifice; and hence, a sense of bravery. In celebrated cases, the power disparity between a whistleblower and the persons or institutions implicated in the wrongdoing clearly also adds to this sense. A "David and Goliath" factor goes to the courage of those who blow the whistle with any appreciation of risk, especially in the face of more powerful forces. While there are examples of victorious whistleblower "Davids," moreover, these are few and far between; more commonly, whistleblowers who survive relatively well are likely to have been neither "high target" nor high profile. In the public domain, also common are cases where even if the whistleblower enjoyed a moral victory, and their disclosure led to action and positive change, they also ended up suffering for the experience—hence, not just a hero, but a "tragic hero," "saint" or martyr as suggested by Grant (2002), above. The famous study of "broken lives and organizational power" compiled by Alford (2001) reflects this commonality. One Australian study of 83 whistleblowers, recruited by word of mouth and newspaper advertisement, concluded that since all reported having suffered, there was no such thing as a whistleblower who did not fit this "non-suffering" stereotype (de Maria, 1999, p. 25).

The problems here again point to the extra gaps between stereotype and reality that apply in the whistleblowing context. Yes, whistleblowers can be extremely courageous, or mildly so, but they can also disclose in circumstances where they face little or no risk, or are ignorant of the risks (especially where disclosure is simply part of their job). Who is the more deserving of public attention and support: the whistleblower who deliberately goes into battle against a huge target and at least has a fighting chance of devising a commensurate defense strategy; or the whistleblower who naively airs what they believe is a routine concern to which management will respond, only to find they have stumbled on the tip of an iceberg of fraud and corruption… also doing the right thing, but with no defense strategy at all, for no real fault of their own? Further, against claims that all whistleblowers suffer in one way or another, the empirical evidence indicates that under many social and institutional conditions, this is far from the case (see Smith & Brown, 2008; Miceli & Near, 2013; Smith, 2014). It may be that whistleblowers whose cases become higher profile are more likely to suffer reprisals or destroyed careers, or vice versa, or both; often these cases may involve more serious wrongdoing or political stakes; and it may be that individuals in these situations can be more accurately identified as heroic, including for taking on or persevering in the face of great odds. However, this does not account for the great proportion of whistleblowers who never end up in any, let alone all of these categories. Are not some of them also likely to be heroes, on this criterion? And yet the chances of them being recognized as such is much diminished, relative to the stereotype.

Together, examining these three factors further reinforces why external and public whistleblowing is more likely to be identified as heroic, being both more exceptional and sometimes higher risk—but also further reinforces why limiting the frame of reference only to public whistleblowing is fraught, since whistleblowers may also only end up on these higher profile paths out of desperation or obsession. Indeed, media and other stakeholders can end up trying to ram particular whistleblowers into a classic hero stereotype, irrespective of reality, when the fit is quite poor—especially where the nature of media discourse itself dictates this stereotype as a method for creating and maintaining the celebrity status in support of particular individuals in the new social media age. This can be seen in media treatment of Snowden (Moretti, 2014), and even in media constructions of the WikiLeaks founder, Julian Assange, on a similar model of persecuted hero, even when he himself was/is an activist publisher rather than a whistleblower (see generally Fowler, 2011). The same dynamic saw enormous media and civil society effort go into constructing Assange's most famous whistleblower, Chelsea (then Bradley) Manning, as a hero, when prosecuted by the US military for disclosing vast quantities of classified material including field logs from the Afghanistan and Iraq wars, battle videos and thousands of US diplomatic cables. Once it emerged that Manning did not know the contents of much of the material before leaking it, and did so for a complex combination of personal reasons, it became clearer that the reality was not one that any classic hero stereotype could usefully fit (see Madar, 2012).

Implications for Social and Policy Responses

In order to divine what kind of more nuanced concept of heroism might better fit a broader cross-section of whistleblowing, in place of classic archetypes or stereotypes, it is important to ask how we want society to understand and perceive whistleblowers—and in particular, how any such labels might help to encourage and protect public interest whistleblowing, so that its crucial value for society can be both recognized and maximized. If the larger part of attempts to identify whistleblowers as heroes is normative rather than descriptive, then what are the actual values of this… and are there any potential costs? As already seen, identification as a hero may be a valid means of enlisting support and aiding protection, but a blind stereotype may be counterproductive if, in fact, it helps legitimate the opposite stereotype of betrayal, and if many, or most individual cases lay poor claims to the key criteria on which hero status traditionally rests.

On one hand, the identification of whistleblowers as heroes (or anti-heroes) on that pattern can be seen as a natural product of a 30-year period in which public, media and political recognition of the role of whistleblowing has expanded, but policy thinking and regulatory efforts to effectively manage whistleblowing have been slow to catch up. For much of this period, relatively little has been known about how to properly protect whistleblowers in a substantive sense, or to normalize whistleblowing as part of regulatory and organizational systems, apart from *ex post facto* legal protections such as compensation, exoneration or prosecution against reprisals in individual cases (see generally Dworkin & Brown, 2013; Vaughn, 2013). This anti-retaliation approach, spearheaded by the USA and copied by many jurisdictions, tends to reinforce the oppositional stereotypes described above by prioritizing a focus on individual whistleblowers, and their legal claims against employers and reprisors. A whistleblower with the luck or resources to be supported by an effective legal and/or political campaign stands to benefit from a heroic characterization, assuming it can be sustained; just as a whistleblower who successfully harnesses that characterization may find that this profile helps provide protection against some forms of reprisal.

Nevertheless, the limitations are plainly many. The bulk of whistleblowers do not have ready access to the legal and political resources necessary to command the legal protections that their actions deserve, even where a supportive legal framework exists. If in the minority who try to go public, then unless they have such a legal or political battle in train, they can struggle to command any attention, let alone support, from the media. Even where they can command it, and claim the hero mantle, this attention and support may be short-lived. Allison and Goethals (2013, p. 41) classify Joe Darby as "heroic" but also highlight the "transitory" nature of this status: "hero today, gone tomorrow." After the public attention subsides, or if a whistleblower fails to gain it but succeeds in drawing even more ire from their organization through the publicity effort, all they may have achieved is a better target painted on their head.

More recently, some countries have seriously embraced the challenge of trying to internalize whistleblowing in their integrity and regulatory arrangements—sometimes in parallel, but also as an alternative to relying on *ex post facto* legal, political and media battles as the main means of securing protection or compensation (Dworkin & Brown, 2013). Increasingly, these structural or institutional approaches also legitimate public whistleblowing to the media, at least as a last resort; but they are plainly aimed at forcing or inducing organizations and regulators to better hear and protect their own whistleblowers in the first place. There are many types of whistleblowing which organizations and regulators can handle well, thus reducing the need for whistleblowers to pursue or be cast into classic but unrealistic hero characterizations. Again, of course, there are limitations. Such approaches are easier to implement in countries with well-developed public integrity frameworks and, especially, employment law frameworks (for example, in the United Kingdom, Ireland or Australia, as against the USA where most employers can still hire and fire "at will"). There will also always be organizations that fail in their whistleblower support duties, or issues that are too hot for organizations and authorities themselves to handle. In these situations, without alternative legal and/or media support, this institutionalization approach can be seen as a trap, in which the whistleblower may be more easily crushed by reprisals for no gain.

The key distinction for present purposes is that, whereas the anti-retaliation approach can benefit from placing the strongest possible focus on the merits and character of the whistleblower—helping explain and perpetuate hero/anti-hero stereotypes—the institutionalization approach seeks to take the focus *off* the whistleblower. Rather than promoting the concept of a whistleblower as inherently noble, brave and exceptional, it presents the whistleblower as simply professional, the process as safe even if not always easy (hence, no bravery required), and its incidence as normal even if ideally infrequent. An important premise is that rather than ascending into a panoply of heroes or saints, the whistleblower by their disclosure passes responsibility to the integrity processes of the organization, or of society as a whole; it is no longer the whistleblower's concern, but a shared one, so that provided it is actually addressed, and the whistleblower is supported and not targeted, their own role has been discharged. Under this approach, encouragement and protection is served by the *least* possible focus on the personal merits and character of the whistleblower among the wider organization or public—even if their actions may indeed be quite heroic, and capable of being celebrated as such.

Together, this discussion of existing research and knowledge highlights the need for a concept of heroism that fits with the social value we place on whistleblowing *generally*, as against a classic stereotype that while familiar and sometimes even accurate in its application to individuals, can also be ill-fitting and counterproductive. For these reasons, application of hero stereotypes to whistleblowing may be as much a hindrance as a help to shaping an improved public discourse and a more effective range of policy responses. What seems to be needed is a concept of "quiet" heroism in which selflessness, bravery and exceptionalism—despite remaining important and sometimes apposite—are also nuanced or replaced with more realistic ideas of what whistleblowing entails, why it is valuable and how it is best encouraged and managed. To identify possible ingredients, however, it is also useful to look directly to social attitudes towards whistleblowing, for evidence which might confirm or throw further light on possible anchors for a more nuanced concept.

Social and Cultural Attitudes

Do citizens see whistleblowing in the type of strongly positive terms that would be consistent with classic hero stereotypes? Alternatively, do they see such reporting of wrongdoing in anti-hero terms, or somewhere in between—and what of those whose pro-social behavior we are analyzing: whistleblowers and potential whistleblowers? Answering these questions is surprisingly difficult, because as yet, little research has been conducted on an international basis which might yield a systematic or comprehensive picture. Many researchers across a range of countries have tended to presume that social attitudes to whistleblowing are likely to be unsympathetic, or more consistent with anti-hero stereotypes (see Vandekerckhove et al., 2014). For example, based on limited evidence, Australia's international reputation is one of a strong "anti-dobbing culture which is contrary to whistleblowing" (Sawyer, 2004) and might even make it a "cardinal sin" (see various sources cited by Hartman et al., 2009, pp. 264–265; Sehgal, 2014). Yet this contrasts sharply with the popularity of the hero stereotype among the mainstream media, and the public support that politicians have presumably sensed, at federal level and in all states, when passing and updating whistleblower protection legislation since 1993.

To get a better initial fix, in 2012 the author and colleagues surveyed the attitudes of random national samples of adults in Australia ($n = 1211$) and the United Kingdom ($n = 2000$), together with a large self-selected sample of individuals ($n = 2622$) from a range of countries through the first World Online Whistleblowing (WOW) Survey.[1] The questions were developed through review of previous instruments, interviews with whistleblowers and media representatives across a range of countries, and consultation within the International Whistleblowing Research Network including a meeting at Seattle University in March 2012. The full WOW Survey consisted of 41 questions, with 10 of these questions used in the Australian and UK random sample surveys, plus demographic questions. The Australian and UK surveys thus afford a statistically representative snapshot of these populations, which share comparable political, institutional and legal traditions. The longer self-selected survey enabled comparison of individuals on a variety of extra attributes and attitudes, including comparison of respondents who had (1) had seen organizational wrongdoing and blown the whistle (whistleblowers, $n = 745$), (2) not seen wrongdoing but said they would blow the whistle if they did (potential whistleblowers, $n = 1538$), or (3) either seen wrongdoing but not blown the whistle, or said they would not blow the whistle even if they did see it (non-whistleblowers, $n = 329$; total, $n = 2622$). Responses were drawn primarily from Australia ($n = 491$), UK & Ireland ($n = 71$), North America ($n = 146$), Europe (predominantly Germany) ($n = 1774$), missing ($n = 140$).[2]

How Well Does the Hero-Whistleblower Stereotype Resonate?

A first conclusion, already reported elsewhere (Brown, Vandekerckhove, & Dreyfus, 2014; Vandekerckhove et al., 2014), is that presumptions that whistleblowing is not popularly supported can easily be misplaced. Indeed, the perception that whistleblowing is culturally unacceptable in a given society may not accord with the reality of how whistleblowing is actually viewed in that society. In both Australia and the UK, only around half of respondents (53 and 47 percent respectively) felt that in their society, it was "generally acceptable for people to speak up about serious wrongdoing, even if it means revealing inside information"—but as shown in Table 19.1, a much higher proportion of respondents (81 percent, in both countries) felt that "people should be supported" rather than punished for revealing wrongdoing, even if it meant revealing inside information. Unsurprisingly, support was even higher among the self-selecting WOW survey sample.

While these results help explain why the broad stereotype of whistleblowers as heroic is likely to resonate with these publics, Table 19.2 helps confirm why that broad stereotype is nevertheless a problematic fit. The perceived acceptability of reporting varies significantly, depending upon who is the target of the whistleblowing. Against presumptions of an anti-whistleblowing culture, acceptability of reporting on persons in authority is high, especially in Australia (again 81 percent; UK 71 percent), but this reduces for reporting on colleagues, and reduces again to only 60 percent acceptability for reporting on family or friends, in line with normal hierarchies of loyalty. The same pattern repeats for all groups among the self-selecting WOW respondents, notwithstanding their stronger support for reporting overall. The results reinforce the context dependency of whistleblowing, discussed earlier.

Further nuances were confirmed when these publics were asked their view on to whom it was most appropriate to reveal wrongdoing, and when. As discussed earlier, the classic hero stereotype is largely born of situations where the whistleblowing has become public and the whistleblower is battling powerful organizations, but anti-hero stereotypes are also triggered if a

Table 19.1 Support for whistleblowing (%) (Q3)

	Statement	Australia (n = 1211)	UK (n = 2000)	World Online Whistleblowing (WOW) Survey			
				W/blowers (n = 745)	Potential w/blowers (n = 1548)	Non- w/blowers (n = 329)	Total (n = 2622)
a.	People should be **supported** for revealing serious wrongdoing, even if it means revealing inside information	81.3	81.2	95.7	96.1	92.7	95.5
b.	People who reveal inside information should be **punished**, even if they are revealing serious wrongdoing	8.5	6.0	1.3	1.2	4.6	1.7
c.	Neither/Don't know	10.2	12.8	3.0	2.7	2.7	2.8
	Total	100.0	100.0	100.0	100.0	100.0	100.0

Table 19.2 Acceptability of whistleblowing in particular circumstances (Q4). Responses to the question: "How **acceptable** do you personally think it is for someone to reveal inside information about serious wrongdoing by each of these different **types of people**?" The table shows percentages responding "acceptable"

	Serious wrongdoing by:	Australia (n = 1211)	UK (n = 2000)	World Online Whistleblowing (WOW) Survey			
				W/blowers (n = 745)	Potential w/blowers (n = 1548)	Non- w/blowers (n = 329)	Total (n = 2622)
a.	**People in charge** of an organization	81.1%	71.1%	95.4%	97.5%	92.4%	96.3%
b.	**Other staff or workers** in an organization	76.8%	69.6%	90.9%	87.0%	79.6%	87.1%
c.	A **family** member or personal **friend** working in the **organization**	59.8%	59.4%	70.5%	62.5%	57.8%	64.1%

whistleblower can be portrayed as having unreasonably eschewed "proper" channels, or as having gone public too late, or too early. When asked which if any of a number of channels represented "the most effective way to get action to stop serious wrongdoing," more respondents selected reporting "to people in authority, via official channels" (Australia, 56 percent; UK, 51 percent) than chose reporting "to journalists or news organizations" (Australia, 17 percent; UK, 19 percent) or directly to the public via new or social media (Australia, 6 percent; UK, 7 percent) (see Appendix Q9). Similarly, Table 19.3 shows that public whistleblowing does have legitimacy, to the extent that a large majority of citizens (Australia 87 percent, UK 88 percent) saw it as potentially acceptable for a whistleblower to use the media *at some stage*. However, 10 percent or fewer considered that the media should be available "as a first option, in any situation," with most

Table 19.3 When should whistleblowing to the media be acceptable? (%) (Q10). Responses to the question: "If someone in an organization has inside information about serious wrongdoing, **when** do you think they should be able to use a journalist, the media, or the internet to draw attention to it?"

		Australia (n = 1211)	UK (n = 2000)	World Online Whistleblowing Survey (WOWS)			
				W/blowers (n = 745)	Potential w/blowers (n = 1548)	Non- w/blowers (n = 329)	Total (n = 2622)
a.	As a first option, in any situation	6.8	9.5	6.8	5.1	5.5	5.6
b.	Whenever there become specific reasons to do so	34.4	33.8	47.4	57.0	55.3	54.0
c.	Only as a last resort, if all else fails	46.0	44.3	42.3	34.0	27.4	35.5
d.	Never	4.8	4.6	2.0	1.0	4.6	1.7
e.	Don't know	8.0	7.7	1.5	2.9	7.3	3.1
	Total	100.0	100.0	100.0	100.0	100.0	100.0

seeing this as only acceptable "whenever there become specific reasons to do so" (Australia 41 percent, UK 43 percent) or "as a last resort, if all else fails" (Australia 46 percent, UK 44 percent).

Further, but more surprisingly, the results from the self-selecting WOW respondents were in a similar direction. Despite their higher support for whistleblowing overall, these respondents were no more likely than the Australian and UK general publics to support whistleblowing to media "as a first option" (6 percent). While this sample was more likely to believe that the media should be approached whenever there were "specific reasons" (54 percent), this was actually least true of whistleblowers themselves (47 percent), who were also more likely to believe the media should be only a last resort (42 percent, as against 34 percent of potential whistleblowers, and 27 percent of non-whistleblowers). For this large sample of whistleblowers, publicity and profile, in the manner associated with hero stereotypes of whistleblowing, does not appear to be the key. Instead, like the general citizenry but perhaps even more so, whistleblowers would apparently prefer to be able to rely on official channels they can trust (Brown, Vandekerckhove, & Dreyfus, 2014).

The Self-Images of Whistleblowers

Finally, the self-selecting WOW respondents in the study were directly asked how they would "generally describe people who reveal inside information about serious wrongdoing to the media," and asked to select one description closest to their view, out of a continuum on the hero/anti-hero spectrum: "heroes," "martyrs," "normal," "misfits" and "villains." While this question was not asked of the general publics in the study, the WOW Survey afforded a longer questionnaire which was also always more likely to capture a larger number of actual whistleblowers and sympathizers. Table 19.4 gives a breakdown of the overall responses, as well as the geographic locations of the main groups of respondents. Overall, while the self-selecting nature of the sample makes it unsurprising that views of whistleblowers would tend towards the heroic, it is striking that as many as 41 percent of respondents chose the neutral descriptor of whistleblowers as simply "normal" rather than taking the opportunity to put them on a pedestal as either heroes or martyrs. The geographic results are also interesting, however. While the differing sizes and compositions of these samples means that no reliable conclusion can be drawn, the fact that 63 percent of North American respondents chose the term "heroes" and only 23 percent chose "normal," as against 40 and 44 percent respectively for German respondents, may indicate that the hero stereotype does hold greater currency in particular contexts. Whether this is a product of particular political and legal systems and discourses, or the other way around, and whether it is necessarily healthy or productive, would be important topics for debate.

Tables 19.5 and 19.6 also reinforce the discussions and results noted above, by showing that even among this mostly pro-whistleblowing group, those who were most likely to view whistleblowers as "normal," rather than heroic, were those who had greatest trust in existing institutions and official channels—consistently with arguments that whistleblowing is best encouraged and recognized by being institutionalized rather than through oppositional stereotypes. In Table 19.5, this is shown by the higher proportion of those who already believe "about the right amount of information is kept secret in organizations" who also saw whistleblowing as simply "normal" (54 percent); and in Table 19.6, by the higher proportion of those who believe that whistleblowing to the media is acceptable "only in the last resort" (46 percent); that is, that whistleblowing is normal *and* that official institutions should be trusted. These results are consistent with previous findings that most of those who believe in whistleblowing are not driven by distrust of institutions, but rather see whistleblowing and institutions as working together. For example, while many of the whistleblowers in the sample do consider media exposure to be the most effective way to get action on wrongdoing (34 percent), even more (at least 44 percent) consider that official channels should be tried first, or should be the only channels used (see Brown, Vandekerckhove, & Dreyfus, 2014).

Table 19.4 Description of whistleblowers (Q27) × country/language groups (%)—World Online Whistleblowing Survey (WOWS). Responses to the question: "How would you generally describe people who reveal inside information about serious wrongdoing to the media? Choose the description closest to your view"

Description	US/Canada (n = 133)	Australia (n = 416)	Germany (n = 1302)	Other (n = 206)	Total (n = 2057)
heroes	62.8%	49.5%	39.8%	53.4%	44.6%
martyrs	12.3%	9.1%	11.0%	8.3%	10.4%
normal	23.3%	38.9%	44.1%	37.9%	41.1%
misfits	2.3%	1.2%	3.7%	0.0%	2.7%
villains	0%	1.2%	1.5%	0.5%	1.2%
Total	100.0%	100.0%	100.0%	100.0%	100.0%

Table 19.5 Description of whistleblowers (Q27) × view of secrecy (Q1) (%)—World Online Whistleblowing Survey (WOWS)

Description	Q1. In the society in which I live ...			Total (n = 2017)
	Too much information is kept secret in organisations (n = 1804)	About the right amount of information is kept secret in organisations (n = 180)	Not enough information is kept secret in organisations (n = 33)	
heroes	47.6%	25.0%	15.2%	45.0%
martyrs	10.4%	8.3%	15.2%	10.3%
normal	39.5%	53.9%	36.4%	40.8%
misfits	2.3%	7.2%	6.1%	2.8%
villains	0.2%	5.6%	27.3%	1.1%
Total	100.0%	100.0%	100.0%	100.0%

Table 19.6 Description of whistleblowers (Q27) × when acceptable to use media (Q10) (%)—World Online Whistleblowing Survey (WOWS)

Description	Q10. When acceptable to use media:				Total (n = 2040)
	As a first option, in any situation (n = 137)	Whenever there become specific reasons to do so (n = 1186)	Only as a last resort, if all else fails (n = 691)	Never (n = 26)	
heroes	64.2%	47.1%	37.9%	7.7%	44.7%
martyrs	6.6%	10.5%	11.6%	3.8%	10.5%
normal	28.5%	40.0%	45.9%	19.2%	40.9%
misfits	0.7%	2.4%	3.5%	7.7%	2.7%
villains	0.0%	0.1%	1.2%	61.5%	1.2%
Total	100.0%	100.0%	100.0%	100.0%	100.0%

Even more strikingly, Table 19.7 shows that the overall result is also the same for those who identify as having reported wrongdoing (whistleblowers), along with those who say they would if they saw wrongdoing (potential whistleblowers). Neither whistleblowers or potential whistleblowers showed any greater desire to seize the heroic or martyrdom labels. It was only non-whistleblowers who varied from this pattern and were less likely to see whistleblowing as "normal"—either because they saw whistleblowers as anti-heroes rather than heroes, or because they were more likely to see them as having suffered as martyrs, either of which would explain these respondents' non-whistleblowing preference.

Finally, as shown in Table 19.8, a view of whistleblowing as simply normal, rather than heroic, was more likely among those whistleblowers who reported that people in authority had treated them "the same" or "well" as a result of their whistleblowing—rather than badly, as most stereotypes presume. Consistently with the earlier discussion, not all whistleblower respondents reported having suffered at the hands of the organization. Indeed it is striking that even among this self-selecting group, 50 percent of those identifying as whistleblowers indicated they did *not* consider anyone in authority to have mistreated them. The fact that such a high proportion of this group saw whistleblowing as simply normal, again indicates not only that successful whistleblowing is possible, but that it may be more possible where treated as part of the professional routine rather than singled out as exceptional, including in the eyes of whistleblowers themselves. It was those who reported mistreatment who were more likely to see whistleblowing as heroism or martyrdom, and less likely to see it as normal; but whether the direction of cause and effect is all one way, or might also be the other way round, demands further study.

Table 19.7 Description of whistleblowers (Q27) × whistleblowing experience (%)—World Online Whistleblowing Survey (WOWS)

Description	Whistleblowers (n = 608)	Potential whistleblowers (n = 1208)	Non-whistleblowers (n = 241)	Total (n=2057)
heroes	43.4%	44.9%	46.1%	44.6%
martyrs	10.9%	9.4%	14.1%	10.4%
normal	41.8%	42.4%	32.8%	41.1%
misfits	3.8%	2.2%	2.5%	2.7%
villains	.2%	1.1%	4.6%	1.2%
	100.0%	100.0%	100.0%	100.0%

Table 19.8 Description of whistleblowers (Q27) × whistleblowing treatment (%)—World Online Whistleblowing Survey (WOWS). Responses to the question: "After you revealed the wrongdoing, how do you feel you were treated by people in authority in the organization?" (Q43a)

Description	Well or extremely well (n = 76)	The same (n = 263)	Badly or extremely badly (n = 340)	Total (n = 679)
heroes	39.5%	43.0%	47.4%	44.8%
martyrs	5.3%	9.5%	14.4%	11.5%
normal	50.0%	43.3%	34.7%	39.8%
misfits	3.9%	3.0%	3.5%	3.4%
villains	1.3%	1.1%	0.0%	0.6%
Total	100.0%	100.0%	100.0%	100.0%

Conclusions

This chapter has drawn on existing whistleblowing research to ask whether, when and why the concept of whistleblowers as heroes is most apposite. In the face of common representations of whistleblowing as inherently heroic, it has discussed the mistakes and disadvantages of assuming that because some whistleblowers can be accurately identified as heroes, this is either accurate or helpful in respect of most, or all, especially when perceived in terms of a classic hero stereotype. Indeed, as seen in the first half of the chapter, the unexceptional nature of much whistleblowing, the complexity of its motivations, and the options for best recognizing it, can all combine to make the "hero-whistleblower" stereotype as much a hindrance as a help in shaping improved public discourse and policy responses. This is because, even though some whistleblowers are certainly heroes on this stereotype, the characteristics of selflessness, exceptionalism and bravery that typically definite heroism can also be a poor fit for much of the whistleblowing that we consider valuable, and which needs to be encouraged and protected. Furthermore, with much expert and media discourse over whistleblowing defined by a self-defeating battle of hero and anti-hero stereotypes, applying the heroism stereotype can end up being counterproductive—either because it is too easy for the un-reality of this status to be exposed, thereby discrediting both whistleblower and whistleblowing, or because it simply assists to paint an even larger target on the whistleblower's head, unless the circumstances are such that increased attention and profile are actually conducive to, rather than corrosive of, the chances of protection.

By reviewing when and why we tend to identify whistleblowers as heroes, and analyzing this in relation to growing research on the reality of whistleblowing behavior and processes, including social attitudes and the self-images of whistleblowers, we have identified that a more nuanced approach may be need to identifying what is (or can be) heroic about whistleblowing, and what may not be, or isn't, or might be better *not* depicted as heroic even when it is. In the second half of the chapter, this was underscored by evidence that public support for whistleblowing, even when high in general, is also context dependent; and that citizens and whistleblowers alike place priority on being able to trust in institutional processes in which whistleblowing can successfully occur, as a matter of routine, rather than necessarily seeing those who disclose wrongdoing placed on a public pedestal for what they have done.

How, then, might the discourse be shifted to escape the battle of stereotypes? These analyses have supported the need to promote whistleblowing as a "quiet" or everyday form of heroism, recognizing that much whistleblowing can and should begin and end with little or no heroism at all. Its ingredients include a recognition that since whistleblowing is to be encouraged for its prosocial effects even when no altruism or selflessness is involved, there are disadvantages in seeking to honor and protect *only* those whose motives appear noble and pure, just as we need to find ways to honor and protect those who blow the whistle, even when it is difficult to characterize as particularly exceptional or brave. Somehow, what are needed are approaches to whistleblowing in which it remains possible to value heroic acts of whistleblowing on that basis, particularly where this is actually conducive to securing protection; but equally to value *all* whistleblowing, whether heroic or not, as a process on which public integrity relies, and in which heroes and non-heroes alike may be better served by protections which do not depend on their conduct being labelled as such. Fortunately, across more and more countries, regulatory arrangements and policy processes are now developing to the point where this more nuanced approach to the characterization of heroism may be ready to evolve, and play its role in support of whistleblowing as a key, ongoing part of social and political integrity regimes.

Acknowledgements

The research for this chapter was made possible by funding from Griffith University, University of Greenwich, and the Australian Research Council through Discovery Project DP1095696 (Griffith University and the University of Melbourne). The author thanks the funding institutions and his project team colleagues at the University of Melbourne, especially Suelette Dreyfus and Emma Osman for data analysis and support.

Notes

1   The Australian data were collected by Newspoll Limited for Griffith University in May 2012. The UK data were collected by ComRes for University of Greenwich in October 2012. The WOW Survey data were collected between May 2012 and April 2013 by Griffith University and University of Melbourne under Australian Research Council Discovery Project DP1095696; respondents were recruited through a range of mainstream and online media and civil society networks.
2   As with other research in this field, the term "whistleblowing" was not itself used, lest it was already associated with any particular stereotype (positive or negative) in the respondent's mind; instead, the questions introduced concepts of organizational membership, inside information, serious wrongdoing, revelation and reporting in a non-leading way, as detailed in the Appendix. Full text of the WOW Survey questionnaire including the common items can be found at https:///whistleblowingsurvey.org.

References

Alati, D. (2015). Cowardly traitor or heroic whistleblower? The impact of Edward Snowden's disclosures on Canada and the United Kingdom's security establishments, *Lincoln Memorial University Law Review*, *3*(Fall), 91–114.
Alford, C. F. (2001). *Whistleblowers: Broken lives and organizational power*. Ithaca, NY: Cornell University Press.
Allison, S. T. & Goethals, G. R. (2013). *Heroic leadership: An influence taxonomy of 100 exceptional individuals*. Abingdon: Routledge.
Brown, A. J. (ed) (2008). *Whistleblowing in the Australian public sector*. Canberra: ANU Press/Australia & New Zealand School of Government.
Brown, A. J., Vandekerckhove, W. & Dreyfus, S. 2014. The relationship between transparency, whistleblowing, and public trust. In P. Ala'i & R. Vaughn (eds), *Research handbook on transparency* (pp. 30–58). Cheltenham: Edward Elgar.
Calland, R. & Dehn, G. (eds) (2004). *Whistleblowing around the world: Law, culture and practice*. London: Public Concern At Work.
De Maria, W. (1999). *Deadly disclosures: Whistleblowing and the ethical meltdown of Australia*. Adelaide: Wakefield Press.
Dozier, J. B., & Miceli, M. P. (1985). Potential predictors of whistle-blowing: A prosocial behavior perspective. *Academy of Management Review*, *10*(4)(October): 823–836.
Dworkin, T. M., & Brown, A. J. (2013). The money or the media? Lessons from contrasting developments in US and Australian whistleblowing laws. *Seattle Journal of Social Justice*, *11*(2): 653–713.
EARC (1991). *Report on protection of whistleblowers*. October. Brisbane: Electoral and Administrative Review Commission (QLD).
Egan, S. W. (1988). Hero or traitor? The ethical dilemma of the whistleblower. M.A. thesis, University of Utah, Salt Lake City, UT.
Fowler, A. (2011). *The most dangerous man in the world: A definitive account of Julian Assange and Wikileaks*. Melbourne: Melbourne University Press.
Fox, R. G. (1993). Protecting the whistleblower. *Adelaide Law Review*, *5*(2), 144.
Grant, C. (2002). Whistle blowers: Saints of secular culture. *Journal of Business Ethics*, *39*: 391–399.
Guardian (2015). The Guardian view on whistleblowers: heroes working in the public interest. Editorial. *The Guardian* (February 12). Retrieved from www.theguardian.com/commentisfree/2015/feb/11/guardian-view-whistleblowers-heroes-working-public-interest.
Hartman, L. P., Elm, D. R., Radin, T. J., & Pope, K. (2009). Translating corporate culture around the world: A cross-cultural analysis of whistleblowing as an example of how to say and do the right thing. *POLITEIA*, *25*(93), 255–272.
Hillon, M. E., Smith, W. L, & Isaacs, G. D. (2005). Heroic/anti-heroic narratives: The quests of Sherron Watkins. *Tamara: Journal of Critical Postmodern Organization Science*, *3*(2), 16–26.

Independent (2015). Apple co-founder Steve Wozniak describes NSA whistleblower Edward Snowden as a "total hero." *The Independent* (May 27). Retrieved from www.independent.co.uk/news/people/apple-co-founder-steve-wozniak-describes-nsa-whistleblower-edward-snowden-as-a-total-hero-10278956.html.

Latané, B., & Darley, J. M. (1970). *The unresponsive bystander: Why doesn't he help?* New York: Appleton-Century-Crofts.

Lewis, D. B. (2001). Introduction. In D. B. Lewis (ed.), *Whistleblowing at work* (pp. 1–9). London: Athlone Press.

Lewis, D. B. (ed.) (2010). *A global approach to public interest disclosure*. Cheltenham: Edward Elgar.

Madar, C. (2012). *The passion of Bradley Manning: The story behind the Wikileaks whistleblower*. London: OR Books.

McCall, J. R. (1989). Whistleblowers: Curse or cure? *National Law Journal* (June), 15.

Miceli, M. P., & Near, J. P. (1984). The relationships among beliefs, organizational position, and whistle-blowing status: A discriminant analysis. *Academy of Management Journal*, 27(4), 687–705.

Miceli, M. P., & Near, J. P. (2013). An international comparison of the incidence of public sector whistle-blowing and the prediction of retaliation: Australia, Norway, and the US, *Australian Journal of Public Administration*, 72(4)(December), 433–446.

Miceli, M. P., Near, J. P. & Dworkin, T. M. (2008). *Whistle-blowing in organizations*. Abingdon: Routledge.

Miceli, M. P., Van Scotter, J. R., Near, J. P., & Rehg, M. (2001). Responses to perceived organizational wrongdoing: Do perceiver characteristics matter? In J. M. Darley, D. M. Messick, & T. R. Tyler (eds), *Social influences on ethical behavior* (pp. 119–135). Mahwah, NJ: Lawrence Erlbaum Associates.

Moretti, A. (2014). Whistleblower or traitor: Edward Snowden, Daniel Ellsberg and the power of media celebrity. *Global Media Journal* Special Issue (June). Retrieved from www.globalmediajournal.com/open-access/whistleblower-or-traitor-edward-snowden-daniel-ellsberg-and-the-power-of-media-celebrity.php?aid=47949.

Olsen, J. (2014). Reporting versus inaction: How much is there, what explains the differences and what to measure. In A. J. Brown, D. Lewis, R. Moberly, & W. Vandekerckhove (eds), *International handbook of whistleblowing research* (pp. 177–206). Cheltenham: Edward Elgar.

Penner, L. A., Dovidio, J. F., Piliavin, J. A., & Schroeder, D. A. (2005). Prosocial behavior: multilevel perspectives. *Annual Review of Psychology*, 56, 365–392.

Roberts, P. (2014). Motivations for whistleblowing: Personal, private and public interests. In A. J. Brown, D. Lewis, R. Moberly, & W. Vandekerckhove (eds), *International handbook of whistleblowing research* (pp. 207–229). Cheltenham: Edward Elgar.

Sawyer, K. (2004). Courage without mateship. Paper prepared for the National Conference of Whistleblowers Australia, Melbourne, 28 November. Retrieved from www.bmartin.cc/dissent/documents/Sawyer04.pdf.

Sehgal, P. (2014). *Whistleblowers: Traitors or heroes? A global perspective*. Proceedings of 26th International Business Research Conference, Imperial College, London, 7–8 April.

Senate Select Committee on Public Interest Whistleblowing (1994). *In the public interest*. Parliamentary Paper No. 148/1994 (August). Canberra: Senate Select Committee on Public Interest Whistleblowing (Australia).

Smith, R. (2014). Whistleblowers and suffering. In A. J. Brown, D. Lewis, R. Moberly, & W. Vandekerckhove (eds), *International handbook of whistleblowing research* (pp. 37–70). Cheltenham: Edward Elgar.

Smith, R. & Brown, A. J. (2008). The good, the bad and the ugly: Whistleblowing outcomes. In A. J. Brown (ed.), *Whistleblowing in the Australian public sector* (pp. 230–249). Canberra: ANU Press/Australia & New Zealand School of Government.

Thomas, H. (2007). *Sick to death*. Sydney: Allen & Unwin.

Vandekerckhove, W. (2006). *Whistleblowing and organizational social responsibility: A global assessment*. Aldershot: Ashgate.

Vandekerckhove, W., Uys, T., Rehg, M., & Brown, A. J. (2014). Understandings of whistleblowing: Dilemmas of societal culture. In A. J. Brown, D. Lewis, R. Moberly, & W. Vandekerckhove (eds), *International handbook of whistleblowing research* (pp. 37–70). Cheltenham: Edward Elgar.

Vaughn, R. G. (2013). *The successes and failures of whistleblower laws*. Cheltenham: Edward Elgar.

Appendix: World Online Whistleblowing Survey items used

Q1. "Inside information" is information that someone has because of their role in an organization—for example, as an employee of a government department or a business, or as a member of an education, religious or community organization. Often inside information is secret or confidential, for good reason. However, often it is also about important things going on within the organization.

Which one of the following comes closest to your view? In [name of country/the society in which I live], too much/about the right amount/not enough information is kept secret in organizations.

Q2. Sometimes, inside information can be about **serious wrongdoing.** This is when a person or organization does things that are unlawful, unjust, dangerous or dishonest enough to harm the interests of individuals, the organization or wider society.

Which one of the following comes closest to your view? In [name of country/the society in which I live], it is generally unacceptable/acceptable for people to speak up about serious wrongdoing, if inside information would have to be revealed.

Q3. Which one of the following best describes what you think should happen in [my/name of country] society? "People should be supported for revealing serious wrongdoing, even if it means revealing inside information/People who reveal inside information should be punished, even if they are revealing serious wrongdoing."

Q4. How acceptable do you personally think it is for someone to reveal inside information about serious wrongdoing by each of these different types of people? [Acceptable/unacceptable/neither or can't say]. To reveal inside information about
   a. serious wrongdoing by people in charge of an organization?
   b. serious wrongdoing by other staff or workers in an organization?
   c. serious wrongdoing by a family member or personal friend working in the organization?

Q6. How much do you agree or disagree with the following statements? [Agree/Disagree/neither/can't say]:
   a. If I observed wrongdoing, I would feel personally obliged to report it to someone in my organization.
   b. If I reported wrongdoing to someone in my organization, I am confident something appropriate would be done about it.
   c. Management in my organization is serious about protecting people who report wrongdoing.

Q9. In different societies, there are different views on the most effective way to get action to stop serious wrongdoing. Which one of these do you think is the most effective way in [your society/name of country]? By reporting the serious wrongdoing:
   a. to people in authority via the official channels
   b. to journalists or news organizations
   c. directly to the general public via internet, Twitter, Facebook or online blogs
   d. some other way
   e. none of the above—in [my society/name of country], there is no effective way to get action to stop serious wrongdoing.

Q10. If someone in an organization has inside information about serious wrongdoing, **when** do you think they should be able to use a journalist, the media, or the internet to draw attention to it?
   a. As a first option, in any situation
   b. Whenever there become specific reasons to do so

c. Only as a last resort, if all else fails
  d. Never.

Q27. How would you generally describe people who reveal inside information about serious wrongdoing to the media? Choose the description closest to your view.
  a. Heroes
  b. Martyrs
  c. Normal
  d. Misfits
  e. Villains
  f. None of the above/Don't know

Q36. In any organization you've been a member of, have you ever seen or had direct evidence of serious wrongdoing?
  a. Yes
  b. No
[If yes:]

Q38. Who, if anyone, did you tell about the serious wrongdoing? Select all that apply.
  a. Family or friends
  b. Work colleagues
  c. People in charge within the organization
  d. People in authority outside the organization (e.g., police, ombudsman, elected representatives)
  e. A journalist or news organization, website or online
  f. Other **(PLEASE SPECIFY)**
  g. I did not tell anyone
[If b–f]

Q43. After you revealed the wrongdoing, how do you feel you were treated by (a) People in authority in the organization

Extremely well	Quite well	The same	Quite badly	Extremely badly
1	2	3	4	5

Part III
Processes of Heroism

20
The Hero's Transformation

Scott T. Allison and George R. Goethals

Stories of heroes undergoing significant transformations are as old as stories themselves. The first known mythical narrative in Western literature, *The Epic of Gilgamesh*, tells the tale of Gilgamesh, the great demigod ruler of Uruk who revels in his invincibility. Gilgamesh terrorizes a city, kills the guardian of a forest, spurns the goddess of love, and slays the mighty bull of heaven. He is reckless, ruthless, and arrogant. Through his friendship with Enkidu and later by his recognition of his own mortality, Gilgamesh experiences loss, becomes humbled, and acquires wisdom about life and love. His personal growth as a hero establishes the precedent of transformation in hero stories, inspiring the development of hero characters in countless fictional tales for over 4,000 years. From Gilgamesh to Luke Skywalker, from Odysseus to Jane Eyre, heroes set out on a journey, transform into new and improved versions of themselves, and in the process encourage us all to follow in their footsteps.

In this chapter, we provide an analysis of human transformation in heroic storytelling and in the lives of everyday people. We describe what a transformation is, why it is important, what causes it to happen, and how it varies from hero to hero. We argue that the hero's transformation is the most central yet most overlooked component of the monomyth of the hero as described by Joseph Campbell (1949) in his classic volume, *The Hero with a Thousand Faces*. Our chapter discusses the ways in which the hero's journey parallels various stages of healthy human development, during which people undergo moral, mental, emotional, spiritual, and physical transformations. We will describe the many triggers, dimensions, processes, and consequences of the hero's transformation. Our concluding thoughts will focus on the role of the hero's transformation in the personal development of the hero and for the well-being of society.

Pervasiveness of Transformation

Transformation is ubiquitous in the natural world. In zoology, the phenomenon of *metamorphosis* describes the radical change from tadpole to frog, caterpillar to butterfly, and polyp to jellyfish. Evolutionary biologists have identified two types of transformations of species: *phyletic gradualism* describes the slow transformation of one species into a new one, and *punctuated gradualism* describes sudden evolutionary shifts.

Similarly, geologists have distinguished between slow, incremental changes in the earth, called *uniformitarianism*, and rapid, violent changes, called *catastrophism*. In the material world, *physical transformations* refer to changes in physical properties that do not produce new substances, as when water transforms to steam or to ice. *Chemical transformations* produce new substances, as when photosynthesis leads to the production of a different set of chemical substances. In climatology, a *tipping point* refers to the irreversible instant at which the earth shifts from one stable state (e.g., an ice age) to another. Once a tipping point has been reached, a transition to a new state occurs. These examples of transformative events in the natural world suggest that transformations vary along the dimensions of speed, type, depth, and timing.

In the social world, transformation is also pervasive. Societies and cultures form, undergo internal change, and dissolve. Transformation is implicated in most of the stages of Tuckman's (1965) classic model describing group development as *forming, storming, norming,* and *performing*. As changes in biological organisms can either be constructive (e.g., mitosis) or destructive (e.g., cancer), so can changes within social entities. Positive transformative movements in collectives promote healthy growth and social unity, as evidenced by the feminist movement, civil rights movement, gay rights movement, and myriad other unifying crusades. Destructive collective transformations exclude and damage segments of populations; examples include Hitler's *Final Solution*, Pol Pot's *Khmer Rouge*, and the massacre of indigenous populations in Australia, New Zealand, and the Americas. Revolutions abound in the political world, with coups aimed at either expanding human rights or dismantling them (Wasserstrom, Hunt, & Young, 2000). Subcultures within larger cultural systems also undergo transformations. These subcultural upheavals can have enduring transformative effects on the greater culture as a whole. Examples include the revolutions that have occurred in the areas of technology (Bostrom, 2006), science (Kuhn, 1962), healthcare (Lee & Cosgrove, 2014), transportation (Crouch, 2004), and music (Reising, 2002), to name but a few.

Psychological transformations have long piqued the interest of scholars and are a central impetus for heroic growth in individuals. Two early seminal works that addressed psychological transformation were William James' (1902/2013) discussion of spiritual conversion in his classic volume, *The Varieties of Religious Experience*, and Sigmund Freud's (1905/2011) *Three Essays on the Theory of Sexuality*, which described life-altering transformative events in childhood. Although Freud suggested that people resist change in adulthood, all subsequent major schools of psychological thought have since proposed mechanisms for transformative change throughout the lifespan. Humanistic theories, in particular, have embraced the idea that humans are capable of a long-term transformation into self-actualized individuals (Maslow, 1943). Recent theories of self-processes portray humans as open to change and growth under some conditions (Sedikides & Hepper, 2009) but resistant under others (Swann, 2012). The current positive psychology movement is now carrying the mantle of illuminating the mechanisms underlying healthy transformative growth in humans (Lopez & Snyder, 2011).

The Mythic Hero's Transformation

Ironically, the founder of heroism science, Joseph Campbell, was not a trained scientist at all but a comparative mythologist who noticed "a certain typical hero sequence of actions which can be detected in stories from all over the world and from many periods in history" (Campbell, 1988, p. 166). Campbell's genius lay in his ability to recognize the complex psychological origins and consequences of the mythic hero's journey. The hero's transformation is one such consequence, and for Campbell it was the centerpiece of the journey. According to Campbell, hero myths "grab you somewhere down inside" and "inspire the possibility of the realization of your perfection, the fullness of your strength" (Campbell, 1988, p. 183). Myths "provide a field in which you can locate yourself" (Campbell, 2004, p. xvi) and they "carry the individual through the stages of life" (p. 9). The resultant transformations seen in heroic tales "are infinite in their revelation" (Campbell, 1988, p. 183). Campbell cites Otto Rank's (1909) observation that "everyone is a hero in birth, where he undergoes a tremendous psychological as well as physical transformation, from the condition of a little water creature living in a realm of amniotic fluid into an air-breathing mammal" (p. 153). This transformation at birth is prescient; it foreshadows a lifetime of transformative journeys for human beings.

Defining the Hero's Transformation

Campbell (1949) described the monomyth of the hero in this way: "A hero ventures forth from the world of common day into a region of supernatural wonder: fabulous forces are there encountered and a decisive victory is won: the hero comes back from this mysterious adventure with the power to bestow boons on his fellow man" (p. 30). This description of the journey points to three distinct transformations: A transformation of *setting*, a transformation of *self*, and a transformation of *society*. The sequence is critical, with each transformation essential for producing the next one. Without a change in setting, the hero cannot change herself, and without a change in herself, the hero cannot change the world. Our focus here is on the hero's transformation of the self, but this link in the chain necessarily requires some consideration of the links preceding and following it. The mythic hero *must* be cast out of her familiar world and into a different world, otherwise there can be no departure from her status quo. Once transformed, the hero *must* use her newly enriched state to better the world, otherwise the hero's transformation is bereft of social significance.

The hero's transformation is essential for the hero to achieve her goal on the journey. During the quest, "ineffable realizations are experienced" and "things that before had been mysterious are now fully understood" (Campbell, 1972, p. 219). The ineffability of these new insights stems from their unconscious origins. Jungian principles of the collective unconscious form the basis of Campbell's theorizing about hero mythology. As Le Grice (2013) notes, "myths are expressions of the imagination, shaped by the archetypal dynamics of the psyche" (p. 153). As such, the many recurring elements of the mythic hero's journey have their "inner, psychological correlates" (Campbell, 1972, p. 153). The hero's journey is rife with social symbols and motifs that connect the hero to her deeper self, and these unconscious images must be encountered, and conflicts with them must be resolved, to bring about transformation (Campbell, 2004). Ultimately, the hero's outer journey reflects an inner, psychological journey that involves "leaving one condition and finding the source of life to bring you forth into a richer or mature condition" (Campbell, 1988, p. 152).

Purpose of the Hero's Transformation

When people embark on the hero's journey, they "undergo a truly heroic transformation of consciousness," requiring them "to think a different way" (Campbell, 1988, p. 155). This shift provides a new "a map or picture of the universe and allows us to see ourselves in relationship to nature" (Campbell, 1991, p. 56). Buddhist traditions and twelve-step programs of recovery refer to transformation as an awakening. In a similar manner, Campbell (2004) described the journey's purpose as a much-needed voyage designed to "wake you up" (p. 12). Below we offer five reasons why transformation is such a key element in the hero's journey:

1 Transformations foster developmental growth. Early human societies recognized the value of initiation rituals in promoting the transition from childhood to adulthood (van Gennep, 1909). A number of scholars, including Campbell, have lamented the failure of our postmodern society to recognize the psychological importance of rites and rituals (Campbell, 1988; Le Grice, 2013; Rohr, 2011). Coming-of-age stories are common in mythic hero tales about children "awakening to the new world that opens at adolescence" (Campbell, 1988, p. 167). The hero's journey "helps us pass through and deal with the

various stages of life from birth to death" (Campbell, 1991, p. 56). Recent research affirms Campbell's assertions about the developmental significance of transformational rites of passage. Imber-Black and Roberts (1998), for example, found that transformative rituals help children learn how to build relationships and distinguish fantasy from reality. In addition, Norton and Gino (2014) have shown that rites and rituals help people gain a sense of control, mitigate negative emotional states, and grow into mature individuals.

2. Transformations promote healing. We have argued elsewhere (Allison & Goethals, 2014, 2016) that the simple act of sharing stories about hero transformations can deliver many of the same benefits as group therapy (Yalom & Leszcz, 2005). These benefits include the instillation of hope; the relief of knowing that others share one's emotional experiences; the fostering of self-awareness; the relief of stress; and the development of a sense of meaning about life. A growing number of clinical psychologists invoke hero transformations in their practice to help their clients develop the heroic traits of strength, resilience, and courage (Grace, 2015). Recent research on *post-traumatic growth* demonstrates that people can overcome severe trauma and even use it to transform themselves into stronger, healthier persons than they were before the trauma (Ramos & Leal, 2013). In biology, there are numerous examples of transformative healing. The phenomenon of *neurogenesis* refers to the development of new brain cells in the hippocampus through exercise, diet, meditation, and learning. This transformative healing and growing can occur even after catastrophic brain trauma. Efthimiou (Chapter 8, this volume) discusses how the hero organism can engage in *regeneration* or *restoration* processes, referring to an organism's ability to grow, heal, and re-create itself. Researchers have recently identified the *Wolverine* gene, which one day will allow people to re-grow lost limbs (Efthimiou, 2015). Medical researchers have also developed methods for transforming leukemia cells into leukemia-killing immune cells, thus ridding patients of cancer (Andrews, 2015). Moreover, the practice of meditation and mindfulness has been found to produce neurobiological changes, such as healthier functioning of the lateral prefrontal cortex, reduced inflammation, and faster recovery from the physical effects of stress (Renter 2014).

3. Transformations cultivate social unity. Campbell (1972) argued that hero transformations "drop or lift [heroes] out of themselves, so that their conduct is not their own but of the species, the society" (p. 57). He cites an essay written in 1840 by philosopher Arthur Schopenhauer, who observed that the transformed individual has moved "from the lesser, secondary knowledge of himself as separate from others" to "the greater, truer truth, that we are all one in the ground of our being" (p. 151). The transformed hero is "selfless, boundless, without ego." Campbell called this new way of thinking a "metaphysically valid insight" (p. 151). In tribal societies, initiation rituals serve as heroes journeys designed to unify novices and elders into a single whole. These rituals often include "a special mutilation which varies with the tribe (a tooth is removed, the penis is incised, etc.) and which makes the novice forever identical with the adult members" (van Gennep, 1909, p. 75). The most meaningful transformations are a journey from egocentricity to sociocentricity, from elitism to egalitarianism (Campbell, 1949; Rohr, 2011; Wilber, 2007). No longer isolated from the world, transformed individuals enjoy a feeling of union with others. Describing the hero's journey, Campbell (1949) wrote, "where we had thought to be alone, we shall be with all the world" (p. 25).

4. Transformations advance society. The culmination of the hero's journey is the hero's boon, or gift, to society. This gift is what separates the hero's journey from simply being a test of personal survival. For the voyage to be heroic, the protagonist in myth must use her newly acquired insights and gifts to better the world (Campbell, 1949; Rohr, 2011). The heroic boon to society follows the successful completion of the individual quest, and so we can say that the social boon is entirely dependent upon the hero's personal transformation that

made the personal quest a success. Hero mythology, according to Campbell (1972), is designed to teach us that society is not a "perfectly static organization" but represents a "movement of the species forward" (p. 48). During the process of experiencing personal transformation, the hero obtains the "elixir" that empowers and enables her to help guide others on their personal transformative journeys. This idea is consistent with contemporary theories of leadership that focus on the role of enlightened leaders to transform their followers, elevating them toward greater levels of motivation and morality (e.g., Burns, 1978, 2003).

5   Transformations deepen spiritual and cosmic understanding. Campbell (1988) observed that the hero's transformation involves learning "to experience the supernormal range of human spiritual life" (p. 152). Myths, he said, "bring us into a level of consciousness that is spiritual" (p. 19). In every hero tale, the hero must "die spiritually" and then be "reborn to a larger way of living" (p. 141), a process that is the enactment of a universal spiritual theme of death being the necessary experience for producing new life (Campbell, 1991, p. 102). Many people report being "born again" by religious conversion to Christ or to Buddha (Lee, 2014). Hero transformations may also supply cosmological wisdom. Ethnographer van Gennep (1909) observed that transformative rituals in early human tribes have "been linked to the celestial passages, the revolutions of the planets, and the phases of the moon. It is indeed a cosmic conception that relates the stages of human existence to those of plant and animal life and, by a sort of pre-scientific divination, joins them to the great rhythms of the universe" (p. 194).

Ten Dimensions of Transformation

As we have noted, transformations can vary on many dimensions. This observation is consistent with Campbell's (1949) acknowledgement that within and across cultures there are many mythological variations of the hero monomyth. Not all transformative hero journeys contain the same stages, dilemmas, archetypal images, and social dynamics. Below we have assembled a list of 10 dimensions on which hero transformations can vary:

1   subject;
2   scale;
3   speed;
4   duration;
5   timing;
6   direction;
7   type;
8   depth;
9   openness; and
10 source.

While other dimensions no doubt exist, we consider these to be among the most important. Below we discuss each of these dimensions in turn.

Subject: Hero or Followers

In the vast majority of hero tales, the protagonist is the primary recipient or target of the heroic transformation. This lone hero is the beneficiary of transformation in hero tales from Beowulf to Harry Potter. In some stories, however, the heroic protagonist remains unchanged throughout the narrative but he or she serves as the catalyst for the transformation in others. Stories of the leadership accomplishments of Susan B. Anthony, Mahatma Gandhi, and Martin Luther King, Jr. are prominent examples of the hero's followers enjoying the fruits of transformation. It is not our claim that Anthony, Gandhi, and King, Jr. failed to undergo a personal transformation themselves. Surely they did. Rather, we observe that some hero stories focus only on the already transformed leader's metamorphic effect on other people.

Scale: Individual, Dyad, Group, or Society

Most hero narratives feature a single individual as the target of transformation. Allison and Smith (2015) have recognized a larger social structure of heroic actors that includes heroes as individuals, dyads, small group ensembles, and large organizations and societies. At times heroic tales feature dyadic heroes as the target of heroic transformation, as seen in stories about Romulus and Remus, Thelma and Louise, and Batman and Robin. The heroic target subject can also be a group or collective, in such as the *Avengers*, the *Monuments Men*, or the *Supremes*. Moreover, as we have noted, an entire organization or society can also serve as the target of the transformative effects of a great individual hero or group of heroes.

Speed: Slow or Fast

Heroic transformations can occur gradually over time, or they can occur with sudden intensity. William James (1902/2013) documented this distinction in his analysis of the varieties of religious conversion. Transformations that occur with great speed appear to be rather rare in real life but are the signature characteristic of heroes in the comic superhero genre. The Incredible Hulk, Wolverine, Ant-Man, and Popeye all enjoy nearly instant physical transformations. In real life, speed is a critical variable in responses to emergency situations that demand a rapid response. A growing body of research on altruism shows that heroic reactions to emergencies occur instantaneously, with any type of deliberative thought actually interfering with the helping behavior (Rand & Epstein, 2014). William James noted that spiritual transformations can occur quickly in the aftermath of crisis situations, or they can unfold gradually over time. There are vast individual differences. Unlike *target* and *scale*, which are discrete variables, the *speed* dimension is best viewed as a continuous variable.

Duration: Short-Lived or Long-Lasting

Transformative effects can be ephemeral in their duration, or they can be longstanding, or even permanent. One might reasonably ask whether an ephemeral transformation is really a transformation at all. Some (potential) heroes may give the impression of change but later demonstrate that change has not occurred. The iconic 1980s television drama *Dallas* featured a villainous character, J. R. Ewing, who repeatedly created the illusion of having been transformed into a heroic character, but inevitably Ewing would revert to his dark ways. Robert Downey, Jr. suffered years of setbacks on his road to recovery from drug addiction before his transformation to sobriety took hold. The character of Atticus Finch in *To Kill a Mockingbird* had long been hailed as a heroic champion of civil rights but the 2015 release of Harper Lee's *Go Set a Watchman* appears to have tainted Finch's reputation. Opinions can often vary about the nature and duration of heroic transformation. St. Augustine's conversion from sinner to saint did not happen overnight and in fact was characterized by many short-lived fits and starts before a permanent change was established. As with the speed dimension, the duration dimension operates as a continuous rather than as a discrete variable.

Timing: Early Life or Late Life

Transformations can occur at any point in life. Early life transformations usually occur in hero stories involving calamitous or severely challenging childhood circumstances, such as those endured by Helen Keller or Malala Yousafzai. At times, people are transformed early in life by extraordinarily positive circumstances, as exemplified by Elvis Presley, Michael Jackson, and others who enjoyed instant meteoric career success. Early-life transformations, whether positive or negative, appear to leave the ill-prepared hero vulnerable to a tragic end. Transformations can be triggered by life-changing external events that can occur at any stage of one's life, or by processes of natural human development. Some models of lifespan development propose multiple transformative changes throughout the entire human lifetime (Erikson, 1994). Other models point to one major transformation in mid-life or late in the lifespan (Jung, 1970; Rohr, 2011). Stories from hospice workers suggest that people's most momentous transformation occurs in the days or moments just prior to death, when the dying finally get honest about their lives, their regrets, and their spiritual place in the universe (Callanan & Kelley 2012). This timing dimension of transformation is also best thought of as a continuous variable.

Direction: The Four Heroic Arcs

In every hero narrative, the hero's transformation follows a specific arc or trajectory. Allison and Smith (2015) have identified four distinct transformational arcs of the hero. First, the *classic hero arc* begins with the hero living life as an ordinary individual, and after being thrust into the journey she becomes transformed into a highly moral or competent hero by the story's end. Bilbo Baggins in *The Hobbit* is a prototypical example of a classic arc. Second, the *enlightened hero arc* showcases a character who is villainous at first but who redeems herself by the story's conclusion. Phil Connors in the movie *Groundhog Day* exemplifies this hero arc. A third heroic arc features the *redeemed hero*, who undergoes two transformations. The hero starts out neutral or positive, descends into villainy, but redeems herself in the end. The character of *Maleficent* in the prequel to *Sleeping Beauty* represents a good example of the redeemed arc. The fourth and final heroic arc features no transformation at all; the protagonist begins the journey as a hero and remains heroic throughout the narrative. This non-transformation characterizes the journey of the superhero. Superman, for example, is just as super at the outset of the story as he is at the conclusion.

Type: Moral, Emotional, Spiritual, Intellectual, Physical, and Motivational

Allison and Smith (2015) identified five types of transformations that heroes undergo. These five types of hero transformations extend Turner's (1966) conceptualization of the vast changes that young people undergo during the coming-of-age rituals in tribal societies. The first type is a *moral* transformation. In film, two examples of heroes who experience moral change include *Casablanca*'s Rick Blaine, who must overcome his hardened heart to side with the Allies, and Han Solo in *Star Wars*, whose motives shift from greed to humanitarianism. The second type of transformation is an *emotional* transformation. These refer to transformations of the heart, and they include heroes who, through adversity, grow in courage, resilience, and empathy. An example is Franklin Roosevelt, whose battle with polio transformed him from an aloof, distant figure to a kind, compassionate leader. A third type is a *spiritual* transformation, describing heroes who experience a life-changing conversion in beliefs about God or the universe. Examples include Louis Zamperini's journey in *Unbroken*, Gautama Buddha's path of enlightenment, the first disciples of Jesus, and Moses's journey in *The Ten Commandments*. Fourth, heroes can undergo *intellectual* transformations, featuring a change in mental abilities or fundamental insights about the world. Coming-of-age stories are excellent examples of such transformations, as in *Huckleberry Finn* and *Ender's Game*.

The fifth type of transformation is a *physical* one, as seen in superhero origin stories in which the hero is an ordinary person until an accident involving exposure to toxins or radiation endows the hero with a superpower. Spiderman, the Hulk, and the Avengers are examples of heroes who undergo physical transformations. Outside the realm of comics, everyday heroes can heroically transform themselves in a physical sense. A notable example is Caitlyn Jenner, whose openness about her transgender procedure helped integrate the LGBTQ community into the mainstream of society. The story of the famous golfer Ben Hogan serves as another real-world example of heroic physical transformation. Hogan suffered grave injuries to his lower body in an automobile accident, and the permanent damage he sustained to his legs actually improved his golf swing and propelled him to achieve greater superstardom. Physical transformations can also precipitate moral transformations, as in the case of Ron Woodroof in the story of the *Dallas Buyers Club*.

Psychologists have only recently begun to understand the link between psychological and physical transformations. Gray (2010) found that people who performed a selfless act actually became physically stronger, demonstrating an embodied component to heroism. Our understanding of physical and genetic transformations is undergoing a revolution (see Carey, 2013). For example, Landers et al. (2009) have identified what they call a *hero gene*, called KIFAP3, which allows sufferers of motor neuron disease to become more resistant to malignant transformation. In this same vein, Shyh-Chang et al. (2013) have identified a type of *superhero gene* called Lin28a, which reverts cells to an embryonic state that allows for the growth of new limbs and organs. Friend and Shadt (2014) have embarked on a *Resilience Project* aimed at identifying unique individuals or "genetic heroes" who have demonstrated exceptional resilience to transformations involving debilitating disease and genetic mutation (Carter, 2014). These and other studies suggest that an epigenetic basis of transformation is becoming a reality (Efthimiou, 2015). The link between the hero's journey and epigenetic processes is now producing new insights about heroic leadership and embodied dimensions of leadership (Efthimiou, 2016).

In addition to Allison and Smith's (2015) five transformations, we propose a sixth one: a *motivational* transformation. Events in one's life can slowly, or often quite suddenly, change one's entire motivational focus in life. Candace Lightner lost her child in an automobile accident involving an intoxicated driver, motivating her to establish Mothers Against Drunk Driving. John Walsh lost his son to a murderous predator and, motivated to prevent similar tragedies, began hosting the television show *America's Most Wanted*. Family members who lose loved ones to gun violence often devote their lives to promoting gun control legislation. Tragedies can beget motivational changes in people who heroically use these tragedies to transform entire societies. We suspect there are more than six types of transformations but we offer these six as a starting point for future scholarly discussions.

Depth: Shallow or Deep

As we have suggested, the degree of transformation undergone by a hero can vary from superficial to profound. This dimension can also refer to the depth of information processing shown by the hero before and during the heroic act. Heroes who devote their lives to a noble cause will allocate considerable thought to their heroic actions. These deep thinkers are leaders of important social movements such as Gandhi, Anthony, Mandela, and King, Jr. At the other end of the continuum are heroes who respond instantly to an emergency situation. These individuals will act heroically with little thought. Research by Rand and Epstein (2014) found that "high-stakes extreme altruism may be largely motivated by automatic, intuitive processes" (see also Kraft-Todd & Rand, Chapter 3, this volume). These investigators suggest that heroic acts may spring from people's tendency to overgeneralize their pattern of helping in lower-stake settings to higher-stake settings. Bystanders with the courage to intervene may have cultivated a helping response "as an automatic default, which then sometimes gets applied in atypical settings where helping is extreme costly."

Openness: Motivation and Ability

We propose that for heroic transformation to take place, a hero must possess the *ability* to change, and sometimes, but not necessarily, the *motivation* to change. This idea is consistent with conceptions of the mythic hero as an individual who is either reluctant or compelled to go on the hero's journey against her will (Campbell, 1949; Peck, 2003; Rohr, 2011). Examples of reluctant heroes abound. Stephen Hawking was forced by ALS to undergo a life-altering transformation. In *The Wizard of Oz*, Dorothy's understanding of home is only made possible after she is swept by a tornado into the Land of Oz. The conversion of Paul the Apostle occurs after he is pitched off his horse by a blinding light. When children in tribal societies reach a certain age, they are thrown into rituals of adulthood whether they want to or not (Turner, 1966). In all these examples, people undergo change only because they are forced by circumstances beyond their control.

Some heroes, of course, do choose to go on the hero's journey. For example, Siddhartha voluntarily leaves the comforts of his castle to seek spiritual illumination. In *The Hobbit*, Bilbo Baggins freely decides to join the thirteen dwarves on their quest to reclaim their mountain. Odysseus decides to fight in the Trojan War and afterward desires to sail home to Ithaca. Throughout history, people have expressed their motivation for transformative change in poetry and in song lyrics, as when country crooner Billy Joe Shaver sang that he was an old piece of coal who aspired to become a diamond ("I'm just an old chunk of coal," 1981). Aspirations for positive change are vocalized by myriad artists such as Johnny Cash in "Folsom Prison Blues," Kelly Clarkson in "Stronger," George Harrison in "Here Comes the Sun," and Martha K. Lankton in "Just a Closer Walk with Thee." Deliberate changes in one's life trajectory usually begin with this motivation to change. Obstacles to such motivation can include an ignorance that one's current non-heroic life needs changing (Campbell, 1949); a slothful laziness about doing what it takes to change (Peck, 2003); a narcissism in one's personality makeup that thwarts any desire to change (Scott, 2012); and even birth-order effects that render first-borns less motivated to take heroic risks compared to later-borns (Sulloway & Zeigenhaft, 2010).

Psychological defenses may underlie people's resistance to going on the transformative journey. Jung (1956) described the *shadow* as the dark, unknown aspects of our personalities that prevent us from transforming into our full potential. According to Campbell (1988), "all of these wonderful poetic images of mythology are referring to something in you," and that your shadow impedes your transformation "when your mind is simply trapped by the image out there so that you never make the reference to yourself" (p. 68). The shadow is "represented as the monster that has to be overcome, the dragon" (Campbell, 2004, p. 73). Although "the shadow is the landfill of the self," it also "holds great potentialities in you" because, if one is fortunate, dark energies build up to the point of *enantiodromia*: a dramatic expression of the shadow as its opposite, an expression so vivid that denial of the shadow is cracked and transformation, however painful, results. Campbell calls this illumination of the shadow an "unheeded demon" that comes "roaring up into the light" (p. 73). The *golden* shadow, moreover, consists of positive aspects of the self, also buried in our unconscious, that we project onto others as hero worship. As we bring the content of our positive and negative shadows into the light, we are transformed. People who undergo such change must have both the motivation and the ability to do so, often through psychotherapy.

Both motivation and ability are often necessary for many transformative life changes to occur. Maslow's (1943) model of hierarchical needs suggests that people can get stuck at lower stages of the hierarchy that focus on the fulfillment of basic biological and security needs. Heroic potential may be suppressed when individuals are afflicted by poverty or safety concerns that prevent their ability to progress upward in the hierarchy toward higher-level goals. Moreover, transformative change may be impossible if people lack the ability to show resilience in the face of adversity (Seligman, 2011b), or if people are unable to derive meaning from adverse circumstances (Frankl, 1946). Another obstacle to one's ability to transform may reside in the absence of good mentor figures who can offer guidance through the hero's journey. Parks (Chapter 23, this volume) offers a more thorough discussion of these and other impediments to heroic action. We now turn our attention to the importance of influence from various sources of transformation.

Source: Internal or External

We distinguish between sources of transformative change that come from within the individual and sources that originate from outside the individual. We have identified four *internal* sources of transformation. First, transformation can be a byproduct of stages of natural human development. An initial transformative event, a sperm cell fertilizing an egg, leads to a zygote transforming into an embryo, which then becomes (in order) a fetus, a baby, a toddler, a child, an adolescent, a young adult, a mid-life adult, and an elderly adult. Accompanying these physical developments are stages of transformative growth in areas of emotion (Trentacosts & Izard, 2006), morality (Kohlberg, 1969; Shweder, Mahapatra, & Miller, 1987), spirituality (Bradbury, 2010), sociability (Erikson, 1994), and various forms of intelligence (Piaget & Inhelder, 1958).

A second internal source of change resides in people's needs and goals. From the perspective of Maslow's (1943) pyramid of needs, an individual is motivated to fulfill the needs at a particular level once lower level needs are satisfied. Once the needs at the four lower levels are satisfied, one is no longer concerned with them or driven by them. In effect, one transitions to higher levels and eventually achieves self-actualization, during which one might enjoy *peak experiences* of having discovered meaning, beauty, truth, and a sense of oneness with the world. Self-actualization has a sort of self-centered mysticism to it. One feels whole, enhanced, and connected. It is also the case that one's needs and motives can shift naturally over time or in response to changes in one's life circumstances. For example, research has found that people who undergo a battle with a deadly disease will undergo a change in their needs, goals, and choice of heroes. This idea of need-based heroism is part of Allison and Goethals' (2014, 2016) *heroic leadership dynamic* (HLD). The HLD explains why people who are fighting cancer will choose new heroes who have successfully overcome the same cancer, why people who play football tend to choose famous football players as heroes and why, whimsically, people who undergo painful divorce may choose King Henry VIII as their hero. As our needs change, transformative role models help us transform ourselves thereby helping us meet our newfound needs.

A third internal source of transformative change is human transgression and failure. People often undergo significant change after being humbled by their "fallings and failings" (Rohr, 2011, p. xv). Joseph Campbell (2004) acknowledged that not all heroic quests end with glorious, heroic success. "There is always the possibility for a fiasco," he said (p. 133). Such fiascos can serve as the grist for a larger transformative mill, producing a kind of suffering needed to fuel a greater hero journey. It is a general truth that for substance abusers to be sufficiently motivated to seek recovery from their addictions, they must reach a profound level of pain and suffering. This state is commonly referred to as "hitting rock bottom." Suffering, according to Rohr (2011), "doesn't accomplish anything tangible but creates space for learning and love" (p. 68). This space has been called *liminal space* (van Gennep, 1909; Turner, 1966), defined as the transitional space between one state of being and an entirely different state of being. In liminal space, one has been stripped of one's previous life, humbled, and silenced. Transgressions, and the liminal space that follows them, are the fertile soil from which heroic transformations may bloom.

Finally, a fourth internal source of transformation is what we call an enlightened dawning of responsibility. This dawning is captured in a simple phrase, composed of ten two-letter words, "If it is to be, it is up to me" (Phipps, 2011). There is a long history of social psychological work devoted to studying the forces at work that undermine the dawning of responsibility in emergency settings (Latane & Darley, 1969). Research has shown that in a crisis a small but courageous minority of people do step up to do the right thing even when there are strong pressures to avoid assuming responsibility. These fearless social aberrants, most of whom are ordinary citizens, are able to transcend their circumstances and transform from ordinary to extraordinary. Whistleblowers are a notable example; they demonstrate the mettle to step up and do right thing at great potential cost to themselves (Brown, Chapter 19, this volume; Lewis, Brown, & Moberly, 2014). Bystander training is now available to cultivate this dawning of responsibility in situations where transformative leadership is needed (Brown, 2015).

In sum, the four internal factors that elicit transformative change are natural development, needs and goals, transgression, and the dawning of responsibility. We next turn our attention to four *external* situational forces that can evoke transformative change. Situations, for example, can trigger emotional responses that transform us. William James (1902/2013) noted that in the context of religious conversion, "emotional occasions … are extremely potent in precipitating mental rearrangements" (p. 77). Emotions need not be negative to induce change. The recently identified emotion of *elevation* can transform people psychologically and behaviorally (Haidt, 2003). People feel elevated after witnessing a morally beautiful act, and this elevated feeling has been shown to produce altruistic acts (Thomson & Siegel, 2013). Similarly, feelings of awe and wonder can be invoked by reading hero mythology (Campbell, 2004) and by viewing spectacular images of natural beauty. Awe and wonder have also been shown to be associated with prosocial behavior (Piff, Dietze, Feinberg, Stancato, & Keltner, 2015). Moreover, empathic feelings have attracted considerable research attention, with dozens of studies demonstrating that exposure to the suffering of others can induce empathy. Empathy, like awe and wonder, can also have a positive, transformative effect on altruistic responses (Williams, O'Driscoll, & Moore, 2014).

A second external source of transformation is the series of trials that all heroes must undergo during their journey. We have referred to suffering as an internal cause of transformation when it results from self-destructive actions, but suffering caused by outside forces can serve as an external source of transformation. Campbell (1988) believed that "trials are designed to see to it that the intending hero should be really a hero. Is he really a match for this task?" (p. 154). The point of greatest danger for the hero is when she enters the *belly of the whale* (Campbell, 1949). The belly can be entered literally as in stories of Jonah and Pinocchio, but usually the belly is a metaphorical place along the journey in which the hero's darkest inner-demons must be "disempowered, overcome, and controlled" (p. 180). For Campbell, the hero's journey truly is an inner task of conquering one's fears and slaying one's dragons. In the sixteenth century, Saint John of the Cross referred to this ultimate trial as the *Dark Night of the Soul*, which describes a state of spiritual desolation that we are called to overcome and is at the heart of the road to enlightenment (Johnson, 1991). Positive psychologists today refer to this transformative process as post-traumatic growth, during which people convert the worst thing that ever happened to them into the best (Rendon, 2015).

A third external source of transformation is the vast hero literature and mythology to which we are exposed throughout our lives. We have argued elsewhere (Allison & Goethals, 2014, 2016) that narratives about heroes, pervasive in all of storytelling from Gilgamesh to the present day, serve as a nourishing catalyst for transformative change. The central premise of the HLD is that our consumption of heroic tales takes place within an interactive system or process that is energizing, always in motion, and drawing us toward rising heroes and repelling us from falling ones. The HLD framework proposes two transformative functions of hero stories: an *epistemic* function and an *energizing* function. Hero narratives supply epistemic growth by offering scripts for prosocial action, by revealing fundamental truths about human existence, by unpacking life paradoxes, and by cultivating emotional intelligence. The epistemic value of hero tales is revealed in Campbell's (1988) observation that hero mythology offers insights into "what can be known but not told" (p. 206) and that "mythology is the womb of mankind's initiation to life and death" (Campbell, 2002, p. 34). The second transformative function of hero tales, focusing on their energizing benefits, provides people with agency and efficacy. Hero narratives promote moral elevation, heal psychic wounds, and inspire psychological growth (Allison & Goethals, 2016).

The fourth external source of transformation is the social environment of the hero. In hero narratives and classic mythology, the hero's journey is populated by numerous friends, companions, lovers, parent figures, and mentors who assist the hero on her quest. We explore these social sources of transformation in greater detail below.

Social Sources of Transformation

In his original treatment of the hero's monomyth, Joseph Campbell (1949) detailed the multilayered social landscape of the hero's journey. The hero is always helped along the journey by the actual, imagined, or implied presence of others. These latter instances involving imagined or implied assistance are rare in storytelling, but they do crop up in stories of lone survival as seen in movies such as *Gravity*, *Cast Away*, *Life of Pi*, and *All is Lost*. Actual encounters with social entities are far more common in hero tales. During the journey, the hero will befriend people, or creatures, who represent qualities that she lacks and must acquire to triumph on her quest. A notable example is Dorothy's encounter with the scarecrow, tin man, and lion, who represent the brain, heart, and courage that Dorothy lacks in *The Wizard of Oz*. Sidekicks are another common source of support for heroes, as featured in the Lone Ranger and Tonto, Batman and Robin, and Han Solo and Chewbacca. Campbell (1949) also discussed the importance of encounters with parental figures; male heroes seek atonement with father figures, and female heroes with mother figures. Campbell also described the hero's brush with lovers and temptresses, who can either assist, distract, or do harm to the hero.

One of the most essential social events of the hero's journey is the arrival of the mentor figure. In classic myth, the mentor is often a magical outsider, an elder, an exotic person or creature whom one would least expect to possess the wisdom needed for the hero to succeed. According to Campbell (2004), the mentor "may be some little wood sprite or wise man or fairy godmother or animal that comes to you as a companion or as an advisor, letting you know what the dangers are along the way and how to overcome them" (p. 116). The majority of people who are asked to name their heroes mention a mentor or coach who had a transformative effect on them (Allison & Goethals, 2011). As legendary football coach Tom Landry observed, a mentor is someone "who tells you what you don't want to hear, who has you see what you don't want to see, so you can be who you have always known you could be" (Farcht, 2007, p. 294). Famous mentors in hero tales include Merlin the Magician giving King Arthur the knowledge to rule England, Yoda helping Luke Skywalker defeat Darth Vader, and Mr. Miyagi training the Karate Kid. Good mentors equip the hero with what she needs, but there can also be bad mentors who steer the hero down a dark path of self-destruction (Allison & Smith, 2015). Examples of dark mentors include the serpent in Genesis 3:4, Sauron in *Lord of the Rings*, Terence Fletcher in *Whiplash*, and Tyler Durden in *Fight Club*.

The temporal sequencing of mentorship is an important element of the hero's journey. Mentors help heroes become transformed, and later, having succeeded on their journeys, these transformed heroes then assume the role of mentor for others who are at earlier stages of their quests. In short, "transformed people transform people" (Rohr, 2014, p. 263). Mentors can have a transformative effect with their words of advice, with their actions, or both. Words can fall on deaf ears but one's actions, attitudes, and lifestyle can leave a lasting imprint. St. Francis of Assisi conveyed it this way: "You must preach the Gospel at all times, and when necessary use words" (Rohr, 2014, p. 263). Many people consider Wesley Autrey, New York's subway hero, to be a mentor figure, not from anything he said but from his one bold, selfless act of saving a man who had fallen on the tracks before an oncoming train (Allison & Goethals, 2013). A mentor can be viewed as a type of hero who enhances the lives of others (Kinsella, Ritchie, & Igou, 2015).

Inasmuch as mentorship is a type of leadership, one could say that the hero's journey prepares people for leadership roles by offering a transformative experience that can be shared later with others. Burns (1978) argued that transforming leaders make an effort to satisfy followers' lower needs (e.g., survival and safety), thereby elevating them for the important work that they—leaders *and* followers—must do together to produce significant higher-level changes. Burns described transforming leadership as individuals engaging each other "in such a way that leaders and followers raise one another to higher levels of motivation and morality" (p. 20). Both leaders and followers will be "elevated" such that the leaders create a "new cadre of leaders" (p. 20). This conception is consistent with Campbell's ideas about the role of mentorship during the hero's journey, with the mentor elevating the hero and preparing her for future mentoring duties. Burns' framework also makes explicit a notion that is largely implicit in Maslow's (1943) model, namely, that the self-actualized person has become an elder, a mentor figure, and a moral actor who wields transformative influence over others. Erik Erikson's (1994) theory of lifelong development makes the similar claim that older *generative* individuals, having been given so much early in life, are now in a position to give back to younger people.

Other theories also point to the transformative effect of mentoring and leadership. Hollander (1995) has proposed a two-way influence relationship between a leader and followers aimed primarily at attaining mutual goals. Hollander defined leadership as "a shared experience, a voyage through time" with the leader in partnership with followers to pursue common interests. For Hollander, "a major component of the leader–follower relationship is the leader's perception of his or her self relative to followers, and how they in turn perceive the leader" (p. 55). Tyler and Lind (1992) have shown that these perceptions are critically important in cementing good follower loyalty. Followers will perceive a leader as a "legitimate" authority when she adheres to basic principles of procedural justice. Leaders who show fairness, respect, and concern for the needs of followers are able to build followers' self-esteem, a pivotal step in Maslow's (1943) pyramid, thereby fostering followers' transformative movement toward meeting higher-level needs.

Mentors and leaders can also use their charisma to exert a transformative effect on their followers. Goethals and Allison (2014) reviewed the transforming leadership of three heroic leaders from the twentieth century whom they dubbed "the three kings": Muhammad Ali, Elvis Presley, and Martin Luther King, Jr. These kings radiated powerful charisma that transformed their followers. All three kings had exceptional personas. All three made an emotional connection with their audiences. All three related and embodied compelling stories. All three enacted theatrical leadership that gave people what they wanted and needed. Two of them, King and Ali, used words, delivered in riveting styles, often touching on religious precepts, to influence their followers' thoughts, feelings, and behavior. The three kings used their charisma to transform others, through both their words and their example.

We conclude this section on social sources of transformation with a brief discussion of divine sources. The human tendency to anthropomorphize their deities, as in Christian references to "Father" and "Son," suggests a social component to faith-based transformation. Heroes from classic mythology and contemporary hero narratives are often transformed by a god, higher power, or supernatural force. William James (1902/2013) was the first scholar to record systematic observations of divinely inspired transformations. He described five transformative effects of believing in a higher power. First, people experience a serenity characterized by "peace," "harmony," and "the loss of all worry." Second, there is "the sense of perceiving truths not known before" with "the mysteries of life" becoming "lucid." Third, there is "an appearance of newness," a freshness of perception that "beautifies every object." Fourth, people enjoy immense feelings of subjective well-being, an "ecstasy of happiness," "love," and "joy." Finally, people experience a feeling of deep connection to others and to nature, "of being in a wider life than that of this world's selfish little interests" (James, 1902/2013, pp. 86–89). Members of 12-step recovery programs are asked to develop a belief in a higher power, as described in the second step, to experience the beneficial, healing effects that William James described. Step 12 even refers to a "spiritual awakening" that members undergo, often described as a transformation of the mind, body, and spirit. Regular attendance at 12-Step meetings is also essential to recovery; there can be no awakening or transformation without face-to-face contact with other members, a fact that underscores the importance of the social basis of transformation.

Hero Characteristics: Pre and Post-Transformation

Early in the hero's journey, the yet-to-be transformed hero is missing one or more important inner qualities that are necessary to triumph on the quest and deliver the boon to society. As Campbell (1988) notes, the pre-transformed hero is an incomplete individual who embarks on the hero's journey "either to recover what has been lost or to discover some life-giving elixir" (p. 152). Our review of the literature on transformation reveals three missing pieces of the neophyte hero who must suffer some sort of death of her former self in order to be reborn into "a richer" and "mature condition" (p. 152). The untransformed hero is missing (1) a sociocentric view of life; (2) an autonomy from the "patho-adolescent culture" in which humans have always lived; and (3) a mindset of growth and change. We note that the route to transformation, requiring the acquisition of these three qualities, bears a striking similarity to Maslow's (1943) pathway to self-actualization, Erikson's (1994) eight-stage model of socio-emotional development, and many other conceptualizations of social, spiritual, and emotional growth (e.g., Gilligan, 1982; Kohlberg, 1969; Levinson, 1986; Plotkin, 2007; Rohr, 2011).

Egocentricity to Sociocentricity

According to Campbell (1988), "when we quit thinking primarily about ourselves and our own self-preservation, we undergo a truly heroic transformation of consciousness" (p. 155). Campbell (2004) believed that one of the central functions of hero mythology is to "get a sense of everything—yourself, your society, the universe, and the mystery beyond—as one great unit" (p. 55). Richard Rohr (2011) calls this "the unified field," borrowing a phrase from Albert Einstein, who sought a unified theory that could explain the entire physical universe. Poet Annie Dillard (2013) described this unified field as "our complex and inexplicable caring for each other, and for our life together here" (p. 9). In most hero narratives, the hero begins the journey disconnected from the world. She is a self-centered, prideful individual whose sole preoccupation is establishing her identity, her career, and her material world. The entire point of her hero journey is to awaken her to the larger, deeper task of thinking beyond herself, to developing communion with everyone and with everything.

Not all human cultures emphasize this connective journey to an equal degree. There is a notable "dichotomy of the egocentric *west* versus the sociocentric *rest*" (Johnson, 2003, p. 91), suggesting that a journey toward sociocentric transformation may be more needed, and therefore more pervasive, in hero tales of Western societies. Still, one encounters deep elements of sociocentric transformation woven in the fabric of Eastern societies. For example, in Buddhism, the *bodhicitta* refers to an awakened mind "that inspires a promise, a vow to advance step by step to help others" (Mercer, 2016). The Bohisattva is an enlightened hero who, through a disciplined path of awakening, acquires an understanding of *dana* (generosity), *sila* (morality), *ksanti* (patience), *virya* (effort), *samadhi* (meditative calm and insight), and *prajna* (wisdom). Doing the right thing becomes effortless and rewarding. Taoist traditions, moreover, view enlightenment as the acquisition of communication, communion and connection with all people and all of nature.

A number of philosophers and spiritual thinkers have distinguished between *dualistic* thinking and *nondualistic* thinking (e.g., Carreira, 2014; Culliford, 2010; Rohr, 2011; Wilber, 2007). The dualistic mind dichotomizes people, things, and ideas, and it is the dominant mode of thinking for the pre-transformed hero. It is "either-or" thinking. In contrast, the nondualistic mind bathes in the mindset of inclusivity; it is "both-and" thinking. Rohr (2011) describes the dualistic mind as wedded to the *seven C's of delusion*: "it compares, it competes, it conflicts, it conspires, it condemns, it cancels out any contrary evidence, and it then crucifies with impunity" (p. 147). Dualistic thinking works for most of us when we are young, carving out our identities and establishing boundaries between "good" versus "bad, and "us" versus "them." Howard Gardner (1995) refers to this thinking style as that of a 5-year-old child, a style that unfortunately many of us never outgrow. For the hero to become unified with the world—the end state of Campbell's (1949) monomyth—dualistic thinking must lead to some type of "falling" or a "failing," setting the stage for transformation toward nondualistic thinking. "The rational mind stresses opposites," wrote Campbell (1991). "Compassion and love go beyond pairs of opposites" (p. 197). Hero mythology does not promote the rational; it promotes the *transrational*, which "transcends all categories of thought" (p. 41) and points to "a breakthrough of the reality of this life [when] you realize that you and that other are, in fact, one" (p. 54).

The journey toward the discovery of the one-ness of humanity may not be a far leap from our natural inborn inclination. Kylie Hamlin & Karen Wynn's (2011) work on infants shows that even newborns express a preference for morally good individuals over selfish ones. Additional research demonstrates that there is a strong genetic basis for performing behaviors aimed at civic engagement and other pro-social causes (Dawes, Settle, Loewen, McGue, & Iacono, 2015). To the extent that we spend the first stages of our lives selfishly building our personal identities and careers, we may be designed to awaken in later stages to our original predisposition toward sociocentricity (Rohr, 2011). Campbell (2001) urged us all to cultivate this greater purpose of forming compassionate unification with all of humanity. He believed this awakening is the central function of hero mythology.

Dependency to Autonomy

Our western culture's preoccupation with safety, security, socioeconomic well-being, and entertainment has led some observers to call the culture "patho-adolescent" (Plotkin, 2007; Rohr, 2011; West, 2008). Much of this patho-adolescence no doubt stems from people's behavior and identity being steeped in consumerism, materialism, competition, violence, and nationalism. Rigid adherence to dualistic thinking may play a role in the maintenance of this culture, but the adolescence goes beyond thinking style to include a misguided belief that the lower-level needs in Maslow's hierarchy are the only needs that ever matter. A person's willingness to deviate from the dominant cultural pattern is essential for heroic transformation. Heroes do the right thing, and do what they must do, regardless of authority, tradition, and consequence. Maslow (1943) called this characteristic *autonomy*. "There are the 'strong' people," wrote Maslow, "who can easily weather disagreement or opposition, who can swim against the stream of public opinion and who can stand up for the truth at great personal cost" (p. 379). Fulfillment of the lower needs in the pyramid is essential for autonomy to develop in individuals. "People who have been made secure and strong in the earliest years tend to remain secure and strong thereafter in the face of whatever threatens" (p. 380).

The world's greatest heroes have been fearless in their autonomy. Jesus of Nazareth was a revolutionary who defied the conventions of his culture and then paid the ultimate price. Other similar examples are Martin Luther King, Jr., Joan of Arc, Malcolm X, Harvey Milk, and Mahatma Gandhi (Wolf & Zuckerman, 2012). Phil Zimbardo has championed the idea that heroes are people with the ability to resist social pressures that promote evil, and that such resistance requires the moral courage to be guided by one's heart rather than by social cues. Zimbardo and other hero activists drive home the point that "the opposite of a hero isn't a villain; it's a bystander" (Chakrabortty, 2010; see also The Hero Construction Company, www.theherocc.com). While the transformed hero enjoys "union with the world," she remains an autonomous individual who can establish her own path in the world that is unfettered by the patho-adolescence all around her. "What a man can be, he *must* be," wrote Maslow (p. 376), expressing an idea consistent with Campbell's (1991) advice to "Follow your bliss" (p. 22). Each of us, according to Campbell (2004), has a unique heroic gift to offer the world, and our life purpose is to conquer our dragons at all costs to find that gift. We do not find our bliss by following a trail blazed by others. Instead, "you enter the forest at the darkest point, where there is no path. Where there's a way or path, it is someone else's path; each human being is a unique phenomenon" (p. xxvi).

Stagnation to Growth

One can be autonomous but not necessarily growing and stretching toward realizing one's full potential. The hero must leave home and venture on the journey to obliterate a status quo that is no longer working. Earlier we discussed the reluctant hero, the person who does not choose to change but is cast onto the hero track as a result of "fallings," "failings," or life-altering circumstances beyond her control. The pre-transformed hero naturally resists change, and thus severe setbacks may be her only impetus to budge. Without a prod, she will remain comfortable in her stagnation, oblivious to the idea that anything needs changing. This obliviousness, and how it is remedied, reflects an important mythic archetype. Fables and fairy tales abound that tell of heroes with a form of amnesia about their true identity. The hero is a person who lacks awareness of her special heritage, her exceptional pedigree. The whole point of the narrative is to demonstrate how, after many arduous trials, she is able to discover her true special nature. We see this pattern in tales of kings and princesses who are oblivious about their royal birthright, and the story centers on how they go about reclaiming that birthright. This narrative of amnesia has had lasting appeal because it speaks to all of us. Every individual, as we have noted, has hidden heroic gifts that beg for discovery.

The hero's journey has been referred to as the death of the false self and the birth of the true self (Rohr, 2011; Sperry, 2011). The false self is one's identity, possessions, and career that one has spent the first half of life building at great cost. Spiritual masters assert that whereas the false self consists of those aspects of the self that are temporary constructions designed to feed the ego, the true self is eternal. One's true self is the spirit or soul, or "the face you had before you were born" (Hori, 2000). The hero's journey marks the death of pretense and inauthenticity, and the birth of the person one is meant to be. Campbell (1988) described the process as "killing the infantile ego and bringing forth an adult" (p. 168). Sperry (2011) has argued that people are so attached to their false selves that they fear the death of the false self even more than they fear the death of their physical self. Our growth can also be inhibited by a phenomenon called the crab bucket syndrome (Simmons, 2012). This syndrome describes the consequences of our entrenchment with our families, our friends, and our communities, and they with us. Any attempt we make to crawl up and out of the bucket is met with failure as the crabs below us pull us back down. For most of us, the hero's journey represents the best way, and perhaps the only way, to escape the bucket and discover our true selves.

As we transform, we need not abandon our old selves in their entirety. Recall that the transformed, nondualistic hero holds a view of the world that *transcends and includes*. This holistic view of one's self and one's values is reflected in Jung's mandala as a creative tension of opposites and as a celebration, and embracing, of one's complexity. Campbell (1991) argued that a healthy, transformed individual accepts and embraces her growth and contradictions. "The psychological transformation," wrote Campbell, "would be that whatever was formerly endured is now known, loved, and served" (p. 207).

Conclusion and Future Directions

This chapter has reviewed the causes, processes, dimensions, and consequences of the hero's transformation. Admittedly, our treatment of these issues has emphasized breadth at the expense of depth, as surely an entire book could be devoted to each of many issues we have raised. Tales of heroic transformations have moved human beings for countless centuries, first via the oral tradition before the advent of written language and then later in plays, novels, and cinema. William James once observed, "Whenever one aim grows so stable as to expel definitively its previous rivals from an individual's life, we tend to speak of the phenomenon, and even *wonder* at it, as a transformation" (James, 1902/2013, p. 70, italics added). James' use of the word "wonder" implies that people are moved by the transformations they see in people, and also that these transformation are a rare occurrence. As did James, we suspect that many people spend their entire lives resisting change, denying the need for it, and suffering as a result of avoiding it (Allison & Setterberg, 2016). As Jung (1945) observed, "There is no coming to consciousness without pain. People will do anything, no matter how absurd, in order to avoid facing their own soul. One does not become enlightened by imagining figures of light, but by making the darkness conscious" (p. 335).

Those who dare to transform, or who are compelled to do so by circumstance, grow into fully developed human beings ready, willing, and able to transform others. The transformed hero represents the pinnacle of human maturity, the state of well-being that allows people to flourish (Seligman, 2011b) and experience eudaimonia (Franco, Efthimiou, & Zimbardo, in press). For Buddhists, the highest state of enlightenment is *nirvana*, a state of bliss when one is reborn into a new life and free from all suffering. For Hindus, this ultimate state of bliss is *ananda*, and for Muslims it is *taqwa*. Peterson and Seligman (2004) surveyed cultures from around the globe and identified 24 universal character strengths that describe the healthiest and most mature human beings worldwide. These character strengths were then grouped into six character virtues: *wisdom, courage, humanity, justice, temperance,* and *transcendence*. The six virtues closely match Campbell's (1949) description of the transformed hero. As a result of their journey, heroes acquire wisdom about themselves and the world; they develop the courage to face their inner dragons; they are in union with all of humanity; they pursue justice even at a cost to themselves; they are humbled and tempered; and they embark on a journey that "opens the world so that it becomes transparent to something that is beyond speech, beyond words, in short, to what we call transcendence" (Campbell, 2014, p. 40).

A promising new direction for research is now unfolding in our understanding of the biological and genetic bases of heroic transformation (Efthimiou, 2015). Recent research has shown that there are more dopamine receptors in risk-takers and far-travelers than in risk-avoiders and homebodies (Dreber, Rand, Wernerfelt, Garcia, Lum, & Zeckhauser, 2011). This finding suggests that a predisposition to venture forth on the hero's journey may be built into some people's systems. There may also be genetic markers for novelty seeking and risk-taking (Thomson, Hanna, Carlson, & Rupert, 2012). Research is also beginning to explore the embodiment of heroism, demonstrating the reciprocal influence of mind and body in producing heroic action (Efthimiou, 2015). Campbell (1988) seems to have anticipated this work, observing that hero myths "were designed to harmonize the mind and the body" (p. 87). Hero myths contain symbolic, metaphorical images representing "the energies of the organs of the body in conflict with each other … The brain is one of the organs" (p. 46).

Our understanding of heroic transformation should be enhanced by the newly emerging transdisciplinary approach to heroism (Allison, 2015; Efthimiou, 2016; Efthimiou, Chapter 8, this volume; Efthimiou & Allison, 2016). This approach emphasizes a holistic perspective that integrates the social and physical sciences within a humanities context. Again, Campbell (1969) understood the significance of an emerging science that incorporates multiple disciplinarity. He conjectured that hero mythology has "succeeded in creating for the human species an environment of sign stimuli that release physical responses" such as joy, anger, tears, pain, and impulsivity. Consequently, "the biology, psychology, sociology, and history of these sign stimuli may be said to constitute the field of our subject, the science of Comparative Mythology" (p. 41). In his book on "happiness genes," Baird (2010) reviews evidence suggesting that we can change our ancestral, evolutionary wiring to a more evolved state. Based on this research, Efthimiou (personal communication, August 1, 2015) speculates that people's aspirations and preparations for doing heroic work can produce surprising concomitant physical benefits. The process of undergoing rigorous hero training "from beginner to intermediate to proficient" could change "our very cellular structure in the process." In short, Efthimiou views heroism as "embodied skill acquisition—something that is embedded and embodied in our very being."

Another ripe area for future research resides in the phenomenon of malignant transformation. Villainous embodied transformation has been demonstrated by Gray (2010) who found that merely thinking about harming another person significantly increased participants' physical strength. Campbell (1988) explained villainy in terms of an inability to bring one's deepest dragons and inner gifts into conscious awareness. He speculated that "consciousness thinks it's running the shop. But it's a secondary organ of a total human being, and it must not put itself in control. It must submit and serve the humanity of the body." If a person "doesn't listen to the demands of his own heart," then he is doomed to villainy (p. 181). Allison and Smith (2015) discuss the many ways that heroes and villains differ in their transformations. Both heroes and villains are wounded in some way, but only heroes find ways to heal the wounds, even when the damage appears irreparable. Heroes transcend difficult circumstances; villains succumb to them. Heroes, moreover, discover their missing inner quality and become transformed. Villains, however, never discover that quality and either stagnate or regress. Heroes attract benevolent mentors; villains either never get mentored or attract dark mentors. Heroes usually participate in all aspects of their journey; villains often "outsource" parts of their journey to henchmen or minions. Finally, heroes are on a journey of becoming in union with the world, whereas villains are on a journey of separation from the world. Malignant transformation has been discussed at length by Zimbardo (2008), who calls it the *Lucifer Effect*.

Campbell (2004) asserted that "a good life is one hero journey after another" (p.133). The wisdom of writers and philosophers, from Homer in 800 BCE to Phil Zimbardo, tells us that we are all called to lead a heroic life. Yet most people are unaware of this fact, or they face impediments that thwart the realization of their heroic potential. If the ultimate goal of the hero's journey is for the hero to bestow the world with transformative gifts, then one would think that the world would be doing everything possible to promote hero's journeys for everyone. Service to others appears to be both the means of achieving personal transformation as well as the consequence of transformation. Kok et al. (2013) found that the practice of loving kindness toward others had positive transformative effects on participants' physiology, and Jenkins et al. (2013) discovered that volunteering to help others is associated with lower depression and lower mortality. Indeed, the best way to transform oneself may be to transform others. Joseph Campbell urged us to "follow your bliss," and ultimately the hero transformation is as much about creating bliss for others as it is for oneself.

References

Allison, S. T. (2015). The initiation of heroism science. *Heroism Science, 1*, 1–8.
Allison, S. T., & Goethals, G. R. (2011). *Heroes: What they do and why we need them*. New York: Oxford University Press.
Allison, S. T., & Goethals, G. R. (2013). *Heroic leadership: An influence taxonomy of 100 exceptional individuals*. New York: Routledge.
Allison, S. T., & Goethals, G. R. (2014). "Now he belongs to the ages": The heroic leadership dynamic and deep narratives of greatness. In G. R. Goethals et al. (eds), *Conceptions of leadership: Enduring ideas and emerging insights* (pp. 167–184). New York: Palgrave Macmillan. doi: 10.1057/9781137472038.0011
Allison, S. T., & Goethals, G. R. (2016). Hero worship: The elevation of the human spirit. *Journal for the Theory of Social Behaviour, 46*, 182–210.
Allison, S. T., & Setterberg, G. C. (2016). Suffering and sacrifice: Individual and collective benefits, and implications for leadership. In S. T. Allison, C. T. Kocher, & G. R. Goethals (eds), *Frontiers in spiritual leadership: Discovering the better angels of our nature*. New York: Palgrave Macmillan.
Allison, S. T., & Smith, G. (2015). *Reel heroes & villains*. Richmond, VA: Agile Writer Press.
Andrews, R. (2015). Scientists can now make leukemia cells kill each other. Retrieved from www.iflscience.com/health-and-medicine/scientists-can-now-make-leukemia-cells-kill-each-other.
Baird, J. D. (2010). *Happiness genes*. Wayne, NJ: New Page Books.
Bostrom, N. (2006). Technological revolutions: Ethics and policy in the dark. In N. Cameron & M. Mitchell (eds), *Nanoscale: Issues and perspectives for the nano century* (pp. 129–152). New York: John Wiley.
Bradbury, P. (2010). Learning and development as a spiritual journey. *Journal of Spirituality, Leadership, and Management, 4*, 62–71.
Brown, S. (2015). How one university uses new-student orientation to talk about sexual assault. Retrieved September 10, 2015 at: http://m.chronicle.com/article/How-One-University-Uses/232603#sthash.hEd4UBzU.dpuf.
Burns, J. M. (1978). *Leadership*. New York: Harper & Row.
Burns, J. M. (2003). *Transforming leadership: A new pursuit of happiness*. New York: Atlantic Monthly Press.
Callanan, M., & Kelley, P. (2012). *Final gifts: Understanding the special awareness, needs, and communications of the dying*. New York: Simon & Schuster.
Campbell, A. (1999). Staying alive: Evolution, culture, and women's intrasexual aggression. *Behavioral and Brain Sciences, 22*, 203–252.
Campbell, J. (1949). *The hero with a thousand faces*. New York: New World Library.
Campbell, J. (1969). *The masks of god: Primitive mythology*. New York: Viking Press.
Campbell, J. (1972). *Myths to live by*. New York: Viking Press.
Campbell, J. (1988). *The power of myth*. New York: Anchor Books.
Campbell, J. (1991). *Reflections on the art of living*. New York: HarperCollins.
Campbell, J. (2001). *Thou art that*. Novata, CA: New World Library.
Campbell, J. (2002). *Flight of the wild gander*. San Francisco, CA: New World Library.
Campbell, J. (2004). *Pathways to bliss*. Novata, CA: New World Library.
Campbell, J. (2014). *The hero's journey*. San Francisco, CA; New World Library.
Carey, N. (2014). *The epigenetics revolution: How modern biology is rewriting our understanding of genetics, disease, and inheritance*. New York: Columbia University Press.
Carreira, J. (2014). *Radical inclusivity*. Philadelphia, PA: Emergence Education.
Carter, S. (2014). *The Resilience Project: A search for unexpected heroes*. New York: Sage.
Chakrabortty, A. (2010). Brain food: The psychology of heroism. Retrieved on September 15, 2015 from www.theguardian.com/science/2010/mar/09/brain-food-psychology-heroism.
Crouch, T. (2004). *Wings: A history of aviation from kites to the space age*. New York: W. W. Norton & Co.
Culliford, L. (2014). *The psychology of spirituality*. London: Jessica Kingsley publishers.
Dawes, C. T., Settle, J. E., Loewen, P. J., McGue, M. (2015). Genes, psychological traits and civic engagement. *Philosophical Transactions of the Royal Society B, 370*, 20150015.
Dillard, A. (2013). *Teaching a stone to talk*. New York: Harper Perrenial.
Dreber, A., Rand, D. G., Wernerfelt, N., Garcia, J. R., Lum, J. K., & Zeckhauser. R. (2011). *The dopamine Receptor D4 gene (DRD4) and self-reported risk taking in the economic domain*. HKS Faculty Research Working Paper Series. Cambridge, MA: John F. Kennedy School for Government, Harvard University.
Efthimiou, O. (2015). The search for the hero gene: Fact or fiction? *International Advances in Heroism Science, 1*, 1–6.
Efthimiou, O. (2016). Heroic leadership embodiment: A sustainable wellbeing framework. *Sustainability Accounting, Management and Policy Journal*.

Efthimiou, O, & Allison, S. T. (2016). Heroism science: Frameworks for an emerging field. Unpublished manuscript, Murdoch University, Perth, Australia.
Erikson, E. H. (1994). *Identity and the life cycle*. New York: W. W. Norton & Company.
Farcht, J. (2007). *Building personal leadership*. Hampton, VA: Morgan James Publishing.
Franco, Z., Efthimiou, O., & Zimbardo, P. G. (in press). The eudaimonics of heroism. In J. Vitterso (ed.), *Handbook of eudaimonic wellbeing*. New York: Springer.
Frankl, V. (1946). *Man's search for meaning*. Vienna, Austria: Verlag für Jugend und Volk.
Freud, S. (1905/2011). *Three essays on the theory of sexuality*. Eastford, CT: Martino Fine Books.
Friend, S. H., & Schadt, E. E. (2014). Clues from the resilient. *Science, 244*, 970–972. doi: 10.1126/science.1255648.
Gardner, H. (1995). *Leading minds*. New York: HarperCollins.
Gilligan, C. (1982). *In a different voice: Psychological theory and women's development*. Cambridge, MA: Harvard University Press.
Goethals, G. R., & Allison, S. T. (2012). Making heroes: The construction of courage, competence and virtue. *Advances in Experimental Social Psychology, 46*, 183–235. doi: 10.1016/B978-0-12-394281-4.00004-0
Goethals, G. R., & Allison, S. T. (2014). Kings and charisma, Lincoln and leadership: An evolutionary perspective. In G. R. Goethals et al. (eds), *Conceptions of leadership: Enduring ideas and emerging insights* (pp. 111–126). New York: Palgrave Macmillan. doi: 10.1057/9781137472038
Grace, J. (2015). The hero's journey of a psychotherapist. Retrieved May 27, 2016 from https://blog.richmond.edu/heroes/2015/09/01/jaime-graces-heros-journey.
Gray, K. (2010). Moral transformation: Good and evil turn the weak into the mighty. *Social Psychological and Personality Science, 1*, 253–258.
Haidt, J. (2003). Elevation and the positive psychology of morality. In C. L. M. Keyes & J. Haidt (eds), *Flourishing: Positive psychology and the life well-lived* (pp. 275–289). Washington, DC: American Psychological Association.
Hamlin, J. K., & Winn, K. (2011). Young infants prefer social to antisocial others. *Cognitive Development, 26*, 30–39.
Hollander, E. P. (1995). Ethical challenges in the leader–follower relationship. *Business Ethics Quarterly, 5*, 55–65.
Hori, V. S. (2000). Koan and kensho in the rinzai Zen curriculum. In S. Heine & D. S. Wright (eds), *The koan. texts and contexts in Zen Buddhism* (pp. 280–316). Oxford: Oxford University Press
Imber-Black, E., & Robers, J. (1998). *Rituals for our times*. Lanham, MD: Jason Aronson.
James, W. (1902). *The varieties of religious experience*. Boston, MA: Bedford.
Jenkins, C. E., et al. (2013). Is volunteering a public health intervention? *BMC Public Health, 13*, 773.
Johnson, A. (2003). *Families of the forest*. Berkeley, CA: University of California Press.
Johnson, R. A. (1991). *Transformation: Understanding the three levels of masculine consciousness*. New York: HarperOne.
Jung, C. (1945). *Alchemical studies*. Princeton, NJ: Princeton University Press.
Jung, C. (1956). *The archetypes and the collective unconscious*. Princeton, NJ: Princeton University Press.
Jung, C. (1970). *The structure and dynamics of the psyche (volume 8)*. Princeton, NJ: Princeton University Press.
Kinsella, E.L., Ritchie, T.D., & Igou, E.R. (2015). Lay perspectives on the social and psychological functions of heroes. *Frontiers in Psychology, 6*, 130. doi: 10.3389/fpsyg.2015.00130
Kohlberg, L. (1969). Stage and sequence: The cognitive-developmental approach to socialization. In D. A. Goslin (ed.), *Handbook of socialization: Theory and research* (pp. 78–99). Boston, MA: Houghton Mifflin.
Kok, B. E., et al. (2013). How positive emotions build physical health. *Psychological Science, 24*, 1123–1134.
Kuhn, T. S. (1962). *The structure of scientific revolutions*. Chicago, IL: University of Chicago Press.
Landers, J. E. (2009). Reduced expression of the Kinesin-Associated Protein 3 (KIFAP3) gene increases survival in sporadic amyotrophic lateral sclerosis. *Proceedings of the National Academy of Sciences, 106*, 9004–9009. doi: 10.1073/pnas.0812937106
Latane, B., & Darley, J. (1969). Bystander "Apathy." *American Scientist, 57*, 244–268.
Lee, B. (2014). *Born-Again Buddhist: My Path to Living Mindfully and Compassionately with Mood Disorders*. Amazon Digital Services.
Lee, T. H., & Cosgrove, T. (2014). Engaging doctors in the healthcare revolution. *Harvard Business Review*.
Le Grice, K. (2013). *The rebirth of the hero: Mythology as a guide to spiritual transformation*. London: Muswell Hill Press.
Levinson, D. J. (1986). *The seasons of a man's life*. New York: Ballentine Books.
Lewis, D., Brown, A. J., & Moberly, R. (2014). Whistleblowing, its importance and the state of the research. In A. J. Brown, D. Lewis, R. Moberly, & W. Vandekerckhove (eds), *The international handbook on whistleblowing research* (pp. 1–36). Cheltenham: Edward Elgar.

Lopez, S. J., & Snyder, C. R. (eds) (2011). *The Oxford handbook of positive psychology*. New York: Oxford University Press.

Martinuza, B. (2015). What's empathy got to do with it? Retrieved September 10, 2015 from www.mindtools.com/pages/article/newLDR_75.htm.

Maslow, A. (1943). A theory of human motivation. *Psychological Review, 50*(4), 370–396.

Mercer, R. (2016). The effortless benevolence of heroic figures in Buddhist traditions. Retrieved from https://blog.richmond.edu/heroes/2016/01/08/the-effortless-benevolence-of-heroic-figures-in-buddhist-traditions.

Norton, M. J. & Gino, F. (2014). Rituals alleviate grieving for loved ones, lovers, and lotteries. *Journal of Experimental Psychology: General, 143*(1), 266–272.

Peck, M. S. (2003). *The road less traveled*. New York: Touchstone.

Peterson, C., & Seligman, M. E. P. (2004). *Character strengths and virtues*. Washington, DC: American Psychological Association.

Phipps, R. (2011). My trip to Melbourne. Retrieved September 8, 2015 from http://quotationsbook.com/quote/35768.

Piaget, J., & Inhelder, B. (1958). *The growth of logical thinking from childhood to adolescence*. New York: Basic Books.

Piff, P. K., Dietze, P., Feinberg, M., Stancato, D. M., & Keltner, D. (2015). Awe, the small self, and prosocial behavior. *Journal of Personality and Social Psychology, 108*, 883–899.

Plotkin, B. (2007). *Nature and the Human Soul*. New York: New World Library.

Ramos, C., & Leal, I. (2013). Posttraumatic growth in the aftermath of trauma: A literature review about related factors and application contexts. *Psychology, Community & Health, 2*, 43–54. doi:10.5964/pch.v2i1.39

Rand, D. G., & Epstein, Z. G. (2014). Risking your life without a second thought: Intuitive decision-making and extreme altruism. *PLoS ONE, 9*. doi: 10.1371/journal.pone.0109687

Rank, O. (1909). *Der mythus von der geburt des helden*. Berlin, Germany: Franz Deuticke.

Reising, R. (2002). *Every sound there is: The Beatles' Revolver and the transformation of rock and roll*. New York: Ashgate Publishing.

Rendon, J. (2015). *Upside: The new science of post-traumatic growth*. New York: Touchstone.

Renter, E. (2014). Meditation alters genes rapidly, triggers molecular changes. Retrieved from http://naturalsociety.com/meditation-alters-genes-says-new-study.

Rohr, R. (2011). *Falling upward*. Hoboken, NJ: Jossey-Bass.

Rohr, R. (2014). *Eager to love*. Cincinnati, OH: Franciscan Media.

Schopenhauer, A. (1840). *On the basis of morality*. Indianapolis, IN: Hackett Publishing.

Scott, L. E. (2012). *The path forward: Surviving the narcissist*. Chicago, IL: E. S. Enterprises.

Sedikides, C., & Hepper, E. G. D. (2009). Self-improvement. *Social and Personality Psychology Compass, 3*, 899–917.

Seligman, M. E. P. (2011a). *Flourish*. New York: Atria Books.

Seligman, M. E. P. (2011b). Building resilience. *Harvard Business Review, 4*, 1–7.

Shweder, R. A., Mahapatra, X, & Miller, J. G. (1987). Culture and moral development. In J. Kagan & S. Lamb (eds), *The emergence of morality in young children* (pp. 1–83). Chicago, IL: University of Chicago Press.

Shyh-Chang, N., Zhu, H., Yvanka de Soysa, T., Shinoda, G. Seligson, M. T., Tsanov, K. M., Nguyen, L. Asara, J. M., Cantley, L. C., & Daley, G. Q. (2013). Lin28 enhances tissue repair by reprogramming cellular metabolism. *Cell, 155*, 778–792. doi: 10.1016/j.cell.2013.09.059

Simmons, A. (2012). *The crab syndrome*. San Antonio, TX: Antuan Simmons.

Sperry, L. (2011). *Spirituality in clinical practice*. New York: Routledge.

Sulloway, F. J., & Zeigenhaft, R. L. (2010). Birth order and risk taking in athletics: A meta-analysis and study of major league baseball. *Personality and Social Psychology Review, 14*, 402–416. doi: 10.1177/1088868310361241

Swann, W. B., Jr. (2012). Self-verification theory. In P. Van Lang, A. Kruglanski, & E. T. Higgins (eds), *Handbook of Theories of Social Psychology* (pp. 23–42). London: Sage.

Thomson, A. L., & Siegel, J. T. (2013). A moral act, elevation, and prosocial behavior: Moderators of morality. *The Journal of Positive Psychology, 8*, 50–64.

Thomson, C., Hanna, C., Carlson, S., & Rupert, J. (2012) The -521 C/T variant in the dopamine-4-receptor gene (DRD4) is associated with skiing and snowboarding behavior. *Scandanavian Journal of Medical Science Sports, 23*, 108–113.

Trentacosts, C., & Izard, C. (2006). Emotional development. In N. Salkind (ed.), *Encyclopedia of human development* (Vol. 1, pp. 456–458). Thousand Oaks, CA: Sage Reference.

Tuckman, B. (1965). Developmental sequence in small groups. *Psychological Bulletin, 63*, 384–399. doi: 10.1037/h0022100

Turner, V. W. (1964). Betwixt and between: The liminal period between Rites de Passage. In *Proceedings of the American Ethnological Society, Symposium on New Approaches to the Study of Religion* (pp. 46–55). New York: American Ethnological Society.

Turner, V. W. (1966). *The ritual process: Structure and anti-structure*. Ithaca, NY: Cornell University Press.

Tyler, J., & Lind, (1992). A relational model of authority in groups. *Advances in Experimental Social Psychology, 25*, 115–191.

van Gennep, A. (1909). *The rites of passage*. Paris: Émile Nourry.

Wasserstrom, J. N., Hunt, L., & Young, M. B. (2000). *Human rights and revolutions*. Lanham, MD: Rowman & Littlefield Publishers.

West, D. (2008). *The death of the grown-up*. London: St. Martin's Griffin.

Wilber, K. (2007). *Integral spirituality*. Boulder, CO: Shambhala.

Williams, A., O'Driscoll, K., & Moore, C. (2014). The influence of empathic concern on prosocial behavior in children. *Frontiers in Psychology, 5*, 424. doi.org/10.3389/fpsyg.2014.00425

Wolf, B., & Zuckerman, P. (2012). Deviant heroes: Nonconformists as agents of justice and social change. *Deviant Behavior, 33*, 639–654.

Yalom, I., & Leszcz, M. (2005). *Theory and practice of group psychotherapy*. New York: Basic Books.

Zimbardo, P. (2008). *The Lucifer effect: Understanding how good people turn evil*. New York: Random House.

21

Moral Transformation
The Paths to Heroism, Villainy, and Victimhood

Amelia Goranson and Kurt Gray

Becoming Heroes: Moral Transformation in Everyday Life

In Pakistan in early 2009, seventh-grade Malala Yousafzai started an anonymous blog with the BBC. In this blog, she discussed the Taliban's growing presence in the Swat Valley. Soon after she began her blog, the Taliban banned girls from schools in the area. Malala wrote about the fighting in the area, her daily life, and her boredom without schooling. Finally, the schools re-opened, and Malala's blog ended. Shortly after this, she was asked to be in a documentary for the *New York Times* and was interviewed on many television programs in the area and around the world. Malala became a Taliban target, culminating in an assassination attempt in late 2012, because of all this publicity. Malala was shot in the head. After months in hospitals and numerous surgeries, Malala made a full recovery. She and her family moved to the UK, where she continues to strongly advocate for women's education. In 2014, Malala became the youngest recipient in the history of the Nobel Peace Prize.

One year after the assassination attempt on Malala Yousafzai, Jeff Smith was trying to remove a stump from his yard in Oregon using his old tractor. His muddy boot slipped off the clutch, and the tractor flipped over. Smith was pinned to the ground, and was having trouble breathing beneath the 3,000-pound tractor. When his two daughters, 14 and 16, heard him screaming, they ran out to help. Seeing that their father could not breathe, they worked together to lift the machine off of their father enough to allow him to breathe until a neighbor was able to remove the tractor with his own heavy machinery (Dolak, 2013).

These two stories, while occurring in vastly different circumstances, display a common theme: ordinary people can do the extraordinary when they do good. More famous examples include Mother Teresa living in extreme poverty to help the needy, Mohandas Gandhi fasting for weeks to free India from colonial rule, and Martin Luther King steadfastly preaching non-violent protest amidst the violence of the civil rights era. These individuals all began as average people, but were *morally transformed* by their circumstances and their goals. Moral transformation is the idea that people shift from one moral role to another simply by changing their self-perceptions from weak to strong. These cases involve the transformation into heroes, but moral transformation also involves journeys that end in villainy and victimhood. This chapter explores the six different types of moral transformation of the self, which are rooted in the theory of *dyadic morality*.

Dividing Up the Moral World

By definition, morality is about good and evil. Scientists and philosophers alike have long argued that we are moral by nature; our sense of morality directs our actions and attitudes (Hutcheson, 1726). Our attention to good and evil seems to come as naturally to us as the capacity to feel hunger and thirst. We notice when others are good to us, and also when they wrong us. We celebrate cultural and political heroes who save entire peoples from downfall, and condemn the villains who harm those among us. Despite their importance in our cultural narratives, heroes and villains do not exist in a vacuum. They become good and evil through their actions upon others. To become heroes, Mother Teresa, Gandhi, and Martin Luther King needed the poor, disenfranchised, and oppressed to help. The presence of these recipients of moral deeds is taken for granted by many theories in moral psychology—but not by dyadic morality.

The theory of dyadic morality suggests that mind perception—the way we ascribe mental abilities to others—is key in deciding whether an action is moral or immoral. We understand all acts with a template of two minds, an agent and patient (Gray, Young, & Waytz, 2012; Schein, Goranson, & Gray, 2015; Schein & Gray, 2015). Agents are heroes and villains, those with the power to do moral or immoral actions. Agents are perceived as having vast pools of willpower and self-control. Importantly, we perceive their actions as *intentional*. Both heroes and villains are intentional agents, but they work in opposition, with villains inflicting harm on suffering victims and heroes working to prevent this harm. Patients, on the other hand, are victims and beneficiaries. They are the receivers of the moral or immoral actions. Patients are perceived as vulnerable feelers. We perceive less intentionality in their actions and see them as more helpless, making the title "patient" quite fitting. These two minds, agent and patient, grow out of the two dimensions of mind perception: agency—the capacity to act and intend—and experience—the capacity for sensing and feeling. These two dimensions of mind perception correspond to the moral dyad, with agents possessing high levels of agency and patients possessing high levels of experience.

Good versus evil and agent versus patient provide a two dimensional space for understanding the moral world. This space contains four cells: hero, villain, victim, and beneficiary. Victim and beneficiary are not meaningfully different, so we will talk about heroes, villains, and victims exclusively in this chapter. Good and evil are separate dimensions, but it is easier to switch between good and evil than between agent and patient. Since heroes and villains both possess high levels of agency, these roles are closer than roles with high levels of patiency. Switching between heroes and villains simply requires a shift in the valence of the agency; a switch to patiency necessitates a transformation from strong and willful to feeling and sensing.

Character and Typecasting

These moral roles, however, are not just perceptions in the moment, but are stable perceptions of individuals. In this way, these roles are like attractor states—dynamic, complex systems of associations that seek preferred modes of behavior based on both internal and external influences (Thelen & Smith, 1996). While we might encounter a large range of ideas—even ideas that conflict with our current perception about any given person—over time, only the ideas that are consistent with our current schema of that individual will be embraced as relevant and credible. Encountering inconsistent information will trigger our attractor states, reinforcing our previously held beliefs and channeling our thoughts and experiences into the narrow range of experiences that are coherent with our attractors. In other areas of psychology, this is thought of as moral character. We care about an individual's character, not just their actions. The fundamental attribution error further reinforces this idea; when viewing others, we attribute their behaviors to who they are as a person, not to situational or environmental factors. In other words, moral judgments are often person-centered.

Person-centered moral judgments focus on moral character. One's character can tell us how moral or immoral the person is likely to behave (Abele & Wojciszke, 2007; Cottrell, Neuberg, & Li, 2007)—will they be a hero when the need arises? Or will they be a villain? At best, someone of good moral character will be actively helpful to us. At worst, they will not be harmful to us. A person of weak moral character, on the other hand, might actively work against us or betray us. People pay attention to others' moral character, as it determines whether an individual will follow through on his or her commitments, stick to his or her values, and keep his or her goals (Blasi, 2005). Our moral character judgments are powerful determinants of our overall impressions of individuals with whom we expect to have a substantive relationship (Goodwin, Piazza, & Rozin, 2014).

Dyadic morality calls this idea that judgments of agents and patients tend to be stable across situations *moral typecasting* (Gray & Wegner, 2009). Gandhi, for example, is not only seen as agentic when he forgoes food or comfort for the greater good, but is permanently "typecasted" as an agent. Once an individual is typecasted into a role, many other characteristics come online, including how we perceive their mind. Typecasting provides us with a template for coherent and stable perceptions of individuals.

Moral Transformation

All moral roles are linked to seeing or being a mind. While mind perception has been studied in regards to others, there is also research to suggest that this type of thinking can be applied to oneself; in other words, when one does a moral or immoral deed, he or she might transform his or her self-perceptions and begin to think of him or herself as more agentic. The power of self-perception has been well studied. The way that we think about ourselves can be a powerful predictor of behavior, as we tend to behave in ways that confirm our self-perceptions (Bem, 1967). Furthermore, the perceptual associations present between moral deeds and agency might actually lead to physical manifestations of agency after one has enacted a moral or immoral deed (Barsalou, 1999; Williams & Bargh, 2008). *Moral transformation* is the embodiment of moral typecasting (Gray, 2010). Mother Teresa, Gandhi, and Martin Luther King, Jr. were not born agentic. Rather, they became agentic through their heroic actions. In performing these heroic actions, their self-perceptions shifted and they began to see themselves as powerful agents of change. Those who help or harm others are likely to see themselves as more tenacious, willful, and better able to withstand discomfort, self-transforming into heroes when the need arises. While we often typecast others in a static role, the moral world is dynamic. Our moral roles can be changed with effort, or under extreme and trying circumstances. Not only can we shift our self-perceptions from good to evil, but we can also self-transform from patient to agent. In fact, we transform from one role to another many times throughout our lives. In this chapter, we will discuss the three moral roles (hero, villain, and victim), and the six different ways we can transform our roles and self-perceptions over our lifetime:

1. from victim to hero;
2. victim to villain;
3. hero to villain;
4. hero to victim;
5. villain to victim; and
6. villain to hero.

From Victim to Hero

Perhaps the most classic story describes the transformation from victim to hero. Mother Theresa transformed from a poor nun to a great helper and servant to the poor. Harry Potter was transformed from victim of his terrible aunt and uncle to a superhero, defeating the evil Voldemort. Even the Virgin Mary was transformed from an ordinary, poor woman to a religious icon after giving birth to Jesus Christ. We see this narrative trope in works of fiction, in our daily lives, and in cultural narratives. It is so common that Joseph Campbell (1949) has developed a formula of sorts for this type of transformation—The Hero's Journey.

The Hero's Journey describes the archetype of the Hero, who achieves high goals on behalf of his or her group. The hero starts out as an ordinary person, but is soon called to action and begins his journey. The hero is tested throughout this journey and is faced with his final challenge, during which he confronts death or his greatest fear. Once triumphant, the hero gets his reward. On his way back, however, the hero comes in danger of losing the reward. When the hero crosses back into his ordinary world, there is one more challenge to overcome. Once the hero makes a sacrifice in order to overcome his final challenge on the way back to his ordinary life, the story is finally resolved. The hero returns home with the reward, and has the power to transform the ordinary world. While variants on this basic trope exist, the basic form of the story remains. The hero starts off as a weaker person, transforms himself into a stronger, more agentic person, and ultimately achieves his goal, allowing him to better the world. The elements of moral transformation are present: the hero, initially a patient, is transformed into a strong, intentional agent full of willpower, ready to achieve his goal and conquer any obstacles that may come in the way of doing so. It is important to note that the hero has not always been heroic. Instead, the hero started off in another role—the villain, or the victim. The hero struggled to gain the strength, skills, and power to achieve his or her heroic feat, and in doing so, completed the process of moral transformation. In fact, our major life changes are often marked by moral transformation of one sort or the other.

The most classic Hero's Journey occurs when people start as victims who are weak in some way. In fact, Dan McAdams' work on the redemptive life narrative suggests that a little adversity might actually be a *good* thing. He finds that highly generative adults tend to identify an instance of suffering in others as very important in their life stories; it seems that finding a suffering patient may help people more easily make the transition from victim to strong, powerful agent (McAdams, 2006, 2013; McAdams & Guo, 2015). Furthermore, he finds that those who score high on self-report measures of generativity are more likely to frame their life narratives in terms of positive, prosocial, and redemptive terms (McAdams, 2013). They are more likely to spin negative events in a positive light and grow from negative experiences into more helpful and happier people (McAdams, Diamond, de St Aubin, & Mansfield, 1997; McAdams, Reynolds, Lewis, Patten, & Bowman, 2001; McAdams & Guo, 2015; Walker & Frimer, 2007). When faced with difficult situations, it seems that these highly generative adults are used to employing their 'redemptive defenses' and self-transform from victims of their situations to powerful agents of positive change.

These findings fit with other areas of psychological literature that suggest that those who strive to make meaning of stressful events (Park, 2010) and those who aim to find the positives in negative situations (Affleck & Tennen, 1996) tend to reap psychological benefits. These benefits range from healthier psychological development and higher levels of well-being to positive outcomes on physical health and wellness (Antoni et al., 2006; Madan & Pakenham, 2014; Nowlan, Wuthrich, & Rapee, 2015). Furthermore, when individuals write about traumatic or emotionally stressful events, the process of writing seems to have both psychological and physical health benefits (Pennebaker, 1997; Pennebaker, Kiecolt-Glaser, & Glaser, 1988; Pennebaker & Seagal, 1999). Increased expression of negative emotions, insight, and narratives indicating insight into causal relationships surrounding the trauma lead to more positive health outcomes (Pennebaker, 1993). Further supporting the idea of moral transformation, those who wrote about traumas displayed lower levels of subjective distress, fewer healthcare provider visits, and better immune functioning (Pennebaker et al., 1988), all indications that writing about traumas could potentially make us not only stronger, but healthier, too.

Even ordinary people who are not purely victims can become more powerful through moral transformation. While it is clear that individuals have the ability to use their willpower for heroic ends, moral transformation suggests that the agentic properties of heroes could translate into physical strength. Indeed, when individuals were given the chance to donate a dollar to charity, they could hold up a hand weight or squeeze a hand grip for significantly longer than those who were simply given a dollar to keep, even after controlling for pre-test strength (Gray, 2010). Furthermore, when individuals wrote a story about either helping, harming, or having a neutral interaction with another person, those in the agentic helping and harming conditions could hold up the hand weight significantly longer than those in the control condition, suggesting that even the opportunity to imagine oneself as agentic can begin to shift self-perceptions (Gray, 2010). It seems that even ordinary people like you and me are prone to moral transformation throughout our lives.

Not only does moral transformation help us get physically stronger, it can help us live longer and decrease our stress levels. In their 1976 study on agency and aging, Rodin and Langer found that allowing elderly people in nursing homes to care for a plant (versus having a staff member care for the plant) and emphasizing their agency through reminders that they are responsible for themselves led to higher well-being, more community participation, and higher alertness among the residents (Langer & Rodin, 1976). Further, other research on caretaking suggests that caretakers tend to have lower mortality rates than the general population, even though they have higher levels of daily stress (R. M. Brown & Brown, 2014; S. L. Brown et al., 2009). These results further suggest that taking care of a feeling patient can make the agent feel stronger, more capable, and more responsible. Thus, increasing both momentary and dispositional agency can engender powerful life changes through moral transformation.

So far, all examples of moral transformation have included a clear action. Sometimes, however, an empty transformation occurs. At times, we may be motivated to see ourselves as heroes lest we face a less flattering reality. The sucker-to-saint effect suggests that, when we have not acted in our own self-interest but someone else has acted in theirs, we retrospectively moralize our actions to avoid feeling like a "sucker" (Jordan & Monin, 2008). Through this process, we attempt to bolster a positive self-image and see ourselves as saints, who simply completed an action for the good of someone else, instead of suckers who blindly worked against self-interest. While it would be easy to feel like a victim after violating our own self-interest, the sucker-to-saint effect suggests that instead, we put ourselves on moral high ground and think of ourselves as heroes. The transformation from victim to hero is a clear case of moral transformation from suffering victim to strong, intentional agent. Unfortunately, not all victims transform in such a positive way.

From Victim to Villain

Most are familiar with the story of Moby Dick's Captain Ahab, who obsessively hunts for the white whale who destroyed his ship and severed his leg. Ahab, clearly painted as the victim of Moby Dick's destruction, searches frantically for revenge on his wrongdoer. Blinded by his need for vengeance, Ahab slowly morphs himself from victim to villain. This becomes clear when Ahab meets Captain Gardiner, who is in search of survivors—especially his son—after Moby Dick destroyed his ship. Ahab lost his leg to this whale, and Gardiner may have potentially lost his son. The difference, however, is that the man's son is not certainly lost. It is possible that, with Ahab's help, the two could find the son and save him from Moby Dick's destruction. Captain Ahab remains too blinded by his rage to help the man, however. He does not choose to search for the son, and instead continues to chase the white whale. While Ahab was presented with a beautiful chance for redemption, to focus his energies on a positive and productive search, he chooses revenge instead. This act of turning from his fellow man, a man who is a victim of the same villain that led Ahab to this fateful journey, changes Ahab from a simple victim of an unfortunate event to a villain obsessed with exacting his revenge at any cost. In this case, gaining a strong sense of moral agency was not used in a positive manner. It is cases such as Ahab's that show the potential for a dark side to moral transformation.

Cases of negative moral transformation occur in real life as well. Eric Harris and Dylan Klebold were not popular in high school. They were involved in theater, video productions, and maintaining their school's computer server. They were the frequent targets of bullying. On the morning of April 20, 1999, the pair entered Columbine High School and shot and killed 13 people, injuring 24 others. These individuals, once victims, transformed into villains.

Ahab and the Columbine shooters illustrate victim entitlement to act selfishly. Some research suggests that, when we feel we have been treated unfairly, we then believe we have endured more suffering than we should have, causing us to behave in entitled or selfish ways (Zitek, Jordan, Monin, & Leach, 2010). In these studies, when individuals thought about a time in the past when they had been treated unfairly, they were more selfish, less likely to help the out the experimenter, and claimed more money than their opponents after a computer "glitch" occurred. When reminded of their victim role, these individuals no longer feel willing to be helpful or prosocial and instead act selfishly, transforming from victim to villain.

Moral licensing can also occur when one is transformed from victim to villain. Moral licensing suggests that sometimes the victim role can cause individuals to feel entitled to behave in less socially acceptable ways. When participants were given the chance to establish that they were not prejudiced or politically incorrect people, they were then more likely to express politically incorrect opinions in the future (Monin & Miller, 2001). After endorsing Barack Obama, others felt licensed to make ambiguously racist statements (Effron, Cameron, & Monin, 2009). These studies illustrate the sense of entitlement that victims can feel, transforming themselves into villains when they act on that sense of entitlement.

Some individuals seem to use the benefits of a victim role to their advantage. In psychological disorders like factitious disorder and malingering, the individual takes on a sick role, consciously producing false symptoms, in order to gain attention and external rewards (e.g., money, drugs, shelter; Huffman & Stern, 2003; Nadelson, 1979). These individuals exemplify an incomplete transformation from villain to victim; while they would like to be seen as victims, they are often seen as frauds and at times were diagnosed as psychopaths, making them more suited for a villain role (Clarke & Melnick, 1958; Spiro, 1968). In these situations, individuals no longer reap the benefits of the victim role and are instead seen as villains. The transformation into a villain does not always start from a place of powerlessness, however. Sometimes, the good intentioned turn their actions from prosocial to antisocial and transform from heroes to villains.

Hero to Villain

Few heroes are more quintessentially American than soldiers. Unfortunately, soldiers are not always heroes, a lesson Americans learned the hard way during the Vietnam War. In March of 1968, the Charlie Company of the Americal Division's 11th Infantry Brigade, stationed in Vietnam, was tasked with eliminating the rebel leaders of the National Liberation Front (NLF). After 7 a.m. on March 16, the troops would storm the village in My Lai. They were told that most of the villagers would be at market at this time of morning and only remaining villagers would be NLF supporters, to be eliminated at any cost. When the soldiers entered My Lai that morning, they killed ruthlessly and without discrimination. Hundreds of men, women, and children were brutally murdered, mutilated, and raped in the streets of My Lai at the hands of American soldiers. Not a shot was fired in retaliation to these attacks.

While this might seem like an extreme example, there are many contemporary examples of heroes using their power for evil in modern society. The torture and abuse by the US Army and

CIA in the Abu Ghraib prison, police brutality stories in the news, and cases of molestation by priests in the Catholic Church are all salient examples of heroes using their agency for evil, morphing their self-perceptions from heroes to villains. Acts like this, by moral agents who have gone against a moral code of "doing what is right," are often termed *moral injury* (Shay, 2014). Moral injury is an especially salient issue in war veterans, exacerbating post-war trauma (Currier, Holland, & Malott, 2015; Farnsworth, Drescher, Nieuwsma, Walser, & Currier, 2014). It seems that this role tension—heroes enacting villainous deeds—causes psychological tension that is difficult to ease, especially after emotionally intense experiences such as war.

Such moral injury can also be understood through the "slippery slope" of unethical behavior that can transpire after small ethical infractions. In this "slippery slope" of unethical behavior, individuals may find it increasingly easy to commit future unethical acts after their first ethical transgression. It is thought that such a slippery slope effect aids in the ability for individuals to morally disengage over time across ethical decisions (Welsh, Ordóñez, Snyder, & Christian, 2015). This moral disengagement process is facilitated through the rationalization and justification of one's questionable conduct (Detert, Treviño, & Sweitzer, 2008). Consider Eliot Spitzer. Throughout his career as New York State Attorney General, and later as Governor, he made ethical governing his goal. To accomplish this goal, he worked to end white-collar crime, securities fraud, computer chip price fixing, and environmental pollution. He campaigned for the legalization of same-sex marriage. Perhaps most notably, however, he was staunchly anti-prostitution and made his negative views of paid sex well known. He not only campaigned to end prostitution in New York State, but also across America and in other parts of the world. In 2008, however, Spitzer was uncovered as a hypocrite, having paid thousands of dollars for high-end prostitutes over the past several months. Such moral hypocrisy can certainly be explained by the slippery slope effect; heroes can transition to villains through ethical infractions that grow gradually larger and more severe. Heroes do not always transform into bad agents, however. Sometimes, heroes become weak.

Hero to Victim

Robin Williams was, to many, an American hero. His stand-up comedy, improvisational comedy, and roles in popular films cemented Williams as a famous and beloved American celebrity. Beyond his career in film and comedy, Williams was also touted as a philanthropist, founding Comic Relief USA and making frequent appearances at fundraising benefits. In his personal life, however, Williams struggled at times with mental health and addiction problems. He was addicted to cocaine for a time and also struggled with alcoholism for many years. In the last year of life, he was seeking care for alcoholism, depression, and anxiety. On August 11, 2014, Williams committed suicide in his home in California. While, on the outside, Williams appeared to be a hero to many Americans, on the inside, he was suffering. In the final months of his life, it is clear that Williams did not feel like a hero. Instead, he perceived himself as the victim of his addictions and physical diseases. Unfortunately, depression and anxiety are often comorbid and both include symptoms such as feelings of helplessness or hopelessness, often exacerbated by alcohol use disorders (Mellentin, Nielsen, Stenager, & Nielsen, 2015; Swendsen, 1997). It is clear that Williams had completed a moral transformation of self during this time of his life; unfortunately, this transformation was one with a negative outcome. Instead of bolstering his feelings of agency and competence, Williams' transformation had more negative outcomes. Not all moral transformations have such negative consequences, but the transformation from agent to patient often has negative outcomes.

Suicide like that of Williams' is not altogether uncommon. While most Americans did not know Williams, he seemed the picture of happiness to many: he was funny, rich, and famous. Sometimes, we cannot know the mental states even of those who are closer to us; those who seem happy and strong may be suffering internally. In fact, socially prescribed perfectionism and perfectionistic self-presentations are both significantly predictive of suicide in adolescents (Roxborough et al., 2012). The relationship between these perfectionistic traits and suicidal behaviors is mediated by social disconnection (Roxborough et al., 2012). This indicates that suicide can sometimes be spurred on from the perceived inability to meet others' expectations, which leads to a decreased sense of belonging (Hewitt, Norton, Flett, Callander, & Cowan, 1998). Perhaps sometimes, when one is cast as a hero, this causes pressure to live up to the expectations of a strong, powerful, infallible hero. This pressure can cause psychological distress, at times transforming people into victims. Unfortunately, the transformation into a victim is not exclusive to heroes.

Villain to Victim

Just as heroes can fall from greatness, villains can lose their power, too. The Muslim Brotherhood was an extremist Islamic party that perpetrated great human rights abuses and restricted religious freedom of Egyptians during the Egyptian revolution in 2011. The president, Mohamed Morsi, issued a temporary constitutional declaration in 2012 that allowed him unlimited power to legislate without judicial oversight or review. He became widely hated and was eventually overthrown by the Egyptian military. After this coup, chaos erupted in Egypt, with authorities cracking down on the Muslim Brotherhood and Morsi supporters. A month after the overthrow, the Egyptian military opened fire on a group of Morsi supporters, killing 120 and injuring over 4,000 people. A few months later, a sit-in of Brotherhood supporters was disbanded using machine guns, snipers, and bulldozers. Snipers even shot individuals trying to enter a nearby hospital to get medical help. Children and teens were killed or injured, and at least one person was burned alive. It is clear that, over time, the Muslim Brotherhood and its supporters were transformed from villains to victims.

These kinds of transformations are not always so extreme. Consider the narrative of Alcoholics Anonymous and closely related groups. Going in to these programs, individuals have often been typecast as villains: fathers who neglect their children in favor of alcohol, mothers who spend money on drugs instead of food, men who get their families in debt because of gambling problems. One might think that, in order to make these individuals believe that they have the power to overcome addiction, the treatment should make the individuals feel that they have control over their own lives. This, however, is not how twelve-step programs like AA are structured. Instead of empowerment, they paint the alcoholics as weak, at the mercy of God. AA preaches the gospel of hitting rock bottom. AA asks its members to let go of ego, to accept that they have no power of their addiction to alcohol, and to pray. Using this method, AA emphasizes to members again and again that the only way through their addiction is to be a powerless victim. Leaving their fate to God, members are stripped of their agency and constantly reminded of their patiency.

Unsurprisingly, doing bad deeds makes us feel negatively. This is abundantly clear in Stanley Milgram's 1963 study on obedience to authority. In the lab, Milgram told his participants that they would be involved in a task with another participant. This other participant was truly a confederate. The participant's job was to administer a test to the confederate, and to shock the confederate when he got the answer wrong. Each time the confederate answered incorrectly, the strength of the shock was increased. Importantly, there was an experimenter in the room with the participant. The experimenter ordered the participant to go on if he started to have doubts about the strength of the electric shocks. When participants shocked the learners, they often expressed great distress at feeling like they were perpetrating villainous deeds, a self-perception that was at odds with their usual vision of themselves. About 70 percent of the participants in the study did not resist the order to keep shocking the learner, and felt like great villains

(Milgram, 1963). When they discovered the true nature of the study, the participants realized that they were victims of the authority figure urging them to keep shocking.

Some individuals seem to need no prompting in order to act like villains. This is apparent in narcissistic individuals. Narcissists have self-enhancing behaviors, inflated self-appraisals, and fragile self-views (Fanti & Henrich, 2014). Narcissism has also been linked to antisocial (Frick, 2009) and aggressive (Ang, Ong, Lim, & Lim, 2009) behaviors in children and adolescents. Narcissistic children tend to bully others more than their non-narcissistic peers (Fanti & Kimonis, 2012). This is exacerbated in children who have low self-esteem. By bullying others, the individual gains power and status, bolstering a positive self-image (Griffin & Gross, 2004; Washburn, McMahon, King, Reinecke, & Silver, 2004). Interestingly, narcissists also report feeling more victimized, perhaps as a result of their fragile self-views (McCullough, Emmons, Kilpatrick, & Mooney, 2003). It seems, then, that many villainous, narcissistic behaviors may stem from an underlying feeling of victimhood.

Furthermore, research from our lab suggests that, in order to decrease blame for one's antisocial actions, one need only play the victim (Gray & Wegner, 2011). In this way, individuals can sneakily use the victim role in order to continue their villainous acts. Agentic heroes are afforded more blame for their actions than patientic victims. Previous agentic deeds typecast an individual as an agent, whether hero or victim, and future punishments are doled out accordingly. When one is typecast as a patient, however, one's victimhood is clearer and they are judged as less capable of earning blame. In this way, villains can make sure they get less blame for their actions when they typecast themselves as victims after their negative deed.

Villain to Hero

Luckily, bad agency can be turned into good agency under the right circumstances. Malcolm Little illustrates this well. Little was born on May 19, 1925. His father was an advocate of black pride and was outspoken about his beliefs. When Malcolm was six, his father died in a streetcar accident that the family believed was a result of his unpopular beliefs. At the age of 13, Malcolm entered the foster system when his mother entered a mental hospital. By age twenty, Malcolm had already been to prison on numerous charges. In prison, he discovered and joined the Islamic religious movement Nation of Islam. It was during this time that the man formerly known as Malcolm Little changed his moniker to Malcolm X. When he was released from prison, Malcolm X quickly ascended the ranks in the Nation of Islam, eventually becoming one of the organization's powerful leaders. In this role, he propagated beliefs about black supremacy, continued segregation, and the belief that Blacks should return to Africa since that is where they came from. He publicly opposed the Civil Rights Movement, belittling their ideas of nonviolent protest and integration of Blacks and Whites in society. Malcolm X propagated the belief that Blacks should use whatever force necessary to defend themselves and take their rightful place as the superior race. During this time of his life, Malcolm X was clearly quite powerful, but used this power for immoral acts.

In the mid-1960s, however, Malcolm X began transforming his self-perception from villain to hero. He left the Nation of Islam and publicly expressed regret for the ideas and actions he supported in his time as a leader in this organization. Malcolm X decided to embrace a different kind of Muslim faith, and began to practice Sunni Islam. During this time in his life, he recanted his former beliefs about racism and founded two organizations for positive social change: Muslim Mosque, Inc. and the Organization of Afro-American Unity. Until his assassination in 1965, Malcolm X promoted more positive social values including Pan-Africanism, Black self-defense, and Black self-determination. Consistent with these values, Malcolm X transformed himself from villain to hero through positive other-centered action by the end of his life.

The transformation from villain to hero is a difficult one. It is well known that bad is stronger than good in the everyday, in major life events, in interpersonal interactions, and learning (Baumeister, Bratslavsky, Finkenauer, & Vohs, 2001). This pattern persists even when controlling for event salience or diagnosticity of the action. Adults possess a strong negativity bias (Ito, Larsen, Smith, & Cacioppo, 1998; Rozin & Royzman, 2001). They not only attend to negative information more than positive information, but also learn quicker when negatively reinforced (Öhman & Mineka, 2001). Given the strong evidence that bad is stronger than good, it seems quite remarkable that some overcome this strong negativity and transform from villain to hero.

Some research, however, supports the idea that whether we attend to positive versus negative information depends on our age. A positivity effect is found in older adults such that they put greater focus on emotion regulation when faced with negative information, allowing them to enhance the positive information they come across and diminish the negative (Mather & Carstensen, 2005). As people age and their time horizons shrink, they tend to focus more on goals promoting well-being and meaning-making (Carstensen, Isaacowitz, & Charles, 1999). Further, our research suggests that this positivity effect has less to do with age and more to do with perceived time horizons. In examining death row prisoners' last statements, prisoners use significantly more positive emotion and less negative emotion words than MTurk workers simulating the experience, and use less negative emotion words than a sample of poetry written by death row inmates (Goranson, Ritter, Waytz, Norton, & Gray, submitted).

There are other ways that individuals come to inner peace after perceived wrongdoing. Research on restitution suggests that when an out-group member observes one of one's in-group members engage in unethical behavior, members of the in-group are more likely to take action to right or make up for these unethical behaviors (Gino, Gu, & Zhong, 2009). Further, not only does restitution encourage individuals to make up for past wrongs, it also increases the likelihood that the offending party will be forgiven (Carlisle et al., 2012). For example, when an individual is given a small portion of the prize in an economic distribution game, they usually feel wronged. Restitution—in the form of a generous distribution in a later round—increases forgiveness more than a simple apology. While the distributor started off as a villain, they were able to redeem themselves in the eyes of their victim after using their agency for good in a subsequent interaction, becoming a hero.

The transformation from villain to hero is not always as easy as just giving your partner a few more tickets in a game, however. Whistleblowers experience the difficulty of this transition firsthand. While involved in a company that may be engaging in some morally or ethically questionable behaviors, these individuals are often conceptualized as villains. If they "blow the whistle" on unethical behaviors, however, they can transform into heroes. This process is not easy. After blowing the whistle, individuals report reduced social support, alienation, and stigma against them as a result of whistle blowing (McGlynn & Richardson, 2014). In their transformation to heroes, these individuals show increased emphasis on moral values and for the welfare of others (Avakian & Roberts, 2012). In becoming a whistleblower, the individual takes on the role of a positive moral agent. In many ways, this transformation from villain to hero is the classic American tale: one of hope and redemption.

Practical Recommendations: Becoming Your Own Hero

Moral transformation can inform every part of our lives. Rarely does life go as planned all of the time. Whether we forget a deadline at work or lose our partner in a tragic accident, we commonly encounter hardships. Our work on moral transformation suggests that if we can turn these unfortunate situations into ones where we become positive agents of change, we can transform ourselves into the heroes of our own lives. Hannah Arendt created the idea of the "banality of evil," the idea that perhaps those who perpetrate great evils in the name of a political or social regime are not necessarily inherently evil or crazy; instead, they might just be ordinary people who accept the dogma of the dominant sociopolitical atmosphere and leaders (Arendt, 1976). They might simply participate in evildoing because they want to be good citizens.

As a counterpoint to this idea, Philip Zimbardo and colleagues have proposed the banality of heroism (Franco, Blau, & Zimbardo, 2011). This idea emerged from the observation that most heroes are simply ordinary people who emerge as heroes in particular situations. If some ordinary people can do extraordinary deeds under the right circumstances, maybe we can create a culture in which we value these good deeds so much that heroism becomes 'banal.' So ingrained would be the impulse to do good when possible that it is downright inconsequential. Encouraging socio-centric action when others are normally passive to create a society in which moral transformation was a normal, everyday occurrence.

In order to be heroes of the everyday, we do not need to run into burning buildings to save people, intervene in fist fights, or dash into the street to save a puppy from being hit by car. Becoming a hero requires moral transformation of the self. Start small. Create a positive feedback loop for yourself; build upon small, prosocial actions that make you feel powerful, helpful, and agentic. Over time, you may start to see yourself as a powerful force of good in the world. Heroes act with good intentions, and these good intentions can have a power in and of themselves to effectively sooth pain or increasing pleasure (Gray, 2012). There are lots of ways to help; both direct and indirect actions can make us feel powerful and heroic for a moment. The recipe for heroism is not simply brute strength, adrenaline, and quick action. Heroes can be kind, caring, and warm.

In fact, research suggests that the most important factor in determining whether another person is seen as good or bad is whether that person is warm and prosocial (Abele & Wojciszke, 2007; Cuddy, Fiske, & Glick, 2008; Fiske, Cuddy, Glick, & Xu, 2002). In interviews with "unsung heroes," Frimer and colleagues found that heroes were caring; they talked about how helping others helped give their lives meaning and structure (Frimer, Walker, Dunlop, Lee, & Riches, 2011; Frimer, Walker, Lee, Riches, & Dunlop, 2012). Helping made them feel fulfilled. They helped not out of obligation, but for the greater good. Heroes' stories were filled with themes of agency, empowerment, redemption, and optimism.

Work on moral conviction suggests that we do hold within us the power for good when we put our mind to it. It seems that passionate moral ideas permeate certain attitudes more than others, and this moral intensity indicates conviction. For example, strong moral conviction predicts resistance to majority influence both publicly and privately on politically charged topics; the strength of moral opposition to torture, for example, predicts their likelihood of conforming to the level of support for torture that others report (Aramovich, Lytle, & Skitka, 2012). Stronger moral convictions contribute to how people relate to authority rulings, such as Supreme Court decisions, with stronger moral convictions promoting less acceptance of Supreme Court decisions as the final word (Skitka, Bauman, & Lytle, 2009). Moral convictions about hot topics in politics predict voting behavior and candidate support, as well as willingness to engage in activism in support of one's political views (Skitka, Morgan, & Wisneski, 2015). Moral conviction has the power to shape behavior, and if harnessed for good, could lead to heroic acts.

Scientific Implications

Work on moral transformation will impact many areas of psychology. Moral transformation has clear implications for the power literature. Power is associated with agency, both positive and negative. Priming participants with high levels of power is found to lead to both prosocial and antisocial action in social dilemmas (Galinsky, Gruenfeld, & Magee, 2003).

Power can lead to some negative social consequences such as decreased participation in group decision-making tasks (Locke & Anderson, 2015), increased risk taking (Anderson & Galinsky, 2006), and increased unethical behavior (Dubois, Rucker, & Galinsky, 2015). In more promising findings from a moral transformation perspective, the powerful can also have higher empathic accuracy (Côté et al., 2011) and tend to gain more power through breaking rules for the benefit of others (Van Kleef, Homan, Finkenauer, Blaker, & Heerdink, 2012). Moral transformation suggests that power can be harnessed for good, and future research might investigate how to harness the power of the good to enact prosocial change.

The power and agency we can harness through good deeds also has broad implications for the self-control literature. Both state and trait self-control could be manipulated with moral transformation paradigms. The current findings on moral transformation seem to suggest that the best way to increase self-control in desired situations may be to increase a sense of agency through doing good deeds. One study examined this phenomenon in preschoolers using a fun paradigm: preschoolers were asked to complete the marshmallow task either with a Superman cape on or with no cape on. Those children who wore superman capes showed the self-control necessary to avoid eating the marshmallow, especially when they heard the directions framed in terms of using Superman's powers to exert this self-control (Karniol et al., 2011). Superheroes are perhaps the quintessential agents; we do not picture Superman crying when he is hurt or feeling pain when he is fighting off Supervillains. Moral transformation suggests that when we make people feel like 'superheroes' of their own lives, we can increase self-control and strength, leading to a whole host of desirable outcomes.

It seems that the answer to the question "are some life events so stressful that they force us to become our best selves?" is "yes!" When confronted with hardship, some individuals tend to rise above and become empowered, become the heroes of their own lives. These individuals, in the course of crafting their own redemptive life narratives, become the agents of their own lives, enacting positive changes and finding the good in their current situations (McAdams, 2006; McAdams et al., 1997; McAdams & Guo, 2015). Transformation is dynamic; it may not be possible to *always* be the heroes of our own stories. It is nearly inevitable that we will have moments of weakness and will sometimes make poor choices. The important take-away from work on moral transformation is that it *can* be harnessed for good. Even if we step off the path to redemption, we can always work our way back, regain our agency, and harness it for good. Through our actions and choices, we write our life stories. Knowledge of moral transformation suggests that we can shape our lives and become powerful, positive agents through the conscious choice to act heroically. Heroism need not always be a harrowing adventure. Indeed, perhaps more commonly it is simply the choice to act prosocially when we could choose selfish action.

Whether we view ourselves as a strong, competent agent or a weak, feeling patient has deep implications for the way that we view, interact with, and interpret the world. Our life narratives are shaped by the way in which we view ourselves. Dyadic morality suggests that the moral world is divided up in agents and patients, and this affects the way that we see ourselves and others. While we cannot always be the heroes of our stories, the current work on moral transformation suggests that even doing a little bit of good can imbue us with a sense of agency and competence, leading to more good deeds. This growing body of literature will have implications for the way that we think about ourselves, about our life events, and about psychological constructs like power, self-control, and aging. While heroes are usually the stuff of fiction and lore, our work suggests that by doing small good deeds, we can become heroes of the everyday, too. Armed with an understanding of dyadic morality and mind perception, we can better understand the causes and consequences of our transitions between hero, villain, and victim roles throughout the lifetime. You may not be Superman, but recognizing the power of moral transformation can help you become Super-you.

References

Abele, A. E., & Wojciszke, B. (2007). Agency and communion from the perspective of self versus others. *Journal of Personality and Social Psychology*, 93(5), 751–763. doi: 10.1037/0022-3514.93.5.751

Affleck, G., & Tennen, H. (1996). Construing benefits from adversity: Adaptational significance and disposltional underpinnings. *Journal of Personality*, 64(4), 899–922.

Anderson, C., & Galinsky, A. D. (2006). Power, optimism, and risk-taking. *European Journal of Social Psychology*, 36(4), 511–536. doi: 10.1002/ejsp.324

Ang, R. P., Ong, E. Y. L., Lim, J. C. Y., & Lim, E. W. (2009). From narcissistic exploitativeness to bullying behavior: The mediating role of approval-of-aggression beliefs. *Social Development*, 19(4), 721–735. doi: 10.1111/j.1467-9507.2009.00557.x

Antoni, M. H., Lechner, S. C., Kazi, A., Wimberly, S. R., Sifre, T., Urcuyo, K. R., ... Carver, C. S. (2006). How stress management improves quality of life after treatment for breast cancer. *Journal of Consulting and Clinical Psychology*, 74(6), 1143–1152. doi: 10.1037/0022-006X.74.6.1152

Aramovich, N. P., Lytle, B. L., & Skitka, L. J. (2012). Opposing torture: Moral conviction and resistance to majority influence. *Social Influence*, 7(1), 21–34. doi: 10.1080/15534510.2011.640199

Arendt, H. (1976). *Eichmann in Jerusalem: A report on the banality of evil*. New York: Penguin Books.

Avakian, S., & Roberts, J. (2012). Whistleblowers in organisations: Prophets at work? *Journal of Business Ethics*, 110(1), 71–84. doi: 10.1007/s10551-011-1148-7

Barsalou, L. W. (1999). Perceptions of perceptual symbols. *Behavioral and Brain Sciences*, 22(04), 637–660.

Baumeister, R. F., Bratslavsky, E., Finkenauer, C., & Vohs, K. D. (2001). Bad is stronger than good. *Review of General Psychology*, 5(4), 323–370. doi: 10.1037//1089-2680.5.4.323

Bem, D. J. (1967). Self-perception: An alternative interpretation of cognitive dissonance phenomena. *Psychological Review*, 74(3), 183.

Blasi, A. (2005). Moral character: A psychological approach. In D. K. Lapsley & F. C. Power (eds), *Character psychology and character education* (pp. 67–100). Notre Dame, IN: University of Notre Dame Press.

Brown, R. M., & Brown, S. L. (2014). Informal caregiving: A reappraisal of effects on caregivers. *Social Issues and Policy Review*, 8(1), 74–102.

Brown, S. L., Smith, D. M., Schulz, R., Kabeto, M. U., Ubel, P. A., Poulin, M., ... Langa, K. M. (2009). Caregiving behavior is associated with decreased mortality risk. *Psychological Science*, 20(4), 488–494. doi: 10.1111/j.1467-9280.2009.02323.x

Campbell, J. (1949). *The hero with a thousand faces*. New York: New World Library.

Carlisle, R. D., Tsang, J.-A., Ahmad, N. Y., Worthington, E. L., Witvliet, C. vanOyen, & Wade, N. (2012). Do actions speak louder than words? Differential effects of apology and restitution on behavioral and self-report measures of forgiveness. *The Journal of Positive Psychology*, 7(4), 294–305. doi: 10.1080/17439760.2012.690444

Carstensen, L. L., Isaacowitz, D. M., & Charles, S. T. (1999). Taking time seriously: A theory of socioemotional selectivity. *American Psychologist*, 54(3), 165–181. doi: 10.1037/0003-066X.54.3.165

Clarke, E., & Melnick, S. (1958). The Munchausen syndrome or the problem of hospital hoboes. *The American Journal of Medicine*, 25(1), 6–12.

Côté, S., Kraus, M. W., Cheng, B. H., Oveis, C., van der Löwe, I., Lian, H., & Keltner, D. (2011). Social power facilitates the effect of prosocial orientation on empathic accuracy. *Journal of Personality and Social Psychology*, 101(2), 217–232. doi: 10.1037/a0023171

Cottrell, C. A., Neuberg, S. L., & Li, N. P. (2007). What do people desire in others? A sociofunctional perspective on the importance of different valued characteristics. *Journal of Personality and Social Psychology*, 92(2), 208–231. doi: 10.1037/0022-3514.92.2.208

Cuddy, A. J. C., Fiske, S. T., & Glick, P. (2008). Warmth and competence as universal dimensions of social perception: The stereotype content model and the BIAS map. In *Advances in Experimental Social Psychology* (Vol. 40, pp. 61–149). Oxford: Elsevier. Retrieved from http://linkinghub.elsevier.com/retrieve/pii/S0065260107000020.

Currier, J. M., Holland, J. M., & Malott, J. (2015). Moral injury, meaning making, and mental health in returning veterans: Moral injury and meaning. *Journal of Clinical Psychology*, 71(3), 229–240. doi: 10.1002/jclp.22134

Detert, J. R., Treviño, L. K., & Sweitzer, V. L. (2008). Moral disengagement in ethical decision making: a study of antecedents and outcomes. *Journal of Applied Psychology*, 93(2), 374.

Dolak, K. (2013). Teen daughters lift 3,000-pound tractor off dad. Retrieved from http://abcnews.go.com/blogs/headlines/2013/04/teen-daughters-lift-3000-pound-tractor-off-dad.

Dubois, D., Rucker, D. D., & Galinsky, A. D. (2015). Social class, power, and selfishness: When and why upper and lower class individuals behave unethically. *Journal of Personality and Social Psychology*, 108(3), 436–449. doi: 10.1037/pspi0000008

Effron, D. A., Cameron, J. S., & Monin, B. (2009). Endorsing Obama licenses favoring Whites. *Journal of Experimental Social Psychology, 45*(3), 590–593. doi: 10.1016/j.jesp.2009.02.001

Fanti, K. A., & Henrich, C. C. (2014). Effects of self-esteem and narcissism on bullying and victimization during early adolescence. *Journal of Early Adolescence, 35*, 5–29.

Fanti, K. A., & Kimonis, E. R. (2012). Bullying and victimization: The role of conduct problems and psychopathic traits. *Journal of Research on Adolescence, 22*(4), 617–631. doi: 10.1111/j.1532-7795.2012.00809.x

Farnsworth, J. K., Drescher, K. D., Nieuwsma, J. A., Walser, R. B., & Currier, J. M. (2014). The role of moral emotions in military trauma: Implications for the study and treatment of moral injury. *Review of General Psychology, 18*(4), 249–262. doi: 10.1037/gpr0000018

Fiske, S. T., Cuddy, A. J. C., Glick, P., & Xu, J. (2002). A model of (often mixed) stereotype content: Competence and warmth respectively follow from perceived status and competition. *Journal of Personality and Social Psychology, 82*(6), 878–902. doi: 10.1037/0022-3514.82.6.878

Franco, Z. E., Blau, K., & Zimbardo, P. G. (2011). Heroism: A conceptual analysis and differentiation between heroic action and altruism. *Review of General Psychology, 15*(2), 99.

Frick, P. J. (2009). Extending the construct of psychopathy to youth: Implications for understanding, diagnosing, and treating antisocial children and adolescents. *Canadian Journal of Psychiatry/Revue Canadienne de Psychiatrie, 31*(12), 803.

Frimer, J. A., Walker, L. J., Dunlop, W. L., Lee, B. H., & Riches, A. (2011). The integration of agency and communion in moral personality: Evidence of enlightened self-interest. *Journal of Personality and Social Psychology, 101*(1), 149.

Frimer, J. A., Walker, L. J., Lee, B. H., Riches, A., & Dunlop, W. L. (2012). Hierarchical integration of agency and communion: A study of influential moral figures. *Journal of Personality, 80*(4), 1117–1145.

Galinsky, A. D., Gruenfeld, D. H., & Magee, J. C. (2003). From power to action. *Journal of Personality and Social Psychology, 85*(3), 453–466. doi: 10.1037/0022-3514.85.3.453

Gino, F., Gu, J., & Zhong, C.-B. (2009). Contagion or restitution? When bad apples can motivate ethical behavior. *Journal of Experimental Social Psychology, 45*(6), 1299–1302. doi: 10.1016/j.jesp.2009.07.014

Goodwin, G. P., Piazza, J., & Rozin, P. (2014). Moral character predominates in person perception and evaluation. *Journal of Personality and Social Psychology, 106*(1), 148–168. doi: 10.1037/a0034726

Goranson, A., Ritter, R. S., Waytz, A., Norton, M. I., & Gray, K. (submitted). Death is unexpectedly positive. Manuscript submitted for publication.

Gray, K. (2010). Moral transformation: Good and evil turn the weak into the mighty. *Social Psychological and Personality Science, 1*(3), 253–258. doi: 10.1177/1948550610367686

Gray, K. (2012). The power of good intentions: Perceived benevolence soothes pain, increases pleasure, and improves taste. *Social Psychological and Personality Science, 3*, 639–645.

Gray, K., & Wegner, D. M. (2009). Moral typecasting: Divergent perceptions of moral agents and moral patients. *Journal of Personality and Social Psychology, 96*(3), 505–520. doi: 10.1037/a0013748

Gray, K., & Wegner, D. M. (2011). To escape blame, don't be a hero—be a victim. *Journal of Experimental Social Psychology, 47*(2), 516–519. doi: 10.1016/j.jesp.2010.12.012

Gray, K., Young, L., & Waytz, A. (2012). Mind perception is the essence of morality. *Psychological Inquiry, 23*, 101–124. doi: 10.1080/1047840x.2012.651387

Griffin, R. S., & Gross, A. M. (2004). Childhood bullying: Current empirical findings and future directions for research. *Aggression and Violent Behavior, 9*(4), 379–400. doi: 10.1016/S1359-1789(03)00033-8

Hewitt, P. L., Norton, G. R., Flett, G. L., Callander, L., & Cowan, T. (1998). Dimensions of perfectionism, hopelessness, and attempted suicide in a sample of alcoholics. *Suicide and Life-Threatening Behavior, 28*(4), 395–406.

Huffman, J. C., & Stern, T. A. (2003). The diagnosis and treatment of Munchausen's syndrome. *General Hospital Psychiatry, 25*(5), 358–363.

Hutcheson, F. (1726). *An inquiry into the original of our ideas of beauty and virtue; in two treatises*. London: J. Darby, A. Bettesworth, F. Fayram, J. Pemberton, C. Rivington, J. Hooke, F. Clay, J. Batley, and E. Symon.

Ito, T. A., Larsen, J. T., Smith, N. K., & Cacioppo, J. T. (1998). Negative information weighs more heavily on the brain: the negativity bias in evaluative categorizations. *Journal of Personality and Social Psychology, 75*(4), 887–900.

Jordan, A. H., & Monin, B. (2008). From sucker to saint moralization in response to self-threat. *Psychological Science, 19*(8), 809–815. doi: 10.1111/j.1467-9280.2008.02161.x

Karniol, R., Galili, L., Shtilerman, D., Naim, R., Stern, K., Manjoch, H., & Silverman, R. (2011). Why superman can wait: Cognitive self-transformation in the delay of gratification paradigm. *Journal of Clinical Child & Adolescent Psychology, 40*, 307–317. doi: 10.1080/15374416.2011.546040

Langer, E. J., & Rodin, I. (1976). The effects of choice and enhanced personal responsibility for the aged: a field experiment in an institutional setting. *Journal of Personality and Social Psychology, 34*(2), 191–198.

Locke, C. C., & Anderson, C. (2015). The downside of looking like a leader: Power, nonverbal confidence, and participative decision-making. *Journal of Experimental Social Psychology, 58*, 42–47. doi: 10.1016/j.jesp.2014.12.004

Madan, S., & Pakenham, K. I. (2014). The stress-buffering effects of hope on adjustment to multiple sclerosis. *International Journal of Behavioral Medicine, 21*(6), 877–890.

Mather, M., & Carstensen, L. L. (2005). Aging and motivated cognition: The positivity effect in attention and memory. *Trends in Cognitive Sciences, 9*(10), 496–502. doi: 10.1016/j.tics.2005.08.005

McAdams, D. P. (2006). The redemptive self: Generativity and the stories Americans live by. *Research in Human Development, 3*, 81–100.

McAdams, D. P. (2013). *The redemptive self: Stories Americans live by* (rev. ed.). Oxford: Oxford University Press.

McAdams, D. P., & Guo, J. (2015). Narrating the generative life. *Psychological Science, 26*(4), 475–483.

McAdams, D. P., Diamond, A., de St Aubin, E., & Mansfield, E. (1997). Stories of commitment: The psychosocial construction of generative lives. *Journal of Personality and Social Psychology, 72*(3), 678.

McAdams, D. P., Reynolds, J., Lewis, M., Patten, A. H., & Bowman, P. J. (2001). When bad things turn good and good things turn bad: Sequences of redemption and contamination in life narrative and their relation to psychosocial adaptation in midlife adults and in students. *Personality and Social Psychology Bulletin, 27*(4), 474–485.

McCullough, M. E., Emmons, R. A., Kilpatrick, S. D., & Mooney, C. N. (2003). Narcissists as "victims": The role of narcissism in the perception of transgressions. *Personality and Social Psychology Bulletin, 29*(7), 885–893.

McGlynn, J., & Richardson, B. K. (2014). Private support, public alienation: Whistle-blowers and the paradox of social support. *Western Journal of Communication, 78*(2), 213–237. doi: 10.1080/10570314.2013.807436

Mellentin, A. I., Nielsen, B., Stenager, E., & Nielsen, A. S. (2015). The effect of co-morbid depression and anxiety on the course and outcome of alcohol outpatient treatment: A naturalistic prospective cohort study. *Nordic Journal of Psychiatry, 69*(5), 331–338. doi: 10.3109/08039488.2014.981857

Milgram, S. (1963). Behavioral study of obedience. *Journal of Abnormal and Social Psychology, 67*, 317–378.

Monin, B., & Miller, D. T. (2001). Moral credentials and the expression of prejudice. *Journal of Personality and Social Psychology, 81*(1), 33.

Nadelson, T. (1979). The Munchausen spectrum: Borderline character features. *General Hospital Psychiatry, 1*(1), 11–17.

Nowlan, J. S., Wuthrich, V. M., & Rapee, R. M. (2015). Positive reappraisal in older adults: A systematic literature review. *Aging & Mental Health, 19*(6).

Öhman, A., & Mineka, S. (2001). Fears, phobias, and preparedness: Toward an evolved module of fear and fear learning. *Psychological Review, 108*(3), 483–522. doi: 10.1037//0033-295X.108.3.483

Park, C. L. (2010). Making sense of the meaning literature: An integrative review of meaning making and its effects on adjustment to stressful life events. *Psychological Bulletin, 136*(2), 257–301. doi: 10.1037/a0018301

Pennebaker, J. W. (1993). Putting stress into words: Health, linguistic, and therapeutic implications. *Behaviour Research and Therapy, 31*(6), 539–548.

Pennebaker, J. W. (1997). Writing about emotional experiences as a therapeutic process. *Psychological Science, 8*(3), 162–166.

Pennebaker, J. W., & Seagal, J. D. (1999). Forming a story: The health benefits of narrative. *Journal of Clinical Psychology, 55*(10), 1243–1254. doi: 10.1002/(SICI)1097-4679(199910)55:10<1243::AID-JCLP6>3.3.CO;2-E

Pennebaker, J. W., Kiecolt-Glaser, J. K., & Glaser, R. (1988). Disclosure of traumas and immune function: health implications for psychotherapy. *Journal of Consulting and Clinical Psychology, 56*(2), 239.

Roxborough, H. M., Hewitt, P. L., Kaldas, J., Flett, G. L., Caelian, C. M., Sherry, S., & Sherry, D. L. (2012). Perfectionistic self-presentation, socially prescribed perfectionism, and suicide in youth: A test of the perfectionism social disconnection model: Perfectionism, social disconnection, and suicide. *Suicide and Life-Threatening Behavior, 42*(2), 217–233. doi: 10.1111/j.1943-278X.2012.00084.x

Rozin, P., & Royzman, E. B. (2001). Negativity bias, negativity dominance, and contagion. *Personality and Social Psychology Review, 5*(4), 296–320.

Schein, C., & Gray, K. (2015). The unifying moral dyad: Liberals and conservatives share the same harm-based moral template. *Personality and Social Psychology Bulletin, 41*(8), 1147–1163. doi: 10.1177/0146167215591501

Schein, C., Goranson, A., & Gray, K. (2015). The uncensored truth about morality. *The Psychologist, 28*(12), 982–985.

Shay, J. (2014). Moral injury. *Psychoanalytic Psychology, 31*(2), 182–191. doi: 10.1037/a0036090

Skitka, L. J., Bauman, C. W., & Lytle, B. L. (2009). Limits on legitimacy: Moral and religious convictions as constraints on deference to authority. *Journal of Personality and Social Psychology, 97*(4), 567–578. doi: 10.1037/a0015998

Skitka, L. J., Morgan, G. S., & Wisneski, D. C. (2015). Political orientation and moral conviction: A conservative advantage or an equal opportunity motivator of political engagement? Retrieved from www.sydneysymposium.unsw.edu.au/2014/chapters/SkitkaSSSP2014.pdf.

Spiro, H. R. (1968). Chronic factitious illness: Munchausen's syndrome. *Archives of General Psychiatry, 18*(5), 569–579.

Swendsen, J. D. (1997). Anxiety, depression, and their comorbidity: An experience sampling test of the helplessness-hopelessness theory. *Cognitive Therapy and Research, 21*(1), 97–114.

Thelen, E., & Smith, L. B. (1996). *A dynamic systems approach to the development of cognition and action.* MIT press.

Van Kleef, G. A., Homan, A. C., Finkenauer, C., Blaker, N. M., & Heerdink, M. W. (2012). Prosocial norm violations fuel power affordance. *Journal of Experimental Social Psychology, 48*(4), 937–942. doi: 10.1016/j.jesp.2012.02.022

Walker, L. J., & Frimer, J. A. (2007). Moral personality of brave and caring exemplars. *Journal of Personality and Social Psychology, 93*(5), 845–860. doi: 10.1037/0022-3514.93.5.845

Washburn, J. J., McMahon, S. D., King, C. A., Reinecke, M. A., & Silver, C. (2004). Narcissistic features in young adolescents: Relations to aggression and internalizing symptoms. *Journal of Youth and Adolescence, 33*(3), 247–260.

Welsh, D. T., Ordóñez, L. D., Snyder, D. G., & Christian, M. S. (2015). The slippery slope: How small ethical transgressions pave the way for larger future transgressions. *Journal of Applied Psychology, 100*(1), 114.

Williams, L. E., & Bargh, J. A. (2008). Experiencing physical warmth promotes interpersonal warmth. *Science, 322*(5901), 606–607. doi: 10.1126/science.1162548

Zitek, E. M., Jordan, A. H., Monin, B., & Leach, F. R. (2010). Victim entitlement to behave selfishly. *Journal of Personality and Social Psychology, 98*(2), 245–255. doi: 10.1037/a0017168

22

The Impact of Heroism on Heroes and Observers

Stories of Elevation and Personal Change

Jeanne Nakamura and Laura Graham

The hero story represents a compelling genre of literature—the hero journey draws readers in with tales of struggle, persistence, triumph, and perhaps transformation. The hero is celebrated, though, not for the journey but for his or her admirable qualities. The heroic figures of myth represent the quintessential hero through the qualities they embody: bravery, competence, persistence, and loyalty among others. The literature on heroism reflects this focus on heroic traits, as much of what is known focuses on the personality characteristics, types, motivations, and perceptions of heroes (e.g., Allison & Goethals, 2011; Blau & Zimbardo, 2011; Kinsella, Ritchie, & Igou, 2015a; Walker, Frimer, & Dunlop, 2010; Zimbardo, 2007). The value of the hero story beyond its dramatic impact is much less emphasized in the investigation of heroes from a psychological standpoint. The effect of heroic action on development of the self and other advances the psychology of heroism through bringing attention to the potential positive effects of heroic stories in people's lives. This chapter focuses on the positive impact of heroic action for two integral aspects of the hero story: the hero, and the audience.

Moral stories of heroism provide an opportunity to examine how moral heroic action might be integrated into the hero's own life. From a narrative psychology perspective, stories represent who we are—we understand our experiences and ourselves by creating a cohesive story complete with themes, characters, peaks, and valleys (McAdams, 2001). Narrative analysis reveals aspects central to one's identity, and can even demonstrate how one attributes a change in the self to a specific event (Pals, 2006). Narrative studies of moral exemplars have shed light on the personality aspects of heroes (e.g., Walker et al., 2010) but have yet to examine the impact of heroism through narratives. Narratives of moral action provide a glimpse into how one understands one's own heroism in the larger context of one's life. Further, narratives of remembered heroism show how one understands such a story as impacting the self. It is through these stories that we may examine how one internalizes heroism, both one's own heroic action and the action of another. Therefore, this chapter asks: How does heroism positively affect the hero through its integration into their self-story? And how do stories of others' heroism positively affect the ordinary people who witness or learn second-hand about heroism and preserve the stories in their memory?

The impact of heroism on witnesses has not gone unnoticed. Allison and Goethals (2011) argue that heroes shape us by providing examples for how to be and behave, "they point the way toward doing the right things and doing them well" (p. 207). This aligns with the finding that lay people draw on heroes as moral models in a time of threat (Kinsella, Ritchie, & Igou, 2015b). It is agreed that heroes exemplify desirable behaviors, but exactly how this impacts others may be explained in part by the emotions they stir, which however has not been empirically examined. Discrete emotions provide an opportunity for understanding reactions to heroism as they are often triggered by social encounters (see Parkinson, 1996) and represent normative responses with defined triggers, appraisals, and behavioral outcomes. Identifying the specific emotion triggered in response to heroism is important for understanding its impact on others.

Moral elevation is the response to witnessing an act of moral beauty (Haidt, 2000, 2003a) and it would be logical to think that this might be a reaction to heroism. Zimbardo (2007) put forth criteria for an action to qualify as heroic: It is voluntary, involves risk or potential sacrifice, is conducted in service to others, and without anticipated personal gain. The selflessness and benevolence of such an act is likely to elicit an emotion for which the trigger is moral goodness—elevation. We examine elevation as a response to heroism, in order to understand how heroism might incite change in those who learn of the hero's acts. Remembered stories of moral heroism can shed light on both the connection between heroism and elevation, as well as the potential transformative effect of heroism.

Currently, there is still debate over how to define "hero" (Allison & Goethals, 2011; Franco et al., 2011; Kinsella et al., 2015a). However, the growing scholarship in heroism has helped to clarify the defining features of heroes. In one prototype study, heroes were identifiable by certain features such as bravery, sacrifice, moral integrity, and risk-taking (Kinsella et al., 2015a). Zimbardo (2007) also emphasized risk and sacrifice as necessary elements for heroic action. Franco and colleagues (2011) argue that although heroes and altruists are similar in behaving prosocially, risk and self-sacrifice are the very factors that distinguish the two. Most heroes align with Colby and Damon's (1992) criteria for being a moral exemplar, and contributions to the heroism literature have been made from moral exemplar studies (e.g., Walker & Frimer, 2007; Walker et al., 2010). In accordance with these conceptions of heroism, we define heroism as exemplary moral action that involves clear physical risk and sacrifice. In doing so we aim to shed light on the impact of moral stories that clearly qualify as heroic.

This chapter illuminates the impact of heroism on the self and others through examining two types of hero stories. The first is the hero's narrative of their own "hero chapter" in later life, and the second is an observer's narrative of a time when they witnessed moral beauty. We use a positive psychology perspective in our in-depth analysis of heroic moral exemplar narratives and through proposing the positive emotion elevation as a specific response to heroism. The first section of this chapter draws on personal narratives of moral heroes in later life to examine how they understand their own heroism and its personal impact. The second section presents moral elevation as a response to heroism and uses narratives of elevation to understand the impact of heroism on the observer. In both sections, we propose that the impact of heroic moral action at its best involves self-transformation. Specifically, the hero chapter is articulated with a theme of self-change, and narratives of elevation reveal that some acts of moral beauty change those who witness such heroism. Finally, we discuss implications and directions for future research.

Moral Exemplars' Stories of Heroism: Social Purpose and Personal Change

Heroes constitute one kind of exemplar population, and researchers have been keenly interested in their embodiment of virtues and strengths such as courage (Goethals & Allison, 2012). Directly relevant to hero research, exemplar approaches have been adopted to study such positive-psychological phenomena as creativity (Zuckerman, 1977; Nakamura & Fajans, 2014), good work (Gardner, Csikszentmihalyi, & Damon, 2001; Nakamura, Shernoff, & Hooker, 2009), and extraordinary moral commitment (e.g., Colby & Damon, 1992). The common goal of these studies is to understand a positive phenomenon through the study of extreme cases that enable elucidation of the phenomenon's defining features by exemplifying them: paradigm-changing scientists, mentors who perpetuate good work, the exceptionally brave, caring, and just. The specific methods often rely on formal nominating procedures, systematic use of comparison groups or within-group analyses, and qualitative approaches (Matsuba et al., 2013). Rather than using exemplar methods solely to study heroes' traits, however, some research on moral exemplars would recommend a narrative approach.

The narrative perspective addresses how individuals construct stories that make sense of their lives, bestowing coherence and direction on their lived experience (e.g., Cohler, 1982; McAdams, 2001; Singer, 2004). In constructing a narrative understanding of their experience—a self-story—individuals form a coherent identity and this evolves over time with new experiences and changing goals (McAdams, 2008). The focus of the present section is on how a hero makes sense of an emergent moral commitment that manifests heroism, integrating it into the self-story or narrative identity.

By definition, narratives about moral heroes and other moral exemplars are stories of what was done for someone or something beyond the self. They focus on what happened to *others*. At the heart of the narrative, the beneficiary of heroism undergoes a change from being endangered, in need, hurt, or stunted towards being safe, sustained, healed, or growing. The moral hero is a powerful agent of positive change—but it is another's change.

In contrast, we ask whether moral heroism is narrated in terms of positive change undergone by the *hero*. That is, against the obvious alternative possibility that heroes may see themselves as benefiting others while de-forming or diminishing the self, we ask whether heroic experience ever is associated by heroes with positive personal change. The evidence in the narrative literature is mixed. In recent years, several studies adopting a narrative perspective have examined moral exemplars or heroes (e.g., Dunlop & Walker, 2013; Dunlop, Walker, & Matsuba, 2012; Walker & Frimer, 2007). This literature has shown that themes of redemption (shifts from bad to good; McAdams et al., 2001) characterize the narratives of moral exemplars. However, closer examination in one study of (young-adult) moral exemplars determined that the distinguishing themes specifically concerned acts of sacrifice that benefit others rather than personally transformative forms of redemption such as growth, learning or recovery (Matsuba & Walker, 2005). Moreover, rather than specifically addressing whether these moral exemplars tell stories of personal transformation through heroic experience specifically, this and other studies have examined how moral exemplars narrate their lives in general. Their goal has been to understand what kinds of people heroes are, rather than how they make sense of their heroic experience.

Further, for the most part (although see Dunlop et al., 2012, and work on generative lives, McAdams & Guo, 2015) these studies have not considered what may distinguish the particular case when moral heroism takes place in the second half of life. This later-life heroism is a major focus of the present section. In addition, when later-life moral exemplars are discussed, older age tends to be conflated with longstanding or lifelong commitment. In past narrative research on moral exemplars (e.g., Dunlop, Walker, & Matsuba, 2012, 2013; Frimer, Walker, Lee, Riches, & Dunlop, 2012; cf. Colby & Damon, 1992), the two have tended to coincide. We instead separate the two, making it possible to compare continuing and first-time older moral exemplars. That is, we compare a long-term moral exemplar, for whom the older-age heroic chapter is part of a history of moral commitment and whose narrative relates it to an earlier heroic chapter, with a second moral exemplar whose older-age heroic chapter is narrated as having no real precedent within his life.

The distinction between age and length of commitment is of particular practical significance in the present socio-historical context, when older adults are entering the traditional retirement years with decades of active life ahead of them and might chart courses of meaningful engagement during these years via either continuity or change from their earlier commitments. The different kinds of later-life chapters narrated by older moral exemplars, and the different ways these chapters are related to the chapters that precede them, provide other people with multiple models of positive aging.

On the conceptual level, we introduce into the narrative study of heroes the explicit consideration of *heroic chapters* and we decouple age from length of heroic experience, inviting attention to two topics concerning the *structure* of heroes' narratives: first-time heroism and older-age (later-life) heroic chapters. Considering the location of a chapter within the larger narrative of a life complements the treatment of recurring narrative sequences, or sets of causally linked events, such as the redemption sequences shown to characterize moral exemplars' personal narratives. More generally, the notion of heroic chapters recognizes that in addition to the isolated heroic act (e.g., running into a burning building to save someone) and lifelong heroic commitment (e.g., a career in firefighting) there are intermediate cases where heroic experience consists in a period defined by a unifying purpose that has an identifiable beginning and some extension in time.

A body of theory and research in the narrative-identity tradition that is relevant to the present examination of moral heroism has addressed people's use of positive personal change to characterize events (Bauer & McAdams, 2004, 2010; Bauer, McAdams, & Sakaeda, 2005; Bauer & Park, 2010; Lilgendahl & McAdams, 2011). For example, Lilgendahl and McAdams (2011) examined causal connections focused on self-growth, in which past events are narrated as leading to clarification of identity, growth of positive relationships, or gaining of wisdom or insight.

In this line of work, some attention has been given to the description of positive personal change by older adults (e.g., Bauer & Park, 2010). It shows that older adults do employ growth themes in making sense of their lives. However, to our knowledge the narrative study of positive personal change has not yet explored the impact of moral heroism. Finally, consistent with our attention to narrative structure, we consider positive change manifested in the narrated life trajectory (e.g., rise, vs. plateau or decline) as well as perceived change in the narrator (e.g., gaining of wisdom). Although most narrative research on positive change has focused on the latter, we view both of these as aspects of narrative identity.

Older Moral Exemplars' Narratives of Heroic Chapters

The database drawn upon in this section is a corpus of semi-structured interviews that focus on the interviewees' successful creation, in the second half of life, of a program addressing a significant social problem (e.g., needs of at-risk populations, environmental threats). These moral exemplars comprised 39 U.S. individuals aged 60 years or older (mean = 69.8 years, standard deviation = 5.4) who had been nominated and received recognition by the nonprofit organization, Encore.org, because they were judged to be running an effective social program that they had created when they were over 50. Interviewees provided accounts of the genesis of the program and how they saw it fitting within the larger story of their life. They were explicitly asked what sacrifices, if any, had been required and how, if at all, they were affected by creating and running it. Interviewees were also asked about high and low points, mirroring questions typically used in narrative studies but pertaining specifically to their social program.

As we have noted, Franco et al. (2011) identified physical risk and secondarily sacrifice as key criteria of heroism, distinguishing it from altruism. Interestingly, in empirically evaluating different theoretical accounts of moral heroism, Walker et al. (2010) in contrast treated all moral exemplars, both the brave and the caring, as moral heroes. Similarly, Colby and Damon (1992) viewed individuals as exemplars of long-term moral commitment based on willingness to accept risk and make sacrifices, even if circumstances had not required them to face physical danger or make major sacrifices. The systematic comparison of moral exemplars who are heroic in Franco et al.'s (2011) terms with moral exemplars considered heroic without risk and sacrifice is a possible area for future research.

Here, in order to be able to examine clear-cut cases of heroism, we identified and will discuss two participants in our study of older moral exemplars who accepted significant physical risk and sacrifice in the process of creating the social programs for which they were recognized. That is, these are moral exemplars whose narratives indicate that they are also heroic by Franco et al.'s (2011) criteria. In Walker and colleagues' (2010) terms, they are individuals who are both caring and brave. The case approach adopted is compatible with seeking an existence proof that heroic chapters can be narrated with positive personal change and then describing those cases if found, to generate possible research directions.

Inspection of the 39 interviews showed that in general the exemplars did not narrate this later-life chapter with reference to physical risk, danger, or harm faced in pursuing their moral commitments. The interviews highlight that the presence of sacrifice is ambiguous. In one sense all of the interviewees had incurred costs from an objective standpoint because of the amount of time, attention, and energy they had selectively invested in the moral commitment, and the associated opportunity costs. In particular, it might be expected that with advancing age and an objectively shrinking time horizon, awareness of these costs might discourage taking up uncertain new undertakings (Carstensen, 2006). However, almost all of the 39 interviewees minimized these costs. More specifically, when asked what sacrifices they had made along the way, some did acknowledge that they regretted foregone time with family but many declined to view opportunity costs as a sacrifice at all. Others minimized these costs by representing them as freely accepted.

The two individuals selected because they unambiguously fit the criteria for heroism also fortuitously contrasted on the dimension of continuity versus discontinuity between later-life moral heroism and their primary career. That is, in one case the previous career had involved moral heroism and in the other case moral heroism was new to later life. Our expectation was that individuals experiencing continuity and discontinuity of moral heroism might constitute extremes with respect to the likelihood of narrating with positive personal change even though both were describing discrete chapters of moral heroism occurring in the second half of life.

We introduce the two cases by describing the social problems they have addressed and indicating why their interviews suggested they qualify as moral heroes based on (a) undertaking risk and sacrifice and (b) making a positive change for others. We then revisit where the heroic chapters fit into their narratives, and turn to the question of perceived *personal* change in their narratives.

Carol Fennelly

In her late forties, Carol Fennelly was a long-time faith-based activist in Washington, DC doing political commentary in print and on radio when someone encouraged her to take up the cause of families disrupted by the closing of a DC men's prison. The incarcerated men were being relocated to another state, hundreds of miles away. The distance would create a tremendous barrier to family visits; even a phone call with a child or other family member would become prohibitively costly. The welfare of male felons—many imprisoned for violent crimes—was a decidedly unpopular cause. But Fennelly concluded that what was happening was "just wrong," from a human perspective. And she knew family ties represent an important protective factor against recidivism. In response to an experience of being called to act ("I just woke up one morning and knew I had to do it"), she described searching for a way to serve the disrupted families, eventually selling her own "dream house" to help fund a program, Hope House, connecting incarcerated men with their children on the outside. It enables prisoners to talk with their children, make recordings of books for them, and reunite in summer camps—at the prison—for a week of art-making, story-telling, and other activities. Remarkably, she has convinced the authorities in high-security prisons to allow the camps and prisoners themselves to participate.

Jeanne Nakamura and Laura Graham

Evidence of Moral Heroism

Risk and Sacrifice

In this current chapter of her life, Carol Fennelly has faced both risk and sacrifice. The physical risk is evident. She runs the summer camps inside high-security prisons with participants who may come from rival gangs and have long records of violence. One prison ("really dangerous") ended the program, despite several successful years, as a safety matter when a guard there was stabbed 31 times at the end of a summer of rioting. However, Fennelly ascribes her success with inmates to the trust generated by always "showing up" and when asked said she has never thought about giving up along the way. In addition, starting the program involved sacrifice. Like other moral exemplars we interviewed, she was comfortable with her single-minded focus on the program. However, she did describe as a sacrifice selling her recently acquired dream home in order to launch the program ("Do you know how hard that was?").

Impact on Others

At the time of the interview, inmates had made 19,000 recordings for their children and attended 34 summer camps. Fennelly, who describes her work as having more highs than lows, related stories that movingly conveyed the program's impact on the men and their families. For example, one child had never seen a photo of her father, yet when she met him for the first time because of the program, she knew him on sight:

> [S]he's 10 years old and a little tiny girl. So we got to the door of the visiting room where we do this camp, and she ran across the room—broke away from me, ran across the room, and jumped into her father's arms and hugged him and kissed him. There was not a dry eye in the room …

Fennelly concluded the story with an observation about the program's impact on the incarcerated men:

> [T]he last day of camp when the dads—[who] are these hardcore, tattooed men—are standing up in tears talking about how much they love their children and how sorry they are … you know at that moment these children have just saved their fathers' lives.

Bo Webb

After serving in the Marines, working in the tool and die trade, and running his own machine shop, Bo Webb described retiring and returning from the Midwest to the mountains of West Virginia, having been "born and raised in a beautiful piece of Appalachia." Within a year he came face to face with the coal industry's mining practice of mountain top removal. A flyover confronted him with the extent of the destruction ("dust and death") hidden behind a ridge: it was "shocking," "surreal," "sad," and "gut wrenching." He "couldn't believe it" and immediately recognized it as monumental and transformative: It "changed everything and I knew that something had to be done." He began by doing research on the problem for a local organization; it became a full-time undertaking. When he turned to action, he encountered roadblocks to addressing the problem locally: The coal industry was powerful, politicians were beholden, people were scared and reluctant. Webb looked outward and ultimately partnered with a scientist in Virginia, devising together an approach inspired by the civil rights movement. Webb and his partners have sought to educate, mobilize grassroots opposition, increase national awareness, and advocate for reform of laws and policies.

Evidence of Moral Heroism

Risk and Sacrifice

Whereas Fennelly could anticipate the risks associated with creating the summer camps and planned them anyway, Webb's moral heroism might be called emergent. In fact, he describes being naïvely optimistic at the outset ("a year from now this will be over, I'll have this done, and be back to gardening"). He did not anticipate the disapproval, shunning, and anger at the hands of community members who perceived him as endangering their livelihoods and welfare by fighting the coal companies. He did not foresee being ridiculed while arguing his case for changing laws and policies. He did not anticipate the death threats he would receive nor the death of a key partner in the fight. Nor did he anticipate how difficult it would be to overcome others' fears and recruit them to the cause. He nevertheless decided he was in it "for the long haul," set his retirement plans aside, and persisted in spite of the risk and sacrifice involved.

Impact on Others

Webb characterizes his work as having more lows than highs but it has had concrete results, notably the successful conclusion of a six-year fight to have a new school built in his community at a safe distance from the mining, and successes in the effort to recruit others to the fight. He notes that "the most rewarding thing that I ever, ever experienced is when someone new stands up and says, 'I'm not going to take this,' and they become active."

Continuities and Discontinuities into Later Life

As noted earlier, the two examples of later-adult heroic chapters differ on the dimension of continuity versus discontinuity with prior experience, a dimension conceptually relevant to the question of whether heroic moral action is narrated in terms of positive personal change. That is, heroic undertakings that occur in mature adulthood might be expected to express stability more than accompany change, so avowals of positive personal change in any story of late-life heroism would offer evidence that it is possible for heroes to view their endeavors as changing them in positive ways. The evidence would be especially compelling in cases of continuity—that is, recurrent rather than first-time heroism.

Fennelly represents one extreme on the dimension of continuity/discontinuity. For her, the heroic chapter in later-adulthood follows an earlier chapter of heroic moral commitment. With respect to the first chapter, Fennelly described moving as a 27-year-old divorced housewife with two small children from California to Washington, DC because she felt "called" to do something for others with her life. After initially working in a faith-based soup kitchen she became an activist and advocate for the homeless as a leader of the Community for Creative Non-violence (CCNV). For 17 years, she and her partner (an influential advocate for the homeless) lived in CCNV's 1,400-bed homeless shelter for men in DC.

This earlier chapter of moral commitment was heroic in Franco et al.'s (2011) sense. CCNV catalyzed positive changes for homeless in DC and successfully raised awareness of homelessness nationally. But the work was filled with risk and sacrifice: Fennelly participated in hunger strikes, was arrested and jailed, and raised her two children in the homeless shelter. She weathered death threats and required police protection after leading an effort to drive drug traffickers out of the shelter. Given this, Fennelly's later-adult chapter constitutes objective continuity of heroic moral commitment.

Webb represents the other extreme: objective discontinuity of the later-adult heroic chapter with prior experience. After retirement, he was "settling in to have a nice, big, beautiful garden and fish and hunt the rest of my life… [and] content doing that"—he loved the natural beauty of Appalachia and envisioned in retirement preserving "the old mountain ways" by teaching them to young people—"but it got interrupted." Webb describes himself as politically conservative with no background in activism ("I was just kind of flying by the seat of my pants").

It should be clear how the two cases provide narratives of three heroic chapters: One first-time early-adult heroic chapter (Fennelly), one later-adult heroic chapter continuous with prior experience (Fennelly), and one first-time later-adult heroic chapter (Webb).

Narratives of Heroic Chapters

Analyzing the three heroic chapters just described, several observations can be made. First, they do illustrate that first-time heroism may be narrated in terms of positive personal change—that is, in terms of positive change in the hero as well as those who benefit from the hero's actions.

One example of narrating a first-time heroic chapter with personal change was provided by Carol Fennelly, who describes the chapter as beginning in adulthood (i.e., she does not begin the story in her youth). Consistent with the canonical hero narrative (Goethals & Allison, 2012), Fennelly narrates her first heroic chapter as one of profound change even though she offers a thread of narrative continuity with her young-adult self (in the shelter, "I always thought, 'I'm just a housewife with 1,400 men in my life'"). She depicts change as occurring via enrichment in two linked respects. She moved from a strong but vague helping instinct ("I was a housewife wanting to do a nice thing") to a capacity for effective action ("I learned how to make it reality"). And, she augmented this instinct to care ("a heart that requires me to respond") with a "sense of justice and rightness." Two other features of her narrative of this first-time heroic chapter also comport with the canonical hero's story from myth, described by Goethals and Allison (2012): She describes initially resisting when she experienced being called and she points to her late partner as contributing to her transformation ("he just taught me everything").

Perhaps more surprising, profound personal change proved to be equally characteristic of the narrative of a first-time heroic chapter that occurred in late adulthood, as seen in Bo Webb's case. Although a strong thread of continuity is provided by the skills from his primary career that carried forward and his deep, longstanding attachment to Appalachia, Webb's narrative depicts extensive positive change later in life in response to a strongly negative event. He articulates transformations in his views of others (you can't expect everyone to see the issue the way you want) and his personal relationships (his activism produced first criticism by others then their pride), as well as tremendous expansion of perspective, knowledge, and skills. Most notably, in Webb's narrative, his self-story had to be revised. The heroic chapter is understood as fundamentally changing his perception of his former self and his former way of acquiring attitudes:

> I had to learn a lot about myself, to be honest about it, because I used to be what I considered conservative … I found that I was being influenced by maybe a news program or by another person … And I look back at that and I realize I've been influenced by that instead of actually learning about it myself. You know? And when you educate yourself as to what's going on around you, then you can become a lot more real and know the truth. So yeah, I've learned to seek the truth …

His narrative is one of unsought growth, later in life, a result of first-time moral heroism:

> [I]t's totally changed my life, totally changed the way I think about the world. It woke me up to the better man—it made a better person out of me, I'll say that. Made me much more aware as to social issues. And how bad it is out there.

In addition to finding that chapters of first-time heroism, in both early and late adulthood, may be narrated with personal growth, we found that even in the context of long-term moral commitment, a new heroic chapter later in adulthood may be narrated in terms of positive change. This was illustrated by Carol Fennelly's second heroic chapter.

On the one hand, Fennelly's narrative of the later chapter conveys continuity, carrying forward gains attributed to the first heroic chapter (organizing skills, familiarity with the population served, and a sense of social justice) as well as what she characterizes as a housewife's priorities ("I care about helping these guys stay together with their children"). Further, this narrative does not describe fundamental transformations like those of her first-time, young-adult heroic chapter. The second heroic chapter nevertheless is narrated as occasioning positive personal change via unexpectedly deep relationships and a sense of community that have evolved with the families served, new capacities (she has developed greater "tact," learning to curb her activist impulse as she works within existing systems), and opportunities for creativity and learning ("every camp we learn something new").

In Fennelly's second heroic chapter positive change is most clearly seen in a different way, however, as the perception of continued rise in the narrated life trajectory during the second half of life. From a narrative-identity perspective, a person is identified with the life that they have led. One way this might be manifested is in conceptualizing positive change in the contour of the path traced by the life as narrated. That is, from a narrative perspective distinctions like meteoric rise, slow but steady gain, peak, plateau, ups and downs, and decline capture the direction and rate of perceived change and situate an individual chapter in the context of the longer path traced in the narrative.

Fennelly herself juxtaposed the two heroic chapters of her life. She acknowledged that her narrative at the end of the first heroic chapter raised the possibility that the best was behind her and a central part of her identity had been lost: "I was thinking when I was there ... this is my life, CCNV. You know? So, when I left there, I mean it was like, 'Oh my God. That was my life. Now I have none. What do I do?'" However, currently she narrates the later-life heroic chapter not as an echo or weaker reverberation, but instead as a destination toward which she had been growing in the past:

> And as I was starting Hope House, I realized that all that [i.e., CCNV]—that was not my life. That was preparation for this life. And this work. So I'm using all those skills that I really honed and learned at the shelter.

Fennelly concluded that rather than having been itself the apex of her life's work, "my last life with homeless people was getting me ready to do *this* work." This conveys how narratives are dynamic, constantly changing as one encounters new experiences that call for revision (McAdams, 2001), even if the peak already seemed determined.

Relevant to the growing number of older adults with decades of active life ahead of them in the traditional retirement years, Carol Fennelly's case also introduces the notion of a positive *recovery sequence*. That is, in part Fennelly's second heroic chapter is narrated as a recovery from the sense of "impotence" she ascribes to her suspension of direct social and political action during her interlude as a political commentator between the two heroic chapters. The narrative of recovery is of general interest because it points to one form of positive role change that people might deliberately craft in their *post-retirement* years if they experience loss of a valued work identity.

Two additional general points about these accounts should be made. First, the beginning of each of the heroic chapters represents a discontinuity in the personal narrative that requires meaning-making (Singer, 2004). In each instance, it was made coherent by narration in terms of felt necessity.

In Webb's case, a contamination sequence in McAdams' sense of good turned to bad (McAdams et al., 2001) was narrated as the catalyst of an instant moral commitment despite there being no precedent for it in his life. That is, the mining that he discovered violated, violently, the vital engagements that had brought him back to West Virginia: the place of his origins, its natural beauty, the loved activities it afforded, the valued traditions and living community associated with it. As he tells it, there was never a question he would act.

In Fennelly's case, the unifying theme in the early and late heroic chapters was the felt necessity imposed by experiencing a "call" to engage. Fennelly explained the calling in the early, first-time chapter as connecting to a vague altruistic instinct; she explained the calling in the later chapter as connecting to an identity, well established by then, as a faith-based, prosocial actor. In the early chapter, in contrast to Webb, accepting the call did not occur instantly; she resisted for some time. In the second heroic chapter, she did not resist the call, ascribing this to the lesson learned in the earlier chapter ("my experience is that if I know something is the right thing to do and I don't do it, bad things happen"). Webb's seeing the degradation of natural beauty and Fennelly's experience of a call both were reconciled through the resolve to act. The duty to answer the call provides the narrative with coherence, they both "did what they had to do." This makes the fact that they eventually ascribe personal change to their hero journey more compelling: they did not accept the challenge anticipating personal gain or growth, yet their narratives reflect a retrospective interpretation of the whole experience as having changed them for the better.

Second, we should draw a conceptual distinction between positive change narrated as a direct result of shouldering and surviving risk and danger versus what we see here, where change is narrated as having been made possible by determined persistence in the heroic undertaking.

These individuals do not narrate change via *the simple fact of heroism*, that is, via accepting and prevailing over risk and danger and/or reflecting upon the feat. For example, they do not say "in steeling myself, taking the risk, conquering my fears, etc., I developed qualities I had not had" or "I learned I had qualities I had not recognized." Rather, they narrate change via *the journey that their heroism allowed to unfold*. In these narratives, Fennelly moved toward populations and places that others shied away from approaching and Webb moved against forces that others held back from confronting. It was by not shrinking from danger that they stayed on the paths of social purpose they associated with personal change. This may be consistent with heroism that entails but is not defined by accepting risk of physical harm. These themes make the chapter heroic, but how they relate to the positive personal change experienced can only be understood within the larger narrative of the journey.

Discussion

The heroic chapters of these individuals' narratives demonstrate that significant moral action, including in later life, may be perceived as leading to positive change not only in the external world, which is its goal, but also in the individual, as a kind of collateral benefit. We found that the narratives were characterized by positive personal change in two different ways: as seen in the individual's growth or betterment as a person and as seen in a continued upward path, rather than maintenance or decline, during the second half of life. The second of these, the perceived trajectory of the life path, is an aspect of narrative identity that has received less attention than recurring themes and causal connections in studies of the personal narratives of moral exemplars.

"First-time" moral heroism to date also has been comparatively neglected in the small narrative literature on older moral exemplars, which instead has focused on older individuals who have sustained a long-term moral commitment into the second half of life. The present exploratory analysis begins to address this gap. These cases hold special interest from the standpoint of positive aging as models for what has been referred to as the *encore career*, a paid or unpaid undertaking after the end of an individual's primary career that addresses a social purpose (Freedman, 2006).

The present cases are also of interest because the unit of the heroic chapter, as contrasted with both lifelong commitments and isolated acts of heroism, may allow new questions to be asked, such as whether first-time heroism is narrated in terms of more fundamental personal change than subsequent heroic chapters in the same personal narrative—regardless of when in a life the first-time heroism occurs. That is, we saw in one case a narrative of fundamental personal transformation as part of a heroic chapter that began after retirement.

Future research also might fruitfully explore a notion of *one-time* heroic chapters (Roderick Kramer, personal communication, February 5, 2016), examining how individuals make sense of (perceived) single acts or episodes of heroism and their aftermath. The challenges of moving forward after such a chapter as well as integrating it into one's identity retrospectively are hinted at in Carol Fennelly's account of her experience during the interlude between her two chapters of heroism.

The case analyses in this section suggest several avenues for future research. For example, researchers might seek to identify factors (e.g., type of heroism) that make it more likely positive personal change will be associated with heroic action in narrative accounts. Research also might address whether the patterns described characterize equally well "non-heroic" moral exemplars (i.e., individuals who did not take on risk of physical harm and make large sacrifices). This would begin to address the question of the differences, if any, between the narrative identities of moral exemplars and moral heroes.

This section has shifted the focus of attention from the impact of heroic acts on their beneficiaries—the usual focus of stories of heroic acts—to their impact on the individuals who perform the acts, as expressed in the heroes' personal narratives. The specific question addressed was whether moral heroes narrate their experience in terms of positive personal change, even when heroism is a chapter in the second half of life, either for the first time or as part of a life of moral heroism. Along the way some readers may have found the narratives of these individuals' heroism inspiring or uplifting. We turn next to this third possible impact of heroic action: the effect of narratives of heroism—and of extraordinary moral action more generally—on their witnesses.

Witnesses' Stories of Heroism: Elevation and Personal Change

The previous section aligns with the growing literature on heroism with a focus on the hero. Finding positive personal change in the narratives of heroes furthers our understanding of the hero and complements other efforts to designate hero types, personality characteristics, motivations, and features of heroic action. However, the impact of the hero story does not end with the hero. Understanding the change prompted by heroism requires a look at those who witness heroic action, and the stories they tell about such heroism.

Literature celebrates the hero and acknowledges the importance of heroes as necessary at the societal level to engender hope and to provide an example worthy of emulation. From a psychological perspective, the reaction in the observer can be better understood by first considering how heroic actions make us feel. In particular, emotions constitute physiological and cognitive states that happen in response to a triggering event (Scherer, 2005). Some emotion theorists emphasize the social nature of emotions and argue that they are often triggered by social happenings and have social implications (Parkinson, 1996), which suggests that emotions are a good start in examining the response to a social event such as heroism. Emotions are not all the same; rather, discrete emotions have distinctive eliciting events, physiology, and appraisals among other defining characteristics. This section aims to identify the specific emotion state that is most distinctive of the response to heroism and use this to understand how heroism impacts the observer. We look toward literature on relevant emotions, those that are inherently moral, and those that are other-praising, to understand the impact of heroism on the observer. We put forth moral elevation as the primary emotion experienced in response to witnessing heroic action.

Although heroes have been defined in several ways, one prominent component to heroism involves moral action (Kinsella et al., 2015b; Walker et al., 2010; Goethals & Allison, 2012). This is true even of lay conceptions of heroism, as one study found that heroes serve as moral models of action (Kinsella et al., 2015b). This moral feature narrows the possible emotions that may be elicited from heroic action. For example, admiration might reasonably be felt towards a hero because of his or her abilities, but this emotion does not entail a moral situation. Admiration is triggered by a non-moral display of great talent, skill, or achievement (Algoe & Haidt, 2009), limiting the possibility that this would be felt following a heroic moral action. In the same vein, inspiration may also be thought of as a response to heroism. Inspiration is often considered a motivational state triggered by anything that reveals new or better possibilities (Thrash & Elliot, 2004) but is not the most fitting response to heroism as it does not require a moral trigger. According to Landis et al. (2009), elevation involves more direct connection to others than inspiration. This aligns with the hero literature as heroism involves connection to others through self–other overlap (Sullivan & Venter, 2005). This defining moral quality also differentiates heroes within the category of admirable others such as role models. Although both are worthy of emulation, role models may be celebrated for their success and achievement in a non-moral domain and need not take risks to qualify as a role model. To the extent that heroes engage in moral action, their observers must experience emotions that are specific to moral situations.

The Moral Emotion of Elevation

Moral emotions are characterized as responses to actions that transcend the direct interests of the self (Haidt, 2003b). According to Haidt (2003b), the defining features of moral emotions are that their elicitors do not directly involve the self, and that they somehow promote prosocial behavior. In his categorization of moral emotions, Haidt (2003b) places moral emotions into four families: the self-conscious family, the other-condemning family, the other-suffering family, and the other-praising family. Specific instances of heroism might elicit moral emotions such as compassion at the plight of another, disgust at maltreatment, contempt, or anger at an injustice. Isolating the heroic action, however, only involves the act of benevolence in light of risk, and onlookers are left with positive emotions toward the hero. Specifically, we look to the other-praising moral emotions family to understand a response to heroism. Gratitude and elevation comprise this family of emotions. Gratitude involves the perception that a benefactor intentionally is benefitting the self (Haidt, 2003b). In the situation of heroism, one who directly benefits from a heroic act might indeed feel gratitude towards the hero if he or she was the recipient of heroic action. This is limited though in describing a general response to heroism as it does not consider those who hear or witness the heroic act but are not a direct part of the story. To satisfy all of the above criteria, we turn to moral elevation.

Elevation is defined as the response to witnessing an act of moral beauty. Haidt (2000) attributes the name of the emotion to Thomas Jefferson, who described how reading about moral acts in literature can create "a strong desire in ourselves of doing charitable and grateful acts also." Elevation is triggered by a moral act of which one is not the beneficiary. It has been distinguished empirically from other, similar emotions such as gratitude, awe, and amusement (Algoe & Haidt, 2009; Siegel, Thomson, & Navarro, 2014; Schnall, Roper & Fessler, 2010). The emotion involves feeling warmth in the chest, tears in the eyes, uplifted, and inspired (Haidt, 2003a). To the extent that heroism is characterized by extraordinary moral acts, elevation represents the most fitting emotional response.

Elevation as a response to heroism is further illustrated when considering the opposite of both elevation and heroism. According to Haidt (2003a) the opposite of moral elevation is social disgust, triggered by a moral transgression that causes us to feel nauseous and want to close the self off, as opposed to feelings of warmth and opening up that characterize elevation. Turning to heroes, Zimbardo (2007) contrasts heroic action with villainous actions humanity is capable of as demonstrated by his 1971 prison experiment. To learn of the maltreatment these participants enacted towards each other causes one to draw inward and feel distaste, or social disgust. One can imagine, however, the feeling that would have accompanied learning that one fictitious prisoner stood up for another and helped despite clear risk—that of elevation.

The contrast between moral elevation and social disgust maps perfectly onto the hero/villain distinction, demonstrating how elevation as a response to heroism provides a complete picture of the effect of heroism. Gray and Wegner (2011) touched upon the relationship between elevation and heroism in their examination of the dyadic structure of moral emotions. They proposed that moral emotions have a dyadic structure and fall along two dimensions: valence (help/harm) and moral type (moral agent/moral patient). Heroes and villains both fall at the moral agent pole of the continuum, as they represent the moral actors. However, heroes are on the "help" end, whereas villains are on the "harm" end. The authors assert that villains elicit disgust and anger, whereas heroes elicit inspiration and elevation. The current endeavor furthers this connection by examining how elevation may be the mechanism through which moral heroism changes others.

How Elevation Changes the Observer

Witnessing an act of moral beauty engenders a change in the observer's views, desires, and actual behavior. Beyond the corresponding feelings and physiological response, elevation also involves a positive cognitive response through feeling increasingly optimistic about humanity as a whole (Algoe & Haidt, 2009). The moral acts cause one to not only think favorably of the moral actor, but also generalize this positive view to humanity. This aligns with theorizing about the importance of heroes for society, heroes make us feel hopeful about the human race (Allison & Goethals, 2011). Elevation is the mechanism through which such positive feelings towards humanity arise. Another integral part of elevation involves the desire to be a better person through moral behavior (Algoe & Haidt, 2009). This is the piece of inspiration specific to morality that is likely triggered when witnessing the actions of a moral hero. Not only does the moral hero elicit an emotional response, but the heroism also motivates the observer to become better.

Empirical research has shown that the effect does not stop at mere desire, but feeling elevated results in actual prosocial behavior. Specifically, elevation promotes a variety of prosocial behaviors such as donation behavior (Thomson & Siegel, 2013), helping behaviors (Schnall et al., 2010), mentoring (Thomson, Nakamura, Siegel, & Csikszentmihalyi, 2014), volunteering (Cox, 2010), willingness to take an unpaid survey (Schnall & Roper, 2012), and organizational citizenship behavior (Vianello, Galliani, & Haidt, 2010). Several of these studies have shown how elevation can result in prosocial behavior that is different from that shown in the elevation trigger. For example, Schnall et al. (2010) induced elevation by showing a clip from *Oprah* involving the kindness of a music teacher to his student, which resulted in participants being willing to stay to complete a complicated math questionnaire as well as help with a tedious task. This suggests that the way in which one is prosocial following elevation is not limited to simply modeling the good act witnessed. Rather, being elevated involves the desire to do something good that is attainable and available to the observer. This is important for heroism given the exceptional nature of heroic acts—it suggests that heroism still motivates prosocial behavior even if replicating the exact heroic act is impossible.

The way in which elevation changes the observer is not limited to views of humanity and increased prosocial behavior. One recent study (Graham, 2015) has revealed through narratives of elevation that some people incur a self-designated change as a result of an elevating event. Specifically, a third of the narratives of elevation were coded for "growth" as represented by a self-designated change directly attributed to the moral act witnessed. From a narrative perspective, the self-change resulting from the elevating event indicates that the observer integrated this event into their own narrative identity. In other words, this instance of witnessing a good deed has implications for who the person is today, despite the fact that they were not directly involved. This transformative effect of moral acts suggests that heroic moral acts might go beyond uplifting one's views of humanity and inspiring others to do good deeds toward actually becoming a better person as a result of an elevating instance.

Moral elevation is a logical answer to the question of how a hero's action affects those who witness or learn of the heroism. It is intuitive that heroic moral action would uplift and inspire us morally. However, the trigger of elevation is not exclusive to heroes. Elevation needs only moral action to be triggered, whereas heroic moral action requires some degree of risk or sacrifice (Franco et al., 2011). Although we might infer that heroic actions are more compelling, it is currently unknown whether or not the elevating stories individuals generate could be considered "heroic" according to our definition. Further, precisely because of the risk and sacrifice entailed, from a social comparison perspective the opposite might be true: instead, heroic actions might be less elevating than other moral actions. We go beyond speculation about the connection between elevation and heroism by looking to data to examine the possibility of a relation and to illustrate what elevating heroism sounds like.

Case of Moral Elevation Narratives

One way to study elevation involves looking to personal elevation memories. Narratives of elevating memories offer opportunities for rich analysis of the features of the elevating stories individuals choose to narrate. In addition, recalling an elevating memory has proven to induce elevation in the moment (Algoe & Haidt, 2009). We examined the frequency of hero narratives as well as the relation of recalling hero stories to the emotion of moral elevation.

The data reported here came from a larger project examining the relation between moral elevation and eudaimonia (Graham, 2015). Participants included 321 adults from the U.S. who filled out an online survey. The survey included a prompt that asked about an elevation memory, which was modeled after a "turning point narrative" (McAdams & Bowman, 2001; McAdams et al., 2006). Participants were asked to think of a situation when they witnessed "an act of moral beauty in which someone or a group of people display the goodness of humanity in a memorable way." They were asked to write in detail about "a specific time when you learned of such an act expressing people's higher or better nature" when they themselves were not the beneficiary of the good deed. The instance didn't require that the person witness the moral act in person, rather it could be something they watched on television, heard about, or read about. A preliminary study confirmed that elevation in the moment was elicited from the narrative prompt.

In order to examine the prevalence of heroism in the elevation narratives, we coded the responses as "heroic" or "non-heroic". Responses that did not involve moral action of another to another were eliminated from analysis. To fit our definition of heroism, we coded narratives as "heroic" if they involved a clear risk or sacrifice. Narratives that mentioned specific heroic words such as "risk, sacrifice, hero, brave" when describing another person's moral action were coded as heroic. In addition, narratives that did not include heroic words were also coded as heroic if the moral situation involved implicit but objective risk or sacrifice in light of danger (e.g., running into a burning building to save a child).

We found evidence of heroic themes in 58 (18%) of the narratives. This is informative for a number of reasons. The prompt did not call for an explicitly "heroic" story, rather, only for a good deed to another. When asked to generate a memory about witnessing good, 17 percent of the individuals came up with a memory about a hero. There are several ways of interpreting this. This could indicate that memories of good deeds without risk or sacrifice are more plentiful and therefore easier for individuals to draw from. This makes sense in light of the fact that heroic acts are extraordinary and therefore maybe there is a smaller memory bank of heroic stories compared to moral stories from which to draw.

Alternatively, research on prototypic hero characteristics suggests a different interpretation. Kinsella et al. (2015a) found that lay conceptions of heroes primarily consist of central hero features including "brave, moral integrity, courageous", whereas peripheral hero features such as "caring, compassionate" aid in the identification of heroes but not as strongly as the central features. That the instruction didn't explicitly ask for a hero story but one that aligns more with the peripheral hero features of "compassion and caring" could have impacted which stories were called forth. However, despite no mention of hero in the instructions, still a sixth of the participants generated hero stories. This indicates that when some think of an example of moral beauty, their mind automatically goes to a story involving risk and sacrifice.

Thirty-one of the elevation narratives explicitly mentioned a specific hero word (e.g., hero, danger, risk, sacrifice, brave). For example, one person describes:

> In the big earthquake in Sichuan Province in China, a child who is only 10 years old saved many lives. I saw this in the news. The boy is so cute and brave. He is the class monitor in his class. When the earthquake came, everyone is very scared and nervous. And many of his classmates and teachers were buried in the collapsed houses. The little hero saved himself firstly and climb out from the collapse classroom [sic]. Then he went back to save others bravely in the aftershock. Many people were moved by him, and so do I [sic]. I will try my best to help others in the future.

Other stories entailed a situation in which there was implicit risk or sacrifice but the participant didn't explicitly use specific hero words. For example, one person remembered:

> When I was little, I heard a story about one of my cousins going out of his way to help a friend. I thought that maybe he gave the friend money, or something else like that, but his generosity went far beyond money. The friend was in need of an emergency liver transplant. My cousin decided to undergo the surgery in order to donate some of his liver to the friend. I was very moved by this story. It made me realize what a true friend my cousin was, and how far he was willing to go to help a friend in need. The liver transplant, while the friend eventually did pass away, prolonged his life for a much longer time than if my cousin had not donated his liver.

Although 17 percent of the elevating stories did qualify as hero stories, the majority did not include an element of risk or sacrifice. Most stories centered around a protagonist who conveyed kindness and generosity through an act of moral beauty that was perhaps unexpected, but involved little risk. For example, one participant described a woman paying for another person's groceries:

> I was shopping at a local grocery store sometime last year, I went into the checkout line and there was an elderly woman about three shoppers ahead of me in the line, the cashier stated her total and the woman was short about 40 dollars. She nervously started looking through her bags and proceeded to take out some essential items. Before she could finish, a nice lady took out her own debit card and covered the whole amount of the lady's grocery bill. I have done that in the past before for a few people but seeing someone else step up like that made me realize that yes there are still good people around.

One way in which the two types of stories were similar was in their capacity to elevate. Analysis revealed that there was no difference between heroic stories and non-heroic stories in the degree to which the study participant was elevated. Elements of elevation can be seen in the content of both types of stories when one mentions a heightened view of humanity or desire to be more prosocial. In the examples from above the non-heroic narrative mentioned that it "made me realize that yes there are still good people around" and one heroic example said, "I will try my best to help others in the future". Both types of stories included instances without trace elements of elevation and simply involved the recounting of an act of moral beauty, either with or without risk.

Regardless of heroic stories not being significantly more or less elevating, it is clear that the heroic action in some cases did seem to be a catalyst of change in the person. This was apparent through the changes in views of humanity and prosocial behavior (the elevating elements highlighted above) but also there was explicit mention of being substantially impacted as a person in some cases. The change in these narratives is directly attributed to the elevating event, long-lasting, and goes beyond wanting to be more prosocial to being motivated to become a better person in general or in multiple domains. For example:

> The biggest event I can remember though was perhaps when I was about six years old and I saw a man push a little boy from my neighborhood out of the way when a wreck happened near his house. There were two cars and they collided head on into each other and he ran over to grab up this little boy that he did not even know and in the process he was hit by one of the cars and suffered a broken leg and a fractured arm. I remember him saying to a paramedic that it was all worth it because the boy was not hurt. It made such an impact on me. Knowing that a stranger truly would risk their life for a stranger. I was inspired to always be the best person I could be.

This change present in some of the moral hero narratives suggests that the influence of heroes on others has the potential to go beyond inspiring one to do good in a similar way despite risk, but toward developing into an all-around better person.

The lack of difference between the hero/non-hero stories in their capacity to elevate and change the observer presents an interesting finding given that a number of viable contrary predictions could have been made. Employing Festinger's (1954) social comparison theory, one might assume heroic stories to be less elevating as they elicit self-comparison as opposed to transcending of the self. Comparing oneself to a "superior other" (e.g., upward social comparison) is often thought to be self-deflating and is related to negative affect and a decrease in well-being (Wheeler & Miyake, 1992). However, the hero narratives in which there was clear social comparison almost always resulted in motivation to be better as opposed to deterring positive change as a result of feeling inferior. For example:

> In New York City a man fell on the subway tracks and another man jumped on the tracks to save him. This happened in 2007 during the winter time. The man I guess had a seizure and when he fell on the tracks the other man jumped onto them [sic] and rolled him into a tiny one-foot space as the train rolled over them. He felt it was the right thing to do. When I read the story I thought how incredibly heroic a stranger would risk his life to save another. I always admire people like that because it is one thing if it is your job (firefighter, doctor, police officer, soldier) you understand the risks you are taking because you have the calling to do so. But when in the moment, when you out of nowhere see a situation like that and decide to yourself that you have to be the one to save them when no one else will takes such courage. Reading stories like this makes me wish that I had that courage, I wish I could be more selfless to strangers. I would do anything to save my family and children,

but risking my life for a questionable stranger takes more courage than I think I have. It has changed me in that I try every day to think I could be that brave of a person and I hope to myself if ever confronted with a situation like this I would do the same thing.

The motivation reflected in the moral hero narratives aligns with an alternative view regarding upward social comparison: that it may lead to hope and inspiration that leads to self-improvement (Lockwood & Kunda, 2000; Wood, 1989). Regardless, the relationship between upward social comparison and negative affect still might prompt one to anticipate moral hero stories to be less elevating.

Another possible prediction involves the idea that moral hero stories might elicit awe as opposed to elevation. Awe involves a challenge to one's current understanding caused by something perceived to be greater than the self (Keltner & Haidt, 2003). Awe may also be "flavored" by other themes including threat (e.g., danger) or exceptional ability. Because heroic moral actions involve extraordinary acts of exceptional ability in light of risk or danger, one might assume that awe is elicited from such actions, and that elevation is specific only to moral actions that are less "awe-inspiring". However, awe is triggered specifically by something perceived as "vast" or "powerful" which does not always apply to the actions of a moral hero. Further, awe is typically associated with feeling lowered or inferior to the trigger (Keltner & Haidt, 2003), which does not align with findings on how heroism involves feeling similar to the hero (Sullivan & Venter, 2005). Although these lines of thinking present viable reasons one may have predicted moral hero stories to be more elevating, the results cannot be explained by either prediction.

In contrast, there are a number of reasons to think that hero narratives may have been more elevating. Research shows that perceived effort of the protagonist in an elevating story is related to higher elevating responses (Thomson & Siegel, 2013). One who does a good deed in spite of risk or danger might be seen as putting forth greater effort, and thus be more elevating. This is apparent through comparing the examples previously mentioned, the hero example in which a child faced danger to save the lives of others might be perceived as high effort, whereas the non-heroic story in which a woman paid for another person's groceries might be perceived as less effort.

Similarly, an argument for hero stories being more elevating comes simply from the compelling nature of such stories. Given that certain elements of stories resonate and entertain more than others (e.g., plot thickening, suspense, drama), one might posit that moral stories with drama and excitement are more elevating because the observer is more engaged in the story, thus experiencing stronger corresponding emotions as a result. The difference in a sense of narrative drama was apparent in the hero narratives as opposed to stories of simple kindness without risk. Many of the hero narratives described rich experiences of witnessing heroes in which the person seemed to be profoundly moved by such action. To the reader, these may arguably be even more appealing and entertaining than the others as the heroic elements add undeniable drama. One woman describes the following scenario:

> I was watching a news story on television about a house fire. The firefighters had been called but had yet to arrive. People on the scene were yelling that there was someone still in the house that had not made it out. A man walking by at the time walked into the burning house and came running out carrying an older man to safety. I was thinking about how this man might die in the fire. I felt nervous looking at the frantic situation. I was watching as the man came out of nowhere to go into the burning building and my heart warmed as I saw his brave and selfless actions. My eyes welled with tears as I saw this man bring the older man out of the house to safety. The situation was also warming listening to newscasters talk about how this stranger acted in kindness and then left as quickly as he

appeared. He wasn't doing what he did for praise or reward, he was just doing the right thing out of his care for someone else. His actions made me want to be brave and hopefully make a similar decision if I were faced with saving someone's life. This event gave me a stronger faith in people.

Although there were apparent differences between narratives as compelling story forms, this element still did not account for the lack of differences in how elevating each story was. In all, heroic narratives are just as elevating as non-heroic narratives, suggesting that moral elevation might be the appropriate response for both moral beauty, and moral beauty in the face of risk or danger.

Discussion

We have proposed that elevation is the most fitting response to witnessing heroism. This is grounded conceptually as heroism is conceived of as involving moral action, which gives rise to a moral emotion. Elevation is the most appropriate emotion given that it is triggered by an extraordinary act of moral beauty of which the self was not a beneficiary. Analysis of elevation narratives revealed that some individuals do think of stories of heroism (e.g., moral acts involving great sacrifice, risk or danger) when asked to write about an elevating memory, even when there is no prompt to think of heroic stories. Despite the potential negative element of risk and danger, the moral hero stories were just as elevating as stories of simple altruism. Further, some of the stories even included the designation of a change in the self as a result of witnessing such heroism.

The results are valuable in showing us that some individuals recall heroic acts when asked to write about an act of moral beauty and that these are on average neither more nor less elevating than their risk-free counterparts. It is possible that for some people, when it comes to moral acts, stories of heroism are most moving and thus they call one forth when thinking about stories that are morally inspiring. Future research might seek to explore if stories of heroism are equally as elevating as altruism for everyone, or if this effect only exists for those for whom benevolence in the face of great sacrifice, risk and danger resonates deeply. However, given the pervasiveness of heroism in literature, movies, and television, it is likely that heroism is compelling for everyone as a story-form, but also equally as moving as altruism.

This chapter presents evidence to suggest that heroism and altruism both elicit the same emotion. Elevation as a response to both heroism and altruism does not negate the definitional and prototypical distinctions between the two kinds of act. Rather, it is their shared component of moral action that inspires in a similar way despite the risk and danger involved in heroism. It is possible that the moral act that defines both is so powerfully inspiring that it doesn't matter if there is risk or sacrifice involved. Not only do these moral acts uplift those who learn of them, but they have the capacity to change people for the better. Through elevation, heroic acts inspire better views of humanity, prosocial behavior, and in some instances, are credited with changing the witness for the better. Although this is true of both heroism and altruism, the absorbing elements of the hero story may be key in facilitating these changes in an indirect way. If the most captivating stories that grab our attention are those that involve goodness in light of danger, then it is possible that hero stories present the best opportunity to elicit elevation.

Conclusion and Future Directions

We have proposed that the story of moral heroism does not end with the heroic action. Rather, stories of heroism are internalized and recounted with an element of personal change. In two lines of analysis we selected cases for study by adhering to Franco et al.'s (2011) definition of heroes as individuals who *incur risk and sacrifice* in the course of successfully meeting others' needs and we drew on the moral exemplar, narrative psychology, and moral emotion literatures to consider the question of whether acting heroically and witnessing heroism (as defined by Franco et al.) are associated with self-reported positive change. Future research comparing moral exemplars who have undertaken risk and sacrifice with those who have not might help clarify the hero construct. Personal narratives of moral exemplars revealed that one's "hero chapter" in later life involves personal change. Stories of others' heroism were found among narratives of elevation, demonstrating how heroic actions may change those who learn of them through elevation. Both ways in which heroism has an impact represent areas in need of further exploration.

Hero narratives provided a unique look into how one conceptualizes one's own heroism. We found that first-time heroism was characterized by personal growth, and that change was even present in a second heroic chapter through the perception that an unexpected life course was charted. Future research could build on this start by determining what types of personal growth are ascribed to heroism and by further examining how the anticipated contour of one's life is affected by heroism. A longitudinal study would shed light on how one's perceived life trajectory continues or is disrupted when an opportunity to act heroically arises. Further, comparing narratives of this type of heroic chapter with narratives of one-time heroic acts would help to determine if stories of positive transformation are specific to this type of heroism or may be generalized to other types.

Elevation as a response to witnessing heroism also provides a rich opportunity for future research. We found that when prompted to tell a story of elevation, some generated stories of moral heroism. Aligning with Gray and Wegner's (2011) theorizing, elevation seemed to be a response to recalling others' heroic acts as these stories were just as uplifting as stories of less harrowing moral beauty. Empirical research could further explore this connection by assessing the effectiveness of a moral heroism manipulation at eliciting elevation in comparison to a standard elevation manipulation. We also found evidence of personal change in narratives about witnessing moral heroism, encouraging future efforts to determine how commonly such change is experienced and the conditions under which moral heroism is most likely to prompt personal change in the observer.

The transformative impact of heroism on both the hero and observer has implications for how we think about heroism. The story of heroism is no longer limited to impact through entertainment or providing a role model. Rather, heroism may be a catalyst for change in the hero despite limiting factors such as age or no intention of change. Those who commit to a moral cause and make sacrifices in the context of risk or danger may be better off in ways they hadn't anticipated. Further, the ability of heroism to inspire those not directly involved suggests that stories of heroism reach beyond their immediate beneficiaries and provide an opportunity of growth for the observer. Heroism invites a positive transformation that transcends the immediate present and lives on in the stories of those impacted by its positive effects.

Acknowledgments

We gratefully acknowledge Encore.org (formerly Civic Ventures), in particular Jim Emerman, Eunice Lin Nichols, and Aireen Navarro Khauv, and the John Templeton Foundation, who made possible the study of moral exemplars on which this chapter draws.

References

Algoe, S. B., & Haidt, J. (2009). Witnessing excellence in action: The "other-praising" emotions of elevation, gratitude, and admiration. *Journal of Positive Psychology, 4*(2), 105–127.

Allison, S. T., & Goethals, G. R. (2011). *Heroes: What they do and why we need them.* New York: Oxford University Press.

Bauer, J. J., & McAdams, D. P. (2004). Personal growth in adults' stories of life transitions. *Journal of Personality*, 72(3), 573–602.

Bauer, J. J., & McAdams, D. P. (2010). Eudaimonic growth: Narrative growth goals predict increases in ego development and subjective well-being 3 years later. *Developmental Psychology*, 46(4), 761–772.

Bauer, J. J., & Park, S. W. (2010). Growth is not just for the young: Growth narratives, eudaimonic resilience, and the aging self. In P. S. Fry, C. L. M. Keyes (eds), *New frontiers in resilient aging: Life-strengths and well-being in late life* (pp. 60–89). Cambridge, UK: Cambridge University Press.

Bauer, J. J., McAdams, D. P., & Sakaeda, A. R. (2005). Interpreting the good life: Growth memories in the lives of mature, happy people. *Journal of Personality and Social Psychology*, 88(1), 203–217.

Carstensen, L. L. (2006). The influence of a sense of time on human development. *Science*, 312, 1913–1915.

Cohler, B. J. (1982). Personal narrative and life course. In P. B. Baltes & O. G. Brim (eds), *Life-span development and behavior* (Vol. 4, pp. 205–241). New York: Academic Press.

Colby, A., & Damon, W. (1992). *Some do care.* New York: Free Press.

Cox, K. S. (2010). Elevation predicts domain-specific volunteerism 3 months later. *Journal of Positive Psychology*, 5(5), 333–341.

Dunlop, W. L., & Walker, L. J. (2013). The personality profile of brave exemplars: A person-centered analysis. *Journal of Research in Personality*, 47(4), 380–384.

Dunlop, W. L., Walker, L. J., & Matsuba, M. K. (2012). The distinctive moral personality of care exemplars. *Journal of Positive Psychology*, 7(2), 131–143.

Dunlop, W. L., Walker, L. J., & Matsuba, M. K. (2013). The development of moral motivation across the adult lifespan. *European Journal of Developmental Psychology*, 10, 285–300.

Festinger, L. (1954). A theory of social comparison processes. *Human Relations*, 7(2), 117–140.

Franco, Z. E., Blau, K., & Zimbardo, P. G. (2011). Heroism: A conceptual analysis and differentiation between heroic action and altruism. *Review of General Psychology*, 15(2), 99–113.

Freedman, M. (2006). The social-purpose encore career: Baby boomers, civic engagement, and the next stage of work. *Generations*, 30(4), 43–46.

Frimer, J. A., Walker, L. J., Lee, B. H., Riches, A., & Dunlop, W. L. (2012). Hierarchical integration of agency and communion: A study of influential moral figures. *Journal of Personality*, 80(4), 1117–1145.

Gardner, H., Csikszentmihalyi, M., & Damon, W. (2001). *Good work.* New York: Basic Books.

Goethals, G. R., & Allison, S. T. (2012). Making heroes: The construction of courage, competence, and virtue. In J. M. Olson & M. P. Zanna (eds), *Advances in experimental social psychology* (Vol. 46, pp. 183–235). San Diego, CA: Elsevier.

Graham, L. E. (2015). The elevated good life: Moral elevation and elevation narratives in relation to eudaimonic well-being. Unpublished manuscript.

Gray, K., & Wegner, D. M. (2011). Dimensions of moral emotions. *Emotion Review*, 3(3), 258–260.

Haidt, J. (2000). The positive emotion of elevation. *Prevention and Treatment*, 3(3). Retrieved from http://journals.apa.org/prevention/volume3/pre0030003c.html.

Haidt, J. (2003a). Elevation and the positive psychology of morality. In C. L. M. Keyes & J. Haidt (eds) *Flourishing: Positive psychology and the life well-lived* (pp. 275–289). Washington DC: American Psychological Association.

Haidt, J. (2003b). The moral emotions. In R. J. Davidson, K. R. Scherer, & H. H. Goldsmith (eds), *Handbook of affective sciences* (pp. 852–870). Oxford: Oxford University Press.

Keltner, D., & Haidt, J. (2003). Approaching awe, a moral, spiritual, and aesthetic emotion. *Cognition & Emotion*, 17(2), 297–314.

Kinsella, E. L., Ritchie, T. D., & Igou, E. R. (2015a). Zeroing in on heroes: A prototype analysis of hero features. *Journal of Personality and Social Psychology*, 108(1), 114–127.

Kinsella, E. L., Ritchie, T. D., & Igou, E. R. (2015b). Lay perspectives on the social and psychological functions of heroes. *Frontiers in Psychology*, 6, 130.

Landis, S. K., Sherman, M. F., Piedmont, R. L., Kirkhart, M. W., Rapp, E. M., & Bike, D. H. (2009). The relation between elevation and self-reported prosocial behavior: Incremental validity over the five-factor model of personality. *Journal of Positive Psychology*, 4(1), 71–84.

Lilgendahl, J. P., & McAdams, D. P. (2011). Constructing stories of self-growth: How individual differences in patterns of autobiographical reasoning relate to well-being in midlife. *Journal of Personality*, 79, 391–428.

Lockwood, P., & Kunda, Z. (2000). Outstanding role models: Do they inspire or demoralize us? In A. Tesser, R. B. Felson, & J. M. Suls (eds), *Psychological perspectives on self and identity* (pp. 147–171). Washington, DC: American Psychological Association.

Matusuba, K., King, P. E., & Bronk, K. C. (eds). (2013). Exemplar research [special issue]. *New Directions for Child and Adolescent Development*, 142(4).

Matsuba, M. K., & Walker, L. J. (2005). Young adult moral exemplars: The making of self through stories. *Journal of Research on Adolescence*, *15*, 275–297.

McAdams, D. P. (2001). The psychology of life stories. *Review of General Psychology*, *5*(2), 100–122.

McAdams, D. P. (2008). Personal narratives and the life story. In O. P. John, R. W. Robins, & L. A. Pervin (eds), *Handbook of personality: Theory and research* (Vol. 3, pp. 242–262). New York: Guilford Press.

McAdams, D. P., & Bowman, P. J. (2001). Narrating life's turning points: Redemption and contamination. In D. P. McAdams, R. Josselson & A. Lieblich (eds), *Turns in the road: Narrative studies of lives in transition* (pp. 3–34). Washington, DC: American Psychological Association.

McAdams, D. P., & Guo, J. (2015). Narrating the generative life. *Psychological Science*, *26*(4), 475–483.

McAdams, D. P., Bauer, J. J., Sakaeda, A. R., Anyidoho, N. A., Machado, M. A., Magrino Failla, K., ... & Pals, J. L. (2006). Continuity and change in the life story: A longitudinal study of autobiographical memories in emerging adulthood. *Journal of Personality*, *74*(5), 1371–1400.

McAdams, D. P., Reynolds, J., Lewis, M., Patten, A. H., & Bowman, P. J. (2001). When bad things turn good and good things turn bad: Sequences of redemption and contamination in life narrative and their relation to psychosocial adaptation in midlife adults and in students. *Personality and Social Psychology Bulletin*, *27*(4), 474–485.

Nakamura, J., & Fajans, J. (2014). Interviewing highly eminent creators. In D. K. Simonton (ed.), *The Wiley handbook of genius* (pp. 33–61). Chichester: Wiley.

Nakamura, J., Shernoff, D., & Hooker, C. (2009). *Good mentoring*. San Francisco, CA: Jossey-Bass.

Pals, J. L. (2006). Constructing the "springboard effect": Causal connections, self-making, and growth within the life story. In D. P. McAdams, R. Josselson, & A. Lieblich (eds), *Identity and story: Creating self in narrative* (pp. 175–199). Washington, DC: American Psychological Association.

Parkinson, B. (1996). Emotions are social. *British Journal of Psychology*, *87*(4), 663–683.

Scherer, K. R. (2005). What are emotions? And how can they be measured? *Social Science Information*, *44*(4), 695–729.

Schnall, S., & Roper, J. (2012). Elevation puts moral values into action. *Social Psychological and Personality Science*, *3*(3), 373–378.

Schnall, S., Roper, J., & Fessler, D. M. (2010). Elevation leads to altruistic behavior. *Psychological Science*, *21*(3), 315–320.

Siegel, J. T., Thomson, A. L., & Navarro, M. A. (2014). Experimentally distinguishing elevation from gratitude: Oh, the morality. *Journal of Positive Psychology*, *9*(5), 414–427.

Singer, J. A. (2004). Narrative identity and meaning making across the adult lifespan: An introduction. *Journal of Personality*, *72*(3), 437–460.

Sullivan, M. P., & Venter, A. (2005). The hero within: Inclusion of heroes into the self. *Self and Identity*, *4*(2), 101–111.

Thomson, A. L., & Siegel, J. T. (2013). A moral act, elevation, and prosocial behavior: Moderators of morality. *Journal of Positive Psychology*, *8*(1), 50–64.

Thomson, A. L., Nakamura, J., Siegel, J. T., & Csikszentmihalyi, M. (2014). Elevation and mentoring: An experimental assessment of causal relations. *Journal of Positive Psychology*, *9*(5), 402–413.

Thrash, T. M., & Elliot, A. J. (2004). Inspiration: Core characteristics, component processes, antecedents, and function. *Journal of Personality and Social Psychology*, *87*(6), 957–973.

Vianello, M., Galliani, E. M., & Haidt, J. (2010). Elevation at work: The effects of leaders' moral excellence. *Journal of Positive Psychology*, *5*(5), 390–411.

Walker, L. J., & Frimer, J. A. (2007). Moral personality of brave and caring exemplars. *Journal of Personality and Social Psychology*, *93*(5), 845–860.

Walker, L. J., Frimer, J. A., & Dunlop, W. L. (2010). Varieties of moral personality: Beyond the banality of heroism. *Journal of Personality*, *78*(3), 907–942.

Wheeler, L., & Miyake, K. (1992). Social comparison in everyday life. *Journal of Personality and Social Psychology*, *62*(5), 760–773.

Wood, J. V. (1989). Theory and research concerning social comparisons of personal attributes. *Psychological Bulletin*, *106*, 231–248.

Zimbardo, P. (2007). *The Lucifer effect: Understanding how good people turn evil*. New York: Random House.

Zuckerman, H. (1977). *Scientific elite*. New Brunswick, NJ: Transaction Publishers.

23
Accidental and Purposeful Impediments to Heroism

Craig D. Parks

Comic book fans know that Spider-Man's most persistent nemesis is not a villain, but rather newspaper publisher J. Jonah Jameson, who not only criticizes Spider-Man's every action in print, but also alleges that Spider-Man wears a mask because he himself is a criminal. Jameson argues that Spider-Man is motivated not by a desire to fight crime, but by a desire for personal glory. He offers a reward for Spider-Man's capture, and hires people to defeat Spider-Man. In issue 10 of *The Amazing Spider-Man* (March 1964), Jameson admits that his dislike of Spider-Man is motivated by a negative comparison: Jameson thinks of himself as a good man, but believes he looks incompetent when compared to Spider-Man. In issue 175 of *The Spectacular Spider-Man* (April 1991), Spider-Man's wife suggests that the dislike stems from Spider-Man's failure to follow the rules of law enforcement, despite the fact that he successfully captures criminals.[1]

Fortunately for the residents of New York City, Spider-Man looks past Jameson's hostility and continues to fight crime. But there are many real-world budding heroes who experience the same treatment but cannot put it behind them. Instead, these people reduce their efforts so that they perform like everyone else, sometimes abandon good works entirely, and occasionally even quit the group. Such reactions are at once expected, understandable, and harmful to the collective welfare. Further, while some of these potential real-world heroes have their own Jonah Jamesons to deal with, others are victims of accidental discouragements: The person who can break up a fight but doesn't, because no one else seems inclined to do so; the man who wants to volunteer at a preschool, but will not, because working with little children is seen as unmanly in his social circle; the driver of an old car who needs help with a breakdown but does not receive it, because of an assumption that it is dangerous to assist low-income individuals.

In this chapter, I will review both accidental and purposeful impediments to the expression of heroic behavior. I define an *accidental* impediment as any social or psychological phenomenon that has the side effect of inhibiting heroism, and a *purposeful* impediment as a phenomenon that is intended to suppress heroic action by someone else. My focus is on everyday heroism. The question of why someone would not act for people caught in an extreme situation, like genocide or mass starvation, is an important one but beyond our scope. The interested reader is directed to Staub (2002) as an entry point for this topic.

Prior Thought on Impediments to Heroism

The idea that those who have the chance to be a hero may be inhibited from taking the opportunity is not new. Shontz and Fink (1959) argued that heroism is a behavior that most people forgo; their explanation for this was that people tend to associate heroism with a degree of discomfort that few will willingly experience. In a study of student volunteers at a mental health clinic, Gelineau and Kantor (1964) found that while most students voiced support for volunteering at the clinic, many refused to actually volunteer, for fear of disapproval from their friends. In his taxonomy of mixed-motive games, Rapoport (1967; see also Harris, 1969) defined a "hero" as someone who performs an action that improves outcomes for all involved, with others experiencing a greater improvement than the actor. Guyer and Rapoport (1969) speculated that, because the action produces a better outcome for others than for self, people given the opportunity to be a hero will rarely take it. To test this, they placed people into one of the two-person, repeated-trial situations of interdependence shown in Figure 23.1. In these situations, people choose simultaneously and without interaction. In each, choices quickly (usually on the first trial) converged on (A, A). When that happens, a unilateral change in choice produces better outcomes for both people. Guyer and Rapoport found that, in the Leader situation, the likelihood of a person switching to (B) after convergence was .75, but in the Hero situation it was only .42. People were thus more willing to act to improve matters when their magnitude of improvement was the best than when others would experience the greatest improvement.

Accidental Impediments to Heroism

Troubled situations can provoke a variety of social responses. Drivers who encounter a car accident find it hard to resist the temptation to gawk, even if the damage is extensive and visually unpleasant (Most, Chun, Widders, & Zald, 2005). People in a troubled situation may express emotions that are considered socially inappropriate, such as laughter (Folkman, 2008). The experience of an emergency can induce feelings of cohesion with one's fellow afflicted, even if those people are strangers (Drury, Cocking, & Reicher, 2009). These responses can, and often do, have a variety of unintended consequences. Rubberneckers at a traffic accident presumably do not mean to inhibit traffic flow. Those who laugh during a funeral service are probably not trying to upset the aggrieved. People who have been evacuated from a burning building have likely not decided that this is a good time to expand their social networks. Yet these often result from the situational experience.

Hero:

		Person 2	
		A	B
Person 1	A	2, 2	4, 3
	B	3, 4	1, 1

Leader:

		Person 2	
		A	B
Person 1	A	2, 2	3, 4
	B	4, 3	1, 1

Figure 23.1 Examples of "Hero" and "Leader" Games

One such unintended consequence that can arise is discouragement of heroic action. In fact, there are a number of common responses to experienced troubles that have been shown to inhibit others from acting to end the troubles. Some are a function of the social environment in which the event occurs; some are related to the potential actor's perception of the situation; and emerging evidence suggests that the physiology of the experience may also suppress heroic impulse. Let us examine each of these in turn.

Social-Environmental Inhibitors

The Bystander Effect

Arguably the most well-known of all accidental inhibitors of heroism is the *bystander effect* first described by Latané and Darley (1968). Basically, the effect arises when a group of people witnesses a negative event unfolding, and the simple fact that there is a large number of potential actors decreases the likelihood that any one specific person will intervene. Importantly, and often overlooked in discussions of the phenomenon, the overall probability that *someone* will eventually help remains constant as the group size changes, but spreading that probability across an ever-larger group reduces the individual probability that Person X will act, and delays delivery of the heroic act. While there has been some controversy surrounding how the effect was identified (see Manning, Levine, & Collins, 2007), research (as well as a number of terrible real-world incidents—for example, the 2009 gang-rape of a girl at a homecoming dance in Richmond, California) clearly documents that a large number of fellow witnesses has some type of inhibitory effect on one's willingness to intervene (Fischer et al., 2011). As such, researchers have tried to determine whether there are certain situations in which it is more or less likely to occur, and whether the likelihood of occurrence can be minimized through intervention.

Much research has looked for boundary conditions of the bystander effect, and happily, there are a number of situations in which groups of witnesses seem relatively willing to help. One of the first empirical studies of bystander intervention (Latané & Rodin, 1969) contrasted pairs of strangers and pairs of friends. Action was more quickly taken when two friends witnessed the distress than two strangers, apparently because strangers misinterpreted each other's initial hesitation as a lack of concern for the distressed person. Levine and Crowther (2008) replicated this friendship effect with a larger group of witnesses. Help is also provided more quickly if the group of witnesses feel cohesive with each other (Rutkowski, Gruder, & Romer, 1983), see the victim as a member of an ingroup (Levine, Cassidy, Brazier, & Reicher, 2002), or will themselves be impacted by the outcome of the situation (Chekroun & Brauer, 2002). Some form of public accountability for one's actions also reduces the tendency to delay helping (Garcia, Weaver, Darley, & Spence, 2009; van Bommel, van Prooijen, Elffers, & Van Lange, 2012). At the individual level, a person is more likely to act, regardless of the behavior of others, if s/he feels competent and confident (Cramer, McMaster, Bartell, & Dragna, 1988), has personally experienced the crisis that the victim is experiencing (Huston, Ruggiero, Conner, & Geis, 1981) or knows someone who has (McMahon, 2010), or has prosocial personality traits (Bereczkei, Birkas, & Kerekes, 2010).

These boundary conditions are all quite plausible for real social situations, giving hope that bystander hesitation is not as pervasive as it may seem. Unfortunately, there is also evidence that hesitance is easily triggered. For example, it can occur in virtual groups merely through observation that no one has provided an immediate response to a posted request for assistance (Voelpel, Eckhoff, & Förster, 2008). Merely imagining being a "face in the crowd" can induce people to be unhelpful on a subsequent task (Garcia, Weaver, Moskowitz, & Darley, 2002), as can being part of a valued ingroup that holds a general "don't get involved" ethic (Baldry & Pagliaro, 2014). Situations that do not seem to be dangerous (Fischer, Greitemeyer, Pollozek, & Frey, 2006) or are stereotyped as nonthreatening (McMahon, 2010) are less likely to provoke intervention by witnesses, as are incidents of female-on-female aggression (Lowe, Levine, Best, & Heim, 2012).

It must be said that some of the demonstrations of how easily bystander apathy is triggered are disturbing. For example, witnesses to a sexual assault are less likely to intervene if the woman is inferred to have invited the attack, for example by being drunk or provocatively dressed; this is especially true for male witnesses (Burn, 2009). Police officers are susceptible to noninvolvement in domestic violence situations if they belong to don't-get-involved ingroups, and those ingroups are made salient (Baldry & Pagliaro, 2014). This is far from an exhaustive list of the conditions under which bystander passivity can occur, but is sufficient to demonstrate that, while witnesses forgoing the opportunity to save the day is not a given, the mindset is rather easily instilled.

The issue of the failure to intervene by observers of sexual assault raises a question of whether bystander apathy can be overcome through training. Indeed, some legal scholars have argued that failure to intervene in a clear emergency should be treated as a liable act (e.g., Bagby, 1999; Benzmiller, 2013), so whether apathy can be eliminated is a critical question. The research has been conducted primarily by those who study assault, as well as experts in youth bullying, another area where witness apathy is common. Regarding bullying, meta-analysis suggests that young people can be taught to take the initiative and help a bullied schoolmate, though the training works significantly better on high-school students than on younger kids (Polanin, Espelage, & Pigott, 2012). Similarly, teaching people to intervene in sexual assault does seem to help reduce the male hesitance to intervene reported by Burn (2009) (e.g., Gidycz, Orchowski, & Berkowitz, 2011), and a large-scale collegiate study of the "Green Dot" violence-prevention training program documents its efficacy at encouraging intervention, even among those who merely hear a presentation from a Green Dot trainer (Coker et al., 2011). These data seem quite encouraging of the prospect of eliminating bystander effects. However, an analysis of the National Crime Victimization Survey suggests that interveners often have misplaced confidence and a flawed understanding of what needs to be done, and end up either having no impact or making the situation worse rather than better; specifically, interveners had a positive impact only 37 percent of the time (Hart & Miethe, 2008). Bullying shows a similar pattern, with a chronic issue being that witnesses will often engage in seemingly innocuous behaviors that actually make things worse (Salmivalli, Voeten, & Poskiparta, 2011).

The Social Environment

A host of factors in the social environment also seem to influence a person's willingness to act heroically. Milgram (1970) recognized this when he undertook to defend city dwellers against charges that they are callous and unfeeling when confronted with needy others. Milgram instead argued that the city itself acts to inhibit helping in its residents, in four ways. First, the crowded nature of the city makes privacy a premium; as such, potential helpers assume that others see their personal problems as private matters for which they do not want intrusion. Next, the dense city has so many people who are in need every day that a potential helper needs to pick and choose when to intervene, or else spend the entire day doing nothing but helping. The unhelpful witness is thus not so much callous as s/he is fatigued. Third, the dangerous nature of a city, relative to a suburban or rural environment, makes its residents especially sensitive to personal harm, leading them to intervene only when the situation is unambiguously safe. Finally, Milgram argued that city dwellers evolve norms of noninvolvement as a way to help deal with the chronic information overload associated with city life, in that ignoring others allows one to focus only on the stimuli that directly impact one's routine.

A number of studies followed in the wake of Milgram's paper suggesting that characteristics of the place at which the problem occurs can indeed impact willingness to act heroically, though tests of Milgram's specific propositions do not seem to exist. Hackler and colleagues (1974) showed that intervention is less likely to occur in high-mobility neighborhoods (i.e., neighborhoods in which people move in and relocate with some frequency), apparently because such neighborhoods have weak communication networks. Importantly, this was true regardless of the affluence of the neighborhood. West, Whitney, and Schnedler (1975) found the racial composition of the location to predict delivery of help, in that intervention took longer to occur when the victim's race did not match the dominant race of the location. Thus Blacks waited longer for help in White neighborhoods than in Black neighborhoods, and vice versa for White victims. Neighborhood deterioration also seems to be a major influence on heroic acts, with a number of studies finding people relatively unwilling to act heroically when the event happens in a resource-poor location (Kullberg, Timpka, Svensson, Karlsson, & Lindqvist, 2010; Phan, Blumer, & Demaiter, 2009; Wagner, Hornstein, & Holloway, 1982). Finally, both experimental (Sherrod & Downs, 1974) and field (Moser, 1988) studies suggest that cognitively overloaded people are relatively unlikely to offer help to others, even if the needed help is easy for the person to provide.

Cultural Norms

At a normative level, certain cultural-subgroup norms seem to dictate against intervention in at least some situations. For example, the "culture of honor" that exists in the American South states that violence is permissible if it is in the service of preserving one's honor. Cohen and colleagues (Cohen, Vandello, Puente, & Rantilla, 1999) had people from the North and South observe and characterize objectively hostile situations, and found the Southerners less likely to see the situation as one that presented a danger and hence demanded intervention. Similarly, Lewis (2003) found strong norms against intervention in domestic violence situations among rural Americans, the norm being grounded in the notion that one should respect privacy and family reputation. Members of collectivist cultures are more likely to conform to nonintervention norms than are members of individualist cultures, even if the situation is one for which help is clearly needed (Pozzoli, Ang, & Gini, 2012). There is also some evidence of ethnic differences in willingness to get involved, with African-American males feeling relatively strongly that nonintervention is generally appropriate (Weisz & Black, 2008).

Perceptual Inhibitors

How one perceives the needful situation can also lead to accidental inhibition of heroism.
These perceptions can be driven by a number of factors, external and internal.

Masculinity

A number of researchers have asked whether a man's decision to intervene is impacted by his sense of masculinity. Many studies find a strong masculine identity can instigate a fear of public embarrassment if the intervention fails, making such men especially unlikely to act (e.g., Carlson, 2008; Leone, Parrott, Swartout, & Tharp, 2016; Siem & Spence, 1986; Tice & Baumeister, 1985). Related to this, men are especially hesitant to intervene in a woman-on-woman conflict in part because they worry how it will look if they fail to end the conflict (Lowe et al., 2012). However, other researchers have found men who see themselves as strong and aggressive to be likely to help, especially when the person in need is a woman (Laner, Benin, & Ventrone, 2001), and still others have found no connection between masculinity and intervention (Eisenberg, Schaller, Miller, Fultz, Fabes, & Shell, 1988). Note also that men who feel emasculated will seek out opportunities to be heroic, as a way to reduce their sense of unmanliness (Holt & Thompson, 2004).

Why might the masculine man be worried about embarrassment? The answer may relate to the stereotype of men as heroic and chivalrous when immediate, emergency situations occur (Eagly & Crowley, 1986). A man who fails to end the emergency would appear to run counter to the stereotype, that is, would appear unheroic and unchivalrous. Negatively violating a stereotype is associated with enhanced negative affect on the part of the actor (Bartholow, Fabiani, Gratton, & Bettencourt, 2001) and globally negative perceptions of the actor by observers (Bettencourt, Dill, Greathouse, Charlton, & Mulholland, 1997), so it is no surprise that the man for whom being masculine is an important trait would try to avoid any demonstration that he is not heroic.

Role Conflict

Related to the masculinity issue is the problem of role conflict. A potential hero may find him/herself in a situation in which one role dictates intervention, while another dictates inaction (Frost, Fiedler, & Anderson, 1983). For example, many studies of police officer stress have shown a key stressor to be the felt conflict between being an agent of help and a rule enforcer (see Burke, 1998). Similarly, workplace supervisors who have a troubled subordinate are often torn between a desire to be supportive and the high-production emphasis of their leadership roles (Hopkins, 1997). In a field study of bullied schoolchildren, Thornberg (2007) found that children who witnessed bullying but did nothing about it sometimes justified their inaction by putting greater emphasis on their role as student ("I can't help because I need to get my work done") than as acquaintance of the victim.

Misperception

Misperception of others' motives and feelings is chronic in social settings. When it occurs in needful situations, it can lead to inaction. For example, Gilovich and colleagues (Gilovich, Savitsky, & Medvec, 1998) showed that witnesses often infer that their concern about the situation is obvious when it actually is not. Because others are apparently not reacting to their worry, witnesses erroneously conclude that the situation is not problematic, and does not require intervention. More generally, people tend to assume that their mistakes are more publicly scrutinized than they actually are, making embarrassment a powerful inhibitor of action, and regrettable inaction a psychologically tolerable mistake (Gilovich & Medvec, 1995). Further complicating matters is that people tend to overestimate their willingness to engage in a potentially embarrassing behavior (Van Boven, Loewenstein, Welch, & Dunning, 2012), which suggests people will exhibit much bravado when speculating on their potential for heroism, but fail to act accordingly when the opportunity presents itself.

Perceived Self-Promotion

The desire for self-esteem, or a self-perception that one is good and a valuable member of society, is likely universal (Greenberg, 2008). The quest for high self-esteem can lead people to engage in a variety of behaviors that do not necessarily have benefit for others. For our purposes, one such behavior is notable. Basking in reflected glory, or BIRGing, is the phenomenon by which a person tangentially associates with successful groups (Cialdini et al., 1976). Think, for example, of people who wear clothing with the logos of successful sports teams. One such type of group is one that performs heroic acts: Lifesaving, damage control, etc. In a field study of search-and-rescue teams, Lois (1999) found that established members of the teams were so concerned about new members being attracted to the group purely for purposes of self-promotion that they would often assign these members menial tasks to make them prove their commitment, even when the new members had valuable skills. Stiff and van Vugt (2008) similarly found that new group members would often be treated with suspicion, even if they had needed abilities and stated that they had no selfish interest in group membership.

Physiological Influences

Might physiology contribute impediments to heroism? A number of theorists have speculated that hesitance to act for the needy is at least somewhat grounded in physiological deficits.[2]

Hormones

Becker and Eagly (2004) suggested that willingness to intervene in risky situations may be influenced by testosterone level, with lower levels of testosterone making one less likely to act. Unfortunately, empirical studies of testosterone and selfless behavior produce findings that are all over the place, with some indeed finding high testosterone associated with selflessness (e.g., Eisenegger et al., 2010), others showing it connected to decreased willingness to help (e.g., Zak et al., 2009), and still others finding no connection at all (e.g., Zethraeus et al., 2009). Reimers and Diekhof (2015) suggest that while the confusion may be due in part to mechanical issues (method of administration of the hormone, sex composition of the sample), the bigger issue is theoretical, in that testosterone has indirect, rather than direct, effects on selfless behavior. Clearly, more research is needed to disentangle the data.

Shirtcliff and colleagues (2009) implicate cortisol in heroism, in that cortisol stimulates activity in the anterior cingulate cortex (ACC), which controls empathic response. Low levels of cortisol would thus make a witness less likely to feel the need to help a distressed person. Related to this, Buchanan and colleagues (2012) showed that victim stress can be acquired by an observer, which then elevates cortisol level in the observer. An observer who does not experience heightened stress from the victim's plight would thus be less likely to feel a need to intervene. Zilioli and colleagues (2014) suggested that testosterone and cortisol work in concert to influence heroic action, with high testosterone inhibiting heroism when cortisol is low, and facilitating it when cortisol is high. Such an idea is consistent with Reimers and Diekhof's (2015) argument that testosterone has only indirect influence on heroism.

Finally, some theorists have suggested that arginine vasopressin, a hormone that seems to play a role in social decision making, may also impact heroic acts (Donaldson & Young, 2008). However, research so far has not supported this notion (Israel, Weisel, Ebstein, & Bornstein, 2012).

Neural Processes

There is some evidence that the neural circuitry associated with helpful responding may differentially activate depending upon characteristics of the needy person. In particular, the experience of shared pain, which is an important contributor to empathic response (imagine, for example, the sensation one feels when seeing someone else hit in the crotch), seems to be dampened when the sufferer is a member of an outgroup (Avenanti, Sirigu, & Aglioti, 2010; Azevedo et al., 2013; Xu, Zuo, Wang, & Han, 2009).

Summary

There are three ways in which a person's heroic inclination might be accidentally suppressed. Features of the social environment, such as the actions of others, norms, and the setting itself, may inhibit the actor. Internal factors can skew the would-be hero's perception of what the situation calls for or what the outcomes might be from a heroic attempt. Finally, physiological influences, apparently beyond the person's control, can act on the brain to direct behavior away from the needy situation.

Purposeful Impediments to Heroism

The previous section details a number of incidental phenomena that can disrupt the intention to act heroically. The everyday nature of these phenomena should give one pause. But, of perhaps greater concern is a second class of inhibitors of heroism, a set of actions that are purposely performed by people in order to squelch heroic inclinations in others. There is clear evidence that people do indeed actively attempt to discourage the helpful. In perhaps the most famous demonstration, Herrmann, Thöni, and Gächter (2008) found some degree of social punishment of highly cooperative people in 16 different countries. In a few countries, punishment of the highly cooperative was more severe than punishment of the highly uncooperative. On the surface, such actions seem ludicrous—why would you want to stop someone from being helpful and beneficent? But as we will see, these actions are driven by real, tangible motivations that have troubling implications for the collective good. The motivations can be broadly characterized as dislike of outgroups; concern about changing standards of normative behavior; stereotypes of the generous; and rule violation.

The Hero as Aider of an Outgroup

A hero obviously cannot control who needs assistance. A philanthropist who wants to pay for a skate park in his town presumably realizes that anyone can use it. What this means is that a hero will often deliver help to someone who others consider an outgroup member. It is well-established that people do not like to see outgroup members receive special benefits, and it is seemingly a nearly universal phenomenon. A vivid example of how widespread outgroup dislike is can be found in Ruffle and Sosis (2006), who documented outgroup hostility among members of a kibbutz when interacting with residents of the nearby town. Importantly for our purposes, there is evidence that people will pressure those who are inclined to help outgroup members to not deliver the help (McCauley & Moskalenko, 2008). As such, one purposeful impediment to heroic action is social pressure to not help an outgroup.

Exactly why people are disinterested in outgroup benefit, and how strongly they dislike the outgroup, remain topics of debate. Originally thought to be at the root of prejudice, outgroup hate is now considered at best a secondary factor (Brewer, 1999; Greenwald & Pettigrew, 2014; see also Halevy, Weisel, & Bornstein, 2012), though it may be a primal influence on the sexual prejudices held by religious fundamentalists (Laythe, Finkel, Bringle, & Kirkpatrick, 2002). An arena in which it seems clearly impactful is within "parochial business networks," whereby business owners in a particular industry will only interact with other business owners who share a common feature (e.g., ethnicity) with themselves (Bowles & Gintis, 2004). Bowles and Gintis give as an example American hoteliers of Asian Indian descent, who share information and make customer recommendations only amongst themselves. Because hotel ownership is such a common vocation among this ethnic group, hoteliers who are not of the group are noticeably impacted by the insularity. At this point, then, the extent to which outgroup dislike will cause someone to react seems primarily situational.

But why does it even occur? Why do we care about what "those people" get? There are at least three different schools of thought on this question.

Competitive Advantage

A key aspect of the evolutionary perspective on social behavior is that social groups compete with each other. This means that one is always looking for a way to advantage one's group relative to another. This sometimes requires engaging in a behavior that incurs personal sacrifice, but also leads to a larger loss for an outgroup, a phenomenon known as *parochial altruism* (De Dreu et al., 2010). Within the context of our discussion, a parochially altruistic act would be to deny needed help to an outgroup, even if that help would have also benefitted one's ingroup. Consider, for example, a city council member who votes against construction of a skate park, even though her constituents' children might want it, because she does not like the skateboarding community. Evolutionary theorists see parochial altruism as a beneficial trait, hence it would be selected for (Choi & Bowles, 2007). There is evidence that people with a strong ingroup identity will be especially supportive of parochially altruistic acts, and encouraging of people who perform them (Ginges, Hansen, & Norenzayan, 2009). Under this point of view, then, we would expect a person who holds a strong ingroup orientation to try to prevent a heroic action directed toward an outgroup member, in order to provide a competitive advantage for his/her group. Not only would the city council member vote against the skate park, she would actively try to discourage other council members from supporting it.

The extent to which a person actively seeks to deny an outgroup is a subject of much debate. An example in support of the notion was reported by Hein and colleagues (2010). They exposed men to a target man who was experiencing painful shocks from electrodes on the back of his hand, and told the observers that they could reduce the target's pain by having some of the electrodes moved onto their hand. People were generally willing to wear some electrodes if the sufferer was an ingroup member, but not if he was an outgroup member. As well, Cikara and Fiske (2012) documented physiological pleasure responses in people who observed a member of a competitive outgroup experience misfortune. In contrast, Halevy, Weisel, and Bornstein (2012) had people play a resource allocation game, and consistently found allocation decisions to be based strictly on what was most beneficial to the ingroup.

Parker and Janoff-Bulman (2013) suggest that whether or not "outgroup hate" is a motivator of action (or failure to act) is determined by whether the ingroup–outgroup distinction is based on morality, with outgroup hate being a motivator only when interacting with a morally different group. In their studies, ingroup–outgroup distinctions were determined either by stance on abortion or support for a sports team. Consistent with their prediction, outgroup hate occurred when one had to interact with people who held the opposing view on abortion, but not when other liked a rival sports team. While this seems to clarify the dynamics of outgroup hate, it should be noted that Hein et al. (2010) also used sport-team preference as the ingroup–outgroup marker. (The specific sports differed—Parker and Janoff-Bulman used baseball, Hein et al. soccer—but it is hard to see why this would matter.) Koopmans and Rebers (2009) suggest that the issue is less a desire to harm the outgroup as it is differential expectations: People expect outgroup members would not be very helpful to them, and so "forward reciprocate" the lack of help to the current situation. Stürmer, Snyder, and Omoto (2005) argue for attraction as the key factor, with people being more willing to help an outgroup member who is attractive, in terms of having desirable physical, intellectual, and/or behavioral characteristics, than one who falls short on these qualities. Whether we purposely avoid heroic action in order to harm an outgroup member thus remains an open question.

Relative Social Comparison

Related to the issue of intergroup competition is perceived advantage, determined through social comparison. Simply put, when evaluating outcomes in an intergroup situation, people tend to focus on relative standing rather than absolute standing. For example, Parks, Rumble, and Posey (2002) had people play a number of trials of a social dilemma game, which required cooperation in order to accumulate substantial outcomes. Halfway through the game, they provided players with feedback on their point accumulation so far. People who were told that they had far exceeded average performance, and had only one person in the session with a greater number of points, nonetheless became significantly less cooperative when the game resumed. These people reacted not to their absolute performance (I'm far above average) but to their relative performance (one person is doing better than me), and responded by being less engaged with the group.

Relative comparison can have some unusual effects on prosocial behavior. It can make people willing to act only on the condition that they also receive a payoff, indeed a larger payoff than the recipient will get. For example, the most common motivation to donate clothing to organizations that service the disadvantaged is the desire to clear space in one's closet (Ha-Brookshire & Hodges, 2009). In fact, not a one of Ha-Brookshire and Hodges' respondents reported "help those in need" as a motivation for their donations. Of particular issue is a type of "kick them when they're down" dynamic that can arise in advantaged groups. This occurs when the group seeks to increase their advantage over the disadvantaged outgroup, thus producing unhelpful, or harmful, behaviors toward the disadvantaged (Dambrun et al., 2006; Grofman & Muller, 1973; McPherson & Parks, 2011).

The relative comparison explanation, then, predicts that a person will attempt to stop a hero when the person perceives the hero's target as already receiving "too much." Leach and colleagues (2002) refer to this as "moral indignation" and note that the perceiver may actually feel that s/he is the one who deserves to be helped. If, for example, a person with a roomy closet was nonetheless thinking to donate clothes to Goodwill, we might expect her morally indignant associates to ask why she would consider doing so, when the poor already have welfare, food stamps, reduced-rent housing, and so on.

Infrahumanization

The principle of infrahumanization refers to perception of an outgroup as being less human than one's ingroup. An aspect of this perception of sub-humanness is a belief that the outgroup is emotionally simple, and experiences only the primary emotions: Happiness, anger, sadness, etc. (Leyens et al., 2000). This perception can lead to the inference that outgroup members in need will not appreciate the help that is delivered, and so there is no reason to be heroic and intervene. Published examples of failure to aid "subhumans" are unfortunately too easy to find. A number of studies have shown that people who are most likely to express unwillingness to aid victims of a natural disaster tend to perceive the victims as subhuman outgroup members: The Japanese who experienced the 2011 earthquake and tsunami were robotic (Andrighetto et al., 2014) or dominance-obsessed (Sun, Zagefka, & Goodwin, 2013); the Haitians who experienced the 2010 earthquake were backward and animalistic (Andrighetto et al., 2014); Black residents of New Orleans did not feel much sorrow or grief over the losses they incurred from Hurricane Katrina (Cuddy, Rock, & Norton, 2007). In a different vein, Wen, Hudak, and Hwang (2007) found that homeless people are often perceived as an "it" by medical professionals, and will be bypassed for care in favor of other patients, even in emergency rooms, on the grounds that they are neither experiencing all that much discomfort, nor will take full advantage of the treatment provided them. (See Leyens, 2013, for a more extensive review of the problem of dehumanization of medical patients.) Finally, Zhang and colleagues (2015) found that those who dehumanize were more likely to favor harsh punishment of an outgroup member who engaged in a drastic action for which there could be multiple explanations (e.g., immigration into a disputed area). Those who see the target of heroism as a subhuman outgroup member would thus be likely to pressure a would-be hero into not acting, on the grounds that the heroism would be wasted.

Social Undesirables

Sometimes, it is not only that "they" are being helped, it is that "they" are being helped despite, in a just-world sense, having brought their misery upon themselves. The most famous example of this mindset was documented by Snyder, Omoto, and Crain (1999), who showed that AIDS-patient volunteers with strong social networks were more likely to end their volunteerism than those with weak networks, because the former were being stigmatized for their efforts by their social circle. The same effect has since been shown with those who help other types of groups that are open to just-world perceptions, like drug addicts and sex workers (see Parks, Joireman, & Van Lange, 2013, for a summary of this research). Snyder and Omoto (2008) suggest that those who volunteer primarily for other-focused reasons (e.g., to contribute to one's community) may be more profoundly affected by the stigmatization than those who volunteer for self-focused reasons (e.g., personal growth).

The Hero as a Norm-Shifter

The second purposeful impediment to heroism has nothing to do with the recipient. Rather, this impediment revolves around the implications of the hero having acted. Simply stated, acting as a hero can serve to redefine what constitutes normal or expected behavior in future similar situations. We have already seen that Jonah Jameson dislikes Spider-Man in large part for this reason: Jameson is concerned that people will come to see Spider-Man's behavior as normal, which means Jameson's good works will eventually be seen as insufficient. If people are truly concerned about a hero causing a norm to shift upward, it follows that they would actively attempt to thwart the hero's actions, or perhaps support the hero only when s/he performs low-key actions, at normal intervals.

There is empirical evidence that people do indeed have concerns that a hero is raising the bar for normative behavior. Parks and Stone (2010) had people perform a cooperative task with simulated others that required both contributing resources toward an entity, and harvesting resources from the entity. Of the others, all gave and took normative amounts except for one person, who gave either maximally or minimally, and took either maximally or minimally. After completion of the task, people were asked to indicate to what extent they would like each group member to remain in the group for a second round. Parks and Stone found that the person who gave much and took little was surprisingly unpopular, almost as unpopular as the person who gave little and took much. Follow-up studies suggested that a reason for this unpopularity was a concern that everyone else would now be expected to be equally selfless in the next round, and that a person who was following a common equity rule would appear to be selfish by way of comparison. (As we will see in the next section, though, this was not the only reason uncovered by Parks and Stone.) Irwin and Horne (2013) replicated this finding, and Bone and colleagues (2014) found weak evidence for it. Related to this, Duffy and Kornienko (2010) were able to induce considerable amounts of contribution in subjects by presenting the contribution task as a "generosity tournament," leading people to compete over who is the most generous among them. (The Giving Pledge program, created by Warren Buffett and Bill Gates to challenge billionaires to publicly commit the majority of their wealth to philanthropy, might be seen as a real example of this.) This suggests that an unusually giving group member will indeed cause others to feel that they have to outdo him/her.

The Hero Stereotyped as a Selfish Person

Interestingly, one inhibitor of heroic action may be a fear of being thought of as a cold and heartless person. On the surface this seems ludicrous—how could someone who puts him/herself out for others be thought callous? In fact, an interesting study by Raihani (2014) offers just such a possibility. He examined contributions to an actual fundraising website and found that donors preferred to remain anonymous when making either unusually small, or unusually large, donations, and preferred to go public when making normative donations. Raihani suggested that the generous wanted to be anonymous out of fear of recrimination for their contribution. The fear may have been driven by concerns about being seen as a norm-shifter, as discussed in the previous section, but it may also have been because of negative stereotypes of the wealthy, specifically that they are cold and hostile (e.g., Fiske, Cuddy, Glick, & Xu, 2002; Kervyn, Judd, & Yzerbyt, 2008). Under this logic, resource-rich individuals who give of themselves are seen not as generous, but rather as trying to legitimize their wealth, and will be called on this by group members who are not rich. Empirical analysis of the motivations for donation to charities indicates that some people indeed donate not because they believe in the value of the charity, but rather to enhance their social reputation (Bekkers & Wiepking, 2011), so there is some basis for skepticism about the hero's motives. Resource-rich people who are truly giving and helpful may well be aware of this perception, and not wanting to be subjected to social punishment, will either act anonymously or not at all. Applying all of this to the notion of suppressed heroism, it is possible that a person who could act the hero will not, out of concern that others will be skeptical of his/her true motivation and accuse him/her of cynical action.

There is evidence that the potential hero should indeed be wary. Critcher and Dunning (2011) showed that observers regularly impute selfish motives into the selfless actions of others, even in the face of considerable evidence that the actor did not gain from the heroic action. Newman and Cain (2014) found that a charitable action that might also have personal benefit is seen as more reprehensible than a similar action that has no charitable benefit. Similarly, Barasch and colleagues (2014) found those who performed a prosocial action in order to enhance their reputation were negatively evaluated by others (though those who performed the action in order to reap emotional rewards were evaluated more positively). Even children as young as 8 years of age are suspicious of people who can possibly realize personal benefits from a selfless act (Heyman et al., 2014). All of this suggests that the potential hero who notices any possible personal gain from his/her heroism might well opt out of action, so as to avoid the attendant social punishment. This, then, becomes another form of purposeful inhibition of heroic action, in that society is distinguishing between "good" heroism (that which is truly selfless) and "bad" heroism (that which provides benefit to the hero).

The Hero as a Cheater

Imagine playing a game of Monopoly. You land on Boardwalk, which someone else owns and on which sit two hotels. You do not have enough money to pay the rent, and all of your properties are mortgaged. By the rules of the game, you have lost and are out. But now imagine that the owner of Boardwalk says that he would like you to be able to keep playing, and so will forgive the rent this time. You can stay in the game.

This is a generous offer. But there is a good chance that you will react adversely to it, because it violates the rules of the game. The violation is in your favor, but it nonetheless goes against how the game is supposed to be played. Similarly, there is evidence that people oppose heroes because they do not do what they are "supposed" to do; they are violating rules of social exchange. Parks and Stone (2010) found this as another frequently given explanation for why people did not want to keep the selfless other person in the group. As well, Parks et al. (2013) suggested that perceived rule-breaking may also contribute to the stigmatization of those who volunteer to work with questionable groups—AIDS patients are "supposed" to be tended to by the AIDS-afflicted, drug addicts by recovering addicts, and so on.

How exactly is the hero breaking a social rule? Specifically, s/he is behaving inequitably, in that s/he is receiving less from the situation than s/he is putting into it. Equity is a fundamental principle of social exchange that is adhered to by at least higher-order nonhuman species as well as humans (see Price & Brosnan, 2012, for a recent review). Violations of equity are thus distressing. Importantly, at least humans often react negatively even when the violation is in their favor. Shaw and Olson (2012) provide a nice recent example of this phenomenon. They had children distribute resources among others and themselves, and found that the children would throw away a leftover resource rather than keep it for themselves, even if it was acceptable to keep the extra resource, if keeping it meant that they would have more than they deserved.

Why would people be averse to equity violations that are in their favor? There are a number of possible explanations. The violation may confound the person's expectations, and thus raise a concern that future events will be unpredictable (Chen & Santos, 2006). Rejection of a personally beneficial violation may be an attempt to signal that one is reasonable and fair (Shaw & Olson, 2012). It may be a byproduct of an emphasis on impartiality, which has been suggested to be a basic human trait (DeScioli & Kurzban, 2009). It may be a response to negative emotions produced by the fact that someone is not getting what s/he deserves (Dawes, Fowler, Johnson, McElreath, & Smirnov, 2007). It may induce feelings of indebtedness, in that we will need to do something nice for the hero in the future (Greenberg & Westcott, 1983). Regardless of reason, the fact remains that people will often react negatively to heroic gestures, on the grounds that the hero is getting shorted on outcomes. The generous owner of Boardwalk in our Monopoly game is not getting the payoff that he deserves, and that is uncomfortable.

How might this phenomenon act as a purposeful impediment to heroism? If the needy person has any of the reactions delineated above, and is in a position to make reasoned decisions, s/he may simply refuse the heroic intervention; the Monopoly player, for example, may just quit the game (Nadler & Fisher, 1986). If the person is not able to refuse, s/he may instead impose psychological costs on the hero. For example, in a study of doctors who purposely work in poor countries under difficult conditions, Al-Dubai and Rampal (2010) found that one of the most common factors causing these doctors to leave for more comfortable environments was patient lack of appreciation for the doctor's efforts. Similarly, Kulik (2006) showed that men who volunteer for social service work are most likely to quit if the recipients do not seem to value their efforts.

Summary

We have looked at four ways in which people can purposely discourage a heroic act by another: Present the action as providing benefit to an outgroup; exert pressure to not deviate from a norm; foster a perception of the hero as a selfish person; and treat the hero as a rule-breaker. It is easy to think of real examples of all of these ways.

Thwarted Heroism versus Cowardice

We have reviewed a number of factors that can prevent someone from acting heroically. It can be argued that many, perhaps most, of these could be overcome fairly easily. Are concerns about the counter-normative nature of heroism really a strong deterrent, given that most cultures tolerate some degree of norm deviance? Are people truly all that concerned about what a group of strangers might think of their decision to intervene in a needy situation? Might "thwarted heroism" just be a manifestation of a deeper trait, cowardice, with cowardly people being on the lookout for features of the situation that would allow them to safely express their fear of intervention? In this sense, there is no such thing as an "impediment to heroism;" rather, there are triggers of cowardice that someone who is cowardly will be sensitive to.

It is interesting to note that a discussion along these lines exists in the philosophy literature.

Basically, the debate centers around whether other-regarding behavior is driven purely by the situation, meaning that any perception of someone as "heroic" is a fundamental attribution error (Harman, 1999), or whether people possess basic, global orientations to help others, with the situation merely serving to activate (or not) the orientation (Miller, 2010). A portion of this debate concerns negative reactions to the needy situation and the ability to alleviate those negative reactions. In particular, Miller (2010) suggests that some people will be attuned to the potential to avoid blame for inaction, and if that potential seems acceptably high, will fail to act. This implies, for example, that people who do not want to get involved would be more aware of the number of other witnesses than people who feel a need to intervene. What appears to be an impediment to heroism instead turns out to be a convenient dodge, or in other words, an expression of cowardice.

The psychology of cowardice has not been examined, which is surprising, given its connotations and clear connections to group behavior, interpersonal relations, psychological trauma, and stigmatization (Walsh, 2014). Evolutionary biologists have found perceived cowardice in others to be a powerful stimulus for punishment and retributive behavior against the coward (e.g., Mathew & Boyd, 2014; see also Campbell, 1982). Soldiers who have been wrongly accused of cowardice report lasting effects of the stigmatization, even after the accusation has been shown to be wrong (Mears, 2013). Felt cowardice has been shown to be a primary contributor to post-traumatic stress disorder in soldiers (McFarlane, 1995). Legal scholars have noted that people who fail to help in a clear emergency are particular targets of public scorn (Hyman, 2006). Given this, it is entirely plausible that those who are disinclined to take a risk and aid a person in need would look for cover in the form of an alternate explanation for why they did not get involved. It may thus be that some instances of apparently external obstacles toward heroism are in fact created by an actor who recognizes a need to get involved, but does not want to, and does not want others to conclude that s/he does not want to. This is an issue worthy of study, as is the more general topic of the psychology of cowardice.

Impediments to Heroism: Conclusions

We have seen that it is quite easy to disrupt heroic intent in others. It can happen accidentally, or it can be done on purpose. The Spider-Mans in our midst will work around and shrug off these obstacles, but more people will refrain from acting, which is a poor outcome for society at large. Three questions immediately arise: Can we teach would-be heroes to recognize and overcome the accidental impediments? Can we discourage the would-be disrupters from acting on their impulse, and be tolerant of heroes? And, to what extent are these events true preventions of heroism versus disguised cowardice?

As to the first question, there is some hope. Though we saw that the accidental impediments can be triggered in quite minimal situations, we also saw that there are situations in which they could activate, but do not (e.g., when a group of witnesses are known to each other). This suggests that at least bystander intervention effects may show a person-by-situation interaction. Such interactions can potentially be exploited for behavior change. As an example, Zettler and Hilbig (2010) showed that employees low on Honesty/Humility can be induced to perform fewer counterproductive work behaviors by changing their perception of the politics of their workplace. It may be that encouraging people to view heroic situations in a different way will make them more willing to intervene. Changing cultural norms, or perceptions of social-environmental conditions, is admittedly a tougher proposition.

The second question is likely harder to address. We saw that others have strong reasons for not wanting the would-be hero to act. Dislike of outgroups, norm deviants, and rule-breakers have all proven resistant to a variety of interventions, and perception of the hero as a selfish person is likely as resistant to change as the many other biased perceptions of others that people maintain. What is needed here is a fundamental change in one's view of selfless action. We somehow need to encourage people to see action for others as at once a higher form of social action, and an action that does not threaten one's own social standing. This is admittedly a tall order.

Finally, what about cowardice? Maybe the concerns we have raised here about thwarted heroism are largely a paper tiger, and the real problem is that many people are simply not brave enough to respond when a need arises. This is an open question that suggests a need for research into the psychology of a purposeful failure to act. Such research would be difficult, but as we have seen, what little we know about cowardice suggests that it is a powerful phenomenon. It would not be surprising if at least some of the instances of suppressed heroism are in fact cover-ups of a preference to not act. While this represents a problem in its own right, discovery that thwarted heroism is less common than it seems would be an important finding.

Final Thoughts

We began this chapter with an example of purposeful poor treatment of a fictional hero. It is not hard to find examples with real heroes and would-be heroes. Mountaineering guides on Mount Everest are so focused on reaching the summit that they discourage members of their teams from stopping to help other climbers who are in distress (Savage & Torgler, 2015). Employees who want to expose systematic wrongs and improve work conditions are inhibited from doing so by threats of co-worker ostracism and stigmatization by colleagues as a traitor (Jackson et al., 2010; Nezlek, Wesselmann, Wheeler, & Williams, 2012). The actor Sean Penn used a small flat-bottom boat to rescue people in the aftermath of Hurricane Katrina, and was said by critics to have brought a camera crew along (he did not) or to have done it in order to promote a new film (he had no films in production) (Heller, 2011). People who are willing to take risks in order to aid others are either being socially pressured to not do so, or paid a social price after having done so.

If we value the Spider-Mans, Sean Penns and whistleblowers of the world, it follows that we need to develop some interventions that promote tolerance, if not support, of would-be heroes. At present psychology offers no such tools. Allison and Goethals (2011) tell us that people enjoy seeing heroes fall almost as much seeing heroes rise. This is troubling, but at least the world has benefitted from the heroism for a period of time. Prevention of heroes is arguably a bigger problem, and one that demands research attention.

Notes

1   All information in this paragraph is taken from the Marvel Comics online repository at marvel.wikia.com.
2   Preston (2013) extensively reviews the neurocircuitry that is recruited in empathic and caregiving response. While damage to, or malformation of, this circuitry would likely influence a person's willingness to act heroically, in this section I confine myself to physiological factors that can fluctuate naturally within and across persons.

References

Al-Dubai, S. A. R., & Rampal, K. G. (2010). Prevalence and associated factors of burnout among doctors in Yemen. *Journal of Occupational Health, 52*, 58–65.
Allison, S. T., & Goethals, G. R. (2011). *Heroes: What they do and why we need them*. New York: Oxford University Press.
Andrighetto, L., Baldissarri, C., Lattanzio, S., Loughnan, S., & Volpato, C. (2014). Human-itarian aid? Two forms of dehumanization and willingness to help after natural disasters. *British Journal of Social Psychology, 53*, 573–584.

Avenanti, A., Sirigu, A., & Aglioti, S. M. (2010). Racial bias reduces empathic sensorimotor resonance with other-race pain. *Current Biology, 20,* 1018–1022.

Azevedo, R. T., Macaluso, E., Avenanti, A., Santangelo, V., Cazzato, V., & Aglioti, S. M. (2013). Their pain is not our pain: Brain and autonomic correlates of empathic resonance with the pain of same and different race individuals. *Human Brain Mapping, 34,* 3168–3181.

Bagby, J. (1999). Justifications for state bystander intervention statutes: Why crime witnesses should be required to call for help. *Indiana Law Review, 33,* 571–597.

Baldry, A. C., & Pagliaro, S. (2014). Helping victims of intimate partner violence: The influence of group norms among lay people and the police. *Psychology of Violence, 4,* 334–347.

Barasch, A., Levine, E. E., Berman, J. Z., & Small, D. A. (2014). Selfish or selfless? On the signal value of emotion in altruistic behavior. *Journal of Personality and Social Psychology, 107,* 393–413.

Bartholow, B. D., Fabiani, M., Gratton, G., & Bettencourt, B. A. (2001). A psychophysiological examination of cognitive processing of and affective responses to social expectancy violations. *Psychological Science, 12,* 197–204.

Becker, S. W., & Eagly, A. H. (2004). The heroism of men and women. *American Psychologist, 59,* 163–178.

Bekkers, R., & Wiepking, P. (2011). A literature review of empirical studies of philanthropy: Eight mechanisms that drive charitable giving. *Nonprofit and Voluntary Sector Quarterly, 40,* 924–973.

Benzmiller, H. (2013). The cyber-samaritans: Exploring criminal liability for the "innocent" bystanders of cyberbullying. *Northwestern University Law Review, 107,* 927–962.

Bereczkei, T., Birkas, B., & Kerekes, Z. (2010). The presence of others, prosocial traits, and Machiavellianism: A personality × situation approach. *Social Psychology, 41,* 238–245.

Bettencourt, B. A., Dill, K. E., Greathouse, S. A., Charlton, K., & Mulholland, A. (1997). Evaluations of ingroup and outgroup members: The role of category-based expectancy violation. *Journal of Experimental Social Psychology, 33,* 244–275.

Bone, J., Silva, A. S., & Raihani, N. J. (2014). Defectors, not norm violators, are punished by third-parties. *Biology Letters, 10,* 20140388.

Bowles, S., & Gintis, H. (2004). Persistent parochialism: Trust and exclusion in ethnic networks. *Journal of Economic Behavior and Organization, 55,* 1–23.

Brewer, M. B. (1999). The psychology of prejudice: Ingroup love or outgroup hate? *Journal of Social Issues, 55,* 429–444.

Buchanan, T. W., Bagley, S. L., Stansfield, R. B., & Preston, S. D. (2012). The empathic, physiological resonance of stress. *Social Neuroscience, 7,* 191–201.

Burke, R. J. (1998). Work and non-work stressors and well-being among police officers: The role of coping. *Anxiety, Stress, and Coping, 11,* 345–362.

Burn, S. M. (2009). A situational model of sexual assault prevention through bystander intervention. *Sex Roles, 60,* 779–792.

Campbell, D. T. (1982). Legal and primary-group social controls. In M. Gruter & P. Bohannan (eds), *Law, biology, and culture* (pp. 159–171). San Diego, CA: Ross-Erikson.

Carlson, M. (2008). I'd rather go along and be considered a man: Masculinity and bystander intervention. *Journal of Men's Studies, 16,* 3–17.

Chekroun, P., & Brauer, M. (2002). The bystander effect and social control behavior: The effect of the presence of others on people's reactions to norm violations. *European Journal of Social Psychology, 32,* 853–867.

Chen, M. K., & Santos, L. R. (2006). Some thoughts on the adaptive function of inequity aversion: An alternative to Brosnan's social hypothesis. *Social Justice Research, 19,* 201–207.

Choi, J.-K., & Bowles, S. (2007). The coevolution of parochial altruism and war. *Science, 318,* 636–640.

Cialdini, R. B., Borden, R. J., Thorne, A., Walker, M. R., Freeman, S., & Sloan, L. R. (1976). Basking in reflected glory: Three (football) field studies. *Journal of Personality and Social Psychology, 34,* 366–375.

Cikara, M., & Fiske, S. T. (2012). Stereotypes and Schadenfreude: Affective and physiological markers of pleasure at outgroup misfortunes. *Social Psychological and Personality Science, 3,* 63–71.

Cohen, D., Vandello, J., Puente, S., & Rantilla, A. (1999). "When you call me that, smile!" How norms for politeness, interaction styles, and aggression work together in Southern culture. *Social Psychology Quarterly, 62,* 257–275.

Coker, A. L., Cook-Craig, P. G., Williams, C. M., Fisher, B. S., Clear, E. R., …& Hegge, L. M. (2011). Evaluation of Green Dot: An active bystander intervention to reduce sexual violence on college campuses. *Violence against Women, 17,* 777–796.

Cramer, R. E., McMaster, M. R., Bartell, P. A., & Dragna, M. (1988). Subject competence and minimization of the bystander effect. *Journal of Applied Social Psychology, 18,* 1133–1148.

Critcher, C. R., & Dunning, D. (2011). No good deed goes unquestioned: Cynical construals maintain belief in the power of self-interest. *Journal of Experimental Social Psychology, 47,* 1207–1213.

Cuddy, A. J. C., Rock, M. S., & Norton, M. I. (2007). Aid in the aftermath of Hurricane Katrina: Inferences of secondary emotions and intergroup helping. *Group Processes and Intergroup Relations, 10,* 107–118.

Dambrun, M., Taylor, D. M., McDonald, D. A., Crush, J., & Méot, A. (2006). The relative deprivation-gratification continuum and the attitudes of South Africans toward immigrants: A test of the V-curve hypothesis. *Journal of Personality and Social Psychology, 91,* 1032–1044.

Dawes, C. T., Fowler, J. H., Johnson, T., McElreath, R., & Smirnov, O. (2007). Egalitarian motives in humans. *Nature, 446,* 794–796.

De Dreu, C. K. W., Greer, L. L., Handgraaf, M. J. J., Shalvi, S., Van Kleef, G. A., …& Feith, S. W. W. (2010). The neuropeptide oxytocin regulates parochial altruism in intergroup conflict among humans. *Science, 328,* 1408–1411.

DeScioli, P., & Kurzban, R. (2009). Mysteries of morality. *Cognition, 112,* 281–299.

Donaldson, Z. R., & Young, L. J. (2008). Oxytocin, vasopressin, and the neurogenetics of sociality. *Science, 322,* 900–904.

Drury, J., Cocking, C., & Reicher, S. (2009). Everyone for themselves? A comparative study of crowd solidarity among emergency survivors. *British Journal of Social Psychology, 48,* 487–506.

Duffy, J., & Kornienko, T. (2010). Does competition affect giving? *Journal of Economic Behavior and Organization, 74,* 82–103.

Eagly, A. H., & Crowley, M. (1986). Gender and helping behavior: A meta-analytic review of the social psychological literature. *Psychological Bulletin, 100,* 283–308.

Eisenberg, N., Schaller, M., Miller, P. A., Fultz, J., Fabes, R. A., & Shell, R. (1988). Gender-related traits and helping in a nonemergency situation. *Sex Roles, 19,* 605–618.

Eisenegger, C., Naef, M., Snozzi, R., Heinrichs, M., & Fehr, E. (2010). Prejudice and truth about the effect of testosterone on human bargaining behavior. *Nature, 463,* 356–359.

Fischer, P., Greitemeyer, T., Pollozek, F., & Frey, D. (2006). The unresponsive bystander: Are bystanders more responsive in dangerous emergencies? *European Journal of Social Psychology, 36,* 267–278.

Fischer, P., Krueger, J. I., Greitemeyer, T., Vogrincic, C., Kastenmüller, A., … Kainbacher, M. (2011). The bystander effect: A meta-analytic review on bystander intervention in dangerous and non-dangerous emergencies. *Psychological Bulletin, 137,* 517–537.

Fiske, S. T., Cuddy, A. J. C., Glick, P., & Xu, J. (2002). A model of (often mixed) stereotype content: Competence and warmth respectively follow from perceived status and competition. *Journal of Personality and Social Psychology, 82,* 878–902.

Folkman, S. (2008). The case for positive emotions in the stress process. *Anxiety, Stress, and Coping, 21,* 3–14.

Frost, D. E., Fiedler, F. E., & Anderson, J. W. (1983). The role of personal risk-taking in effective leadership. *Human Relations, 36,* 185–202.

Garcia, S. M., Weaver, K., Darley, J. M., & Spence, B. T. (2009). Dual effects of implicit bystanders: Inhibiting vs. facilitating helping behavior. *Journal of Consumer Psychology, 19,* 215–224.

Garcia, S. M., Weaver, K., Moskowitz, G. B., & Darley, J. M. (2002). Crowded minds: The implicit bystander effect. *Journal of Personality and Social Psychology, 83,* 843–853.

Gelineau, V. A., & Kantor, D. (1964). Pro-social commitment among college students. *Journal of Social Issues, 20,* 112–130.

Gidcyz, C. A., Orchowski, L. M., & Berkowitz, A. D. (2011). Preventing sexual aggression among college men: An evaluation of a social norm and bystander intervention program. *Violence against Women, 17,* 720–742.

Gilovich, T., & Medvec, V. H. (1995). The experience of regret: What, when, and why. *Psychological Review, 102,* 379–395.

Gilovich, T., Savitsky, K., & Medvec, V. H. (1998). The illusion of transparency: Biased assessments of others' ability to read one's emotional states. *Journal of Personality and Social Psychology, 75,* 332–346.

Ginges, J., Hansen, I., & Norenzayan, A. (2009). Religion and support for suicide attacks. *Psychological Science, 20,* 224–230.

Greenberg, J. (2008). Understanding the vital human quest for self-esteem. *Perspectives on Psychological Science, 3,* 48–55.

Greenberg, M. S., & Westcott, D. R. (1983). Indebtedness as a mediator of reactions to aid. In J. D. Fisher, A. Nadler, & B. M. DePaulo (eds), *New directions in helping: Recipient reactions to aid* (pp. 85–112). New York: Academic Press.

Greenwald, A. G., & Pettigrew, T. F. (2014). With malice toward none and charity toward some: Ingroup favoritism enables discrimination. *American Psychologist, 69,* 669–684.

Grofman, B. N., & Muller, E. N. (1973). The strange case of relative gratification and potential for political violence: The V-curve hypothesis. *American Political Science Review, 57,* 514–539.

Guyer, M. J., & Rapoport, A. (1969). Information effects in two mixed-motive games. *Behavioral Science, 14,* 467–482.

Ha-Brookshire, J. E., & Hodges, N. N. (2009). Socially responsible consumer behavior? Exploring used clothing donation behavior. *Clothing and Textiles Research Journal, 27*, 179–196.

Hackler, J. C., Ho, K. -Y., & Urquhart-Ross, C. (1974). The willingness to intervene: Differing community characteristics. *Social Problems, 21*, 328–344.

Halevy, N., Weisel, O., & Bornstein, G. (2012). "In-group love" and "out-group hate" in repeated interaction between groups. *Journal of Behavioral Decision Making, 25*, 188–195.

Harman, G. (1999). Moral philosophy meets social psychology: Virtue ethics and the fundamental attribution error. *Proceedings of the Aristotelian Society, 99*, 315–322.

Harris, R. J. (1969). A geometric classification system for 2 × 2 interval-symmetric games. *Behavioral Science, 14*, 138–146.

Hart, T. C., & Miethe, T. D. (2008). Exploring bystander presence and intervention in nonfatal violent victimization: When does helping really help? *Violence and Victims, 23*, 637–651.

Hein, G., Silani, G., Preuschoff, K., Batson, C. D., & Singer, T. (2010). Neural responses to ingroup and outgroup members' suffering predict individual differences in costly helping. *Neuron, 68*, 149–160.

Heller, Z. (2011). The accidental activist. *New York Times Style Magazine* (March 25). Retrieved August 4, 2015 from http://tmagazine.blogs.nytimes.com/2011/03/25/the-accidental-activist/?_r=0.

Herrmann, B., Thöni, C., & Gächter, S. (2008). Antisocial punishment across societies. *Science, 319*, 1362–1367.

Heyman, G., Barner, D., Heumann, J., & Schenck, L. (2014). Children's sensitivity to ulterior motives when evaluating prosocial behavior. *Cognitive Science, 38*, 683–700.

Holt, D. B., & Thompson, C. J. (2004). Man-of-action heroes: The pursuit of heroic masculinity in everyday consumption. *Journal of Consumer Research, 31*, 425–440.

Hopkins, K. M. (1997). Supervisor intervention with troubled workers: A social identity perspective. *Human Relations, 50*, 1215–1238.

Huston, T. L., Ruggiero, M., Conner, R., & Geis, G. (1981). Bystander intervention into crime: A study based on naturally-occurring episodes. *Social Psychology Quarterly, 44*, 14–23.

Hyman, D. A. (2006). Rescue without law: An empirical perspective on the duty to rescue. *Texas Law Review, 84*, 653–738.

Irwin, K., & Horne, C. (2013). A normative explanation of antisocial punishment. *Social Science Research, 42*, 562–570.

Israel, S., Weisel, O., Ebstein, R. P., & Bornstein, G. (2012). Oxytocin, but not vasopressin, increases both parochial and universal altruism. *Psychoneuroendocrinology, 37*, 1341–1344.

Jackson, D., Peters, K., Andrew, S., Edenborough, M., Halcomb, E., ... & Wilkes, L. (2010). Trial and retribution: A qualitative study of whistleblowing and workplace relationships in nursing. *Contemporary Nurse, 36*, 34–44.

Kervyn, N. O., Judd, C. M., & Yzerbyt, V. Y. (2008). You want to appear competent? Be mean! You want to appear sociable? Be lazy! Group differentiation and the compensation effect. *Journal of Experimental Social Psychology, 45*, 363–367.

Koopmans, R., & Rebers, S. (2009). Collective action in culturally similar and dissimilar groups: An experiment on parochialism, conditional cooperation, and their linkages. *Evolution and Human Behavior, 30*, 201–211.

Kulik, L. (2006). Burnout among volunteers in the social services: The impact of gender and employment status. *Journal of Community Psychology, 34*, 541–561.

Kullberg, A., Timpka, T., Svensson, T., Karlsson, N., & Lindqvist, K. (2010). Does the perceived neighborhood reputation contribute to neighborhood differences in social trust and residential wellbeing? *Journal of Community Psychology, 38*, 591–606.

Laner, M. R., Benin, M. H., & Ventrone, N. A. (2001). Bystander attitudes toward victims of violence: Who's worth helping? *Deviant Behavior, 22*, 23–42.

Latané, B., & Darley, J. M. (1968). Group inhibition of bystander intervention in emergencies. *Journal of Personality and Social Psychology, 10*, 215–221.

Latané, B., & Rodin, J. (1969). A lady in distress: Inhibiting effects of friends and strangers on bystander intervention. *Journal of Experimental Social Psychology, 5*, 189–202.

Laythe, B., Finkel, D. G., Bringle, R. G., & Kirkpatrick, L. A. (2002). Religious fundamentalism as a predictor of prejudice: A two-component model. *Journal for the Scientific Study of Religion, 41*, 623–635.

Leach, C. W., Snider, N., & Iyer, A. (2002). "Poisoning the consciences of the fortunate": The experience of relative advantage and support for social equality. In I. Walker & H. J. Smith (eds), *Relative deprivation: Specification, development, and integration* (pp. 136–163). New York: Cambridge University Press.

Leone, R. M., Parrott, D. J., Swartout, K. M., & Tharp, A. T. (2016). Masculinity and bystander attitudes: Moderating effects of masculine gender role stress. *Psychology of Violence, 6*, 82–90.

Levine, M., & Crowther, S. (2008). The responsive bystander: How social group membership and group size can encourage as well as inhibit bystander intervention. *Journal of Personality and Social Psychology*, *95*, 1429–1439.

Levine, M., Cassidy, C., Brazier, G., & Reicher, S. (2002). Self-categorization and bystander non-intervention: Two experimental studies. *Journal of Applied Social Psychology*, *32*, 1452–1463.

Lewis, S. H. (2003). *Unspoken crimes: Sexual assault in rural America*. Enola, PA: National Sexual Violence Resource Center.

Leyens, J.-P. (2013). Humanity forever in medical dehumanization. In P. G. Bain, J. Vaes, & J.-P. Leyens (eds), *Humanness and dehumanization* (pp. 167–185). New York: Psychology Press.

Leyens, J.-P., Paladino, P. M., Rodriguez-Torres, R., Vaes, J., Demoulin, S., Rodriguez-Perez, A., & Gaunt, R. (2000). The emotional side of prejudice: The attribution of secondary emotions to ingroups and outgroups. *Personality and Social Psychology Review*, *4*, 186–197.

Lois, J. (1999). Socialization to heroism: Individualism and collectivism in a voluntary search and rescue group. *Social Psychology Quarterly*, *62*, 117–135.

Lowe, R. D., Levine, M., Best, R. M., & Heim, D. (2012). Bystander reaction to women fighting: Developing a theory of intervention. *Journal of Interpersonal Violence*, *27*, 1802–1826.

Manning, R., Levine, M., & Collins, A. (2007). The Kitty Genovese murder and the social psychology of helping: The parable of the 38 witnesses. *American Psychologist*, *62*, 555–562.

Mathew, S., & Boyd, R. (2014). The cost of cowardice: Punitive sentiments towards free riders in Turkana raids. *Evolution and Human Behavior*, *35*, 58–64.

McCauley, C., & Moskalenko, S. (2008). Mechanisms of political radicalization: Pathways toward terrorism. *Terrorism and Political Violence*, *20*, 415–433.

McFarlane, A. C. (1995). The severity of the trauma: Issues about its role in posttraumatic stress disorder. In R. J. Kleber, C. R. Figley, & B. P. R. Gersons (eds), *Beyond trauma: Cultural and societal dynamics* (pp. 31–54). New York: Plenum Press.

McMahon, S. (2010). Rape myth beliefs and bystander attitudes among incoming college students. *Journal of American College Health*, *59*, 3–11.

McPherson, S., & Parks, C. D. (2011). Intergroup and interindividual resource competition escalating into conflict: The elimination option. *Group Dynamics*, *15*, 285–296.

Mears, D. S. (2013). The Catch-22 Effect: The lasting stigma of wartime cowardice in the U. S. Army Air Forces. *Journal of Military History*, *77*, 1025–1054.

Milgram, S. (1970). The experience of living in cities. *Science*, *167*, 1461–1468.

Miller, C. (2010). Character traits, social psychology, and impediments to helping behavior. *Journal of Ethics and Social Philosophy*, *5*, 1–36.

Moser, G. (1988). Urban stress and helping behavior: Effects of environmental overload and noise on behavior. *Journal of Environmental Psychology*, *8*, 287–298.

Most, S. B., Chun, M. M., Widders, D. M., & Zald, D. H. (2005). Emotional rubbernecking: Cognitive control and personality in emotion-induced blindness. *Psychonomic Bulletin and Review*, *12*, 654–661.

Nadler, A., & Fisher, J. D. (1986). The role of threat to self-esteem and perceived control in recipient reaction to help: Theory development and empirical validation. *Advances in Experimental Social Psychology*, *19*, 81–122.

Newman, G. E., & Cain, D. M. (2014). Tainted altruism: When doing some good is evaluated as worse than doing no good at all. *Psychological Science*, *25*, 648–655.

Nezlek, J. B., Wesselmann, E. D., Wheeler, L., & Williams, K. D. (2012). Ostracism in everyday life. *Group Dynamics*, *16*, 91–104.

Parker, M. T., & Janoff-Bulman, R. (2013). Lessons from morality-based social identity: The power of outgroup "hate," not just ingroup "love." *Social Justice Research*, *26*, 81–96.

Parks, C. D., & Stone, A. B. (2010). The desire to expel unselfish members from the group. *Journal of Personality and Social Psychology*, *99*, 303–310.

Parks, C. D., Joireman, J., & Van Lange, P. A. M. (2013). Cooperation, trust, and antagonism: How public goods are promoted. *Psychological Science in the Public Interest*, *14*, 119–165.

Parks, C. D., Rumble, A. C., & Posey, D. C. (2002). The effects of envy on reciprocation in social dilemmas. *Personality and Social Psychology Bulletin*, *28*, 522–534.

Phan, M. B., Blumer, N., & Demaiter, E. I. (2009). Helping hands: Neighborhood diversity, deprivation, and reciprocity of support in non-kin networks. *Journal of Social and Personal Relationships*, *26*, 899–918.

Polanin, J. R., Espelage, D. L., & Pigott, T. D. (2012). A meta-analysis of school-based bullying prevention programs' effects on bystander intervention behavior. *School Psychology Review*, *41*, 47–65.

Pozzoli, T., Ang, R. P., & Gini, G. (2012). Bystanders' reactions to bullying: A cross-cultural analysis of personal correlates among Italian and Singaporean students. *Social Development*, *21*, 686–703.

Preston, S. D. (2013). The origins of altruism in offspring care. *Psychological Bulletin*, *139*, 1305–1341.

Price, S. A., & Brosnan, S. F. (2012). To each according to his need? Variability in the responses to inequity in non-human primates. *Social Justice Research, 25*, 140–169.

Raihani, N. J. (2014). Hidden altruism in a real-world setting. *Biology Letters, 10*, 20130884.

Rapoport, A. (1967). Exploiter, Leader, Hero, and Martyr: The four archetypes of the 2 × 2 game. *Behavioral Science, 12*, 81–84.

Reimers, L., & Diekhof, E. K. (2015). Testosterone is associated with cooperation during intergroup competition by enhancing parochial altruism. *Frontiers in Neuroscience, 9*, 183–201.

Ruffle, B. J., & Sosis, R. (2006). Cooperation and the in-group-out-group bias: A field test on Israeli kibbutz members and city residents. *Journal of Economic Behavior and Organization, 60*, 147–163.

Rutkowski, G. K., Gruder, C. L., & Romer, D. (1983). Group cohesiveness, social norms, and bystander intervention. *Journal of Personality and Social Psychology, 44*, 545–552.

Salmivalli, C., Voeten, M., & Poskiparta, E. (2011). Bystanders matter: Associations between reinforcing, defending, and the frequency of bullying behavior in classrooms. *Journal of Clinical Child and Adolescent Psychology, 40*, 668–676.

Savage, D. A., & Torgler, B. (2015). *The times they are a changin': The effect of institutional change on cooperative behavior at 26,000 ft over sixty years*. New York: Palgrave Macmillan.

Shaw, A., & Olson, K. R. (2012). Children discard a resource to avoid inequity. *Journal of Experimental Psychology: General, 141*, 382–395.

Sherrod, D. R., & Downs, R. (1974). Environmental determinants of altruism: The effects of stimulus overload and perceived control on helping. *Journal of Experimental Social Psychology, 10*, 468–479.

Shirtcliff, E. A., Vitacco, M. J., Graf, A. R., Gostisha, A. J., Merz, J. L., & Zahn-Wexler, C. (2009). Neurobiology of empathy and callousness: Implications for the development of antisocial behavior. *Behavioral Science and Law, 27*, 137–171.

Shontz, F. C., & Fink, S. L. (1959). A psychobiological analysis of discomfort, pain, and death. *Journal of General Psychology, 60*, 275–287.

Siem, F. M., & Spence, J. T. (1986). Gender-related traits and helping behaviors. *Journal of Personality and Social Psychology, 51*, 615–621.

Snyder, M., & Omoto, A. M. (2008). Volunteerism: Social issues perspectives and social policy implications. *Social Issues and Policy Review, 2*, 1–36.

Snyder, M., Omoto, A. M., & Crain, A. L. (1999). Punished for their good deeds: Stigmatization of AIDS volunteers. *American Behavioral Scientist, 42*, 1175–1192.

Staub, E. (2002). The psychology of bystanders, perpetrators, and heroic helpers. In L. S. Newman & R. Erber (eds), *Understanding genocide* (pp. 11–42). New York: Oxford University Press.

Stiff, C., & van Vugt, M. (2008). The power of reputations: The role of third-party information in the admission of new group members. *Group Dynamics, 12*, 155–166.

Stürmer, S., Snyder, M., & Omoto, A. M. (2005). Prosocial emotions and helping: The moderating role of group membership. *Journal of Personality and Social Psychology, 88*, 532–546.

Sun, S., Zagefka, H., & Goodwin, R. (2013). Predictors of intergroup concern for disaster victims of the Japan earthquake. *Asian Journal of Social Psychology, 16*, 152–157.

Thornberg, R. (2007). A classmate in distress: Schoolchildren as bystanders and their reasons for how they act. *Social Psychology of Education, 10*, 5–28.

Tice, D. M., & Baumeister, R. F. (1985). Masculinity inhibits helping in emergencies: Personality does predict the bystander effect. *Journal of Personality and Social Psychology, 49*, 420–428.

Van Bommel, M., van Prooijen, J.-W., Elffers, H., & Van Lange, P. A. M. (2012). Be aware to care: Public self-awareness leads to a reversal of the bystander effect. *Journal of Experimental Social Psychology, 48*, 926–930.

Van Boven, L., Loewenstein, G., Welch, E., & Dunning, D. (2012). The illusion of courage in self-predictions: Mispredicting one's own behavior in embarrassing situations. *Journal of Behavioral Decision Making, 25*, 1–12.

Voelpel, S. C., Eckhoff, R. A., & Förster, J. (2008). David against Goliath? Group size and bystander effects in virtual knowledge sharing. *Human Relations, 61*, 271–295.

Wagner, S., Hornstein, H. A., & Holloway, S. (1982). Willingness to help a stranger: The effects of social context and opinion similarity. *Journal of Applied Social Psychology, 12*, 429–443.

Walsh, C. (2014). *Cowardice: A brief history*. Princeton, NJ: Princeton University Press.

Weisz, A. N., & Black, B. M. (2008). Peer intervention in dating violence: Beliefs of African-American middle school adolescents. *Journal of Ethnic and Cultural Diversity in Social Work, 17*, 177–196.

Wen, C. K., Hudak, P. L., & Hwang, S. W. (2007). Homeless people's perceptions of welcomeness and unwelcomeness in healthcare encounters. *Journal of General Internal Medicine, 22*, 1011–1017.

West, S. G., Whitney, G., & Schnedler, R. (1975). Helping a motorist in distress: The effects of sex, race, and neighborhood. *Journal of Personality and Social Psychology, 31*, 691–698.

Xu, X., Zuo, X., Wang, X., & Han, S. (2009). Do you feel my pain? Racial group membership modulates empathic neural responses. *Journal of Neuroscience, 29,* 8525–8529.

Zak, P. J., Kurzban, R., Ahmadi, S., Swerdloff, R. S., Park, J., ... & Matzner, W. (2009). Testosterone administration decreases generosity in the ultimatum game. *PLoS One, 4,* e8830.

Zethraeus, N., Kocoska-Maras, L., Ellingsen, T., von Schoultz, B., Hirschberg, A. L., & Johannesson, M. (2009). A randomized trial of the effect of estrogen and testosterone on economic behavior. *Proceedings of the National Academy of Sciences, 106,* 6535–6538.

Zettler, I., & Hilbig, B. E. (2010). Honesty-humility and a person-situation interaction at work. *European Journal of Personality, 24,* 569–582.

Zhang, H., Chan, D. K.-S., Teng, F., & Zhang, D. (2015). Sense of interpersonal security and preference for harsh actions against others: The role of dehumanization. *Journal of Experimental Social Psychology, 56,* 165–171.

Zilioli, S., Ponzi, D., Henry, A., & Maestripieri, D. (2014). Testosterone, cortisol, and empathy: Evidence for the dual-hormone hypothesis. *Adaptive Human Behavior and Physiology, 1,* 1–13.

24
Heroic Empathy
The Heart of Leadership

Ronald H. Humphrey and Laural L. Adams

What compels people to risk their lives for complete strangers, not just once but many times over? Perhaps it is heroic empathy, a compassionate identification with others combined with a bias towards action. U.S. Coast Guard rescuers provide an ideal example of this. Every year they save 3,000 lives, often putting their own lives in danger while so doing (Phillips & Loy, 2003). For example, Patrick was fresh out of his aviation survival technician training program when he demonstrated heroic empathy (case example based on Humphrey, 2013; Phillips & Loy, 2003). A fishing boat had sent an emergency call to his base in Kodiak, Alaska. One of the boat's crew members had been badly injured, his arm almost cut off. Without a quick rescue, the crewman would die. To complicate matters, it was night time, and the raging snow storm meant visibility would be especially poor. The 25-foot waves would make landing on the boat difficult and dangerous. Undeterred, Patrick let himself be lowered from the helicopter towards the boat. A huge wave hit the fishing boat, causing a steel girder to smack into Patrick. Back on the helicopter, the flight attendant thought that the girder might have killed or seriously injured Patrick, so he quickly hoisted him back up. Patrick was aching but avowed himself fit for duty.

The pilot wondered if the bad conditions meant the rescue should be called off. The decision was Patrick's, and he knew that calling off the rescue would mean the injured fisherman would die. Patrick decided to try again, this time with a new plan. Instead of dropping straight into the boat, Patrick had the helicopter swing him along the waterline towards the side of the boat. This meant that Patrick would be swamped with freezing cold seawater during the big waves, but the plan worked and Patrick was able to board the boat and rescue the fisherman. The fisherman lived as a result of Patrick's bravery and competence.

The above case illustrates three of the defining characteristics of heroes. According to Goethals and Allison (2012), heroes are courageous, competent, and virtuous. This matches well with the seven characteristics that the U.S. Coast Guard looks for in recruits:

1 intelligence;
2 high energy;
3 self-confidence;
4 continual learning;
5 compassion;
6 courage with a bias toward action; and

7   character.

(Phillips & Loy, 2003)

Obviously characteristic 6, courage with a bias toward action, matches with being courageous. Characteristics 1–4 match with competence, and compassion and character match with virtue.

It is this special combination of courage, competence, and virtue that separates heroes from others. Courage, like that shown by Patrick in the U.S. Coast Guard case, is characteristic of many types of heroes, and certainly many people would not be brave enough to jump out of a helicopter into a winter storm at sea. However, courage by itself is not enough. A person may perform a risky behavior, and thus act courageously, but unless this risk is taken on behalf of a moral purpose it is not a heroic act. As Goethals and Allison (2012, p. 186) state, "First and foremost, heroes are people who do something that is moral." Extreme sports enthusiasts, race car drivers, and other dare devils risk their lives for thrills, but they are not heroes according to this moral standard. However, it must be admitted that they may be seen as heroes by their fellow enthusiasts, as heroic status is in many ways in the eyes of the beholders (Goethals & Allison, 2012). Perhaps their followers find some way to attach a moral purpose to these pursuits, for instance, by believing that these activities develop courage, self-confidence, and discipline, or are a worthy life goal (i.e., living ones' dreams for adventure). However, when risky behaviors endanger others the actors may even be seen as villains instead of heroes. For example, when people drive recklessly on public roads. Thus overall a moral purpose is still one of the key defining characteristics of courageous heroes.

Support for the dual roles of bravery and moral purpose is provided by the study by Kinsella, Ritchie, and Igou (2015). Among the 8 features they found that were central to prototypical perceptions of heroes, the three features seen as most prototypical of heroes are *brave*, *moral integrity*, and *courageous*.

Competence is also crucial to heroes. Heroes need to be competent enough to achieve their moral purpose and to aid those they are trying to help. This is clearly shown in the U.S. Coast Guard case discussed earlier. Patrick had to have the skills to carry out a dangerous and difficult mission in order to achieve his moral purpose, rescuing the injured fisherman. Carrying out tasks that are easily performed by most people, no matter how important, is not enough to garner one attributions of heroism. As Goethals and Allison (2012) observed, heroic status is more likely to be given to those who overcome obstacles and task difficulties that would defeat the average person. Heroes are often depicted as struggling against almost overwhelming odds, and their heroic status is conferred when they finally succeed through their competence and ingenuity. People tend to have sympathy for underdogs (Allison & Burnette, 2009; Allison & Goethals, 2008). Indeed, underdogs are particularly likely to be accorded heroic status, provided they go on to win (Kim et al., 2008). An important exception to this is in the case of martyrs, who may not personally succeed in achieving their goals, but who inspire others to take up the cause and the struggle.

Although history books and popular culture are full of heroes who have performed truly outstanding achievements, it must be recognized that many people are heroes in the eyes of their friends and family members. Indeed, Allison and Goethals (2011) conducted a national survey of adults, and they asked respondents to list heroes. They found that 32 percent of the heroes listed were family members. In their open-ended explanations of their choices, participants were grateful for the generosity their heroic family members showed, and they appreciated the sacrifices that their family members made and the struggles that they went through in order to help them out.

Although courage and competence are two of the three key characteristics of heroes, the moral purpose, often accompanied by self-sacrifice and struggle, is at the heart of heroism. It is this moral purpose that motivates the heroic behavior and that makes heroes willing to endure struggles and persevere in the face of obstacles. In this chapter we will develop the argument that empathy is one of the core motivating forces behind moral purpose and heroic action. This emphasis on empathy is consistent with Goethals and Allison's (2012) view of the origins of moral thinking as it relates to heroes. They draw upon the work on moral development in children by Kohlberg (1969; Kohlberg & Hersh, 1977). According to Kohlberg's model, moral development depends on being able to take the perspective of other people. At the first level in Kohlberg's model, the pre-conventional stage, children are concerned with rewards and punishments and their own self-interests. As the children gain in the ability to perceive others' perspectives, they move to the conventional level, where they consider social norms, authority figures, and other social groups' standards for behavior. Kohlberg believed that most people remained at the conventional level of morality and only a few progressed to the highest level, post-conventional morality, which requires a deeper level of empathy. As Goethals and Allison (2012) put it, life experiences may push or pull people into thinking more deeply about others' needs and perspectives, and thus into the post-conventional stage. The ability to perceive others' thoughts, feelings and needs is the essence of cognitive forms of empathy and thus empathy is crucial to moral development and virtue.

Hoffman (2001) has also related empathy to moral development, and reasons that empathy is a major motivator promoting caring and justice. He maintains that our empathic instincts had great survival value and thus lead to the development of an empathy instinct or trait. Groups of humans that had empathic concern for each other survived and propagated more than those that did not, thus leading to ever greater levels of empathy among humans.

Further support for the role of empathy in heroism is provided by Goethals and Allison's (2012) study of heroic traits. They used a trait listing and sorting methodology to discover how students perceive heroes. They found that the list of traits sorted into 8 clusters: Caring, Charismatic, Inspiring, Reliable, Resilient, Selfless, Smart, and Strong. Relevant to this chapter, the first cluster, Caring, includes the traits compassionate, empathic, and kind. As we shall see from the later review of the literature on empathy, empathy's role in heroic behavior may be even greater than this suggests.

What is Empathy?

Empathy is commonly defined "as the ability to comprehend another's feelings and to re-experience them oneself" (Salovey & Mayer, 1990, pp. 194–195). This definition recognizes that there is a cognitive component to empathy, which is the ability to perceive and recognize another's feelings. And it also recognizes that there is an affective component, which is where one feels to at least some degree what others are feeling. Over the years various philosophers and social scientists have emphasized one aspect of this or another. The origins of the empathy concept go back to 1873, when the term Einfühlung (translated to "empathy") was invented by Robert Vischer to explain how someone "feels into" another's emotion (Titchener, 1999). Since then, a variety of conceptualizations have emerged, with Batson (2009) listing 8 different forms of empathy.

In a classic description of the empathic process, Katz illustrates how an empathetic response is "triggered by cues in the conversation or by impressions we receive of the state of mind or feeling of the other person":

> We assimilate this information without being aware of doing so. We pick up the signals through a kind of inner radar and certain changes in our own emotional states make themselves felt. We mimic the other person and in the excitement of our spontaneous response our attention is almost completely absorbed.
>
> (Katz, 1963, p. 5)

Katz further maintained that this process results in the empathizer expressing recognition and acceptance of the other person's needs and emotions, and that this acceptance has a reassuring effect on the other person. Perhaps this is one reason why empathic listening is a keystone of many types of therapy (Rogers, 1975). Some scholars have even gone so far as to assert that empathy is "the fundamental competence of social awareness" and "the sine qua non of all social effectiveness in working life" (Goleman, Boyatzis, & McKee, 2002, p. 50).

The distinction between cognitive and affective empathy is important because it is possible for someone to recognize what others are feeling without sympathizing with them or sharing their emotions. Modern neurological research has verified that the cognitive and affective empathic processes are separate and distinct (Cox et al., 2012; Decety, 2011). This has important implications, both good and bad, in terms of willingness to perform heroic behaviors on behalf of others. As will be shown in a later section, people are more willing to help another person when they identify with them and are feeling affective empathy. Thus affective empathy may be a powerful catalyst to heroic behavior. However, heroes often operate in emotionally tense settings, where many people are prone to panic, personal distress, or emotional hijacking (Goleman, 1995). Heroes need enough empathic detachment to regulate their emotions to perform at their best.

Affective empathy has been depicted as an "other-oriented emotional response elicited by the congruent welfare of someone else" (Batson, 2009, p. 418). Affective empathy occurs from a "bottom up" process whereby people first imitate the emotions they are witnessing by activating "mirror neurons" that mimic the emotions being observed (Kilner & Lemon, 2013). This is an automatic process that occurs before conscious awareness, and thus is largely uncontrolled by higher thought processes. This automatic form of empathy may have physiological effects, including on heart rates and breathing patterns, and may influence emotional states as well (Critchley et al., 2004; Vignemont & Singer, 2006).

In contrast, cognitive empathy is a "top-down" process more susceptible to conscious control. Conceptualizations of cognitive empathy differ somewhat, in that some count awareness of others' emotions, thoughts and perspectives without any sharing of emotions as a type of cognitive empathy (sometimes this is simply known as perspective taking). However, others consider cognitive empathy to be a sharing of another's emotions coupled with an awareness that one is feeling the emotions for different reasons than is the person being observed (for a review of different conceptualizations of empathy from a neuroscience perspective, see Decety & Meyer, 2008). In this case, cognitive empathy involves an awareness that the emotions they are witnessing in others are not their own emotions. Thus cognitive empathy involves less of an identification with the other party and a lower sharing of emotions.

Cognitive empathy can be influenced by focus of attention and by a variety of workplace or environmental factors that direct one's attention towards others (thus increasing empathy) or towards oneself or other non-social features of the environment (Batson, Eklund, Chermok, Hoyt, & Ortiz, 2007). This suggests that training programs can promote empathy by getting people to focus their attentions on the needs of others. Studies have shown that people can learn to be higher on cognitive empathy (although not affective empathy) (Dziobek et al., 2008). For example, empathy training programs have helped clinicians become better at diagnosing patient problems and helped them establish better overall doctor-patient relationships (Dow, Leong, Anderson, & Wenzel, 2007). Following on from this, it also suggests that the impulse to help others, perhaps in a heroic way, could also be influenced.

Empathy, Prosocial Behavior, and Heroic Behavior

Empathy is often regarded as an internal mental and affective process best assessed by either physiological measures or self-reports of internal states. Nonetheless, empathy can also be considered from a behavioral standpoint—does someone act in an empathic way towards others? In other words, does the individual exhibit prosocial behavior or good organizational citizenship? Empathy is often used as an explanation for these prosocial behaviors, and this approach is known as the empathy-altruism hypothesis (e.g., Batson et al., 2007). Prosocial behavior can consist of simple acts, such as donating small sums of money to charity, helping others out with their work, or similar acts of generosity and good will. At the high end of this spectrum, we can consider heroic behaviors as among the ultimate forms of prosocial behaviors, since it may involve risking one's life to help others.

Meta-analyses have confirmed the empathy-altruism hypothesis (Eisenberg & Miller, 1987). People who scored higher on empathy were more likely to perform prosocial behaviors and were also more cooperative and more socially competent. The results were similar regardless of whether empathy and prosocial behavior was measured using questionnaire measures of both, or whether measured in simulations that actually gave participants a chance to act prosocially. Interestingly, even measures of empathy based on observations of the facial features of the participants showed support for the empathy-altruism hypothesis.

Why is it that empathy predicts prosocial behavior? Scholars who take an evolutionary perspective argue that empathy emerged because it helped people survive during difficult times (Preston, 2013). By acting empathically towards a member of their species in distress, they help the species as a whole survive (Hoffman, 2001).

Empathy and Heroic Self-Sacrifice

Going back to the question asked at the beginning of this chapter, why is it that some people are willing to behave heroically and risk their careers, their freedom, their health, and even their lives to help others? The empathy literature may help answer this question, because the research shows that empathic people are more likely to make personal sacrifices to help others. Studies on empathy have shown that people high on empathy are willing to perform altruistic behaviors even when they come at a cost in terms of time or money (Joireman, Daniels, George-Falvy, & Kamdar, 2006). Heroic behavior, risking one's life, can be seen as the ultimate end of this altruistic, self-sacrificing continuum.

As Goethals and Allison (2012) so vividly depict in their summary of the literature on heroes, self-sacrificing behavior and risk-taking are part of the hero mythology and prototypes. As they observe, a dramatic illustration of the importance of self-sacrifice concerns the effects of being assassinated on perceptions of presidential greatness. Simonton (1994) found that being assassinated was equivalent to spending four years leading the nation through wartime. Presidents who risked their lives in well publicized events prior to being president also seem to have a boost in perceptions of greatness. George Washington risked his life during battle several times, and was well-known for being among the last to retreat. His aides had to retrieve him during one retreat. At other times, he rode his famous white horse in front of the troops and in clear sight of the enemy, defying enemy fire. Teddy Roosevelt, another president rated high on greatness, risked his life in various well-known episodes throughout his career. He endangered his life while fighting corruption in city hall, and in his most famous event personally led the troops up San Juan Hill during the Spanish–American War. Later, he risked his life, and seriously damaged his health, exploring a previously unexplored river in Brazil. These true-life exploits all contributed to his almost mythological heroic status.

It is perhaps not surprising, given the importance of self-sacrifice, that this theme is well-reflected in the lives of the four presidents given special recognition in the form of the Mount Rushmore National Memorial. One, Abraham Lincoln, led the nation through civil war and was assassinated as well. George Washington and Teddy Roosevelt both personally risked their lives in combat and were well-known for their bravery and boldness. Thomas Jefferson was not known for his exploits on the battlefield, but as a revolutionary his life was on the line, and if the revolutionaries had lost the war it was well-known that he would have been hung as a traitor.

Equally important, the four presidents on Mount Rushmore were also known for their compassion and empathy for others. George Washington demonstrated his compassion for his troops during the tough times and harsh winter at Valley Forge (Humphrey, 2013). While his troops were at Valley Forge, roughly 3,000 (out of 11,000) soldiers perished from frigid temperatures, lack of food, and sickness. Washington demonstrated his empathy for his troops by sharing their harsh conditions. He supervised the construction of shelters to protect his troops from the cold, and he was one of the last ones to move into a shelter. Abraham Lincoln was known for his humble, self-effacing manner, and gentle humor. More importantly, he devoted his life and career towards helping out those less fortunate than himself. Although not known for being humble, Teddy Roosevelt devoted his career just as much towards helping those less fortunate. Although from a wealthy family, he campaigned for reforms that helped the poor and middle class, and in his personal interactions with others he showed a keen interest in the lives of others no matter what their background. Thomas Jefferson was also from a privileged background, but he too campaigned to give everyone the right to pursue liberty and happiness. Jefferson was such a soft touch to his friends that he frequently ended up in financial difficulties because of the money he loaned out with little reassurance of being repaid.

The altruistic behaviors shown by the Mount Rushmore presidents are typical of those high on empathy. Empathy is a powerful motivator of altruistic behavior even when it comes at great personal cost and sacrifice. The presidents also illustrate how individual personal sacrifice facilitates the survival of the group, as maintained by the sociobiologists discussed earlier. Each of the presidents acted on behalf of the larger society, and their societies grew and prospered as a result.

The particular type of empathy shown by heroic leaders may be especially important. Many empathy measures and conceptualizations of empathy have been developed by clinical psychologist and other counsellors. Because of these clinical origins, many conceptualizations of empathy focus on negative emotions—the sort displayed by those seeking professional help. In addition, empathy is often described as a one-way process, whereby the counsellor listens and the client emotes his or her feelings. However, Kellett, Humphrey and Sleeth (2006) argued that this conceptualization of empathy is not particularly appropriate for leaders. First, if the negative emotions are transferred to the counsellor (a common problem in therapeutic settings) then the counsellors become depressed or in other ways feel badly. In contrast, leaders need to display confidence and optimism during difficult times (Humphrey, 2008; Humphrey, Pollack, and Hawver, 2008). Thus empathy measures designed for leaders need to take into account the need for positive emotions. Second, empathy is often described as a passive, one-way process in which the listener receives the emotions from the speaker. Leaders, in contrast, have to take an active role and stimulate the sharing of emotions. Rogers (1975) most famously described therapeutic empathy and listening as a highly active process because of the effort it takes to understand someone else. Leaders need to take this active role if they are to understand the needs of their followers. However, they must also engage in shaping and influencing their followers, particularly when their followers are feeling pessimistic about their chances to succeed (Humphrey, 2008; Humphrey et al., 2008). This is why Kellett and her colleagues described their interactive empathy scale as a two-way influence, in which leaders are both influenced by their followers' emotions, but also influence their followers' emotions as well through their common empathic bond (Kellett et al., 2006). As they maintained, leaders need to take the initiative in creating the empathic bond with and among their followers.

The above conceptualization of empathy is also consistent with the shared leadership view that leadership is a multiway process (Pearce & Conger, 2003). According to the shared leadership perspective, leadership in modern organizations occurs at every level, and top leaders need to be influenced by their followers, and grant their followers opportunities to take initiative and demonstrate leadership. This is because knowledge is widely distributed in organizations, and decision-making authority and leadership needs to shift to whoever has the most knowledge and expertise about the problem at hand. From an empathic viewpoint, an empathic bond among followers and leaders would make them more willing to accept each other's viewpoints and goals. When people share an affective empathic bond, they feel to at least some degree what the other person is feeling, and this can help them understand the needs and desires of the other party. Even cognitive forms of empathy mean that the empathizer has at least an awareness of the needs, feelings, and viewpoints of the other party.

It is far easier to empathize with others when they are similar to us in terms of age, social class, background, dress and looks, and overall lifestyle. When people are similar to us, it is easier to imagine ourselves in their situation. With high levels of similarity, we may even have been in their situation before, or may even be currently experiencing it ourselves. When people share and experience common situations, the levels of empathy may be strong enough to promote lifelong bonds and high levels of mutual admiration and liking. This is one reason why wartime buddies, despite enduring high levels of stress and horrific conditions, often feel empathy and warm feelings for each other, and many stay in touch throughout their lifetimes.

The common sense observation that it is easier to empathize with others who are like us has been confirmed by research (Decety & Jackson, 2004; Preston & Hofelich, 2012). In part, this is because similarity primes cognitive mechanisms that make it easier to imagine ourselves in others' circumstances (Chambers & Davis, 2012). Without "walking a mile" in others' shoes, as the adage goes, it is hard to fully imagine ourselves in someone else's situation. This is what makes the empathy and care for the less privileged so remarkable among leaders like Washington and Teddy Roosevelt, whose privileged upbringings placed them far above those they dedicated their lives to helping. Like his relative Theodore, FDR also grew up in luxury. However, as a young adult he contracted a crippling case of polio, and it is possible that FDR's deep compassion for the poor and helpless was forged in the fire of his own crisis and personal tragedy.

Charismatic Leadership, Empathy, and Heroism

The above conceptualization of empathic heroes has some strong overlaps with depictions of charismatic leaders, suggesting that empathy and heroism are two major components of charismatic leadership. The original concept of charisma was in line with the view of heroes as truly exceptional and special (Goethals & Allison, 2012). Weber (1924/1947) used the term charisma to refer to leaders with special gifts and powers; the word charisma is derived from the ancient Greek word meaning "divine gift" and literally referred to religious leaders who had gifts of miracles from god. Weber applied it to political leaders who had extraordinary impact on society, often by leading major social movements. According to Weber, these charismatic leaders awed their followers through their special gifts of oratory and leadership, and made their followers feel that their charismatic leader was far above them in talents and abilities.

However, later scholars began to develop a little more skepticism as to the divine origins of charisma and of the view that only truly exceptional individuals can have charisma (Shamir, 1995). These scholars argued that other leaders can also have charisma even if they are not transforming the world in the way that charismatic leaders like Moses or Churchill did. They began to develop models of charisma that emphasized rhetorical techniques, such as the use of "we" statements to create perceptions of a common identity (Shamir, Arthur, & House, 1994; Shamir, House, & Arthur, 1993). This emphasis on we statements suggests that charismatic leaders need to create a sense of an empathic bond between them and their followers.

Because it is possible to learn rhetorical techniques, scholars in this tradition take more of a behavioral approach, rather than a trait approach, to leadership (Conger, 2011; Conger &

Kanungo, 1987). Thus this approach emphasized the various behaviors that lead others to attribute charisma to a leader. As Conger, Kanungo, and Menon (2000, p. 749) state, "charismatic leadership is distinguished from other forms by the followers' perceptions of the manager's formulation of a shared and idealized future vision as well as his or her effective articulation of this vision in an inspirational manner." Note that this approach keeps some of the emphasis on social movements or change, and also emphasizes a shared bond in the form of a common future. The focus on rhetorical techniques that create perceptions of special abilities or at least of leadership qualities is still there. This perspective accords well with the view that heroes have competence and high ability (Goethals & Allison, 2012).

Models of charisma also emphasized the role of crisis situations in garnering attributions of charisma (Conger, Kanungo, & Menon, 2000; Halverson, Murphy, & Riggio, 2004; Pillai, 1996). After all, it is hard to believe that someone is truly exceptional if he or she is solving merely routine problems. It is only when leaders solve crisis situations or other problems that baffle us are we willing to grant them the superior status of charisma. Crisis situations call for the soaring inspirational language typical of charismatic leadership (Bligh, Kohles, & Meindl, 2004). Empathy also plays a role in crisis situations, and of course crisis is when heroes are most needed. In crisis situations heroes need to be sensitive to the needs and wants of their followers. Without empathy, successful and wealthy people may be uncaring when others lose their jobs due to economic crisis situations. With empathy, they may be motivated to use their wealth, knowledge, and skills to help others. Whereas empathy helps them understand why help is needed, courage and heroic behavior may be needed to take action.

Although early theories of charisma emphasize crisis as a necessary precursor for awe-inspiring attributions of charisma, it must be acknowledged that later models argue that charismatic attributions may also be granted during times of great opportunities, or when people achieve extraordinary feats that astound others (Conger, 2011). This accords with the view of sports leaders or other outstanding achievers as heroes (Goethals & Allison, 2012). A high tech computer programmer who makes a vast fortune almost overnight, or a top athlete who sets a world record, may be seen as charismatic heroes in the eyes of their followers. When these heroes display empathy by contributing to society as well, their heroic status is often enhanced, which is why so many professional sports teams take time out from their televised broadcasts to highlight charitable actions by their players. Lance Armstrong, before his fall from grace, achieved world-wide hero status in part because the charity he founded, Livestrong, raised roughly a billion dollars for charity.

So far, the view espoused in this chapter has largely covered heroic empathy from the individual perspective (i.e., from the view that empathic leaders have special abilities, such as high levels of empathy, courage, and competence, that makes them stand out). However, as we will see in the next section, empathic heroes are also socially constructed and owe much to organizational and societal factors that predispose others to see them as heroes, and that facilitate their empathic and heroic actions.

How Empathy Makes Heroic Leadership Possible

As Goethals and Allison (2012) so vividly depict in their summary of the literature on heroes, self-sacrificing behavior and risk-taking are part of the hero mythology and prototypes. Other research has identified the benefits and rewards that are exchanged between leaders and their followers, but heroic leaders are characterized by selflessness and self-sacrifice. In order to avoid rendering the relationship between heroic leaders and followers as merely transactional, we employ a theoretical framework, namely, distributed cognition (DC) that positions heroic leaders in the larger context of the organization and in the system in which the organization resides. This enables us to underscore the role that empathy, particularly cognitive empathy, has in giving rise to heroic leaders and their acts. In the remainder of this chapter, we examine how other researchers have used a DC approach to understand the dynamic socio-cognitive properties of complex organizations and articulate what we believe this approach reveals about the nature and function of heroes in organizations.

Woodrow Wilson once said, "I not only use all the brains I have, but all I can borrow" (1914/1979). He understood the important role that followers play in leaders' success, and in this case, he was particularly aware of relying on their cognitive competencies. Heroic leaders play important roles in organizations, but they do not accomplish their great feats alone. As Barack Obama noted during the 2012 presidential elections,

> [I]f you've been successful, you didn't get there on your own … If you were successful, somebody along the line gave you some help. There was a great teacher somewhere in your life. Somebody helped to create this unbelievable American system that we have that allowed you to thrive. Somebody invested in roads and bridges. If you've got a business—you didn't build that. Somebody else made that happen.
>
> *(C-SPAN, 2012)*

His comments, directed at small business owners, spurred a flurry of debate over the self-sufficiency of the stalwart entrepreneur, over the locus of a leader's success, and seemed to garner Obama both criticism and praise. Just how dependent are great leaders on their followers? Further, what role does empathy play in this relationship?

In Chapter 15 of this handbook, Dana Klisanin draws our attention to the collaboratively constructed nature of the hero in the networked age. Further, Zimbardo, Breckenridge, & Moghaddam (2013) underscore the fact that the definition of the hero construct varies, with some conceptions anchoring the hero as an exceptional individual and others emphasizing that heroic feats can come from ordinary individuals in everyday circumstances. The idea of the "banality of heroism" (namely, that the heroic impulse exists in each of us) has been advanced to oppose the terrifying idea of the "banality of evil" proposed by Hannah Arendt (namely, that evil has been rendered supremely ordinary, and Adolf Eichmann's deeds and subsequent trial served as evidence) (Franco & Zimbardo, 2006). This scholarship, along with Barack Obama's commentary to small business owners emphasizing our interdependence, suggests a growing tension around the idea of locating heroism within the exceptional individual. Yet, even these arguments and hypotheses have not gone far enough to reveal the well-spring of heroism that can be made available to all of us. Alternatively, the DC approach paves the way for recognizing where heroism comes from and how one might foster the "heroic imagination," as described by Blau, Franco, and Zimbardo (2012). A DC approach to heroism can help us recognize the co-constructed nature of heroism in order to begin to understand how to deliberately structure organizations that encourage what Franco and Zimbardo call "the high watermark of human behavior."

Further, a DC approach reveals how circulating representations of "heroes" and heroic acts are dependent on organizational members' capacity for empathy. Both leaders' and followers' empathy enables the potential for leaders to emerge in these social structures. This empathy also enables ideas of heroic action to perpetuate, which then structure organizational members' responses to the challenges they face in their organizational contexts. As we discuss below, this theoretical framework helps address the fact that while interactions between leaders and their followers provide each with benefits, researchers are uneasy about qualifying this mutuality as quid pro quo exchanges that are purely transactional in nature (Messick, 2005). As the literature on heroism reveals, heroes do not engage in heroic acts for self-serving ends. In fact, heroism is consistently defined in terms of selflessness and self-sacrifice (Kinsella et al., 2015). DC provides an alternative theoretical framework through which to examine the apparent contradiction between the leader-member exchange literature and the research on heroic leadership. It also enables us to capture the coherence and evolution of heroism as a practice embedded in organizations. Specifically, we explore how multidirectional interrelating between leaders and followers, which is founded on members' capacity for empathy, both enables and constrains the opportunities for heroes to emerge in organizations. A DC framework reveals that cognitive empathy plays a role in constructing systems of practice (Halverson, 2003) that enable the emergence of heroic leaders who possess the traits, such as intelligence, compassion, and competence, ascribed to such leaders. Followers and leaders alike have roles in perpetuating these traits. This perpetuation occurs through complex systems of representation, such as, for example, stories of heroic deeds that become part of organizational lore. From a DC perspective, even deeds themselves serve as signifiers of preferred organizational behavior, functioning to reify the types of behaviors and goals endorsed by the organization (or endorsed by the larger social system in which these organizations reside). These various forms of representation, both internal and external, function to reify the ever-evolving conception of the hero and structure both followers' and leaders' activities. Below, we describe the foundations of distributed cognition, emphasizing a broad definition of artefacts, those inscriptive tools that enable the offloading of cognition from individuals to the systems in which they participate.

Distributed Cognition

Distributed cognition has evolved from the mid-1980s out of the cultural historical psychology of Vygotsky, whose book *Mind and Society* influenced social science researchers to consider that individual cognition is offloaded into the environment through both social and technological means (Hutchins, 2000). Hutchins, a cultural anthropologist who studied how navigational symbols and tools enabled large navy ships to navigate in tight, shallow waterways and expansive seas, believed that contemporary cognitive theories tended to be disembodied, subordinating the fact that cognition is distributed in systems and occurs in both agents and the material world (Hutchins, 1995). According to Hutchins, the coordination of individuals, artifacts and the environment produces a system of practice in which participants work towards shared goals by distributing their cognitive efforts, not just across a system's members, but through its technologies as well. Practices are forms of technologies (what the Greeks referred to as *technē*, or craft). For example, speaking to large audiences, comporting oneself with confidence, and framing one's message as inspirational are practices we often associate with heroic figures. But chief among these technologies are forms of representation that precede actors, whether leaders or followers. For example, Hutchins explains how the cognitive work of navigation was at one point in history offloaded to the sextant and the celestial array of stars; both were representations of one's bearing at sea and both were interpreted by sea-goers, extending their cognition via these mediational means.

This emphasis on the propagation of representational states across media suggests that thinking and ideas can be located in many mediums and communicated through a variety of semiotic tools. For example, the recognition and awareness of the presence of another can be understood as offloaded to the simple gesture of the wave. This approach broadens the phenomena one studies in order to understand organizations. As Hutchins explains, "The emphasis on finding and describing 'knowledge structures' that are somewhere 'inside' the individual encourages us to overlook the fact that human cognition is always situated in a complex sociocultural world and cannot be unaffected by it" (1995 xiii). Given that distributed cognition looks for a "broader class of cognitive events and does not expect all such events to be encompassed by the skin or skull of an individual" (Hutchins, 2000, p. 2), where might cognitive empathy fall in such a framework and how might it function in relation to propagating representations of the hero and heroic acts?

We tend to think of the ways in which heroes and heroic leaders are represented in external media, such as films, books, video games, organizational lore, and striking images. Yet, representations are also found internally in the mind, and the DC approach encourages a holistic analysis of how these internal representations are coordinated with external ones to construct systems of practice. Representations that exist in the mind are often referred to as knowledge structures, and the most commonly researched knowledge structures are schemas, scripts, and frames. An example of a commonly circulated schema is the construct of the doctor. The script that accompanies a visit to the doctor would include expectations about how the interaction and the activities during the appointment will unfold. Formerly, a common frame for doctor-patient interactions held that the doctor possessed the authority on the nature of the body and bodily experiences, but with the access to information via the internet, this frame has shifted and patients now claim relatively more expertise over their own subjective bodily experiences and commonly recognize doctors' limitations (Adams, 2014). It is easy to see that external representations, meaning the more modern depictions of doctors that circulate, have helped to reify these expectations and even to structure both patients' and doctors' actions. One might compare, for example, renditions of the doctor by painter Norman Rockwell during the early-to-mid 19th century as the fatherly and compassionate authority figure with the depiction of Dr. House on the TV series *House, MD*, the detached and idiosyncratic expert who works his teams of specialists to puzzle out the difficult mysteries of the body. However, there is no research on heroism or heroic leadership that links internal forms of representation to the circulation of the hero construct (Goethals & Allison, 2011). Yet, Emrich (1995) in his work on leadership has distinguished the variables about which people might construct such schemas: people tend to have theories about what traits leaders possess, how they behave and the nature of their agency. These factors might be usefully employed to flesh out existing schemas for heroic leaders.

However, there is yet another form of internal representation that has a profound effect on the circulation of the hero and the heroic leader, both through society and the organizational systems that operate within it. Mental models can be understood as cognitive representations (Bezemer & Kress, 2008; Thibault, 2004). Mental models are "small-scale models" (Craik, 1943) or symbolic representations that we construct in our heads to help us reason through the complex nature of the world. A type of mental model familiar to most people is the mental map, which contains spatial representations of geographies through which users can navigate in their heads. Another familiar everyday context for mental modelling that most people will recognize involves reasoning through how to get a large piece of furniture through a door, a problem "usually solved by mentally simulating turning over a geometrical structure approximating the configuration of the piece of furniture through various rotations" (Nersessian, 2002, p. 150). People construct mental models of others in order to anticipate their responses to certain situations (Adams, 2014). Adams found that mental models are dynamic, enabling a "thinker" to imagine how another person might respond to a particular context. The mental model itself is comprised of objects, both abstract and conceptual, relationality between these objects, and forms of dynamism applied to "run" the model. Mental models are multimodal constructions in that they that employ representational modalities afforded by "mind," such as force, image, and affect; their design reveals the thinker's tacit values and assumptions. Mental models are used to work through "problem spaces" and when those spaces involve predicting other people's behavior, we tend to model others responding to the situational variables we think are significant to them. In this way, these situational factors become significant to us, and our mental models provide us with a range of potential responses we think influential others would consider legitimate. Research suggests that reflecting on our mental models of others (or on our models of specific challenges and problems) can enable us to extend our reasoning, critically evaluate our assumptions and expand the range of responses available to us (Adams, 2014).

Previous methods to research the modelling of other people and their imagined responses have relied on discourse analysis, talk-aloud protocols, and semi-structured interviews; the results revealed that people constructed models of others who would evaluate their performance (Adams, 2014). Specifically, people frequently construct mental models of others in order to imagine how they might respond to their work (in this case, passages of writing) in order to self-correct (Adams, 2014). More importantly, these dynamic, opinionated imagined others could be either a person in real life with which the participant regarded as a critic, a mentor who "spoke to them" to provide advice and recommendations that the participant then followed, or even someone they admired but had never met. Participants tended to imagine these figures providing them with constructive (sometimes even harsh, but well-intended) criticism. Many people regard their role models as heroes, and ideally, one's mentor doubles as one's role model. However, the DC approach has not yet been used to investigate the mental models we create of our heroes and mentors. Research investigating traits of heroic leaders suggests that people will model those whom they believe to be competent to evaluate their performance (Goethals & Allison, 2011) and those who are designated to evaluate them (e.g. supervisors or teachers who evaluate subordinates or students).

How do we model these heroes for whom we have such great regard? The "eight great traits" that Goethals and Allison have identified are likely components of respondents' dynamic mental models, which are far more holistic and responsive than the list of traits or typologies of heroes suggests. However, how dynamic and manipulable are these models? Under what conditions are we motivated to invoke mental models of heroes that function to reassure us or even perhaps to provide us with constructive criticism or vocal advice? Do people model heroes' responses to unique situations in order to anticipate how their hero will behave under certain circumstances so that they can mimic their heroes' behaviors and do people wonder how their heroes (particularly those who serve as role models) will evaluate their actions?

These questions warrant additional investigations. However, it is likely that we mentally model heroic leaders to both anticipate how they will act in the contexts that, as Campbell explains, gives rise to heroic acts (Campbell, 1988). These internal representations are coordinated and work in tandem with the representations of heroes that circulate in the systems in which we participate. They work to reify and perpetuate the cultural repository of images we have of heroes. According to a DC framework, the distinct representations of heroic leaders in medicine provided earlier each arose in part by our shared expectations but also continued to shape those expectations. Further, in addition to providing us instructions on how to "act the part" in certain contexts, mental models carry ideological cargo (Adams, 2014). Mental models of critics, mentors or heroes function to shape our values. Campbell (1988) suggests this when he so playfully points out that as a boy, he had an angel on one shoulder and a devil on the other, each whispering in his ear. He explains that all those who participated in his religious education "concretized" the forces of good and evil in these two forms, and it had a profound influence on his behaviors. While he would not explain it in the same terms, these concretized mental figures had circulated externally as shared representations, and once they had been shared with Campbell in his boyhood, they enabled him to model and assess acts based on values associated with his Catholicism.

Importantly, these representations are enabled by cognitive empathy. As discussed earlier in this chapter, cognitive empathy is the top down process of imagining others' emotions. Emotional responses are context specific and people are able to predict how their leaders or followers might feel in certain contexts. For example, we might predict a heroic leader that responds to news of an alliance with others as ecstatic or as deeply disappointed, depending on the context. These predictions, based on contextual variables, suggest people are constructing mental models of heroes that include affective components. These affective components of our mental models arise from our capacity for cognitive empathy, for modelling affect in relation to situational variables. These emotional states play important roles in how one responds to a situation. Thus, our ability to construct mental models that factor in our affective states (Adams, 2014) allows leaders to anticipate their followers and followers to predict their leaders.

According to a DC framework, these internal representations produced by both heroic leaders and followers work in tandem with representations in other forms of external media. For example, while an organization might be considered a relatively closed system (Coleman, 1988), organizations exist within the larger framework of national and global collectives. Mental models of heroes circulate throughout these systems via external artifacts and signifiers to help shape the actions of leaders and to help followers set expectations for their behaviors. This circulation of representations is similar to an instruction manual for the heroic leader, yet it appears in pieces and the instructions are widely distributed across the system. For example, the *Star Wars* movies, through the character of Han Solo, have instructed massive numbers of viewers that the "mercenary figure" might require nothing more than the right context to instigate a profound sense of heroic purpose (Campbell, 1988). Such a lesson instructs us all that while we may foster economic relationships with our organizations, it is possible to experience a deep connection to them and their aims, even at a great cost to ourselves. This figure of the mercenary-turned-hero has the power to turn organizational leaders into heroic leaders by enabling them to mentally model the possibility of responding to situations not for personal gain, but out of deep obligation to "do the right thing." It is only by way of our capacity to mentally model Han Solo's situation that we understand that in the beginning, he is not emotionally committed to the cause for which he is recruited, but later we understand the deeply satisfying rewards of the emotional ties to which he has committed himself. It is through such instruction contained in the heroic form of Han Solo that we can begin to understand our reluctance, both as researchers and as human beings, to relegate the relationship between leaders and followers as mere exchanges. A DC framework allows us to understand that our participation in organizations is richer and more complex.

Conceptions of the hero vary across culture and context. Yet, the conceptions of the hero form a constellation of sorts. As such, they serve as a repository of the range of possible heroic acts. Culture itself has been theorized from a DC perspective as the distribution of beliefs across members of society (Schwartz, 1978) with later researchers devising quantitative models of cultural patterns (Romney, Weller, & Batchelder, 1986). Organizational cultures arise in part from individuals' acts, and those serve to represent and reify the conceptions of heroic action, but so too will artefactual renditions, such those that occur in organizational lore. Additionally, policies and procedures, which may not speak directly to heroism, will nonetheless frame what is considered exceptional behavior in a particular context. One only has to consider performance evaluation guidelines to see how these kinds of artifacts go ahead of us to circulate and propagate conceptions of exceptional leaders in organizational contexts.

Lastly, the DC framework begs the question, what conclusions are we to draw from the propagation of scholarship on the "everyday hero"? Is it that scholars who research this topic are capturing (i.e. representing) a phenomenon that circulates among us or is it that these scholars themselves are participating in coalescing cultural forces through representation, forces that with enough momentum participate in propagating the cultural material through which to make possible the hero in us all? More likely, there is a recursive relationship between scholarship and practice that results in a tipping point (Gladwell, 2006), a historical moment that brings forth cultural change. Franco and Zimbardo's (2006) work on the hero provides an example of the scholar's agency in the larger cultural system: they assert, "We believe it has become necessary to revisit the historical meanings of the word, and to make it come alive in modern terms.... [I]t is possible to foster ... the development of a personal heroic ideal. This heroic ideal can help guide a person's behavior in times of trouble or moral uncertainty." These scholars capture the yearning we have for the meaningful journeys that Campbell (1988) dedicated his life to exploring through the power of myth. Campbell himself has propagated much of the cultural material that today inspires many individuals, both leaders and followers, to embrace our ordinary lives as heroic quests.

Conclusions

From this review we can see that empathy is a prime motivator for heroic behavior. Empathy has numerous positive effects on heroic leaders. To begin with, empathy can help potential heroes realize when others are in distress. In cases of emergency, distress may be evident, but when social problems become widespread and endemic, such as poverty or slavery, unempathetic people may not recognize the suffering of others. Even more crucially, empathy is what motivates leaders to take risks on behalf of others, even to the extent of sacrificing their own lives. Research has supported the "empathy-altruism hypothesis" using a variety of methodologies. Sociobiologists have argued that empathy is a key motivator for heroic action, and that empathic behavior helps groups survive even when individuals sacrifice their own lives for the greater good.

Empathy may also help heroes become more effective leaders by helping them establish empathic bonds that unite them with their followers. This helps heroes emerge as leaders, which then allows them to mobilize resources to take action. Charismatic leadership theory emphasizes risk-taking self-sacrifice, a compassion for others, and an awareness of others' needs and wants. This suggests that heroic empathy may be a key component of charismatic leadership. A closer integration of the two literatures, charismatic leadership and heroic leadership, may prove beneficial to both. Charismatic leaders are usually inspiring speakers, and they know how to get recognition and public acclaim. Empathy may help people who perform heroic acts get recognized as heroes and achieve heroic status, regardless of whether they are seeking such status. Although heroic status is in some ways in the eyes of the beholder, people who display empathic concern are more likely to be recognized as heroes.

People need heroes. Empathic heroes may serve important roles for organizations and societies, thus people and institutions create heroes when necessary. Numerous people do heroic things every day, but few are held up to the public as role models and celebrated as heroes. When organizations hold up people as heroes, it is because heroic myths and stories motivate their followers to achieve their organization's mission. Thus heroic stories serve valuable functions for organizations and societies. Although heroes are often described as individuals with exceptional courage and abilities, heroic behaviors are distributed throughout organizations. The glorification of particular people as heroes serves as a useful way of transmitting an organization's values and mission to its followers. However, we must not forget that generous and self-sacrificing behavior, and empathic kindness, is the birth right of every human, and not just a special few.

Because of the close linkage between empathy and heroic behavior, organizations that require heroic behavior need to stress the empathic side of their mission, and encourage empathic behavior among their members. This can sometimes be a difficult task in organizations that require high levels of courage and physical bravery, because these organizations sometimes promulgate a macho form of bravery and physical toughness. However, as a DC approach reveals, deliberately circulating representations of organizational members' heroic behavior in ways that highlight empathy—in other words, celebrating empathy and heroism together—has the power to instruct members' responses to situations that require heroism. Organizations such as the U.S. Coast Guard know the importance of empathy and character to their mission. As the literature on heroism demonstrates, moral purpose is at the heart of heroic behavior, and heroic empathy is at the heart of moral purpose.

References

Adams, L. L. (2014). Theorizing mental models in disciplinary writing ecologies through scholarship, talk-aloud protocols, and semi-structured interviews. Doctoral dissertation, Bowling Green State University, Ohio, USA.

Allison, S. T., & Burnette, J. L. (2009). Fairness and preference for underdogs and top dogs. In R. M. Kramer, A. E. Tenbrunsel, & M. H. Bazerman (eds), *Social Decision Making: Social Dilemmas, Social Values, and Ethical Judgments* (pp. 291–314). Hove: Psychology Press.

Allison, S. T., & Goethals, G. R. (2008). Deifying the dead and downtrodden: Sympathetic figures as inspirational leaders. In J. B. Ciulla, D. R. Forsyth, M. A. Genovese, G. R. Goethals, L. C. Han, & C. L. Hoyt (eds), *Leadership at the Crossroads*, 181–196. Westport, CT: Praeger.

Allison, S. T., & Goethals, G. R. (2011). *Heroes: What they do and why we need them.* Oxford: Oxford University Press.

Batson, C. D. (2009). These things called empathy: Eight related but distinct phenomena. In J. Decety & W. Ickes (eds), *The Social Neuroscience of Empathy* (pp. 3–16). Cambridge, MA: MIT Press.

Batson, C. D., Eklund, J. H., Chermok, V. L., Hoyt, J. L., & Ortiz, B. G. (2007). An additional antecedent of empathic concern: Valuing the welfare of the person in need. *Journal of Personality and Social Psychology*, 93(1), 65–74.

Bezemer, J., & Kress, G. (2008). Writing in multimodal texts a social semiotic account of designs for learning. *Written communication*, 25(2), 166-195.

Blau, K., Franco, Z., & Zimbardo, P. (2012). Fostering the heroic imagination: An ancient Ideal and a modern vision. *Psi Chi Journal*.

Bligh, M. C., Kohles, J. C., & Meindl, J. R. (2004). Charisma under crisis: Presidential leadership, rhetoric, and media responses before and after the September 11th terrorist attacks. *The Leadership Quarterly*, 15, 211–239.

Campbell, J. (1988). *The power of myth* (with B. Moyers). New York: Anchor.

Chambers, J. R., & Davis, M. H. (2012). The role of the self in perspective-taking and empathy: Ease of self-simulation as a heuristic for inferring empathic feelings. *Social Cognition*, 30(2), 153–180.

Coleman, J. S. (1988). Social capital in the creation of human capital. *American Journal of Sociology*, 94, 95–120.

Conger, J. A. (2011). Charismatic leadership. In A. Bryman, D. Collinson, K. Grint, B. Jackson, & M. Uhl-Bien (eds), *Sage Handbook of Leadership* (pp. 86–102). Thousand Oaks, CA: Sage Publications.

Conger, J. A., & Kanungo, R. N. (1987). Toward a behavioral theory of charismatic leadership in organizational settings. *Academy of Management Review*, 12, 637–647.

Conger, J. A., Kanungo, R. N., & Menon, S. T. (2000). Charismatic leadership and follower effects. *Journal of Organizational Behavior*, 21, 747–767.

Cox, C. L., Uddin, L. Q., Di Martino, A., Castellanos, F. X., Milham, M. P., & Kelly, C. (2012). The balance between feeling and knowing: Affective and cognitive empathy are reflected in the brain's intrinsic functional dynamics. *Social Cognitive and Affective Neuroscience*, 7(6), 727–737.

Craik, K. J. W. (1943). *The nature of explanation.* Cambridge, UK: Cambridge University Press.

Critchley, H. D., Wiens, S., Rothstein, P., Ohman, A., & Dolan, R. J. (2004). Neural systems supporting interoceptive awareness. *Nature Neuroscience*, 7(2), 189–195.

C-SPAN (2012). President Obama campaign rally in Roanoke. July 13. Retrieved August 13, 2012 from www.c-span.org/video/?307056-2/president-obama-campaign-rally-roanoke.

Decety, J. (2011). Dissecting the neural mechanisms mediating empathy. *Empathy Review*, 3(1), 92–108.

Decety, J., & Jackson, P. L. (2004). The functional architecture of human empathy. *Behavioral and Cognitive Neuroscience Reviews*, 3(2), 71–100.

Decety, J., & Meyer, M. (2008). From emotion resonance to empathic understanding: A social developmental neuroscience account. *Development and Psychopathology*, 20(4), 1053–1080.

Dow, A. W., Leong, D., Anderson, A., & Wenzel, R. P. (2007). Using theater to teach clinical empathy: A pilot study. *Journal of General Internal Medicine*, 22(8), 1114–1118.

Dziobek, I., Rogers, K., Fleck, S., Bahnemann, M., Heekeren, H. R., Wolf, O. T., & Convit, A. (2008). Dissociation of cognitive and emotional empathy in adults with Asperger syndrome using the Multifaceted Empathy Test (MET). *Journal of Autism and Developmental Disorders*, 38(3), 464–473.

Eisenberg, N., & Miller, P. A. (1987). The relation of empathy to prosocial and related behaviors. *Psychological bulletin*, 101(1), 91.

Emrich, C. G. (1999). Context effects in leadership perception. *Personality and Social Psychology Bulletin*, 25(8), 991–1006.

Franco, Z., & Zimbardo, P. (2006). The banality of heroism. *Greater Good*, 3(2), 30–35.

Gladwell, M. (2006). *The tipping point: How little things can make a big difference.* New York: Little, Brown.

Goethals, G. R., and S. T. Allison. (2012). Making heroes: The construction of courage, competence, and virtue. In M. Olson & M. P. Zanna (eds), *Advances in experimental social psychology* (Vol. 46, pp. 183–235). San Diego, CA: Elsevier.

Goleman, D. (1995). *Emotional intelligence*. New York: Bantam Books.

Goleman, D., Boyatzis, R., & McKee, A. (2004). *Primal leadership: Realizing the power of emotional intelligence*. Boston, MA: Harvard Business School Press.

Halverson, R., (2003). Systems of practice: How leaders use artifacts to create professional community in schools. *Education Policy Analysis Archives*, *11*(37).

Hoffman, M. L. (2001). *Empathy and moral development: Implications for caring and justice*. Cambridge, UK: Cambridge University Press.

Humphrey, R. H. (2008). The right way to lead with emotional labor. In R. H. Humphrey (ed.), *Affect and emotion: New directions in management theory and research* (pp. 1-17). Charlotte, NC: Information Age Publishing.

Humphrey, R. H. (2013). *Effective leadership: Theories, cases, and applications*. Los Angeles, CA: Sage.

Humphrey, R. H., Pollack, J. M., & Hawver, T. H. (2008). Leading with emotional labor. *Journal of Managerial Psychology*, *23*(2), 151–168.

Hutchins, E. (1995). *Cognition in the wild*. Cambridge, MA: MIT Press.

Hutchins, E. (2000). Distributed cognition. In *International Encyclopedia of the Social and Behavioral Sciences*. Oxford: Elsevier Science.

Joireman, J., Daniels, D., George-Falvy, J., & Kamdar, D. (2006). Organizational citizenship behaviors as a function of empathy, consideration of future consequences, and employee time horizon: An initial exploration using an in-basket simulation of OCBs. *Journal of Applied Social Psychology*, *36*(9), 2266–2292.

Katz, R. L. (1963). *Empathy: Its nature and uses*. London: The Free Press of Glencoe.

Kellett, J. B., Humphrey, R. H., & Sleeth, R. G. (2002). Empathy and complex task performance: Two routes to leadership. *The Leadership Quarterly*, *13*(5), 523–544.

Kellett, J. B., Humphrey, R. H., & Sleeth, R. G. (2006). Empathy and the emergence of task and relations leaders. *The Leadership Quarterly*, *17*(2), 146–162.

Kilner, J. M., & Lemon, R. N. (2013). What we know currently about mirror neurons. *Current Biology*, *23*, R1057–R1062.

Kim, J., Allison, S. T., Eylon, D., Goethals, G. R., Markus, M. J., Hindle, S. M., & McGuire, H. A. (2008). Rooting for (and then abandoning) the underdog. *Journal of Applied Social Psychology*, *38*(10), 2550–2573.

Kinsella, E. L., Ritchie, T. D., & Igou, E. R. (2015). Zeroing in on heroes: A prototype analysis of hero features. *Journal of Personality and Social Psychology*, *108*(1), 114.

Kohlberg, L. (1969). Stage and sequence: The cognitive developmental approach to socialization. In D. A. Goslin (ed.), *Handbook of socialization theory and research* (pp. 347–380). Chicago, IL: Rand McNally.

Kohlberg, L., & Hersh, R. H. (1977). Moral development: A review of the theory. *Theory into Practice*, *16*(2), 53–59.

Messick, D. M. (2005). On the psychological exchange between leaders and followers. In D. M. Messick & R. M. Kramer (eds), *The psychology of leadership: New perspectives and research* (pp. 81–96). Mahwah, NJ: Lawrence Erlbaum.

Nersessian, N. J. (2002). The cognitive basis of model-based reasoning in science. In P. Carruthers, S. Stich, & M. Siegal (eds), *The cognitive basis of science* (pp. 133–153). Cambridge: Cambridge University Press.

Pearce, C. L., & Conger, J. A. (eds). (2003). *Shared leadership: Reframing the hows and whys of leadership*. Thousand Oaks, CA: Sage Publications.

Phillips, D. T., & Loy, J. M. (2003). *Character in action: The U.S. Coast Guard on leadership*. Annapolis, MD: Naval Institute Press.

Pillai, R. (1996). Crisis and the emergence of charismatic leadership in groups: An experimental investigation. *Journal of Applied Social Psychology*, 26(6), 543–562.

Preston, S. D. (2013). The origins of altruism in offspring care. *Psychological Bulletin*, *139*(6), 1305–1341.

Preston, S. D., & Hofelich, A. J. (2012). The many faces of empathy: Parsing empathic phenomena through a proximate, dynamic-systems view of representing the other in the self. *Emotion Review*, *4*(1), 24–33.

Rogers, C. R. (1975). Empathic: An unappreciated way of being. *Counseling Psychologist*, *5*(2), 2–10.

Romney, A. K., Weller, S. C., & Batchelder, W. H. (1986). Culture as consensus: A theory of culture and informant accuracy. *American Anthropologist*, *88*(2), 313–338.

Sadri, G., Weber, T. J., & Gentry, W. A. (2011). Empathic emotion and leadership performance: An empirical analysis across 38 countries. *The Leadership Quarterly*, *22*(5), 818–830.

Salovey, P., & Mayer, J. D. (1990). Emotional intelligence. *Imagination, Cognition, and Personality*, *9*(3), 185–211.

Schwartz, T. (1978). The size and shape of a culture. In F. Barth (ed.), *Scale and social organisation* (pp. 215–252). Oslo: Universitetsforlaget.

Shamir, B. (1995). Social distance and charisma: Theoretical notes and an exploratory study. *The Leadership Quarterly*, *6*, 19–47.

Shamir, B., Arthur, M. B., & House, R. J. (1994). The rhetoric of charismatic leadership: Theoretical extension and a case study. *Leadership Quarterly*, *5*, 25–42.

Shamir, B., House, R. J., & Arthur, M. B. (1993). The motivational effects of charismatic leadership: a self-concept based theory. *Organization Science*, *4*, 577–594.

Simonton, D. K. (1994). *Greatness: Who makes history and why*. Guilford Press. Thibault, P. (2004). *Brain, mind and the signifying body: An ecosocial semiotic theory*. London: A. & C. Black.

Titchener, M. (1999). *The cultural origins of human cognition*. Cambridge, MA: Harvard University Press.

Vignemont, F., & Singer, T. (2006). The empathic brain: How, when, and why? *Trends in Cognitive Sciences*, *10*(10), 435-441.

Weber, M. (1924/1947). *The theory of social and economic organization* (A.M. Henderson & T. Parsons, Trans.; T. Parsons, Ed.). New York: The Free Press.

Wilson, W. (1914/1979) Remarks to the National Press Club (20 March 1914). In A. Link (ed.), *The Papers of Woodrow Wilson*. Princeton, NJ: Princeton University Press.

Zimbardo, P. G., Breckenridge, J. N., & Moghaddam, F. M. (2013). "Exclusive" and "inclusive" visions of heroism and democracy. *Current Psychology*, *32*(3), 221–233.

25

Heroic Leaders and Despotic Tyrants

How Power and Status Shape Leadership

Anika Stuppy and Nicole L. Mead

When one thinks of a hero, one thinks of a leader. Leaders are an integral and coveted part of social life because they are essential for navigating their groups through murky waters and troubled times. When they succeed in doing so, they are raised up by the group and become a hero in their followers' eyes. From a young age, most people dream about becoming leaders of their group, perhaps even the world, in part because they strongly desire the many benefits that are bestowed upon leaders. In return for bestowing valuable resources upon leaders, followers expect that leaders use their influence for the good of the group (e.g., van Vugt, Hogan, & Kaiser, 2008).

Unfortunately, not all leaders use their position of privilege equally. Some use it for the betterment of others, while others use it for shameless self-enrichment. As an example of the former, Abraham Lincoln (former President of the United States) maneuvered an entire country through difficult times, worked selflessly to inspire his followers, and consolidated conflicts. Such examples highlight the great potential that leaders can have for acting as a hero. Yet other leaders grossly misuse their influence to exploit adherents for personal gain. Abusive tyrants such as Joseph Stalin (former General Secretary of the Soviet Union), Kim Jong-un (the supreme leader of the Democratic People's Republic of Korea) or Baschar al-Assad (President of Syria) act in stark contrast to the ideal of heroic leadership. Abuse of power is not limited to extreme cases. Relatively milder cases of ill-suited leaders (or mini tyrants) are prevalent in every-day life, as suggested by the finding that only half of all American employees were satisfied with their boss (Conference Board, 2010).

Which factors determine whether leaders use their influence to elevate others (thereby acting as a hero) or themselves (thereby potentially acting as a tyrant)? In this chapter, we sketch a simple yet comprehensive framework which can help explain when and why leaders behave in desirable or undesirable ways. To do so, we elucidate how two seemingly similar yet very different aspects of social hierarchies—status and power—can influence leadership. We then build on these differences in social hierarchies by examining how individual motivations toward prestige and dominance interact with structural forms of social hierarchies to influence leadership behavior. Finally, we examine how leaders react to power and status threats.

A second aim of this chapter is to provide practical guidance. Knowledge about status and power helps to sort out undesirable candidates who strive to hoard the social and material benefits of power for themselves. It also helps to clarify how social hierarchies and leadership positions can be managed structurally in order to maximize the benefits and minimize the detriments of leadership (see also Hersey & Blanchard, 1993; Northouse, 2015).

This chapter is organized as follows. The first half of the chapter theoretically differentiates status and power. We describe why power and status were selected throughout evolutionary history, identify empirically validated antecedents of power and status, and discuss the nature of power and status hierarchies in modern societies. The second half of the chapter examines how power and status relate to leadership outcomes. We explore why a person who is respected may be easily awarded power, and how being awarded structural power independently of status often fosters self-oriented behavior in the intended leader. Lastly, we discuss theoretically and practically relevant moderators that identify when and why structural power can produce heroic leaders.

Power and Status: Two Core Dimensions of Social Hierarchy

Hierarchies are a universal feature of social life. In established groups, such as neighborhood communities, peer groups, and work teams, researchers have observed rank orders of varying stability (Bernstein, 1981; Buss, 1996; Eibl-Eibesfeldt, 1989; Mazur, 1985). In new groups, people who were previously unacquainted immediately started to sort out a social ranking system (i.e., more outgoing and attractive students were ranked higher in perceived respect, influence, and prominence by their peers; Anderson, John, Keltner, & Kring, 2001). These findings suggest that humans implicitly strive to construct hierarchies (Barkow, 1975).

Throughout evolutionary history, hierarchies facilitated group survival because they helped groups solve survival problems. During famines, war, or other challenging times, it was functional for the group to have the skilled, high-ranking members tackle the complex tasks while the lower-ranking members followed (Eibl-Eibesfeldt, 1989; Halevy, Chou, & Galinsky, 2011; Ridgeway & Diekema, 1989). When they succeeded in fighting off immediate dangers, subordinates doubly rewarded the victors: respect and admiration were showered on the heroic leaders, which in turn gave them status, money, estate, and mates, which in turn gave them social power. Hence, power, status and leadership behavior are closely intertwined since ancient times.

This section begins by outlining why evolution shaped status and power for social stratification. Subsequently, we highlight individual differences that have been identified as antecedents of high social status and high power. We end this section by outlining the nature of power and status hierarchies in modern society and discuss how high-status and high-power individuals influence their peers.

The Evolutionary Roots of Dominance and Prestige-Orientations, and How they Relate to Power and Status

In the ancestral past, having power and status facilitated survival (Henrich & Gil-White, 2001). As such, evolution has selected two distinct motivations and strategies that enable humans to ascend the social hierarchy. Dominance is characterized as a self-oriented motivation/strategy in which individuals manipulate others for the purpose of gaining influence and resources. Group members oriented toward dominance used physical violence, force, and coercion to gain control over desired resources and secure reproductive success. Although having power does not necessarily entail the ill-treatment of others, the present-day definition of power captures the desired outcome of a dominance-oriented strategy—namely, control over valued resources (Keltner, Gruenfeld, & Anderson, 2003; Magee & Galinsky, 2008).

While some people are indeed primarily motivated toward power for the sake of power itself, others seek power as a tool to realize other objectives. Those who seek power just because they enjoy having it often use the dominance strategy to secure power and, as leaders, will prioritize protecting their power over other tasks (Maner & Mead, 2010). However, others strive to realize goals that are far more important to them than the quench for power. For instance, Nelson Mandela (former president of South Africa) strongly desired to improve his peers' welfare. He managed to obtain power without harming others—hence not by applying the dominance strategy—and used the influence that power entailed to benefit the powerless.

In contrast to dominance, which is primarily a self-oriented strategy, the Mandela example may illustrate what is called prestige orientation, which is a relatively more other-oriented motivation and confers benefits on both the individual and the group. In the past, groups conferred prestige and respect upon individuals who used valuable skills to help their group achieve important outcomes (Henrich & Gil-White, 2001). Ingratiating with respected and skilled group members enhances the skills of the less proficient and abbreviates the otherwise tedious learning processes. It also provides fitness advantages for the esteemed individual, as prestige strategies are often met with social and material rewards from group members. Indeed, to this day, social status is defined by the degree of respect and admiration granted to a person (e.g., Ridgeway & Walker, 1995).

Prestige and dominance describe motivations towards status and power and corresponding strategies to obtain status and power. Because of the survival benefits conferred to those who successfully pursued strategies toward dominance and prestige, those distinct motivations may be hardwired and fundamental to humans. Those strongly motivated to dominate or be admired put effort into securing these social outcomes when encountering peers (Cheng, Tracy, Foulsham, Kingstone, & Henrich, 2013). As such, it may be the case that these motivations serve as a foundation for the power and status hierarchies that are defining features of human social life.

Notably, although prestige and dominance may have evolved as distinct motivations to serve different functions, they are deeply intertwined. Personality measures reveal that prestige and dominance motivations are moderately correlated, as one would expect (e.g., Maner & Mead, 2010; Mead & Maner, 2012). As such, they may be predictive of some outcomes, such as motivation towards positions of leadership. However, as will be revealed later in the chapter, they are highly predictive of whether people use power in heroic or abusive ways.

The social structures of status and power are also often confounded in the real world. Wealth is a good illustration of this problem. On the one hand, the wealthy are powerful because they can pay others to obey their will. On the other hand, wealth can garner admiration and respect among peers. Possessions signal being successful in life, especially when "true" competence is hard to observe (Cheng & Tracy, 2013; Henrich & Henrich, 2007). Socioeconomic status (SES) is hence neither a measure of only status (Han, Nunes, & Drèze, 2013) or only power (Dubois, Rucker, & Galinsky, 2015) as it confounds these constructs. The case of wealth exemplifies how power and status can often blend in the real world. As we will illustrate later in this chapter, status and power are even mutually reinforcing: Power can breed status, and having status can breed power—further increasing these constructs' overlap.

Antecedents—Individual Differences that Bring about Social Status and Power

To get a better understanding of the nature of power and status, it is informative to know who typically winds up in these positions. Past research identified personality traits, motivations, physiological characteristics, and acquired skills that correlated positively with having either status or power (Table 25.1). However, these characteristics do not exclusively boost either status or power—they often trigger both. For instance, skill and expertise can give rise to power and influence, because others depend on that person's abilities and knowledge. At the same time, knowledge fosters status because people admire knowledgeable peers (see also Anderson & Cameron, 2014 for a thorough discussion of the antecedents of power and status).

Table 25.1 Antecedents of Power and Status

Antecedents of power

Trait	Category	Relation to power	Source
Dominance	Motivation/interpersonal strategy	Dominance describes the motivation to obtain power. Dominance is also an interpersonal strategy in which power is obtained via force and the selfish manipulation of group resources.	Henrich and Gil-White (2001) Hawley (1999)
Need for power	Motivation	High need for power correlates with desire to control resources.	McCelland (1975)
Testosterone/gender	Physiological	Higher baseline testosterone/being male positively correlates with dominance and power.	Johnson, Burk, and Kirkpatrick (2007)
Physical strength and size	Physiological	Physically stronger and taller individuals are perceived as more powerful and they occupy more powerful positions.	Judge and Cable (2004)

Antecedents of status

Trait	Category	Relation to status	Source
Prestige	Motivation/interpersonal strategy	Prestige describes the motivation to obtain status. Prestige is also an interpersonal strategy in which status is obtained by engaging in behavior that heightens esteem in the eyes of others (e.g., cooperation, generosity)	Henrich and Gil-White, (2001) Willer (2009) Griskevicius, Tybur, and Van den Bergh (2010)
Extraversion	Personality	Extraversion is positively correlated with status attainment at first encounters. In the long run, extraversion can hurt status.	Anderson et al. (2001) Bendersky and Shah (2013)
Agreeableness	Personality	Moderate trait agreeableness is positively related to status attainment.	Anderson et al. (2001) Cheng et al. (2010)
Self-monitoring	Personality	High self-monitors adapt their behavior in ways that elicit status. For instance, they exchange resources strategically such that others perceive them as generous.	Flynn, Reagans, Amanatullah, and Ames (2006)
Attractiveness	Physiological	Attractiveness positively correlated with social status	Anderson et al. (2001)
Ethnicity	Physiological	Being white is positively correlated with social status.	Berger, Cohen, and Zelditch (1972) Lin, Kwan, Cheung, and Fiske (2005)
Intelligence/knowledge	Trait and acquired skill	Intelligence, competence, and expert knowledge are positively correlated with social status.	Gintner and Lindskold (1975) Sorrentino and Boutillier (1975) Littlepage, Schmidt, Whisler, and Frost (1995) Ridgeway (1987)

The Nature of Status and Power Hierarchies in Modern Society

Prestige and dominance strategies evolved because they were functional for survival in groups (Henrich & Gil-White, 2001). Until today, these two motivations toward social rank influence how hierarchies are formed and how individuals react to the endowment of power. While the nature of prestige and dominance *motivations* was conserved, the characteristics of power and status *hierarchies* may have been transformed radically. This section discusses why modern societies created roles and positions that award structural power and/or status. Afterwards, we outline which form of social influence results from structural power and status.

Power and Status Hierarchies in Modern Society

Leader-follower relationships entail an essential tension (e.g., van Vugt et al., 2008). Although group members recognize the need for leaders, the benefits they bestow on leaders and the control they give up to leaders leaves followers vulnerable to exploitation (van Vugt, 2006). Indeed, plenty of power-holders abuse their influence and mistreat their subordinates (Kipnis, 1972; Tepper, 2000). This research confirmed lay observations about the corruptive nature of power. (As covered later in the chapter, recent research has gone beyond this overly general picture, identifying conditions under which power does and does not "corrupt.") Given painful experiences with past abusive leaders, some groups began to take preventive measures to change the nature of power.

Many modern societies now restrain and structurally define power to prevent its abuse (Lasswell & Kaplan, 2013; Mahoney & Thelen, 2010). Regulations define how, and to what extent a single person exerts power. To illustrate, police officers can incarcerate people, impose financial penalties, and use physical violence only in clearly defined circumstances. Another alteration concerns the stability of resource-control. In ancestral societies, power positions were quite unstable and superiors had to defend their resources by aggressing against subordinates who were motivated toward their power (Henrich & Gil-White, 2001). Nowadays, many powerful positions are relatively stable, allowing power-holders to focus on leading the group rather than protecting their power (Maner & Mead, 2010; Mead & Maner, 2012; van Vugt et al., 2008).

While many societies have modified how resources are controlled, the psychology of prestige conferral seems to have changed very little. Until today, the most competent, skilled, and cooperative group members (e.g., star-athletes and outstanding managers) attain high social status (Cheng et al., 2013; Henrich & Gil-White, 2001). As covered later in the chapter, it may be that status processes have changed much less than power processes because the latter but not the former tends to be abused upon conferral.

Social Influence from Status and Power

Both the powerful and the respected exert influence in their group (Anderson & Shirako, 2008; Cheng et al., 2013). Because the relationships between the powerless and the powerful, and those high and low in status are qualitatively different, social influence takes on different forms.

A powerful person is influential because the asymmetry in resources creates dependence. Low-ranking group members comply with the demands of those who control possessions, knowledge, and/or skill in order to safeguard benefits (e.g., money or livelihoods) or avoid punishment (e.g., physical welfare, being deprived of the resource; Cheng, Tracy, & Henrich, 2010; Cheng et al., 2013). Dependency relationships are ubiquitous: Subordinates abide to orders to get bonus payments; IT specialists pressure their employer for a raise because the company depends on their knowledge. Power relationships can be similar to trading relationships in which goods and services are provided in exchange for the power-holder's resource. Subordinates do not freely defer, as in the case of status (Henrich & Gil-White, 2001), but their deference is contingent on a resource.

Powerful leaders make followers comply by administering punishments and rewards. Notably, this form of leadership lowers subordinates' intrinsic motivation. When people worked to avoid reprimands or secure a raise, they perceived their tasks and duties as less enjoyable which lowered work quality and job-satisfaction (Gagné & Deci, 2005). Eventually, this could force powerful leaders to monitor and patronize their employees. This encumbers the leader and puts followers under stress. Taken together, leaders who mostly steer through influence (instead of status) seem somewhat dysfunctional.

High-status leaders exert influence because others look up to them. Followers want to attain the approval, affection, and friendship of the prestigious because they are attractive interaction partners (Cheng et al., 2013; Henrich & Gil-White, 2001). To improve relationship quality, followers will comply with the wishes of esteemed leaders. Furthermore, prestigious individuals are perceived as competent, making their suggestions seem valuable (Maddux & Rogers, 1980; Kahle & Homer, 1985; Shamir, House, & Arthur, 1993). For instance, a heroic, high-status leader like Mahatma Gandhi (leader of the Indian independence movement) exerted influence without coercion. Inspired followers tried to resemble his ideals because they admired him. These arguments suggest that status can put people on a pedestal, turning their actions and opinions into guidelines for those of lower rank.

High-status leaders do not lead by applying a carrot-and-stick approach—they inspire their followers. Pursuing intrinsically set goals motivates followers to work harder (Gagné & Deci, 2005). Future research should continue to disentangle how power and status as orthogonal leader characteristics influence relationship and interaction quality between subordinates and superiors.

From Status to Power

In the real world, people often enjoy power and status simultaneously. In both naturalistic and laboratory based groups, those who were well liked and respected also controlled the resources (Barth & Noel, 1972; Carli & Eagly, 1999; Guinote, Judd, & Brauer, 2002; Hewstone, Rubin, & Willis, 2002; Sidanius & Pratto, 1999). In other words, status may be an antecedent of power because people often want to give control over resources to those they like and admire. Historic examples illustrate how easily respected veterans ascend the political ladder. Charles de Gaulle (former president of France) was the single French general who successfully fought back German troops in the Second World War. His heroic actions proved his bravery and patriotism, boosting his prestige among the public. He was elected president of France immediately after the war. Similarly, 39 out of 44 US presidents had—often quite successful—military careers before taking office. In this section, we trace the routes from status to power. At the end of this section, we discuss cases in which dominance-motivated people may strategically strive for status and thus use status as a means towards the end goal of having power.

Status Can Pave the Way to Power

People with high social status can become powerful because peers voluntarily endow them with control over resources. This is not always a passive or indirect process. Quite often this occurs because high-status individuals pursue socially accepted ways to access resources. In an experimental setting, the prestigious were generous towards their partner and gave up short-term personal gain (Blader & Chen, 2012). Notably, this promotes dependency and influence in the long run because the partners will feel the need to reciprocate (Flynn, 2003; Gurven, Allen-Arave, Hill, & Hurtado, 2000; Wedekind & Braithwaite, 2002). Furthermore, prestigious individuals initiate and participate in cooperative transactions by forming alliances, collaborating, and returning favors (Cottrell, Neuberg, & Li, 2007; Griskevicius et al., 2007; van Vugt & Iredale, 2013; Stiff & van Vugt, 2008). While these strategies are effective for securing high resource outcomes in non-forceful ways, they serve a second purpose. Generosity, reciprocation, and prosocial actions actually increase prestige (Bateson, Nettle, & Roberts, 2006; Milinski, Semmann, & Krambeck, 2002). Hence, in contrast to the dominant who prioritize accumulating resources at all costs, including costs to the group (Blader & Chen, 2012), those striving for prestige use strategies that provide resources and gain the affection of others. The concern about their social esteem makes them prioritize relationship quality over short-term personal gain.

High-status people put effort into gaining resources but they also receive them without any action from their side. Perceived status activates expectations about the person's capabilities (Magee & Galinsky, 2008; Nisbett & Wilson, 1977). These expectations can change the way low-status individuals interact with an esteemed counterpart and result in a self-fulfilling prophecy (Berger & Conner, 1974). In an experimental setting, participants believed they took part in a gamble with a bogus opponent of either low or high social status (a student with a very high or very low GPA respectively). At the end of the game, this bogus high-status opponent had earned a larger share of money (Thye, 2000); merely because participants believed the high-status person was more capable than they were. This evidence suggests that status helps to gain control over resources simply because peers believe the high-status person should have more resources.

In a similar vein, groups perceive a prestigious individual's possessions and assets to be more precious which promotes power. Expectation states theory suggests that the status value of an actor spreads to exchangeable objects (Berger & Conner, 1974; Lovaglia, 1994, 1997). For instance, products that were designed or produced by famous actors or athletes will achieve higher prices and revenues because of their association with the esteemed person (Elberse, 2007). Experimental evidence supports this reasoning. In a gambling experiment, subjects could exchange their own blue poker chips for either purple poker chips associated with a higher status partner or orange chips associated with a lower status partner. Participants tried harder to acquire the purple chips, assumed they were generally more important than orange chips, and forwent profit to obtain them (Thye, 2000). These findings illustrate the many advantages of social status. The prestigious have a relatively easier time obtaining material wealth and are passively bestowed with resources by their peers.

High-status paves the way to gaining material resources but it also facilitates social power—having control over others. Followers expect their prestigious peers to be competent enough to take over difficult leadership tasks (Bruins, Ellemers, & De Gilder, 1999; King, Johnson, & van Vugt, 2009; van Vugt et al., 2008) and they have good reasons to believe that they will indeed make great leaders. Status signals intellectual competence, social competence, and commitment to the group's values, all of which would help tackle the leadership duties of solving complex coordination tasks like distributing workload, monitoring deadlines, and resolving disputes. Additionally, respected individuals seem to endorse norms and values that forbid the abuse of power (Fragale, Overbeck, & Neale, 2011). Because status partly emerges by repeatedly observing a person cooperate, followers might infer that this person will adopt a benevolent and fair leadership style.

And indeed, when given a free choice, group members often place their most prestigious members in powerful leadership positions. Participants who made high-quality comments (Gintner & Lindskold, 1975; Sorrentino & Boutillier, 1975), were perceived as experts (Bottger, 1984; Littlepage et al., 1995; Ridgeway, 1987), donated to charity (Milinski et al., 2002), and made large contributions to a public fund (Willer, 2009), were all more likely to be placed in influential positions by their peers. High-status candidates often prove worthy of the responsibility they are given. Historic examples illustrate that esteemed people in powerful positions turn out to be heroic leaders. Nelson Mandela endured 27 years in prison for his political beliefs. Accepting this great personal sacrifice for his moral convictions earned him respect and admiration around the world. After being released from prison, Mandela was elected president of South Africa with a landslide win. He continued to use his political power as a heroic leader, continuously working to benefit the nation's poorest.

High-status group members seem to be great candidates for leadership positions and their peers recognize their potential. However, under some circumstances status can be a poor indicator of a person's intentions and character. Historic examples demonstrate how initially respected and esteemed people used their power in destructive ways. For instance, Josef Stalin possessed great charisma and was able to quickly surround himself with followers and admirers. However, he turned into a tyrant as soon as he was given power. The question emerges: why is prestige sometimes not a good indicator of a person's competence and moral character? The next section discusses how some people use status as a way to seize power.

When Status is Used Strategically to Accumulate Power

Group members prefer to entrust power to those they respect, admire, and generally like. As such, people who desire power may strategically pursue status in order to clinch power. To elucidate the difference between genuinely and disingenuously pursuing prestige, narcissism will be contrasted with prestige motivation.

Narcissism

Narcissists can possess great charm and are often well liked on first encounters (Back, Schmukle, & Egloff, 2010). In part, this is because narcissists are preoccupied with feeling great and wonderful and so they can radiate self-confidence and self-assuredness, known as the grandiosity dimension of narcissism (Ackerman et al., 2010). Narcissists streamline their appearance and behavior, for instance by dressing neatly, being funny, smiling, and standing self-assuredly, to gain others respect and admiration (Back et al., 2010). Their desire to be admired and popular makes them act in ways that please others to gain social status. However, status might be awarded prematurely. Research indicates that in the long run, narcissists are actually disliked by their peers (Paulhus, 1998). Why might this be the case?

Narcissism can have a dark underbelly: the entitlement/exploitation dimension of narcissism has been linked to a strong aspiration for power and superiority (Ackerman et al., 2010; Brown & Zeigler-Hill, 2004) and interpersonally harmful outcomes such as disparagement of others, rape, and aggression (Bushman & Baumeister, 1998; Exline, Baumeister, Bushman, Campbell, & Finkel, 2004; Watson & Morris, 1991). Evidence suggests that some narcissists strategically accumulate status in groups to prepare the ground for obtaining power. They initially conceal their dominance motive because they know that others disapprove of it (Watson, Grisham, Trotter, & Biderman, 1984). Cultivating status and tempering dominance motivations may be functional strategies as narcissists have been successful in securing leadership positions in groups (Brunell et al., 2008).

However, in the long run, the socially toxic consequences of the entitlement/exploitation dimension may unfold upon attainment of power because power gives people the freedom to act on underlying motives that are socially distasteful (Mead, Baumeister, Stuppy, & Vohs, 2016). To summarize, narcissists can appear as competent and likable initially. Because they quickly accumulate prestige on first encounters, others might think of them as ideal candidates for leadership positions (Back et al., 2010; Rosenthal & Pittinsky, 2006). However, when they are in power, their strong drive for dominance might be unleashed—resulting in the feared tyrant instead of the imagined hero.

Prestige Motivation

Prestige motivation describes the authentic concern to gain others' respect, esteem, and affection. Unlike narcissists, who use status as a stepping stone on their way to power, those seeking prestige pursue status as a goal in itself—they do not necessarily also want power. Indeed, research demonstrated that status is an emotional reward that is different from any material resources (Emerson, 1972).

At first blush, it seems promising to measure prestige motivation or social status when selecting candidates for a powerful position. Evidence suggests that those who want to gain approval act as successful and desirable leaders (Blader & Chen, 2012; Fragale et al., 2011). Additionally, when endowed with power, those highly motivated toward prestige used their influence for the good of the group rather than to maintain their power (Maner & Mead, 2010). Although this initial evidence is promising, it behooves researchers and practitioners to keep in mind that there is a moderate but consistent positive correlation between prestige motivation and dominance motivation. Hence, when studying or selecting based on prestige motivation it is important to be careful with conceptualization and measurement. For example, when trying to staff leadership positions, implicit measures of prestige and dominance that are less prone to be biased by self-presentational efforts might be better indicators of a candidate's true motivational underpinnings (Schultheiss, Campbell, & McClelland, 1999).

The role of prestige motivation in leadership is currently underexplored and provides ample possibilities for future research. Initial evidence suggest that prestige-motivated leaders secured better group outcomes (Blader & Chen, 2012), acted in the best interest of the group (Mead & Maner, 2012) and were perceived as warmer by subordinates (Fragale et al., 2011). However, for a balanced discussion, it is important to look at the potential drawbacks of status-oriented leaders. It may be that leaders who are overly concerned with the needs of the group may have a leadership style that seems opportunistic and lacking directedness. This may even pave the way for dominance-motivated people to disrupt the social group and overthrow the leader to gain power. The field would benefit from continuing to investigate which circumstances allow prestige-oriented individuals to become successful and heroic leaders.

From Power to Leadership

Heroic leaders are central and valuable figures in the social realm. They protect their groups from harm and work towards securing better life outcomes for their followers. Identifying circumstances that make leaders act as heroes is thus a worthwhile endeavor. In this section, we first discuss *action-orientation* as a broad psychological outcome of power and outline how it relates to leadership behavior. Afterwards, we identify structural and individual differences that determine if a power-holder will act heroically or tyrannically. Essentially, we outline how threats to power and threats to status can prompt leaders to harm subordinates because it helps them protect their individual power.

Can Structural Power Produce Tyrants?

Structural power positions have been argued to trigger a state of action-orientation (Galinsky, Gruenfeld, & Magee, 2003) arguably because having control over resources enables individuals to realize personal goals without coordinating with others. For example, powerful people perceived that they could realize their goals more easily (Guinote, 2010) and were more likely to take action towards their goal (Galinsky et al., 2003). They approached others more (Anderson & Berdahl, 2002), made first offers in negotiations (Magee, Galinsky & Gruenfeld, 2007), and even produced better application letters for a job (Lammers, Dubois, Rucker, &

Galinsky, 2013). While there is initial evidence suggesting that an action-orientation might benefit status because it makes people more proactive (Kilduff & Galinsky, 2013), action-orientation may be a rather ambiguous outcome of power.

Depending on the individual's goals and motivations, the feeling that one has the power to act can be used to hurt or help followers (Cheng et al., 2003; Galinsky, Magee, Rus, Rothman & Todd, 2014; Maner & Mead, 2010). Ample evidence suggests that feelings of autonomy foster egoism and disregard for dependents and subordinates. Those made to feel powerful were indifferent to other's feelings (Galinsky, Magee, Inesi, & Gruenfeld, 2006; Van Kleef et al., 2008). They put less cognitive energy into understanding other's behavior—even in delicate situations: Judges produced less complex judgments when they were in more powerful positions (Gruenfeld & Preston, 2000). The powerful blandly violated politeness norms by interrupting others when talking, taking more cookies from a plate, and eating with their mouth open (Brown & Levinson, 1987; Keltner et al., 2003).

More detrimental to status is the fact that power-holders often seem to prioritize themselves over others. In the workplace, a considerable amount of bosses act like tyrants—not leaders (Barrington & Franco, 2010). Why does structural power tempt people to abuse it?

One argument has been that, because of the many benefits of power, the powerful are motivated to maintain a power-distance gap between themselves and their subordinates (McClelland, 1975; Maner & Mead, 2010; van Vugt et al., 2008). In other words, powerful people abuse their power in order to protect it from others. For example, when leaders were given a position of unstable power—and hence, they could potentially lose their power to other group members—they used their power to protect their position rather than to help the group (Maner & Mead, 2010). In contrast, when power was stable and absolute, such detrimental behaviors were not observed.

When Does Awarded Power Produce Heroic Leaders? Moderators of the Effect of Power

Having structural power entails the tempting possibility to misuse one's influence to accumulate personal gain rather than securing the group's welfare. However, not everybody who is given control over others becomes corrupted. Prominent historic figures like Abraham Lincoln or Nelson Mandela, and everyday examples of esteemed bosses and supervisors (Conference Board, 2010), suggest that some power-holders do act as benevolent leaders and even heroes. This section examines individual differences and structural features of power—how positions are awarded and designed—that moderate how influence is exercised. Lastly, we discuss how threats to power and status influence the power-holders behavior.

Individual Characteristics

Dominance Motivation

As discussed earlier: those motivated to dominate are those who desire power the most. At their core, dominant people want to accumulate resources to establish a power gap, create dependent relationships to subordinates, and make sure others stay inferior (Barkow, 1989; Ellis, 1995; Henrich & Gil-White, 2001). Dominance-oriented power-holders took strategic actions that harmed the group goal just to maintain control and influence over their subordinates (Case & Maner, 2014; Maner & Mead, 2010; Mead & Maner, 2012). For instance, they excluded a highly skilled team member that could have helped the group progress because they did not want their superiority to be threatened. Prestige-oriented power-holders on the other hand kept the rival in the group because they prioritized their team's welfare over their own (Maner & Mead, 2010).

Testosterone is the physiological antecedent of a dominance motivation. High or rising circulating testosterone has been linked to bossy behaviors in adult males (Mazur & Booth, 1998). Moreover, testosterone and dominance have a circular relationship in which dominant behaviors reinforce testosterone levels and vice versa (Mazur & Lamb, 1980). Trait testosterone levels predict who is drawn to power positions and who tries to avoid them. Participants with low testosterone levels did not desire power and felt uncomfortable and insecure when given power (Josephs, Sellers, Newman, & Mehta, 2006). Potentially, these people could make great leaders because they are not preoccupied with maintain the power gap but instead prioritize the group's progress. However, these findings illustrate that sometimes those with the right mindset and personality for influential jobs shy away from these positions which gives leeway for dominant individuals to take over.

Goals

The power-holder's norms, values, and goals will shape how power is exerted. Andrew Carnegie (an American industrialist) for instance, grew up poor but ascended to one of the richest citizens of the US. His own social advancement let him realize the importance of education and equality and prompted him to use his large fortune for philanthropic causes (Wall, 1989). Hence, those who have the "right" mindset will prioritize their follower's needs over personal wishes.

Multiple studies illustrate how structural power brings out the best in kindhearted people. Power-holders high in relational self-construal and empathetic concern divided resources fairly between themselves and others. Their concern for others made them act just as fairly as participants endowed with status in this study (Blader & Chen, 2012). They also tried to take other's perspective more (Gordon & Chen, 2013). In a similar vein, communally oriented power-holders divided workload equally while the exchange-oriented made their counterpart do the majority of work for a group assignment (Chen, Lee-Chai, & Bargh, 2001). Lastly, as mentioned, individuals with a prestige motivation, or who associated having power with having prestige, used power for the good of the group rather than to protect and increase their own power (Maner & Mead, 2010; Schmid Mast, Jonas, & Hall, 2009). In conclusion, a person's goals moderate the effects of power on interpersonal behavior and codetermine leadership style. It is advisable for practitioners to assess personality traits that tap into other-orientation when selecting candidates for influential positions. Implicit measures that circumvent self-presentational efforts seem especially useful.

Structural Characteristics

Accountability

Making power-holders accountable for their behavior heightens their concern for the needs and wishes of their subordinates. Accountability mechanisms make sure that a superior's decisions are identifiable and the subject of critical evaluation (Grant & Keohane, 2005). For instance, companies closely monitor how managers spend their project budgets by installing internal revision teams that scrutinize irregularities in budget allocations. In experiments, inducing feelings of responsibility led the dominant to both rein in their selfish desires and display community-minded behaviors such as volunteering (Winter & Barenbaum, 1985). Accountability also prevented power-holders from taking credit for successes and blaming failure on their subordinates (Rus, van Knippenberg, & Wisse, 2012). Essentially, liability forces even dominance motivated power-holders to be concerned about their status. Because their actions are evaluated regarding their value for the group goal, power-holders will try to meet their subordinates' expectations in order to avoid punishment for misconduct.

The Basis of Power

Superiors exert a more functional, goal-oriented leadership style when the stability of their power is conditional on their group's performance. For instance, managers' structural power is often tied to performance outcomes. If performance objectives are missed, a manager could lose his job or be denied a desirable bonus. This prompts power-holders to be tuned towards the needs of their employees and show superior individuation ability and task-orientation (Galinsky et al., 2014; Overbeck & Park, 2001, 2006). Practitioners are advised to tie the stability of power to overall group performance. This ensures that superiors prioritize to lead their team towards success and prevents them from becoming absorbed in power struggles.

Empowering subordinates to decrease the absolute power gap is another way to prevent abusive leadership. Nowadays, power dynamics are often somewhat reciprocal. To illustrate, while professors issue grades and award recommendations that can determine a student's career path, students give course evaluations that can influence a professor's likelihood to be promoted. Superiors will be more attuned towards their group's needs and wishes—and hence more concerned about being liked and respected—when their subordinates exert control over their outcomes.

Threat

Legitimacy Threat

Legitimization practices exist to justify a leader's superior power towards the inferiors. In the ancestral past, positions of power were often inherited which provided legitimization through birth right. In the case of kings and other royalty, power was even "approved by god." In today's society, power is often legitimately constituted via a democratic voting system. Essentially, legitimization facilitates prestige conferral because it underlines the admirable skills, knowledge, and traits that justify why the person exerts control over others. Subordinates perceive that the person was put in power for a reason: either due to some supernatural power, an inherited right, or superior skills and knowledge.

Superiors who attained power illegitimately have low social status in the eyes of followers. Illegitimacy implies that they do not possess the traits that would justify that they exert influence over other's life. Accordingly, it is more likely that those at the bottom strive to overthrow unauthorized power-holders. Research demonstrated that those low in rank took action to change the status-quo when they perceived the power hierarchy to be illegitimate (Martorana, Galinsky, & Rao, 2005). Illegitimacy also affects the power-holders behavior: If rulers felt that they did not deserve the power they were bestowed, they became inactive, hesitant, and more self-critical (Lammers, Galinsky, Gordijn, & Otten, 2008; Lammers, Stapel, & Galinsky, 2010). Still other research demonstrates that a threat to legitimacy made power-holders demean their subordinates, partially in an attempt to restore threatened feelings of self-worth (Fast, Halevy, & Galinsky, 2011). Taken together, illegitimate rulers have high power but lack social status. Whether being disliked and disrespected makes rulers aggress or socially withdraw is probably moderated by individual traits. In any case, power that begets status prevents effective leadership. Within a large organization, employees that exerted control over others but lacked prestige were involved in more coworker-conflicts than any other combination of power and status (Anicich, Fast, Halevy, & Galinsky, in press). Practitioners are advised to make the legitimization for their power-holders explicit such that working relationships are not undermined by power quarrels.

Stability Threat

When rivals challenge the current power-holder, the stability of the hierarchy is threatened. When they fear to lose their influence in the group, some power-holders use a primitive coping mechanism—the dominance strategy—to reassert their position. This entails applying brute force and violence to trump the rival. For instance, when Vladimir Putin (president of Russia) was criticized and ridiculed by a female activist group (Pussy Riot), he protected his power (and status) by sentencing the women to harsh prison sentences. Aggression could indeed be functional because it evolved in part as a strategy to coopt other's resources (Buss & Duntley, 2006; Tooby & Cosmides, 1988).

Will all threatened leaders act like Putin and pursue dominance strategies to protect their power? Previous research showed how a threat to power made leaders demean and tease their subordinates and express anger (Frijda & Mesquita, 1994; Georgesen & Harris, 2006; Howard, Blumstein, & Schwartz, 1986; Keltner, Capps, Kring, Young, & Heerey, 2001). They do so in order to reassert control over resources and widen the power gap. However, a new stream of research discovered that threat does not trigger aggression in all types of leaders and against anybody. Rather, only dominance motivated superiors who have a strong interest in preserving their power take strategic action that harm their rivals (Maner & Mead, 2010; Mead & Maner, 2012; Case & Maner, 2014). The dominance-motivated but not the prestige-motivated excluded skilled rivals, withheld information from their group, and prevented their subordinates from forming bonds and alliances. Notably, they selectively hurt the most competent and hence most threatening individual, not the group on a broad basis.

In the long run, dominance is a dysfunctional strategy to confront power threats. In today's world, where status and legitimacy are important to maintain power positions, dominant behaviors deteriorate a person's prestige even more (van Vugt, 2006). A coercive superior with tarnished status will further destabilize the power hierarchy. As discussed earlier, power-holders that are low in status are disliked and appear illegitimate (Anicich et al., in press). This motivates members to leave the group or revolt against the dominant leader (Martorana et al., 2005; van Vugt et al., 2004).

Although highly competent and skilled in-group rivals can threaten both a leader's power (e.g., as the rival might try to get hold of the powerful position) and status (e.g., as subordinates might divert attention to the rival, and start conferring prestige to him or her), research is mute as to which one is more problematic for leadership behavior group functioning. Future research should explore whether prestige-oriented leaders prioritize to regain their subordinate's affection by working harder for the group instead of strategically harming rivals to secure power. Furthermore, scholars should test whether rivals that exclusively threaten power or status trigger tailored coping strategies in leaders and how this interacts with trait motivations.

Intergroup Competition

A very different form of threat that high-power individuals face is the hazard of a rivaling outgroup. When competing against another group, powerful individuals suppress selfish motives and prioritize to achieve the best possible outcome for their team. Intergroup competition leads power-holders, independently of their motivation for dominance or prestige, to aggress against the outgroup and support their ingroup as much as possible (Maner & Mead, 2010; Mead & Maner, 2012). Those who attack and defeat external rivals will accumulate prestige because they signal devotion to the group's goals (Halevy, Chou, Cohen, & Livingston, 2012). This mechanism underlines why power holders are often transformed into great leaders and even heroes in times of war or natural catastrophes. George W. Bush's (former president of the United States) popularity rankings skyrocketed after he declared war to those responsible for the 9/11 terror attacks. Great Britain celebrated Winston Churchill (former prime minister of the United Kingdom) as a hero for leading British troops to victory in the Second World War. When the commander's abilities and goals are put to the test and he proves capable of securing the group's survival, he will achieve high social status.

Many external threats afford leaders to act in ways that harm their ingroup in the here and now but secure group survival in the long run. For instance, in times of economic crisis, managers have to enforce salary cuts or collective dismissals to prevent bankruptcy. Prestige-oriented leaders now face a difficult dilemma: They need to cause momentary suffering in order to secure group-survival in the long run. Future research could explore how prestige and dominance motivated leaders will handle this tradeoff. It is conceivable that prestige-oriented leaders delay painful but necessary decisions because they want to protect their image. On the other hand, it is also conceivable that they will make the difficult decisions that are needed because they are not concerned with keeping their high-ranking position. Dominance-motivated leaders may be quicker to make harsh but necessary changes. However, it is also possible that they neglect the needs of the group during times of crisis in order to solidify their power. Given the competing possibilities and the importance of these answers for practical and theoretical knowledge, it behooves researchers to continue uncovering the answers to these tough questions.

Conclusion

This chapter started off by differentiating power and status theoretically. Evolution brought about dominance and prestige based hierarchies because they help groups cope with survival challenges. Until today, prestige and dominance—hence desire to be high up in the status and power hierarchy—are central features in human's motivational portfolio. Even though power and status are often correlated and conflated in the real world, scholars should be mindful about their theoretical differences.

The second half of this chapter discussed linkages between status, power, and leadership outcomes. First, status and power are antecedents of leadership. Humans want those whom they like and respect to take control over group outcomes because they hope they will act as heroes. However, it is often those who desire to dominate that end up having power (Anderson & Kilduff, 2009; Cheng et al., 2010; Lord, de Vader, & Alliger, 1986) because they take strategic actions that lure others into bestowing power on them. Second, prestige and dominance are motivations that shape how leaders use their power. Prestige-motivated leaders had their followers' best interests in mind and came close to the ideal of heroic leadership. They behaved fairly (Blader & Chen, 2012), and stayed focused on the group goal instead of monitoring and controlling rivals (Maner & Mead, 2010; Mead & Maner, 2012). Third, the interaction between power and status shapes leader's actions. Leaders that lack status, for instance because they are seen as illegitimate, destabilize hierarchies (Martorana et al., 2005). Especially dominant leaders will then try to stabilize the rank-order in dysfunctional ways, potentially exacerbating the problem and harming their subordinates (Maner & Mead, 2010). To summarize, superior's *trait* and *state* concern for power and status explains many divergent leadership outcomes.

This chapter furnished suggestions to help practitioners detect potential heroic leaders and design more functional leadership-roles. First of all, indirect measures are advisable to assess the strength of candidates' dominance motivations. As mentioned, dominance is often concealed because others disapprove of it (van Vugt et al., 2008). Practitioners should avoid giving power to the dominant as they might set aside group goals to secure and increase personal power. Second of all, we recommend to design influential positions such that power is contingent on status. Transparent legitimization, accountability mechanisms, and built-in co-dependencies between managers and subordinates serve this purpose. Work teams will be more stable and functional when employees respect, and admire their supervisors.

We hope that this chapter will inspire researchers to further disentangle the differential outcomes of power and dominance, and status and prestige, respectively and to examine them as separate constructs in the future. It also seems promising to expand the current framework by including even other individual difference factors. Especially the interaction between dominance motivation and other individual traits provides ample possibilities for future research. For instance, it remains puzzling why many real-world leaders undermine and circumvent existing structural power constraints even though their power is currently not threatened. Many real-world cases illustrate how the most influential and high-ranking people evade taxes, bribe government officials, enforce nepotism, and pad their expense accounts. Apparently, some power-holders constantly strive to aggrandize and monopolize power for other than functional reasons (Kipnis, 1976). The individual difference factors that cause the desire for power to be unquenchable are still in the dark.

References

Ackerman, R. A., Witt, E. A., Donnellan, M. B., Trzesniewski, K. H., Robins, R. W., & Kashy, D. A. (2010). What does the Narcissistic Personality Inventory really measure? *Assessment, 18*(1), 67–87.

Anderson, C., & Berdahl, J. L. (2002). The experience of power: examining the effects of power on approach and inhibition tendencies. *Journal of Personality and Social Psychology, 83*(6), 1362.

Anderson, C., & Cameron, J. (2014). Personality and status attainment: A micropolitics perspective. In J. T. Cheng, J. L. Tracy & C. Anderson (eds), *The psychology of social status* (pp. 99—117). New York: Springer.

Anderson, C., & Kilduff, G. J. (2009). The pursuit of status in social groups. *Current Directions in Psychological Science, 18*(5), 295–298.

Anderson, C., & Shirako, A. (2008). Are individuals' reputations related to their history of behavior?. *Journal of Personality and Social Psychology, 94*(2), 320.

Anderson, C., John, O. P., Keltner, D., & Kring, A. M. (2001). Who attains social status? Effects of personality and physical attractiveness in social groups. *Journal of Personality and Social Psychology, 81*(1), 116–132.

Anicich, E. M., Fast, N. J., Halevy, N., & Galinsky, A. D. (in press). When the bases of social hierarchy collide: How power without status drives interpersonal conflict. *Organization Science*.

Back, M. D., Schmukle, S. C., & Egloff, B. (2010). Why are narcissists so charming at first sight? Decoding the narcissism–popularity link at zero acquaintance. *Journal of Personality and Social Psychology, 98*(1), 132.

Barkow, J. H. (1975). Strategies for self-esteem and prestige in Maradi, Niger Republic. In T. E. Williams (ed.), *Psychological anthropology* (pp. 373–388). The Hague: Mouton.

Barkow, J. H. (1989). *Darwin, sex, and status: Biological approaches to mind and culture*. Toronto, Canada: University of Toronto Press.

Barrington, L. & Franco, L. (2010). I can't get no … job satistfaction, that is. Conference Board Annual Job Satisfaction Survey, January. Retrieved from www.conferenceboard.ca/e-library/abstract.aspx?DID=3372.

Barth, E. A., & Noel, D. L. (1972). Conceptual frameworks for the analysis of race relations: An evaluation. *Social Forces, 50*(3), 333–348.

Bateson, M., Nettle, D., & Roberts, G. (2006). Cues of being watched enhance cooperation in a real-world setting. *Biology Letters, 2*(3), 412–414.

Bendersky, C., & Shah, N. P. (2013). The downfall of extraverts and rise of neurotics: The dynamic process of status allocation in task groups. *Academy of Management Journal, 56*(2), 387–406.

Berger, J., & Conner, T. L. (1974). Performance expectations and behavior in small groups: A revised formulation. In J. Berger, T.L. Conner, & M. H. Fisek (eds). *Expectation states theory: A theoretical research program* (pp. 85–109). Cambridge, UK: Winthrop.

Berger, J., Cohen, B. P., & Zelditch Jr, M. (1972). Status characteristics and social interaction. *American Sociological Review, 37*(3), 241–255.

Bernstein, I. S. (1981). Dominance: The baby and the bathwater. *Behavioral Brain Sciences, 4*, 419–457.

Blader, S. L., & Chen, Y. R. (2012). Differentiating the effects of status and power: a justice perspective. *Journal of Personality and Social Psychology, 102*(5), 994.

Bottger, P. C. (1984). Expertise and air time as bases of actual and perceived influence in problem-solving groups. *Journal of Applied Psychology, 69*(2), 214.

Brown, P., & Levinson, S. C. (1987). *Politeness: Some universals in language usage*. Cambridge, UK: Cambridge University Press.

Brown, R. P., & Zeigler-Hill, V. (2004). Narcissism and the non-equivalence of self-esteem measures: A matter of dominance?. *Journal of Research in Personality*, *38*(6), 585–592.

Bruins, J., Ellemers, N., & De Gilder, D. (1999). Power use and differential competence as determinants of subordinates' evaluative and behavioural responses in simulated organizations. *European Journal of Social Psychology*, *29*(7), 843–870.

Brunell, A., Gentry, W. A., Hoffman, B. J., Kuhnert, K. W., & DeMarree, K. G. (2008). Leader emergence: The case of the narcissistic leader. *Personality and Social Psychology Bulletin*, *34*(12), 1663–1676.

Bushman, B. J., & Baumeister, R. F. (1998). Threatened egotism, narcissism, self-esteem, and direct and displaced aggression: Does self-love or self-hate lead to violence? *Journal of Personality and Social Psychology*, *75*(1), 219.

Buss, D. M. (1996). Social adaptation and five major factors of personality. In J. S. Wiggins (ed.), *The five-factor model of personality: Theoretical perspectives* (pp. 180–207). New York: Guilford Press.

Buss, D. M., & Duntley, J. D. (2006). The evolution of aggression. In M. Schaller, J. A. Simpson, & D. T. Kenrick (eds), *Evolution and social psychology* (pp. 263–286). New York: Psychology Press.

Carli, L. L., & Eagly, A. H. (1999). Gender effects on social influence and emergent leadership. In G. N. Powell (ed.), *Handbook of gender and work* (pp. 203–222), Thousand Oaks, CA: Sage.

Case, C. R., & Maner, J. K. (2014). Divide and conquer: When and why leaders undermine the cohesive fabric of their group. *Journal of Personality and Social Psychology*, *107*(6), 1033–1050.

Chen, S., Lee-Chai, A. Y., & Bargh, J. A. (2001). Relationship orientation as a moderator of the effects of social power. *Journal of Personality and Social Psychology*, *80*(2), 173–187.

Cheng, J. T., & Tracy, J. L. (2013). The impact of wealth on prestige and dominance rank relationships. *Psychological Inquiry*, *24*(2), 102–108.

Cheng, J. T., Tracy, J. L., Foulsham, T., Kingstone, A., & Henrich, J. (2013). Two ways to the top: Evidence that dominance and prestige are distinct yet viable avenues to social rank and influence. *Journal of Personality and Social Psychology*, *104*(1), 103.

Cheng, J. T., Tracy, J. L., & Henrich, J. (2010). Pride, personality, and the evolutionary foundations of human social status. *Evolution and Human Behavior*, *31*(5), 334–347.

Conference Board. (2010). *I can't get no ... job satisfaction, that is: America's unhappy workers*. New York: The Conference Board.

Cottrell, C. A., Neuberg, S. L., & Li, N. P. (2007). What do people desire in others? A sociofunctional perspective on the importance of different valued characteristics. *Journal of Personality and Social Psychology*, *92*(2), 208.

Deag, J. M., & Crook, J. H. (1971). Social behaviour and "agonistic buffering" in the wild barbary macaque Macaca sylvana L. *Folia Primatologica*, *15*(3–4), 183–200.

Dubois, D., Rucker, D. D., & Galinsky, A. D. (2015). Social class, power, and selfishness: When and why upper and lower class individuals behave unethically. *Journal of Personality and Social Psychology*, *108*(3), 436.

Eibl-Eibesfeldt, I. (1989). *Human ethology*. Hawthorne, NY: Aldine De Gruyter.

Elberse, A. (2007). The power of stars: Do star actors drive the success of movies? *Journal of Marketing*, *71*(4), 102–120.

Ellis, L. (1995). Dominance and reproductive success among nonhuman animals: A cross-species comparison. *Ethology and Sociobiology*, *16*(4), 257–333.

Emerson, R. M. (1972). Exchange theory, Part I: A psychological basis for social exchange. *Sociological Theories in Progress*, *2*, 38–57.

Exline, J. J., Baumeister, R. F., Bushman, B. J., Campbell, W. K., & Finkel, E. J. (2004). Too proud to let go: narcissistic entitlement as a barrier to forgiveness. *Journal of Personality and Social Psychology*, *87*(6), 894.

Fast, N. J., Halevy, N., & Galinsky, A. D. (2012). The destructive nature of power without status. *Journal of Experimental Social Psychology*, *48*(1), 391–394.

Flynn, F. J. (2003). How much should I give and how often? The effects of generosity and frequency of favor exchange on social status and productivity. *Academy of Management Journal*, *46*(5), 539–553.

Flynn, F. J., Reagans, R. E., Amanatullah, E. T., & Ames, D. R. (2006). Helping one's way to the top: self-monitors achieve status by helping others and knowing who helps whom. *Journal of Personality and Social Psychology*, *91*(6), 1123–1137.

Fragale, A. R., Overbeck, J. R., & Neale, M. A. (2011). Resources versus respect: Social judgments based on targets' power and status positions. *Journal of Experimental Social Psychology*, *47*(4), 767–775.

Frijda, N. H., & Mesquita, B. (1994). The social roles and functions of emotions. In S. Kitayama, & H. R. Markus (eds), *Emotion and culture: Empirical studies of mutual influence* (pp. 51–87). Washington, DC: American Psychological Association.

Gagné, M., & Deci, E. L. (2005). Self-determination theory and work motivation. *Journal of Organizational behavior*, *26*(4), 331–362.

Galinsky, A. D., Gruenfeld, D. H., & Magee, J. C. (2003). From power to action. *Journal of personality and social psychology*, 85(3), 453–466.

Galinsky, A. D., Magee, J. C., Inesi, M. E., & Gruenfeld, D. H. (2006). Power and perspectives not taken. *Psychological Science*, 17(12), 1068–1074.

Galinsky, A. D., Magee, J. C., Rus, D., Rothman, N. B., & Todd, A. R. (2014). Acceleration With Steering The Synergistic Benefits of Combining Power and Perspective-Taking. *Social Psychological and Personality Science*, 5(6), 627–635.

Georgesen, J., & Harris, M. J. (2006). Holding onto power: Effects of powerholders' positional instability and expectancies on interactions with subordinates. *European Journal of Social Psychology*, 36, 451–468.

Gintner, G., & Lindskold, S. (1975). Rate of participation and expertise as factors influencing leader choice. *Journal of Personality and Social Psychology*, 32(6), 1085–1089.

Gordon, A. M., & Chen, S. (2013). Does power help or hurt? The moderating role of self-other focus on power and perspective taking in romantic relationships. *Personality and Social Psychology Bulletin*, 39, 1097–1110.

Grant, R. W., & Keohane, R. O. (2005). Accountability and abuses of power in world politics. *American Political Science Review*, 99(01), 29–43.

Griskevicius, V., Tybur, J. M., Sundie, J. M., Cialdini, R. B., Miller, G. F., & Kenrick, D. T. (2007). Blatant benevolence and conspicuous consumption: when romantic motives elicit strategic costly signals. *Journal of Personality and Social Psychology*, 93(1), 85.

Griskevicius, V., Tybur, J. M., & Van den Bergh, B. (2010). Going green to be seen: status, reputation, and conspicuous conservation. *Journal of Personality and Social Psychology*, 98(3), 392.

Gruenfeld, D. H., & Preston, J. (2000). Upending the status quo: Cognitive complexity in US Supreme Court justices who overturn legal precedent. *Personality and Social Psychology Bulletin*, 26(8), 1013–1022.

Guinote, A. (2010). Power and goal pursuit. *Personality and Social Psychology Bulletin*, 33(8), 1076–1087.

Guinote, A., Judd, C. M., & Brauer, M. (2002). Effects of power on perceived and objective group variability: evidence that more powerful groups are more variable. *Journal of Personality and Social Psychology*, 82(5), 708.

Gurven, M., Allen-Arave, W., Hill, K., & Hurtado, A. (2000). "It's a wonderful life": Signaling generosity among the Ache of Paraguay. *Evolution and Human Behavior*, 21(4), 263–282.

Halevy, N., Chou, E. Y., Cohen, T. R., & Livingston, R. W. (2012). Status conferral in intergroup social dilemmas: Behavioral antecedents and consequences of prestige and dominance. *Journal of Personality and Social Psychology*, 102(2), 351–366.

Halevy, N., Chou, E. Y., & Galinsky, A. D. (2011). A functional model of hierarchy: Why, how, and when vertical differentiation enhances group performance. *Organizational Psychology Review*, 1(1), 32–52.

Han, Y. J., Nunes, J. C., & Drèze, X. (2013). Signaling status with luxury goods: The role of brand prominence. *International Retail and Marketing Review*, 9(1), 1–22.

Hawley, P. H. (1999). The ontogenesis of social dominance: A strategy-based evolutionary perspective. *Developmental Review*, 19(1), 97–132.

Henrich, J., & Gil-White, F. J. (2001). The evolution of prestige: Freely conferred deference as a mechanism for enhancing the benefits of cultural transmission. *Evolution and Human Behavior*, 22(3), 165–196.

Henrich, N. S., & Henrich, J. (2007). *Why humans cooperate: A cultural and evolutionary explanation.* Oxford, UK: Oxford University Press.

Hersey, P., & Blanchard, K. H. (1993). *Management of organizational behavior: Utilizing human resources.* Upper Saddle River, NJ: Prentice-Hall.

Hewstone, M., Rubin, M., & Willis, H. (2002). Intergroup bias. *Annual Review of Psychology*, 53(1), 575–604.

Howard, J. A., Blumstein, P., & Schwartz, P. (1986). Sex, power, and influence tactics in intimate relationships. *Journal of Personality and Social Psychology*, 51(1), 102–109.

Johnson, R. T., Burk, J. A., & Kirkpatrick, L. A. (2007). Dominance and prestige as differential predictors of aggression and testosterone levels in men. *Evolution and Human Behavior*, 28(5), 345–351.

Josephs, R. A., Sellers, J. G., Newman, M. L., & Mehta, P. H. (2006). The mismatch effect: when testosterone and status are at odds. *Journal of Personality and Social Psychology*, 90(6), 999–1013.

Judge, T. A., & Cable, D. M. (2004). The effect of physical height on workplace success and income: preliminary test of a theoretical model. *Journal of Applied Psychology*, 89(3), 428–441.

Kahle, L. R., & Homer, P. M. (1985). Physical attractiveness of the celebrity endorser: A social adaptation perspective. *Journal of Consumer Research*, 11(4), 954–961.

Keltner, D., Capps, L., Kring, A. M., Young, R. C., & Heerey, E. A. (2001). Just teasing: a conceptual analysis and empirical review. *Psychological Bulletin*, 127(2), 229–248.

Keltner, D., Gruenfeld, D. H., & Anderson, C. (2003). Power, approach, and inhibition. *Psychological Review*, 110(2), 265–284.

Kilduff, G. J., & Galinsky, A. D. (2013). From the ephemeral to the enduring: How approach-oriented mindsets lead to greater status. *Journal of Personality and Social Psychology*, 105(5), 816–831.

King, A. J., Johnson, D. D., & van Vugt, M. (2009). The origins and evolution of leadership. *Current Biology, 19*(19), 911–916.

Kipnis, D. (1972). Does power corrupt?. *Journal of Personality and Social Psychology, 24*(1), 33–41.

Kipnis, D. (1976). *The powerholders.* Chicago, IL: University of Chicago Press.

Lammers, J., Dubois, D., Rucker, D. D., & Galinsky, A. D. (2013). Power gets the job: Priming power improves interview outcomes. *Journal of Experimental Social Psychology, 49*(4), 776–779.

Lammers, J., Galinsky, A. D., Gordijn, E. H., & Otten, S. (2008). Illegitimacy moderates the effects of power on approach. *Psychological Science, 19*(6), 558–564.

Lammers, J., Stapel, D. A., & Galinsky, A. D. (2010). Power increases hypocrisy moralizing in reasoning, immorality in behavior. *Psychological Science, 21*(5), 737–744.

Lasswell, H. D., & Kaplan, A. (2013). *Power and society: A framework for political inquiry.* Piscataway, NJ: Transaction Publishers.

Lin, M. H., Kwan, V. S., Cheung, A., & Fiske, S. T. (2005). Stereotype content model explains prejudice for an envied outgroup: Scale of anti-Asian American stereotypes. *Personality and Social Psychology Bulletin, 31*(1), 34–47.

Littlepage, G. E., Schmidt, G. W., Whisler, E. W., & Frost, A. G. (1995). An input-process-output analysis of influence and performance in problem-solving groups. *Journal of Personality and Social Psychology, 69*(5), 877–889.

Lord, R. G., De Vader, C. L., & Alliger, G. M. (1986). A meta-analysis of the relation between personality traits and leadership perceptions: An application of validity generalization procedures. *Journal of Applied Psychology, 71*(3), 402–410.

Lovaglia, M. J. (1994). Relating power to status. *Advances in Group Processes, 11,* 87–111.

Lovaglia, M. J. (1997). Status, Emotion, and Structural Power. In J. Szmatka, J. Szmatka, & J. Berger (eds), *Status, network, and structure: theory development in group processes* (pp. 159–178). Stanford, CA: Stanford University Press.

Maddux, J. E., & Rogers, R. W. (1980). Effects of source expertness, physical attractiveness, and supporting arguments on persuasion: A case of brains over beauty. *Journal of Personality and Social Psychology, 39*(2), 235.

Magee, J. C., & Galinsky, A. D. (2008). 8 Social hierarchy: The self reinforcing nature of power and status. *The Academy of Management Annals, 2*(1), 351–398.

Magee, J. C., Galinsky, A. D., & Gruenfeld, D. H. (2007). Power, propensity to negotiate, and moving first in competitive interactions. *Personality and Social Psychology Bulletin, 33*(2), 200–212.

Mahoney, J., & Thelen, K. (2010). A theory of gradual institutional change. In J. Mahoney & K. Thelen (eds), *Explaining institutional change: Ambiguity, agency, and power* (pp. 1–37). Cambridge, UK: Cambridge University Press.

Maner, J. K., & Mead, N. L. (2010). The essential tension between leadership and power: when leaders sacrifice group goals for the sake of self-interest. *Journal of Personality and Social Psychology, 99*(3), 482–497.

Martorana, P. V., Galinsky, A. D., & Rao, H. (2005). From system justification to system condemnation: Antecedents of attempts to change power hierarchies. *Research on Managing Groups and Teams, 7,* 285–315.

Mazur, A. (1985). A biosocial model of status in face-to-face primate groups. *Social Forces, 64,* 377–402.

Mazur, A., & Booth, A. (1998). Testosterone and dominance in men. *Behavioral and Brain Sciences, 21*(03), 353–363.

Mazur, A., & Lamb, T. A. (1980). Testosterone, status, and mood in human males. *Hormones and Behavior, 14*(3), 236–246.

McClelland, D. C. (1975). *Power: The inner experience.* Hoboken, NJ: Wiley-Blackwell.

Mead, N. L. Baumeister, R. F., Stuppy, A., & Vohs, K. D. (2015). Why does power corrupt? Power unleashes narcissism. Unpublished Manuscript.

Mead, N. L., & Maner, J. K. (2012). On keeping your enemies close: Powerful leaders seek proximity to ingroup power threats. *Journal of Personality and Social Psychology, 102*(3), 576–591.

Milinski, M., Semmann, D., & Krambeck, H. J. (2002). Reputation helps solve the "tragedy of the commons." *Nature, 415*(6870), 424–426.

Nisbett, R. E., & Wilson, T. D. (1977). The halo effect: Evidence for unconscious alteration of judgments. *Journal of Personality and Social Psychology, 35*(4), 250–256.

Northouse, P. G. (2015). *Leadership: Theory and practice.* New York: Sage.

Overbeck, J. R., & Park, B. (2001). When power does not corrupt: superior individuation processes among powerful perceivers. *Journal of Personality and Social Psychology, 81*(4), 549–565.

Overbeck, J. R., & Park, B. (2006). Powerful perceivers, powerless objects: Flexibility of powerholders' social attention. *Organizational Behavior and Human Decision Processes, 99*(2), 227–243.

Paulhus, D. L. (1998). Interpersonal and intrapsychic adaptiveness of trait self-enhancement: A mixed blessing?. *Journal of Personality and Social Psychology*, *74*(5), 1197–1208.

Ridgeway, C. L. (1987). Nonverbal behavior, dominance, and the basis of status in task groups. *American Sociological Review*, *52*(5), 683–694.

Ridgeway, C., & Diekema, D. (1989). Dominance and collective hierarchy formation in male and female task groups. *American Sociological Review*, *54*(1), 79–93.

Ridgeway, C. L., & Walker, H. (1995). Status structures. In K. Cook, G. Fine, & J. House (eds), *Sociological perspectives on social psychology* (pp. 281–310). London, UK: Pearson.

Rosenthal, S. A., & Pittinsky, T. L. (2006). Narcissistic leadership. *The Leadership Quarterly*, *17*(6), 617–633.

Rus, D., van Knippenberg, D., & Wisse, B. (2012). Leader power and self-serving behavior: The moderating role of accountability. *The Leadership Quarterly*, *23*(1), 13–26.

Schmid Mast, M., Jonas, K., & Hall, J. A. (2009). Give a person power and he or she will show interpersonal sensitivity: the phenomenon and its why and when. *Journal of Personality and Social Psychology*, *97*(5), 835.

Schultheiss, O. C., Campbell, K. L., & McClelland, D. C. (1999). Implicit power motivation moderates men's testosterone responses to imagined and real dominance success. *Hormones and Behavior*, *36*(3), 234–241.

Shamir, B., House, R. J., & Arthur, M. B. (1993). The motivational effects of charismatic leadership: A self-concept based theory. *Organization Science*, *4*(4), 577–594.

Sidanius, J., & Pratto, F. (2004). Social dominance theory: A new synthesis. In J. T. Jost & J. Sidanius (eds), *Political psychology: Key readings* (pp. 315–332). New York: Psychology Press.

Sorrentino, R. M., & Boutillier, R. G. (1975). The effect of quantity and quality of verbal interaction on ratings of leadership ability. *Journal of Experimental Social Psychology*, *11*(5), 403–411.

Stiff, C., & van Vugt, M. (2008). The power of reputations: The role of third party information in the admission of new group members. *Group Dynamics: Theory, Research, and Practice*, *12*(2), 155–166.

Tepper, B. J. (2000). Consequences of abusive supervision. *Academy of Management Journal*, *43*(2), 178–190.

Thye, S. R. (2000). A status value theory of power in exchange relations. *American Sociological Review*, *65*(3), 407–432.

Tooby, J., & Cosmides, L. (1988). *The evolution of war and its cognitive foundations*. Institute for Evolutionary Studies Technical Report 88-1. Retrieved from www.cep.ucsb.edu/codirectors/codirectors/case2014/Tooby%20publications%20for%20Bio-Bibliography/008%20The%20evolution%20of%20war%20and%20its%20cognitive%20foundations%20(1988).pdf.

Van Kleef, G. A., Oveis, C., Van Der Löwe, I., LuoKogan, A., Goetz, J., & Keltner, D. (2008). Power, distress, and compassion turning a blind eye to the suffering of others. *Psychological Science*, *19*(12), 1315–1322.

Van Vugt, M. (2006). Evolutionary origins of leadership and followership. *Personality and Social Psychology Review*, *10*(4), 354–371.

Van Vugt, M., & Iredale, W. (2013). Men behaving nicely: Public goods as peacock tails. British *Journal of Psychology*, *104*(1), 3–13.

Van Vugt, M., Hogan, R., & Kaiser, R. B. (2008). Leadership, followership, and evolution: some lessons from the past. *American Psychologist*, *63*(3), 182–196.

Wall, J. F. (1989). *Andrew Carnegie*. Pittsburgh, PA: University of Pittsburgh.

Watson, P. J., & Morris, R. J. (1991). Narcissism, empathy and social desirability. *Personality and Individual Differences*, *12*(6), 575–579.

Watson, P. J., Grisham, S. O., Trotter, M. V., & Biderman, M. D. (1984). Narcissism and empathy: Validity evidence for the narcissistic personality inventory. *Journal of Personality Assessment*, *48*, 301–305.

Wedekind, C., & Braithwaite, V. A. (2002). The long-term benefits of human generosity in indirect reciprocity. *Current Biology*, *12*(12), 1012–1015.

Willer, R. (2009). Groups reward individual sacrifice: The status solution to the collective action problem. *American Sociological Review*, *74*(1), 23–43.

Winter, D. G., & Barenbaum, N. B. (1985). Responsibility and the power motive in women and men. *Journal of Personality*, *53*(2), 335–355.

26

The Intersection of Purpose and Heroism

A Study of Exemplars

Kendall Cotton Bronk and Brian R. Riches

Purpose and heroism are conceptually overlapping constructs. Both heroic and purposeful acts are intentionally performed as a means of being of service to the world beyond the self. In this way, heroic and purposeful acts share both elements of transcendence and a goal orientation. These constructs are so closely related in fact, that some have defined one in terms of the other. For instance, scholars have defined heroism as "an individual's commitment to a noble purpose, usually aimed at furthering the welfare of others, and involving the willingness to accept the consequences of achieving that purpose" (Jayawickreme & Di Stefano, 2012, p. 165; see also Becker & Eagly, 2004; Campbell, 2008; Franco, Blue, & Zimbardo, 2011). In this conception, purpose is the essence of heroic action.

In spite of their conceptual similarities, little has been written about how these constructs overlap and how they differ. As a result, it has been unclear how these constructs might interact and if the promotion of one may influence the development of the other. Learning more about this relationship could have important implications for fostering both of these socially desirable and personally beneficial constructs. To that end, this chapter seeks to illuminate the nature of the relationship between purpose and heroism. In it we propose a framework that features two routes through which these constructs intersect. In one, which we term *purpose-guided heroism*, the development of purpose precedes heroic action, and in the other, which we call *heroism-guided purpose*, heroic action precedes the formation of a purpose in life. Following our theoretical explanation of this framework, we profile two real life heroes whose experiences exemplify these different linkages. First, though, we provide brief overviews of heroism and purpose.

Heroism

A leading conception of heroism proposes that a hero *is a person who knowingly and voluntarily acts for the good of one or more people at significant risk to the self without being motivated by reward* (Zimbardo, 2007). This definition includes several key components, including significant risk, voluntary action, self-transcendent motives, and no expectation of reward. Risk, including physical and social risk, makes heroism a distinct form of altruism (Franco, Blau, & Zimbardo, 2011). Heroes include civilians who rescue others from burning buildings and in so doing risk their lives, and whistle blowers who reveal corruption in the workplace and in so doing risk their job, income, and social standing (Franco et al., 2011; Franco & Zimbardo, 2006; Zimbardo, 2007). Many classical and modern perspectives also consider great sacrifices to be examples of heroic action (Kohen, 2013). Accordingly, individuals who set aside their own well-being to help others may be considered heroes.

In addition to including some element of significant risk, heroic action must also be completed knowingly and voluntarily. That means that someone who accidentally bumps a person out of the way of an oncoming car would not be considered a hero, and neither would someone who was coerced into assisting another. While both of these situations may result in positive outcomes, they are not voluntary, and therefore they are not examples of heroic action.

Heroism also requires that individuals act for the good of others or causes beyond the self. Heroic action is motivated by a desire to help another person, aid a group of people, or contribute to an issue in the broader world; it is not intended to help the self. In this way, heroic action involves an element of self-transcendence.

Finally, heroic actions are performed without any expectation of personal reward or gain. While in some cases heroes are recognized for their efforts, recognition or compensation does not motivate their behavior. Instead, heroic action is motivated by a desire to help another or advance a cause, not by a desire for personal gain.

Based on this conception of heroism, anyone can be a hero if presented the opportunity. However, individuals who take heroic action (e.g., voluntary, risky action for the good of others) are rare (Franco & Zimbardo, 2006). A recent news story underscores the uncommon nature of heroic action. In Beaverton, Oregon a woman nearly burned to death in her car as six individuals stood by watching and videotaping the incident. Only one young man, a teenager, came forward to help, and in so doing, risked his life but, according to police, very likely saved hers. Following the incident he noted that what surprised him were not the flames coming from the car but the fact that no one else stepped forward to help (Paz, 2015).

Purpose in Life

Similar to heroism, purpose is defined in part by a commitment to act in ways that benefit the world beyond the self. Historically definitions of purpose have varied, but in the past decade a consensus has emerged: *a purpose in life represents a stable and generalized intention to accomplish something that is personally meaningful and at the same time leads to productive engagement with some aspect of the world beyond the self* (Damon, Menon, & Bronk, 2003). This definition includes three important elements. First, a purpose is a highly meaningful, long term goal. Like a compass guiding a vessel, it serves as a personally significant, far horizon aim that directs more short term objectives. Second, a purpose in life is not just a dream or an aspiration, but instead it is something individuals actively engage in working toward. Engagement is typically evident by the investment of time, energy, and effort in pursuit of the aim. Finally, in addition to being personally meaningful, a purpose in life is also relevant to the broader world. This is an important point; along with the goal-oriented criterion, this beyond the self criterion differentiates purpose from the related *meaning* construct. Any activity that is personally significant can be said to be meaningful, but only those enduring aims that are also of consequence to the broader world can be said to represent purposes. Accordingly, a walk in the woods may be meaningful, while working to preserve the environment may inspire an enduring sense of purpose.

Similar to research on heroism, research on purpose has increased dramatically in the past decade. Researchers have concluded, for example, that individuals tend to find purpose in giving back to their communities, helping their families, living in accordance with their religious beliefs, and serving their countries (Bronk, 2013; Damon, 2008). In some cases, purpose drives engagement in these activities, and in other cases people discover purpose through their involvement in these activities; in still other cases a budding purpose directs individuals to a particular activity that turn out to be highly meaningful (Bronk, 2012; Hill, Sumner, & Burrow, 2014).

Empirical studies have also determined that purpose and meaning are critical to optimal development across the lifespan. For instance, researchers have identified purpose as central to positive youth development (Benson, 2006; Damon, 2004, 2008; Lerner et al., 2005; Shek, 1992), adult flourishing (Seligman, 2011), and healthy aging (Pinquart, 2002). Purpose is also inversely related to loneliness (Paloutzian & Ellison, 1982), boredom (Fahlman et al., 2009; Drob & Bernard, 1988; Bargdill, 2000), depression (Bigler, Neimeyer, & Brown, 2001), and anxiety (Bigler, Neimeyer, & Brown, 2001) and is positively related to hope (Mascaro & Rosen, 2005), happiness (French & Joseph, 1999; Lewis, Lanigan, Joseph, & de Fockert, 1997), and life satisfaction (Bronk, Hill, Lapsley, Talib, & Finch, 2009).

In most cases, purpose is associated with positive affect (King, Hicks, Krull, & Del Gaiso, 2006; Noblejas de la Flor, 1997). However, studies find that in at least some circumstances, especially parenting (Umberson & Gove, 1989) and caregiving (Marks, Lambert, & Choi, 2002), the presence of purpose is not consistently associated with positive emotions. While adults may not always find parenting or caregiving particularly enjoyable, they do tend to derive a deep sense of meaning from these activities. It seems likely that the same pattern of results could hold for at least some heroes who are guided by a broader purpose in life. Serving others in a heroic fashion may not always be pleasant or fun, but it is likely to be highly meaningful.

Purpose among Heroes

Based on these definitions, it is clear that purpose and heroism share some core features. For instance, both are evidenced by goal-oriented activities. Neither purposeful nor heroic deeds are completed accidentally or unintentionally; instead both are voluntarily performed and deliberately executed. Individuals guided by a purpose in life reflect deeply upon the things that matter most to them, and their actions are carefully considered to align with their long term aims (Damon, 2008). Similarly, when heroes make seemingly instantaneous decisions to aid others, they are likely doing so based on a longstanding belief, about the importance of assisting others, that they considered much earlier in their development (Damon & Colby, 2015). Because they have already thought about the significance of helping others, they do not need to reconsider its importance when the opportunity to act accordingly arises; instead, they just act. In other words, though heroic actions may seem reflexive, we argue that they are more likely based on a carefully constructed value system considered earlier in life.

Another feature shared by both purposeful and heroic acts is the motivation behind their performance. Both acts are spurred, at least in part, by a desire to contribute to the world beyond the self. Rather than being driven by purely self-focused motives, these acts are intended to help another person, a group of people, or to advance a personally meaningful cause.

These constructs also share a focus on unpleasant sacrifice. Heroism is risky and the pursuit of purpose can be messy and difficult (Zimbardo, 2007). Yet, in spite of the obvious personal cost, individuals engage in these acts because they are important.

While these constructs are similar, they are not one and the same. They differ in that whereas a heroic deed could be a one-time act, purpose inspires an enduring commitment to action. Also, whereas a heroic act necessarily features some element of risk, a purpose in life need not, and whereas a heroic act is necessarily focused on aiding another or others, a purpose in life may be motivated by a desire to progress toward a broader array of social aims. For instance a purpose in life may be evident among individuals who seek to contribute to artistic or spiritual pursuits or to create new musical or structural forms.

Clearly heroism and purpose overlap though they describe distinct phenomena, and though empirical research examining the relationship between purpose and heroism is scant at best, we propose that a Venn diagram accurately and succinctly illustrates their relationship. Not all people with a purpose in life act heroically (consider individuals who quietly but earnestly strive to raise children who will become productive citizens, for instance), and not all heroes are guided by an enduring purpose in life (consider a woman who instinctively grabs a small child out of the way of an oncoming car). However, in at least some cases, the two constructs overlap; some individuals who act heroically do so because they are guided by an enduring purpose in life, and some individuals who have acted heroically derive such meaning from the experience that they end up developing a lasting sense of purpose.

More specifically, we offer a framework that features two ways purpose and heroism can overlap. The first, which we call *purpose-guided heroism*, proposes that the existence of an enduring purpose in life readies individuals for heroic action. Individuals with purpose may be more likely than others to act heroically because they are more likely to recognize opportunities for heroic action. Individuals with purpose have clearly defined values and beliefs (Damon, 2008), which means they know what matters to them and why. As a result, when something happens that violates a deeply held belief, they do not have to wonder if they should act. They know. Individuals who do not view the world through a lens of purpose may ignore or miss entirely opportunities for heroic action.

Not only are individuals with purpose more likely to recognize opportunities for heroic action, but they are also better prepared to act on them when the opportunity arises. Individuals guided by a purpose in life tend to develop social networks and practical skills that help advance their personally meaningful aims, and these same relationships and capacities arm them with the resources required for heroic action (Bronk, 2012; Burrow & Hill, 2011). Leading a life of purpose can essentially make someone a hero-in-waiting (Zimbardo, 2007).

The last way purpose can facilitate heroic action is through moral commitment. The same moral sense that undergirds some forms of purpose can lead individuals to act heroically when the situation presents itself. A careful review of the definition of purpose reminds us that not all forms of purpose are moral (Damon, Menon, & Bronk, 2003). A purpose in life may represent *any* stable and generalized intention to act in ways that are personally meaningful and significant to the world beyond the self. Mother Teresa, who cared tirelessly for the poor and infirmed, was guided by a caring purpose, but at the same time the individuals who flew airplanes into the World Trade Center and Pentagon on 9/11 were also likely guided by a purpose, in this case a destructive one. Similarly, not all heroic acts are moral (Campbell & Moyers, 1991). While it is beyond the scope of the present chapter to try to distinguish moral from immoral pursuits, a variety of philosophical traditions guide us in how to do this.[1]

Although not all forms of purpose are moral, clearly some are formed by a strong sense of moral commitment. In these cases, we argue that the same moral commitment that leads individuals to pursue a noble purpose in life compels them to act heroically when afforded the opportunity. A purpose in life often stems from an individual's sense of identity, and when purpose and identity are intertwined, actions consistent with one's purpose in life become more likely (Bronk, 2011; Erikson, 1968, 1980). For instance, compared to others, individuals who find purpose in standing up to injustices would be more likely to act heroically when they witness another's rights being violated. Because they have already thought deeply about the importance of equal rights, they do not need to spend time reconsidering how they feel about this issue. Instead, when the opportunity arises, they are likely to act (Damon & Colby, 2015). In this way, the same moral beliefs that inspire a purpose in life can spur heroic action.

Taken together, the presence of purpose helps individuals recognize opportunities for heroic action and prepares them to act when the opportunity arises. A purpose in life, in this case, serves as an important foundation for heroic action.

The second way these constructs may overlap occurs when a heroic act inspires an enduring commitment to purpose. Individuals may be thrust into a position where they are presented with the opportunity to act heroically, and perhaps because of the contextual particulars—a personal relationship or some other external force—they engage. This is not to say that the heroic action is involuntary. Heroic action by definition is always a choice. But it can be encouraged by external factors, and as a result of an extrinsically motivated action, an intrinsic motivation for a larger cause may be borne. In the case of *heroism-guided purpose*, a heroic act serves as a springboard for the development of an enduring purpose in life. A heroic deed can inspire a lasting commitment to a purpose that was not present before the individual took action. It may be that acting heroically enables individuals to see the world in a new light or it may be that acting heroically alerts individuals to injustices of which they were previously unaware. Either way, the experience of heroic action can provide the basis for the development of a long-lasting purpose in life.

To this point we have discussed the framework in fairly abstract terms, but below we examine exemplars of heroism and purpose, and we explain how their lives demonstrate our proposed model. First, we profile Archbishop Oscar Romero, who risked his life fighting on behalf of the impoverished in El Salvador. His heroic actions were consistent with and inspired by a long held purpose in life, and in this way he illustrates *purpose-guided heroism*. Next, we profile Miep Gies, one of the people who helped hide Anne Frank and her family during the Holocaust. While Gies was not politically active to begin with, the act of protecting the Frank family radicalized her and filled her with a lasting purpose in life. Accordingly, her actions illustrate *heroism-guided purpose*. We start with Oscar Romero.

Exemplars of Purpose and Heroism

Oscar Arnulfo Romero

In 1917, Oscar Romero was born in a small village in Ciudad Barrios in the San Miguel department of El Salvador (Brockman, 1989). His family was not particularly wealthy. Nor were they particularly religious, but in spite of this, neighbors remember Romero as a studious and pious child. He attended public school until third grade, all that was offered at the time, and then was sent to study privately under a teacher until he was thirteen (Brockman, 1989).

Upon finishing his education, Romero's father wanted him to apprentice to become a carpenter, and he did for a time, but he really wanted to attend seminary school (Brockman, 1989). This yearning was not a surprise to people who knew young Romero; he was frequently seen praying at local churches. At thirteen, Romero left Ciudad Barrios to attend San Miguel minor seminary. For a young boy from a remote village, this was a significant move (Brockman, 1989). Leaving home to join the seminary represented an early step toward pursuing what would eventually become his purpose in life. Like other adolescent exemplars of purpose, Romero found himself on a productive and meaningful path from a young age (Bronk, 2011).

In 1937, following his education at the San Miguel minor seminary, he moved to the national seminary in San Salvador. He received his licentiate degree in theology in 1941 and was ordained as a Catholic priest in 1942 (Brockman, 1989; Erdozaín, 1981). Later on, Romero wrote "the nucleus of my life is to witness the love of God to humans and of humans among themselves… I have tried to follow the supreme shepherd, Jesus Christ, who directed his love to all" (Romero & Brockman, 1984). This was clearly his purpose in life, and though he did not write about it until later, it was evident early in his life. In fact, Romero's purpose was apparent in decisions he made throughout his childhood, adolescence, and young adult years. It guided his school and career choices, and it became even more evident in the work he would do in the next twenty years as a priest, a church administrator, an editor for a local newspaper, and a director for Alcoholics Anonymous.

These different roles put him in contact with a variety of people, including members of the working poor. He learned that wealthy landowners were paying workers less than the minimum wage. Because of this, workers were engaged in a losing battle against the government backed landowners, and the army regularly resorted to violence to maintain control over the impoverished citizens (Brockman, 1989; Erdozaín, 1981). At this time, the Catholic Church typically worked closely with members of the local government and Romero, along with other church leaders, supported the ruling class. However, following the Second Vatican Council (1962–1965), the church's support of the government began to wane, and the previously conservative Romero, guided by his personally meaningful belief in God's love, began to change, too.

In 1974 Romero was appointed Archbishop of San Salvador. His writings at this time show him becoming increasingly skeptical of the ruling class' practices (Romero, undated; Brockman, 1989). The government-sanctioned violence against the poor "undermined Romero's trust in the good will of the authorities" (Romero, undated; Brockman, 1989). As he began to acknowledge the unfair treatment the poor people in San Salvador were receiving, he became increasingly moved to fight against it. Following the assassination of his friend and mentor, Jesuit Father Rutilio Grande in 1977, Romero began to take more dramatic action opposing the government and supporting the poor, as Father Grande had done before him (Romero, undated; Brockman, 1989). Archbishop Romero continued to refine and enact his sense of purpose as he became an "outspoken opponent of injustice and defender of the poor" (Romero, undated). Archbishop Romero's ideas regarding God's love and how it should play out in the world around him evolved as he learned about the plight of the poor. The slow but steady development of his commitment mirrors the experience of other young people who led exemplary lives of purpose (Bronk, 2011).

Romero continued his fight on behalf of the poor into 1980, when a new government took over. He pleaded with members of the army to stop killing their brethren, and reminded them that they need not obey immoral orders. In his last speech in March of that year, he spoke directly about his now clearly defined purpose in life. He preached about how he sought to bring all people—rich and poor, oppressed and oppressor—together in Christian unity. He wanted people from all stations in life to work together to promote social justice. He preached about "a liberation that includes, above all, respect for the dignity of the person, the salvation of the people's common good, and transcendence, which looks before all to God, and from God alone derives its hope and its force" (as cited in Brockman, 1989).

His words in pursuit of unity, liberty, and justice for the poor put him at great risk. He knew he could be jailed, tortured, or even killed for what he was saying, but his commitment to his purpose superseded his concern for his own well-being. "I want to assure you," he said during his homily on November 11, 1979, "that I will not abandon my people but that together with them I will run all the risks that my ministry demands" (Romero & Brockman, 1984, p. 100). As a result of his words and deeds, Archbishop Romero was branded a communist and a troublemaker and was pressured to back down from his platform (Brockman, 1989; Erdozaín, 1981; Romero & Brockman, 1984). However, far from it, he persisted and even intensified his efforts. His controversial sermons and speeches made Archbishop Romero a hero.

Although members of the government had tolerated Archbishop Romero's contrary perspective early on, they became increasingly concerned about his growing and outspoken support of the poor. This final speech served as a critical tipping point in their opinion of him. The day after he gave this speech, while conducting mass at the altar, Archbishop Oscar Romero was assassinated by a man with close ties to the government (Brockman, 1989; Erdozaín, 1981; Garrett, 2010; Renderos, 2010).

In a variety of ways, Archbishop Romero's purpose in life prepared him to act heroically when the opportunity arose. Whereas others may have been able to turn a blind eye to the suffering of the poor, Archbishop Romero was not. His purpose in life, demonstrated in the Episcopal motto he selected when becoming a bishop, "Sentir con la Iglesia" or "To Be of One Mind and Heart with the Church" (Brockman, 1989), made him particularly sensitive to the unfair treatment a segment of the local population was receiving. He could not ignore it. He recognized that heroic action was needed, and he acted.

Additionally, like other exemplars of purpose, Archbishop Romero developed social and practical resources that enabled him to act heroically. Many individuals with purpose find mentors who help them pursue the aims that matter most to them (Bronk, 2011), and Archbishop Romero was no exception. During his ascendancy in the church he befriended several people, including Father Grande, who helped him recognize the need for action and taught him how to engage effectively. Additionally, as a result of his purpose, Archbishop Romero found himself in a position to act. Had he continued to work as a carpenter he would not have had the platform from which to protest with authority, but as an Archbishop, he did. In these ways, his enduring purpose in life facilitated his heroic action.

It is also evident that the same moral sense that undergirded Archbishop Romero's purpose in life also inspired his heroism. His desire to share God's love with all people sharply contrasted with the injustices he saw being unfairly directed toward the working poor in his community, and he committed himself to improving the situation. Archbishop Romero's moral commitment to the sanctity of life was a key component of his purpose:

> Nothing is so important to me as a human life. Taking life is something so serious, so grave—more than the violation of any other human right—because it is the love of God's children, and because such bloodshed only negates love, awakens new hatreds, makes reconciliation and peace impossible.
>
> *(Cited in Brockman, 1984)*

This moral commitment inspired Oscar Romero's speeches and sermons from early in his career until the time he died, and it was this same moral commitment that gave him the fortitude to stand against those who would harm him and the people for whom he cared.

Archbishop Romero developed a meaningful purpose early in life, which inspired and prepared him to act heroically when the opportunity was presented. Accordingly, he serves as a fitting example of *purpose-guided heroism*.

Miep Gies

Whereas Archbishop Romero was deeply religious, Miep Gies was not. During her childhood she attended church, but the horrors of the Second World War and the Holocaust stole her faith. In spite of their different orientations to religion, both Gies and Romero represent exemplars of heroism and purpose. Miep Gies exemplifies the second proposed linkage between these two constructs.

The story of Anne Frank and her time spent hiding in the secret annex during the Second World War is well known, but the story of the people who helped hide Anne and the others is less familiar. Four individuals and two of their spouses served as the hiders' lifelines; visiting the secret annex daily, they brought food, clothing, and news. In addition to bringing the things required to keep those in hiding alive, the helpers also offered emotional support and encouragement, which turned out to be every bit as essential. They filled this role in spite of the great risk inherent in doing so. Under Nazi law, helping Jews was punishable by jail time, deportation, and even death.

One of the helpers was Miep Gies. Born Hermine Santruschitz in Vienna, Austria in 1909, she moved to the Netherlands when she was ten-years-old. When she was five, the First World War broke out, and as a result of food shortages that endured over the next five years, Hermine became undernourished and ill. She was one of many children suffering in 1920, so—remarkably—as part of a foreign aid program, along with a group of Austrian children she boarded a train bound for the Netherlands, where a foster family she had never met before took her in.

Though she was only supposed to stay for three months, she remained in the Netherlands permanently. She grew close to her adoptive parents, brothers, and sister, who lovingly gave her the Dutch nickname, Miep. Gies "took to Dutch life quite naturally," and in her autobiography, she reports that her childhood was a happy one (Gies, 1987, p. 20). She describes her childhood home as a place where "almost always, lively children filled the air with shouts and laughter; if they weren't playing games, they were whistling upward to call their friends out to play" (p. 15). As an adolescent, she developed an appreciation for classical music and a polite interest in politics, but neither she nor her adoptive family was politically active.

In 1933 Gies was twenty-four and looking for work. Jobs were hard to come by at this time, but as luck would have it, she found a posting for a jam maker at a local company called Opecta. When she arrived for her interview she met Otto Frank, who was new to Amsterdam and struggled to speak Dutch. He was relieved to learn that Gies spoke German, his native tongue, and after a brief conversation, he hired her. Over the years, Gies and Frank developed a close friendship. Gies met Frank's family, his wife, Edith, and his two daughters, Margot and Anne, and on the weekends she often joined the family for dinner. Among other things, Frank and Gies discovered they shared a similar perspective on politics. Like many in the Netherlands, both were deeply opposed to Hitler, who had recently seized power in Germany. However, though Gies opposed Hitler, she was not engaged in political activities, and, as she wrote in her autobiography, she "had never felt strongly one way or another about Jewish people" (p. 27).

As the Nazis marched across Europe and into the Netherlands, it became clear that Jewish families, including the Franks, were not safe. Almost daily, the Germans began imposing new laws on the Jews: First they had to register as Jews through a census; later they had to wear a yellow star identifying them as Jews; and, eventually they were rounded up and taken away in buses and trains never to be seen or heard from again. Otto and his family rightfully feared for their safety. Like many other Jews in Amsterdam at the time, they decided to go into hiding. Frank asked Gies, "are you willing to take on the responsibility of taking care of us while we are in hiding?" (Gies, 1987, p. 79). Without hesitation and with the full knowledge of the risks involved in doing so, Gies agreed. For more than two years, risking great personal harm and even death, Gies faithfully cared for her friends. She did not expect anything in return because of course they had nothing to give. In fact, she did not tell anyone except her husband, Jan Geis, what she was doing. Jan supported Miep's decision to help the Franks, and he did the same, visiting them as often as he could. In her tireless and dangerous support of the Frank family, Gies was a hero.

Though Gies was not politically active prior to her act of heroism, the experience of caring for her friends changed her and her husband. Like Miep, Jan Gies was aware of political issues but not politically active before this experience, but months into helping hide the Franks, he joined the Dutch Resistance, and later still Miep and Jan decided to hide a Jewish man in their apartment.

The stress involved in the work they were doing was tremendous. Gies wrote,

> It was strange, but sometimes when I felt I was at the end of my strength, I'd push myself just a little bit further, and tapping into a reserve energy I didn't know I had, I'd find that I could summon more strength and endurance as the situation demanded.
>
> *(Gies, 1987, p. 131)*

She worried constantly about falling ill and getting caught. If something happened to Gies it was not just she who would suffer but the eight desperate people who relied on her as well.

Tragically, and in spite of the tremendous effort that Gies and the other helpers put forth, the Franks and their friends in hiding were eventually discovered. Soon after the Franks were taken away, Gies entered the hiding place and gathered the pile of papers she knew to be Anne's diary. She immediately stashed them in her desk with every intention of returning them to Anne when she was released. That day never came as all of those who hid in the secret annex, except Otto, perished.

Gies was devastated by the loss of her friends, and the experience changed her in a profound way. She did not want her friends to be forgotten, and ensuring that their legacy endured provided her with a lasting sense of purpose. She traveled worldwide giving talks about hiding the individuals in the secret annex, she wrote a book about her experience called *Anne Frank Remembered*, and she took a leading role, along with Otto and some of the other helpers, in establishing the Anne Frank House. "A day never goes by that I do not think about what happened" (Gies, 1987, p. 217).

Another way Gies ensured that the Holocaust was not forgotten was to respond to letters written to her by school children who read her book and Anne's diary. The transcript of her responses, posted on the Scholastic website, reveals that Gies "felt really grateful for the opportunity to help" the people hiding in the secret annex: "It brought a lot of sense to our lives. It is always nice to feel needed by other people. This, at least, is my understanding of living a worthwhile life" (Scholastic, 1997).

In an interview, Gies was asked if she would help the Frank family again—knowing that she could not save them. Gies explained that she would do whatever she could. Her efforts extended the young Anne's life by two years, and during that time she wrote her influential diary. That alone made the effort worthwhile.

Joseph Campbell, who wrote extensively about the heroic myth, noted that meaning is often discovered as a result of the hero's journey, and this certainly seems to have been the case for Gies (Campbell, 2008; Campbell & Moyers, 1991). Through her heroic act, her purpose was revealed. Her heroic deed inspired an enduring sense of purpose that remained a part of her life until she died at one hundred years of age.

Helping to hide the Franks and others opened Gies' eyes to the experience of the Jews during the Second World War. She witnessed up close the persecution they suffered, and when she stayed overnight in the secret annex one night, she experienced firsthand the fear of being discovered. Had Gies never met the Franks, she might have been able to turn a blind eye to the whole thing. She could have easily continued with her life and ignored the plight of the persecuted people. This certainly would have been safer, and had she not befriended Otto Frank and been asked to help hide his family and friends, she may well have chosen this course of action, as most other people did. It has been estimated that "less than one half of 1% of the total population under Nazi occupation" worked to preserve the lives of innocent Jews (Midlarsky, Jones, & Nemeroff, 2006, p. 30). But by acting, Gies' eyes were opened and she could not close them again. Her heroic actions inspired a sense of purpose that guided the rest of her life, and in this way, her life exemplifies the experience of *heroism-guided purpose*.

Conclusion

In this chapter, we propose that while not all people with purpose become heroes and not all heroes lead lives of purpose, in many cases, purpose and heroism overlap. In particular, we propose a framework in which purpose and heroism intersect in two ways. First, in the case of *purpose-guided heroism*, individuals possess a clear sense of purpose that leads them to act heroically when the opportunity presents itself. Archbishop Romero found purpose in seeking to share God's love with all people and in helping people share that same love with one another. In the lack of respect and dignity shown to the working poor in his country of El Salvador, Archbishop Romero saw his value of love being violated, and he spoke up. In a series of heroic speeches and sermons, he encouraged those in power to treat the poor more fairly, and in so doing he risked his well-being, his reputation, and ultimately his life. Being inspired by God's love and seeking to share that love with others made him sensitive to how people treated one another, and the personal relationships and practical skills he cultivated on his path to purpose prepared him to act heroically when given the opportunity.

Heroism-guided purpose represents the second way these constructs can overlap. It is evident when individuals act heroically and are changed as a result. The experience of Miep Gies illustrates this phenomenon. Though she was not politically active early in her life, helping hide the Frank family inspired a purpose that endured in her later life. Helping hide her Jewish friends revealed her purpose. It focused her attention on an issue that she had not previously considered, but that turned out to be highly meaningful to her. She found purpose in ensuring that the memory of those who hid did not fade and in promoting tolerance and the humane treatment of all people.

Fleshing out the links between purpose and heroism reveals important nuances about the nature of both of these important constructs. As a result of better understanding their points of intersection we know more about purpose and heroism as important constructs in their own right. However, beyond this, the exercise has important practical implications as well. As mentioned before, heroism is rare (Midlarsky et al., 2006), and a variety of endeavors seek to make heroism more wide spread (e.g. the Giraffe Project, www.giraffe.org; the Hero Construction Company, www.heroconstruction.org). The theoretical model proposed here suggests that an as of yet unexamined path to heroism could involve first fostering purpose. A handful of studies find that while purposes in life ultimately come from within, intentional efforts can encourage their formation (Koshy & Mariano, 2011). Interventions and programs that cultivate purpose may encourage individuals to better identify opportunities to act heroically and prepare them to do so if and when the opportunity presents itself.

Additionally, given that heroic acts can lead to the development of purpose, it might be useful to encourage individuals to reflect on the meaning of their heroic experiences after the fact. Given that few people engage in heroism, this intervention would be smaller scale and likely tailored to heroes. Some heroes, particularly wartime heroes, end up suffering from post-traumatic stress disorder (Friedman, 2014), and rather than focusing on just helping these individuals bounce back from the trauma associated with their heroic deeds, perhaps therapists, counselors, and psychologists could encourage them to find a larger meaning and purpose in their actions. Doing so could help promote post-traumatic growth along with purpose (Tedeschi, Park, & Calhoun, 1998).

We believe the *purpose-guided heroism* and *heroism-guided purpose* framework aids our understanding of these constructs and points to potentially useful ways of fostering both purpose and heroism; however, this framework also highlights the need for additional research. Empirical studies that directly examine the relationship between purpose and heroism are needed. These studies should seek to address a myriad of questions that this framework raises. For instance, how common are these different linkages? Is it the case that purpose more commonly precedes heroism or vice versa? Does the timing of events determine which linkage is more likely? In other words, does heroism typically precede purpose among younger individuals, as it did for the young Gies, and vice versa among older individuals, as it did for the older Romero? Are there other ways in which purpose and heroism interact? Do different cultural contexts encourage purposes that are more likely than others to lead to heroic acts, or are particular acts of heroism more likely than others to engender an enduring sense of purpose? Is the experience of heroism different for people with purpose? Are people who have the opportunity to both lead a life of purpose and act heroically better off than those who either act heroically in the absence of purpose or who lead a life of purpose but never get the chance to act heroically? As with most papers that propose a theoretical model, this one raises more questions than it answers, but we believe this is a useful outcome as these two constructs—purpose and heroism—warrant additional investigation and have important implications for the well-being of all people and all communities.

Note

1 The interested reader is directed to Damon, Menon, and Bronk (2003) for a discussion of some of these traditions.

References

Bargdill, R. W. (2000). The study of boredom. *Journal of Phenomenological Psychology, 31,* 188–219.
Becker, S. W., & Eagly, A. H. (2004). The heroism of women and men. *American Psychologist, 59*(3), 163.
Benson, P. L. (2006). *All kids are our kids: What communities must do to raise caring and responsible children and adolescents* (2nd ed.) San Francisco, CA: Jossey-Bass.
Bigler, M. Neimeyer, G. J., & Brown, E. (2001). The divided self revisited: Effects of self-concept clarity and self-concept differentiation on psychological adjustment. *Journal of Social and Clinical Psychology, 20,* 396–415.
Brockman, J. R. (1989). *Romero: A life.* New York: Orbis Books.
Bronk, K. C. (2011). A grounded theory of the development of noble youth purpose. *Journal of Adolescent Research, 27*(1), 78–109. doi: 10.1177/0743558411412958
Bronk, K. C. (2012). A grounded theory of youth purpose. *Journal of Adolescent Research, 27,* 78–109. http://dx.doi.org/10.1177/0743558411412958.
Bronk, K. C. (2013). *Purpose in life: A critical component of positive youth development.* New York: Springer Publishers.
Bronk, K. C., Hill, P. L., Lapsley, D. K., Talib, T., & Finch, W. H. (2009). Purpose, hope, and life satisfaction in three age groups. *Journal of positive psychology, 4*(6), 500–510.
Burrow, A. L., & Hill, P. L. (2011). Purpose as a form of identity capital for positive youth adjustment. *Developmental Psychology, 47,* 1196–1206.
Campbell, J. (2008). *The hero with a thousand faces* (17th ed.). Novato, CA: New World Library.
Campbell, J., & Moyers, B. (1991). *The power of myth.* New York: Anchor Books.
Damon, W. (2004). What is positive youth development? *The Annals of the American Academy of Political and Social Science, 591,* 13–24.
Damon, W. (2008). *The path to purpose: Helping our children find their calling in life.* San Francisco, CA: Jossey Bass.
Damon, W., & Colby, A. (2015). *The power of ideals: The real story of moral choice.* New York: Oxford University Press.
Damon, W., Menon, J., & Bronk, K. C. (2003). The development of purpose during adolescence. *Applied Developmental Science, 7*(3), 119–128.
Drob, S. L., & Bernard, H. S. (1988). The bored patient: A developmental existential perspective. *Psychotherapy Patient, 3*(3–4), 63–73.
Erdozaín, P. (1981). *Archbishop Romero, Martyr of Salvador.* New York: Orbis Books.
Erikson, E. H. (1968). *Identity: Youth and crisis.* New York: Norton.
Erikson, E. H. (1980). *Identity and the life cycle.* New York: Norton.
Fahlman, S. A., Merce, K. B., Gaskovski, P., Eastwood, A. E., & Eastwood, J. D. (2009). Does a lack of life meaning cause boredom? Results from psychometric, longitudinal and experimental analyses, *Journal of Social and Clinical Psychology, 28*(3), 307–340.
Franco, Z., & Zimbardo, P. (2006). The banality of heroism. *Greater Good, 3*(2), 30–35.
Franco, Z. E., Blau, K., & Zimbardo, P. G. (2011). Heroism: A conceptual analysis and differentiation between heroic action and altruism. *Review of General Psychology, 15*(2), 99–113. doi: 10.1037/a0022672
French, S., & Joseph, S. (1999). Religiosity and its association with happiness, purpose in life, and self-actualization. *Mental Health, Religion, & Culture, 2,* 117–120.
Friedman, M. J. (2014). PTSD history and overview. Retrieved July 26, 2015 from www.ptsd.va.gov/professional/PTSD-overview/ptsd-overview.asp.
Garrett, L. (2010). *Expectations for change and the challenges of governance: The first year of President Mauricio Funes.* Washington, DC: Center for Democracy in the Americas. Retrieved from http://democracyinamericas.org/pdfs/El_Salvador_Funes_First_Year_Report.pdf.
Gies, M. (1987). *Anne Frank Remembered: The story of the woman who helped to hide the Frank family.* New York: Simon & Schuster.
Hill, P. A., Sumner, R. A., & Burrow, A. L. (2014). Understanding the pathways to purpose: Examining personality and well-being correlates across adulthood. *Journal of Positive Psychology, 9,* 227–234.
Jayawickreme, E., & Di Stefano, P. (2012). How can we study heroism? Integrating persons, situations and communities. *Political Psychology, 33*(1), 165–178. doi: 10.1111/j.1467-9221.2011.00861.x

King, L. A., Hicks, J. A., & Krull, J., & Del Gaiso, A. K. (2006). Positive affect and the experience of meaning in life. *Journal of Personality and Social Psychology, 90*, 179–196.

Kohen, A. (2013). *Untangling heroism: Classical philosophy and the concept of the hero*. New York: Routledge.

Koshy, S. I., & Mariano, J. M. (2011). Promoting youth purpose: A review of the literature. *New Directions in Youth Development, 132*, 13–30.

Lerner, R. M., Lerner, J. V. L., Almerigi, J. B., Theokas, C., Phelps, E., Gestsdottir, S. Naudeau, S., Jelicic, H., Alberts, A., Ma, L., Smith, L. M., Bobek, D. L., Richman-Raphael, D., Simpson, I., Christiansen, E. D., & von Eye, A. (2005). Positive youth development, participation in community youth development programs, and community contributions of fifth-grade adolescents: Findings from the first wave of the 4-H study of positive youth development. *Journal of Early Adolescence, 25*(1), 17–71.

Lewis, C. A., Lanigan, C., Joseph, S., & de Fockert, J. (1997). Religiosity and happiness: No evidence for an association among undergraduates. *Personality and Individual Differences, 22*, 119–121.

Marks, N. F., Lambert, J. D., & Choi, H. (2002). Transitions to caregiving, gender, and psychological well-being: A prospective U.S. national study. *Journal of Marriage and Family, 64*, 657–667.

Mascaro, N., & Rosen, D. H. (2005). Existential meaning's role in the enhancement of hope and prevention of depressive symptoms. *Journal of Personality, 73*(4), 985–1013.

Midlarsky, E., Jones, S. F., & Nemeroff, R. K. (2006). Heroic rescue during the Holocaust: Empirical and methodological perspectives. In *Strengthening research methodology: Psychological measurement and evaluation* (pp. 29–45). Washington, DC: American Psychological Association. doi: 10.1037/11384-002

Noblejas de la Flor, M. A. (1997). Meaning levels and drug abuse therapy: An empirical study. *International Forum for Logotherapy, 20*(1), 46–51.

Paloutzian, R. F., & Ellison, C. W. (1982). Loneliness, spiritual well-being, and quality of life. In L. A. Peplau & D. Perlman (eds), *Loneliness: A sourcebook of current theory, research, and therapy*. New York: Wiley.

Paz, V. (2015). Teen saves woman from burning car as onlookers record video. *KSL* (July 21). Retrieved from www.ksl.com/?nid=1286&sid=35584736.

Pinquart, M. (2002). Creating and maintaining purpose in life in old age: A meta-analysis. *Ageing International, 27*(2), 90–114.

Renderos, A. (2010). El Salvador publicly marks Archbishop Romero's killing for first time. *Los Angeles Times* (March 24). Retrieved from http://articles.latimes.com/2010/mar/24/world/la-fg-salvador-romero25-2010mar25.

Romero, Ó. A. (undated). Archbishop Oscar Arnulfo Romero biography. Retrieved from www.un.org/en/events/righttotruthday/romero.shtml.

Romero, Ó. A., & Brockman, J. R. (eds). (1984). *The Church is all of you: Thoughts of Archbishop Oscar A. Romero*. San Francisco, CA: Harper.

Scholastic (1997). An interview with Miep Gies. Retrieved June 20, 2015 from http://teacher.scholastic.com/frank/tscripts/miep.htm.

Seligman, M. E. P. (2011). *Flourishing: A visionary new understanding of happiness and well-being*. New York: Free Press.

Shek, D. (1992). Meaning in life and psychological well-being: An empirical study using the Chinese version of the purpose in life questionnaire. *Journal of Genetic Psychology, 153*, 185–190.

Tedeschi, R. G., Park, C. L., & Calhoun, L. G. (1998). *Posttraumatic growth: Positive transformations in the aftermath of crisis*. Mahwah, NJ: Lawrence Erlbaum Associates Publishers.

Umberson, D., & Gove, W. (1989). Parenthood and psychological well-being: Theory, measurement, and stage in the life course. *Journal of Family Issues, 10*, 440–462.

Zimbardo, P. (2007). *The Lucifer effect: Understanding how good people turn evil*. New York: Random House.

27

Heroism and the Pursuit of Meaning

Jeffrey D. Green, Daryl R. Van Tongeren, Athena H. Cairo, and Nao Hagiwara

Abraham Lincoln visited the city of Richmond on April 4, 1865, just two days after Confederate forces evacuated. Though he was hated by most residents of the Confederate capital, he was treated as a near deity by others. The African American residents of Richmond who had been freed just the day before clamored to see him, and many sought to touch "Father Abraham" because it made their freedom feel real. Just days prior, General William Tecumseh Sherman met him personally for the only time, and later asserted, "Of all the men I have met, he seemed to possess more of the elements of greatness, combined with goodness, than any other" (Goodwin, 2005, p. 713). Lincoln would be assassinated a few days later, and his Secretary of War Edwin Stanton pronounced his entry into the pantheon of heroes: "Now he belongs to the Ages."

We propose that essential components of heroism and heroic actions are embedded in meaning and virtue. That is, our central thesis is that heroes and heroic behavior are intertwined with virtue and with finding meaning or purpose in life. Abraham Lincoln is an archetypal hero. We argue that it was his singular commitment to the cause of reunifying north and south, and finding his life purpose in this cause, that sustained his efforts and forged a hero. Moreover, his virtuous character likely conferred additional meaning to him and elevated his actions to the heroic; his "greatness combined with goodness" was more properly *greatness (heroism) created by goodness*. Lincoln saw this supremely important goal of ending the Civil War and uniting north and south through in his lifetime, and indeed gave his life for it. He continually rallied and inspired others to his cause, such as in the Gettysburg Address:

> It is for us, the living, rather to dedicate ourselves to the great task before us … that we here highly resolve that these dead shall not have died in vain—that this nation, under God, shall have a new birth of freedom—and that government of the people, by the people, for the people, shall not perish from the earth.
>
> *(Lincoln, 1863)*

Before we expand on our thesis regarding heroes and meaning and virtue, we turn briefly to definitional matters.

Definitions

Defining heroes and heroism is a challenge, and some emphasize that heroism, like beauty, exists in the eye of the beholder (Allison & Goethals, 2014). However, most beholders would agree that heroes and heroic actions go beyond garden-variety friendliness or helpfulness; rather, they are characterized by a constellation of traits that represent the best in humanity. Prior research supports this idea that heroes can be conceptualized along several "noble" dimensions. One poll of college students suggested that heroes were likely to be described by eight characteristics (the "Great Eight"): *intelligent, strong, selfless, caring, charismatic, resilient, reliable,* and *inspiring* (Allison & Goethals, 2011). We note the obvious overlap with virtues: one could make the argument that six or seven (all but intelligence) of the traits are virtuous. Many heroic exemplars easily can be matched with several, if not all, of these dimensions. Lincoln, for instance, appears to embody all eight characteristics (Allison & Goethals, 2011): his selfless and intelligent blame-taking regarding his cabinet members' poor choices, his caring for disabled soldiers, his charismatic and inspiring speeches, and his resilience and strength in the face of an exhausting and protracted Civil War.

Though heroes may embody any or all of these characteristics, we also have evidence that certain characteristics might be considered more prototypical of heroism than others. A follow-up study (Allison & Goethals, 2011) found that students rated *inspiring* and *selfless* as the most important hero characteristics, reflecting the meaning-enhancing qualities of heroism and the notion that heroes generally help others at their own expense, often in the face of physical peril (Franco et al., 2011). A more recently published poll found similar ascribed characteristics of heroes. Participants were asked what they thought heroes were like and what they do. A cluster analysis of responses found that heroes were thought to be *protecting* (saving, acting against evil), *enhancing* (inspiring, providing morale), and *moral modeling* (making the world better; Kinsella, Ritchie, & Igou, 2015, study 2). Another study found that participants thought that heroes generally fulfilled a protective function more than would regular leaders or role models. Heroes can protect in many ways, from physically saving another person from harm, to offering guidance and wisdom (Allison & Goethals, 2011). These conceptualizations of heroes also can inspire hope about the goodness of others.

Thus, though there is no clear-cut definition of heroes, there appear to be some crucial, empirically-supported themes that emerge from theorizing and empirical work to date. Heroes typically are seen as impelled by other-oriented rather than selfish motives (though sometimes a transformation must occur first in the hero), usually in order to protect others. They make or are willing to make a significant sacrifice or pay a price, which perhaps is why more noble motives are required, such as risking one's life for others. Their deeds also are considered extraordinary in their effects, more so than general acts of helpfulness or prosociality (Becker & Eagly, 2004; Allison & Goethals, 2011; Franco et al., 2011); saving an ant is not heroic, but saving a busload of children is. Such actions square well with definitions of virtuous or moral behavior (Fowers, 2005, 2012; Haidt, 2007), which highlight how moral actors often forgo selfish desires and incur costs—perhaps even risking their lives, in the case of heroism—for the benefit of others. That is, moral or virtuous behavior involves putting others before oneself, so heroic actions are virtuous behaviors enacted on a large stage, with large potential costs, but also powerful results.

Meaning similarly is a slippery construct, so there is value in defining it at different levels (Heintzelman & King, 2014). At a very basic (social-cognitive) level, meaning is broadly defined as "expected associations" among constructs (Heine, Proulx, & Vohs, 2006). For example, ice is supposed to be cold, fire is supposed to be hot, and oranges are supposed to be, well, orange. Definitions on this level help us make sense of the world: warm ice would be *senseless*, and talking about cold fire or a purple orange would be considered *nonsense*. In this way, meaningful associations may help fulfill psychological needs of understanding and of having control over our environment (Stevens & Fiske, 1995). However, such rudimentary explanations of meaning likely do not fully account for the rich and motivationally powerful effects of understanding meaning in more abstract ways (Heintzelman & King, 2014). Accordingly, others have broader definitions of meaning. For example, Steger and colleagues (e.g., Shin & Steger, 2014) define meaning as the combination of coherence (i.e., understanding how life's events and one's identity fit together) and purpose (i.e., orienting life toward something greater than oneself), and others (Heintzelman & King, 2014) have identified a third feature of meaning: significance (i.e., one's life makes an important contribution to humanity). Intrapersonally, we seek to have integrity among the various aspects of and events in our lives by seeking coherence. Interpersonally, individuals are focused on transcending the self and connecting with a larger group or bigger goal through purpose, which involves making productive, enduring contributions to the world and leave us feeling significant (Bronk & Riches, Chapter 26, this volume).

We agree that meaning in all its forms or levels is critical for intra- and interpersonal well-being. Research has amply demonstrated how even mundane violations of meaning (e.g., a blue banana, a transmogrifying experimenter—replacing one researcher for another without participant awareness; Proulx & Heine, 2008) have psychological ramifications and result in compensatory efforts to restore meaning and regain psychological equanimity. However, there appears to be something special about achieving personal meaning (e.g., making sense and finding coherence in life events) in ways that facilitate seeking and finding purpose or significance in life (e.g., making lasting and positive contributions to the world). Perhaps the best way to illustrate linkages between heroism and meaning is to take a dynamic approach to the hero narrative.

With this in mind, we next examine how the search for meaning is imbued within classic hero narratives and psychological processes associated with heroism. Specifically, we discuss how heroes and heroic stories confer meaning through several domains, particularly through social connection and understanding of the world.

"Walking With Destiny": Meaning-Making in the Hero Narrative

Essential components of heroism and heroic actions are embedded in meaning and virtue, particularly the hero narrative. The unfolding hero narrative or script is emphasized by hero researchers (e.g., Goethals & Allison, 2012), inspired in part by Joseph Campbell's (1949) groundbreaking theorizing about transcultural elements of the hero story. This unfolding drama lends itself to examining a central role for meaning. Meaning researchers have identified the dynamic nature of how individuals seek and defend meaning, which nicely maps onto the hero narrative. The hero story unfolds over time to reveal important truths. Heroes typically wade into unfamiliar territory (often literally), encounter strange and sometimes overwhelming situations, enlist help from others (mentors, partners), and eventually acquire a new skill or trait that helps them ultimately to be victorious (Goethals & Allison, 2012). In many cases, heroes are underdogs (Vandello, Goldschmied, & Michniewicz, Chapter 18, this volume), so less is expected of them initially, heightening the drama, such as when it appears that evil is almost certain to triumph over good.

Frodo in the Lord of the Rings is beloved in part because he may exemplify the ultimate underdog hero journey. It seems impossible to believe that a half-sized hobbit could venture into the very heart of evil (Mordor) and defeat a nearly omnipotent and omniscient foe.

Luke Skywalker's journey in the Star Wars films follows this script very closely. He is an orphan stuck in a desolate and backward planet, and the rebellion against the Evil Empire comes to his doorstep. Before he knows it, he has a wise mentor and some bold companions, is learning about the Force and his particular sensitivity to it, is rocketing across the stars to perform courageous acts, and is poised to become one of the most important heroes in the galaxy.

Turning to real life, Abraham Lincoln also is an underdog hero. Even history buffs often forget that before being elected president, Lincoln was a mere state senator, mocked for his backwoods background as well as his gangly and unattractive appearance. He had never won a national election, though he had lost a US senatorial one. As president, he was immediately faced with a country riven in two over slavery. Reconciliation via either peace or war appeared exceedingly difficult.

Winston Churchill's underdog hero path had many similarities to Lincoln's. Churchill was a failed politician; for example, as secretary of the admiralty he was ascribed the lion's share of the blame for the First World War Gallipoli disaster. Churchill had a speech impediment and a possible drinking problem, and he was largely ignored and even mocked in Parliament—clearly seen as a has-been politician who would never again wield real power. This political ostracism occurred in large part because he incessantly warned the nation, particularly the pacifists in Parliamentary leadership, that Hitler was a megalomaniac whose ambitions would not be sated and whose promises could not be trusted. Named England's prime minister at the outbreak of the Second World War, Churchill appeared to be in a dismal situation as England was isolated at the edge of Europe and hopelessly outnumbered and outgunned by Germany's forces. But the night after meeting with the King and becoming Prime Minister, Churchill wrote in his diary, "I felt as if I were walking with destiny, and that all my past life had been but a preparation for this hour and for this trial ... I thought I knew a good deal about it all, I was sure I should not fail" (Churchill, 1948, p. 667).

What enabled Lincoln and Churchill to become heroes and arguably some of the finest political leaders of the modern age? Joseph Campbell suggests that heroes must "follow [their] bliss," and act authentically—and we would add meaningfully (cf. Osbon, 1991, p. 8). In order to help the world, heroes may need to better understand themselves and their gifts, conquer fears and doubts, and often go against majority opinion or social norms. The conviction that one was "walking with destiny"—that one's purpose and significance in life was now set forth—surely played a critical role for both Churchill and Lincoln.

Meaning permeates hero narratives. Seeking meaning often leads heroes into those unfamiliar environments and to ask deep transrational questions (Allison & Goethals, 2014). Who am I? What are my capabilities? How might Good triumph? How can this Evil be defeated? Might I or must I play a role in this cosmic drama? Heroes in the making and underdogs seek to make sense of themselves and their world and to forge an identity of good or virtue in the process. The ultimate end, of course, relates to meaning in life: the hero finds life purpose through her or his actions. By extension, consumers of these narratives also receive a story about purpose or how life or the universe works (or should work). These types of pressing existential questions likely overlap with *deep meaning*, or a rich and lasting understanding of one's role in the larger scope of the universe and the human narrative. Engaging with deep meaning is existentially unsettling, in part because insufficiently satisfying answers about one's role (e.g., if you really think about it, life seems rather meaningless) may elicit considerable anxiety.

For instance, one way in which heroic narratives provide *epistemic wisdom* (Allison & Goethals, 2014), or answers to questions of deep meaning, might be within the domain of mortality salience. Terror management theory (TMT) suggests that we are particularly vulnerable to deep-seated anxiety and dread when considering our own mortality. Many of the institutions and processes that we consider "uniquely human"—culture, worldviews, self-esteem—help to buffer against this anxiety. Participation in these institutions reaffirm our connection to others and our symbolic immortality—our belief that we will live on through our deeds or relationships with others after we die (Greenberg et al., 1990; Rosenblatt, Greenberg, Solomon, Pyszczynski, & Lyon, 1989). Hero stories are concrete examples of how a hero's deeds live on in the hearts and minds of later generations after the hero's death, and provide guidance for what behaviors are most praised and remembered in one's unique culture, thus providing meaning and vanquishing the anxiety espoused by the inevitability of death. Because heroes inherently face great challenges and threats to meaning, they also exemplify how best to cope with the challenges that everyone faces at some point. Moreover, the behavior endemic to heroic stories often reflects central, cherished worldviews and thus may provide relief from the existential anxiety of death (Allison & Goethals, 2014).

However, many meaning researchers propose that mortality-related terror is merely one way in which meaning needs can be fulfilled. According to the Meaning Maintenance Model (MMM; Heine et al., 2006), meaning is derived from any significant, expected, and coherent associations and connections. These associations can be within oneself (resolving a contradiction or flaw), in the world (good should be victorious), or between the two (e.g., affirming close relationships). Humans are inveterate meaning-makers who are driven to construct meaning (life lessons, insights, relationships) from even the most senseless or overwhelming tragedy or challenge.

In contrast to TMT, the MMM proposes that loss or disruption of meaning in any realm of life leads individuals to attempt to restore it through any domain possible, even if it is unrelated to the domain of lost meaning. People typically engage one of four avenues or domains of meaning: self-esteem, certainty or closure, belongingness, and symbolic immortality (Heine et al., 2006). For example, if one feels threatened in one area, such as certainty, compensatory meaning can be gained in one or more of the other three areas in order to restore equilibrium. This notion of *fluid compensation* is amply demonstrated empirically in related realms, such as the self-affirmation literature (Steele, 1988). From this perspective, heroism may provide meaning through several conceptual domains. As we elucidate in the following sections, heroic stories can provide examples of symbolic immortality and cherished worldviews, but they also may bolster relational bonds with others and inspire meaning-seeking in the face of challenges. Answering questions of deep meaning is difficult, but heroes embrace this challenge of seeking their deep meaning, often wrestling with how they fit in the world, as their journey progresses. Moreover, part of the allure—and perhaps part of what makes heroes so heroic—is their desire, and perhaps their eventual ability, to seek answers regarding their deep purpose, even in the face of uncertain circumstances, terrible obstacles, and threats of death. Not only are their actions heroic, but their personal quest for meaning, deep meaning, is motivational and inspiring.

There Are No Heroes in a Vacuum: Social Connection

The social nature of heroes is almost self-evident. Very rarely may a hero emerge in a social (or literal) vacuum, such as Sandra Bullock's character in the film *Gravity*, lost and adrift in space and trying desperately to get back to earth. But these stories appear to lack several critical elements of the typical hero story. In the case of *Gravity*, the Bullock character does nothing for others, but simply survives. Similarly, those who take extraordinary risks, such as BASE jumpers, or who set records like Charles Lindbergh, are admired for their amazing feats but typically are not labelled heroes. There is neither a moral element nor an other-oriented element. The making of heroes appears to be an archetypal process involving interactions with several other important figures in one's life as well as larger community that is affected by the hero's choices. Very often, they start at a rather un-heroic place in their lives, lacking the confidence or the social conscience to act for a group (e.g., Joan of Arc, Harry Potter, Han Solo). As they develop a sense of identity and purpose, they often benefit from the guidance of a wise elder (e.g., Socrates, Dumbledore, Obi-Wan Kenobi). Through their noble actions they often save other individuals or groups (e.g., Oskar Schindler, Indiana Jones) and their interactions with those they help or lead can also shape their perspective and choices (e.g., Oskar Schindler).

Meaning-making similarly is typically a social experience. In spite of the fact that some emphasize very individual quests for meaning (e.g., Burns, Jackson, Tarpley, & Smith, 1996), such as a monk living a solitary existence, meaning nearly always is embedded in family, community, and culture. Many writers suggest that social connection is a primary vehicle through which we search for and find meaning (Frankl, 1959; Heine et al., 2006). Consequently, our greatest heroes are the ones who appear to affect the largest communities, like Lincoln, Gandhi, Churchill, and Mandela. Heroes, then, are not simply successful individuals, but those who are continuously extraordinary and make a lasting and positive impact on others.

Heroes provide meaning in life through many social avenues: they remind us that we might be remembered after death, that our actions can directly benefit future generations, and in some cases even that we are connected to God or other religious entities. All of these meaning-providing features also help to vanquish the fear of death through the provision of symbolic immortality (Heine et al., 2006); in this way, heroes are lauded as admirable models of excellence to whom we should aspire to emulate as a way to conquer our own death-related terror (Rosenblatt et al., 1989). Similarly, morality in general can be thought of as inherently social. Though there may be elements of morality for an individual in isolation (e.g., Jesus admonishing that a thought is equivalent to an action), some have proposed that morality evolved to help us live in groups, or even that morality requires at least one other person (Gray, Waytz, & Young, 2012). In fact, some have argued that "moral thinking is for social doing" (Haidt, 2007). That is, our moral cognitions and judgments orient us toward actions that benefit the well-being of others, even at a cost to ourselves. Moral behavior allows us to live in groups and helps regulate intragroup and intergroup social interactions. However, morality necessarily implicates that one person is the victim (i.e., moral patient) and one person is the offender (i.e., moral agent) (Gray & Wegner, 2009). Heroes must be virtuous, and their virtuous behavior often is relationally focused: saving the lives of others, rescuing or reuniting separated loved ones, or providing freedom or equality for a large number of people. Next we discuss how virtues which confer positive psychological benefits also enhance bonds of social connection with others.

Heroes Overcome and Transcend Obstacles, which Confers Meaning

Relatedly, the hero narrative almost always starts with a gap: the hero is callow, untested, selfish, or prideful. The hero may face temptation. The opportunity to make a significant sacrifice may be taken, or avoided. At this juncture, tension builds. We interpret this process of fixing a flaw or overcoming an obstacle as exercising virtue. In our work, we've discovered that acting virtuously appears to confer meaning. Usually, this meaning acquisition is in the context of relationships, as in the case of the meaning maintenance model (Heine et al., 2006).

Research has demonstrated this process more directly with meaning as well. We (Van Tongeren & Green, 2010) adapted a popular paradigm for cognitively activating or priming a certain concept by presenting words subliminally (in a fraction of a second) and then assessed individuals on one or more of the domains of meaning. While individuals directed their attention to the center of a computer screen, several words were presented in the periphery (corners of the screen) for 50 milliseconds. Half of the individuals were presented with words related to meaninglessness (e.g., chaos, empty, futile), whereas the other half were presented with a matched set of control words (e.g., curved, echoes, furnace). Participants were not aware that words had been flashed, much less able to identify them. In one experiment, those who experienced the words about meaninglessness reported being more religious and having more meaning in life relative to the control group. In other words, they appeared to compensate for this meaning threat by simply asserting meaning. A second experiment assessed all the domains of meaning proposed by the MMM and found that those exposed to the meaningless words reported having higher self-esteem, higher need for closure, and greater symbolic immortality relative to those in the control group. When meaning is threatened, people quickly and efficiently begin reconstructing meaning by asserting that life is meaningful in myriad ways: they have more positive attitudes toward themselves, seek certainty, and imagine that their contributions will be important and long-lasting. They also report feeling more belonging with their social groups. Thus, in the wake of threats, people are motivated to recover lost meaning through various avenues—heroes may choose paths that are more socially productive.

Underdogs may feel this meaning threat acutely. Their flaws may be highlighted by new characters or situations revealing themselves. They respond by seeking meaning through saving another or even the world (a dramatic example of symbolic immortality) or by protecting or rescuing a vulnerable victim or group (belongingness). Luke Skywalker, who already had lost his family as well as a newly discovered but cherished mentor, becomes the symbol of the Rebellion against the seemingly invincible Empire. What could exemplify symbolic immortality better than destroying an object called the Death Star? Similarly, Lincoln and Churchill felt that the very survival of their respective nations—which would live on after them and be beacons of democratic government—were at stake. Studies of lay individuals suggest that underdogs generally are scrutinized regarding how meaningful their struggles are: individuals perceive underdogs' struggles as highly identifiable and worthy of sympathy, but only when they are also relevant and consequential (Kim et al., 2008).

Relatedly, heroes may exert extraordinary effort to move past their previous limitations. The first critical step is to not give up in the face of initial failure or overwhelming odds, which requires the virtues of persistence and self-regulation (see below). This persistence to reach new levels of success confers self-esteem and thus increases meaning. Regarding the motive of certainty, many heroes begin their journeys uncertain of themselves and the world around them. But as they make choices to overcome personal and external obstacles, they gain wisdom, enhance self-concept clarity, and increase self-efficacy. For instance, Harry Potter began his wizarding career very uncertain of his abilities or even his true nature. Upon gaining entrance to Hogwarts, he was told he could do well either in the heroic house of Gryffindor or the conniving house of Slytherin. Harry was sorted into Gryffindor because he wanted to uphold central traits of bravery and integrity rather than cunning. Throughout his life he continuously chose to remain consistent in his values and fought evil even when tempted by arch-nemesis Voldemort to give up. Similarly, Lincoln's heroic efforts to manage disparate political factions and a series of incompetent generals via patience, good humor, and the power of his eloquence was in the service of uniting north and south—perhaps the ultimate in the nation's belongingness since its foundation.

"Greatness Combined with Goodness": Meaning and Virtue

We previously articulated the four sources or domains of meaning according to the Meaning Maintenance Model. We propose a fifth domain of meaning: *virtue*. Virtue, defined broadly as the regulation of selfish impulses for the benefit of others' well-being (Fowers, 2005, 2012; Haidt, 2007), may provide a strong sense of meaning. We've found that when people act virtuously, they report higher meaning in their lives (Emmons, 2003). We do hasten to add that these domains of meaning are not entirely separate. For example, the sociometer literature proposes that self-esteem acts primarily as a gauge of how accepted we feel (Leary, 2005). Thus, self-esteem and belongingness are inextricably linked and empirically correlated. Our proposed additional pillar of meaning, virtue, may similarly be correlated with other pillars such as self-esteem or symbolic immortality. Below, we articulate some of the recent research linking acting virtuously to enhanced meaning in life.

Meaning via Forgiveness

Forgiveness is an especially appropriate avenue to examine the seeking and protecting of meaning. Forgiveness is often described as the process by which individuals replace negative emotions such as avoidance and anger toward a transgressor with more positive emotions such as compassion (Worthington, 2005, 2006). Forgiveness is often (but perhaps not always) a pertinent theme in the hero's journey: are they motivated by revenge (e.g., Batman's quest to avenge the death of his parents through the eradication of evil in Gotham) or will they offer forgiveness of villains by empathizing with the common humanity? (As an aside, we note that forgiveness and justice are not mutually exclusive; heroes can bring foes to justice but mercifully not end their lives.) Some of the most profound examples of heroes involve extending forgiveness even when it is not sought, such as Pope John Paul II forgiving his would-be assassin or many victims of the Nazi concentration camps forgiving their persecutors. Justice and revenge may in many respects be the easier choice, whereas extending forgiveness may be the more courageous and heroic choice. That said, some heroes may eschew forgiveness entirely and still be considered heroic, such as in the case of Batman. One interesting avenue of future research may be to identify potential differences in forgiving and unforgiving heroes and the types of psychological needs they help provide in individuals.

On the other hand, sometimes potential heroes are the ones who need to ask for forgiveness. This may get at the heart of the missing factor in the hero journey that hero scholars emphasize, and may also take courage. One of Harry Potter's principal friends and allies, Ron Weasley, abandoned him during a dark time, but later reappeared, asked for forgiveness, and played a critical role in Harry's victory over evil. Sometimes the forgiveness process takes a particularly long time to unfold. Jean Valjean, the hero of *Les Misérables*, begins and ends his hero's journey with acts of forgiveness. After being released from prison, he stole silver candlesticks from a priest. After catching him, the priest forgave him and even gave him the silver, telling him to use it for good. The priest's actions shattered Valjean's worldview and motivated him to change his identity (breaking his parole) and to become a new, better man. A decade later in the midst of a war, Valjean in turn forgave and showed mercy to his greatest enemy, the police inspector who had been pursuing him all those years (Hugo, 1887/1987).

An offense in a close relationship is another clear example of a meaning threat or violation: cherished others are not supposed to hurt the ones they love. But granting forgiveness typically yields both physical and psychological health benefits (Davis, Green, Reid, Moloney, & Burnette, 2015). Might it also confer meaning? In two studies, we (Van Tongeren et al., 2015) found that granting forgiveness does indeed lead to increased felt meaning in life. One study found an association between offering forgiveness and perceived meaning in life. However, this correlational evidence could suggest that those with meaning actually are more likely to offer forgiveness, rather than forgiveness leading to meaning. Therefore, in a second study, we conducted a six-month longitudinal study in which both partners reported offenses and forgiveness or unforgiveness of those offenses every two weeks. We measured offenses both nomothetically (a fixed set of 20 offenses that participants regularly reported on as having experienced or not by their partner) and ideographically (participants wrote about and rated the most significant personal offenses occurring the last two weeks). These offenses ran the gamut from being disrespectful to being emotionally or physically unfaithful. Those who granted more forgiveness across the time periods subsequently reported more meaning in life. Furthermore, the benefits seemed to be particularly potent for individuals whose partners had been relatively prolific offenders. Put another way, low forgiveness in the wake of more partner offenses led to lower meaning in life. There can be a downside to repeated forgiveness if an offender is not willing to make amends or change his or her ways: victims can feel like doormats and experience an erosion of self-respect (Luchies, Finkel, McNulty, & Kumashiro, 2010). However, if the relationship is not permanently ruptured, forgiveness restores hope and renders the future viable, which restores meaning that is embedded in our close relationships.

It would be interesting to investigate whether *seeking* forgiveness also provides meaning in life. Our view is that it would. Research suggests individuals who transgress against another are often motivated to restore their sense of self-esteem (e.g., through compliance; McMillen, 1971) and when feeling guilty are motivated to restore their relationship with the person they hurt (Baumeister, Stillwell, & Heatherton, 1994). If the petition for forgiveness is granted by the partner-victim, meaning almost certainly will be enhanced via increased self-evaluation or relationship satisfaction (Van Tongeren, Green, Davis, Hook, & Hulsey, 2016). However, even if the victim refused to forgive, the offender may experience increased meaning for having made an attempt to right a wrong and restore the relationship. For instance, autobiographical narratives of transgressions are more likely to include accounts of apologies and attempts to repair the relationship when individuals recall being an offender rather than a victim, suggesting that offenders place a high value on these repair attempts (Baumeister, Stillwell, & Wotman, 1990; Zechmeister & Romero, 2002). We do have empirical evidence that a virtue related to (perhaps a precursor of) seeking forgiveness leads to increased meaning: that of humility.

Meaning via Humility

We have obtained some indirect evidence for the proposition that humility may confer meaning. Humility involves restraining the self in some way by holding a more moderate and accurate view of oneself. As such, it represents a step away from self-aggrandizement or elevation away from others, and back toward the group or community. This relational approach to conceptualizing humility (Davis et al., 2011) has demonstrated relationship-enhancing properties, such as promoting forgiveness (Van Tongeren, Davis, & Hook, 2014). We (Van Tongeren, Stafford, Hook, Green, Davis, & Johnson, 2016) conducted three studies in which humility reduced negative attitudes, behavioral intentions, and overt negative behaviors towards members of religious outgroups. These various manifestations of outgroup derogation are classic examples of defensive reactions to psychological threat, such as threat to meaning or awareness of one's death. For example, one study subliminally activated the concept of humility via very rapid presentation of humility-related words (e.g., humble) versus neutral words (e.g., height) in a control condition. Participants wrote about a cherished social or cultural value, which then was ostensibly criticized by another participant who did not share the same value. In an alleged unrelated subsequent study, these participants had the opportunity to administer hot sauce to the critical other, who was known by the participant to dislike spicy food. Humility apparently inhibited the aggressive act of administering hot sauce relative to the control condition. Thus, this pattern seems consistent with restoring or acquiring meaning, though that has not been directly validated empirically.

Meaning via Prosociality

Allison and Goethals (2014) emphasize the role of hero schemas (a constellation of heroic traits) or scripts (the aforementioned hero narrative) in guiding behavior and inspiring others to act heroically. Central to these schematic models of heroism is the heroic deed, which almost invariably involves helping others, either directly (e.g., rescuing others in need) or indirectly (e.g., working for social change). A violation of these schemas would constitute a meaning violation and elicit the same compensatory processes as other sources of meaning. For instance, heroes like Luke Skywalker or Batman are often motivated to take up arms against a greater evil after failing to save someone they love. Anticipation of such violations (e.g., the experience of dissonance or guilt) might motivate heroism, such as when an individual chooses to engage in a heroic action (e.g., saving a child from an oncoming bus) because not intervening would be a violation of one's moral code. Oliner and Oliner (1988) describe rescuers of Jewish citizens during the Holocaust were generally "more sensitive than others to violations that threaten their moral values," perceiving what was happening to the Jewish people as "destructive of the very fabric that gives their lives order and meaning" (pp. 250, 251).

As we stated previously, heroic behavior appears in many ways to be a subset—a more extreme version—of prosocial actions. People typically view heroic deeds as having three elements: unselfish motivation for the action, a significant cost or risk to the hero, and a significant beneficial effect for others (Allison & Goethals, 2011; Becker & Eagly, 2004; Franco et al., 2011). Prosocial actions may or may not be motivated by other-oriented emotions such as empathy, and there often is little to no risk or cost to the actor. In addition, the effects could be felt in minor ways and by smaller numbers of people. Despite being positive, helpful behaviors, these typically are not what people think of when they think about heroic action.

Some of our research highlights the relationship between prosocial behaviors and meaning in life, suggesting that virtuous or moral behaviors may even confer a sense of meaning in life (Van Tongeren, Green, Davis, Hook, & Hulsey, 2016). A recent survey of Americans also suggests that those who describe themselves as "givers," or those who report more time taking care of others, also report higher meaning in life. In contrast, perceiving oneself as a "taker" was unrelated to perceived meaning (Baumeister, Vohs, Aaker, & Garbinsky, 2013). Interestingly, Baumeister et al. (2013) did not always find that helping was correlated with meaning. Those who were non-parents did not report any association between meaning in life and helping children—suggesting those who help children regularly for their job, rather than through family bonds, may not typically feel greater meaning because of it. These findings suggest that helping behaviors that are motivated by morals or empathy may be more likely to lead to increased meaning. Similarly, heroic actions, done voluntarily and for an unselfish reason, may also be particularly meaningful (Allison & Goethals, 2014). However, this hypothesis remains to be tested directly.

Meaning via Self-Control

Self-control or self-regulation is a critical component of the hero's journey, and this self-control may be especially critical when exercising virtue (or restraining evil, which sometimes may involve restraining one's own selfish impulses). Indeed, as Allison and Goethals (2014) asserted, "redeeming ourselves through effort and achievement or through moral commitment requires self-control," and similarly, many of the traits ascribed to heroes also require self-control such as selflessness, resilience, and reliability (p. 107). Self-regulation is the effortful altering of one's behavior from what is easy and desirable. This relates to both action and inaction; inhibiting the impulse to lash out at someone or to give in to temptation requires self-control just as persisting in an unpleasant task or making a sacrifice does. Research over the past two decades has revealed that self-regulation draws from a common source of energy that is depleted when it is used, like a muscle (e.g., Baumeister & Vohs, 2012). Hence, after exercising self-regulation, individuals are in the state of ego depletion and will typically fail at subsequent self-regulation efforts (Baumeister, Bratslavsky, Muraven, & Tice, 1998; Finkel & Campbell, 2001). No matter what the specific first task is, such as inhibiting an emotional response, solving complex problems, or avoiding eating delicious food, a second, unrelated task is likely to be compromised. A classic study compared individuals who either avoided eating delicious, fresh-baked cookies or indulged in those cookies in an ostensible taste test. Those who ate the cookies were not ego depleted, and they persisted more than twice as long on a problem-solving task relative to those who successfully avoided eating the cookies but became ego depleted in the process. The good news is that self-control capacity can be restored after enough rest or even strengthened with regular practice and training (Muraven, Baumeister, & Tice, 1999).

In this way, self-regulation may be the *fuel* that allows people to move from being potential heroes to actual heroes. In fact, we've argued elsewhere (Green & Van Tongeren, 2012) that self-regulation could be considered the "master virtue." That is, many of the virtues like patience, perseverance, and humility appear to require self-regulation in order to overcome our "natural" tendencies to be impatient, give up, or act selfishly. For instance, self-regulatory ego depletion has been associated with less willingness to help others (DeWall, Baumeister, Gailliot, Maner, 2008), greater aggression (DeWall, Baumeister, Stillman, & Gailliot, 2007), and greater dishonesty (Mead, Baumeister, Gino, Schweitzer, & Ariely, 2009). Thus because heroes engage in selfless, patient, and just behavior even in the face of hardship, when psychological research would expect people to act most selfishly, we believe self-regulation holds an important place in the constellation of heroic traits.

Henry Morton Stanley, the famed African explorer who located a lost missionary with the famous quip, "Dr. Livingstone, I presume," is an embodiment of research findings regarding strengthening or extending the stamina of self-control. He endured unspeakable hardships and lost many of his men on several trips into the heart of Africa. For example, an expedition followed the Congo River to the sea for several months, but lost two thirds of the men. Stanley was the only surviving European. His endurance and persistence in these expeditions can be traced to his childhood. From a young age, Stanley worked hard at developing discipline and virtue. He practiced keeping his room scrupulously clean, and his handwriting neat. Even on his arduous expeditions, Stanley insisted on shaving every morning (Baumeister & Tierney, 2013).

Although no direct evidence exists supporting this notion, one implication of the literature on self-control may be that people who engage in self-control more often may be more likely to engage it during potentially heroic situations. The earliest empirical work long-term strengthening of self-regulatory resources revealed that individuals who worked on their posture and recorded everything they ate for two weeks exhibited heightened willpower after a laboratory ego depletion task (Muraven et al., 1999). More in-depth work by different research teams had individuals exercise self-control over several weeks in areas such as regular workouts or more disciplined study habits. These folks not only improved in their target areas, but in the other areas of their lives. For example, those who regularly worked out also got more responsible and disciplined with their money (e.g., Oaten & Cheng, 2006). Thus, though people differ in their dispositional levels of self-control, they can make lasting changes, and these changes will be associated with success and work and school as well as greater happiness and self-esteem (de Ridder, Lensvelt-Mulders, Finkenauer, Stok, & Baumeister, 2012). We note that a virtue cannot be described as a virtue unless there is consistency over time. A partner is not faithful and an employee is not honest unless they eschew temptation every time they face it, day after day, year after year. We can strengthen the self-control muscle in a particular domain (including most virtues) until it becomes a habit.

We see self-regulation as especially critical in two areas of the hero's journey. The first is *temptation*. Heroes often go through a testing, like Jesus Christ in the desert with Satan thrice tempting him. Usually this test involves a choice between what is self-enhancing versus what is beneficial for a group (the latter being a transcendent, moral action which should confer meaning by connecting the hero to something greater). In this respect, many hero stories may be a bit unrealistic from a scientific standpoint because the hero may already be ego depleted on his or her journey. However, there is some research in which significantly increasing motivation somehow allows individuals to persist and exercise greater than expected self-control (Muraven & Slessareva, 2003). Snapping at a co-worker or taking undue credit for a group endeavor may be avoided after reflecting on long-term goals and increasing motivation to achieve those goals. Perhaps a hero whose motivation is increased (such as by reflecting on his or her desire to save others in need) is able to exercise greater self-control than previously, and thus reaches a more exceptional goal.

The fallen hero typically fails due either to hubris or to failed self-regulation, or both. While stories often illustrate how close a hero comes to failure and tragedy (Allison & Goethals, 2011), it often takes only a single failure in order to disqualify the potential hero. This failure could be action, such as killing a villain in a moment of blinding rage, or inaction, such as not responding to the plight of a victim. Examples abound in both the real world and in film and literature of a single episode of cheating unraveling a marriage, or a single loss of temper leading to death or imprisonment. New York Governor Eliot Spitzer had a distinguished record as a lawyer and politician, but was discovered to have used an escort service and resigned after just one year in office. Celebrated golfer Tiger Woods fell from public grace after his extramarital affairs were revealed. Redemption for heroes also often involves personal commitment to self-regulate in order to change and help others, such as in the case of Betty Ford's work to overcome her drug addiction and support for treatment centers to help others do the same (Allison & Goethals, 2011). If needs for meaning are met through domains of control and understanding over one's environment (Heine et al., 2006; Stevens & Fiske, 1995), self-regulation may play a direct role in meaning-making by allowing heroes to show how we all can achieve difficult goals and succeed where we used to fail through hard work and perseverance.

The second critical area in the hero's journey is when extraordinary effort is required, such as when a hero faces great costs or sacrifice for the benefit of others. This taps into the idea of ego depletion. How can the hero or would-be hero exercise this extraordinary effort when it has not occurred before? One way we seem to expand our capacity is via self-affirmation (Schmeichel & Vohs, 2009), such as reflecting on our values. Those heroes who are aware of their critical choice point may be affirming their values, providing additional motivation and ability to persevere. We suspect others, such as mentors and family members, can also provide this boost by affirming us. Obi-Wan Kenobi told Luke that the Force was strong in him, and Winston Churchill's wife Clementine regularly wrote encouraging letters to him that bolstered his resolve. The hero's mentor also may help the hero develop the habit of self-control via effortful training. We recall the notion that heroes are highly competent as well as highly moral; many presumably have spent a good bit of time building up their self-regulation muscle.

Self-regulation often is a highly social process. For instance, outside the scope of heroism, researchers have found that romantic partners who are depleted are less likely to accommodate (inhibit a destructive response) when their partner behaves badly (Finkel & Campbell, 2001), and self-control failure is associated with more violent impulses and thoughts toward one's romantic partner (Finkel, DeWall, Slotter, Oaten, & Foshee, 2009). With this in mind, we must refer to the social context in order to get the best picture of self-regulation, virtue, and meaning for the hero or would-be hero. Very recent work has pointed to the importance of relationships in exercising self-control. Transactive Goal Dynamics Theory proposes that two more individuals can exercise self-control jointly, as a single system (Fitzsimons, Finkel, & vanDellen, 2015).

What does this mean for heroes or even the casually virtuous? Close others can provide direct support in helping reach an individual, dyadic, or group goal. Many hands may lighten the load and reduce ego depletion. Close others may increase motivation to succeed. They might provide self-affirmation or positive mood, which have been shown to ameliorate the effects of extended effort. As stated previously, heroes develop in large part through their relationships with friends, mentors, and teachers along their journey. These mentors and partners on heroic journeys may be especially helpful in the context of self-regulation. Moreover, this assistance may be particularly crucial when the difficult tasks are virtuous ones. Once the journey begins, however, the initial steps may begin to be self-reinforcing, as the individual feels increased meaning in life, and starts to see beneficial changes in the group or community. A journey begins with a single step, though, and that first step for the would-be hero might be the most difficult from a self-regulation standpoint. Moreover, self-regulatory efforts can often enhance the well-being of others. Although it requires self-regulation to meet personal goals (e.g., forgoing ice cream during a diet to achieve a target weight), sometimes self-regulatory efforts directly benefit others (e.g., waking up early to care for a child so one's partner can exercise, spending time listening earnestly to a friend in need despite the desire to take a nap). Such actions add value to relationships and enhance meaning (Van Tongeren, Green, Davis, Hook, & Hulsey, 2016). We hope that future research empirically tests several of these points.

In conclusion, although little empirical work directly ties self-regulation to heroism, we believe self-regulation may play a critical role in the meaning-making process that heroes engage in as well as exemplify for others. Self-regulation is required for the truly virtuous actions that heroes engage in, particularly acting virtuously in the face of hardship, and acting selflessly when there is a significant personal cost. Future research is needed to understand better whether self-regulation is necessary for heroic meaning, and how self-regulation is inherent in meaning-making for individuals.

Meaning via Gratitude

Recent research has highlighted the importance of feeling and expressing gratitude in maintaining positive relationships and personal well-being, and there are many reasons to think that heroes are more likely to feel gratitude as well. Feelings of gratitude are positive and invigorating, and can be distinguished from conceptually similar states like indebtedness, which emphasize one's lower position of power to the debtor (Mathews & Green, 2010; McCullough, Kilpatrick, Emmons, & Larson, 2001). Gratitude is a "relational virtue," a behavior and mindset which works to strengthen and repair interpersonal relationships (Davis et al., 2013). Gratitude predicts greater positive affect, a sense of connectedness with others, and helping (Emmons & McCullough, 2003). Gratitude is evoked when we know someone has done something good for us when they did not have to, and promotes a desire to not only repay the benefactor, but also be closer to them (Algoe & Haidt, 2009; McCullough et al., 2001). Heroes often inspire gratitude from others, and this feeling may increase the salience of one's meaning in life through an increased sense of closeness and belongingness (Kleiman, Adams, Kashdan, & Kiskind, 2013). Experimental work has shown that writing notes of gratitude increase meaning relative to those in a control condition who wrote about their plans for the week (Van Tongeren, Green, Davis, Hook, & Hulsey, 2016). Heroes also may feel more grateful to others and for their available resources because of their tendency to be other-oriented, and thus their gratitude may motivate additional virtue. Take for instance the notable example of James Harrison, an Australian man diagnosed with a life-threatening illness at 14. Although he recovered, his treatment required him to receive almost two gallons of donated blood in order to survive. Full of gratitude toward the unknowable number of people who helped him with their blood donations, he vowed to donate as much blood as possible in order to give back. So, at the age of 18 he began donating blood every few weeks, and has been doing so for the last *60 years*. Harrison's heroic impact goes beyond normal blood donations, however: in a serendipitous twist, his blood has an extremely rare antibody which is necessary to treat a disease called Rh incompatibility in pregnant women. Because of this antibody, Harrison's donations have been estimated to have saved the lives of over two million babies at the time of this publication, and he plans to keep giving until he is no longer able.

In short, one avenue for creating and sustaining personal meaning is acting virtuously, and the virtues of humility, prosociality, self-control, and gratitude may be virtues that confer meaning or purpose. However, the search for or defense of meaning may in some cases prevent the birth of heroes or even birth villains.

Does Defending Meaning Create Heroes or Villains?

Social psychology literature is replete with examples of how individuals defend the self-concept from threat (Alicke & Sedikides, 2009). For instance, they prefer flattering over critical or accurate feedback (Hepper, Hart, Gregg, & Sedikides, 2011), derogate the source of negative feedback (Fein & Spencer, 1997), and eschew opportunities to learn accurate but unflattering facts about themselves (Sanitioso, Kunda, & Fong, 1990). These self-concept defenses occur both consciously and unconsciously (Alicke & Sedikides, 2009). We previously discussed how defense of meaning may also occur largely outside of conscious awareness. That is, fluid compensation may occur in situations in which our meaning or view of the world is somehow challenged, even subliminally (Van Tongeren & Green, 2010).

What does this mean for heroism? It means that people often face key points in their lives in which their world is upended. These points constitute meaning threats. Unfortunately, the default response is to defend meaning—and thus to fail to learn or grow or act heroically. That is one reason why heroes are rare. But others may have the resources with which to cope with the meaning threat and change or grow in some way. Virtues themselves may be an affirmation of sorts: People typically value being seen as moral (Aquino & Reed, 2002), and are motivated to live up to socially bound expressions of virtue within particular cultures (Fowers, 2012). One way of responding to meaning threats is to reaffirm those values—likely moral or virtuous values—that individuals desire to see in their own identity and which are supported by prevailing social norms—as a way of restoring a sense of meaning. Thus, virtue affirmation may be one (positive) response to violations of meaning.

However, this process of meaning restoration does not always yield prosocial outcomes. It appears that individuals also often engage in self-serving cognitive gymnastics when meaning is threatened. There is ample indirect evidence of this in how individuals process information. They readily embrace information that aligns with their existing beliefs (particularly existential beliefs), but go to great lengths to discredit information that challenges their existing beliefs (Lord, Ross, & Lepper, 1979; Nyhan & Reifler, 2010). This process has been called confirmation bias (among other names) and helps to explain why individuals are surprisingly resistant to attitude change regarding centrally held or cherished attitudes, even in the face of rather powerful countervailing evidence. Even asking people to consider information in an unbiased fashion has no discernable effect (Lord, Lepper, & Preston, 1984). So we are not likely to be persuaded to change our gods, our political views, or our sports teams.

We suspect that these central beliefs are especially resistant to change because they are imbued with meaning; to change these beliefs is to change our worldview. If we admit that our worldview may not be completely accurate, at least through the concession that even a mundane aspect of our belief system is flawed, then we may question the veracity of our entire worldview, including existentially pressing issues such as beliefs regarding the afterlife and the purpose of human existence. As a way to maintain absolute and unwavering faith in their constellation of beliefs, people are motivated to discount disconfirming information, and, more radically, eliminate alternative viewpoints and dismiss or derogate the individuals who hold them. Closure and certainty are one of the foundations of meaning, according to the MMM, so questioning central beliefs may necessarily result in reduced felt meaning in life. Perhaps in some respect heroes are heroes because they are willing and able to endure meaning threats. They are open to new experiences and new ways of thinking and are willing to undertake a painful cognitive journey (that may accompany a painful physical journey). Finding meaning via other sources may help in this regard, consistent with MMM theorizing. For example, a mentor or love interest may provide a meaning boost via self-esteem or belonging that gives the would-be hero strength to change her thinking and worldview.

One of the most heroic acts may be the cognitive transformation needed to reconsider an arch enemy to be a potential friend who can be redeemed, as Luke Skywalker did with his father Darth Vader in Return of the Jedi ("I sense good in you"). The central thesis of Doris Kearns Goodwin's Pulitzer Prize-winning book *Team of Rivals* is that Lincoln had the courage and humility not to demonize vanquished political enemies, but to recognize their gifts and put them in his cabinet, even though some would continue to sharply criticize him behind his back or even make overtures at running against him in 1864. Allison and Smith (2015) discuss key differences between heroes and villains, and one sharp distinction is that heroes discover a missing inner quality, whereas villains do not. Identifying and fixing such a flaw likely constitutes a meaning threat, so this theorizing is consistent with our argument.

There may be a point in someone's life that serves as a trigger moment or hero crossroads. The choice may not always be between acting like a hero and failing to act (and being just another ordinary person). In many cases, the other divergent path may be that of a villain. That is, defensive reactions to maintain meaning—to bolster one's worldview even when faced with disconfirming evidence—may actually lead to antisocial or harmful actions. For example, people more readily disparage or even mistreat outgroup members when they feel psychologically threatened (see Greenberg et al., 1990; Rosenblatt et al., 1989). Meaning systems are helpful to provide structure and order in the world, answer questions about the nature of humanity and the potential purpose of life, and guide actions by explicating the moral standards for right living. However, the content of a meaning system matters greatly—we have argued elsewhere (Van Tongeren et al., 2011) that for meaning systems to effectively manage existential anxiety and not promote evil or villainous acts, they should provide certainty (i.e., have relatively concrete claims), confer meaning that transcends death (i.e., extend the meaning and significance of one's life and actions beyond the grave), and value all human life (i.e., recognize the importance of each life as equal and worth protecting). Certain constellations of beliefs may provide certainty and death-transcendent meaning, but may do so by dehumanizing another group or promoting violence (e.g., Nazi ideology). Perhaps the valuing of all human life is one important distinguishing feature that separates heroes from villains. Moreover, such responses are often magnified under threats against one's meaning system.

In the face of identity threat, individuals may increase collective self-esteem by derogating out-group members (Branscombe & Wann, 1994). A soldier whose identity is closely bound to either his nation or a higher code of honor could choose to save an enemy combatant's life or follow his orders. This dilemma is illustrated clearly in the story of Franz Stigler, a German pilot in the Second World War who came upon a wounded American bomber, piloted by Charles Brown, struggling to reach friendly territory. Instead of following his orders and shooting the defenseless Brown out of the sky, Stigler thought of his code of honor, and guided Brown safely back to Allied territory. After the war, the two reunited and became close friends.

Heroes are treasured individuals because they affirm our meaning structures (Allison & Goethals, 2014). Heroic stories, or basking in the glory of real-life heroic successes (e.g., sports teams) can bolster social identity (Allison & Goethals, 2011), which may subsequently bolster meaning via increased self-esteem (Proulx et al., 2006). Heroes themselves may have their meaning affirmed through their own actions. Heroes who provided physical assistance reported feeling a spontaneous, overwhelming drive to help immediately (Becker & Eagly, 2004). Joseph Campbell asserts that "the heroic life is living the individual adventure" (Osbon, 1991, p. 8): the heroic journey is itself thought to be a search for personal identity and meaning in life, and to truly help others heroically, individuals must affirm their sense of self.

Though there is little extant empirical work linking heroes and meaning-making, we have proposed that there are ample possible connections, and we urge researchers to investigate empirically many of the points we have raised. Investigating these connections will yield a fuller understanding of both heroes and how they are made as well as how individuals construct meaning. Virtuous behavior appears to be the critical connection. Morality confers meaning, and extraordinary morality creates heroes. Seeking meaning and affirmation of meaning via virtuous behavior may be a key to unlocking the latent hero that exists in all of us.

References

Algoe, S. A., & Haidt, J. (2009). Witnessing excellence in action: the "other-praising" emotions of elevation, gratitude, and admiration. *The Journal of Positive Psychology, 4*, 105–127.

Alicke, M., & Sedikides, C. (2009). Self-enhancement and self-protection: What they are and what they do. *European Review of Social Psychology, 20*, 1–48.

Allison, S. T., & Goethals, G. R. (2011). *Heroes: What they do and why we need them.* New York: Oxford University Press.

Allison, S. T., & Goethals, G. R. (2014). "Now he belongs to the ages": The heroic leadership dynamic and deep narratives of greatness. In G. R. Goethals, S. T. Allison, R. M. Kramer, & D. M. Messick (eds) *Conceptions of leadership: Enduring ideas and emerging insights* (pp. 167–183). New York: Palgrave Macmillan.

Allison, S., & Smith, G. (2015). *Reel heroes and villains: Two hero experts critique the movies (Volume 2)*. Midlothian, VA: Agile Writer Press.

Aquino, K., & Reed, A., II (2002). The self-importance of moral identity. *Journal of Personality and Social Psychology, 83*, 1423–1440.

Baumeister, R. F., & Tierney, J. (2013). *Willpower*. New York: Penguin Books.

Baumeister, R. F., & Vohs, K. D. (2007). Self-regulation, ego depletion, and motivation. *Social and Personality Psychology Compass, 1*, 115–128.

Baumeister, R. F., & Vohs, K. D. (2012). Self-regulation and the executive function of the self. In M. R. Leary & J. P. Tangney (eds), *Handbook of self and identity* (pp. 180–197). New York: Guilford.

Baumeister, R. F., Bratslavsky, E., Muraven, M., & Tice, D. M. (1998). Ego depletion: Is the active self a limited resource? *Journal of Personality and Social Psychology, 74*, 1252–1265.

Baumeister, R. F., Stillwell, A. M., & Heatherton, T. F. (1994). Guilt: An interpersonal approach. *Psychological Bulletin, 115*, 243–267.

Baumeister, R. F., Stillwell, A. M., & Wotman, S. R. (1990). Victim and perpetrator accounts of interpersonal conflict: Autobiographical narratives about anger. *Journal of Personality and Social Psychology, 59*, 994–1005.

Baumeister, R. F., Vohs, K. D., Aaker, J. L., & Garbinsky, E. N. (2013). Some key differences between a happy life and a meaningful life. *Journal of Positive Psychology, 8*, 505–516.

Becker, S. W. & Eagly, A. H. (2004). The heroism of women and men. *American Psychologist, 59*, 163–178.

Beedie, C. J., & Lane, A. M. (2012). The role of glucose in self-control: Another look at the evidence and an alternative conceptualization. *Personality and Social Psychology Review, 16*, 143–153.

Branscombe, N. R., & Wann, D. L. (1994), Collective self-esteem consequences of outgroup derogation when a valued social identity is on trial. *European Journal of Social Psychology, 24*, 641–657. doi: 10.1002/ejsp.2420240603

Burns, C. T., Jackson, L. M., Tarpley, W. R., & Smith, G. J. (1996). Religion as quest: The self-directed pursuit of meaning. *Personality and Social Psychology Bulletin, 22*, 1068–1076.

Campbell, J. (1949). *The hero with a thousand faces*. New York: Pantheon Books.

Churchill, W. S. (1948). *The second world war, Volume 1: The gathering storm*. Boston, MA: Houghton Mifflin.

Davis, D. E., Hook, J. N., Worthington, E. L. Jr., Van Tongeren, D. R., Gartner, A. L., Jennings, D. J. II, & Emmons, R. A. (2011). Relational humility: Conceptualizing and measuring humility as a personality judgment. *Journal of Personality Assessment, 93*, 225–234.

Davis, D. E., Worthington, E. L., Jr., & Hook, J. N., Emmons, R. A., Hill, P. C, Bollinger, R. A., & Van Tongeren, D. R. (2013). Humility and the development and repair of social bonds: Two longitudinal studies. *Self and Identity, 12*, 58–77.

Davis, J. L., Green, J. D., Reid, C. A., Moloney, J. M., & Burnette, J. (2015). Forgiveness and health in nonmarried dyadic relationships. In L. L. Toussaint, E. Worthington, & D. Williams (eds), *Forgiveness and health: Scientific evidence and theories relating forgiveness to better health* (pp. 239–253). New York: Springer Publishers.

de Ridder, D. T. D., Lensvelt-Mulders, G., Finkenauer, G., Stok, F. M., & Baumeister, R. F. (2012). Taking stock of self-control: A meta-analysis of how trait self-control relates to a wide range of behaviors. *Personality and Social Psychology Review, 16*, 76–99.

DeWall, C. N., Baumeister, R. F., Gailliot, M. T., Maner, J. K. (2008). Depletion makes the heart grow less helpful: Helping as a function of self-regulatory energy and genetic relatedness. *Personality and Social Psychology Bulletin, 34*, 1653–1662.

DeWall, C. N., Baumeister, R. F., Stillman, T. F., & Gailliot, M. T. (2007). Violence restrained: Effects of self-regulatory capacity and its depletion on aggressive behavior. *Journal of Experimental Social Psychology, 43*, 62–76.

Emmons, R. A. (2003). Personal goals, life meaning, and virtue: Wellsprings of a positive life. In C. L. M. Keyes & J. A. Haidt (eds), *Flourishing: Positive psychology and the life well-lived* (pp. 105–128). Washington, DC: American Psychological Association.

Emmons, R. A., & McCullough, M. E. (2003). Counting blessings versus burdens: An experimental investigation of gratitude and subjective well-being in daily life. *Journal of Personality and Social Psychology, 84*, 377–389. doi: 10.1037/0022-3514.84.2.377

Fein, S., & Spencer, S. J. (1997). Prejudice as self-image maintenance: Affirming the self through derogating others. *Journal of Personality and Social Psychology 73*, 31–44.

Finkel, E. J., & Campbell, W. K. (2001). Self-control and accommodation in close relationships: An interdependence analysis. *Journal of Personality and Social Psychology, 81*, 263–277.

Finkel, E. J., DeWall, C. N., Slotter, E. B., Oaten, M., & Foshee, V. A. (2009). Self-regulatory failure and intimate partner violence perpetration. *Journal of Personality and Social Psychology, 97*, 483–499.

Fitzsimons, G. M., Finkel, E. J., & vanDellen, M. R., (2015). Transactive goal dynamics. *Psychological Review, 122*, 648–673.

Fowers, B. J. (2005). Defining virtue. In B. Fowers (ed.), *Virtue and psychology: Pursuing excellence in ordinary practices* (pp. 27–54). Washington, DC: American Psychological Association.

Fowers, B. J. (2012). Placing virtue and the human good in psychology. *Journal of Theoretical and Philosophical Psychology, 32*, 1–9.

Franco, Z. E., Blau, K., & Zimbardo, P. G. (2011). Heroism: A conceptual analysis and differentiation between heroic action and altruism. *Review of General Psychologist, 15*, 99–113.

Frankl, V. E. (1959). *Man's search for meaning*. New York: Buccaneer Books.

Galliot, M. T., Baumeister, R. F., DeWall, C. N., Maner, J. K., Plant, E. A., Tice, D. M., Brewer, L. E., & Schmeichel, B. J. (2007). Self-control relies on glucose as a limited energy source: Willpower is more than a metaphor. *Journal of Personality and Social Psychology, 92*, 325–336.

Goethals, G. R., & Allison, S. T. (2012). Making heroes: The construction of courage, competence, and virtue. *Advances in Experimental Social Psychology, 46*, 184–235.

Goodwin, D. K. (2005). *Team of rivals*. New York: Simon & Schuster.

Gray, K., & Wegner, D. M. (2009). Moral typecasting: Divergent perceptions of moral agents and moral patients. *Journal of Personality and Social Psychology, 96*, 505–520.

Gray, K., Waytz, A., & Young, L. (2012). The moral dyad: A fundamental template unifying moral judgment. Psychological Inquiry, 23, 206–215.

Green, J. D., & Van Tongeren, D. R. (2012). Self-regulation and a meaning-based approach to virtues: Comments on Hampson's Habitus. *Edification, 6*, 19–23.

Greenberg, J., Pyszczynski, T., & Solomon, S., Rosenblatt, A., Veeder, M., & Kirkland, S. et al. (1990). Evidence for a terror management theory II: The effects of mortality salience on reactions to those who threaten or bolster the cultural worldview. *Journal of Personality and Social Psychology, 57*, 308–318.

Haidt, J. (2007). The new synthesis in moral psychology. *Science, 316*, 998–1002.

Heine, S., J., Proulx, T., & Vohs, K. D. (2006). The meaning maintenance model: On the coherence of social motivations. *Personality and Social Psychology Review, 10*, 88–110.

Heintzelman, S. J., & King, L.A. (2014). (The feeling of) Meaning-as-Information. *Personality and Social Psychology Review, 18*, 153–167.

Hepper, E., Hart, C. M., Gregg, A. P., & Sedikides, C. (2011). Motivated expectations of social interactions in positive feedback. *Journal of Social Psychology, 151*, 455–477.

Hugo, V. (1887/1987). *Les Misérables*. New York: Signet Classics.

Inzlicht, M., & Schmeichel, B. J. (2012). What is ego depletion? Toward a mechanistic revision of the resource model of self-control. *Perspectives on Psychological Science, 7*, 450–463.

Kim, J., Allison, S. T., Eylon, D., Goethals, G., Markus, M., Hindle, S., & McGuire, H. (2008). Rooting for (and then abandoning) the underdog. *Journal of Applied Social Psychology, 38*, 2550–2573.

Kinsella, E. L., Ritchie, T. D., & Igou, E. R. (2015). Lay perspectives on the social and psychological functions of heroes. *Frontiers in Psychology, 6*, 130.

Kleiman, E. M., Adams, L. A., Kashdan, T. B., & Riskind, J. H. (2013). Gratitude and grit indirectly reduce risk of suicidal ideations by enhancing meaning in life: Evidence for a mediated moderation model. *Journal of Research in Personality, 47*, 539–546.

Leary, M. R. (2005). Sociometer theory and the pursuit of relational value: Getting to the root of self-esteem. *European Review of Social Psychologist, 16*, 75–111.

Lincoln, A. (1863). The Gettysburg address. Gettysburg, PA, November 19. Retrieved from www.abraham-lincolnonline.org/lincoln/speeches/gettysburg.htm.

Lord, C. G., Lepper, M. R., & Preston, E. (1984). Considering the opposite: A corrective strategy for social judgment. *Journal of Personality and Social Psychology, 47*, 1231–1243.

Lord, C. G., Ross, L., & Lepper, M. R. (1979). Biased assimilation and attitude polarization: The effects of prior theories on subsequently considered evidence. *Journal of Personality and Social Psychology, 37*, 2098–2109.

Luchies, L. B., Finkel, E. J., McNulty, J. K., & Kumashiro, M. (2010). The doormat effect: When forgiving erodes self-respect and self-concept clarity. *Journal of Personality and Social Psychology, 98*, 734–749.

Mathews, M., & Green, J. D. (2010). Looking at me, appreciating you: Self-focused attention distinguishes between gratitude and indebtedness. *Cognition and Emotion, 24*, 710–718.

McCullough, M. E., Kilpatrick, S. D., Emmons, R. A., & Larson, D. B. (2001). Is gratitude a moral affect? *Psychological Bulletin, 127*, 249–266.

McMillen, D. L. (1971). Transgression, self-image, and compliant behavior. *Journal of Personality and Social Psychology, 20*, 176–179.

Mead, N. L., Baumeister, R. F., Gino, F., Schweitzer, M. E., & Ariely, D. (2009). Too tired to tell the truth:

Self-control resource depletion and dishonesty. *Journal of Experimental Social Psychology, 45,* 594–597.

Muraven, M., & Slessareva, E. (2003). Mechanisms of self-control failure: Motivation and limited resources. *Personality and Social Psychology Bulletin, 29,* 894–906.

Muraven, M., Baumeister, & Tice, D. M. (1999). Longitudinal improvement of self-regulation through practice: Building self-control strength through repeated exercise. *Journal of Social Psychology, 139,* 446–457.

Nyhan, B., & Reifler, J. (2010). When corrections fail: The persistence of political misperceptions. *Political Behavior, 32,* 303–330.

Oaten, M. & Cheng, K. (2006). Longitudinal gains in self-regulation from regular physical exercise. *British Journal of Health Psychology, 11,* 717–733.

Oliner, S. P. and Oliner P. M. (1988). *The altruistic personality.* New York: The Free Press.

Osbon, D. K. (ed.) (1991). *A Joseph Campbell companion: Reflections on the art of living.* New York: HarperCollins.

Proulx, T., & Heine, S. J. (2008). The case of the transmogrifying experimenter: Affirmation of a moral schema following implicit change detection. *Psychological Science, 19,* 1294–1300.

Rosenblatt, A., Greenberg, J., Solomon, S., Pyszczynski, T., & Lyon, D. (1989). Evidence for a terror management theory: I. The effects of mortality salience on reactions to those who violate or uphold cultural values. *Journal of Personality and Social Psychology, 57,* 681–690.

Sanitioso, R. B., Kunda, Z., & Fong, G. T. (1990). Motivated recruitment of autobiographical memories. *Journal of Personality and Social Psychology, 59,* 229–241.

Schmeichel, B. J., & Vohs, K. D. (2009). Self-affirmation and self-control: Affirming core values counteracts ego depletion. *Journal of Personality and Social Psychology, 96,* 770–782.

Shin, J. Y., & Steger, M. F. (2014). Promoting meaning and purpose in life. In A. C. Parks & S. M. Schueller (eds), *The Wiley Blackwell Handbook of Positive Psychological Interventions* (pp. 90–110). Malden, MA: Wiley Blackwell.

Steele, C. M. (1988). The psychology of self-affirmation: Sustaining the integrity of the self. *Advances in Experimental Social Psychology, 21,* 261–302.

Stevens, L. E., & Fiske, S. T. (1995). Motivation and cognition in social life: A social survival perspective. *Social Cognition, 13,* 189–214.

Van Tongeren, D. R., Davis, D. E., & Hook, J. N. (2014). Social benefits of humility: Initiating and maintaining romantic relationships. *Journal of Positive Psychology, 9,* 313–321.

Van Tongeren, D. R., Green, J. D., Davis, J. L., Davis, D. E., Worthington, E. L. Jr., Hook, J. N., Jennings, D. J. II, Gartner, A. L., Greer, C. L., & Greer, T. W. (2011). Meaning as a restraint of evil. In J. H. Hellens (ed.), *Explaining Evil: Vol 3, Approaches, Responses, Solutions* (pp. 203–216). New York: Praeger.

Van Tongeren, D. R., Green, J. D., Davis, D. E., Hook, J. N., & Hulsey, T. L. (2016). Prosociality enhances meaning in life. *Journal of Positive Psychology, 11,* 225–236.

Van Tongeren, D. R., Green, J. D., Hook, J. N., Davis, D. E., Davis, J. L., & Ramos, M. (2015). Forgiveness increases meaning in life. *Social Psychological and Personality Science, 6,* 47–55.

Van Tongeren, D. R., Stafford, J., Hook, J. N., Green, J. D., Davis, D. E., & Johnson, K. A. (2016). Humility attenuates negative attitudes and behaviors toward religious outgroup members. *Journal of Positive Psychology, 11,* 199–208.

Worthington, E. L., Jr. (ed.). (2005). *Handbook of forgiveness.* New York: Brunner-Routledge.

Worthington, E. L., Jr. (2006). *Forgiveness and reconciliation: Theory and application.* New York: Brunner-Routledge.

Zechmeister, J. S., & Romero, C. (2002). Victim and offender accounts of interpersonal conflict: Autobiographical narratives of forgiveness and unforgiveness. *Journal of Personality and Social Psychology, 82,* 675–686. doi: 10.1037/0022-3514.82.4.675

28
Psychopathy and Heroism
Unresolved Questions and Future Directions

Brett A. Murphy, Scott O. Lilienfeld, and Ashley L. Watts

When he was a baby, Andy McNab was abandoned in a shopping bag in front of a hospital and subsequently adopted. He did poorly in school and engaged in petty crimes as a juvenile. His life changed, however, when he joined the British Army at the age of sixteen. During his career, he excelled in the art of warfare, eventually leaving the military in 1993 as a member of the British Special Forces, having been awarded numerous medals for military heroism. Since then, he has written best-selling books about his war experiences, expanded his career into the business world, and is currently with his fifth wife.

One of his books, co-written with psychologist Kevin Dutton, is entitled *The Good Psychopath's Guide to Success: How to Use Your Inner Psychopath to Get the Most Out of Life*. McNab is a self-professed psychopath who openly credits his successes to his psychopathic traits, such as his reduced feelings of empathy and fear (Dutton & McNab, 2014). He argues that psychopathic traits can help us achieve success in life, and perhaps even allow us to act heroically when the situation calls for it. As McNab explained, "If I'm in a hostage situation I'd rather have a psychopath coming through the door than anyone else because I know he's going to be completely focused on the job in hand" (Merz, 2014). In his view, the capacity for cold-blooded killer instincts can be a tremendous advantage not just for psychopathic persons, but for those around them, at least in certain cases.

McNab's idea may understandably strike many readers as counterintuitive, even implausible. Whereas heroes are thought of as moral exemplars, psychopaths are typically cold, callous people without much moral conscience. It is difficult, at first glance, to see what the two groups of individuals could have in common. Yet McNab's conjecture is not new, as several scholars have theorized that certain psychopathic traits may sometimes be conducive to heroism, or at the very least adaptive in some cases (e.g., Lykken, 1995). Depending upon the situation, selected characteristics of psychopathic individuals, such as reduced physical or social fear, impulsivity, or emotional callousness, may allow them to successfully act when others do not, even perhaps in heroic ways. At the same time, other features of psychopathy, such as a deficient moral sense, may militate against the likelihood of heroism. In this chapter, we explore potential relationships between heroism and psychopathic traits while illuminating both the bright and dark sides of heroism.

What is Psychopathy?

Few psychological terms generate as much concern and fear as "psychopath," and often for good reason. Psychopathic personality (or psychopathy) encompasses a variety of behavioral, interpersonal, and emotional traits including lack of empathy, reduced capacity for guilt and remorse, willingness to lie and cheat, and manipulativeness. Psychiatrist Hervey Cleckley (1941/1988), who was the first to systematically describe psychopathy, portrayed the prototypical psychopath as a paradoxical figure, one who appears outwardly charming, confident, and likeable, but is also severely lacking in empathy, remorse, and impulse control (see also Hare, 1993; Hare & Neumann, 2008). Moreover, psychopathic individuals are often so adept at masking their emotional and moral abnormalities that they can come across as normal, caring, or even prosocial individuals (Book et al., 2015; Cleckley, 1941/1988). They can at times be ruthless social predators, however, and are often highly skilled in their exploitative behaviors.

Many writers describe psychopathy in language that implies that it is categorical (i.e., that there is a clear line separating psychopathy from normality). In contrast, most research demonstrates that psychopathy is underpinned by one or more dimensions of personality traits that blend imperceptibly into normality (e.g., Edens, Marcus, Lilienfeld, & Poythress, 2006; Guay, Ruscio, Knight, & Hare, 2007), suggesting that it can be profitably studied in nonclinical (e.g., student, community) settings given that these traits appear to be continuous among these samples. Along these lines, increasing evidence suggests that psychopathy is not a monolithic construct, but instead is a constellation of multiple (at least three) separable dimensions (Benning, Patrick, Blonigen, Hicks, & Iacono, 2005; Lilienfeld, Watts, Smith, Berg, & Latzman, in press); an individual may be substantially higher or lower on one dimension than on another. Importantly, elevated levels of any one of these constituent dimensions does not psychopathy make. Rather, psychopathy is likely to emerge at elevated levels of most or all of these dimensions; different combinations of these dimensions will likely result in different interpersonal manifestations and flavors of functional impairment.

One prominent conceptualization, the triarchic model of psychopathy (Patrick, Fowles, & Krueger, 2009), describes these traits in terms of three separable dimensions: boldness, meanness, and disinhibition. The *boldness* dimension comprises heightened social potency, a willingness to take risks or take on challenges, and elevated emotional resilience. *Meanness* comprises callousness, cruelty, and predatory behaviors, and *disinhibition* comprises impulsivity, distrustful hostility, and emotion dysregulation (Patrick & Drislane, in press). Related to the *boldness* dimension, substantial research has indicated that psychopathic individuals tend to have a reduced capacity for fear (e.g., Lykken, 1957; Patrick, Bradley, & Lang, 1993; Sadeh & Verona, 2012) and perhaps anxiety (Derefinko, in press; cf. Watts, Lilienfeld, & Patrick, in preparation), or even a broader propensity to be insensitive to threat. The boldness dimension of psychopathy is probably the most obviously theoretically relevant to heroism, whereas the disinhibition facet may be related to some heroic acts, especially more impulsive forms of heroism. In contrast, the meanness dimension is less obviously relevant and may instead lower the odds of heroism, given its association with diminished empathy and guilt.

Partly because of the fear deficits associated with psychopathy, Lykken (1995, p. 118; see also Lykken, 1982) theorized that "the hero and the psychopath may be twigs on the same genetic branch," sharing a predisposition to relative fearlessness that could manifest in either socially praiseworthy or socially blameworthy behaviors, depending upon other variables, such as a history of effective parenting. At first glance, this hypothesis may understandably strike many readers as unlikely. How could psychopathy, which is typically associated with malevolence and amorality, be associated with heroism, which represents the pinnacle of meritorious human behavior? Could there possibly be a relationship between lacking moral feelings and engaging in risky acts that serve others?

These questions are actually a collection of many subquestions:

- Are psychopathic traits correlated with running into a burning building to save a girlfriend?
- Are they correlated with diving into a dangerous river to rescue an elderly stranger?
- Are they correlated with being a police officer?
- Are they correlated with being the kind of cop who will risk his career, and perhaps his life, to expose corruption among his colleagues?
- Are they correlated with being highly visible leaders in social justice movements?
- Are they correlated with donating a kidney anonymously to a stranger?

The answer to each of these questions is likely to be different. Moreover, the answer to each question may sometimes be yes, and sometimes no, depending on numerous factors.

As noted earlier, psychopathy encompasses a variety of traits (Lilienfeld et al., 2015), which may relate differentially to the many conceptual flavors of heroism. Whether any psychopathic features will be excitatory of, or inhibitory of, heroism will depend radically upon the situations and motivations that are involved. Herein, we explore the various aspects of psychopathy and the contexts in which psychopathy may lend itself to heroic actions and, conversely, where it may not. Since Lykken (1995) advanced his suggestion that psychopaths and heroes may be "twigs on the same genetic branch," a small body of research has examined this potential association (e.g., Smith, Lilienfeld, Coffey, & Dabbs, 2013), but this field of research is still nascent. As a result, in this chapter, we aim to raise far more questions than answers and to stimulate further research.

Psychopathy: Diagnostic and Assessment Issues

The origins of the *boldness* dimension (Patrick et al., 2009) emerged in Cleckley's (1941/1988) classic descriptions of psychopaths, in which he identified superficial charm and low levels of nervousness as indicators of the disorder. Furthermore, he commented on the psychopathic individual's apparent normalcy, writing that "everything about him is likely to suggest desirable and superior human qualities, a robust mental health" (p. 339) and "regularly we find in him extraordinary poise rather than jitteriness or worry (p. 340)." Today, most researchers view psychopathy as a constellation of personality traits and allied behaviors. On the one hand, psychopathic individuals may display ostensibly adaptive or socially desirable features, such as charm, competence, likeability, and sangfroid. On the other hand, however, they may also exhibit certain maladaptive behaviors, such as impulsivity, recklessness, and coldheartedness, which often give rise to antisocial and criminal behaviors. This confluence of seemingly oxymoronic features likely predisposes to both adaptive and maladaptive features (Lilienfeld, Watts, & Smith, 2015).

Most psychopathy research has been conducted with incarcerated individuals, who have committed criminal acts and have been unable to escape detection and confinement (Lilienfeld, 1994). Perhaps as a consequence, most psychopathy research has focused largely on socially "unsuccessful" populations. Moreover, because those in prison have limited opportunities for heroic behaviors, the potential link between psychopathy and heroism may have been largely overlooked. The most extensively validated measure of psychopathy, the Psychopathy Checklist—Revised (PCL-R; Hare, 1991/2003), is designed to assess psychopathic traits in criminal populations and includes a lengthy interview assessment as well as review of case files. Recent factor analyses suggest that the PCL-R can be subdivided into four facets: *interpersonal* characteristics, such as superficial charm and deceitfulness; *affective* characteristics, such as low empathy and lack of remorse; *lifestyle* characteristics, such as impulsivity and irresponsibility; and *antisocial* characteristics, such as poor aggression control and adult criminal outcomes (Hare,

1991/2003). The PCL-R does not explicitly measure relative fearlessness or boldness, but there is some evidence that it indirectly assesses such traits, especially in its interpersonal facet, which comprises narcissism and glibness (Neumann, Johannson, & Hare, 2013; Venables, Hall, & Patrick, 2014).

Despite the focus of most researchers on imprisoned psychopathic individuals, many or perhaps most, psychopathic individuals are probably not institutionalized, and roam freely through society (Hall & Benning, 2006). As Hare (1993) argued, incarcerated psychopaths "represent only the tip of a very large iceberg" (p. 115). Partly related to the seeming adaptiveness of some psychopathic traits, such as boldness, theories regarding psychopathy have long touched on the controversial concept of the "successful" psychopath, the individual who is able to navigate freely and effectively in the world despite high levels of psychopathic traits (e.g., Ishikawa et al., 2001; Lilienfeld, Watts, & Smith, 2015; Mullins-Sweatt et al., 2010; Widom, 1977). Several authors have argued that psychopathic individuals may even be overrepresented in some vocations, such as politics, business, law, and extreme sports (Babiak & Hare, 2006; Babiak, Neumann, & Hare, 2010; Lilienfeld et al., 2015).

To study psychopathy in non-institutionalized populations, a number of self-report measures have been created in recent decades, including: the Psychopathic Personality Inventory—Revised (PPI-R; Lilienfeld, Widows, & Staff, 2005); the Triarchic Psychopathy Measure (TriPM; Patrick, 2010); the Levenson Self-Report Psychopathy scale (LSRP; Levenson, Kiehl, & Fitzpatrick, 1995); the Self-Report Psychopathy Scale—III (SRP-II; Paulhus, Neumann, & Hare, in press); the Elemental Psychopathy Assessment (EPA; Lynam et al., 2011; Lynam et al., 2013); and at least a half dozen other measures. Some of these measures explicitly assess boldness traits, whereas most of the others appear to assess these traits indirectly (Lilienfeld, Smith, Sauvigne, Patrick et al., in press).

The most widely cited self-report measure, the PPI-R (Lilienfeld et al., 2005) and its predecessor (Lilienfeld & Andrews, 1996), encompass three higher-order dimensions: *Fearless Dominance* (PPI-FD); *Self-centered Impulsivity* (PPI-SCI); and *Coldheartedness* (PPI-CH) (Benning et al., 2003). PPI-FD consists of the subscales of Social Influence; Fearlessness; and Stress Immunity; individuals with high scores on this dimension are typically bold, dominant, and may be a pillar of confidence in challenging situations. PPI-SCI consists of the subscales of Rebellious Nonconformity, Blame Externalization, Carefree Nonplanfulness, and Machiavellian Egocentricity; individuals with high scores on this dimension are typically impulsive, irresponsible in various ways, and self-serving in their thoughts and behaviors. PPI-CH, which is a standalone dimension that consists of only one subscale, assesses callousness and lack of empathy and guilt (Benning et al., 2003).

Similar in conceptualization to the PPI and the PPI-R, the Triarchic Psychopathy Measure (TriPM; Patrick, 2010), which was designed to capture the triarchic model of psychopathy discussed earlier, has begun to attract substantial research attention in recent years. It consists of three dimensions: *Boldness*, *Disinhibition*, and *Meanness*. The *Boldness* dimension is approximately equivalent to the PPI-R dimension of *Fearless Dominance*; the *Disinhibition* dimension is approximately equivalent to the PPI-R dimension of *Self-Centered Impulsivity*, and the *Meanness* dimension overlaps primarily with the PPI-R *Coldheartedness* dimension, with a lesser contribution from the PPI-R *Self-Centered Impulsivity* dimension (Drislane, Patrick, & Arsal, 2014; Sellbom & Phillips, 2013). Because of the high degree of overlap between PPI-FD and *Boldness* in the triarchic model, the two are often referred to interchangeably; recent work has described PPI-FD in terms of the boldness construct (e.g., Lilienfeld, Watts et al., in press), a convention generally followed in this chapter, although reference to FD is typically reserved for specific cases in which boldness was measured by PPI-FD.

Table 28.1 Psychopathic Personality Inventory Dimensions

PPI dimension	Fearless dominance	Self-centered impulsivity	Coldheartedness
Acronym	PPI-FD	PPI-SCI	PPI-CH
Subscales	Fearlessness Stress Immunity Social Influence	Carefree nonplanfulness Machiavellian egocentricity Rebellious nonconformity Blame externalization	Coldheartedness
Approximate equivalent in triarchic model of psychopathy	Boldness	Disinhibition	Meanness (which also overlaps with PPI-SCI)

Psychopaths: Heroes and Criminals?

Following upon the conjectures of Lykken (1982, 1995, 1996), the boldness traits associated with psychopathy are probably the most obvious potential source of connection between psychopathy and heroism. The capacity for doggedly facing intimidating challenges, for stepping up and taking the lead, and for taking risks that others might not are all conceptually related to heroism. Several studies described in this chapter (Patrick, Edens, Poythress, Lilienfeld, & Benning, 2006; Smith et al., 2013) provide evidence that, at least in some contexts, boldness is associated with heroism.

Given that many acts of heroism are generated by rapid impulses, with little or no time for reflection (Rand & Epstein, 2014), it is also possible that disinhibition is sometimes related to heroism (for evidence that disinhibition is related to intervening to help others when other bystanders are present, see Van den Bos, Muller, & Van Bussel, 2009). The impulsivity associated with psychopathy, especially in conjunction with relative fearlessness, may make psychopathic individuals more likely to tackle a hijacker, rush at a mugger, jump into a torrid river, or take any number of no-time-to-think actions that are involved in some heroic acts. The evidence for this relationship, from the few relevant studies that have been conducted (e.g., Patrick et al., 2006; Sandoval et al., 2000; Smith et al., 2013), is mixed, but intriguing research questions remain. For instance, disinhibition traits may be positively related to impulsively heroic acts, but negatively related to heroic acts that are deliberative or require sustained commitment. It is also possible that disinhibition relates more to spectacularly risky acts of heroism than to more everyday acts of heroism.

At the outset, it is difficult to imagine that tendencies towards meanness or coldheartedness would be associated with most prototypical acts of heroism, or with altruistic acts more broadly. Even if boldness and disinhibition traits may often be related to heroism, meanness traits and heroism probably run counter to one another in many or most situations, as noted earlier. This may not always be the case, however. For instance, lack of empathy and shallow emotionality might be associated with some forms of heroism, such as being willing to use violence or intimidation against others in emergency situations or desiring to enter into professionally heroic occupations like law enforcement. One study (Falkenbach & Tsoukalas, 2011), described in more detail later, found that psychopathic traits were positively associated with being a police officer but, as is the case with correlational data, direction of the causal arrow between the two could not be established. In particular, serving as a police officer and the concomitant exposure to crime and violence could potentially make a person more coldhearted over time. In contrast, coldhearted individuals, or psychopathic individuals more broadly, may be drawn to occupations in which they are permitted to carry a gun and exercise officially-sanctioned dominance over others. Although the role of causality is less understood, we suspect that the manifestation of psychopathic traits and allied behaviors is a product of both of these processes. In sum, different dimensions of psychopathy may be associated with heroism, but perhaps in ways that depend heavily upon the context and motivations associated with different forms of heroic behavior. Research is still extremely limited, but there is rich potential for exploring these questions in future studies.

Heterogeneity in Heroism: Differing Conceptualizations

"Hero" is an interpersonally subjective term; different people celebrate different heroes. Some have noted that the term is "radically ambiguous" in modern usage (Gill, 1996, p. 98): heroism is, as they say, in the eye of the beholder (Allison & Goethals, 2011). In many cases, one person's hero is another's *bête noire* (Franco, Blau, & Zimbardo, 2011; Jayawickreme & DiStefano, 2012). For instance, Justin Bieber, Lady Gaga, Madonna, Donald Trump, Kanye West, and Edward Snowden all have admirers who regard them as heroes, whereas others dislike or even abhor them. Similarly, Lyudmila Pavlichenko, the young female sniper who recorded more than 300 kills during the Second World War, was officially designated as a "Hero of the Soviet Union" and celebrated in the United States, but she was hated by the Nazis and their allies. Or take Chris Kyle, a United States Navy SEAL depicted famously in the film *American Sniper*, who was celebrated by many Americans but reviled as a "psychopath" or "sociopath" by many others (e.g., comedian Bill Maher) who found his proclaimed "love" of killing "savages" (Kyle, McEwen, & DeFelice, 2012, p. 4) to be highly disturbing. Even renowned heroes like Gandhi, Martin Luther King Jr., and Abraham Lincoln were disdained by many in their own times; indeed, all three were assassinated. Heroes are *typically* reflections of group (or subgroup) cultures and mores, not necessarily universal exemplars. This ambiguity potentially opens some doors for a relationship between psychopathy and heroism, as heroes can potentially be individuals that some others consider morally repugnant.

In addition to the arguably polarizing nature of the term "hero," there is remarkable heterogeneity in the way that humans view heroic acts. Although heroism is in part subjective, some acts are almost universally regarded as heroic, though, such as rescuing a child from being attacked by vicious animals, pulling an injured person from a burning vehicle, stepping in front of a person to take a bullet for him or her, and so on; others, however, are not ubiquitously regarded as heroic (e.g., suicide bombing as a religious demonstration). Although the former acts represent only a tiny sliver of the universe of heroic actions, they have received a heavy share of public acclaim and research.

Heroism and Psychological Research

Trait versus State Debate

Some have argued that heroic actions are frequently more causally related to the particularities of the evoking situations than they are to stable personality traits. For instance, Zimbardo (2007, p. 485) argued that "The banality of evil shares much with the banality of heroism. Neither attribute is the direct consequence of unique dispositional tendencies; there are no special attributes of either pathology or goodness residing within the human psyche or the human genome. Both conditions emerge in particular situations at particular times when situational forces play a compelling role in moving particular individuals across a decisional line from inaction to action." Others have adopted a more dispositional approach, arguing that personality traits play some role in predicting which people engage in extreme acts of heroism, even if the evoking situation is the proximal mover (e.g., Smith et al., 2013). Nonetheless, personality traits seem to play less of a role in more impulsive prosocial acts and a more pronounced role in more deliberative, sustained prosocial commitments (Walker, Frimer, & Dunlop, 2010). More stable personality traits, such as depth of moral conviction or certain dispositions relevant to psychopathy, are perhaps more likely to assume center stage when someone deliberates and then commits to a difficult course of action, as opposed to when someone impulsively engages in a no-time-to-think heroic act.

This trait versus situation debate raises the possibility that the most important distinction among different forms of heroism is whether heroes deliberated about the costs and benefits of their actions. Responding impulsively to an unexpected event may be entirely different than spending time ruminating about a course of action and then making a brave decision, although it is unknown whether these broad classes of behavior stem from overlapping personality underpinnings. The heroism of, say, the Freedom Riders, who knowingly and willingly risked their lives to protest Jim Crow, may be entirely different from the heroism of the random bystanders who may have impulsively jumped in to defend them when they were being assaulted by angry mobs. This distinction between deliberative and non-deliberative heroism appears to have been neglected in much of the recent scientific literature, although it may be a matter of degree as opposed to kind.

Definitional Issues

Although the words "hero" and "heroism" are familiar to all of us, and the archetype of the hero is deeply embedded in popular culture (Kinsella, Ritchie, & Igou, 2015), scholars have long struggled to devise conceptualizations and definitions that can be effectively used for theorizing and research. Some define "hero" according to how the word is used colloquially. This position is consistent with a "family resemblance" perspective in which one defines a "hero" according to a motley crew of overlapping similarities, in which no one feature is common to all (see Rosch & Mervis, 1975; Wittgenstein, 1953). This dizzying array of operationalizations of the term "hero" might be best summarized as "one who is viewed by others as an exemplary person or as a person who has performed some exemplary deed or deeds."

Beyond that, heroism seems to imply that someone has gone above and beyond the typical range of human experience in some way, or has done something unusual that few other people ever do. This broad and perhaps nebulous definition encompasses a large diversity of types of heroes. Zimbardo (2007, pp. 468–471), for instance, elaborated 12 types of heroes: military and duty-bound heroes; political or military leaders; martyrs; whistleblowers; bureaucracy heroes; civil heroes; religious figures; adventurers; underdogs; Good Samaritans; politico-religious figures; and last, but certainly not least, scientific heroes. Even that list is still quite under-inclusive; for instance, it leaves out musical and artistic heroes, sports heroes, educational heroes, and so on. At the same time, this list may also be unduly lengthy and might eventually be condensed into more parsimonious categories using factor analytic approaches. For instance, the primary distinction among types of heroism may lie largely in one broad dimension, such as impulsive versus deliberative heroic acts.

Becker and Eagly (2004, p. 164) defined heroes as "individuals who choose to take risks on behalf of one or more people, despite the possibility of dying or suffering serious physical consequences from these actions," going on to say: "It is the acceptance of risk to one's life that calls for valor or courage and thus transforms prosocial behavior into heroism." Others have expanded heroism beyond physical risk-taking (e.g., Franco et al., 2011; Smith et al., 2013). For instance, Jayawickreme and DiStefano (2012, p. 165) defined heroism as "an individual's commitment to a noble purpose, usually aimed at furthering the welfare of others, and involving the willingness to accept the consequences of achieving that purpose." Nevertheless, this definition may exclude many acts of heroism because it implies significant cognitive reflection that may be entirely lacking in many rapid reflex, impulsive acts of heroism (e.g., jumping in front of a moving vehicle to save a child).

Franco et al. (2011, p. 100) offered a definition that allows for both physical and non-physical risks, but also stated that "across all forms of heroics, the actor must transcend considerable fear to act decisively." This definition, although inclusive in many regards, would probably exclude heroic acts committed by psychopathic individuals given that most psychopathic individuals are characterized by unusually low levels of fear (Lykken, 1995). Furthermore, if heroism requires the presence of fear, which is somehow overcome, then many acts of impulsive, "no-time-to-think" heroism may not be counted as heroism.

Psychopathy and Heroism: Theoretical Implications and Research Findings

Although each of the aforementioned definitions offers a unique and perhaps valuable perspective, we argue that no one definition yet encompasses the vast variety of heroic behaviors. Several characteristics, however, are relatively common in research, each of which bears important implications for the role of psychopathy in heroic behavior. Here, we describe various characteristics that are particularly germane to the potential link between psychopathy and heroism. In turn, we discuss research findings relevant to these theoretical notions, primarily limiting our discussion of relevant research within the scope of impulsive versus deliberative heroism.

Impulsive versus Deliberative Heroism

Impulsive Heroism

Many heroic actions are impulsive, with individuals spending little or no time reflecting upon the risks and benefits of their actions. The teen who pulls a stranger from a burning car, the bystander who rushes in to disrupt a mugging, and the passerby who dashes into the street to save a child from being run over all perform their heroic actions with little time to contemplate what they are doing. For the most part, they simply act on impulse (Rand & Epstein, 2014).

The Carnegie Hero Fund Commission is an excellent resource for investigating extreme cases of non-deliberative heroism. To qualify as a Carnegie Hero Medal Recipient, a civilian must voluntarily risk his or her life to an extraordinary degree in an attempt to save the life of someone else (not including a child or someone else for whom they are responsible). The database of summaries on the Carnegie Hero Fund Commission website (www.carnegiehero.org) evidences a wide variety of daring rescue attempts, including some in which the rescuer perished. Studies utilizing transcripts of interviews with these Hero Medal Recipients indicate that the actions of these kinds of heroes were almost entirely rapid and intuitive, with little if any deliberation involved (Rand & Epstein, 2014). By and large, these heroes act first and think later.

The Carnegie Hero Fund Commission records indicate that men perform the overwhelming majority (82–91%) of these kinds of impulsive heroic acts (Becker & Eagly, 2004; Rand & Epstein, 2014), perhaps consistent with findings that males possess lower levels of trait fear and higher levels of trait impulsivity than do women (Cross, Copping, & Campbell, 2011). This male slant would probably be even more exaggerated if police officers, firefighters, armed services personnel, and other individuals could qualify based upon acts performed within the course of their professional duties. Interestingly, multiple studies of these kinds of heroic rescues have observed that the male heroes are disproportionately of lower socio-economic status (Johnson,

1996; Lyons, 2005). One hypothesis put forth to explain this finding is that lower SES men have less ability to attract women and are, therefore, more likely to take risks to gain the admiration of women (Lyons, 2005); alternatively, perhaps higher SES individuals have lower empathic or protective propensities (see Piff et al., 2010; Piff, 2014; Stellar, Manzo, Kraus, & Keltner, 2012).

Because the situation plays such a large role in the causes of impulsive heroic acts, and because extreme heroic acts are so uncommon, Zimbardo (2007, p. 487) argued that "heroic behavior is rare enough not to be readily predictable by any psychological assessments of personality." Because of this difficulty, some researchers have tried to assess this element of personality by measuring less extreme, more common impulsive acts of "everyday heroism," such as breaking up fights in public or assisting an injured stranger (Lilienfeld, 1998; Patrick et al., 2006; Sandoval et al., 2000; Smith et al., 2013). Although these kinds of acts may only involve relatively little risk to the helper, they are assumed to bear a family resemblance to more extreme, prototypical acts of heroism (Smith et al., 2013). Nevertheless, whether this presumption is true remains an open question. In this vein, we are only aware of one measure of "everyday heroism," the Activity Frequency Inventory (AFI; Lilienfeld, 1998), which has been used in a small number of studies to uncover correlates of heroism, particularly in relationship to psychopathy (Patrick et al., 2006; Smith et al., 2013). Troublingly, though, there is limited evidence indicating that self-report measures of these kinds of heroic acts may not be very predictive of actual heroic behaviors in experimental designs in which individuals are presented with an opportunity to act courageously (Baumert, Halmburger, & Schmitt, 2013).

Impulsive heroism may emerge from rapid empathic or protective impulses, with benefitting another as the main motivation. In contrast, impulsive heroism may also emerge from something more like an instinct to chase "glory" or gain social reputation. Individuals, men in particular, may be influenced by heroic impulses that have evolved as a way to signal positive qualities and gain social reputation or attractiveness. This hypothesis is consistent with "costly signaling theory," an influential evolutionary biology model of risky behavior (Grafen, 1990; Zahavi, 1975). According to this model, some risky behaviors can signal to potential mates that a male is highly fit from an evolutionary perspective. Consider male Arabian babbler birds, who compete to be the group sentinel, watching out for predatory birds from the treetops. Serving in this role makes the male sentinel the most likely to be eaten, but also earns him preferential access to female mates (Zahavi & Zahavi, 1997). Similarly, some human males may take what appear to be substantial risks, like competing in county rodeos, partly to signal to females that they are good evolutionary "bets." If so, some impulsive heroic acts, especially among males, may be aimed more at *appearing* good than actually *being* good, whether or not this kind of motivation is consciously in the mind of the hero. Costly acts, risky prosocial acts, or both, may, in this view, be connected to social dominance, attractiveness, social reputation, and so on.

Although research with humans is limited, some studies have provided suggestive evidence that brave acts of impulsive heroism are a high risk but high reward proposition, especially for men. For instance, multiple studies have indicated that people who engage in physically brave acts, particularly men, are more attractive to potential mates (Farthing, 2005; Kelly & Dunbar, 2001). Moreover, there is some indication that bravery increases men's attractiveness to prospective partners more than does global altruism, especially for short-term sexual relationships (Kelly & Dunbar, 2001). For example, Rusch, Leunissen, and van Vugt (2015) found that Second World War soldiers who were awarded the Medal of Honor sired more offspring than other Second World War veterans, even though the non-heroic veteran sample lived longer. In two other studies, Rusch and colleagues (2015) found that women rated hypothetical men who were war heroes as more attractive than other veterans (but there was no effect for men rating women who were war heroes).

In other words, bravery may in general be "sexier" than kindness, perhaps particularly in men. If these rewards are great enough, especially from a reproductive point of view, then this kind of costly signaling may help to explain at least some of the causal origins of impulsive heroism. Moreover, if the costly signaling theory of heroism reflects psychological reality, and if there are indeed major sex differences in this regard, this model could account for the massive gender disparity in impulsive heroism. If this perspective is close to the truth, it could help to explain how psychopathy could be positively associated with impulsive heroism, even though such acts may appear at first glance to be contrary to the psychopathic person's strong allegiance to self-interest.

Impulsive Heroism and Psychopathy

A small number of studies have examined the relationship between psychopathic traits and impulsive forms of heroism. In an initial analysis of 103 male inmates, Sandoval et al. (2000) observed no significant relationships between AFI scores (Activity Frequency Inventory, a self-report measure of "everyday" heroism; Lilienfeld, 1998) and the PPI or any of its subscales, suggesting that psychopathy was not associated with everyday acts of heroism, at least among prisoners. Nevertheless, these authors did not examine the PPI higher-order dimensions, which emerged in the research literature several years later. Remedying this omission, Patrick and colleagues (2006) found that the PPI-FD higher-order dimension was significantly positively correlated with scores on the AFI among prisoners, whereas PPI-SCI was significantly negatively related to this measure of lower-level everyday heroism.

In later studies, with two undergraduate samples, one community sample, and a sample of U.S. Presidents rated by biographers and other experts, Smith et al. (2013) explored the relationships between the PPI and PPI-R, one the one hand, and the AFI, on the other. In the first undergraduate sample ($n = 124$), PPI-FD was significantly associated with AFI scores, whereas PPI-SCI was not; PPI total scores were also positively correlated with the AFI. Similarly, in a community sample ($n = 457$), PPI-FD and total scores were significantly positively correlated with AFI scores whereas PPI-SCI scores were not. In this community sample, similar results were found for the triarchic model of psychopathy, with Boldness being positively correlated with everyday heroism, whereas Meanness and Disinhibition were not.

In another undergraduate sample ($n = 125$), however, only PPI-SCI was significantly positively associated with everyday heroism, whereas PPI total scores and PPI-FD scores were not (Smith et al., 2013). In this second undergraduate sample, AFI scores were positively correlated with delinquent behavior and with antisocial personality disorder features, which included a longstanding history of lying, cheating, and stealing. This second sample differed from the other two samples in being primarily male, whereas they were primarily female, although gender was not a statistically significant moderator in any of the three studies (Smith et al., 2013). In the presidential sample, which naturally suffered from reduced statistical power ($n = 42$), there was some evidence that PPI-FD, as derived from regression equations using the facets of the Revised NEO Personality Inventory (NEO PI-R; Costa & McCrae, 1992), was associated with a history of war heroism by presidents prior to their inaugurations (Smith et al., 2013); PPI-SCI was not significantly associated with war heroism.

Although the evidence from the studies presented by Smith and colleagues (2013) was mixed, the overall pattern of findings provides some support for the hypothesis that psychopathic traits are positively associated with impulsive heroism. At the subscale level, the PPI Social Potency scale (now termed Social Influence) was most consistently correlated with everyday heroism. The PPI Fearlessness subscale, in contrast, was less consistently related to impulsive heroism (Smith et al., 2013).

Although Lykken's (1982, 1995) hypothesis regarding the relationship between psychopathy and heroism was founded on the idea that both might reflect a heightened immunity to fear, these findings raise the intriguing possibility that the link between psychopathy and heroism may be less related to physical fearlessness and more related to social dominance. This kind of link would align well with the "competitive altruism" hypothesis of heroism put forth by McAndrew and Perilloux (2012), as it may be that social dominance or social potency are more related to costly signaling for social gain than are other traits, like fearlessness. Importantly, Patrick and colleagues (2006) did not find consistent evidence for the positive relation between everyday heroism and PPI-SCI, suggesting that the impulsive personality features tied to psychopathy were not consistently associated with heroic behavior among this prison sample.

Another, albeit more provisional, piece of evidence for the role of fearlessness in heroism derives from research on an extensively studied middle-aged woman, S.M. S.M., who lives in Iowa, suffers from a rare condition known as Urbach-Wiethe disease, which results in bilateral calcification of the amygdalae, symmetrical brain structures that play an integral role in fear processing, but likely the processing of emotions more broadly. S.M. is remarkably fearless; for example, she shows dramatically impaired recognition of facial expressions of fear and little or no emotional response to normally fear-provoking stimuli, such as snakes, spiders, horror films, and theme characters in haunted houses (e.g., Adolphs, Tranel, Damasio, & Damasio, 1995). Interestingly, S.M. has anecdotally been described as "heroic" (Feinstein, Adolphs, Damasio, & Tranel, 2011, p. 36).

To investigate this impression systematically, our laboratory, in conjunction with colleagues at the University of Iowa, recently administered a set of questionnaires to SM, including indices of fearlessness, psychopathy, and heroism, including the AFI (Lilienfeld, Tranel, Reber, Hamann, Sauvigne, Murphy, Smith, & Watts, in preparation). Consistent with previous reports, SM scored substantially (2 to 3 standard deviations) above the mean on measures of fearlessness, including PPI-FD, although she was not markedly elevated on other features of psychopathy. Consistent with the hypothesized link between fearlessness and heroism, SM scored approximately three standard deviations above the mean on the AFI, suggesting a strong tendency to engage in everyday acts of heroism compared with typical adults. Although based on a single case report and hence of unclear generalizability, these tantalizing findings are consistent with the possibility that fearlessness can predispose to heroism (e.g., Lykken, 1982). The limited research published regarding the relationship between psychopathy and impulsive heroism is mixed, but generally seems to point to the Boldness traits as primarily responsible for whatever relationships might exist, whereas the other dimensions of psychopathy, such as Disinhibition and Meanness, seem to be less related to heroism. The literature, though, remains limited, so there is substantial room for future research to explore these potential relationships.

Deliberative Heroism

Not all heroes engage in their good deeds impulsively. Many heroic actions involve substantial premeditation, sustained commitment, or both. Holocaust rescuers, who risked their own lives in order to hide and shelter Jews, are perhaps the most prominent exemplars of this kind of heroism (e.g., Midlarsky, Jones, & Corley, 2005; Suedfeld & de Best, 2008). Not only did they have time to consider their choice initially, they then remained committed to their decision over long periods of time, even years in some cases, despite obvious and serious personal risk. This kind of heroism has been on display many times since the Holocaust, such as in the case of Hutus who risked their lives to hide and shelter Tutsis during the Rwandan genocide. It is also manifested in a wide range of other situations: whistleblowing; some humanitarian work; various forms of civil disobedience (e.g., diner sit-ins during the American Civil Rights movement); and an expansive range of other acts of moral courage.

Deliberate Heroism and Psychopathy

Given that psychopathy is characterized not only by lack of empathy and moral conviction, but also by irresponsibility and unreliability (Cleckley, 1941/1988), sustained moral commitments of this variety would seem to be incompatible with psychopathic traits. To some extent, this kind of non-impulsive heroism can be observed in many other situations. Consider individuals who go into war zones, sites of infectious disease epidemics, and other dangerous environments to provide humanitarian aid to those who are suffering, in turn risking their lives for compassionate causes. Alternatively, consider individuals who donate their kidneys to complete strangers, accepting pain, fear of surgery and potential complications, and life interruption for the sake of helping someone in need.

In one study comparing a group of individuals who donated kidneys anonymously to strangers with a group of matched controls, Marsh and colleagues (2014) found that the kidney donors exhibited lower PPI-SCI scores than comparison participants (these low scores were particularly marked for the PPI Blame Externalization and Machiavellian Egocentricity subscales). Interestingly, the two groups were not significantly different on PPI-FD scores. They also observed that the kidney donors had significantly greater right amygdala volume and greater amygdala responsivity when viewing fearful faces, compared with controls (Marsh et al., 2014). This pattern is opposite to that typically observed in psychopathy, which is associated with reduced amygdala volume (Pardini, Raine, Erickson, & Loeber, 2014; Yang, Raine, Narr, Colletti, & Toga, 2009) and reduced amygdala responsivity when viewing fearful faces (Marsh & Blair, 2008). The authors hypothesized that extraordinary altruists and psychopaths may lie on opposite ends of an empathic caring continuum, but noted that "extraordinary altruism may represent the inverse of only *some* components of psychopathy, but not other components such as social dominance or impulsivity" (Marsh et al., 2014, p. 15,039, emphasis added). Many individuals willingly risk pain, sickness, or injury to presumably follow the call of compassion, but highly psychopathic individuals are unlikely to be of this ilk.

The risks involved in deliberative heroism need not be physical. This kind of heroism can emerge in the context of other forms of risk, such as social (e.g., losing friends) or financial (e.g., being fired). The fraternity brother who stands up to condemn his peers' hazing rituals, the employee who takes the lonely stand of calling out her superiors for unethical behavior, the child who stands up in defense of her unpopular and bullied classmate, and the honest cop who crosses the "thin blue line" to expose corruption among his colleagues, all perform acts of deliberative heroism. To some extent, these acts bear a family resemblance to the actions of Holocaust rescuers and other highly risky manifestations of deliberate heroism.

Difficult conceptual questions arise in cases in which an individual makes a deliberate choice to put himself or herself in a vocational position of heightened physical risk, ostensibly to serve a greater good. For instance, how should pursuing a career as a police officer or firefighter be understood from a scientific view of heroism? What about joining the Navy SEALs or the Secret Service? To some extent, the answer probably relates to individuals' motivations and to their actions in the line of duty, rather than to merely the professional decision itself.

The findings of Falkenbach and Tsoukalas (2011) are of some relevance in this regard. They compared the PPI scores of criminal offenders with those of police officers, firefighters, and other individuals who are involved in high-risk, prosocial occupations. They observed that the professional hero group obtained higher PPI-FD and PPI-CH scores. In other words, in this sample, police officers exhibited higher boldness traits and, perhaps surprisingly, higher coldheartedness traits, than criminal offenders. Although the causal arrows between psychopathic traits and serving as a police officer are incapable of being ascertained, such findings may indicate that some forms of deliberative heroism are positively associated with some psychopathic traits, such as social dominance and callousness. If so, such relationships may exist primarily with regard to forms of deliberative heroism that are socially acclaimed, not to deliberatively heroic acts that put individuals at risk of being rejected by friends, family, coworkers, and so on.

At least some forms of deliberative heroism are strongly related to, and perhaps synonymous with, what has been referred to as "moral courage." Authors have defined "moral courage" in a number of similar ways, such as "the ability to use inner principles to do what is good for others, regardless of threat to self, as a matter of practice" (Sekerka & Bagozzi, 2007, p. 135); "speaking up or taking on behalf of what one believes is right...in situations that may feel social or physically risky or unsafe" (Bronstein et al., 2007, pp. 661–662); and "facing the particular fears and dangers arising from the possibility that one will be punished (broadly speaking) for taking a moral stand" (Pianalto, 2012, p. 167). Although these definitions have much in common, they frequently differ in whether "moral courage" must take place in the face of risks from other people (e.g., being fired, being executed) or whether the risks can be non-social (e.g., contracting Ebola). As is the case with research regarding heroism, an unusually small amount of research attention has been accorded to "moral courage" (Osswald et al., 2010). One finding that has emerged in several studies, however, is that moral courage may be associated with heightened self-esteem or self-assurance (e.g., Bronstein et al., 2007), offering a potential linkage to the social dominance sometimes observed in psychopathy.

Just as impulsive heroism may be capable of being assessed using less extreme forms of impulsive heroism, by means of the AFI (Lilienfeld, 1998), deliberative heroism may similarly be measured by using less extreme, more common forms of such behaviors. For instance, Bronstein and colleagues' Moral Courage Scale (2007) includes items such as "If I see someone being picked on or bullied, I try to stop it," "I try to get others involved in thinking and taking action on important issues," and "If my friends all think something is okay to do, I go along with it, even if I'm not sure it's the right thing." Another example is the Professional Moral Courage Scale by Sekerka, Bagozzi, and Charnigo (2009), intended for use in workplace settings, which includes items such as "I hold my ground on moral matters, even if there are opposing social pressures," "I act morally even if it puts me in an uncomfortable position with my superiors," and "When I encounter an ethical challenge I take it on with moral action, regardless of how it may pose a negative impact on how others see me." Nevertheless, neither of these moral courage scales appears to have received extensive construct validation.

Other scales used in altruism research may be valuable for exploring deliberative heroism, even if they do not relate as directly to courage. For instance, both the Prosocial Moral Reasoning scale (Carlo, Eisenberg, & Knight, 1992), which is appropriate for use with children and adolescents, and the Altruistic Moral Judgment Scale (Midlarsky et al., 1999) assess the extent to which individuals approach decisions whereby they can benefit someone else, but only at a cost to their own self-interests. These latter measures may be particularly helpful in accounting for other-serving and self-serving motivations in regard to deliberative heroism.

Where deliberative heroism is driven by empathic concern for the suffering or needs of others, traits such as coldheartedness and low empathy, which are centrally relevant to psychopathy, are probably negatively correlated with such acts. Although heroism can sometimes be propelled by compassion, it may also be propelled by sensitivity to justice and fairness, disdain for corruption, love for equality or liberty, or any number of other moral principles, as well as other emotional impulses such as anger and resistance to authority. Although psychopathic individuals tend to have weaker moral convictions, which would generally make them poor candidates for being moral courage exemplars, psychopathic traits such as rebellious nonconformity and distrustful hostility might actually make them more likely to engage in deliberatively heroic acts in some contexts. Interestingly, early work using bystander intervention paradigms revealed that nontraditionalism was a predictor of willingness to intervene in emergences (Latané & Darley, 1970). Psychopathic individuals are less easily cowed and more willing to take on challenges, which might lead them to be willing to resist authority in some positive ways, just as it makes them more likely to resist in negative ways.

When deliberative heroism is driven primarily by dominance, reputation, or attractiveness motivations, we could hypothesize that certain psychopathic traits, especially boldness, would be positively correlated with heroism. As noted earlier, although, disentangling these motivations is exceedingly difficult.

Other Characteristics

Risk

Despite continued controversy regarding the definition of heroism, it seems clear that an element of *risk*, or the presence of bravery or courage, is part of what separates heroism from other forms of altruism, and heroes from leaders and role models, in the perceptions of lay observers (Kinsella, Ritchie, & Igou, 2015; Rankin & Eagly, 2008). Consistent with this view, researchers tend to conceptualize heroism in terms of risk or self-sacrifice (e.g., Becker & Eagly, 2004; Franco et al., 2011). In other words, heroism is not merely doing great good for others, it is doing good when it requires sacrificing, or at least risking, the self-interests of the hero. Given that psychopathy is marked by high levels of egocentricity (Hare, 1993), individuals with marked levels of psychopathic traits would presumably be less willing to act altruistically when doing so conflicts with their self-interests.

Empathic and/or moral value motivations

Some have also suggested that motivation, though difficult to discern, is important in defining heroism (Jayawickreme & DiStefano, 2012). Because deliberative heroism appears to encompass a much broader range of potential acts and decisions, the motivations at play are likely to be much more diverse. On a general level, however, different forms might be susceptible to being distinguished by empathic concern. For instance, Holocaust rescuers, individuals who donate kidneys to strangers, and children who stand up for bullied classmates, may generally be moved to act, at least to some extent, by empathic concern. Other kinds of deliberative heroism, such as when a cop blows the whistle on corruption in the police force, may be less motivated by empathy and more motivated by other principles and emotions, such as justice sensitivity and moral outrage.

Prosocial acts can, of course, be motivated by empathy and attachment to principles and values (Batson et al., 1988). This kind of behavior may arise from a strong empathic impulse in some cases, whereby the hero abruptly resonates with another who is under threat. Alternatively, this kind of behavior may also stem from instincts evolved from kin altruism or reciprocal altruism (Johnson, 1996). In other words, heroism may emerge from an empathic or moral instinct, aimed primarily at benefiting others or serving values that one holds dear.

Research regarding empathy-related deliberative heroism provides limited, but revealing, trait-level information. In a study comparing Holocaust rescuers with comparison groups of Holocaust bystanders (neighbors of rescuers who did not engage in rescue activities) and prewar immigrants, Midlarsky, Jones, and Corley (2005) found that these rescuers were particularly characterized by extremely high levels of altruistic moral reasoning and feelings of social responsibility, but also by heightened empathy and propensity to risk-taking. Other studies have similarly observed that Holocaust rescuers are characterized by heightened empathy and strong attachments to moral principles (London, 1970; Oliner & Oliner, 1988; Suedfeld & de Best, 2008; also see Fagin-Jones & Midlarsky, 2007). Another study assessing moral courage in a large sample of German students, with a focus on discrimination, revealed that moral courage was positively correlated with empathic concern and negatively correlated with social dominance orientation (Labuhn, Wagner, van Dick, & Christ, 2004); this trait profile would appear to be largely inconsistent with psychopathy.

In a slightly different take, a longitudinal study with adolescents found that although low-cost prosocial behaviors (e.g., "I really enjoy doing small favors for people I do not know") were predicted by empathic concern, higher-cost prosocial behaviors (e.g., "I volunteer in programs to help others in need, like food or clothes drives.") were more predicted by the endorsement strength of moral values (Padilla-Walker & Fraser, 2014). Similarly, in another study, Niesta Kayser and colleagues (2010) found that willingness to sign a public petition, with full name and address included, condemning the existence of a German far-right political party was not significantly associated with empathic concern, but was substantially positively correlated with the strength of individuals' moral principles and their willingness to resist group pressure and engage in civil disobedience. In sum, empathy-related heroism may be motivated not only by empathy, but by the degree to which individuals hold strongly internalized moral values and principles, and are willing to resist group pressure.

Although psychopathic traits are associated with increased willingness to take risks, the overall characteristics of these kinds of heroic rescuers are largely incompatible with psychopathic traits. Indeed, if heroic acts require *genuine caring or moral intent*, then psychopathic traits would be nearly guaranteed to run counter to heroism given psychopathic individuals' deficits in empathy and conscience. As Hare (1993, p. 26) noted, "psychopaths are intraspecies predators who use charm, manipulation, intimidation, and violence to control others and to satisfy their own selfish needs. Lacking in conscience and in feelings for others, they cold-bloodedly take what they want and do as they please, violating social norms and expectations without the slightest sense of guilt and regret." The unusually low empathy of psychopathic individuals would seem to all but guarantee that they would not risk or sacrifice themselves out of loving kindness for others.

It is, however, theoretically possible for an individual to be largely devoid of empathy and deep emotions, yet have a *heightened moral "code"* of some kind, even if that code is unconventional. Numerous studies have indicated, however, that psychopathy is associated with generalized reductions in morality (Aharoni, Antonenko, & Kiehl, 2011; Glenn et al., 2009; Dolan & Fullam, 2010), and also with a decreased importance of moral concerns in their self-concept (Glenn et al., 2010). More specifically, Aharoni and colleagues (2011) found that psychopathy was significantly negatively associated with two domains of morality, preventing harm and desiring fairness. Importantly, however, psychopathy was not significantly associated with three other types of morality: respect for authority, ingroup loyalty, and purity/sanctity, suggesting that psychopathy is not associated with more agentic or deontological (or emotional) forms of morality. Hence, the results from these studies suggest that psychopathy is probably not correlated with heroism stemming from strong moral convictions.

Self-enhancement

Heroism can also, however, be motivated by a desire to enhance one's reputation or attractiveness among others, which may be particularly relevant to psychopathy. From this theoretical perspective, many apparently altruistic acts, risky or otherwise, can be understood as competitive rather than selfless, with individuals jockeying to attain a heightened reputation or standing among others. This behavior is sometimes referred to "competitive altruism" (Roberts, 1998) or generalized altruism (Trivers, 1971). This competitive, self-serving motivation may extend beyond common forms of altruism and intrude into heroism, as some theorists argue that heroic acts may often emerge as high-risk/high-reward attempts to gain reputation and resources, serving as costly signaling behaviors that can elevate the individual above competing others (McAndrew & Perilloux, 2012). In other words, even when it may appear that the individual is clearly sacrificing his or her self-interests, rather than engaging in a low-cost altruistic act, the behavior might still be motivated, whether consciously realized or not, by a desire to appear "high quality" in the view of others. Along these lines, a number of studies have indicated that willingness to help others, perhaps particularly in men, is greater when the helping act is witnessed by others, when there is an audience for one's goodness (for a meta-analytic review, see Eagly & Crowley, 1986; for an example, see Bereczkei, Birkas, & Kerekes, 2010), whereas other studies have pointed to some prosocial acts as driven by egoistic motivations for status, reputation, attractiveness, and the like (Griskevicius et al., 2007; Griskevicius, Tybur, den Bergh, 2010), again perhaps especially for men (e.g., Barclay, 2010).

A desire for social reputation can even motivate heroism in cases in which the individual is taking a stance that is rejected by most of society, so long as it improves one's social standing within a subgroup of people. For instance, a man may engage in radical leftist protest activities, risking arrest and going against the norms of the broader society, while being motivated by a desire to win allies and romantic admirers among his fellow radical leftists. Within any subgroup, there may exist a hierarchy of power or admiration, and there will often be individuals seeking to climb in status among the subgroup.

Relatedly, a number of studies have found that, among some individuals, high levels of prosocial behavior co-exist alongside high levels of aggressiveness (e.g., McGinley & Carlo, 2007), and another study reviewed earlier found that heroism was positively associated with antisocial behaviors in two nonclinical samples (Smith et al., 2013). In the theoretical framework presented by Hawley (1999), both prosocial and antisocial/coercive acts can be understood as strategies to gain social dominance and control relative to others. Consistent with this position, Hawley and colleagues have repeatedly observed that many of the most socially dominant individuals in groups tend to engage in high levels of prosocial and coercive behaviors (Hawley, Little, & Pasupathi, 2002; Hawley, Little, & Card, 2007, 2008; Hawley & Geldhof, 2012). Engaging in prosocial actions does not necessarily mean that one is kind-hearted; some individuals do good for others primarily to make themselves look good in the eyes of others, or to otherwise gain social power.

If some acts of heroism entail possible social payoffs, psychopathy may actually be positively associated with them in some cases. Perhaps psychopathic heroism may be due more to the social benefits that can accrue from such acts than to genuine caring or a strong moral compass. For instance, multiple studies have indicated that Machiavellian traits, which include a ruthless and cynical willingness to take advantage of others, are associated with heightened willingness to engage in prosocial behavior in social contexts in which it will be witnessed or rewarded, as compared with situations in which it will be anonymous or less rewarded (Bereczkei et al., 2010; Berger & Palacios, 2014); that is when there is an advantage to engage in prosocial behavior instrumentally. Interestingly, Machiavellian traits are moderately correlated with psychopathy (McHoskey, Worzel, & Szyvarto, 1998), and the two constructs, along with narcissism, comprise what some personality researchers term the "Dark Triad" (Paulhus & Williams, 2002). Of particular importance to the relationship between psychopathy and heroism, White (2014) observed that psychopathic traits and low levels of empathy were substantially positively correlated with the motivation to engage in publicly observable prosocial acts, but negatively correlated with the motivation to engage in prosocial acts that are not publicly observed or which do not carry any benefit to them.

These studies support the possibility that heroic and other altruistic acts may actually be positively correlated with psychopathy, so long as there is a potential payoff for the psychopathic person. From the standpoint of the outside observer, it may be nearly impossible to know what kinds of motivations lead particular individuals to engage in specific altruistic or heroic acts. Psychopathic individuals, who tend to be manipulative and cunning, may rely on this lack of transparency to accrue the self-serving benefits of seemingly altruistic behaviors. Moreover, many or most heroic acts may be multiply determined; they may be a reflection of a person's moral conviction, desire to be admired, empathy, split-second protective impulses, or some combination thereof.

Conclusions and Future Directions

Although the research is preliminary and somewhat mixed, it suggests that certain psychopathic traits, especially those relevant to boldness, are potentially relevant to impulsive heroism. In contrast, evidence for the role of other higher-order dimensions of psychopathy (e.g., disinhibition and meanness) is inconsistent. Further research is needed to elucidate these potential connections.

For instance, it would be valuable to examine psychopathic traits in samples of impulsive heroes, such as Carnegie Hero Medalists, in comparison with non-heroic samples. Although it is possible, as suggested by Zimbardo (2007), that these kinds of acts are primarily situational rather than dispositional in origin, certain personality differences may help to explain why some people engage in sensational acts of impulsive heroism whereas others do not. We hypothesize that the former individuals would be elevated on boldness traits, similar to what was found with everyday heroism in Smith and colleagues (2013) and Patrick and colleagues (2006), and perhaps also higher levels of disinhibition, lower levels of meanness, or both.

Virtually no research has explored the relationship between psychopathy and deliberative heroism. As a starting point, it would be informative to explore the relationships between measures of psychopathy and moral courage, either using one of the currently available questionnaires or a better-developed new self-report measure. Extending such inquiry to diverse samples of deliberative heroes, such as humanitarian aid workers in conflict zone, would be revealing.

Beyond that, it would also be valuable to further explore potential connections between psychopathic traits and heroic vocations, such as firefighting and law enforcement. Ideally, such research would measure psychopathic traits among individuals who are entering such occupations, rather than among individuals who have already served for long periods of time, to shed light on temporal directionality. It would also be valuable to measure hypothetical interest in these vocations among students and compare these levels of interest among individuals with differing levels of psychopathic traits.

One of the most important areas of future research regarding psychopathy and all forms of heroism involves finding ways to disentangle the multifaceted motivations underlying heroic acts. To some extent, this goal could be accomplished by including measures of genuine altruism, such as the Prosocial Moral Reasoning scale (Carlo, Eisenberg, & Knight, 1992) and the Altruistic Moral Judgment Scale (Midlarsky et al., 1999), which measure the degree to which people are willing to engage in altruistic acts even when the negative costs to the self are clear.

In sum, Lykken's (1995, p. 118) influential hypothesis that heroes and psychopaths are "twigs on the same genetic branch" continues to be intriguing, but it remains a conjecture in need of further corroboration. This paucity of corroboration is more a matter of absence of evidence than of evidence of absence, as much of the necessary research remains to be conducted. Given the substantial heterogeneity of both psychopathy and heroism, however, it seems exceedingly unlikely that a better understanding of psychopathy alone will be sufficient to unlock the longstanding mystery of why certain individuals behavior heroically. Clearly, not all psychopathic individuals are heroic, and many exceedingly heroic individuals are not remotely psychopathic. At the same time, if the admittedly modest amount of research on this provocative linkage is any guide, it seems plausible that certain features of psychopathy, especially those relevant to social potency, fearlessness, and perhaps disinhibition, play a causal role in at least certain forms of heroism. If so, psychopathy may turn out to be one small but nonetheless critical piece in the large and complex jigsaw puzzle of heroism. The construct of psychopathy has the potential to powerfully inform heroism research, illuminating both the bright and dark sides of various manifestations of heroism.

References

Adolphs, R., Tranel, D., Damasio, H., & Damasio, A. R. (1995). Fear and the human amygdala. *The Journal of Neuroscience, 15,* 5879–5891.

Aharoni, E., Antonenko, O., & Kiehl, K. A. (2011). Disparities in the moral intuitions of criminal offenders: The role of psychopathy. *Journal of Research in Personality, 45*(3), 322–327.

Allison, S. T., & Goethals, G. R. (2011). *Heroes: What they do and why we need them.* New York: Oxford University Press.

Babiak, P., & Hare, R. D. (2006). *Snakes in suits: When psychopaths go to work.* New York: Regan Books.

Babiak, P., Neumann, C. S., & Hare, R. D. (2010). Corporate psychopathy: Talking the walk. *Behavioral Sciences & the Law, 28*(2), 174–193.

Barclay, P. (2010). Altruism as a courtship display: Some effects of third party generosity on audience perceptions. *British Journal of Psychology, 101*(1), 123–135.

Batson, C. D., Dyck, J. L., Brandt, J. R., Batson, J. G., Powell, A. L., McMaster, M. R., & Griffitt, C. (1988). Five studies testing two new egoistic alternatives to the empathy-altruism hypothesis. *Journal of Personality and Social Psychology, 55*(1), 52.

Baumert, A., Halmburger, A., & Schmitt, M. (2013). Interventions against norm violations: Dispositional determinants of self-reported and real moral courage. *Personality and Social Psychology Bulletin, 39*(8), 1053–1068.

Becker, S. W., & Eagly, A. H. (2004). The heroism of women and men. *American Psychologist, 59,* 163–178.

Benning, S. D., Patrick, C. J., Hicks, B. M., Blonigen, D. M., & Krueger, R. F. (2003). Factor structure of the psychopathic personality inventory: Validity and implications for clinical assessment. *Psychological Assessment, 15*(3), 340–350.

Benning, S. D., Patrick, C. J., Blonigen, D. M., Hicks, B. M., & Iacono, W. G. (2005). Estimating facets of psychopathy from normal personality traits: A step toward community epidemiological investigations. *Assessment, 12*(1), 3–18.

Bereczkei, T., Birkas, B., & Kerekes, Z. (2010). The presence of others, prosocial traits, Machiavellianism: A personality× situation approach. *Social Psychology, 41*(4), 238–245.

Berger, C., & Palacios, D. (2014). Associations between prosocial behavior, Machiavellianism, and social status: Effects of peer norms and classroom social contexts. *Journal of Latino/Latin American Studies, 6*(1), 19–30.

Book, A., Methot, T., Gauthier, N., Hosker-Field, A., Forth, A., Quinsey, V., & Molnar, D. (2014). The mask of sanity revisited: Psychopathic traits and affective mimicry. *Evolutionary Psychological Science, 1*(2), 91–102.

Bronstein, P., Fox, B. J., Kamon, J. L., & Knolls, M. L. (2007). Parenting and gender as predictors of moral courage in late adolescence: A longitudinal study. *Sex Roles, 56*(9–10), 661–674.

Carlo, G., Eisenberg, N., & Knight, G. P. (1992). An objective measure of adolescents' prosocial moral reasoning. *Journal of Research on Adolescence, 2*(4), 331–349.

Cleckley, H. (1941/1988). *The mask of sanity: An attempt to clarify some issues about the so called psychopathic personality* (5th ed.). St. Louis, MO: Mosby.

Costa, P. T., & McCrae, R. R. (1992). Normal personality assessment in clinical practice: The NEO Personality Inventory. *Psychological Assessment, 4*(1), 5.

Cross, C. P., Copping, L. T., & Campbell, A. (2011). Sex differences in impulsivity: a meta-analysis. *Psychological Bulletin, 137*(1), 97–130.

Derefinko, K. J. (in press). Psychopathy and low anxiety: Meta analytic evidence for the absence of inhibition, not affect. *Journal of Personality.*

Dolan, M. C., & Fullam, R. S. (2010). Moral/conventional transgression distinction and psychopathy in conduct disordered adolescent offenders. *Personality and Individual Differences, 49*(8), 995–1000.

Drislane, L. E., Patrick, C. J., & Arsal, G. (2014). Clarifying the content coverage of differing psychopathy inventories through reference to the Triarchic Psychopathy Measure. *Psychological Assessment, 26*(2), 350–362.

Dutton, K., & McNab, A. *The good psychopath's guide to success: How to use your inner psychopath to get the most out of life.* London: Transworld Publishers.

Eagly, A. H., & Crowley, M. (1986). Gender and helping behavior: A meta-analytic review of the social psychological literature. *Psychological Bulletin, 100*(3), 283.

Edens, J. F., Marcus, D. K., Lilienfeld, S. O., & Poythress, N. G. (2006). Psychopathic, not psychopath: Taxometric evidence for the dimensional structure of psychopathy. *Journal of Abnormal Psychology, 115,* 131–144.

Fagin-Jones, S., & Midlarsky, E. (2007). Courageous altruism: Personal and situational correlates of rescue during the Holocaust. *The Journal of Positive Psychology, 2*(2), 136–147.

Falkenbach, D., & Tsoukalas, M. (2011). Can adaptive traits be observed in hero populations? Presented as a poster at the 4th Biennial Meeting of the Society for the Scientific Study of Psychopathy, May 19–21, Montreal, Canada.

Farthing, G. W. (2005). Attitudes toward heroic and nonheroic physical risk takers as mates and as friends. *Evolution and Human Behavior*, 26(2), 171–185.

Feinstein, J. S., Adolphs, R., Damasio, A., & Tranel, D. (2011). The human amygdala and the induction and experience of fear. *Current Biology*, 21, 34–38.

Franco, Z., Blau, K., & Zimbardo, P. (2011). Heroism: A conceptual analysis and differentiation between heroic action and altruism. *Review of General Psychology*, 15, 99–113.

Gill, C. (1996). *Personality in Greek epic, tragedy and philosophy: The self in dialogue*. Oxford: Clarendon Press.

Glenn, A. L., Iyer, R., Graham, J., Koleva, S., & Haidt, J. (2009). Are all types of morality compromised in psychopathy? *Journal of Personality Disorders*, 23(4), 384–398.

Glenn, A. L., Koleva, S., Iyer, R., Graham, J., & Ditto, P. H. (2010). Moral identity in psychopathy. *Judgment and Decision*, 5(7), 497–505.

Grafen, A. (1990). Biological signals as handicaps. *Journal of Theoretical Biology*, 144(4), 517–546.

Griskevicius, V., Tybur, J. M., Sundie, J. M., Cialdini, R. B., Miller, G. F., & Kenrick, D. T. (2007). Blatant benevolence and conspicuous consumption: When romantic motives elicit strategic costly signals. *Journal of Personality and Social Psychology*, 93(1), 85.

Griskevicius, V., Tybur, J. M., & Van den Bergh, B. (2010). Going green to be seen: Status, reputation, and conspicuous conservation. *Journal of Personality and Social Psychology*, 98(3), 392.

Guay, J. P., Ruscio, J., Knight, R. A., & Hare, R. D. (2007). A taxometric analysis of the latent structure of psychopathy: Evidence for dimensionality. *Journal of Abnormal Psychology*, 116(4), 701.

Hall, J. R., & Benning, S. D. (2006). The "successful" psychopath. In C. J. Patrick (ed.), *Handbook of Psychopathy* (pp. 459–475). New York: Guilford Press.

Hare, R. D. (1991/2003). *The Hare Psychopathy Checklist–revised*. Toronto: Multi-Health Systems.

Hare, R. D. (1993). *Without conscience: The disturbing world of the psychopaths among us*. New York: Simon & Schuster.

Hare, R. D., & Neumann, C. S. (2008). Psychopathy as a clinical and empirical construct. *Annual Review of Clinical Psychology*, 4, 217–246.

Hawley, P. H. (1999). The ontogenesis of social dominance: A strategy-based evolutionary perspective. *Developmental Review*, 19(1), 97–132.

Hawley, P. H., & Geldhof, G. J. (2012). Preschoolers' social dominance, moral cognition, and moral behavior: An evolutionary perspective. *Journal of Experimental Child Psychology*, 112(1), 18–35.

Hawley, P. H., Little, T. D., & Card, N. A. (2007). The allure of a mean friend: Relationship quality and processes of aggressive adolescents with prosocial skills. *International Journal of Behavioral Development*, 31(2), 170–180.

Hawley, P. H., Little, T. D., & Card, N. A. (2008). The myth of the alpha male: A new look at dominance-related beliefs and behaviors among adolescent males and females. *International Journal of Behavioral Development*, 32(1), 76–88.

Hawley, P. H., Little, T. D., & Pasupathi, M. (2002). Winning friends and influencing peers: Strategies of peer influence in late childhood. *International Journal of Behavioral Development*, 26(5), 466–474.

Ishikawa, S. S., Raine, A., Lencz, T., Bihrle, S., & Lacasse, L. (2001). Autonomic stress reactivity and executive functions in successful and unsuccessful criminal psychopaths from the community. *Journal of Abnormal Psychology*, 110, 423–432.

Jayawickreme, E., & DiStefano, P. (2012). How can we study heroism? Integrating persons, situations and communities. *Political Psychology*, 33, 165–178.

Johnson, R. C. (1996). Attributes of Carnegie medalists performing acts of heroism and of the recipients of these acts. *Ethology and Sociobiology*, 17, 355–362.

Kelly, S., & Dunbar, R. I. (2001). Who dares, wins. *Human Nature*, 12(2), 89–105.

Kinsella, E. L., Ritchie, T. D., & Igou, E. R. (2015). Zeroing in on heroes: A prototype analysis of hero features. *Journal of Personality and Social Psychology*, 108(1), 114.

Kyle, C., McEwen, S., & DeFelice, J. (2012). *American sniper: The autobiography of the most lethal sniper in U.S. Military History*. New York: William Morrow.

Labuhn, A. S., Wagner, U., van Dick, R., & Christ, O. (2004). Determinants of civil courage: Results of a questionnaire study. *Zeitschrift fur Sozialpsychologie*, 35(2), 93–102.

Latané, B., & Darley, J. M. (1970). *The unresponsive bystander: Why doesn't he help?* New York: Appleton-Century-Crofts.

Levenson, M. R., Kiehl, K. A., & Fitzpatrick, C. M. (1995). Assessing psychopathic attributes in a non-institutionalized population. *Journal of Personality and Social Psychology*, 68, 151–158.

Lilienfeld, S. O. (1994). Conceptual problems in the assessment of psychopathy. *Clinical Psychology Review*, 14, 17–38.

Lilienfeld, S. O. (1998). Fearlessness, antisocial behavior, and heroism. Unpublished manuscript.

Lilienfeld, S. O., & Andrews, B. P. (1996). Development and preliminary validation of a self-report measure of psychopathic personality traits in noncriminal population. *Journal of Personality Assessment*, 66(3), 488–524.

Lilienfeld, S.O, Smith, S. F. Sauvigne, K., Patrick, C. J., Drislane, L., Latzman, R. L., & Krueger, R. (in press). Is boldness relevant to psychopathic personality? A meta-analytic review of non-PCL-based psychopathy measures. *Psychological Assessment*.

Lilienfeld, S.O., Tranel, D., Reber, J., Hamann, S., Sauvigne, K. C., Murphy, B. A., Smith, S. F., & Watts, A. L (in preparation). Fearlessness, psychopathy, and heroism: A single-case report of a patient with bilateral amygdala damage.

Lilienfeld, S. O., Watts, A. L., & Smith, S. F. (2015). Successful psychopathy: A scientific status report. *Current Directions in Psychological Science*, 24(4), 298–303.

Lilienfeld, S. O., Watts, A. L., Smith, S. F., Berg, J. M., & Latzman, R. D. (in press). Psychopathy deconstructed and reconstructed: Identifying and assembling the Personality building blocks of Cleckley's chimera. *Journal of personality*.

Lilienfeld, S. O., Widows, M. R., & Staff, P. A. R. (2005). Psychopathic Personality Inventory TM—revised. *Social Influence (SOI)*, 61(65), 97.

London, P. (1970). The rescuers: Motivational hypotheses about Christians who saved Jews from the Nazis. In J. Macaulay & L. Berkowitz (eds), *Altruism and helping behavior* (pp. 241–250). New York: Academic Press.

Lykken, D.T. (1957). A study of anxiety in the sociopathic personality. *Journal of Abnormal and Social Psychology*, 55(1), 6–10.

Lykken, D. T. (1982). Fearlessness: Its carefree charm and deadly risks. *Psychology Today* (September), 20–28.

Lykken, D. T. (1995). *The antisocial personalities*. Hove: Psychology Press.

Lykken, D. T. (1996). Psychopathy, sociopathy, and crime. *Society*, 34, 29–38.

Lynam, D. R., Gaughan, E. T., Miller, J. D., Miller, D. J., Mullins-Sweatt, S., & Widiger, T. A. (2011). Assessing the basic traits associated with psychopathy: Development and validation of the Elemental Psychopathy Assessment. *Psychological Assessment*, 23, 108–124.

Lynam, D. R., Sherman, E. D., Samuel, D., Miller, J. D., Few, L. R., & Widiger, T. A. (2013). Development of a short form of the Elemental Psychopathy Assessment. *Assessment*, 20, 659–669.

Lyons, M. T. (2005). Who are the heroes? Characteristics of people who rescue others. *Journal of Cultural and Evolutionary Psychology*, 3(3–4), 245–254.

Marsh, A. A., & Blair, R. J. R. (2008). Deficits in facial affect recognition among antisocial populations: a meta-analysis. *Neuroscience & Biobehavioral Reviews*, 32(3), 454–465.

Marsh, A. A., Stoycos, S. A., Brethel-Haurwitz, K. M., Robinson, P., VanMeter, J. W., & Cardinale, E. M. (2014). Neural and cognitive characteristics of extraordinary altruists. *Proceedings of the National Academy of Sciences*, 111(42), 15,036–15,041.

McAndrew, F., & Perilloux, C. (2012). The selfish hero: A study of the individual benefits of self-sacrificial behavior. *Psychological Reports: Mental & Physical Health*, 111, 27–43.

McGinley, M., & Carlo, G. (2007). Two sides of the same coin? The relations between prosocial and physically aggressive behaviors. *Journal of Youth and Adolescence*, 36(3), 337–349.

McHoskey, J. W., Worzel, W., & Szyarto, C. (1998). Machiavellianism and psychopathy. *Journal of Personality and Social Psychology*, 74(1), 192.

Merz, T. (2014). Why psychopaths are more successful. *The Telegraph* (May 7). Retrieved from www.telegraph.co.uk/men/thinking-man/10788449/Why-psychopaths-are-more-successful.html.

Midlarsky, E., Fagin Jones, S., & Corley, R. P. (2005). Personality correlates of heroic rescue during the Holocaust. *Journal of Personality*, 73(4), 907–934.

Midlarsky, E., Kahana, E., Corley, R., Nemeroff, R., & Schonbar, R. (1999). Altruistic moral judgment among older adults. *International Journal of Aging and Human Development*, 49, 39–53.

Mullins-Sweatt, S. N., Glover, N. G., Derefinko, K. J., Miller, J. D., & Widiger, T. A. (2010). The search for the successful psychopath. *Journal of Research in Personality*, 44, 554–558.

Neumann, C. S., Johansson, P. T., & Hare, R. D. (2013). The Psychopathy Checklist—Revised (PCL-R), low anxiety, and fearlessness: A structural equation modeling analysis. *Personality Disorders*, 4, 129–137.

Niesta Kayser, D., Greitemeyer, T., Fischer, P., & Frey, D. (2010). Why mood affects help giving, but not moral courage: comparing two types of prosocial behaviour. *European Journal of Social Psychology*, 40(7), 1136–1157.

Oliner, S. P., & Oliner, P. M. (1988). *The altruistic personality: Rescuers of Jews in Nazi Europe*. New York: Free Press.

Osswald, S., Greitemeyer, T., Fischer, P., & Frey, D. (2010). What is moral courage? Definition, explication, and classification of a complex construct. In C. L. S. Pury & S. J. Lopez (eds), *The psychology of courage: Modern research on an ancient virtue* (pp. 149–164). Washington, DC: APA.

Padilla-Walker, L. M., & Fraser, A. M. (2014). How much is it going to cost me? Bidirectional relations between adolescents' moral personality and prosocial behavior. *Journal of Adolescence, 37*(7), 993–1001.

Pardini, D. A., Raine, A., Erickson, K., & Loeber, R. (2014). Lower amygdala volume in men is associated with childhood aggression, early psychopathic traits, and future violence. *Biological Psychiatry, 75*(1), 73–80.

Patrick C.J. (2010). Triarchic Psychopathy Measure (TriPM). Retrieved April 9, from www.phenxtoolkit.org/index.php?pageLink=browse.protocoldetails&id=121601.

Patrick, C. J., & Drislane, L. E. (in press). Triarchic model of psychopathy: Origins, operationalizations, and observed linkages with personality and general psychopathology. *Journal of Personality*.

Patrick, C.J., Bradley, M.M., and Lang, P.J. (1993). Emotion in the criminal psychopath: Startle reflex modulation. *Journal of Abnormal Psychology, 102*(1), 82–92.

Patrick, C. J., Edens, J. F., Poythress, N. G., Lilienfeld, S. O., & Benning, S. D. (2006). Construct validity of the psychopathic personality inventory two factor model with offenders. *Psychological Assessment, 18*, 204–208.

Patrick, C. J., Fowles, D. C., & Krueger, R. F. (2009). Triarchic conceptualization of psychopathy: Developmental origins of disinhibition, boldness, and meanness. *Development and Psychopathology, 21*(3), 913–938.

Paulhus, D. L., & Williams, K. M. (2002). The dark triad of personality: Narcissism, Machiavellianism, and psychopathy. *Journal of Research in Personality, 36*(6), 556–563.

Paulhus, D. L., Neumann, C. S., & Hare, R. D. (in press). *Manual for the Hare Self-Report Psychopathy scale*. Toronto: Multi-Health Systems.

Pianalto, M. (2012). Moral courage and facing others. *International Journal of Philosophical Studies, 20*(2), 165–184.

Piff, P. K. (2014). Wealth and the inflated self: Class, entitlement, and narcissism. *Personality and Social Psychology Bulletin, 40*(1), 34–43.

Piff, P. K., Kraus, M. W., Côté, S., Cheng, B. H., & Keltner, D. (2010). Having less, giving more: The influence of social class on prosocial behavior. *Journal of Personality and Social Psychology, 99*(5), 771.

Rand, D. G., & Epstein, Z. G. (2014). Risking Your Life without a Second Thought: Intuitive Decision-Making and Extreme Altruism. *PLoS ONE, 9*(10), e109687.

Rankin, L. E., & Eagly, A. H. (2008). Is his heroism hailed and hers hidden? Women, men, and the social construction of heroism. *Psychology of Women Quarterly, 32*(4), 414–422.

Roberts, G. (1998). Competitive altruism: from reciprocity to the handicap principle. *Proceedings of the Royal Society of London B, 265*(1394), 427–431.

Rosch, E., & Mervis, C. B. (1975). Family resemblances: Studies in the internal structure of categories. *Cognitive Psychology, 7*(4), 573–605.

Rusch, H., Leunissen, J. M., & van Vugt, M. (2015). Historical and experimental evidence of sexual selection for war heroism. *Evolution and Human Behavior, 36*, 367–373.

Sadeh, N., & Verona, E. (2012). Visual complexity attenuates emotional processing in psychopathy: implications for fear-potentiated startle deficits. *Cognitive, Affective, & Behavioral Neuroscience, 12*(2), 346–360.

Sandoval, A. M. R., Hancock, D., Poythress, N., Edens, J. F., & Lilienfeld, S. (2000). Construct validity of the Psychopathic Personality Inventory in a correctional sample. *Journal of Personality Assessment, 74*(2), 262–281.

Sekerka, L. E., & Bagozzi, R. P. (2007). Moral courage in the workplace: Moving to and from the desire and decision to act. *Business Ethics: A European Review, 16*(2), 132–149.

Sekerka, L. E., Bagozzi, R. P., & Charnigo, R. (2009). Facing ethical challenges in the workplace: Conceptualizing and measuring professional moral courage. *Journal of Business Ethics, 89*(4), 565–579.

Sellbom, M., & Phillips, T. R. (2013). An examination of the triarchic conceptualization of psychopathy in incarcerated and nonincarcerated samples. *Journal of Abnormal Psychology, 122*(1), 208.

Smith, S. F., Lilienfeld, S. O., Coffey, K., & Dabbs, J. M. (2013). Are psychopaths and heroes twigs off the same branch? Evidence from college, community, and presidential samples. *Journal of Research in Personality, 47*(5), 634–646.

Stellar, J. E., Manzo, V. M., Kraus, M. W., & Keltner, D. (2012). Class and compassion: socioeconomic factors predict responses to suffering. *Emotion, 12*(3), 449.

Suedfeld, P., & de Best, S. (2008). Value hierarchies of Holocaust rescuers and resistance fighters. *Genocide Studies and Prevention, 3*(1), 31–42.

Trivers, R. L. (1971). The evolution of reciprocal altruism. *Quarterly Review of Biology, 46*(1), 35–57.

Van den Bos, K., Müller, P. A., & Van Bussel, A. A. (2009). Helping to overcome intervention inertia in bystander's dilemmas: Behavioral disinhibition can improve the greater good. *Journal of Experimental Social Psychology*, *45*(4), 873–878.

Venables, N. C., Hall, J. R., & Patrick, C. J. (2014). Differentiating psychopathy from antisocial personality disorder: A triarchic model perspective. *Psychological Medicine*, *44*(5), 1005–1013.

Walker, L. J., Frimer, J. A., & Dunlop, W. L. (2010). Varieties of moral personality: Beyond the banality of heroism. *Journal of Personality*, *78*(3), 907–942.

Watts, A. L., Lilienfeld, S. O., & Patrick C.J. (in preparation). The fearlessness model of psychopathy: A meta-analytic and conceptual review.

White, B. A. (2014). Who cares when nobody is watching? Psychopathic traits and empathy in prosocial behaviors. *Personality and Individual Differences*, *56*, 116–121.

Widom, C. S. (1977). A methodology for studying noninstitutionalized psychopaths. *Journal of Consulting and Clinical Psychology*, *45*, 674–683.

Wittgenstein, L. (1953). *Philosophical investigations*. Oxford: Basil Blackwell.

Yang, Y., Raine, A., Narr, K. L., Colletti, P., & Toga, A. W. (2009). Localization of deformations within the amygdala in individuals with psychopathy. *Archives of General Psychiatry*, *66*(9), 986–994.

Zahavi, A. (1975). Mate selection: a selection for handicap. *Journal of Theoretical Biology*, *53*, 205–214.

Zahavi, A., & Zahavi, A. (1997). *The Handicap Principle: a missing piece of Darwin's puzzle*. New York: Oxford University Press.

Zimbardo, P. (2007). *The Lucifer effect*. New York: Random House.

29

The Courage of One's Moral Convictions

Exploring the Two Sides of Heroism

Ronnie Janoff-Bulman and Prerana Bharadwaj

Heroism is often associated with grand physical feats that involve rescuing another in serious trouble: saving a potential drowning victim struggling in deep water or jumping onto subway tracks to pull a person to safety. The decision to intervene appears to be quick and immediate, and the assumption of risk is apparent. Drowning victims flail and tax the strength of the strongest of swimmers, and the possibility of an oncoming train is ever-present for the rescuer who jumps onto train tracks. These rescuers are clearly heroes. The morality of their acts seems obvious, and they take great risks to help an unknown other.

When three young Americans and a British businessman thwarted the attack of a gunman on a French passenger train, they pointed out afterwards that their actions were "just gut instinct ... It wasn't really a conscious decision" (Yoeli & Rand, 2015, p. SR10). Having reviewed transcripts of interviews with past winners of the Carnegie Medal for heroism, awarded to those who take extraordinary risks to save or attempt to save the lives of others, Yoeli and Rand emphasize that heroes almost uniformly describe their behavior as intuitive and fast rather than carefully reasoned; this was the case even when the heroes actually had some time to stop and think. The researchers concluded, "It is striking that our brute instincts, rather than our celebrated higher cognitive faculties, are what lead to such moral acts" (Yoeli & Rand, 2015, p. SR10). Apparently the trick to acting heroically is not to think too much, in which case self-preservation might override the impulse to help.

Our interest is in those who do have plenty of time to think about their behavior—who deliberate, override the drive for self-preservation, and decide to engage in moral acts in the face of known risks. Their heroism involves less immediate, more principle-based behavior reflected in prolonged acts of moral courage and resistance. These are people who have strong moral convictions, and their behavior is based on these convictions; that is, they have the courage of their moral convictions. In the first part of this chapter we will explore moral convictions as a basis for heroic action. Our focus will then be the links between morality and heroism; we will propose that heroic behavior may not begin with moral convictions, but rather these convictions may develop gradually and reinforce increasingly risky, moral behavior. Based on recent work on morality and moral convictions, we will then turn to a consideration of the dark side of heroic behavior and will conclude with some caveats regarding the truest forms of heroism.

Principle-Based Heroism

Heroism involves morality, for heroic acts are those that help others or defend a moral principle (e.g., Franco, Blau, & Zimbardo, 2011). These acts of "social heroism" (Franco et al., 2011) typically occur over an extended period of time, and they can be private as well as public behaviors. Private acts might include hiding and thereby saving members of victimized groups during genocides, or secretly running a network of safe houses, as abolitionists did with the Underground Railroad in mid-19th century America. These are courageous acts that can be successful only if the heroes remain unidentified. In contrast, public protests—for civil rights, for example—can only be successful if they attract a wide enough audience that can ultimately be swayed—and in turn sway—those in power. Interestingly, when it comes to moral acts, people can typically rest assured that their behavior will be met with social approval; this is surely the case with immediate acts of physical heroism. Yet the more extended, deliberative instances of principle-based heroism are generally met, at least initially, with social disapproval (see Osswald, Greitemeyer, Fischer, & Frey, 2010). Included in this type of heroism are rescuers and resisters (see Oliner & Oliner, 1988, on "rescue altruism" and Shepela, Cook, Horlitz, Leal, Luciano, Lutfy, Miller, Mitchell, & Worden, 1999, on "courageous resistance").

Those who saved the lives of Jews during the Second World War were clearly rescuers. Many know of Mies Giep, a Dutch woman who hid Anne Frank and her family. Other exemplars of heroic acts of rescue include Feng-Shan Ho, Dimitar Peshev, and Irena Sendler. Feng-Shan Ho was consul-general of the Chinese embassy in Vienna during the Second World War, and in acting against his superior's orders, he issued visas to Shanghai and saved the lives of approximately 2,000 Austrian Jews. Dimitar Peshev opposed Bulgaria's pro-Nazi cabinet and, as Minister of Justice and Deputy Speaker of the National Assembly, prevented the deportation of Bulgaria's 48,000 Jews. The heroism of Irena Sendler saved the lives of approximately 2,500 Jewish children. As a member of the German Social Welfare Department, she had permission to enter the Warsaw Ghetto to check for typhus. Sendler smuggled Jewish children out of the ghetto in suitcases, boxes, trams, and ambulances, and she was consequently imprisoned and tortured by the Nazis.

Resisters represent a second category of heroes whose moral acts are extended over time. These are individuals who engage in risky, typically public actions to promote a moral cause. Well-known examples include Martin Luther King and Nelson Mandela, who led nonviolent resistance movements in their heroic work for equal rights. Aung Sun Suu Kyi, too, relied on nonviolent resistance in her heroic effort to promote democracy in Burma. The more anonymous freedom riders who risked their lives in the South in the 1960s were heroes as well; beginning in 1961 they rode interstate buses into the U.S. South to explicitly challenge the non-enforcement of Supreme Court decisions that found segregated buses to be unconstitutional. They also sat in mixed racial groups in restaurants, at lunch counters and in hotels to protest racial discrimination. The nonviolent freedom riders were often arrested, but the greater risks were the violent white mobs that attacked them. Of course not everyone would regard the behaviors of Martin Luther King, Nelson Mandela, Aung Sun Suu Kyi and the freedom riders as heroic. That is, the perception of heroism rests in part on the degree to which people endorse the moral principle being defended, an issue we address later in this chapter.

For both rescuers and resisters, there is a potent recognition of others' harm-doing, the essence of immorality (see Gray, Young, & Waytz, 2012), and a deep commitment to minimizing or eradicating it—whether harm to the victims who are being rescued or harm in the form of discrimination and/or mistreatment of those the resisters are fighting for. Their behaviors are unquestionably moral. The behaviors also reflect great courage, because there is a recognition that powerful entities have the fearsome ability to retaliate against them. It is the accepted risk and great personal costs that turns these moral behaviors into heroism (see, e.g., Allison &

Goethals, 2011). Heroes are willing to sacrifice their own safety and security to act altruistically or reinforce a moral position. From a philosophical point of view, such heroic acts are regarded as superogatory—they are clearly good acts, but they are not morally required. The heroism derives from the discretionary nature of the risks that are undertaken; people are not required or even expected to engage in behaviors that threaten self-preservation or engender social rejection. The risks of heroism often involve physical harm, but typically also include social risks such as ostracism and loss of status that follow from countering strong social norms (e.g., Franco et al., 2011; Glazer & Glazer, 1989; Osswald et al., 2010). It is one's moral conviction that enables an individual to accept this risk or, rather, provides the courage to accept the risk and act heroically.

Heroism and Moral Conviction

Moral convictions are a very distinct type of attitude. The study of attitudes has long been a central focus of research by social psychologists, with attitudes defined as positive and negative evaluations of attitude objects (Eagly & Chaiken, 1993). Sometimes these evaluations reflect subjective preferences such as favorite foods or clothing styles, in which case they are simply a matter of personal taste and individual discretion. Sometimes they reflect socially shared conventions (see Nucci, 2001; Turiel, 2002) that suggest how things are typically done in one's group; such shared views are often represented in rules and laws that apply to one's community, but not necessarily to others outside the group. Yet there is another type of attitude that is believed to apply to all, regardless of group boundaries; these involve morality and are viewed as universal (see, e.g., Hare, 1981; Kant, 1786/1947; Turiel, 2002; also see Haidt, Rosenberg, & Hom, 2003).

Work by Skitka and colleagues has provided a rich understanding of moral convictions, which are very strong attitudes based on the perception of morality and immorality (Skitka, Bauman, & Sargis, 2005; Skitka, 2010); these convictions are not simply moral judgments, but involve moral mandates or imperatives that reflect core beliefs about right and wrong. Moral convictions differ from other attitudes, and not only because well-known attitude constructs such as attitude importance, strength, extremity, and certainty do not capture the essential nature of these evaluations (see Skitka, 2010, for a review). They are believed to be not only universal, but absolute as well; they are "experienced as facts about the world" (Skitka et al., 2005, p. 896). Although we may know that others hold a different moral position, we nevertheless believe they are wrong and should share our moral perspective. In evaluating positions based on moral convictions, there is only right and wrong—no continuum of "rightness" (Parker & Janoff-Bulman, 2013; also see Gray & Wegner, 2009; Skitka et al., 2005).

Moral convictions reflect potent beliefs about how things should be, and they involve strong emotions and more intense affect than is experienced with very strong non-moral attitudes (Skitka et al., 2005; Rozin, Lowery, Imada, & Haidt, 1999). This is particularly apparent in the moral outrage, contempt and disgust felt in response to violations of one's moral convictions (see, e.g., Haidt, 2001, 2003). Moral convictions are also experienced as autonomous, in the sense that they do not depend on external sources such as authorities or established groups. Those with moral convictions believe they have mandates that release them from having to follow or obey others, including authorities (e.g., Skitka, Bauman, & Lytle, 2009; see Skitka, 2010 for a review). Research has found that those with moral convictions are more likely to resist majority influence and consensus information (Hornsey, Majkut, Terry, & McKimmie, 2003; Hornsey, Smith & Begg, 2007); indeed they continue to maintain their conviction even in the face of strong pressures to conform. Importantly, people are likely to reject authorities when they violate their moral convictions.

Particularly important for an understanding of heroism is the strong motivation associated with moral convictions; as Skitka (2010) writes, they "are experienced as motivational guides ...

[and] a unique combination of factual belief, compelling motives, and justification for action" (p. 270). Moral convictions carry with them potent "shoulds" or "should nots" that not only motivate behavior, but provide a justification for one's behavior as well. Given that heroism involves substantial risk, the motivation to act must be particularly strong for such behavior to occur. Moral convictions are what enable a person to resist the dominant forces and risk the consequences. The courage to act derives from a moral conviction to do the right thing. Thus, as Skitka (2010) points out, "moral convictions can protect against obedience to potentially malevolent authorities" (p. 267).

Moral convictions seem to involve certainty about one's position and certainty about the need to act; a strong belief in the truth value of one's view coupled with motivational force suggests the ready path from moral convictions to the courage to act—and ultimately to heroic action. The moral mandate, or moral imperative, to act on one's moral convictions provides the strength to endure risks and withstand possible painful repercussions from those with the power to retaliate.

Origins of Moral Conviction

Past studies of rescuers and resisters point to some traits that may be important in characterizing heroes. A high tolerance for risk and fearlessness are mentioned (see, e.g., London, 1970; Oliner & Oliner, 1988; Staub, 2003; Tec, 1986), but of course this tells us little, because they necessarily follow from the acts themselves, which are risky. Other traits include openness to experience, resistance to group pressure and justice sensitivity, as well as empathy and a sense of competence and self-assurance (see Osswald et al., 2010, for a review). The traits seem like a grab bag of factors that are subsumed by a combination of the words "moral" and "conviction"—that is, some combination of moral concern joined with a strong commitment to act on these concerns.

When we think of heroes and the necessity of moral conviction in resisting an easier behavioral path, we likely think about people who seem to have moral clarity and strong convictions from the start—people likely to be perceived as different from you and me—as extraordinary—that is, born heroes. Heroism is not the stuff of everyday life; rather, heroism is extraordinary. We therefore assume the characterological makeup of heroes is extraordinary as well. In judging cause and effect, humans typically rely on a resemblance criterion (see Nisbett & Ross, 1980), a somewhat crude form of the representativeness heuristic (Kahneman & Tversky, 1973) whereby we believe causes and effects are similar, and big events thus have big causes: "When confronted with large effects, it is to comparably large causes that we turn for explanations" (Nisbett & Ross, 1980, p. 252). The resemblance criterion helps account for the popularity of conspiracy theories in accounting for important outcomes. And it seems that heroic acts, too, must be the choice of truly remarkable human beings—surely not ordinary mortals like ourselves.

Immediate heroes who jump onto train tracks to rescue a child or swim out in rough seas to rescue a struggling teen are responding to strong social cues, but seem to have dispositions that enable them to take great risks in that moment; they immediately, seemingly automatically, accept the risk. In contrast, in the case of extended social heroism, the process of rescuing or resisting takes place over time, and interestingly—and perhaps surprisingly—social psychological research suggests that it need not begin with extraordinary people with remarkable characters. In the end, these rescuers are in fact remarkable and extraordinary, but their heroic behavior may represent the end of a process that began in a relatively mundane fashion.

Certainly there are some extraordinary people who had moral vision and strength from early on; these are people with remarkable characters and very strong moral convictions who set out from the start to rescue victims and resist malevolent groups or authorities. The exemplars presented earlier may well be such people. But it is important to recognize that moral conviction, and the moral clarity it involves, may also be created over time—that is, it can involve a process of learning by doing that may actually start without any sense of strong moral purpose or principled morality. This is a process that entails a gradual transformation of motives. Here the initial motivation is not grand and heroic; there are no strong moral convictions that initiate heroism, but rather far more ordinary human motivations—in fact the stuff of ordinary mortals like ourselves. Somewhat akin to foot-in-the-door processes (Freedman & Fraser, 1966; Burger, 1999), taking small, moral steps can produce increased commitment, which over time can build to heroic acts, in much the same way that great cruelty is best accounted for by a process of gradual steps along a continuum of destruction (Staub, 1989, 2003).

Just as the foot-in-the door phenomenon is based in self-perception, consistency, and commitment (Burger, 1999), so, too, is the process that converts relatively ordinary moral behaviors into extended acts of heroism. The freely chosen initial behavior sets the rescuer or resister on the heroic path by fostering a self-perception of the kind of person who engages in such moral behavior; here people infer their attitudes by examining their behaviors (Bem, 1967). In addition, the absence of sufficient external justification creates pressure to find a justification for behavior (see Festinger, 1957, on cognitive dissonance) and produces a concomitant increase in commitment; as Brickman (1987) notes, "intrinsic values come from actions: behavior creates value rather than vice versa" (p. 68). Increasing risk serves to strengthen one's moral self-perception and commitment to a consistent course of behavior, because acts engaged in despite risks are increasingly perceived as freely chosen and intrinsically valuable. Justification for the behavior is likely based not only on one's own praiseworthy nature, but on the increasing value of the people one is helping or the moral principle defended. The upshot is strong moral conviction that fosters and maintains heroic behavior.

As Staub notes, people learn by doing; that is, they learn as a result of their own actions (Staub, 1979, 1989, 2003). In the case of harm-doing, people increasingly devalue their victims, and this facilitates worse treatment and even violence; the perpetrators increasingly come to see themselves as willing and able to engage in cruelty and violence (Staub, 2003). This is a process of increasing dehumanization of the victim and desensitization of the perpetrator. The moral conviction involved in heroism can involve a parallel gradual process that instead entails increasing humanization of the victim and sensitization of the helper to the moral imperative of helping. Once perpetrators begin to harm, harm-doing becomes more probable; inhibitions against cruelty and violence diminish. Similarly, once rescuers begin to help, further helping becomes more probable, and possible risks become less likely to inhibit further altruistic behavior.

In the case of rescuers, heroism often begins with a request for help by another, rather than with a strong initial motivation to help others in need. The truly extraordinary actions of Raoul Wallenberg illustrate the absence of an initial intrinsic motivation to engage in extraordinary acts of heroism. In 1944 Wallenberg was dissatisfied with his career. He was Swedish and working in an import-export business with a partner who was a Hungarian Jewish refugee. Given this connection, he was approached by a member of the American War Refugee Board to go to Hungary as a Swedish diplomat to try to save the lives of Hungarian Jews being sent to their death at Auschwitz. Wallenberg agreed to go. At the time there apparently wasn't a guiding motive in his life, but this provided him with a strong sense of responsibility (Staub, 1978, 2003).

Ultimately Wallenberg subordinated everything in his life to the cause of saving Jews in the Second World War (Marton, 1982). By issuing "protective passports" that identified bearers as Swedish subjects awaiting repatriation, he prevented the deportation of Hungarian Jews; these passports weren't legal, but they looked official and were generally accepted by the authorities, who sometimes sought bribes. Wallenberg also rented and declared diplomatic immunity for over 30 buildings in Budapest, where he safely housed Jews. It is estimated that Wallenberg may have saved the lives of as many as 100,000 Hungarian Jews.

More typically in the case of rescuers, the request for help comes not from a government agency, but simply from a friend or acquaintance who needs help. This was the case in the Second World War, when Jewish families sought help from neighbors. The empathic response to provide aid in an up-close-and-personal interaction could set courageous resistance in motion and over time establish a moral conviction to save a family and defy authorities. Having helped someone they knew, some people continued to help despite great personal costs and sacrifices.

The gradual path to heroism may begin with small moral acts based in empathy, with another asking for help, but can even start with more self-interested motives that over time, through one's own actions, transmute into heroic behaviors reflecting strong moral convictions to do the right thing. In this regard, a particularly interesting example is Oskar Schindler, a German industrialist who saved the lives of 1200 Jews who worked in his factories (Crowe, 2004). At the beginning of the Second World War he made millions profiting from the war, and by the end he had spent every penny he had to save the lives of the 1200 Jews. This was a man who was truly heroic, but whose path to heroism began with a less than heroic motivation—that is, his own desire to make a profit. He was a member of the Nazi Party and collected information for the Nazi government. In 1939 he obtained an enamelware factory in Krakow, Poland, and the majority of his workers were Jews. He was motivated to keep his factory running and was initially able to use his connections to shield his workers from deportation and death in the concentration camps. Over time, however, as he behaved in ways to protect his workers, initially out of self-interest, he increasingly took risks to save them. He gave the Nazi officials larger and larger bribes and gifts and even convinced officials to allow him to move his factory to Sudetenland, which kept his workers from the gas chambers; 1200 Jews traveled to Sudetenland with him in October 1944. Though classified as an armaments factory, the plant produced just one wagonload of live ammunition in just under eight months of operation, but presented bogus production figures, and served to keep the Jews alive. Schindler continued to bribe officials until the end of the war to prevent his workers from being killed. In the end he was so committed to saving his Jewish workers—as opposed to making a profit—that he ultimately spent his entire fortune on bribes and black market purchases for his workers. Oskar Schindler died penniless in 1974 and was buried in Jerusalem on Mount Zion (Crowe, 2004).

In short, heroism need not begin with strong moral convictions, but instead may reflect an evolution from small acts of helping or resistance to extraordinary acts of moral courage that involve great personal risk and sacrifice. The "Righteous Among the Nations" is an honor bestowed by the Israeli government in recognition of non-Jews who risked their lives during the Holocaust to save the lives of Jews. To date just short of 25,000 men and women from every walk of life have received this honor for their heroism. Some of these heroes were no doubt extraordinary from the start, but it seems likely that many of these thousands of rescuers experienced the transformative effects (i.e., increasing moral conviction and courage) of helping neighbors, friends, or countrymen in need. They may have started out like you and me, and a request from a neighbor or friend set them on an extraordinary course to heroism.

The Other Side of Heroism

It is both inspiring and humbling to read about the lengths to which some people have gone to help others and defend a moral position. In either case, it is moral conviction, with its mandate to do the right thing, that helps account for the courage to accept the severe risks associated with heroic acts. Sometimes the moral conviction is there from the start; sometimes it develops over time as a consequence of people's actions. Paradoxically, however, it is also moral conviction that can help us recognize a darker side of heroism—a side we typically don't associate with heroism. Here we need to familiarize ourselves with additional aspects of moral conviction, and of morality more generally.

In fully describing the nature of moral convictions, Skitka (2010) maintains that they are actually both reassuring and "terrifying"; that is they can lead people to resist malevolent authorities, but they are also "associated with the rejection of the rule of law, and can provide a motivational foundation for violent protest and acts of terrorism" (p. 267). Yes, moral convictions provide the motivational force, or courage, to act when others sit back, to resist cruel policies, and engage in moral behavior. However moral convictions are also associated with greater intolerance of attitudinally dissimilar others; we seek social and physical distance from those whose moral convictions differ from our own and display very low levels of cooperativeness towards them (Skitka et al., 2005; also see Haidt et al., 2003). In other words, they are a barrier to conflict resolution. In addition, and importantly, moral convictions are associated with more violent means to achieve ends consistent with one's convictions (Skitka et al, 2005; Skitka & Mullen, 2002). They facilitate rejection of authorities, but also rejection of the proper rule of law. In a study by Skitka and Houston (2001), for example, participants viewed vigilantism and due process of law as equally fair in leading to the death of a murder defendant when there was strong moral clarity about the defendant's guilt.

Of course if we all shared the same views of morality and moral issues, this dark side of moral convictions would be not be apparent. However, despite the presumably self-evident nature of rights and wrongs in our own minds, it is nevertheless the case that such "facts" may elude us and people differ in their views of morality and immorality. Thus strong moral convictions reside on both sides of the debates about abortion, gay marriage, welfare, gun control, and the progressive income tax, among other social issues. Each side regards its own perspective as moral and the other as immoral, but this only serves to illustrate the darker problems associated with moral convictions. They provide people with the motivation, justification, and courage to act in spite of great risks, but the acts themselves are a reflection of an individual's own moral principles. And if we relied on community sanctioning as the proper criterion for assessing morality, we would essentially eliminate the possibility of heroism in the interests of social change, as in cases of heroic resistance. Such resistance aims to change the norms sanctioned by the larger given community.

Recent psychological work on morality has expanded the domains associated with morality (see, e.g., Haidt, 2007, 2012; Janoff-Bulman & Carnes, 2013; Rai & Fiske, 2011). Morality has traditionally been regarded as dealing with helping and fairness (see, e.g., Kohlberg, 1981, 1984), but the influential work of Haidt and colleagues (Graham, Nosek, Haidt, Iyer, Koleva, & Ditto, 2011; Haidt, 2007, 2012) on Moral Foundations Theory (MFT) includes not only the individualizing moral foundations of Care and Fairness, but the binding foundations of Authority, Loyalty, and Purity. The individualizing foundations focus on the rights and welfare of individuals, whereas the binding foundations focus on the group and serve to strengthen the collective. The binding foundations are endorsed more strongly by political conservatives than liberals (Graham, Haidt, & Nosek, 2009; Haidt & Graham, 2007), leaving liberals without a binding morality in MFT. In addition to the interpersonal moralities of helping, fairness, and not harming, Janoff-Bulman and Carnes (2013) include intrapersonal moral principles (self-restraint and industriousness) as well as two group-based, binding moralities in their Model of Moral Motives (MMM). The two binding foundations are Social Order, which is endorsed by conservatives, and Social Justice, which is endorsed by liberals (Janoff-Bulman, 2009; Janoff-Bulman & Carnes, 2013; Janoff-Bulman, Sheikh, & Baldacci, 2008). Social Order subsumes Haidt's three binding foundations (Authority, Loyalty, and Purity), in that each is essentially a means of achieving the conformity and norm adherence sought through a focus on Social Order. Social Justice endorsers emphasize communal sharing in the interests of greater egalitarianism in the distribution of resources and rights. Opposing views of abortion, gay marriage, gun control, welfare, and the progressive income tax reflect differences in endorsement of distinct moral principles. Gay marriage, for example, is a matter of Social Justice for liberals, whereas it defies Purity and Social Order for conservatives.

Thus when Kim Davis refused to issue marriage licenses to gay couples in her role as county clerk in Rowan County, Kentucky, she was heralded as a hero by the Religious Right. Her defiance of the Supreme Court and jail time for contempt led her attorney to compare her to Martin Luther King Jr. for her act of conscience, and Davis's supporters compared her to Rosa Parks for her civil disobedience.

The murder of Dr. George Tiller in Kansas was no doubt the act of a person whose actions were based in strong moral convictions about abortion. Dr. Tiller provided abortions and care to thousands of women in Kansas. For years Dr. Tiller and his clinic were targeted by antiabortion groups. The father of four and the grandfather of 10, Dr. Tiller was shot in the head by Scott Roeder while he was in church in Wichita, Kansas.

Timothy McVeigh's bombing of a Federal building in Oklahoma, bombs in public transportation in London and Madrid, gunning down innocent bystanders in Paris, flying planes into the World Trade Center—these acts were all likely based in moral convictions, perceived as justified and right, and chosen in spite of the known risks involved. Although clearly regarded as heinous crimes by those who share our own view of morality, these actions nevertheless were likely viewed as heroic by those who shared the perpetrators' moral worldviews.

In their book *Virtuous Violence*, Fiske and Rai (2015) claim that violence ranging from everyday acts to large scale atrocities are typically based in strong moral motives. Even genocide is regarded as a moral act by those who support the killings; it is believed to be required to purify the perpetrator group, which is "polluted" by the presence of the outgroup in their collective (Chirot & McCauley, 2006). Decontamination of the ingroup from outgroup pollution was the moral motivation of the Holocaust, the Cambodian genocide, the purges of Stalin and Mao, the extermination of the Huguenots by the Catholics, and the massacre of the Tutsis by the Hutus (Fiske & Rai, 2015, p. 209). And, as Ginges and Atran (2009; Atran 2010) argue, the motives of terrorists are fundamentally moral as well; the terrorists believe they are doing "right." In their research, Ginges and Atran (2009; also see Ginges, Atran, Sachdeva, & Medin, 2011) have shown that support for violent acts of terrorism and war are usually driven by moral motives and not by self-interest (e.g., desire for reward in the "next life"), instrumental motives, or material incentives.

As Steven Pinker writes:

> The world has far too much morality. If you added up all the homicides committed in pursuit of self-help justice,[1] the casualties of religious and revolutionary wars, the people executed for victimless crimes and misdemeanors, and the targets of ideological genocides, they would surely outnumber the fatalities from amoral predation and conquest.
>
> *(Pinker, 2011, p. 622)*

Heroism and Morality: A Few Caveats

For us to achieve better, healthier societies that can counteract evil, Zimbardo (2007) has argued for fostering a "heroic imagination," which is essentially a mindset that involves accepting risks and sacrifices to help others in need or "in defense of a moral cause." Few would contest the "goodness" involved in helping those in need, but as we discussed above, there are many instances when the "goodness" of a heroic act lies only with those who share the "hero's" moral worldview. A focus on altruism might seem like a good place to start, but it can lead us down a murky path. After all, when a fanatic pro-lifer shoots a doctor who performs abortions, he says he is helping the unborn fetus. Those who engage in genocide believe they are benefiting their society. Simply fostering a heroic imagination is likely to fall short of creating the kind of societies Zimbardo no doubt has in mind. Given that heroism seems based in moral convictions, some caveats regarding the morality-heroism link may enable us to fine-tune our understanding of heroism.

One obvious difference between the light and dark sides of heroism is whether the heroic acts involve harm to others. Killing an abortion provider or engaging in terrorism may be based in strong moral convictions and involve the acceptance of risk, but in defending the perpetrators' moral worldviews, the violent actions counter a fundamental—perhaps *the* fundamental rule— of group living, which is "do no harm" (Gray et al., 2012; Janoff-Bulman & Carnes, 2013). Although the perpetrators no doubt believe they are avenging harm-doers, their very acts seem to make use of immorality to further their personal view of morality. The ends don't justify the means, and in defending one set of moral principles, these individuals also increase suffering with their violent acts.

Gray, Young, and Waytz (2012) maintain that the essence of immorality is harm-doing, and recent empirical work supports this claim (see, e.g., Gray, Schein, & Ward, 2014). The famous footbridge and trolley problems seemed to stymie philosophers for years, because the outcome of the two scenarios is the same—moving a switch to redirect a trolley results in killing one and saving five lives, and similarly pushing a person off a footbridge to stop a trolley results in killing one and saving five. Yet in the former (switch) case the overwhelming majority of respondents, regardless of age, gender, or nation, regard the action as morally acceptable, whereas when it comes to pushing someone off a footbridge, the pattern is reversed—the overwhelming majority of people find it morally unacceptable (see, e.g., Greene, 2013). Importantly, Greene and colleagues (Greene, Sommerville, Nystrom, Darley, & Cohen, 2001) note that the footbridge activates parts of the brain associated with emotion, whereas such emotion is absent when considering whether to pull the switch and redirect the trolley. Put another way, at a very fundamental level we not only know, but feel it's wrong to fatally harm an innocent other, even if it results in saving five other lives.

In discussing rescuers and resisters, our focus was on people who did not engage in harm-doing. Rescuers clearly helped others, and the resisters relied on nonviolent means of defending their moral position. The willingness to resist violence in defense of a moral cause is actually advantageous. More specifically, recent work on violent versus nonviolent resistance in the last century has found that nonviolent resistance is actually far more effective than violent resistance in bringing about desired ends (Chenoweth & Stephan, 2011; Stephan & Chenoweth, 2008). In accounting for their findings the researchers noted that nonviolent campaigns are regarded as more legitimate and therefore produce greater participation, which in turn puts greater pressure on authorities. Also, violent responses by authorities to violent resistance is apt to be regarded as justified, whereas such violent responses to nonviolence are regarded as unjustified and are likely to backfire (Chenoweth & Stephan, 2011; Stephan & Chenoweth, 2008). As Fiske and Rai (2015) write regarding civil disobedience more generally, "Refusing to adopt violent means to resist the authority, even when they suffer violent retribution for their transgressions, the resisters delegitimate all violence, and hence delegitimate the policies and practices that can only be enforced with violence" (p. 278).

The violent responses of authorities to the nonviolent resistance during the civil rights movement in the American South clearly served to sway public opinion and increase popular support for an end to racial discrimination. On March 7, 1965, some 600 marchers headed out of Selma towards Montgomery, the state capital. Almost immediately Alabama State Troopers and local police violently attacked the marchers with tear gas and billy clubs, leading to the hospitalization of 50 people. The events of "Bloody Sunday" were televised around the world and had an impact on American popular opinion about racial injustice. Martin Luther King called for supporters to come to Selma to march for voting rights, and following a second symbolic march on March 9, 3200 people left Selma on March 21 on a third and final march, this time with federal protection. When they reached Montgomery on March 25, the marchers were 25,000 strong; and less than five months later the Voting Rights Act of 1965 was signed into law.

In acknowledging the value of nonviolent resistance and positing that harm-doing and violence belie heroism, we nevertheless recognize the links between violence and heroism in the popular imagination, particularly in heroic acts associated with war. As Fiske and Rai (2015) note, throughout history warriors have been regarded as virtuous. Unfortunately a discussion of the morality of war is beyond the scope of this chapter. Of course on the battlefield it is likely to be a case of kill or be killed. Nevertheless, it is worth noting that when medals are awarded for heroism in war, they are awarded for taking risks "beyond the call of duty," and these typically involve courageous acts that rescue or save the lives of fellow soldiers. Devotion to the others in their unit leads soldiers to take great risks, and even die themselves; soldiers report that they can't bear letting their fellow soldiers die (e.g., Wong, Kolditz, Millen, & Potter, 2003; also see Fiske & Rai, 2015).

Regardless of context, violent acts involve dehumanization of the victims (see, e.g., Bandura, 1999; Haslam, 2006; Fiske & Rai, 2015; Staub, 1989). By seeing their targets as less than human, perpetrators can maintain their own moral self-image. They have placed the victims outside of their moral universe (Opotow, 2005) and thereby unworthy of human care or concern. This aspect of harm-doing provides a natural link to a second caveat regarding heroism. That is, truly heroic acts serve to expand our moral universe. To understand the importance of this qualification, it is helpful to take a closer look at the nature of morality and its limitations.

Morality is fundamentally about the ingroup—protecting and providing for others similar to us. From the perspective of both biological evolution (see, e.g., Wilson, 2012) and cultural evolution (see, e.g., Richerson & Boyd, 2005), morality developed to facilitate ingroup functioning. Our ingroup can be based on family ties, shared activities, ethnicity, religion, nationality, or any other criterion that might affect our perceived similarity to another. The greater the perceived similarity, the greater the morality in our treatment of others; ingroup members readily constitute our moral universe.

This tribal orientation is already evident in human infancy. Thus in recent studies with 9 and 14 month olds, researchers found that infants clearly preferred puppets that helped similar others and hindered dissimilar others (Hamlin, Mahajan, Liberman, & Wynn, 2013; also see Mahajan & Wynn, 2012). In these studies perceived similarity was based on food choices or choice of mitten color, with similar puppets presumably choosing the same food or mitten as the infant, and dissimilar ones choosing the other food or mitten offered. The findings are consistent with a growing literature indicating that infants prefer others from familiar social categories (see, e.g., Bar-Haim, Ziv, Lamy, & Hodes, 2006; Kinzler, Dupoux, & Spelke, 2007). As Hamlin et al. (2013) write, "it seems likely that infants' tendency to notice and prefer similarity is related to emergent intergroup biases" (p. 593).

This preference for others similar to us (i.e., the ingroup) is apparent in diverse research findings. We are most likely to experience empathy in response to others' suffering when they are close, familiar others (de Waal, 2008), and empathy for ingroup members is often associated with strong feelings of Schadenfreude toward outgroup members (see Cikara, Bruneau & Saxe, 2011). We are also most likely to provide help to similar others (e.g., Krebs, 1975; Batson, Turk, Shaw, & Klein, 1995). Ingroup favoritism is a robust finding in the social psychological literature (see Brewer, 1999, for a review), and this favoritism arises even when based on the most shallow, arbitrary criteria (see, e.g., Brewer, 1979, on the minimal group paradigm). When our group engages in torture, we see it as moral; when an outgroup engages in the same behavior it is perceive as immoral (Tarrant, Branscombe, Warner, & Weston, 2012). Research by Cohen, Montoya, and Insko (2006), based on a database of preindustrial societies from across the globe, found that loyalty to one's own group was strongly associated with greater aggression and violence toward outgroups. The co-occurrence of ingroup altruism and intergroup hostility has been labelled "parochial altruism" by evolutionary theorists (Bernhard, Fischbacker, & Fehr, 2006; Choi & Bowles, 2007).

Our parochial, tribal tendencies imply constriction of the moral universe, so as to benefit most the members of our ingroup. We believe that the truest forms of heroism would counter such partiality and would serve to expand the moral universe. In this way dissimilar, unfamiliar others would be the recipients of help, care, and protection. Groups that are stigmatized and deemed inferior in a given society would be defended and shielded from harm. The altruistic acts of the men and women who sheltered and saved Jews during the Second World War are exemplars of this orientation. Interestingly, Monroe (1996) argues that the quality that seemed to best distinguish those who rescued Jews from non-rescuers was the sense of "belonging to one human family" (p. 205). Of course this perspective may have evolved over the course of their heroic helping, but nevertheless reflects an acceptance of the "other" in one's moral universe.

Those whose work aims at equality and rights for all also represent a perspective based in moral expansion. The work of resistance is aimed at eliminating differences between ingroups and outgroups; its goal is equal rights and treatment for those who are stigmatized and subordinated by the dominant society. The work of heroic resisters reflects an "ethical mode of reasoning," which Singer (2011) argues expands the moral circle to a universalist view that involves equal concern for all human beings (also see McFarland, Brown, & Webb, 2013, on "identification with all humanity").

Heroism is based in moral conviction—a certainty about one's own moral position that motivates and justifies courageous actions that involve personal risk and sacrifice. The positive connotations associated with heroism break down when we realize that there is a dark side to moral convictions—and to heroic acts as well. In defense of their moral positions, people have not only helped outgroup members, but murdered them as well; and both would be regarded as heroes by those who share their moral worldviews. In considering heroism, and the development of a heroic imagination, we should be cognizant of the dark side of moral convictions and reserve heroism for certain types of moral acts—those that serve to expand the moral circle. Killing and harm-doing by their very nature constrict the moral circle by eliminating the victims from inclusion; in contrast, the work of rescuing and nonviolent resistance by their very nature expand the circle. In concluding, the words of Pinker once again seem particularly apt:

> Though the net contribution of the human moral sense to human well-being may well be negative, on those occasions when it is suitably deployed it can claim some monumental advances, including the humanitarian reforms of the Enlightenment and the Rights Revolutions of recent decades. When it comes to virulent ideologies, morality may be the disease, but morality is also the cure.
>
> *(Pinker, 2011, p. 622)*

Note

1 Pinker defines self-help justice as violent retaliation that does not involve state intervention, such as vigilantism, frontier justice, and culture of honor retaliation.

References

Allison, S. T., & Goethals, G. R. (2011). *Heroes: What they do and why we need them.* New York: Oxford University Press.

Atran, S. (2010). *Talking to the enemy: Faith, brotherhood, and the (un)making of terrorists.* New York: HarperCollins.

Bandura, A. (1999). Moral disengagement in the perpetration of inhumanities. *Personality and Social Psychology Review, 3,* 193–209.

Bar-Haim, Y., Ziv, T., Lamy, D., & Hodes, R. M. (2006). Nature and nurture in own-race face processing. *Psychological Science, 17,* 159–163.

Batson, C. D., Turk, C. L., Shaw, L. L., & Klein, T. R. (1995). Information function of empathic emotion: Learning that we value the other's welfare. *Journal of Personality and Social Psychology, 6*, 300–313.

Bem, D. J. (1967). Self-perception theory. In L. Berkowitz (ed.), *Advances in experimental social psychology* (Vol. 6, pp. 1–62). New York: Academic Press.

Bernhard, H., Fischbacker, U., & Fehr, E. (2006). Parochial altruism in humans. *Nature, 442*, 912–915.

Brewer M. B. (1979). In-group bias in the minimal intergroup situation: A cognitive-motivational analysis. *Psychological Bulletin, 86*, 307–324.

Brewer, M. B. (1999). The psychology of prejudice: Ingroup love or outgroup hate? *Journal of Social Issues, 55*, 429–444.

Brickman, P. (1987). *Commitment, conflict, and caring*. Englewood Cliffs, NJ: Prentice-Hall.

Burger, J. M. (1999). The foot-in-the-door compliance procedure: A multiple-process analysis and review. *Personality and Social Psychology Review, 3*, 303–325

Chenoweth, E., & Stephan, M. J. (2011). *Why civil resistance works: The strategic logic of nonviolent conflict.* New York: Columbia University Press.

Chirot, D., & McCauley, C. (2006). *Why not kill them all? The logic and prevention of mass political murder.* Princeton, NJ: Princeton University Press.

Choi, J.-K., Bowles, S. (2007). The coevolution of parochial altruism and war. *Science, 318*, 636–640.

Cikara, M., Bruneau, E. G., & Saxe, R. R. (2011). Us and them: Intergroup failures of empathy. *Current Directions in Psychological Science, 20*, 149–153.

Cohen, T. R., Montoya, R. M., & Insko, C. A. (2006). Group morality and intergroup relations: Cross-cultural and experimental evidence. *Personality and Social Psychology Bulletin, 32*, 1559–1572.

Crowe, D. M. (2004). *Oskar Schindler: The untold account of his life, wartime activities, and the true story behind the list*. Cambridge, MA: Westview Press.

De Waal, F. B. M. (2008). Putting altruism back into altruism: The evolution of empathy. *Annual Review of Psychology, 59*, 279–300.

Eagly, A. H., & Chaiken, S. (1993). *The psychology of attitudes*. Fort Worth, TX: Harcourt, Brace, & Janovich.

Festinger, L. (1957). *A theory of cognitive dissonance*. Stanford, CA: Stanford University Press.

Fiske, A. P., & Rai, T. S. (2015). *Virtuous violence*. New York: Cambridge University Press.

Franco, E. F., Blau., K., & Zimbardo, P. G. (2011). Heroism: A Conceptual analysis and differentiation between heroic action and altruism. *Review of General Psychology, 15*, 99–113.

Freedman, J. L., & Fraser, S. C. (1966). Compliance without pressure: The foot-in-the door technique. *Journal of Personality and Social Psychology, 4*, 195–202.

Ginges, J., & Atran, S. (2009). What motivates participation in violent political action: Selective incentives or parochial altruism? *Annals of the New York Academy of Sciences, 1167*, 115–123.

Ginges, J., Atran, S., Sachdeva, S., & Medin, D. (2011). Psychology out of the laboratory: The challenge of violent extremism. *American Psychologist, 66*, 507–519.

Glazer, M. P., & Glazer, P. M. (1989). *The whistleblowers: Exposing corruption in government and industry*. New York: Basic Books.

Graham, J., Haidt, J., & Nosek, B. (2009). Liberals and conservatives use different sets of moral foundations. *Journal of Personality and Social Psychology, 96*, 1029–1046.

Graham, J., Nosek, B. A., Haidt, J., Iyer, R., Koleva, S., & Ditto, P. H. (2011). Mapping the moral domain. *Journal of Personality and Social Psychology, 101*, 366–385.

Gray, K., & Wegner, D. M. (2009). Moral typecasting: Divergent perceptions of moral agents and moral patients. *Journal of Personality and Social Psychology, 96*, 505–520.

Gray, K., Schein, C., & Ward. A. F. (2014). The myth of harmless wrongs in moral cognition: Automatic dyadic completion from sin to suffering. *Journal of Experimental Psychology: General, 143*, 1600–1615.

Gray, K., Young, L., & Waytz, A. (2012). Mind perception is the essence of morality. *Psychological Inquiry, 23*(2), 101–124.

Greene, J. (2013). *Moral tribes*. New York: Penguin Press.

Greene, J. D., Sommerville, R. B., Nystrom, L. E., Darley, J. M., & Cohen, J. D. (2001). An fMRI investigation of emotional engagement in moral judgment. *Science, 293*, 2105–2108.

Haidt, J. (2001). The emotional dog and its rational tail: A social intuitionist approach to moral judgment. *Psychological Review, 108*, 814–834.

Haidt, J. (2003). The moral emotions. In R. J. Davidson, K. R. Scherer, & H. H. Goldsmith (eds), *Handbook of affective sciences* (pp. 852–870). Oxford: Oxford University Press.

Haidt, J. (2007). The new synthesis in moral psychology. *Science, 316*, 998–1002.

Haidt, J. (2012). *The righteous mind: Why good people are divided by politics and religion*. New York: Pantheon Books.

Haidt, J., & Graham, J. (2007). When morality opposes justice: Conservatives have moral intuitions that liberals may not recognize. *Social Justice Research, 20*, 98–116.

Haidt, J., Rosenberg, E., & Hom, H. (2003). Differentiating diversities: Moral diversity is not like other kinds. *Journal of Applied Social Psychology, 33,* 1–36.
Hamlin, J. K., Mahajan, N., Liberman, Z., & Wynn, K (2013). Not like me = bad: Infants prefer those who harm dissimilar others. *Psychological Science, 24,* 589–594.
Hare, R. M. (1981). *Moral thinking: Its levels, method, and point.* Oxford: Oxford University Press.
Haslam, N. (2006). Dehumanization: An integrative review. *Personality and Social Psychology Review, 10,* 252–264.
Hornsey, M. J., Majkut, L., Terry, D. J., & McKimmie, B. M. (2003). On being loud and proud: Non-conformity and counter-conformity to group norms. *British Journal of Social Psychology, 42,* 319–335.
Hornsey, M. J., Smith, J. R., & Begg, D. I. (2007). Effects of norms among those with moral conviction: Counter-conformity emerges on intentions but not behaviors. *Social Influence, 2,* 244–268.
Janoff-Bulman, R. (2009). To provide or protect: Motivational bases of political liberalism and conservatism. *Psychological Inquiry, 20,* 120–128.
Janoff-Bulman, R., & Carnes, N. C. (2013). Surveying the moral landscape: Moral motives and group-based moralities. *Personality and Social Psychology Review, 17,* 219–236.
Janoff-Bulman, R., Sheikh, S., & Balducci, K. G. (2008). Mapping moral motives: Approach avoidance, and political orientation. *Journal of Experimental Social Psychology, 44,* 1091–1099.
Kahneman, D, & Tversky, A. (1973). On the psychology of prediction. *Psychological Review, 80,* 237–251.
Kant, I. (1786/1947). *Fundamentals of the metaphysics of morals.* New York: Longmans.
Kinzler, K. D., Dupoux, E., & Spelke, E. S. (2007) The native language of social cognition. *Proceedings of the National Academy of Sciences, USA, 104,* 12,577–12,580.
Kohlberg, L. (1981). *Essays on moral development: Vol. I. The philosophy of moral development.* San Francisco, CA: Harper & Row.
Kohlberg, L. (1984). *Essays on moral development: Vol. II. The psychology of moral development.* San Francisco, CA: Harper & Row.
Krebs, D.L. (2008). Morality: An evolutionary account. *Perspectives on Psychological Science, 3,* 149–172.
London, P. (1970). The rescuers: Motivational hypotheses about Christians who saved Jews from the Nazis. In J. Macauley & J. Berkowitz (eds), *Altruism and helping behavior* (pp. 241–250). New York: Academic Press.
Mahajan, N., & Wynn, K. (2012). Origins of "us" vesrus "them": Prelinguistic infants prefer similar others. *Cognition, 124,* 227–233.
Marton, K. (1982). *Wallenberg.* New York: Random House.
McFarland, S., Brown, D., & Webb, M. (2013). Identification with all humanity as a moral concept and psychological construct. *Current Directions in Psychological Science, 22,* 194–198.
Monroe, K. (1996). *The heart of altruism: Perception of a common humanity.* Princeton, NJ: Princeton University Press.
Nisbett, R. E., & Ross, L. (1980). *Human inference: Strategies and shortcomings of social judgment.* Englewood Cliffs, NJ: Prentice-Hall.
Nucci, L. (2001). *Education in the moral domain.* Cambridge: Cambridge University Press.
Oliner, S. P., & Oliner, P. M. (1988). *The altruistic personality.* New York: Free Press.
Opotow, S. (2005). Hate, conflict, and moral exclusion. In R. J. Sternberg (ed.), *The psychology of hate* (pp. 121–153). Washington, DC: American Psychological Association.
Osswald, S., Greitmeyer, T., Fischer, P., & Frey, D. (2010). Moral courage. In E. Kals & J. Maes (eds), *Justice and conflicts* (pp. 391–405). Heidelberg: Springer-Verlag.
Parker, M. T., & Janoff-Bulman, R. (2013). Lessons from morality-based social identity: The power of outgroup "hate," not just ingroup "love." *Social Justice Research, 26,* 81–96.
Pinker, S. (2011). *The better angels of our nature: Why violence has declined.* New York: Viking.
Rai, T. S., & Fiske, A. P. (2011). Moral psychology is relationship regulation: Moral motives for unity, hierarchy, equality, and proportionality. *Psychological Review, 118,* 57–75.
Richerson, P. J., & Boyd, R. (2005). *Not by genes alone: How culture transformed human evolution.* Chicago, IL: University of Chicago Press.
Rozin, P., Lowery, L., Imada, S., & Haidt, J. (1999). The CAD triad hypothesis: A mapping between three moral emotions (contempt, anger, disgust) and three moral codes (community, autonomy, divinity). *Journal of Personality and Social Psychology, 76,* 574–586.
Shepela, S. T., Cook, J., Horlitz, E., Leal, R., Luciano, S., Lutfy, E., Miller, C., Mitchell, G., & Worden, E. (1999). Courageous resistance: A special case of altruism. *Theory and Psychology, 96,* 787–805.
Singer, P. (2011). *The expanding circle: Ethics, evolution, and moral progress.* Princeton, NJ: Princeton University Press.
Skitka, L. J. (2010). The psychology of moral conviction. *Social and Personality Psychology Compass, 4,* 267–281.

Skitka, L. J., & Houston, D. A. (2001). When due process is of no consequence: Moral mandates and presumed defendant guilt or innocence. *Social Justice Research, 14*(3), 305–326.

Skitka, L. J., & Mullen, E. (2002). The dark side of moral conviction. *Analyses of Social Issues and Public Policy, 2*, 35–41.

Skitka, L. J., Bauman, C. W., & Lytle, B. L. (2009). The limits of legitimacy: Moral and religious convictions as constraints on deference to authority. *Journal of Personality and Social Psychology, 97*, 567–578.

Skitka, L. J., Bauman, C. W., & Sargis, E. G. (2005). Moral conviction: Another contributor to attitude strength or something more? *Journal of Personality and Social Psychology, 88*, 895–917.

Staub, E. (1978). *Positive social behavior and morality, Vol. 1: Social and personal influences*. New York: Academic Press.

Staub, E. (1979). *Positive social behavior and morality, Vol. 2: Socialization and development*. New York: Academic Press.

Staub, E. (1989). *The roots of evil: The origins of genocide and other group violence*. New York: Cambridge University Press.

Staub, E. (2003). *The psychology of good and evil: Why children, adults and groups help and harm others*. New York: Cambridge University Press.

Stephan, M. J., & Chenoweth, E. (2008). Why civil resistance works: The strategic logic of nonviolent conflict. *International Security, 33*, 7–44.

Tarrant, M., Branscombe, N. R., Warner, R. H., & Weston, D. (2012). Social identity and perceptions of torture: It's moral when we do it. *Journal of Experimental Social Psychology, 48*, 513–518.

Tec, N. (1986). *When light pierced the darkness: Christian rescue of Jews in Nazi-occupied Poland*. Oxford: Oxford University Press.

Turiel, E. (2002). *The culture of morality: Social development, context, and conflict*. Cambridge, UK: Cambridge University Press.

Wilson, E. O. (2012). *The social conquest of earth*. New York: W. W. Norton

Wong, L., Kolditz, T. A., Millen, R. A., & Potter, T. M. (2003). *Why they fight: Combat motivation in the Iraq war*. Carlisle Barracks, PA: Strategic Studies Institute.

Yoeli, E., & Rand, D. (2015). The trick to acting heroically. *The New York Times* (August 30), p. SR10.

Zimbardo, P. G. (2007). *The Lucifer effect: Understanding how good people turn evil*. New York: Random House.

Index

Abu Ghraib 24, 358, 407
ACT UP/NY 253–60
Adams, J. 316–17
Adams, L. 13, 469–72
agency 4–5, 11, 121, 124, 126–7, 139, 211, 220, 291, 296, 469, 471; communion and 112–15, 130–1; embodied 153–6; emergency of heroic leadership and 89, 92–5; moral character and 100, 109, 112–15; relational developmental systems (RDS) metatheory and 92–4; transformation and 390; 402–12
AIDS/HIV 133, 233, 251, 253, 255–6, 259, 448–9
Albayrak, T. 165, 167
Alcoholics Anonymous (AA) 408
Alford, C. F. 362
Algoe, S. B. 26, 125, 254, 259, 318, 428–30
Ali, M. 391
Allison, S. T. 3–8, 10, 12, 141, 143–51, 156–157, 295, 310–11, 424, 459–61, 515–16, 521; capacity for morality 222; death positivity bias 319; fall of heroes 452; family members as heroes 328; Great Eight traits of heroism 6–7, 21, 93, 123, 153–4, 158, 206–7, 218, 293, 303, 320, 470, 507–8; heroic leadership dynamic (HLD) 4, 6, 25, 139, 143–4, 149–51, 154–6, 258, 388–9; hero mythology and prototypes 463, 466; heroes vs. villains 520; identification with struggle 344–5; on Joe Darby 357–8, 364; self-control 516; taxonomy of heroes 24–5; transparent heroes 277, 333; witnesses of heroism 417
Allport, G. 99
altruism 20–2, 60, 93–5, 130, 146, 148, 270, 429, 433; altruistic suicide 65; calling and 327, 426; competitive altruism 46, 535, 539; deliberative heroism and 537; digital altruism 285; empathy-altruism hypothesis 463–4, 472; gender and 83; helper's high and 156; heroic altruism in Nazi Europe 203–23; heroic risk-taking and 74, 310, 330, 418, 420, 434–5, 495, 538; heroic sacrifice and 310, 330, 418, 420, 434, 538; heroic transformation and 384, 386, 389; heroism and 74–80, 82–5, 310, 330, 418, 420, 434–5, 495, 538; offspring care model of 77–9, 83–5; parochial altruism 446; psychopathy and 529, 533, 535–41; "pure" altruism 68–9; spiritual leadership and 302, 303, 308; whistleblowing and 358–9, 361–2, 371
Altruistic Personality Project 204
American Civil War 131, 197, 463, 507–8; *see also* Lincoln A.
Anand, V. 171
Anderson, V. L. 208
Anthony, S. B. 384, 386
Apollo 13 space mission 187, 190–1, 197
Ardelt, M. 11
Arendt, H. 100, 220, 410–11, 467
Aristotle 103, 108, 143
Arnett, J. 266
Aronson, E. 344
Asch, S. E. 131, 220, 251
Assad, B. 476
Assange, J. 363
Augustine of Hippo 384
Aung San Suu Kyi 23, 29, 31, 65, 113, 548

Babbage, C. 44
Bakan, D. 112, 113
banality of evil 4, 100, 139, 148, 156–8, 220, 286, 410–11, 467, 530
Bandura, A. 94, 140, 172, 173, 253, 273, 321, 323
Barclay, P. 10
Bardi, A. 176
Batson, C. D. 170, 176, 205, 206, 216, 461–3, 538

Index

Baum, S. K. 219
Baumeister, R. 3, 6, 274, 516
Baumert, A. 11
Bazerman, M. H. 171
Becker, S. W. 19, 20, 27, 76–7, 89, 147, 206, 318–19, 444, 521, 531
Begley, S. 150
Bell, A. G. 44
Bellah, R. 324–5
Bem, D. J. 102, 403, 551
Bennis, W. 186, 198
Bentham, J. 103
Beowulf 2, 383
Berglas, S. 350
Berkowitz, M. W. 91–3
Bharadwaj, P. 13
big game hunting 40–1
Biswas-Diener, R. 264
Black Lives Matter 396, 351
Blau, K. 1, 20, 89, 139, 205, 251–2, 259, 283, 286–7, 289, 295, 318, 330, 332, 333, 348, 411, 467, 495, 548
Blum, L. A. 103
body *see* embodied cognition; embodied consciousness; embodied heroism; embodied wisdom
Bornstein, M. H. 95
Bowles, S. 445
Brandtstädter, J. 89
bravery 20–3, 26, 31, 37, 42, 93, 101–11, 217, 230–1, 262, 264, 277, 316, 320, 322, 347–8, 351, 357–8, 361–2. 364–5, 371, 417–21, 431–4, 460, 463, 472, 481, 513, 533, 538
Brickman, P. 551
broad-minded affective coping (BMAC) 30
Bronfenbrenner, U. 90
Bronk, K. C. 13
Bronstein, P. 537
Brown, A. J. 12
Brown, A. M. 44
Brown, B. 223
Brown, C. 521
Brown, S. D. 328
Buchanan, T. W. 444
Buddhism 120–1, 130, 328, 381, 383, 385, 392, 395; *see also* Dalai Lama
bullying 31, 143, 166, 214, 222, 406, 409, 536–8; bystander effect and 441; cyber-bullying 289, 293; moral courage and 166, 264; role conflict and 443
Burkhard, B. 11
Bush, G. W. 128, *129*, 244, 488
bystander apathy/effect 14, 31, 77, 81–2, 100, 166, 168, 170–2, 175–7, 359, 440–1, 529
bystanders 20, 24–5, 251–2, 264, 289, 451, 531–2, 537; bystander training 389; Holocaust and 204, 208, 209–23, 387, 538; moral courage and 166, 168, 172, 175–7; opposite of a hero 394

Cahill, M. B. 126, 132
Cairo, A. 13
Callina, K. S. *see* Schmid Callina, K.
calling: call to engage 426; everyday heroes and 333–4; heroism and 3, 327–34, 432; higher calling 3, 307, 310, 358; identity striving and 276; work as 12, 245, 324–7
Campbell, J. 8–9, 19, 25, 142–3, 147–9, 151–2, 156, 231, 470–1; hero monomyth 3–4, 6, 310, 317–18, 339, 379, 381, 383, 390, 393; meaning 509–10, 521; purpose 503; transformation 379–83, 387–96, 404
Canadian Medal of Bravery 101, 103–4
career development 316–34; future research 331–3; heroism and 317–24; work as a calling 324–31
Carello, C. 153–7
Caring Canadian Award 101, 104, 106, 111
Carlyle, T. 1–4, 7–9, 13
Carnegie, A. 486
Carnegie Hero Medal 36, 38, 42–3, 47, 59, 76, 95, 216, 532, 541, 547
catch-22 situations 189, 190
Ceaser, D. 331
CEOs 121, 268, 270, 300, 308, 361
character development 88–96, 146
charisma 11, 130, 132–3, 332, 391, 483; etymology 2; and Great Eight attributes of heroism 6, 21, 93–4, 123, 126, 153, 207, 293, 303, 320, 461, 508; charismatic leadership 2, 186, 391, 465–6, 472
charitable giving 51–2, 63, 129, 292
Charlie Hebdo massacre 186, 223
Chemero, A. 140–1
Choosing Wisdom (film) 235–7, 241–5
Chrisley, R. 149
Churchill, W. 465, 489, 510–11, 513, 518
Cikara, M. 446
civil heroes 5, 22–4, 90, 287, 289, 531
Civil Rights Movement 132–3, 264, 380, 384, 401, 409, 422, 535, 555; *see also* King, M. L., Jr.
Civil War *see* American Civil War
Cleckley, H. 526–7, 535
Clinton, H. 350
cognition: cognitive dissonance 222, 551; distributed cognition (DC) 13, 466–72; dual process model 59, 68; embodied cognition 143, 145–6, 148–9, 157; epiphany experience 259; moral cognition 108, 115; social heuristics and 58, 64–5, 68–9
Cohen, D. 442
Cohen, T. R. 556
Colby, A. 96, 106, 111, 210, 217, 220, 418, 420, 497, 498
Columbine school shooting 406
coming-of-age stories 381, 385–6
communion 100, 104, 109, 112–15, 126–7, 130–1, 392–3
competence 23, 44, 80, 82, 93, 121, 130, 207,

562

232, 245, 273, 304, 329, 340, 344, 385, 407, 412, 417, 440, 459–62, 466–8; incompetence 245, 253, 350, 438, 513
Condren, M. 11
Conger, J. A. 466
connectors 132–3
Conway, P. 20–1, 26
Cooper, C. 361
Corley, R. 204, 538
correspondence bias 126
Corrigan, J. 126, 132
Costa Concordia disaster 187, 189–90
costly signaling theory and 36, 40–6, 49–53, 75–6, 533–4; heroism judgment as costly signaling 49–50; signaling intelligence 44–5; signaling physical abilities 41–3; signaling wealth and resources 43–4; signaling willingness to help 45, 50
courage: existential courage 262–80; moral courage 165–78, 206–7, 213, 217–20, 222–3, 264–5, 394, 535, 537–8, 541, 547, 552; physical courage 264
Crandall, R. 24
crisis, heroism in times of 185–99; action strategies 194–8; Apollo 13 mission 187, 190–1; *Costa Concordia* disaster 187, 189–90; definitions and theories of crisis 187–9; economic crisis 187, 191–4; examples of 189–94; future research 198–9; situational dynamics of crisis 187–9
crowd theory 2
Csikszentmihalyi, M. 11, 156, 265, 286, 295, 301
Cyberhero archetype 285–6, 289–93

Dalai Lama 25, 120–1, 124, *125*, 126, 130, 219
Dallas (television series) 384
Dallas Buyers Club 386
Daman, J. 208
Damon, W. 96, 106, 111, 210, 217, 220, 418, 420, 497, 498
Darby, J. 24, 357, 364
Darley, J. M. 77, 81, 100, 165, 167, 168, 170, 220, 251, 359, 389, 440, 537
Darwin, C. 2, 50–1
Davidai, S. 343
Davis, K. 554
Davis, M. 51
Dayal, P. 283, 289
de Gaulle, C. 481
de St. Aubin, E. 110
de Waal, F. 77, 556
Decter-Frain, A. 11
despotic tyrants and despotic power 3, 476–90; accountability and 486; dominance motivation and 485–6; evolutionary roots of dominance and prestige-orientations 477–8; from power to leadership 484–9; individual differences and 478–9; intergroup competition and 488–9; legitimacy threat and 487; moderators of the effect of power 485–9; narcissism and 483; power and status 477–83; power and status hierarchies in modern society 480–1; prestige motivation and 484; social influences on status and power 480–1; stability threat and 488
DeSteno, D. 277
deviant heroes (activists and artists) 249–60; *see also* social heroism
Di Stefano, P. 495, 531, 538
Diaz, J. 62–3
Diamond, A. 110
diffusion of responsibility 81, 172, 220; *see also* bystander apathy/effect
Dik, B. 12
Dillard, A. 392
dispositions and predispositions 126, 171–4, 176, 211, 212, 215, 218–23, 324, 330, 393, 395, 517, 526, 530–1, 541, 550; moral heroism and 11, 102–5, 107–8, 111, 115; situationism versus 9, 100–4
distributed cognition 468–72
dualistic thinking 393–4
Dunbar, R. I. M. 42, 533
Dunlop, W. L. 104, 112, 113, 318–19, 411, 417, 419, 531
Dweck, C. 277
Dyck, A. 166

Eagly, A. H. 20, 27, 76–7, 89, 147, 206, 318–19, 444, 521, 531
Earhart, A. 25
ecological psychology 140, 153–5, 157
economic crisis 187, 191–4, 466, 489
education and socio-cultural change heroes 31–2
Efthimiou, O. 1, 4–5, 11, 296, 382, 386, 395–6
Eichmann, A. 100, 467
Einstein, A. 392
Eisenberg, N. 173–6, 205, 211
elevation 121, 132, 254–5, 258–9, 308, 389–91, 418, 427–35, 476, 515
Ellsberg, D. 142, 146, 147
embodied cognition 143, 145–6, 148–9, 157
embodied consciousness 11, 139, 141, 144, 149, 157–8
embodied heroism 139–59, 386, 396; hero organism 148–59; heroic body 144–8; heroism as state of consciousness 141–4; multi-disciplinarity, and 140–1
embodied wisdom 314
emerging adults 114, 266–7, 275–9
Emerson, R. M. 484
Emerson, R. W. 196
Emmons, R. A. 270
emotional intelligence 150, 153, 158, 300, 390
empathy 13, 36, 69, 77, 80–1, 84, 109, 168, 176, 231, 234, 235, 242, 271–2, 344, 513, 516; definition of 461–2; dispositional empathy 176; empathic harm aversion 67; heroic empathy 459–72; Holocaust rescuers and 208,

211–16, 218–19, 221–2; hormones and 444; moral conviction and 550, 552, 556; moral courage and 168, 176; psychopathy and 525–9, 533, 535–40; spiritual leadership and 303; transformation and 385, 389, 412
Emrich, C. G. 369
Engel, G. L. 152, 153
enlightenment (Buddhist) 385, 389, 393, 395
Enlightenment Era 103, 107, 557
environmental justice 331
epiphany 254–5, 258–9
Epstein, Z. G. 47, 59, 193, 384, 386, 529, 532
Erikson, E. 4, 266, 267, 311, 385, 391–2
everyday heroes 68, 438, 471, 533–5, 541; callings and 333; embodiment and 142–3; media and 52; moral courage and 11, 165–78; transparent heroes as 25
evolutionary biology and psychology 3, 4, 10, 36–53, 379–80, 451, 533; fitness benefits 3, 36, 38–40, 46–7, 49, 63, 75, 78; group selection 64; helping and 38–9; homology 11, 79–84; ingroup bias/loyalty 64–5, 122, 349, 445–7, 448–9, 549, 554, 556–7; justice and 60–3; kin selection theory 3, 36, 38, 53; offspring care model of altruism 77–85; pacifism and 65–8; paradox of heroism as altruism 74–7; punishment 3; reciprocity 53; self-interest 58–69; solidarity and 63–5; tag-based cooperation 64; vested interest 3; *see also* prosociality and prosocial behavior
evolutionary neurobiology 74–85
existential courage 262–80; courage research 263–4; identity striving in emergent adults 266–7; identity striving as 265–6; inductive research approach 267–9; methodological implications 278; practical implications 278–9; profiles in 269–75; theoretical implications 275–8

Fagin-Jones, S. 11, 204, 206–9, 213–19
Fairey, S. 125
Farthing, G. W. 42
Fennelly, C. 421–7
Fink, S. L. 438
Fischer, P. 166–8, 172, 537
Fiske, A. P. 554–6
Fiske, S. T. 446
Flanagan, O. 103, 108
Fleeson, W. 104
Flow Genome Project 151, 156–8
Fogelman, E. 213, 215
foot-in the door- phenomenon 213, 551
forgiveness 111, 235, 238–41, 410, 513–15
Fosha, D. 150
Franco, Z. 1, 4–8, 11, 20, 22, 24, 89–92, 94, 139, 141, 146–8, 150, 156–8, 167, 205, 251–2, 259, 286–7, 289, 295, 310, 318, 330, 332–3, 418, 420–1, 434–5, 467, 471, 532
Frank, A. 212, 499, 501, 503, 548

Frankl, V. 276, 327, 388, 511
Frazier, J. A. 342
Fredrickson, B. L. 30, 276
free will 9–10, 142
Fremont, E. 11
Freud, S. 2–3, 344, 380
Frey, D. 166–8, 172, 537
Friedman, P. 208, 223
Friend, S. 140, 386; *see also* Resilience Project
Frimer, J. A. 5, 11, 103, 104, 106–14, 219, 220, 318–20, 411, 418–19, 531
Fruchtl, J. 19
Fry, V. 216
functions of heroes 25–7

Gallagher, S. 141, 142, 143, 145, 155
Gandhi, M. K. 25, 31, 50, 59, 65, 68, 94, 123, 251, 287, 304, 30, 328, 384, 386, 394, 401–3, 481, 511, 530
Ganz, I. 204, 210–12
Garcia, M. 125
Gardner, H. 265, 275, 393
Gash, H. 20–1, 26
Gates, B. 43, 262, 448
Gelineau, V. A. 439
generosity 42–7, 75, 91, 94, 123, 126, 328, 392, 431, 445, 448–50, 460, 463, 472, 481–2
Genovese, K. 81–2, 220
Gestsdottir, S. 92
Gies, M. 212, 221, 499, 501–3
Gilgamesh epic 379, 389
Gilligan, C. 103
Gilovich, T. 343, 443
Gino, F. 171, 382, 410
Gintis, H. 445
Giraffe Heroes Project 23
Gladwell, M. 133, 344, 471
Gneezy, U. 52
Goethals, G. R. 3–8, 10, 12, 141, 143–51, 156–7, 295, 310–11, 424, 459–61, 515–16, 521; capacity for morality 222; death positivity bias 319; fall of heroes 452; family members as heroes 328; Great Eight traits of heroism 6–7, 21, 93, 123, 153–4, 158, 206–7, 218, 293, 303, 320, 470, 507–8; heroic leadership dynamic (HLD) 4, 6, 25, 139, 143–4, 149–51, 154–6, 258, 388–9; hero mythology and prototypes 463, 466; on Joe Darby 357–8, 364; self-control 516; taxonomy of heroes 24–5; transparent heroes 277, 333; witnesses of heroism 417
Goldschmied, N. 12
good Samaritans 7, 8, 24, 76, 318, 330, 531
Goodwin, D. K. 520
Goranson, A. 12
Graebe, F. 213, 214, 221
Graham, J. 69
Graham, L. 12
Grant, C. 358, 360–1, 362

gratitude 13, 26, 31, 428, 519
Gravity (film) 390, 511
Gray, K. 12, 140, 386, 396, 429, 435, 555
Great Eight traits of heroism 6–7, 21, 93, 123, 153–4, 158, 206–7, 218, 293, 303, 320, 470, 507–8
great man theory of heroic leadership 1–4, 7, 9, 120
Great Recession of 2007 187, 191–4
Green, J. 13
Greitemeyer, T. 166–8, 172, 537
Groundhog Day (film) 386
Gundlach, M. J. 168, 170, 174
Gushee, D. P. 208, 210, 215
Guyer, M. J. 439
Gyatso, T. *see* Dalai Lama

Hackler, J. C. 442
Hagiwara, Nao 13
Haidt, J. 24, 26, 122, 125, 147, 254, 259, 389, 418, 428–30, 433, 512, 553
Haldane, J. B. S. 38
Halmburger, A. 11
Hamilton, W. D. 36, 38, 49, 75
Hamlin, K. 393
Hannah, S. T. 91–2, 94
Hardman, K. 36
Hare, R. D. 526, 527, 528, 538, 539
Harrison, J. 519
Harry Potter (fictional character) 25, 339, 383, 403–4, 511, 513–14
Hartshorne, Hugh 100
Hawking, S. 387
Hawley, P. H. 205, 540
Hayes, Chris 48
health, wellbeing, and rehabilitation heroes 30–1
Hegel, G. W. F. 19, 142
Hein, G. 446
helping behavior 11, 59, 62, 206, 211, 223, 252, 337, 384, 429, 516; moral courage and 165, 167–8, 170–2, 174, 176
Hemingway, E. 362
Hero Construction Company 31, 143, 394, 504
hero functions framework 20, 26–7; enhancing 26–7; moral modeling 27; protecting 27
hero gene 386
hero identification 28
hero judgments 39, 48–51
hero narratives 417–35
hero organism (HO) 4–5, 11, 139, 145–6, 148–58, 296, 382
hero worship 1–2, 13, 387
heroes, types of 24–5; classic heroes 25, 361, 363, 365, 371, 385, 404, 509; cyberheroes 285–6, 289–93; deviant heroes (activists and artists) 249–60; enlightened heroes 385, 392; folklore/fictive heroes 37; Holocaust rescuers 79, 81, 203–23, 499, 515, 535, 536, 538, 552; intellectual heroes 44, 53; medical heroes 229–46; moral heroes 99–116; networked heroes 283–96; prototypical heroes 3, 37, 141; redeemed heroes 386; traditional heroes 8, 23, 24, 27, 291, 295, 318; tragic heroes 8, 25, 318, 361, 362; transforming heroes 8, 25, 318; transitional heroes 6, 8, 25, 318; transitory heroes 8, 24–25, 27, 318; transparent heroes 8, 25, 27, 277, 318, 333; transposed heroes 8, 25, 318; trending heroes 8, 24, 318 underdogs 7–8, 12, 251, 319, 339–52, 509–13; whistleblowers 356–71; *see also individual entries*; heroism
heroic chapters 418–27, 435; *see also* hero narratives
heroic empathy 459–72; charismatic leadership and 465–6; distributed cognition and 468–72; empathy defined 461–2; empathy's role in heroic leadership 466–8; prosocial behavior and 462–3; self-sacrifice and 463–5; *see also* empathy
heroic failure 186–7, 189–90
heroic imagination 4, 10, 186, 252, 259, 286, 295, 333, 467, 554, 557
Heroic Imagination Project 31, 143
heroic influence 8, 10, 24, 29–30
heroic leadership dynamic (HLD) 4, 6, 25, 139, 143–4, 149–51, 154–6, 258, 388–9
heroic self-efficacy 4, 253, 259; *see also* self-efficacy
heroism: adaptive everyday ethical behavior and 58–69; calling and 3, 327–34, 432; career development and 316–34; central and peripheral traits 6–7, 22–4, 431; character development and 88–96; definitions of 5–7, 20, 37, 43, 167, 530–2; embodied 139–58; as embodied skill acquisition 143, 396; emergent heroism 5, 59, 62–3, 65, 68, 423; evolutionary perspectives on 36–53, 58–69, 74–85; existential courage and 262–79; impediments to 438–52; impulsive versus deliberative 532–8; meaning and 507–21; in medicine 229–46; metaphors of 4–5; moral character and 99–116; moral convictions and 547–57; moral courages and 165–78; in networked society 283–96; neurobiology of 67, 74–85, 157, 158; non-adaptive explanations of 46–7; objective approach to defining 5–6; principle-based heroism 548–9; psychopathy and 525–41; purpose and 495–504; relational developmental systems (RDS) and 88–96; situationist/situationalist approach 4, 7–8, 9, 11, 13, 20, 100–4, 185, 187–9, 319–20, 331–2; social heroism in everyday life 249–60; subjective approach to defining 6–7; sustained heroism 5, 59, 63, 65, 68; in times of crisis 185–99; *see also* heroes, types of
heroism science 1–14, 139, 142, 145–6, 149, 151, 155, 158, 284, 286, 360–1, 380; rise of 140–1; themes of 9–10

Index

Hilfiker, D. 231–2, 236
Hippocratic oath 65
Hitler, A. 50, 113, 203, 209, 380, 502, 510
HIV *see* AIDS/HIV
Hobbit, The 385, 387
Hoffman, M. L. 211, 461, 463
Hoffman, T. 361–2
Hogan, B. 386
Hollander, E. P. 391
Holocaust 100, 501, 503, 554
Holocaust rescuers 79, 81, 203–23, 499, 515, 535, 536, 538, 551–2; demographics 207–12; implications and future research 220–3; moral exemplarity and 220–1; personality variables 215–18; situational variables 212–15; social responsibility and 216
Homer 22, 231, 387, 396
Hopson, J. 166
House (television series) 469
Howard, J. A. 173
Hrdy, S. 77
Huneke, D. K. 212–15
humility 3, 11, 13, 28, 106, 221, 233–4, 238–9, 245, 301, 451, 515–16, 519–20
Humphrey, R. 13, 464
Hutchins, E. 468

identity striving 262–80; courage research and, 263–4; emergent adults and 266–7; as existential courage 265–6; inductive research approach 267–9; methodological implications 278; practical implications 278–9; profiles in existential courage 269–75; theoretical implications 275–8
Igou, E. 4, 6–7, 10, 93, 295, 318, 391, 418, 428, 431, 460, 467
Ihle, C. 36
impediments to heroism 438–52; accidental impediments 439–45; bystander effect 440–1; cheating and 449–50; cultural norms 442; hormones 444; masculinity 442–3; misperception 443; neural processes 444; norm-shifting and 448; outgroups and 445–8; perceived self-promotion 443–4; perceptual inhibitors 442–4; physiological influences 444; purposeful impediments 445–50; role conflict 443; selfish person stereotype 448–9; social environment 441–2; thwarted heroism versus cowardice 450–1
incentives 45–6, 50–3, 123, 554
infrahumanization 447
ingroups 64–5, 122, 340, 349, 441, 445–7, 448–9, 549, 554, 556–7; *see also* outgroups
Insko, C. A. 556
Invisible Children 131
Islamic State 203, 223, 293

Jackson, K. T. 302
Jackson, M. 121, 385

James, W. 1, 4, 19, 32, 106, 145, 380, 384, 389, 391–2, 395
Jameson, J. J. 438, 448
Janoff-Bulman, R. 13, 111, 446
Jayawickreme, E. 495, 531, 538
Jefferson, T. 428, 463–4
Jenner, C. 386
Jesus of Nazareth 25, 318, 328, 358, 393, 404, 499, 512, 517
Jewish Foundation for the Righteous 207
Joan of Arc 394, 511
Jobs, S. 262
John Paul II, Pope 514
Johnson, A. 392
Johnson, D. D. P. 46
Johnson, M. 5, 139–40, 142, 144–8, 153
Johnson, R. A. 305, 389
Johnson, R. C. 538
Jones, A. 24
Jones, E. E. 349, 350
Jordan, M. 48, 121
Josie King Foundation 233
Joy, W. B. 147
Jung, C.: archetypes theory 3, 9, 142, 285, 289; collective unconscious 301, 381; transformation 387, 395; wounded healer 231, 313
justice 58–69, 91–2, 103, 166–9, 171, 175–6; environmental justice 331; moral courage and 166–8, *169*, 171, 175–6; social justice 127–8, 143, 285, 296, 425, 500, 527, 553; underdogs and 345–9

Kafashan, S. 10
Kant, I. 103, 117
Kantor, D. 439
Kanungo, R. N. 466
Karsky, J. 217
Katz, R. L. 461–2
Kaufman, J. 63
Kaulesar, B. 67
Keller, H. 309, 385
Kellett, J. B. 464
Kelly, J. A. 133
Kelly, S. 42, 533
Keltner, D. 24, 433
Kennedy, J. F. 95, 128, 129
Kim, J. 341, 342, 349
Kim Jong-il 113
Kim Jong-un 476
King, M. L., Jr. 23, 31, 50, 94, 121, 124, 126–8, 133, 219, 251, 264, 287, 304, 328, 384, 386, 391, 394, 401–3, 530, 548, 554, 555
King, S. 233–4
King, W. F. H. 249
Kinsella, E. 4, 6–7, 10, 93, 140, 152, 295, 318, 391, 418, 428, 431, 460, 467, 508, 531
Kirby, K. E. 330
Klapp, O. E. 7, 19, 25, 27

Klisanin, D. 12, 467
Kohen, A. 5, 7, 496
Kohlberg, L. 103, 105–8, 120, 461
Kohlreiser, G. 223
Kok, B. E. 396
Kony, J. 131, 283, 287
Kotler, S. 156–7
Kraft-Todd, G. 10, 51
Kramer, R. M. 12
Krassnitzky, O. 146
Kubler-Ross, E. 313
Kuhl, U. 173
Kyle, C. 530

Lady Gaga 24, 530
Landau, M. J. 24, 148–9
Landers, J. E. 386
Latané, B. 77, 81, 165, 167, 168, 220, 251, 359, 389, 440, 537
Latour, B. 283
Lau, E. 12
Le Bon, G. 2
Le Grice, K. 381
leadership: charismatic leadership 2, 186, 465–6, 472; heroic leadership 2–4, 10, 25, 88–96, 154–8, 185–99, 210, 245, 258, 303, 310, 386, 388, 391, 466–72, 476–7, 482–4, 489; relational developmental systems (RDS) and 88–96; spiritual leadership 12, 120, 300–14; *see also* heroic leadership dynamic (HLD)
Leary, D. 4
Lebuda, I. 11
Lee, B. H., 112, 113, 411
Lent, R. W. 328
Lerner, R. 91, 94, 146
Les Misérables 514
Lester, P. B. 94–5
Lewis, I. 316–17, 319, 322–4, 328–9
Lewis, S. H. 442
Lightner, C. 386
Lilienfeld, S. 13
Lincoln, A. 131, 197–8, 463–4, 476, 485, 507–11, 513, 520, 530
Lobel, T. 145, 153–4
Lois, J. 443
Lopez, S. J. 263
Lord of the Rings 390, 509
Lykken, D. T. 526, 527, 529, 532, 534–5, 541

Maddi, S. 265
Maleficent 385
masculinity 2–3, 22, 28, 231, 442–3
McAdams, D. P. 102, 108–10, 404, 417, 419–20, 425–6, 430
McCain, J. 95, 96
McCallum, R. 149
McLaughlin, J. 316, 317
Machiavellianism 536, 540
McIntyre, S. 48

McNab, A. 525
McVeigh, T. 554
Magnusson, D. 101
Maher, B. 530
Malcolm X 394, 409
Mandela, N. 23, 25, 31, 106, 113, 128, 251, 386, 478, 482–3, 485, 511, 548
Mansfield, E. 110
March on Washington 278
Marsh, A. 83, 536
martial heroes 5, 22–4, 90, 205, 249, 287
martyrs 7, 8, 24, 128, 130, 230, 250, 318–19, 362, 368, *369*, 370, *370*, 460, 531
masculinity 442
Maslow, A. 3–4, 278, 380, 387–8, 391–4
Matsuba, M. K. 101, 107, 114
mavens (trusted experts) 132–3
May, M. 100
May, N. 11
May, R. 278
Mayr, E. 77
Mead, N. 13
meaning and heroism 507–21; defending meaning 519–21; definitions of heroism and meaning 507–9; meaning-making in the hero narrative 509–13; meaning via forgiveness 513–15; meaning via gratitude 519–20; meaning via humility 515; meaning via prosociality 515–16; meaning via self-control 516–19; obstacles and 512–13; social connection and 511–12; virtue and 513–19; *see also* purpose and heroism
Meaning Maintenance Model (MMM) 511–12, 520, 553
medical heroes 229–46; heroic leadership in medicine 244–5; hero's journey and 233–4; path from adversity to wisdom 237–9; physician mistakes and 231–3; post-traumatic growth and 234; responses to medical error 239–44; wisdom in medicine 234–6; wounded hero archetype and 229, 231
Menon, S. T. 466
mentors 3, 110, 115, 242, 310, 327, 388, 390–1, 396, 419, 429, 470, 500–1, 509, 513, 518, 520
Merleau-Ponty, M. 139, 141–4, 147–8, 150–2, 156, 158
metaphor 19, 25, 30–1, 107, 125, 145–6, 231, 236, 395; metaphors of heroism 4–5
metaphoric identity mapping (MIM) 31
Miceli, M. P, 166, 170, 172, 174–5, 178, 357
Michniewicz, K. 12
Midlarsky, E. 204, 206–9, 213–19, 221, 503, 504, 537, 538, 541
Mikula, G. 171, 176
Milgram, S. 81, 95, 100, 133, 219, 250, 251, 408–9, 441–2
Milk, H. 394
Miller, L. 12
Miller, W. 68

Index

Moby Dick 405
Monroe, K. 216, 219, 557
Monteiro, L. H. 150–1
Montoya, R. M. 556
moral character 11, 99–116, 218, 347, 402–3
moral convictions 482, 547–57; darker side of heroism and 552–4; everyday heroes and 171–2, 174–5, 178; heroism and 549–50; moral transformation and 411; origins of 550–2; principal-based heroism 548–9; psychopathy and 531, 535, 537, 539–41
moral courage 165–78, 394, 535, 547, 552; bullying and 222, 537; definition of 165–7, 537; existential courage and 264–5; future research and practical implications 176–8; heroism of 167; of Holocaust rescuers 206–7, 213, 217–20, 223; identity and 264–5; integrative model of 167–76; medical heroism and 231; psychopathy and 537–8, 541
Moral Foundations Theory (MFT) 69, 553
Moral Heroes 23
moral heroes and moral heroism 11, 99–116, 120–33; Carlyle's classes of heroes and 8; developmental roots of 110; developmental trajectories of 113–15; evidence of 422–4; first-time vs. older age heroic chapters 419–27, 435; followers and 120–33; foundation for 108; group benefits from 122–3; hero creation and 123–7; influence on others 429–32; integration of agency and communion 111–12; judgment-action gap 107–8; moral stories and 417–21; redemption and 110–11; selection of heroes and 6; transcendence and 105–7; varieties of 103–5; whistleblowers as 358
moral modeling 10, 26–7, 418, 428, 508
moral transformation 401–12; becoming your own hero 410–11; character and typecasting 402–10; hero to victim 407–8; hero to villain 406–7; scientific implications 411–12; victim to hero 403–5; victim to villain 405–6; villain to hero 409–10; villain to victim 408–9; *see also* transformation
morality, dyadic 401–3, 412
Morsi, M. 408
Mount Rushmore National Monument 463–4
Moya, P. 141–4, 152
Muller, P. A. 171, 529
Murphy, B. 13
Mustaro, P. N. 150–1
Mycoskie, B. 122

Nakamura, J. 12
narcissism 2, 126, 387, 409, 483–4, 528, 540
Nazi Germany 6, 79, 203–23, 320, 501–3, 514, 521, 530, 548, 552; *see also* Holocaust; Holocaust rescuers
Near, J. P. 166, 170, 172, 174–5, 178, 357
Nelson, L. D. 343

Nelson, S. D. 150, 152
nepotism 49, 53, 490
networked society 283–96; digital altruism 285–6; future of 292–6; psyche of networked hero 289–92
neurobiology 67, 74–85, 157, 158
new heroism 142, 147, 151
Niesta Kayser, D. 168, 176, 539
Nietzsche, F. 1, 2
Nixon, E. 133
Nobel Peace Prize 50, 96, 120, 122, 124, 130, 132, 401
nonviolent resistance/protest 65, 68, 69, 409, 548, 555–7
Norton, M. I. 350
Nucci, L. P. 91–2
Numan, M. 78

Obama, B. 124, 125–6, 129, 130, 132–3, 349–50, 406, 467
observers, impact of heroism and heroes on 417–35; elevation 418, 428–35; first-time vs. older age heroic chapters 419–27, 435; future directions 434–5; moral elevation narratives 430–4; moral exemplars' stories of heroism 418–27; social purpose 418–27; witnesses' stories of heroism 427–30
Occupy Wall Street 295, 351
O'Connor, W. 12
Oedipus 25
Oliner, P. M. 203–4, 206, 208–16, 218, 515
Oliner, S. P. 77, 81, 111, 203–4, 206, 208–16, 218, 320, 515
Osswald, S. 166–8, 172, 537
ostracism 22, 39, 90, 123, 264, 357, 452, 510, 549
outgroups 64, 122, 128, 444–7, 450, 451, 488, 515, 521, 554, 556–7; *see also* ingroups
Owens, J. 11

pacifism 58, 60, 65–9, 510
Paldiel, M. 214, 221
parenting 221–2, 497, 526

Park, C. L. 329
Parks, C. 12–13
Parks, R. 23, 24, 31, 132, 133, 554
Patrick, C. J. 527–9, 533–5, 541
Pavlichenko, L. 530
Payne, C. R. 94, 167, 186
personal sacrifice 13, 20, 22, 24, 58, 126, 128–30, 324, 330–1, 446, 463–4, 482
personality: characteristic adaptations 102, 108, 220; dispositional traits 102–5, 107–8, 111, 115; life narratives 102–3, 108–11, 220, 320, 332, 404, 412; *see also* dispositions and predispositions
Peterson, C. 262, 264, 395
philanthropists and philanthropy 43, 51–3, 76, 156, 216, 270, 407, 445, 448, 486

physical characteristics of heroes 23–4
physical feats of heroism 37, 547, 550; *see also* rescuers
physical intelligence (PI) 139, 145–6, 153–6, 158
Pinker, S. 66, 116, 554, 557
Pittman, T. S. 349
Pitts, R. C. 105
Plato 107, 143
Plews-Ogan, M. 11, 233
portraits of heroes 124–5
post-traumatic growth 234, 235, 382, 389, 504
post-traumatic stress disorder (PTSD) 150, 451
pratfall effect 344
presdispositions *see* dispositions and predispositions
Presley, E. 124, 385, 391
Preston, S. 10–11, 463
principle-based heroism 548–9
Pritchard, M. 208, 221
Pritchard Junior, R. 36
prosociality and prosocial behavior 59, 62, 88–90, 110–11, 115, 122, 126, 440, 447, 449; altruism and 418; awe/wonder and 389; career development and 325, 330–1, 334; costly signaling theory and 36, 40–6, 49–53, 533–4; despotic leaders and 482; deviant heroes and 251, 253, 259; everyday heroism and 172, 174, 176; evolution and 36–8, 46–7, 52–3, 77, 79–80, 83–4; fitness benefits of 36–8; helping and 38–9; hero narratives and 147–8, 404; heroic empathy and 462–3; heroism as extreme form of 37; heroism science research and 9; Holocaust rescuers and 205, 210–11, 215–16, 218, 221–3; impact of heroism on observers and 425, 428–9, 432, 434; kin selection and 36; meaning and 515–16, 520; moral courage and 165–7; psychopathy and 526, 531, 533, 536–41; punishment and 39; reciprocity and, 38–9; selflessness versus 358–9; transformation and 389–90, 404, 406, 411–12; vested interest and 39; whistleblowing and 371; *see also* altruism
protecting 7, 10, 20, 22–3, 25–7, 31, 37, 93, 165–6, 170, 173, 175, 508, 513
prototype theory 105
psychopathy 13, 83, 311, 406, 525–41; definition of psychopathy 525–7; diagnostic and assessment issues 527–8; empathy and 67, 525–9, 532–3, 535–40; future directions 541; heterogeneity in heroism and 530; impulsive versus deliberative heroism 532–8; psychopaths as heroes or criminals 529–30; research 530–40; risk and 538–9; self-enhancement and 539–40; trait versus state debate 530–1; triarchic model of psychopathy 526, 528–9, 534
punishment 38–40, 53, 60–1, 123, 232–3, 250, 366, 409, 445, 447, 449, 451, 461, 480–1, 486, 501, 537

pup retrieval 78–80, 83–4
purpose and heroism 495–504; definition of heroism 495–6; definition of purpose 496–7; exemplars of 499–503; purpose among heroes 497–9; *see also* meaning and heroism
Pury, C. L. S. 263–4
Putin, V. 113, 488

racism 177, 406, 409
Rai, T. S. 554–6
Rand, D. G. 10, 47, 59, 193, 384, 386, 529, 532
Rank, O. 380–1
Rankin, L. 286
Rapoport, A. 439
rationalization structures 171
Reagan, R. 122, *125*, 127–8
reciprocal causal influence 9
reciprocity 49, 51, 53; benefits, 40; direct reciprocity 38–9, 60–1, 63–4, 69, 123; indirect reciprocity 38–9, 61, 64; strong reciprocity 75, 77
redemption 109–11, 385, 405, 410–12, 419–20, 518
regulatory focus 29
relational developmental systems (RDS) metatheory of character development 11, 88–96, 146; definitions of leadership and 89–91; development of leadership and heroism 94–5; overview 88–9; role of agency 92–4
reputational benefits and rewards 43, 46–7, 49, 51–2, 62–3, 65, 68–9, 75
rescuers 20, 24–5, 36, 38, 40, 74, 79–81, 104, 189, 192, 195, 231, 264, 283, 291, 316–17, 320, 323–4, 452, 459, 495, 527, 532; *see also* Holocaust rescuers
Resilience Project 140, 158, 386
resiliency 3, 6, 13, 21, 30, 93, 123, 130, 139–40, 152–4, 158, 196, 199, 207, 273, 277, 293–4, 303, 320, 382, 385–6, 388, 461, 508, 516, 526
resource holding potential (RHP) 66
Richards, R. 277
Riches, B. 13, 112, 113, 411
Righteous Among the Nations honor 205, 552
Ritchie, T. 4, 6–7, 10, 93, 295, 318, 391, 418, 428, 431, 460, 467
Rockefeller, J. 43
Rocky film franchise 339, 343, 347
Rodin, J. 77, 405, 440
Rogers, C. 278
Rohr, R. 388, 390–1, 392, 393, 394
Romero, O. A. 499–501
Roosevelt, E. 106
Roosevelt, F. D. 385
Roosevelt, T. 463–5
Rosenbaum, R. 312
Rosenblatt, J. 78
Rotella, A. 10
Rowley, C. 361
Rustichini, A. 52

Index

Saskin, M. 311
schadenfreude 346–7, 556
Schindler, O. 217, 511, 552
Schmid C. K. 91, 94, 146
Schmitt, M. 11
Schnedler, R. 442
Schneirla, T. C. 78
Schoenewolf, G. 6
Schopenhauer, A. 9, 382
Schulweis, H. 204
Schwartz, B. 20
Schwartz, S. H. 112, 173, 176
Schwarzenegger, A. 24
self-actualization 3, 24, 380, 388, 391–2
self-control *see* self-regulation
self-discrepancy theory 29
self-efficacy 4, 94, 169, *173*, 253, 259, 273, 320–1, 323–4, 326, 513
self-esteem 340, 350–1, 391, 409, 443, 510–15, 517, 520–1, 537
self-interest 51, 58–69, 205, 245, 320, 349, 358, 405, 461, 534, 537–9, 552, 554
self-regulation 30, 92–3, 270, 273, 513, 516–19
self-sacrifice 7, 20, 22–3, 25–6, 310–11, 418, 460, 472, 538; audience response to 129; central characteristics of heroism 7; empathy and 463–7; Holocaust rescuers and 207, 208; as proximate mechanism 36; solidarity and 58–60, 64, 68; suicide bombers and 130; whistleblowers and 358, 361
Seligman, M. E. P. 262, 263, 264, 388, 395
Sendler, I. 25, 207, 548
September 11, 2001, terrorist attacks 128, 131, 150, 264, 488–9, 498, 554
Settersten, R. 266–7
Shadt, S. 140, 386; *see also* Resilience Project
Shackleton, E. 195
Shelp, E. E. 263
Sherlock Holmes (fictional character) 25, 37
Sherman, S. 12
Shimizu, A. 12
Shinseki, E. 96
Shirtcliff, E. A. 444
Shontz, F. C. 438
Shyh-Chang, N. 386
Simmons, J. P. 343
Simonton, D. K. 463
situationist/situationalist approach to heroism 4, 7–8, 9, 11, 13, 20, 100–4, 185, 187–9, 319–20, 331–2
Skitka, L. J. 166–7, 171–2, 174–5, 549–50, 553
Sleeping Beauty 385
Sleeth, R. G. 464
slippery slope effect 171, 407
Smith, D. 199
Smith, G. 3, 5, 7, 8, 384, 385, 386, 390, 396, 520
Smith, J. 401
Smith, J. R. 253
Smith, S. F. 533–4, 540, 541
Smith, W. L. 361, 363
Smyth, B. 141–2, 144, 147, 148, 150–1, 156, 158
Snowden, E. 48, 115, 285, 289, 358, 360, 361, 363, 530
Snyder, E. E. 342
social comparison theory 29–30
social contagion 131–3
social heroes/heroism 8, 22–4, 90, 141, 146, 205–6, 287, 289; calling and 329–31; civil disobedience and 251–4; deviant heroes (artists and activists) 249–60; elevation and 254–5, 258–9; epiphany and 254–5, 258–9; heroic imagination and 252, 259; moral conviction and 548, 550
social heuristics 10, 58–69; justice and 60–3; pacifism and 65–8; Social Heuristics Hypothesis 47; solidarity and 63–5
social identity theory 121, 277, 340
social learning 58–9, 94–5
social media 12, 131–2, 146, 286–7, 291–3, 296, 363, 367; Facebook 43, 132, 288–9
social responsibility 207, 216, 219, 222, 302, 538
sociopathy 530; *see also* psychopathy
solidarity 58, 60, 63–5, 68–9
Sommers, S. R. 350
Sparks, A. 10
speeches of heroes 126–31
Spencer, H. 9
Sperry 394
spiritual leadership 300–14; heroism in 303–4; impact of 300–1; training program in 304–13; transcendence and 301–3, 309–11
Spirituality Mind Body Institute (SMBI) 304–14
Spitzer, E. 407, 517
Stacey, D. 11
Stalin, J. 7, 476, 483, 554
Stalker, C. 330–1
Stanford prison experiment 95, 100, 205, 220; *see also* Milgram, S.
Stanley, H. M. 517
Star Trek 196–7
Star Wars 379, 385, 390, 471, 509, 511, 513, 513, 518, 520
Staub, E. 107, 204, 206, 207, 217–20, 223, 264, 438, 551
Stephens, J. 149
stereotyped behavior in non-human animals 77–9
stereotypes (human) 333, 346, 347; gender 208, 443; of heroes 20–4, 448–50; of heroic whistleblowers 356–71; Jewish 211, 216, 218, 219
Stigler, F. 521
stigma 340, 346, 350, 410, 448–9, 451–2, 557
Stockdale paradox 196
Streater, K. 277
Stuppy, A. 13
Su, S. 11
suicide 273, 289, 330, 407–8; altruistic suicide 65;

cyber-bullying and 293; physician-assisted 172, 175; physicians and 232, 233; suicide bombers 6, 90, 130, 286, 530
Sun Tzu 231
superhero gene 386
superheroes 23, 25, 37, 42, 289, 291–2, 384–6, 404, 412, 438, 513–15

taxonomies of heroes 7–8
technology 156, 278, 283–96, 314, 380, 468
Ten Commandments, The 385
Teresa of Calcutta (Mother Teresa) 25, 59, 113, 124, 304–6, 309, 328, 401–3, 438, 448, 451–2, 498
terror management theory (TMT) 510–11
testosterone 444, 479, 486
Thalidomide crisis 187, 194–5
Thalys train attack 547
Thornberg, R. 443
Tiller, G. 554
Tillich, P. 265
Time magazine's Person of the Year 295–6
titles and awards of heroes 124–6
To Kill a Mockingbird 384
Tolstoy, L. 9
traditional heroes 8, 23, 24, 27, 291, 295, 318
tragic heroes 8, 25, 318, 361, 362
Traits that Transcend 207, 218
transcendence 2, 8, 105–7, 301–3, 309–10, 395, 495–6, 500, 517, 521
transcendent heroes 8, 25, 318
transcendent summons 325, 327–8, 331, 334
transfigured heroes 8, 24–5, 318
transformation 379, 396; becoming your own hero 410–11; character and typecasting 402–10; dependency to autonomy 393–4; egocentricity to sociocentricity 392–3; future directions and implications 395–6, 411–12; hero characteristics before and after 392–5; hero to victim 407–8; hero to villain 406–7; hero's transformation defined 381; moral transformation 401–12; mythic hero's transformation 380–3; in the natural world 379–80; pervasiveness of transformation 379–80; purpose of the hero's transformation 381–3; psychological transformation 380; social sources of transformation 390–2; in the social world 380; stagnation to growth 394–5; ten dimensions of transformation 383–90; victim to hero 403–5; victim to villain 405–6; villain to hero 409–10; villain to victim 408–9; *see also* moral transformation
transforming heroes 8, 25, 318
transitional heroes 6, 8, 25, 318
transitory heroes 8, 24–5, 27, 318
transparent heroes 8, 25, 27, 277, 318, 333
transposed heroes 8, 25, 318
trending heroes 8, 24, 318
Trivers, R. 38, 60, 75, 539

trolley problem 555
Trommsdorff, G. 92
Tubman, H. 24
Turiel, E. 107
Turnbull, M. 48
Turner, V. W. 385
Turvey, M. T. 153–7
Tutu, D. 132
Twain, M. 29
tyrants *see* despotic tyrants and despotic power

Unbroken 385
underdogs 7–8, 12, 251, 319, 339–52, 460, 509–13; appeal of 340–1; complementary justice and 347–8; definition of 340; fragility of support for 349; as heroes 351–2; hope and 342–4; identifying with 344–5; justice and 345–8; self as 349–51; unexpected and 341–2
Universal Declaration of Human Rights (UDHR) 286–7, 296
U.S. Coast Guard 459–60, 472

values 28–30, 205, 289, 361, 363, 395; aesthetic values 147; career development and 321–5, 329–31; deviant heroes and 251–3, 256–7; family and parental values 211–12; Holocaust rescuers and 205, 210–13, 216, 218, 220–2; moral values 165–7, 170, 173–8, 218; sacred values 11, 126–8, 130; social and cultural values 20, 21, 25, 27, 92–3, 112–13, 115, 121, 125; spiritual heroism and 300–9, 314
van Bussel, A. A. L. 171, 529
van Gennep, A. 381, 382, 383
van den Bos, K. 171, 529
Van Ittersum, K. 94, 167, 186
Van Tongeren, D. 13
Vandello, J. 12
Vanstone, R. 11
Varese, F. 214–15
Vietnam War 406
Vygotsky, L. 468

Wade, G. H. 147, 156
Walker, L. J. 5, 11, 103, 104, 106, 112–14, 219, 220, 318–20, 411, 418–19, 531
Wallenberg, R. 217–18, 551
Walsh, J. 386
Wansink, B. 94, 167, 186
warmth 23, 130, 210–11, 222, 428–9, 478, 480–3, 488, 518, 550
Washington, G. 21, 463–4
Watkins, S. 361
Watts, A. 13
Waytz, A. 176, 402, 512, 548, 555
Webb, B. 422–6
Weber, M. 2, 465
Wegner, D. M. 403, 409, 429, 435
Weick, K. E. 190, 276
West, S. G. 442

Index

whistleblowing 7–8, 12, 356–71, 389, 452, 531, 535; altruism and 20, 358–9, 361–2, 371; moral courage and 166, 168, 170, 172–4, 177, 178, 264; risk-taking and 192, 318, 356, 357, 359–63; self-images of whistleblowers 368–9; social and cultural attitudes 367–70; as social heroism 24, 206, 251, 264; transformation from villain to hero 410; whistleblowers as heroes 357–71; World Online Whistleblowing Survey (WOWS) 356–7, 365–70, 373–5
Whitney, G. 442
WikiLeaks 363
Williams, L. A. 277
Williams, R. 407
Wilson, W. 467
wisdom 20, 25, 27, 60–2, 143–5, 286, 307–9, 311, 313–14, 379, 383, 420, 508, 513; embodied wisdom 314; epistemic wisdom 510; medical heroes and 233–45; transformation and 390, 393, 395–6; Three-Dimensional Wisdom Model 234–5
Wise, J. 63
Wizard of Oz The 387, 390
Woods, T. 25, 518
Woodward, C. 263–4
WorldCom 361
wounded hero archetype 229, 231, 313

Wozniak, S. 358, 360
Wu, A. 232, 236
Wynn, K. 393

Yad Vashem 203, 205–8
Yaish, M. 214–15
Young, L. 402, 512, 548, 555
Yousafzai, M. 96, *125*, 128, 132, 385, 401

Zahavi, A. 36, 40, 533
Zahavi, D. 141, 142, 143, 145, 155
Ziemke, T. 149
Zimbardo, P. 5, 20, 89, 186, 266, 276, 471; banality of evil/heroism 4, 100, 139, 148, 156–8, 220, 286, 410–11, 467, 530; definition of heroism 167, 295, 318, 394, 467, 495; heroes-in-training/waiting 143, 158, 498; heroic acts 325, 418, 496, 533, 541; heroic imagination 4, 10, 252, 259, 286, 333, 467, 554; Lucifer Effect, 396; new heroism 142, 147; obedience to authority (Stanford prison experiment) 95, 100, 205, 250, 429; situationist view of heroism 7–8, 157, 187, 283, 319–20, 331–2; social heroism 24, 146, 251–2, 259, 287, 330, 548; taxonomy of hero types 7, 24, 287, 289, 329–30, 332, 531
Zuckerberg, M. 43